# BOOKS BY

# C. L. SULZBERGER

<table>
<tr><td>A Long Row of Candles</td><td>1969</td></tr>
<tr><td>(American Heritage) History of World War II</td><td>1966</td></tr>
<tr><td>Unfinished Revolution: America and the Third World</td><td>1965</td></tr>
<tr><td>The Test: de Gaulle and Algeria</td><td>1962</td></tr>
<tr><td>My Brother Death</td><td>1961</td></tr>
<tr><td>What's Wrong with U.S. Foreign Policy</td><td>1959</td></tr>
<tr><td>The Big Thaw</td><td>1956</td></tr>
<tr><td>Sit-Down with John L. Lewis</td><td>1938</td></tr>
</table>

# A Long Row of Candles

# A LONG ROW OF CANDLES

MEMOIRS AND DIARIES
[ 1 9 3 4 – 1 9 5 4 ]

## C. L. SULZBERGER

*The Macmillan Company*

Library of Congress Catalog Card Number: 69-10642


The Macmillan Company
Collier-Macmillan Canada Ltd., Toronto, Ontario

Printed in the United States of America

FOR JESSICA

*My First Granddaughter*

# Acknowledgments

I wish to express my deepest thanks to Susan Sevray and Eda Pallier for helping to prepare and edit this manuscript and to Marina, my wife, for reading it with a critical eye.

I acknowledge permission from *The New York Times* to reprint here certain material included in dispatches to that newspaper; permission from Mrs. George Bainbridge, Doubleday & Co., Inc., and the Macmillan Company of Canada, Ltd., to quote the lines from *Rudyard Kipling's Verse: Definitive Edition,* on page 792; permission from Harcourt, Brace & World, Inc., to quote C. P. Cavafy's "Candles," from *The Complete Poems of Cavafy,* trans. by Rae Dalven; and permission from General Louis Fortier to quote from his letter to me of November 12, 1942.

I also thank Benjamin Welles for letting me reprint some paragraphs from a letter written on March 30, 1967; Paddy Leigh Fermor for providing his version of George Morton's SOE song and Lord Hartwell and Winston S. Churchill for allowing me to publish a copy of a personal and Top Secret telegram composed by the senior Winston Churchill (edited in his writing but never sent); also for authority to publish the documentation of Prime Minister Churchill's handwritten deal with Stalin on the Balkans.

CLS

# Contents

# L'Envoi

Personal recollections are published for various reasons: the desire to make money; a wish to amplify history's footnotes; ill-disguised vanity; or compulsive indiscretion, the kind of thing that makes a secret rare. I confess, in descending order, to the first three of these attributions.

The bulk of this and subsequent volumes is made up of a reporter's notebook. For years, indeed decades, it was never kept with the idea of publication. Blessed with an unusually bad memory, I jotted down remembrances of conversations or events I thought might be of future journalistic use.

Until long after this particular memoir (which runs into late 1954), it never occurred to me that the notes I took would be of interest to anyone but myself. They were merely filed away for eventual use in dispatches and/or columns, listed chronologically or cross-indexed by subject.

Sometimes such notes were compiled because a particular event was unusual or pleasant—for example, crossing the Khyber Pass by Afghan bus, conveying a secret request for alliance from Tito to the King of Greece or flying over the South Pole (to be recounted in a later volume). But, for the most part, these are simply jottings on what important people of my lifetime had to say, jottings without pretense to style.

It is a question of the prominence of the sayers and how their comments related to current events or future history, not what I had to say about them. This was not a consciously "public" diary, and that limiting factor is more than evident in the ensuing pages.

Anything the reader will find of interest in the major portion of this book (diaries from 1945 on) is of interest solely because of the persons whose opinions were expressed, not because of the way I have recounted such opinions. There was at no time in my mind—at least until a date far more recent than 1954—a thought of recording words for anyone's use but my own.

Much later, when friends remarked that my diaries covered a long period, a wide area, and included talks with many figures of more than passing importance, I began to ponder publication. By then it was too late to think of reworking the raw material of journalism into a more elegant literary form.

I have been surprised, on going through my diaries, to find both how much I noted and how much I omitted. Thus, for example, I jotted down observations concerning the features, dress or eating preferences of various persons who appear in these pages. Yet, when General Eisenhower (in the locker room of the St. Germain golf club, during the summer of 1951) offered to sell me some property next door to his Gettysburg farm and to have a retired general who looked after his own estate also keep an eye on mine, I made no record of this generous suggestion (which I, perhaps foolishly, declined).

Until 1946 I took all notes myself. Subsequently I was blessed with secretaries whose increasing talents and understanding made it easier for me to keep a record—and also, if anything, made me lazier and more abrupt in annotating dialogues.

Now that I suddenly find these records filtering through the necessary editorial procedures, being at times tithed for the sake of surviving interest, I feel appallingly indiscreet. Is it fair to attach to the names of men and women old, dead or agreeably forgotten, opinions that no longer apply to an evolving world?

This matter of propriety bothered me in compiling *A Long Row of Candles* until I acknowledged to myself one salient fact. If distinguished diplomats like Harold Nicolson or famous ministers like André Malraux can publish their recollections, why not a modest newspaperman?

And, in all sincerity, I think I have allowed a decent lapse of time between what once was private between me and those with whom I talked and the sharing of that wealth. Unlike the associates of the late President Kennedy who raced across his warm grave into print, I have permitted the tolerant winds of time to cool off secrets now exposed, secrets that really never were very great.

During my time a newspaperman's life was splendid, above all that of a foreign correspondent, and the years covered in this particular volume were almost all spent in reporting from abroad. Nowadays Washington has become the gravitational center for American journalism and the television screen is gradually easing newspapers into the ashcan.

The current theory is that anyone who can describe a fire in Kansas City can analyze a crisis in Jugoslavia. Language, experience, knowledge and what used to be called culture are being sacrificed to speed. Two minutes time on TV is more effective in this age of cybernetics than the months spent by Henry Morton Stanley in tracking down Dr. Livingstone for the old *Herald* last century.

When young men ask me for advice on how to become a foreign correspondent I tell them today: "Don't." It is like becoming a blacksmith in 1919—still an honorable and skilled profession; but the horse is doomed.

For a full decade in the following account I was in charge of the foreign service of *The New York Times* traveling around the world and organizing the way in which our correspondents reported its occurrences. I came into the job by accident, the accident of war.

In my time a real reporter still worked hard for scoops and gave few damns for authority or convention. My friend Ben Welles, to whom I give the accolade "a real reporter," wrote me in 1967 (when moved by a column I had written about the departure from France of SHAPE headquarters):

> I thought of the night we sat on the floor of your bedroom in the Metropole, Brussels, and clued [Senator] John Sherman Cooper into the picture alongside nice old Bech [prime minister of Luxembourg]. . . . of the ten days in Lisbon (NATO's most famous ministerial meeting) with Cian and Anne and Mike Hoffman [Cian—Camille Cianfarra—went down with the *Andrea Doria* in 1956. Anne McCormick, who wrote the column I now write, died in 1954. Hoffman, a fine newspaperman, has become a banker].
>
> The nights spent driving out to Estoril with Byroade [an ambassador and assistant secretary of state] to wean a story out of him; of the night in the Lisbon *fado* joint where I got my hair-cut and Cian backed half a mile down the one-way street and we all got potted and threw confetti as the right righteous Portuguese plutocracy glowered at the Yankee savages.
>
> And especially the morning bull sessions in the College of Civil Engineering where coach CLS would give us the growl: "Goddammit, you guys, I don't want to see an agency piece on the front page for ten days. Cianfarra, you go after those eyeties and get your hands on their documents . . . Hoffman, see what your economists have got to say . . . Welles, you oughta know a couple of colonels from SHAPE who'll leak if you pour enough booze into them. . . . I'll take the Greeks; they're all Marina's cousins anyway."
>
> Good days, boss. They don't come like that anymore.

No Ben; they don't. *Où sont les neiges d'antan?*

At my time of life when one has had the recent experience of naming a granddaughter and cutting the fat from an overstuffed diary, when one looks forward still to mustering sufficient energy to write books dreamed of years ago, odd recollections stir, amid fond memories.

The relations between men of one nation and another vary according to their coincidence in time. I have often regretted that the political vagaries of my generation have made it so hard to develop real friendships with Russians and Chinese, two peoples for whom I have particular admiration and affection.

And what is it that makes for special bonds between individual countries at certain moments of history? What strange destiny can turn Americans from savage enemies to trusted friends of Germans, Japanese and Italians, all within a brief span of years?

Why, one wonders, do the French—above all other Europeans—pay such high regard to food and drink? And why, also, are they the world's least boring (if often most irritating) people? What is it in Britain's inherited genes that produces snobbism, reticence and enormous, understated courage?

Why is it also that the French, with their intellectual genius, know nothing of self-government and prefer to throw away constitutions instead of amending them? (They have so far had fourteen.) Or, for that matter, how does it happen that the greatest respecters of constitutional law, the British, have no written constitution at all?

How does a nation earn contemporary repute, good or bad? For years the Rumanians were regarded as supine; and yet, in recent time, they have shown an enviable spirit of audacity.

In early 1940 I visited General Weygand's *Armeé du Levant* and, among the exuberant Spahis, Goumiers and Légionnaires I noted hundreds of slant-eyed little Vietnamese, carrying stretchers or waiting on table. "Why," I asked, "are all the Annamites service troops?"

The answer: "They can't fight." (Yes, the Vietnamese!)

I remember when the Arabs told me the Jews couldn't fight and I remember when the Jews told me the Arabs couldn't fight.

Napoleon always maintained that the essential element for an officer was luck. I am convinced that luck, rather than talent, is the greatest asset of a newspaperman.

It has been my fortune to play bad golf, bridge or chess with Eisenhower, Harriman, Nixon, Bohlen and Couve de Murville. I have lunched in Dulles' honor at the Quai d'Orsay and heard him obfuscate the French language. I have interpreted between Turkish officers and Soviet diplomats and, for that matter, at a most private luncheon between an American ambassador and future prime minister of France.

By chance I have become acquainted with divers famous men from de Gaulle (whom I have known a quarter of a century) to Tito, Chiang Kai-shek, Khrushchev, Nasser, De Gasperi, Castro and the Duke of Windsor, a clutch of Communists and a wallet of kings. Over the decades I have worked on all seven continents including Antarctica.

There is no doubt in my mind that the man I most admired among those I met was Winston Churchill. Churchill had the qualities of a poet and a pirate; I can ask no better mixture. Among public figures, de Gaulle alone had equal courtesy of manner.

I made a habit of asking great men who most influenced them in their lives and have found an odd melange, from an obscure American commander in Panama (for Eisenhower) to Tito (for Nasser: "He showed me how to get help from both sides without joining either").

It has been my fate to see men stand up unyielding to adversity. I have been lucky enough to visit secret EOKA conspirators in Cyprus and the Algerian FLN; and I have heard a heavy Communist prison gate clang shut behind me as I was taken to talk with Archbishop Stepinac in his gloomy cell.

By rare privilege I can boast that among my close friends have been some of the finest public servants the United States produced since the glowing eighteenth century: Chip Bohlen, Averell Harriman, David Bruce, Larry Norstad; all honest, versatile, sensitive, brave and patriotic men. I am proud to come from the same land as they and to inhabit the same moment in time.

And, in contemplating my own diary, I remember how inaccurate diaries can be. Once I played cards with Eisenhower, Harriman, Gruenther and Dan Kimball, United States Secretary of the Navy, while all discussed the memoirs of James Forrestal, first Secretary of Defense. They had attended a meeting referred to in the book and each agreed that Forrestal's account was wrong. But when I asked what, then, was the true version, all promptly disagreed among themselves.

When one consciously reviews one's own small part in history, that of observer, a worm with a notebook, only then can one see how history casts its own shadow before it. Thus, as early as the spring of 1954, the United States was on the brink of war in Indochina; and that war, as I write this, has not yet ended—although it never officially began.

Also, one finds when remembering things past that history can sweep up those who do not deliberately seek to lead it. I am still certain Eisenhower never really wanted to be President. Indeed, just before his nomination in Chicago, he was threatening not to run if the Republicans didn't change their platform.

I sometimes wonder if politicians understand other people or their role in time; or, for that matter, whether people or time itself truly understand most politicians. Too often through the years I have heard the same man contradict himself with outrageous sincerity.

Religion plays a massive role in shaping human lives and yet I am flabbergasted at the lack of purity I have detected among religious leaders with whom I have talked from the temples of Europe to the cathedrals of Asia. In almost all of them I found more interest in Caesar's domain than in God's.

The greatest lesson I have learned is that, despite Marxist worship of events and trends, it is men who influence history by their will; and Churchill, de Gaulle and Tito have confirmed this view. The giant (although de Gaulle has more than once assured me that "the age of giants is over") can make history, but the pretender is overwhelmed by it.

This, of course, is but an introduction to a book of memoirs and diaries which, in itself, running a few volumes of enormous length, constitutes a kind of verbal diarrhea. Here I see no point in artificially protracting the disease.

May I only summarize by saying these things. Rule A for a newspaperman is that "leaks" are the food of the trade; and over the years I have found that, as with the best drinks, the leak always fizzes from the top. The desire for indiscretion at the upper level seems compelling. Rule B is that ideology or nationality have nothing to do with the niceness or non-niceness of a man; goodness is an inner quality reserved to no creed or race.

Finally, as the reader will discover, a large amount of time and space are spent in that vague area still known as the Balkans. Why? Because it is a region I loved and love for its vigor, poetry and charm, the valor of its people and the persistence of its beauty. Also because there I left my youth and found my wife. *Vale!*

# A Long Row of Candles

# I

# A FOND AND

# SPECIAL LIGHT

THE GREEK POET CAVAFY SAW LIFE AS A ROW OF CANDLES. When he entered his Alexandrian church he looked into the past and wrote:

> The days gone by remain behind us,
> a mournful line of burnt-out candles . . .
> I do not want to look at them; their form saddens me,
> and it saddens me to recall their first light.

For most of us, when we look backward at the row of candles in our minds, they glow with a fond and special light they never in reality attained. It is not the sputtering vision of Cavafy but that of another poet, Edna Millay, whose candle burned so brightly that she knew it would not last the night. Whose does? The question is an impertinence and the night is long.

Yet, if we can approach its gloom, recalling the tapers of our own existence, rendered splendid by affectionate memory, why is that not itself an excellent thing? My own life is more remarkable in indulgent recollection than ever it was in fact. Nevertheless, for me this does not tarnish it, for it was mine.

My origins are American, middle class and Jewish. I was related to but never possessed money. My father died young and on the threshold of success. I remember him as a vigorous man who wished me to understand him and never succeeded. He had a sharp temper, which, in later years, I found I had inherited.

I was brought up in great comfort, helped by my grandfather and my uncles, taught patriotism, virtue, a deep respect for education and little about religion. Much later I appreciated that, in some circumstances and by some people, Jewishness was considered a handicap. While I was at college Hitler seized power in Germany and started his dreadful persecutions. I took a course at Harvard Divinity School on the history of the Jews and was impressed and disturbed by the persistence of anti-Semitism throughout time.

My childhood was spent in the countryside not far from New York. I learned to fish, skate and play the usual games. Although I was often and seriously ill this had no inhibiting effect but merely drove me to books. Before I reached my teens I was familiar with most of the conventional classics that I, at least, have ever read.

Those were splendid times. I wonder, in this era of the locker-room civilization, how many boys have the fun I did. There was a seemingly vast field behind our house where we played baseball and constructed a clubhouse of odd boards and logs. Sometimes in the summer I visited a farm in the Berkshires where I caught trout in a nearby stream, stickleback in a well, raised rabbits and learned how to trap woodchucks. We were near a lumber mill whose piles of waste sawdust provided admirable terrain for tunnels and secret caves.

Americans, being ardently republican, like to claim aristocratic antecedents. We are all descended from European lords, Irish kings, African rulers or Indian chiefs. I am told I am entitled to two escutcheons. Should this be true it would imply that some of my Jewish forebears courted favor with the feudal bosses of their time. One ancestral branch, the Hayses, chose three hares as an emblem; another, the Peixottos, three fish. This pleases me for I am an eager, if poor, shot and ardent angler.

My mother's family never bothered to trace its modest origins, seeming merely to bubble out of Illinois, where mother was born, Colorado and Tennessee. Through father's mother, however, we boasted prouder roots.

One paternal branch fled to Holland from the Spanish Inquisition in 1492. It remained in Rotterdam until the end of the seventeenth century when it came to North America. According to my grandmother, six Haes brothers built a boat, loaded it with family and livestock, and sailed it to the Colonies. All the male descendants were named Hays and most of them abandoned the Jewish faith.

In 1732 my particular ancestor settled in Westchester County, outside New York City, and remained there until the Revolution. George Washington used his farmhouse as a headquarters. It was subsequently attacked by the British Colonel Tarleton and later burned down, in 1779, by some of Tarleton's Tory friends. My ancestor was offered the choice of relocating on Manhattan Island, in what is now known as the Silk Stocking District, or at a village named Pleasantville, elsewhere in Westchester. He chose Pleasantville, believing the prospects more favorable. I have never been a financial genius myself.

The son of this gentleman, Jacob Hays, became the last High Constable of New York. Hook-nosed, heavy-set, he gained renown by a direct manner of administration and the fact that he never armed himself with more than his gold-headed staff of office. Grandma, a frail woman, contended that once he encountered two famous lawbreakers, bashed their heads together and carted them off to jail. This legend gave her immense satisfaction. Jacob's cousin, Benjamin, was known as "Uncle Ben, the Jew, the best Christian in Westchester County." His was then the only Jewish family in all Westchester, a county today filled with the estates and country clubs of wealthy coreligionists. Another ancestor settled in Curaçao. His descendants came to New York in 1807 and produced a more intellectual line including physicians, a diplomat and a journalist, Benjamin Franklin Peixotto. Peixotto was editor of a Cleveland paper and unwisely supported his friend Senator Stephen Douglas for the presidential nomination. Lincoln won.

The Sulzbergers were a modest clan from the South German region that borders Switzerland and the Lake of Constanz. In the first half of the nineteenth century they came to the United States and settled as far apart as Philadelphia and Arkansas. The snobbish Hayses thought it a comedown when one of them married my grandmother.

I went to school just outside New York and completed my education at Harvard where, because of father's death, reduced circumstances forced me to earn part of my keep. During one year I catalogued library books and spent more time reading than filling out cards. Engaged in this pleasant task I acquired curious bits of learning including acquaintance with the civilization of the Toltecs. This helped me to win the poetry prize of $175 with a derivative offering called "The Red Land," about early Mexican Indians. Much later it also gave me special entree to Jacques Soustelle, distinguished French archaeologist who successively became de Gaulle's wartime intelligence chief, de Gaulle's cabinet minister, and civilian inspirer of de Gaulle's enemies, the Secret Army Organization, or OAS. Soustelle had spent some years in Central America, and we used to discuss his dream of writing a novel called *Hungry Wolf, the Portrait of a Toltec Gentleman.* Hungry Wolf in Toltec is Nezahualcoyotl, who was my great university hero. He wrote fine poetry which, as a king, he commanded to be recited to the orchestral accompaniment of conch horns and kettledrums. If anyone mispronounced a word or struck the wrong note his heart was cut out.

My college life was not remarkable, but I can make it sound as if it had been. Jim Agee, who became a minor literary classic, took me on the *Advocate,* oldest American university magazine. Eventually I became president. With five roommates I lived in its new building, which we induced the trustees to buy after an alcoholic dinner. (I saw to it that undergraduate officers prepared themselves for this persuasion by first drinking two ounces of olive oil.) Our life was exuberant. One morning I awakened to discover tattoos on three separate places. Two of these, fortunately, were on my feet. I wore them off by going barefoot in the summer.

Eventually I discovered more money was to be made selling newspapers than by reading Toltec on the sly. The New York *Herald Tribune* had an annual competition. The man who sold most subscriptions at Harvard was awarded a prosperous franchise. My uncle was then vice-president (and soon to be publisher) of *The New York Times,* the *Tribune's* rival. However, this did not inhibit me and I managed to win the competition easily. I advised prospects they would be better informed by reading the comments of Walter Lippmann than those of the *Times'* columnist, Arthur Krock. Years later, when I had joined the *Times,* Krock generously forgave me. Not so the *Herald Tribune;* when its circulation staff discovered their Harvard agent was related to the opposition I was politely fired. An assistant manager had prior consultation with the *Times* and agreed I should share the franchise of that paper with a reluctant classmate who previously held this all alone.

In those days I never entertained the idea of going into any branch of journalism. I fancied myself a poet and had been encouraged in this illusion by T. S. Eliot and Conrad Aiken, both of whom were temporarily attached to Harvard. I used to play furious Ping-pong with Aiken on the long *Advocate* oaken council table. Aiken was a pudgy, friendly man who had acquired great skill at table tennis in England, when he and his wife had kept warm by dressing in many sweaters and batting celluloid balls. Eliot accepted me in a special course for fifteen pupils. We were illumined by his brilliant mind. Even in 1933 he forecast that Hemingway would be regarded as the Kipling of his time. Kipling was then seen as "square." Ultimately, Eliot predicted, both would find equal literary rank. Timid and withdrawn as Eliot was in class, he had a talent for banging the piano and singing a huge number of limericks, some of which I suspect he had written himself. I liked him despite the fact that he gave me a poor mark on my term paper. Its subject was: "The Undergraduate Poetry of T. S. Eliot."

I loved poetry and thought I had talent. I submitted a poem to a magazine published by the distinguished S. Foster Damon. At that time I was under the influence of Apollinaire, who had written in a form called the calligram, printed in lines devised to fit the shape of the subject, like a mouse with a tail trickling into tiny words or syllables. One night I bought a bottle of bootlegged Metaxa brandy, drank half of it, carefully slit a vein in my left arm, applied a pyjama cord tourniquet, dipped in an old-fashioned pen, and composed a neatly printed masterpiece entitled "Calligram in Blood." Professor Damon sent it back with this note: "Dear Mr. Sulzberger: Your contribution has been tasted by all members of the editorial board. This is a poetry magazine and not a butcher shop."

Harvard is a rich intellectual pudding not easy to digest. For a time I studied astronomy but found myself stumped by higher mathematics. I then moved into art history and wrote a long paper on El Greco (before Spain), a subject on which there was only one real authority, Willumsen. I borrowed all copies of his book from the libraries of Cambridge and Boston and kept them out until my paper had been graded, hoping thus to hamper the critical abilities of my teachers. This was not overwhelmingly successful. I shifted to the English Renaissance. I did not overwork and, to my horror, learned at a dance in my senior year that my tutor was placing bets I would not graduate. I rode back to college in a tail coat, and began a thesis on John Donne's reasons for taking orders in the Anglican church. My conclusions were that he was poor, married, knew nothing of birth control, and needed a job.

In my field it was necessary to get honors in order to receive a diploma. The ultimate test was an hour-long oral examination by an assemblage of professors. This comprised two parts: any chosen topic which the student could select himself and prepare for; and a general conversation designed to ascertain the scope of knowledge acquired. I knew there was little I could do to make up for my general ignorance on the Renaissance so I spent all my preparation on the first topic. My special subject was the relationship between Cardinal Wolsey and the Vatican in the year 1529. By the time I had finished I could virtually recite what the Cardinal had eaten for breakfast on any particular day.

I decided it might be wise to look the part of a serious student. Although it was glowing spring and I used to row, I gave this up and stayed out of the sun to develop suitable pallor. On my last night I could study no more, so I bought a selection of comic strips and remained up until dawn reading them. I then put on a black suit, added a black tie so that my interrogators might suspect I was not only serious or ill but also perhaps in mourning.

I was received by six professors who regarded me kindly, offered me a cigarette and, after a few minutes quizzing on Wolsey, assumed that I knew the subject. Then one of them, seeking a gambit to open broader exploration, asked me what I considered the best poetry of the English Renaissance. There is a special god who looks after idiots, drunkards and unprepared students, and he inspired me to say: "The Mother Goose rhymes." I went on to improvise haphazardly about Banbury Cross and Elizabethan processions and how the first things one learned came out of Mother Goose and how, furthermore, these might also be the last things remembered as one rolled over towards the grave. The pedagogues knew much about Renaissance literature but little about nursery rhymes. They dismissed me after ten minutes and awarded me top mark, enabling me to graduate with high honors.

I was named to Phi Beta Kappa, to the astonishment of several friends who gave me an applejack breakfast on the day of induction to this learned fraternity. The breakfast produced a major embarrassment. I was sitting in the front row of capped-and-gowned scholars, facing rows of proud parents when, while A. Lawrence Lowell was making his last public address as Harvard's dignified president, I slumped to the platform behind him, passing out for the only time in my life. Two classmates carried me solemnly off stage and hid me until I had recovered. My mother spotted one on his return and rushed to inquire what had happened. "It isn't anything serious," she was told, "only appendicitis."

When I left Harvard in 1934 I hadn't the vaguest idea of how to make a living. I was only certain I would never enter the grubby newspaper business in which I had family connections. First I tried to get a job as forest ranger in Arizona through a friend in the Department of the Interior. It seemed to me that riding horses about the Tonto Rim, which I already knew, fishing and occasionally spotting fires was an excellent way of spending time while writing poetry. My friend, however, advised he could not help unless I used political influence, of which I possessed none. Those were the tail-end days of the Great Depression. I was then offered a post as editor of a high-brow literary magazine which seemed suitable until I discovered my pay would be drawn from the publication's profits which were then running at an average of minus $50,000 a year.

At this point I determined to join a book publishing firm. Max Perkins, the brilliant editor of Scribner's whose tolerance was renowned, received me kindly. He had no job available, but promised one a year hence if I would spend the intervening time on an out-of-town paper learning how to copyread and edit. This seemed boring but understandable. Through a friend in the advertising business I obtained an introduction to the Scripps-Howard chain, which offered to hire me on a trial basis in Pittsburgh for $25 a week. Thereafter it never occurred to me to leave the newspaper trade.

Few less well-equipped reporters have ever arrived on a strange job in a strange city. I was twenty-one years old and could barely typewrite by the hunt-and-peck system with one finger of one hand. I knew nothing about journalism except that I disapproved of it as tedious. I had never even acquired the habit of reading any newspaper including those I sold.

My city editor, Larry Fagan, was a gentle man with a heart of cornmeal mush but, like many of his peers, he sought to mask this under a ferocious exterior. He had coronary trouble and his doctor had forced him to cease smoking the cigars he loved. Therefore, instead of smoking them, he ate them. He would stride around the city room in shirt sleeves, his face seemingly contorted by brown rings of nicotine stain at each corner of his mouth. The more excited he became the more rapidly he devoured the butt.

Larry first assigned me to rewrite little squibs telephoned in from regional correspondents, items about cats choking on mice or the birth of triplets. One day, as I was casually pecking these out with a timid fore-finger, I looked around and saw him regarding me, arms across his little belly, the end of a cigar disappearing fast. "Sulzberger," he hollered in a loud voice, "you'd better learn how to type." I immediately started to use two fingers, one on each hand. I still do this today, but the rate of speed has improved.

Pittsburgh was a vigorous, ugly city in those days and I relished it. In the center of the coal and steel districts of Pennsylvania, West Virginia and Ohio, it was filled with tough workers, many of them unemployed, who had immigrated from Italy and Central Europe. It had a huge Negro popula-tion, largely concentrated in a district that bordered the Italian quarter and, since Mussolini was blatantly preparing to attack Ethiopia, there existed bitter racial feeling along the frontier between them. At the time of the heavyweight championship fight between Joe Louis and Primo Carnera, a photographer named Louis O'Dille took me on a drinking tour with him in this frontier area. We bet as much money as we could afford, being given generous odds on both fighters by emotional backers in each bar; by bal-ancing wagers it was impossible not to win.

I lived for some months in the YMCA, finally moving to a modest boarding house run by the granddaughter of a Civil War general. This cost me $3.50 a week. I rode the trolley to and from work, found a place where I could get an adequate breakfast for 11 cents and harnessed my appetite at other meals. Many of us used to lunch with an assistant city editor at a former speakeasy whose proprietor could neither read nor write. He had trouble distinguishing between ten- and twenty-dollar bills but he had been an expert and audacious bootlegger, served good food, put out free Tom and Jerries at his bar over the Christmas season and loaned us money when we were broke.

My heavier drinking was done in the poor quarters of town. The cheap-est and most effective potion was known as a Heater and Cooler. This, served in separate glasses, comprised four ounces of what was called beer and two ounces of what was called whiskey. The standard price at the places I frequented was 10 cents but I found one bar that charged only a nickel. For less than a quarter one was ready to face anything including the cold and Mr. Fagan.

Each year the Carnegie International Exhibit of Modern Painting was held in Pittsburgh. This was the great artistic event and the big annual assignment of our art editor, an elderly gentleman who dreamed of writing the great American novel and spent much time drinking in preparation. Some weeks after my arrival, the press preview of The Carnegie fell due. The editor had disappeared somewhere with a bottle.

"Sulzy," summoned Mr. Fagan. "Do you know anything about art?" "Not much, sir." "But you went to Harvard, didn't you?" "Yes, sir." "Okay, you take on that damned paint show."

I attended the preview and, on my tour, was struck by a painting of Salvador Dali that was for sale and had not been bespoken. I therefore went to Mr. O'Connor, the gentleman who conducted us critics around and asked if he thought I could buy the Dali. He inquired what price I was ready to pay. I offered $350. I had a hundred dollars in the bank, which I could produce as a down payment, and was prepared to borrow the rest, repaying at the rate of $12.50 a week. Mr. O'Connor gravely said he would transmit my proposal to Dali and, to my delight and his astonishment, it was accepted. For many weeks, I lived on half-salary. But, first in the YMCA where it rested on the foot of my bed, then on the wall of my boardinghouse, I had the enormous pleasure of looking at one of Dali's finest works.

Dali himself wrote me several letters, invited me to visit him in Catalonia and explained his theories including his concept of the painting I had bought, entitled "Enigmatic Elements in Landscape." This, he said, represented a portrait of the ghost of Jan Vermeer of Delft dressed in a bullfighter's costume. He also told me the masters who had most influenced him were Vermeer, Velasquez and Meissonier.

The surrealist was then a magnificent artist who had not yet become what I consider a phony. However, he shortly came over to the United States and sold himself to mammon. A few years later I called on him in Paris and he received me in a velvet dressing gown, his dark studio hung with heavy velvet curtains. He was doing what he called a portrait of Freud.

My own picture had a particular history. In early 1938, when I became a foreign correspondent, I left it with a girl friend in Washington. Some time later, I went broke in Bulgaria and cabled my friend collect, asking her to sell the Dali for whatever she could get and to wire me the money in Sofia.

In early 1942, when I came home with my new wife, the dealer who had handled the transaction told me the painting had been bought by Thomas J. Watson, one of the wealthiest men in America. I wrote to Watson asking if I could buy the Dali back. He wished to know why and I explained that I had been temporarily destitute. Watson said that the same thing had once happened to him. He now had an impressive art collection but had once been forced to sell his first purchase, which he later bought back. He resold me the Dali, minus the dealer's percentage, a generous gesture. It now hangs in my Paris house, valued at $50,000.

This brief excursion into culture was not representative of my Pittsburgh life. It was still the day of the itinerant newspaperman, tough, expert, hard-drinking, who drifted from one job to another, always finding work because of his competence, quitting when he became bored or fought with the boss. They were a fine, proud professional lot and I am sorry their day is gone. A particular friend, the drama critic, was a red-haired, homely former Colorado track layer who kept one bottle in his desk drawer and another in his coat locker. I could tell when he had been inspecting either. At such a moment his walk changed into an airy jig and he would softly sing a tune beginning:

> Oh children see the honest man,
> A-coming down the lane.
> Oh let us swipe his pocketbook
> And steal his watch and chain.

Fagan designated me receptionist for freaks and eccentrics ranging from Jugoslav terrorists to seers and visionaries. One day a gentleman was sent to my desk and promptly stripped off his shirt. He then asked me to write my name on his back. I did so, and was surprised to see that, as a result of some peculiar urticarial condition, the words rose up on his skin a half inch high. The gentleman's name was Pete Hensel. His last regular employ had been with a circus. I headed his story:

> YOU DON'T NEED A PEN AND YOU DON'T NEED A PENCIL
> TO WRITE YOUR JOHN HANCOCK ON MR. PETE HENSEL

and thought, as the limerick goes, that was one up for me.

One colleague was a modest little editor whose happy demeanor concealed an obsession with death. He took out insurance policies on reporters assigned to fly on assignments—with himself as beneficiary. He also claimed the right to witness all executions. Murder was a popular avocation among the violent and racially mixed miners and mill workers of depression days, and on each fatal occasion Bill would take off for the death house at the State Penitentiary. Electrocutions occurred in the early morning. On the preceding evening the victim was given his choice of menu from what was regarded as a Lucullan last supper. Every morning, in time for our first edition, we would receive a detailed description of how well the prisoner had dined. Then we would wait for further news. Bill, unfortunately, was fascinated by the process of killing but unable to face it without prior alcoholic refreshment. As a consequence he never achieved his great dream of consciously witnessing these grim events. Always a rewrite man would concoct, under Bill's by-line, a vivid description derived from agency dispatches.

Only once did Bill himself carry out his assignment. He did not actually see the execution but he borrowed the carbon copy of the story written by an associate from another paper, added a great many adjectives and compiled a masterful piece. He was disappointed when this was not published. "What the hell goes on?" he asked Fagan when he got back. "Nothing much, Bill," said the city editor. "Damned good yarn too. Trouble was the guy was fried yesterday, not this morning." Bill had recovered consciousness twenty-four hours too late.

I started as a police reporter on a beat including the Allegheny County morgue. This was always well tenanted for, with three rivers tempting the discouraged to suicide and with a vigorous population addicted to Heaters and Coolers, many bodies were brought in to be laid out for identification. The coroner's staff of frustrated doctors who had never made the grade took pride in artistic preparation of their displays. They had two basic sets of make-up, one for Negroes and one for whites, with contrasting shades of cream and powder with which to adorn a corpse. Downstairs was a tank for the deposit of "floaters" taken from the rivers in a condition too poor to be exhibited. After a short period they were, if unclaimed, disposed of by the city. But upstairs was a large room with tiled floor bordered by slightly inclined, flat, glass-topped cases. Into these, the better preserved bodies, adorned with cosmetics, were wheeled, with all but their gaudy faces covered by sheets.

The Pittsburgh morgue was in an imitation Gothic building of gray stone kept at agreeably cool temperatures. As a consequence, during the hot summer, many people from nearby offices would come in at lunchtime to munch their sandwiches. Sometimes they brought along the wife and kiddies to view the current exhibits. I was always fascinated by the air of eager anticipation with which they wandered, chatting, from display to display, presumably seeking an acquaintance.

Once I was assigned to the trial of a certain Jennie Viscount accused under a Pennsylvania statute banning "necromancy or incantation" for profit. Mrs. Viscount was a witch in the neighborhood of Johnstown. She could lay down spells for as little as a dollar. For a larger fee she took one customer to a cemetery where she exhumed a heart, stuffed with pins, wrapped in ribbon and encased by cardboard. This was handed to Mr. Patsy Schultz, the Johnstown fire chief, who confessed to "feeling pretty tough ever since."

During my first and unusually cold winter, with a savage wind thrusting down the river valleys, I was told to investigate the way in which Pittsburgh cared for the hordes of unemployed who, despite a city ordinance forbidding beggars, were panhandling in the streets. I equipped myself with old windbreaker, torn flannels and down-at-heel shoes and set out for ten days as a hobo. Meeting several agreeable bums on my first morning, I was guided to one of the four principal flophouses where we bedded down. There I registered under the name Richard Simon, reckoning that if perchance I encountered an acquaintance who hailed me by my nickname, Cy (Si), no one would be surprised if I turned around.

The flophouses were not luxurious. Each late afternoon as we signed in, we were stripped, our clothes were put through delousing chambers, and we were handed dirty-looking flannel nightgowns and seated at long tables for the evening meal of bread and soup. Then we retired to enormous barracks, usually containing from three hundred to five hundred double-decker iron beds, arranged in rows, almost touching each other, and reeking of humanity. My first night was enlivened by an insane Hungarian neighbor who suffered from the illusion that he was upside down. He carefully crawled headfirst under the blanket, depositing his feet upon the pillow. The lights were turned out at nine o'clock. Our dormitory was illuminated by blue flashes of trolley wires, reflected off the snow outside. I can still remember those vast, splayed feet outlined beside my face, while their owner chuckled inside his cocoon.

The second day, unaccustomed to the techniques of this life, I had left my shoes beside the bottom bed below me and they were stolen. A huge Irish ex-pugilist, with hair growing down to his fingernails, saw me padding about. First he located the thief, a sullen Croat to whom he gave one bash, and returned my property. Then he admonished me that shoes were precious and I should sleep with them under my head. He became a begging colleague whose experience was invaluable. He had once been a sparring partner of a heavyweight named Ernie Schaaf who, at that time, fought the up-and-coming Joe Louis. The two of us were allowed free in Schaaf's ringside corner to watch our champion—beaten to a pulp.

One day I went down for breakfast and handed in the ticket for my deloused clothing to find that a leg of my trousers had been burned off at the knee. The delouser was a very hot room in which the garments, hung on iron hangers, rotated slowly. My hanger had turned fiery red with unfortunate results. The social worker in charge gave me a pair of frayed miner's dungaree pants.

I always kept a nickel with me, tied in the corner of a handkerchief so that, in case of arrest, I could telephone my paper and ask for help. But I never needed this, being artfully instructed on begging and how to keep an eye out for the police. I generally teamed up with the Irishman and a young man from California. The Californian, bumming his way East to visit a married sister, carried a special treasure in his pocket, a pair of clean lisle socks so that he would appear well dressed on arrival.

I discovered that the wealthier quarters of Pittsburgh were also the stingiest. When sighting the approach of someone clearly preparing to request a dime, horrified ladies would cross the street to avoid him. This was by no means true in the lower middle-class areas. People who were themselves not far from destitution invariably showed great generosity and this shamed me in my false position. On New Year's Eve, in a bleak snowstorm, I was shivering along with my California friend when we took temporary shelter in an Italian delicatessen. The proprietor gave us each a dollar and treated us to dinner of red wine and salami sandwiches.

It was easy to make five dollars a day by tactful begging, a knack I seemed to come by naturally. Being also on a reporter's salary, I thought it only moral that I should desist after acquiring this daily sum. Sometimes I would slip home to my boardinghouse, take a bath, then go down to the

cellar and smear myself with fresh dirt from the coal bin. And in spare
hours I played checkers in a flophouse with an Englishman whose besetting
sin was drink. He claimed to be a graduate of Eton.

I was a tenant of each major hostel and gradually became acquainted
with a disagreeable social phenomenon. The labor movement, under
Roosevelt's New Deal, was restive and self-confident. There were increasing numbers of strikes in our area. The distressed employers therefore
turned for help to strikebreaker organizations and they, in turn, recruited
from our midst. Outside each flophouse agents sought to sign us up, offering good pay and fanciful working conditions. They would load volunteers
into trucks and drive them off to battle with the picket lines. The ordinary
rank-and-file strikebreakers were called "finks" and their commissioned
officers were "nobles." These "nobles," as is usual with mercenaries, were
able to take care of themselves. Once they had conducted their troops
through flying stones into fortified factories where they pretended to work,
they used to organize crap games with loaded dice. They coerced the finks
into these affairs and won their earnings back.

Some time afterward I was assigned by Fagan to cover a strike against
the city's largest dairy. Strikebreakers delivered milk by convoying trucks
and beating up interfering pickets. I copied down the license numbers of
these protective cars, seeking to identify the operating gangs, until I was
caught by a gentleman named Whitey, a well-known "noble," who
took me into a garage and threatened to beat me to pieces. I talked
loudly with a confidence I did not feel about the power of the press and
was finally delivered to the dairy vice-president's office. He telephoned
Fagan, who summoned me back. The *Press* refused to write anything about
Whitey's activities because the dairy was a large advertiser.

Still later, when I was working in Washington, I again met some of these
gentlemen when they were subpoenaed by a Senate committee investigating
their activities. I then discovered that Whitey's boss was a former war hero
named "Eat-Em-Up-Alive" Jack. "Eat-Em-Up-Alive" testified that when
he brought his troops to force a northern New York picket line his employer accompanied him to the battlefield in an open car. "Eat-Em-Up-
Alive" arose in the tonneau and, as the strikers let loose, he turned to his
employer saying: "Boss, between you and me I didn't know there was so
many bricks in North Tonawanda."

I left Pittsburgh after a happy year when I fell in love with the mistress
of one of my colleagues, a long, lithe, elegant girl with long black hair, long
retroussé nose, prominent cheekbones and lovely mouth. We moved into a
two-room basement flat in Greenwich Village and lived there very happily
for a month. She was eight years older than I and good-natured enough to
ignore my demands for marriage.

She had a magazine job and each day, after she went to her office, I
worked feverishly on a novel. My only interruption came from children to

whom I always gave candy and who lived in neighboring buildings that abutted on our common garden between an experimental theater and a tiny house owned by Edna St. Vincent Millay. In the evenings D. and I cooked dinner and then investigated the line of bars between Lee Chumley's and Jack Delaney's.

I finished the book just as my money ran out; so I got an assignment in the Washington bureau of the United Press. During my final two days the agony of parting was heightened by the fact that I had to read my novel. I never showed it to anyone. For twelve hours, page by page I fed it into the open fireplace, occasionally helped by my candy-chewing friends. It takes a long time to burn a manuscript.

Having bought my ticket to Washington, I decided to keep $20 and spend the rest on a farewell evening on the town. We returned home full of drink and fell sleepily into bed. At 2 A.M. there was a terrible crash echoed immediately by another. D. leapt out of bed. I followed a moment later to find her former admirer, who had burst through the glass doors that separated us from the street, in the process of flooring her with a left hook. Still only semiconscious, I went for him. D. picked herself up and rushed hollering into the night.

I could vaguely hear her outside summoning help, the police, fire department, screaming in a nightgown. The neighborhood, used to unexpected interruptions, paid no heed.

The reason for her anxiety was that the interloper, apart from journalism, had spent two years in the prize ring. Fortunately, however, he too had apparently been touring local bars. In the end, we were both utterly exhausted. D. came back and suggested coffee. Sober and oddly bored, he went home. The next day, after a hectic farewell, I went to say goodbye to my aged grandmother. She remarked that I looked unusually well but asked about a scrape on the cheek and a large scab on the left ear where I had been bitten. I explained that I had been on a hunting trip with a friend.

D. wrote me twelve delightful letters and then disappeared.

Washington, late in 1935, was an agreeably self-centered city, electrified by President Roosevelt. Even then it was a journalist's paradise, despite a munificent salary of $30 a week. With the help of Harrison Salisbury, my first UP overseer, I found a flat in Georgetown comprising a handsome sitting room, a somewhat smaller bedroom with closet, antiquated bath and what was called a kitchenette. It was elegantly furnished with imitation antiques and two suits of armor. There was no electricity. The only lighting was in gas jets. The outside board at the base of my closet was missing and when I carelessly threw my shoes, they landed out on the street.

One night a college roommate came to stay and I gave him an enthusiastic party. A UP reporter, an earnest fellow who has since become a professor, got hopelessly drunk. We laboriously dressed him in armor, wired the hinges shut, stood him in the corner and forgot him. My former roommate and I eventually retired. I had warned my guest about the intricate lighting system but he awoke during the night, turned the gas jet on, lit a match and there was an enormous explosion. This revived the forgotten friend, still standing unconscious and encased in iron. He fell with a strident crash and we extricated him by cutting the fasteners with a can opener.

In those days I used to play softball Sundays with friends on a nearby Maryland estate. One of the players had been Dartmouth baseball captain. When the New York Yankees came to face the Washington Senators they included a third baseman formerly on the Dartmouth team, so we invited several of them to a Sunday game. That night I gave a splendid party. However, while I was busily typing an advance piece for early editions, some of the Yankees thought it would be amusing to drop bottles out of the window and their aim was not professional. While neighbors' protests were coming in, Salisbury—who was there—discovered it was difficult to edit my work because I had forgotten to put paper in the typewriter.

The UP was entrancing. I had been told by the head office in New York that I should not expect large pay, only experience and a by-line. It was a good system from the UP viewpoint. I received two raises of $2.50 each, before I left in early 1938, each time after covering the biggest story in the United States and threatening to resign. Not all UP "staffers," as the management referred to us, were so easily contented. One teletype operator told me of a reporter in Boston who was given very little pay but was rewarded by being called night bureau manager. There were only two men in the bureau, himself and the day bureau manager. After some years the night bureau manager became displeased with his status so he got very drunk.

Wire services operate complex teletype networks that extend right across the United States but there are certain key relay stations. For example, news going South is funneled directly to Atlanta and news going West is funneled directly to Kansas City. At each junction it is re-edited or cut, then forwarded. In between, all teletype machines are automatically linked. If something outstanding occurs, the bureau transmitting can break into the entire circuit, at least as far as Atlanta and Kansas City, by throwing a master switch and stopping the regular flow of copy. Five bells ring out on a one-line "flash" which is immediately followed by three bells and a brief bulletin summarizing the occurrence. According to my informant, the night bureau manager broke into the circuit with the following information.

(FIVE BELLS ! ! ! ! !) FLASH—BOSTON—CHRIST ARRIVES IN SECOND COMING.

Then, to the assembled editors who habitually gather around teletypes when the bells ring:

(THREE BELLS ! ! ! ! !) (UP)—BOSTON, THIS WILL ANNOUNCE THE RESIGNATION OF JOHN SMITH, UNITED PRESS NIGHT BUREAU MANAGER.

I started out for UP as assistant to our Treasury correspondent, charged with picking up unimportant handouts and looking in at the Commerce Department, the Federal Reserve Board, the Securities and Exchange Commission, the Bureau of Internal Revenue and the Board of Tax Appeals. I knew nothing about finance and unwittingly started a run on the French franc as a result of information provided by a helpful friend.

The Treasury Department, then administered by Secretary Henry Morgenthau, Jr., a serious gentleman, was famous for its press room where reporters from all over town gathered to play simultaneous games of bridge, poker, fan-tan and pitch. Our number included two extremely bibulous individuals, one of whom worked for *The New York Times*. When the latter was unaccountably absent one day I was assigned by my press room colleagues to write his comment on an unprecedentedly large peacetime borrowing. I compiled this with great care after the UP desk told me it wanted only fifty words, and sent a column and a half to the *Times* bureau, over the absentee's signature. The *Times* published this under his by-line on the front page. Late that night I was awakened by telephone and summoned into the bureau to match the *Times* piece. It was no good protesting that I, in fact, had written it; nor, for that matter, that I had not kept a carbon copy.

As a general fill-in, I often helped out at the State Department where we were represented by a weather-beaten Don Juan who had lost a leg years before in the wreck of a locomotive. One early morning I was called by Salisbury who told me to hurry to the State Department because Monty was ill. I went to the old State, War and Navy Building, found there was nothing urgent at hand, then telephoned Monty at home. A grouchy voice answered: "I lost my goddamned leg." I reported this fact to the other reporters; they were entranced. We decided to freeze all State Department news, leaving one of our number to answer calls, and embarked by taxi for Monty's house. He was lying in bed, eyes bleary and bloodshot, quite unable to move. The missing artificial limb was usually fastened just below the right hip and its absence therefore caused unusual inconvenience. We urged him to recollect what he could of the previous night's adventures, then separated into search parties. Eventually we discovered the member under the bed of a blonde, but we never did discover how Monty got home.

At twenty-two, when the world is still one's oyster and none of its pearls chancrous, a man is eager for knowledge and experience. The UP provided both. I covered intricate stock manipulations, unraveled by the

SEC. I discussed monetary transactions with solemn members of the FRB, managing to hide the glaze of boredom that dimmed the back of my eyes. I recounted the previsions of State Department experts who assured me Hitler would never move on Austria because he feared Mussolini. I wrote about tax peculations. A friend who headed the Bureau of Air Commerce allowed me to ride with him and pilot strange new planes. One had wings that folded up and we drove it along Constitution Avenue.

I flew through a hurricane to Norfolk in a Navy Fighter loaded with Red Cross medicines and, in that flooded city, watched the wind lift the corrugated roof from a house across the street, moving it twenty feet, then, minutes later, picking it up in gentle fingers to replace it, only slightly askew. I covered Roosevelt's press conferences and those of the laconic, courteous Secretary of State, Cordell Hull. When the President sought to pack his Supreme Court, I induced an august justice to break tradition and give me an unprecedented interview. But my big break came when the reporter covering Labor, ineffably bored with the subject, persuaded the office to let him write features instead. I was offered his assignment.

At that time, hard on the heels of NRA—the famous Blue Eagle, or National Labor Relations Act—trade unions took a massive leap forward and were busily organizing in the wreckage of a gravely shaken, backward social structure. John L. Lewis, head of the coal miners, had seceded from the traditionalist American Federation of Labor and created his Congress of Industrial Organizations. The CIO was then regarded as quite revolutionary. It rebelled at the AF of L system of forming unions by crafts and, instead, built massive horizontal syndicates including all workers engaged in any single industry or, for that matter, even on its peripheries.

Lewis, a man of imagination, intelligence and tremendous ruthlessness, was by far the outstanding labor figure of his time. He was a bulky, powerful, animalish man with pointed eyebrows, like the ears of a fox, leonine mane, and a soft, feline walk. His brain was swift but he liked to speak in long, ponderous sentences and was given to old-fashioned phrases and lengthy quotations from the Bible. He enjoyed jokes and had a sudden chuckle.

Lewis seized the opportunity offered by the New Deal and rode its wave to a position of unprecedented authority. He introduced fresh techniques, including the sit-down strike. He was a fine orator with a sonorous Welsh voice that I have heard equaled only by Aneurin Bevan on the wild Waunpound Heath in the country common to the two men's ancestors. Lewis was also a shrewd politician and gloriously ambitious. All this made him for me a man of peculiar fascination.

I came to know him well. I spent much time sitting around his United Mine Workers office, chatting with his henchmen, including a tough trio made up of his brother, Denny Lewis, and two toughs, Ora Gassaway and Ray Edmundson, who embellished my knowledge of craps. Frequently

John L. himself would call me in to chat. He told me about his past and about his future dreams. Despite his upsetting influence upon the national scene, he was at heart a conservative. He had once been offered the post of Secretary of Labor by the Republicans. He mistrusted Roosevelt and later broke with him. He enjoyed fighting, having once been a heavyweight contender and later acquiring middle-aged fame by knocking down the chief of the carpenters' union.

Lewis had a diabolical gift for mimicry, a cruel tongue and a limitless sense of opportunism, but he was also kind and surprisingly gentle. He adored his brilliant daughter Kathryn, an intellectual graduate of a snooty eastern college who, unhappily, was cursed with a gland affliction that made her enormously fat. This in turn produced a hidden bitterness. Once she helped her father devise a blueprint showing how the mine workers could theoretically seize the United States government by *coup d'état*.

Lewis organized one industry after another and called a succession of marvelously disciplined sit-down strikes. He was seen as a devil by most employers and many editors who charged him with inciting insurrection. All this provided excellent copy. My first big chance came when the CIO, clamping its fist around the automobile industry, called a sit-down at General Motors. The auto workers were then headed by Homer Martin, a former Baptist preacher who claimed fame as a hop-skip-and-jump champion. But Lewis was the man who ran the strike and conducted the negotiations that won it. And Lewis took me with him to Detroit.

The UP placed me in charge of its task force covering this event, which was producing banner headlines from coast to coast. This was my first major story and I worked twenty hours a day. Gassaway got me a hotel room down the corridor from John L. and each night, after lengthy talks with Michigan's Governor Frank Murphy, federal mediators and General Motors tycoons, Lewis would hold a press conference before retiring. I would then go to his room and he would not only tell me what had really happened but would act it out. He wore long woolen underwear in which he strode up and down, puffing a cigar, first imitating the motor company's suave Alfred Sloan and Knudsen, a burly Dane whom he would caricature: "But vy vait, pliss?" He would ruffle his hair and ape the accents of Murphy, then patently seeking high national office by means of a successful settlement. He would end his performance sitting on the edge of a chair, his great belly hanging out and straining the buttons of his union suit, with mincing gestures and high-pitched voice mimicking the frantic telephone calls from Frances Perkins, the unfortunate lady Secretary of Labor.

Knudsen and Sloan were friendly and helpful but they were helpless against Lewis's ruthless tactics, encouraged by White House tolerance. They respected enjoinments to secrecy imposed upon the negotiators. This alone was of immense aid to Lewis, who violated the code whenever he saw fit. And Murphy was the prisoner of his own ambition. Once I called upon him and he received me, worn out with fatigue, lying in bed. He talked about his personal future while his hands lay idly before him, one on an open atlas displaying a map of the Philippines, the other on a newspaper article attacking Roosevelt's court plan. He had already been Governor of the Philippines and would be nominated to the high tribunal.

The strike was conducted with panache and efficiency. In a plant at Flint, previously concerned with fabricating exterior furnishings of cars, the workers, guarded by their own pickets and state troopers, organized a special assembly line which produced leather-sewn blackjacks on each of which was attached the famous tag, "Body by Fisher." Later these achieved value as souvenirs.

After winning the General Motors battle and then at Chrysler, Lewis proceeded swiftly to magnify his power. He moved into steel, the key to America's economy in the thirties. The United States Steel Corporation was governed by one cardinal social principle: It would never recognize or deal with a union. Despite turmoil elsewhere, Big Steel remained adamantly loyal to this tenet that had, in the past, caused bitterness and bloodshed from Birmingham to the Great Lakes.

When US Steel was formed in 1901 as the nation's greatest trust, it adopted the following policy: "We are unalterably opposed to any extension of union labor and advise subsidiaries to take firm positions when these questions come up." Later, Jim Crawford, mayor of Duquesne, Pennsylvania (near Pittsburgh), admitted: "Jesus Christ himself could not speak in Duquesne for the AF of L." The infuriated workers used to call Crawford "Toad."

In 1936 Lewis took over the Amalgamated Association of Iron, Steel and Tin Workers from the battered AF of L and began an organizing campaign under Philip Murray, a genial Scotsman who was to become chief of the CIO. The steel industry announced it would "oppose any attempt to compel its employees to join a union or to pay tribute for the right to work." John L. cut out this notice and tacked it to his paneled office wall. That same autumn, in Washington, he met Myron Taylor, dignified chairman of US Steel, and the two subsequently began a series of highly confidential talks in Taylor's New York mansion. By the beginning of March, 1937, these meetings had led to the outlines of a collective bargaining agreement. Lewis telephoned from New York late one night and, to my astonishment, told me: "You can write that before sundown tomorrow the United States Steel Corporation will have announced a contract with the United Steel Workers of America."

In American sociological terms, this was as amazing as, less than three years afterward, the Hitler–Stalin Pact was to international affairs. And, since the negotiation had been clandestine, the editors of papers buying UP service were even more surprised when my sensational dispatch arrived in their offices next morning. I was sworn not to reveal my source so all I could do, entirely on my own authority, was to announce the apparently impossible and describe terms I said would be published that very day. Throughout the country, afternoon papers printed this news under big headlines. But there was no hint of confirmation and Lewis's own office would admit only that he was out of town. US Steel said nothing. Inquiries were telephoned to UP by worried publishers and, one by one, they began to play down the report or drop it from later editions. Shortly after sundown, however, when the last afternoon papers had been distributed, an unheralded press conference was called by Taylor. There, with Lewis beside him, he announced the contract. The UP flooded me with congratulations. I demanded a raise and was awarded $2.50 a week.

Whenever possible, Lewis followed a technique similar to that once taught by American Communists and called: "How to unseat a mounted policeman without hurting the horse." He won his battles and then proceeded to make friends with the employers he had defeated. John L. himself used to tell me: "I am not a Republican; I am not a Democrat; I am not a Fascist, a Communist or a Socialist. I am for labor and I will go with anyone who will work for me in this cause." Lewis was a significant phenomenon. By his ability to seize a favorable opportunity to lead a movement that was almost revolutionary in its speed and scope, he made a large mark on twentieth century American history. What he achieved no longer seems remarkable for we have become accustomed to more mature labor–capital relations, but in his day he was regarded as a kind of contemporary Danton or Bakunin.

It was also fun, if less inspiring, to cover the rival AF of L. The AF of L always chose comfortable sites for its conventions and executive council meetings. I attended one of the former in Denver where I used to dine regularly in a famous steak house with an intellectual unionist named John Frey. I was interested to find a labor boss who was a connoisseur of rye whisky and who introduced me, moreover, to Black Velvet, a drink concocted of champagne and stout. At that convention the reporters decided to enjoy their surroundings. Normally we were fiercely competitive and used, at moments of crisis, to assign underlings with piles of nickels to occupy and hold available all public telephones so that we could manage time scoops on our flashes. But Denver was too agreeable for strife.

One of our number, who has since become a member of Alcoholics Anonymous, failed to arrive in time for the opening session, so we took turns writing stories under his signature and filing them to his paper. After a three-day search we found him in a hotel room whose floor was covered with peanuts. Naked from the waist up, he was propped before a mirror, shaving. On the bed, cracking nuts, lay Denver's only policewoman.

By 1937 I had begun to look around for new fields. The UP sent me forms inquiring whether I wished to work abroad but I had foolish misconceptions of what this involved. I thought of foreign correspondents as distinguished, elderly gentlemen who spoke difficult tongues without accent, carried canes and hobnobbed with cynical statesmen. When I was asked to list my linguistic abilities I shyly registered none and was always bypassed in selections. I had, in fact, spoken some French and German since childhood, thanks to governesses and summers abroad, and later I was aghast to find how bad the average foreign correspondent is at languages.

The moment of decision was more or less forced upon me. It had become known that I was a friend of Lewis and since he was then very much in the world's eye a publisher asked me to write a book on him. I agreed but my bureau chief quite properly pointed out that the subject was contentious and the UP reserved the right to see and approve the manuscript before it appeared. I disliked this thought; therefore, on most cordial terms which have remained so through the years, I left the press agency.

It took me exactly ten days to write *Sit-Down with John L. Lewis,* perhaps the worst book ever printed. Nevertheless, it served a useful purpose in my life. I sold a section of it to *The Saturday Evening Post* for what seemed an incredibly large sum, obtained a passport, bade farewell to my family and departed for Europe. That was more than thirty years ago. I have never since lived in the United States.

I sailed for England on a little steamer, half freighter and half passenger vessel, that took ten days to cross the ocean, docking up the Thames in London. The trip was pleasant. The ship's doctor, as is often the case, was a most agreeable man who enjoyed playing poker. He organized a game which included myself, the male half of an American dancing team and an English jockey returning with the savings of a lifetime on Havana tracks. The doctor was accustomed to prescribing whisky for almost any known ailment and showed concern for our health. I won a great deal of money and, in fact, had to make a small present to the jockey to help him complete his journey.

# 2

---

# TALES FROM THE

# VIENNA MORGUE

LONDON WAS MY BASE UNTIL JUST BEFORE THE MUNICH AGREEMENT in October, 1938, when Britain and France paved the dreary road to their own decline. I became enormously fond of the English, a paradoxical people, more shy than arrogant, humorous, hospitable and immensely brave if too diffident to admit as much; and obstinate although they worship compromise. At that time the Germans officially decided the British were otiose and soft, thanks largely to Joachim von Ribbentrop's shallow observations as ambassador and subsequent foreign minister. One had only to join in their masochistic way of life to see what an idiot Ribbentrop was. When I opened my wardrobe in a well-known Jermyn Street hotel, a bathtub fell out on a hinge and smacked me on the head. The toilet in a huge castle where I spent the weekend was a plush-covered armchair that didn't flush. Central heating was internally administered and the cuisine startling. In Scotland I was introduced to haggis, a mixture of oatmeal and offal, which reminded me of the Frenchman who said: "At the first taste I thought it was ordure; at the second taste I wished it was."

At this time I held no regular job and accepted various writing assignments. An American magazine asked for an article on Ambassador Joseph P. Kennedy whom I had known in Washington when he served on the Securities and Exchange and Maritime Commissions. He greeted me warmly and placed his staff at my disposal, requesting only that I show him my piece in advance so he might correct factual errors.

Kennedy talked freely and most interestingly. He said: "I can't expect to live out the ordinary span of life because I've been living too hard. I know I'll die young. Therefore, after this job, I want to quit public life. I want to

establish my older sons firmly enough so they can look after the younger
children." Alas, Joe, junior, was killed during the war; Jack was assassinated after he became President; and Bob was murdered while campaigning for that office.

My inquiries indicated that nevertheless the ambassador had personal
ambitions and well-placed Washington friends wrote asserting these were
limitless. I noted in my diary: "Kennedy says he has received approaches
suggesting he run for the presidency. Claims he will not run because he
loves his family too much. His present job is bad enough for the children
without absolutely ruining them."

A very highly placed member of the government in Washington wrote
me—on the condition that I not mention his name—the following analysis:

> As for Joe Kennedy, you probably know all about him because of his
> gift for charming newspapermen into writing such reams as are usually
> reserved for occupants of the White House or the electric chair. So far,
> he has evinced no public aspiration for either. However, he has received
> a great number of letters from Americans announcing they will vote for
> him if he runs for the presidency in 1940. He has also been sounded out
> by certain political sources. He told a friend of mine he wouldn't dream
> of taking such a job because it would be too tough on his family. He told
> me:
> "I'm not a good candidate. I'm no good at going out and asking the
> public to vote for me. So far, I've managed to keep hold of my personal
> independence and I've never given the presidency a serious thought. I
> will go back to business when I finish here. The last time I went back to
> public office (as chairman of the maritime commission) I didn't go back
> for glory."
> Here is what a friend of his says, a fellow who knows him well and
> who, in addition, is an extremely influential person in Washington: "Joe
> is intensely interested in public affairs but equally interested in his own
> power, position and promotion. Generally speaking, he likes to do a
> spectacular job and move on as he did with the SEC and, less success-
> fully, with the maritime commission. I think he has had his eye on a
> Cabinet post in Commerce or, preferably, in the Treasury." [I showed
> this to Kennedy and he says "bunk."]
> "Neither seemed to be available when he was receptive. Then his
> mind turned to an ambassadorship. He probably sensed the possibility
> of war and increasing importance and popular interest in foreign devel-
> opments. The social prestige of the position probably weighed signifi-
> cantly with him." [Says Kennedy: "Social prestige never did matter,
> why now?"]
> "I think he did feel that the position would mean a great deal to his
> wife and children. Joe seldom plans to stay in any position long. But I
> don't know that he has set any time limit [on London]. That might
> depend upon his being asked to take up an equal or higher post here—
> his accomplishing something definite in his job abroad. From his early

experience as a speculator, Joe has learned that it is a good thing to get out as well as sell out when your stock is riding high. Joe has been written about as a possible candidate in 1940; Joe is too smart to get out on a limb. Yet he is smart enough to seize an opportunity if it comes his way. I am by no means trying to run him down. But I think one must make an emotional rather than an intellectual analysis of Joe. And a psychoanalysis of the greatest of men is likely to find explanation in the simplest emotional forces.'

Kennedy feels this analysis is unfounded, in many respects. "I never thought about an ambassadorship," he says, "and this offer came as a complete surprise. I was offered the Secretaryship of Commerce but I didn't want it. The only reason I went back to Washington was to tackle the dirty job of staring off the Maritime Commission and we feel that our report on the situation was a good start. When I'm through with this post, I'm through with public life. I've been working hard and I went to get my sons off right in the world."

Joe Kennedy is known as a loyal Roosevelt man and he is personally fond of the President. However, he criticizes some of the chief executive's left-wing advisors and certain policies, particularly in the realm of taxes. In England, he has occasionally ventured blunt remarks. He told a group of Oxford students that, if United States bonds went down another 10 per cent, every insurance company and bank in the country would go bust.

It is said that the President likes to rib Joe about his friendly rivalry with Bullitt. They tell this story about London: one day Kennedy supposedly rushed to the transatlantic telephone with a hot piece of news. "Joe, you're slipping," the President is alleged to have said. "Bill Bullitt told me that two days ago."

Kennedy was then highly popular in England and had not yet been attacked as an "appeaser," a label attached to him when war came and British intelligence tapped his reports to Washington. In 1938 his extrovert charm and gay family had captured public imagination.

The ambassador disliked parts of my article, above all reference to his own presidential ambitions, and warned me, when I refused to change it: "You know, the publisher of that magazine is a close friend of mine. I'll see to it your piece is never printed."

I stood by my statements and mailed the manuscript to the United States. Weeks later, when I was in Prague, the proofs were forwarded. The piece had been so altered it almost seemed as if the ambassador had written it himself and all reference to his political views or aspirations was gone. I cabled a protest and asked, at least, that my signature should be removed. It was too late.

In those days I saw much of John Strachey, the brilliant Harold Laski, and other British Socialists to whom I had been given introductions by American labor leaders. Strachey lived very plainly in the top half of a modest house near the London zoo. His study contained only a desk, table, two chairs, a bookcase and a bed without bedspread. Tall, dark, heavy, maculate, reputed then to be pro-Communist, although later he became minister of defense, he struck me as ill at ease. But he spoke with delicate lucidity and enjoyed discussing the American trade union movement, always concluding: "The CIO must win or all is lost in the USA."

Laski was a more ebullient, vatic talker with a rich mine of complaints. He suspected fascists everywhere. They were in the "officer class" of London's metropolitan police. They were serving as *agents provocateurs* in Admiralty workshops. In America they had begun to sprout: the late Huey Long, Mayor Hague of Jersey City, Governor Talmadge of Georgia, Father Coughlin in Michigan, Tom Girdler and Henry Ford in industry. A conversation would go about like this:

L: My friend, maybe there isn't yet a real Fascist Party in the States. But your ruling class will fight before it yields its privileged position.

FRIEND: That seems exaggerated. In England at any rate there's already Mosley and a Fascist gang. And there isn't really any danger, is there?

L: Mosley is intelligent in a way. But he's also a fool. And his following is ridiculous.

FRIEND: Well then?

L: The danger is in the government itself. That's where you find the gentlemanly kind of fascism. Fascists in incipient form.

A Harvard classmate had a house in Westminster, near Sir Oswald Mosley's headquarters, so I used to go around to listen and collect propaganda brochures. It was weird to hear for the first time the malefic nonsense that democracy was doomed, that decisions could only be taken by authority, that the English and the Germans were of the same blood stock and destined for a brotherly fate. With more conviction than logic I was advised, with the sequence of a metronome: "We're not anti-Semitic, only anti-Jewish. We believe in complete religious tolerance and we have no racial policy. But we are against Jews because they have attacked our movement."

An ex-dockworker named John Brown organized a splinter faction of this unhealthy movement and I often saw him: a confused, orotund but somehow sympathetic figure. Red-faced, sharp-featured and rather ratty, Brown wanted to return England to the old days of yeoman society. He claimed the Chamberlain government symbolized a "foreign policy of cowardice" but he admired fascism, above all the Italian form, and wanted to "revitalize" democracy. He, too, disliked the Jews but would assure me with a sad look: "There are some Englishmen and Greeks who are worse."

The organized English Fascists proved incompetent. I turned to Laski's bogeymen, the exponents of "gentlemanly" fascism. These were symbolized in the public mind by what was known as the Cliveden Set.

Cliveden, country seat of the Astors, was frequently the informal meeting place of English leaders who thought Hitler should be accommodated and prodded eastward against Russia. They were not evil but misguided; they scarcely represented what was best in the British character.

Lord Lothian, later ambassador to Washington and associated with this group, invited me for a weekend at his lovely Norfolk castle, Blickling, an immense and beautiful estate with private deer park, golf course, heath and woodlands in the center of which sat Blickling itself, a splendidly proportioned building containing a collection of Van Dycks, Holbeins and Gainsboroughs. I was met by a chauffeur who showed ineffable disdain when he discovered me stepping out of a third-class carriage and carrying a cardboard suitcase. Only his impeccable training permitted him to remove this gingerly from my hand. It was a large house party and included two well-known Cliveden figures, Lady Astor and Geoffrey Dawson, editor of the then obsequious *Times* of London. One guest, an elderly lady, spent her time in the garden studying Debrett's and Burke's *Peerage,* looking for unusual names. The finest belonged to a country parson called Tollemache-Tollemache-Plantagenet-Plantagenet. There was also an elderly general who ran through the rose bushes before breakfast, dressed in long underwear.

The first afternoon Lothian suggested golf. I nervously hooked my way among the roebuck nibbling in the rough. Lothian was an expert and managed to keep pace from bush to bush while assuring me in serious tones that I should not believe the rot I heard about the Cliveden Set. "There's no such thing," he said: a brilliant man, but not convincing. He spoke admiringly of the Nazi youth movement and confided: "Really, the young German male specimen is exceptional. I wish we had a similar movement for a fitter Britain."

A few days later Lady Astor invited me to lunch with Dawson and Sir Samuel Hoare, whose name doesn't glow in history. I noted: "Lady Astor swats people on the behind to get them moving and refers to her husband as Jakie. Hoare is quiet and handsome while Dawson is short, heavy, smug, conceited, snobbish and pompous. I must say both Dawson and Hoare give the impression of being bored admirers of the Germans."

My inquiries proved nothing except that some Englishmen of considerable importance were prepared to tolerate Nazi horrors and the danger Germany represented to Europe in the hopes that Hitler would eventually turn his greed to Russia, leaving the tight little island alone. By this time I had heard so much about fascism without myself experiencing its ghastliness that I decided to inspect its morbid laboratory. I chose Austria.

For this purpose I needed more regular attachments than a free-lance status. North American Newspaper Alliance gave me credentials, agreeing to accept articles, and Lord Beaverbrook's *London Evening Standard* hired me as a piece-rate correspondent with the additional guarantee to pay well for special features in a space I shared with Dean Inge, a clergyman known as the Gloomy Dean. I got visas and tickets to Vienna and Prague. Then I called on Jan Masaryk, son of the first Czech President, envoy in London and future foreign minister. Half-American, Masaryk was large and hearty, with bluff manner and a fondness for slang. Under a mask of swingeing toughness he was sensitive, highly cultivated, loyal and a noble patriot. He was also a good friend with a special gift for hospitality, preferring to cook complicated dishes himself while he entertained chosen companions. I became devoted to him over the years, in London, Moscow, Prague and Paris, both in defeat and victory. He always gave me wise counsel. This fine man was the victim of a Communist *coup d'état* in 1948. The official story was that he jumped to death from his apartment in the Czernin Palace when visited by secret police. I have reason to believe it was not suicide.

Before me, while writing, is a report made by SDECE, then a branch of the French Secret Service, classified as TRÉS SECRET and marked for reference purposes A/11.0/21.1/4903/526.454/25.2.7. This claims a certain Dr. Teply was summoned to the Czernin before dawn on March 10, 1949, where he was met by agents of two Czech police, the STB and SNB. In the courtyard, under a blanket, lay the body of Masaryk dressed in pyjamas with different colored top and bottom. The corpse showed bruises, scratches and other signs of violence.

Dr. Teply found the wound of a 7.65 caliber bullet in the back of Masaryk's neck, ringed by powder burns indicating the shot had been fired from immediate range. He also noticed heel injuries that looked as if they had come from hammer blows. The hands were marked as though by a vigorous fight. The body was carried upstairs to Masaryk's flat where Teply was joined by two Communist ministers, Nosek and Clementis. The doctor found the apartment in total disarray, bottles broken and furniture overturned. Nosek smoothed the covers and Jan's body was laid on the bed. The window ledge bore traces of human excrement. Teply observed that this indicated the man had already been dead or dying when he crossed the sill. However, Nosek announced: "This is suicide." Looking at Teply, he warned: "You haven't seen or heard a thing." A few months later Dr. Teply died. It was stated he had given himself a wrong injection.

How strange to recapture lively, gnomic conversations with Masaryk in the London of 1938, when Czechoslovakia's mortal illness was beginning; and then to think of his fiendish end in the wake of what seemed victory. Jan warned me in his legation that Hitler already coveted Czechoslovakia and was looking further eastward. He urged Lord Halifax, British foreign secretary, to invest 100,000,000 pounds in Eastern Europe to keep it out of the Nazis' economic orbit. He added: "Chamberlain thought Czechoslovakia was a contagious disease only a few weeks ago. The English have been muddling through. That isn't enough; it's time they learned." Although Rumania was a Czech ally in the Little Entente, King Carol had complained to Masaryk: "I can't let the Bolsheviks march through my country." "Do you think they're going to ask?" was Masaryk's reply. It was a march through Rumania to Prague that prepared the way for his own eventual death.

Masaryk said to me something very prescient for early 1938:

There is always the possibility of a rapprochement between Germany and Russia. That's why Marshal Tukhachevsky was shot. He was trying to get along with the German General Staff. We always say, why leave Russia out of the game? If both Germany and Russia are isolated, they are bound to get together. If a banana seller can't sell his bananas at one end of the street, he goes to the other end, doesn't he? Hitler is crazy and you can't trust him. Ribbentrop is a stupid boor with illusions. He is nothing but a wine salesman who thinks he is a duke. He doesn't realize he is an accident, like myself [Jan's favorite apology for success—which he modestly attributed to the fact that he was the first Czech President's son].

As for Henlein, the boss of our Sudeten Nazis? He's a nice, small fellow, stupid and fond of publicity. I told him: "Henlein, now you are like Greta Garbo. But if you ever become a gauleiter you'll be just like the woman who cleans out a hotel shithouse!"

Jan gave me letters, including one to President Beneš, and I took off for Vienna. That city had already been reduced to provincial status as capital of Nazi Germany's Ostmark. In an overheated third-class car, filled with torpid farmers, redolent of dung and wearing green homespun with swastikas in their lapels, I was assured by my companions that freedom was a luxury the world could ill afford. This platitude was already fecund.

In Vienna I lodged at a hotel on Singerstrasse whose manager greeted me with "Heil Hitler" and the ridiculous salute the Nazis imagined was Roman. Posters bore the Führer's picture and libraries were filled with works by him or extolling him. Most stores displayed signs saying "Aryan shop," or "This Jew is already in Dachau," or "This Jew ought to be in Dachau." I went to St. Stephen's cathedral and saw a uniformed man grab a young woman from the steps and march her along, followed by a jeering crowd. Inside many people silently prayed. Later on I discovered this was commonplace and that some worshippers were devout Catholics who had been officially classified as Jewish under the Nuremberg Laws

The atmosphere of this famous, ancient city combined the less pleasant features of menagerie and charnel house. I have since heard much about the charm and *gemütlichkeit* of Austrians and, indeed, often encountered it. But in those days it was absent. I felt enraged as a Jew and disgusted as a human. The capital seemed mesmerized by the mad theorems, silly features and basilisk eye of Hitler.

John Wiley, United States consul general, did a magnificent job although

his hands were tied by American red tape and his charity was blocked by
Nazi tergiversations. A courageous, warm-hearted man, he drafted a niece
and her girl friend to help his overworked staff, which included a future
ambassador, Freddy Reinhardt. They sought to send words of encouragement to the long lines always waiting outside in the vain hope of acquiring
American visas.

Wiley's agents had pieced together a vivid picture of the terror. Boxcars
taking anti-Nazis from Vienna to Munich and the Dachau concentration
camp were coming back stained with blood and clotted with chunks of flesh
and hair. Jews who couldn't find the means to emigrate were told: "Well,
there's always the Danube." That filthy river was charged with corpses.

An Englishman I knew was arrested and briefly held because his office
boy, a Peeping Tom, had discovered in the urinal that the boss was circum-
cized. One evening in a movie the lights flashed on and I was puzzled to see
a Brownshirt rise and announce: "It stinks here." Policemen checked everyone's papers, looking for non-Aryans.

In the agony of this lowering and denigrating atmosphere, I still had gay
moments for a reason of singular cruelty: Vienna contained many attractive women who knew they were ultimately doomed. Some of these poor
creatures attached themselves to any American and often proposed marriage. They suffered the sad illusion that a wedding certificate automatically
entailed a United States passport. Others, wiser or deprived of hope,
merely wished to be carefree while awaiting the Brown Death. I met a
young baroness with one Jewish grandfather who had been halted on the
road to Budapest where she was to meet her husband. She had not heard
from him since and concluded: "He's either a coward or a fool." She was
feverishly spending her fortune on such frivolities as hats and always insisted on paying when we went out together. "I want to leave nothing
behind." she would say. "I shall live vividly. And then I shall die."

I visited a soup kitchen where 12,000 terrified Jews were fed each day
by the Israelite community while blackshirted SS guards mocked and kept
the queues in military order. Many of these people were farmers from the
Burgenland over whose villages the Nazis had hung black flags and posted
placards: "Jews enter here at risk of life."

Of the people I then knew perhaps the strangest was an American reporter named Robert Best, a tragic eccentric who turned traitor. After the
war he was captured and sentenced to federal prison. He died there in
1952. But when I knew him he was helpful, ingenious and brave. Best was
a familiar sight in Vienna. Each night he sat at the same café wearing a
broad-brimmed hat. He drank heavily and was rumored to take drugs.
When talking, he had a weird habit of rolling his eyes entirely up so that
the pupils vanished in his head and only the whites remained. His two
closest associates were a secretary and a mistress. The secretary, once tried
for murdering her husband, had used her pretty legs to advantage in court

and was acquitted by a sentimental jury. She later wrote her memoirs and became a journalist. The mistress was an Austrian aristocrat who probably introduced Best to dope. He loved her and decided not to return to the United States in the exchange of civilians after Pearl Harbor, becoming instead a Nazi propagandist.

All I can say is I liked Best and heard various tales of how he had helped acquaintances to elude the Nazis. We often spent evenings together, starting late in the Café de l'Europe and ending with bean soup in the Augustinerkeller. My German was then quite passable and Best's was perfect. We would sometimes sit at long wooden tables in beer cellars waiting until the Brownshirts and Blackshirts clattered around hanging their hats, coats, dirks and belts on coat racks, then slipping in beside us. Best would start up a conversation with the German Nazis. Pretty soon, as they slurped beer, he would have them admitting it was hard to watch their efficient orderliness fouled up by the sloppy Austrians. Meanwhile I would prompt the Austrian Nazis to confess resentment at the Prussians who sought to lord it over them. In this way we managed to promote excellent rows.

Best helped me arrange the most distrained experience of my life. He found a corrupt official who handed on a bribe to the caretaker of the Jewish section in the city morgue so that I could be left alone there checking records. After dinner one night I took a street car to the Zentral Friedhof where, inside the gate, I was met by a small man in black coat and hat. He had two days growth of beard and his breath stank of onions. He accepted an envelope containing money, led me through a building to a long room and nervously shut the door. I can still hear the sound of that clicking lock. Despite my experience with Pittsburgh corpses, I was terrified.

Having been warned against lights, I took a torch from my pocket and looked around. On a large desk I found two ledgers in which were handwritten entries listing the name, date and cause of death for each of the morgue's customers. Beyond, through an arch, was an oblong chamber where I could see the outline of many tables bearing flat objects covered with sheets. I checked five of these bodies by the numbers pinned to their coverings and compared my observations with the ledger listings. All five were recorded as suicides and, in the case of three, it was difficult to judge if this diagnosis was, in fact, exact. On pulling back the sheets, it was obvious that the other two, at any rate, had been beaten to death. I have never known a man to kill himself by punching out his own eyes.

My torch disclosed shelves on three walls like those in a library. These contained rows of black pots resembling the noses of artillery shells except that the points were cut off flat so they could stand on end. They were remarkably light and seemed made of plastic. I examined several. Into the tin lids were stamped names and dates as, for example:

No. 1732. Städt Bestattungsamt München. Frank, Fritz. Hochschüler. *5.7.11 Wien 14.1.38 Dachau. F.B. 4.6.1938

This, being interpreted, meant that student Fritz Frank, born in Vienna July 5, 1911, had died twenty-seven years later at Dachau and was given a state burial, which meant cremation. With a faint, rustling sound, I put back the urn containing his ashes and was struck by how little a man's body weighed when the problem was scientifically reduced.

In this shriekingly silent atmosphere, I remained several hours, keeping as busy as possible in order not to yield to jangling nerves. I remembered Ambrose Bierce's story of a similar vigil, a corpse that moved, and a survivor who fled with sudden, snow-white hair. Before dawn there was a prearranged scratch on the door. The little man let me out, escorting me to the gate. I asked him about the urn collection: they were unclaimed bodies. Presumably all relatives were already dead.

Through the translucent night, I walked home. The city was strangely silent in the absence of those boot tramps that seem to give the Teuton special pleasure. Nevertheless, the smell of fear—a strange, intangible smell—pervaded everything. A needle-sharp cloud slid across the gibbous moon. That day I left by train for Prague, hiding papers and notebooks under my shirt and belt in case of prying customs guards. However, they proved jovial and incurious.

It was my intention to write a sensational series of articles but I was not aware that I had suffered a traumatic experience from which it would take weeks to recover. There is something solid, like a dumpling, about a Czechoslovakian hotel and yet, whenever I sat down to my typewriter, secure in the illusion of sanity and comfort, my mind blanked and I began to retch. I tried long walks as a remedy but this didn't work and I broke out in a tremendous rash. What technical name psychologists give to this condition I do not know but I was unable to master it and finally chucked the project, writing nothing. This was neither courageous nor helpful to those I wished to aid by describing the Nazi brutishness. However, I shed it, all of it, and rode off to Carlsbad with a Czech major, focusing my attention on the lovely grain and hop fields of Sudetenland and the new troubles they obscured.

Until that season, Carlsbad had been a fashionable vacation spot for the rich. Henlein's Nazi movement and rumbles from Germany had frightened away the normal custom. The only other clients in my hotel were an unfortunate dime-store heiress and her train. Carlsbad was already developing a familiar swastika look, thanks to Henlein's agitations, and I could scarcely have imagined the next time I was to see the town, eighteen years later, it would be filled with privileged, fat Russians, obediently lurching and belching their way round and round the medicated springs.

Back in Prague, filling up with foreign correspondents flapping their portables like vultures, Hugh Baillie, head of UP, offered to rehire me for more than twice the salary he had paid me in Washington. I preferred to keep my free-lance status unless war came, so we drew up a contingency agreement on that basis. In Vienna I had seen a city already swamped by misery; Prague was different. Intellectually, one knew disaster was inevitable unless the Czechs had the courage to face it all alone, because neither Britain nor France would help. Alas, this was not in their character. A patient, stubborn, stolid people, their great hero was that literary delight, the Good Soldier Schweik, who had muddled up the Austrian Army in World War I but who never dreamed of anything more audacious than good-humored passive resistance.

Prague is one of Europe's loveliest towns, with graceful bridges, baroque buildings and delicate alleys. I spent sunny afternoons in the wooded outskirts and evenings in riverside clubs and restaurants. The night spots were filled with pretty girls who had fled the Viennese ossuary or been frightened out of Budapest. I was accepted in a circle centered about Rudolf Thomas, editor of the capital's German-language paper and a violent anti-Nazi. He and his wife were great friends but had separate emotional lives. Her lover had just died and Thomas possessed a beautiful young Swedish mistress named Ingrid whose closest chum was a red-haired Viennese actress who became a special friend of mine. Frau Thomas treated Ingrid and V. as daughters and we all used to sit around drinking plum brandy in tiny crystal glasses and listening while liberal authors, philosophers and politicians glumly forecast the disaster that eventually clattered down. After the Munich sellout, Thomas and his wife shot themselves. Ingrid fled to Stockholm. I was told later that she, too, committed suicide. With luck I was able to get V. out of the country, via Poland, and she went to the United States where she became a moderately successful actress.

One bright summer afternoon I walked across the ornamented bridge above the placid, gleaming Vltava, filled with paddle boats, to the Hradčany Palace where Beneš made his office and paid a farewell call upon the president. Edvard Beneš was a simple, decent, thoughtful, upright man who, thanks to Masaryk's introduction, had been kind enough to receive me several times despite the onerous pressures of that moribund season. Had he been truly supported by his allies, instead of callously doublecrossed, he might have been a doughty leader. Unfortunately, he was betrayed; and he lacked that flare, that nexus with invincible foolhardiness which marks the difference between national hero and unhappy symbol of defeat. Had Beneš, for example, been reckless Serb instead of prudent Czech, had he pushed the disaster button with his own pudgy finger, disregarding his reluctant allies, history might have taken a different swerve.

Beneš was a pink-faced, earnest little soccer player, fit, light-footed, humorless, with chilly blue eyes. He had already once before endured the excruciating trial of listening to foreign counselors in World War I when he was diplomatic secretary to Thomas Masaryk, head of the exiled Czechoslovakian movement and eventually his country's first President. From this hard period he had learned calm optimism, resolve, a mildly serious manner of speaking and perhaps too great a respect for size in the scale of international power. He could never have been a Tito.

I told Beneš I was planning to return to London and asked what he intended to do, now that Hitler had made it plain he would move into the Sudetenland, come what may, and Britain and France were confining themselves to weary words of advice. For an instant the President regarded me in silence, a slight wrinkle on his brow. Then he rose to his diminutive height, walked to the right of his great desk, seized a pointer and, like a schoolteacher in a geography lesson, rolled down an enormous map of Central Europe. "Here," he said, "here" and "here," designating Czech and German cities.

"If Hitler bombs Prague," he said with cold precision, "I shall bomb Berlin. If Hitler bombs Pilsen, I shall bomb Nuremberg. If he bombs Bratislava, I shall bomb Vienna. We have an air force too and it is good." He then proceeded to recite military figures: the production of Skoda and other munitions factories; statistics on the serving army and reserve divisions; strategy and tactics. He claimed the fortifications facing Germany were impregnable, despite fifth column activities in Sudetenland, and that defense positions opposite Nazi Austria were rapidly assuming shape.

"We, too, have our own Maginot Line," he said, "and I remain confident in my allies. France is my ally and France has Europe's strongest army. England has an air force that must frighten Hitler. I am confident in my allies. But if by any chance they fail to move, I shall force the game. Do not mistake me. That means world war. France is our partner and France will come to our aid—whatever the English say or do. France knows its responsibilities and obligations. You know, we have entirely too many Sudeten Germans in our country, thanks only to French insistence at the Versailles Conference. However, the French are with us. We have this in common: we are democracies and we hate the Nazis. But even if they weren't, we are prepared to fight. We could hold off Hitler many weeks while the West makes up its mind. I repeat: I shall force the game."

What a vainglorious boast. His spirit and resolution were in the end eroded by a crumby French government, headed by Daladier and Bonnet, and its British friend, Chamberlain, supported by the Cliveden Set. When the crunch came, Beneš only whimpered and Czechoslovakia sagged while the world washed its hands in dismay. Nevertheless, after his inspiriting lecture, which impressed me greatly, I asked Beneš for some personal advice.

"Supposing war does come," I inquired, "what would you suggest I do? You were once a journalist. I am twenty-five years old, without a reputation, and there are famous correspondents everywhere. Jan Masaryk told me to ask your counsel. What is it?"

"Go to the Balkans, Cyrus," Beneš said. "There is nobody in the Balkans. That will be the most interesting place. The other side of the Axis—the West knows little about it."

In September I returned to England to make arrangements with UP as war correspondent if the blowup came. They agreed to pay me $75 a week from the moment of outbreak until two weeks after an armistice. Fog-bound London was digging pitiful trenches in its parks, stumbling towards destiny and displaying neither the vigor nor intensity that carried it out of disaster's pit when trouble came. September 16 Churchill, alas not yet in power, warned his sluggish countrymen: "England has been offered a choice between war and shame. She has chosen shame and will get war."

I crossed to Paris on the ferry-train, sharing a compartment with a Greek deputy who smelled of garlic. The porter whispered to me: "Them South Americans don't never open the windows. You'll need a gas mask in there." Gas masks were much on the public mind. A slight mist hung over Dover and searchlight fingers moved gently inside it. The Channel was quiet and greasy as if awaiting its first consignment of dead.

Psychologically, at that moment, the French seemed encouragingly different. At the end of September, 1938, Paris brimmed with strutting Gallic self-confidence even if this didn't reach the seat of government. Stocky *poilus,* chickens slung about their necks on strings and wine bottles protruding from their pockets, were kissing their girls goodbye. In an earthy way they seemed invincible. How odd to recollect that within one year all this electricity ran out of France and crossed over into England. When Daladier bought time by sacrificing his Czech allies, he spiritually castrated the French. But the English, when they saw their folly, were strangely transmogrified from a nation of sleepwalkers into their more accustomed role of buccaneers.

I entrained for Basel, sitting up all night chatting with young Germans called home to their regiments. It was not easy to find space. Thousands of tourists, refugees or neutrals were scrambling about while governments seized much of the normal rolling stock to move their troops. In Basel I got a third-class seat in a wooden carriage destined for Zagreb, Belgrade and the Balkans. Eight of us squeezed into the compartment. Two were Croatian nuns returning to their convent, apple-cheeked ladies with peasant figures not wholly disguised by their ample robes. Each had huge wicker-work suitcases which provoked eager curiosity every time we crossed a frontier. At that tense moment the customs was rigid and both inspectors and fellow passengers peered carefully into the sisters' private belongings. Nobody knew just what nuns wore beneath their habits and there was unabashed interest in finding out.

We finally reached a hamlet called Mallnitz, in German-occupied Aus-

tria, where our train was shunted to a siding to make way for troop transfers. We sat glumly looking at loads of gray-clad Nazi soldiers rumbling
past. A modest station buffet offered sausages, black bread and beer. Unfortunately, after I had bought my ticket in Basel, I had only one $10 bill
left and it was not my intention to spend it before I got to Belgrade. This
halt in Mallnitz posed an unexpected problem: how long would we stay
there and how long could I go without eating? I was determined not to
change my bill for worthless German marks.

The first night one of the nuns removed her wimple, produced a small,
handkerchief-sized pillow, leaned upon it and promptly went to sleep. Everybody else took off their shoes. It was raining outside and cold. A tobacco merchant in one corner, jut-jawed, low-browed and grizzled, kept
muttering in a mixture of Serbian and German: "It's a swindle. Everything
is a swindle." He insisted we would be interned for the duration. At meal-
times my companions would leave the train. To stop thinking about their
healthy appetites I moved into an empty second-class compartment and
began to typewrite. The conductor complained this was against the rules
but I reminded him the railway was also breaking its contract by keeping
me in Mallnitz. At the end of the first day there was a timid knock on the
door and the two nuns peered in, head-by-head, asking if I wasn't hungry. I
assured them I was on a diet. Next day, at lunchtime, there was another
timid tap. The door slid open and in they came, smiling like healthy
angels, bearing a tray loaded with bread, sausages and beer. I thanked
them and promised to send a contribution to their convent after I got to
Belgrade—which I did.

After two days the station master announced through cupped hands that
Hitler, Mussolini, Chamberlain and Daladier had met in Munich and
agreed to keep the peace. After some hours the train was pushed back on
the main line and we chugged off to the Balkans, passing a sign at Villach:
"The most southern city of the German Reich greets the Führer."

In Jugoslav mountain villages crowds were demonstrating, waving flags,
patriotic emblems and hand-printed posters damning Hitler. They sang in
clear, mellifluous voices. Some of them wept. I had a feeling of freshness,
vigor and intensity. In the Slovenian capital of Ljubljana, a farewell party
was bidding Godspeed to a tipsy, blond Czech. I noted:

His friends carry him to the train on their shoulders, all singing sponta-
neously and beautifully. Meanwhile another man stands and watches the
small woman with him lift an enormous, heavy suitcase over her head to
the compartment window. The engines keep chuffing. Raw-boned soldiers, wearing squat, boat-shaped caps, stand silently while crowds of
young Slovenes interrupt their songs with occasional cheers for Czechoslovakia, Beneš and democracy. Finally the drunken Czech kisses all his
friends goodbye, male and female, and climbs aboard, wearing a corsage
of wild flowers which he scatters to the sobbing, shouting group
below.

# 3

## WHERE ANYTHING

## COULD HAPPEN

## AND GENERALLY DID

ND NOW, LIKE SOME DELIGHTED OLD TURK WITH HIS HUBBLE-
bubble pipe, reclining on a divan with sweet memories, I shall
relax and reminisce about the Balkans. For that was a fine time
and a fine place to be. The Balkans, which in Turkish means "mountains,"
run roughly from the Danube to the Dardanelles, from Istria to Istanbul
and is a term for the little lands of Hungary, Rumania, Jugoslavia, Albania,
Bulgaria, Greece and part of Turkey, although neither Hungarian nor
Greek welcomes inclusion in the label. It is, or was, a gay peninsula filled
with sprightly people who ate peppered foods, drank strong liquors, wore
flamboyant clothes, loved and murdered easily and had a spendid talent for
starting wars. Less imaginative westerners looked down on them with secret
envy, sniffing at their royalty, scoffing at their pretensions, and fearing their
savage terrorists. Karl Marx called them "ethnic trash." I, as a footloose
youngster in my twenties, adored them.

In my day I came to know their kings and Communists; to argue with
their priests and politicians; to love their princesses and their dancing girls.
I learned to speak three of their languages, badly but fluently, accompanied
four of their armies, was expelled from two countries and fled two others
before advancing Nazi hordes. In the Balkans I was bombed, bullied,
coddled, arrested and enticed. Once I took a letter from one group of
revolutionists to another, suggesting a joint uprising in Bulgaria and Jugoslavia. Another time I bore a message from a Communist to a king, calling
for alliance. In the Balkans I left part of my soul and found my wife.

I traveled bold peaks and furtive valleys, where the god Pan once ran wild and bearded priests later led regiments in battle—going by train, foot, airplane, boat, car and horseback. On an Albanian autobus I sat wedged on a bench between a goat and a man with a blunderbuss. I was approached by spies, plotters and dictators, was cajoled by poetesses, listened to ancient songs played on one-string fiddles by blind bards, learned to dance the czardas and the kolo, became addicted to varnish-tasting wine, saw big men falter, little men rise, and made friends and enemies who have endured through life. I met slippered Serbs, fierce Magyars, hawk-featured Ghegs, sullen Tosks, Szeklers, Kutzo-Vlachs and gypsies.

Most of the gypsies, alas, now are gone, burned in Hitler's ovens as inferior stock. Ah, how they featured in the Balkans of my time: clever enough to nail horseshoes to a flea, sleep with open eyes, sell you the air; filled with wild music their menfolk played on accordions and violins and their dark-haired women sang as their graceful hands beat tambourines. There were gypsy tribes all over, leading special, feckless lives. In Jugoslavia it was still their custom for the father to buy his son a bride, testing her value by sleeping with her first, while a crone sang to the waiting groom: "Oh, my girl, stupid little one! Oh, that you may be crazy after me! Oh, just a little lamb after his mother! Hey Johnny, listen daddy. Just see what happened to her this morning."

A few years before my arrival the United States was represented by a language professor as its minister in Belgrade and on one St. George's Day, the gypsy fete, he saw a gathering of the tribes in the marketplace near his legation. He stopped off to chat and they were much impressed that America had sent "a gypsy" as envoy to Jugoslavia. Flattered, he invited their three principal kings for coffee and discovered, only after they had left, that two of his most valued rugs were missing.

In the Homolje region of East Jugoslavia lived a people called the Dubokans. The Dubokans celebrated Whitsun with a demonic dance from which, one by one, the womenfolk fell out unconscious, screaming: "Great Lord, do not burn me, do not roast me." Their men then bore them to a nearby stream where, through crossed knives, they spat wormwood and garlic water on their faces. Peasants in parts of Serbia named their sixth child Vuk, which means wolf, because witches were reputed to eat the sixth-born and feared wolves. Mourning women were represented by the cuckoo, which had lost its only brother and constantly lamented him. In remote areas custom required mothers to bear their babies on the hard ground, with fairies as their godmothers and beech leaves as their blankets.

In Macedonia women wore bulky sashes because, in the past, Turkish commanders had instructed their soldiers not to rape the pregnant. In arcane Dubrovnik, its belly full as of wine, few old families were left because, when as Ragusa, long an Adriatic republic proud as Venice (which gave its name to a fine sailing ship, the Argosy) it fell to the Austrians, the nobles made a pact to have no more children until their city should regain its freedom. Nearby at Ulcinj, on the Albanian border, was a colony of Negroes, descended from escaped Turkish slaves. One, named Musta, was recaptured by a corsair but fled again to freedom and in Ulcinj his relatives celebrated by cooking three cauldrons of halva, an oriental sweet. Musta died in 1900 at the age of 124. A mulatto descendant was a captain in the Jugoslav Royal Guard whom I used to see each late afternoon, strolling along the main street, dangling his sword and ogling the girls.

Many of the Royal Guard, tall men who wore pastel uniforms with short, fur-trimmed jackets and boots, came from Montenegro, a tiny land tenanted by giants. Their last king, Nikola, was called *gospodar,* or boss, by his subjects. In World War I, when Montenegro was still independent, it fought the Austrians and its soldiers boasted: "We and the Russians are invincible; together we are 150,000,000 strong."

In Slovenia a colony of Germans at Gottschee, speaking a medieval dialect, opposed Jugoslavia's French alliance and would have nothing to do with anything French because, in Napoleon's time, they had been plundered by his *cuirassiers*. In Macedonian Ochrid stood a tower from which Czar Samuel, a Bulgar, had leapt when his army returned from Constantinople, chained together as prisoners, one eye in each hundredth head, the others totally blinded. The tower had been built to stand firm by walling a live maiden in its masonry as a sacrificial deodand.

In Bosnia they still regretted the last king, Stjepan Tomasević, executed in 1463 by a Turkish commander who captured him two times by the same ruse and sneered: "Only a fool gets bitten twice by a snake from the same hole." And in Zagreb, capital of Croatia, there was a stone where Matija Gubec, leader of a peasant revolt, had been seated on a red-hot throne by the Hungarians. One church dignitary who attended went mad, screaming as Gubec died: "Blood, blood, blood."

The Jugo, or South, Slavs are vain (indeed megalomaniac) poets, brave, sly, generous, vital, intensely proud of their long and sanguinary roll of battles, most of which they lost. Theirs was a country of violence and long memories.

When I reached this vibrant nation immediately after Munich, it was ruled by a regent, uncle of the boy-king whose father had been murdered and whose grandfather, a scholar who translated John Stuart Mill's *On Liberty*, succeeded to the throne only after his adherents had chopped up the previous tenant and cast his body on a dung heap. The prime minister was an over-confident dictator named Milan Stojadinović, large, bland, mustachioed, then trying unsuccessfully to form his own fascist party, green shirts, salute and all. He called himself *vodža,* or leader, until, to his astonishment, he was removed by Prince Paul.

I had been recommended to a modest hotel where I obtained a room for $1 a day, and everything smelled of strong sausage. Covered with flea bites,

I started to wander about Belgrade, an ugly city with which I fell in love. Belgrade is situated on a height where the Danube and Sava rivers meet and dominated by a medieval Turkish fortress called Kalemegdan. This contained a museum with old weapons and a blood-stained uniform of the last assassinated king.

The capital was a delightful peasant town. It smelled of fog, sweat and meat. Hundreds of wagons rattled through, drawn by horses adorned with jingling bells. In the early morning droves of oxen shuffled by. There was a constant squeak from the few automobiles, each of which carried two horns, one to scare people and animals and the other, a hand bulb, to be sounded once, twice or three times depending on which direction the driver intended to pursue. Country farmers, wearing slippers upturned at the toes, boat-shaped hats and homespun pants and jackets, greaved and gallooned with thick, gaily-knitted woolen socks, strode silently along followed by their obedient womenfolk bearing bundles.

In the evenings I dined with friends at simple restaurants called *kafanas,* eating skewered mutton or spiced, skinless sausages and onions, and sweet oriental pastries, drinking enormous quantities of red wine, and *šlivovica,* a colorless plum brandy. There was a pellucid white wine, made forty miles away at Smederovo, which we used to consume there, under the walls of an old Danubian castle, because it lost its savor if brought even the short distance to Belgrade.

In the *kafanas* febrile orchestras played and gypsy girls danced and sang wailing songs. As a token of appreciation it was the custom to stand up and hurl your glass at the wall. Each *kafana* had one or two employes whose only job was sweeping up the rain of glass. Wine was cheap. The ordinary bill amounted to more for glassware than its contents. On some evenings I saw thirsty students with no more money pass around eau de cologne.

In the Triglav, a dingy place with a renowned, lambent fiddler, I often sat with a group of youngsters discussing their plans for raising insurrection. They showed me pictures of themselves doing secret military training in the wooded countryside. One of them, Slobodan Princip, was the nephew of Gavrilo Princip who slew Archduke Franz Ferdinand in 1914 and started World War I. All subsequently became high officers in Tito's Partisan army.

I soon found that Beneš had been absolutely right; there were no American journalists in Belgrade; there was plenty of news; and everyone was helpful about passing it on. Within a few days I had replenished my pocketbook with funds from the *London Evening Standard.* As the only American reporter, I was, furthermore, well received by the small United States legation headed by an experienced minister, Arthur Bliss Lane. His principal assistant was a charming young man named Robert Joyce with a scintillating, ebullient, beautiful wife. We used to golf together on the nine-hole course outside Belgrade which had been opened by the Prince Regent, who drove the first ball while wearing a black bowler hat.

One day, when Mrs. Lane and Peggy, their daughter, were away, I invited the minister and the Joyces to dine. I had thought carefully about which of my customary haunts might be most suitable and finally made reservations in a grill where a small boy squatted in the window turning spits. The proprietor bowed, escorted us to our table and produced some splendid red wine and what was proudly known as "Serbian caviar," a concoction of eggplant and red pepper. Then, beaming with pleasure, he served a roasted little pig. Lane was presented with the choicest piece, the hind end, which sat squarely on his plate, curled tail protruding upwards. The minister turned a saffron color. He made unconvincing efforts to move his knife and fork around. Finally he explained he was suffering from a digestive disorder and had had a sudden seizure. He asked if we would mind returning with him to the legation. There, the minister seemed to think the best medicine was brandy, in copious amounts.

Belgrade was filled with Albanians, tall, lithe men in leggings and white skull caps. They came each autumn to chop wood and, when they had saved enough money, went back to their southern villages to buy wives. It required four years chopping to get a good mate. The Albanians always looked for especially healthy women because, if one wife died, it meant working four more years to buy another.

I spent afternoons sitting on a bench in the Kalemegdan Park studying Serbian and eating large purple grapes. The proverbs delighted me: "Fight like a devil for your freedom; then live in it like a saint." "Be humble, for the worst thing in the world is of the same stuff as yourself. Be confident, for the stars are of the same stuff as yourself." I found few Serbs who lived like saints and none who were humble. I read about witches. In Montenegro, squamous hags flew off on broomsticks for meetings on copper threshing floors, anointing themselves under the armpits with toad gravy and mare's milk butter, saying: "Let me catch neither thorn nor bow but go straight to trouble-stirring threshing floor."

In the evenings, there was always an agreeable clatter of horse and oxen hoofs on cobbled streets, the whining horns of river steamers, the wails of accordion and tambouritza music starting up in the *kafanas.* Diagonally across from my hotel was the office of *Politika,* Jugoslavia's best newspaper, owned by a family named Ribnikar with which I was very friendly. Vladislav Ribnikar, editor-in-chief, was married to a Czech woman who was a secret Communist; he eventually also entered the party. After the Nazi occupation in 1941 he hid Tito in his house, and later joined the Partisans, becoming vice-president of the first Communist regime. He was a quiet, sardonic, gamboge-colored man. He showed me how the censorship operated. Normally, editors knew without instruction which subjects were taboo. Occasionally specific memoranda arrived, for example, saying:

"Do not print anything against Germany." However, Ribnikar published fake dispatches purporting to originate in China and describing conditions there in such a way that readers knew they referred to Jugoslavia. The censors couldn't complain.

One evening when we were drinking Turkish coffee in his office, Vlada told me the last *hajduk* had just been killed. This was big news in Jugoslavia where *hajduks* were a special symbol of courage and contempt for imposed authority. They had variously been guerilla chieftains, robbers, Robin Hoods, who stole from the rich and gave to the poor, all of whom first developed the habit of fighting central authority when it was Turkish. In latter days the *hajduks* were really nothing but romantic Dillingers but they had their special mystique and each district boasted of its former *hajduks*. In the fourteenth century, when caught, they were hanged upside down. Later the Turks adopted the practice of roasting or impaling them. But they persevered, assuming the role of folkloric heroes; with luxuriant mustaches, belted pistols and heavy hanjar cutlasses. Old men claimed the government owned the highroad but the *hajduk* owned the forest. Vlada told me the last of these excellent thugs, Pavle Dokić, had now died violently. While dodging gendarmes in the mountainous Homolje, Dokić raped a shepherd girl who stabbed him in the privates; so he killed her and shot himself, leaving behind a diary which said in part: "I will have a step like a youth and I will travel like a hero and will feed like a wolf. I will be like God in heaven for now we have remained, only us two, He in heaven and I on earth. As we *hajduks* say, so it must be and there will always be us *hajduks,* for the forest without *hajduks* cannot be, as heaven without God."

The *hajduks,* despite their crimes, had been popular but the gendarmes were detested. Many gravestones were simply marked: "Killed by the murderous hands of the gendarmes." The gendarmes and their associates, the grim political police, played a special role. When not dealing with outright banditry they concentrated on stamping out conspiracy of which there was an adequate amount, coming from secret right-wing societies and even more abundantly from the left.

Although allied to France, Jugoslavia was already beginning to flirt with the Axis powers and this caused popular resentment. Its government banned Communists and didn't even recognize the Soviet Union's existence. The last Czarist minister, a gentleman named Strandtmann, lived in the old Russian legation and still enjoyed diplomatic privileges twenty-one years after the Bolshevik Revolution. Some White Russian *émigrés* had found employ in the police where they specialized in hunting down suspected Marxists. Their enthusiasm in this task was unrestrained and those interrogated were frequently prepared for questioning by having hot, hardboiled eggs inserted in the pits of their strapped-down arms.

One evening I went to the house of a liberal university professor named

Dragoljub Jovanović who had just been released from jail. Jovanović was a haggard man bothered by keloids. He told me his house had been surrounded by policemen in the early morning darkness and that several then burst through the window. He protested: "I am a deputy in parliament." Roaring with laughter, one gendarme replied: "Well, if Hitler can enter Czechoslovakia, we see no reason why we cannot enter the home of a deputy. The western democracies are dead."

A high school teacher named Ilija Petrović called on me. Petrović had studied English literature at Columbia and worked in the United States Library of Congress. Since returning to Jugoslavia he had become a secret Communist and was an old familiar of the prison system. He was still limping because his feet had been horsewhipped. Petrović told me a White Russian, who directed his interrogation, started with the observation: "Oh, I particularly like professors because they are my colleagues." When it was over, he offered Petrović a cigarette and helped him brush off his clothes. Ilija claimed he had been hanged by the hands with a brick attached to his testicles, had a knotted cord tightened about his head, and was thrust into stinging acid.

I could not know how accurate these frightful tales were, but I did come to realize the dictatorship was hated and one could sense the rumble of discontent. A friend of mine was a deputy from the ruling party and strongly supported the premier. He had recently run for re-election in his Serbian farm district and was startled, as he climbed the wooden platform, to notice that many grim, mustachioed peasants before him, scowling, arms akimbo, had pistols tucked in their sashes and unpleasantly hostile expressions. So he abandoned his proregime speech and told the audience: "vote for me and I will protect you against the evil people in Belgrade." He won.

Petrović took me to a meeting of secret Communists who boasted: "Lenin predicted Spain would be the first country after Russia to go Communist; and Serbia will be the last; because we Serbs are individuals and real democrats and we love our land." Pondering this odd communist boast, I walked home through the gathering darkness. Peasants were standing in the alleys selling slabs of roast pumpkin on metal sheets lying above charcoal fires. Two old men had the butts of ancient pistols sticking out of their belts. Looking through the windows of houses in the poorer quarter, I could see families gathered around the supper table lighted with candles. In the windows of restaurants suckling pigs and chickens turned on spits above charcoal fires by little boys. Many of the peasant carts were pulled by mares with colts tagging alongside.

At the end of November I went to Zagreb, capital of the Catholic province of Croatia where the Croatian Peasant Party was all-powerful. It was headed by Vlatko Maček, who detested the Serbs and was thinking of secession. Like Stojadinović in Belgrade, he was also in touch with Axis agents. Zagreb, a pretty town with a splendid gothic cathedral, was filled with signs saying *"Zivio Zbor," "Zivio Ljotić."* "Zivio" means "long live" and "Zbor" was the Fascist Party of a man named Ljotić. I noted: "You can smell which way the wind is blowing. Zagreb is much more European looking than Belgrade and the influence of Hitlerian Europe is creeping in. There are nice buildings, fine-looking shops, few peasants on the streets and a general atmosphere of well-dressed prosperity. Everyone is getting ready for Christmas: red boxes of candy, Saint Nicholases wearing bishops' mitres. Even the skewbald horses here are bigger and fatter and look better treated than the seedy Belgrade steeds. But the American consul tells me the situation is deteriorating and there are more and more swastikas."

Maček proved to be an unimpressive-looking, gnomish man with glasses, shrewd, stubborn face, simple clothes and no necktie. I was told he had been the first intellectual to join the Peasant Party, years earlier, and tried to hide this fact by seeking to appear uncouth. Maček said he had no faith in national elections, and would refuse to send deputies to the next parliament. He intended to fight for complete autonomy. He savagely attacked Stojadinović as a liar who never kept his promises, whose gendarmes killed opponents and whose agents controlled the press. He hinted that if he could gain no help elsewhere, he was ready to accept German or Italian aid to achieve his aims. "If France and England lose interest," he warned, "then we are certainly in the German orbit. Democracy cannot collapse here; it has never existed."

I telephoned a story on this interview to London and was soon thereafter visited by a plainclothesman, who told me I was no longer welcome in Jugoslavia. My visa was invalidated and I was conducted to the railway station and placed on a train for Fiume, the nearest Italian town. In Fiume I called on the Jugoslav consul to demand permission to return. I spent several days waiting, consulting the embarrassed diplomat, going to Italian movies and finally was advised it had all been the mistake of an excessively zealous Zagreb official. I received a new visa and embarked on an Adriatic coastal steamer loaded with turkeys.

We cruised by lovely Dalmatian islands and villages, unloading and loading cargo while the turkeys, to my intense astonishment, kept up a low whistling chorus. On election day, December 11, the ship arrived in Split where I was met by a former diplomat named Berislav Andjelinović. As we walked down the jetty I noticed policemen picking up bodies near the waterfront. "What's going on?" I asked Andjelinović. "Nothing," he replied with mild astonishment. "Today is election day. We always kill more men in an election than the Greeks do in a revolution," said he proudly.

He later became a Cetnik, grew a long beard, and joined the forces of Draža Mihailović. Then he escaped to Cairo, was for a time a minister in the *émigré* government, changed sides and returned as a Tito partisan. He had once served as a Jugoslav diplomat in the United States. Before going to Washington, he spent a day in New York. Andjelinović was taken to the top of the Empire State Building. He stood in silence, regarding the city below. "What do you think?" asked his friend. "Ah, what a wonderful city to destroy," said Berislav.

Split is a magnificent town built into the ruins of the Roman Emperor Diocletian's summer palace; and Dubrovnik, girded by a round wall, at the juncture of craggy mountains and the Adriatic, is one of the world's architectural diadems. I traveled inland to Mostar, in Herzegovina, and Sarajevo, the Bosnian capital, with an antique dealer named Mustafa Hassanović who introduced me to the Moslem political leaders. Many South Slavs had been converted to Islam by the Turks and their community had political importance as a balance between the Orthodox and Catholics. Sarajevo was the center of Jugoslav Islam and there, in its *čaršija* or bazaar, one saw masses of turbaned priests, tarbooshed men, women in shrouds and black gauze veils. The city was undergoing its annual visitation by special traveling Moslem priests who called themselves "beadles" and whose business was saving people's souls. I discussed this trade at length with one of them, an old Arab named Said Emir Akkad, while we sat in the home of Mustafa's father and the Said, playing with a string of prayer beads, dressed in light blue gown and turban, sipped his syrupy coffee. He came to Europe each winter to arrange to take the prilgrimage to Mecca on behalf of any rich pious men who had died before they, themselves, had had a chance to make the holy trip. Said Emir would contract with relatives or friends to substitute for the departed and make the necessary prayers. He received 100 pounds sterling for each client. He asked if I knew anyone in the United States who might need the services of a Mecca "beadle."

Said Emir Akkad and another "beadle" named Hossein Effendi, a merry old soul with a face like a shriveled drumhead, invited me to visit them in the Moriča Han, a sixteenth-century caravanserai still doing business as a hotel. There were six "beadles" in the city at the time. We used to chat together and drink glasses of *salep,* a hot distillation of saffron and spices. Some of the younger "beadles" were attracted by the follies of Sarajevo. They often attended *kafanas* where there were dancing girls as well as music, and Mustafa pointed out to me that, during the "beadles" season, the girls were generally plumper and tunes more caterwauling than usual, in order to suit oriental tastes.

Sarajevo, despite its bleak association with political murder, was a peaceful-looking hill town, dotted with minarets. But it, too, pullulated with trouble. One evening in a restaurant, I noticed a vociferous argument at one table. Quite calmly, all the officers and almost everyone else put on their coats and departed with their ladies. The place became virtually empty, sullen, gravid, when, of a sudden, a savage fight started. Bottles, knives, chairs, tables were brought into action while the manager peeped furtively from a doorway. When I left, the place was a shambles. Next day I asked Mustafa's father, one of the chiefs of the Moslem community, why the police had not intervened. "That would have been foolish," he replied: "As it was, nobody was even killed."

Shortly before Christmas I went back to Split and boarded another boat headed southward to Albania.

# 4

## HAMLET AMONG

## THE EAGLE MEN

H AD SHAKESPEARE SITUATED *Hamlet* INSTEAD OF *Twelfth Night* in Illyria, the following might seem more appropriate; for Albania is the ancient Illyria and, when I arrived there at the end of 1938, the last act of a *Hamlet* in fancy dress was in its denouement.

Albania is a craggy, small land wedged between the Adriatic, Jugoslavia and Greece. Its people have been bastardized by centuries of war with Slavs, Greeks, Turks and Latins. Yet there are still two dominant tribal groupings, in the South, the Tosks and, in the North, the Ghegs. Among the latter are clans called Malissori, or mountain men, bird-featured, lean; known for their bravery, their cupidity, and the preference they accord to robbery over work. The Ghegs are, or then were, infinitely courteous, pursuing complex canons laid down in the thirteenth century by a sage named Lek. This, among other things, specified the laws of blood feud. If any man in the clan was killed, it became the duty of his nearest male relative to slay the murderer. Politeness, however, dictated that the murderer be received in an enemy's home, amiably entertained for the night, and given a fair start next morning before the hunt resumed. And there were subsidiary codicils. Thus, for example, no one could shoot another's dog while there was still light enough to see a blade of grass between the feet. Albanian herd dogs are huge, vicious and hungry.

Albania's language bears no resemblance to other human speech. Unlike Finnish, it cannot even be identified as belonging to a linguistic family. It is said to derive from the tongue of ancient Illyria whose bold queen placed chains across a river to keep conquering Roman galleys from rowing up.

This language is known as Shqip and the Albanians called themselves Shqipetars, which means "sons of the eagle," Eagle Men. When one saw a fierce, aquiline chieftain riding to market on a donkey, bearing his gun, while behind walked his women carrying bundles, one could understand the origins of the word. The men were blond, lean, handsome and many looked as if they could have stepped from the House of Lords. The women were lovely until they reached a mature age—around twenty-four. Work did not improve their beauty and their lot was work, while the men protected them, hunting beasts or each other.

After the Turks were expelled from Albania they left a chaos of tribes and religions. In the South, near Greece, were Greek Orthodox Christians; in the North a minority of Roman Catholics. Between were the Moslems, among whom the little-known Bektashi sect was powerful. The Bektashi had originally been a warrior fraternity whose priests provided chaplains for the Sultan's Janissary corps. The Janissaries themselves comprised, for the most part, sons of Christian families under Ottoman domination. These regiments were favored and, guided by the ambitious Bektashi, became a compact revolutionary force in Turkey. When the sultans decided to rid themselves of this recurring menace, they dissolved the Janissaries and exiled their Bektashi confessors to Albania.

There the Bektashis still had many *tekkes,* or monasteries. I visited that of their supreme chief, Myrteza, the Grand Baba (great grandfather,) in Kruja, a fortified stronghold of the famous King Skanderbeg of whom it was said, at his death: "The world will never again know such a lion." The Baba was a fine old fellow with shrewd eyes, horny hands and gray spade beard. His girdle was the color of blood, wound about his robes and containing a mystical crystal object. He also had a green turban encircling his *tac,* or ornamental white stovepipe hat.

The great grandfather and his abbots told me their first holy man, Hadji Bektash Veli, had founded the order in the thirteenth century. They were a tolerant sect who, unlike most Moslems, drank alcohol, ate pork, and regarded other religions with friendliness. Drink was a part of the religious ceremonial and the Babas would sit around sipping raki while musicians played stringed instruments and sang: "Tears of blood flow from thine eye; let it go round again, that rose-colored cup." One Bektashi poem, recited to me by Baba Myrteza of Kruja as we drank raki in the monastery, said: "My mystery none ever comprehended: To all creatures I was brother."

After the Turks were expelled in 1912 a German princeling, Wilhelm of Wied, became Albania's ruler but he resigned, preferring the rank of major in the Kaiser's army, a more peaceable profession with a better chance of advancement. He was followed by a short-lived republic in which the dominant figure was a bishop named Fan Noli, who later fled to Boston, Massachusetts.

In 1938 Albania was an independent monarchy ruled by King Zog the First (and last). Zog's original name was Ahmed Bey Zogu. He had been chief of the Gheg clan of Mati and as such had been educated in both

Constantinople and Vienna: a striking figure, tall, mustachioed and with the swinging gait of a mountaineer.

Ahmed Bey Zogu held political office under Fan Noli and decided to take over power himself. He went to Jugoslavia, and Belgrade furnished him with gold and mercenaries including White Russian officers looking for money and adventure. With a rag-tag, bobtail army, Ahmed Bey marched into Albania, conquered it and established himself as president. Eventually he named himself King Zog.

Ambition is an infectious disease. One of Zog's sisters, Nafije, had married another nobleman named Tsena Bey Kryeziu. Tsena Bey was sent as Albanian minister to Belgrade but Zog heard rumors that his brother-in-law, having learned the arts of conspiracy, was planning a coup himself. Zog packed Tsena Bey off to Prague, more placid, less accustomed to gunmen, and also further away. However, Zog heard further disturbing rumors and, at that point, a court official told me, the King started inquiries for a discreet unemployed, expert marksman. A polylingual student named Agiadh Bebi was found.

Fortified by three glasses of brandy, Agiadh Bebi shot Tsena Bey dead as he was dining in Prague in 1927. Unfortunately, Agiadh Bebi was a better shot than plotter and the Czech police easily captured him. Zog feared the young assassin might be indiscreet at his trial so further inquiries were made for another marksman, more adept at evasive action. When Agiadh Bebi appeared in a Prague courtroom he was drilled by an assassin's assassin who promptly disappeared. The assassin's assassin surfaced in Jugoslavia where he began to drink heavily and, when tipsy, talked too much. Word of this reached Tirana. Within a short time, an assassin's assassin's assassin was discovered. He killed the assassin's assassin and disappeared. I was never able to learn any more about the assassin's assassin's assassin.

King Zog's court included Tsena's widow and his other sisters, with whom I danced one night at the last regal ball. They wore splendid gowns largely composed of sequins and what I took to be curtain rings.

Since the king had only recently married, his heir was still Prince Tati, son of Tsena Bey, who had become sixteen, legally a man, shortly before my arrival in Albania. Zog was exceptionally fond of Tati and pampered him. Tati's favorite pursuit was driving a red sports car as swiftly as possible down and around the one grand boulevard leading out of Tirana. This impressive avenue had been laid out by Italian engineers. Broad, gleaming and well surfaced, it was only about a mile long.

Tati seemed to admire his affectionate uncle. Nevertheless, at sixteen, he was automatically subject to the blood feud obligations of any honorable Albanian gentleman, and friends of his father, the late Tsena Bey, began to whisper reminders to him. There was no legal proof that Zog had hired the assassin but this was widely assumed to be the case. In Shakespeare the ghost of Hamlet's father appears on the palace battlements to instruct his son. No ghost appeared on the nonexistent battlements of Zog's modest pink villa. *Hamlet* played differently among the Eagle Men. Tati was only tormented by innuendo and by hints of what was to be expected in a land whose social ethic was the Canon of Lek. This specified: "Blood vengeance, slaying a man according to the laws of honor, must not be confounded with murder. Murder starts a blood feud."

As a result of this background the poor little prince who, like all Albanians, loved firearms, was deprived by royal order of his guns. A friend said to him: "Never shoot a woodcock; I'll give you a feather." Fortunately for Tati and for Zog there was not any final act to the drama. In the spring of 1939 Queen Geraldine produced a boy baby named Skander, after the famous hero, and two days later the monarch and his family fled the country before Mussolini's troops.

I found Albania a giddy place. Its brio and bravura, the flamboyance of its people with their tight, white pants, white skullcaps and little vests of black, still mourning Skanderberg's death, helped camouflage the penury of life. There was no railway and only a few roads. I traveled by horse, foot, bus, automobile, and when I left it was by rowboat, across the stormy lake of Ochrid. The only flights I made were in the plane of the Italian consul general, a colonel, at Valona, spotting landing fields for the invasion that was soon to come.

I encountered strange customs. In the northern clan of Mirditi, run by a Christian chief, girls could speak to no man except a relative for fear of ostracism. The polite greeting to a lady was "Strength to your arms" and the accepted reply was "Sugar to your mouth, we bow with honor." A doctor told me 30 per cent of the cases in Tirana's hospital were knife and gunshot wounds. At villages near Scutari in the North the following exchange was customary:

PEASANT: Welcome to our home and share with us what God has willed us, even if it be salt and bread.
c.: God help you and, as they say, may your chimney be higher.
p.: Have you been able?
c.: Little by slowly.

Edward Lear, the humorist and painter, visited Albania in the nineteenth century and reported a conversation as sounding like: "Dort beer, dort bloo, dort hitch, hitch beer, blue beer, beer chak, dort gatch." This is not an inaccurate description.

The country folk still had pagan legends and chthonian gods. They spoke of the Dif, a twelve-foot giant of the underworld who fancied human flesh, and of the Thopch, a dwarf. Difs were as tall as pine trees with black beards falling to their knees, filthy as boars and covered with lice. They stole innocent women to fan the flies away when they slept in midsummer heat. One gypsy tribe worshipped God but called him Devil. Rufai dervishes howled and stuck skewers in their cheeks but didn't bleed. If a woman died, her grave was dug deeper than a man's because it was assumed her sins were greater.

The hands and feet of corpses were tied, the eyes and mouth closed. At night, watchers sat beside the dead with lit candles. If a cat jumped over the body, the soul was transmogrified into a ghost. An ordinary, cat-less soul remained in the owner's house forty days and then flew out as a butterfly. Corpses were buried with a coin in the mouth to pay debts in the next world. When a man fell from his horse it was advisable to spray honey and avoid the vengeance of spirits called White Girls. The best antidote to evil spells was a mixture of lead poured molten into cold water, to which was added the saliva of a stork and the blood of two killed brothers. The patient's face was washed in this concoction while someone recited: "Become ye water and salt." A recommended cure for typhus was sugar and frog guts, placed warm on the sufferer's head.

The Kapedan or chief of the Mirditi, Mark Djon, was a gentleman who dressed in traditional Albanian fashion from the waist down and like a European from the waist up. He claimed he could raise five thousand fighting men on three day's notice, detested Zog and was conspiring with the Italians. Once when I walked with him through Tirana, the Kapedan, wearing tight Albanian leggings, well-cut jacket and derby hat, began making scurrilous remarks about Zog. Right behind us strode a striking figure in a handsome cloak. "Won't he hear what you're saying?" I inquired. "Oh, never mind him. That is my personal bodyguard."

The favorite Mirditi song began: "Let us fight as it is our custom." They also sang: "I am a man from Mirditi and I do not surrender; my ancestor was a cutting sword." Or again: "Tell mother that her son got married; and if she asks what kind of bride, tell her he got three bullets in his chest."

Tirana was an overgrown village of shacks, bazaar stalls and little minareted mosques. It contained few buildings of note apart from a simple, Italian-built hotel and the Parliament, once an officers' club, which bore the explicit sign: "Deputies will please check their guns." Only on the outskirts was an unpretentious suburban quarter of modern houses where most diplomats lived and where the king and his sisters had palaces which would, in any other town, have passed as bourgeois villas. The streets were invariably muddy; there were few cars and many donkeys. Transport for the rich was the four-wheeled carriage. Hundreds of these had known better days in Vienna and Budapest before World War I and were now clustered in the capital, a kind of old droshkies' cemetery.

Fortunately, in these rural surroundings, I became friendly with a rufous-haired Austrian girl who had a lithe figure, the striking name of Zerline, and few inhibitions. Zerline was there with a party of Hungarians. She enjoyed accurate recollection of her past triumphs which, considering her youth, were remarkable. Zerline would confide to my astonished ears: "I was very successful in Paris. In Venice they ran after me in the streets crying *la rozza, la rozza.* In Lucerne there was the nicest English boy. He was tall and good-looking and he came down to breakfast every day with his Byron under his arm. But he was a Christian Scientist and I couldn't stand that. After all, there is a limit. He still writes me but I tell him I could never marry anyone who believes such silly stuff. It isn't manly."

How airy and original a companion she was in the viscid Albanian mud.

Tirana had been built in the seventeenth century by the Turks, who named it for a victory at Teheran. It was magnificently located with mountains on three sides, covered with snow in winter time. Life, apart from the hotel or legations, was exceedingly simple. Skewered meat and rice was the basic menu of anything calling itself a restaurant. The city sounded of braying donkeys and the mantic exhortations of muezzins calling the faithful to prayer. It smelled of mud and Turkish coffee grounds.

Albanians loved gambling so much that it was outlawed except for a few days at the start of each year when everyone bet on almost any game of chance. Peddlers erected rudimentary roulette wheels, spinning arrows in circles against a penciled paper background of numbers. There was little else in the way of amusement. Zog was said to show three movies a day in his palace for the benefit of his family.

On a bus trip to Valona I waited hours in a cold, windswept village. A crowd had formed a circle about a poor man who lay on the frozen mud, gasping, racked by abrasive coughs, while children casually played beside him, whipping scraps of paper along with sticks. One friend squatted next to the invalid and cradled his head from time to time. Finally the man died. Nobody said a word. The children played, the friend left; so did everyone else; and the body lay alone. When my bus took off, it was still there. At Kavaje, south of Durazzo, was an agricultural boarding school run with American missionary funds. The students were so undernourished that after each vacation, spent at home with families who lived on corn bread and yogurt, they were given a preschool rest of several days and stuffed with food in order to face the next term's work.

Zog was an absolute ruler. He told one foreign diplomat: "Don't bother to talk with my ministers. They're only servants. If you want anything, come and see me about it." But behind him shadowy figures contested for influence. One, General Josef Seredji, known as "Sefa," was reputed to be the principal pro-Italian in the royal entourage. Another man of major importance was called Abdurrahman Mati and came from the same clan as his sovereign. There was even gossip that he was Zog's real father. The king was openly devoted to him. When Zog's mother was alive she had insisted on supervising the cooking of his meals to prevent any poison plots. It was believed that Abdurrahman had assumed the role of food tester after her death. Abdurrahman was called by diplomats the "Rasputin of Albania" and by less-educated people the "Black Spot." He was the great enemy of Seredji, who would say: "When old Abdurrahman dies, be sure and bury him deep." The bazaar claimed that whenever Zog received the chief of a rival clan, the Black Spot sat behind a curtain with two cocked revolvers. When he first arrived in Tirana, Abdurrahman had been poor but his wealth grew substantially. He had a useful way of sending particularly tough carpenters to mend the fences around his estates and somehow they always managed to move them several yards out in all directions as part of the repair process. Those who protested suffered for their audacity.

A particular enemy of Abdurrahman, and a friend of General Seredji, was an Italian named Giovanni Giro. Giro was a Fascist bravo who had taken part with Mussolini in the original march on Rome. He was an engaging, tubby ruffian with everted personality. I used to visit him at his house which was watched by a private bodyguard and a vicious black dog attached to a chain. Giro's assignment was conspiracy. He paid off many clan chieftains and gave me personal introductions to some, including the redoubtable Djon of the Mirditi tribe.

It was clear Giro had not known many Americans but was strongly impressed by Hollywood gangster films. Whenever I called he would produce a bottle of gin, and no glasses; then he would gurgle great swigs and pass the bottle in what he imagined to be the approved fashion. He was full of excellent and mysterious tales. He used to boast: "That rascal king respects me enough to see me dead. You have noticed my precautions," referring to his guard and monstrous dog. Giro told me: "If you have an enemy in this barbaric land, there is a simple way to eliminate him. First you look around for some veteran criminal wanted by the law and hiding in the mountains. It is not hard to establish contact. Then you tell him you will bribe the proper authorities to insure he will remain at liberty, if he assassinates the man you want out of the way. And then, of course, you give him a hundred gold napoleons."

Gold was still the established currency. The first time I dined at the home of Radoje Janković, Jugoslav minister, whom I had known as consul general in New York, he asked me if I played poker. I soon found myself at a table with my host, Albania's Foreign Minister Libohova, and Fuat Togay, the Turkish minister, while the ladies politely retired. As in many European countries the game was played with a stripped deck of thirty-two cards—minus everything below sevens—and only four sat at table. I was startled when the other three players pulled out chamois leather bags. There were no chips in sight. Janković noticed my surprise. He remarked politely, "Let me stake you. Tomorrow we can settle." And he opened his chamois bag, pouring a mass of gold coins on the table: sovereigns, napoleons and louis d'or. These were the only chips used. I played with care.

Janković was a fine chap: a massive, tall Serb with magisterial manner,

white hair, heavy gestures, huge voice, and the gout. He had flat, sly eyes
with brows like the ears of a startled wolf. He was given to fustian statements. In my presence he once told the appalled Italian minister: "We will
exterminate you if you ever dare make war on us. We will poison the rivers
running into Italy in the North. And we will poison the Adriatic sea. Our
brilliant scientists make cultures of things like cholera; watch out for us, I
warn you."

For Janković, conspiracy was the essence of life. Night after night,
sitting up over the brandy he so much relished, he told me the vivid tale of
murders in which he himself had been involved, starting in 1903 when
Janković took part in the plot that overthrew Serbia's ruling Obrenović
dynasty. He was then a young officer loyal to Captain Dragutin Dimi-
trijević, called "Apis," the bee, because he had a white bald spot on his
head. "Apis" was a great intriguer who later organized a secret society
called "Union or Death" which became known as the Black Hand. He was
finally shot in 1917.

Janković and other nationalists disliked Queen Draga, consort of the last
Obrenović, and considered her frivolous. After a dance at the officers'
casino they armed themselves and at two o'clock one May morning broke
into the palace and overpowered the guard. They searched it room by
room. One of the conspirators outside suddenly hollered: "There he is. He
just looked out the window." The King and Queen were hiding in a tiny
antechamber obscured by curtains. Janković and Apis shot the lock from
the door, rushed in and fired several times. When the bodies fell, both
dressed in short silk nightshirts, the Queen's violet, the King's rose colored,
they were heaved out of the window on to a pile of fertilizer. Janković used
to smack his lips with pleasure at the recollection.

He joined Apis's Black Hand and assisted the Bosnian youths, headed
by Gavrilo Princip, who murdered the Hapsburg archduke in Sarajevo.
Later he marched through Albania to the sea with the defeated army of old
King Peter Karageorgević. He told me the Ghegs used to raid the retreating
Serbs for arms and "When we caught them we tied them to trees and a
sergeant would go down the line and cut their throats. We had no bullets to
spare. I never saw an Albanian wince or turn his head."

Janković was admirably chosen for his mission in Albania. He was an
inveterate plotter; and so, alas, were others in his legation. His military
attaché, a Croatian colonel, was later assigned to the Belgrade general staff.
Two days before Hitler attacked Jugoslavia in April, 1941, he flew to
Vienna in a stolen plane with a satchel full of plans. He had been a secret
member of the Croatian Fascist Party.

One night, when we dined alone after his family went to Belgrade on
holiday, Janković got rather drunk. "Come with me," he commanded,
twitching his cicatrized face. Bearing a lantern, he stomped goutily down
into the cellar of his residence where, beside an antiquated stove, stood a

huge, old-fashioned safe. He opened this with several keys, then reached inside and pulled out a box of papers. "See what a swine that Zog is," said the minister. He proceeded to show me receipts from the Albanian king for funds received from Jugoslavia. Some, dating back to his presidential days, were signed A. Zogu; the others merely Zog or Zog R. One was for $60,000; others for various amounts in gold coinage, listed generally as "Napoléons" or "Napoléons d'or." "The pig," said Janković. "We receive nothing in return. And he also takes money from the Italians, the British and the Greeks. What can you do with a man like that, a man who calls himself a king?"

Having himself been a regicide, Janković showed no respect for royalty. He sneered: "I set my staff to calculating, in terms of what we pay him, how often that rascal Zog tells the truth. We reckon he lies 53 per cent of the time." This is an interesting diplomatic statistic. I sought to persuade the minister to let me photograph some of his receipts but a cunning look came into his eyes. "Ah no, my friend," he murmured in a rumbling voice. "That drunk I am not! Nor ever will I be." He slammed the creaking strongbox door and guided me upstairs. As I walked to my hotel across the melting mud, I saw the first seasonal storks flying in against the moon and coming to rest on Tirana's tumble-down chimneys.

One day I drove to Scutari with Janković, who wished to visit his consul. On the southern shore of a lake by the same name, which borders Montenegro, Scutari was the capital of old Illyria. Atop its citadel was a fine castle built by the Venetians and from whose crenellations you could still imagine the cataphracts of battle. It was a sleepy town, Turkish-looking but a Roman Catholic center. I wandered about while Janković did his consular business. Then he took me to lunch in the home of a local Bey. From the outside, his house appeared dilapidated but we entered a realm of antique luxury: divans, low chairs, Turkestani and Afghan carpets. The Bey, a grave old gentleman, had studied in Paris and gave us an exquisite, European meal. After lunch he showed us his pictures, including, I found to my astonishment, a Rembrandt. "You are surprised," he admonished, stroking his white beard and looking for all the world like one of the Dutchman's own venerable models. I was.

Later, in the seaport of Valona, I met two other amiable diplomats. The Jugoslav consul was a monstrously big Serb, more than six foot six, who detested Albania, sneered at the Italians whom he was assigned to outwit, and fancied himself a poet. Many years afterwards he arrived at my Paris office bearing a manuscript as large as the New York telephone directory, written in careful Cyrillic script. He wanted me to arrange for its publication in the United States and assured me: "This is the finest poem ever written in any Slavonic language. It will make both you and me famous. Those fools in Belgrade do not recognize greatness when they see it."

Godjevac, the consul, was much involved in the routine business of

granting visas to the hundreds of Albanians who wished to walk to Jugoslavia and cut wood in order to purchase wives. Once as I sat with him
while, one after another, these peripatetic Lochinvars, clutching their white
skull caps, stood answering his questions, he asked a skinny Tosk: "Do you
know what country this man comes from? He comes from America. From
the United States of America. Have you heard of it?"

"Yes," said the Albanian.

"And where is it?"

The Tosk scratched his head. "About three months' walk," he answered.

Godjevac's Italian colleague was an army colonel named Salvoni. His
principal function was to prepare for eventual Italian seizure of Albania
and he made no mystery about it. He took me in his Savoia-Marchetti on
flights through the bleak Acroceraunian range, describing emergency landing fields in the valleys below. We ourselves landed at both Kortcha and
Argyrocastro, towns I was next to inspect, thanks to the courtesy of the
Greek Army, in the winter of 1940–1941 after the Greeks had reversed a
Fascist invasion.

Britain and the United States were represented in Albania by diplomats
who might have been considered odd if for no other reason than that they
eschewed conspiracy. The British maintained their legation at Durazzo,
some twenty miles from the capital. When their minister, an aging oriental-
ist named Sir Andrew Ryan, had important business he was forced to climb
into his venerable Rolls Royce and bump over potholes to Tirana. He
preferred to avoid the ordeal, maintaining official contact by a miserable,
single-strand telephone and sitting in the garden with his energetic wife.
The American minister, a southerner named Hugh G. Grant, was not of the
diplomatic profession. He came from Alabama and had worked for Senator Hugo Black before that distinguished politician was named to the Supreme Court by President Roosevelt. At the time, a Pittsburgh newspaperman unearthed the fact that Black had once been a member of the Ku Klux
Klan. Grant was sent to Tirana *en poste*.

He was a quiet, humorless individual who worked hard reporting
minutiae that distressed the one career code clerk attached to the legation,
a gentleman from Maine who looked forward only to the retirement that
awaited him when he left Albania. "Who the hell cares?" the clerk would
grumble, "what the lead editorial in *Shtypi* has to say about China?"

The Grants lived simply in their brick legation. Meals were rarely graced
with wine and the menu was generally of American canned food. They
respected that old-fashioned tradition which called for them to address
each other as Mr. and Mrs. It was startling at table, when the minister
asked, "Mrs. Grant, would you pass the salt?" Grant always referred to the
king as "His Majesty," even in private conversation.

I must herewith interrupt the sequence of this tale to recount events that
occurred in April, after I had gone, but which directly involved the

Ryans and the Grants. While in Albania I had become persuaded that Mussolini intended to grab the country. The Italians themselves, from Giro to Salvoni, were blatantly indiscreet about their activities and intentions. Nevertheless, I had been warned not to attempt to cable dispatches on this subject from Tirana and that foreigners' mail was inspected and held; therefore I would be wise to refrain from any predictions until I had crossed the border. I confined myself to descriptive features and, alas, when I went to Jugoslavia and wrote dispatches forecasting a Fascist invasion, these were considered too alarmist, unjustified by what the Foreign Office knew, denied by what Rome was saying, and therefore unpublished by my editors.

On Good Friday, 1939, when Durazzo was already feeling the agreeable zephyrs of spring, Sir Andrew Ryan awoke to the explosion of shells in his garden. For some days coded cables had been arriving but these had piled up, for the most part not deciphered, because Sir Andrew had generously given Easter leave to his two aides, a lepidopterist who took off for the Albanian hills and a lonely youth who had made for the fleshpots of Rome. The envoy was therefore unaware of urgent, last-minute warnings from London. He called Grant on the tenuous telephone and, when this proved dead, Lady Ryan climbed into the ancient Rolls and drove to Tirana to discover what was happening. While Grant and Lady Ryan were conferring, they noticed a caravan of cars driving eastward. It contained much of the national gold reserve and the royal family. A few Albanian units pretended scattered resistance to the Italians, gaining sufficient time for Zog to cross over into Greece before his country subsided into occupation. Grant insisted on staying on for months although Washington did not recognize the Italian conquest. One of his last tasks was to regain for the American school at Kavaje two cows stolen by the fence builders of Abdurrahman Mati. In Rome the following September, just after he left Tirana, Grant asked me for a newspaper job. I saw no opening. He returned to Washington and was promptly named minister to Siam.

His hero, Zog, stayed in Greece a while, and then wandered about England, Egypt and France, where he finally died. During the war, when guerrilla movements were springing up in the Balkans, a Zogist band fought the Germans and Italians under the leadership of a brave Albanian named Abbas Kupi. He, unhappily, was smashed by the Communist Partisans who still run Albania. I have always thought that a great wasted slogan was: "For King and Kupi" (pronounced "Kewpie").

The King spoke German with his queen, a lovely Hungarian countess from an impoverished branch of the Apponyis. She achieved royal position accidentally. After Zog made himself sovereign, he sent envoys around Europe in search of eligible brides. Initially charged with this mission was

a dark, oily-haired gentleman named Martini, the king's master of cere-
monies, who introduced his master to various young ladies from Italy and
Hungary. Finally, Kol Kotchy, a deputy, showed the ruler photographs of
Geraldine, who was then working in a Budapest museum. Her mother, the
Brooklyn-born Gladys Steuart, then wife of a French lieutenant colonel
named Girault, was eager to press the match. So Kotchy brought a certain
Hungarian general Gitzy to Tirana to arrange the details.

The marriage was romantic and ceremonious. Many of the Queen's
relatives arrived to contribute to the splendor. One, Count Tony Apponyi,
dazzled everyone by adorning his plump figure in green satin and tight
breeches. He remained in Tirana to supervise his niece's financial affairs. I
used to drink with Apponyi, who boasted: "We brought a real girl down
here—not a café dancer like that Teleki," referring to the daughter of a
rival Magyar family. The count persuaded Zog to buy back several of the
Apponyi estates lost after World War I but got into trouble with his royal
master by announcing one day in his cups: "The only gold around here
that Zog hasn't yet grabbed is on the scales of the fish in the palace pond."
I last saw Apponyi in Budapest at the end of 1940. I was preparing to
drive into so-called Slovakia, created by Hitler from the rump of Czechoslovakia, and Count Tony wanted to come along as a freeloader to look at
his lost lands. I declined.

Certainly the grandest experience of my Albanian visit was the last royal
ball given by King Zog and Queen Geraldine, an occasion that took place
New Year's Eve and showed off in full splendor the panoply of the Zogist
court. I borrowed a tail coat from a diplomat of such junior rank that he
had not received an invitation and joined the procession of hired carriages
forming before my hotel: Apponyi with his jaded American wife; two
cousins of the last Turkish sultan; the Rumanian minister, eagerly describing the day's woodcock hunt to the uninterested and blind Greek chargé
d'affaires; a Budapest munitions salesman; and the Italian press attaché
who, curiously, doubled as Dutch consul. It was raining. Trains of donkeys
stumbled through the mud and, across the way, earnest little men in white
fezzes were playing roulette beneath an umbrella, watching a rusty spinner
wobble over a crudely ciphered piece of cardboard.

My carriage was particularly antique and leaky. The driver pulled a
rubber awning over my lap but the trip was slow and damp. The horse
stopped four times, refusing to continue until the angry driver got out,
slushed through the mud, and kicked, punched, dragged heavily at the bit.
Outside the palace it was still drizzling and rain shone on the faces of the
royal guards, lined up at the portico in plum-colored uniforms, mountain
men from the King's own district of Mati. They stood stiff and sturdy, with
right forearm laid along waist in Albanian salute, palm facing earth.

When I left my hat and coat, the attendant gave me, in addition to a
check, a lottery ticket. While I tried to figure out what this was for, a

squadron of ushers and officers swarmed around and I sidled along with them, ending up in a reception room, rectangular, about sixty by a hundred feet, with a high ceiling. On one wall hung a portrait of the King's late mother. Across, sitting upon a dais, was the guard's plum-colored band. Everyone stood in awkward groups: parliamentary deputies, cabinet ministers, a few foreigners' wives. There was a sprinkling of heavily decorated officers, including Zog's White Russian mercenaries wearing Czarist uniform with ribbons of St. George's cross.

At half-past eleven word seeped in that Zog was coming. A crowd rose on tiptoe to peer over the 320-pound deputy from Berat. The entourage filed past rapidly: King, Queen, family, diplomats and then the rest of us more or less pell-mell, down a stone staircase and into a sizeable salon along one wall of which, burning merrily, was a row of the pot-bellied stoves you find on American farms. The room had been an outdoor tennis court but was subsequently enclosed to take care of gatherings of this order. The walls and ceiling were wood. During the King's marriage, they almost caught fire from the heat of movie cameramen's lights. The board floor was covered with thick oriental rugs. On the walls hung dozens of brocaded, velvet Albanian cloaks, displayed in the shape of butterflies; dark blue and dark red, arabesques with profligate gold and silver thread. Collections of weapons were strung up intermittently: damascened swords and inlaid pistols set out in figures of "Z" to honor the King. A long line of tables, forming an elbow, followed the left-hand wall and the further end of the room. They were laden with gold plate, coruscant Bohemian crystal, candelabra, food and wine.

The royal family gathered at the corner of a table, eating and chatting while the diplomatic corps made a hubble-bubble around them. At midnight, the electric lights faded out and candles left a soft glow. In the distance, through the windows, I could see a few lanterns on the hillside. The King picked up a goblet of champagne and, in Albanian, said: "Happy New Year to everyone in my home and everywhere." He kissed the Queen while the assemblage clapped. Janković muttered in French: "I could do that."

When the lights returned, people began to wave lottery tickets like the one I had received. Somebody took my orange ticket and gave me a bundle. Inside I found a blue woolen muffler, brown socks, necktie and fancy handkerchief. Everybody got a present. Other men had shirts and ties done up in packages; bolts of material for suits; sweaters, suspenders. The women received fancy underwear, stuff for dresses, perfume, bunny rabbits containing pockets crammed with lingerie.

The King and Queen slipped out and conversation rumbled in an undercurrent of mixed languages: Albanian, Turkish, Greek, Serbian, French, German, Italian, English. An elderly man, obviously ill, huddled in a chair, holding his head. The Queen's boy brother, done up in his first tail coat, told a guard to bring the fellow a glass of water. Then dancing started; the King's two nieces were very popular.

While I stood at the edge, hugging my gift package and regarding the ball, Dr. Libohova, the foreign minister, appeared with news that the King wanted to talk with me so I parked my bundle and followed, past two stiffly saluting guards, under a heavy hanging of draperies, into a small foyer. At the back was a Christmas tree with lights and spangles and still further behind a painted sky arrangement with big golden stars. Zog and Geraldine were standing together; he about six feet tall, slender, with reddish brown hair and mustache, light blue eyes, a small chin, dressed in plain military uniform with stiff white shirt and collar, black four-in-hand tie; she in white dress with ermine cape; diamond ear pendants, necklace and coronet.

My audience was very dull and in court Albanian—a most polite language, translated through the royal interpreter. The King said he was glad to see me again, that President Roosevelt was a very wonderful man and that he'd like to wish President Roosevelt a Happy New Year and how he, having heard so much of it from his traveling sisters, would like to go to America himself. And so on. When he was done, I bowed, shook hands again, and departed backwards, bowing intermittently as instructed by the court chamberlain. This produced disaster. I backed into a velvet curtain which came tumbling down on my head. Extricated by the foreign minister and a servant, and noticing a broad grin on the Queen's face, I sidled out like a crab.

People were still eating: champagne, *foie gras,* salads, ice creams, devoured beneath chandeliers of glittering lighted candles—and all in a famished land. I was astounded to watch clansmen stamping out their burning cigarettes on lovely Persian rugs. There was a lottery and three big prizes were awarded: a silver coffee set with tray, a silver filigreed clock, and a leather case. Janković, resplendent in gold-braided uniform, developed gout and offered me a lift. Outside the rain had stopped. The same guards were standing there but looked wilted. One was unable to stifle a yawn. As I went through the palace gate, I noticed the outline of two minarets standing up against the snowy mountain sides in the moonlit distance. A cab driver was beating his horse on the nostrils and a few gypsy children still begged at the royal entranceway.

In 1939, I left Albania by bus from Tirana to Elbasan, bumping hour after hour along the slushy track jammed against a peasant in sheepskin jacket and white cap who carried a blunderbuss that kept jabbing me in the ribs. I could not edge away from him for next to me on the other side was an unhappy goat. Two benches ahead sat an Albanian gentleman who spoke French and we chatted over the rumbles and thuds until, in Elbasan, at the end of the journey, he invited me to lunch in the principal restaurant. After a time a friend of his arrived and, to my surprise, started to talk with

me in German. With coffee, a third man sat down, exchanged a few remarks in Albanian, looked at me with a fixed gaze and suddenly asked in
good American accents: "Weren't you in the class of '34 at Harvard?" He
had been a day student, an Albanian-American, now teaching in Elbasan
under government contract.

From Elbasan I caught another bus over the mountains to Pogradec on
the Lake of Ochrid that divides Albania from Jugoslav Macedonia. Lacus-
trine Ochrid is fierce and lovely. It was once called Lychnis by the Greeks,
who say Pan dwelled there with his shepherds. Pogradec itself had little to
recommend it. But I could not get out, for the road to Jugoslavia was
blocked by snow and a blizzard was raging. After hours of haggling, I
persuaded two fishermen to take me across the lake in their rowboat so, on
a glum morning, with wind whipping sharp flakes into our eyes, we set off
into the gray distance. The fishermen were nervous and refused to deliver
me at the town of Ochrid, on the Jugoslav side, because they said patrols
would shoot at us. They claimed the Jugoslavs were notoriously bad shots
but feared their aim might be sufficiently disconcerted by the storm to be
dangerous.

Therefore they proposed to deposit me on the southeastern shore near
the frontier. They guided their awkward barge to the chosen point and I
was happy to leave its wet and shaky confines. I paid them four gold
sovereigns and clambered out with my baggage. As the boat withdrew into
the blizzard, a Jugoslav frontier guard emerged, dressed in long greatcoat,
his cap pulled over his eyes, pointed his rifle and demanded to know my
business. I explained I was going to the monastery of Sveti Naum. It was
too late to hope to get to Ochrid and the Serbian monasteries were famous
for their hospitality. The abbey of Sveti Naum was a renowned institution
on a site that had first been endowed by Justinian and later named for one
of the first three saints who preached Christianity to the Slavs.

The soldier grunted. He was persuaded by the gift of a sovereign to
abandon his post, sling his gun over his back, pick up my suitcase and
typewriter and guide me a couple of miles through the snow to my destination. As we arrived two priests on donkeys were trotting up to the gate,
their beards stiff with frost, and they let me in, summoning the abbot.

The *iguman,* or abbot, was a paladin of a prelate, huge, black-gowned,
black-hatted with curled, iron beard and the demeanor of God the Father.
He took my hand graciously between his enormous paws, offered the
monastic hospitality like some grave lord, and ordered one of his monks to
carry my luggage to a neat little room. A maid servant appeared, somewhat
to my surprise in this austere male haven, and lit a fire of faggots. Then I
dined on *čevabčiči,* the peppery, sausage-shaped Serbian hamburgers, and
raw onions, together with the abbot and six monks. Afterwards he invited
me to his chambers for *šlivovica* and talk.

This was an anxious experience. Mr. Grant, in Tirana, had given me a carton of American cigarettes and the *iguman* relished their taste. He puffed and puffed, exhaling with sweet pleasure, and we quickly destroyed one bottle of plum brandy; he called for another. As this bibulous pontifex drank, some of the liquor dribbled down his hirsute face. He would lean forward as I politely held a light for his Lucky Strike; but the constant flow of alcohol and conversation produced an aura of unsteadiness and, time and again, small forest fires ran across the edges of his beard. Unconcerned, he patted these out with his massive hand as if it were the most natural gesture. The poor old abbot was worried about the future. A godless generation showed distressing lack of interest in the holy life. The ancient monastery now contained but 10 per cent of its monkish contingent. The *iguman* regarded this as a sign of sad and atheistic days; time was to prove him right.

Next day it was no longer snowing and the abbot arranged for me to ride through the drifts to Ochrid, guided by a servant on another horse and with my bags strapped to a mule. It was clear and bright with only feathery noise-shadows as chunks of snow slid gently off the pine tree branches when we glided by. To the left extended the long spread of lake, its incredible depth indicated by a dark purple penumbra. Archaic fishing boats, shaped like black triangles with high, clumsy prows, scuttled over the deep like awkward crabs.

I spent several days in Ochrid, examining its frescoes and Byzantine churches. They were not in good condition. Moslem soldiers of Marshal Franchet d'Esperey's Allied army had picked out the eyes of aureoled saints with bayonets as they advanced from Salonika in World War I. Daws, ravens and bats sheltered amid high corners of desolate basilicas. This was once a boastful city, capital of the Bulgarian Czar who sought to take Constantinople back in medieval times and killed himself when his army came back blinded and in chains.

An elderly, threadbare Macedonian attached himself to me as guide, a gentleman named Jovan Popostefanović. He told me that when he was born the Turks still ruled and his name was written in Macedonian style as Vane Popostefanija. After the first Balkan War, the Bulgars came and decreed that he must spell his name Ivan Popstefanov. Following the Second Balkan War he was instructed by the Serbs to assume his present style of nomenclature. "Alas," said Jovan, "such is the fate of our dear Macedonia. No wonder the rest of the world calls stew a Macédoine. We do not even any longer know our names, we the nation whose Alexander conquered the world's entirety. When will we smash our fetters and gather round our capital in Solun?" (which, incidentally, is the Greek port of Salonika). Popostefanović harbored no hope that he himself would see that splendid day: a toothless crock with fevered gums who no longer had a finer occupation than to pull his worn, fur-collared coat about him and stare at edifices of the past. Everyone in Ochrid called Jovan "the Old

One." He complained: "In my youth I spent money lavishly and I was known as 'Vanka the Fantastic.' And now I am 'Jovan the Impoverished,' 'the Old One.' "

I left Ochrid by bus across the forbidding mountains that engirdled it. We proceeded slowly, as every few miles there was a drift and all male passengers had to descend and help the driver shovel the creaking vehicle through. In front sat a cheerful soldier with his girl. She had a ghastly toothache. Her jaw was wrapped in a woolen scarf and she leaned her head against his bumping shoulder, sobbing constantly and moaning, *"Kuku majka, kuku majka;* ah woe, my little mother!" Finally we came to a complete halt in a village called Gostivar. Snowbound, we spent the night sitting before the fire of an inn while waiting for an army detachment to clear the road.

Eventually I reached Skoplje, capital of Jugoslav Macedonia, an attractive, dilapidated town with a clashing, jabbering row of bazaar stalls and many mosques whose minarets thrust eagerly towards the sky. A gypsy whose *kafana* I patronized told me his people had no interest in who ruled Macedonia or in the name of which God. "There are $77\frac{1}{2}$ religions in the world," he explained, "ours is the half." He persuaded his daughter to sing "The Girl in the Red Chemise," the Romany wedding plaint, describing the bride's traditional virginity test. Young couples, she advised me, always exchanged sugar and honey so they would learn to be sweet to each other.

From Skoplje I sent dispatches predicting that Italy would seize Albania. My London editor disbelieved me and I earned little from my journalistic jeremiad. So I wandered on to Sofia where a friend had offered me the use of his small apartment, an occasion suited to my penury.

# 5

## THE CHERRY
## TREE GUN

THE BULGARIANS ARE GLUM, UNLUCKY PEOPLE, TOUGH AND DOUR, priding themselves for some strange reason on being "the Prussians of the Balkans," a title not many would crave. They are excellent soldiers but generally manage to choose the wrong side in war. One of their early kings, Krum, made a drinking cup of his rival's skull which neither improved the taste of nightcaps nor brought its owner fortune.

Through no desire of their own, the Bulgarians have had their name attached to the Bogomil heresy, which taught that Satan was Christ's brother, and to the ugly sin of buggery (bulgary). All their neighbors detest them. One old story goes accordingly: A Serbian peasant had lived a noble, upright life. So, one day, God leaned over the gold bar of Heaven and said: "Jovan, you are the best Serbian peasant I have ever seen so I have decided to do for you anything you want. But remember, Jovan, whatever I do for you, I shall do twice as much for Ivan, the Bulgarian peasant who lives across the stream. What do you want?" Jovan removed his fur *kalpak* hat, scratched his locks, and finally said: "All right, God. Take out one of my eyes."

The Bulgars are Europe's best gardeners, earnest, hard-working and endowed with the green thumb, but not even the gardeners have much luck. A special treaty, based on barter, was signed by Sofia and Budapest in 1937. Under this, hundreds of Bulgarian market gardeners were sent to Hungary to till the plains and the Hungarians exported dozens of beautiful dancing girls to cheer up Sofia nightclubs. The gardeners' earnings were impounded in Budapest and the dancing girls' earnings were impounded in Sofia; then exchanged against each other. However, the gardeners never even saw the girls.

There is something deeply touching about the Bulgarians' drear destiny. Whatever the Bulgars set their minds to seems to go wrong. When they revolted against their Turkish overlords in the nineteenth century, they needed artillery but didn't even have an iron foundry. They made a cannon from a cherry tree, reinforced by wrapping the hardwood barrel with wire. The first time it was fired, it exploded. This tale became the subject of Bulgaria's most famous novel. It isn't even a good book.

My own Bulgarian luck seemed quite tainted. I arrived with a few gold sovereigns tied in the corner of my handkerchief, a habit I was to continue until after the war ended, having learned in Albania that simple people may best be induced to help by money they can taste. This knowledge was often useful in hiring water buffalo to haul my car out of Balkan mud, bribing telephone operators to give my calls priority and prevailing on hotel porters to find accommodation.

When I first reached Sofia my store of gold was embarrassingly small and I was forced to arrange the cabled sale of my Dali picture. While I was in Bulgaria two wars broke out, in Albania and in Greece. Once I was arrested in Sofia and cast into a cell with my friend Jim Gaul because we had dispossessed two drivers of their droshkies, mounted the horses, and staged a clattering midnight race down the capital's main thoroughfare. When an official came to let us out, Jim undiplomatically blacked his eye; so back we went. Another time I was jailed in Plovdiv because my terrier removed the seat of a policeman's pants. This action, incidentally, was acclaimed in the Turkish press. They said an American dog knew better than the British government just how Bulgarians should be treated.

In a sense the Bulgarians, whose Balkan range gave the peninsula its name, are the most pathetic of the Balkan peoples. Although they had boasted two periods of Medieval splendor and dynamism, they then disappeared into history for generations. A Slovakian scholar discovered a mass of Slavic-speaking peasants in Turkish Europe who called themselves Bugars and identified them as the Bulgars. I used to play golf with a few friends who had sunk nine cans in a sheep pasture near a village called Bugarov. We called ourselves the Royal Bugger-Off Golf Club and the greatest hazard was a pack of vicious dogs.

The Bulgarians derived many customs from their neighbors. They adopted the Serbs' folk hero, Kraljević Marko. Their church came from Greek orthodoxy although it turned anti-Greek and chauvinistic. I used to drink an ancient wine called Melnik, a heavy, purpureal draft from a southern village by that name. Melnik, founded in the twelfth century, had been a place to which the Byzantine emperors exiled troublesome nobles and they brought with them the vanities of the court including its scented wine. The Turks, too, left their mark. Rich men in villages were still called Čorbadjia after the Turkish for meat eater. And, as I began to learn the language (half-way between Serbian and Ukrainian), I found it contained many common-sense proverbs from Turkey, as for example: "A silver saddle makes the horse no better"; or: "Begged meat is bitter to eat."

When I started to travel around, I found quaint local customs. Women refused to take part in village plays, having learned obscurity under the Turks, and men played the female roles, but refused to shave off their mustaches, instead pomading them white. Girls in the hinterland took love potions and wore bat wings in their girdles. Near Pirin it was said a friendly species of dragon roved, looking like human beings covered with lizard scales and flying precisely four feet off the ground. At Sozopol, near the Turkish border, a fanatical sect danced on glowing, red-hot embers.

For some strange reason, the Bulgars are Europe's finest murderers. Even in my day visitors to the Sobranja, or parliament, were searched for firearms. When the Italians, Hungarians and Croat nationalists collaborated in arranging the assassination of Jugoslavia's King Alexander, accomplished at Marseille, the deed was done by a hired Bulgarian, nicknamed "Vlado the Chauffeur," a confirmed vegetarian because he considered it cruel to kill animals. The Bulgarian Macedonians had a terrorist brotherhood called IMRO (Internal Macedonian Revolutionary Organization) whose aim was to recapture from the Jugoslavs and Greeks their part of Macedonia. IMRO had a skull-and-crossbones insigne and swore members to allegiance over a Bible and revolver.

Its most famous chieftain was Ivančo Mihailov, who made money for guns by operating ten opium factories. Mihailov was adored by a certain Menča Karničev but he agreed to marry her only on condition she kill his rival, which she did.

During the worst IMRO days of the 1930s the standard fee for an assassination was $20. In 1933 the Sofia ministry of interior announced that anyone who feared for his life might hire bodyguards of good character provided they were duly registered. This custom of expressing political views with force had been long established. In 1895 an unpopular politician named Stambulov was slain in a peculiarly vicious way. Stambulov habitually wore a vest of chain mail so his murderers hacked off his arms in a Sofia street. He took three days to die. Sir Harold Nicolson recalled how, as a boy, when his father was a diplomat in Bulgaria, he stared in the window of a Sofia shop at a pickle jar containing Stambulov's fingers. Another politician, named Stamboliski, was captured by his enemies who stuck him with knives, then made him dig his own grave, cut off his hands and ears, shot him, and finally chopped off his head.

Possibly such methods of expression inhibited opinion; Bulgaria did not have an impressive record of self-government. Its first independent king, Ferdinand (known as "the Fox"), retained for himself 90 per cent of all bribes received by the state for loans or armaments contracts, giving only one-tenth to his ministers. King Boris, the ruler when I was there, was a tricky man whose hobby was to drive locomotives, whose ambition was to gain more territory, and who finally joined the Axis and died in mysterious fashion.

Russia was the mystical attraction for the Bulgars, perhaps because they were not truly Slavs. The main street of Sofia, named for a czar, looked like a Russian stage setting with its green, onion-domed church, glazed bricks and palace sentry boxes, striped as in some Muscovite ballet. The favorite saying when anything went wrong was *"Čičo Ivan ot Mockva sliza ot Dunava"*—Uncle Ivan from Moscow is coming up the Danube—to help out. The popular hero was Georgi Dimitrov, a Bulgarian who taunted Goering at the Reichstag fire trial, later became head of the Comintern and was prime minister of his communized country when he died.

I liked Sofia because it was picturesque, the people were friendly and it was cheap. My first day there I entered a tidy restaurant with clean white paper on the tables and ordered an excellent meal including a small carafe of wine. This, with a 20 per cent tip, cost 9 American cents.

I often visited the modest *Sobranja* (parliament) where I talked with political leaders including a fine democratic chief blessed with precisely the same name as the venerated, if absent, Communist Georgi Dimitrov. Dimitrov the Democrat was smuggled out of Bulgaria in 1945 with American aid when agents of his namesake were about to seize him. I also became a close friend of the agrarian, Grigor Vassiliev, who will reappear later in these pages when he used me as the pawn in a plot to stage simultaneous revolutions in Bulgaria and Jugoslavia. Vassiliev was a tall, lanky man with sandy gray mustache, sallow complexion and a potato-shaped nose. His wife, a Macedonian with IMRO family connections, had a good deal of money but Grigor slowly dissipated this fortune. He was an inveterate, and bad, gambler. Nevertheless, he was agreeable, hospitable and blessed with two strikingly pretty daughters.

The capital park was featured by flocks of crows and a prepossessing swimming pool. When the pool first opened, a delighted public swarmed in; several days later a corpse floated to the surface. Frequently I met with friends at one of the numerous cafés near this park. Regardless of party, all united in wanting a Greater Bulgaria, praising Mother Russia, and condemning the government. George Rendel, the British minister, explained that the administration had been Turkish for so many centuries that it became a patriotic habit to damn any regime at all.

Poor Rendel—he was having a hard time. After Munich, as war's likelihood increased, Britain had decided to expand its propaganda. One after another speaker was sent to Sofia until Rendel complained: "All they do is to describe what a great and wealthy country England is. At the same time we do nothing to help poor little Bulgaria. The result is invariably disastrous. I have just requested the Foreign Office to cease sending British Council visitors."

There were several nightclubs in Sofia, notable for bad champagne and remarkably attractive Hungarian dancing girls, brought in under the trade agreement with Budapest. One night, while I was sitting with one of these, the manager appeared, obsequiously wringing his hands. "I have an unusual offer," he said. "It is now midnight. You may stay on one more hour and drink all the free champagne you wish. But then you will have to depart and leave her behind," said he, nodding at my partner.

He explained that the Japanese chargé d'affaires had been reassigned and, with a compatriot, wished to hire the entire place, orchestra, girls and all, for the night—apparently, the owner reasoned, an old Japanese custom. All the customers accepted—and subsequently moved on to a similar establishment. Afterwards I learned the two Japanese had finally been carried upstairs to their legation car at 6 A.M. and been taken home unconscious. This was the most notable Sofia orgy until, more than a year later, the American minister, George Earle, smote a German on the head with a bottle of champagne.

The night of April 6, 1939, I went to the Cathedral of St. Alexander Nevsky for Easter services. An enormous crowd, redolent of incense and garlic, stood, holding lighted candles, regarding an ornamental bier in the central nave. We filed out behind the bier, borne by priests in chasubles and dalmatics adorned with gorgeous orphreys, carrying lighted candles homeward while the massive bells tolled. Next day I learned Mussolini had at last invaded Albania. The American legation told me the United Press in London had been calling me all night. I telephoned Webb Miller, then UP's star, and he said the agency wished to apply my war-plus-two-weeks contract; would I go to Albania as correspondent with King Zog's army? I requested permission to hire an airplane—or there would be no more army. Webb asked New York and by the time he called back, Zog had fled. I was told to proceed to Athens where the brave Albanian monarch was heading.

# 6

---

# THE CASE OF THE

# LOUD-SPEAKING

# CORPSE

F OR ONE DAZED, BRIEF INSTANT THE TRAVELER WHO FOR THE FIRST
time reaches Greece on a bright spring day is disappointed. Where
is the loveliness of which he has heard so much rhetorical praise?
There is neither the patterned geometry of fair France nor the green tidiness of England or forest Germany; not even the grandeur of American
ranges thrusting to eternity. Then, in one sudden flash it strikes. *Thauma!*
This is pure beauty: land, sea and sky, each perfect in itself and perfectly
composed. And once this truth encompasses, one is lost. I speak with the
nostalgia of experience; for it is in Greece that I found my wife, in Greece
that my son was born, and in Greece that I made the home where I shall
spend my fading days.

In Greece the perplexing world of nit picks assumes due proportions. I
learned this as I swam in the soft Aegean, boated to the islands, or strode
through Attica across the worn slopes of Parnes, Pentelicon and Hymettus
where bees distill such a sweet and spiritual honey.

One learns to contemplate amid the fragrance of thyme, rosemary,
terebinth and lavender, pondering old goat-gods and musical fairies as,
finding their way from barren, stony soil come broom, poppies, flax, sea
lavender, and camomile daisies and, despite the inhospitable earth,
tamarisk, alder, agave, judas trees, quinces, pears and apricots, emerging
among the pines and wise old olive trees, brushed by tender, seasonal
winds.

The cuckoos sing; the dove and quail begin to flutter northward; and one forgets daily problems, gazing from temple ruins to distant peaks where even now one faintly hears pagan deities munch their bread of asphodel with carious teeth. The silver groves, the carefully terraced vineyards, the bell-jangles of browsing flocks, the notes of the herdsman's double flute, the mewing of gulls circling inland in search of insects, the kestrel swoop among cypress trees brooding over generations of noble dead; the wheeling of pigeons and the whisper of imagined lyres; the bray of donkeys, the clatter of shrill voices; the hooting of miniature owls at eventide, the soft rustle of pine-needled feet; the gabble-gabble of ceaseless talk and always sea sounds, the flurrying tides and rustle of waves that tumble upon each other beneath the sun and under the silent rising of the moon.

I rode into this perpetual vitality with a little French reporter from the Havas Agency who, apart from being an affable companion, was the most notable trencherman I ever met. Maurice was little interested in Albanian issues, Athenian politics, bawling bazaars, or the flamboyant royal guard, dressed in tasseled red slippers, embroidered jackets and white fustanella skirts. His attention was focused on the menu presented at a coastal tavern whose name he had shrewdly obtained before our arrival and where, clutching fork and knife with equal firmness, he introduced me to baby cuttlefish, Byzantine stuffed grape leaves and groupers snatched from their sea caves and immediately grilled, and resinated wine which, since the age of Homeric voyages when it was stored in pine-tarred kegs among the oarsmen's feet, has tasted delightfully of turpentine.

Athens was in a frenzy. The Greeks held Italy in contempt but were forced to respect Mussolini's pompous boasts that he could muster eight million bayonets. And they feared Hitler, leaning from Austria into the Balkans. Lincoln MacVeagh, the scholarly American minister, said:

> Now they are really between the devil and the deep blue sea. The Axis armies and their puppets are moving to the border. The English fleet is stretched along the coast. Saturday midnight, at the Easter service, everyone was nervous. The Fascists had finished taking Albania. After the service General Metaxas [the dictator] summoned the British minister, Sir Sidney Waterlow. Metaxas was pale. Almost in tears, he warned Waterlow the Greeks would fight if an inch of their soil were violated. Now the British know these people mean business. If necessary, they will have to do something. That would mean world war.

Spy scares at that time were rife. These assume a gorgeous hue in a volatile land like Greece but by far the most gaudy incident involved a certain Italian named Vicenzo Caivano who had just been arrested. Caivano lived in Istanbul. Some years previously he had married a Greek woman from the Piraeus, Athens' harbor and port-of-call for visiting naval squadrons. The Caivanos bought a house in Piraeus and shuttled between there and Turkey where he had a business.

In 1937, after Signora Caivano died, her widower asked the mayor of Piraeus for permission to erect a chapel in her honor. Normally the area was restricted. But Caivano was given authority to build. He hired necessary master builders and constructed a modest church with a subterranean vault. His wife's embalmed corpse was shipped from Istanbul in a bronze coffin, its berouged face showing under a glass panel affixed at the head. The special interment ceremony was attended by the Archbishop of Athens.

Whenever he was in Piraeus Caivano made a practice of communing in the chapel for two or three hours daily. He always wore deep mourning and was regarded as slightly insane. No servants remained with him long because he insisted on eating alone with a place set for his wife whose glass he would solemnly clink. British intelligence, equipped with more modern instruments than its Greek counterpart, tipped off Athens that coded wireless transmissions were being monitored in Piraeus. Greek direction finders triangulated the source in the vicinity of the chapel. One night, when Caivano was in Istanbul the building was searched, walls tapped and screened with mine detectors. Then the casket was pried open. Inside, separated by a partition from the mummified head, the investigators found a high-powered transmitting set. When Caivano returned to the Piraeus they laid a trap and arrested him in the vault.

There was another wholly nonmilitary incident at this time. A Greek sea captain was hailed into court by an insurance company on suspicion of having scuttled his caïque in order to collect an inflated evaluation. His defense was brief and unabashedly to the point. "Masters," said he to the judges. "I was carrying a cargo of cheese to Alexandria. But my ship was old and the timbers had worn thin. My ship was also filled with rats. The rats were notably voracious and they ate their way through the cheese. But it was very salty cheese, a *kasseri,* and this made them thirsty. When they got through the cheese to the bottom of the boat they heard the water slipping by outside going glug, glug, glug. *Thée-mou,* my God, when they heard this agreeable noise it drove them mad with thirst; and they ate through the hull of my caïque to get to the water below. Thus, *gamoto,* my ship sank."

The electricity of the Albanian crisis ran rapidly out. MacVeagh told me a mobilization order was ready to be issued, but added:

Mobilization is tricky here. Greek characteristics continue through the ages. Metaxas knows he has his enemies. Remember, before they fought the Persians at Plataea, some of the Athenians wanted to sell out in order to oust their leader. This government fears mobilization might permit a group of soldiers to try and throw Metaxas out.

MacVeagh was astute and managed with remarkable acuity to base predictions of future events on Greek historical characteristics. He foresaw an eventual Italian ultimatum and he also foresaw refusal by Greece to accept it. He foresaw a successful national defense at a time when most of his diplomatic colleagues predicted immediate disaster. A year and a half before Mussolini invaded, MacVeagh said to me:

> If war comes, Greece must in the end be on England's side. There is some pro-German feeling, above all among monarchists. Metaxas himself graduated from German war academies, where he was called "little Moltke." But were Greece to join the Axis, even if this Axis won the war, Greece would lose its freedom and become a virtual colony. With the English she is safe. England has no aspirations here. Even if, during a long war, the Greek government should be driven from the country, in the end Greece would recover its independence.

This was brilliant prophesy. Two years later, the Greek government and royal family would be in exile, their land brutally occupied. But government and king returned, and to such complete independence that soon they were to go to the brink of war with England, their greatest ally, over the nasty Cyprus question.

In those days I first met Metaxas and King George II. The dictator was a pudgy, small man with pale, pasty face, spectacles, and not the slightest physical attribute one normally associates with a general or ruthless autocrat, both of which he was. Despite his unimpressive appearance and volatile Hellenic blood, he was cold-blooded, unemotional, and could be impassively brutal. He was hated by most Greeks. Yet, when he had the courage to say *oxi* (no) to an Italian ultimatum in October, 1940, and when he showed his military genius by organizing an effective defense, he earned respect and admiration. As for King George, he was a fluent gossip and decidedly amusing although he had no talent for popularity among his ebullient compatriots. The ruler insisted tactlessly on regarding them as foreigners; to most Greeks he was aloof and remote. They disliked his choice of mistress more for the fact that she was brunette than for the fact that she was English, and therefore foreign, muttering: "At least he could have found a blonde."

I filed several dispatches for the United Press, realizing that the term of our contract would be short since all fighting had ceased in Albania and the Italians had stopped at the Greek frontier. Zog had been quietly urged to move on to Rumania where King Carol accorded him royal honors, much to the fury of Carol's cousin, Wilhelm of Wied, formerly brief tenant of the throne of the Eagle Men and then in Bucharest.

To inquire into Albania's fate I went up to the border north of Janina where everyone was discussing what they would do to the "macaroni eaters." The Greeks had reinforced their frontier garrison. All Epirus was on a war footing. Janina, a sleepy Turkish-looking town, was enlivened by cavalry officers trotting up to cafés, tethering their horses and sitting down to play backgammon.

I boated on the green, sluggish lake, mirroring sclerotic mountains, where a nineteenth-century Ottoman pasha, Ali, called "the Lion," had drowned womenfolk in sacks. Before heaving them into the water, he coated the sacks with sugar in order to insure that death came sweetly.

I managed to slip into Albania through a frontier post called Perati. There I found pathetically seedy Albanian troops still wearing hand-me-down Italian uniforms once furnished at cut-rates to Zog by a munificent Rome. They had ripped Zog's "Z" emblem from their caps; that was the only difference, and they appeared no more ferocious on Mussolini's behalf than they had proven in the name of their former ruler. The Italian officers with whom I spoke were disconsolate. "Those Greeks," said a captain from Bari. "They are so provocative. They keep pointing guns at us and making derogatory remarks."

During that agitated spring I saw much of A. C. (Shan) Sedgwick of *The New York Times* and met his nineteen-year-old Greek niece Marina, a slender girl with dark, iridescent hair and glowing eyes. She moved with secret grace, stood like a marigold and wafted the scent of lemon-fragrant verbena.

To a jaded man of twenty-six Marina seemed but a sweet infant agreeably adorning her uncle's home when she came from her mother's country house to spend the night. Once, when I invited them to lunch, at the last instant Shan and his wife Roxane couldn't come and I found myself tête-à-tête with Marina. Months later she confessed this was the first time she had been allowed to take a meal alone with a man. I offered her a dry Martini which she seemed to drink with pleasure. As we grew to know each other, this became a standard preliminary when we dined. Only long afterwards, the day of our wedding, did Marina confess she hated all alcohol, above all dry Martinis; she had feared putting me off by seeming a teetotaler. We have been married almost a quarter of a century and she has never touched one since. This, dear reader, is the way Greek women since Circe have entrapped their men.

In May when the most generous interpretation of my UP contract—war (in Albania) plus two weeks—drew to its peaceful conclusion, I restored relationships with the *Evening Standard,* and took off on a long motor trip: to Thermopylae, Delphi and the hyaline Gulf of Corinth with its sanctuaries for the earth mother, Gaia, and the earth shaker, Poseidon. The breeze rippled the wheat and the black skirts of shepherds moving their flocks to the mountains for summer pasture. Indeed, the heights of Arcadia are the crossroads for the splendidly named Greek winds: Tramontana, Levantes and Ponentes from North, East and West; Batis the gentle evening blow and the strong-fingered Meltemi, whipping waves in the Gulf of Argolis where I was to settle in years to come.

At the tip of the Peloponnesus, not far from the cave where Charon ferried customers across the river Styx, archaeologists had just found the palace at Pylos of Nestor, tamer of horses, who fought the war against

Troy. It was hot and dusty. Only the first faint outlines of his steep citadel had yet been uncovered above the grain-bearing plain. Aided by straw-bound carafes of retsina, the mind's eye could still see there, in the soft evening, Nestor, lord of chariots, seated with his sons, roasting the flesh of oxen on spits, pouring wine from golden cups, annointing themselves with chrism and regarding the length of famous halls, patrolled by soldiers with good ashen spears.

I flew to Candia in Crete, El Greco's home, and walked to Cnossus beneath a broiling, half-African sun to examine the bright frescoes of tiny-waisted women somersaulting over bulls' horns. I took a bus to Canea, by acrid charcoal ovens and villages filled with huge Cretans, Greece's best fighters (or so they boast), wearing black turbans, blue double-breasted vests, red sashes, boots and baggy black bloomers. I hired a mule and rode from Rethymno up the rocky trail to Arkadi, a monastery perched above a chasm filled with sweet-smelling herbs. There, five hundred Cretans had shut themselves up to fight the Turks and blew themselves to pieces when the wall was breached.

The *igumen,* in black beard, black gown and black velvet cap, invited me for lunch. Somewhat astonished, I found the jolly monks surrounded by ladies, many of them with black curly hair, straight noses, light blue-gray eyes and little waists, resembling the bull tumblers of Cnossus. A bearded ruffian in strange peaked hat, folded over like a pirate's, served us bitter *raki,* goblets of wine, fish, eggs, goat cheese and fresh honey while the girls cuddled beside their amiable priests. Occasionally the *igumen* turned aside with a mephitic belch and spat into the corner. That evening he showed me a caseful of skulls in a recondite chapel and then, through a trap door, an entire floor paved with still more skulls: the martyrs to the Turks. That night I rode down through a thunderstorm and bathed naked on an interminable beach beneath the limpid stars.

Back in Athens I found a telegram from my uncle, proprietor of *The New York Times,* asking me to fly to London for a "business consultation." There I dined with him and his former managing editor, Frederick Birchall, and they invited me to join the *Times.* I refused. They then proposed that I undertake a special survey of Balkan communications available in case of war. I agreed to this if it did not interfere with my *Standard* arrangements. Old Birch plied me with drink and, at what he judged the propitious moment, said: "Well, laddy, at least if you won't come with the *Times* now, will you give us first option if war comes?" At this point Uncle Arthur tactfully left.

I felt in a strong bargaining position. Already I had such an understanding with UP, while Columbia Broadcasting System had tendered a similar offer at much larger pay. Finally there were no other available American reporters in the Balkans; I had acquired fairly extensive experience, spoke French and German and had learned to burble in Serbian, Albanian and

Bulgarian as well as two personal demotic tongues that I call "Foreign" and are all that remain now that my linguistic lobes have atrophied. In Latin Foreign I can still, with the aid of gestures, find my way from Cadiz to Constanza and, in Slavic Foreign, from Sušak to Samarkand. With this background I asked of Birch: what would he offer and in what capacity for a contingency contract with the *Times?*

"What is the UP figure?" he inquired, suddenly looking more like managing editor than friend. I demurred. I told him the CBS offer was unusually handsome. "But nobody in his right mind wants to broadcast," said Birch with evocative gestures. "Those words vanish with the wind. I am suggesting that you work for the finest newspaper in the world. If war comes I'll make you bureau manager for all the Balkans at $100 a week; and you can terminate the contract two weeks after an armistice, if you are fool enough." I had no desire to join a family enterprise but was ruefully forced to agree it happened to be a remarkable paper. Nevertheless, Birch's offer was financially unappealing and I had learned to bargain in Tirana poker games and Sarajevo bazaars. Damning me as impertinent and avaricious, Birch finally met my salary terms. In little more than three months, when Hitler attacked Poland, the contract was applied. By the time World War II ended I headed the *Times'* entire foreign service so I never exercised my two-week option to get out.

The day after our conversation, I said goodbye to Birch and Uncle Arthur, disengaged from UP and CBS, and flew to Turkey to start my communications study.

# 7

## THE WAR WAIT

I SPENT THE SUMMER OF 1939 IN TURKEY, HUNGARY AND RUMANIA
completing my communications investigation and reporting for the
*Standard* and North American Newspaper Alliance. That August I
settled in Bucharest to wait for war.

Turkey, my initial point of inquiry, was dominated by one obsession,
Russia. This had little to do with communism as such. Mustapha Kemal
Ataturk, after his revolution, accepted certain socialist ideas and even
collaborated gingerly with the Soviets. But Russia remained an unchanging
enemy. Turkish mothers still warned naughty children to watch out or the
"Moskva" would get them.

Ataturk, a remarkable leader, had died a few months earlier, a brave, farsighted but dissolute and heteroclitic patriot. His first revolutionary prime
minister, Rauf Bey Orbay, introduced me to a physician who had attended
the dictator as he lay ill with cirrhosis. "He saw us doctors talking in a
corner," said the physician, "and he asked: 'What's the matter? Are you
afraid to tell me the truth? You think I drink too much? Well, I shall not
touch another drop. Forever.' It was hard for us to say: 'Ghazi, now you
drink two bottles of alcohol each day. Can you not cut down to one; and
then slowly reduce the ration?' 'No,' he insisted, 'I shall drink no more.'
Had he accepted to taper off, he might have lived another year or two. He
had vitality, that man."

Rauf was himself an unusual individual. A naval officer, he commanded
a famous raiding cruiser and also arranged for a tinpot submarine to deposit
Azzam, later head of the Arab League, behind enemy lines in Libya during
the 1911 Italo-Turkish war. Rauf was promoted admiral and finally named
navy minister during World War I, signing the armistice on behalf of the

74

last Sultan. Then he fled eastward to Anatolia where Kemal had raised the
standard of revolt. He became first premier of the revolutionary republic.
Rauf broke with Ataturk later and spent years as a refugee in France. For
a time he supported himself by rowing a boat. He finally returned to
Turkey and, during World War II, became ambassador to England.
Honest, courteous, modest, gifted with an impeccable memory, he refused
to write his intensely interesting memoirs, always saying: "Let history speak
for itself. I shall be content with whatever small footnote is allotted to me."
Strongly knit, burly, with furrowed brow and kindly wrinkles at the corners
of his eyes, Rauf became my close friend over the next twenty years. The
Turks say "A cup of coffee commits one to forty years of friendship." I
must have consumed a thousand little cups of mocha with Rauf.

Ever since they had settled around the glaucous Sea of Marmora the
Turks had been torn between East and West. When the Ottomans took
Constantinople in 1453, the conquered Greeks decided: "Rather the turban
in Constantinople than the hat of a Roman Cardinal" and accepted Ottoman
rule. The Sultans adopted Byzantine ambitions and sybaritic customs, adding their own harems filled with eunuchs and officiated over by a master of
the girls, a chief nightingale-keeper and a keeper of the parrots. For four
centuries they ruled a multiracial state: Greeks, Serbs, Bulgars, Rumanians, Albanians, Bosniaks, Jews, Gypsies, Egyptians, Berbers, Negroes, Arabs, Armenians, Kurds; a state in which the Turks themselves
were a permanent minority. Despite the predominance of Islam, numerous
other faiths were permitted: Orthodox, Roman Catholic, Copts, Nesto-
rians, Jacobite-Syrians, devil-worshipping Yezidis, Samaritans, Druses and
the moon-worshipping Sabaeans on the banks of the Tigris. Of the orthodox Patriarchs of Constantinople, one hundred forty were deposed, forty-
one resigned, three were poisoned, two murdered, one beheaded, one
drowned, one hanged, one strangled; and yet the patriarchy continued
through all Turkey's convulsions and still remains active in Istanbul. During the seventeenth century an Albanian Grand Vizier named Köprülü
decided to use the clever Greeks of Constantinople's Phanar to administer
those portions of the empire where the stolid Turks had difficulty collecting
taxes. The system worked with remarkable success and explains the origin
of many Rumanian princely families with old Byzantine names.

Mahmud II sought to "Europeanize" this agglomeration. He ended the
fantastic Asiatic dress of heavy turbans, silken and cambric robes and
replaced these with the frock coat and a hat he considered very "western,"
now known as the fez. When Ataturk took over he regarded the fez as a
backward, oriental symbol. In 1925 he ordered every male Turk to appear
in occidental headgear. There were few hatters in the realm, apart from fez
makers, and the embarrassed ruck of peasants suddenly appeared in every
imaginable covering from stiff bowlers and straw boaters to women's Paris

bonnets. An Egyptian diplomat came to a reception wearing a fez and Ataturk slapped it off.

Byzantine corruption was difficult to erase. The uncle of a friend paid license fees and fines for a dog over a period of nineteen years although he never owned such an animal; this was simply a means of gaining permission to serve drinks in his restaurant after hours.

In Istanbul with its lovely mosques, the handsome structures of Sinan, that fine architect of the Ottoman renaissance, and florescent, unparalleled vistas, I settled in a cheap hotel called the Londra from which I could look down on the Golden Horn.

In those days Davut, a Persian Jew, owned a small shop in the bazaar. Tall, fluent, modest, with amiable, hook-nosed face, Davut received from agents (to most of whom he was related) extraordinary objects from the bazaars of Central Asia. Always ready with syrupy coffee or minted tea and endless founts of rumor, Davut had a special price for each customer and preliminary haggling was his private pleasure. He was ready to supply almost anything. Once I heard him tell a distinguished American, "Today I have something particular for you: a sixteen-year-old Tartar virgin." Davut had been "wiped out" many times by fire, taxes and restrictive legislation. I have listened to him as he complained in catatonic tones that all his savings had vanished. Yet Davut still managed to maintain membership in Istanbul's most costly yacht club.

In Istanbul sixteen centuries of empire piled on empire in ramshackle hodgepodge, rimmed by rushing waters and jerry-built filth, pierced by the thrust of minarets, and hiding the stolen treasures of three continents. I spent hours in the bazaar, savoring its odd smells and listening to the hurly-burly where cobblers, metal workers and peddlers vied. I scrambled among the scaffoldings of St. Sophia, basilica of Holy Wisdom, with a brilliant old American archaeologist named Whittemore who uncovered the magnificent mosaics and crawled around the dome like a human fly. And I ate at Pandeli's, a bare restaurant with long wooden tables whose drunken Greek proprietor served customers only what he thought each deserved.

Although it was summer and the government had scuttled to the seaside, I went to Ankara, an old Hittite stronghold on the pastel-shaded, dusty Anatolian plateau, which Ataturk had chosen as seat for his new republic: a clattering boom town whose citizens, in those days, discouraged visitors from inspecting the ancient ramparts with their fanes to pagan deities and tumbling walls with the nests of roosting storks; they preferred the modern to the quaint from which they were struggling to emerge. In Ankara I consulted radio and telephone technicians, foreign office functionaries, editors of the muzzled press, and had a long talk with a young woman named Sabiha Gökchen, Ataturk's adopted daughter. She received me in the pretentious little house he had bequeathed her: a small, agreeable, dumpy girl with brown hair, honest blue eyes, sturdy ankles and immense feet. Sabiha was a symbol of Turkish womanhood liberated by the Kemalist revolution, first aviatrix of her country, Turkey's Amelia Earhart. As a regular air force officer, she had enthusiastically bombed Kurdish villages during one of that irascible people's uprisings. "I like bombing and machine-gunning," she confided, after serving me sour cherry juice and homemade cookies. She headed a flyers' school in Ankara and dreamed of organizing an "Amazon squadron" among the first generation of Turkish girls to shed the bloomer and the veil.

Ankara was then a hot, dusty, Anatolian town. In the indigo evenings, beneath the crescent moon and star of Moslem fanions, one could look out toward the barren east from which jangling, barbarous horse-borne armies with their horse-tailed pashas, baggage camels and their bashi-bazouks, had clattered from Central Asia into Europe.

The only decent hotel was a modest establishment called the Ankara Palas, across the street from the old parliament. This looked so much like the average conception of a Turkish bath that two Americans once wandered in bearing towels and were arrested for offending the state. The most comforting feature of the capital was a restaurant named Karpić after its Russian-Armenian proprietor. Old Karpić, a heavy, bald, large-featured man who served splendid caviar, *šašlik* and Kiev cutlets, had been endowed by Ataturk so Ankara would have one eating place to cheer up foreign diplomats, disgruntled when they had to abandon Istanbul.

The biggest event that summer was military, which is not surprising as the Turks are par excellence a warrior nation. Besieged by arms merchants from rival nations, they were then trying to make up their minds on the most suitable infantry helmet. The choice had narrowed down to the German *pickelhauber* or the British Tommy's basin. A test was carried out before competitive attachés. Steel hats were placed on the granitic Anatolian scree and delighted Turkish officers hacked, shot and battered at the two designs. Much to Britain's delight, the English version was chosen. For some strange reason this has great psychological importance; it is usual that armies wearing similar helmets tend to band together in time of war.

I flew from Turkey to Budapest in an old Junkers. No one spoke of anything but Hungary's territorial claims. *"Nem, nem soha*—no, no, never" was the national slogan—a blank refusal to accept the Trianon Treaty, which, after World War I, had truncated the country. The Nazis were making evident headway with both the German minority and Magyar conservatives who looked forward to another war.

The Magyars have vitality, intelligence, grace; so, for the foreigner and for the prosperous, Budapest was a fine place, gay and effluent with talk, music and flirtation. In the cafés, where journalists, writers and intellectuals gathered daily, they discussed Sandor Petöfi, a nineteenth-century poet-patriot who wrote that dogs were always well looked after and wolves starved; but only wolves were free.

The feudal differences between land-rich aristocrats or favored bourgeois and the little peasants who tilled vineyards or rode herd on the great
*pusztas* (plains) were more marked than in other Southeastern European
states. The rich were for the most part tall, distinguished men with graceful, well-dressed ladies. Only the German minority of Swabian settlers sent
in as frontier guards against the old Turkish invaders were well-built,
sturdy representatives of the impoverished classes. But, so obsessed was
everyone with the desire to claim lost territories, feelings of social discontent seemed wholly obscured. And the good food, heady Bull's Blood wine,
apricot brandy, intellectual arguments and the plethora of lovely girls made
Budapest a marvelous center for any young bachelor's inquiry.

I was helped in my Budapest survey for *The New York Times* by its
local representative, Elizabeth de Pünkösti, a delicate, sensitive woman
whose connections were so widespread in all circles that she never needed
to leave her comfortable apartment in order to learn what was going on.
Poor Elizabeth—her parents had committed suicide during the brief Communist Republic of Bela Kun after World War I, and she was to kill herself
in World War II.

The last lap of my survey was in Rumania where I decided to wait out
the start of what was by then so apparently an inevitable war. Because of
the uncertainty of my stay I moved from a hotel to a small pension where I
was accorded two rooms in considerable comfort and where I completed
my report for Birchall.

In the same pension lived a huge American named Tulipp, an agent for
the United States Treasury's antinarcotics service. The Balkans are studded
with farms that grow opium as a cash crop. They are also blessed with an
opulent tradition of lawlessness and a gift for smuggling. The area was
therefore a fine laboratory for T-Men assigned to track the dope trade at its
source.

Tulipp told me that once, in India, he found himself without funds and
hired out as bodyguard to a corpse being shipped to Europe from Bombay
in a sealed barrel of brandy. He tapped the keg and drank it up during the
tedious journey. I was to encounter him time and again in various guises.
During the war, I saw him wearing the uniform of a navy commander.
Another time, in Beirut, he was fashionably adorned in the tailor-made
garb of war correspondent and proclaimed that he represented *Country
Gentleman*.

In 1939 Tulipp was well-known in the better Balkan bars. One would be
clutching a glass in solitary thought when, even without turning, one could
feel a tremendous shadow slip across the threshold. This sensibility would
be confirmed by pressure on the back from a hand the size of a snow
shovel. "Now don't move," came a rumbled whisper, as if it were possible
to escape that ponderous hold. "And don't recognize me. I will shortly
introduce myself." This he would then proceed to do: sometimes as Johnson and sometimes as du Pont and sometimes as Papadopoulos, depending

on circumstance. And Tulipp, a generous man, would set about buying drinks. As the hours passed, his confidence would commence to resonate about the room. "I'm here on a hot trail. We're closing in on Popescu, cocaine merchant. At least he calls himself Popescu. I've followed him from Skoplje. Now I'm prepared to strike. His real name is Lucci. The haul will be big. Very big [to me]: I'll let you know when you can write the story." Tulipp's voice would by now be thundering—a booming, resonant bass. By the time he had finished these confidences designating his proposed victim to everyone in the bar, Popescu-Lucci would have completed his Rumanian deals, converted profits into hard currency, dined leisurely, and departed for distant points. A few days later, with admirable persistency, Tulipp would resume his search.

Bucharest was delightfully depraved. When the *Times* had paid me for my report, I moved to the gaudy Athenée Palace Hotel to enjoy my wait for war. This was a comfortable establishment with excellent service, fine food, luxurious accommodation, a corrupt staff always seeking to change a customer's money at black market rates, and continual competition by ladies of easy or nonexistent virtue to share the warmth of a client's bed. There was small opportunity for the ample population of paid prostitutes because of enthusiastic rivalry among amateurs of all classes, from princesses down. One night when I discreetly tottered home with an actress of my acquaintance I found, to my embarrassment, a handsome young chambermaid sleeping peacefully on my pillow.

Thank heavens I first knew Bucharest in the days of my youth and in its own spiritual decrepitude. The Czar of Russia once sneered: "Rumania: it's not a country; it's a profession." Because of its foppish officers, in sharply cut uniforms, corsets and cosmetics, the Rumanian army had a dismally low reputation. Nevertheless, in World War I, when these officers fled at the battle of Marašešti, the sturdy Rumanian peasantry chewed up attacking German divisions. After World War II I asked my friend, General Hans Speidel, who had commanded various mixed Axis contingents and became Field Marshal Rommel's chief of staff: "Which among all the non-German troops were the best soldiers: the Finns, the Croats, the Hungarians?" "None of them," he said: "the Rumanians. Give them good leadership and they are as good as any you'll find."

The Rumania of those days was a striking testimonial to that old Balkan proverb: "The fish stinks from the head first." The government was lazy, crooked, unreliable and unbelievably avaricious. Graft was the great leaven. The very first official I met pulled open a drawer in his desk, exposing packets of foreign money, and sought to bribe me. When I declined he asked what black market rate I was receiving for my dollars, an odd question since it was illegal to change currency except at approved banks. I told him what the Athenée Palace porter gave me. "Why that man's a crook," he scoffed. "I'll give you 15 per cent more."

If ever a land deserved revolution it was Rumania. King Carol was later to assure me Rumanians were truly democratic because the peasants uncovered their heads and clutched their forelocks when he passed! He was an immoral, selfish man. When he finally fled his country in 1940, he managed to abscond with considerable personal wealth, and his mistress, the red-haired, violet-eyed Magda Lupescu. She had a cozy way of looking after him in an affectionate and almost maternal manner and, to his credit, he remained loyal to her even in adversity.

There were few decent politicians apart from the upright, courageous Iuliu Maniu, a Transylvanian, who had helped during World War I to create Czechoslovakia. He tried to give a proper voice to the peasants whose holdings were small and whose productivity was limited because they didn't know their jobs.

At that time a particular peasant hero named Petrarca Lupu claimed to have spoken several times with God the Father. A picture of himself during one of these colloquies was painted outside his house, God wearing a vast white beard from which only his hands and feet protruded. Petrarca became a dream symbol of the poor farmers who hoped for divine intercession to aid their cause so persistently ignored by mundane administration. There was a story that when the German field marshal, Mackensen, stormed into Rumania during World War I he spent the first night in a peasant's house and was amazed to discover no toilet. He summoned his unwilling host who said: "If we had toilets we would be invading Germany, not you us."

Despite its loveliness, Rumania simmered with hatreds. Anti-Semitism was rife, fanned by tradition, the Germans, Hungarians and Russians, and a local Rumanian Fascist band called the Iron Guard. At Cernauţi the British Council, a cultural and propaganda organization, did boom business teaching English to Jews who then promptly tried to emigrate to Palestine. The Rumanians detested their own debased wealthy classes. The Greek Phanariote princes appointed by the Turks had always been servile to the Sultan's representatives and embraced their robes in public; but they made the indigenous Boyar nobility carry them from one room to another and kiss their hands and knees. The Rumanians also hated their neighbors, the Bulgars, Hungarians and Russians; and they feared and resented the powerful Germans. The Russians had a well-justified reputation for plunder. General Kutuzov boasted he would leave the Rumanians "only their eyes to weep."

I found it joyful to travel about the rolling, fertile countryside, with its green fields, banked flowers and espaliered orchards, its purling streams, mountains and forests. I conceived an affection for the hospitable Rumanian peasants, an affection I still retain. I motored through Transylvania, the land of vampires, witches, love potions and animals gifted with supernatural powers, where bastards are sweetly called "children of the flowers" (hippies please note).

From Bucovina (the Beech Forest) to Transylvania (Ardeal—the hill section) and down to the Danube marshes lay a fascinating land with wild life varying from sturgeon to antediluvian flamingo. In Moldavia I heard a shepherd sing: "Of the murder thou shalt not tell them; only say I married a proud queen." And in Oltenia, at Easter, girls prayed: "From the great lords and ladies, from the goats and the ewes, even from the little birds and the stars, let love be taken and given to me."

In Carpathian churches, the portals were sheltered by overhanging eaves and the plaster walls on each side were painted with bright scenes of heaven and hell. The devils and damned always seemed to enjoy themselves more than the saints and angels. I started a collection of icons depicting merry demons (a collection I was later forced to leave in Wehrmacht hands). The Rumanians had a curiously resigned and amiable relationship with death, regarding it eye-to-eye without much horror. I was told of a peasant widow who, at her husband's funeral, made the following simple speech when the priest had finished his prayers: "Oh death, begin your work of corruption at his back, then his legs, then his chest; oh death, leave his face until the last for it was handsome."

I returned to Bucharest at the end of August, and one night a Jugoslav diplomat invited me to dine with two young lady friends. The gentleman used his diplomatic advantages for amatory purposes. He spoke excellent Rumanian and was also fond of gypsies. He therefore regularly visited the gypsy market and, when he spotted a lovely, dark-haired maiden, made arrangements with her father involving a handsome amount of baksheesh. The girl would then be installed in a small apartment T. rented for this purpose, furnished with an unscrupulous housekeeper. This beldam saw to it that the young lady was well scrubbed, medically inspected, and generally broken in. By the time T. had lost interest in his previous conquest, he would take the newest love shopping, bedecking her with the finery available in Bucharest, which called itself the Paris of the Balkans. With this humble Casanova and two of his sloe-eyed ladies, I sat beneath eucalyptus trees strung with lights while fiddlers played haunting lays and we drank white Wallachian wine into the early morning. That morning World War II began: September 1, 1939.

I received an urgent telephone call from Berlin. It was Birchall. "Laddy," he shouted over the wire, "you're on. Set up a Balkan bureau and communicate with New York. Cheerio."

# 8

# JACKALING

THE JACKAL OF OUR ERA IS THE WAR CORRESPONDENT. HIS FUNC-
tion is to describe in all its horror how men kill each other, in
what manner they die and for what cause they imagine. His own
and the censor's prejudice combine to see that this is done in glowing terms.

*"Il popolo e una bestia,"* wrote Tommaso Campanella. It is the war
correspondent's role to clothe this beast in glamor. The war correspondent
does not justify his trade by killing, although some are killed themselves.
He is the passive participant in an active chase.

Even the most venturesome of this breed, among whom I was never
numbered, can depart the scene when it suits him or his editor. He need not
bare his breast indefinitely for the sake of duty or of chauvinism although I
have known brave, true war correspondents who died unnecessarily only to
confirm a fact. I have also seen others write dauntless eyewitness accounts
from safe headquarters or even bars. It is an odd trade, in some cases best
practiced by a literary coward while the unstylish hero dies little mourned
in a time of mass dying.

Before the end of the war at my own unembarrassed convenience I saw
some aspects of an intolerable tragedy in which 9,000,000 soldiers were
slaughtered and thrice that number of civilians while I, describing vignettes
of holocaust, have never killed a man myself. This, in our age, is an
anomaly. I have never been an officer nor commanded a proper soldier
although I have held the "assimilated" rank of captain in four armies,
American, British, Greek and Jugoslav. In the last instance, my credentials
were signed by a king.

At various times and in various conditions I accompanied the troops of
Hungary, Bulgaria, Greece, Jugoslavia, Russia, Britain and the United

States plus contingents from Poland, France, Canada, South Africa, New Zealand and Brazil. I have seen their dead and I have also seen dead Germans and dead Italians in varying attitudes and in varying climes, frozen stiff with bright red blood, rotting with brown blood in the heat; some with throats eaten out by dogs and others with throats bitten out by human beings.

The very process of autobiography which is, alas, instinctual, is also in itself the essence of immodesty. The mind coats past deeds with romance or with sentiment, diminishes embarrassments or forgets them in entirety, attaches to small events the grandeur of personal involvement, takes comfort in tiny vanities and warmth in remembered pleasures. I have not desired or sought adventure, being by nature a peaceful man and the contrary of audacious. Most humans are born with a limited reservoir of courage and unless this reservoir is nourished by secret, inner streams, it runs out. My reservoir ran out early. Even today, having experienced two crashes, when I climb into an airplane I remain a firm believer in the law of gravity. Circumstance projected me into a weird life for which I was never really suited, much as the cowardly moth is driven to the fascination of flames.

And, although war's spastic clutch did not reach out and seize me in my Balkan fastness for many months after I joined *The New York Times,* war dominated the thoughts of all I encountered for almost six full years, even before I was personally caught in its senseless grip and sought—seeing it, tasting it, watching it—to follow vainly in the footsteps of the first great journalistic pioneers of battle, Calisthenes and Xenophon.

Most of the war I spent to the east and south of Hitler. I was in Bucharest when it started and in Moscow when it ended, being carried on the numberless hands of an immeasurable and uncontrollable mob of Russians along the great Red Square. I flew to England after V-E Day on the plane of General Hap Arnold, the first aircraft to make the trip across battered Germany and direct from Moscow to Prestwick.

The war was so entirely terrible that one's brain, regarding it later as through time's reversed telescope, sees only dimly remembered details. Like millions of soldiers and civilians, but always in relative comfort and comparative safety, I was bombed, shelled and shot at. I hunted submarines in the Mediterranean in cheerful seaplanes, participated as an idle passenger in the terrible mass bombing of Cassino, fled advancing German armies by automobile, sailboat and train, and hounded them happily with divers Allied forces once the dreadful tide had turned. In Jugoslavia, I was taken out by a trigger-happy patrol with the intention of shooting me and, in the same crumbling land, was briefly jailed as a spy. I escaped court-martial by the British in Greece, a process compounded of pompous lunacy and throttling red tape, for the simple reason that the British were driven out by the Nazis before they could make up their muddled minds. When the general commanding these chair-borne boobs learned of the incident he personally accredited me to all forces at his disposal—land, sea and air—for I had once done him a most useful favor.

This, alas, is the way a war correspondent tends to look back on a war whose ghastliness has already receded into history; it is I, I, I, and petty little incidents, while the true horror of it and all its filth and waste have vanished in a cloud of mental dust.

As soon as I had been hired by Birchall I flew to Belgrade to arrange a central command post from which to coordinate reports from our various correspondents between Ankara and Budapest. Not only did I like Belgrade; I realized early that it had a vitality not shared by other southeastern capitals and would inevitably figure large in the history then proceeding to unfold.

You will find that the South Slavs impinge frequently on this book because they have impinged frequently on my life: the chaotic, anarchic and fascinating assortment of peoples who have been quarreling among themselves since they first moved into the Balkans from the Russian steppes and who are still quarreling today about what they know as Marxism. As a matter of fact their demigod, Karl Marx, had no use for them. He wrote of the South Slavs: "This ethnic trash always becomes and remains until its complete extermination or denationalization the most fanatic carrier of counterrevolution, since its entire existence is nothing more than a protest against a historical revolution." That wry opinion, since shared by Stalin and by Mao Tse-tung, has done little to diminish the self-confidence of the Jugoslavs, who today insist they are the world's true Marxists; only, I fear, their dogma may have been written by Groucho, not Karl.

When I arrived in Belgrade, for the first time financially fat, I proved my status by moving into the Srbski Kralj, best hotel in town. The Srbski Kralj (Serbian King) was a large, old-fashioned, rather dingy building on the border of the Kalemegdan Park which made up with good food and affable service for its somewhat outmoded physical comforts. It was one of the finest places I have ever inhabited. The night porter and the bartender, a gentleman named Milan, rivaled each other in providing amiable feminine company for lonely bachelors. Milan, a stocky, bald, little Serb, was both a marriage broker and procurer on the side. He arranged a happy wedding between an Englishman and a handsome peasant girl, the daughter of a friend. And he always furnished a minimal number of drinks to the ladies of little virtue who graced his bar evenings and were, when custom was available, dispatched by Milan or Milutin, his porter colleague, to the visitor's room.

The telephone operator was charming. Her ingenious persistence could locate a client anywhere in town when a long-distance call came. She also managed to secure connections with Rome, Berne or even London despite the complications caused by the fact that the trunk lines crossed through Germany. I made it a habit to give her a box of candy every month.

The hotel was filled with munitions merchants, black market operators and spies. One of the former, an immense American gorilla, arrived dramatically from Turkey, where he had been selling aircraft. I first met him at a cocktail party just after he had been received by Prince Paul, the regent. He was wearing an extraordinarily hideous, badly cut suit of orange Balkan homespun and massive, bright yellow shoes. Noticing the attention provoked by his costume, he explained the circumstance.

M., the munitions merchant, knew when he left Turkey that he had to be in Belgrade by four o'clock the next afternoon so he decided not to risk the uncertain air connections and took the Orient Express from Istanbul. At dinner that evening he found himself seated across from a striking Rumanian brunette. He struck up an acquaintance successfully lubricated by drink, made an assignation and, later on, wearing green pyjamas and bathrobe, strode through to the next sleeping car where he spent the night in the lady's compartment. Being a man of discretion and experience, he departed courteously at 6 A.M. To his horror, when he went to the end of the car and flung open the door, he found himself staring at an empty expanse of rapidly receding track.

The train had split into two sections at the Turkish border. M.'s car, in the first section, was speeding merrily ahead—with his clothes, his luggage, his passport, his papers and his hopes for a successful contract with Prince Paul. With no other choice, M. descended grimly when the train reached Sofia at seven o'clock. He borrowed a coin from the startled station master and called up the home of his agent in the Bulgarian capital. "Get down here in a hurry," he barked, "and bring with you the largest suit, shirt and shoes in Sofia." The astonished agent explained that no stores opened until nine o'clock. Shortly before ten he came with a suitcase and found the unshaven M. sulking on a bench and surrounded by inquisitive Bulgars. M. changed rapidly, drove to the American legation and explained the problem. A call was put through to Jugoslavia and instructions given to remove his baggage from the *wagon-lit* before it rattled on into Germany. Then the minister gave M. a temporary passport and arranged for him to fly to Belgrade. He arrived just in time to keep his royal appointment and had come to the cocktail party from Beli Dvor, Prince Paul's White Palace. He decided to tell his story rather than permit the impression that he dressed that way by choice.

The black market operators and spies of the Srbski Kralj were frequently one and the same. Jugoslavia's dinar had plummeted since the Nazis invaded Poland and everyone was seeking dollars. One agreeable gentleman who presented himself as a Czech refugee kept hanging around. He offered all kinds of services from a high exchange rate to the company of his lovely blonde wife. Fortunately the chief of police, a friend of mine who later was executed by the Tito regime, summoned me to his office and warned that the "Czech" was an agent of Hitler's Abwehr (intelligence service).

The Jugoslavs did their best to say and do nothing that might offend either belligerent side. The Belgrade press amused itself with accounts of a local hero, Milovan Savović, who ate an entire forty-two-page Sunday newspaper on a bet, having on previous occasions devoured a Latin grammar, a Moslem fez, thirty unshelled eggs, and a raw rabbit including its teeth and fur.

During this period I acquired a car and a dog. I bought a Mercedes from Andrew Tarnowski, a Polish count, who had loaded his possessions into a fleet of automobiles and driven southward to Rumania and Jugoslavia. The dog, a three-month-old wire-haired fox terrier named Felix, was also Polish. He belonged to a diplomat named Czerwinski who, suddenly impoverished, was anxious to sell Felix. One day I was at a friendly craps game. The puppy showed intense interest in the dice and also stole champagne from all glasses on the floor beside the gamblers. These dual passions intrigued me and I took the dog instead of cash. Thereafter Felix traveled all over with me, insisted on his drink each afternoon (either champagne or vermouth-and-soda), was wounded by bomb splinters in Greece, escaped to Turkey and finally died in Egypt.

I flew with Felix to Rome, still a neutral capital, and settled at the Hotel de Russie, just below the Borghese Gardens where the agreeable servants would amuse themselves with my terrier while I worked. In the mornings I wandered about with an Italian girl, visiting each day a chosen section discussed in whatever chapter of Gibbon I happened to be reading. Afternoons and early evenings I worked at the *Times* office where Herbert Matthews, the bureau manager, had given me space to set up a Balkans desk.

In Rome Felix made clear the persistency of his alcoholic tendencies. In some strange way he had learned to tell time and always at six he would begin to make a nuisance of himself, barking, scratching and begging until I had ordered him his cocktail; and always he insisted on something bubbly which I served in a large ashtray. The only way I could get back at him was after I discovered that his favorite dog biscuits, expensive morsels that came in a tin round box, were extremely tasty. I would munch these loudly to his intense rage.

One day I learned Mussolini was to make an important speech in the Forum. I went, just after lunch, with Felix and Norman Alley, a renowned newsreel cameraman who had filmed the Japanese bombing of the American gunboat *Panay*. We arrived early and found a place to stand just before the podium from which the Duce was to address the throng. The area had been strung with loud-speakers and there were several microphones on the platform. Thousands of people gathered and, when Mussolini suddenly burst through with a group of frantic Blackshirts, stretching forth his right arm in the fascist salute, everyone began shrieking, *"Duce! Duce! Duce!"*

When he ceased his salute and commenced to speak, Felix was unaware of the change. He continued to shout, his barks echoing far more loudly than Mussolini's voice because of our nearness to the microphones. Finally, a flying squadron of *fascisti* descended on the three of us and, despite Felix's efforts at self-defense, expelled us physically from the outdoor auditorium.

I have always believed the Duce bore a grudge against Felix for this insult. His son-in-law, Count Ciano (whom he later executed) took part in only one air raid during World War II. That was the first bombing of Salonika where I was blown out of bed and Felix was wounded by splinters, an incident from which he never entirely recovered. I suspect he was the principal target assigned to Ciano's squadron.

I stayed in Rome throughout the autumn writing minatory pieces about "Russia's dramatic return to European affairs" thanks to Stalin's deal with Hitler and their joint partition of Poland. I fulminated about "expansion of Soviet influence in the southeast of the Continent" and "Rumania again wondering if some day it will be engulfed in a Slavic sea" and observed that "taking the long view of things, there are many who see Stalin reverting to the policies of Peter the Great. Peter initiated the Russian quest for warm-water ports, which brought many wars to the Baltic region and the Balkan peninsula."

When the *Times* finally created a special office in Berne to relay foreign dispatches, I quit Rome and flew back to the Balkans. In Belgrade I interviewed Stojadinović, the big, mustachioed prime minister who was trying to develop a fascist organization of his own and who imagined he was about to become a fixture—until the Prince Regent dumped him. Stojadinović, as is the wont of aspirant dictators, tried to camouflage his ambitions. He insisted his program was based on Roosevelt's New Deal. Years later I was to hear various two-bit military tyrants insist they were aping General de Gaulle.

During that winter I frequented a group of young Jugoslav patriot-conspirators. Later on, all became high-ranking officers in Tito's Partisan army and one of them, Lolo Ribar, was a member of the party Politburo. We often met in a smoky little *kafana* called the Triglav where, amid wailing violins and squealing gypsy singers, we sat, smoked, drank wine and I listened while they told me what they planned if Hitler attacked Jugoslavia. They had formed a small military group and sympathetic army officers had given them a few rifles with which they trained in the wooded countryside.

One friend, mentioned earlier, a lean youth with wavy hair and lantern jaw, was named Slobodan Princip, nephew of the Gavrilo Princip who assassinated Franz Ferdinand, Archduke of Austria, precipitating World War I.

Slobodan used to boast that the French called his famous uncle *"le* PRINCIPE *de la guerre."* He liked to pronounce his name in the French manner. Slobodan would dolorously recall that Uncle Gavrilo, imprisoned in the Bohemian fortress of Theresienstadt, suffered tuberculosis and a fungus growth on one arm which had to be amputated; he had twice tried to hang himself with a towel before he finally died in 1918. These grim memories gave him maenadic pleasure. Slobodan himself, as a Partisan colonel in Bosnia, was captured by the Italians and died before a firing squad shouting patriotic slogans.

The organization to which these youngsters belonged called itself the "Youth Movement for the Defense of the Country" and was, I learned later, a subsidiary of the clandestine Communist Party. Its members carried little flags bearing the slogan: "We will defend our frontiers." Slobodan and Lolo assured me: "Although we oppose terrorism as a method, we have the same strength and fighting spirit as did Gavro [nickname for the elder Princip] and the youth movement of his days. We will defend our country to the end against all who aggress. They may kill thousands of us but we will win. We will win because we are free men." (The word Slobodan means "free man" in Serbian.) This irrefragable spirit, I must say, helps explain the success of Tito's guerilla army against the Axis and also Jugoslavia's refusal to become Stalin's satellite. All but one of these friends died during World War II. Poor Lolo was killed by a German bomb as he was about to take off on a liaison mission to Allied headquarters.

In Bulgaria I found in late 1939 that, despite Hitler's victory in Poland, "The Soviet Union is the constant subject of conversation in Sofia's cafés . . . that mystical and impractical force, pan-Slavism, is far from a dead letter. . . . The Russian aim is to use Bulgaria for all it is worth in an effort to expand Soviet influence in the Balkans and to renew Moscow's traditional push toward Mediterranean outlets."

In Turkey a similar obsession was carefully veiled. Prime Minister Saraçoglu had gone to the USSR and was told Russia wanted to "recover" the Caucasus districts of Kars and Ardahan which, indeed, she later claimed formally as soon as World War II had ended. The Turks said no. Saraçoglu confided to me that Rumania was then trying to get the soggy Balkan Entente (Turkey, Greece, Jugoslavia and Rumania) to form a neutral bloc; but the Turks rather wisely placed little stock in the idea. They considered Rumania too weak and too obviously menaced by both Germany and Russia. They preferred to leave the Entente weak and imprecise, filled with legal loopholes that vitiated obligations to help threatened members. The Jugoslavs agreed. One Belgrade official admitted: "What can we do? Prince Paul favors England; the army favors France; the government favors Germany; the people favor Russia."

The Jugoslavs, or rather Prince Paul, had changed governments. The quiet, arcane and disinterested Regent, who was more concerned with collecting art and living in Florence than with governing anarchic Slavs, had simply ousted Stojadinović and placed him under house arrest. To succeed him he named a saturnine half-gypsy trickster called Dragiša Cvetković, a sleezy, caricatural Balkan statesman. Cvetković sent for me shortly after his appointment. He asked me, washing his weak hands in the air, if I wouldn't please interview him and write a "nice" article.

Later, through his girl friend, whom I knew, the prime minister tried to buy Felix from me. He had been told wire-haired fox terriers were very chic. I informed his embarrassed aide the price was $1,000. "But isn't that excessive, even for a very chic dog?" inquired the aide. I kept Felix.

Cvetković's name will not glow in history. He signed a pact with Hitler in 1941. His reputation for financial honesty was limited. After her divorce, his first wife attracted attention by appearing on a balcony in their home town Niš, throwing small change to a crowd that rapidly assembled below, hollering: "Here, I return to you some of the money my ex-husband stole from the people." Then she turned around, lifted her skirt, and exposed her ample behind, shouting: "This is what he really thinks of you."

In Budapest people were still more concerned with Germany than Russia. A Nazi movement, dressed in black jackets, trousers and high Hussar boots, was increasingly in evidence. This was derided by opponents as the "mounted chimney sweeps." But the Hungarians, like their hated Rumanian enemies, didn't want to be swamped by a sea of Slavs. Their primary aspiration was to regain territories lost in World War I. This led them to the disaster of siding with the Axis and being swallowed by the Soviets. Magyar stomachs proved bigger than their eyes.

In Budapest I lived (with Felix) in the Dunapalota Hotel, a sign of my lofty *New York Times* status which had whipped me from the beer and sausage of a free-lance to the champagne and *foie gras* congruent with big-paper prestige. Count Csaky, Hungarian foreign minister, was also a resident of my hotel. I often chatted with him over brandy and coffee in the evenings before locking up Felix and going off to investigate nocturnal amusements along the upper Danube valley. Csaky was a small, perfectly mannered aristocrat with an old-fashioned conscience, pro-German but anti-Nazi sympathies, an admiration for monarchy, London tailors and what was called the "English gentleman." He had an almost demential fear of Russia and a vague hope that the United States might help Budapest in the European power balance. Csaky told me one night that Germany had made a secret deal with Rumania guaranteeing that country's frontiers in exchange for economic and political concessions. The poor man took an umbrageous view of a Berlin guarantee for Transylvania.

I was fascinated by Budapest. Mornings I would breakfast by the window, watching ice floes tumble down the Danube, a subject of intense interest to both sides in the war. The Germans were hoping to develop barge traffic upstream, availing themselves of Rumanian petroleum, Jugo-slav and Bulgarian grain and meat; the Russians were hoping to penetrate Central Europe's trade pattern and, for the first time, to gain a seat on the Danubian Commission that governed the river; and the British were trying to frustrate both attempts. Special crews of English daredevils had been sent to mine the great arterial river. These saboteurs were theoretically disguised as special diplomatic attachés and businessmen.

Normally, after breakfast I would walk Felix to Elizabeth de Pünkösti's house for discreet analysis of all the chromatic rumors she had acquired; she did not like discussing these by telephone. Then I would join friends at some café for intense debate on the world's events which Central Europe always regards from the assumption that it is the navel of the universe. Afternoons I would see officials and editors, then deposit Felix with a hotel bellboy before beginning the evening's round during some phase of which, with scribbled notes as a text, I would dictate the news by telephone to my paper.

I often dined on Margaret Island, cold, gloomy, but attractive, in the middle of the Danube, or in one of the many gypsy taverns on the west side of the river, devouring paprika dishes and wines from the southern vine-yards while fiddlers rent the air. Sometimes I would go with a gaggle of companions to one of the several fancy nightclubs where I learned the czardas, a Magyar dance. More than once I stayed with my friend Ed Kennedy of the Associated Press, until the orchestra folded up its instru-ments and then, with some gay dancing partner, wandered out into the gathering dawn for a breakfast of goulash. At the Arizona, snappiest of the nightclubs, the scenery was enlivened by a beautiful girl named Nagy Emmy. Nagy (pronounced Nadj) means "large." I had first heard of Emmy from Bob Joyce who spent a weekend in Budapest and came back raving about her. I presented a brief note of introduction which didn't seem to make much impression.

Our first conversation went like this.

CLS: Don't you remember Joyce? He says he knows you and likes you.

NE: I speak English.

CLS: I know. Beautifully. But doesn't the name Joyce mean anything to you?

NE: Your name is Joyce?

CLS: No.

NE: You like champagne?

CLS: No.

NE: Why?

CLS: It gives me hay fever.

NE: I like champagne.

CLS: I know.

NE: I want champagne.

CLS: You can't have any.

NE: Why?

CLS: The sight of it gives me hay fever.

NE: [Settling for an Alexander cocktail] Your name Joyce? What's your first name?

CLS: George.

NE: I like you Georgie. You dance?

CLS: No. Don't you know another fellow named Joyce? Tall. Dark hair. Invested 400 pengoes in you. Comes from Belgrade, Jugoslavia.

NE: I like to go to Jugoslavia.

CLS: He's an American also.

NE: I like Americans. Can I have champagne? [Turning to my companion, Kennedy] What's your name?

EK: Joyce.

NE: You brothers?

Poor Emmy; stupid, beautiful, amiable, sleek, pard-like, I saw her off and on for months and came to adore her inane analogues: a delightful, hungry, lazy animal, a sort of Gaia, earth goddess of the Danube valley. She disappeared during the war.

Ed Kennedy, then beginning a distinguished career, was a lean, sad-looking fellow with humorous eyes, excellent wit and much gusto. He went on to head the AP staff in the North African and French campaigns and achieved the greatest scoop of World War II by announcing the armistice of Rheims in May, 1945. He did this by the simple process of advising the censors, who had been forbidden to release the news until it was coordinated with Moscow, that he intended to violate their restrictions since clearly it was not a breach in security. The war was over. The censors said they had shut off all means of transmission. So Ed picked up a military telephone in Paris, asked for the London exchange, gave the number of the AP office there, and dictated the news. For this he was rewarded by AP with discharge.

The rival United Press had done better by its reporters in World War I. Roy Howard, a young correspondent who flashed word of a premature and phony armistice, later became head of UP and boss of the Scripps-Howard chain. Another UP employee, whom I shall call "Smith," had an even gaudier success. Smith was stationed in Vienna in 1918–1919 when the Austrian capital was rife with speculation of an impending *putsch*. Each day, after filing their dispatches, the foreign correpondents would meet for nightcaps and to exchange chimerical rumors about impending coups. One night Smith, horribly drunk, sat down at his typewriter. That was all he remembered until, early next morning, he was awakened by sharp knocking on his door. A uniformed official commanded him to appear immediately at the central telegraph office. While dressing, he recollected dimly that, before tottering home, he had sent some sort of cable.

When he arrived at the central telegraph office he saw several colleagues standing with sullen expressions. He was handed a sheaf of cables: CONGRATULATIONS WORLD SHATTERING SCOOP; MAGNIFICENT BEAT THANKS; FINEST JOURNALISTIC FEAT OF CENTURY, signed by his employers. He then discovered what had happened. After leaving his companions he had produced an alcoholic farrago from the rumors they had been discussing and, in a daze, filed a dispatch based on these bottle-dreams. An hour later a *putsch* did in fact occur. The conspirators' first move was to seize the telegraph office and prevent all news from leaving Austria. Smith's account was far from accurate; but it contained the essential "fact"—a coup had taken place. Smith immediately and permanently forswore alcohol. Eventually he became publisher of an important American newspaper. No such luck, alas, for the honest, maligned and shabbily treated Kennedy.

In December, 1939, I decided to go to Slovakia where Hitler had installed a totalitarian and viciously Nazi regime. I invited Kennedy to come along. Washington did not diplomatically recognize Slovakia; it even refused to acknowledge its existence. The enraged Slovaks therefore made unnecessary difficulties about visas. When they finally relented, we had to find a chauffeur above Hungary's military age limit and a car permitted to leave the country. This we did, discovering the worst driver in all Central Europe, a gentleman who enjoyed turning completely around, releasing the wheel, in order to carry on political argumentation with his passengers while his automobile, a huge and venerable Daimler, chugged heavily down the road.

When Czechoslovakia was partitioned, the Führer allowed the Poles and Hungarians to grab chunks. Budapest had acquired the easternmost province of Ruthenia, or sub-Carpathian Ukraine, an area since seized by Russia. The capital, called Uzhorod by the Czechs and Ungvar by the Hungarians, was our first destination. When we had finally survived the convoluting road to Ungvar we found a furtive, rural town under stern military rule. The officers commanding the administration had little sympathy for the press; they refused to see us.

Ungvar was jammed with new nightclubs and crammed with Budapest dancing girls dispatched to console the occupying forces. In order to inform the great American public, Kennedy and I began a tour of these nightclubs. We rapidly acquired a vast amount of information, some of which was printable, from the nubile young ladies who had become mistresses of generals and colonels and who really knew what was going on. The moment came, around three o'clock in the morning, when I decided to retire with this knowledge. Ed, engaged in journalistic endeavors, flatly refused to go, so I left him with a well-informed blonde. First, however, to be sure he was not cheated, I paid the bill for both of us and added an extra bottle of champagne to keep Kennedy fueled. When I awoke, I found Ed completely naked, unconscious, kneeling beside his cot; he had not quite been able to crawl inside. I shook him hard; I enveloped his head in a cold, damp towel; I slapped his cheeks and pounded his back. At last he stirred, opened one eye part way, regarded me with distaste and said: "The biggest bed in the whole damned world. She had the biggest bed in the whole damned world. Why didn't I stay there?"

We bumped grouchily over the frontier, into Slovakia with its border guards and customs agents sporting swastika armbands. Ed finally turned to me and said: "Well, at least I can tell you this. They thought I was drunk when I left that nightclub. The manager tried to cheat me. He sent another bottle of champagne. He was trying to jack up the bill. Hah! Thought I was drunk. I insisted on a new bill without champagne." "You what?" I shouted. "You mean you paid that bill all over again? That manager is the only honest man in Ruthenia. Now, you alcoholic fool, you've succeeded in corrupting him."

We rolled by coruscating streams along the western slopes of the Carpathians until we reached a country town called Prešov where, just after ordering a lunch of sausages and beer, we were arrested and frog-marched to the central barracks. There three Slovaks, in black, storm-trooper uniforms with *haakenkreuz* insignia, began to interrogate us in the presence of a fourth man in mufti. Within a short time it was evident the fourth man was both German and the local Gestapo representative.

The interrogation took place in German, which Kennedy did not speak. Occasionally the Slovaks exchanged remarks in their own language which, thanks to my grounding in "Slavonic foreign," I could follow. We were accused of being smugglers and English spies. We were asked about our origins and connections. When I listed my religion as Jewish (in fact I am an atheist) the inquisitors were taken aback; not by the fact that I might be Jewish but that an English spy should be so stupid as to announce it. Then, to our delight, one of the Slovaks called in a seedy individual who swore he had been brought up with Ed in Kassa (Košice), near the Hungarian border, that they had gone to school together and that Ed was a well-known Magyar terrorist. Kenedi, pronounced the same as Kennedy, is a common Hungarian name. This allegation was too much. We burst into roars of laughter. Even the Gestapo man began to look embarrassed. After all, a Hungarian spy who could speak no Danubian language was a different thing from an agent of British Intelligence. Finally, after some hours of idiotic and forensic questioning, we were released.

From that moment until we reached Bratislava, the Slovakian capital, we were followed by a police agent who was presumably the only Slovak capable of counterespionage against the English. He was not difficult to identify. Wherever we ate or drank, at the next table would be a gentleman avidly reading a newspaper which obscured his face. When we drove along the road we were, to the undisguised anxiety of our chauffeur, closely followed by a small Tatra car. When we walked through the streets of a town or village, a man with hat brim pulled low over his bowed forehead scuttled along behind us. We knew it was always the same agent for the simple reason that he had red hair and a black patch over one eye.

The two main German papers of Bratislava, *Grenzbote* and *Deutsche Stimmen,* covered their front pages with sensational articles that had little to do with news being featured elsewhere in the world, the sinking in Argentina of the raider *Graf Spee.* Slovak readers were alarmed by a bannered account that began SECRET SERVICE *unter uns! Die Wühlarbeit des Englischen Geheimdienstes in der Slowakei Geschlossene Abwehrfront des Slowakischen und Deutschen Volkes"* (Secret service amongst us; the undermining in Slovakia by British Secret Service; the common defense front of the Slovakian and German peoples).

This entertainment inconvenienced us when we arrived at the city of Zilina and Ed instructed the driver to take us to the AP's local string correspondent. The stringer looked out of the window when he heard our ring and saw us standing before his door. He shouted to us to go away and refused to answer our knocks or, afterwards, our telephone calls. The poor man was frightened silly. So we drove on towards Bratislava, followed by our red-headed, one-eyed friend, whose persistent presence rendered our own chauffeur so nervous that he skidded off a snowy bridge and wrecked the car. From gawking peasants we managed to hire three teams of horses to haul us back on the road. To our astonishment, the Daimler was able to limp along, protesting, at fifteen miles an hour until we installed it in a capital garage.

In Bratislava the red-haired agent was replaced by a female accomplice whose figure resembled a dumpling and whose face looked like a buttered moon. She pretended great friendship, spoke a rather recondite form of English, provided us with a mass of misinformation, arranged appointments with truculent members of the puppet government and, for good luck, produced several agrarian politicians who joined in denouncing Hungarian landlords, starting with Count Anton Apponyi.

I spent that winter of my content wandering backwards and forwards through my journalistic empire. Felix was a faithful companion on most of these trips although sometimes, when the prospect of his presence seemed likely to exceed his normal nuisance value, I left him in Belgrade with a half-breed, wire-haired friend, Slatko (Sweet) Joyce. Traveling with Felix was hazardous for he had odd habits in addition to his fondness for fizzy alcoholic drinks. I used to chain him to the door handle in the back seat of my Mercedes convertible. One day, when we were driving through Bulgaria with the top down, he developed a peculiar rage against a goat tethered by the wayside. Musing, I was suddenly struck by oppressive silence, looked about and saw no Felix, only an empty collar dangling from a chain. I turned around, drove back, and found him tormenting the infuriated animal.

Another time he escaped in the royal forest outside Belgrade where I was illegally stalking pheasants. I did my best to summon him without calling attention to myself, for the woods were filled with soldiers and gendarmes. When night fell, I had to stop the search. Days passed and I could find no trace of Felix. At last, guided by the advice of Vlada Ribnikar, its editor, I advertised in *Politika* and offered a sizable reward. To my amazement some days later a rotund, rubbery gentleman arrived at the Srbski Kralj towing on a cord a filthy, grease-stained dog that showed much glee on seeing me. The gentleman was a clown who had found Felix in a village outside Belgrade where his circus was performing on bazaar day. He had adopted the terrier, hoping to teach him tricks, but in this he was deceived. I paid the reward, bought Felix a drink and popped him in the bathtub.

Early 1940 was a time for secret diplomacy in the Balkans. Mussolini held a clandestine meeting with Csaky. Prince Paul met Rumania's Carol at the frontier town of Vrsec for what was supposed to be a shooting party. The Italians seemed to be trying to produce a common front in Southeast Europe aimed openly at Russia but also indirectly at Germany. And on February 2 the Balkan Entente (Jugoslavia, Turkey, Greece, Rumania) held a foreign ministers' conference in Belgrade. This was a dismal affair. Berlin and Moscow had completed Poland's partition and the gallant Finnish resistance to Soviet aggression was showing signs of collapse. All Europe's little lands feared the bell would soon be tolling for them and yet, as their semibreve of calm drew to a close, they could do no more than reaffirm hopes to avoid the storm while their statesmen made oily, pleonastic speeches that did not manage to obscure their mutual mistrust.

For me the most agreeable aspect of the conclave was the arrival of Anne O'Hare McCormick, who then wrote *The New York Times* column that became mine after her death in 1954. Anne was one of the wisest, nicest women I have ever known. Already over sixty, she still retained boundless energy and feminine charm. With plain, merry face, square jaw and upturned nose, she radiated warmth and kindness; everyone loved her and, what was important for a journalist, also confided in her. As always, Anne was accompanied by her elderly husband who had suffered a stroke some years past and was but a shadow of his former courtly self; yet she adored him and never traveled without him, pretending to rely upon his counsel. She would not even dictate one of her perceptive articles without Frank standing beside her, often in a tiny telephone booth, gravely turning the pages. A delightful, memorable pair: I salute them both.

When they arrived at Belgrade's suburban station after a train trip from Rumania, Anne descended, embraced me and began to chatter like a machine gun shooting platinum bullets while poor Frank stood in puzzlement before a mound of luggage, objurgating equally puzzled Serbian porters. When we rescued him and led him to my car he turned with an air of grave knowledge and said: "Aha. Jugoslovakia. Tell me, Cy, who's president now?" Anne chided him affectionately: "Stop teasing the boy, Frank. You know Jugoslavia's a kingdom."

The Entente ministers agreed to renew their meaningless pact and praised Italy for its "nonbelligerent" attitude although everyone suspected the Duce would scramble into the war if Hitler gained a success when he struck at France. I celebrated the end of the conference with the McCormicks and a group of Italian reporters who, although forced to wear Fascist emblems to keep their jobs, were fervently pro-Allied. First we went to a White Russian nightclub called the Kazbek where a tubercular beauty sang curdling love songs while a Cossack did kneebends and spat knives into the floor. Then we went to the Dardanelles, a Moslem hangout where the main feature was a dual belly dance. As an almost naked lady writhed, a mustachioed gentleman with hypertrophic nose and baggy red bloomers kept time, flashing on and off a light hidden in a sensitive area of his pants.

After the conference, I flew to Italy and the Middle East to survey Mussolini's famous North African army. In Trieste I found twenty-six German ships sheltering from the British Mediterranean fleet, the first tangible sign I had encountered of the blockade. In Rome I found the Italians worrying almost equally about new Soviet and new German threats in the Balkans. In Tripoli and Benghazi I found strutting Fascist troop contingents led by bored officers who were just as friendly as they proved to be later in British prisoner-of-war camps. They amused themselves by Corybantic flirtations with the faded European ladies who graced the shabby hotels and who had come to Libya as a retreat, a kind of elephants' burying ground for their professional hopes. The only positive thing I acquired in Libya was a first-class case of malaria.

As soon as I was able to move, I flew to Cairo, an exact replica of Hollywood representations of World War I in the days of Allenby: streets jammed with lorries in tawny desert camouflage, hordes of turbaned and befezzed peddlers, guides and idlers in long white gowns, snappily uniformed English guards officers and sloppy New Zealanders and Australians who refused to salute; a symbiosis of the martial and the miserable. My purpose was to assay relative strengths of military forces in the eastern Mediterranean. I lunched with the British commander, General Jumbo Wilson, who gave me introductions to his officers in mandated Palestine and to the French in Syria and Lebanon and who then sent me off across the Sinai desert by army transport. I was accompanied by a buck private who sat politely in front beside the driver, his rifle pointed ominously back at me. He was being transported to Damascus to testify in a trial of Arab terrorists who had kidnapped him a year earlier. This soldier, a North Irelander, told me he intended to identify any Arab brought into the courtroom as one of his captors, whether or not this was the case, because "They're all a bunch of dommed bondits."

I interviewed commanders in Jerusalem, Damascus and Beirut. General Weygand, the snippy little chief of France's Levant army, spoke with distaste of the British, contempt for the Americans and assured me France would smash Hitler that very spring. He also talked of a possible Allied attack through the Caucasus against the Russian oil fields near Baku and Grozny. However, he admitted that the Turks, with whom he had discussed that project, showed remarkable lack of enthusiasm. Weygand had six divisions of impressive-looking troops and boasted of their putative power. His own conceit and the *élan* of his staff were high. I noted the latter seemed to congregate each night in an establishment known as the Kit-Kat Club which featured a callipygian Finnish dancer wearing only three rhinestones.

The Levant army never launched the campaigns planned for it. Weygand went back to France where he played a major role in engineering the surrender. The troops he left behind fought but one engagement—against the British and Free French in 1941. They were defeated.

From Aleppo, in North Syria, I boarded the Taurus express for Ankara accompanied, as usual, by Felix, who was attacked by a one-eared, bobtailed Turkish cat while inspecting a lamppost in the Adana railway station and who jumped into my arms, followed promptly by this descendant of ancient Hittite lions.

In Ankara I had the first of many meetings with Franz von Papen, former chancellor of Germany who did so much to help Hitler into power and then ambassador to Turkey. The last time I ever saw him was in the prisoners' dock at the Nuremberg War Crimes trial. Papen was a smooth, well-mannered, erect gentleman, charming, interesting to talk to, with a strange chiliastic belief in his own political resurrection. He constantly referred to "when I was chancellor" and implied a hope that some day he might regain that post. At one point he rapidly observed there had been a change in American public opinion "since my last visit to the States." He did not smile. (Papen left the United States in a hurry during World War I when, as assistant military attaché, he was charged with promoting the Black Tom sabotage case.) The ambassador had a large map of Russia on his desk. I asked him why he was so interested in a country which, to all intents and purposes, was then Germany's cobelligerent. He looked at me coldly and, without answering, inquired why the United States wanted to amend its Neutrality Act.

In March, 1940, while I was in Ankara, the Turks feared the flattening of Finland would free Russia to make new claims against Balkan states including the Turkish provinces of Kars and Ardahan, which, indeed, Stalin was to demand before the war ended. Prime Minister Saraçoglu, a tricky but shrewd statesman, discerned a grand Berlin maneuver designed to drag Italy into the conflict and direct the course of Russian imperialism toward the Middle East. "There," he told me, "a war of movement could be staged and the advantages of Italy's strategic mid-Mediterranean position could endanger Allied communications."

I flew to Rumania where I had a recurrent attack of malaria while dining at the American legation. The minister helped me from the table, sent me home and dispatched his physician, who proved to be a German lady. She gave me numerous blue pills and the unusual instruction to drink as much alcohol as possible. When she left, I weakly summoned a waiter and ordered three whiskies. The very first taste made me ill. Every time I opened my eyes and saw those hideous drinks, I felt like dying. To the bewilderment of the waiter, I summoned him again and told him to take the poisonous stuff away. I was to have malaria many times again but I avoided that remedy. I think the German woman must have been a Nazi.

I left Bucharest by train shortly before Easter and troops, released for holiday leave, thronged in at every station. I had a first-class ticket but this did me no good; each seat and inch of space was taken. I stood in the corridor, wedged amid a dense mass of garlic-smelling soldiery. When we halted, still more conscripts tried to scramble in and, if they failed, they smashed the windows, climbed through and lay along the heads of their companions. This was most interesting but I suffered two torturous inconveniences. I was forced to hold Felix squirming in my arms. After a time he ceased fulminating at my neighbors and settled down to sleep in resigned discomfort but there was no means of heeding his natural calls and he was forced to discharge on me and the gentleman beside me.

This in itself was bad enough; but, even worse, it provoked inevitable conversation with my neighbor, a school teacher in civilian life who ardently admired the works of Edgar Allan Poe. Without surcease he recited to me and the slumbering Felix that dreary poem, "The Raven," in sonorous Rumanian, filling my ears with tedious euphonies and covering my face with a patina of spit. To this day I can still remember: *"Raspunse corbul niciodaţa"* (quoth the raven nevermore).

In Belgrade the former dictator, Stojadinović, had been placed under house arrest as part of a move to crack down on Germanophiles, who tended to support him. Nazi propaganda cells were being searched out and secret orders had been issued by General Nedić, the war minister, to resist invasion no matter what contradictory orders might be heard on the radio. The Jugoslavs were alarmed by the Führer's Scandinavian thrust although they confided: "Thank God that as long as the war had to spread, it spread once more to the North." The Nazis were extending their control over the vital Danube; gloom had set in, and few observant people did not feel that a tidal wave would sweep the Balkans before the final peace was signed.

On April 18, although it was supposedly forbidden, I visited Stojadinović in his suburban house, simply pushing past the bewildered soldiers guarding his gate. The former dictator greeted me with surprise and pleasure, the first strange face he had seen since his sequestration. Stojadinović was not yet accustomed to the idea that he had been thrust from power. He said Prince Paul's police had seized his papers including correspondence with Hitler and Mussolini. He claimed he had been trying to arrange Jugoslav-Bulgarian friendship by backing Sofia's claims to territory from Rumania and Greece, a rather sour way of improving Balkan relationships since Jugoslavia was allied to both proposed victims. Stojadinović said: "Clearly this was a sound basis to arrange things. We would have to yield no territory. The Turks supported me." He was furious with Cvetković, his successor, always referring to him only as "that gypsy from Niš."

Before I left, he asked me to take messages to Stoičo Mušanov, speaker of the Bulgarian Sobranje (parliament), and Tatarescu, the Rumanian premier, assuring them he was "now a democrat." "What sort of a democrat?" I asked the pseudo-Fascist. "I am for disciplined democracy," he said. "We cannot have the same sort of democracy they have in England. English parliamentary debates are one thing. In our country a parliamentary debate works like this: First they disagree with you. Then they call you names. Then they shoot you." I asked him why, if he now thought democracy had some merits, he didn't try it when he was prime minister. "One must govern as one can," he answered.

That spring of 1940, as the poppies came out under the fruit blossoms and the cruel winter winds, Bora and Kossova, subsided, Hitler invaded Norway and Denmark. The Balkan countries breathed more easily because they thought this reduced immediate German pressure. But when the Scandinavian campaign turned to total victory and then, on May 10, 1940, when the Nazis thundered through the Lowlands and past France's Maginot Line, a great gloom fell.

As an immediate result Jugoslavia developed a guerrilla syndrome embracing various factions. All the irregular conspiratorial societies that have featured South Slav history began to make preparations. Old Comitadjis and Serbian Cetniks—veterans who hadn't done more than drink and gossip since 1918—began to meet amid ineluctable clouds of café smoke. One hangout was Belgrade's seedy Hotel Balkan where grizzled heroes of the Turkish wars sat tugging their hispid mustachios, fur hats jammed down over their ears, drinking numberless cups of thick, syrupy coffee. The word Cetnik, soon again to become renowned, literally means "bandit" but had a glorious legend attached to it in Jugoslavia.

I wrote about the Cetniks that May: "These will be formed into units of six each, dressed in peasant costume and armed with hand grenades. They will serve primarily to cover retreats and combat parachutists and isolated military attacks. Their organization has been placed in the charge of a leading strategist named Mihailović." This, of course, was the famous Draža Mihailović who became leader of the Royalist resistance during Jugoslavia's occupation. He was then a general staff colonel, close to the officers' group that, within a year, was to plot with British Intelligence agents to oust Prince Paul and a government that had yielded to Axis pressure.

Mihailović urged the war minister to organize purely Serbian military formations because "we cannot count on the Croats" and it was an open secret that an air force general, Borivoje Mirković, was conspiring with Serb officers, above all General Dušan Simović, air commander, to prepare a possible *coup d'état*.

There was growing contact between the plotters and British agents including the military and air attachés, Lieutenant Colonel C. S. Clarke and Wing Commander A. H. H. MacDonald, a lean temerarious Scot. Clarke had started his assignment clumsily; he attempted to bribe Colonel Zarko Popović, Jugoslav director of military intelligence, with a generous sum of dollars. Popović ignored this *faux pas* with bitter serenity and agreed to give Clarke names of Axis agents if he would exchange results.

While the Nazi cerement was being drawn over France, Churchill asked his minister of economic warfare, Hugh Dalton, to set up what was called the Special Operations Executive, or SOE, a "department of dirty tricks" to conduct subversion and sabotage. Dalton's men began to congregate in Belgrade, some assigned as attachés, some as temporary legation secretaries, others recruited from the English business colony. One would see them each noon taking a preprandial *šlivovica* with friends: Hanau, who was to be strangely murdered in Cairo; Bailey, later parachuted to Mihailović's guerillas; Masterson, already charged with organizing opponents of Prince Paul's regency for emergency action. The air was obnebulated with murky schemes. After one meeting in nearby Zemun with Mihailović and potential putschists, MacDonald introduced me to the puissant Cetnik, a thin, intellectual-looking man with glasses. I never met the guerrilla chieftain again although I was in direct radio contact with him during the Nazi occupation and he invited me to parachute to his forces, a plan frustrated by SOE.

That first war summer, while the Axis drums snored elsewhere, we became accustomed to fevered activity by German and Italian "tourists" and businessmen. The British intrusion was more subtle. One group of newcomers was charged with sabotaging Danube barge traffic. Sandy Glen, a bland, bespectacled stockbroker engaged in this endeavor, later was landed behind Axis lines in Albania and Norway and then sent to Rumania, establishing the first liaison with Marshal Tolbukhin's troops.

Another group was preoccupied with espionage and propaganda in Albania. Julian Amery, who subsequently became a cabinet minister but was still a slender youngster, not yet twenty, was involved in this intriguing task. Julian induced Parker, my Belgrade stringer, to quit journalism and accept the job of proconsul (*sic*) in Skoplje, capital of Jugoslav Macedonia and nearest city to Albania. Parker was later expelled as a result of Axis pressure, provoked by articles I had written after I took a trip along the Jugoslav-Albanian border with him and he showed me Italian maps including as Albanian great chunks of Jugoslavia and Greece.

Another odd English spy, then in Belgrade, whom I shall call Smith, was a naturalist by profession and had been an officer in charge of a labor battalion with the Allied forces that advanced into the Balkans from Salonika at the end of World War I. Smith learned to speak Serbian as his troops dug their way northward and he became friendly with several of the redoubtable Cetniks who, in 1940, were beginning to reassemble at the Hotel Balkan to plan desperate deeds. Smith seemed to spend singularly little time chasing insects and one day a clandestine Fascist brochure attacked him, claiming he had been sent by London to organize Jugoslav locusts to destroy the wheat crop. Poor Smith—he called a solemn press conference and publicly denied he was organizing locusts.

That May was beautiful and nervous. A fresh wind blew up the Danube valley, clear and clean like the horns coming in at the start of a Brahms second movement. The plum trees blossomed and wheat burst to the surface in the broad river flatlands. But Hitler's troops were again clanking forward and everyone talked only of war. The head of Jugoslavia's Croatian Peasant Party announced the Croats would "fight like lions" should their land be invaded. One year later, when this pledge was tested, they fought like dogs—against their own government's forces. A Serbian patriotic organization attacked the Germans for contributing 100,000 reichsmarks to a flood relief fund, saying the money had been "stolen from our brother Czechs and Poles." It continued: "Brothers, let your strong fists be always ready so that you are prepared for justice and truth at any time." Prince Paul began to call up troops and some of the country's few tanks rumbled to depots outside the capital. I wrote on May 13: "There is a growing conviction in the Balkans that Italy will be in the war very soon." Two days later I added: "Information was received here today through official channels that Italy has definitely resolved to enter the European war on Germany's side." Within a month Mussolini had jumped on the back of crippled France.

Jugoslavs love intrigue and conspiracy. The Sokol society of young athletes announced that its 300,000 members, who spent most of their time singing and doing physical jerks, were preparing to fight fifth-column threats. My youthful Communist friends—Ribar, Princip, Dedijer and the others—speeded up their amateurish military maneuvers in nearby forests. An underground Fascist organization chalked signs and slogans in the cities.

Belgrade absorbed more and more meaty Teutons wearing motorists' caps and ill-fitting tweeds. The Nazi in charge of German tourist and trade missions, a great blood pudding of a man, was believed by the British to be in charge of Hitler's espionage. I visited him in his office one day and asked him to comment on this rumor. *"Ach, mein lieber Herr Sulzberger,"* said he with jovial humor, *"ich bin nur Himmelspion.* I am only a spy of the

Heavens, keeping a watch on the skies and hoping they help this dear country produce a generous grain crop for us to buy."

Mussolini, that querulous scavenger, scrambled into the war and France fell with a thud. The Serbs, who dominated Jugoslavia's officer corps and administration, were stunned. They loved the French and had clung to the hollow legend that France had Europe's finest army. One Sunday Charles Clarke, the British military attaché, took a solitary stroll in the woods outside Belgrade. He encountered a tall, old peasant, striding down the path in his leggings, upturned slippers and sheepskin hat, beating a pig to market with his crook and hollering: *"Hajde,* Churchill; get along there, Churchill." This was too much for Clarke. He marched up and demanded: "Did I hear you correctly? Do you call that pig Churchill?" The Serb answered, somewhat bewildered: "Yes, he's my last hope."

I flew to Budapest and Sofia and found the Hungarians and Bulgarians clamoring for revision of their boundaries. One Sofia official boasted to me: "Around Paris they are tearing up the shameful peace treaties of 1918, including that of Neuilly, where were hammered out the chains placed around Bulgaria's neck." The British minister confided: "Germany could take over this country in twelve hours through its fifth column of 'merchants of military age' and the people they have bought."

In Sofia, my friend Grigor Vassilev, a politician with two pretty daughters, invited me to his house one night for dinner. The dinner was exceptionally lavish, even for Grigor's hearty tastes. First he gave me a great deal of *slivovova* which came from an ancient barrel on his wife's Macedonian estate. Then, at table, I surprisingly found myself seated between the two girls, a rare event as Grigor was strict, old-fashioned, and preferred to keep his womenfolk out of sight. The girls were agreeable and flirtatious and we had that rare thing in Bulgaria, two bottles of burgundy. At the end Grigor and I retired with Turkish coffee and French brandy.

It was perfectly clear that something was up. Grigor, a tall, sallow man who bore considerable physical resemblance (I discovered later) to the famous Soviet traitor, General Vlassov, was leader of the Agrarian Party but not always a serious political factor. When he detected in me a sufficiently expansive mood, he asked: "You are going to Belgrade tomorrow?" "Yes, to get my car and dog." "You will do me a small favor?" "Of course." "It is only a matter of taking a letter." "Think nothing of it."

At this point Grigor poured another drink and seemed a trifle uneasy. "Maybe," he said, "I should tell you it is for Milan Grol [a Jugoslav Democratic politician]." "O.K. That's all right." "I want you to hand it personally to Grol." "Certainly." "However," and here his long Adam's apple gulped, "I must advise you that it would be better for the police not to see it."

Even my bemused senses caught an oddness in this affair. I told Grigor: "Damn you, now I've said I'll do it; the least you can do is show me the letter since there's something obviously fishy in it." He went to his high desk, unlocked a drawer, took out an unsealed envelope and read the document. It was an elaborate proposal for simultaneous revolutions in Jugoslavia and Bulgaria which would oust their royal rulers and proclaim a unified South Slav republic. I sobered rapidly, regarding the Cyrillic scrawl as if it were a lapidary inscription on my tomb.

Next day I rode nervously to Belgrade, the letter tucked in my underpants. I was positive the customs guards and militiamen who inspected our passports and compartments on each side of the border must surely have been tipped off and envisioned an immediate future filled with bastinadoes and firing squads. Nothing happened; but as soon as I reached the Jugoslav capital I called Grol and told him I must see him on a matter of extreme importance.

Somewhat quizzically he received me in the comfortable study of his house. I handed him the letter, he affixed his glasses and began slowly to read. As each second passed his already lemon-colored face grew more pale and his pendulous lower lip sagged. His hands began to tremble and the more they trembled the greater his difficulty in reading the message. At last he finished, his hands absolutely palsied. He looked across at me with an expression of fear and horror, as if I were some ghastly afrit. "I am going to burn this right away," he said. "Grigor must be out of his mind. Now leave. Leave right away. And never tell anyone about this. Never tell anyone. If I am asked if I know you, I shall deny it." I left. Grol, who, unlike most Serbs, was excessively cautious, later played a pitiful puppet role in the effort to arrange a postwar coalition government between Tito and the *émigré* regime to which Britain and the United States were committed.

Traveling southward to Turkey, I motored through the fragrant Bulgar rose farms. In Plovdiv, birthplace of Philip of Macedon, a wheel came off my car. While this was being repaired by a blacksmith, who skillfully hammered out emergency bolts, my dog Felix bit a gendarme in the behind, removing the seat of his pants. This event delayed me another twelve hours and I crossed the border after dark, losing myself on the dirt roads of Turkish Thrace and, to my dismay, coming under rifle fire in the fortified area known as the Chatalja Line.

I found the Turks pleasantly calm. They rather admired the Germans but detested their Soviet cobelligerents and new Italian allies. They were alarmed by the sudden rush of Bulgarian revisionism and bitter at the English for not being sterner in their attitude to Sofia. A leading newspaper, whose proprietor had heard of Felix's Plovdiv incident, wrote an editorial commending him and saying: "London should heed this dog. He knows how to treat Bulgarian officials."

I scuttled to Rumania, whose weak-kneed regime was dissolving amid a sudden spate of anti-Allied palmodes. The foreign minister announced that Rumania was "advised by all her friends and allies" to cede Bessarabia to a Soviet ultimatum "in order not to start a war in these parts of Europe." Officially permitted anti-Semitism broke out and I wrote from Bucharest: "Rumors continue to circulate about an impending political and military pact with the Reich." The Balkan Entente, so carefully devised by France, was breaking up on France's tomb.

Rumania's regime tried desperately and obscenely to survive. It renounced the Anglo-French protective guarantee of April 15, 1939. Greenshirted Iron Guard fascists reappeared, causing a Jugoslav diplomat to observe: "They remind me of unripe tomatoes—green outside, red inside." The King called the Iron Guard to power and pudgy Nazi "tourists" began to fill the capital. For the first time I began to hear Germans talking openly of a coming war with the Soviets although they were still cobelligerents. On July 3, 1940—almost a year before that disastrous campaign started—I wrote from Bucharest: "The Germans are confident that in a war with Russia they could defeat the Soviet army . . . There are some reports here—which cannot be confirmed—that Nazi troops have been moving East recently. There are similar reports that a German military mission may come here," Sir Reginald Hoare, British minister, gave a farewell luncheon for the families of twenty-eight petroleum officials who had been helping the Rumanians exploit their wells and who had been expelled. After lunch ten were arrested. Before their ultimate release, some had been strung up by their thumbs and others whipped on the soles of their feet. All over the country the murder of Jews began.

At Salzburg and Vienna, Italian and German statesmen drew a new map for Southeast Europe and the Russians, aware they were being edged out, explored the possibility of closer relations with Jugoslavia, Bulgaria and even Rumania, which they had just amputated. It was possible to read the writing on the wall: the Hitler-Stalin pact was cracking. July 27 I wrote: "It is obvious to all that the chief enemy, as seen from Rome and Berlin, is Soviet Russia."

The Axis press started a series of personal attacks which were to continue throughout the war. Virginio Gayda, Mussolini's main propagandist, denounced me as a "tarantula creeping from capital to capital spreading poison and alarm." The Rome *Messagero,* Leghorn *Telegrafo* and Milan *Corriere della Sera* accused me of "ridiculously tendentious statements." And the Vienna edition of Hitler's personal organ, *Voelkischer Beobachter,* ran a special banner headline on its front page calling me a *hetzagent* or "hate agent." Despite this, I had trusted friends in the Axis camp who passed on useful information.

One, who later became Rome's ambassador to Britain, offered to drive me personally out of Jugoslavia on the eve of the Axis attack—although he knew this would endanger his family and ruin his career. Two others did everything they could to help Marina, by then my fiancée, in occupied

Greece. Gino Tomajuoli, one of my closest Italian friends both then and now, had earned a reputation for singular bravery during the Ethiopian War by leading forays far in the van of the Duce's regular army. After the Germans invaded Russia, he was assigned to accompany a Bavarian infantry regiment as war correspondent during the difficult 1942–1943 winter campaign. The regiment lost so many officers as it fought its retreat backward through the snows near Kharkov, that the colonel asked Gino, an experienced soldier, to take command of a company. Each dawn and dusk they were attacked by mounted Cossacks firing automatic weapons. Although the Cossacks lost heavily, there were always more next day. The ground was firmly frozen and it was impossible to dig trenches. To shelter at night, the regiment built cabins using corpses as logs. Gino was wounded, abandoned, and picked up by the Russians, who left him to receive medical attention at a collective farm. By sheer chance the pharmacist was an elderly physician who had studied in Florence before the Revolution. He was so delighted to find an Italian that, when his patient was cured, he arranged with local partisans to have him smuggled back to the German lines.

In mid-summer 1940 Gino asked me to meet him in Budapest so he could tell me about an Axis conference in Salzburg and Vienna. He had spent a long evening with Count Ciano, Mussolini's son-in-law and foreign minister, and Ciano told him that Rumania was about to be carved up once again; also that the Duce was preparing to invade Greece from Albania. An English agent in Belgrade, later murdered on a mission to Tito, confirmed the latter. I predicted to my paper (August 3, 1940): "Further partition of Rumania under the auspices of her good friends, Germany and Italy, is at hand." Ten days later I added: "It was reported here tonight that three Italian troop transports had crossed the Otranto Straits to land detachments of troops at Durazzo, Albania." I rushed southward to Athens.

On August 15 an Italian submarine torpedoed and sank the cruiser *Helle*, second largest ship in the Greek fleet, as she lay at anchor off Tinos island, which was celebrating a religious festival. General Metaxas, the Greek dictator, called up 40,000 reservists and announced Greece would fight if attacked and would "rely on the Greek people to resist with courage."

However, when no disaster came, I had to leave Athens to attend the impending Rumanian surgery. In Belgrade I prepared my car by installing a spare gas tank, fitting it out with two ropes, jacks, extra tools and vulcanizing kits, then took off for Budapest with Felix for the Hungarian army's comic-opera occupation of Transylvania. I carried several tire-patches and was rarely inconvenienced more than a half hour by horseshoe nail punctures.

I had had a huge black steel tank affixed to the rear of the car, able to carry enough fuel to get from Hungary to Turkey. There were few roadside garages then, even in villages. When the regular supply was running short, I would halt, take out a short length of rubber hose and an empty ten-gallon can and siphon it full, then empty the can by funnel into the regular tank. If one got stuck in mud or snow, it was rare to find automotive power available to haul one out; there were few cars and fewer tractors in the Balkans. One had to negotiate with peasants to hire a team of horses, oxen or water buffalo. For this purpose I carried, tied up in corners of my handkerchief, fifteen or twenty gold sovereigns. The Balkan countryfolk would do almost anything for gold, which they used to adorn their wives' necklaces and bracelets.

That was a time and place where such formalities as uniformed war correspondents, conducting officers and the trappings of military journalism were still unknown. I applied at the Budapest foreign ministry for documents permitting me to go to the Hungarian staging point at Debrecen, near the Rumanian border; but I learned then and there to expect nothing but trouble if one caters to bureaucracy.

Count Csaky, the foreign minister, summoned me for a lecture about some pieces I had recently written. He categorically forbade me to accompany the Transylvanian expedition. I replied that, in such a case, *The New York Times* would print nothing about this great event. Csaky was naive enough to believe me and relented. Poor fellow, he was at heart a decent man. Less than a year afterward, he committed suicide when Hungary blithely ignored the Jugoslav Pact of Eternal Friendship and joined Hitler in his invasion.

On September 5, 1940, the Hungarian army moved across the Rumanian border. I had toured Transylvania a few months earlier with a charming Rumanian princess who claimed the province contained only a handful of Hungarians. My less lovely military escort was determined to prove the contrary.

The advance started from Debrecen, a cattle town on the edge of the Hungarian *puszta,* or plain, renowned for horse fairs and excellent sausages. I accompanied the informal press cavalcade to a village called Biharkerezstes where I pretended to have a mechanical breakdown. After despairing grumbles, the official in charge had to move along according to plan with the rest of my colleagues. I waited in a field so advancing troops could pass, finally taking off when I was sure I could move independently and as a free agent.

The occupation of Transylvania was a shambles. The Rumanians made no stand; they simply retreated, ripping up roadways and telephone lines, destroying the meager fortifications of the Carol Line, pulling down bridges. Rumanian nationals who didn't move eastward with their troops stayed furtively under cover so that, in truth, the population did assume a certain Hungarian air as we marched through, the sturdy little flat-faced soldiers, looking like leftovers from Attila, striding behind handsome, tall blond officers on horseback, dressed in London-tailored uniforms. This contrast stressed the feudal gap in Hungarian society.

Much of the occupying force was soon tipsy since villagers kept running out with buckets of wine. The infantry, largely garlanded with flowers, continually shouted: *"Eljen Magyar Honved! Eljen Magyar Honved!* Long live the Hungarian Army." This was usually followed by hoarse screams: "Forward to Bucharest!" Had the Rumanians tried to oppose this parade they could have caused much trouble because so many rifles were spiked with roses and artillery, limbered, was festooned in blossoms. Behind the army came trucks loaded with gendarmes wearing Beau Brummell hats crested with cock feathers. I accompanied this parade as far as Transylvania's capital, Cluj under the Rumanians, which promptly assumed its Hungarian name, Kolozsvar.

Felix proved a useful companion. In the village of Banffy Hunyad I was billeted in a prosperous peasant's house. Six of us were assigned to one room which contained a huge double bed and a narrow chaise longue. I immediately stretched out on the chaise longue with Felix's chin about my knee. A young lieutenant thought the fairest division of sleeping space would be four on the bed and two on the divan but Felix proceeded to growl and I assured him the dog was vicious. The lieutenant retreated to the groaning bed.

Next morning I took off for Kolozsvar along a side road leading through a bog. I got stuck in a soft patch and held up the advance of a mechanized brigade which didn't dare ease past me for fear of being truly swamped. The high point of the performance was a victory parade in Kolozsvar (Cluj) where Admiral Horthy, the hefty Hungarian Regent who possessed neither fleet nor throne, rode on a broad-backed white horse, dressed in World War I naval uniform. Historians have tended to be gentle with Horthy. I personally met him only twice and thought him a stuffy old fool. When he was liberated from his Nazi caretakers at the end of World War II, he was placed in an interrogation center that went under the code name of ASHCAN and I was privileged to read secret accounts of his remarks. In official questioning Horthy was exceedingly polite and faithfully pro-Western. Then he would meet colleagues like von Papen in the camp yard and stroll about under the trees confiding what fools the Americans were and how easily they could be tricked. Neither Horthy nor Papen knew that almost each leaf was wired and that their confidences were being taken down.

It was impossible to cable a dispatch describing this fandango because the Rumanians had ripped out all communications; so I decided to drive back to Debrecen from where I could telephone our office in Berne, Switzerland. I started off with the top down on my convertible maroon and black Mercedes, Felix barking gaily at everyone; but soon a heavy rainstorm burst. I had just finished putting up the top and was climbing into the car when the military policeman of an advancing Hungarian unit told me the road was blocked to civilians. In those days I wore my hair *en brosse,* had no glasses, and had on a rather military looking trench coat. Furthermore, my car was spattered and its clearly non-Hungarian plates were obscured by mud. So, in my best German, I barked at the MP, told him not to be obstructive, that "the Colonel" had ordered me to proceed this way. I did.

It was a bumpy journey over miles of recently sabotaged road, with battalion after marching battalion forced grumpily to swing over to the side and make space. Near the old Hungarian border, I had a flat tire. By then it was night and I had to replace and patch by the headlights. The rain had brought out billions of tiny, almost white young frogs and they were hopping all over the road and me in one gray, ghostly, agitated blanket. Felix was terrified and shivered in the car. When we started off again, it was to a curious greasy noise as, mile after mile, we squashed along the frog-carpet.

Scarcely had I telephoned my reports when the unpopular King Carol fled Bucharest in a special train bearing his most valuable possessions, his mistress and assorted toadies.

By then the Bulgarians were also preparing to devour their piece of Rumanian flesh. I reached Sofia in the third week of September and, bored with the eccentricities of Felix, left him behind and relied upon the care of a Bulgarian major named Bolkonski who, with his carefully oiled cavalry boots, Russian-type uniform, handsome, dark features and Slavic moodiness, reminded me of his Tolstoyan prototype. Bolkonski drove with me to the port city of Varna on the Black Sea, which was to serve as the base for occupying that part of Rumania's Dobruja province awarded to Sofia by the Germans. Four divisions had been assembled outside Varna under the command of General Georgi Popov, who had been presented with the necessary white charger by the citizens of Dobrič. The Dobruja, which was inhabited by a medley of Bulgarians, Rumanians, gypsies, Russians and Tatar remnants of the Golden Horde, produced considerable wheat and had begun to achieve fame as a beach resort. Queen Marie, the royally lecherous Rumanian, had caused her heart to be buried in its little capital, Balčik.

On September 21 the great operation began. An impressive cavalry charge across the old border line had been scheduled. Several squadrons of horsemen formed up, and, as the old frontier post was knocked down, a scrawny Bulgar priest, his beard scented with garlic, started spraying holy water over the high command. This ceremony caused the steeds of Popov and Colonel Antonov, commander of the vanguard, to bolt and, as the distinguished officers lurched abruptly into the beloved province, seeking to keep their stirrups, the rest of the cavalry thundered behind. Bolkonski, cursing merrily, drove me in afterward aboard a German scout car while a battle fleet of antiquated Bulgarian vessels steamed along the coast. It was an exceptionally hot day. Trumpets sounded; horses and a few armored vehicles wandered across the steppe amid high wheat and sunflowers. Men in lambskin kalpaks and women with heavily embroidered aprons and headdresses weighted with coins of the Russian, Austrian, and Ottoman empires stood in the villages smiling.

When we got to Balčik I discovered that everyone, including foreigners, was expected to take part in the formal victory parade so, carrying my coat jacket in one arm, my portable typewriter in another, with the sweating Bolkonski striding beside me in his cavalry boots, I marched behind a delegation of German and Italian officers and newspapermen, all of them shouting in various languages: "Down with the Little Entente!" "Down with the Balkan Entente!" "Down with guaranties!" Peasants began to dance along the curbs. Gypsy children ran in and out of the lines, stretching forth their hands and yammering "baksheesh, baksheesh." Our distinguished delegation was halted before the reviewing dais where the newly appointed Bulgarian mayor screamed hoarsely: "Now let us hope that our country will be enriched not only by golden Dobruja but also soon by the level plains of Thrace and the blue Aegean." In less than a year Bulgarian troops entered Greece.

I returned to truncated Rumania, somewhat dizzied by the events of the past month. The new sovereign, young King Michael, had no time to rally his bewildered and corrupted nation. Fascist momentum gained daily. On September 27, while I was dining at an outdoor restaurant, two peculiarly nasty Fascist journalists rushed up boasting that Berlin, Rome and Tokyo had just signed a Tripartite Pact. "What do you Americans think about that," one asked, as they sat down uninvited and helped themselves to wine. "All I can say," I replied, "is that when the Allied victory parade is held it will include a Rumanian contingent. As usual you will change sides."

The foreign office issued an odd communiqué for a land that had until recently been a protected friend of the Allies. It said: "We go with the Axis; we go with the Axis right up to the hilt."

October 4 Hitler met again with Mussolini and I wrote from Belgrade: "Many diplomats believe German occupation of Rumania is not excluded." The next day I wrote: "Italian troops have continued to move into Albania. . . . It would seem that Greece and Rumania remain the only countries immediately threatened." I flew back to Bucharest; it was a Hobson's choice with Athens. Germany began Rumania's military occupation on October 11, among other things taking over two floors of the hotel where I stayed, ordering the pro-French owner to hang the Nazi flag over the entrance or to hang there himself, should he refuse. The indignant but terrified American chargé d'affaires was ousted from his apartment on one requisitioned floor.

The occupation was blatant but reporters were ordered to say nothing about it. We were warned all that would be passed on the censored telegraph lines and monitored telephone was reference to the presence of a German "military mission." Nevertheless, I was able to write:

The German military mission here is, to say the least, ubiquitous. One air division of the mission is arriving at Ploesti. Units of a Panzer division have been seen [fifty-one words censored]. It was scarcely necessary to issue a communiqué to let the inhabitants of Bucharest know there was a mission here. At one moment thirty-five of the mission's uniformed officers were standing in the lobby of the Athenée Palace Hotel tonight; one dining room was entirely occupied by them while an overflow of ten tables was seated in another dining room.

Unit by unit I noted where the "mission" was being stationed and added: "General Hansen arrived today. He also was present with the German military mission to Rotterdam last spring." Rotterdam, of course, had been destroyed.

The Nazis, in their *pickelhaube* helmets, carefully established control points at key sectors in Bucharest and set up machine gun posts that did much to dampen the city's normal *joie de vivre*. Some of my friends went into hiding; others began to cultivate Axis acquaintances. A few days before the last Englishmen left Bucharest their local chief of intelligence, an immense young man, sidled up beside me at the Athenée Palace bar and asked in muttered tones if I wouldn't carry information in and out of Rumania to and from his "representatives" and otherwise "help the cause." I was startled. There were at least twenty uniformed German officers in the bar. But D. didn't seem abashed. He handed me six golfballs as a token of good faith. Golfballs were then as rare in Southeast Europe as snowballs in hell. I told D. I couldn't work for him but gave him the name of a Jugoslav air force officer who had important connections in the airline linking Bucharest and Belgrade. I only asked D. to keep my name out of the affair. Some days later, when I was playing golf in Belgrade with an Italian diplomat, my Jugoslav officer friend hollered across the course: "Hey, what's the idea of telling British intelligence I'd work for them?"

The last British left Bucharest October 14, leaning out of the train that took them to Constanța and shouting to tearful Rumanian friends: "Keep the flag flying." I went back from the station to the Athenée Palace bar and had to fight my way through the press of uniformed German colonels and generals. They were most affable and insisted on confiding their Führer's intention of invading Russia. I found this hard to believe if only because it was such an ill-kept secret. Nevertheless, I wrote: "Germany slammed Europe's back door in Russia's face at Vienna last August and she bolted it fast when she began to occupy Rumania. Now Berlin begins to fill out its Balkan *Lebensraum* and there is small place therein for Rome, none for

Moscow . . . the Germans boast that when the day comes the Reichswehr will go through the Soviet army 'as a knife cuts a potato.' "

That was eight months before Hitler attacked Stalin. I left Bucharest a few days later, taking a bus to Giurgiu on the Danube River and crossing to the Bulgarian side in a freezing open barge. I took the amiably old-fashioned train to Sofia and settled in. A friend brought Felix over from Belgrade and we moved to the second-class hotel because the rather modest Number One hostelry, perhaps aware of Felix's dislike for Bulgars, quite refused to have him.

During 1940–1941 the United States was represented in Bulgaria by an unusual minister named George H. Earle. Earle was not of the career service. He had been Governor of Pennsylvania, where I first met him in Pittsburgh under somewhat flamboyant circumstances. I had been assigned to interview the governor, arrived at his hotel one morning, and found him, wearing candy-bar-striped pyjamas, engaged in a game of hearts with David Lawrence, a Democratic party boss who later became the state's chief executive himself. Earle courteously invited me to join the game, at which he proved to be expert.

Earle was a large, powerful man, rather handsome, with wavy hair and cold blue eyes. He was extremely fond of feminine company. Before he had been in Sofia long he was often seen with a beautiful Hungarian blonde, one of the many dancing girls exchanged against Bulgarian market gardeners in the commercial treaty of which I have written earlier. This young lady, A., often dined with the minister, me, and my own long-legged friend, Madeleine, a former goose girl from Kiskunfelegyhazar. When Earle was subsequently sent as naval attaché to Istanbul, A. arrived there on contract with Taksim's nightclub. A British officer was assigned to investigate her. He found she was reporting to both the Abwehr and Sicherheitsdienst, the principal Nazi intelligence branches.

Perhaps indiscreet and certainly unorthodox, Earle was nevertheless a true friend, quite fearless and a gay companion. The only thing I had against him was a miserable little heteroclite dachshund that had a nasty habit of tiptoeing up behind one and nipping off a piece of leg. I solved this problem once and for all by drop-kicking the animal across the room; afterwards it treated me with respect.

Earle was fond of animals and I arranged for him to get a cheetah, six feet from tail tip to nose, that belonged to a Latvian-Norwegian couple in Jugoslavia who were moving to South America. The minister had a special cage constructed in the American legation courtyard and when the cheetah was installed, he bravely entered the cage with a large piece of beef and was photographed for the Sofia press. Admiration for Americans was enhanced. Unfortunately, when the Bulgarians joined the Axis and Earle had to leave, he bequeathed his pet to the King. The monarch was less interested in feline friends. He placed Pussy in a zoo and there during a meat shortage she died.

At that time the United States had virtually no intelligence service and President Roosevelt asked General Wild Bill Donovan to study the problem. Donovan toured Europe, coming to Sofia where Earle took him on a nocturnal tour. Somehow our future espionage boss lost his passport. Discreet inquiries were made and the document was returned with the explanation that it had been found in a gutter. I have little doubt that it had been well inspected and photographed beforehand by German "tourists."

Earle ultimately acquired renown from a nightclub incident. He was sitting companionably with friends when a pugnacious Nazi, looking straight at the American minister, made insulting remarks about the United States and ordered the band to play the *"Horst Wessel Lied."* George may not have been a smooth diplomat but he was a man of action. He picked up a bottle of champagne and smacked the Nazi on the head, a gesture not calculated to win admiration in the State Department but which hurt neither him nor his country among the rustic Bulgars.

After we went to war Earle asked his old friend Roosevelt to send him to Istanbul as naval attaché. A. promptly used her connections to get transferred from Sofia but George, in the meantime, fell violently in love with an attractive Belgian girl whom he eventually married. I used to see a good deal of him whenever I went to Turkey. He lived in a quaint apartment, cluttered up with gems and caged birds, for both of which he had developed a sudden passion. I often went with him to the bazaars where he searched for new acquisitions. My chum Davut kept a small boy on the alert and, whenever George was in the neighborhood, the lad would run back and report. Davut immediately placed higher-price tickets on any item he thought the naval attaché might wish, in order to start at an advantage in the inevitable sessions of bargaining.

In Sofia Earle and I spent much time together with A. and Madeleine. A. was clever and both sang and danced well. Madeleine, who was six feet tall, wholly lacked in talent but was adorable and beautiful. She had been a dentist's assistant after quitting her geese and an entrepreneur with a cavity hired her merely to grace the end of a chorus line because she was quite as lovely as she was nice. We had known each other for months.

Madeleine and I spent an agreeable fortnight walking, talking and picnicking with Felix in the hills outside Sofia, and I waited in her nightclub evening after evening drinking bad champagne, often with Earle, for her exceptionally dull performance to end. It was pleasant despite the glowering political atmosphere. On October 22 I wrote: "The possibility of a German occupation of Bulgaria is the principal topic of conversation." Two days later I added: "The chief difficulty here is that the press, the police and the army are now all more or less in German hands."

The Danube Commission, which supervised the famous river's traffic, admitted Russia as a member for the first time and was scheduled to meet in Bucharest with a Soviet delegation on October 28. I purchased a ticket to return there but our Hungarian friends had told Earle the twenty-seventh was my birthday and he persuaded me to stay so he could give me a party. The four of us had a rather uproarious night. Some time before dawn on the twenty-eighth the telephone rang and the whispered voice of our new stringer in Belgrade, Ray Brock, came indistinctly over the bad long-distance connection, speaking softly like feathers in a wound: "Italy has invaded Greece."

Madeleine packed my few belongings while I called in all directions. Panayotis Pipinellis, the cool-headed, diminutive Greek envoy who was to become his country's foreign minister and premier, got dressed, went to his legation and personally stamped a visa in my passport. Earle insisted I should take his car, an enormous official Cadillac, and have his chauffeur drive me not only to Greece but as far as I wished to go inside that embattled country. I accepted the offer partially, explaining I would happily be driven to the frontier but that I could not see the possibility of putting a charge on my expense account for one destroyed Cadillac plus a dead Bulgarian. I paid my hotel bill, Madeleine rode with me as far as the streetcar terminus at the city's end, and then Felix and I started down the long, long road to Greek Macedonia, behind an ashen, terrified driver. We finally got to the border where, much to his relief, I dismissed the chauffeur and started off on foot carrying a suitcase in one hand and a typewriter in the other, Felix romping alongside. The border authorities were charming, if perplexed, and soon we were trudging on. I continue the account by quoting from a letter I wrote shortly afterward:

Pretty soon we were able to bum a ride in a military auto as far as a joint called Siderocastron where I made pals with a tough little major who is commandant of the district and about whom more later. Eventually, with Felix in my arms, I got on a troop train bringing the boys in from Thrace and Macedonia and, jammed in with hundreds of them, began to bump towards Salonika. We were in boxcars and there was a complete blackout so the smell was more concentrated as I always find that if I can't see, I smell better; and that was certainly confirmed.

At Salonika it was pitch black and raining; we got there after eight hours' shaking; and I finally persuaded a Greek guy who was also looking for a hotel to find the way for me. We had to walk three miles through the rain and finally got there by the Braille System. The hotel wasn't bad except that it was on the waterfront a few yards from the port facilities and my room was on the top floor. There wasn't much to write about the first couple of days but I gathered together some news our man in Athens wasn't able to get out and slipped it by the censor right under his nose through some devious trickery. The censor was a son of a bitch. He spoke no English so we had to prepare telephone messages in French. Furthermore, he was renowned as one of the most pro-German and pro-Italian citizens of Salonika but there was nothing to be done about it. After about three days I had been working until 4 A.M., was worn out, and was awakened at nine by an air raid alarm. I walked out on my top floor balcony where I had an admirable view. I didn't see any planes—just heard the racket of antiaircraft and saw the puffs in the sky. Then there was an all clear and I went back to bed. I figured it must have been practice.

At a quarter to ten there was another alert and I rolled over in bed, being dog tired, and Felix rolled over on my feet when Wes Gallagher of the Associated Press [later head of AP] came rushing in naked and said as how this time it was the real thing since he had just seen a bomb burst in the water just before the hotel; and then he disappeared. While I was trying to absorb all this in my somewhat befuddled mind there was a terrific bang overhead which sounded just as if someone had placed a large base drum on my cranium and then socked it. The windows, the shutters, and pieces of wall all went flying around, my bed overturned and I landed on the floor in a heap. I crawled out through the door, which Gallagher had fortunately left open, and just as I got into the hall on my hands and knees there was another smack and the wall began quivering a bit while large chunks of plaster came down and I lay on my belly next to the wall wondering if it would fall. It didn't. There were some more explosions going down the street. I didn't have much time to get scared but I can assure you I felt pretty green by then.

I went back into my room and shook the concrete and glass out of my clothes and took them into the hall to get dressed and then, in the company of Gallagher who was also dressing in the hall, inspected the damage. The two bombs had busted up the corner of the hotel in which I was living. In the next room had been an English captain ordered to stay in bed with a bad case of dysentery. He stayed in bed until the double door arose and imbedded itself like an arrow in the wall right above his head. Then I believe his dysentery was cured for he left and I never saw him again. On the floor beside the destroyed bathroom was a large cylindrical object covered with plaster which Gallagher and I knowingly examined and spurned with our feet, deciding it was a hot water boiler torn loose by the explosions. Later on we learned it was a two-hundred-kilo bomb that had fallen through the roof but failed to explode.

Felix had completely disappeared and I went down to look for him. I went out the back door and around and saw that another bomb had landed right next to the bar on the street and blown the entire place out but fortunately it was not the cocktail hour. There were several small craters on the street in front and the swinging door had been mangled. Right in front of the hotel were three dead fishermen and in the harbor was a fellow who had been pulling like hell in his rowboat to get away from the shore: A bomb had landed next to him and he was standing in water up to his waist with no boat in sight but the two handles of the oars still sticking out trying to row but moving nowheres. I went through the place where the front door had been before and found Felix behind a large crowd fighting for space beneath the porter's desk.

Then with Gallagher and Stokes of Reuters walked up the street to get the hell away from the waterfront and we were joined by a most hysterical "Hunky" dancing girl who did not look very good at all and who was heading rapidly for the mountains. Soon two of her colleagues rushed past, with pale faces and smeared lipstick. There were a few corpses here and there and lots of wounded horses walking around dragging large sections of gut behind them but no one would shoot them. One little man with no expression was calmly smoking a cigarette butt picking up small pieces of flesh and sticking them in a cardboard box; I don't know what he intended to do with them.

We went to the consulate and announced to the consul, a jerk who had been living ten miles out of town since the start of the war, that he was going to have to find a place for us to live whether he wished or no. There were a few fires in the town and lots of buildings knocked down. Just then there was another alarm and we retired into the cellar shelter of the vice consul's home nearby—a hell of a nice guy named Ed Gullion [later American ambassador to the Congo]. This brings up an interesting sidelight. One day during a raid, the consul was separating papers, taking them from one safe to put in another since they were moving the consulate out of town. A raid sounded and he shouted to Gullion who was also in the office, "Here Gullion, put those papers away," and beat it down the stairs like a rabbit.

They bombed the town pretty heavily for three days during which time we lived out at the American college, a joint run by a nice old pair of missionaries named Riggs who object to swearing so that my legs were black and blue where they had been kicked by Gallagher, who acted as guardian of my language. The censorship was blown up, the censor vanished, and a large piece of shell caught a cop sitting by the window in the back and killed him; unfortunately our pal the censor escaped unscathed. But we couldn't file a single thing for five days and the censor, when we located him, said we couldn't send a word except what was in communiqués even if we were hit by bombs and since communiqués were issued in Athens we would have to go to Athens to send them.

All this time we were having to walk about town since everything including cars, horses and bicycles had been mobilized and three times we had the pleasure of being in the general staff headquarters when raids came and had to go into their badly constructed cellar to wait them out while the planes looked for it—and never found it although the only dive bomber the "Eyeties" used came over there once but missed. The rest of the time we spent jumping in and out of trenches which were not so popular since a bomb hit one and killed sixteen.

Gallagher and I tried getting out to Bulgaria to send our tale. We persuaded a sixty-nine-year-old screwball American named Alethea Pattison to drive us up to the border in her old Ford car for fifty bucks. I drove and, by following the tactic of stepping on the gas whenever a soldier popped out in the road to ask for papers, got all the way up to

Siderocastron where we were stopped by a whole platoon. We spent the night there and I found my old pal the major who was beginning to practice the English he had once learned as a traveling salesman in the Midlands and next day he drove us to the border; but when we got there they refused to let us across since we hadn't any papers. So back we went to Salonika.

Some years afterward Muki Windischgraetz, an Italian from Trieste, told me he had taken part in the raid in which Felix was wounded, the first of what Salonikans called their *blitz*. This was the only World War II mission led by Ciano. Poor Felix did not wholly escape. The combination of bomb splinters and shock gave him a nervous breakdown from which he never recovered. From then on, whenever he heard a siren—whether fire engine, ambulance, air raid or all clear—he either jumped into my arms or hid under the heaviest piece of furniture. He lost his strength and, in 1942, was bitten by a scorpion in the desert west of Cairo, dying soon thereafter.

Having been frustrated in our attempts to tell the world what had happened to Salonika, Gallagher and I flipped a coin to see which of us would stay and which would go to Athens. We gave each other copies of our stories and I, having won, took off on the slow, uncertain rail journey. It lasted two days and nights, sitting on the floor of a corridor, and every time aircraft flew overhead the train stopped and the lot of us were ordered ignominiously into the bushes. I must give Gallagher full marks: on the second day he managed to get a telephone connection out of Greece and dictated my dispatch right after his own.

I stayed in Athens about three weeks, renting an apartment from Marina's mother, a duplex whose top floor was occupied by an attractive English girl. Marina had become a lieutenant-nurse and worked immensely long hours at the military hospital in the capital, moving in to the Sedgwicks' from the country. She was given the nasty job of carrying out buckets of amputated hands and feet once wounds and frostbite had begun to do their dreadful work at the front. Tense, yet glowing with energy and patriotism, she still managed to come with me to *tavernas* on her evenings off.

Reporting was a nuisance. The censorship was rigid on both military and civilian affairs. Telephone calls abroad were carefully monitored and the first digression from approved, censored texts broke the circuit. The blackout was total and the best way to and from the censorship and telegraph offices was by bike, sometimes on the handlebars of a cycle pedaled by one of our young office boys, who, until they were mobilized, included Marina's brother and cousin. The official spokesman who gave daily military briefings was George Seferiadis, a delightful and cultivated poet. He subsequently became Greek ambassador to London and won the Nobel Prize for literature under the name George Seferis. George didn't know the faintest thing about strategy, tactics or war. He could only smile helplessly, shrugging his shoulders, when any questions were asked.

In those days Fancy Dan arrangements for uniformed, shepherded war correspondents had not yet been made. When we were finally able to talk our way into going to the front, everyone was on his own. I finally managed to obtain a car with Patrick Maitland of *The Times* of London and David Walker of Reuters. Two army chauffeurs were assigned to us, peasants, who spoke no known language, didn't know how to drive and who were respectively named Christ and Evangelus. Both had a habit of stopping in every village we went through to have a snack and a drink. Christ started driving but hit two cars in ten yards so we placed the entire burden of responsibility on Evangelus. This worked all right until about forty kilometers south of Larissa where the car stopped. Christ got out, borrowed a shepherd's crook and started poking all the insides of the car with it. Evangelus partially undressed, then lifted up the hood of the car and bored in like a gopher hauling out parts and scattering them on the road. This process went on for an hour while all our expostulations could do nothing.

Then an English courier came by and we got his driver who spoke Greek to work. He pulled Christ and Evangelus out of the car, put the parts back in, poured some gasoline and off we went. At Larissa we found a chauffeur who drove well and spoke English so we sent Christ out for some cigarettes, giving him 100 drachmas and, while he was gone, off we went with the new driver. We got stopped that night at a little place called Kalambaka because the chauffeur's papers weren't in order but we finally argued ourselves out of that by the use of much whisky. I saw a batch of Italian prisoners there eating soup with their hands; a difficult feat. They were all officers and all came from Florence: one was a philosophy professor, two were lawyers. I wanted to ask them if they knew any of my friends.

The Greek army in Albania was based on the Epirote capital of Janina where Ali Pasha had once drowned his wives in sugar-sweetened sacks. This pleasant town had become a base for the dilapidated but courageous forces that blunted Mussolini's initial armored thrust and were now shoving the Italian divisions northward and backward into the snows of the Acroceraunian range. The atmosphere was much that of an early twentieth-century Balkan War. Most guns and much transport were drawn by horses. Truck convoys of reinforcements arrived with flowers stuck in their rifles. The Italians had almost total control of the air but the British gallantly sent up a squadron of Gladiator biplanes. These had to be helped on their muddy take-offs by ground crews running along with the tails on their shoulders until they gathered speed. When the Royal Air Force finally got some Hurricanes into action they swept the skies.

The Italians had struck through the valleys and along the roads with their tinny tanks but, once the Greeks stopped them, they counterattacked along the ridgecombs, taking along their dismantled Schneider-Danglis mountain guns and pounding frightened enemy concentrations below. Often patrols, especially the tough evzones who parade in peacetime wearing pompom slippers and white kilts, would slip along the thorny brush at night, moving one blanket ahead of another to deaden the crackles and calcareous echoes, attacking outposts with knives and, when these got stuck, using their hands and teeth. I saw one forward prisoner-of-war cage containing several Italians with neck wounds from such encounters. Two delighted evzones, finding I was American, gave me a postcard of themselves, arms around each other's shoulders, on which they had written: "To Mister Cyrus from his brave Greek friends, Janni and Costa, who keep their teeth sharp by brushing them with Kolynos toothpaste."

I was astonished and impressed by the combination of Greek courage and skill. Their bravura expressed itself in fantastic ways. One ancient plane of the tiny air force, with a crew of two still riding in old-fashioned open cockpits, used to drop shoes, rocks and bottles on the Italians in low-level swoops once their bomb-loads were gone. After being pinned down by several rounds of artillery plus a Savoia Marchetti, I had coffee one evening with the corps commander, a tubby but resolute gentleman. "How did you feel?" he asked. "Scared out of my wits." "A Greek is never frightened." This cockiness infected the small group of reporters allowed to wander about the rocky front. There was great competition among the English, who specialized in stories beginning "I." One night, on handing in my dispatch to the censor, I noticed on top of the heap a dispatch from an Australian commencing: "I am the first correspondent to cross the Albanian border swinging on the end of a rope." The Australian subsequently built himself some reputation as a fiction writer.

The durable Greeks, supported by pack howitzers and a small but effective British air unit, worked their way along the crests and deep into Albania, chasing the Italians out of southern and eastern towns and establishing themselves on the wild shores of Lake Ochrid where satyrs once tootled pipes. It was pathetic to see the little Italian corpses, looking especially small and cold, and batches of prisoners, not in the least bit martial, wanting only to get out of the Acroceraunian cold. Frostbite was beginning to take more victims than artillery.

Signs of Mussolini's bombast were everywhere: posters reading: "Long Live Imperial Italy" and "I recognize no Obstacle." On one makeshift grave a Fascist poet painted in tar on the board cross a tribute to his dead comrade: "In the shadows of the Mountains of Epirus, Under a rude cross, You have found eternal glory." As always in war the dead were surrounded by scraps of letters from home: "My dearest son, I salute you in the name of the Virgin and pray you will be back with us in time to celebrate your birthday. I send you 150 lire that you may remember the love of your beloved father and mother." The wind often blew into our encampments bits of plumage—from jaunty Bersaglieri hats.

Despite the cruelty of freezing weather which caught both sides ill-equipped, and despite the rantipole savagery of close-quarter fighting, a certain camaraderie seemed to prevail between the Mediterranean peasants and fishermen then engaged in killing one another. Both prayed continually to the Virgin Mary. Although she appeared differently to the Western and Eastern Catholic religions, each shared the same fevered affinity. She was often reported, dressed wholly in black like any Greek island girl, as an apparition above one or other isolated unit on a peak. When the frightened Italians were captured they were relatively well-treated. It was common to see a Greek officer on muleback, rifle across knees, riding down the road behind two prisoners while all three chatted amiably over shared cigarettes.

A friend of mine, a major from an old military family, organized a kind of commando to raid behind the Italian lines. He told me with gusto: "We were picked men with picked guides and we traveled by night. We slept in the forests and lived off wild boar, bread, cheese, olives, carrying grenades, rifles and bayonets and ammunition. Four of us carried the parts of two machine guns. Always within two days march were two mules loaded with more supplies. We were all disguised as peasants and our faces were blacked. We struck suddenly and swiftly, dynamiting their bridges and roads and descending on village gendarme stations. There were no wounded. We killed all the enemy we met and those of us who could not come back with us will never return. Seventeen are still there."

I returned to Belgrade to pick up my Mercedes and drove it nonstop back to Athens, over terrible roads and heavy snowdrifts, so I could spend Christmas with Marina. The year ended on a note of optimism. Greek submarines sank three Italian troop transports and the army held its initiative despite the bitter weather in the Acroceraunians and heavy Italian reinforcements. We wound up 1940 with a maenadic New Year's Eve party at the King George Hotel bar, jammed with British air crews on leave. In spite of the blackout it was very gay—the last Athenian jamboree for years. An American friend kept squirting champagne over everyone. I threw him downstairs and broke his arm.

# 9

---

# ANNUS MIRABILIS

OR ME 1941 WAS A STRANGE KIND OF *annus mirabilis*. IT WAS CON-
sumed by a series of disasters but during it I fell in love, and by the
time it ended the Germans had met their first massive defeat in
Russia, a blow from which they never recovered, and the United States
had entered the war, insuring Hitler's defeat.

During that extraordinary year I experienced various adventures. I tried,
unsuccessfully, to save the life of our string correspondent in Rumania who
had been sentenced to death. I was expelled by the Germans from Bulgaria
and driven by their armies from Jugoslavia and Greece. I was forced by the
Wehrmacht to evacuate Moscow with the diplomatic corps and much of
the Soviet government. For my reports I was offered . . . and then had my
name withdrawn by my paper . . . a Pulitzer Prize. But by January 1942 I
was (and still am) happily married and the Allies had started to swim the
tide of victory.

Britain began to commit itself gingerly but increasingly to Greece's fate.
I flew down to Crete on a bomber to investigate tales I had heard of a
dashing commando that staged raids against Italian outposts in the
Dodecanese Islands (then governed by Rome) and reports of a mounting
British show of force. The plane bounced down at what might be called the
world's oldest airport, for it was from a mountain just a few miles away
that Icarus launched his difficult flight toward the sun. I then bummed a
ride to Canea on the back of a truck. That city hadn't changed since my
last visit two years earlier, despite a few bombing raids. But there was one
striking difference—the marked prevalence of British fighting forces and
equipment. The commando, I discovered, contained several Spanish Re-

publican refugees who enjoyed carving Italians with their knuckle-duster knives.

After lunching in their officers' mess on whisky, beer and bully beef, which makes a fine meal, I started off with a naval intelligence officer along the seacoast road past bivouacs of Scottish troops and lines of enormous black-booted, baggy-pantalooned, black-capped, bearded Cretans seeking to join up at recruiting centers.

We visited the ramshackle village port of Suda Bay, a most important prize in Crete and one of the Mediterranean's naval jewels. Suda Bay had been the scene of a constant game of cat and mouse since the Italian attack. The place frequently hummed with Italian planes, usually so high up that one could only hear the faint noise of their motors. They almost invariably swooped down from the same mountain point to bomb.

The Royal Navy was much in evidence, its men mostly with long beards looking like Gilbert and Sullivan actors. They had their own little taverns where they drank strong Cretan wine, a heady mixture which it would take a chemist to analyze. This was reinforced by a daily ration of His Majesty's Jamaica rum, refreshing for a landsman  The sailors improvised bathtubs out of stone coffins found in the neighborhood.

I attended one party in the house of the mayor of a hamlet near the bay. When it started, a full moon was coming out of the Aegean, and when it ended the moon was falling through olive groves to Africa. The beach lay along the side of the water like snow and the slim shapes of warships stood out against the horizon. In the distance naval shore parties were filing from a tavern beside a former prison. It had until recently contained three unusual tenants: an admiral and a general who had fought on the wrong side of the last Greek revolution and a murderer working out a thousand-year sentence. The admiral and the general were again serving the colors; the murderer moved to another jail.

Nearby, detachments waited on the alert beside their shore batteries and antiaircraft guns. They watched the rising moon spray the shore and the fleet with light and looked around for the Germans who already fulminated in the Mediterranean sky. The mayor summoned his guests about the table and set forth a pig that had been roasted from teeth to tail, a turkey and a chicken and several gallons of black-colored wine. The harbor master handed a plate with enough food for three men to Lieutenant Commander Douglas Duff, a Scotsman with opulent red beard, a neck so big he couldn't wear a collar but draped it in a muffler, a face like Henry VIII, an appetite like Gargantua and the nickname of Falstaff.

Duff had been born in Argentina and was the sole survivor of a torpedoed ship during World War I. He became a monk for two years and then entered the Black and Tan police in Ireland. He claimed that he was a Knight of Malta, a papal count, a bishop of the Assyrian Church and a member of the general staff of Lawrence of Arabia; that he spoke Turkish,

Arabic, Amharic, Kurdish and Assyrian. He fought with the Druses against the French and with the Assyrians against the Kurds.

In Cairo and Beirut I had known a Syrian chieftain named Shahabandar who was murdered in 1940 and Duff once served as his assistant, helping him hang two Arabs down a well for torturing a Jew. Duff was court-martialed but released. He helped an adamantine Arab surgeon in scientifically decapitating culprits and amputating their right arms with the aid of anesthetic and scalpel, thus combining the advantages of modern science with the usages of tribal custom.

Duff was adored by the children of Western Crete. He fed them sweets and stole milk from ship's stores, which the mayor then distributed. A vast man, he weighed some three hundred pounds. Once, when he tried to fly to Alexandria in a flying boat—one of the largest aircraft then existing—he couldn't get in. He was strong as a bull. A junior officer told me Duff had picked up a man and thrown him through a door six feet away. When a dud bomb fell in Suda he ordered the space cleared of men and dug it out himself.

Other guests included a scorbutic lieutenant who had been a jockey. During his last race the battle for France began and he ran dinghies back and forth to Dunkerque evacuating troops. Another was the local priest—a fine old man with black beard and long hair done up in a bun, deep eyes and a biblical mien, who had fought the Turks. The food and wine disappeared, largely down Duff's enormous maw. The priest's daughter, a black-eyed girl with the hour-glass figure peculiar to Crete since the days of Minos, began a song.

*"Matia, matia, matia, mou,"* she sang, "your eyes are like a bay in which the water is not rippled by the wind, fear not the sailor who sails in these waters. *Matia, matia, matia, mou,* love now for ye may no longer be able to love later."

Falstaff replied with a fleering, bawdy ballad that nobody understood, though it was well received. Aeneas, a fisherman, came in with his wife and one of the officers walked about on his hands, while another danced a hornpipe. "God aid the democracies and their cause," said the mayor. The priest imparted a blessing. "Mr. Mayor," said an officer, "we are proud to be your ally."

I inspected the seedy defenses set up around airfields and key points by Major General Gambier-Parry, the amiable but unimpressive British commander whose mess I attended. Of the latter experience I best remember a moment when dinner was served after an enthusiastic cocktail party and a Christian Scientist, whose emotions were perhaps affected, passed out in the onion soup. A colonel, engaged in conversation with Gambier-Parry, lifted the cheese-covered face from the bowl and set it gently on the table without interrupting his story. At the end he said: "Can't let the beggar drown, you know." From Crete I took a tour hunting submarines aboard an RAF Sunderland so enormous that it resembled a gymnasium.

Gunners perched in far corners while I regarded them from a cot on which I had stretched out. The only thing we shot was gulls.

That January the short, fatherly-looking Greek dictator, General Metaxas (known as "Little Moltke"), died and, despite his widespread unpopularity, there were great demonstrations of sorrow. His refusal to knuckle under to Mussolini had turned him into a symbol of national unity. With ugly rumors seeping down from the North where Germany's presence was ever more blatant, an undercurrent of fear replaced the euphoria of initial victory.

*The New York Times* had had a series of string correspondents in Rumania since the regular incumbent, a Hungarian Jew, wisely decided to leave for the United States. The job was handed on by one stringer to another and was then held by a Dutchman whom I had not yet met. I was startled to learn that he had been arrested and was being held incommunicado, charged with complicity in the murder of a Nazi major. I promptly departed for Bucharest to save him.

Unfortunately, I could do nothing. Rumanian officials refused even to receive me. The United States minister, a conventional stuffed shirt, argued it was impossible to act since the man's legal position was too complicated. Although, indeed, he worked for an American newspaper it was on a part-time basis; his country was occupied and therefore had an unusual diplomatic status; every inquiry he had tentatively attempted was rebuffed.

The poor stringer was executed. At last I departed, feeling helpless, furious and ashamed. For $25 our military attaché, Major (later General) John Ratay, bought me a marvelous fur-lined, fur-collared second-hand coat to brave the open boat crossing the Danube to Bulgaria. (Incidentally, General Mark Clark offered me $1,000 for the coat three years later in Italy. I didn't sell.) Ratay drove me down to the river port to say farewell. A Poznanian Pole by birth, he spoke English with a German accent, which had caused the French to follow him meticulously around the front during World War I. He knew the Germans well and was convinced they would attack Russia that spring, and smash it. He was right on the first count.

In Sofia the process of Nazi colonization was proceeding fast. Hundreds of Germans dressed in civilian clothes and carrying light baggage, with smooth soapstone faces and cornflower blue eyes, had begun filtering into Bulgarian Dobruja. No uniformed Nazi troops had yet entered but extensive preparations for military occupation were proceeding. Germans in ski clothes could be seen supervising the strengthening of roads and the shoring up of bridges. Quantities of gasoline were brought to the airports.

During February's last days the Germans began a formal entry into Bulgaria. For me, one of the first results was a governmental order to depart. I was checked out across the frontier and never again saw Bulgaria under non-Communist rule. Elizabeth de Pünkösti was soon to kill herself in Budapest and Maria Popilieva, our correspondent in Sofia, was about to start a terrible series of ordeals in successive Nazi and Communist prisons. I did see her after the war, in 1956: half-blind, terribly poor, solitary and suspicious, a furtive shadow of her rosy, cheerful self.

When I got back to Belgrade, more and more foreigners were convinced that Jugoslavia would soon cave in. I believed that the tough, pepper-eating Serbs who reeked of onions and downed copious quantities of klekovača (a drink tasting like piano varnish), were ready to defend their country. On the premise that the government wouldn't cede or, if it did, that it would be thrown out by a people who preferred to fight, I made many large wagers. Alas, when it came time to collect, most of the losers had disappeared amid the hecatomb and, anyway, the dinar wasn't worth the paper it was printed on.

Curiously enough, despite the swirling gloom, I had a most enjoyable time. I was carefree, fear-free; my newspaper paid me enough to live quite merrily and I was surrounded by excellent journalistic stories. Although I was involved with the lovely Marina in Athens far, far more than I consciously realized, I still had a charming Belgrade girl, tall, blonde, radiant, with long blue eyes, long hair, long limbs, like some goddess of the Adriatic Sea. She is still, I am glad to say, thriving happily and a true friend.

As torrential March began I was tipped off that Anthony Eden, British foreign secretary, was secretly visiting Greece. I rushed to Athens and had a long talk with that elegant and courageous statesman who quizzed me about Jugoslavia. He was both surprised and pleased when I assured him the people would fight and would oust any government seeking to prevent them. Eden told me Britain had offered the late General Metaxas an expeditionary force but the dictator had refused unless 200,000 well-equipped men were promised. Now, with no such precise stipulations, the British were sending what they could to Metaxas' successor. However, Turkey could not be relied upon to help against the impending German thrust.

Britain's expedition was under Sir Henry Maitland Wilson, the corpulent general known as "Jumbo" whom I had already known in Egypt and who had led a victorious assault on Libya. (Jumbo later told me he first learned of his Greek assignment from Eden, Sir Archibald Wavell and Sir John Dill, chief of the Imperial General Staff, when they deplaned at Benghazi, advised him of his new task, promising him fourteen divisions. In the end he got less than three.)

The first elements of Wilson's force were accompanied by nattily uniformed war correspondents and conducting officers, equipped with their own communications, transport and censorship. I resented this intrusion on the easy Balkan journalistic rubric but soon realized I could not function unless I too were accredited to this martial organization. Therefore, with unforeseen and negative consequences, I applied.

The officer in charge of the veteran reporters flown up from the Middle

East and the new Balkan recruits clamoring for service was a delightful, heavy-drinking major named Evan Alban. Alban was remarkable for the fact that, wherever he found himself, one could be certain that something potable was in the near vicinity; also, because he had lost an eye and always wore a black patch. He may not have been the press's most intellectual tutor and, I may say, was of no use to me when I became involved in a network of troubles. Nevertheless, I liked him. He possessed humor and a philosophy that was well stated in Belloc's jingle he taught me:

> One cannot hope to bribe or twist,
> Thank God, the British journalist.
> But, seeing what the man will do
> Unbribed, there's no occasion to.

The Greeks stood firm against mounting pressures. Often I would sit with Shan Sedgwick in the beer garden of a brewery, watching long lines of British transport and imperial troops trundling up the highway from the port of Piraeus. All this looked enormously impressive to our innocent eyes. But the German manager of the garage where I kept my Mercedes in repair scoffed and assured me: "When the time comes the Wehrmacht will go through this like a knife." The Nazi military attaché, who spoke impeccable English, attired himself in tweeds and somehow managed to intrude into a British encampment, a fact that only became known when his report to Berlin on the secret legation radio was monitored and decoded. Pictures of the Allied disembarkment were published in *Signal,* the Wehrmacht magazine.

Everything was in hiatus, a period of tense waiting. Marina and I occasionally went to a nightclub (they now closed very early) where the high point of each evening's performance came when a sentimental, mustached and enormous English officer, wearing well-tailored uniform, would pick up a single rose, hold it between his massive hands, and waltz solemnly around the floor while the orchestra played louder and other customers cheered.

On March 8 it was made brilliantly plain that Greece would fight to the end despite oppressive German threats on the northern border and despite heavy Italian reinforcements in Albania. George Vlachos, most influential editor in Athens (father of Eleni Vlachos, who became renowned much later for opposing the colonels' dictatorship of 1967), published an open letter to Hitler in the carefully censored press. This said:

> And now you wish us to say farewell to those [the British allies] whom the Italians brought here. So be it. Let us say it. But to whom? To the living. But how can we throw out the dead? Those who died on our mountains. Those who, wounded, fell to earth in Attica and drew there their last breath. Those who at a time when their own country was in flames came to Greece and fought there, died there, and there found their graves. Listen, Your Excellency, there are deeds which cannot be

done in Greece, and that is one of them. We cannot throw out either the living or the dead. We will throw out no one, but we shall stand here upright by their side until the day when sunshine breaks through the storm.

What would your army do, Your Excellency, if instead of horses and artillery we sent to receive them on the frontier our twenty thousand wounded in their bloody bandages? But no, that cannot be. Small or great, that part of the Greek army which can be sent there will stand in Thrace as they have stood upon Epirus. There they will await the return from Berlin of the Runner, who came five years ago to light the torch at Olympus [for the 1936 Olympic games in Germany]. We shall see this torch light a fire, a fire that will light this little nation which has taught all other nations how to live and which will now teach them how to die.

Mussolini flew to Albania and took personal command of his forces. Wounded veterans, sitting at Athens cafés beneath the late winter sun, heard the rumor: "The Nazis have demanded that all British leave, that we make peace with the macaronis." I visited the German legation, which was still allowed to function, and talked with a Nazi diplomat whom I was to know years later as a representative of Bonn to NATO. He said with unctuous regret: "We have great admiration for Greece but you must remember the Führer's promise to combat England wherever Englishmen are to be found."

That spring, the Belgrade government finally knuckled under to Nazi pressure. Prince Paul, the elegant, art-loving Regent, was forced, to his distaste, to grant Berlin permission for its armies to cross Jugoslavia. Lane, the American Minister, tried to prevent this concession but Paul told him sadly, "You big nations are hard. You talk of our honor but you are far away." On March 25, in Vienna, the Jugoslavs adhered to the Axis Pact.

The English had long been preparing for this possibility and acted with admirable promptness and efficiency. Leopold Amery, a cabinet member, urged the Serbs on the BBC, "Will you let your people become once more a subject race?" London's intelligence agents, including the two air attachés, Hugh MacDonald and Tom Mapplebeck, conspired feverishly with General Mirković of the Jugoslav air force and officers of the Royal Guard. They, in turn, contacted Colonel Mihailovic, with whom MacDonald had been in touch for months. Meantime Hugh Dalton, head of London's Special Operations Executive (SOE), a cloak and dagger outfit, told his Belgrade representative, an oil man named Tom Masterson: "Use all means to raise a revolution." On March 27 the plotters struck, spreading violent slogans: "No war without the Serbs," "Better grave than slave," and "Better war than a pact."

The *coup d'état* worked with surprising success. It was made in the name of young King Peter (who had not yet attained his majority and was still subject to his uncle, the Regent). Peter's signature was forged to a document making the air force commander, General Dušan Simović, prime minister. A voice resembling the King's broadcast over the radio that Peter had taken over power. Prince Paul and his wife, the beautiful Greek Princess Olga, were sent to Athens and later to South Africa. Simović dispatched a military mission to Moscow seeking aid. Early on April 6, a Soviet-Jugoslav treaty of friendship was signed. Stalin cynically canceled this and severed his new diplomatic relations when Jugoslavia was overrun.

As soon as word of the coup reached euphoric Athens I decided to rush north. It was obvious Hitler would strike back at this affront. I intended to drive my Mercedes for it was far from certain the Jugoslav army could provide any transportation and my car was by then completely equipped for almost any Balkan hazard. Unfortunately, when I went to the garage to pick it up, I found the Mercedes had been neatly telescoped by my future brother-in-law who borrowed it and aimed it accurately at a bus. However, the efficient if lugubrious Nazi garage owner repaired it quickly. I took off with Patrick Maitland two days later. Since the British army's bureaucratic muddle had not yet even answered my application to be accredited as war correspondent, I felt no need to advise Alban and his minions; nor did I.

We drove steadily northward over awful, pocketed, muddy roads, jammed with the battered trucks and horse-drawn wagons on which the Greek supply system depended. Occasionally we slept by the roadside, wrapped against the night wind in an army blanket. I was optimistic. Having successfully pinned my faith on the Serbian people's political instincts, I now counted on their martial talents. From Bitolj, at the head of the Monastir Gap in southern Jugoslavia, I sent a dispatch beginning: "Judging from available indications a terrific Allied attack on Albania is now distinctly probable and could result not only in an Axis disaster of at least the magnitude of Dunkerque, but conceivably in Italy's elimination from the war." Alas, how tragically wrong I was!

Sir John Dill flew to Belgrade hoping to coordinate defenses but Simović, thinking some form of appeasement might conciliate the Nazis, refused to sign a military convention. He did send his deputy chief of staff to confer with Wilson and the Greek commander, General Papagos, at Bitolj. However, they agreed on nothing. The German armies in Hungary and Bulgaria feverishly altered their dispositions, the Luftwaffe flew in extra squadrons, and it was clear that Hitler would give the Jugoslavs no choice except to fight for their lives. Indeed, at 2:30 P.M. on the very day of the *coup d'état* the Führer issued Directive Twenty-five to smash Jugoslavia.

While a traumatic mobilization started, I rushed about Belgrade getting permission to accompany the army on what I so hopefully imagined would be an Albanian Dunkerque. Simović, the prime minister, gave me the only war correspondent's credentials I believe were granted for that brief campaign: a special visa authorizing me to join the attack in Albania but which required the stamp of each corps commander in the military districts en route. I instructed Ray Brock, a hefty and courageous Texan who had succeeded Parker as our local representative, to stay with the government wherever it went. Then we waited.

Two days before the Axis onslaught Gastone Guidotti, the charming Italian chargé d'affairs (later ambassador to London), invited me for lunch. He was a close friend and his heart was firmly on the Allied side even though, in response to Ciano's orders, he had to wear in his lapel a Fascist emblem. Gastone's house was deserted. He had packed off his wife and daughters and sent most of the furniture with them. However, he gave me a superb meal, followed by excellent cognac in his barren sitting room. Then he said with some embarrassment: "Cy, it is no secret what is about to happen. And I must tell you as a friend that we and the Germans have been instructed to look for you as soon as we are able. Seiler of the German legation· has already spoken to me of this. Won't you let me help? I don't want you to get caught. Will you permit me to drive you in my car to any frontier you choose?"

This was a remarkable offer. In order to save me Gastone was proposing to risk his own career and perhaps the safety of his family. I thanked him warmly but assured him I had made my own arrangements. (When next I saw Gastone in London, after Mussolini's fall, he told me the Gestapo had come to him shortly after their arrival in Belgrade and asked: "Where is your friend, the Jew Sulzberger?" Quite truthfully he replied he didn't know.)

April 4 I jotted in a copybook I had bought with the intention of keeping a diary, an intention that didn't last long:

Broke my only pair of glasses and went to an optician to buy a new pair. He was reluctant but I insisted that he should get them ready today. I don't think there is much time so there is no point having a more careful job done but receiving the spectacles too late.

Hugh MacDonald got another cable from Athens. It was from the British military authorities. They told him to "order" me to return to Greece immediately to face charges that I had violated my agreement as an accredited correspondent by going to Jugoslavia, I told Hugh they should go climb a tree. I am not an accredited correspondent because they have taken so long in going through the red tape of my application that I never had any reply. I came up here to cover a war. It is obvious the Germans are not going to let the March 27 *coup d'état* go by unpunished. Hugh agrees with me 100 per cent and is entirely on my side.

Late April 5 I filed my last dispatch from Belgrade, telephoning from the office of my friend Corrado Sofia, correspondent of Stefani, the Fascist official news agency. He dictated a highly slanted article to his Rome office.

I dictated a wholly different account to our relay station in Berne. Then we clinked glasses of *šlivovica,* shattered them on the floor and said good-bye. I next saw him during the summer of 1944 in Allied Rome.

I packed my car with bread, sausage, cheese, *šlivovica,* bought two tires on the black market, and then dressed in ski clothes, the nearest thing I had to rough equipment. In one pocket of the car I stuck a Belgian revolver I had taken from a dead Italian officer in Albania and loaded another pocket with ammunition. Then I stood on the balcony of my hotel room at the corner of the Kalemegdan, which was being used as an arsenal, watching long lines of peasants shuffle in one gate to pick up uniforms and rifles, and march out another singing: "Listen, girl I love, Hitler has come to our frontiers but the Serbs are standing there with guns to see how many ribs the Germans have." Their Slavic voices were strong and resonant. The moon was full: ideal bombing weather.

Lou Fortier, American military attaché, had tipped me off that I had better start for Albania soon. Therefore, around 1:00 A.M. April 6 I paid my hotel bill, changing hundreds of dollars to cover immense telephone charges. (Before dawn the Srbski Kralj, with all that wealth inside, had burned to the ground.)

The English, knowing of my plans, had asked me if I would take one of their "diplomats" from Budapest as far as Bitolj (where the road forked southward to Greece and northwestward to Ochrid, springboard for the Albanian attack). Before meeting my passenger, I dropped by to say good-bye to Lane. He was playing a desolate game of poker with Fortier and two businessmen. They invited me to take a hand. I played for two hours, winning great quantities of dinars, none of which were to do me more good than the proceeds of my bet on Jugoslav politics or my payment to the Hotel Srbski Kralj. Finally, I said farewell and drove off. (It was weeks before I heard of Lane again. His house was bombed but he and his staff, despite several narrow escapes, all behaved excellently. For his part, Lane had been informed of my death. He sent me a telegram in Turkey that May when he discovered the news was premature.)

Lines of cars were parked outside the British legation. I drew up and was introduced to Ben, the hulking young man who was hitchhiking in the direction of Greece. He proved to be a calm, resourceful, agreeable companion. I do not give his real name simply because I was soon to discover that he worked for British Intelligence (indeed, he was later parachuted back into Jugoslavia on a mission), is alive, and still, when I last heard of him, attached to the same profession.

We had a hard time threading our way out of town amid marching troops and their incredibly slow, lumbering ox-drawn munitions carts. At a hill some miles out, where a World War I monument stands, there was a noise like the purring of distant cats and another noise like the far-off tearing of silk. At Kraljevo, a Serbian town, we learned that formal war had started with the dive-bombing of Belgrade, an operation that brought 17,000 deaths.

From Austria, from Hungary, from Bulgaria (but not, be it noted, from reluctant Rumania, a former ally) Wehrmacht and satellite troops poured into Jugoslavia and swiftly disintegrated the cocky Serbs. Croat Fascists led mutinies against the Belgrade regime, Croat officers flew off to Germany with secret plans, Croat paramilitary organizations joined the invaders. Only seven of the thirty-one divisions theoretically at Simović's disposal ever took part in active fighting.

I stopped at Kraljevo and again at Sremska Mitrovica where the British had important lead and zinc mines. The commanding general of the Ibar division assured me twenty-seven German planes had been destroyed over Belgrade. Somewhat encouraged and in an enormous hurry to join the Albanian onslaught, I pressed on without sleep. The drive was bumpy and increasingly fatiguing. Horse-drawn Jugoslav military transport had left so many additional· shoe nails on the road that all told, before crossing the Greek border, I was forced to change tires fourteen times, removing the tubes and patching them, often while Nazi planes slid overhead. At night our headlights were covered with black cloth through which only the faintest slit of light was permitted.

Finally, worn out, I turned over the wheel to Ben, giving him what I thought were precise road directions. I dozed off and Ben promptly took a wrong turning, heading toward a strip of the Bulgarian border where, unknown to us, an Axis thrust was in the process of being mounted. When the noise awakened me I found we were grinding along a dry creekbed and, before I had time to complain, a Jugoslav soldier popped out of the bushes, nervously pointing his rifle. He was bewildered to discover two strangely attired foreigners, one of whom pretended to speak no Serbian at all. The sentry summoned two companions and, hands up, they ordered us out of the car. When my revolver and ammunition were discovered there was evident consternation. Hands still up, a rifle in Ben's back and a Schmeisser in mine, we were ordered to unit headquarters, having to balance nervously over a bridge that consisted of a barkless wet log stretched across a brook.

The lieutenant in charge of the outpost, already alarmed by the gathering Nazi attack, promptly concluded we were spies. The radio had been filled with warnings about agents and paratroopers in all kinds of disguise. Therefore, with little waste of time, he told us we would have to be shot. I argued vigorously against this decision and gave emphasis to my logic by pointing out that there were two bottles of *šlivovica* under the rear seat of my Mercedes. A private was dispatched to confirm this report. First one, then the other bottle, was subsequently broached. Finally the lieutenant was persuaded to read my permit from General Simović (which he could barely do) and to hear my translation of a document designating Ben a British King's Messenger. As things happen among the Serbs, the atmosphere changed swiftly. Amid embraces and toasts we finished the *šlivovica* and were then escorted back to our car. Eventually we departed in the waning moonlight amid a jovial salvo, the only amiable shots discharged on that cruel border.

Before dawn we were again arrested in the road junction of Stara Kača-nik, a Turkish-looking village with mosque and wooden-porched low houses. The Jugoslavs were concentrating artillery and some of their few trucks there prior to pushing off westward for the great Albanian offensive. However, before we were allowed out of the local jail, where we spent the next few hours, the commander was turning his guns around and unlimbering them against the Germans clambering up behind from the east.

The jail consisted of a single moldy cellar where a very hard-nut colonel was already in the process of interrogating other suspected spies hauled in off the road. These included a British diplomat (who survived to become an ambassador), a Jugoslav girl and two Englishmen I had never seen before. We greeted each other rather cheerlessly. The colonel sent for shears from the blacksmith's forge, announcing his intention of opening all the sealed, padlocked Foreign Office bags which his prisoners, standing on official protocol, refused to unlock. To my horror, the contents of the pouches were emptied on the damp floor and included one English major's uniform, two radio transmitters and receivers, small arms and other unusual diplomatic equipment. Immediately the colonel decided we were obvious fifth columnists and again the same conclusion: firing squad. I was beginning to feel like Alice before the decapitation-minded queen.

By then Ben and I had acquired a certain amount of experience in hysterical command posts. After infinite argument and earnest persuasion we induced the colonel to use his hand-cranked military telephone line to Skoplje where there was a British consular officer. He might, if found, be able to identify our companions (although it seemed to me that Talleyrand himself would have had a difficult time explaining the diplomatic equipment dumped on the floor in a heap). Finally, after hours, mostly taken up with locating the Skoplje consul, we were released.

The colonel, increasingly bored with the whole procedure and much more interested in the battle forming up along his rear, had told Ben and me we could go but we resolved to stay until the entire party was freed. When that moment came, the colonel ordered the truculent guard from the door, turned to us and said:

All patrols along the gorge running south from here have been ordered to shoot on sight any car resembling yours [the English diplomat's, a huge Horscht]. I cannot countermand these orders. Our field communications are inadequate. All I can do is send a sergeant along to explain. If anyone stops you, he will vouch that you are all right. I will give him a written note. But take care. Good luck.

Our friends, pointing out that their group included a woman, quite properly proposed they should carry the unhappy sergeant. Furthermore, they suggested that our car go first because theirs was much more powerful and could easily keep up with us. This arrangement was not entirely attractive since there was nothing to identify my Mercedes to the trigger-happy Serbs. As Ben and I took off in the morning clamor, I told him, while the enormous Horscht rumbled a discreet hundred yards behind: "If you even see a single leaf rustle, raise your hands high and shout." From there on his performance resembled a jumpy jack-in-the-box. Nevertheless, we got through the gorge. Once we had reached the open, wider spaces, the Horscht whizzed past, disappeared in a cloud of dust, and we never saw it again. Wearily, I suggested we lie down beside the road and sleep.

When we awakened and had nibbled some sausage, we headed towards Skoplje. The city was undergoing an uninterrupted aerial bombardment. There were no Jugoslav fighters and the only apparent opposition to the Junkers and Heinkels came from a few pitiful machine guns. Here and there cheerful gendarmes and soldiers lay in slit trenches, popping away excitedly with rifles and boasting to one another. "I got one. I'm sure I got that one."

In Skoplje, capital of Jugoslav Macedonia, we were picked up by nervous security forces and taken to an old Roman dungeon. Everywhere there was chaos: tangles of telegraph wires; heaps of masonry; corpses of humans and animals; immense quantities of glass; a cacophony of noises; screams, thuds, shouts, blasts and the whine of bombers, bark of guns. At last I was conducted to military headquarters where I had to get my papers stamped by the corps commander. He proved to be a small, resolute Serb with a boil on the back of his neck which made him open his high, old-fashioned uniform collar and protrude his neck like a chicken. As he examined my permit he calmly munched a piece of dry bread and onion and assured me that despite the bombings, all along his front the situation was excellent. Four hours later Skoplje was in German hands.

Instilled with putative confidence by the general, I gassed the car at his fuel depot and we headed for Veles, a sleepy town which we had to traverse in order to cross the boiling Vardar River and start the climb toward the Albanian ranges. I was horrified, on approaching Veles, to find that both its bridges had been bombed. The road bridge was absolutely out. Fortunately, the railway span was still standing although part of it was on fire and the way was blocked by rubble and tangled wires. Ben and I cleared a passage and drove shakily through the embers.

Veles was empty. The main street had been well shaken up, covered with glass and pocked with bomb holes. Many buildings were blazing brightly. At the outskirts we came upon a parade of refugees hurrying out along the high Pelargonian Plateau. Two hours later Veles was in German hands.

Still further on lorries, loaded with troops, were heading in the direction of the Babuna Pass. This famous strategic feature blocked the twin entrances to Greece in the south, via the Monastir (Bitolj) Gap, and to Albania in the West, via the road around Lake Ochrid. The Babuna Pass was a vital military position that could easily be held a considerable time by determined defenders. None were in sight as we wound upward around its hairpin turns.

When we reached Bitolj (formerly known as Monastir) I dropped Ben at the hotel and rushed off to corps headquarters although it was already dark. The senior duty officer told me I would have to return next morning to see the corps commander. Since there was nothing else to do but await the next stamp on my permits, I joined Ben for a heavy dinner and our first decent sleep in nights, a sleep the urgent need of which had been underscored that day when I dozed at the wheel and only woke up as the Mercedes was teetering along a forty-five-degree embankment. Next day I jotted down these notes:

> This morning I awoke at 7, intending to go up to Ochrid and Struga and thence into Albania around Lake Ochrid. At 9 I went to army headquarters and found a few minor officers and some civilians busily packing things in cases. I insisted the general must be there, but they told me he had already evacuated.
>
> Not more than an hour after midnight the commanding general had ordered the military evacuation of Bitolj. At 8 A.M. civil evacuation— including such bureaus as the National Bank—was ordered. The chief of police was told to remain in the Grand Hotel and surrender the town.

It was hard to believe that the Babuna Pass and Monastir Gap were being abandoned without any effort at resistance. Nevertheless, the chief of police personally confirmed to me his instructions to hand over when the Nazis reached Bitolj. Months later King Peter told me the area commander was a traitor.

Prevented by a craven command from carrying out my plan to join in an Albanian offensive which, as it turned out, never materialized, I decided to head for Greece. In the confused muddle near our hotel I spotted Ben by his huge height. He told me that so far he had been unable to find a ride so I picked him up together with a Bosnialk engineer and four other refugees and slowly, the car straining under its excessive load, we rumbled southward.

There was no one on either side of the crumbling dado that marked the abandoned frontier. A few miles inside Greece we came across the tail-end of an intact Jugoslav division. They immediately clustered around us clamoring: *"Gdje Engleski,* where are the English?" To my astonishment, although Luftwaffe bombers hummed overhead, the retreating soldiers still had canvas over the muzzles of their battery of fine, mobile, up-to-date antiaircraft guns.

Just outside Florina, the northernmost Greek city, I dropped our consignment of refugees and drove to a tidy tent encampment above which flapped a Union Jack and before which stood a guard of neat, trim, English tommies, all approved Kipling style. This turned out to be the forward British position, commanded by an impressive brigadier who received us delightedly, eager for news.

This eagerness, alas, soon faded when we told him what we knew. He had no other first-hand information because of the breakdown in military communications with Jugoslavia. He asked where I thought the Germans were. I surmised they were already over the Babuna Pass and that he would be seeing them before the sun was down.

The brigadier reacted calmly. He summoned his operations chief, and, in our presence, dictated a succinct dispatch to rear headquarters requesting that any spare armor be sent immediately to his support. He then offered us some whisky, bully beef and pickles. When the dispatch rider eventually chugged back on his motorcycle, the brigadier read his message, then handed it to me without comment. One tank and two Bren carriers were being sent to help him. Not long afterwards his unit was wiped out by German panzers. Churchill mentioned its courage in a gloomy summation of the Balkan battle.

Collapse was immediate and total. Jugoslavia's martial repute was only later rehabilitated by Marshal Tito's famous guerrilla movement which began organized resistance after Hitler's invasion of Russia. On the advice of the Serbian Orthodox Patriarch Gavrilo, King Peter and his entourage flew to Greece April 14. The next day he was followed by Generals Simović and Mirković plus several air force officers and some of the national gold reserve. Although Mirković spoke no English, he was subsequently given general's rank by the British in the Middle East. The Nazi ambassador in Moscow demanded that Russia terminate its recognition of the Belgrade regime. The calcareous Vyshinsky, a good man for the job, called in Ambassador Gavrilović and told him the Kremlin no longer considered Jugoslavia existed as a political entity.

I wanted to stay in Florina and write my dispatch on Jugoslavia but the brigadier begged me to go to Jumbo Wilson's headquarters, assuring me it was urgent to tell the commander all we knew since the whole campaign was obfuscated. He told me Wilson was now established at Elassona, behind Mount Olympus, so I agreed to drive there.

Rather to my surprise, as soon as we got past the sentries at Jumbo's command post and were placed in the hands of an officer, Ben asked the latter: "Is there anybody here from MI 6?" I then realized for the first time just whom he was working for. Ben was taken off one way and I went the other, being conducted to Colonel Stanley Casson, Wilson's theater intelligence chief. Casson recalls the encounter as follows in his book, *Greece Against the Axis:*

In the evening a bustle outside our mess tent indicated still another arrival. It proved to be Si (sic) Sulzberger, the correspondent of *The New York Times,* who had dashed for his life from the bombs at Skoplje and narrowly escaped being shot a dozen times as a spy. I was not surprised at this when I saw him, because he was wearing dilapidated plus fours and above them a so-called golfing coat of white leather [actually a ski jacket] that looked all the world like the correct wear for a professional spy. But he had much news for us. . . . From what he told us and from other sources it was clear that Jugoslavia was as near total collapse as a country could well be.

Wilson, despite the enormous pressure on his forces, was resolute, friendly, intelligent. Poor man, he will never secure his fair place in history. His war was a series of lost causes. When he served as Wavell's field commander and won great victories in Libya, Wavell got the credit (the reverse of what happened when Montgomery was Alexander's field commander at El Alamein). Wilson was sent to Greece with only a fraction of the forces promised him. Yet he managed a respectable evacuation after Jugoslavia's disintegration smashed his plans. Later in the war he told me, when his commandos had been forced to abandon the Dodecanese Island of Cos, "I suppose that henceforth I'll be known as the Wizard of Cos."

Mark Chapman-Walker, the general's aide-de-camp, was ordered to produce whisky while Wilson quizzed me. I never confessed to either of them subsequently that, had I not known I was among friends, I would have suspected a poison plot. It certainly wasn't whisky. But I told Jumbo all I knew and answered his searching questions as best I could. When I was through I asked his help. I explained about the mess I was in with the British press authorities. He pooh-poohed this and told me to pay no attention. I then asked for assistance in transmitting my dispatch, pointing out it was already far too late; that it was probably the first eyewitness account of the Jugoslav debacle and therefore of intense world interest. Wilson instructed Chapman-Walker to make arrangements with the signal corps center at Larissa for me to have a military line to Athens for as long as I required. He then bade me farewell. The next time I saw him was in Cairo.

At Larissa the Royal Signals were helpful and efficient, locating Shan Sedgwick immediately. Although glad to learn I was safe, he was appalled to hear my voice and even more appalled that I was calling from a British military center. "For God's sake," he screamed into the telephone, "I'm glad you're alive but what are you doing? Everyone's looking for you. They want to arrest you here. And court-martial you." I reassured him, saying I had just seen the commanding general and was calling on his specific authority. Shan took down my dispatch. However, when he submitted it to the censors that night, they curtly refused to send it on.

My car was looted while I was dictating in Larissa. When I finally got to

Athens I found the Greek front collapsing everywhere. German armor from Jugoslavia had pierced its center and already an air of incipient chaos was evident. Legations were burning their state papers and the bright spring air filled with smoke. A crisscross of contradictory orders demoralized the dissolving armed forces, part of which were actually demobilized in the middle of the fighting.

Nevertheless, there were heroic incidents. Colonel Papamarcakis, a Cretan commanding at Perithori, was ordered to surrender after a token show of resistance. He summoned his men, told them of the order and offered them a chance to leave. All stayed and all were slain with their commander. When Fort Rupel, near the Bulgarian border, was attacked by Nazi dive bombers and artillery, a wounded sergeant announced in the dressing station: "Listen men, we must hold them with our teeth." The Germans finally blasted their way into the position and found chalked upon the wall: "At Thermopylae the Three Hundred were killed. Here the Eighty will fall defending their country."

Marina was heartbroken at her country's fate but still grimly working in her hospital, now overflowing with wounded. She told me of two youngsters lying side by side in her ward. One recounted to her:

> We were up on the Bulgarian border when the Nazis started their advance. Their infantry came forward in a psychological attack, standing up straight as gods while we lay behind our rocks, feeling smaller and smaller as they approached. Finally Christo said: "These cannot be men or they wouldn't stand up that way. It isn't right. Do you think that our bullets won't hurt them?" So I said: "I don't know. We must try." And we shot; and two of them went down. Then another two; but there were so many. Then another soldier said: "The Germans are nothing but a bunch of chauffeurs. If you get them out of their machines you find they're no damned good."

Back in befuddled Athens, I realized the full extent of my difficulties with the British army bureaucrats. Exaggerated rumors of my sins had spread through the anarchic town and even old friends cut me dead. I could send no stories through the censorship. Captain Hugh Laming, Alban's assistant, told me court-martial proceedings were being drawn up.

At first I was simply flabbergasted by the stupidity. I pointed out that: (1) I had not been accredited by the British authorities, thanks to their own slowness, and therefore was not under their authority; (2) although I had mentioned—without giving figures or estimates of strength—that there were British forces in Greece, their presence had already been reported in the world press and photographed for the official German army publication; (3) the charge that I had visited the front without permission was nonsense as the Greek front was the Jugoslav rear. I added that the C. in C., General Wilson, supported me on all counts.

These contentions made singularly little impression. I became thoroughly angry and took steps of my own. The minister of the interior, Maniadakis, a very tough individual called "the Greek Himmler" by his enemies, knew me well. I often lunched with him on beans, bread and wine in the GHQ mess at the Grande Bretagne Hotel. I therefore called on this squat, big-eared Cretan and explained my plight. He listened silently, then gave orders to the telephone service, which was under his control, that my dispatches should henceforth not be liable to any censorship and that I should be connected with every long-distance number I requested. He merely asked me not to be "too indiscreet."

The British military were already making preparations to evacuate accredited war correspondents and MacVeagh, the United States minister, urged me to go along. I refused. Instead, I inquired about among caïque owners and located a redoubtable sponge-fishing captain named Mikhali Pantelis. I hired Pantelis at a fee of 2 gold sovereigns a day while waiting plus 100 sovereigns when needed for actual departure. I instructed him to secrete his boat in a cove near Raffina, northeast of Athens, to load it with fuel for his auxiliary engine, water and some food, and to report to me twice daily, ready to move with minimal notice.

Thus I felt confident that I could do my job and could also wind it up on my own terms without stooping to accept the help of nincompoops who had picked a needless quarrel in the midst of disaster. As a matter of fact, when word of my preparations got about, one member of the British legation staff asked if I would take him along when I decided to go; he had more faith in my arrangements than those of the Royal Navy. I happily agreed but he chose the navy in the end (at his minister's behest). Later he was parachuted back to the Greek guerrillas as a liaison officer and was shot dead by a sniper.

For days I was so preoccupied by the onrush of doom and with professional affairs that I gave little thought to my own deep personal problems. The Sedgwicks prepared to leave on a British ship carrying diplomats to the Middle East and, one evening before their departure, Shan asked me with old-fashioned embarrassment just what my intentions were toward his adored niece. I assured him they were strictly honorable. However, I hadn't thought beyond that point.

After her uncle and aunt embarked I talked things over with Marina. I wasn't really certain I wished to marry at that time, nor did she, for her part, want to leave. Furthermore, Pantelis had told me I should merely carry a few clothes and be prepared to swim to Turkey from the coast because he doubted if he could actually land. He advised me not to take Marina because of what he described as the Turks' "hostile attitude." "Let the lady join you later," he suggested. Marina said we should both reflect further on whether we wished to wed. Meanwhile she didn't want to leave her mother at that tragic moment. No one, at that time, could imagine the

Germans, who had proclaimed such admiration for the Greeks, would behave with anything other than civility. There was not yet any hint of the merciless savagery Nazi occupation would bring. I therefore decided to leave Marina behind and she could join me abroad if we were still so resolved. Marina accepted this idiotic judgment with demure and courageous sympathy.

Metaxas' successor, Prime Minister Korizis, committed suicide. The government dissolved and many ministers began evacuating. I burned my files so as to leave nothing that might embarrass either Marina's mother (whose apartment I had rented) or the Sedgwicks. I had already left behind in Belgrade my little collection of devil-bearing ikons. My other valuable possessions, an excellent set of golf clubs and my Mercedes, were to stay in Greece. I have often speculated on what brave souls may have been killed with fragments of my melted-down matched irons, the finest I ever possessed.

Dan Deluce of the AP, who had his lovely wife Alma with him, missed the tobacco ship on which they planned to sail to Turkey so he asked if they could get a hitch out on my boat. I warned about Mikhali's forebodings but agreed they had little choice. Walter Bosshard, a doughty Zurich correspondent who looked like an old-fashioned Swiss mercenary, also requested a ride.

On our last night, when it was evident the time had come and I had given Pantelis instructions to be ready to leave at dawn, I took Marina out for a farewell dinner in Costi's, then Athens' finest restaurant. She wore a saucy, tassled hat, ate lobster soup, pretended gaiety and, as a token of fortune, gave me her little ruby ring. All that night we talked about the past and wondered about the future. In the morning she gave me our usual breakfast of figs, walnuts and goat cheese. I told her to rejoin her mother in the country and, above all, to stay out of Shan's and my apartments. Oddly enough, the day the first Axis forces entered Athens, an Albanian I had befriended and who claimed to be a refugee, showed up at my flat dressed in an Italian major's uniform, demanding to know my whereabouts.

The other correspondents were duly evacuated with the British forces. They were shepherded by Alban to the Peloponnesus and ultimately boarded a naval convoy under heavy German fire. The journalists on that retreat composed the following theme song:

> A one-eyed old major lay plastered;
> And as in the stable he lay, he lay,
> His batman said: "Wake you old bastard,
> They're starting the *blitzkrieg* today."
>
> Oh give me my belt and my braces;
> Oh give me my bottle of gin, of gin;

> Oh hand me my bloody revolver;
> And let the damned battle begin!

In a field near Nauplion, a colleague informed me, the insouciant Alban balanced carefully on a small wall with a bottle sticking out of his pocket. He addressed the assembled reporters and conducting officers, including Laming, while the Germans divebombed the vicinity. "Gentlemen," he said, "and ladies [including by a nod the blonde Greek cabaret dancer who had tagged along], you will move off in double file. You will not break ranks if attacked. You will carry your wounded with you and leave your dead behind." And then, turning to his assistant: "Laming, bring up the rear and see that none of the buggers escape."

My own departure was more quiet. Marina helped load my little Mercedes with a suitcase, a portable typewriter, and Felix, who had disgraced himself by biting a child the previous day, thus adding a rabies scare to the general hysteria. I kissed her farewell. The last thing I saw in the mirror as I drove away was that lovely slender figure standing like a flower in the door, a waving handkerchief, a smile, and sad brown eyes brimming with tears.

The voyage proved neither desperate nor eventful. Mikhali took aboard several demobilized pilots bound for their island homes. It was fair smooth weather but, because of the Luftwaffe, we sailed mostly in the dark. Our wake was phosphorescent, reflecting brilliant stars. Except for the occasional thunder of a plane, the atmosphere of peace and tranquility was almost oppressive.

At sunrise we hove to in sheltered bays while Bosshard, the indomitable Swiss, concocted remarkable meals from canned goods and Metaxas brandy. Pantelis, an incurable optimist, kept urging me not to forget to support Greek claims to Libya, after Italy's defeat, because Libya possessed the best sponge-fishing grounds. As a reminder, he gave me a grimy card printed in French: *"Michel Pantelis, exportateur d'éponges."*

We dropped off air force crews at Andros and other islands, finally reaching Chios, where Marina's family had dwelled in old Byzantine days, famous for its licorice-tasting mastic resin. When we put in for water at a village on the southern shore, a fisherman came up and said: "We fought as bravely against the Germans as against the Italians. But we cannot go on forever. Tell America we fought well. She should know where our hearts are, still on the side of freedom. We will now suffer; but we have faith. Our struggle has not been useless." Mikhali added: "I know that in the end everything will be all right. We Greeks are little people but we have big hearts."

Pantelis had originally warned that he might have to drop us at the harbor town of Chios itself, some miles directly across from Turkey, but would arrange for a small boat to row us near the coast. However, he was astonished to find Chios near anarchy. Two cabinet ministers and a former mayor of Athens were already bidding competitively for any kind of transportation across the strait to Turkey. So, in the end, Mikhali seized his courage and took off, after a night of uncertainty, heading for the harbor of Tchesme. Hesitantly, he sailed along, mile after mile and, when he found he was not greeted by gunfire, finally deposited us at the mole.

The Turks were unused to Swiss and American passports and perplexed when we turned out an assortment of small arms, ammunition, and hunting knives. Finally they decided to ignore their regulations and to greet us with warm courtesy. They summoned a rickety autobus to take us on to Izmir. There we put up in an extraordinary, old-fashioned hotel run by a sleek but hospitable Arabian Nights character whose salon was filled with divans and who looked as if he kept a catamite in the cellar. He fed us enormous pilaffs and actually discovered a telephone connection to Istanbul, no mean feat.

By the time I actually touched Turkish soil my soul began to gnaw. Only then did I realize the extent of my mistake in leaving Marina behind. I knew from the hollowness swelling inside that she really meant far more to me than I had hitherto suspected, more than anyone I had ever known or, indeed, was ever again to know. The more I thought the more vividly I saw in my mind's eye that deeply poignant image of Marina waving farewell from her doorstep.

Therefore, as soon as I had managed to send from Izmir my first uncensored dispatch about the entire fiasco, I returned to Tchesme. Displaying a fistful of my remaining sovereigns I persuaded two oarsmen to ferry me back to Chios. In a little rowboat, each pulling a long sweep, we set off towards Greece. I sat in the stern, silent. Half-way across the channel my Turks became cautious. They mumbled to each other, growled at me and started to turn back. I pulled my revolver from the pocket of my fur coat and began to fiddle with it. Hastily they resumed course.

Chios had not yet been officially occupied. I rushed to the village post office and composed a telegram to Marina telling her to get ready; I was coming. But it was too late. The message actually got through, the last from her ancestral island while it was still free, and I later learned she had indeed prepared for my arrival. But it never materialized. I could get no transport back in the direction of the mainland. Bitter at my folly, I sent a spate of further messages to Athens, but they might as well have been filed directly into oblivion. The Nazis had lowered an impenetrable silent curtain.

With my last gold I hired another rowboat back to Turkey when word came that a caïque-load of Germans was heading for Chios. By that time the chaotic atmosphere of our first visit had been replaced by leaden, frightened silence. I sat on a narrow seat, sharp with the spicules of sponges, while the boat turned, slewing, yawing, and one sullen Turkish sailor pulled, making the oarlocks creak as we lumbered into the wind.

Never, I glumly realized, could I again make so terrible an error; nor have I ever again missed Marina so much.

When I returned to Izmir I found a message from New York asking me to go to Ankara and install a new transmission system along lines I had recommended in my report two years earlier. I proceeded to the capital as fast as I could and was delighted to find many friends, including Geoffrey and Ruth McDermott from Sofia. Unlike most of their compatriots, they greeted me with true warmth. Only afterwards did I learn from Commander Wolfson, chief of British intelligence for Turkey, that as a consequence of my row with the press officials in Athens a signal had been sent from London warning against me as a dangerous character.

At that time *The New York Times* was having immense difficulty transmitting dispatches over the antiquated Turkish telegraphic system. Messages were delayed as much as forty-eight hours. Consequently, after some negotiation, I made a deal to hire the government radio for a modest sum every night, after 2 A.M., when it had ceased broadcasting. I arranged to have my articles precensored by a censorship that officially didn't exist and I then began to dictate my articles to monitoring offices we had established both in New York and Berne, Switzerland.

When one dictates over the telephone and there is a difficult word one spells each letter with a familiar symbol to insure correct understanding. For example, if there is some strange name such as Erzurum (a Turkish city), one will dictate: "E-for-Edward, R-for-Robert, Z-for-Zebra," and so forth. I applied this system to the radio but, whenever the letter M occurred I would never say the obvious "M-for-Mother." It was always "M-for-Marina." And it was "D-for-Dora" (her mother), "A-for-Athens," "G-for-Greece." At least, I was determined, Marina should have the chance to know I was thinking of her even if, as I had discovered, mail service with occupied Greece was completely interrupted.

May 1, 1941, was her twenty-first birthday. I learned, later, that she and some friends, her mother and grandmother, were sitting gloomily around the radio in her country house trying to gather crumbs of information from the distant outer world. Suddenly they heard a familiar voice pronouncing: "M-for-Marina." The phrase was repeated many times. They were struck by the fact I found it curiously necessary to employ mnemonic words. The next night, at precisely the same time, there were many more Ms, As, Gs and Ds, all carefully spelled out. It was evident I was trying to say something on the distant Anatolian plateau. Marina's neighbors were Eugene Vanderpool, an American archaeologist, and his wife, Joan, who remained in Greece throughout the occupation (although Gene was later incarcerated by the Germans). Joan sat down with Marina and Dora to work out an elaborate code that could be fitted to my broadcast pleonasms.

This contained precise instructions covering various contingencies and was a highly practical device. If, for example, I said "M-for-Marina" it meant she should try and leave Athens as swifty as possible and join me in Turkey. If, on the other hand, I said "M-for-Mother" it meant she should remain there for awhile until the situation had clarified. If I said "M-for-Moscow" it meant things were too nebulous and, for the nonce, she should not contemplate escape. If I said "A-for-Alexis" (her brother) it meant I had received the code. If I said "S-for-Sedgwick" it meant her uncle and aunt were all right. And so forth—intricately tabulated on several tightly composed sheets of paper.

This document was given to the kindly Turkish minister on the eve of his departure from Athens and he brought it with him to Ankara. Immediately the proportion of "M-for-Marinas" in my dispatches multiplied by geometric progression. But there was no way for Marina to communicate again. Only occasionally someone would elude the Nazi barriers, slip out of Greece and inform me that she still kept her nightly vigil by the radio.

Other news from Athens was glum and worrisome. Food shortages were getting rapidly worse as Greece, a country that lived by sea trade, was cut off from normal resources. The Italians, who were treated contemptuously as Hitler's jackals, tried to lord it over the Athenians. When Colonel Nick Craw, American air attaché, became involved in a successful fight with three of them, he was rapidly given the accolade of public hero. Poor Nick—he was uselessly killed by French bullets during the 1942 North African landings and lies buried in Morocco, awarded the Congressional Medal of Honor for bravery against our oldest allies.

The Germans drove the British out of Crete in a savage airborne assault that cost them heavily but which also proved the lack of British preparations on an island they should have been able to hold. At the time a large German plane, damaged in the fighting, crashed by the public toilets of Phaleron, outside Athens. Word spread: "There was a Nazi pilot who knew just where to go."

That summer a considerable group of reporters assembled in Turkey. There were the refugees from Greece, including Deluce, Bosshard and myself, the refugees from Jugoslavia sent out via Budapest and including Ray Brock, who became our permanent Turkish correspondent, and an assortment of others. We waited like vultures for further German assaults in Cyprus or the Middle East, or for a possible attack on Russia. For the first time in its long history, Ankara became an important international listening post.

We Americans taught the British how to play baseball (softball) and, aided by some excellent athletes, they didn't do badly. I reached the quarter finals of the (not very distinguished) Turkish national tennis championships, but tripped, flubbed and fumbled when President Inönu showed up. In the evenings we dined at Karpic's, bribing the Rumanian orchestra to play anti-German songs, and played a version of charades in the Ankara Palas bar. Old Karpic, a bald, egg-headed Armenian, always personally served Felix, taking him quietly to the garden and placing a large silver platter of bones and entrails before his delighted nose. Late each night, after the national program closed down, Brock and I dictated our dispatches to Berne. I instructed him in my private code so he might be able to communicate with Marina if I moved on.

So many journalists clustered in provincial Ankara that, to cover events properly and avoid stumbling over each other, we divided into two competitive teams, assigning sources and holding briefings every afternoon. Bosshard and I, who were on the same team, visited von Papen regularly because we knew him and were neutrals. I also saw the British ambassador, Sir Hughe Knatchbull-Hugessen, a charming man whose principal claim to fame, unfortunately, was as the dupe of one of World War II's most successful spies, his own Albanian valet who operated for the Germans under the name of Cicero. Cicero, by duplicating Hugessen's keys, was able to photograph top secret papers including the main strategic decisions of the Cairo, Teheran and Yalta Conferences. Another minor spy, we discovered later to our horror, was an American broadcaster who regularly informed the Soviet embassy.

Turkey's neutrality and central position made it a marvelous news center. From Ankara we were able to report the pro-Nazi coup of Rashid Ali's Iraqi officers and how the British broke it up before Germany could establish its own regime. The young Regent, Prince Abdulillah, sought refuge in our Baghdad legation and Paul Knabenshue, a courageous and resourceful American diplomat, hid him under the rug of his official car and drove him to the Royal Air Force base at Habbaniyeh where a handful of British held out until reinforcements came. We also managed to get out detailed news on the tragic little war between Vichy and Gaullist-French-plus-British in Syria and the Lebanon.

Despite these sideshows, it became increasingly plain that the big story shaping up was friction between Germany and Russia. The depredatory partners who had carved up eastern Europe denied anything was amiss but I could not forget what Nazi officers had told me earlier in Bucharest. From Finnish, Vichy French, German and Spanish sources, to say nothing of the cautious but well-informed Turks, it appeared more and more likely that a break was imminent. On June 14 I wrote:

> German and Russian relations seem to have approached a crucial point, according to reliable diplomatic information, and sensational developments may be looked for in a very short time. . . . The German and Russian armies have completed enormous concentrations on their common frontier . . . the reason for apparent tension between the two powers is believed to be Germany's desire to get control of the wealth of the Ukraine and the Caucasus in order to reinforce the Axis position for a long war.

At dawn on June 22, Hitler attacked.

Immediately every newspaperman applied for a Soviet visa. The Russians accepted our applications with stony, uncommunicative expressions and advised us to wait. This was a restless undertaking as our offices pressed for action. We invented a vodka-orange juice cocktail later known as the Screwdriver, the only way of swallowing Turkish *"votka."* We wearily watched interminable nightclub acts in Karpic's and the Ankara Palas. Occasionally I played bridge with Inönu and a handsome old Britain admiral named Kelly who had been rushed to Turkey as a diplomatic agent. Kelly was one of two famous seagoing brothers known to the service as "Kelly the Good" and "Kelly the Bad." A destroyer was named after the former but my friend, Kelly the Bad, was assigned the more hieratic function of manipulating pasteboards. He and Kelly the Good had not spoken for years but a story was told of Kelly the Bad's last meeting with his renowned brother. The Bad Kelly was strolling down Piccadilly en route to his club when he saw the Good Kelly walking briskly toward him. The Good Kelly cut him dead. The Bad Kelly halted, tapped him on the arm and said: "Sir, I believe you knew my mother."

I received occasional letters smuggled from Marina.

I hear Turkish women are all horribly ugly and fat and nasty, all round???? . . . You remember that night in Costi's, when you asked me to go away with you? That night I thought the world would stop. But it didn't. I got to thinking and thinking and decided not to come, pretending to myself that it was my mother and my duty to my country and my people. Eyewash. I knew all along that it was because I was scared to death of losing you, not in the way that I would if you left, but in a deeper, more terrible way, if I came with you . . . at a time when you needed your freedom most. Now I figure that if I don't come to you I've lost you anyhow, while if I do, I have a fair chance of success; if I fail things won't be worse. I've fixed all my papers and now I'm looking all over Athens for someone with whom I could travel, be he the public hangman if necessary. (P.S. Love to Felix. Thank God I didn't keep him. He would have starved.)

This period was a dreadfully frustrating one. I was unable to do anything about either my personal or my professional life. On July 1 I asked von Papen, as a gambit, if he didn't think Germany had already lost the war. To my astonishment he failed to make an indignant denial—despite the enormous advances during the Nazi offensive's initial week.

Colonel Zarko Popović, who had been chief of Jugoslav military intelligence before going to Moscow for a brief tour as military attaché, told me an odd tale. He had come to Ankara, after the Soviets broke relations with his government in April. He said that on March 23, four days before the Belgrade *coup d'état* which overthrew a pro-German regime, he had attended a reception at the Japanese embassy in Moscow for the representatives of all Axis and neutral states. The Japanese ambassador, General Tatakawa, approached him and said, "I must offer you my congratulations. Your country is the latest member of the Tripartite Pact."

Popović replied, "Excuse me, but you must not confuse me with the Bulgarians. I am Jugoslav." Tatakawa persisted. He said: "Your country has agreed to sign. You will soon be with us." Popović vigorously denied that such a thing was possible, and spoke so loudly that he attracted the attention of other guests, two of whom, Colonel Aschenbrenner, the German air attaché, and Major Flodstrom, the Swedish military attaché, joined the conversation. Aschenbrenner asked why he was so vehement in assailing the pact.

Popović answered "Because, Colonel, my country is not a harlot. The army will never accept anything that brings dishonor upon the nation. We do not want war, but if you force our hand, as you have in the case of Bulgaria and Rumania, then you will find that we shall certainly fight you. We shall fight in the knowledge that for the moment the weight of the German army must beat us, but we still prefer death to shame, and in the end you will be defeated."

Next day Flodstrom came to see Popović in his flat and asked why he has been so rude to Aschenbrenner. Popović said sternly: "Because he insulted my people in suggesting that they would submit to their enemies as easily as Bulgaria and Rumania." Flodstrom was impressed. He confessed to pleasure at the shock which this defiance had given to the German. Incidentally, Popović assured me the Russians would have been entirely ready for a major war in October, 1941.

By the middle of July I knew positively Marina was trying to get out and had arranged the necessary permits. However, at the same moment, I received a Soviet visa. This astonished me because no other correspondent was granted one (including the American we later discovered was working for Moscow) and I had been writing hostile, anti-Stalinist articles.

*The New York Times* had kept a representative in Russia throughout the bleak years when there were no diplomatic links with the United States. This man, a talented writer and brilliant conversationalist named Walter Duranty, had been highly regarded by the Kremlin. He was instrumental in furthering the recognition that followed Roosevelt's election in 1932. Duranty, a friend of mine, was witty, spry, flamboyant and energetic although he had a wooden leg. I knew him in Bucharest where he had great success with the ladies. He was eventually replaced and the last of our correspondents in Moscow, a testy, vain Englishman named Gedye, had persuaded the *Times* to withdraw him and close down the bureau because he was bored and stymied by rigid censorship. Possibly the Russians were as eager as the *Times* to reestablish a reporter from the most influential American paper.

In any case, I hastily made my preparations to depart with Dragomir Bogić, a Jugoslav diplomat who was returning to Moscow after that capital had restored relations with his government. The opportunity presented itself when the Turks undertook, as neutrals, to exchange a trainload of

Axis diplomats coming from the USSR against a trainload of Soviet diplomats coming from Germanized Europe. They permitted Bogić and myself to join the Russian party.

I left Felix with the McDermotts, who possessed his great friend, a Sealyham named Ian that closely resembled a sausage dipped in hair tonic. Geoffrey and Ruth promised to take care of Marina when she eventually showed up and Ray Brock undertook to maintain the flow of code messages in nightly *New York Times* broadcasts. Little did I know that, almost as I was entraining on this long trip, Marina was approaching the final stage of her infinitely more complicated voyage.

I learned afterwards that her mother refused to let her travel alone but she had finally found two friends who were engaged to Greek naval officers in the Middle East. The three pretty girls approached a romantic German officer in the permit section who promptly said: *"Ach, wie schön,"* and gave them the necessary papers, stamps and signatures. The girls then had to have these approved by the Italians and Bulgarians.

At this point a deaf old Greek colonel named Melas, high up in his country's military intelligence and an old family friend, descended suddenly upon her. It would be her patriotic duty, he explained, to carry a message to allied headquarters in Cairo. And this was a very complex, very important message, cosmic in its secrecy. It must be committed entirely and accurately to memory. She had, the colonel knew, but two days prior to her departure. During those two days, said Melas, Marina must memorize his information. He then handed her, with instructions that they must eventually be burned, a series of detailed documents: reports on German troop dispositions, specifications on headquarters sites, news of airforce movements and naval concentrations. As he left her, Colonel Melas said: "I cannot be held responsible if these papers are discovered on you. Certainly, and quite properly, you will be shot."

Marina spent her final forty-eight hours studying. Her mother and her remarkable old grandmother tested her on every detail, making her recite this homework as she paced up and down the bearskin rug spread before the hearth. Then, when she had everything letter perfect, with fine feminine absent-mindedness she wrapped the documents in her best silk nightgown and packed them in the only suitcase she was allowed to take.

The three girls rode a Lufthansa plane to Bulgaria because there was no direct connection with Turkey. En route they passed through German military and Gestapo customs at Salonika. They landed in Sofia where they were cursorily examined by Bulgarian customs assisted by the Gestapo's local branch. Then they took the train to Istanbul and, on the border, again went through meticulous Axis eyes. In no case was their baggage opened. But Marina was not worried. In Sofia she slept in her second-best nightgown. She didn't fully unpack her bag until she arrived in Istanbul. Then she fainted.

As a matter of fact, Alexis, her brother, attached to RAF intelligence, first learned of his sister's arrival in Turkey when a colleague indiscreetly showed him reports of a successful bombing raid. To these were appended the message: "According to target data provided by Marina Lada."

Marina and Felix stayed with the McDermotts for weeks. Finally Shan Sedgwick, by this time installed as *Times* correspondent with British Ninth and Tenth Army headquarters in Jerusalem (a rather fictional force designed to take over Iran, Iraq and Syria), prevailed upon her to join Roxane and himself. Shan, who was about to become my uncle, wrote my *Times* uncle, Arthur, saying:

We expect Marina and Felix here shortly. Marina was certainly well looked after by some very good friends of Cy's and ours who are attached to the British embassy in Ankara, but all the same some sprouting Victorianism in us makes us feel that it is more suitable for a young girl, left stranded financially and hard hit emotionally, being away from her family, to remain with her aunt and uncle. Besides, I frankly feel that Turkey is none too safe a haven for any proven enemies of the Axis. I'm not at liberty to tell you now by letter, but some day you will hear of the exploits of this niece of yours, how she threw her own little monkey wrench into the mighty cogs of the archfiend's war machine and you will be thrilled indeed.

I may digress now to tell you that Marina is the nicest, the sweetest, least complex girl I have ever known. She is a walking beatitude. I give this as my fixed opinion and make no excuses for prejudice. I have in fact watched her grow up. As a child she seemed incapable of any unkind sentiment. Humanity was her distinction and still is. She sheds goodness and grace. During those dreadful last days in the life of her country she bore up remarkably, allowing no personal consideration to interfere with her duties as a nursing sister.

When I finally left Turkey, the McDermotts gave me a splendid farewell party and then brought Felix down to the railway station to see me off. One of Ankara's favorite evening occupations was seeing people off. I climbed into an old-fashioned *wagon-lit* compartment next to the enormous Bogić, already drunk as some grandiose Serbian Vojvod. He was traveling back to his post with several huge crates of food, wine and whisky, protected by two loyal legation servants.

Bogić was a delightful character. He told me his career had been set back when he once rode a horse up the stairs and into the Belgrade officers' club. The only improbable aspect it seemed to me was that a large enough horse could be found to carry him. He swore he would not drink any more whisky until we got to Mineralnyi Vodi in the Caucasus where Narzan (a sparkling water) comes from. As things turned out, he stuck to his promise. We reached Mineralnyi Vodi just after dawn. It was boiling hot, but Bogić sat up, sent his servants out to buy all available Narzan and got beautifully drunk.

All told, from Ankara to Moscow, the trip took eleven days, July 19 through 29. We went by wide-gauge train to Erzurum, from there by motorcade to Sarikamish in Turkish Armenia, then by Soviet train to Leninakhan, another train to Tiflis (Tbilisi), then Baku and finally, after an interim, by slow stages to Moscow. I had nothing to do except practice making myself understood to my Russian companions in a pigeon-pie of Serbian and Bulgarian which came out as scrambled Ukrainian. So I kept a diary, part of which follows:

Bogić, Jugoslav chargé d'affaires in Moscow, is returning to reopen the legation there. The Russians broke off relations and expelled the staff after the German attack. Dragi is a huge, fat Serb, so enormous that on the trip out from Russia to Turkey, he suffered a great inconvenience. From Kars to Erzurum there is a narrow-gauge railway with small cars. The trip took over twenty hours and Bogić was too fat to get through the door of the toilet. With us, we have two Serbian servants of the legation. One is a former village gendarme. He is paid in dollars, but he continually changes these dollars into dinars because, he says, "That is the money of my country and, Bogami, why should I not have my own money?" I am afraid he will not have a penny when the war ends.

Erzurum, our first stop, is a serrated jumble of stone houses. We drive off in dilapidated buses toward the Turkish Caucasus, our party including a group of Soviet diplomats from various embassies and legations in Germany and Axis occupied countries. One of them, Fomin, a thin, blond man, who was first secretary in Berlin, is very amiable and speaks good German.

After a dusty, bumpy ride, we stop beside a brook, under a great cluster of jagged peaks, topped by the ruins of an old castle. Everyone washes, drinks and eats grapes. The only trees for miles are a type of cottonwood, by the banks of the stream.

In Turkish Armenia, we pass occasional filthy stone or mud huts. A soldier roughly pushes a woman out of the way. Now we are entering cool green woods. We are met by a car filled with Turkish army officers who take us to spring of ice-cold natural soda water where we fall on our stomachs and drink. This is a region for bear and wolf. Snow comes early in October.

We stop at the town of Sarikamish and we are given a big dinner; it is about two miles from the railroad station. The mess hall is small and our party is large, so we eat in two shifts. There are many speeches which have to be translated from Turkish to French, French to German, German to Russian and vice versa. This requires much time and means a lot of vodka is consumed.

The colonel commanding the garrison becomes quite chummy after the vodka, since Bogić and I are acting as interpreters for the French-German link and drink our way through both sittings of the dinner. All the Turkish officers appear very pro-English and pro-Russian. They praise the Red Army, Stalin and the Turkish and Russian Revolutions. They toast "Down with Hitler." This is quite a comparison to the atmosphere in Ankara. They are very angry with the Nazis because a German diplomatic party just passed through on its way back to Berlin from Moscow. The Turks made great efforts to lay on a dinner for them, but Ambassador von Schulenberg failed even to come.

After the second sitting and a few extra drinks, the colonel says: "You are an American and therefore a good mechanic. Drive us back to the railway station." I am drunk enough to accept the challenge. The vehicle is an old German Borgward half-track with no less than six shifts. Eight drunken Turkish officers pile in singing with the colonel, Bogić, and me. A private cranks it up and we bump across country in glittering moonlight, singing all the way to the station where the Turks give us vodka, ignore the Russians and hold up the train for another hour of drinking before they pour us aboard. Finally, we roll on toward Kars. A young Turkish lieutenant from Istanbul points out sights in the dark. He speaks fairly good English. At Kars we have tea. We can discern great treeless rolling hills and a grim gray castle fortress on a hilltop. Then we rumble toward Russia past the round castle of the medieval Armenian capital, near the frontier. We have had three different railway gauges: European, Decauville and Russian.

At the border we wait in a field, unloading our luggage in order to change to a Soviet train. The Russians, glad to be back in their native land, gather together around a man who produces an accordion and they begin to sing army and peasant songs. Tractors are working in the fields. In the heat, the wheat harvest is almost in. Red Army soldiers are exercising nearby.

The soldiers have excellent boots and, compared to Turks, their uniforms are of good quality. They wear strange forage caps like khaki sailor's hats with the brims turned down. After a long wait, we start off for Leninakhan, passing an armored train pulling flat cars loaded with military vehicles. This is a contrast to all the tales you used to hear in Europe: about the ragged Russians who entered Poland; about the ragged Russians who entered Bessarabia.

Leninakhan, in Soviet Armenia, is right behind snowcapped Ararat where Noah landed his ark. The customs examination there is tedious but very friendly. Proko and Krsto, our Jugoslav servants, have some sausage wrapped in Turkish papers. The guards take the papers and rewrap the sausages in Soviet journals. They take my revolver (a souvenir from Albania) and ammunition, but promise to send it back to Moscow. [They didn't.] I have no rubles and those which Bogić expected to have sent by telegram haven't arrived. Some local government employee (his job isn't quite clear) gives me seven hundred rubles in exchange for an IOU payable at the American embassy in Moscow. "But with the Germans in Smolensk," says Dragi, "we may never get there."

We take a carriage from the station to the Zentralni Gostionitza and get a room for four (Proko and Krsto included). Krsto is feeling poorly. He has a bad stomach. The Turkish doctors have told him to take only tea. This makes him frightfully hungry and every two days he eats a lot of sausage and drinks a lot of vodka. Then he feels poorly all over again. The toilet in the hotel is filthy but there is water to wash in. Bogić and I have lunch: sour flat beer, tea, rice, *shashlik* (broiled chunks of lamb on a spit), eggs, cheese, onions. It's our first meal of the day and costs 44 rubles (officially one dollar equals $5\frac{1}{10}$ rubles).

We wander about town looking for a public bath because there is none in the hotel. The public bath is booked up until 7:45 P.M. so we poke about the few shops, containing hardly anything but cheap suitcases, cloth, chinaware, small statues of Lenin. Old peasants in caps and smocks sit behind the counters calculating prices on wooden bead abacuses. The churches all have their crosses up. Squadrons of soldiers march up and down; they march very smartly and salute well. They are singing.

> Our force is growing stronger.
> The War has brought us closer together,
> And our hearts are now one entity.
> Our breasts are full of anger.
> Fire from all guns.
> Smash the enemy to destruction.
> > Hey-hey battery,
> > Blast more merrily.
> We'll shatter the Fascist armor.
> There will be no mercy
> From our shells.

During the evening I sit on the stoop of the hotel watching the crowds while waiting for an automobile which has promised to take us to the station. One by one, about twenty-five airplanes take off from a field behind the town and fly away, lights showing. There is no blackout here. The people are strolling about the main square like the *corso* crowds in Italy or the Balkans. They look neither destitute nor affluent. The soldiers are the only ones who are really well dressed; they are exceedingly smart. There are numerous tall, fierce-looking, brown Armenians. Gangs of boys playing in the streets stop every now and then to watch the soldiers. Wrinkled old men sit under the street lamps reading Armenian papers. There are a few handsome, well-groomed, made-up women soldiers; specialist auxiliary categories. A handful of old peasants in ragged fur coats and sheepskin hats wanders past.

Inside the hotel I drink beer, strange, sour stuff, with an Armenian

Intourist representative from Erivan. The Armenian speaks good English; he learned it from the American Near East Relief and he worships the United States. His ambition is to go there some day. He showed Saroyan around when he came to the Armenian Republic. He says he used to listen to my broadcasts to *The New York Times* from Ankara every night.

We go on to the station at train time. It is hung with garish banners and all red decorations, brave slogans, anti-Hitler posters, pictures of Soviet leaders. There is a monstrous, gilded statue of Lenin. Women and children are sleeping wherever they can find space. Booted, blond Russian and dark Caucasian soldiers are singing magnificent songs. Pictures of Stalin, Kalinin, Molotov and Gorki hang in the station office. A big rat runs across the floor.

Finally we get aboard the train and take a compartment for four; it is a sleeper but not *wagon-lit;* there is no bedding, no blankets, pillows; but it is a *soft* compartment; not a *hard* one with only board beds like the other cars.

We rumble on through the night towards Tiflis. These Russian trains always start with a terrific banging jerk; obviously as much rolling stock as possible is hung on to each engine, making more locomotives available for military trains. In the morning we are going through green gorges, valleys, mountains and plains of Georgia. Corn, sunflowers, green vegetables, melons, cucumbers, wheat are growing by the tracks. At each station there are hawkers crying: "Good plums, good, good, good" and crowds of men standing about in sheepskin *kalpaks,* peasant women in orange shawls, old men carrying woven, patterned saddlebags. The train is jammed and some travelers going on short hops hang on to the car steps. There is a railway car, abandoned on a thirty-foot length of track with neither beginning nor end, with a family living in it. Pickle vendors come through the train. The wheat harvest seems to be all in.

## TIFLIS, BAKU, ROSTOV, *July 24–25–26, 1941*

TIFLIS is a big, sprawling, hot town under an arid mountain supporting a funicular railway. Fine bridges span the dirty, gray Ura River. Soldiers including women stroll along the broad streets. All signs are in both Georgian and Russian. The outlook is peaceful; there are hardly any cars, most of them having been mobilized. In the main church, with open door, a woman is praying by the altar where lighted candles are burning.

Leaving Tiflis the train slides on interminably, passing through steaming flatlands and stinking marshes into Azerbaijan. In the distance, dim mountains are outlined. The heat is great and the air is heavy. At Azerbaijan one feels at the western fringe of the orient with its filth, its colorful cloths, dark eyes and faces of Turks, Kurds, Lazes, Armenians, Georgians, Circassians, Azerbaijanis, Persians, Jews. Many men are wearing colored caps. It makes you think of all kinds of little pleasures as you roll along slowly: Altin, the Turkish liqueur, with small gold leaves floating in it; the amber colored Georgian wine.

Along the flats by the Caspian Sea one almost suffocates in the dead, sticky, hot, salt air. Peasants stand beneath the burning sun wearing heavy sheepskin hats. Everybody makes their own tea on the train; there is a samovar in each car. All the time, sweating men are wandering through the corridors in their pyjamas. The pathetic little conductor lives in a hard boarded half-compartment next to a filthy toilet. He emerges from time to time to brew tea on the samovar.

At Baku, one is overwhelmed by the mixed smell of sea-salt and petroleum. When we get to the station it is blacked out and we gobble a hasty meal. People wander up and down the platform in their pyjamas. Talking pigeon Russian with soldiers, I find them extremely friendly and inquisitive. One says to me: What are you? I say: American. He asks me what I do and I say: I am a journalist. He asks me what paper I am with and I say *The New York Times*. A man in a white smock interrupts and asks me what the circulation is. I say 2,000,000, wishing it were. He boasts in reply: Our *Pravda* has 2,500,000. He concludes the conversation by asking if I ever read *The Daily Worker*.

All day long, Friday, July 25, we proceed slowly northward along the Caspian with innumerable stops. At each stop, women and little boys and girls hawk small fried fish, crayfish, tomatoes, melons, cucumbers. To the East is the calm flat sea. We hold up for one day as oil trains pass us on the way North. Now we begin to see the flat, round fur turbans of Dhagestan. Fields are increasingly full of sunflowers. Automatic reapers have started to take in the wheat harvest.

On the morning of July 26, we leave Dhagestan and the Caspian on the way to Ordzhonikidze. Proko buys a chicken for lunch from one of the peasant hawkers. A new conductor serves tea. At one stop, a one-legged beggar comes through the train. I give him a ruble. He says: I thank you for respecting me. Proko points out the window and says: As soon as we cross the Caspian Sea, we come to the Finnish frontier. A woman peasant passes through the train inviting the passengers to buy her more than excellent ice cream.

The green fields of the upper Don Basin are rich and flat. There are huge slag piles beside the coal mines. The coal seams are covered by thick plains of wheat. No alcohol is on sale in the railroad stations. At Orel there are trainloads of material and wounded. Nurses wander around in dark blue uniforms. The soldiers vary from sturdy tough-looking veterans to dirty boys. Many are undersized. Their uniforms are worn and filthy. Women are working everywhere—in the fields, as signalmen on the railway. We halt at Tula, where our passports are again examined, and in the night we hear the sound of machine gun practice. Noisy recruits are training. At dawn of July 29 we finally reach Moscow.

# I O

## STALIN AT BAY

THE SOVIET CAPITAL PRESENTED A QUITE EXTRAORDINARY SIGHT those vivid lengthy summer days. It had been extensively camouflaged by a corps of artists working with the Red Army command. The enormous Bolshoi Theater was hung with a drapery that sought to give it the appearance of a georgic village with little wooden houses peeking out from the penumbra of trees. Surfaces of the principal squares were carefully painted to look like rural communities and forests. It was forbidden to walk across these spaces for fear of disclosing their secrets to intruding reconnaissance planes.

I saw a little boy ride into such a plaza on his home-made scooter constructed of two boards and the wheels of one roller skate. A bulky policeman, with absolutely no expression on his face, walked up to the lad, cuffed him, and broke the scooter across his knee while passersby looked on in silence, their eyes mirroring apodictic hatred. The city was filled with soldiers in summer uniforms, many of them wounded. Although Moscow had been bombed several times and the air raid sirens and thunder of flak batteries were a nightly feature, little damage had been done. However, not long after my arrival, one bomb sliced off a corner of the Bolshoi and left its great camouflage curtain flapping foolishly in the evening breeze.

Bogić, who was met by an official car, dropped me at the National Hotel where I had arranged a reservation through the Associated Press. This fine, old-fashioned hostelry, next door to the American embassy chancery and across from the Red Square and the Kremlin, was by far the best in Moscow. I was given Leon Trotsky's old suite of two huge rooms with monstrous, plastron chandeliers, heavy curtains, the furniture of a deluxe mortuary and the largest grand piano I have ever seen.

The food, both in the National and the Metropole, to which I subsequently moved, was still ample and delicious, including quantities of the best caviar, game such as hazel hen (*ryabchik*) with cranberry sauce (*klyukhva,* a synonym for craziness) and heavy pastries. There were supplies of Caucasus and Crimean wines and brandy. Some nights we dined at the Aragvi Caucasian restaurant which, although it looked and smelled like the men's lavatory of a subway station, was famous for its *shashlik.* All this luxury was soon to fade from the scene. By December one was lucky to get enough soup, bread and what we called "motorized compote" because of the worms actively competing for the fruit.

On the first day I called upon the head of the Press Department in the Commissariat for Foreign Affairs (Narkomindel), a gentleman named Palgunov. Palgunov was a hard-working, unimaginative, humorless bureaucrat, small, ruffled, with suspicious eyes peering out from spectacles with lenses like the bottoms of milk bottles. He had the virtue of speaking French so that I was able to establish direct intellectual contact but it was rare that the message seemed to get through. His stubbornly nit-picking approach to journalistic needs infuriated me; yet he controlled access to all appointments as well as the censorship apparatus, from which there was no appeal.

One simply submitted a dispatch, received what was left of it, marked up by the censor's crayon, then took it to the telegraph office (telephones were forbidden) and sent it off even, as was frequently the case, if it made no sense at all, being composed of verbless sentences and headless paragraphs. I remember transmitting one descriptive piece about a front visit starting (after Palgunov's myrmidons had finished): "Passed through a village of houses." Henry Shapiro of the UP wrote a bland article about Soviet trade that was held up for weeks. He finally elicited the information that it had been killed for attempting to transmit military information. Shapiro had mentioned imports of dyestuffs. This was taken by a censor who spoke putative English to mean weapons (stuff to make people die).

Palgunov welcomed me tepidly to Moscow. He explained how to file dispatches and told me it was necessary to stamp each page with the special *New York Times* bureau stamp. I remarked that we had closed down our bureau a couple of years previously, therefore had no stamp. He calmly advised me to have a new one made. Where, I asked? He gave me the address of the only shop in Moscow where these could be obtained and added, somewhat dimly, that it had been blown up in a recent bombing raid. I inquired what he expected me to do. He said that was my affair.

Fortunately, Henry Cassidy of AP let me send dispatches to his London office for transmission to New York, using the AP stamp until, many weeks later, I was able to obtain one of my own. He also helped me find an efficient secretary, Tania Sofyana, daughter of a Czarist general whose family was originally of Crimean Greek extraction. Sofyana, a hard-working, friendly, exceedingly fat woman (who was to lose forty pounds during the starvation of the next two years) spent a long time in one of Stalin's Kazakhstan concentration camps. She boasted of this experience because her camp included many distinguished sufferers and this had a certain snob appeal for her.

I shared an automobile with Quent Reynolds of *Collier's,* who arrived in September, and Philip Jordan of the London *News Chronicle.* This car was originally driven by a pimply young Finnish-American named Oswald Pale whose father had come to Russia during the depression and exchanged his passport for a job. In September Oswald was exiled to Siberia for fear that, as a Finn, he might develop fifth column tendencies. (Poor Oswald was incapable of even standing up to a cockroach.) He was followed by a succession of short-lived replacements, all of whom were sent East one by one because they had German minority or Baltic connections.

Working in Moscow was dreary and difficult. One had to have every available newspaper translated (and the list of those available was small, including no non-Moscow journals or technical publications) and to attend unutterably dull press conferences. When we asked to go to the front we were taken to collective farms and factories. We were not permitted to send anything that had not originated in an official press conference or a Soviet publication. As a result, the news we dispatched concerning military operations was invariably late, incomplete and overoptimistic.

This system forced the outside world to depend for its information on Berlin's claims and the jumbled reports assembled by reporters in neutral capitals like Berne where *The New York Times'* own representative, a former copy boy, produced some truly Münchausen-like masterpieces. He blew up the Dnieper Dam several days ahead of the Russians. He had Stalin execute Marshal Timoshenko (who at this writing, twenty-seven years later, is still alive). In a formidable military maneuver, he concentrated so many Wehrmacht soldiers on the Kerch Peninsula that I calculated they would have had to be carrying each other piggyback.

Despite frustrations, I was forced to work seven days a week, eighteen hours a day. A batch of censors, including a pleasant young man named Kozhimyakho, conspired to hamper our journalistic efforts. When I received a cable from Marina in Ankara, shortly after my arrival, I began to wire her daily. Kozhimyakho, a handsome young man, was much intrigued. He pointed out that Marina was a Russian saint and that Lada (her maiden name) was a pre-Christian Russian goddess of spring. He begged me to bring her photograph to his office. When I did so, it elicited friendly admiration but no favored treatment for my dispatches. Poor Kozhimyakho—he was killed the following spring while conducting reporters on a front tour.

The foreign press corps was a strange motley, ranging from Erskine Caldwell, the novelist, and his photographer-wife, Peggy Bourke-White, to assorted Communist correspondents for party papers around the world, correspondents, I may add, who received no favors as compared with us but were, indeed, far worse treated. Among the latter was a nice, scholarly Spaniard named Jesus Hernandez Tomas who had been a member of Spain's Communist Central Committee and minister of public education in Negrin's Republican government during the Civil War. He hated Russia and finally succeeded in getting himself smuggled to Mexico where he became a used car dealer.

Very few Russians were allowed to mix with the tiny foreign colony. I did manage to become acquainted with a handful. They included the famous Mikhail Borodin. Borodin had been sent to China as Stalin's representative with Chiang Kai-shek. Chiang finally expelled him and he fell into disgrace. Having nothing to do and being deeply worried about his son, a soldier (who later was killed), he used to come by often and sit drinking vodka, a gloomy man with dark, hooded face, talking about America (where he was born) and China.

I came to know three writers well: a playwright named Afinogenev, a Ukrainian satirist named Evgeni Petrov and Ilya Ehrenburg, fulgurous in propaganda but a rather dismal novelist. I liked Afinogenev and Petrov immensely and actually drank *pyom na brüderschaft* with the latter, an old Slavic ritual that made us blood brothers. Evgeni, big, strong, swart, with sardonic expression and pointed satanic features, was an army colonel and did all he could, quite unsuccessfully, to try and help me to the front. He was killed at the Sevastopol Battle in 1942. Afinogenev was blown up by a Moscow bomb in December, 1941.

Ehrenburg, whom I liked least, perhaps because he was craven vis-à-vis authority and alternated in manner between unctuousness and arrogance, was nevertheless helpful. He was highly cultivated and spoke beautiful French. He invited me several times for meals in his small but (for Moscow) unusually comfortable apartment with its good French pictures and excellent food and wine. Ehrenburg had lived in Paris after the Russian Revolution writing thrillers in which the villain was always a Red Guardsman. As if he were letting me peep at a pornographic photo, he loaned me his early satire *Julio Jurenito* in French with his own appended French comments. Through Ehrenburg I also came to meet Alexis Tolstoy and Mikhail Sholokhov. Tolstoy, related to Russia's most famous author, was a talented writer himself. Large and flabby-looking, he hewed close to the Kremlin line which involved him in acrobatic troubles. He had just finished a minatory novel about Peter the Great, lambasting him, and sent it to the Kremlin, when he learned that Stalin's line had changed and that the Soviet dictator now admired Peter as a nationalist. So Alexis sat down and started a lauding biography of the old Czar. As for Sholokhov, who later was awarded the Nobel Prize for his wonderful series on the Don Cossacks, he stayed out of trouble by remaining drunk. Once I sat next to him at lunch.

He was pickled to the ears. I remarked that he had been luckier than Tolstoy and less obscene than Ehrenburg in pursuing his literary career. "Yes," he chuckled, regarding me with a bleary stare, "because I drink like a shoemaker."

Moscow didn't present the aspect of a sorely threatened city whose outer limits were not too far from the raging battlefront. Its population gave the impression of going about its work with unusual seriousness, called on to perform special tasks necessitating extraordinary effort and attention. The prevailing calm reflected something fundamental in Muscovite temperament, perhaps based on the old Russian proverb: "The maggot gnaws the cabbage but it dies before it's done." There seemed increasing confidence that the old cabbage would surfeit yet another maggot.

There were many militiamen, wearing steel helmets; most of them carrying rifles. Numerous people walked about with gas masks slung over their shoulders. Security regulations were excessive, famous museums were unvisited and cameras banned. Sight-seeing objectives such as Lenin's Tomb and St. Basil's Church were closed. Sandbags lay everywhere. Once, at night, I was arrested for "smoking ostentatiously."

Posters drawn by the best artists and caricaturists appeared on thousands of walls, saying such things as: "Pure Aryan blood is respected in a cow; pure-blooded Prussian cattle are better than all other breeds; Germans don't respect either Einstein or Heine but only cows and bulls because a cow has a bright brain and a healthy soul; but from Heine and Einstein there aren't any calves and there isn't any milk." Pictures illustrated rejoicing Russian and British pilots halting momentarily in the air over Berlin to shake hands; or uniformed nurses caring for soldiers under fire on the field of battle; or Stalin gravely reading the latest news exactly like a broker looking at the ticker tape.

It was usual to see truckloads of soldiers swinging down the streets chanting in the remarkable voices common to the Slav peoples, hortatory choruses like:

The storm breaks over our fields.
Clouds come down to earth to greet the uninvited guests with rains of fire.
The hour has struck, Comrade Soldier.
And not once and not twice we've taught our enemies to keep off the Russian steppe.

Or:

Enemy raiders roared toward Leningrad
but there were strongly met and came to grief
Enemy, stay away from Leningrad.

Mass meetings of women, or workers, of Communist Youth were staged to inject vigor into production. Stakhanovite (speed-up) experts were hon-

ored equally with brave soldiers. Civilian cooperation was encouraged
through such organizations as fire wardens. Authors, ballerinas, young
girls, old men, worked in squadrons during raids to stamp out each incendiary as it sputtered on rooftops.

Until September food was plentiful in markets and restaurants. Under
the wartime system, white-collar workers were given cards allowing them
fixed rations that were sometimes not available but could be supplemented
at costlier, crowded free markets to which peasants brought their goods.

The theater, art and literature maintained prewar standards. There was
an unusual number of books in stores, because of less provincial demand
now that large elements of the population were bearing arms. Newspapers
were snatched up by long queues awaiting new editions outside the kiosks.
While, after Hitler's initial and astounding blows, no giddy optimism was
evident, people kept reminding each other Britain and America were supporting them. Then they would add: "Moscow is the capital of Russia.
How can Russia be crushed?"

The diplomatic corps was almost as ill-informed and frustrated as the
correspondents corps although it dwelled in more comfort. Each ambassador and service attaché was ostentatiously followed by the secret police
(NKVD). Their telephones were tapped, bugging devices were placed in
their homes and offices, hardly any Russians save stooges and *agents
provocateurs* visited them. Even the most important had difficulty in obtaining appointments with leading Soviet figures (and these, because of
Stalin's odd working habits, were mostly night appointments). When diplomats entertained they were forced to entertain each other.

The best known envoy was Sir Stafford Cripps, an ascetic, vegetarian
British socialist, sent to Moscow on the assumption this bias might help
him in a Marxist capital. Of course, it did the reverse; English lords and
American millionaires were a more popular class type. Isolated and often
alone, Cripps spent much time communing with his excellent Airedale. He
knew so little about what was going on that he was in London at the time
of Hitler's attack, having reckoned his mission a failure. I saw Cripps
occasionally, as he was a kind man, but I found his personality chilly, his
intellectuality overrated. He looked like a rheumy American Pilgrim Father, minus the broad-brimmed black hat, and despite his loyal admiration
for fruit juice and carrots, his sticky eyes and pendulous nose quite unfairly
gave the impression of a reformed alcoholic. He served his country loyally
in Moscow, India and as chancellor of the exchequer during the post-war
Labor government. Nevertheless, when regarding him, I could never forget
the famous Churchillian quip: "There but for the grace of God goes
God."

Lawrence Steinhardt was the American ambassador. A political appointee, he was undoubtedly clever, as he demonstrated by establishing
warm, indeed, confidential contacts with the Japanese, then in a position to

know a great deal about what was going on. But Steinhardt was not popular. When he and his wife entertained (before the Axis invasion; she left in 1941), Ambassador and Mrs. Steinhardt and ranking guests were served French wines and Narzan, a bubbly mineral water. The rest received Soviet wines and tap water from the same bottles. Even a visitor without the palate of a *tastevin* could recognize Moscow water, which is not fizzy and is highly chlorinated.

The American correspondents did not like or trust him although, one by one, he sought to curry their individual favor. On September 4 I noted: "Together with three other reporters called on Steinhardt at 2 A.M. to find out about his interview with Stalin. He told us a compote of lies. Steinhardt is trying to get away on 'vacation.' Washington authorities want him to stay. When we indicated to the ambassador that we knew as much (through indiscreet nonadmirers on his staff), he complained: 'You boys are crucifying me.' " I regret these ignoble recollections because, once Steinhardt was out of Russia's psychotic atmosphere, he was very nice to me. When he was ambassador in Turkey and Czechoslovakia, I stayed with him. Poor man—he died as envoy to Canada afterwards, burning up in his embassy plane.

The United States military attaché was Ivan Yeaton, a hearty, agreeable, ill-informed professional officer of Scandinavian extraction who reminded me of the old saw: "What's dumber than a dumb Englishman? A bright Swede." From the first day he was convinced the Soviet army and air force had been destroyed, that the war was over on the Eastern front. When we were ordered out of Moscow he assured his colleagues that the special train would never escape the Nazis' iron ring around the capital.

There were other, more colorful and certainly better informed members of the foreign diplomatic corps. Mohammed Said, the Iranian ambassador, had served in Russia several times, spoke the language well and knew the people. With suave subtlety and astonishing acuity he managed to sort fact from fiction.

My favorite envoy was the Afghan, a sleek, sleepy, dark, plump relative of his country's royal family. The Afghan estimated that an assignment to Russia was an unnecessary hardship requiring ingenuity to overcome. He assigned his principal assistant to keep him in agreeable feminine company. As a result, he acquired a gypsy girl friend who, as he might have suspected, was also working for the NKVD. She disappeared, not long after he had confirmed this suspicion. Weeks passed; the NKVD began to worry about its lost agent. Finally a ranking official called on the Afghan and asked if he had ever known a Miss So-and-so. "Indeed, yes." "Well, perhaps you could tell us what became of her?" "Certainly," said the Afghan, "come with me." He took the NKVD inspector to his garden, pointed among the shrubs. "There she is, down there," he said with a smile of pleasant satisfaction. The nonplused secret policeman left. Eventually, the Afghan was transferred to another post.

Another distinguished member of the Moscow foreign colony was Father Leopold Braun, an Augustinian friar from the United States who was assigned as chaplain to the French embassy. The Roosevelt–Litvinov accord which restored Russo-American diplomatic relations in 1933 provided that an American priest could hold this post in order to satisfy the religious requirements of foreign Catholics.

Braun was a tough, intelligent, wiry, fearless man. He lived in a tiny, cold flat guarded by a ferociously Russophobic dog. I often dined with the two of them on vodka, bread and sprats, a not very enjoyable but highly inexpensive species of septentrional sardine. Braun certainly merited Soviet suspicions of his behavior. Once, when I was talking to him about news from the front and he showed himself remarkably well informed, I asked him how he knew so much. Uninhibitedly, he said: "There aren't many Catholics in the Red Army, mostly from European provinces Stalin seized. But some of them come here on leave. I confess them." Braun was heartbroken that his rather ugly church had been gradually stripped of all its altar ornaments, chasubles and holy decorations. Each time there was a robbery and he complained, the NKVD informed him it was sorry but there were many hoodlums about: "Don't you know, there's a war on?" When de Gaulle visited Moscow in 1944 and announced his intention of going to Sunday services, all the missing valuables were suddenly restored—by the NKVD.

If daily life in Moscow was notably unamusing at the time, it seems funny in retrospect. I noted one day:

> The Archbishop of Canterbury sent a telegram wishing success and good luck to the Patriarch Sergei. The British ambassador refused to deliver it on the grounds that this would mean Sergei's immediate end. The ambassador's answer to the archbishop implied that Canterbury should not expect Stalin to recognize religion any more than Canterbury would recognize communism.
>
> Recently a member of the British air mission got drunk, met some Russian men and prostitutes, walked home with them just after an air raid, saw a house on fire, plunged in (still drunk) and put it out. He was hailed by a group of volunteer fire workers who carried him home on their shoulders. The chief of the firemen took off his Order of Lenin and pinned it on the Englishman. The airman has since been terrified this decoration would be officially conferred upon him, causing him trouble in England.

Almost each night was punctuated by air raids. These were not very damaging because of the extraordinarily wasteful but effective defenses around the capital. The Moscow area was divided into squares and as soon as enemy planes intruded into one of these mapped regions, every single gun of every caliber stationed inside the square pointed up and let go with all available ammunition. This managed to cripple some raiders and certainly gave spiritual solace to the Muscovites. They were vastly impressed by the hail of shell fragments that, having been aimed up, were brought down by gravity, chunking around the heads of people still abroad in the streets. It was certainly an inspirational sight to watch aircraft pinned by searchlights over the center of the city. Skinny and Peggy Caldwell, who were doing broadcasts as well as photographs and had to move around often after dark, obtained from the authorities weird, broad-brimmed basin helmets that looked like the head armor of medieval Japanese *ronin*.

In hotels it was a fixed rule that every tenant had to go to air raid shelters whether he wished or not. The chambermaid and a militiaman checked up from room to room, searching behind drapes, beneath beds and in closets for those who preferred sleep. Shelters became places of distinct social interest. There were special havens for superior personnages: Stalin had his own in the Kremlin; and there was one for distinguished visitors, which was made available to Harry Hopkins. But even for those further down the classless society's scale, one could find stimulus in the structure of protection.

The National shelter was proud of its chic clientele. I enjoyed myself there playing bridge with a Leningrad essayist, dominoes with another writer who had quenched fifteen incendiaries since the attacks on Moscow began, poker with a Polish general and, at the moment when one high explosive hit across the yard, shaking our antiquated structure, was engaged in a contest of homemade anagrams with a party of English prisoners just escaped from Germany.

The Metropole shelter had more local color. It was situated in a sprawling, barrel-vaulted cellar along the walls of which triple-decker wooden bunks had been erected. These generally were jam-full of temporary residents, including hundreds shepherded in from the crossroads above, many of them magnificently drunk. Three decades of Soviet dictatorship had in no way dampened their liking for talk and debate. They would sit in their upper bunks, hollering, weeping, drinking, farting, and belching, while watching chess games staged by fellow shelterers below, arguing about the correctness of the players' strategy and puffing clouds of acrid smoke from their *papyrossi* cigarettes. Whenever a chess kibbitzer became too assertive a debate would start concerning his right to speak freely.

In the Metropole I was much taken one day by a stocky man, dressed in what was obviously homemade French uniform, beret, breeches, puttees and all. He strutted with a peculiar Gallic cockiness. His name was Pierre Billotte and he was a French captain, son of a famous general, who had been taken prisoner of war by the Nazis. Pierre had escaped in spring, 1941, was interned by the Russians and released soon after Hitler's attack.

A dynamic, formidably intelligent and most agreeable man, he was sent by convoy from Archangelsk to England. There he became de Gaulle's chief of staff, was promoted to general, and eventually became a cabinet minister in postwar France. He is still one of my closest French friends.

In September, after the Russians had staged a successful counterattack against the Germans, bringing in Siberian troops to punch a hole in Nazi positions around Smolensk, the authorities at last permitted some of us to visit the front. The trip was carefully supervised by functionaries and political commissars. They were obviously instructed to keep us out of danger, to overfeed us, and to inject us with alcohol beyond the normal call of journalistic duty. We soon learned that the only way to meet the latter threat was to appoint a drinking champion for each meal, allowing him to respond to all toasts and then carrying him around from point to point until he recovered sufficiently to resume his work and his eventual position on our vodka order of the day. On this unusual expedition, where the liver was exposed to greater dangers than the heart or brain, I kept a diary:

ON THE RUSSIAN FRONT, *September 17-22, 1941*

WE sleep in one large room of a schoolhouse. All through the cold night men stir restlessly as the sound of exploding shells echoes over the hard ground. In the early morning, a sharp breeze comes through the chinks. While we are washing up, a barber shaves the officers. Drive off to a chilly village under fire of German batteries. A few women and old men are pitching hay from a wagon into a barn. Some geese huddle on the green.

Ahead of us, in a truck, are soldiers with their greatcoat collars up, some with mantles over their forage caps, carrying bayoneted rifles. We cross a corduroy road in a forest swamp. Near by, horse-drawn howitzers move across the plain. A Junkers 88 lies smashed in a field. Its landing gear is busted, its propellers smashed. The bulletproof glass in its cabin is stippled with holes.

The heavily forested region explains how guerrillas can operate. Off the main highway, the roads are terrible. However, a good deal of truck transport, mixed with horses and wagons, plunges through the mud. Squads of soldiers work on the roads. The wind runs through the evergreen woods in great gusts. A truck slushes down a forest road bearing pieces of a shot-up Russian plane. The frost has already begun and leaves are red. This may bring bad luck to the Germans.

Now we are at Sadova, a recent battlefield where much equipment was captured. This includes half-tracks, medium tanks and field pieces. To my delight, I find two Borgward half-tracks, like the one I drove in Turkey, with front wheels on tires and ten rear wheels on caterpillars. There is a burned-up gun hauler. The Russians knocked out thirty batteries here and captured fourteen other guns. The countryside is not very scarred; this appears to have been a war of movement.

At dusk we pass a steaming camouflaged kitchen, which makes us hungry. We drive through a village wrecked by shell fire. There is a hole in the church and several in the school. Most buildings are smashed. Trees are down. The roads in the fields are pitted with shell craters and rimmed by hastily dug trenches. The woods are lacerated and torn by shells, dotted with huge bomb craters. Amputated trunks were knocked off by Russian artillery (the tree tops fell westward). There are piles of dead birches cut by the Germans to camouflage their batteries in an open field.

Russian tanks are dug in in pits on the edge of the woods. Quite a lot of German equipment has been turned against the Nazis by these tough-looking officers and men. In the center of the forest we dine on a table with white cloth. The waiters wear white jackets over their uniforms. Our host is the divisional commander, Colonel Mihail Dodonov, a handsome fellow. Just as we sit down, a twin-tailed Dornier flies directly overhead on reconnaissance through puffs of antiaircraft fire. Bomb fragments echo in the trees. A radio loudspeaker placed on a branch broadcasts Russian songs.

The division's political commissar, Roussanov, says this Siberian unit has never retreated. It came into line July 15. On July 19 and 20 it engaged in battle on the Podshchuchie salient of the Smolensk sector and smashed a large group of German troops, destroying fifteen tanks and causing 15,000 German casualties. Although steadily bombed by the Luftwaffe, it moved forward on a front between three and four kilometers wide. Some Germans, according to prisoners, went crazy because of the artillery fire; they are horrified by the power of Russian guns.

I visited several sod-covered dugouts, containing three beds (benches cut in the earth) a shelf for rifles, and electric light wired to a battery. The sod roof is supported by poles. Steps are cut down from the outside. The soldiers have excellent rain cloaks. Pouring rain turns the horrible roads into a mess of mud. Gangs in waterproof mantles are working to get traffic through. A special truckload of soldiers with shovels comes along with our convoy to push us out of difficulties. Overhead, slow, small biplanes (U-2) transport the wounded to the rear.

We lunch at a Sovkhoz (state agricultural factory) where cheese and jam are made. It is situated on a hill, above a stream, and has been converted into a small hospital. Afterwards, we pass a convoy of trucks stuck in the mud near a huge shell crater. A tractorized troop carrier hauls a gas truck up a slippery hill. Telephone lines are being strung. Infantry keeps marching by: Russians, Siberians, Kazakhs, Uzbeks, Turkmenians and Ukrainians. Overhead, clouds of birds swarm south. We come to the gutted ruins of Dorogobuzh, now badly bombed, where we sleep on piles of straw.

That evening is my turn on the vodka rotation list. The Russians like to

drink competitively and, after the usual toasts, a glass is placed before me
and another before a major general, then equal drinks are measured out.
We each destroy two bottles of vodka and are well into a horrible variety
of Crimean brandy when my adversary passes out. He is carried to his
straw mattress and spends most of the night vomiting over himself. Some
hours later he wakes up, lights a *papyrossi,* and sets his bed on fire. I try
to find my way out to take a leak, miss the door, and almost break my fist
on the concrete wall before a kind sentry helps me. Thank God my turn is
over.


Breakfast on cold fish, cutlets, vodka and mashed potatoes. Our brigade
commissar, whose boasts have led us to call him "the killer," says he was
at the battle of Dniepropetrovsk, and the Germans lost heavily. I wonder.

Vernon Bartlett, always eating raw mushrooms, has to rush off after
breakfast to do what the English call "a rear." A peasant comes along and
stares. Bartlett tries to get him to go away by explaining that he is a
member of Parliament. This only excites widespread curiosity. The peasant
brings up an admiring throng of friends and soldiers.

We are a weary group. During his sleep, Philip Jordan, long wisps of
hair falling all along his face, shouts out in an anguished voice: "Where the
hell are we?" Alexander Werth, in dogskin coat, looks like a depraved
madman. A. T. Cholerton, of the *Daily Telegraph,* his beard full of straw,
spends most of the night searching for his handkerchief and glasses. The
correspondents' "Soviet" meets and loudly disagrees every dawn and dusk.
Cholerton spoils our appetite each breakfast by nibbling raw fish which he
holds by the tail, getting oil and bones mixed up in his beard.

A scholarly looking colonel with rimless spectacles takes charge of us
and promptly loses the way. Our brigade commissar, the killer, in spite
of his spick-and-span new uniform, cannot recognize aircraft. He keeps
calling out alarms when Soviet planes pass overhead, brandishing his
clearly unused Mauser. A T-34 medium tank turns by us over a wet field
and then up the road, plowing through the mud at about thirty miles an
hour. I suspect no other friendly foreigners have yet seen this impressive
Soviet weapon.

The road is marked with bomb holes all the way to Yelnia, past a field
marked with infantry trenches and occasional graves with red stars set on
top. Yelnia was clearly the scene of sharp fighting. The fields are pitted. A
half-track bakery wagon, filled with black loaves, is overturned. Yelnia was
a bastion of the German offensive and is now utterly ruined.

The German trenches are full of ragged clothes, gas masks, sheepskin-
lined coats, dud shells, hand grenades, empty ammunition boxes. The Russians took the outer trench with a bayonet charge. Rain pools in the

trenches are stained with blood. The battlefield smells. A decaying hand
sticks out of the mud. For the most part, the Russians just pitched German
dead into shellholes. Their own dead were collected and put in mass
graves.

Two peasant boys are digging in the ruins of a house. This is one long
road of desolation. Everything is penetrated by the slightly sour stink of
death. A hunchbacked old woman scrambles along madly. Her nerves were
shocked in the bombing and she always carries bundles in her hands because she had just set two bundles down in order to run, when she was
stunned in an air raid.

Four Messerschmidts fly overhead as we examine a wrecked Skoda
reconnaissance car stuck in the bushes. Nearby is an abandoned Soviet
airfield littered with bomb racks. A Russian antitank gun camouflaged in a
clump of trees is protected by a guard. When the Germans quit Yelnia they
burned every important building and locked the few remaining Russians in
the church.


Soviet artillery—Defense Commissar Joseph Stalin's "god of war"—is
superior to the German in this sector. The Germans have recently been
losing twice as many men and five times as much equipment as the Russians on this front. Now that autumn has turned everything into one
morass, the Nazis are forced to use horses for transport and artillery, thus
losing the maneuverability that was their great initial advantage. Their rear
is unsafe and constantly subjected to partisan raids from the forests. The
war here has been transformed. The Nazis are rushing up winter supplies
and stores of skis from Norway. The cold already is descending and the
winds are hustling huge rain-loaded clouds across the horizon. Soviet soldiers gazing across the slopes repeat the ancient proverb, "A Russian's
meat is a German's poison."

Lieutenant General Vassily Sokolovsky, forty-three years old, a husky,
square-jawed, long-nosed man of grave demeanor, is chief of staff on the
front. (Later he became a marshal and Red Army Chief of Staff.) He says:
"The Blitzkrieg, in its essentials, has been transformed into blitz-destruction
of German men and materials. This began at Smolensk. The Blitzkrieg has
developed into a continuous grinding of the German war machine. The
process resembles Verdun, but in terms of ten or one hundred times the
destruction, because of the increased efficiency of new machines, such as
tanks and airplanes. Our artillery is master of the field."


Three parachutists are swinging down against the setting sun as the last
plane taxis to rest and the ground crew covers it with pine boughs.
These are only practice leaps, the general explains. The general, a sturdy

man in fleece-lined flying suit and kepi, is Gyorgi Zacharoff, thirty-one
years old. He has been decorated three times and has taken part in major
battles. By trade he is an agricultural chemist.

These snub-nosed planes decked in boughs are Ilyushin and Yak fighter
bombers. They are light, snappy and seem ready to spring out at you. They
have just returned from Smolensk, where they bombed an airdrome, starting a dozen fires and banging up Nazi officers' quarters. One has a shell
hole in the wing into which you can put your arm right up to the shoulder,
but the plywood and fiber held together.

Second Lieutenant Alexei Roden, nineteen, who flew this plane, is wearing a fur-lined flying vest. He says a formation of ten planes made the raid,
diving from 10,000 to three hundred feet. He got it in the wing at 1,000,
but carried out his assignment. It shook him up, but he managed to get
through. "It was a surprise. Their fighters never got up." It is dark now and
a breeze strums through the branches and the plane's landing gear. They are
armed with rockets fixed beneath the wings. Zacharoff personally stages a
firing test from a parked plane.

Night has come, thick and starless, and we bump along the rutted road
to Vyazma, the town whose famous gingerbread once was nibbled by
Napoleon's soldiers. Awakened in jerry-built two-story hotel, by the crash
of antiaircraft fire and that terrible screaming noise of falling bombs. Every
one does a racing dive onto the hallway floor, like frogs leaping into a
pond. Bombs blast all the windows out.

At night, after dining in the officers' mess, a schoolhouse, the colonel
says: "I have a surprise—some Fascist prisoners [they always call them
Fascists here]. You made their acquaintance this morning when they
bombed you. Our fighters shot them down."

The door opens. Three young Germans pause on the threshold, click
their heels and salute. They sit in the center of the room, side by side, clad
in rumpled flying suits. On the right is Rudolf Taeuse, twenty-five, blond,
faintly mustached. He stares impassively. His left arm is in a sling. In the
center is Walther Rasek, twenty-two, surly. He has a bandaged arm and his
head is swathed. Only the right eye is visible and it burns fiercely. Beside
him sits Josef Trocha, twenty-six, a diminutive radio operator, clutching
his flier's cap.

Rasek glowers and blurts out he has bombed London. He sounds like
the *Voelkischer Beobachter:* "We will win the war. We had to fight England, but we did not know we had to fight Russia. We are not worried
about the United States; it is far away. We only attacked London after
Berlin was bombed. Germany had to fight. We are too small. We need
colonies. We learned in school about colonies. It is our duty to fight."

And in the cold morning light, in a treeless field where sprout the earliest
shoots of winter wheat, is a plane spread-eagled into the earth. For hundreds of feet are strewn pieces of wreckage—broken propellers, chunks of

engine, wheels, strips of the metal covering. The glass nose of the cockpit is cracked. There are holes in the engine covers, holes in the wings and a hole in the little plate that says "Dornier Werke–Junkers–88A." A big Russian sentry pulls up his greatcoat collar and rubs the armored fuselage with his boot. "It is a great bird," he says. "Yes, it is a great bird, but we knocked it down."

This trip carefully assured that we saw no real action but could not manage to hide valuable impressions. More and more women's detachments were in evidence. I saw numbers of the fast, low-silhouetted T-34 tanks that were to become so famous and endured as a standard weapon right through the Korean war and even Vietnam. And I saw well-made Yak and Ilyushin aircraft, the latter armed with eight rockets each as General Zacharoff demonstrated on a three-kilometer range. (I also met Sokolovsky, who became one of Russia's most renowned soldiers, a highly trained, competent officer.)

The atmosphere in the capital became first weary, then tense. Fewer and fewer able-bodied men were evident in civilian clothes, more and more wounded limped about the streets. Successive kinds of food became short and, although forbidden by law, the first beggars appeared.

Already in August the Japanese correspondents, who had to work from the same small press room as ourselves, were instructed to send all dispatches in English to tighten up security. One evening I could not help noticing on the typewriter of Hatanaka, the affable little *Asahi* representative, a carbon copy of this message to his editor: "AWAITING FAVORABLE NEWS REREMITTANCE PLEASE."

Distinguished visitors arrived: Averell Harriman, Lord Beaverbrook, eventually Harry Hopkins and Anthony Eden. They brought encouraging promises of matériel, some of which was already coming along the hazardous northern convoy route and some of which would soon be sent through Iran, which the British and Russians had occupied to ensure that vital avenue of access against Nazi agents who were inciting the Persian tribes. When the first P-40 fighters turned up from neutral America to aid the hard-pressed Soviet air force, 120 Russian pilots were certified competent to fly them. Solos were made twenty-four hours after initial instruction.

Late that summer, Moscow decided to make use of the surviving Polish officers and men scattered around prisons in the USSR after the 1940 round-up when Russia joined Germany in the partition of Poland. I say "surviving" because, as we were slowly to discover, an enormous number of Polish officers had been massacred by the Russians in the gloomy Katyn forest.

Soon after he was released from the Lubyanka prison, General Wladyslaw Anders, selected to command this new Polish force, received me at his country's reestablished embassy. In August, Anders had been moved to a more comfortable cell, barbered, saluted and treated with sudden courtesy. It was evident from his amplified diet that the NKVD was trying to fatten him up, preparatory to releasing him.

Anders, a stern-looking former cavalryman, was still using a cane when I talked with him. His wounds from the 1940 campaign had not yet entirely healed. I noted:

> He is about six feet tall, bald with remaining hair very close cut, thin, well set-up, rather handsome, very emotional (tears come into his eyes as he speaks of the sufferings of his men), spick and span in well-cut uniform made by an NKVD tailor right after he got out of prison. As soon as he was released his decorations were returned and he again wears them.
>
> In World War I, fighting under the Czar, Anders' cavalry unit captured the only German general taken by the Russians. Anders was named commander-in-chief of the new Polish army in Russia by Sikorski while he (Anders) was still in prison. He is decidedly anti-Soviet but still more violent against the Germans. In that respect he typifies much of Eastern Europe. After the Polish-Soviet accord was signed in London, Anders was released and began to organize a Polish army.
>
> Anders first knew of Germany's attack when he heard the thud of bombs not far from his cell. Shortly after that the jailer appeared and asked if there was anything he could do for his leg. Anders said he had been there more than a year and nobody had troubled about him; he saw no reason to change. The jailer persisted. Then Anders said: "I know why you are so interested. Because Russia is at war now."

By mid-October it was evident a new crisis had begun. The German offensive took off from Smolensk and started down the main highway for Moscow. It broke through major defense systems and only by mobilizing militiamen and police, who had hitherto been guarding public buildings and directing traffic, did Stalin manage to plug the gap. Women and school children were set to work digging trenches and earthworks on the capital's outskirts. The diplomatic corps was unofficially informed that it shortly would be moved farther east. The correspondents were told nothing. I conferred with Arch Steele of the *Chicago Daily News,* and we tried to make arrangements for an emergency automobile trek of our own. But the last of my succession of chauffeurs disappeared and took the car along.

Finally, on October 15, we were officially ordered to get ready for swift departure. It was snowing heavily. We gathered that evening at the American embassy residence. Each foreign colony met together for its own transportation. We assembled in the Spaso ballroom, dressed in winter clothing and carrying ill-assorted hand baggage. Colonel Yeaton rushed around assuring everyone in his booming voice that the idea was asinine since the Germans had already closed a circle around Moscow. Nevertheless, leaving behind in charge of American property two diplomats, Llewellyn Thompson (later ambassador to the USSR) and Fred Reinhardt (later ambassador to Egypt and Italy), we loaded into official cars and took off through silent, snowy streets.

Uneasy signs of cracking discipline had already started to spread. When the NKVD and militia were withdrawn to defend the highway where the Germans were now within sight of Moscow's Khimke water tower, the first hints of mob rule appeared. Bakeries and food shops were looted. Thousands of people scrambled to the railway stations or headed out of town on trucks and carts. Some fifth columnists, who were shot, included directors of factories who ordered their workers to break up machinery with hammers and then flee.

That night, every inch of the Kazan railway station was jammed with humanity: old women and children huddled around bundles; old men clustered in corners, waiting in the hope that ticket queues would eventually open again; limping wounded shepherded by nurses; expressionless reinforcements with knapsacks and rifles. Everything smelled of cabbage and sweat despite the penetrating cold. There was a black-out, save for torches and lamps. We filed clumsily toward our assembly point, the station restaurant, picking our way over mounds of sleepers. In the dim shadows I made out occasional familiar figures: the fur-hatted Cripps with his frightened Airedale; the enormous Bogić; Ehrenburg, Lozovsky; ballerinas, actresses; the Japanese, drinking vodka; all the *haut monde* of the disintegrating Soviet world. It was a scene from Gorki illustrated by Bosch.

The train, which headed off into a five-day blizzard early on October 16, bore a singularly famous human cargo. Had there not been a persisting curtain of thick snowflakes, it surely would have been attacked next dawn by the Luftwaffe, which was pounding the access routes in an effort to stem the tide of Siberian reinforcements. However, one could see no more than three or four yards, as if peering through skimmed milk.

We passed long trains on sidings, also heading eastward and loaded with the machinery of evacuated factories. Beside the trackbeds lay occasional heaps of rusting machinery, cast off for priority consignments. Now and then trains of Siberian reinforcements, wearing fur hats and long greatcoats, loaded into box, passenger and open flat cars, rattled glumly in the direction from which we had come.

I doubt if history has ever seen an odder group of travelers. In one car were leading members of the world Communist apparatus, the Comintern, including Raymond Guyot and Dolores Ibaruri, better known as *La Pasionaria*. In another were prominent Soviet writers: Ehrenburg, Petrov, Afinogenov. In still others were the main apparatus of the Soviet government, except for key members ordered to stay in the Kremlin by Stalin's side. Two "soft" cars (each compartment including four berths) were reserved for diplomats and correspondents.

Amid the confusion I managed to scramble into a compartment with

Reynolds, Cassidy and Alice-Leone Moats, an attractive *Collier's* writer
with whom we had all flirted, until one gloomy evening when we compared
unsuccessful notes and bitterly decided she must be the oldest living virgin.
Moatsie took charge of the rest of us who immediately began a nonstop
poker game. At moments of fury she would descend from her upper berth,
drive us into the corridor, and sweep out accumulated cigarette butts,
scraps of paper and crusts. Steinhardt joined the game and stayed for
immensely long sessions. This insured that our group had favored attention
from Charlie Thayer, the brilliant and amusing young embassy secretary in
charge of feeding and lubricating the American contingent. Steinhardt possessed the first small traveling radio I had ever seen and from it we learned
the Germans had broken through Moscow's defenses. "Come on," roared
the enormous Reynolds, "deal."

Tension lifted when Panayotis Pipinellis, the tiny, immaculate Greek
ambassador who had arrived in Moscow just in time to catch the evacuation train, tapped on our door and bowed his way in politely to shake
Steinhardt's hand. He was dressed in formal frock coat, and, not having
had time to pay his official courtesy calls in the disintegrating capital, was
making effective use of our extraordinary train. I asked Pipinellis, whom I
had known in Sofia and Athens: "Do you still insist that you are always an
optimist?" Drawing himself gallantly up to his full height of five foot two,
he answered: "Yes, 110 per cent.

None of us knew much about Kuibyshev. Before the Revolution, it had
been called Samara. This fact made it easy for anyone so inclined to cable
his office that we were keeping an appointment with John O'Hara—except
that the Moscow cable office refused to accept messages after the evacuation order. Samara had been the site of many battles between the Czar's
troops and Tatar hordes. Camel trains used to unload there after tedious
journeys from the Turkestan steppes. Although it had been renamed for
Valerian Kuibyshev, head of the first Five-Year Plan, we soon found it had
not changed much from its early role as Europe's backdoor to Asia. On
October 26 I wrote in my diary:

Kuibyshev is still in the halfway stage of making ready to care for its
new population. The provincial theater before long will open its doors
to the finest ballet and opera artists; the Bolshoi Theater troupe left
Moscow last week and will resume its regular winter program here.

Although we have been here only a moment, as it were, and nothing
else is organized, NKVD guards have been established for all the foreign
diplomatic chiefs of mission despite the incredible shortage of cars. Two
cars are regularly parked outside the new temporary American embassy
building here. One of them is the ambassador's. The other one belongs
to NKVD snoops.

As rapidly as possible this temporary capital is being organized like
Moscow. *Propusks* (official passes) are needed everywhere—in the
Kuibyshev foreign office just as in the Moscow Narkomindel. The Rus-

sians are incredibly bureaucratic-minded. They even drop *propusks* to the Germans in an effort to convince them that this gives them permission to desert.

I know of one instance of a German deserter who was sent to a prison camp in the USSR and set to forced labor with other prisoners, foreign and Russian. One day the camp commandant read some long instruction in the Russian language which actually warned all prisoners not to go beyond a certain area. No boundaries were marked, but those who understood Russian knew what was meant. The German didn't understand and he walked past the forbidden zone in order to relieve himself. A guard rushed up and, when the German was only a yard away from him, shot him in the stomach and left him to die.

This was told to me by a British air gunner—one of two in Kuibyshev. They were from a party of eighteen who fought as volunteers in Finland. After the peace between Finland and Russia, they tried to get home. They couldn't cross Norway which had been occupied by the Germans. They were trying to sneak through Estonia when they were caught by the Russians and put in the prison camp. They claimed they were brutally treated and underfed. Early this month for the first time they got a break—although England and Russia have been allies since June. They were ordered to report at the camp headquarters. They were not told why. They were put on a train with a guard and told they were being sent to Moscow—but not why. Finally they were released and shuttled on to Kuibyshev.

All through this month anti-British feeling has been growing. There are constant murmurs against the lack of sufficient British aid, the failure of the British to create a diversion in the West. Strangely enough, there is apparently no resentment against the United States. Genya Petrov, the famous Russian author, who is a good friend of mine these days, told me on October 24 that the Russian people were "notably disgusted." He got drunk in the Grand Hotel where we were working on a bottle of whisky our assistant military attaché had given me. Genya tried to pick a fight with some RAF officers who had come down from Murmansk where they had been showing Russian pilots how to fly British planes.

Petrov tugged at his revolver (he was wearing his colonel's uniform) and tried to shoot them. Fortunately, although he is very powerful, he was so plastered I was able to prevent any damage. Two more drinks passed him out. Earlier he had said that while the British papers talk of aid to Russia, one listens to such BBC communiqués as "Today two British bombers raided Boulogne." He claims he is convinced the British could and should have made a landing on the continent of Europe this autumn but were too selfish and were afraid of the German army despite the fact that it had been so weakened by the Russians.

Afinogenev, the famous Soviet playwright, agrees, adding that the Russian papers now mention British aid as seldom as possible "so as not to incite the people" and that Russia realizes she has got to face this job practically alone. Both Petrov and Afinogenev have made it plain several times they suspect neither Britain nor America will help Russia if she is attacked by Japan.

KUIBYSHEV, *October 27, 1941*

DRUNKS curled up asleep in gutters, staggering in the arms of companions, fighting, weeping or singing are a frequent sight; it's the same here as in Moscow.

Discipline is cracking around Moscow: newspaper reports of executions, of food store managers fleeing with food, or employers telling employees they can go and take away state property. There are reports of the liquidation of anti-Soviet groups that had been attacking automobiles. It is inevitable that hordes of wild children will become common again as they were fifteen years ago following the vast forced evacuation. The streets of Kuibyshev are full of tough, dirty youngsters in their middle teens.

Most of the law and order units of the NKVD have now reassembled here, having moved on from Moscow. Many were apparently evacuated to this city days before the diplomats. A government store has already been established for foreigners where they can buy food. So far, sugar, chocolate, biscuits and carrots are the principal things to be purchased. Intourist has begun making a check-up on who among us has paid his hotel bill in Moscow and who has not.

This city, swollen with an excess population, who are miserable as the cold winds of Asia start blowing, is full of long queues outside the food stores and the few cafes. It is evident that mobilization is going on here. The streets are full of raw recruits with bundles—mostly young lads in their teens. More and more soldiers are coming to town, and officers in gray fur caps. Contingents of privates sing as they march. Four medium antiaircraft guns on wheels have been sunk into pits outside the main government building.

Last night two telegrams were delivered to me in my room in the same envelope. One of them was from Marina. The other, extremely long, was to the Soviet foreign office from its embassy in Tokyo and was in code. I took it over through a blizzard. This is surely a good example of the carelessness with which the government operates at all levels. It is probable the foreign office is going to have to wait many extra hours for what may be vital information during a time of crisis in Japan.

One of the first signs of the contemplated evacuation of Moscow was the closing down of several telegraph windows in the main telegraph office and the moving of personnel to Kuibyshev. Incidentally, I notice that all computing done at the telegraph office windows here is on abacuses. Words are counted and ruble payments figured out on these ancient machines.

KUIBYSHEV, *October 28, 1941*

AMERICAN air experts arriving from England are tremendously impressed with the Russian pilots and Soviet organization which they say is frequently superior to that of the British. They say there are ample numbers of trained pilots but not enough aircraft. When the first shipment of Tomahawks was about to arrive at Archangelsk, Lieutenant John Alison went up to supervise the preparation of a field meeting specifications. He was taken by the Russians to a large mud swamp. They pointed this out to him and when he said it would be difficult to prepare, the Russians merely asked him what were the necessary requirements in terms of runways and what was the time limit by when everything had to be ready. After he told them, they called out thousands of forced laborers and had the field ready in short order.

When the planes arrived and were assembled, Alison asked for pilots to learn how to use fifty aircraft. One hundred twenty turned up. In England only seventeen had turned up for a similar program. These Russian pilots were eager and experienced. After twenty-four hours of preliminary instruction the first pilot took off on a solo flight. He made a perfect take-off, then maneuvered around and finally landed. He reported: "Everything is all right, but the generator is broken." Examination of the plane proved he was right. Generators are the weak point of Tomahawks (P-40s). New generators were later shipped out. Alison says that in England, by way of contrast, the pilots are sloppy, slower to learn and cracked up a couple of planes. The Russians learn very well and quickly adapt themselves to new machines and the reading of English words on their instruments.

Alison says there are few American bombers here yet. These use American bombsights and bomb racks, which requires the constant shipment of bombs from the United States. It was found easier to do this than to change to Russian bomb racks in order to use Russian bombs.

Medicine. Soviet medicine and operating techniques are very good, but Western ideas of sterilization do not prevail. Thus, foreigners have seen operations where all the instruments were sterilized and then a nurse reaches with prongs for a knife and takes it in her bare hand to give to the surgeon. The Russians have several world-famous doctors and are well up on plastic surgery and blood transfusion. At an animal hospital in Moscow when the Steinhardts' sick dog had to be killed, the Russians had a new painless and instantaneous rectal syringe for the job.

Constantine Oumansky, Soviet ambassador in Washington who is now here, went to Moscow early this week to try to find a plane for the United States. He failed. He then wired Steinhardt to ask if Steinhardt could help arrange his (Oumansky's) transportation out via train. This is quite incredible because Oumansky is being replaced as ambassador by Maxim Litvinov. Apparently nobody has told him yet.

In October the Russians revised their estimates on the number of planes they would require from the United States and Britain. Their new and higher estimates are based on the loss of factory districts to the Germans and the transferral of other factories to the east, which is making them unproductive until their output is reestablished. The I-18 fighter factory in Moscow is now being rapidly dismantled and moved east.

W. A. Wood, an elderly American engineer, has been in Russia since several months before the war. He is paid a salary of $18,000 a year by the Soviet government and a generous expense allowance. He is a great expert on copper tension and on armaments. Despite this he has had scarcely anything to do. He used to spend all his time in Moscow sitting in the Hotel Metropole talking with the floor supervisor.

Several weeks ago a Russian colonel whom he had known visited him and explained that the Russians were running short of shell bands and having great difficulty keeping up the supply. Wood thought a while and then said to the colonel that in such-and-such a factory in Leningrad the Russians had two machines of such-and-such a type for the manufacture of boiler tubings. Wood suggested that with the change of a few essential dies the Russians would be able to make so many thousands of shell bands daily with these machines, and he sketched out rough designs. The colonel thanked him and left. Wood never heard from him again. Later he found out his recommendations had been followed, but they never asked Wood's help—although he had offered to go up himself and make the alterations.

The few correspondents here have invented a song to the tune of "The Volga Boatman," which we sing with much sorrow every night over the empty bottles:

*Nichevo, njet; nichevo, njet; njet, njet, njet; nichevo, njet.*
*Njet maslo; njet jajce; njet boumaga;*
*Njet banjo; njet pirozhnye;*
*Njet koffee; nichevo njet.*

(There isn't anything, nothing, nothing. No butter, no eggs, no paper, no banjo, no hamburgers, no coffee; nothing.)

After the government left Moscow there was a great wave of nervousness there and considerable individual pilfering and looting and breaking into stores, although there were no mass riots. The militia seemed to disappear, and the guards were even drawn away from in front of the American embassy. Later Stalin restored order and the militia reappeared. Strict military discipline was instituted. Now calm is returning. Several food stores have been opened to relieve the queues and stop grumbling among the masses. Nevertheless, the press continues to report executions and prison sentences for infringements of discipline. The director and five other administrators of the Moscow circus fled in a truck with large sums of money during a circus performance at Moscow. A want order has been issued for all of them. If found, they will be sentenced by a military tribunal.

On October 27 Steinhardt told me that the British have prepared to fight if necessary for the protection of the Caucasus oil districts.

I must say the wording of the Soviet communiqués is really ridiculous. Thus, for example, a communiqué will say, "Our troops abandoned Viasma last night. Fighting continues in the direction of Viasma."

One of the most unpardonable features of Russia is the constant and enormous waste of time in queues. Thousands of man-hours of labor are spent that way, and it naturally creates discontent. Everything has a bottleneck. This loss certainly cannot even be balanced by the overtime "slave labor" of the prison camps.

All the foreign reporters lived in an old-fashioned wooden hostelry, by far Kuibyshev's best, which boasted the name "Grand Hotel." It was like the provincial inn in an Aksakhov or Dostoievsky novel, crowded, warm (the double windows were never opened) and redolent of cabbage, both cooked and digested. The Russians did their very best for us and the roster of nonjournalistic guests was distinguished. At the time I was there it included Oumansky (Soviet ambassador to Washington), Anders (commander of the Polish army), several ambassadors and the delegation of the Outer Mongolian People's Republic. There was only one toilet for each floor. We did our best to use it before the untutored Mongols.

I shared a room with Cassidy, an agreeable, intelligent journalist. One morning when we both had hangovers I heard an incredible noise right outside. After I could no longer stand the booms I pulled open the door and stared: abysmal silence. As soon as I retired to bed the noise began again. I rushed to the door, looked about: silence. Then I looked down and focused dully on a diminutive Mongolian boy who had been playing with his sister. He had a voice like the bull of Bashan. I succeeded in frightening the children back into their habitat across the hall, squeezed in one room with all the other Mongolians.

When we first arrived and descended to the dining room, the Narkomindel and NKVD had managed to prepare glorious menus: game, fowl, caviar, wines, cheese, fruit, and so on. Within three days this façade had disappeared. We subsided to bread, beer, soup. Soon an event like the appearance of pickled tomatoes at the Foreigners' Shop was of major importance. Ehrenburg commented sourly in his memoirs:

> Foreign correspondents . . . lived at the Grand Hotel, drank a lot and occasionally treated Petrov and me to whisky and soda. They were sure that in a month or two Hitler would conquer the whole of Russia, and sometimes comforted themselves and us with the thought that the struggle would continue in Egypt or India. When the news came of the Japanese attack on Pearl Harbor, the Americans in the Grand Hotel came to blows with the Japanese journalists.

Everyone has a right to his own recollections but this simply wasn't true. My blood brother Petrov shared every drop of whisky I ever laid hands on (not many, I confess); we were all pro-Red Army, and our relations with the Japanese were quite affable. I remember, on the day of Pearl Harbor, the courteous Hatanaka, who lived on the same floor, bowing, smiling, and saying: "So sorry, we sank your fleet this morning. Supposing we are at war."

I expressed skepticism about both reports. Nevertheless, after struggling through hip-high snow to our temporary embassy in a schoolhouse, I learned from Mike Michela, assistant military attaché, that Hatanaka was right on each count. Washington went through the formal moves of declaring war on the Axis, including Bulgaria. Sofia's regretful envoy, Stamenev, formerly King Boris's counselor and an old friend and Grand Hotel neighbor, sent me a magnificent assortment of royal cigarettes together with a little note explaining it wasn't his fault.

Kuibyshev was never designed to function as a national capital. The first afternoon we were there, Steele and I explored the shabby town. The main church was hung with an enormous cloth poster championing the virtues of atheism. The main cinema displayed a film in which a nasty Jesuit priest seduced a peasant girl. Next day the poster was gone and the film had been changed. But police action could not obscure Kuibyshev's dreariness.

The Volga soon froze solid and, after that, trains of double-humped Bactrian camels in their long winter wool padded solemnly across from the Asiatic side to unload sparse goods in the Kuibyshev bazaars. The wind started to form in distant Mongolia or the Altai mountains on China's frontier, took off slowly and gathered force hurrying westward over the steppes. By the time it reached us it was formidable. Snow piled up soon and thick. The reporters had last seen their cars in Moscow and improved their flabby physiques by trudging through drifts, occasionally chest high, to the temporary foreign office, press office, embassies, and eventually to the overburdened telegraph office. I sent one two-thousand-word cable at urgent rates (50 cents a word) via Stockholm because it contained some hot exclusive news I managed to get past the censor. It took a week to reach New York.

Considering the strain everyone was under, it seems astonishing on looking back how well the claustrophobic foreign colony seemed to get along: writers, generals, diplomats, air force officers, Communist agitators, Japanese, Americans; even Genya Petrov, who tried to shoot some RAF pilots simply because they were in British uniform, was happy to drink with English diplomats once he had finally sobered up. Incidentally, I learned early that no Russian could drink half as much whisky as vodka, although few regretted the attempt.

One man I came to know well was George Andreichin. George was a Bulgarian peasant who had been adopted by King Ferdinand at a time the crown was seeking popularity by sponsoring poor lads. Andreichin became a Socialist, while still living in the palace. The King regretfully sent him off, giving him a good head start over his secret police. George went to the United States, became involved in the "Wobbly" movement (International Workers of the World), was arrested during postwar "Red menace" days, and was furnished bail by William Bullitt, subsequently first United States ambassador to the Soviet Union.

Andreichin jumped bail and headed off for Revolutionary Russia, the goal of every young revolutionist. He took a train in Western Europe and, sitting in a third-class compartment, rattled across the brand new country of Czechoslovakia when the door rolled open and in came a sturdy, bearded old gentleman in huntsman's costume, bearing a shotgun and game bag. "George," said the huntsman, throwing his arms around him. "Your Majesty," said George. He rode mile after mile recounting his adventures to the Bulgarian King.

Once he reached Russia, George so ingratiated himself with Leon Trotsky that he became the first defense commissar's private secretary. Years later, during the great Stalinist purge, he was arrested and told by the NKVD: "Citizen Andreichin [it was always a mark of disfavor when a Communist was called "Citizen" instead of "Comrade"], you are going to be charged anyway but I will give you your choice. Do you wish to be arraigned as a Trotskyite or as an American agent?" George replied that it was well known he had been Trotsky's secretary and also that he had later been assigned to develop close relations with Americans. He opted for the latter accusation.

He was sent to a labor camp in the Far North whose arduous regime tested even his Bulgarian peasant's constitution. The prisoners learned about the Axis invasion from new inmates, including former and future allies. Andreichin was finally summoned to the commandant's office, told nothing, but placed in charge of a guard and sent to Moscow. He was released by the chief of the Lubyanka just in time to be evacuated to Kuibyshev. I saw Andreichin often in Kuibyshev and occasionally in Paris after the war, when he was a delegate to various international meetings including the peace conference. During the late 1940s, he disappeared again—into a Bulgarian Communist prison. This time he was older—and he died.

There were rare sights of interest along the desolate Volga valley, apart from the unhappy Polish army being regrouped at a Tatar village called Buzuluk. A few new factories were being thrown together in sheds housing machinery evacuated from the Ukraine and the industrialized regions near Moscow and Leningrad. I visited one of these, a Leningrad plant whose equipment had been incorporated into a small Kuibyshev ordnance establishment.

On November 10 Steinhardt was finally able to get away on his long-delayed "vacation," taking out with him Maxim Litvinov, former commissar for foreign affairs and newly named ambassador to the United States.

Poor Oumansky wasn't told until the last moment that he would not return
to his Washington post.

Two weeks later I had a long talk with Cripps and jotted in my diary:

He is a difficult man to figure out. He is perspicacious but I also have a
feeling he is somewhat devious. Certainly the reputation he acquired for
having foreseen war between Germany and Russia is wholly unmerited.
He was back in London trying to give up his job as a hopeless mess
when Hitler attacked.

Cripps said Churchill is "sentimentally excellent" about Russia but
"politically bad." He said Churchill's famous first speech after the German attack on Russia had been drafted together by Churchill, Cripps
and John Winant, American ambassador in London. Churchill then read
it emotionally to Winant and Cripps with tears streaming down his
face.

Cripps predicted that despite the current offensive against Moscow
the Germans will not capture the Soviet capital. He points out they were
much nearer to Leningrad and then, when the tough fighting began
there, were unable to take it. Should Moscow fall, the Germans will not
go on further, Cripps thinks. He admits that General Mason-Mac-
Farlane, his military expert, is less certain about this. Cripps says the
southern German thrust is the most serious. However the Russians are
pushing two drives west of Rostov. Timoshenko has two reserve armies
at his disposal.

Cripps said he had great admiration for Stalin. Stalin faces major
decisions constantly—things like the total evacuation of cities, the destruction of the Dnieper Dam, the moving of the Baltic or Black Sea
fleets.

I noted in my journal:

A year ago Cripps made a British offer to Russia including recognition of Soviet tenure of the Baltic states, gold and the promise of a
certain amount of shipping. Cripps said the Russians remained discreetly
secret about this offer. Yet the BBC broadcast it. The Russians were
furious and never even replied.

Cripps says Anglo-Soviet relations now are extremely strained and
difficult. Beaverbrook's recent trip here was a fiasco. Cripps says: "He
didn't understand the Russians and I told him so. His approach was
wrong. Georgians and Armenians like Stalin and Mikoyan are Asiatics
and appreciate and expect bargaining. If you give them anything for
nothing, they think you are being foolish and weak. Beaverbrook took
all the cards out of my hands."

When the Russians are angry, their propaganda completely ignores
Britain, and they contemptuously refer to the Anglo-German war as a
separate thing, implying that Russia and Britain don't even have a
common enemy. The Russians fear that we wish to see Russia weaken
Germany and then Britain plus Germany would turn against Russia; or
at any rate that the Anglo-American powers would just be glad to see

both Russia and Germany weakened. A great number of British policy makers do feel that way. The armed services in Britain are distinctly anti-Russian.

The Russians want to know what we intend to do in Europe, and they mistrust British intentions. Churchill absolutely refuses to consider the terms of settlement. Cripps said "the Atlantic Charter is no bloody good at all." It means nothing to the Baltic or the Balkans. "Now is the time to make our plans clear. Russia expects to be bargained with and can be bargained with now. Later she may be stronger, and should her army march into Berlin, I can tell you what sort of Europe we will have. Before the peace conference there must be an agreement on a settlement in Europe between the United States, the Soviet Union and Great Britain."

On November 25 I saw Anders again and he talked at length, saying: "I am not an orator or a diplomat but a soldier. I speak in simple words." (He spoke French, but also is fluent in German and Russian.) He was still leaning on a cane. He said that when he took over his job some of the Poles were in prison, some in concentration camps, some in forced labor camps. He said that the Polish-Russian accord changed everything:

On the day I was named commander-in-chief I was in prison. That evening I was given an apartment and a motorcar and all possible comforts.

When in prison I always spoke openly on the international situation with the NKVD officials. Therefore it was easy to continue such conversations afterwards. It was not difficult to make them understand the necessity for the Polish army. There were tremendous difficulties in reassembling people dispersed all over European and Asiatic Russia. I didn't even know the places where they were. Orders sent to Soviet officials from Moscow were not always respected in the provinces. There are many small bureaucrats who don't understand what is happening and don't wish to believe that people in jail should be released.

The Soviet army, after surviving the brutal shocks of summer, had started to reform. The gap between commissioned and other ranks became ever wider. Pay was doubled for wartime. Officers received a one month's pay bonus before going to the front and a 25 per cent bonus while in the lines. All ranks were granted tax exemptions, reduced rents and free transportation. Almost twenty new elite Guards divisions were created with double pay plus a 50 per cent bonus for officers.

One felt desperately confined, picking up bits of information of that sort and filtering them through a muddle-headed censorship with maximum effort and minimum result while a massive new battle was starting up in Moscow. General Zhukov, who had begun to emerge as the most brilliant of the new generation, easing aside the old marshals—Budenny, Voroshilov, Timoshenko and Shapozhnikov—seemed to have seized the offensive around the capital. Judging from reports we heard, he was having signal success. Only on December 13, after the Germans had already started to reel backward, were a few of us allowed to fly to Moscow.

We took off at 10:45 A.M. on a Soviet copy of an American DC-3 in the roof of which a gun turret had been inserted, protected only by some kind of plastic glass. A young soldier in fur cap and mittens stood on a make-shift wooden platform wielding a Lewis gun. The turret was so badly constructed that snowflakes kept pouring through it into our icy plane. The airfield was snow covered and windy when we rattled off on our four-and-a-half-hour flight.

The first three hours were routine, sitting along two benches facing each other. Passengers who became airsick simply rose and vomited into one of two large gasoline tins placed in the center aisle. The frequency of this occurrence encouraged me to look out the window. This was all right until half-way to Moscow when we began to really hedge hop instead of flying at the usual fifty-foot altitude which Soviet pilots then used to facilitate navigation, following highways and railroad lines.

It was only after I stared through the blizzard and suddenly saw steeples and factory chimneys whizzing by overhead that I turned my eyes inward and closed them. There was another plane in our convoy, containing Soviet officers and one foreigner. It ran into a railway train, bouncing off a box car and losing a wing against a telephone pole before coming to rest in a snowdrift. Everyone tottered out and, as might have been expected, the only person injured was the foreigner, a military attaché.

I wrote in my diary:

It was fascinating to motor through Moscow and notice that there had been no change since mid-October. All the way from the airport to the Hotel Metropole where I was again installed there was not a single sign of bombing. The hotel manager said to me when I entered:
"I told you when you left that you would be back soon. Here you are. Welcome. We showed those Fascists. Hitler can't take Moscow. His men have been finding that out for months. But now even he, living as he does in a daze, must know it too."

Moscow had a gala atmosphere, now that it knew the Germans were being driven from the iron circle gripping its outskirts. On my first morning back, the sun rose propitiously, shining on placid white streets, filled with deep drifts because most of the usual women snow cleaners had been assigned to more urgent tasks. It was a Sunday and numerous drawn-looking Muscovites, behaving with inordinate gaiety, bustled about on their shopping, jesting at the latest posters ridiculing the retreating Germans.

The Ballet announced a gala performance. Soldiers back on leave ambled along with their wives, girls or mothers. Uniformed peasant lads from the provinces got their first awed glimpse of the Kremlin's crenelated walls and the snow-laden, bulbous turrets of magnificent St. Basil's Church.

Along the broad avenues cavalrymen riding in pairs patrolled their beats, for the city still was under martial law. At each corner stood infantrymen—usually noncommissioned officers—still on the alert with bayoneted rifles. Readiness remained the watchword. Overhead was the constant drone of fighter patrols in the bright, clear sky, and occasional flights of bombers roared back from the west. Repair platoons were taking care of the amazingly slight bomb damage in rapid fashion that kept Moscow relatively unharmed despite the Luftwaffe's persistent efforts.

All morning long I strolled about the streets, regarding cheerful crowds. There were fewer children playing with sleds and skis than in normal times. There were more women. There were more soldiers: infantrymen in fleece-lined leather coats with yellow fur *kalpaks;* women auxiliary workers in skirted uniforms with gray squirrel caps; provincial levies wearing quilted jackets, mittens, boots and spiked woolen forage caps emblazoned with the red star; Cossack officers in gay dress costumes, with blue capes, spurred knee-boots and high astrakhan hats, strutting about with girls on their arms.

As I walked along the sidewalk, a talkative and grinning young man with one extra drink under his belt grabbed my arm. "You are happy," I said. "Why?" "It is Moscow," he said. "Here we are in Moscow."

A woman I know, who had just come back to the capital, explained: "I am glad to have seen this day. You foreigners cannot understand. Of course, my family is not here. Most of my friends are gone. But this is Moscow. If you foreigners could only understand what that means."

There were more beggars and I was appalled when a poor woman spurned the 10 rubles ($2) I offered her, asking only for bread—which I didn't have. The black-out remained total and it was forbidden to smoke outside at night.

Many miles to the west, beaten German troops were retreating slowly, harried by the Russian cavalry and pounded by heavy artillery, which Stalin once called the god of war. Passing constantly through the streets of Moscow were Red Army trucks, staff cars and motorcycles on their way to the front.

I visited the six Americans who had stayed behind during the hardest period: Thompson, Reinhardt, John Morgan and Harold Waddell, embassy clerks; John Leiono, embassy building superintendent; and Father Braun, who had conducted his regular services, although all windows of his chapel were shattered by bombs.

Thompson and Reinhardt volunteered to remain behind to carry out necessary duties when most diplomats were requested by the Soviet government to go to Kuibyshev. Their main job was packing and shipping eastward property of Americans and Britons, whose interests they looked after, and reporting on the situation in the capital.

Thompson and Reinhardt more or less ran the foreign colony. The Afghan embassy, the Spanish (*émigré* Republican) legation, the Bulgarian legation (Bulgaria didn't declare war on Russia), the Turkish embassy and the Japanese embassy all left representatives behind and, until America entered the war, Thompson looked after them. He supervised food distribution for eighty Soviet citizens—United States and British embassy employees and their families. He and Reinhardt managed to get seven carloads of American and British property packed and shipped east.

They took Finnish baths, went to theaters when possible, listened to the radio and entertained their foreign colleagues. Once, to see what it was like, they sheltered for the night in a subway car prepared for diplomats by the Swedes. The rest of the time they stayed in bed during raids. Every Saturday afternoon they staged American movie shows for the staff and other foreign representatives.

Thompson and the others lived in Spaso House where they amused themselves with preparations for a skating rink on the front lawn. When the city's water supply was temporarily threatened, they stored water in all bathtubs and froze it in metal wastebaskets to prepare for siege. They even converted into a mobile privy an old Rolls Royce limousine that had once belonged to Lady Paget, the British philanthropist, cutting a hole under the rear seat.

Back in the Metropole the correspondents were given a special mess where everyone ate at one table and, although we grumbled about the food given us by Jack, the harried manager, he did his best. We had an enormous amount of legwork, not having located our cars or drivers and being forced to wade through the snow to the telegraph office with our dispatches. But this was slight payment for the privilege of being back once more at the heart of a true story and, within two days, we were at last allowed up at the front.

I was fortunate enough to be taken to the army of a new star on the Soviet horizon, Lieutenant General A. A. Vlassov, who was then at the peak of his career. He had become Zhukov's most successful field commander and was swinging a wide arc around and through the German sector north and northwest of Moscow, past Klin and Volokolamsk.

Little did anyone suspect that Vlassov would finish his dazzling career as World War II's highest-ranking traitor. He was captured in July, 1942, and, later that summer, agreed to recruit an army for Hitler from among the hundreds of thousands of war prisoners the Nazis had taken. He ended up by briefly liberating Prague with his puppet troops, then retreating ahead of the onrushing Red Army and yielding himself to General George Patton's American forces. Patton turned him over to the Soviets, who hanged him.

Vlassov was then a national hero: a big man, about six foot three with his height further accentuated by his high, general's lambskin *kalpak*. He had a long up-turned nose and thick glasses. When one stood talking to him outside, his nose rapidly acquired a small snowdrift of its own and his glasses fogged. I have a snapshot, showing him towering over one of his division commanders, General Korol, who was a good six feet.

The trip was fascinating but savagely cold. I carried a bottle of vodka in one pocket of my fur-lined coat and wore elbow-length tank driver's mittens, given to me by Genya Petrov, that were both lined and covered with sealskin. We only had time to eat once a day and were billeted where luck would have it. But it was an exhilarating experience. Hitler's first major defeat. I wrote:

For intervening periods the only sound one hears along this battle-front is the constant shuffle of infantry and horses, the snow-muffled whir of tractors, tanks and trucks and the thud of artillery. And if one waits that, too, becomes more distant as again horse teams and tractors hitch up their guns and howitzers and resume their westward trek. Ever so often, in the surrounding thickets, there is a rattle of machine guns; the mopping up proceeds.

The ground is strewn with clusters of abandoned guns, tanks and trucks where rear-guard stands were made; litters of munition cases, used cartridges, machine guns and staff cars. This desolate landscape evinces the usual tragic scars of war—burned houses, ruined churches; and a ghastly touch is added by occasional corpses of men and horses, their blood instantly frozen bright red, dragged from the road and dumped in the fields, stretching stiff limbs starkly toward heaven. Here and there the mantle of new snow masks grim shapes that can only be suspected.

One is struck by the resemblance of the snowy, littered Russian landscape to that depicted by Meissonier in his version of Napoleon's famous retreat. The difference in more than a century of inventions appears to be reduced before the bare enormity of nature.

The gap is bridged by the Russians themselves, who are using everything from cavalry and horse-drawn sleighs to powerful new tractors from the Stalin factory to haul their attacking strength. I have noticed in the Soviet arsenal everything from brand-new self-propelled guns to old Howitzers, stamped with the Czar's double eagle and the dates 1914, 1915. Vast quantities of ammunition and tank fuel are hauled up on horse-drawn sleighs.

Drive through mantled woods in a snowstorm, past occasional stranded tanks. Soldiers, rifles still on their backs, are atop telephone poles restringing wires; field communication lines are strung along the ground. The roads are far smoother in the snow than the last time I was at the front, in muddy September. Returning peasants glide past in sleighs.

Frozen German bodies sprawl stiffly in the snow by crippled enemy tanks and trucks. Past a formation of intact, frozen Nazi tanks, a detachment of soldiers rides to the front in sleighs. Snow-spattered horses munch hay by an abandoned German antitank gun. A wounded horse stands shivering in a field; field guns thud across the hillside. A helmeted and hooded cavalry detachment with sabers swinging rides by a long train of wagons and trucks and marching men. Mechanics work on Russian tanks parked near trees. A white-helmeted infantryman begs a match.

In the snow Vlassov arrives. He is a giant and wears a high gray fur *kalpak* with a red top. He says he has just dispatched mobile and ski units to take Volokolamsk; the vanguard already is cutting off the last line of the Nazi retreat. Vlassov explains that another force is attacking Volokolamsk from the south, and because of the thick forests to the west the Nazis cannot escape. "They are trapped, I think," he says.

Columns and columns of infantry—tired, tough veterans with hard-bitten faces—slog along at post-haste march, bending under the weight of automatic rifles and dragging heavy metal ammunition cases in the snow; fatigued, strong, weather-beaten men. Behind come more tanks with commanders looking out of turrets, wiping smoke-blackened faces; more field guns with crews asleep, precariously balanced on carriages, white-washed helmets askew.

At the end of the line is a brisk young lieutenant with a fur cap under his helmet. "Who are you?" he asks, pointing a rifle, when I try to take pictures. I explain. "Oh!" he says. "American. We will take Berlin." And off again, down the long road over the snow.

I got back to Moscow after three stimulating days and had the enormous task of writing an immensely long dispatch, page by page, taking each page to the censor, getting it stamped, then trudging through snow to the telegraph office so as to get the story moving; then returning to the Metropole to write another page and repeat the performance. It was pitch black outside and the streets were blocked with snow.

By this time I felt I had done my job for *The New York Times* and had earned the right to leave Russia and get married. Edwin (Jimmy) James, my managing editor, was a genial, good-natured friend but devoted to journalism first and last. Years later he told me every foreign correspondent ought to be castrated before going abroad so he'd keep his mind on his work. Jimmy, who was certainly not castrated and had had a rich sex life in his days overseas, had no desire to help me. He was under the impression that I was giving him excellent service and therefore played that watchful waiting game so well known to Roman generals and American managing editors. I decided to become master of my own fate, return to Kuibyshev and rehire Ralph Parker, our former Belgrade stringer.

When I got back from Moscow there had been such a heavy snowfall that Kuibyshev airport was cut off from town. I spent a night and day playing *atchko* and dominoes with Russian pilots. *Atchko* is a game I commend to all diplomats assigned to Russia: it is illegal to deal off the top of the deck. Dominoes is the same as the American version, played with exceptional gusto. Each domino was slapped down on the table with a terrific bang. Sitting beside a wood stove, their fleece-lined flying suits beside them, slap, the flyers would go: "It's yours, Comrade Lieutenant." And again, slap, slap, while a bomber rolled in from a practice run or a transport came tearing up the drifts after a nine-hour flight from Tashkent. Slap, and "Now you Americans know who will be stabbed in the back, eh, comrade!" Finally a truck, with the blade of a plow fastened to the front, came inching through the drifts.

Parker, disconsolate and embittered by the death of his first wife and her baby and not yet wrapped up in the affairs of Valentina, the NKVD colonel with whom he eventually sought solace, was now at work in Kuibyshev for *The Times* of London. Without asking New York's permission I simply rehired him for our paper. I told him I would notify New York and instruct him when to start filing the moment I could find passage out.

I used my last few days in a desperate search for transportation and wired Marina to expect me, probably in early January. When, among my farewell calls, I said goodbye to Anders, he was feeling enraged. Polish soldiers coming in on trains from all over the USSR were being callously treated. Sixteen starved corpses were found in one box car when it was opened on arrival. Anders had compiled a precise list of five thousand missing officers and was suspicious of their fate. (We later found out they had already been shot in Katyn.)

Finally I obtained a seat on a plane bound for Teheran, wired James and handed over to Parker. The passengers included Johnny Alison, Hub Zemke, a young United States Air Force instructor who later became a general, plus two British ambassadors, Knatchbull-Hugessen from Ankara and Sir Reader Bullard from Teheran, who had been in Moscow to confer when Anthony Eden saw Stalin. We bounded off the snowy Kuibyshev airport and took off at about the height of a tall man for Astrakhan where we spent our first night.

I knew Astrakhan had been the world's caviar capital so I rushed to the retail shop where there was a small queue. When my turn came I ordered two kilos (almost four and a half pounds) of the best, gray-green, esturgeon. By the time my tins had been filled and sealed, Hugessen and Bullard arrived. They were furious to find there was no more and insisted I share with them. "Gentlemen," I said. "Apart from the fact that both of you have access to all the caviar you want in Ankara and Teheran and apart from the fact that I believe in the old American rule, first come, first served, I am getting married next week and this is for my wedding party. Sorry."

The creaking Russian DC-3 had limited range and our second night was spent at Baku. There, in a small dining room reserved for foreigners, I was startled to find several English friends from Rumania, all wearing officers' uniforms. They had been sent to Baku, the petroleum capital, on a rush mission when it seemed as if the Germans might overrun the wells. As oil experts, they were assigned to instruct the Russians in demolition methods. Since then they had been kept in a comfortable Baku isolation ward, shepherded by NKVD officers, and given nothing to do. They had no prospect of a job, since the Nazi offensive was thrown back, but nobody wanted to take the responsibility of releasing them.

Next morning, the last day of 1941, we took off again. Even over the jagged Elburz range that separates the Iranian plateau from Soviet Azerbaijan, our pilot carefully kept only a few yards above the surface of the earth, making the journey like a roller coaster. At last, on a starry New Year's Eve, we landed at Teheran, the first lighted city I had seen for months, looking gay, friendly, warm and civilized. I summoned a carriage driver, who spoke Russian, and clip-clopped happily off to the modest Firdowsi Hotel, which looked to me like a combination of every Ritz in the world. Before greeting the New Year, I drank a whole bottle of champagne—alone.

# I I

# GOD MAKES

# AN EXCEPTION

THE PERSIAN SUN ROSE BRIGHT AND AUSPICIOUS ON 1942, THE year of my marriage, a marriage that has bloomed ever since. But even Teheran presented bureaucratic complications. I had to pre-occupy myself with red tape requirements and military permits for travel to Jerusalem where Marina was living with the Sedgewicks. The entire Middle East was under British Army control.

I wired Shan to make arrangements for the wedding and to expect me soon. At my end, I needed help on wedding presents and here I was most agreeably aided by the niece of a friend, a beautiful girl named Firouzé (turquoise). Firouzé had once been the Shah's girl but her political appeal among Iranian tribes or international royalty did not rival her sex appeal as a marriageable factor. She had lustrous black hair, brows, eyes; a lithe figure, long nose and mouth and spoke French perfectly but with a soft and wholly ungallic lilt, as if it were the language of Omar Khayyam. In every way she resembled a houri from some medieval Islamic poem. Firouzé saw to it that I acquired for Marina various items of jewelry, material and a magnificent old velvet vest, sewn with pearls. In the evenings we dined on Iranian caviar and *shashlik,* discussing the future and looking at the star-dusted sky above the towering Elburz range. We were young and opti-mistic.

On January 4 the young Shah received me: a quiet, courteous, solemn and rather timid youth. Firouzé had mischievously warned that he would bum any cigarettes I had. I was surprised when he did. He was even more surprised to discover they were Iranian. "I always smoke American ciga-rettes," he said.

Mohammed Reza Pahlevi, then twenty-two years old, had suffered greatly. His father, a tough, self-made cavalry sergeant, had been forced to abdicate by the British and Russians. He himself had seen his country occupied by the two countries Persians most feared. (Indeed, swastikas were then painted on many Teheran walls and hawkers sold pictures of Hitler in the bazaar.) I noted:

I rode up to the palace in a drozhky drawn by two skeletal white horses. The driver was apparently terrified of driving into the palace gate, although this had been explained to him by the proprietor of the Hotel Firdowsi. Three times he drove past it; then I shouted at him to turn around, and he went back. The carriage stopped and an enormous stream poured from both horses' pizzles as an officer rushed up to inquire who I was and what I wanted. Then a butler from the palace came out and informed him it was all right, and I walked into the gate past two guards, one with a bayoneted rifle, the other with a long silver mace. It was like the garden of a villa of some size, with a dog playing in the gravel path. The modern-style building had marble walls.

Inside, I left my hat, coat and gloves on a table and the *chef de protocol* for the court greeted me. After a chat and a cup of tea, he led me upstairs to the Shah's office, opened the door, introduced me and left. The Shah shook hands, expressed polite pleasure at seeing me, and waved me over to a small couch where I sat beside him. He is a brown-faced boy with a graceful carriage, but not handsome; he has brown eyes, somewhat curly black hair, sensual but not too thick-lipped mouth, a good jaw, a rather fleshy hooked nose and nice brown eyes. He is about five feet nine inches tall and very slender. He was wearing a light khaki uniform with a crown on either shoulder.

The Shah referred constantly to Iran as an "occupied" country. He seemed to resent more than anything that Iran was not accorded the right to defend itself with English and Russian aid, but was only guaranteed protection. He said, there was no excuse for the Anglo-Soviet occupation, that the numbers of Germans and Italians could have been easily handled.

He said that German and especially Japanese propaganda had been very effective, that the Japanese never mentioned themselves in their broadcasts but referred to the Germans and what they would do for Iran and Islam. Axis propagandists always depicted Hitler as a Moslem and a descendant of the Prophet, born with a green belt around his middle.

In those days Teheran was an agreeable, rather rustic backwater. The first great hoist into modernity came when the United States established its Persian Gulf Service Command. But in early 1942 there were few foreigners, apart from a handful of British officers and the diplomatic colony, and the pace of life was leisurely. There were none of the huge new buildings that now lower over the capital and the humble Firdowsi was the only hotel recommended to non-Asiatic travelers. Bazaars and antiquarians had ornate carpets, diamantine jewels and delicately painted miniatures to offer.

I took the famous southward bound Trans-Iranian Express that creeps through endless tunnels to the oil ports of the Persian Gulf. At Ahwaz I descended and was taken in charge by a British major who fed and lubricated me at the officers mess and gave me a hut with latticed Indian charpoy bed on which to sleep. Most officers and men in the Iran–Iraq area were from the Indian army.

The cold wind whistled across the featureless, azoic desert, and jackals howled throughout the spacious night. Next day I joined a truck convoy bound for Basra, in Iraq, sitting next to a turbaned Punjabi driver smelling of rancid ghee. We rumbled beside lackadaisical gangs of Iranian men and women working on the road, across parched flats, past dead jackals and live gazelles and sand grouse, scattering into the shifting mirages. Across from Basra I was surprised to find gondolas floating on the murky green water of the Shatt-al-Arab where the joined Tigris and Euphrates flow into the Persian Gulf.

From Basra I rode a troop train up to Baghdad, a disappointing city, cold in winter, dusty and infernally hot in summer. While waiting to arrange the next onward lap, I was well looked after by my hotel bartender, an affable gentleman named Jesus, and the American legation and British embassy, both of which were eager for any first-hand Russian tidbits.

General Nuri as-Said, prime minister and dominant figure on the Iraqi scene, told me he would join the alliance against Germany in exchange for American economic aid. He said:

> We are allies of Britain. We have already severed relations with Germany, Italy and Japan. We are helping Britain in all her needs and therefore believe we are entitled to have the United States lease-lend clauses apply to us. Iraq has ample grounds for a grudge against the Axis. Rashid Ali and other traitors wanted by the government are sheltered in Germany. There they are protected and paid. Axis broadcasters in the Arabic language are constantly attacking our government and the royal family in the most insulting terms. No nations can keep quiet before such insults.

Poor Nuri—in 1958 there was another uprising in Iraq, this time a left-wing, not right-wing, one and this time successful. The monarchy was ousted and both Abdulillah and Nuri were butchered, their bodies dragged through the streets by jeering mobs. Nuri had been a dignified and effective politician. He received his first officer's commission from the Turks before World War I but was always an Arab nationalist. At the end, he grew careless and overconfident and was destroyed by the power of a new movement he had underestimated, Nasserism.

From Baghdad I took a Nairn pullman bus to Damascus and Beirut.

The Nairn line was then a formidable communications system operated by two New Zealand brothers who had been in Allenby's World War I army and stayed on to make their fortunes. They developed a transdesert route across which one could ride relatively comfortable cars and buses, stopping off for refreshment at oases and petroleum pipeline pumping stations. When World War II came they made a bonanza out of British military transport.

At the Beirut terminal Sedgwick was waiting in British officer's uniform (as a war correspondent) with sheepskin jacket, a big smile on his face but a worried look in his eyes. By the time we got to the St. Georges Hotel I knew why he was anxious. Would I, he inquired, be very much opposed if instead of being married in Jerusalem by a civil ceremony we were wed in Beirut by a Presbyterian chaplain? Not at all, I assured him; but why? Then he told me.

As soon as Marina learned that I would arrive in early January she and Shan set about arranging our nuptials. Since Marina was Greek Orthodox while I was Jewish-born but by practice a thoroughgoing atheist, she and the Sedgwicks thought the simplest thing was a civil ceremony. Unfortunately, they discovered that under the complicated law governing Palestine, still a League of Nations mandate administered by Britain, only British subjects could thus be married.

They were not depressed by this complication. Shan reasoned that since Jerusalem possessed both a Greek Patriarch and a Grand Rabbi, some sort of deal could be made. He and Marina first called on the Patriarch who was exceptionally affable and expressed himself ready to perform the service personally—until he discovered the groom was not even a Christian. Then, most regretfully, he protested that he was forbidden by canonical restrictions to approve. Slightly alarmed, Shan and Marina visited the Grand Rabbi. He was also enthusiastic; nor did he seem perplexed by the fact that Marina was not Jewish. He simply explained that all she must do was accept conversion and embark on a course of Talmudic studies which should not take more than a year or two. Afterwards, of course, she would have to convince a rabbinical board she had not been converted solely for reasons of love.

This second disappointment produced a shock since by then I had wired from Teheran that I was actually en route. Frantically, Shan suggested that perhaps we could persuade some friendly mullah or imam to officiate in a Moslem ceremony. Marina drew the line: "I'll be damned if I'm blacked out behind a veil for anyone."

At this stage Shan had to go to Beirut for a story and was sitting mournfully in the officers club, contemplating the bottom of a whisky glass, when a colonel he knew clapped him on the back and asked: "What's the matter, Sedg? Why so glum?" Shan told him. "Why that's all right," said the colonel. "Didn't you ever think of Doc Scherer? The American chaplain. I'm sure Scherer will do the job." So Sedgwick called upon this courteous, deeply sincere United States missionary. Scherer was a Presbyterian minister who then wore uniform as an accredited chaplain with the British forces in the Levant territory of Free France. Scherer said not to worry, he would handle everything.

To Shan's relief, I was amused and delighted. We rushed to the motor pool and commandeered a car and driver for Jerusalem.

After endless hours on the winding mountain road we entered the New City and arrived before a small, gray stone house where the Sedgwicks and Marina had taken rooms. An instant later the door flung open and there was Marina: radiant. Beside her, hopping up and down like a mad cricket, was Felix.

We were married January 22. Shan went ahead to arrange for an official American witness from our legation because the United States consul general in Jerusalem, a routine-minded bureaucrat, had warned him the marriage would be illegal. Indeed, he kept saying this anyway for months afterward. Marina and I wondered if it wouldn't be fun some time to have a strictly legal wedding with our children bearing her bridal train.

Roxane Sedgwick, Marina and I drove to Beirut on the morning of the twenty-second. We stopped for lunch in Haifa and were almost late because we became entranced by the restaurant's slot-machine. We drove along the lovely seashore through the crusader town of Acre, past ancient Tyre and Sidon and found Shan pacing up and down outside the St. Georges chewing his mustache. He was feverishly distraught. His New England sense of propriety wouldn't even permit us to go to our room together to wash. Finally, after what seemed an age to him, he drove us to Dr. Scherer's pleasant apartment. The minister was waiting with his wife and Bill Porter, a skinny young vice-consul from the American legation, who was our witness and best man. Bill was then just at the start of a career in which he became a highly distinguished ambassador.

Scherer, a tall bespectacled man with pleasant, homely face, graven with lines of sympathy and humor, was wearing uniform covered by his ministerial cassock. He greeted us with grave affection and then invited Marina and myself into his study. There, more nervous than we, he explained that it was highly unusual for a man in his position to marry two people of other religions. The only service he knew was Presbyterian. He hoped we would not mind if he used this for the ceremony. Nevertheless, he intended to preface it with a special apologia which he read: "Dear God. I know I am departing from custom and, as it were, stepping out of my bailiwick today as I join these two young people in wedlock. But you are undoubtedly aware of all the trouble that exists nowadays on earth. I can only assure you that their two hearts beat as one."

Marina hadn't even time to brush away a tear when the minister rushed us into his sitting room and there married us before a small altar he had erected on a table. Afterwards Mrs. Scherer produced a cake. It was not a very splendid wedding but it was the nicest I have ever heard of and I think it meant more to all concerned, not just the bride and groom, united after so much time and so many adventures. We spent that night in Beirut. A moon reflected on the old Phoenician Bay and waves slapped below.

Next day we moved to the King David Hotel in Jerusalem in order to give our wedding party. Thanks to Shan there was plenty of booze and thanks to my obstinacy in Astrakhan there was plenty of caviar for our friends. Unfortunately, because of wartime rationing, we ran out of bread.

That was a carefree and joyful period even though Jerusalem already seethed with an undercurrent of hatred between Arabs and Jews, both preparing their ultimate private war. I have never liked the world's most famous, ancient city. Beautiful as it is, for me it has always been a visible expression of human aversion. One can see hate rising from its rosy-stoned hilltop as tangibly as one can see mystical passion rising above El Greco paintings of Toledo.

A few days later we went up to Turkey, by the slow Taurus express train from Tripoli, taking along Felix and his old friend, Slatko Joyce, whom I had recovered from his Cairo caretaker and was returning to his new owner, Ray Brock. (Dear Reader: never share a sleeping compartment for forty-eight hours with two wire-haired fox terriers.)

In Ankara we heard ghastly news. A friend who had just slipped out from Greece told us:

Today we don't discuss food. We cannot bear the subject any longer. The streets are full of peddlers selling sweets on folding tables. They cost between 30 and 50 drachmas each. These sweets are made of beans from the carob tree and ersatz cream whitened with marble dust. Newspapers warn the people against buying these because of stomach trouble. The carob bean was formerly used as pig feed. In Ommonia Square vendors are selling sausage for cut-rate prices, as well as livers and giblets. They are made of dog, cat and rat meat. There are epidemics of ptomaine poisoning. Walking any day through Athens' main streets you can see beggars lying on the ground. Passers-by spread handkerchiefs on the faces of those who are dead. That's the only way to tell them from those who have fainted from weakness.

I was told of the following conversation between the German commandant and the mayor of occupied Athens:

MAYOR: Our people are beginning to starve; you are taking our food away and we cannot live.
COMMANDANT: How many are starving?
M.: Only five or six daily now; but soon it will be a hundred times that.
C.: You have something to look forward to. In Poland four hundred are starving daily.

M.: Why do you treat us so?

C.: You Greeks, by your stubbornness, have set us back three months. You must pay.

When we got back to Palestine I motored to Transjordan for a talk with the Emir Abdullah, head of the Hashimite family, ally of Lawrence of Arabia, descendent of the Prophet and ruler of a large but barren principality. (Abdullah, like that other wise Arab leader, Nuri as-Said, was murdered after the war.) The Emir was wearing a tan gabardine robe, white *kafiya* (head dress) held down by a gold and silver *igal* (band), with heavy, gold-handled dagger, sheathed in gold, thrust into his belt. He was a handsome, bearded man with sad face. Speaking Arabic, which his private secretary interpreted, he denounced his adversary, the exiled Grand Mufti of Jerusalem, calling him an enemy of the Arab people. The Grand Mufti, Haj Amin al Hussaini, had endorsed the 1941 Iraqi uprising against the British. One of the Mufti's kinsmen slew Abdullah years later.

The Emir said: "The Mufti is merely a wrecker and destroyer. He quit his mosque while he was respected and not injured in any way. Only his wish to destroy impelled him to quit Palestine, Syria and Iraq in succession. The Arab world is now convinced that he deals with the Italians and sold himself to them for gold."

Soon after our marriage I had told Marina I thought it my duty to go home and join the American forces. I pointed out that, since she could not be with her mother, it would be best for her to stay with mine. We headed for Cairo to arrange a flight back across Central Africa and the South Atlantic. In Cairo I found a curious Hollywood atmosphere. One could sit on the terrace of Shepheards or the Continental and see, filing past, soldiers in British, New Zealand, Australian, French, Polish, Greek, Jugoslav uniforms; even an occasional American attaché from General Maxwell's new mission. One had a deceptive, impressionistic feeling of a vast alliance.

Headquarters were swollen with staff officers. Neither these *pongo* colonels nor the tough little Tommies had much use for the Egyptians and relations were decidedly poor. The British made no effort to disguise their contempt while the unhappy Egyptians wanted no part of a war in which they were theoretically neutral but really occupied and forced to do the bidding of a principal belligerent. At all movies, following British custom, the Egyptians concluded performances with the national anthem; the audience stood to attention and, if it knew the words, sang. Cairenes sometimes marveled at the enthusiasm of the Tommies who were, in fact, chanting with powerful accents: "Oh we're black-faced bastards but we dearly love our King; *Qwais katir,* gonorrhea, King Farouk, King Farouk."

About all the British had left at that epoch was their courage and their sense of humor. This was before the days of Alexander and Montgomery and troops went into battle singing: "We are the King's Armee. No Bloody good are we. We cannot shoot; we cannot fight; we cannot do PT" (physical training). One distinguished regiment, Queen's Household Cavalry, was popularly known as the Mena House Cavalry after the Pryamids resort hotel. The current riddle went: "Why hasn't Rommel met the main British force? Because he's not a member of the Cairo Turf Club."

A. M. Hassanein Pasha, Farouk's chief of cabinet and the man who had been charged with his education, told me the bitter story of deteriorating relationships. Hassanein was a polished, cultivated man of the world, an explorer, pilot, connoisseur: tall, thin, gracious; very much the old-fashioned Egyptian gentleman. He said that King Farouk had been a handsome, intelligent boy but developed badly. He had increasingly strained relationships with Sir Miles Lampson (later Lord Killearn), originally British high commissioner and, since 1936, when Egypt theoretically became fully independent, British ambassador.

Hassanein contended that the overbearing manner of the massive Lampson had contributed to Farouk's intense inferiority complex which was already expressing itself in various disagreeable ways including a kind of *Arabian Nights* sex mania. One day Hassanein invited Marina and me for lunch, an elegant affair until we got to the dessert which looked like vanilla ice cream but was exceedingly gummy to chew. When our host caught us glancing at each other he explained with a smile that this was a favorite delicacy, chicken ice cream. It proved to be exactly that: made of frozen, shredded white meat. Fortunately, I have never had it since.

After lunch Marina was sent home in his car for a siesta and Hassanein gave me a briefing. He said Farouk now so hated Lampson that he always referred to him as "the professor" or "the schoolmaster." Lampson tried unsuccessfully to force Egypt to declare war on the Axis. In January, 1942, without informing Farouk, who was on a trip to Aswan, Lampson bullied the government into breaking relations with Vichy France. This was highly unpopular because of French prestige in Egypt. Lampson then pressed to have the pro-British Nahas Pasha made prime minister, presumably expecting he would declare war.

When nothing happened, Lampson moved in a most unambassadorial way. At 9 P.M. on February 4 a British battalion supported by thirty armored cars surrounded the palace and Lampson, accompanied by the British commander in Egypt, called on the King demanding he appoint Nahas. He said, according to Hassanein, who was present: "Majesty, I want an answer to my request." Farouk replied: "I sent you my [negative] response at six o'clock." Lampson then said the British cruiser *Ajax* was waiting in Alexandria, implying it would take off the King if he did not yield. Farouk buckled. He answered: "Since I love my country and wish to avoid bloodshed, I will call Nahas and ask him to form a cabinet of his own choice." Hassanein then interrupted: "But, Sir Miles, this is in direct violation of the [Anglo-Egyptian] treaty." Lampson said brusquely: "Pasha, I am not here for discussion but to get an answer."

This kind of behavior created savage hatred for Britain among many Egyptians. Hassanein told me the British C. in C. had once sent Farouk an Italian regimental standard captured in the Western Desert. The King pompously seized it, cast it on the floor, stamped upon it and screamed: "These fools will never conquer my country." I asked Hassanein which "fools" Farouk meant, the Italians (whom the Egyptians also hated) or the British. "Both," Hassanein replied sadly.

The United States was then represented in Cairo by a very astute public servant. Alexander Kirk, the minister, was a rapier-thin, exquisitely dressed dandy with the manner of an eighteenth-century fop but under this he concealed a tough, hard-boiled mind and was unabashed in expressing his opinions to Washington. He showed me several messages he had sent the State Department describing the critical military and political situation in Egypt and warning of irreparable disaster if the Nile Valley were to fall. He urged swift and strong American help to our British allies in this theater.

In early April we finally managed to get the proper priority and climb abroad an American DC-3 taking off on the first lap of the long journey home. We spent one night at Omdurman, where Kitchener defeated the Sudanese dervishes, then flew across the French Chad territory to Kano, a walled Moslem city of Northern Nigeria, and on over steaming jungle to Lagos.

In Lagos, where we had to wait three days, we were housed in the unimpressive little Palm Tree Hotel on Apapa Road, almost encompassed by jungle. This had originally been owned by a prosperous Nigerian who was buried nearby beneath a tombstone on which was graven: "Here lies Adjikidji, agent for the internationally renowned Singer Sewing Machine Company." The Palm Tree was quite as delightful as its new proprietor, a friendly gentleman named Littlewood who confessed he had left England "because the police back home want you to walk on only one side of the street." He took us on strolls through the dank undergrowth, discovering orchids for Marina, and led us through Lagos where, all day and all night, native drums beat and, on one fiesta, we watched weirdly clad masked dancers jerk through the narrow streets and flagellate each other with whips. Also staying in our hotel were a Russian admiral and a Russian general, each with his English-speaking NKVD aide, who were on the first technical purchasing mission sent to Washington. The poor men suffered from the extreme heat and Marina and I did little for allied relationships. There was only one bath and it happened to be next to our room. We kept cold water running in the tub; one of us would sit in it, reading for hours, until the other's turn came to be admitted with a code knock.

Finally a Pan American Clipper arrived, sailing like a great destroyer through the gray and immensely humid sky. The passengers boarded a launch: the four Russians, a Canadian acting as agent for the Chinese government, the British colonel in charge of Nigeria's police force, and a three-man South African mission headed by John Martin, an elderly publisher and gold magnate said to be Smuts' *éminence grise*. A band of honor, sturdy black men with black and red uniforms and pompom hats, tootled us off while the colonel stood in the bow, sweating profusely, sun helmet under his arm, saluting like "Sanders of the River."

The flying boat took off like a lumbering whale and Marina and I stretched my fur-lined coat on the floor of the empty rear and slept. We spent one night at Belem, Brazil, another at Trinidad and still another at San Juan, Puerto Rico, always drinking rum punches with Martin, listening to tales of the Rand gold rush and the Boer War. When we finally reached New York it was gleaming cold in an exceptionally late spring snow flurry. Marina walked off the plane into my mother's arms, embarrassed by her little white tropical dress, bare legs and sandals, drawn with what we fancied was airsickness and soon discovered was pregnancy. Marina lost the baby but she recovered fast and completely, as twenty-three-year-old girls so happily do.

Uncle Arthur, who then published the *Times*, called me into his office one day and told me I had been recommended for the Pulitzer Prize on foreign correspondence and that, thanks to the system then prevailing (a stacked deck with Arthur Krock of our Washington bureau in a powerful position on the award committee), it was certain I would receive it. However, the *Times* had also put in Louis Stark, an aging labor specialist, for a prize. Krock had advised Uncle Arthur the paper could have either award, but not both. He was sure I would understand if the paper withdrew me; I was young, and old Lou was not well. I agreed, of course, although with some regret and a certain amount of bewilderment about the system of prize-giving. Krock, himself, got three Pulitzer prizes during his career.

Two years later Uncle Arthur, apparently somewhat absent-mindedly forgetting the first affair, which dealt with my 1941 reporting, told me I had been put up for the 1943 prize (in 1944) for my dispatches on Tito's Partisan movement but again had been withdrawn, this time to insure that a series of editorials on the teaching of history would receive the award. The subject interested my aunt greatly and my uncle was sure I would understand. I reflected sadly that nepotism, in my case, meant being disfavored. I never did get a Pulitzer Prize although I was given a special citation in 1952 for a 1951 interview with Archbishop Stepinac in his prison cell. The citation was Krock's kindly way of repaying hospitality; Marina and I had taken him and his wife on an automobile tour of Italy. He, not the *Times*, submitted my name personally.

That year of 1942 the Greek embassy in Washington offered me the Military Cross, which I politely declined, feeling I had done nothing to justify it. I had already declined a similar proffer of the Jugoslav Order of St. Sava and was later to decline the Greek Order of the Phoenix and, twice, the French Legion of Honor. It is my credo that acceptance of decorations of this sort from foreign governments is equivalent to wearing a badge of prostitution. Looking back on these episodes I am minded of de Jouvenel's observation in *La République des Camarades:* "The victories one gains over oneself are, it is said, the most beautiful but rarely the most advantageous."

In mid-April I went down to Washington and was persuaded both by friends in the Army and the *Times* that I would be more useful as a war correspondent than as a warrior. I have since questioned my own judgment and decision.

Lou Fortier, by then secretary of the Combined Chiefs of Staff, asked me to talk about Russia to a group of War Department intelligence officers including John Ratay (soon to be a general) and Colonel Truman Smith, former military attaché in Berlin. They quizzed me closely, going over a huge map of the USSR, and asked me to stick my neck out and predict what would happen that year (1942). I forecast the Germans would mount an offensive only on the southern front, would get to the high range of the Caucasus and as far as Stalingrad on the Volga, then would be forced to fall back. That November 12 Fortier wrote me (and I still have the letter framed):

> As events proceed in Europe and North Africa, my mind goes back to April of this year when you dropped into my office at the Combined Chiefs of Staff and I asked you your opinion of Russian capabilities for 1942. As you may recall, we had a little informal gathering with Truman Smith, Herman Kramer and John Ratay. Inasmuch as you had visited the German-Russian front in the fall of 1941, you were asked to express your opinion as to the probable turn of events on that front during the current year. I must say, old top, that your "crystal gazing" fell into the class of good educated guessing. I remember your prophesying that the Germans would attack only on the southern front and that while the drive would go east and southeast, the Russians would be able to hold Stalingrad and prevent the Germans from crossing the Caucasus. You seem to have learned considerable military tactical and strategical calculations. At any rate, your estimate hit the 1942 German effort on the nose.

While my forecast turned out to be pleasingly accurate, Fortier is the only one of the officers present at our discussion who did not vehemently disagree. Lou, who had graduated from France's *Ecole Supérieure de Guerre,* had been one of those who believed in the excellence of the French Army and was heartbroken to discover how wrong he was. All the others were persuaded that nothing could stop the combined power of the Wehrmacht and Luftwaffe. They assured me I was naive to think Russia could endure another summer of Nazi pressure.

I was asked to summarize all my impressions in a report which I dictated April 15. This said in part:

Depending on Russia's strength after the war, it is my belief that she definitely intends to get back the Baltic states, Bessarabia, part of Poland, and the 1941 Finnish frontier. I believe she intends to try and gain a paramount diplomatic influence (greater than that of the Czar) in the Balkan slavic states and will encourage the Jugoslavs to demand a large piece of Albania and Trieste. She undoubtedly has also got her eye on a safe egress to the Atlantic, but her methods and ambitions will be dependent upon her position vis-à-vis the United Nations. I don't think for a minute she will agree to withdraw her troops from the southern Caspian seacoast and northern Iran.

Events proved I was wrong about northern Iran, although Moscow did manage to get a revision of the Caspian frontier. Events also proved I was wrong about Albania. For the rest, I believe the forecast was not inaccurate, even including the reach towards the Atlantic by establishing a common frontier with northern Norway.

When I returned to New York I underwent a series of physical examinations, discovering I had the gout and bad eyes, both of which have plagued me ever since. The occulist was puzzled when he examined me. "Were you wounded in the head?" he asked. Certainly not, I told him. Then, as an afterthought, he examined the glasses the Serbian occulist had hurriedly made for me in April 1941. "That's what it is," he said. "The left lens is so incorrect that it has twisted all the muscles of that eye. It will never get much better."

In July, with new spectacles and Marina finally recovered and frisky, I thought it time for a delayed honeymoon. I had had no holiday since the war started, September 1, 1939. The only serious problem was financial. A large movie producer asked me to call at his New York office and made the surprising suggestion that I write the scenario for a war picture on Russia. I declined, saying I had neither the time nor the experience. He then astonished me by offering $10,000 if I would simply allow my name to be used as author of the script, even though I would not have to do a moment's work. This was so patently dishonest that I refused indignantly. I wonder if I would be so innocent today.

The problem was settled when *Life* magazine ordered a Soviet piece which I could in all honesty write and which was sufficiently well paid to finance our honeymoon. For this I had proposed Montana to Marina and she seemed enthusiastic, liking the idea of mountains and proclaiming that she had ridden horseback often in her childhood. We took off for Glacier Park and spent three days in the lodge there while a pack train, cook and guide were assembled. During our wait I took Marina out on the hotel golf course and tried to get her interested in the game. She was far happier picking flowers.

Marina's brief encounter with golf caused her momentary horror. During my weeks with the Greek Army in 1940 and later in Athens, I had acquired a small vocabulary of Greek oaths that, to her embarrassment, I occasionally used when irked, for example, at bad service in a restaurant; we would invariably find the offending waiter was a Greek. Marina begged me to teach her at least one equivalent American phrase. In deep secrecy, swearing her to discretion, I whispered: "Niblick." From then on I would occasionally hear her mutter "Niblick" if she dropped a suitcase on her toes. I had forgotten this when, on my first Montana round of golf I soon landed in a trap. This was still before irons were known only by their numbers and I sadly told the caddy: "Give me a niblick." Marina was aghast. She came running out of a field of flowers muttering: "How can you talk that way?"

We took off, four people and six horses. The first day's ride was more than twenty miles. As Marina stumbled from her mount that evening, confessing her previous acquaintance with horses had been somewhat less than she had told me, she blazed: "If I didn't have to ride this damned thing back again I'd divorce you right away."

Those were glorious weeks. We forgot the war, the occupation of Greece, even that her brother was in an Italian jail. The Germans were at El Alamein and Stalingrad when we disappeared into the Rockies; they were still there when we emerged. We caught all the trout we wanted including a fourteen-pound Mackinaw I took at the mouth of the Kootenai River. Marina, not impressed, gave him to a forest ranger. We saw hundreds of brown bear, a few grizzlies and quantities of moose. One day Marina was busy in our tent while I fished nearby. She heard something at the entrance flap and, without looking, said: "Any luck?" Getting no answer, she turned, saw an embarrassed, hornless moose, and disappeared shrieking under the tent's back wall.

From Montana we went to an uncle's house in the Adirondacks and by the time we got back to New York, fit, happy, brown as berries, I knew it was time to get to work. My assignment was roving chargé d'affaires for the *Times* in the Middle East, Turkey and Russia so I decided the best thing would be to go straight back to Cairo. It was clear the Allies had been building up for an offensive to drive Rommel out of Egypt.

I got my American war correspondent's papers immediately but when I applied for accreditation to the British forces I was refused on the ground that I had been disaccredited in Greece. When I reached London later, I saw Colonel Edgworth-Johnson, chief of that section of the War Office, and made him extract my dossier from his files. This was curtly marked "disaccredited" with the date and "application refused" with another date. I challenged Edgworth-Johnson to show me reference to when my accreditation had first been granted, pointing out it was difficult to disaccredit someone not accredited.

The bureaucratic delay dragged on and I occupied myself as best I could in Washington. I jotted in a notebook:

On November 10, 1942, Justice Felix Frankfurter bet me a meal in the best restaurant for himself and wife, myself and wife and a new hat for the winning wife that this would be the last winter of the war (1942-1943).

Frankfurter said he had asked Byrnes (then Supreme Court Justice, later economic boss, former Senator) if the President had called for a declaration of war the day before Pearl Harbor what the vote would have been. Byrnes estimated that at least two-thirds of Congress would have been in opposition.

November 11, twenty-four years after an armistice ended World War I, I had a long talk with Secretary of State Cordell Hull, I noted:

Hull appeared very old and frail but full of vigor. At times, when he was angry (such as when he talked of Wendell Willkie and "interference by rabble-rousers" with United States policy) he swore, using the word "Christ" frequently.

He attributed the improvement of the situation in Africa to careful United States policy towards Vichy, which permitted the spadework to be prepared.

In 1933, the President asked Hull how he felt about recognizing Russia. He replied with a brief memorandum stating that although the idea was extremely unpopular in the nation at that time it was essential for two reasons. The first reason was less important: that the United States and Russia had always had friendly and cooperative relationships. The second reason was that he foresaw a period of great trouble in the world and it would be well to have Russia on our side.

I asked Hull whether he thought there would be a true postwar co-operative peace without full Russian participation and he said No. Then I asked him if he foresaw Russian cooperation and he said: "Russia has the alternative to live alone, armed to the teeth as she has been almost constantly since the days of Catherine the Great (although not always securely enough armed) or to become a full part of the world, to make and receive concessions in a mutual international cooperative scheme. Our policy has been and will continue to be one of seeking to build up trust abroad especially, in this case, in Russia. I hope that Russia will see the light and will take its full part in an ordered world after the war."

In the end I solved my bureaucratic problems. Jumbo Wilson was in the Middle East, soon to be commander-in-chief. I sent him a message and he had me accredited to him personally, stipulating that this accreditation should be valid for all forces under his command, army, navy and air. However, because of the contretemps with the British over credentials I had lost an enormous amount of time; Montgomery's dazzling Libyan offensive got under way and Eisenhower staged his landing in Morocco and Algeria. I therefore flew to London and arranged for Marina to follow as soon as possible. She still had a Greek passport so Washington could not prevent her departure, as it did for American women. In fact, Marina would have kept her Greek citizenship indefinitely had she not eventually become bored by having to wait in one line at each border-crossing while the children and I were placed in another, quicker queue.

Marina also had her officer's identification card as a lieutenant-nurse in the Greek forces and this was to prove invaluable in getting her around a war that was crisscrossed with military barriers. The only trouble was that I could fly to England on an Army Air Force transport while Marina had to come by convoy. Several ships in her formation were lost to U-boats but her Dutch captain reassured her saying, "You don't need to worry. You'll never know if anything hits us. We're carrying explosives."

# 12

## HITCHHIKING

## AROUND THE AXIS

I ARRIVED IN ENGLAND SHORTLY AHEAD OF MARINA, LUMBERING through the North Atlantic storms in her slow and dangerous convoy. My clipper landed in the Shannon River of Ireland, and from Foynes we drove through a gay landscape: plenty of fat sheep, many little pony carts drawn by stocky plump horses; thatched and sod-roofed carriages; peat bogs; and at last Limerick, a severe, stone, cold gray city on the banks of the Shannon. The small inn where I stayed was a cozy place with a peat fire going and a barmaid busily serving drinks. Two Irish soldiers were working hard consuming them when I arrived; both emphatically pro-German.

In London, where Marina joined me, we dwelled in great splendor at the Savoy Hotel in a huge room lined with picture windows looking out upon the Thames. The Savoy, which had been shaken up by the Luftwaffe, was rather empty and river rooms were not at a premium. Marina and I enjoyed our stay—her first in England—and even the food, about which everyone complained, seemed agreeable. Those were the days of Lord Woolton's potato bread (Woolton was food minister) and "macon," imitation bacon that came from frozen New Zealand sheep. Occasionally we had the treat of an omelet from swan's eggs poached from the King by an air marshal friend who lived in a houseboat. Legally, swans and their progeny belong to the crown.

While waiting to arrange Marina's papers for the next step onward to Cairo, I busied myself writing about occupied Europe. Apart from the horror, and feral cruelty of the Nazi empire, I was struck by how absurd it was. Jugoslav friends gave me a copy of an order published by the German authorities in Slovenia, which had been incorporated into the Reich, teutonizing the inhabitants by decree. With German thoroughness, acceptable translations for all Slavic names were listed. Thus, for example, anybody with the first name of Agapit had to call himself Julius. Bogoljub became Theophil, and Bogomil turned into Gottlieb. Bojan was ordered to change to Hermagoras, and Zlatica to Aurelia. What absolute boobs the Germans are, I thought.

I lunched with Claude Cockburn, whom I had known in 1938. He was still a Communist and working for the *Daily Worker* but it was evident his politics were changing fast. Cockburn was then as always brilliant and amusing.

He spoke of Harold Macmillan, a strong man and very pro-de Gaulle, who had gone as British minister to North Africa. Macmillan was a great drinker, known to call for a magnum of Scotch. Recently, when told he might be on the next royal honors list, he said: "Good. I shall call myself Lord Puck of Pook's Hill."

While I was in London Jan Masaryk invited me for dinner and told me, after postprandial cognac, that the Czech government had accused the Poles of refusing to admit that Teschen was seized by them in an aggressive Munich method; that Poland still coveted this province. What squabbles at such a time! The Poles were proving obdurate on the Teschen question, and Czech-Polish relations in London had deteriorated.

Masaryk was broadcasting home every two weeks. On Christmas he had made a sentimental talk about Prague and what he longed to do there after the war (walking the streets, and so forth). The Communists attacked him for expecting people to risk their lives listening to the forbidden radios hearing such "sentimental slush." Their view was: the Czechs must now rise, and kill.

Otto, the Hapsburg pretender to Austria, sent his chief adjutant, Count Czernin, to Masaryk. Jan, who could be exceedingly scurrile, told him: "Write this down and take it to your boss: 'If Otto leaves me alone, I will leave him alone. If he steps on my toes, I'll kick his royal arse.' Write that down." Czernin was a Czech citizen.

On February 18 Beneš, once again an *émigré* (he had been right-hand man to Dr. Thomas G. Masaryk in preparing the Czechoslovakian Republic during World War I) told me he had been forced to conclude this time that minority questions in central and eastern Europe must be radically settled after the present conflict. His light blue eyes blazing, the stubborn little President who had, alas, failed in a pinch when he let France and Britain sell him down the river in 1938, said:

> I believe that the minority questions of Central and Eastern Europe should be settled this time radically and definitively. We established independent nations but we did not definitely settle minority problems. Germany and Hungary used minorities as their tools and fifth columnists. I think that now we should begin after this war by reestablishing

independent nations and definitely settling questions of their frontiers and, after coming to a decision, completing it by effecting transfers of populations.

Of course this meant uprooting all central Europe. Yet, with bitter serenity, Beneš said:

When we decide this and do it, and only then, will we have a basis for the reconstruction of nations in a larger confederation. I think that if we do not settle first of all and definitively questions of minorities and frontiers, we shall have the greatest difficulties in settling the questions of bigger confederations or commonwealths of nations.

In the future it should not be possible in Europe either to create by the use of minority treaties or minority laws a special State in another State and prepare a large fifth column for a period of crisis or war as we have seen it happen in the present war. We must base national rights on human rights alone, as you do in the United States.

I asked Beneš if he meant by the above that all Germans should be expelled from Czechoslovakia's Sudetenland province and all Hungarians from Slovakia and Ruthenia. "Yes," he said grittily, "surely as many as possible." I then inquired whether he would be ready to cede Ruthenia to the Soviet Union, which generally referred to the area as Ukrainian (sub-Carpathian Ukraine). "Certainly not," he answered. History, unfortunately, was to prove him wrong even before his death in a sternly communized Czechoslovakian satellite of Moscow. Although thousands of Germans and Hungarians were expelled, thousands also stayed on and Ruthenia was snatched by Moscow without even a single murmur from Beneš.

Later I saw General Wladislaw Sikorski, prime minister of the fugitive Polish government who was to die not too long afterwards in a tragic airplane crash. Sikorski, who managed to retain his *sang-froid* while discussing the worsening relationship with Russia, acknowledged:

For the moment, I cannot deny that there are great differences with the Soviets. However, these can and must be overcome. The great technical successes the Red Army is now having will eventually cease. The Polish-Russian frontier of 1,400 kilometers is not only a Polish question but a question for all democracy. The Polish frontier regions with Russia have neither strategical nor economic importance for the USSR.

Despite all the difficulties now, an understanding is quite feasible. The present frontier is the result of an original compromise between the Russians and the Poles. If there is an ethnic minority in Poland it is not Russian. And the reason there is a minority is because we never tried to denationalize it.

Sikorski was a deeply sincere man, more flexible than he sounded and not, like so many Eastern European *émigrés*, an excessive orator. His subsequent death was a major loss.

In March I prepared to go on to North Africa and, eventually, the Middle East. Before my departure, Major Jules Dubois, acting executive officer for the American chief of staff, G-2 (Intelligence), sent a message on to Allied headquarters in Algiers, saying:

Mrs. Sulzberger is traveling with a passport under the name of Tatiani Marie Sulzberger. The Greek government is sending her to Cairo to perform some confidential work for the Greek department of information. Mrs. Sulzberger is a lieutenant in the Greek army nurses corps. Ambassador Biddle [American envoy to all *émigré* governments in London] has received a letter from the Greek information chief here requesting the highest possible priority for Mrs. Sulzberger. Mr. Sulzberger will inform General McClure in person about the confidential mission with which Mrs. Sulzberger is charged.

This was, I may confess, blarney but everything had to be maximized to obtain air priorities. I went ahead of Marina and paid for the blarney when the tail of my aircraft hit a house in Ireland. However, by a miracle no one in the blacked-out airplane was injured (we were all in seats facing backwards). After a few days' wait I flew on to Port Lyautey, a United States Navy airbase in Morocco. I spent a few days in Rabat and Casablanca, largely devoted to arranging to forward my lieutenant-wife on her "confidential mission." Happily, I found two *New York Times* friends serving as Air Force officers and they undertook to guarantee her passage. When I reached Algiers I discovered that Ed Kennedy and Dan Deluce were living in a magnificent house with several other AP reporters. They promised to look after Marina while I went to Tunisia.

At that time Montgomery's British army was hammering the Mareth Line, last Nazi defense to the east, and Patton's Second Corps was trying to break through from the west. I joined the latter in the neighborhood of a Tunisian hamlet called El Guettar.

I was with a small outfit on the Gafsa-Gabes highway when two army sergeants, a thin Devonshire boy named William Brown and a slight youngster named Joseph Randall, of State Center, Iowa, shook hands in midafternoon and slapped each other's backs. That was the way the British, coming from El Alamein, and the Americans, coming from the American east coast via Morocco and Algeria, met on the invious African continent. The scene was astonishingly tranquil, taking place on a road running through barley and wheat fields at the foothills of the Mannaou Mountains. A yellow British armored scout car followed by two others saw some dull green vehicles approaching and when bowl-shaped helmets hove into view of their binoculars, Brown said: "Those are Jerries." Fortunately, an instant later someone shouted: "No, by God, they're Yanks." The Americans accelerated, arrived and hugged their new-found friends, confiding: "We're glad to see someone else besides squareheads." When Montgomery's liaison officers arrived that evening at our encampment they casually asked: "Have you Yanks got any beer?"

As the Allies began to round up increasing packets of German prisoners among the arid, stony djebels, I heard one Nazi complain that many prisoners were being put in the custody of Indian troops by the British. An English officer cut him short: "In the first place they're better than any European troops going and anyway you should be flattered because they're the original Aryans."

I rode back from Tunisia, once I heard Marina had arrived, in a plane including Colonel (soon to be Brigadier General) Elliott Roosevelt, the President's son, and a load of detonators for antipersonnel bombs. Back in Algiers I had my first good talk with General Eisenhower, the Allied commander, a pleasant, informal, surprisingly young-looking man. He wanted to treat all his war correspondents exactly like officers on his own staff, trusting them with the most confidential information and secret plans, so as to be sure they would not unwittingly give something away in speculation because they didn't know its importance. He complained that he had been unfairly treated by the American press because of his administrative policies in liberated North African territory but insisted his job was to get on with the war and to insure order and maximum stability in his rear, not to make political decisions that would affect the future. This was particularly true with respect to the internecine quarrels among the various French factions, above all the Gaullists and anti-Gaullists. Eisenhower impressed me by his sincerity, decency, tolerance and ability, when needed, to take swift decisions. I didn't think he was as easy-going as he looked with his wide grin, amiable blue eyes, and little snub nose; but he had a most informal way about him. He pointed at his nose and said: "You know, the Germans tell the Arabs I'm a Jew—like Roosevelt." Eisenhower said his greatest concern was to stress the complete national equality of all Allied forces serving under him and to emphasize the total integration of his headquarters. "I don't mind if someone gets angry and calls another officer a son of a bitch," he said, "But I'll send him home if he calls him an English son of a bitch."

Back in Algiers I found Marina ensconced in the AP villa, happily acting as housemother to Kennedy, Deluce, *et alii*. We had a splendid reunion. Next morning, when I arose and came downstairs, I found Dan, a lanky six foot three, standing asleep, propped in a corner, on one leg like a stork. I would never have believed this possible and have never seen such a performance repeated by anyone.

Thanks to Dubois's letter, I got priority for the two of us on a DC-3 flying to Cairo. Marina, whose Greek Orthodox superstitions run deep, was apprehensive when our party (all the rest were military) was joined by Archbishop Spellman of New York on one of his indefatigable visits to troops. (The Greek Church still maintains its bias against Rome.) We spent a night in Tripoli, which I had last seen under the Italians, and when we got to Benghazi, Shan Sedgwick joined us, smelling of garlic and wrapped in a fleece-lined coat. Marina and the archbishop were both given special latrine facilities at the heavily cratered Benghazi field—separate-but-equal hulks of shot-down German Junkers aircraft. Our skipper let Spellman handle the controls for a while in the air. I wrote a not very humorous story about the archbishop qualifying as a sky-pilot. This was killed by the censorship as "military information."

In Cairo I established a combined home-and-*New York Times* office in two large adjoining rooms of the Continental Hotel, overlooking a park filled with vermilion shrubs. I hired Gerda Smith-Ross, the charming wife of a British Intelligence officer, as secretary. She looked after the group of us: Sedgwick, Leslie Nichols, Ramses Massif, a young Egyptian (now a high official of the United Nations), and an interpreter named Sharif.

I was glad to get back into the Arab-Balkan mixture of which Cairo was the focal point. By the spring of 1943 Dalton's SOE had spread out various tentacles including holding companies for guerrilla operations. Through our friends working under these umbrellas in Greece, Jugoslavia, Albania and even Rumania and Bulgaria, I was able to keep an eye on occupied East Europe.

That Easter Marina and I were invited to luncheon by Prince Lotfallah, a wealthy Christian Arab who lived in one immense palace and rented others of equal splendor to the British for use as headquarters. The meal for about eighteen people was served on gold plates by a retinue in the Lotfallah livery. The feature was a paschal lamb borne by four servants on a huge golden platter and twice marched around the jubilant table.

After we returned to the Continental late that afternoon I left Marina, summoned Sharif, called a taxi, and told the driver to head out of town. When we reached a filthy village, I ordered a halt and told Sharif to follow me down an alley. At the first dried clay hut, without windows and with open door, I poked my nose in and saw a woman, half a dozen scabious children, some chickens and a baby lying on a heap of rags.

One of its eyes festered and was crawling with flies. I suggested to the mother that trachoma was easily curable and she should take her baby to a clinic. She seemed embarrassed. Sharif had a long, earnest conversation. Finally he explained: "It isn't trachoma. You see, under our law any healthy boy, when he grows up, has to do military service. But his father needs this one in the fields to help draw the plough. So his mother put his eye out with a pin." At that point, reflecting on Lotfallah's princely luncheon, I knew there had to be an Egyptian revolution.

In May I left Marina and once again headed for Moscow. I drove slowly across the Sinai Desert and Palestine, over the Lebanon and Syria to Iraq, talking with the bickering political leaders. One of Emir Abdullah's ministers, a courtly scholar named Samir Rifai, quoted to me a verse from Ibn an-Mu'tazz: "The Pleiades in the latter part of the night resemble the opening of a silver-studded bridle." He told me that an Arab prided himself most on three things: the birth of a boy, the emergence of a poet, and the foaling of a mare. He spoke at length about the emergence in Arabia of three great religions, Judaism, Christianity and Islam, because of the proximity of man and the eternal, the nearness of the stars, the lack of any insignificant trifles to deflect philosophical contemplation. Then he added: "Now I fear tranquillity is gone. There are times of bitter trouble ahead, of killing."

From Baghdad I traveled to a barren place, called Qhanaqin, near Iraq's frontier and started an extensive hitchhike from there to Teheran. The British were running truck convoys across Iran to supply their occupying forces and provide material for shipment to Russia. I wanted to see what Iran was like and how the convoy system worked. It was enjoyable but I discovered the Iranian and Punjabi drivers from the Indian army were more dashing than skillful. Two trucks were wrecked under me. Nevertheless, on my trek I encountered boar hunts in jeeps, cockfights between trained wild chukar partridges, Afridi commandos who spoke no English and probably the best crap-shooting chaplain in the United States Army.

To remember this "Burma Road," starting under a nimbus of hot desert dust and already dotted with wrecked lorries, graves of drivers, carcasses of donkeys, cows and vicious sheep dogs, I kept a diary all the way across the formidable Zagros Mountains to Qazvin, the transferral point where supplies were dumped in a Russian depot. This read:

Starting in Baghdad in an Indian railway car, which a British major constantly squirted with an Iraqi Flit called *"Imshi"* (Arabic for scram) and on which all manner of insect life seems to thrive, the beginning of the trail was already steaming in the 6 A.M. sun. Breakfast in an English colonel's jerry-built house with a swallow perched in a nest above the table. Pink-beaked gray partridges run in and out, pecking at sugar on the floor. Some officers train these birds for cockfights.

A security officer comes in, complaining of a fire lit by bandits near the ordnance dump. Yesterday a Polish sentry was shot by a camp robber and a posse is off with old-fashioned irons, after the culprit. There is still constant trouble with looting and smuggling frontier tribesmen.

The town signs are in Polish, English, Arabic and Iranian in this Tower of Babel. Streets are filled with a mixture of all, including square-faced Slav women uniformed as ATS and flat-hatted, flat-visaged Ghurkhas from the Tibetan frontier. I arrange passage on a dilapidated Dodge truck loaded with sacks of wheat. It is driven by a diminutive Iranian gentleman named Akhbar who looks as if he has just emerged from a medieval Persian miniature and handles a car accordingly.

While skinny, bearded Akhbar turns the truck, we are checked off by a friendly Russian who proudly proclaims that his wife speaks English. Rattle past dumps of tires, steel bars and sacks of grain with steering wheel bound to dashboard by wires, self-starter busted, and ignition working by twisting of loose wires; windshield, scarred by bullet holes, throws off occasional splinters.

Desert rises by slow ridges toward Zagros Range, hazy under the hot sky. Faded paper roses with which Akhbar has decorated his cap flop despairingly. Dry yellow rough valleys like parts of Arizona.

Road gangs of ragged men and women slowly tarring highway with rollers of empty gasoline barrels. Intermittent, untended patches of wheat ready for harvest, although the country borders on famine. Oasis of green by a swift-running stream as road winds upward toward snow-spattered mountains. Handsome walled, palm-ringed cluster of spacious buildings by a hideous town of mud huts. Great shaggy goats grazing in the scrub near buttresses of old fortress.

Crooked beggar in rags bends over, bowing to Allah and screaming for baksheesh. Never before have I seen such rattletrap trucks as these vehicles driven so badly at such speed over such atrocious roads. Among many admirable Iranian gifts to civilization mechanical science does not figure. By the seventh wrecked truck, passed a caravan of fierce, dark gentlemen on horses. Appallingly steep grade rises on cliff above river valley. Huge truck hurtles from other direction, just managing to careen past Akhbar.

Turgid green trout stream rushes by a cluster of flowers like rhododendron in an upland glade. Grouchy English army driver in lorry pushes a wrecked vehicle before him while its Iranian chauffeur grins. Another mud-brick village by a stream with storks stretching on roof-tops and roses rambling in the shade. In hollow beneath high pass, leaf-bowered roadside café serves Iranian drivers on tables and benches draped with Oriental rugs, while others squat on haunches in orchard grove.

Pass convoy of lorries bearing Afridi commandos wearing turbans instead of usual green commando berets. On a steep, sunny pass Akhbar smashes up truck nicely, leaving it with radiator boiling over, fender dented in, wires dangling in all directions and gas tank leaking: he cranks energetically but nothing happens.

An hour later an Indian army Studebaker loaded with Punjabi troops offers a hitch. Akhbar mournfully accepts baksheesh and proceeds to squat gloomily by the road. Beside a broken-down village by a poplar grove is an Indian troop bivouac, near a refreshment truck lettered: "TEAD—the soldier's drink." Pass eleventh wrecked truck in a hundred miles, this one smashed below a cliff on a hairpin bend.

The business of bumming a new ride starts early after breakfast. A trailer-truck is discovered going in the right direction and I am loaded with my kit on top of great bags of peanuts bound for Russia. The Iranian driver, named Ali, wears a black karakul hat with sky-blue center. Ali proves that he is better than the average native chauffeur but with the major fault of coasting down all hills out of gear despite his seven-ton load.

We pass ancient rock carvings on a sheer cliff and continue through a green, stork-filled valley fringed by snowcapped crags. We reach a little garden grove beneath trees grouped about a circular pond. Grinning children douse the dust clots off the wheels with gas cans of water, demanding baksheesh. Ali squats in the shade by a waterside café, eating sour milk and herbs.

Above snow level we cross the divide and Ali coasts downhill, gathering speed and taking the sudden bends at a crazy pace. At the entrance to an old stone bridge is a large truck parked nearly athwart the road, with a native driver bent over the wheel, asleep. Here the British supply line joins the main highway of America's Persian Gulf Service Command in a sizable, shabby town. We unload and the movement control officer calls the nearby United States Army camp which sends a jeep along with two sergeants, excited about a successful gazelle hunt. They hunt in pairs; one drives cross-country after a herd while the other plugs away with a rifle.

A captain who used to boss a Newark trucking line invites me to sleep in his mud and straw-walled, canvas-topped hutment. We eat fried gazelle.

Sleep on my fur coat, waking up at 4 A.M. Today's convoy is already taking off and the broad trailer-truck is loaded with metals in the dark. The driver, a West Virginia farm boy, says he drives six hours every day hauling a heavily loaded truck and trailer. The short-handed units must get the stuff through to Russia. The driver, hitching his leather rifle case over the brake, says: "We got lots of Polacks and Russians in our bunch and they seem to be getting on pretty good with them Russkies."

We climb the pass through a winding river gorge. Groves of aspen grow beneath great brown thumbs of rock. Behind us wind dozens of heavy trucks, all marked with insignia in English, Persian and Russian. The driver grouses: "It takes a strong back and a weak mind to make a good truck driver." We pass a wreck folded up like an accordion and covered with the heavy rolls of barbed wire it was carrying. "The trouble with this place," says the driver, "is that there ain't nothing to drink except this lousy weak wine at six bits a bottle. I ain't seen any American beer since the case I swiped two months ago."

These drivers all call themselves "jockeys" and have erected in their camp a "jockey tent" with a radio, books and home-made furniture, including card and dice tables. One of the most popular figures among them is a gray-haired chaplain with an artistic knack of handling the dice. "Yeah," says the driver, "I suppose he wants to build a church with all our dough. He's a pretty good guy and we like him. He can throw the bull just as good as any of the rest of us."

The driver ruminates: "It was real hell last winter. If you think it's bad now you should have seen it then. We couldn't see ten feet ahead in the blizzards and we damn near froze sleeping in the trailers and using our lamps for heat. The trailers swung from side to side in a cockeyed way on the ice and it sure was dangerous. But except for these Iranians we don't have much casualties, and although some of our outfit have overturned their trucks they have been pretty lucky in escaping."

We descend and pass by a couple of boar hunters in a jeep. Details of military police in command cars and jeeps, armed with rifles, keep the trucks down to the thirty-five-mile speed limit and enforce the safety rules. At the end of the line we reach Qazvin, where our load of metal will be handed on to the Russians. Here signs are in Russian only. Red Army men stroll about clad in summer uniforms and carry tommy guns. Set in the background of a rotting, ancient, mud-built city wall, topped with petal-shaped crenellations, are two green-topped mosque domes. Beggars wander about the streets as we get into the command car for the final trip to Teheran. We sweep out past lean, dirty beggars and mountaineer porters across a fine valley replete with wheat and herds of grazing camels. "It's good to get out on a road that isn't blocked," says the major. "This is a tough racket and I sure hope the Russians like us. They ought to."

In Teheran I stayed with Major General Donald D. Connolly, commander of the American Persian Gulf command. An officer with no previous diplomatic experience and a fairly brusque manner, he did his best to get on with the Russians. I attended various informal gatherings in his basement filled with interpreters, which he called "collations." There was plenty of drink and talk. At one, Connolly said, looking at the Soviet superintendent of Iranian railways (for the Red Army) and tamping his pipe: "You fellows, Colonel Vorobey, have been lousy in rail clearance until recently. We have been piling up stuff at our railheads and depots much faster than you have been moving it north."

Vorobey, a tall, dark, lean fellow, gulped a vodka and waved his hands at the interpreter. "General," he said, "you are a good man and you are only holding back 5 per cent of the stuff we want. But you [and here he hugged Colonel Paul Yount, American director of railways], you are keeping back 15 per cent." Vorobey, grinning hugely at his joke, proceeded to search the stocky Yount's pockets.

Lieutenant Colonel Makarov, a blond Muscovite who joined the Red Army during its fledgling civil war days at the age of fifteen, interrupted this conversation by suddenly throwing back his head and, in a gradually expanding and sweet voice, chanting the virtues of Stenka Razin. Naval Captain Shinkov, neat, chubby and bald-headed, with the tiniest of white mustaches, joined in the chorus. *"Chort vozmi,"* shouted a thick-set Red Army tank major with scarlet lines running athwart his broad gold epaulets, "give us an American song." And, lamely, in the wake of the fine Slavic tonal efforts, someone struck up with "Drink to Me only With Thine Eyes."

Connolly, a grim-faced, gray-haired man, had enough of the gaiety. He pounded the table separating him from Vorobey and said: "We won't make any phony promises to you but I am telling you we will give you fellows more every month and you had better be ready to take it away. We are here for one thing and one thing only. We are here to deliver the goods to Russia and we are not interested in anything else—economics, politics, or international diplomacy. I am not going to get mixed up in any of those things. I have told it to you Russians. I have told it to the British. I have told it to the Iranians."

"Gospodin General, he is a very good man," said Vorobey in pidgin English. "May our aid to Russia flow like this," said an American captain pouring a long drink. "And like German blood," added a sulky-looking Russian, wounded at Dniepropetrovsk.

While I waited for the infrequent shuttle flight to Moscow, I wandered around town and dined as often as possible with Firouzé, picking her up at the walled compound of her house and rattling in a fiacre to hillside taverns. She still delighted me with her tinkling risibility but she also told me serious things. A civil war was taking place between the Iranian army and the powerful Qashqai tribe. An Iranian colonel and his troops had been captured by the tribesmen south of Shiraz and there was alarm that if the government didn't soon stamp out the rising there might be more trouble with the Bakhtiaris, another clan.

The Russians had started to ship abroad through Teheran well-printed propaganda designed to prove that freedom of religion existed in the USSR (which was, of course, untrue). Moscow had closed down the Godless League and its atheist magazine, *Bezbozhnik* (godless), claiming the publication had to be curtailed because of the shortage of paper; but plenty of paper was used to produce the new pamphlets in English and French on church activities. Curiously enough one large book purporting to show free religion was printed on the presses of *Bezbozhnik* and (by mistake) stamped accordingly.

The Americans were appalled by Russian toughness. A drunken Soviet officer was arrested by British MPs and turned over to the Russians. The next day a note of apology was sent to the Persian government and the British mission by the Red Army's local command. The note said rather curiously that the officer would have been severely reprimanded "but unfortunately he died during the night." Connolly told me a veteran Soviet pilot accepted delivery of one of the P-39s we had been furnishing to the Russians. They were assembled in Iran and flown up by Soviet pilots. This poor character ran his plane into a mountain. Connolly decided it would be a nice gesture to put on a special funeral. The American commander and some of his chief officers showed up for the service, but the Russians only sent a minor official. This official arose and spoke: "Stalin said a soldier must know his weapons. Obviously this pilot did not. And he committed the unpardonable crime of smashing up a valuable plane." That was all. There was embarrassed silence among the Americans.

I flew back to Moscow just as Stalin startled the entire Marxist world by announcing the dissolution of the Comintern, the international organization that controlled all Communist parties and molded their policies according to Kremlin dictates. By this time I had a new secretary, Tania Sofyana having quit the *Times* because she disliked Parker. Her successor, Nadja, was heartbroken by the news. Although bitter against the Stalin purges and the prewar brutality that had caused so much death and suffering, she still remained a devout Party member. Her husband had been terribly wounded while fighting against the White Guards during the postrevolutionary civil war. Now she came to me, tears streaming down her face, asking: "What does it mean? What did we fight and suffer for if it now can be erased by one ukase?"

On May 19 Joseph E. Davies, former ambassador to Moscow, arrived on a special mission from President Roosevelt. Davies, who had written a distorted memoir called *Mission to Moscow* that had been made into a movie, had the words *Mission to Moscow* emblazoned in English and Russian on the sides of his plane. He brought along a copy of the film to be shown at the Kremlin. Admiral Stanley, the regular ambassador who had succeeded Steinhardt, was furious about the Davies visit and enough of a frank old seadog so that he could not successfully mask his pique.

Davies told me he had a secret letter from Roosevelt to Stalin. This was an invitation to hold the first East-West summit meeting. He talked with me at Stanley's residence and kept referring to "my good friend, Ambassador Stanley," in a way that made the admiral cringe. I noted:

Davies said that on the way up he stopped at Stalingrad and was shown around the ruins. He said he had placed a wreath on the mass grave which has been set aside as a memorial. He said he made a brief, unprepared speech. I asked: "What did you say, Mr. Ambassador?" He replied that he could not recall because the speech had not been prepared in advance. Then he interrupted himself and added, "Oh, wait a minute. Stamm may have something." His nephew, Lieutenant Stamm of the Navy, who was traveling with him as his aide, reached into his pocket and pulled out a typewritten copy of the "forgotten" speech.

An excerpt from my diary:

Moscow, *June 7, 1943*

Today I heard a story that gives me the creeps. When Stalin gave a dinner for Davies at the Kremlin, a movie was shown, as is the general custom. Believe it or not, it was *Mission to Moscow*. Davies had brought a special reel with him. Apparently even the members of the Politburo snickered when they saw themselves represented in this ridiculous picture.

To my intense disappointment, working conditions for a reporter had not improved despite the perceptibly better military situation. It was the same old business of rewriting Soviet press dispatches, scrabbling about for tidbits from the diplomats, most of whom knew little, and arguing endlessly with the Soviet authorities who neither allowed visits to the front nor permitted interesting interviews. One knew that the Red Army was better, that all the old officer traditions, even the shoulder-board *pogony* epaulets of the Czar were back, and that, despite the end of the Comintern, the Red Army was directing highly efficient partisan movements in occupied Europe. A Russian friend gave me an officers' handbook which specified rigid saluting, and even forbade commissioned ranks from carrying luggage or parcels.

I wrote military commentaries based on expertise I didn't possess and almost all of which were hatcheted to death by the censors. I lunched twice at Ehrenburg's who pendulated between friendship and hostility. Later, in his memoirs, he confided that Lozovsky had warned him: "It's best not to frequent the Americans at all." And once again I sat next to the sodden Sholokhov at a meal; I marveled that he could drink so much without apparently affecting his health.

Uncle Arthur came to Moscow on an inspection trip for the American Red Cross and was entertained lavishly although he accomplished little. The foreign commissariat gave him a lunch at its guest house where Vyshinsky told me civil servants would soon again be given ranks and uniforms, just as under the Czar. There was also an official dinner of ten courses in the banquet hall of the National Hotel. As we stuffed ourselves with caviar, sturgeon, Kiev cutlets, beef stroganov, salads and the complicated desserts of the excellent Russian cuisine, famished-looking waiters tucked scraps in their pockets. Food was still very tight. I saved my breakfast each day for Nadja, except for the tea, and she carefully wrapped it in newspaper to take home to her children. Often, looking like a starved harpy, she would stick a finger in the jam and lick it.

One night a Soviet architect named Alexandrov gave a tremendous party for the diplomats and invited us. Poor Alexandrov—he lived in a squalid room far from the magnificent apartment where he was assigned to entertain on behalf of the government's propaganda and culture divisions. The apartment was filled with icons, handsome furniture, ecclesiastical monstrances, tapestries, drapes. There was an excellent orchestra and all the prettier young ballerinas of the Bolshoi chorus. We ate, drank and sang until morning, finally staggering out into the summer sunlight. When Alexandrov had seen us off with courtly gestures he slunk back to the sordid reality of his own furtive life.

I visited the New Maiden convent in whose cemetery Stalin's wife, Allilujeva, was buried beneath a lovely marble headstone. I trudged through long evenings investigating Moscow's innumerable alleys and noted:

Among the signs of hard times has been the rise in the price of vodka which shot up from 15 to 60 rubles a bottle. Vodka serves as *valuta* or a valuable like foreign currency. In the winter when there is no firewood, you can always get some with vodka. There are queues at the curious Moscow Cocktail Bar because it can get vodka. Officers on leave are full of money, but there's nothing for them to buy, and sometimes they pay as much as 400 rubles for a bottle.

The Cocktail Bar, incidentally, sold for stiff prices mixed drinks, based on vodka, including cherries, plums, cucumbers. The favorite was called a Cowboy Cocktail.

Irritated as I was at the regime and the incredible bureaucracy which frustrated all efforts to work seriously, I could not help cherishing an enormous affection for and sympathy with the Russian people. On June 20 I wrote in my diary:

Today I visited the Yalokhov Church for the 10 A.M. Sunday service. Dozens of poor old beggars, men and women, line the entrance asking for kopecks. This is the largest functioning church in Moscow. It was crowded with hundreds of peasant women in shawls, men, old and young, children. Standing behind me were an army captain and a woman army doctor in uniform. One is impressed with the magnificent vestments of the bearded priest; incense; crowds weaving and bobbing, praying and bowing, kissing icons, holding children up to kiss them; the beautiful singing led by a swaying, shaven-headed man in a Russian blouse; pitiful, tiny, faithful women with bowed heads draped in kerchiefs, their eyes mirroring little happiness.

Finally, after my last request to travel had been refused, either to Leningrad or to the front at Kursk, where it seemed there might soon be a big battle, I had an awful row with Palgunov. He spoke good French and I was able to make plain my opinion in abrupt and accurate fashion, calling him an *"espèce de morpion mécanique."* He merely stared above his thick-lensed spectacles, saying nothing but glowing like a hot samovar. Soon the censorship of my dispatches was even tougher; I resolved to leave.

Eddy Rickenbacker, the World War I American flying ace, had come to Moscow in his own B-24 bomber on a liaison and propaganda mission and Rick agreed to take me out with him to Cairo. On a July morning, before dawn, we stood on an airfield near Moscow. It was still so cold at that time of day that one's breath bellied forth as in winter. There was a full crew and no room in the plane but I spread my fur-lined coat in the bomb bay, after extracting a promise from Rick that no one would absent-mindedly open it. There I stretched out to sleep as we swayed gently through the summer air like a canoe. We flew nonstop to Habbaniyeh in Iraq, then an unheard of feat of endurance, refueled and were in steaming Cairo late that afternoon.

Marina had accepted a cocktail invitation out near the Pyramids at the home of Richard Casey, the Australian who was Britain's minister of state in the Middle East. Drinks were served on a terrace. Although I drank nothing but orangeade, the heat was so overwhelming by contrast with the climate I had just left, that I passed out and came to with Marina holding my wrist anxiously while the lovely Crown Princess of Greece (later Queen) Frederika, mopped my brow with a damp napkin. I stayed in bed three days.

By this time the Jugoslavs and Greeks were fighting with each other just as much as they resisted the Axis, and the Hungarians were trying to get out of a war now evidently turning sour. Count Stephen von Bethlen, a well-known Conservative, sent word secretly to the Allies that he could guarantee an invasion of Hungary would not be resisted locally if Budapest were not bombed and if the return of Transylvania and Slovakia were promised. This arrogant suggestion was, of course, spurned and Prime Minister Kallay savagely criticized Bethlen, saying: "You steered the car down a steep grade, destroyed the brakes and threw away the steering wheel, and now you want me to get it on a new road."

The British changed their policy and established liaison missions with the Communist Partisans in Jugoslavia and Greece, thus granting a form of *de facto* recognition that had hitherto been reserved to royalist guerrillas.

It was also becoming apparent that there would be violence in the post-war Middle East. I wrote: "Already determined factions of Jews and Arabs (in Palestine) are secretly engaged in preparations for militant action. Arabs and Jews have been buying arms and ammunition. The Jews also are building a formidable secret force." Moshe Shertok (later Israel's Foreign Minister Sharett), head of the Political Department of the Jewish Agency in Palestine, warned: "It would be wrong to consider the Jews incapable of deeds of despair if driven to extremes of exasperation."

Friends in Turkey had sent me detailed accounts of a capital levy against non-Moslems in that country and begged me to expose it. I went to Ankara and discovered persecution specifically aimed at the active Greek, Armenian and Jewish minorities who were being economically wiped out and then, to make matters worse, ruthlessly drafted into work battalions and sent on forced labor.

The new Turkish law, Varlik Vergisi, was an obvious reflection of the Nazi influence that gained strength after Hitler's invasion of Russia. The Allies were so worried about jeopardizing their position in neutral Turkey that they failed to protest and instructed their censorship, extending across the Middle East to North Africa and England, that all news of the Varlik was to be banned. After I reached Ankara I discussed this situation with Steinhardt, who had become our ambassador there. He pretended to disapprove of this monstrous law that was literally wiping out the Christian and Jewish minorities but professed himself unable to get Allied censorship elsewhere lifted. He added: "Of course, the Turks will ban any stories on the subject." (He had helped arrange the Allied censorship of Varlik news.)

I decided to act on my own. First I made a careful survey of the Varlik. Then I wrote several dispatches which, as I expected, were held up. Selim Sarper, a tough, highly educated Heidelberg graduate who was later Turkish foreign minister, summoned me to see him at the press section of the foreign office. "These are false," he said to me, slapping copies of my articles on a table before us. "You are merely making trouble for yourself by trying to send such calumnies. Furthermore, as you know, it has been arranged that no rumors of this nature can be transmitted by reporters from elsewhere. Your authorities are aware of the danger of trouble-making for the Allied cause."

I took my passport out and opened it to my Soviet visa which, fortunately, was still valid. "Selim," I said, "I know there is a stop on the subject of the Varlik in all allied areas. Nevertheless, I know you are a reasonable man. As you can see from this passport I can go to Moscow as soon as I wish. I doubt very much if the Russians would care whether I wrote the truth—or greatly magnified it—on this subject. In fact, they don't care very much for Turkey these days."

"Let's be reasonable," said Sarper. Next day he asked me to join him in the office of Prime Minister Saraçoglu. Line by line we went over my articles. Finally, after hours of debate, they agreed to send them off from Ankara.

A government newspaper I quoted set forth the Varlik's philosophy:

There are persons who have not fully comprehended the great changes that have taken place throughout the world and in Turkey during the last twenty-five years. The majority of these people are not foreigners, but persons whom the Ottoman Empire has left us as a heritage. They call themselves Turks and we have not yet been able to liquidate them. . . . By the liquidation of the above-mentioned people we mean the liquidation of a mentality. If they are our subjects, let them tuck up their sleeves and swing the hoe; if they are foreigners, let them leave this country.

When my series was printed it created a stir and the government hastened to withdraw the Varlik. The labor camps were closed down and, although no repayments were made, future levies ceased. Within a matter of weeks I received heartfelt messages of gratitude.

Despite this internal cancer, Turkey was a curious island of tranquillity so far as the war itself was concerned and therefore a focal point for espionage. George Earle, who had come from Bulgaria as naval attaché, told me he had been approached by both von Papen and Admiral Canaris, head of the Abwehr (Germany's secret service), claiming they had a plan to assassinate Hitler and set up a provisional government and would Earle please ask Roosevelt for his support against Russia in exchange. The main

gimmick seemed to be American abandonment of its unconditional surrender formula. Earle claimed he had written Roosevelt about this but
never received a reply. I was skeptical about Earle's direct contact with
von Papen and, above all, Canaris—although I did believe he might be in
touch with von Lersner, a friend of Papen who worked in the German
embassy cultural section. Both through the British, who were probing for
anti-Nazis in the German apparatus, and through Peters, the German journalist I later helped out of a Turkish prison, I knew Hitler had many
opponents in Turkey working with some kind of underground headed by a
former burgomaster named Goerdeler. Occasionally I saw anti-Nazis, the
most famous among whom was Ernst Reuter, then a refugee but later
mayor of West Berlin. I was given a few letters signed by Goerdeler and in
his handwriting to "prove" the sincerity of his opposition.

At that time, our Army Air Force, from a base in Libya, had bombed
Ploesti, the Rumanian oil field and refining center, and absorbed very
heavy losses. Five Congressional Medals of Honor were awarded. Some of
the planes had managed to limp away as far as Turkey where surviving
crews were well cared for by the Turks. They were, of course, eager to get
back to their units and I was asked to help smuggle one B-24 pilot over the
border when I took the Taurus express to Syria. He got false papers from
the embassy and a ticket to the south Turkish city of Adana. Then he
slipped into my compartment and I hid him in the berth, having first
generously tipped the conductor, and stood talking to the latter at the door
when Turkish customs inspection began; it passed me by with a cursory
glance.

I was back in Cairo when Italy surrendered.


CAIRO, *September 10, 1943*

I have gotten into a hell of a row with British censorship. Four days
ago I had lunch with several members of the *émigré* Greek government.
They were discussing the proposed new armistice Italy is about to sign.
The Greeks as well as other Allies are naturally being consulted. Prime
Minister Tsouderos afterwards showed me a draft copy of the armistice
agreement and I confirmed its details with King Peter. This is all Top
Secret and has not been announced. However, I have worked in Algiers
enough to know what a terrible communications jam is going to arise. I
was scared our story might get held up too long to make the paper.
Therefore, on September 7 I wrote a very brief dispatch giving the main
terms of the proposed armistice. I brought this down to Colonel Stevens,
chief British military censor, and told him to hang on to his hat; that the
story I was about to give him was merely to be approved and then held
by his office until the armistice was announced. I explained that I merely
wanted to send this piece from Cairo to backstop our staff in Algiers.
Steve understood completely. He sent my story up to General Scobie,

Jumbo Wilson's chief of staff. Scobie was astonished that the news of the armistice had leaked. Nevertheless, he played ball, approved the story and sent it back to Steve to be held.

On September 8 the armistice was announced by Eisenhower in Algiers, and Steve released my story immediately. To my astonishment—and also to the great embarrassment of Steve and Scobie—Eisenhower did not announce the terms but merely the fact that a cease-fire had been signed. Naturally I had not foreseen this eventuality. I had addressed my dispatch to NYKTIMES LONDON. The British, violating international cable regulations, held my story up in London and refused to forward it to New York. Yesterday a cable marked "MOST SECRET. OFFICER ONLY" was sent from the chiefs of staff to the commanders in chief, Middle East. A friend gave me a copy of this cipher message which was marked "MOST IMMEDIATE." This, when decoded, said:

1. Cable was received in London last night for *New York Times* from Cairo giving alleged text of armistice terms. It has been stopped here but may have been routed some other way as well as through London and, if so, stop should be imposed.

2. Strictest instructions should be issued to censors to prevent recurrence of such releases which endanger success of operations.

I had not knowingly sought to evade censorship here. Nevertheless, a big investigation is on. All kinds of colonels who have been paying little attention to me have been calling up suggesting drinks and meals, and I have already been visited by a couple who casually asked where I got my story. Stevens told me the same is happening to him.

Six Greek guerrilla representatives, flown out by the SOE chief there, Brigadier Myers, and accompanied by Major David Wallace, a British diplomat who had been parachuted back to Greece (where he was later killed), came to see me: three Communists (Tsimas, Roussos and Despotopoulos) and one then fellow traveller (Tsirimokos) from the Communist-led ELAS; a right winger (Pyromaglou) from Colonel Zervos' conservative EDES; and a liberal (Kartalis) from the center faction, EKKA. It was fascinating to hear them argue their political differences in a Cairo hotel, waving their hands and shouting. Nevertheless, they claimed they were now joined under a single command and would take their orders from Jumbo Wilson, Middle East commander. The pact, unfortunately, proved worthless. ELAS gobbled up EKKA and then destroyed EDES, a tougher nut, thus clearing the path for eventual civil war.

A Jugoslav lieutenant colonel, Mladen Zujuvić, whom I had known in Belgrade and who had been with Mihailović's *četniks,* also visited me. He brought the first detailed information I had received on the glamorous Communist Tito, who was forging an increasingly powerful resistance against both the Axis and Mihailović. On Oct. 13 I wrote:

"Zujuvić says Tito is really Josip Broz, a Slavonian. Mihailović had met Tito face to face in the late autumn of 1941 when Tito and some of his officers came to Mihailović's headquarters at Ravna Gora. They met in a little peasant hut. Draža ordered his guard out of the hut but Tito and his officers insisted that their guard, armed with rifles, should remain. When Mihailović asked, 'Why do you keep your guard?' one of Tito's officers replied, 'We have nothing to hide from them.' Everyone gave his name except for Tito who, when asked, replied merely 'Tito.' Major Mišić of Mihailović's side asked 'Gospodin Tito, why don't you give your name? Everybody else does. What are your reasons?' Tito replied, 'It will be known one day.' "

In those days I saw a great deal of Jugoslavia's young King Peter who inhabited a modest villa in a not very fashionable quarter, wore the uniform of his air force, but was not permitted to play the active role he desired. He was watched over carefully by the British and prevented from either returning to his country, as he professed to wish, or from exerting much influence on a situation that had already begun to develop into open civil war between the claimants to Hitler's fading power. On Oct. 15 I wrote:

"Lunch with King Peter today. He has told Mihailović: 'I haven't been very satisfied that he has been fighting enough. I also gave him directions to avoid any conflicts with the Partisans from his side and only to fight if he is attacked.'

"Peter claims there cannot be a settlement in Jugoslavia until there is complete British-American-Russian understanding. He saw Eden yesterday noon and told him that if the Russians would restrain the Partisans, Mihailović would follow British desires in terminating the civil war. Eden said he regretted but Britain did not feel it could defend Mihailović's actions in the forthcoming conference with the Russians (at Moscow).

"Peter complained that M.O.-4 (the British intelligence agency handling these Balkan operations for SOE), held up all messages to him (King Peter) from Mihailović between the dates of August 4 and September 29 and only brought the accumulated batch of telegrams to him yesterday, a half-hour after Eden had left."

CAIRO, *October 16, 1943*

SAW King Peter again today. He now says he is working on a scheme to have the few Jugoslav "Liberators" (American B-24s) organized into a flight that would parachute him into the country.

Afterwards I saw David Balfour, now a British major attached to Ambassador Rex Leeper's mission to the Greek *émigré* government. David has been all kinds of things in his career, but I suspect only, in the end, an intelligence agent. He was a Greek Orthodox priest until just before the Italians attacked in 1940 and confessor to the royal family. He next showed up with beard shaved off in a major's uniform.

He tells me a real civil war broke out in Greece October 8. The struggle is between the ELAS (Communist) and the EDES (rather Royalist). ELAS grabbed most of the Italian arms when they surrendered last month at the time of the armistice.

CAIRO, *October 16, 1943*

SECRETARY Hull is in town *en route* to Moscow for a foreign ministers' conference. This is the first time Hull has ever been in an airplane, but he took it okay. Years ago the Secretary was caught in a tunnel in a train and almost suffocated, and since then has had bad claustrophobia.

I saw Admiral Jack Duncan (naval attaché in Russia) in his hotel room. He is off at dawn with the Hull outfit. He is very furious and claims we are giving the Russians everything they ask for. Duncan saw Harry Hopkins a week ago in Washington. Hopkins said how clever the Russians were; they had persuaded the British to resume the Murmansk convoys. Jack adds, "We will lose some more American ships and get nothing for it."

On the eve of the Moscow conference, my own feeling is that the British are willing to agree to almost any Russian demands in Europe but not in Iran. We seem intransigeant, but with an election coming up next year we might grant the Russians much in exchange for bases in Siberia against Japan.

CAIRO, *October 17, 1943*

TODAY for the first time I was able to send the story of the Greek civil war—after a five-day fight with the censors. I can see why they were chary. An MO 4 officer named Hubbard, a New Zealander, has been shot by ELAS. Colonel Sarafis, now commander-in-chief of ELAS, used to have a small guerrilla band of his own. He was captured by ELAS and led around their villages as a prisoner like a monkey with his wrists tied together and drawn by a cord. After much mockery he was asked to become their commander-in-chief.

David Wallace came to lunch today. He operates under the name of "Edgar" inside Greece. He is just back from England where he saw Churchill and Eden. He said Churchill has an enormous globe at Chequers, too big to fit into 10 Downing Street. It has a glass measuring apparatus, David says. In his presence Churchill carefully measured the distance between Mountbatten's and MacArthur's headquarters. "Sixty-six hundred sixty miles," Churchill said. Then he looked at David and asked, "Do you think that's far enough apart?"

David said he spent a day with his wife Prudence, together with Eden and his wife. His basic conclusion was, 'The very great have no idea of

security." They talked over the most secret details of everything in front of
the wives, whose ears were sticking out like donkeys'.

David is attached to the British Embassy, to the *émigré* government
and also to MO-4. He has been loaned by the Foreign Office as the personal representative of Ambassador Rex Leeper, and as such he was parachuted into Greece. All his messages were to be sent by MO-4 to Leeper as
Leeper's property. When David got back to Cairo, he found that not a
single one of his telegrams had been given to Leeper by MO-4. MO-4 pretended that because they were understaffed they were behind in decipher-
ing. David investigated personally and found that thirteen telegrams had
been decoded and marked for distribution to MO-4 in Cairo and London;
none to Leeper. The Foreign Office is furious.

David is trying to help me get sent to Greece with him but says he is so
unpopular himself with MO-4 that he doubts if anything can be done.


CAIRO, *October 19, 1943*

WALLACE says Churchill's policy toward the Greek King is that Britain must be just to him and in no sense make it harder for him because he
was Britain's ally and left his country as a result. However this does not
mean Britain wants to impose him on Greece; merely to give him his due
chance.

Frank MacAskie (a British intelligence major from A-Force who was
twice captured and was imprisoned with my brother-in-law) says Archbishop Damaskinos will act as Regent of Greece until the King returns.
The King will be told he cannot expect Britain's armed support to go back.
Today a message is being sent to Damaskinos telling him all this.


CAIRO, *October 21, 1943*

ON October 19, 1943 Eden and Hull met with the Russian leaders in
Moscow and the British dropped all pretense of supporting Mihailović in
Jugoslavia. They did a complete about-face, coming out strongly for Tito's
Communist Partisans. The United States did nothing about this switch,
which Hull couldn't pretend to like, because we had conceded to Britain
over-all conduct of Eastern Mediterranean affairs in exchange for Churchill's support of our unconditional surrender formula.


CAIRO, *November 9, 1943*

MAJOR Louis Huot of OSS has come back to Cairo for a couple of days.
According to him, since he went on his reconnaissance to Jugoslavia, he
has had great success in his job of supplying Tito.

Huot claims that Fitzroy Maclean (British chief of the mission to Tito) is very angry at him. I asked Louis how my chances of getting in to Tito were. He said that Sandy Glen had stuck up for me in a meeting on the subject with Major General Gubbins (SOE). Huot also said Tito wants me—especially since I have recently been attacked by Mihailović.

I took Huot to lunch with King Peter and he complained bitterly of "betrayal." However, when Louis assured him that Tito was more nationalist than Communist and that he (Huot) was certain no deal had yet been arranged that precluded a postwar monarchy, the young King took heart. Incidentally, with Peter's urgent approval, Huot promised once again to see if he couldn't get me to Jugoslavia. This time he swore he would ask neither OSS nor its superior, the British SOE for permission, but would smuggle me in on one of his flotilla of small boats.

The big Middle Eastern event of 1943 was a series of summit conferences held in Cairo and Teheran. As president of the Middle East War Correspondents group I was placed at the head of a committee that sought to obtain somewhat better facilities for the press than the unpromising blackout threatened in the name of security.

The conferences dealt with various crucial war and postwar matters. The Cairo meeting agreed to strip Japan of its empire and reduce its territorial status to that existing prior to 1895. The Teheran meeting achieved basic accord on a 1944 Anglo-American invasion of France. Finally, after Teheran, Churchill summoned Inönü down to Cairo for what amounted to a diplomatic Dutch rub. He bawled out the cautious Turks for insufficient aid to the Allied cause.

CAIRO, *December 1, 1943*

TODAY I had a talk with Richard G. Casey, an Australian who is British minister of state for the Middle East. Casey predicted that if a fight starts in Palestine it would repeat in a small scale the prewar battle between Jews and Arabs. The Jews would win the first round but the final struggle would turn out otherwise. The British would not let complete chaos develop. Casey complained: "You can't deal with Jews. You can make an agreement on a settlement; but then next week they come around and ask for more." (He was later Lord Casey and Governor General.)

Casey told me British policy would prefer to see a Greater Syrian State developed—including Syria, the Lebanon, Palestine and Jordan. However, the Jews refuse to accept a minority status in such a country.

Casey—and this is strange for an Australian—then added: "One power should run this part of the world. The British would be willing to pull out from the Middle East if the United States wished to run the area. But there has been no indication of such a desire."

Casey was frank enough to acknowledge he had insufficient influence to improve conference liaison with the daily press. The entire affair was being run by British and American security experts, obsessed with protecting the lives of their principals. Indeed, as it turned out later on, Roosevelt went to stay at the Soviet embassy in Teheran because the Russians had got wind of a plot by the Nazi Sicherheitsdienst to assassinate the allied leaders.

I did manage to arrange a few briefings for the increasingly irritated reporters but these were a dismal failure. The first officer to appear in our press room, an American major who was supposed to discuss Roosevelt's policy, showed up drunk, and, with an idiotic fleer, began things by saying brightly: "I thought you guys would be a bunch of Ay-rabs." Field Marshal Smuts, South African Premier, gave us the luminous assurance: "Everything is in order and moving toward the inevitable conclusion."

We sent message after message to Roosevelt and Churchill, to Harry Hopkins and Eden, all of whom were isolated by barbed wire and guards in the region of Mena House and the Pyramids. The response was negative. General Vinegar Joe Stilwell, Chiang Kai-shek's American subordinate and implacable enemy, arrived at my hotel room quite by surprise and spent two bitter hours criticizing Chiang for corruption, incapacity and inordinate ambition.

By December 3, with the whole world hungry for information and the press choked by frustration, I drafted telegrams to Elmer Davis, of the OWI in Washington, and Brendan Bracken, minister of information in London: "Middle East war correspondents unanimously express in strongest possible terms their complete dissatisfaction with fashion in which public relations and press facilities of great power conferences been managed."

The replies were discouraging. From Washington:

Russell Barnes [O.W.I., chief in Cairo], Sulzberger and correspondents committee from Davis: Your comments on recent conferences are appreciated and are being studied with care. This office hopes to be able to recommend in consultation with information agencies of Allied governments more satisfactory arrangements hereafter.

From London:

C. L. Sulzberger, chairman, Allied Press Committee, Cairo—I am obliged by the message you sent me from the Middle East war correspondents. I must make it clear however that comment on the press arrangements made in Cairo must be sent to the minister of state resident in the Middle East and to the British ambassador under whose authority the publicity arrangements were made. . . . Bracken.

Apart from an engraved silver cigarette case graciously given me by the other correspondents as a reward for beating my head against the bureaucratic wall, the one reward I received for my efforts was a long talk with Churchill. This was the first time I had occasion to meet the British war leader. First he gave a press conference that was disappointingly flensed of fact and stuffed with platitudes; but then Lampson, the British ambassador, was kind enough to arrange for me to have a drink with the Prime Minister. I noted that he seemed extremely fatigued and spoke in a tired voice. He was wearing a tan suit and brown shoes. He had a heavy gold chain in his waistpocket. He solemnly shook hands, invited me to sit down, and reminded me that his grandfather Jerome had been an owner of *The New York Times*. Churchill reviewed with evident satisfaction the plans he had helped so much to materialize, not only for victory but also for safeguarding its permanence. He was prepared to take an even money bet that the Germans would not be able to last out the present winter. He continued:

> In Palestine there should be enough room for both Arabs and Jews. I personally, as you know, have been Zionist from the beginning. But I believe there is enough for all. I have helped the Arabs and put Feisal on the throne of Iraq, Abdullah in Amman. Some people tend to underrate the great services of the Jews. They have made cities in Palestine where there were hamlets and orange groves where there was nothing but glistening sand. Their money flows in from abroad available for developments which would not otherwise exist.

I must confess I was always grateful to Lampson for arranging this conversation.

My attempts to join either the Greek or Jugoslav guerrillas came to naught. I sent new messages to both Tito and Mihailović. Before disappearing from the theater (he had excited both the anger of SOE and the jealousy of his superiors in OSS), Huot told me the British insisted on keeping me out because they thought I knew too much about the Balkans.

# 13

## THE EDGE OF THE

## WHIRLWIND

SOE, THEN RUN BY A HARD-BOILED GROUP OF CYNICS, INCLUDED many young English romantics who delighted in daredevil monkey-shines behind German lines. They usually arrived there at the end of a parachute or were set ashore by submarines. The Cairo element of this collection of adventurers specialized in Balkan operations and had its own song. The original version was written by one of their number, George Morton, but later was revised by Patrick Leigh Fermor (who gained fame by capturing the German commander of Crete and taking him away to Cairo). Leigh Fermor's version of the SOE anthem goes accordingly:

> We've got hundreds of mugs
> Who've been trained as thugs
> And now they're at the money of the Greeks and the Jugs;
> And the man at the helm
> Is a peer of the Realm.
>
> > But nobody's using us now
> > Nobody! Nobody!
> > Nobody's using us now
>
> We've got a Partisan itch
> But there's Mihailović
> And the Foreign Office never seems to know which is which
> We're the talk of the town
> We'd better close down.
>
> > But nobody's using us now

> Nobody! Nobody!
> Nobody's using us now.

After Italy's surrender, which reacted like violent yeast in the fermenting Balkans, I resolved to make every effort to get into Jugoslavia or Greece, by plane, parachute, submarine or any available means. I received credentials with the assimilated rank of captain in the Jugoslav and Greek armies. My Jugoslav papers were signed by King Peter. I sent word to both Tito and Mihailović of my desire to join them as a reporter. I also tried to get similar word to the Greek guerrillas but they were so disorganized and their leadership was so obscure that this was difficult. In the end, for each country, I was forced to rely on approval by SOE, because Allied responsibility in the East Mediterranean and East Europe had been conceded to Britain by Roosevelt at the Casablanca Conference.

SOE persistently vetoed my plans. Some personal friends like Commander Sandy Glen (for Jugoslavia) and David Wallace (for Greece) did their best to push my case. Major Louis Huot of the American OSS, who had organized a fleet of small boats to cross the Adriatic with supplies for Tito, also tried unsuccessfully. The Kings and governments of Jugoslavia and Greece argued for me. Mihailović sent word he would receive me with open arms. I received a similar invitation from Tito with a personal letter signed by the vice-president of his Partisan regime, Vladislav Ribnikar, assuring me of a warm welcome. I made arrangements to take the parachute training course at a British camp in Ramat David, Palestine, the moment approval came; but nothing happened.

Instead I fretted in Cairo, comforted by Marina, going to endless parties attended by gay British staff officers with red tabs on their collars, with the increasingly obscene young King Farouk inevitably standing in a corner scowling or trying to ogle some pretty girl. I had to make do with second- or third-hand tidbits of news from the increasingly active and internecine Balkan Wars.

In the end I decided to go to Italy, still hoping I might find some way of slipping across the Adriatic when opportunity presented. I flew to Oran where the commander of a Free French cruiser invited me on a troop-ferrying trip to Naples. I received the following highly classified letter:

ABOARD, January 15, 1944
VERY SECRET

*Duguay Trouin*
Commanding Officer

Dear Sir,

I have the privilege of asking you to embark aboard the *Duguay Trouin* Sunday, January 16 at 4 P.M. (local time).

The *Duguay Trouin* will be lying in the big pier of Mers-El-Kebir, easily accessible to automobiles.

I am pleased with the thought of having you and your comrade aboard my vessel, where you will find lodging and food; I will do my best to render your sojourn the least uncomfortable possible.

With best regards,

Sincerely yours,

(signed) T. de Quièvrecourt

P.S. It would be wise if you would bring with you some paper for a particular use; it has become unobtainable, and my stock is exhausted. I apologize for this detail.

Four days later I reached Naples and noted in my diary:

NAPLES, *January 19, 1944*

AMUSING trip aboard the *Duguay Trouin*. I was given the admiral's cabin, a magnificent stateroom with its own sitting room-office, including a huge desk, and large private bathroom with a fine bathtub. *Duguay Trouin* was built in the 1920s primarily as a cruising vessel to take cabinet ministers and admirals on visits around the French empire. That's why I had such a magnificent suite. I must say it was quite a contrast to the accommodation for North African troops being shipped to the Italian front. They were huddling all over, on decks, in passageways. They just rolled up in blankets, sea-sick as dogs, and slept where they could. The whole ship stank with vomit by the time we reached Naples.

One day I was walking on deck talking with a French army major during gunnery practice, a chap called "Thamys" whose real name was Tchenkelli: a Russian-Georgian who had been an officer in the French Foreign Legion. After the fall of France, he escaped by having himself sewn up in a coal sack. He eventually got to London and joined the Free French whose Croix de Lorraine he wore. As we were chatting, two French corporals walked by. They were each wearing de Gaulle insignia. Thamys stopped them and asked where and when they had obtained their Croix de Lorraine. They had bought them in Oran the previous week. Thamys ordered them to take them off and throw them into the sea. Then, he dismissed them with a stern salute. I asked why. He replied: "We are going to have plenty of trouble after the war. It will be necessary to know who is really for us and who is not. They have no right to that insignia because they did not earn it."

I was delighted by the ship's song, *"Chanson du Duguay Trouin,"* which was affixed to the ward room wall. This went accordingly:

> *Quand on est marin de France,*
> *D'un de nos pays brillants,*
> *Sous le ciel bleu de Provence,*
> *Soit à Brest ou bien à l'Orient*
> *On est fier de son navire,*

*De son ruban aux lettres d'or,*
*On crane un peu quand on peut dire:*

REFRAIN

*Et voilà le Duguay Trouin,*
*Chantons bien fort ce gai refrain,*
*Fiers nous portons sur nos rubans,*
*Le nom de notre bâtiment;*
*Joyeux marins, joyeux bateau,*
*Fier bâtiment, pavillon haut,*
*Que bien que vieux tout l'monde admire,*
*Ce fait plaisir quand on peut dire:*
*Je suis sur le Duguay Trouin.*

2 ÈME COUPLET

*Lorsqu'étant à Alexandrie,*
*Pour mériter un sourire,*
*Cueillant une fleur jolie*
*Pour faire un doux cadeau pas cher*
*En l'offrant on pouvait dire,*
*En revenant de Ziziria,*
*A celle de Sidi-Gaber:*

When I reached Caserta, enormous royal palace of the Kings of Naples and Sicily where General Mark Clark then had his Fifth Army headquarters, there was a big commotion. In an effort to outflank the stubborn German defense line based on Cassino, an amphibious landing was being made southwest of Rome at Anzio and Nettuno. I was invited to go along with the commander-in-chief, Sir Harold (later Lord) Alexander. I took the following notes:

Went up to the Anzio beachhead today with Alexander on his first visit. We traveled together on the destroyer *Kempenfelt;* I joined Alexander at Caserta. Early in the morning I had stumbled through darkness over the plowed fields to his private train where I waited in his office, a regular railway car containing two tables surrounded by red upholstered armchairs. On one of these tables, above which is fixed a map, is an American radio and field telephone.

Alexander came in and very cordially invited me to breakfast with him and his chief of staff. Then we drove down to Naples where we boarded *Kempenfelt* and zigzagged off through the bay, cutting high plumes of spray because it was pretty windy. One after another, we passed swaying, heaving convoys heading up to the beachhead.

General Al Gruenther, Clark's chief of staff, was in the party. While we were standing upon the bridge chatting, he told me that Alexander is "most unassuming and a very good listener." He described him as very friendly and pro-American. Gruenther, a small, taut, intellectual man, said Alexander was extremely unhappy about the Rapido situation

where we have been held up and gotten rather a bloody nose. He said
Alexander was quiet, mild-mannered, slightly shy and lives modestly in
a mobile billet despite the fact that he could commandeer any villa in
the splendiferous Caserta headquarters region.

Gruenther described the Anzio landing with much enthusiasm. He
said: "We prevented the Germans from knowing of the expedition
largely by the use of our air power. This operation will be studied in the
future. Nevertheless the Germans have been very skillful. They have
already brought reinforcements up to the high ground and are massing
there, although they are probably not yet ready for attack."

Had a good lunch with Alexander, Gruenther and General Brian
Robertson on roast beef and Yorkshire pudding. I was rather amused,
talking with Alexander, to note that he was reading Schiller's poetry in
German. I asked him why, and he said he thought he had better polish
up his German; he would be needing it one of these days—in occupied
Germany, Robertson kept worrying whether Alexander wasn't being
indiscreet.

Alexander impressed me as being thoroughly dauntless and spry for
his age (fifty-one). Some of the American officers and men he visited
complained to me that his red hat band seemed to draw enemy fire in the
rather constricted area. When I questioned him afterwards Alex admitted this was perhaps so but, on the other hand, he wanted the men to
see that their commander went right up into the front line. He liked to
advertise this fact with the red band—unlike our American theory under
which officers wear helmets, both for safety and so that, at any distance,
they are indistinguishable from GIs.

Anzio was really rather a disaster. It didn't achieve its objective of
turning the Nazi line. Even Alexander displayed less warmth toward the
Americans once the initial advantage of surprise wore off and the beachhead became a dead end. Subsequently he was to complain:

For some inexplicable reason General Clark's Anglo-American forces
never reached their objectives, though, according to my information
later, there was nothing to prevent their being gained. Instead Mark
Clark switched his point of attack north to the Alban Hills, in the
direction of Rome. If he had succeeded in carrying out my plan the
disaster to the enemy would have been much greater; indeed, most of
the German forces south of Rome would have been destroyed. I had
always assured General Clark in conversation that Rome would be
entered by his army; and I can only assume that the immediate lure of
Rome for its publicity value persuaded him to switch the direction of
his advance.

Alas, I can fully confirm the implications of Alexander's remark. I spent
most of the next three months in and around Cassino and often talked to
Clark, a rangy, hawk-featured man who looked much like the sheriff in a
Wild West movie. Clark was fearless but he never impressed me by his

brilliance and he was certainly obsessed with vanity. I used to visit his trailer headquarters at times, when he played an evening round of bridge with Gruenther. He always talked about "When I take Rome." Once, when I had been complaining to him about the particular stupidity of his Fifth Army censors, he put his long arm around my shoulder and said: "Cy, when we make our breakthrough I want you to ride in a jeep with me. I'll see to it when we get there that you can tell the world just how Mark Clark took Rome."

After the Anzio landing Fifth Army headquarters moved into a large olive grove below the rocky village of Presenzano. It was even colder in tents than in the stone attics of the Caserta Palace. Jock Whitney, an Army Air Force lieutenant colonel, discovered a couple of cases of Strega, a sweet Italian liqueur, at Benevento, and gave me several bottles. Strega is not the best drinking liquor but it was a lot safer than the fake Pisanti brandy then available in Naples markets and responsible for filling hospitals with paralyzed GIs. I used to keep a bottle under my camp cot, which was always covered with my Rumanian fur coat. When I awakened before dawn I would sleepily reach underneath, pull the Strega into my fur-warmed nest, take a big slug and stagger out for the day's events. That was the coldest South Italian winter of this century.

Although most of the time I quartered with American troops I frequently managed to supplement the excellent American breakfasts by visiting British units for lunch or dining with the gourmet messes of Free French General Juin. Everything was relatively nearby along the Rapido and Sangro River lines where American, British, New Zealand, Indian, Canadian, French, Polish and eventually Brazilian forces stretched across the craggy South Italian peninsula.

Clark took a terrible drubbing from the German defenders when he tried to send the thirty-sixth (Texas) Division across the Rapido. The survivors had to fight their way out of a Nazi trap including mine fields and machine gun crossfire to swim back across the icy river:

The Allies could not call in their artillery against the enemy's machine guns because Allied troops were scattered about in small units all over. They stuck there, tossing their grenades and getting blown out of one hold after another. . . . As they attacked and attacked again, more men slumped through the field, hunched under the weight of their assault boats, suddenly cascading upward as mines exploded. They stumbled in the water, scrambling up the steep four-foot banks. Just beside the Rapido, four men lay in a communications post, praying.

It was a noisy, messy, bloody affair. For the first time in my experience I heard American GIs muttering to each other of mutiny. Clark had his reputation permanently damaged in Texas, home state of most of the thirty-sixth Division's soldiers. Texas negated his chances of being named first ambassador to the Vatican when President Truman considered such a move after the war.

On January 27, 1944 I had a long, interesting talk with Gruenther, Clark's brilliant chief of staff, at the new Presenzano headquarters. I noted:

> Gruenther received me in his trailer office, simply fitted out with a bed, a few maps, a desk, a couple of chairs, a telephone and a collection of books, almost all of which were on military matters. There was also the latest copy of the *Infantry Journal*. He is quiet-voiced, mild-mannered, with pale face, high forehead, long thin nose; generally a rather Renaissance Florentine face. He has a remarkably quick mind and is an expert on bridge, being called in to referee tournaments. He wears long sideburns.

He boasted of the amphibious success at Anzio but added sourly: "You know, Eisenhower says that when he dies he wants his coffin to be an LST or an LCT because they are so important and his life has been so wrapped up in them."

Several times I visited Juin on the sector linking the Fifth and Eighth Armies. Brigadier General Theodore Roosevelt, Jr., son of the rough rider President, was then American liaison officer with the Free French, an admirable, exceedingly brave, rather hard-drinking patriot. He was an old friend of my uncle and wrote him:

> Cyrus came up last night. He is a very fine fellow. I'd met him before but not to know him. The family resemblance is extraordinary. It's not only physical but mental as well. He went up front with Jim and me while our attack developed this morning. . . . We're fighting over the toughest country I've known in battle. On our right, where we are it's severely cold and every mile stands on end.

I spent February wandering around the Cassino position, flying over it, and crawling into that part of the battered city we had captured. I often visited one armored combat team whose commander glowered at his mud-bogged tanks and wished he could barter them for mules. I watched bombs fall on Cassino from an American B-25 that spearheaded an enormous air raid with signal lack of success, managing, among other things, to blow up part of Juin's headquarters. My plane deposited me at the most forward American landing field where I had arranged for a jeep to rush me forward and investigate the results of a raid in which I had participated myself. It was a disappointing experience. We had knocked down our own temporary bridges and blasted such huge holes in the wet valley that American troops, pulled back before the bombing, couldn't even return to their earlier positions.

The First German Parachute Division, under General Heidrich, fought magnificently and made the best possible use of their Cassino bastion.

Heidrich, a fat cigar smoker who fancied he looked like Churchill, tried to talk with every Allied officer captured by his troops—before the prisoners were sent northward to captivity. Our casualties were heavy. I remember the horror of seeing American boys lying in the mud of Purple Heart Valley, their throats eaten out by ravenous dogs. By February 15 Doc Ryder, the tall, scholarly commander of the American Thirty-fourth Division, told me his rifle companies had suffered 65 per cent casualties.

Under his command was a magnificent Japanese-American battalion known as the Puka-Puka, Nisei from California and Hawaii. They fought to prove they were even better Americans than their comrades but they suffered terribly from cold. It was poignant to see their little boots lying about, shed from frost-bitten feet. One day I saw a platoon creeping up past a German lieutenant being led to a prisoner-of-war cage. "But they're Japanese," said the German. "Sure," answered the American sergeant escorting him. "Didn't you know they was on our side? Or do you believe everything Goebbels says?"

One night I watched a detachment of Moroccan Ghoumiers, big, knife-fighting Berbers in long robes, moving past a campfire surrounded by Nepalese Gurkhas. The little Gurkhas, famous also for their knife-fighting ability with sickle-shaped kukris, stared silently. All one could see was the whites of the eyes of one group of mountaineers respectfully peering at the others as they shuffled past.

The Gurkhas, diminutive men who adored football and war, were ferocious and skillful. It seemed impossible that they could do so much damage with their small knives. There was a legendary tale of a Nazi, dodging a kukri and boasting: "Ha, ha, you missed." Replied the Gurkha: "Shake your head and see." The Gurkhas made a redoubtable name for themselves after a night attack against German positions around the Benedictine Abbey of Monte Cassino, when they were cut off and isolated on a height called Hangman's Hill. Each day we would watch planes zoom over their position to drop supplies from multicolored parachutes. Every drop was followed by loud bursts of firing as the Gurkhas struggled to acquire their equipment and the Germans sought to stop them.

The Cassino battle was particularly fascinating because it was static; the lines barely changed and one even learned which particular house was occupied by whom. Sometimes one could sit on a height and see units deployed against each other almost as if watching a medieval battle.

The Allies were in an odd position vis-à-vis the Italians who were neither friend nor foe although some of their troops were tried out in line (and did badly). A *Soldier's Guide to Italy* distributed among our forces said: "You and your outfit have been ordered to invade and conquer an enemy country—Italy" (although an armistice had already been agreed upon). It continued:

Until these people have laid down their arms, *they are the enemy.* . . .
Italy has never before been the enemy of America or Great Britain. In
the past she has always been our friend and she fought as our ally during
the Great War. The policy of Britain and America, therefore, is to treat
the Italians differently from the Germans. . . . Don't therefore think that
you are going to find it easy to pick up a respectable girl in Italy without
running the risk of a first-rate row, and remember that a number of
Germans came to an untimely end through trying.

By February 15 the Allies decided to destroy the historic Abbey of
Monte Cassino, founded by St. Benedict. The bombardment and shelling,
then advertised as the heaviest ever concentrated against a single building,
had been preceded by showering of leaflets counseling everyone in the
Abbey to leave. British General (later Field Marshal) Harding told me
defensively: "Nothing in war is ever as good or as bad as first reports
indicate. But my information is the Germans have definitely been using the
Abbey and we have to deal with it as an enemy position."

During this period of the war I became involved in a spate of heavy
gambling. One day, when I was particularly filthy I jeeped down to Caserta
for a bath; I ran into a Harvard classmate, Jimmy Parton, then a lieutenant
colonel on General Eaker's staff (later a prominent magazine publisher).
Parton invited me to Eaker's luxurious quarters for bath and dinner and
the general asked if I played poker. I was soon involved in a game with
Eaker, Whitney, Parton, General Tooey Spaatz, Army Air Force commander in England, and Brigadier General Elliott Roosevelt. The latter pair
had flown down in response to a challenge. Eaker, an excellent player
(unlike Spaatz), used to fly parchment documents to England taunting the
"Spaatzwaffe," a defiance Tooey was rarely able to refuse. I took several
hundred dollars away from that first encounter so, in the future, whenever
there was a game, Eaker would give Parton advance orders to find me and
bring me back; he didn't like money leaving camp. However, what I won in
poker I frequently lost back in early morning backgammon games in the
tents of Whitney or Parton, set up in the garden behind the palace.

As a result of these competitions, I spent a certain amount of time
around Mediterranean Allied Air Force (MAAF) headquarters and came
to know the handsome young one-star general, Lauris Norstad, who later
became Supreme Commander at NATO. Norstad was greatly interested in
the Balkans and wanted to swing across to that peninsula, merely holding
enough of Italy to protect our airfields, and to seal off East Europe before
the Russians gained control.

Later in February my Jugoslav friend Dedijer received permission to
visit me at Fifth Army. I was embarrassed when he was not allowed to call
on any Allied staff officers or even to attend press briefings. It was assumed
a Communist ally was a security risk. I took him to the front as a passenger. He was enormously impressed by American equipment but I don't
suppose the Cassino battle seemed especially intense to him.

That winter I received a personal letter from Vlada Ribnikar, vice-president of Marshal Tito's provisional government, inviting me again to join the Partisans. It said (in French): "My wife joins me in expressing her joy at hearing that you are prepared to rejoin our Army of National Liberation."

I started new plans for a Jugoslav foray. First I went down to Caserta and Naples to visit Allied diplomatic agents in the hope of enlisting their aid. Freddy Reinhardt shrewdly suggested I might get help from the Balkan Air Force, an Allied enterprise under an RAF commander named Bill Elliot. For a few days I managed to get myself accredited to this outfit, known as "BAF," and when I got to Bari hoped to be taken either to Jugoslavia or Albania. As usual, SOE stepped in and had this unusual accreditation canceled.

While in Naples I saw Count Carlo Sforza, the renowned anti-Fascist who was to become Italian foreign minister. Sforza told me Italy was prepared to give the Dodecanese Islands to Greece and suggested that Fiume, an Adriatic port claimed by Jugoslavia, should be turned into an international zone to house a new League of Nations. He wanted a free port in Trieste under joint Italian-Jugoslav-Austrian-Czechoslovak-Hungarian administration. He added:

I do not believe in the future of colonies. The moment will come when it will not pay to have any colonies. But I think it would not only be ungenerous but unwise to take from a democratic Italy her own pre-Fascist colonies. There is a supreme necessity to avoid creating new myths about injustice and violence.

He even wanted to hang on to Libya. None of this impressed me any more than did Sforza himself, a large, bearded man, blinded by his own fantastic conceit. I was always puzzled by the way he clung to his aristocratic title after the Italian Republic suggested such ranks be dropped.

In early April I called on my old Polish friend, General Anders, who had established a headquarters at Campobasso and then spent some time with his troops, fighting under the British along the Sangro front. There was something deeply touching about this force, which had been constituted in the Soviet Union, from prison camps, and brought across the Middle East to Italy. Their battle song was that of General Dabrowski during the Napoleonic wars: "March, march, Dabrowski, from Italy to Poland." Equipped with American and British material, they replaced their manpower losses with Polish draftees who escaped from the German army.

They were a cheery lot and enjoyed experimenting with such British items of food as bully beef, turning this into the equivalent of spiced Polish dishes. One day I went with a patrol that hoped to supplement the regular diet with trout from the Sangro River by dropping in grenades. Unfortunately, they touched off some mines and got into bad trouble. These Poles finally took Cassino in a fierce assault that May. Anders sent for me to attend—but I was no longer in Italy. His heroic corps left hundreds of dead behind, now grouped in a semicircular cemetery behind Monte Cassino Abbey, perhaps the loveliest, simplest burial ground I have ever seen.

I also visited the Canadians and Indians, then holding the Adriatic flank of the Eighth Army. The Canadians, ingenious soldiers, were famous for the alcohol stills they had devised from pipes of tin cans and in which they cooked local wine into a kind of brandy called "Steam." One Canadian sergeant was known as CPR (Canadian Pacific Railway) because he "always has steam up." The Indians were located in a flat before the German-held heights and reached by two routes respectively known as "The Mined Road" and "The Mad Mile" with Nazi artillery zeroed in on both. They were posted with signs *"Rasta band hai"* (road closed) as all instructions were in Urdu. The Indians amused themselves with the German patrol dogs by distributing peppered food or taking bitches in heat on counterforays. Eighth Army quartermasters had a difficult time providing pork for Hindus, beef for Moslems, rum for Sikhs, ghee for everybody and small-boy sized shoes for the Gurkhas.

On April 10 I started my next fruitless effort to get to Jugoslavia by visiting Josip Smodlaka, Tito's elderly foreign minister, then staying in a village south of Bari. I showed him Ribnikar's letter and he gave me advice on how to get across to the Adriatic Island of Viš, on one of the small boats used by the Partisans. He also had much to say about Tito's National Liberation Movement, claiming it wasn't seeking to impose any specific form of government or political doctrine and would leave these questions to free choice after the war. The Tito government, however, he said, definitely desired to see establisment of a federated state among the southern Slavs and hoped Bulgaria would adhere.

I found Smodlaka in a comfortable Italian farmhouse. On the doors of the barn were painted four slogans: *"Zivio drug Tito"* (Long Live Comrade Tito); "Long Live Comrade Stalin"; "Long Live Churchill"; "Long Live Roosevelt." We talked in French, which Smodlaka spoke fluently.

Following Smodlaka's advice, I went to Monopoli, a small Adriatic fishing village then used as a transit base for Tito's supplies. There were some American light tanks on the wharf, several Partisan officers in red-starred caps and occasional pictures inscribed in Croatian: "Marshal of Jugoslavia, Comrade Josip Broz-Tito." A young woman Partisan named Sonja Leontić introduced me abroad a small steamer, armed with Breda machine guns and commanded by Lieutenant Božo Borčić. While I was showing him my letter from Ribnikar and telling him of Smodlaka's counsel and Tito's invitation, an English security officer and two NCOs came aboard. They ordered me ashore for interrogation. Poor Borčić said: "It is always you can't touch this and you can't touch that. Everybody is pro-Partisan now and there is a volume of words on the radio, but we need help."

This more or less put period to my efforts to return to Jugoslavia. Slim Farish, head of the American mission to Tito, said he'd see if he couldn't work out some way of cutting corners. But nothing came of it. SOE eventually agreed that one correspondent and one photographer, selected by lot, should be allowed into Jugoslavia; my name was not that chosen.

Later that spring I sent by wireless a series of specific questions to Mihailović, the Cetnik commander and Tito's enemy. Replies were subsequently transmitted to the *Times* via King Peter's embassy in Washington. Mihailović said he didn't believe it possible to unite his forces with those of Marshal Tito in view of "past unsuccessful efforts to achieve such unity. However, if a third Jugoslav general were found whom both the Partisans and his own forces could accept, he would be willing to place himself under the command of that third leader."

The wind-up was coldly logical and infinitely sad. Mihailović did in East Europe what the Gaullist organization was ordered to do in West Europe: It lay low to keep an army in being for the day of an Allied landing. Tito, meanwhile, grabbed the initiative and fought the Axis, regardless of Nazi retribution which, brutal as it was, only drove survivors to the Partisan cause. And there never was in Jugoslavia an Allied landing such as that which came to France. The only foreign troops to arrive were Russian. Tito's forces hunted down Mihailović and captured him in the early summer of 1946, months after World War II had ended. Mihailović said, as he was sentenced to death: "Destiny was merciless towards me when it threw me into the most difficult whirlwinds. I wanted much, I began much, but the whirlwind, the world whirlwind, carried me and my work away."

# I 4

## DIVIDING

## THE SPOILS

THAT APRIL LARRY NORSTAD WAS KIND ENOUGH TO OFFER ME A hitch to Cairo and I sat locked in, alone in the tail-gunner's compartment of his B-25, ruminating while bouncing through the upper air. I was glad to get back: Marina was again expecting a baby and we planned to move from the Continental to an apartment of our own.

However, I couldn't escape Balkan intrigue, even if I also couldn't get into the Balkans. Rival representatives of the Jugoslav Partisans and Cetniks, the Greek EAM and EDES, made a kind of headquarters of our two-room hotel suite. Partisans would come in with photographs of grinning men holding knives and standing over a basket filled with human eyes. These, the Partisans swore, had been gouged out by Cetniks. Later, another knock on the door and royalist friends would pile in while I shoved the Partisans into our bedroom to show their trophies to Marina. The Cetniks would then produce identical pictures, telling me these represented Partisan brutality. Marina was scarcely pleased by the turmoil that burst in and out of her room. I have long been surprised that our first child, Marinette, wasn't born a monster.

Cairo, like Algiers in the Western Mediterranean, had by then become primarily an intelligence service capital. The war itself had long since passed it by but, until Athens was liberated, I could think of no other base in which to keep my little family. SOE (the Special Operations Executive of British Intelligence) was responsible for a network of subversive warfare actions in Eastern Europe similar to the Special Operations Branch of the American OSS set up in Algiers to stir up southern France prior to the Allied invasion.

I mention the administrative background of these chthonian intrigues because the British half was in charge of the area with which I was most concerned, East Europe. Before World War II ended, despite my difficulties with this apparatus, two high-ranking British intelligence officers approached me unsuccessfully seeking jobs on *The New York Times* after I had been placed in charge of our foreign correspondents service. I observed that the *Times* was not prepared to give "cover" to agents.

By this time it was evident that power plays had already started in the Balkans. Pro-British and pro-Russian forces were beginning to quarrel about the postwar balance and the United States, thanks to abandonment of any claim to direct interest in East Europe, was in a weak position. I began to take increasing notes as I traveled around and kept these in a more orderly file, thanks to the efficient Gerda Smith-Ross in Cairo. The story begins accordingly:

CAIRO, *April 24, 1944*

SOPHOCLES VENIZELOS, son of a great statesman, resigned as prime minister of the Greek *émigré* government last night.

I saw Venizelos this morning. He started talking about the pro-Communist mutiny of the Greek fleet in Alexandria Harbor. After three ships had been seized, Admiral Vulgaris raised his flag on the *Saktouris* and summoned the other ships to obey or face the threat of force. They surrendered at 8 o'clock last night. The military revolt was largely ended by 6 o'clock Tuesday morning. Venizelos resigned feeling his job was done.

CAIRO, *April 26, 1944*

TODAY I had an extremely interesting talk with Ambassador Lincoln MacVeagh, American envoy to the *émigré* Greek and Jugoslav governments. He is particularly intelligent with a great knowledge of history and a realistic approach to diplomatic affairs.

MacVeagh, very worried about the Eastern Mediterranean (an English sphere) where we have no concrete policy, suggested to Roosevelt in the early spring of 1944 that the Allied expedition which goes to Greece must at least be headed by an American General since we suffer neither from fear of Russia nor distrust of Britain. The idea was turned down. Mac-Veagh would like to see real buffer states between Russia and England (there is no other European power) established in the Balkans, with the U.S.A. actively aiding.

At the Cairo Conference Roosevelt and Churchill decided that King George of Greece could return as a truly constitutional monarch without real powers; they do not understand the Balkans except through Western minds.

Churchill is now personally responsible for Britain's Jugoslav and Greek policies and it is hard for the Foreign Office to advise him and keep him from blurting out difficult remarks.

In January, 1944, Molotov told the British ambassador the USSR had no interest in Greece and no comprehension of Greek affairs. Yet in early April the Russian press and radio suddenly plunked for the EAM guerrillas and Novikov, Soviet ambassador in Cairo, presumed to tell MacVeagh who would be a good man as Greek premier, who would not.

Although the United States is associated with British mistakes in the Balkans, we are still the best liked of the great powers there; Russia is feared, Britain mistrusted.

CAIRO, *May 9, 1944*

I TALKED for an hour and a half with King George of Greece. He was very gossipy, as always. Among other things, he said:

Smuts was the first instigator of the idea of a Balkan "second front." He is deeply disappointed that it is not coming. America backed the idea heartily at first. Later Washington changed its mind and dropped its support but plans for it were carried out much further in the United States than in Britain. Why, asks George, did Marshall relegate Eisenhower to the command of the invasion of Europe instead of taking it over himself as planned? Smuts was so gloomy about abandoning the Balkan front and putting it in the West "that I had to spend forty-eight hours cheering him up."

BEIRUT, *May 17, 1944*

UNDER British guidance the Greek *émigré* government and representatives of guerrilla organizations in the country are having a meeting near here. Prime Minister George Papandreou told them: "The situation of our country is an inferno. The Germans are killing. The Security Battalions are killing. The guerrillas too are killing. Everyone is killing and burning. What is going to be left of our unhappy country?"

TEL AVIV, *June 6, 1944*

TODAY the Allies landed in Normandy. Of all places, I spent D-Day in a British concentration camp at Sarona, near Tel Aviv, which used to be a German settlement. It is now filled with Axis internees plus one Greek, my friend Elly Papadimitriou, who is suspected by British Intelligence (probably with some reason) of being a Communist and who is certainly a left-wing agitator. Nevertheless, Elly is a nice girl, a rather good poet and generally amusing. As a Greek she is absolutely furious at being kept with

Germans and Italians and demands at least to be sent to a Greek monastery. We were all gathered together in the main common room of the camp to listen to a broadcast of General Eisenhower's announcement as the invasion commenced; the same announcement that was broadcast to France, Germany and other nations of Europe. It was rather interesting to see Elly sitting between the British camp commander, whom she hates, and myself, and to have all of us surrounded by Germans and Italians who took the announcement absolutely deadpan.

CAIRO, *June 19, 1944*

INTERESTING conversation today with Kippy (S. Pinckney) Tuck, American ambassador in Egypt.

The situation in Egypt is showing many signs of approaching crisis as in 1919 when hundreds of fellahin who arose were shot. The fellah can take just so much and then he revolts. The government is corrupt, crooked, dishonest. In the old days of Kitchener and Cromer, if an Egyptian politician or public servant was believed to be corrupt, he was immediately ordered out by the British. Now, under Killearn (ex-Lampson), the government, itself riddled with graft and crookedness, is strongly supported by the British. Killearn was instructed to prevent any disorder of any sort in Egypt which might interfere with the war effort, and he has done so— although bluntly and tactlessly and at the sacrifice of moral honesty. The Wafd government is dishonest and finished, and there is no evident successor to it. Nahas hates the King and vice versa. Killearn considers the King a cheap bumpkin, a young poppycock, and the King loathes Killearn.

CAIRO, *June 23, 1944*

ONCE again I have been having a hell of a time with the British about a story. On June 19 I submitted a piece to the censorship which began:

Initial steps toward outlining zones of "initiative" in the Balkan peninsula have been agreed upon by the British and Soviet governments, under which Greece is definitely recognized by Moscow as within the British military sphere of influence and Rumania is likewise recognized by London as within the Soviet Union's military sphere of influence.

The story was submitted to the military censorship which passed it on to the political censorship. Kit Steel, in charge of these things, demanded to know where I got the information. I refused to give even a clue.

As a matter of fact, I got it from MacVeagh, who is furious and wanted the news of this private deal between London and Moscow, dividing up Eastern Europe, to be known. Churchill was shown a copy of the story cabled in code from Cairo, and he is reported to be enraged.

I was to learn later that on June 23, 1944, Churchill drafted a "Personal and Top Secret—Prime Minister's Personal Telegram" to Lord Moyne, who had replaced Casey as minister of state for the Middle East. The message, which was corrected in the Prime Minister's own handwriting and classified as "Personal and Private," made no effort to deny the information I had obtained. However, recalling that his own grandfather had been a former *New York Times* owner, he asked me to be most careful about using it and urged me to consult Moyne in advance. Churchill contended the Anglo-Russian deal was only temporary, that it was in no sense a permanent arrangement for spheres of influence. Curiously enough, after all the precautions of classification and the trouble taken by the Prime Minister to amend the telegram in his own hand, it was never sent. I now possess a copy.

The importance of the Anglo-Soviet deal cannot be exaggerated. First Roosevelt conceded to Churchill the control of Anglo-American affairs in East Europe and the East Mediterranean, apparently as an exchange for British acceptance of the politically popular (in election year America) policy of unconditional surrender. This arrangement itself was so secret that, months later, Secretary of State Hull summoned the British ambassador, Lord Halifax, to complain that certain equipment had been sent by London to Turkey without first consulting Washington. With some embarrassment, Halifax said the action accorded with the Casablanca agreement. Hull himself had never heard of it.

Then, using his personal representatives such as F. W. Deakin, Fitzroy Maclean, David Wallace and his (Churchill's) son Randolph, the Prime Minister personally took charge of Britain's East European policy. In 1943, before the Teheran Conference, he decided to make the switch on Jugoslavia. In the spring of 1944 he instructed Eden to negotiate the spheres of influence pact described above.

The final outcome of the partition occurred during October, 1944, when Churchill met Stalin in Moscow and wrote out a formula carving up the Balkans. This foresaw that in Rumania (spelled by Churchill "Roumania") the Russians would have 90 per cent authority, the "other allies" 10 per cent; in Bulgaria the Russians would have 75 per cent and "the others" 25 per cent; in Hungary and Jugoslavia the split would be fifty-fifty. Churchill spelled it "Yugo Slavia." In exchange Britain (plus the United States) would have a 90 per cent hold in Greece and the Russians only 10 per cent.

This is precisely what happened. The Russians took over in Rumania, Bulgaria and Hungary and squeezed the minority share of influence reserved to the other Allies down to zero. They also, initially, took over in Jugoslavia. For three years Moscow ruled the Belgrade roost. But in 1948 Jugoslavia split with the Soviet Union, thanks to its own determination. Despite the fact, however, that a Communist army seized temporary control of almost all Greece during a civil war, Stalin never directly supported the rebellion.

In concluding my account of this episode, I would like to add the following: Britain's traditional policy was to prevent any European power from bursting through to the East Mediterranean via Greece or Turkey. This policy was reasserted by Churchill in the wartime bargain with Stalin that insured British dominance of Greece. However, by 1947 London discovered itself so impoverished that it could no longer afford the burden. Washington assumed it openly in the Truman Doctrine. That was how the United States first inherited a precise overseas territorial commitment outside our hemisphere, a habit that was to grow rapidly.

I flew back to Italy and drove to Rome where I was given a heartwarming reception by my old friends, Tomajuoli and Alfio Russo, who pawned silver and other possessions to give me a magnificent party. The odd groceries, cigarettes and liquor I was able to distribute from Army PX supplies was fractional recompense. I have always been impressed by the staunch faithfulness of Italian friendships.

While in Rome I heard that the Ardeatine catacombs, where more than three hundred Italian hostages had been slaughtered by the Nazis, were about to be opened. I decided to take with me to the dismal scene an American colonel who maintained that reports of German atrocities were manifest propaganda.

We drove out on a baking hot day and scrambled through the hole that had just been opened into the cave of abomination. The stench was unimaginable. Each batch of prisoners had been machine gunned, falling on top of its predecessors. Some victims were not yet dead when Nazi engineers blew in the entrances.

The colonel said nothing as we jeeped back into Rome but from then on I noticed a striking change in his references to the Nazis. I sent my uniform out to be dry-cleaned and my clothes to be laundered. Nevertheless, that night I awakened, overwhelmed by the oppressive Ardeatine stench. It came from my shoes which I had failed to put outside for fear they might be stolen.

That same summer the mining of the Danube was supervised *sur place* by my old friend Commander Sandy Glen of the Royal Navy who, with a wireless operator, was parachuted to Niš, Jugoslavia. After the advancing Red Army broke through the Galaţi Gap, Glen decided to make personal contact with the Soviet forces to prevent them from blowing themselves up on British mines. He worked his way from a Tito Partisan unit to a Soviet regiment, commanded by Colonel Sucharnikov, and achieved, amid much alcoholic refreshment, what was really the first meeting of British and Soviet troops in Europe.

Sandy told me subsequently:

We soon saw a German officer being escorted down the road. Our Russian lieutenant, who boasted he had killed 150 Nazis, rushed off, seized the German, and before I knew what he was doing, fired seven bullets into him. Later we ran into a batch of three dozen more prisoners. The lieutenant wanted to be hospitable and said we could each shoot six of them. He was most disappointed when their guard showed evidence that they had all turned themselves in with "surrender tickets" and thus couldn't be slaughtered. The lieutenant apologized that we were being deprived of our fun because of foolish bureaucracy.

In July I went to Bari in order to see Lieutenant Colonel Linn M. Farish, senior American officer with the Anglo-American (Fitzroy Maclean) mission to Tito.

BARI, *July 19, 1944*

SLIM FARISH has been in and out of Jugoslavia since September, 1943. This year he took a trip into the Serbian area and saw a good deal of the villages which support Draža Mihailović and his Cetniks. Slim is first class, a tall, rangy Californian.

He is in his forties and broke his hip when he tried to learn parachuting the first time. He has been very emotionally involved in Jugoslavia. For a long time he thought the Partisans were angels and the Cetniks were devils. This, in reverse, is the attitude of some of my friends with Mihailović. None seems to realize they merely like the Jugoslavs. They develop empathy with the people, not their ideologies. Slim only recognized this after he took his trip into Serbia. He is now frightfully over-tired and wrought up. One night we were sitting drinking in his hotel room when the moon came up and he grabbed a tommygun and started to shoot at it. He has had too much. His final brilliant and classified report urged that we try to put an end to the civil war there as soon as possible. This said, in part:

"I, personally, do not feel that I can go on with the work in Jugoslavia unless I can sincerely feel that every possible honest effort is being made to put an end to the civil strife. It is not nice to see arms dropped by one group of our airmen to be turned against men who have rescued and protected their brothers-in-arms. It is not a pleasant sight to see our wounded lying side by side with the men who had rescued and cared for them—and to realize that the bullet holes in the rescuers could have resulted from American ammunition, fired from American rifles, dropped from American aircraft flown by American pilots. At one time I worried because America was not getting the proper recognition for her participation in supply operations. Now I wonder—do we want it? The issues in Jugoslavia are ones which will have to be faced in many parts of the world. The Jugoslavians with their wild, turbulent, strong-willed nature have abandoned reason and resorted to force. Is this the shape of things to come? Are we all of us sacrificing to end this war only to have dozens of little wars spring up which may well merge into one gigantic conflict involving all mankind?"

P.S.—Slim Farish was killed in Northern Greece not long after the above was written. The plane carrying his small group and their supplies found the guerrilla airfield, located the fire pattern and then dropped the supplies first. While circling again in order to come back and drop the men, the plane crashed into a mountain. After this event, procedure was changed; men were dropped first.

Late in 1944 the whole Axis alliance began to come apart. Italy had defected in 1943; the following year Rumania and Bulgaria sued for peace. The Rumanian Prince Barbu Stirbey sought a settlement with the Allies in lengthy secret talks. When these faltered, young King Michael staged a *coup d'état* in August, arresting the pro-Nazi Marshal Antonescu and arranging the basis for a cease-fire. This soon showed signs of following the Churchill-Stalin formula—90 per cent Soviet control.

I came back to Cairo for the birth of my daughter, who arrived on September 11, 1944. During the period of Marina's expectancy we often dined with General Ben Giles, American theater commander, a golfing companion who also often invited us for dinner when he had rich American oil concessionaires ready for sacrifice on the poker table. Marina would quietly read while the execution proceeded; or wander about looking at Ben's weird wall decorations. These included fake photographic montages, devised by his Signals division, which showed Giles (life-size) standing beside rows of dead rabbits hanging from a beam and magnified to the dimension of wolves. When Egyptian friends noticed these naturalistic pictures on the walls, they would ask: "What kind of game is that?" "Rabbits," Ben would say, "Texas jack rabbits." Egyptians were impressed by the American dream.

Before flying back to New York on urgent business I noted:

CAIRO, *September 22, 1944*

CAPTAIN BILLY Moss told me how he and Paddy Leigh Fermor captured General Kreipe (German commander of occupied Crete) together. They planned the operation for months. Moss tried twelve times to join Paddy, who was already in Crete. Finally he got in by motor launch. When they had successfully kidnapped Kreipe, he got quite terrified and actually went gray before they got him to Cairo. He fell off a donkey and broke his shoulder. He also fell off a cliff. Moss and Leigh Fermor wore German uniforms during the actual kidnapping. The Germans found this out later on, so the two of them know they'll be shot if they are ever captured during the war.

Paddy fell ill after the operation, so Billy went in alone this summer.

He only returned last month. His mission was to attack the headquarters of a division of Panzer Grenadiers. He carried a bottle of germ fluid which could give tertiary syphillis to five hundred men if mixed with their food, and kill them in forty-eight hours. He was dressed in Cretan costume and lay in a hole two hundred yards from the German general's headquarters. However, that general had gone to Athens where, as it turned out, he was captured by guerrillas and shot.

Moss is a tall, blond kid, rather intellectual, who is half-Russian. He is a member of the Grenadier Guards. He speaks perfect Russian, and one of his jobs has been to get Russian deserters out of German prisoner-of-war groups. He usually works in Cretan clothes. He is a casual fellow and, although obviously rather a cold-blooded killer, dislikes morbid discussions and cannot eat an animal if he has seen it killed. He told me the British in Crete turned over their prisoners to local guerrillas who slaughter them.

Leigh Fermor, a most talented writer, was guest of honor at a victory dinner tendered to him and Billy by Jumbo Wilson after they had whisked the grumbling Kreipe off to Cairo. At the dinner he complained of pains in his arm and the King of Greece, sitting next to him, had to cut his meat. Next day he was sent to hospital; the doctors diagnosed infantile paralysis. Fortunately, it turned out to be something less vicious and he soon recovered to continue an entertaining career.

CAIRO, *September 24, 1944*

MAJOR GENERAL Ben Giles told me at dinner the other night that the shuttle bombing agreement between the United States and Russia is now off. We demanded bases nearer the front after the Russians had moved it westward. The Russians refused. We have cut off all build-up of matériel to Poltava.

Jimmy James requested me to return to New York and help plan post-war foreign coverage of *The New York Times*. I had agreed to join the paper only in case of a war and for the period of hostilities plus two weeks. However, James offered me the job of chief Foreign Correspondent in charge of all our overseas coverage. I was not yet thirty-two and I accepted. James told me that, as far as he was concerned, he would back any project I suggested and, if I was right, he would give me credit; if I was wrong, he would fire me. While waiting the judgment of events he would endorse all my recommendations to the publisher, my uncle. This suited me fine.

I suggested that we should deemphasize London as a capital that used to dominate *New York Times* news; put more correspondents in Asia and Africa; prepare for trouble in the Middle East and India; keep one man in

Greece and Turkey and another in the Balkans to the north, because they would be ideologically separated; that separate coverage be arranged for central and East Europe and that we should make every effort to insure our foreign correspondents spoke the language of the country to which they were assigned. For ten years I ran the *Times* foreign service, and I like to think it was a forward-looking branch of the newspaper that had more than its normal share of scoops; also, that I stuck up for my reporters as loyally as James supported me.

I resolved to wind up the war with the Russians. The Red Army had borne the heaviest burden and would obviously be the first to enter Berlin. I hoped that I could manage somehow to be with it. First I went to London, Paris and Rome to consult with correspondents. Then, to facilitate my plan, I persuaded Joe Davies, the American diplomat, to send a letter on my behalf to Molotov. He wrote:

> You will doubtless recall that on the occasion of my visit with Marshal Stalin and you at the Kremlin, I spoke of Mr. Sulzberger, who was a correspondent of *The New York Times* then in Moscow, and his desire to fly over the battlefront. The matter was left with the suggestion that you would take it up with the military authorities and see if it was feasible.
>
> I then said that I had a very great respect and admiration for Mr. Sulzberger, and felt that he was a friend of the Soviet Union. He is now very anxious to have an interview, if it is possible, with Marshal Stalin.

I had hoped not only to see Stalin but to obtain his approval of my plan to accompany his army to Berlin. Nothing, alas, came of this careful planning. But when I flew back to Cairo, en route for Russia, to spend Christmas with my wife and new daughter, I was brimful of optimism.

## 1945

THE year began in Cairo, where I still kept a small apartment for my wife and baby daughter. I saw the war out in Moscow, wandered through France and liberated Europe. My family then came westward via Greece. For a time we inhabited a huge suite in the Ritz Hotel, Paris, while it was a generals' billet and cost nothing. When it was derequisitioned I couldn't afford to stay, couldn't find an apartment, therefore moved to London, renting the Westminster House of the novelist, Mrs. Belloc-Lowndes. It was Queen Anne—and hadn't been repaired since.

### CAIRO, *January 2, 1945*

I learned that Sir Hughe Knatchbull-Hugessen, British ambassador to Turkey, signed a secret armistice for the Allies with the Hungarians. It provides that when "the proper time" comes Hungary will turn against the Germans as Italy did. The accord was signed late at night, September 9,

1943, on a boat in the Bosphorus, but was never activated. The Nazis occupied Hungary March 19, 1944. In September, 1944, Admiral Horthy slipped a general into Italy asking for another secret pact before the Russians thrust in. The Allies decided not to trust him.

CAIRO, *January 9, 1945*

THE most interesting murder trial in years starts tomorrow—the case against Lord Moyne's assassins, members of the secret Stern Gang in Palestine. The Stern Gang dates from the early war days. Its founder, Abraham Stern, was a member of the extreme Zionists, who worked for a Jewish State including all Palestine and Transjordan.

The accused admit they are members of the Fighters for Freedom of Israel (Stern Gang) and had been instructed to come to Egypt from Palestine to murder Moyne because, representing Britain, he was carrying out a policy against the interests of Jewish nationalists. Moyne was shot as he left his car outside his house in Zamalek, Cairo.

CAIRO, *January 10, 1945*

THE two accused gave their names as Eliahu Bet-Tsouri and Eliahu Hakim. Bet-Tsouri: brachycephalic, red-haired, blue-eyed, sturdy, was wearing a brown coat, with sports shirt. Hakim: dark, tall, Arab-looking. Both smiled as they came in. British security officials everywhere, some in fezzes.

Allied correspondents, all in uniform, attended. To our astonishment we were not permitted to take notes. The British feared propaganda speeches would be reported and eventually smuggled out past censorship. No doubt about the propaganda. Several times during the first day's proceedings befezzed Egyptians sitting in front of me turned to each other and muttered as the young assassins spoke: "If we had 100 boys like that the British would be out of Egypt in a week."

Hakim:

Moral law guarantees the right and duties of every nation. We are accused of killing Lord Moyne. We accuse the government of which he was minister of killing hundreds of my brothers and sisters. Where is the law which will bring Lord Moyne's government to trial when even the law of the country doesn't consider our national rights?

At 1:15 P.M. on November 6, I stood with my companion with our two bicycles outside Lord Moyne's residence. Lord Moyne arrived at one-thirty and the car entered the grounds. We stepped toward the car. An officer got out of the car from one side and the driver from the other. I stood in front of the officer and ordered him to stand still and to lie on the ground. I went to the car, opened the door and pointed my pistol at

Lord Moyne. I noticed that there was a lady beside him and I took care
not to hurt her. I shot three times at Lord Moyne. At the same time I
heard shots coming from the direction of my colleague. We drove off
quickly. When we reached the main road, at the bridge near Zamalek,
an Egyptian constable came after us. He raised his hand to stop my
companion. Although the opportunity was there to murder him I did not
do so. I fired at his motorcycle. The constable passed me and my companion fell from his bicycle. This again presented another opportunity to
kill the constable, but I did not do so. I tried to escape, but I was
arrested.

ANKARA, *February 4, 1945*

I flew up by RAF because I learned from General Ben Giles (American
commander, Middle East) on the golf course yesterday that Stalin, Roosevelt and Churchill are meeting in Yalta, Soviet Crimea. Giles told me a
Navy courier plane stops in Turkey on its way to the Crimea. I messaged
Harry Hopkins via Army Signals requesting permission to be flown in and
am now waiting. The meeting is top secret and there hasn't been a word
published.

(P.S. I never did get there.)

CAIRO, *February 20, 1945*

GILES had us for dinner. Said he had been given instructions on the
Roosevelt meetings with the Arabs under the most super-secret wraps. No
one was to know anything. When he met Secretary of State Stettinius at a
small military airport far from Cairo, with only an aide, Stettinius asked:
"Where are the photographers?" Ben explained there were none because of
secrecy. "Get some," Stettinius ordered. He waited for an hour in the
hot discomfort until an army sergeant arrived. Then he had himself
snapped leaving the plane, explaining: "This is a historic moment."

TEHERAN, *March 7, 1945*

TODAY I again saw the young Shah, Mohammed Reza Pahlevi. He claims
Iran deserves complete and sympathetic recognition by the United Nations
and above all by the Great Powers for the part she has played in the
Second World War as "a faithful ally since 1941." That seems like a
rather strange argument. Iran was occupied by Soviet and British troops.

MOSCOW, *March 11, 1945*

JOHN Davies, the new secretary at the American embassy in Moscow,
told me a fascinating story while we were together in Teheran waiting for a

plane to Russia. He had been political adviser to General Stilwell in China and had a rather serious run-in with Major General Pat Hurley, the new American ambassador to China.

According to Davies, the Chinese Communists, who have the seat of their government at Yenan, formally requested the United States government to turn over to them all arms and munitions captured by American forces from the Japanese. The purpose is stated to be to enable Communist troops and guerrillas to increase their activities against the Japanese occupying forces.

Apparently the United States accepted this idea, but Chiang Kai-shek, who heads the Chungking Kuomintang government, has refused to permit shipments of this material across China to Yenan territory. Chiang is afraid the Communists will get too strong.

MOSCOW, *March 23, 1945*

THE two young assassins of Moyne were hanged yesterday in Cairo. It is strange how much sympathy they won among Egyptians. Despite the Arab–Jew row, they share mutual hatred of Britain.

Press reports say: "The killers went to the gallows unflinchingly, singing the Hebrew death lament. They protested only that they had not been warned in time to write farewell letters."

MOSCOW, *March 23, 1945*

GEORGE Kennan is Harriman's Number Two at our embassy, a brilliant man but resentful that Harriman hid from him everything connected with Yalta. Kennan argues that the relationship between Russian public feeling and official policy, between motive and action, between cause and effect, is a jealously guarded secret of state. This subtlety often makes invisible the movement of Soviet society.

The war was far more costly to the population than the purges, but easier on the bureaucracy. National self-confidence was immeasurably increased. War pulled regime and people together and strengthened faith in the future. Says Kennan:

It revived the hope, latent in every Russian soul, that the scope and daring of the Russian mind will some day overshadow the achievements of the haughty and conventional West. It dispelled some of the suspicion, equally latent in every Russian soul, that the hand of failure lies heavily over all Russian undertaking.

Stalin will logically seek to increase the power and prestige of the Russian state in the world. A good guess is he will seek to increase fixed capital and maintain the military establishment rather than rapidly improve living standards. After the war, it is probable the Kremlin will revert to the basic program of military industrialization in which it was engaged from 1930 to 1941.

Moscow, *March 26, 1945*

RATHER to my astonishment I was able to send a pretty good scoop today and the censor passed it. I obtained a copy of the *Handbook of the Composition of the Fleets of the World for 1944* printed by the Red Navy press in Moscow and Leningrad, the Soviet equivalent of *Jane's Fighting Ships*.

As a result I wrote that the British battleship *Royal Sovereign* and the United States cruiser *Milwaukee* have been handed over to the USSR under lend-lease agreements by London and Washington and are now operating in the Russian Fleet under the respective names of *Archangelsk* and *Murmansk*. The *Archangelsk* is the largest capital ship in the Soviet fleet.

Moscow, *March 26, 1945*

THE strangest job I ever heard of anyone having here is a man who was "political commissar of a relay team" before the war.

There was not much enthusiasm among returning Russians liberated by Allied armies. Some tried to cut their throats on the way home. One jumped off a ship in the Dardanelles but the Turks picked him up. Some jumped overboard as their ship neared Odessa. Many begged not to be shipped home. When they reached Odessa, thousands were placed in camp for six months and then they will be sorted out.

Moscow, *March 26, 1945*

THE ban on listening to foreign radio stations has been lifted, and the government is now returning radios to the people and permitting them to tune in to the BBC and other foreign programs. This is clearly a mark of self-confidence, as I observed in a dispatch today, but that observation was eliminated by the censor.

Moscow, *March 27, 1945*

THE East European leaders are starting to come here to make obeisance as the war nears its end. Saw Masaryk and Beneš. Masaryk very cynical and sad. He has little faith in being able to keep Czechoslovakia from being Communized. He deeply mistrusts Fierlinger, the Czech envoy. Jan is droopy. Beneš, on the other hand, seems quite businesslike and relatively optimistic. So embittered by what the French and British did to him at Munich, seven years ago, that he seems willing to put some trust in Russia.

Beneš said he was "neither entirely satisfied nor entirely dissatisfied" with his visit. Stalin told him there was absolutely no thought of setting up any sort of puppet German government (like the Hungarian one).

Before leaving London Beneš got a written pledge from the British that they would support the pre-Munich frontiers including Ruthenia. He got an oral pledge from the United States. My feeling is that Czechoslovakia may be shoved a bit West, giving it some German territory as "ancient Slavonic land." Poland is getting up to the Oder. Beneš said, "Czechoslovakia would be ready to absorb such additional lands if it was later decided by the allies this would be for the good of Europe and the general peace." As for Ruthenia, for the moment Beneš says it is Czechoslovakian. But, "if the people there really want it they can join the USSR." He seems to know the wind is plainly blowing that way.

MOSCOW, *April 5, 1945*

TODAY I had a talk at the Narkomindel with Maxim Litvinov, vice-commissar for foreign affairs and for many years commissar. His most recent important assignment, after being replaced as foreign commissar by Molotov in 1939, was as wartime ambassador to Washington. I saw him in his office where he received me in very friendly fashion. I have known him for four years, and he appeared more bitter, unhappy and aged than I have ever seen him. He is white, lined, nervous, fat and uneasy. He was wearing the new uniform of Soviet government officials. He looked rather less like a general than anybody I have ever seen. His gray uniform was rumpled and unpressed and there were food stains on the lapels. He was extremely frank but obviously pessimistic about the world situation, and it was entirely clear that he is not being consulted on any important decisions.

He said he is now working solely on postwar problems, with the exception of reparations. Also, that nobody listens to his advice or pays any attention to him. He seemed utterly convinced things were developing badly among the Allies and for a world security organization.

He thought the San Francisco Conference to form the United Nations Organization had been called too soon. There are too many problems still.

Litvinov seemed cut off from all news. To my knowledge he did not know Tito was coming here, although at the time I spoke with him Tito was due at the airport. I do not believe he knew the Japanese pact would be publicly denounced in two hours' time and that Molotov has already spoken to Satō.

He complained bitterly about the behavior of the press bureau and censorship. He said that he always liked to talk frankly with correspondents; he could only speak as a private individual and very much off the record. "Things were different when I was in Washington," he said.

The situation is developing badly. First, he said, the Allies make a mistake and rub the Russians the wrong way; then the Russians make a mistake and rub the Allies the wrong way.

He was a regular Jeremiah, full of gloom. He didn't say so outright, but he seemed to think worse trouble was coming. A bitter, cynical old revolutionary, isolated and alone; he knows he's had it.

Moscow, *April 8, 1945*

THIS afternoon had the rare privilege of visiting the Kremlin and I wangled it so that John and Patricia Davies could come along. How odd that (1) it is such an unusual thing to be allowed to see what would be a public monument anywhere else, and (2) that I had to get permission to bring along Allied diplomats. I've been in the Kremlin briefly for meetings of the Supreme Soviet but have always in the past been confined to the meeting halls.

It is a splendidly, gloomily grandiose place. The treasures inside are fabulous and yet at the same time they show the barbaric nature of Russia, its strange and cruel contrasts, its religious mysticism: the heavy old coaches and sedan chairs, the vast lumbering sleighs, the Oriental armor, the rooms where Ivan and Peter murdered their own families. One feels both the strength and the terrible weaknesses of Russia here; and yet one is magnetically attracted to this overpowering combination.

Moscow, *April 13, 1945*

I saw Averell Harriman twice during the past ten days. Harriman was extremely disturbed about the trend of Russo-American relations. He looked poorly and had a tic in his right eye, a sort of wink. He felt the situation was very bad and approaching a critical, if not breaking, point. The Russians wanted everything their own way in Poland and were in no mood to compromise; nor were we. They did not understand that a two-thirds vote was needed in the Senate for a security league approval, and this would never be obtained for a phoney organization. He had also been instructed by Washington to protest on Rumania.

At about two o'clock this morning, Harriman learned of Roosevelt's death (which occurred at 11:45 P.M., Moscow time). Immediately he went to see Stalin. Stalin was clearly moved by Roosevelt's death and worried about its implications. He held Harriman's hand for a perceptible time, saying nothing. Then, with Molotov present, they talked. Harriman wished to explain how very important to the American situation and therefore to the international situation this tragedy was. He put it up to Stalin point-blank that Russia must cooperate strongly now. Stalin clearly recognized this, and a number of problems were settled right then and there. Stalin wanted to know all about Truman. Fortunately, Ed Flynn, who knows Truman well, had been here a month before and had told Harriman much about him. Harriman told Stalin, on the basis of this, that Truman was a middle-of-the-road New Dealer, on excellent terms with the Senate, an able man determined to carry out Roosevelt's policies, and, though not experienced in foreign affairs, was a man who chose good advisers and listened to them.

Russo-American relations are a constant tug of war. The Russians strain us to the breaking point and then ease up. During the first few days of April they suddenly commenced giving Harriman smiles instead of gloom. He is going home in a few days for a quick report on the situation to Truman. Then he will probably come back to discuss Poland.

Moscow, *April 15, 1945*

TODAY for the first time I saw Marshal Tito. He received me this morning in the Jugoslav embassy which has been awarded to his movement by the Russians. He is a stocky man of medium height and rather good-looking, with blue eyes and a resemblance to Goering. He was wearing the marshal's uniform the Russians had flown in to him last year. He was very friendly. Although we had a long conversation, there remained much ground to be covered and he asked me to come and see him in Jugoslavia. He told me he knew I had been trying to get there during his campaigns but was blocked by the British.

We started talking in my pidgin Russian and Serbian. I asked him if he would mind shifting to German. He said he preferred not to speak that language (which is really a native tongue for him) and, thank goodness, called in an interpreter. Tito looked rather tired but cocky and satisfied. It was pretty coony of him to arrange his return by train since he was violently air sick all the way up here for six and a half hours.

Tito said that his frontier claims *of the moment* were now known. He wants Southern Carinthia, including Klagenfurt to which he refers as a Slovene city; all of Istria including Fiume; all of Gorizia including Trieste. I doubt if Macedonia will be an issue for some weeks anyway; maybe not until they get Greece ripe for trouble.

I asked him if now that he has his treaty with the USSR he wanted to sign pacts with all or any of his neighbors. Not at this time, he said.

He had asked for—and obviously was positive of receiving—permission to hold a military zone of occupation in Germany. He specifically used the word Germany (Nemachka) rather than Austria but I am confident he was referring to Carinthia.

He gave me a few interesting details about his life. He was captured, severely wounded, in 1915 by the Russians while fighting in the Austro-Hungarian army. He remained in Russia during the Revolution and civil war until 1920 and married here. He fought on the Bolshevik side (Bolshevik is his word) but played no major role. In 1920 he went back and was a metal worker in Zagreb, Kraljevica and other Croat towns. He played an active role in the metal workers' syndicate. In 1928 he was arrested and was in "hard" prison for six years. In 1929 he managed to get his son, Zharko (born in Jugoslavia in 1924) to the USSR. He was released in 1934 and resumed his metal work and also became extremely active in the affairs of the Jugoslav Communist Party. He was never in Spain during the Spanish Civil War. However he played a "role," according to him, in organizing traffic of supplies and men to the Loyalist side.

Tito claims he had never been in the Soviet Union between 1920 and 1944. He was here on a secret visit for "a few days" in the autumn of 1944. That, he says, is the only time prior to this official visit. I see no reason to disbelieve him since he was quite honest in all other facts on his life which I am in a position to check.

(P.S. Much later—on April 16, 1959, *Komunist,* a Jugoslav magazine, published some Tito recollections including: "In January 1937 I arrived in Moscow . . . where the Comintern asked me to be responsible for Jugoslav affairs.")

Moscow, *April 15, 1945*

TONIGHT I had dinner and a long talk with Harriman. He is just about to leave for Washington for talks on the Polish situation and then to go to San Francisco for the conference on a world security organization.

One thing interested me particularly. He told me he would consider his mission as ambassador successful only when Soviet troops were actually committed against the Japanese in the Far East. I expressed amazement and said I thought it would be the task of American diplomacy to do everything possible to prevent the Russians from joining in against the Japanese because of the obvious postwar consequences. Harriman disagreed sharply—but in a friendly fashion.

He told me he felt the United States has two alternatives in policy—either complete isolation or partnership in a security league. We have taken no steps for any other policy. We don't know where our interests are. We ignore the Balkans. Roosevelt had no interest in them when he made the Casablanca deal with Churchill. (Harriman refers here to the deal in which Roosevelt gave Britain authority to command all Eastern European and Eastern Mediterranean operations in exchange for British agreement on unconditional surrender policy). He doesn't think unconditional surrender was a good policy except for local American consumption. There is no such thing as unconditional surrender.

Averell says we must notify the Russians just where we will *not* permit them to go. Otherwise, there will be trouble. He is convinced the USSR is not as strong internally as many people think. The structure of the state is far weaker than we realize in the United States. We exaggerated—after suddenly deciding that Russia would not collapse in a few months, we turned to the other extreme.

MOSCOW, *April 16, 1945*

ATTENDED Tito's reception yesterday evening. Everyone drinking heavily. Tito invited me to down a few vodkas with him and Marshal Budenny, a squat figure who was pouring it down between his handlebar mustachios.

Tito introduced me to Milovan Djilas, the tough, moody Montenegrin who has attracted Stalin's affection by his reputation as a guerrilla and his ability to recite poetry. Djilas looked at me stonily, said: "Ah, you are the American who writes that our Tito is slaughtering Serbian peasants with American rifles." He turned his back. Tito chuckled, pounded me between the shoulders and said: "Don't pay any attention to him."

MOSCOW, *April 17, 1945*

PAT Hurley, who is on his way to China as our ambassador, saw Stalin from 10 P.M. until after midnight last night. Hurley was asking Soviet cooperation in resolving Chinese differences. This evening he invited me for a drink at Spaso. Leaning against the mantel, glass in hand, he said Stalin was in a receptive mood. Hurley claims he said Stalin had an unfair advantage, because Communist cells are allowed to operate in America but no democratic cells are allowed to operate here. He thought freedom was a logical necessary development of history and that any progressive country would face that fact. Stalin disagreed. He laughed. Hurley replied that after all Stalin could only judge by Russia and Russians. Stalin laughed again. Hurley curiously maintains that he had far less difficulty selling the idea of a free and united China to Stalin than to Churchill. "I had no trouble with Stalin," he boasted. "He played ball." Personally, *I* would trust Churchill.

MOSCOW, *April 23, 1945*

I have been trying steadily and with total lack of success to get to Berlin by one or another means. Palgunov, of the press bureau, is hopelessly uncooperative, perhaps because of the time I called him a "mechanical crab." There is no other avenue of approach. My only real writer friends, Afinogenev and Evgeni Petrov, are dead. A. was killed by a bomb in Moscow, late 1941. E., who was a true pal and a Red Army colonel, was shot down near Sebastopol in 1942. So I went to see Ilya Ehrenburg, whom I know fairly well and don't like, to ask if he could try and arrange for me to go to Berlin as a war correspondent for *Red Star,* the only hitch being that the *Times* should have simultaneous right to print my dispatches. Ehrenburg was quite pleasant, gave me a remarkably good lunch with French wine in his modest but comfortable flat. He explained that the Soviet troops call it "French *Kvass*" (yeast cider) and trade it off in huge crates for vodka. He said he'd inquire of *Red Star* on my behalf. I am not optimistic.

Moscow, *April 24, 1945*

THIS evening there was a meeting of the Supreme Soviet (Russia's parliament), the first of the war with Soviet soil completely free of Axis invaders, the eleventh in history and the first in years to which foreign newspapermen were admitted. We were carefully checked in at the Kremlin main gate and even our typewriters searched by NKVD to be sure they weren't concealing bombs. The meeting was slated for 7 P.M. but started an hour late.

The reporters were placed in a box to the right of the dais where Stalin and his Presidium sat, Stalin wearing a fawn-colored uniform with the decoration of Hero of Soviet Labor. He was applauded a long time on entering. This is probably the closest I'll ever get to him (about fifteen feet) because I have never heard any further about my 1943 request for an interview (through Joe Davies) except that he'd be glad to answer any questions in writing, which I refuse to do; I'm not going to set up pins in a propaganda bowling alley for him. When I wrote Molotov on this I was told again Stalin would answer any letter I write. But I'm not writing.

Stalin and the delegates rose in tribute to Roosevelt. On one side of me sat a huge man (obviously NKVD), tough-looking with tattoos on his hairy hands, extremely stupid. I kept asking him: "What paper do you work for, Comrade?" to his embarrassment and the snickers of his NKVD colleague on my other side.

Moscow, *April 27, 1945*

LONG talk with Kennan, chargé d'affaires in Harriman's absence, about the ideological development of Communism. He said the first real opposition battle in the Communist Party was in 1904 when the Bolsheviks and the Mensheviks split on the question of whether it should be a small elite or mass party. Lenin decided a small conspiratorial party was more effective.

"That was when they buried democracy in the Soviet Union," says Kennan.

When Lenin had his stroke, Stalin's position was not paramount. Lenin's testament said Stalin was not the man to succeed him. Lenin considered Stalin coarse, crude and cruel; he felt he would be too rough. Stalin had no intellectual or political authority. He operated on fear. His opponents were the brilliant ones. Radek and Bukharin were among the brainiest men in the whole world. Radek was sort of a court fool for Lenin, very arrogant and fresh. He had a terrifically quick tongue and enormous education and intelligence.

Men like this had no respect for Stalin. They considered him a rough-and-tumble bouncer from the Caucasus. He was never a brain of the party; he was not very well educated. He had a deeply suspicious, dark, Asiatic mind. He was known to be vindictive. He had a genius for power in the true Asiatic way. The others mocked him and the jokes got back to him. (Incidentally, that may help to explain why jokes about Stalin in Russia are so very, very rare.)

Trotsky began accusing Stalin of having no plans for the future; saying he could not make up his mind. Stalin got fed up and moved fast. He exiled Trotsky and sent most of his followers to Siberia. He then ordered the state planners to get busy and lay out a program. Out of this grew the first Five-Year Plan. It was, in effect, really a phony.

Ever since 1926 the State Planning Commission drew up regularly one-year and five-year plans. These were called the "control figures for national economy." Two five-year plans were ready by 1928. In 1928 Stalin decided to publicize one of these plans more in order to offset the charges that he was without any plans. Stuart Chase picked up this propaganda and proceeded to dramatize the plan. This gave Stalin ideas. He gave it a shot in the arm and called it a terrific program. This went over big abroad along the lines, "The Soviets have discovered planning."

MOSCOW, *May 1, 1945*

THE May Day parade in Red Square was massive but despite the excitement on the eve of victory, the usual strict guards were out and nobody was admitted without a permit. The people couldn't see their own parade.

I saw old Litvinov standing below the diplomatic bleachers. I asked him why he wasn't allotted a seat. "I was," he said dourly. "But I prefer it down here with the masses." The way he said "masses," it was in quotes. His pale, ugly face looked thoughtful and sad; none of the exuberation of a magnificent triumph. He never once looked up at Stalin and his lieutenants standing atop Lenin's tomb. He just stared out at the long rows of cannon and marching troops.

LONDON, *May 14, 1945*

I came back to the West a few days ago. I was in Moscow during the
rather incredible celebrations of V-E Day. The Soviet radio announced
the German armistice only when it was official and had been signed by
their military delegate. When it became known in Moscow, people began to
pour out of their homes in all kinds of costume from pajamas to fur coats
to rags. They came out by the thousands. There was a good-sized crowd in
front of the British embassy, but the assemblage before the American
embassy was enormous. This may be because our embassy is right off Red
Square and the Kremlin, or it may be because we are emotionally far more
popular than the British. At any rate, the Moscow authorities kept sending
out new squads of NKVD police. But the crowd was too massive for them.
It is the only demonstration I have ever seen in Russia which was so huge
that the police didn't matter. By the time a hundred new policemen showed
up, there were five thousand more people. They pushed and swayed in all
directions, demonstrating sheer joy. I doubt if America has ever been
applauded with such tremendous enthusiasm in Russia before. I came out
of the embassy shortly after George Kennan, chargé d'affaires, made a
speech in Russian to the crowd. I was picked up by hundreds of jovial and
sympathetic hands and tossed and carried around until I could shake myself loose.

It was hours before the police could restore order and drive the poor
Russians back into their groove. But it was done; the machine began to
grind again.

I left on General Hap Arnold's private plane, which had come on a
special shuttle mission to Moscow. I wanted to take my files in order to
write a series of articles about Russia. I asked our embassy if they would
send them out by pouch. As usual, the red tape boys were in the ascendancy. Joe Phillips said they could send them only if they could first
read my notes and approved them, which would certainly take days. I said
the hell with it.

In the end I got a number of large American embassy envelopes and
some sealing wax, put my files in, sealed them and stamped the wax with
an old Turkish gold coin I happened to have as part of my emergency fund.
The seal, therefore, was in Arabic and quite incomprehensible to the
NKVD.

I put on my war correspondent's uniform and long fur-lined, fur-collared
coat. I have always worn the regular American officer's hat with an eagle—
I must have looked like a pretty high-ranking officer. When I went out with
the crew—I was the only passenger—I carried the envelopes under my
arm. A rather polite colonel from the NKVD asked me what I had. I told
him I was not privileged to discuss the matter, walked onto the plane and
we took off. It was easy as pie. We were supposed to fly to Scotland by a

devious route via the Mediterranean. However, thank God, we had no
Russian navigator aboard. We went up high and then our skipper said the
hell with it and set a path straight across the southern Baltic and northern
Germany, and we made a nonstop flight to Prestwick, disregarding all
Russian threats. At Prestwick I was able to bum a ride on a British plane
down to London.

My first night, Mikolajczyk and Stanczyk, the Polish democrats, came to
see me in my hotel and spent hours drinking, talking, and cussing the
Russians. They both swore they would never go back to Warsaw because
Poland was becoming a Russian satellite and there was nothing to be
done.

LONDON, *May 16, 1945*

IN the first dispatch of my Russian series I said the USSR would attack
Japan in about ninety days from V-E Day. The admiral in charge of British
censorship, Thompson, called up and asked if I was sure of my facts. I said
I was but had written it "on my own" so it could look speculative. He
passed it. But a stupid editor, although it was passed by the chief theater
censor personally, resubmitted the dispatch to Washington under United
States voluntary censorship (which doesn't apply to material already approved abroad). As a result, it was killed.

# 15

## IN THE WAKE

## OF THE WAR

THROUGH GENERAL TED CURTIS, AIR CHIEF OF STAFF IN EUROPE, I have been shown some of the Allied interrogations. Goering was interrogated by Warburg, German Jew, now American officer. He had met Goering long before the war in Sweden, on various parties. Goering never recognized his interrogator but was puzzled by his exquisite German and his intimate knowledge of Goering's Swedish movements.

Goering told us that Hitler always hoped he could come to terms with Britain until Churchill became Prime Minister. At various times Hitler considered invading Iceland, Greenland, Gibraltar, Malta, the Azores. In early 1945 Hitler planned to renounce the Geneva Conventions and thus end desertions by depriving deserters of legal protection, giving himself a free hand against Allied prisoners, starting a barter exchange for human lives.

Goering planned a Luftwaffe surprise attack on the British fleet in Scapa Flow in 1939 but Hitler cancelled it. Goering then hoped to move through Spain and grab Gibraltar, then seek a negotiated peace in 1941 before the war with Russia. He said: "I knew we could defeat the Russian army. But how were we ever to make peace with them? After all, we couldn't march to Vladivostok."

In March, 1945, Goering planned a mass bombardment of all Soviet electric power stations under the code name "Eisenhower." Hitler overruled this to attack the Oder River bridges.

Goering concluded that air forces alone can't bring a great nation to its knees because an air force "cannot occupy." He said his greatest Luftwaffe losses started when Hitler ordered his bombers to transport supplies to Paulus at Stalingrad. "There died the core of the German bomber fleet," he said.

PARIS, *June 24, 1945*

CAPTAIN Rudolf von Ripper, an old friend from the Italian campaign, took me to a party *chez* Marie-Laure de Noailles. Vicomtesse de N. has a fantastic painting collection: a hodgepodge mixture where you can see a Bérard hanging next to a Rubens, a Dali beside a Goya, a Burne-Jones and a Picasso. She also has many of Rip's etchings, from his anti-Nazi prewar days. He worked two years on the drawings; they were stolen by Nazi agents, so he sat down and did them all over again on copper plates.

It was quite a party because Rip's wife has just come down from Sweden after several years in Ravensbrück concentration camp. He is delighted to see her—because she brought the news she is willing to divorce him. He celebrated by drinking a lot of champagne and then eating the glasses with a terrible grinding noise. Claims green tastes best.

PARIS, *July 22, 1945*

SAW Dr. Vladimir (Vlatko) Maček here, our first talk since 1938 when I was expelled from Jugoslavia because of it. The famous Croatian Peasant Party leader is living in a boardinghouse waiting for a British visa. He fled Zagreb May 6 with his family. He said:

Tito's government is trying to introduce a complete Communist dictatorship. The Croatian Peasant Party is considered Public Enemy Number One in Croatia. I probably would have been arrested by the Partisans had I not left in a hurry. During the four years while I was interned by the Germans in Croatia I saw how the Partisans were lowering an iron curtain over Jugoslavia so that nobody could know what went on behind it.

(P.S.—much later: Although there are rumors Goebbels used it, this is the first time I've seen mention of the phrase "Iron Curtain" with reference to Communist East Europe. I published Maček's phrase July 23, 1945. Churchill made it famous in 1946.)

Maček is now sixty-six: pale face, white hair and mustache, frail, colorless, fishy eyes, metal-rimmed spectacles. As in Zagreb, in Paris he wears no necktie, an effort by this bourgeois to appeal to his peasant clientele.

LONDON, *July 27, 1945*

THIS is the day after the British election in which labor gave Churchill a terrible drubbing. I went to see King Peter this morning in his modest two-room suite at Claridge's.

He received me in his bedroom. Queen Alexandra was sitting up in bed in a bed jacket and their ten-day-old son was lying in a basket covered with silk beside the bed. Princess Aspasia, Alexandra's mother, kept popping in and minding other people's business. She did, however, succeed in obtaining some liquor from what she called "the wine cellar"—a closet in which Peter had a few bottles stored away and she managed to shake up some pretty good Martinis. She kept telling me and Peter that she hoped to have a great deal of influence on Peter when he got his throne back. Peter told me that he had to play his hand very cautiously now, but that he still felt that his people would back him if they were given free expression and that he hoped that the Allies would stay by his pledge of this. He told me that President Truman had sent him a letter three days previously promising that he would do his best to see to it that full liberty prevailed in Jugoslavia.

I asked Peter to give me an interview on the effects of the British elections on his position. He was rather reluctant but the influence of a Martini, the insatiable ambition of Princess Aspasia, and the prodding of Queen Alexandra who was most anxious to get a description of the baby published, made him change his mind.

I had to leave then because I had a luncheon engagement and he asked me to come back in the afternoon to finish the interview. I told him I could return only after my appointment with King George of Greece. Aspasia, who hates George, was very intrigued. She asked me to come right away without bothering to telephone, because she wanted to know everything about "Georgie."

I saw King George of Greece at three-thirty o'clock. He seems to be doing rather better than Peter, but, after all, he has been a refugee before. He has a big comfortable office suite in Claridge's.

George, who was dressed in civilian clothes, wearing rimmed spectacles, was friendly as always and full of gossip. If he were not a king, he would be the kind of fellow people call upon at the last minute to fill up a dinner party or a celebrated gossip columnist in the American press.

He was convinced neither his position nor his plans had been changed by the British elections, that Stalin spoke perfect French(!), that he, George, was constantly being visited by Communist agents, that American businessmen were vitally interested in developing chromium and lead mines in Greece. Every time I talk to him, he impresses me as an amiable idiot without any feelings for Greece, its people or for politics. He seems to think of Greece as of a potential area for exploitation by J. P. Morgan & Company. George is obviously determined to get to Greece at the earliest moment.

I returned to King Peter and finished the interview. Aspasia was most anxious to know what "Georgie" had said, but I did not tell her because she talks too much.

Peter was very interested to know my impression of Tito. I told him Tito was very intelligent, able, brave, but also a fanatical Communist. He felt communism and the closest possible link to Russia was the only salvation for Jugoslavia, with the result that he was upholding a dictatorial form of government.

LONDON, *July 28, 1945*

LUNCHED with Jan Masaryk, Czechoslovakian foreign minister. The last time I saw Masaryk was in Moscow. He looks a lot happier and fatter here. Masaryk said he had spent a long time last night with Bevin and Bevin had assured him he would not accept the post of foreign minister because it would divorce him too completely from Labor Party activities and the trade union movement. He wished to be chancellor of the exchequer. Before midnight Attlee announced that Bevin was his foreign minister.

I asked Masaryk why he was so unhappy when I saw him in Moscow last spring. He admitted the Czechoslovakian Communists were making things pretty tough for him.

PARIS, *July 31, 1945*

VLADO Dedijer passed through here en route to Belgrade from San Francisco, where he was on the Jugoslav delegation. He read me part of his Partisan diary. He says this was written in bad light, between long marches, on a few children's notebooks bound together by a Partisan friend and protected against rain in a linen sack fabricated of cloth from a shotdown Axis airplane.

Dedijer asserts that prior to the Mihailović attack against Partisanheld areas in Serbia in autumn 1941, a British military mission headed by English Captain Bill Hudson (*nom de guerre* of "Marko" and later sent to Poland) arrived in Jugoslavia. Dedijer claims that arrival of this mission precipitated the Mihailović attack on Tito and that "Captain Hudson knew well in advance about Cetnik preparations to attack the Partisans."

PARIS, *August 24, 1945*

GERTRUDE Stein kindly invited me to tea: a fat, most amiable old woman who lives in a strange combination of sloppy comfort and a modern art museum with her friend, the cozy, hideous Alice Toklas. Stein is writing a new novel, *Brewsie and Willie,* about GIs and how they worry and how she worries about them and how they worry together about their worrying:

"Are we isolationists or are we isolated is what I want to know," she said, munching excellent cookies. She went on:

I am worried. And the GI is terribly worried. He is quite as worried as I am. We are quite worried together. I am worried as they are worried and they are worried as I am worried. I am trying to get our worries down in my new novel. It is written simply as those boys talk. I know them well and what goes on in their minds.

I am completely drowned in the American army and I eat, think and sleep GI so my French friends are disgusted with me. I am almost the only American woman in civilian clothes these boys see and I am an older woman and many of them talk to me as if I were their mother. I pick them up in the street and bring them home to talk.

The GIs are worried. Their minds are being deadened. They lack spiritual courage. They lack interest in home politics except locally. They don't believe anything is true. It is kind of a dark picture. Compared to Europeans they don't take any active interest in things. They have a leadership complex. I say to them: "Can any of you lead yourselves? Do you all have to be told?"

They are beginning to feel this thing in themselves but they haven't any religion any more. You don't see any Bibles around like you did after the last war. They worship efficiency and only efficiency and maybe subconsciously they're puzzled because Germany, which was the most efficient country in Europe, has "gone West" [been destroyed]. I was on a plane with some soldiers. I asked them if they had any Bibles with them. One soldier said: "Why do we need Bibles? If you have a good ground crew your plane stays up." They all know the percentages of error and they figure, "What has God got to do with it?" They feel these things subconsciously and it makes them sad. The French ask me: "Why are they so sad?" I say they've been away so long and they're homesick and they're young. And the French say: "But they don't look young."

At the same time, when all Europe is going left our boys are terribly conservative. They're more conservative than anyone on earth. That's one thing that makes them nervous. They dimly realize the Germans were all these things.

PARIS, *August 28, 1945*

SAW Duff Cooper, British ambassador, for a *tour d'horizon*. Duff is not altogether pessimistic about France. He says the French have a great gift for recovering from wars. They have lost many wars before and have always recovered quickly. France is still mainly an agricultural country and grows a large share of what it needs. "If Great Britain had been overrun, I doubt if we could ever have recovered, because we depend so much upon our production and our shipping."

PARIS, *August 28, 1945*

HAD a long chat with young Prince Abdulillah, Regent of Iraq, now en route back to Baghdad from the United States. He says Iraq will never agree to increased Jewish immigration into Palestine or Truman's views on a Jewish National Home there. Abdulillah is no strong man. Rather feckless. He is driving slowly to Naples where a British cruiser will ferry him and his Rolls Royce to Istanbul.

PARIS, *August 30, 1945*

SAW Léon Blum this afternoon. He says de Gaulle will be the next prime minister but after that temporary government, he doesn't know what will happen. Blum, who is in remarkably good spirits and radiating energy, received me in his office in the Présidence du Sénat, where he was having tea with his wife and friends.

He denied that he had committed himself not to accept the premiership if the Socialists win the elections. He would take it but would prefer not to, since he wants to retire. Says he is tired.

Blum is extremely happy about the Socialist victory in England, which has strengthened the position of Socialists here.

Blum says he always remembers that it is America which liberated France and that he hopes the French people will never forget this.

LONDON, *September 8, 1945*

SAW Jan Masaryk at the apartment he still maintains in Westminster Gardens. He cooked dinner for us—one of his favorite hobbies. Expert and elegant chafing dishes brought in by a butler. He says, "I am a somber, depressed optimist" about the situation in Czechoslovakia and somewhat less optimistic about Europe. There has been a lot of trouble between the local population and the Russians and between the Russians and each other. Recently, forty Russians were killed in an intramural scrap near Bratislava. Many Russian units without officers are living and raiding like francs-tireurs around the country.

Masaryk intensely dislikes the Poles. Czechoslovakia still claims Teschen and also an area of former German Silesia around Glatz, but the Poles ain't giving. He describes the Soviet ambassador, Zorin, as "a jerk" and says the real boss of the Russians is a man named Tchichaev who is counselor of the embassy and is actually the NKVD chief. There is just enough (barely) food in the country after the Russian troops get through living off the land.

LONDON, *September 10, 1945*

SAW Stettinius this morning. He is most eager to get American attention centered on the United Nations Organization. A decision will be made within the next month on where UNO will sit.

The Russians still adamantly oppose Geneva, and the only other site in Europe is Copenhagen. America is taking a completely open attitude on this question, but there seems to be a growing desire to put the UNO permanently in the United States or Canada. Russia, China and the South American countries would like this.

LONDON, *September 12, 1945*

DINED last night with Ben Cohen, counselor of the State Department and one of Byrnes' principal colleagues on the American delegation. He is very worried about East Europe. One of the great difficulties is that America does not wish to support either pro-Russian or pro-British governments in that area, but does not see how independent, free regimes can be installed. He heard a report that Russia may demand a naval base in the Red Sea.

Chatted with Byrnes and then with John Foster Dulles, Republican adviser. Later, had a couple of drinks in his hotel apartment with Dr. Chaim Weizmann, who is asking Byrnes to receive him to discuss Palestine. Weizmann says if nothing is done to clarify this question by November 1, bloodshed will start—probably begun by the Jews.

LONDON, *September 14, 1945*

LAST night I dined with Maynard Barnes, diplomatic representative to Bulgaria. He said the American secret service managed to steal a telegram in which the Bulgarians were advised of a conversation between their ambassador in Moscow and the Narkomindel. In that conversation the Bulgarians asked the Russians if they thought the Anglo-Americans would be able to force a Mikolajczyk upon Bulgaria. The Russians replied cynically "What if they do? It did not do them much good in Poland, did it?"

LONDON, *September 18, 1945*

MOLOTOV said today (in an interview at the Soviet embassy):

It is just and fair that those Italian territories which belong to the Croatians and the Slovenians should be turned over to them. As regards territories which are Italian in their character, it is proper for Italy to keep them. We shall try to obtain just decisions on Istria and Trieste.

On East Europe, he commented:

We feel, and we have sufficient grounds for this, that in Rumania, Bulgaria and Hungary there exist democratic governments enjoying the confidence of an overwhelming majority of the people of these countries. We feel that it is a great merit of these governments that they have established order and tranquillity, which did not exist in those countries before these governments were set up.

You, as well as I, know well that not everybody is pleased with the existing governments of Bulgaria and Rumania, but I don't think that there are any governments with which everybody is pleased.

We Soviet people think that there are countries in which the question of a change of government is not only right, but urgent, but we do not think that this applies to Rumania, Bulgaria or Hungary.

It is said that there are no eternal governments. That is correct. It applies even to the governments of Bulgaria, Hungary and Rumania. I want to add that national elections are about to take place soon in Bulgaria and Rumania, and subsequently in Hungary. They will be conducted on the basis of universal suffrage and secret ballot.

If, in their elections, those countries take advantage of the experience of England, or other democratic nations, who can object to this?

LONDON, *September 19, 1945*

AT lunch today Byrnes said "peacemaking is not a sensational process; it is a wearisome, tiring thing."

He indicated the type of bargaining that goes on. At Potsdam the United States wanted a Russian commitment that Italy could eventually join the United Nations. Russia wanted a huge sum in reparations to be paid in gold, art treasures and foreign currency. Molotov wouldn't take the former, Byrnes wouldn't take the latter (art and identifiable property). Molotov could do nothing. Byrnes saw him at the end and said he was going home. He wanted action on three things all connected and all together. In the end Stalin said he didn't like Byrnes' methods but he would act. He agreed to the Italian proposition but struck out a reference to Spain. Byrnes agreed to let Stalin have a higher reparations figure (15 per cent instead of 12½ per cent).

LONDON, *October 6, 1945*

AZZAM Bey (Abdul Rahman Azzam), secretary general of the Arab League and old personal friend, called me around today and explained that to his regret he couldn't go through with the scheme he'd cooked up with Weizmann and in which I was middleman. Both men knew I was a friend of the other. After various conversations the Zionist leader and the Arab leader agreed it might be useful if they could meet (they never have) and consult in secrecy. I offered them my house in Barton Street. Guaranteed to get everybody there even including Mrs. Stuart, our housekeeper, out on any day if they gave me advance notice. I would give each of them a key and they could just go in and meet in an empty house.

They were both intrigued. But Azzam told me he had had second thoughts. "I am followed by the British," he said, "and I assume Weizmann is also. If anyone sees me going into your house—and then Weizmann—they can ruin me. One picture of such an event and I could be blackmailed out of all influence. I am sorry but you can see the point, my friend."

Too bad. It might have been useful. I see no way of avoiding the Palestine storm.

LONDON, *October 11, 1945*

SAW King Peter yesterday afternoon. He wanted advice as to whether he should issue a statement on the resignation of Dr. Subašić and Sutej (the non-Communists) from Tito's cabinet. I counseled that he wait until it was officially announced.

He told me that when he had Subašić as a guest for dinner in Italy in 1944, Field Marshal Alexander, Field Marshal Wilson, Duff Cooper and several other distinguished gentlemen were there. During the course of the conversation someone happened to mention fertilizers. Subašić embarrassed the King by launching into a loud discourse on the subject, stating that on his farm in Jugoslavia he always used human fertilizer and had trained his servants to spread it in the fields. Peter saw Wilson and Alexander shaking with laughter.

Later in the day Averell Harriman said: "We must recognize the fact that we occupy the same planet as the Russians, and whether we like it or not, disagreeable as they may be, we have to find some method of getting along."

LONDON, *October 15, 1945*

FROM a letter to a friend:

Now that the dear old United Nations have decided to abandon Geneva to the Swiss, I resolved to give up the hectic black marketing of Paris and have finally found a little house near Westminster Abbey which is quaint and old and all that and also has only one bath, no, repeat no, central heating and mice. Ah well, it will be like the Balkans. Come and stay with us any time. We'll put you folks up in the nursery with the rat traps; there is also a male (demaled) cat who isn't very well housebroken. The address, for future reference, is 1 Barton Street, Westminster, SW 1.

I'm going to Paris to pick up wife, baby, secretary, luggage, files, etc. and bring them back next week. Then we'll be settled for six months or so—that is Marina will—I must resume my travels and am going to Scandinavia early next month.

Our London house belongs to Hilaire Belloc's sister, a fat old lady, always in black, always with a pint of brandy in her huge handbag.

When she mentions "the war" she means 1870 (born in France). She regards Churchill as a young comer and attended his wedding as a friend of his mama's. One room in the house is stacked full of her books— including endless copies of her best-selling *The Lodger*.

LONDON, *October 15, 1945*

LUNCHED with Harold Laski. He said that at Yalta when the subject of trusteeships came up, Churchill announced "I did not come here to see the fumbling fingers of fifteen nations prying into the British heritage."

In the afternoon I saw Stettinius. Stettinius quite evidently is delighted that the UNO seat will be in the United States. He obviously favors San Francisco. He claims that Noel-Baker, the British delegate, is still trying to round up votes to get the assembly to move the site to Geneva and that if he fails in this he is going to try and have it established in New York, to keep it nearer Europe. Noel-Baker is responsible for the rumor that Eisenhower may be selected as Secretary General of UNO in order to give the impression it would thus be under American control and should not be placed in the United States.

LONDON, *October 24, 1945*

ATTENDED the baptism of Alexander, Crown Prince of Jugoslavia, in Westminster Abbey. Certainly the only time the old Slavonic of clerical Serbia has echoed through the Abbey. The Patriarch of Jugoslavia officiated together with the Archbishop of Canterbury. George VI, King of England, carried the baby three times around the baptismal font while the Patriarch was tossing incense merrily around. Alexander howled like a stuck pig when he was dipped in a basin of cold water. The King looked exceedingly embarrassed and held the baby as if it were a hot egg.

"Doth thou," the officiant asked the sponsor "renounce Satan and all his work and all his angels, and all adoration of him, and all his pomp?" The "officiant" was the Patriarch. The "sponsor" was George VI. When the officiant instructed King George: "Blow and spit at him," Alexander squealed.

Incidentally, it is a curious commentary that the Patriarch was allowed in England for only two weeks and was told that if he overstayed his visa he might be subject to a labor draft.

LONDON, *Early November 1945*

EARLY in November I had lunch with Air Marshal Sir John Slessor. He told me it was his idea that Great Britain should train the Jugoslav air force. Later, he went down to South Africa on a visit. When he returned to the Mediterranean (where he was deputy air commander), he saw Eden and Churchill, who had just returned from talks with Stalin. These talks arranged that Russia would have a sphere of interest in Eastern Jugoslavia but that Britain would have a special sphere along the Adriatic Coast. He immediately proposed to Eden that the RAF should be put in charge of training the Jugoslav air force. Eden cabled approving the idea to Sir Archibald Clark-Kerr, ambassador in Moscow, but it was already too late. The idea never was put into practice.

Gusev, the Soviet ambassador here, is a former secret policeman of the NKVD. He is a ruthless, trusted Bolshevik. The first non-NKVD job he had was as Minister to Canada. His brother, another NKVD man, was political commissar for the Black Sea fleet. He made the mistake in 1941 of calling Captain Wyberg (head of the British navy mission to the Black Sea) a liar. Later on, when the British took up a series of points with Stalin, point Number Thirteen on the list was a request for a formal apology from Gusev. Stalin replied that this was not of interest since Comrade Gusev was no longer in his post. Gusev had been liquidated.

During the war, Sandy Glen tells me, the Royal Navy conducted a curious experiment. Some crazy professor had the idea that Eskimo kayaks would be good landing craft for commando raids because, although they turned over, they did not sink. He suggested, they should be filled with Ping-pong balls. The swimming pool of a London club was selected for experiments and armed sailors were placed as guards at the swimming pool door, so that no club members could intrude. Twenty naval ratings were selected for experiments. They spent several days half drowning in the swimming pool. The sum of 18,000 pounds were spent for Ping-pong balls alone. Two ratings were drowned in the North of England before the kayaks were abandoned.

LONDON, *November 9, 1945*

LUNCHED today with Rebecca West. She told me that when Churchill first arrived at Harrow as a boy, he saw a small youngster standing next to a pool of water and pushed him in. The youngster was Leopold Amery, who, many years later became a member of Churchill's cabinet. Amery, somewhat older than Churchill, was a famous athlete at Harrow. When Churchill recognized him as he emerged, he apologized and said he had not realized it was the famous Amery who was small for his age, but like his father Lord Randolph Churchill, who was also small, was a great man. Amery was pleased by this flattery. They became life-long friends.

OSLO, *November 14, 1945*

INTERVIEWED Foreign Minister Trygve Lie in an antechamber of the grim, ugly stone-built Storting today. Lie is a fattish, stocky, ruddy-faced man with thinning black hair, blue eyes and large, very red ears. Like almost all Norwegians he indicates a definite anti-Swedish bias. They don't feel that Sweden did enough to help them and that the Swedes reacted wrongly when Norway was invaded. Said Lie:

> I don't like the idea of a Scandinavian bloc. We will work together with the Swedes and the Danes but not as a bloc. A bloc is more like an organization. We don't wish to go that far. A Nordic bloc—we don't like the word Scandinavian at all—would be no help. Maybe the big powers would misunderstand it and think it might be directed against them. As for the Finns—they are in the position of being in the corner more or less. They were at war with the Allied powers.
>
> If it can be done within the framework of the United Nations Charter—and recognized by all the big powers and blessed by them—we would join a Western coalition. But if there were any objection by any one of the big powers [obviously meaning Russia] we would have to reconsider the situation.
>
> We would like to work together with Sweden, Denmark, Iceland and even Finland, developing our common laws, our Nordic laws accepted by the parliaments in the different countries. We could also improve our cooperation in matters of aviation, films, cultural questions and the rights of nationals in each other's countries.
>
> As for an Atlantic bloc—the idea was discussed in 1940 and 1941. But it is no time to raise this question. There are too many difficulties between the Big Three. Harmony between the Big Three is most important of all—more important than San Francisco or the Atlantic Charter. The Atlantic bloc would be the best bloc though. It would include the United States, Canada, Ireland, Great Britain, France, Sweden, Norway and even the USSR as well as other countries.

I next saw C. J. Hambro, president of the Storting. This is the highest political position in Norway—right after the King and above the prime minister. Hambro is a heavy, white-haired, smiling charmer, an international figure who spent much time in Geneva and the various capitals of the Western world.

He said King Haakon VII recently told him "I'm just the hat placed on a chair to show it's occupied." He said the King can only exercise the veto power together with a majority of his cabinet; no majority, no veto. He said the King's personality, however, could be an important influence and that he served as advisor to his successive governments with the advantage of continuity of experience.

Hambro added: "The Communists and the Socialists are competing in being loyal right now. But there is an old Norwegian saying—there is never much love lost between two thieves in one market."

OSLO, *November 15, 1945*

SPENT an hour this morning with King Haakon VII. His palace is well situated on a small hill, comfortable, electrically heated, but ugly. It was built early last century. The atmosphere is quite informal. The cloakroom attendant willingly accepted a tip.

Haakon received me in his office. He is very lean and tall. He was dressed in an admiral's uniform, wearing two rows of ribbons. His office is cluttered with naval souvenirs like torpedo warheads, ship bookends, etc. His desk was a mess of newspapers, books, papers and dozens of family snapshots. He sat in an armchair and talked steadily for an hour. He waves his hands in a curious, loose way like flippers and his body is very agitated while he talks. He has thin, balding, gray-tan hair and light blue eyes, a turkey neck and wrinkled skin. His face is fairly youthful for his seventy-three years and the skin on his hands remarkably pink and young.

He complained that the government was making a three-day holiday of the fortieth anniversary of his reign and this was a waste of time; the people had taken too many holidays, they should wait for his fiftieth anniversary. The King did not strike me as extra bright but he is very amiable. He belongs to another age. He said he advised his government not to be irked about small nations not being invited to make international decisions. In accented but excellent English he said: "I tell them it is just like in school and they shouldn't get complexes. In school the senior boys make all the decisions and then tell the younger boys. The younger boys may complain and they may have very sensible ideas, but the senior boys say it's too bad, all the decisions have been made and it will be done accordingly."

He talked continually of Norway as if it were his property. He said "I have millions of pounds in England and dollars in America, but I can only spend it there. I would like to pay off debts in Sweden."

He criticized de Gaulle although recalling that he was the "only" Frenchman to resist and we needed him. He said de Gaulle had a big-power complex but "we must say to him, show us if you are a big power, and he can't." De Gaulle should have tried to organize a bloc of small nations led by France and including Holland, Belgium, Denmark and "myself" and then insisted on speaking as a unit in international councils. But it was now too late because France was committed to attempts to be "big."

At first he talked in alarmist fashion about Russia, indicating a great desire to see an Anglo-American coalition. Then he shifted and said the Russians had behaved well here largely, he thought, because the Norwegians had treated their forced labor prisoners so well and given them food under the Germans.

Haakon indicated considerable pique with the Swedes. He said Sweden had sought to keep communication with Germany open while Norway wanted the seas open, therefore they clearly had divergent interests. It was up to Swedish public opinion to change things. Haakon said that the Nordic (he hates "Scandinavian" because he thinks the world always believes that to mean Swedish) nations can work harmoniously together in nongovernmental senses.

He has a complex that Americans used to think of all Norway as "Quisling." This has changed now, he says. He was glad when the resistance began to organize in Norway because "I could keep my back stiffer" in London after that.

He complained that Norwegian workers were not working hard enough and were asking for too big raises and vacations. The railway workers were trying to get four weeks' vacation in summertime just when traffic was heaviest.

He said he never acted in any way except through his government. He did not like to even advise his government unless and until he was sure what public opinion wanted. All this time he was continually grinning in a friendly way, waving his hands which looked much bigger than they were because of the huge naval cuffs, and talking incessantly.

He thought the big powers didn't really sit down and talk over the problems which really faced them but dodged them for the sake of amiability. But the small poor nations couldn't intervene because they weren't "seniors" in the school.

OSLO, *November 16, 1945*

THE difficulties of living in Norway are manifold still. Even newsprint, though plentiful, is rationed in order to be able to export for foreign exchange—very short because of the shipping insurance tie-up.

A friend of mine has a house near Halden that she is getting into shape. She called in a cabinet maker to make some furniture, impossible to buy. He said he had no materials. She got coverings sent from Stockholm and stuffing. She obtained timber. When this was given to him he said he still couldn't do it. He had no thread or nails. Fed up, she said: "Go to hell." "I would like to," said he. "I've had enough of this world."

The returned *émigrés* are out of tune. They cannot keep in touch with the constant political conversations. They don't know many of the names mentioned; the papers are full of local news. They feel stultified like Hambro.

People are not working. They took vacations all summer long. People said: "Why not? We were occupied five years." Or: "Why should we work and earn more money when there's nothing to buy?"

The old literary figures are dim. Knut Hamsun is under virtual house arrest. Sigrid Undset went to America via Japan shortly before Pearl Harbor. She wrote a book on her travels praising the Japs and criticizing the Russians. Her lectures in America were not a success. She is a devout Catholic convert and made the mistake of comparing Hitler and Luther which did not build up her stock in Lutheran Norway. The most promising young poet, Nordahl Grieg, lost his life fighting in the air force from England.

Returning *émigrés* claim people are smaller, maybe undernourishment. Agnes, a friend, joined a secret resistance movement. Each weekend she and some others went to the country where they operated a transmitter sending news of ships and cargoes to England. In March, 1945, the Germans caught them and shot two of her boyfriends. She was taken and questioned twenty-two hours. Her hands tied behind her, she was almost drowned in a bathtub. She thought she was done for but refused to answer questions. She tells the story simply, sees nothing heroic about it, not even the possibility that she might have saved herself by blabbing. She was in concentration camp when liberation came. She wouldn't want to have been anywhere else that day.

*Peer Gynt* at the National Theater, shows restless, dissatisfied, wandering, poetic Norwegian spirit. Sad beautiful waterfall rushing sound of Norwegian language used by Ibsen. Ghastly, realistic trolls.

Sound of buzz saws and smell of fish everywhere. Ate whalemeat hamburgers at Telle's restaurant: not a delicacy.

STOCKHOLM, *November 19, 1945*

THIS afternoon I saw Osten Unden, Swedish foreign minister, a plain, medium-sized man with brown hair, a strong face, black-rimmed glasses and a simple, pleasant manner. He said: "Sweden is not yet a member of the United Nations Organization. We are quite prepared to accept membership, but, of course, that must first be agreed to by Parliament."

Unden said Sweden had no alliances with any countries and opposed participation in any bloc:

We don't consider the idea of a Western bloc wise. We hope for general world collaboration without special blocs. Blocs would be dangerous. If separate political camps develop in the international organization a balance-of-power struggle might start that would be unhealthy.

We want no Nordic bloc and we do not like the idea of an Atlantic bloc. We wish to place all our faith in the United Nations Organization. Sometimes we are in a position to understand the different views and actions of the big powers more objectively than they themselves. For example in America there appears to be discontentment with certain Russian actions. But perhaps sometimes they do not realize how their own actions may provoke suspicion in Russia. Small states sometimes may take a more impartial view of the big-power actions. I hope in the new United Nations, when political questions are discussed, that the views of the small nations may be helpful.

STOCKHOLM, *November 20, 1945*

SAW Crown Prince Gustav Adolf (later King Gustav VI Adolf) this morning at his office in the palace. He is a tall, plain, genial-looking man with spectacles, pale face and colorless brown hair, who might be president of an American insurance company and looks something like a Grant Wood painting. He was very friendly but not interesting. He told me his father, the King, was ill. He said Sweden was doing its part in helping the countries of liberated Europe but that it did not wish to advertise this in a boasting fashion.

STOCKHOLM, *November 20, 1945*

THIS afternoon saw Count Folke Bernadotte, the King's cousin and president of the Swedish Red Cross and the Swedish-American Society: tall, distinguished but not handsome, ruddy face and graying hair. He is conceited and self-assured. He is proud of a book sent him by Poland consisting of a dedication and then merely a list of names of Poles he saved from concentration camp deaths.

Bernadotte has invited General Patton to come here November 29 which he thought was Thanksgiving (it's actually November 22). The American legation is furious that it wasn't informed. Patton was going to come by destroyer but the legation squashed that and he's coming by train.

Bernadotte said:

There's no doubt such a thing as a war crime exists but it is wrong to try high officers such as Keitel and Kesselring merely for preparing their country as best possible for war. In a military job one must do as much as one can to build up one's forces. As for diplomats such as von Papen, they could be considered war criminals if it is proven they violated international law. If a diplomat follows instructions violating international law rather than risking his career to refuse to obey them he could be classified as a criminal. Similarly an officer might risk death in order to avoid violating the Hague conditions but it is sometimes difficult to know where the lines are drawn.

He could consider mutiny to avoid shooting prisoners. But if he is merely following orders from above which are later considered criminal he should not be tried for war crimes.

I am positive Hitler is dead. I believe Himmler helped him on his way. I last saw Himmler early April 24 and he told me Hitler was either already dead or would be inside forty-eight hours and that I would hear the Führer had died bravely fighting on the Berlin barricades.

He said Himmler at the last moment had refused to accept his advice to capitulate on all fronts after the Western Allies had refused a separate peace and had actually arrested General Schellenberg, who had been escorting Bernadotte. However, Schellenberg had brought an astrologer with him, and when the astrologer counseled that it would be the best thing for Himmler and Germany he changed his mind.

STOCKHOLM, *November 22, 1945*

PREMIER Albin Hansson told me today he favored restoration of the Socialist (Second) International and that negotiations to revive this moribund body were going on among European Socialist parties. He commented: "We have always collaborated with our sister parties abroad. The Second International has a headquarters in London (not Brussels) and hopes to revive its efficiency, which I favor." Hansson, a short, stocky man with a pink face, has been premier longer than any other democratic chief of government in modern Europe.

HELSINKI, *November 23, 1945*

ARRIVED at lunch time Friday, November 23, after calm flight from Stockholm in an old Junkers 52. The Finns have no regular foreign air service; the Russians won't permit it. This was a special plane returning after bringing some Swedes to Stockholm.

We landed thirty or forty miles north of Helsinki and took a train on which we had to stand or squat as all seats were filled. The first thing I noticed was the very large number of women wearing black mourning.

There is plenty of paper. The bottom sheet on hotel beds is paper, changed daily, made of the same stuff as towels in public lavatories in America. There are plenty of books published because of the available paper. The Akademiska Bokhandeln is one of the largest book shops in Europe. The Finns like to write and read and adore theater. The women have no jewelry. They wear poor leaden-looking metal rings. They turned in their gold in 1940 to buy arms.

HELSINKI, *November 27, 1945*

FINLAND is receiving just treatment from the Soviet Union, Foreign Minister Carl Johan Enckell told me:

The Russians are respecting our independence entirely. They are adhering rigidly to the armistice terms. Of course the economic conditions of the armistice were heavy. Certain clauses of the armistice limited our freedom of action, such as the ban on the use of diplomatic codes in our foreign service, but these have now been repealed since the Germans departed.

Enckell, an elderly diplomat of long experience, talks English thickly but fluently. He has white hair, beard and mustache, thick dark eyebrows, prominent ears and a tired expression. In his office he wears striped pants, dark coat and spats. He is proud of the list of famous men he has known, including Lenin.

Describing Finland's foreign policy, he said:

Our intention is to seek entry into the United Nations Organization as soon as the peace treaty is signed. But we do not know when this will be. We could sign peace at any time. But certain larger political questions involving the great powers interfere and they apparently first wish to agree on treaties of peace with other countries.

Enckell said Finland desired neither bilateral alliances nor participation in geographical blocs. "The question of an alliance with the USSR has not been raised," he said. "It has not been suggested by either side."

HELSINKI, *November 28, 1945*

FINLAND'S Communist Party favors an alliance with the Soviet Union as soon as a peace treaty is signed, opposes participation in a Scandinavian or Nordic bloc and hopes Finland will be admitted to the United Nations Organization. This foreign policy platform was outlined to me by Ville Pessi, forty-three-year-old metal worker, who, after having spent ten years in prison for political activity, is now general secretary of the party. Pessi, a neat, well-dressed man with a strong, kindly face from which a couple of front teeth are missing, and a friendly manner, was in his office, guarded by a gendarme.

STOCKHOLM, *November 30, 1945*

HAD a chat with General Patton last night. Bernadotte invited me for a drink with him prior to the Swedish dinner in his honor (as a former Olympic team member). Patton, whom I hadn't seen since Tunisia (1943), rapidly had a bit too much—which did nothing to diminish his immodesty. He has gotten into trouble by silly statements in Germany and shows his resentment.

After dinner, he made a speech and, at the end, expressed the hope that "we all will stick together—America, Britain, Germany." There was a hush. His aide, with much embarrassment, made his way rapidly up behind the speaker's table and whispered to him. "No," said Patton. The aide whispered again. "All right," said Patton, "I mean France." Many of the Swedes seemed rather pleased by the slip.

COPENHAGEN, *December 8, 1945*

COPENHAGEN is bustling, busy with Christmas shopping. People complain there is nothing in the stores. In a sense there are shortages (like shoes, tobacco, coffee) but it is a fat city still, despite the vacuum cleaner treatment of the Germans. There are some complications with ration coupons but despite this there is plenty to drink, the best food in Europe (butter, steak, pork, cheese). Huge Jutland horses pull carts loaded with barrels of Carlsberg and Tuborg beer. The great shortage is fuel. There is no hot water even in the best hotels. There is a curfew at 10 P.M. in public places to save electricity.

COPENHAGEN, *December 8, 1945*

THE Danish government would regard with favor a plebiscite in the North German province of Schleswig on whether parts of the historically contested region wished to join Denmark in the future. According to Premier Knud Kristensen:

> Although at the moment there is no basis for moving the border, South Schleswig is historically an old Danish province. We sincerely hope it can develop its natural culture, schools and language freedom. Then, perhaps, in the future, there may be a basis for shifting the frontier.

Schleswig has been a bone of contention for centuries. Viscount Palmerston in 1864 said that only three persons understood it: himself, who had forgotten the explanation, a professor then in a lunatic asylum and a dead prince.

LONDON, *Mid-December, 1945*

CAME back from Scandinavia like Santa Claus. In Stockholm I had acquired my first two suits since 1941. Randolph Churchill, whom I met there on his way back from Russia, introduced me to a twenty-four-hour (Hong Kong type) tailor who not only produced in that time (from excellent English materials, sold during the war against needed supplies) but, because I had to leave, delivered them to my hotel in Copenhagen. Only trouble: Randolph has Edwardian tastes and I ended up with lapels on the vests.

Got loads of stuff for Marina and the baby in Stockholm, a paradise for shopping. In Copenhagen a Danish friend gave me a ham (uncured) but warned me I'd have to pay duty in England, if I could get it in at all. I decided to take no chances. Slung it around my neck on a cord and wore it under my massive, Rumanian coat that extends right down to my ankles. I got in all right.

To our horror we discovered, however, when we looked up in a cook-book how to cure it, that this process requires immense quantities of beer, among other things. Alas, there is no Tuborg here. Wonder how the ham will fare on our kitchen floor in a tub of the insipid brown water now called "beer."

LONDON, *December 17, 1945*

HAD tea with King Peter this afternoon. He has just moved into a new house at 41 Upper Grosvenor Street and gave up his rooms at Claridge's. This used to be the Jugoslav embassy. However, his aide-de-camp, Major Pawson, persuaded the owner to rent it to him cheap and the Jugoslav (Tito) government is very angry.

Peter says he has been getting the cold shoulder from the British since the Jugoslav elections and Tito's declaration of a republic. Mihailović is still in Jugoslavia with about 14,000 troops split up in various areas with some mobile equipment. He hopes to get some radio equipment to Mihailović. He claims there are about 50,000 Jugoslavs outside the country who could fight for him and that he is trying to have them all concentrated in Austria or in Italy. He would like to see the United States tell Tito it would grant no economic aid to Jugoslavia and at the same time he would like to see America give a $3 million loan to Greece in order to show Tito how much we disapprove of him. He believes the only way he can get back is by an armed *coup d'état* which could only take place at least six months after Russian troops are withdrawn not only from Jugoslavia but also from Bulgaria, Rumania and Hungary. This can be done without precipitating a war and the main thing would be to capture the telephone center in Belgrade and other principal government buildings. He claims Mihailović's couriers regularly walk to the sea coast with letters and can make the round trip between Mihailović's headquarters and Naples in about two months. The last news he had from Mihailović was as of six weeks ago. He would like outside aid in his plotting from an organization like the OSS.

I am afraid that not only has King Peter had it but that he is beginning to realize it at last. He says neither Britain nor America is going to recognize the Tito government at present, but that they are not going to withdraw *de facto* recognition.

LONDON, *December 21, 1945*

DINED with Randolph Churchill. He was quite meek. Said he wants to go into politics as a career and is only continuing his newspaper work because he needs money. Says it is difficult for him sometimes to reconcile his "dignity" as an Englishman and a Churchill with his reporting. He hopes to be Prime Minister some day.

LONDON, *December 22, 1945*

DINED with Adlai Stevenson, his wife, Andrei Gromyko (Soviet ambassador to Washington and delegate to the UNO Preparatory Commission here) and Wilder Foote, who works for Adlai. Marina sick in bed and couldn't come.

Stevenson is a most agreeable, talkative liberal; witty, amusing but rather weak. He doesn't lack for ambition and seems to be searching for some goal. He is Stettinius's Number Two and since the former has now gone, after promising me an extensive interview, Adlai suggests he'll be happy to substitute. I can't say his name is very well known.

Wilder, incidentally, used to run a small-town printing shop in New England that produced the *Harvard Advocate* when I was its president (1933–1934).

The dinner was simple, good, agreeable. What amused me was that Mrs. Stevenson (a somewhat gauche woman) had managed to produce a gorgeous Virginia ham in Spartan London. Gromyko took a huge portion; but then he talked a lot and never got around to eating it. When seconds were passed he calmly helped himself to another great slab. Then he continued talking. He never did eat it. Everyone looked ruefully at his plate as it was taken away, above all Stevenson.

Adlai says Churchill told him UNO headquarters should be either in Geneva or in Marrakesh (which Churchill has come to love as a result of wartime visits).

The United States delegation to PRECO (the Preparatory Commission for UNO) has asked the State Department (says Adlai) to investigate the attitude of the Liberian delegation which includes one Liberian Negro and one white Dutchman. It has voted against us on many issues. There is a suspicion it is tied up with the Firestone Rubber Company but nobody knows what Firestone's "foreign policy" is.

Stevenson believes small nations in UNO are not eclipsed and have the opportunity of gaining enlightment by their example to the big powers. He says UNO is of course predominantly a big-power organization because "this is a big-power world."

Stevenson said UNO had to have its headquarters north of the Mason and Dixon line in order to allow colored delegates full freedom. UNO can guarantee the freedom of its membership at its headquarters, but the United States must be educated to such concepts of democracy. There is some talk about Boston being selected as headquarters.

I suggested Berlin should be UNO's seat. "Why," asked Gromyko. "Because," I continued, "it is the best example of what happens without international order. You should build a round tower as headquarters and each floor should have a wide balcony all around it. Then, if there is any disagreement, the statesmen can adjourn their talks and go out and see what happens when statesmen disagree." Stevenson smiled. Gromyko grunted. No one thought I was serious. But I was.

LONDON, *December 30, 1945*

TONIGHT I sent off a long dispatch based on an interview with Stevenson. His basic points:

1. By establishing its site in the United States, UNO will learn much from the example of "vibrant democracy" and Americans will themselves be educated in tolerance and understanding of other peoples.

2. Contrary to the belief of some skeptics, the rights of small nations are much greater under UNO than they would be with no UNO.

3. The Big Five, in order to give UNO a good start, must act with restraint and as examples to the rest of the world, but the very organization of UNO exerts far more compulsion on them to do so than there would be without such a body.

4. The "will to peace" cannot be legislated and must be fostered and developed among the Big Three and the Big Five who, after all, do represent the major aggregation of world power with or without UNO.

5. The experiment of UNO is expected to be of momentous consequence to the world as was the federal Constitution of the United States.

6. Above all, UNO must prevent its members from ever dividing into two camps over any issue.

Stevenson said "the choice of the United States as the site for UNO eradicates the ghosts of Geneva, which are unhappy for some states. It also constitutes recognition of the historical migration of the center of gravity in political affairs to the New World. America, which lies between the Orient and the Occident, becomes, indeed, the center of world policy for peace."

LONDON–NEWHAVEN–DIEPPE–PARIS, *January 3–4, 1946*

TRAIN from Dieppe to Paris. A Corsican woman on the way back to Ajaccio after seven years boasted that her father made the best *vin rosé* in the world. She said the Corsicans hate the Italians, are dissatisfied with the French but don't want independence.

A seventeen-year-old French sailor, has been sailing in the English merchant marine since he was a cabin boy. He is going home to the Touraine but hopes to put to sea again soon in an English or American ship. He loves New York because it is so *riche*.

An American major, a medic, a heart specialist in Brooklyn, has a Bronze Star and wants to go home. He is bored silly. His hospital is filled mostly with venereal disease cases plus gunshot and knife wounds from fights.

Three British civilians, all middle-aged, wearing bulging battle dress with green tabs, work for a large electric company which has loaned them to the

British government. Their job is to go over German installations to evaluate equipment for reparations. They don't even look at factories that are listed as 50 per cent or more bombed. Scrap experts go over those for chromium and other alloys.

PARIS, *January 5, 1946*

SAW Miguel Maura this afternoon. Maura comes from a well-known Spanish royalist family, the brother of a duke. He was minister of interior in 1931 when the King left. He quit Spain two months after the Civil War started and has been in Paris ever since.

He maintains that Largo Caballero shares his views completely, that Prieto agrees with him. However, he describes Negrin as "Moscow's man" and crooked. He claims Negrin brought 40 million pounds out of Spain with him and has never accounted for any of it, that he is now a millionaire.

Maura would like to see Franco ousted immediately by great power action and a government set up including all shades of opinion from monarchists to anarchists but excluding the Communist Party. He says if the Communists were included that it would mean another civil war; everything must be done to avoid this.

This government would then determine by plebiscite whether Spain should be a republic or a monarchy. He says Don Juan agrees with this procedure. Maura is convinced the people would vote for a republic and there would be no bloodshed.

PARIS, *January 5, 1946*

SAW Maurice Thorez this afternoon, a stocky, red-faced former miner who is now boss of the French Communist Party and minister without portfolio in de Gaulle's cabinet. He was wearing a rumpled blue suit and a red tie with stickpin. He received me in his comfortable office in French Communist headquarters.

He said the Communist Party was for complete independence of Syria and the Lebanon and that de Gaulle was committed to this by treaty. However, he said, the Anglo-French accord on the Levant was not clear and it was uncertain when troops would be pulled out of the Lebanon. The accord provided that all troops would be pulled out of Syria first with the French "regrouping" in the Lebanon and the British in Palestine. The British, contrary to the agreement, were "regrouping" in the Lebanon. As a result there were now four English soldiers to each French soldier in the Lebanon. The French have protested to the British about this. The Lebanese are protesting to everyone. He said France wanted to keep a base in Beirut to protect its special interests until UNO took over the guard in the

Middle East. The French did not want to get out of Lebanon until the British cleared out of Palestine—and Thorez also insinuated they should get out of Egypt, Iraq and Transjordan.

Thorez was very optimistic and thought the Communist Party next spring would have a majority to take over the government. If the old system had been adhered to, the Communists should have been given the task of forming the present government because they were the majority. As premier he would complete the task of nationalization (at present only half done in banks, railways, and so on). He favored credits for the army. He is against all blocs. He would like UNO and alliances with each of the Big Three. France is a big power still but not in the grandiose way de Gaulle thinks. France has no business interfering in the Balkans. Thorez would be delighted to see communism in every country in Europe—it is his life dream—but he would not try and promote it by interference if he came in. He would oppose Fascist governments like those in Spain and Greece, however.

Thorez insists de Gaulle is not allowing the Party a role commensurate with its strength and popularity. The Communists nevertheless remain with de Gaulle in principle on separate administration for the Ruhr before Germany is unified, but disagree on frontiers. Thorez says (like all other Frenchmen) that France has been invaded three times and the huge industrial potential of the Ruhr must be taken from German hands.

Thorez says people erroneously believe Tito and Groza are strong because the Red Army is in their countries and points out that despite the Red Army the Communists didn't do well in Austria and Hungary. The British and Americans are in France but communism has the dominant political party. The Communists insisted that coal be given to the people— and it was; that jobs and food be given to them. France and the USSR are the only European countries which have brought their coal production to prewar levels. He claims 75 per cent of the miners are Communists and "they work under our direction." He insists that if a Communist government is formed it will adhere strictly to democratic forms and is in no way dictatorial.


PARIS, *January 7, 1946*

I saw Largo Caballero, former premier of Spain, this afternoon. He appeared considerably aged by his German captivity, but vigorous. He is a pink-faced, white-haired, short, spry individual who speaks atrocious French.

He has the same approximate opinions as Maura who, he says, has no influence. He favors a compromise transitional regime and says the Supreme Court of Spain, which is the least compromised responsible body in Madrid, could help the transition.

Franco should hand over power to a Government formed by the Supreme Court Magistrates and other functionaires and representatives. Then Franco, the Falange leaders, and the most responsible generals should leave Spain. The Falange and similar institutions should be dissolved. All civil liberties would be restored, political prisoners released and Republican *émigrés* permitted to return. A referendum should be held to decide whether Spain becomes a monarchy or a republic.

Caballero says he is anxious that Don Juan make no deal with Franco and asserts the Pretender himself favors a referendum on the monarchy.

PARIS, *January 8, 1946*

SAW Colonel Dewavrin this morning. His office is on the fourth floor of a freezing cold apartment. In the anteroom, a German corporal is in charge of bringing up an occasional scuttle of coal.

Dewavrin, who used to be known as Colonel Passy, is head of the French secret service: a nice-looking bald young man with a record for bravery, determination and cruelty. I asked him if he could tell me anything about rumors that Communist ammunition caches are being distributed around France. He said he had his own personal opinion on the subject but that he confines his activities to foreign matters and knows nothing about what goes on in France itself. He suggested I see the minister of the interior. Obviously, he was lying since it is well known the DGER is alert on these matters, and the very manner of his smile indicated he knew I knew he was lying.

PARIS, *January 9, 1946*

VISITED André Malraux, now de Gaulle's brilliant minister of information. He is extremely nervous and rather dissipated looking: very thin, with dark shadows under his eyes and a long nose and face. He smokes American cigarettes constantly and refuses to sit down, walking about all the time.

He said he had no time to write these days. He is very assertive and sure of his opinions. He told me he knew Tito in Spain. He said Tito operated under the name of "Antonio" and was political commissar to Division Commander Lukacs. Lukacs was a Hungarian who became a general in the Russian army. He said Tito had a good record, that he spoke Russian with Lukacs and that he knew Spanish. (I don't believe Tito was ever in Spain.)

Malraux said all political parties in France were extremely weak, which was a sign of feeble conditions in France these days. The strength of the Communists was greatly exaggerated.

He said Thorez had gone to Russia in 1939, through Switzerland, aided by the Germans. Thorez is a very brave, vigorous, religious Communist, as compared with Tito who is a military Communist. Florimont-Bonte, Thorez's press man, is a former theological student who is very highly trusted by Moscow.

For the last elections the Communist Party made an alliance with the Radical-Socialists. The Radical-Socialists then had one leader left with popular support, Herriot. Herriot had become violently anti-de Gaulle after returning to France and decided to do anything to beat the general. Herriot found that the alliance worked against him. The Radicals lost thirty-five seats to the Communists. The Communists ate the Radicals and are now trying to do the same thing with the Socialists.

Malraux thinks the Communists do not wish to really get power in France. He does not foresee any Communist effort at an armed *coup d'état*. What the Communists want is to gain control of the Assembly and subject the administrative and executive powers of the President to the orders of the Assembly. Then they wish to insist on a pro-Russian and anti-American policy. If the President refuses to carry this out, they will withdraw their support.

Right now the Communists are insisting on a prewar type of governmental philosophy with the executive powers controlled by the assembly. The crisis on military credits is minor compared to this. De Gaulle wants an American-type democracy and more executive power for the president. Malraux expects a very serious crisis long before May when the constitution will be completed. He does not know whether de Gaulle will resign and form his own party or not. He says it is possible but not probable. Not even de Gaulle knows yet what he will do. (De Gaulle walked out eleven days later.)

Malraux contends there is little Marxism in France today. *L'Humanité* is a militant left-wing Jacobin paper, not Marxist.


NEUCHATEL, SWITZERLAND, *January 10, 1946*

DRIVE up from Paris. In Dijon, Hotel de la Cloche still requisitioned and filled with bored GIs. At gas pump outside, six somewhat pathetic-looking German POWs, without any American supervision, tinker with car and fill its tanks. They seem well enough taken care of and cheerful.

Everyone in the towns and villages retires early. The restaurant keepers are suspicious of all foreign-looking customers—they might be black market inspectors. A sign on the Swiss frontier customs hut says especially tough examinations have been ordered to reduce smuggling.

Stop for the night at Neuchatel. Have a beer with two GIs from a PX outfit. One bought four watches on his first day and is very proud of them. The other says: "We ran into a sharper at Geneva. My buddy bought all his watches but I danced with his girl." In Berne it's the same story; half the GIs have more than one watch strapped to their wrists and compare them with others in shop after shop. They are extremely polite and seem to be slightly bewildered by this brief return to civilian life.

BERNE, *January 17, 1946*

I've got the whole story on the July 20, 1944, assassination plot against Hitler but cannot write it yet. Allen Dulles, who headed the OSS in Berne during the war, is saving this material for a book he plans to publish. Too bad. I have the complete OSS report text. May get permission to publish soon. The OSS boys in Berne also told me:

> In January, 1944, a contact had been established through the American military attaché's office in Turkey with the underground German movement of Karl Goerdeler. Goerdeler agreed to come out and meet an American emissary and plan for an actual revolt and assassination of Hitler. The only man of a selected list made available to him in whom he reposed complete trust was Alexander Kirk, then minister in Egypt. Kirk refused to go, contending he could not intervene in another man's (Steinhardt's) territory.

BERNE, *January 18, 1946*

TODAY I received a cable from Connie Peters, Lundwall, Limnhamn, Sweden. She asks me to help her husband Richard Peters, a German, who is interned in Turkey (says she) "because of his work as a journalist on the American list of the people who are not to be free." She says he has a visa for Sweden as soon as he is free. I knew Peters as a journalist in the Balkans and Turkey and he always struck me as a decent, nice, conservative, scholarly guy, no Nazi. His wife, a Swede, has a brother in the RAF. I checked with X-2, OSS, and found Peters listed as suspected of espionage in Greece and Turkey and with at least two aliases. But the photo in the dossier was of an obviously different man!

Friends have let me again peruse the files of interrogations of distinguished prisoners in the "Ashcan" camp in Luxembourg, including Franz von Papen, former chancellor and later German ambassador in Ankara; and Admiral Horthy, former regent of Hungary. They were officially interrogated by American officers and then allowed to wander around and talk to each other in the prison yard. All trees, fences, and so on were filled with recording devices so we could check their private remarks against official conversations.

Papen said Ribbentrop had sought to induce the Turks to sign a pact with Germany in exchange for the German promise of Syria and Palestine (which the Germans didn't own). Papen opposed this. The Turks anyway replied they didn't want any land; this violated Ataturk's testament and they wished only their present domains. Papen said Ribbentrop in Moscow agreed to give Russia half of Poland and the Baltic states.

Horthy in an "Ashcan" conversation, when he thought he was unheard, described Roosevelt as the "arch-enemy" and said the war would have been won (by the Axis) two years ago but for him. The old fool tried to tell American officers in other conversations that he rated well with Roosevelt and that he had written a letter to him; that it was too bad Roosevelt died just before he could send it. He also claimed to have written Stalin on how Hungary should cooperate with the Russians—but he never sent that one either.

GSTAAD, *January 19, 1946*

DINED with Grigore Gafencu, former Rumanian foreign minister. He is in good health but has aged since I last saw him in 1940. He says Ana Pauker is the real Communist boss of Rumania and that Patreceanu is not so important. Gafencu has just finished another book, hopes to go to England and America.

GSTAAD, *January 20, 1946*

LONG talk in his chalet with the exiled Belgian King Leopold, a rather handsome, weak-faced man with blond-brown hair and slightly watery eyes. His wife is extremely pretty. Leopold speaks excellent English, but complains he is out of practice. He was wearing checked sports jacket, red necktie, ski pants and ski boots. His two sons, who were playing outside, are nice-looking boys who kissed him as soon as he appeared.

Leopold said he had prepared a book setting forth his entire wartime case including documents. He did not wish to publish this until after the coming elections in order to avoid influencing the vote. Leopold showed enormous interest in Spain and wanted to know if I thought Don Juan had a chance of getting back. He hoped that, following the general elections, parliament will pass a law permitting a national plebiscite on the question of his return and pledged himself to abide willingly by the result. He added, furthermore, that should the Belgian people vote for his return they could select any form of political government they wished under a monarch, whether conservative, socialist or even communist. Leopold said:

> I don't want to impose myself in any way or to go against the desires of the Belgian people. I wish to remain a constitutional monarch, faithful to the constitution and to my oath to respect the spirit of the constitution, which is democratic. The interests of the country naturally transcend my own.
> I am by right the King of the country and I shall abdicate only if I know that this is the wish of the majority of the people. So far there have been no indications that such is the wish of the majority.

It is most disagreeable to me to be continually made to appear the contrary from what I actually am. Since 1940 the politicians have always tried to present me as a Catholic conservative monarch. My personal ideas are completely different. I am for progress and social reform. Ever since I succeeded my father, I have tried to favor social reform. I think my father was much appreciated by all parties, including Socialists, who respected him and knew his ideas. I was brought up by my father and have the same ideas.

I must emphasize my intentions. The first duty of a constitutional monarch is to remain above and out of all parties and never to favor one more than another.

But no government can compel my abdication—this can be done only by the people. Last July the government asked me to go. I refused. There must be a new law permitting a referendum or plebiscite and I will abide by its decision. There will be no hesitation. Furthermore, the question of my return has nothing to do with the type of political government Belgium would have. I have often heard reports that the King of the Belgians is no true democrat. I refuse to accept that.

In past years our governments have included Socialists, Liberals and Catholics. I have always been in touch with the Socialists. All our governments for more than twenty years have included Socialists. And the best proof that a completely socialistic type of government can exist under a monarchy may today be seen in England.

ROME, *January 22, 1946*

MOTOR down to Italy, near Como. Driver talks of the partisan groups. He says they do nothing but raid and rob now and occasionally parade around. A GI escort is needed to pass at night along a stretch south of Genoa where partisan robberies are frequent. . . . Gangs of boys live in the towns by beggary, thievery and black marketing. . . . Milan looks bare and gloomy in the snow; but the middle class is well dressed and the stores fairly full. Little reconstruction is under way yet. In almost all damaged buildings busted windows are replaced by boards or paper and even in the streetcars the window panes are boarded.

ROME, *January 23, 1946*

TODAY I saw Baron Albrecht von Kessel in Vatican City. Kessel was counselor of the German Vatican embassy, headed by Ambassador von Weizsäcker. Twelve of them are interned in a Vatican guest-house including von Braun, the junior secretary. They are being kept in the Vatican until they receive a safe-conduct back to Germany. Such a safe-conduct, according to Kessel, was offered by the Allies in August and then withdrawn on American instructions. A safe-conduct, he says, means they would go back to Germany and be interrogated but not arrested.

Kessel is a tall, thin Silesian landowner and Junker, slightly effeminate, with curved nose and thick lips. He complains that the Russians are bolshevizing Germany, the Americans are demobilizing, and the English are the only fair administrators in their zone.

Kessel, who was smoking Lucky Strike cigarettes and complained the black market price was going up as the number of American troops in Italy declined, lives fairly well. He played a part in the plot against Hitler which culminated on July 20, 1944. He explained:

I joined the conspiracy in 1937. I was never pro-Nazi. However, at first I felt we must give them a chance in a democratic way. In 1937, I had a long talk with a cousin of mine, Count Schwerin. There was a group of old school friends and foreign ministry people with whom we got together. In 1938 we became very active. We were closely associated with the Kreisau circle. General Halder joined the plot and actually in 1938 an assassination conspiracy was worked out. When we heard the news that Chamberlain was coming to Germany, it was called off.

I was a great friend of Admiral Canaris, chief of the Abwehr, and intellectual director and political boss of the conspiracy. General Beck was the top leader, but von Witzleben was the boss. General Halder was the chief of staff. Canaris was the man with the civilian contacts. There was also a group around Schacht that was in our opposition. Von Weizsäcker was then under secretary of state and I was his aide-de-camp. I always received the latest news of the international situation and my job was to pass this on to Canaris and von Witzleben.

At that time Goerdeler was in contact with us, but the ties of the conspiracy had not yet been strongly knit. The news I gave Canaris was passed on to the Goerdeler and Schacht groups. My job was liaison. During the war I was transferred to Geneva where I was in contact with Gisevius, who was a member of the Schacht group, although he worked for the Abwehr. Schacht felt strongly that the Nazi regime had to be overthrown.

In 1943 I was called to Rome by von Weizsäcker to join his Vatican embassy because I was a friend of his and I had already been an attaché here from 1930 to 1932 and knew the ropes. I saw Goerdeler and Stauffenberg last in December 1943. They told me the plot to overthrow Hitler would take place in January 1944. It didn't. Then I saw Trott zu Solz in Venice, in May 1944, shortly before the Allies took Rome. He said the conspiracy was still continuing but he could not give me a precise date for the assassination of Hitler.

I had no contacts here with the Allies but had been instructed to do what I could to obtain assistance. However, the Allied embassies in the Vatican were firm on the unconditional surrender line and I couldn't contact them. I think if the Casablanca meeting had not adopted the unconditional surrender formula, we would have overthrown Hitler within six months of the battle of Stalingrad. Trott zu Solz had already had conversations in Stockholm seeking encouragement from the British, but this word never came.

Goerdeler was a great friend of Beck, the wise old leader of the movement. Beck would have been Reichspräsident and he insisted that Goerdeler, who was very courageous and active, should be his chancellor. Ulrich von Hassel or old Count von Schulenburg would have been foreign minister. The core of the conspiracy was Beck, General Oster, General Olbricht, Goerdeler, and von Witzleben. Halder was a great sympathizer. We represented all shades of political opinion except for the Communists. We did not trust the Communists because we could not trust Russia and because we did not know what links the Communists had with the Nazis.

Von Papen definitely sympathized with us. After the capture of Paris it was my job to check files of the *Deuxième Bureau* in Paris. There I found a copy of a telegram sent to Paris in November 1939 by the French military attaché at Ankara. I have sent an affidavit concerning this telegram to the court at Nuremberg. The telegram said Papen had just seen President Ismet Inönü and suggested that peace should be signed immediately or everything would be destroyed. Ismet agreed, but said he believed nobody could make peace with Hitler. Von Papen then said, "Then we must get rid of Hitler." Von Papen always saw members of our group when he came to Berlin. I kept a copy of this telegram to show von Papen who came to Berlin shortly afterwards and von Papen said, "Of course I said that."

ROME, *January 24, 1946*

TODAY I saw Premier Alcide De Gasperi, also acting foreign minister, a rather strange looking man with thick lips, heavy spectacles, pleasant, grave demeanor. Devoutly religious, De Gasperi is especially close to the Vatican. He comes from the North and before World War I was in the Austrian parliament under the old empire.

He said: "No democratic government signing away Trieste could last and a resurgence of the worst form of nationalism would be inevitable." But he was ready to cede the Dodecanese and hoped, as a result, to restore good relations with Greece. He foresaw an Austrian demand for the Alto Adige but feels especially strong against any cession there because of his birthplace, Trento.

Rather to my surprise, De Gasperi made a strong plea for the Italian colonies. He said:

Either these are to be taken away for punitive reasons—and it has been said that the Allies do not wish a punitive peace—or our contribution must be recognized. We appeal to the United Nations Organization to study our pre-Fascist contributions in North Africa. We gave a constitution to Libya before Mussolini.

One should not question our morality or our capacity to govern. We would like a UNO commission to go to Libya and judge our work. We sent Venetian peasants to Cyrenaica to win back the desert. Mussolini pulled them out during the war and, when the Italians withdrew, the

desert returned. The natives have demonstrated that they cannot cultivate the land. I want to rebuild ancient Africa, which requires people
who wish to emigrate, and there are no others. Even Tunisia is full of
Italians.

ROME, *January 24, 1946*

THIS afternoon I saw Burton Berry, our representative in Rumania.
He says that when Harriman arrived after the Moscow conference of the
Council of Foreign Ministers he was quite cocky, claiming the conference
was a great success—especially on Rumania. After ten days in Bucharest
he was no longer so assertive.

The British blocked ex-King Carol's passage from Brazil to Europe. But
the Rumanian Communists and Russians, who hope to use the cynical
Carol, are still working for it. The French Communists have put heavy
pressure on the French government to grant it. Carol doesn't want to hurt
his son Mihai, but figures Mihai will have another chance later.

The Moscow conference was a sell-out and the American mission staff
in Bucharest wanted to resign *en bloc* but decided it would do no good.

ROME, *January 26, 1946*

THIS morning I had an audience with Pope Pius XII. Strode through a
series of corridors and past a waiting room where hundreds of people,
largely soldiers, were waiting for a general audience. The old corridors,
lavishly painted and with anterooms furnished with thick carpets and
oriental rugs and hung with portraits and mosaic pictures of former pontiffs,
were filled with Swiss guards, gendarmes in nineteenth-century uniforms
with bayoneted rifles, and chamberlains and honorary functionaries who
work a week of the year and wear magnificent uniforms with spurs and
medals.

When the Pope came into the room where I was waiting, two functionaries almost prostrated themselves. We shook hands and he began to chat.
He is a tall and exceedingly thin man with a yellow face, hawk nose,
glasses and a slightly bewildered expression (too many audiences).

I told him I had spent a lot of time in Russia where I knew Father Braun
well, and wondered if he thought there was any chance of an understanding
between the Vatican and the Kremlin. He knew Braun. He said he thought
that at present there seemed no opportunity to compromise Soviet materialism with religion. However, in the end, he trusted in divine providence.

There was more chitchat. He asked me if I would like a souvenir. I said
yes. He called to some clerical lackey who whipped out a paper packet
including a cheap leaden medallion of the Pope and a small lithographed
picture something like the old-fashioned cigarette card of baseball players.

He gave this to me and then blessed me and all my family making the sign of the cross above my head.

He ducked into the next room where a line of American officers and WACs was kneeling. As I walked by I saw a poor Pole standing there with whom I had chatted before he had spent five years in Dachau and looked it.

ROME, *January 26, 1946*

YESTERDAY I had drinks with Ambassador Alexander Kirk. Kirk thinks Byrnes is awful and that we have given far too much away to the Russians; we should state our minimal demands with a time limit and tell the Russians "people just don't do things that way." The resultant effect on their inferiority complex would do the trick. Kirk says he would never go to Russia as ambassador, he wants to retire; but he wouldn't mind going to Moscow as representative of Sears Roebuck or Montgomery Ward. The OWI should confine its propaganda to distributing Sears Roebuck catalogues. If enough American gadgets were distributed in Eastern Europe it would undermine Soviet Russia. Of course all this with his tongue in his cheek.

ROME, *January 26, 1946*

THIS noon I had a long talk with Prince Umberto, Lieutenant General of the Realm. Saw him in the Quirinale Palace, filled with saluting, heel-clicking guards. Chatted first with his aides-de-camp, one a parachute lieutenant whose only operational jump was to occupy surrendered Cephalonia and who was captured by the British at Alamein, the other a naval officer who was sunk twice during the war. Umberto is a pleasant weak-faced young man, nearing baldness, tall, with a soft kindly Italian visage, whose English is not quite as good as one would expect, although fluent. He is no impressive personality. Afterwards I had a long chat with the very friendly cockeyed General Adolfo Infante, his chief adjutant, whose children were educated in America and England and who lived in America some time. He looks like a restaurant keeper in Pittsburgh.

Umberto told me that should the Italian people vote to retain the monarchy, it is understood he wishes to remain above politics and is equally willing to reign without political interference over any government of any political complexion, Communist, Socialist, liberal or conservative. If they vote for a republic, he will be quite happy to abide by any such decision. Like Leopold; the time for royal arrogance is past.

ROME, *January 27, 1946*

BRITISH and American soldiers receiving 400 lire to the pound and 100 lire to the dollar are widely engaged in black marketing. Furthermore, over 100,000 Polish soldiers here are frequently regarded by Italian workers as potential mercenaries of the right. Many Italians are so poor that despite their hunger they find gifts of food worth selling on the black market. Even normally, elementary education ceases in Italy at the age of eleven. As a result, thousands of children are fascinatedly working for black market peddlers.

One of the difficult questions in Rome is the strict limiting of the electric light supply which is often not realized by Allied soldiers and officers living in requisitioned buildings exempted from the restriction. American Congressmen staying at the Grand Hotel always receive a better supply of hot water.

De Gasperi, the first clerical premier of united Italy, governs a very disillusioned country where for the most part only the rich or the dishonest are comfortable. The lower middle class has been especially hard hit by inflation.

ROME, *January 27, 1946*

TODAY I saw Guglielmo Giannini, editor of *l'Uomo Qualunque* and founder of the Common Man Society, a most discussed political movement in Italy today. Giannini is unusually tall and broad for an Italian: about six foot, with sandy blond hair. He wears a monocle, which is clearly affected because he takes it off to read. He carries a riding crop with a lead knob and wears a Browning automatic pistol in a holster on his right hip. I doubt if that would do him much good because it took him about two minutes to untangle it from his fat behind when he wanted to show it to me.

Speaking in a mixture of pidgin French and English, Giannini said:

I am persuaded that you cannot administer a state without politics but that this should be done only by men who know other trades and professions, and who do not earn their living by politics.

Mussolini, by a process of mental deformity, began to consider himself not a man but Italy. Abroad, he caused attacks on himself to be attacks on Italy. This was not just. The same is true in Russia—Stalin is Russian but Russia is really another thing.

Now, in Italy there is a useless discussion on whether we should be a republic or monarchy. The really important thing is the administration and reconstruction of the country. We want this done, and we don't care whether it is done by a president or by a king. My basic program is this. We should have an administrative state. It would operate public functions like utilities, police, water systems, but it would leave us free. It should have no right to declare war for any reason, even in case of an invasion. That must first be approved by the Chamber of Deputies. The administrative state should be based on a division of power between the executive, legislative and judicial as described by Montesquieu and Jefferson.

We have among the masses of common men all the necessary men to run such a state. The average man knows how. The banker is a common man. So is the tailor. The administrators must know how to do something else well. They must not only live on politics. Politics should be a duty and not a money-making pursuit.

NAPLES, *February 1, 1946*

ON January 28 I drove to Naples. Reconstruction of Southern Italy is showing signs of progress. In every village the bricks and stones have been sorted from piles of rubble and neatly stacked up. The orange and lemon groves, the latter thatched against the cold, are bearing fine fruit, beside flowering almond trees and mimosas. The winter is mild compared with the savage cold wet season of this time two years ago when the bitter fighting was on. There is more transport. Buses are operating and, in Rome, they are supplemented by dinky little trucks with board benches. Outside Naples the Toonerville trolleys with two or three trailers each are jammed with people. The stores are filling up with leather, glass and other craft work, pottery.

NAPLES, *February 3, 1946*

AT lunch today Alf Nester, American consul general at Palermo, says the Mafia is reorganizing in Sicily. It is strong for law and order and cooperating against bandits with the gendarmes. It is strong for Sicilian autonomy, economic reform and to use Sicilian tax receipts for Sicily's benefit. The bandits and die-hard independence forces are numerically small but raising a lot of hell. Early last year a few hundred got away when the army closed in on the revolt. They have worked with various bandit bands and killed and robbed a lot. They are well armed. Many gendarmes have been shot and the police force is small and terror stricken.

MARSEILLE, *February 7, 1946*

ARRIVED here this morning after two nights and one day aboard the *Gripsholm* from Naples. Aboard, among others, were our ambassador to Athens, Lincoln MacVeagh, and minister to Saudi Arabia, Colonel Bill Eddy.

Eddy is very sour on the British and clearly sponsors the Arab view on Palestine. He tells me that some ten thousand Jews have applied for visas to leave Palestine without success and that censorship prevents this from being known. He says General McNarney's adviser on Jewish affairs has shipped American army planes loaded with agitators and propaganda printed in Germany direct to Palestine. Some were forced down at Cairo and General Giles impounded them and arrested passengers and crews, sending them back to Germany.

Eddy, the son of a missionary and brought up at Sidon, speaks excellent Arabic. He is a cousin of Harold Hoskins. He was in the Marines in World War I and walks with a bad limp. This war he was with OSS at Tangiers and elsewhere and did a fine job in helping prepare the North African landings and in setting up secret intelligence centers inside France.

He interpreted between Roosevelt and Ibn Saud at the conferences in Egypt aboard an American warship. It was a striking meeting. Ibn Saud is six foot four, missing one eye, his legs weakened by many wounds. He said to Roosevelt they were twins, each suffering infirmities. Roosevelt said that however Ibn Saud had legs which could take him around and he had to depend on a chair. Ibn Saud said yes, but he was never sure if his legs would get him there. Roosevelt said he had a twin to his chair and would give it to Ibn Saud. He did, which delighted the King. Roosevelt also gave him a plush-seat C-47 with a bed in the corner. Roosevelt had been briefed not to smoke before Ibn Saud. Before lunch, Eddy took the King down while Admiral Leahy took the President in his own lift. Roosevelt stopped the elevator on the way down and smoked two cigarettes before lunch.

Eddy says Saud, Ibn Saud's eldest son, is to succeed him. Ibn Saud has already told that to his sheikhs. If the situation is as it is when he dies this will work out without disorder. But if it changes there might be tribal wars. Feisal, the next son, smokes and drinks on the sly. Nobody knows if his father is aware of this.

MARSEILLE, *February 7, 1946*

GENERAL John Ratay has given me his suite in the Grand Hotel. This is a tough town. There are continual shootings, especially of Americans. Girls going out with Yanks are often ducked in a pond. There are widespread holdups and victims are frequently stripped.

Ratay lives in a villa owned by playwright Edmund Rostand's sister. He is a crabbed old guy (only in his fifties but has high blood pressure). He is retiring, going home in two days on a "sea-train," a ship which carries trains. He wants to wander around the United States, which he has rarely seen in the last twelve years.

He says he and General W. fought for an invasion of the west coast of France in July 1943. The Germans were so committed in Russia they would have let us through and sought a negotiated peace even if the Allies had lost Egypt. General W. finally changed his mind. Ratay says Eisenhower is responsible for the loss of army discipline; that he is catering to the GIs for political reasons; that he hopes to be offered the presidential nomination next time by both parties and will accept the strongest. He thinks we should have invaded the Balkans.

Ratay has entertained many personages here, including Churchill. Churchill said he hoped America would put all German military equipment in depots "so the German divisions can use them when the time comes."

# 16

## THE LAST

## FASCIST STATE

BARCELONA, *February 10, 1946*

I LEFT MARSEILLE BY TRAIN FOR NARBONNE. THERE ONE CHANGES into a dinky "omnibus" train to Cerbère and the Spanish border. The almond trees, mimosa are in bloom. The platanes are carefully trimmed. Along some beaches are signs of Axis beach defenses against the Allies—pillboxes, trenches, barbed wire, small gun turrets. On the train is a bitter old man with a taste for poetic language who describes the beauties of France, which he compares favorably with the rest of the world. He says only the descendants of the Gallic tribes are truly French, not the Normans or the Franks. He deplores giving the vote to women and says the only days worth living were before 1914. Women are fools and radicals, he says.

There is also a young girl lieutenant, Colette, who fought in the FFI and was given a *croix de guerre*. She is now secretary to the general at Perpignan. She advises me to get off at Perpignan for the night as I have missed the train into Spain. The conductor confirms this, so I leave my baggage at the Grand Hotel and then have a couple of armagnacs at the central café with Colette. She comes from Nimes. Her father is angry about her being in the army. She should be married, with children, he says (she is twenty-three). She wants adventure. She was engaged in underground work smuggling people to Spain when arrested by the Vichy police. After three months she was sent on forced labor to Germany. She was with three thousand other women at Königsberg working on roads. Every so often a few women were taken out to breed for the Nazis. During air raids they were not allowed to use shelters. She escaped to Berlin and got away from there with false papers during an air raid. She got back to Nimes where she joined her brother in the Maquis.

BARCELONA, *February 10, 1946*

THE first man I met on the train from Port Bou was a secret police agent, a handsome, well-dressed young man with the telltale trench coat. They ordered 100,000 trench coats for them and that is the way they can usually be detected here where that item of clothing is by no means as common as in the rest of the world.

MADRID, *February 11, 1946*

LUNCH with Walt Butterworth, chargé d'affaires, and Phil Bonsal, first secretary, of the United States embassy. Bonsal estimates that about 70 per cent of the people represent the defeated elements in the Civil War and want a change in government. However, the mode of change is difficult. Nobody wants another war. Too much blood was shed. Butterworth, who is a southerner, says it takes a southerner to fully understand this civil war. More than a million Spaniards were in arms on both sides, excluding foreigners. More were killed behind the lines than at the front. Whether rightly or wrongly Giral and his followers are held directly responsible for hundreds of mass murders, for the naval mutinies and assassinations of many officers. There would be blood if they came back. Hiding away small arms in Spain is traditional.

MADRID, *February 14, 1946*

TODAY I was talking with my secretary, Concha. Her father is an army doctor, a lieutenant colonel who was invalided in Morocco in 1921. He is a moderate Republican. He was "forced" to head the Palace Hotel hospital in Madrid during the Civil War. He is barely able to work now because of Falangist opposition. Her mother is a strong, proud, conservative Catholic who adored her son. He was an army officer sent to Morocco in the Foreign Legion, then to Russia in the Blue Legion, as a "red." Although he has a bad heart they wouldn't invalid him home until too late. He returned and died. C. was engaged to an American but her mother refused to permit it because he was divorced. The choice for Spanish women is either a virtual convent or whoredom. Because she smokes and drinks slightly, Spaniards think she is immoral. The last time she went to confession she recounted her minor sins. The priest asked if she was a repentant. She said NO. She might fool the priest but she couldn't lie to God. So the priest has since refused her communion. She doesn't dare tell her mother.

MADRID, *February 14, 1946*

I saw J. of our legation whom I used to know in Bucharest. He said the smell of the jail at Puerto del Sol is overpowering. People live in caves fifteen minutes from the palace. Poor itinerant families beg and seek work all over Spain. There are thousands of jobless who cannot get Falangist approval and yet road repairs are woefully slow for lack of labor. To get a maid, before you can even put an ad in the paper it must be approved by the Falange and they must approve the maid. (In Barcelona theaters won't sell you a ticket unless you show some form of Falange emblem of which you can buy paper versions from peddlers.) To advertise for a lost pair of spectacles you must pass the script in several copies through the censor. There are many graveyards near prisons where bodies of prisoners are dumped at night.

MADRID, *February 15, 1946*

HAD coffee *chez* Don Pio Baroja, the famous Basque novelist. The regime bans publication in Spain of almost all Baroja's work, despite the fact that it is internationally renowned and has been translated into many foreign languages.

Baroja is an old man, not in the best of health, who lives simply in Madrid because, thanks to censorship, his income has been drastically cut. During the Civil War he took no part. He was briefly arrested by Carlists in Navarre and then went to France. He returned to Spain, establishing residence with his sister in Madrid in 1940 and has been working quietly on his memoirs ever since. The fourth volume of these memoirs will be ready for publication this year. Since it hasn't yet reached politically difficult 1936 it should give the censor no headaches.

All of Baroja's most famous work was published before his return to Madrid. New editions cannot be published here. If old editions turn up, one can surreptitiously buy them in bookshops with blank paper wrappings around them. New editions continue to be published in Latin America.

Baroja says the cultural censorship does not limit itself to his works. Indeed, during the earlier days of the current regime, some literary wits contend there was serious discussion as to whether Don Quixote should be considered a Red. Famous classical works such as *La Celestina* by Francisco de Rojas are still on the banned list.

Baroja has some strange disease, is always cold, wears his beret and overcoat indoors all day.

MADRID, *February 16, 1946*

THE black market is officially condoned by the Falange, which apparently okays those who can sell cigarettes at a buck a package. Stuff of that sort comes up from Casablanca and from Lisbon. The transport shortage is terrible. Thus apples rot at San Sebastian while they command a top price in Madrid. Ham sells for a fraction in the South of what it gets in

Madrid. They can't get things around. The Falange has its fingers in every-thing from brothels on up. Catholic church has immense investments some of which are not too clean.

### MADRID, *February 16, 1946*

THERE are countless stories to the effect that Spain asked and received of God everything but good government. The Spanish press is so appall-ingly bad that even Lojendio, the new press chief, complains there are no good journalists. The reasons why are obvious: censorship and prison. The system for foreign correspondents has some similarities with Russia—all questions in writing first, fear of anyone to give an interview unless Franco has first done so, late night cabinet meetings but no information on whether there is communiqué or not.

### MADRID, *February 18, 1946*

ALL today packs of hoodlums and stumblebums of the party (students, not in uniform) have been parading around the street hollering *"Russia no, Franco si"* and offering to beat up those who don't give the Falangist salute. They are the worst looking bunch of fascist thugs I've seen since the Iron Guard—a pimply, seedy-looking assortment and an insult to the grace and dignity of this proud country.

### MADRID, *February 18, 1946*

THEY tell this story now. God had heard a lot about what was going on in Spain and he heard things were tough. So he sent St. Peter down to investigate and make a report. He waited and waited but Peter never came back. So God sent St. Paul down to look into the situation and to ascertain what happened to Peter. But God waited and Paul never came back. He took a great decision and decided to send Jesus to Spain. And Jesus never came back. So he called in the two thieves and told them it was imperative to find out what was the matter. They went to Spain. They never came back. Finally, God looked through his roster and found an insignificant but very small little saint and told him he simply had to make a report. So the saint was back shortly. "Jesus, Peter and Paul are in prison as 'Reds,' " said he. "And the two thieves are members of the Falange."

### MADRID, *February 19, 1946*

TODAY I lunched with a thirty-three-year-old man who operates under the name of Felipe and who is chief of the propaganda section in Spain for the clandestine Communist Party. He is a well-dressed, prosperous-looking youth with glasses and a small mustache. He was brought up as a bad Catholic; the son of working people trying to edge into the middle class. He studied at medical school for two years until the Civil War came, when he was mobilized into the Republican army. He was a member of the Socialist Youth which united with the Communist Youth. He became a Communist. He rose to battalion political commissar. After the war he fled to France and traveled around South America before he secretly came back to Spain. His family does not know he is here.

We ate in a restaurant opposite the main bull ring. Establishing contact was rather Hollywood. I had had a letter (from France) which I had delivered to someone in Madrid. I was advised yesterday to be in front of my hotel at 11 A.M. A perfectly respectable middle-aged man came by for me in a taxi and chatted about trivia in French as we drove along. He left me at a street corner and a girl picked me up there and took me in a bus to another district of the capital. There I was picked up by another man in a taxi who delivered me to the bull ring restaurant where Felipe introduced himself. All to avoid the police.

Felipe explained in excellent French that the party's Central Committee (of which Dolores Ibaruri, *La Pasionaria,* is the chief) had a three-man delegation in the underground here. All are less than thirty-four years old. Felipe is the member of the trio in charge of agitation propaganda. He says the Party has an active membership of about 25,000; 3,500 in Madrid.

Most of the propaganda circulated is printed in Spain. Only larger items are smuggled from abroad, all coming now from France although in the past from Latin America. They are smuggled by regular couriers, persons with fake diplomatic passports, stowaways.

The Communists have a very small quantity of arms. That is their biggest weakness. "But we are going to solve this problem" and bring them in, presumably from France. There are between nine thousand and twelve thousand guerrillas of all sorts in Spain today. The majority are Communists or under their influence. Each guerrilla is aided by about two or three people. But the movement is not bigger because of the arms shortage.

The Big Three of the Party in Spain are known to Party members as the *"Delegacion."* The Party runs things from Toulouse, which they regard as the acting capital of Spain. Giral is expected to set up residence there.

Should Franco make a deal and quietly hand over the government to Don Juan, the Communists will take no precipitate action. First they wish to study the objectives and program of the new outfit. They have nothing either for or against Don Juan as an individual. However, in April, 1931, the Spanish people made clear their views on the monarchic question. Therefore it is evident the CP is flatly against a monarchy as such. Nevertheless the Party seeks a peaceful solution. It is ready to negotiate with monarchists and all groups opposing Franco. It wishes to form a representative government provisionally and then submit the final governmental form to a popular decision by plebiscite. However, the Party will not accept a plebiscite except after Franco's disappearance and the establishment of representative provisional government. And no Communist could take part in a Don Juan government.

Asked if Moscow or Madrid came first Felipe said: "I am first a Spaniard—above everything. I want to defend my fatherland but I do not wish an aggressive fatherland."

Despite its weakness he says the CP is the strongest opposition party. "It is the center of anti-fascist activity. The number of active militants is small but our supporters number in the hundreds of thousands. The longer Franco stays in now, the better, because the Communists are skillful at organizing underground while none of the other opposition parties are. So the Communists will eat up the rest."

We chatted quite affably for about three hours. Before departing, Felipe (who insisted on paying the bill) asked if I would take a letter to his wife. I agreed. He reached into his pocket and took it out; the envelope was addressed to a woman in Mexico. Probably a forwarding address and dummy name.

MADRID, *February 19, 1946*

YESTERDAY evening I saw General Juan Beigbeder, former foreign minister, former governor of Morocco, one of the earliest plotters in the Civil War, a Franco supporter who was pro-Allied, now a monarchist. He denounced America as hypocritical. Franco could not have won the Civil War without American oil and British commercial credits—despite the so-called embargo.

MADRID, *February 20, 1946*

TODAY I saw Franco: a small, dainty, fat little man with natty uniform, big red sash, good boots. He is very neat, has a plump, weak olive face and a rather youthful, slightly pathetic smile. He looks as little like a dictator as did Metaxas. He is clearly sincere and strikes me as a bit of a fool. Certainly he is very vain. He has very effeminate hands, which he waves about a lot. He loves the sound of his own voice. Baron de las Torres who interpreted is a terrible translator. He confuses everything in English and I received the impression he did the same in Spanish.

The Pardo is lovely, filled with fine Madrid carpets and beautiful eighteenth-century tapestries with gorgeous fresh colors. On the way back in the car with Dolosquaga of the foreign ministry we passed still battered University City where there are no visible signs of reconstruction. We saw a couple of red bereted Falange militia although Franco had assured me this had been dissolved. D. himself identified them. Moorish guards with

flowing blue uniforms and lances on fine steeds are colorful guards at the
Pardo.

The Generalissimo talked earnestly and at length, continually emphasizing points with his nervous, small hands. He said,

> When the Spanish people are consulted on their future form of gov-
> ernment, I believe they will accept the monarchical method which they
> recognize as more stable than the republican. Of course, when the time
> for such a decision comes, the Spanish people can have another type of
> republic different from previous ones, if they so choose. However, I am
> a monarchist. The traditional methods of Spain are monarchic. A mod-
> ern form of monarchy could achieve the methods of a presidential re-
> gime and still conserve the advantages of stability.

Admitting that his own government could be regarded as "transitional,"
he would give no clue as to when such a "transitional" period could terminate. He said that would depend entirely on the course of events.

Speaking of that unknown day when he would complete his functions as
chief of state, the Caudillo said: "That will be my happiest day—when I
no longer need worry about the problems or future of my country."

He continued: "Some of the people who sought to interpret the Falangist
movement as the exclusive operating force in the government have been set
to one side. Others have been reabsorbed into other movements and
bodies, such as the Cortes."

I asked Franco if, however, he regarded himself as head of the Falange
as well as chief of state. His answer was:

> As the head of state, I am also head of the Falange. But it is now a
> different Falange.
>
> Many foreigners misunderstand the Falange's role in Spain. It was
> never a political party. It was merely a feeling which represented the
> spirit of our cause in the Civil War. Elsewhere it might have been called
> a national front. Foreign propaganda has misinterpreted the Falange's
> real position.
>
> The whole country was contained within and represented by the
> Falange movement. Spain had been almost exhausted by political bick-
> ering and the Falange represented an end to this situation and a search
> for order and prosperity.
>
> In other countries, such as France and Italy, one sees efforts by
> various party leaders to join in a common program which is continually
> upset by personal dissatisfactions and bickerings from those leaders. But
> here in Spain we join people together at the base and not at the top. All
> the Spanish people want the same thing. The most representative idea of
> the Falange is anticommunism.
>
> One must be aware that the domination of the Liberal party put Spain
> back fifty years vis-à-vis the rest of the world. That is why Stalin said
> Spain was the European country best prepared for Communism. During

the past century we have had four civil wars and revolutions. We lost our middle class. By 1936 the consumption and production of the Spaniards were far beneath the rest of Europe. That is why the Falange movement evolved to give the country a chance for progress. It was the first step in social security, but our social reforms have placed us in the top rank of the world.

I asked if he believed in the principles voiced in the Atlantic Charter and if so, whether they shouldn't be applied in Spain. He replied:

Yes, the principles are sound. My aim is to apply them basically as far as possible. But these principles must truly be practiced everywhere. I understand that some nations have complained they aren't being practiced towards them.

You may recall that Spain once had a great empire. As we saw the emancipation of our colonies in America we feared that, perhaps, such a trend was too early, but we regarded the process as a mother watching her beloved daughters leave home.

At heart we are a peaceful nation. And now we see that other nations, as a result of this war, are increasing their territories at the expense of other lands. Such a process can pave the way to another war.

I reemphasize Spain's peacefulness. We have remained out of the last two world wars and we don't wish to increase our territory. We can only hope that others will learn this lesson. And as far as the Atlantic Charter goes, internally the people must take care to distinguish real democracy from false democracy and not to permit loose governmental fabric which allows the Trojan horse of communism to enter. We have had a sad experience in the past and we know what communism is and that we must prevent it.

You must realize that following our Civil War—which ended seven years ago—it is difficult to restore all the liberties as may be done in other lands which have not had civil wars of their own. We certainly don't want to give permission for parties to work openly for another Civil War. This is a delicate situation.

I asked Franco why, seven years after the end of the Civil War and nearly a year after the end of the European war, semimartial law still prevailed in Spain. He replied: "There is no martial law here. Courts and laws are functioning in a normal fashion as they did in the past. There is not a single person in prison who has not been tried and found guilty by a civilian court." (Nonsense!)

I asked the Caudillo what was the position of the Falange party's militia. He answered, "The Falange militia does not exist now. It was dissolved except for four or five battalions two years after the Civil War. Those remaining battalions were dissolved almost three years ago and only Boy Scout-types of movements remain."

MADRID, *February 23, 1946*

A curious incident. I got ahold of the catechism used in most Spanish schools today. It is the seventeenth edition of *"Nuevo Ripalda"* as published in Barcelona this year by Editorial José Vilamala. Among other things little children are forced to learn is that principal errors condemned by the church are, in this order—naturalism, Darwinism, atheism, pantheism, deism, rationalism, protestantism, socialism, communism, syndicalism, liberalism, modernism, masonry.

This catechism favors censorship and says it is a grievous sin to subscribe to "liberal" newspapers. Nevertheless, a note in the text specifically states that there can be a reason for reading part of a liberal newspaper: for example, the stock exchange reports—an odd aspect to the religious instruction of young Spaniards.

(P.S. Two weeks later: I reported the above in one of my dispatches on Spain and even included photostatic copies of parts of the text. Our heavily Catholic bullpen refused to print the article in *The New York Times*. Fortunately, there was no coordination with our syndicate; and the article was printed by other newspapers. I have begun to get bleats from nuns and monks scattered around the United States.)

NUREMBERG, *March 6, 1946*

HAVE attended a couple of sessions of the War Crimes Trial. There are dozens of correspondents here, still wearing uniform, all living in a pencil manufacturer's fake castle where his arms (two knights tilting with huge pencils) are displayed everywhere. Nuremberg is a dismal wreck.

The first session was a strange experience. My seat was up in front of the courtroom and as I walked down the corridor, the prisoners filed in on the other side of the barrier, accompanied by their guards. Von Papen happened to be just across the low wooden barrier from me—only a few feet away. We nodded, as if to say, let's have a chat as soon as we've shaken hands with the hostess. Then he turned left to sit down, adjust his earphones. I turned right.

Extraordinary when looking at the group and remembering the horror that most of them actually took part in and all were in one or another way connected with.

Today I had a long talk with Supreme Court Justice Jackson, the American prosecutor (whom I have known since the Mellon tax trial in Pittsburgh).

He thought the German defense very bad. If a good lawyer like Frank Hogan had been defending, he first of all would have offered Goering two choices of defense—either he would play the hero and say: "I did it all because Germany deserved a place in the sun; I had to be ruthless with those who opposed me; it was for my country's good; I am not sorry save that we lost." Or he would have tried to prove that Goering had been opposed to Hitler all along; had deliberately worked for peace, and so forth. But Goering is trying neither line. By the evidence of Generals Bodenschatz and Milch, trying to show how he worked for peace and sought to aid Jews, he has cut from under himself the props for a great heroic speech using the trial as a sounding board for propaganda. That had been greatly feared by Jackson.

Jackson said:

> This trial is setting precedents for international common law which will outlast any crises in international organizations. Mankind is applying and developing codes of conduct and law for humanity itself as an entity and regardless of nationality. All countries involved in this proceeding are learning from each other—even Germans are receiving an education in law and justice. Furthermore, we are establishing a method which may well prove useful for future courts of international settlement. International law and morality is the basis for this process and not separate national legal structures.

WÜRZBURG, *March 9, 1946*

WÜRZBURG was wiped out at the end of the war by an RAF fire raid made in conjunction with the advance of American ground forces. The German commander, an old Nazi, was served an ultimatum by the Americans, telling him to surrender the city or else it would be destroyed. He spurned the ultimatum and then fled. He was gone before the first British planes arrived. (The citizens of Würzburg are still looking for him.) Würzburg lies in a hollow. A spring breeze was blowing, and the incendiary bombs created a fire which almost totally destroyed the city in the course of one night.

I was delighted to find the following posted in American headquarters:

HEADQUARTERS
203 AntiAircraft Automatic Weapons Rn (SP)

APO 227, US ARMY

9 March 1946

Letter order)
No        2)

The Soviet government is an ally of the United States of America and you are, individually and collectively, representatives of our government. I will not tolerate any disparaging remarks against our Allies to the German people.

I do not hate the German people. My policy in regard to dancing and social gathering should indicate that fact to you. But I cannot forget that the sun can never set upon the grave of some American soldier. From Pearl Harbor and Bataan to the Elbe, your buddies are lying dead because of the Nazi party and the evil machinations of Hitler and his gang. If you are a Catholic, stop to remember that the Nazi party persecuted hundreds of nuns and priests and tried to frame them on immorality charges. If you are a Protestant, think of Pastor Niemöller. If you are Jewish . . . Just do not let your *fräulein's* opinion influence yours. She has been reared in an atmosphere of hatred and intolerance of all the nations of the earth except for the master race we have just whipped.

Millions of Russian soldiers and civilians died to save OUR SKINS. Just remember that. If propaganda causes you to hate Russians, stop and think. They died for YOU TOO. If you want to fight again, encouraging these *fräuleins* that we hate Russia is a good way to get things going. Those were the good old days, yes? Standing in the tracks all day in the bitter cold, dirty, hungry, tired. Firing off the line of departure. Making river crossings. Sweating out barrages. It's cold in Russia. Remember that.

In case you think I'm a pinko and you want to write a letter to the B-Bag, let me forestall you. In political thinking I am a conservative Southern Democrat. An ancestor of my name was killed in the War of the American Revolution. But the Russians are our allies. They have guts. They kept hordes of jerries off of us and, by God, I never want to fight again. Think it over. You have been warned.

FRANK W. EBEY<br>
Ebey                                   Lt. Col. CAC, Cmdg.

BERLIN, *March 17, 1946*

TODAY Lieutenant General Lucius Clay, Eisenhower's deputy, commander of the Army of Occupation, told me the American administration is hampered because "we have not the best quality in trained men."

In the Russian zone there is a Soviet drive to consolidate the Socialist and Communist parties. Considerable pressure is being brought on the Social Democrats. In the American sector of Berlin Communist officials encourage the merger plan of Communists and Socialists.

Relations between Americans and Russians have remained very friendly. Zhukov is a strong military man. Sokolovsky is an intelligent deep-thinking man who values friendship with the United States more than gains in Iran or world revolution. Both are in favor of recovery in Russia with friendly allies at the expense of world revolution.

BERLIN, *March 17, 1946*

IN the Soviet sector of Berlin the Russians are working strongly against Social Democrats who oppose union with the Communist party. There are five phases of pressure: (1) A dinner with much vodka to the prospective persuadee. (2) An invitation to come to a political discussion with the Russian commandant—without vodka. (3) A correct but firm visit from the NKVD. It is asked: "Why are you against union? Be careful. We are watching you." (4) Leading Social Democrats are removed from their jobs. This is a big warning. (5) Disappearance. The number of those who disappear is not great. But when the fact is known, everyone else is terrorized.

BERLIN, *March 18, 1946*

I have completed a survey of the United States military government. We are doing a moderately good job, considering our lack of experience.

We held elections long before the Germans were ready. They had neither the necessary education nor the necessary background to vote intelligently. They did not want to vote nor did their leaders. But we forced the process in order to turn over responsibility *too fast.*

Many Germans who really know and like democracy feel we are walking out on them. The Nazis are lying low. In the too-near future we will leave, and these democratic Germans will be treated as collaborators have always been treated.

We are taking great steps to demilitarize Germany by taking away arms and physically disrupting industry. But so far as doing anything about leading German minds to democratic ways of thinking, we haven't scratched the surface.

### Good and Bad Things in Military Government

*Bad:* (1) It has failed miserably in education. (2) It has a woeful lack of austerity and as a result a probable loss of faith among the Germans. (3) MG gets too many directives through Germans rather than from American officers, who should hand them down to our MG detachments before the Germans receive them. (4) MG in the field feels the higher echelons do not know the German people. They talk with leading clergymen, educators and politicians. But the men down on a *Landkreis* level say, "We know the Germans better and we do not have the same hopes for the German people or the same trust in them as the higher echelons who are turning everything over too fast." (5) American white soldiers and officers talk disgustingly about American Negroes in the Army in front of the Germans.

*Good:* (1) The de-Nazification program is well planned and at last is being well executed. (2) The Army is perhaps the first such organization in history to live on its own food. (3) The Germans are impressed by Army services for troops, the obviously high standard of American living and the complete freedom demonstrated in the *Stars and Stripes*.

A much-decorated young officer told me American policy is paradoxical. It tells us to step on and to democratize the Germans at the same time. Combat troops can do the former but not the latter.

Good roads and good plumbing are the best German propaganda on the adolescent GI mind.

LONDON, *March 30, 1946*

KING George of Greece told me he was convinced the elections tomorrow would show the great majority supports him and he sees no reason to continue postponing the plebiscite until 1948. He hoped the British would keep their troops in Greece. He could not understand why the government in Greece did not publicly state the fact that British troops are there as a result of an agreement made with him long ago.

George said one leading minister is spending a sum of 800,000 gold sovereigns purchased by the Greek government to back the drachma at 20,000 to the pound, and that this figure is pocketing some of the profit. He said the British Foreign Office asked him to make a public statement calling upon all Greeks to vote in an orderly way, but that after he wrote it, they refused to permit its publication.

LONDON, *April 15, 1946*

LONG conversation this afternoon with Ambassador Winant. He is leaving shortly and looks forward to his job as American representative to the Economic Council of UNO. However, he had hopes of being Secretary General.

Winant says it is impossible to sign separate peaces, even if the Foreign Ministers Council meeting in Paris fails. He thinks the United States will try to use the promise of a big loan to Russia for bargaining purposes.

Winant considers Molotov a difficult man to deal with—too "provincial" and not sufficiently interested in the world picture. He thinks Stalin definitely keeps an eye on public opinion in America and is impressed by the growing anti-Russian feeling there.

LONDON, *April 18, 1946*

HAD lunch today with Colonel Bill Bailey who is a secret service operative of the British government. He headed a British mission sent by SOE to Mihailović between Christmas 1942 and the third week of September 1943, when Brigadier Armstrong arrived. By profession he is a mining engineer who went to the Balkans in 1927 for Chester Beatty. He was sent back to Jugoslavia when the war started under the cover of "retired businessman."

Bailey says Tito was a much smarter tactician and politician than Mihailović. Armstrong was a pretty silly routine-minded soldier. He instituted a system of regular meetings three times a week with Mihailović. Bailey had to translate. The first topic raised by Armstrong at each meeting was, "Where is my kit? What is the matter with your discipline?" One day, Armstrong's soap was stolen by a Cetnik and, to Bailey's embarrassment, at that morning's staff meeting Armstrong insisted that Mihailović should look into the matter of the lost soap. Mihailović sent his batman to get his knapsack and took out a piece of soap which Bailey had actually given him. He handed it to Armstrong. Armstrong said, "Thank you," putting the soap in his pocket, but added: "This does not put an end to the matter and the question of discipline." Bailey refused to translate this and Armstrong charged him with insubordination.

Bailey thinks we should have made flat commitments to Mihailović. We should have said: "You must attack and blow up such and such a bridge or objective and in exchange we will give you either so much supply from the air, so much money, radio propaganda support, or a promise of backing at the peace conference." We did nothing.

LONDON, *April 22, 1946*

HARRIMAN arrived today. He says he had great doubts about Byrnes, after September, and would not have accepted a diplomatic post again, but Byrnes has increased in stature. He is a much stronger man now and knows more about foreign affairs.

Harriman believes the Russians will stand firm at Paris until the last minute and then give in. He thinks Stalin is having a difficult time "selling" the people on his new heavy industry and armament Five-Year Plan. The Russians would much prefer to get more consumers' goods, but Stalin seems to think this generation of Russians is going to suffer anyway and therefore he must make Russia very strong very quickly. When the European war ended, Stalin felt he could do anything with his three hundred divisions, but the atomic bomb has changed that. Harriman says we are not going to yield at Paris.

Later, I had drinks with Hector McNeil, undersecretary of foreign affairs. He said that last September when the Greek Regent was in London, the British government was not only talking of giving the Dodecanese Islands to Greece quickly, but also Cyprus. However, England received intelligence reports pointing out that if a coup established a Communist government in Greece, bases on the Dodecanese Islands and Cyprus would be granted to the Russians, so the negotiations stopped. McNeil says British troops will remain in Greece for several more months. He does not want the King to go back for at least two years.

LONDON, *April 23, 1946*

TODAY, Bevin told me he hoped India would remain in the British commonwealth as a free member for the sake of its security and to avoid civil war. Civil war in India could start a world conflict.

Bevin said Russian policy towards China in Manchuria was a great mistake and might push China and Japan to unite as a huge Asiatic power.

He does not want a quick settlement of European peace so much as a just settlement and is prepared to see some form of *modus vivendi* in Italy and the Danubian countries rather than an unfair peace.

PARIS, *April 25, 1946*

BACK in Paris for the Big Four Foreign Ministers Council that is to set up peace conferences with Germany's partners—not Germany. Russia is claiming Libya but we refuse any more than free port rights for Moscow in Tripolitania. We offer a Big Four alliance (United States, USSR, Britain, France) under the United Nations organization.

Secretary Byrnes has been accompanied here by Senator Arthur Vandenberg (Republican) and Senator Tom Connally (Democrat) to gain Congressional support. We want a treaty binding the victors to keep Germany and Japan subservient and disarmed for twenty-five years.

PARIS, *May 7, 1946*

SAW Bedell Smith, new ambassador to Moscow. He said there can be no Big Three meeting, except in Moscow. Stalin told him he cannot travel now, because of doctor's orders. Although he looks well, he is getting old and is forced to keep a strict diet.

Stalin told Truman Russia has no intention of going to war with Turkey. Smith says that because of the bad state of Russian communications, the USSR could not support more than forty or fifty divisions on the Turkish frontiers. Therefore the Turks can defend themselves pretty well, if they have an air force.

Smith asked Stalin how much further does Russia intend to expand her frontiers. Stalin replied "only a little further." He refused to elucidate.

Smith considers Molotov the most irritating man in the world. He says at least Vyshinsky is human and shows his emotions. It is Smith's guess that when Stalin dies, the likely order of succession would be: Zhdanov, Andreiev, Malenkov.

Although Zhukov is an old friend of Smith's, now that he is in Moscow, he is a little reluctant to show such friendship. Smith brought a present for Mrs. Zhukov. Zhukov asked if he would not mind sending it through the foreign liaison section of the war ministry.

Shvernik is very worried about the veterans' problem in Russia and talked to Smith at length about it. Many Red Army men are resentful about going back to work in factories. All returning soldiers are given an enforced reorientation course—several weeks for non-Communist Party members, and about four months for Party members. Part of this "course" is virtual solitary confinement.

Smith thinks the Russians want to get their troops back to the Oder–Neisse line. He is convinced there will be no war with Russia. The Russians are too weak. They have no air force. It will take them much more than twenty years to build a good fleet, no matter how hard they try.

PARIS, *May 12, 1946*

TODAY I lunched, walked and had a long talk with Ben Cohen, counselor of the State Department. He said: "While some people speculate on the advantages of replacing Molotov there is this to be said, despite his irritating qualities. Under Stalin and Molotov the USSR has professed at least an interest in international cooperation. This must be encouraged and it is much better than if the USSR merely announced it would henceforth openly adopt an isolationist attitude."

Trieste is an exaggerated issue. We cannot defend it. It is hard for the diplomats to be as firm as the public would like them to be—particularly when the public would refuse to go to war to keep Trieste in Italian hands. There is some idea in the American delegation to make it a free city like Danzig under UNO.

Cohen thinks we may have to use the Lausanne treaty as a basis for Straits revision. We must recognize that Russia still has age-old aspirations towards the Mediterranean and is now for the first time really strong.

We can't plot permanent peace. What we would like to do is to try and insure a sort of armistice or temporary peace for twenty-five years in the hopes the situation would ease during that time and a new generation could continue the peace with a new plan.

LONDON, *June 5, 1946*

HAD a chat with King Peter this afternoon. He says he is writing a book called *I Came to England,* which will discuss his early education and which is intended to embarrass the British government. He thinks it is an even-money bet that in seven years he will be back on his throne and Tito will be out, but he adds: "It is a good thing I am a young man."

LONDON, *June 12, 1946*

HAD a long talk this morning with Field Marshal Lord Wilson. Jumbo is a pretty convinced liberal. He says Mihailović is guilty of collaboration and his officers knew for a long time that Mihailović was playing ball with Nedić. We should get rid of the King of Greece and the King of Italy. They are both tainted with fascism and we fought this war to end fascism.

He says it will be difficult to defend the Middle East if Britain cannot have a base in Cyrenaica. Even Cyrenaica is difficult because there is not enough water there. Perhaps the best way to defend the Middle East would be by airborne troops from Kenya or from Britain. However, there are great difficulties because it requires two-and-a-half airforce men, including ground crews, to move one airborne soldier. He said there is great Anglo-American interest in the Canadian maneuvers. He recently told the Canadian general staff they would have to unlearn all their lessons of this war. They must prepare for a defense against an attack from the Northwest.

He does not think Russia could fight a war for twenty-five years. Therefore, we must make our plans on a twenty-five-year basis. The Russians are grabbing all the German scientists they can find, in order to make long-range preparations for new weapons, airplanes and navy.

Jumbo thinks the United States is making a great mistake reducing its armed forces too quickly and leaving only one big army in the world—Russia's.

TRIESTE, *July 10, 1946*

STAYING with Bob and Jane Joyce (he is American political adviser to General Airey, military commander of the free territory). The American commander is General Moore whose Eighty-eighth Division I was with when it first went into line near Cassino. They are a much matured snappy outfit now.

Strange group of locals centers around Piero (Momo) Janesich, a jeweler and gentleman about whom various tales circulate. He wears a monocle, is an amateur pilot, and has been reported to be an agent of almost every country; a distinguished-looking nineteenth-century type.

With him, on a lovely little estate, live old Prince Hugo Windischgraetz and his wife, Princess Lotte. W. is blind, bitter and reactionary. He has had to give up all his great holdings in the Austro-Hungarian empire, first after World War I, the vestiges now. He considers Woodrow Wilson a greater devil than Lenin because Wilson inspired the creation of Czechoslovakia and Jugoslavia where his lands and castles were. His two sons, Fritzy and Muki, and Muki's pretty new wife are here. Muki, who was in the Italian air force, took part in the raid led by Ciano which blew up my room in Salonika and wounded my dog in 1940. He remembers the raid well; not as well as I do.

TRIESTE, *July 11, 1946*

RIOTS and shooting every day, Slavs against Italians. Just before lunch the sky is so filled with bricks and stones that it looks like the Battle of Crécy. Then time off for *pasta* and a long siesta. A curious schedule.

The mayor is an amiable, paunchy individual. He perspires as he eats fresh-caught *scampi* from the Adriatic. Outside there is no longer any noise because the rioters have returned to their homes for lunch. The mayor says: "It is terrible. I am perfectly certain terrible things are going to happen." His wife adds: "But not until late this afternoon. Now they must take their siesta."

In the alleys shopkeepers are sweeping up broken glass and peering from behind store shutters preparatory to resuming business. Near the waterfront two toughs are tracing *"Hočemo Tito"* (We Want Tito) in the dust on automobile doors.

ROME, *July 14, 1946*

DE Gasperi told me he will ask the peace conference for a plebiscite in the area of Trieste and Venezia Giulia. Either Italy or Jugoslavia would take over the entire disputed region, depending how the majority votes. "I shall appeal for this under the promises of the Atlantic Charter," he said. "We do not accept the principle of internationalization [for Trieste]. But aside from that, the boundaries of the projected free state virtually sever Trieste's communications with Danubian countries and its economic hinterland."

ATHENS, *July 26, 1946*

FLEW back to Athens just in time for the arrival of my son David. Last night Marina, Dora and I took a horse-drawn coach from our house in Maroussi to Kephissia for dinner. The pains started. We rushed Marina to the clinic and David showed up. Although Dora and her mother, Maria, both echoed the doctor's assurance it was a boy, I went and looked for myself. He was, is!

The situation is bad. Last night I wrote: "The maintenance of law and order over large areas of Greece is deteriorating to such an extent that a condition of growing anarchy appears imminent in certain regions." Armed bands are forming again in the mountains and in much of the hinterland. The Communist supporters are strong right in and around Athens.

PARIS, *July 27, 1946*

PRIME Minister Tsaldaris, who heads the Greek delegation, flew me to Paris on his plane, thus allowing me to get back for the opening of the peace conference (for treaties with Italy and the Axis satellites). It was a slow DC-3. I was dozing away when I smelled something like a bad fuel leak. I looked up and saw, just in front of me, Nadine Tsaldaris (his wife) knocking herself out with a handkerchief dipped in a bottle of chloroform. Strangest *mal de mer* system I ever saw. All the way to Paris she kept waking up and putting herself to sleep.

PARIS, *August 3, 1946*

HAD drinks with Byrnes this afternoon (Truman's own bourbon whisky, 7½ years old, made in Kentucky, sold by Hotel Muehlebach, Kansas City). Byrnes says the committees at this conference are most unimportant. Any subject can be brought out from committee to the floor. Byrnes wants a two-thirds majority recommendation by the plenary session to be automatically accepted by the Big Four.

Byrnes has no use for Australian Foreign Minister Evatt who is mishandling the ideals of the small nations. He has great admiration for Canada's Mackenzie King.

Byrnes endorses Spaak's speech calling for a pledge by each of the Big Four to accept a two-thirds recommendation by the conference. He is only sorry Bevin is not here to play ball with him. He implies Attlee isn't much help.

Byrnes will propose that UN troops be put in Trieste when that area's fate is settled. Byrnes wants to get other troops in so there's no danger of a war between the East and West over that area. Tito might try a coup regardless of Russian warnings and then the Russians might be drawn in to help him.

Byrnes feels the more hell raised by the small powers the better. They will realize what he's been up against. Also it will build up his position and help strengthen his arguments on disagreed issues. Then he can get to work behind the scenes "in the jury room."

Byrnes says the Greeks asked him for a $6 billion loan on the grounds that America needs a friend there and a friend must be worth something after all. He's a little fed up with the Greeks.

Byrnes resents all the committees for "justice" for Italy, Greece, and so on. He asks why there shouldn't be a committee for a just peace for the United States.

PARIS, *August 10, 1946*

A couple of days ago I bumped into Tom Connally's wife and she said: "The Senator's very hurt with you, Cy. You always go see Art Vandenberg and you never see Tom." I confessed I had been remiss and asked if she thought it would help if I asked him to lunch. She said, yes. So I booked a private room at LaRue's yesterday and then asked Mrs. C. if she'd help on the menu. She suggested dry Martinis, steak, French fries. Kind of tough since none of them are available; but LaRue's played ball (black market) and I had the two Connallys, Raymond Offroy of the Quai d'Orsay (who speaks good English) and myself. "Old Tawm" cheered up a bit with the cocktails but still seemed somewhat sulky, although looking most impressive with his black string tie and white mane of hair. When the consommé was followed by a real steak, he warmed perceptibly. After a few munches he turned to me solemnly and asked: "Cy, where's Westphalia?"

"Why, in Germany, Senator." "They signed a treaty there, didn't they?" (Offroy was watching, fascinated, awaiting a clue to American policy and wisdom.) "Yes, sir, the Treaty of Westphalia. It ended the Thirty Years War in 1648."

"Yup," said Tawm. "That's where Napoleon was whipped." Offroy gulped.

PARIS, *August 11, 1946*

GEORGE Andreichin invited me for dinner with Vassili Kolarov, Bulgarian prime minister and former head of the Comintern, a tough, squat little man. George, who is Trotsky's former secretary and spent years in a Soviet jail, was also once the adopted son of King Ferdinand.

Our conversation was heavy and entirely devoted to Bulgarian claims and protestations of democratic innocence. To lighten things up, George told Kolarov I had just come back from Greece where my son was born. "What did you name him?" asked Kolarov. "Basil the Bulgar Slayer," said I (Basil being the famous Greek emperor and savior of Constantinople). George roared with laughter. Kolarov was furious.

Next day George sent me a huge box filled with various kinds of Bulgarian cigarettes.

BELGRADE, *October 11, 1946*

SINCE Shan Sedgwick has no transportation in Athens and we had a spare jeep in the Rome bureau, I am driving it down to Greece from Italy and across Jugoslavia, which gives me a chance to see what's going on. It is a fairly edgy period. The Jugoslavs have shot down two loaded American transport planes when they strayed off course. Tension is very high. Several

American newspapers have been calling for war. Djilas announced on the state radio that if I came to Jugoslavia he would have me hanged as a friend of Mihailović. Mihailović is, of course, dead but several of his Cetnik bands are said still to be roving in Serbia and parts of Macedonia and Bosnia.

Trieste, where I picked up Bob Low (of *Time*) as a companion, is taut and there are frequent riots between Slavs and Italians. It is very much an occupied city with the Eighty-eighth Division and the British on a war footing all the way along the frontier.

At the border we were eyed with sullen suspicion by the Jugoslav military who grudgingly let us pass after examining our visas for an inordinate amount of time. We rumbled over the good Italian roads of Istria (now Jugoslav) and down the Ljubljana Gap into old Jugoslavia and dirt roads, spending the first night at Ljubljana, where the air was one of furtive impoverishment.

Next day rattled on to Zagreb, which seemed cold and forbidding with nothing in the shops. Everyone, even people on the hotel staff, whispered to me that Archbishop Stepinac is the great local hero. He is in jail, of course. Drove on to Belgrade and passed parties of youngsters working on what is supposed to become a broad new highway. They are all called Youth Volunteers and I have no doubt some are volunteers—some aren't. In Belgrade, which doesn't look nearly as battered as I had expected, Shelley Patterson, wife of the ambassador, put us up. He is away. I feel somewhat cut off. Did find a few old friends including Predrag and Viri Milojević who carefully instructed me that if I came by car I should be dropped three blocks away, come only in the dark, see if I was being followed, and use a special knock on the door. They have grim tales of dictatorship and secret police terror:

> Vlado Dedijer, now a big shot, intimate of Djilas and in Tito's inner circle, was walking down the street, saw an old friend, greeted him: "What are you doing out of jail?" Next day the friend disappeared.
>
> Old Mrs. Popović, mother of General Koča Popović, the chief of staff, who used to be a very rich bourgeoise, keeps telling friends: "I don't know anything about politics but there must be something wrong with this regime. I have three sons and they make the stupidest of them chief of staff." (Nikola, Koća's brother, is a refugee abroad.)
>
> Djilas's wife is a diehard Communist named Mitra Mitrović. The children sing a song: *"Ya sam Mitra, proletair, nosim samo solitair"* (I am Mitra the proletarian; I wear only diamonds).

There are no more gypsy orchestras in Belgrade, although it is obviously untrue that all gypsies were liquidated by the Germans because one can still see enough of them around the country. The capital seems to have one *kafana* as compared with the dozens which existed before the war. Many of the restaurants of Belgrade are now messes for institutions—for example, the staffs of newspapers. But old touches are still here, such as Albanian woodcutters and corner chestnut venders.

Printing presses serve the state. Thus, there is a booklet on Archbishop Stepinac, *The Thousand Sins of Little Aloysius,* published by a library called "Kerenpuh." This includes cartoons depicting the archbishop and the Catholic clergy as friends of torturers, Axis stool pigeons, executioners and so on. One shows Stepinac washing the feet of a foul-looking Ustashi cut-throat, whose hands are dripping blood and who asks the archbishop to wash the blood off his hands also. Another shows the archbishop blessing some butcher-types, slaughtering unidentified figures.

On September 26 Tito said in a speech: "We arrested Stepinac and we will arrest everyone who resists the present state of affairs whether he likes it or not. We prosecute anti-National Front elements. Whether these elements are from clerical ranks or any other profession they will be held responsible."

BELGRADE, *October 14, 1946*

IN the spring of 1945 Tito had promised to see me and when I got to Belgrade I sent word that I was here and hoped he remembered. I must hand it to him. Despite the horrible relations between our countries he agreed to receive me—although we are on the verge of a break.

He saw me in his villa and when I was taken into his office, not a very large room, he was wearing his full marshal's uniform, including black boots and all. He greeted me coldly, his handshake lacked any friendliness, and he reminded me that it was only because he was a man of his word and also because he knew that I was an old friend of Jugoslavia that he made an exception and received me. He waved me to a chair and then started walking ponderously up and down, up and down, delivering himself as he did so of a tirade against the United States and the hostile West.

However, I had a friend in the room, Tiger, his large old German shepherd dog. Tiger was an SS dog captured by the Partisans during the war and retrained as Tito's personal pet. Tiger was lying sprawled out on the rug in front of his master's desk. And his liver clearly wasn't functioning; perhaps his digestive tract was more used to *wurst* than *čevabčiči;* or perhaps he was simply very old. At any rate, as the dictator strutted about expostulating, Tiger, his eyes half open, with a quizzical expression lay there farting loud and clear. At last I couldn't help grinning. Tito looked at me shrewdly a moment, his light blue eyes gleaming. Then, without a word, he walked to the desk, pushed a button. An aide entered. He muttered to him. A moment later, in came a tray with glasses and *šlivovica.* Still without a word, Tito poured out glasses. Then he suddenly smiled, lifted his hand in a toast, and the storm vanished. We had an agreeable and interesting talk. Here are some excerpts:

We will never collectivize. Our farmers have a cooperative system.

The Communist Party is the leader of the National Front, which it constituted and created. Other parties were taken in. Although not listed, it is in the National Front. It is unnecessary to list it with the other parties of the Front. I want to add the following. The National Front was not created by formal agreement between parties as in other countries. In our case it was created during the war. During the fight against the enemy the Communist Party proclaimed the Front to all honest citizens without respect to their parties—the democratic ones as well as those not so truly democratic—and all had free entry. Following this declaration by the Communist Party the Front was created from below by the masses. It is only afterward when the leaders of other parties saw that most of their members had joined that they issued statements agreeing to the Front. Since no appeal was necessary to the Communist Party there was no need for the Communist Party to be registered. Maybe you think that now the Communist Party is in a way illegally within the National Front. There is absolutely no illegality.

The opposition does not represent any considerable element which could raise any obstacles to the program of the National Front. I know that there is an opposition and that it often employs illegal methods. I know it will never become stronger—only weaker. We do not envisage any change in our attitude towards the opposition or any change in our measures against it because we know their methods are discredited before the masses of the people.

I inquired: "What is the origin of your name, 'Tito'?"

Answer: "This is not a *nom de guerre*. I took it before the war as my illegal name in party work. It is just an ordinary Croatian name. I have had other names such as Rudi and Georgi."

KOZANI, GREECE, *October 21, 1946*

AFTER completing my dispatches from Belgrade I got the jeep overhauled for roads ahead (at the American embassy garage) and then Low and I took off. I had been summoned by the chief spook at the British embassy and warned there were rumors an attempt would be made to assassinate me in the mountain passes to the south where there are said to be Cetnik bands still wandering (anti-Tito) so that a plot could be camouflaged. There are too many rumors around here. I paid no attention save to borrow a Colt forty-five revolver from the American military attaché. This would be of no use except to protect the jeep and against ordinary holdups (I have a few gold coins such as I always carry in the Balkans; for it is the only currency the peasants value). I obtained an official gun permit that (in Cyrillic script) says I am authorized to carry Colt forty-five (serial number)—"Death to fascism long live the people." I hung the revolver from a wire hook behind the dashboard. Also obtained through Tito's office a permit to cross into Greece via the Monastir Gap (Bitolj–Florina), which is a forbidden area.

As far as the border the journey was uneventful except for the shaking we took on the God-awful roads. It was so cold that we bought black sheepskin hats at Paračin. All along the way but especially around Niš we saw gangs of German prisoners of war marching to work or laboring in the wreckage. Slept in Niš and Skoplje (which I last saw two hours before the Germans captured it in April, 1941), then Bitolj. We had a complicated time getting from Bitolj to the actual frontier, just a few miles away, because the road was barred with troops and barriers, but the document from Belgrade worked magically.

At the actual border the colonel in command was very doubtful. He agreed that the document gave us permission to enter Greece but warned that it was too risky. Quite apart from the fact that he said all North Greece was engulfed in anarchy and civil war, he said the frontier zone had not been crossed since the Germans came through on their way out of Greece in 1944 and none of the minefields they had laid had been removed. When we insisted, he very kindly put some soldiers to work filling sandbags and we packed them in tight along the floor of the jeep, the gearshift sticking out, a small hollow for the pedals, so we would have some protection against blast. I tightened the wire by which we had affixed a Stars and Stripes to the front and told Low if he saw anything budge to holler and get his hands up fast. Then we ground off very slowly, about four miles an hour, slithering down the weed-grown dirt path.

No mines, fortunately. But half-way through no man's land we saw little figures ahead disappearing into what later turned out to be slit trenches and dugouts. They must have imagined a jeep, with windshield down (against mine fragmentation) and two fur-hatted occupants, the forerunner of some attack. There were a couple of warning shouts and I halted. We sat there with our hands up. A patrol slunk furtively towards us, covering each other, until they got near enough for me to shout *"Demisiographos Amerikanos."* There were hollers of joy and about ten of them clambered aboard the poor jeep, patting us on the back, grinning, waving their Sten guns. We lumbered on into Greece. There was no frontier post to stamp our passports, or any civilian authority. The commanding officer assigned a young captain to ride with us into Florina and take us to headquarters there.

We spent the night in Florina and then set off for Kozani despite warnings from the garrison commander that we should wait for the next armed convoy (in two days) because most of the area was uncertain, at best, or in the hands of Communist "bandits." Now we are in Kozani and stuck for an indeterminate period because the commanding general simply won't let us go on. "For our sake," he says.

I am assembling my notes here. Some of them (from Belgrade on down in Jugoslavia):

In Skoplje I was told the present government in Jugoslav Macedonia is about as popular as any government could be and is certainly the most popular this area has ever had. Before the war the Macedonians had nothing. Now they have a little "blood and sweat" if nothing else. There was no problem of a *bourgeoisie* or an aristocracy. The Balkan wars removed the Turks. The last war removed the Serbs. The end of the war removed the Bulgars. Now the Macedonians control their own destiny.

Since August there has been a great deal of military activity and troop reinforcements have been pouring in. Numerous rumors about huge motorized and mechanized formations rumbling through the night and large formations of airplanes flying in the dark on unknown missions. It all sounds a little too Balkan to be true.

The leader of the Macedonian opposition to Tito is a man from Prilep named Metodi Andonov or "Cento," which was his *nom de guerre* as a Partisan. He has been arrested and is now in prison awaiting judgment. He was a loyal Partisan during the war but never a Communist. He wants an independent Macedonia owing no allegiance to Belgrade whatsoever. His supporters in the area of Resen revolted and had to be put down with bloodshed.

Government headquarters in Skoplje are in the old provincial governor's or Banovina building, which today is like a scene out of the first weeks of the Russian Revolution in 1917. Its corridors are filled with hundreds of plain people, bewildered peasants, ragged petitioners. The offices are bare and for the most part not very well furnished.

In one of these I interviewed Ljupčo Arsov, vice-president of the Federated People's Republic of Macedonia. His superior, Lazar Koliševski, president of the republic, was out of town. Arsov is thirty-seven and looks younger. He has brown hair and eyes and a nice ready smile. He denied that the Macedonian Republic had more autonomy than the other Jugoslav Republics. He said there was no official or unofficial secret committee, which was supposed eventually to govern all of Macedonia, including the Greek and Bulgarian sections. "There is no need for that," he said.

# 17

---

# CIVIL STRIFE

# IN GREECE

ATHENS, *October 25, 1946*

THE FIFTEENTH GREEK DIVISION HAS ITS HEADQUARTERS AT Kozani. It struck me as a particularly useless outfit, if one can judge by its headquarters. There was immense confusion and the general did not know what was going on; the colonels did not even know where the general was. The only contact with either Larissa or Salonica was by armed military convoy. Even when we left, the chief of staff warned me not to go by road to Larissa. I had no trouble at all.

Armed patrols are sent out in trucks to keep the road clear but it would be my guess that they go about two miles down the road and sit around until it is time to go home again. I passed one military convoy going north, while making my way south. It contained about fifteen or twenty vehicles, including four armored cars with hatches down and guns ready for action.

For some curious reason the armored cars were in the middle of the convoy instead of at the beginning or end. All but one of the other vehicles were trucks filled with soldiers carrying rifles or stens and with one Bren gun or machine gun in each truck at a minimum. In front of this convoy was an old civilian truck filled with women including children. That would be the first vehicle to hit a mine.

The leader of the right-wing bands from Larissa South is named Sourlas. He has two brothers. I saw one of them whipping around on a motor cycle. They appear to specialize in beating up unarmed anti-Royalists. I talked with a British nurse working for UNRRA in Larissa. She said the jails are full and are horrible. While inspecting one hospital she complained that there were two badly wounded men who were receiving no attention, but she was warned not to complain any more. They were leftists. They died. Almost all the hospital cases were gunshot, knife or mine explosion wounds.

ATHENS, *October 26, 1946*

TODAY I had a long talk with King George. It was the first time I have seen him since his return to Greece. He is kind of fidgety and asked me to come in the back door of the Palace on Theohari Street, from which I was smuggled into his office in front. He was sitting alone looking rather insignificant in his study, which is a modest room. A fire was going.

He is obviously very lonely and extremely uncertain as to what he should do or what is going to happen in his country. As usual he is full of all sorts of rumors about what the Russians are up to—some of them correct and some of them obviously false. He is convinced the Jugoslavs are training left-wing Greeks and Slavs from Greece and slipping them across the border. He says the Jugoslavs are now sending in arms. This is done by a special Russian outfit working in Jugoslavia and Albania where there are two Russian brigades and considerable Russian equipment. He says there is a special school in Jugoslavia where left-wing Greeks are trained. (This later proved true.)

He complains of the stupidity of the Greek politicians. He has been talking with them for the last two days in an effort to form a new cabinet. He says they all have the same program, but one does not like the mustache on another's face and another one does not like the necktie that the fourth one wears, and they never seem to be able to get together.

King George is delighted because he feels the United States is now taking an ever-increasing interest in Greece. He says Byrnes gave him great encouragement when he came back. The King is trying to interest American business as well as British business in making private investments. He would like an Anglo-American company to clear the obstructions in the Corinth Canal and widen it. He would like an American company to build a highway from Athens to Salonica and says there is a company which could do this at the rate of three miles a day, making a good solid concrete highway, like an American highway. But while he has all these grandiose schemes he does not seem to realize that no sensible private investor is going to pour dollars or pounds into a mess like this and he does not seem to have the vaguest idea of how to straighten it out—just complains about what the Russians are doing.

He has a phobia about communism which embraces many more people than true Marxists. He seemed quite disappointed when I told him things in Jugoslavia were a lot better than the outside world expects and although I told him I did not think the Jugoslavs had many troops massed in the south he was skeptical. He thinks it will be difficult to dislodge the EAM guerrillas in the north during the winter because it will be just as hard on the Greek army as on the guerrillas. Judging from the Greek army I saw in Kozani and Larissa, they will never do the job alone. I asked him why he had not asked the British for a dozen flail tanks so that he could clear mined stretches of road. He said he would

ATHENS, *October 28, 1946*

HAVE been staying with the family in Marina's little house in Maroussi. Marina and Nursie are quite unconcerned about the chaos. Yesterday when I drove home from Athens I had to take the back road. Alexis (my brother-in-law) called me at Sedgwick's and said lots of shooting was going on in front of the house near the main road. But all was quiet when I got there. Things seem to move in a tragi-comic way and change from hour to hour.

Big tragedy today. The damned jeep, having been brought all the way from Rome through Jugoslav anarchy and a Greek civil war, was stolen. We parked it just by the British embassy where there are both soldiers and armed police. Furthermore, had a thick, heavy chain and padlock around the wheel and removed the distributor cap. Nevertheless, when we went for it, it was gone. Not even a grease spot. Reported the theft to the police who shrugged their shoulders wearily and predicted we'd never see it again. There is a roaring black market in all kinds of automobile parts and the jeep is already surely being taken apart and sold piecemeal to help cannibalize other stolen vehicles.

DHAHRAN, SAUDI ARABIA, *November 30, 1946*

ARAMCO geologists, poking around in the sand among lizards, vipers, gazelles and incalculable numbers of flies, have already discovered huge strikes of oil along the coastal strip of Al Hasa, in Abqaiq, Dammam, Qatif and Abu Hadriya. The concessions which Ibn Saud has leased are possibly the most valuable mineral rights ever explored.

A big American refinery has been built on a sandspit at Ras Tanura, which is already loading United States naval tankers for points as far away as Manila and a Bahrein refinery processes 120,000 barrels daily pumped eighteen miles under the Persian Gulf from Ibn Saud's hidden store of wealth. A new Transarabian Pipeline Company (incorporated in Delaware) is planning to construct a twenty-six-inch line more than a thousand miles westward to the Mediterranean, probably to Haifa or Beirut. A modern harbor is planned at the stinking little Saudi Arabian village of Dammam across from a swampy island that once, long ago, was the center of the pearl fishing industry. The first eighteen miles of a standard-gauge railway have been blueprinted for the steaming coastal region. This would be the first railway in the country since Lawrence of Arabia and his Arab guerrillas destroyed the pilgrim line from Damascus to Medina during World War I.

With oil prospectors, refinery architects and construction engineers have come pioneers of a streamlined age, bringing complex equipment into a land which still largely lives an Old Testament life. The United States Army has built an enormous airport at Dhahran.

At Abqaiq, 140 Americans live in air-cooled barracks and little drab houses beside a growing hamlet of more than a thousand Arab workers who are learning the lesser skilled jobs of handling drills, pipes, valves and hoists. At Ras Tanura, the children of Aramco workers and executives look out across the sand beach at white-sailed dhows heading down the Persian Gulf towards Madagascar and India, loaded with Qatif dates or Bahrein pearls. Six-wheeled trucks with squat sand tires slip over the dunes beside groups of camels grazing off *dikaka,* a scrub which not even a goat would relish. In huts near Dammam and Dhahran *bedou* tribesmen with bobbed, oiled curls of hair squat in the evening over messes of mutton and rice, hoarding up their weekly pay before returning to the nomadic life of the hinterland.

Modernization is retarded by the strictly conservative and fundamentalist religious traditions of Saudi Arabia. Its Wahhabi dynasty frowns on smoking, drinking and other modern fads, good or bad. The religious courts of the Koran are still *the* law. Thus, for example, when Ibn Saud wished to lay a telephone line from Mecca to Jidda he met strong objections among the old judges of the Ulema (religious courts).

It was only when the old King commanded a chapter of the Koran to be read over the new-fangled instrument that his religious counselors saw its value and withdrew their objections. Ignorance is still rife and perhaps 95 per cent of his subjects are illiterate, the social system is strictly feudal, the machine age is just making its first indentations. In many regions the arrival of the airplane predated the arrival of the wheel.

The law is that of the Koran as first set down by the Prophet, interpreted by his holy successors, and strictly applied by Wahhabi fanatics. It is stern and, according to Western concepts, exceedingly harsh. Even old Ibn Saud himself was hailed before a court not long ago. A conservative Arab brought charges that the sovereign was violating the Koran by selling land to the infidel, in this case Aramco. The King removed his golden headdress and argued before the Ulema, carefully citing Koranic texts, that he was obeying Mohammed in seeking to improve the land as best possible. He was acquitted. Immediately he donned his headdress and clapped his accuser into jail.

The rigorous penalties of Saudi Arabian law appear crude. Adultresses are stoned to death. Thieves have their hands chopped off and the stumps plunged into burning oil, which serves as an effective if excruciatingly painful cauterizer. Yet Arabs are horrified at the idea of imprisoning thieves for years; they consider their own punishment code more humane. Furthermore, they point out that its harshness is required by the geographical situation. A vast desert land cannot be filled with police. They contend that a *bedou* can leave a bag of gold in the desert and it will remain untouched until he returns because of the rigorous punishment code.

Since the State Department is firmly opposed to extraterritorial rights, American companies operating in Saudi Arabia are scared of the possibility that some day one of their employees is going to run afoul of this legal code. It is generally understood that speed launches would slip any American, who got into trouble at the Persian Gulf installations, across the water to Bahrein. Once two technicians, requested to repair some electric wires at the Emir's palace in Dammam, got drunk (against the country's law) and entered the official's home reeling and smoking cigars. They were chased out by an alert secretary but, on their way home, beat up an Arab who later accused them of robbing him. The American consul was able to obtain permission for them to sleep outside the jail, on camp beds, while he sat watch over them. When they were tried, the judge accepted their oath that they had not stolen; it was rendered on the Bible, instead of the Koran. He ruled that it was not illegal for foreigners in Saudi Arabia to be drunk as long as they imbibed in their own homes. The two were expelled.

Aramco doctors have obtained permission from the Emir of Al Hasa to slightly humanize the system of amputation for thievery. Now the cleaver used in the region is kept in a sterilizer in an American hospital at Dhahran. When Saudi Arabian officials send for it, the doctors know what's going to happen. A medic goes along and, before the victim is punished, the doctor injects an anesthetic. After the amputation, instead of cauterization in boiling oil, the culprit is taken to the American hospital where the wound is treated and sewn up.

If oil drills get stuck some four thousand feet below the earth, the Moslem crew, which may often include liberated black slaves from Oman, usually concludes that a *Djinn* has clutched the tool and *Mashallah*, praise God, it will be released—as eventually it is. What did, however, astonish the wary *bedou* was the miracle of chicken incubators. Most Western improvements, no matter how complex, are casually accepted, from the airplane to the icebox. A new language is growing up. Thus, although those who employ the words have no real idea what they mean, *guwwah kahrabaa-iyyah shadiidah* means "high voltage." The first wheelbarrows brought to the country were gracefully accepted; but the workers took the wheels off and carried loads in the barrows themselves. I visited Emir Abdul Muhsim bin Abdullah bin Jiluwi who, on the one hand, rang on an electric pushbutton to call for coffee; on the other hand it was brought by a black slave and outside the council room the emir's bodyguard squatted with sabers crossed on the floor to protect their lord.

I spent the day with King Abdul Aziz Ibn Abdur Rahman Al Feisal Al
Saud of Saudi Arabia. Early this morning I drove with the Syrian who is
Foreign Minister in Jidda (Mecca is the King's capital) to the white pillar
marking the frontier of Mecca—beyond which the non-Moslem is not permitted to pass. Then we got out of the car at Shumaisi, which is a small
stop-off beside the Hudaybiya mosque on the road from Jidda to Mecca. It
was at the Hudaybiya mosque that the Prophet Mohammed signed his first
treaty with the unbelievers. There is an ancient cemetery through which we
walked, not even knowing we were strolling over graves because the
Wahhabi sect permits no effigies or images and there were just some un-
marked rocks atop the graves. (Arm in arm with Sheikh Yussuf Hussein,
the foreign minister, I walked a few yards beyond the demarcation line
against the infidel.)

After realizing this was not where Ibn Saud proposed to set up a tent city
to receive me, we went back a couple of miles to Hadda, which is a
resthouse on the pilgrimage route just a little outside Mecca. Mecca itself is
hidden behind a range of stark peaks. Hadda is a place on the fringe of a
green oasis near Wadi Fatima, named for the Prophet's daughter. Some
tents had already been erected by the time we got there, although it was
still early morning. They were filled with comfortable chairs and luxurious
Oriental carpets. New tents were constantly being put up and furniture was
being unloaded from trucks driven out from Mecca. There were several
companies of soldiers in khaki, wearing green headcloths and drilling in
anticipation of their sovereign. Servants and slaves were broiling large
panniers of food on fires beyond the tents.

Ibn Saud drove up in a Mercedes Benz cabriolet, which is his favorite
car. It was given to him by Adolf Hitler. The King of England gave him a
Daimler but he apparently feels more comfortable in the Mercedes in
which he sits beside the driver. He moves with great difficulty nowadays
and suffers from all kinds of illnesses which leave him stooped, halt and
lame. Despite that, bent over as he is, he is still over six feet in height.
They say he was six feet, six inches in his youth. He is a massive man
although now it is largely fat. I would guess that as a youngster he probably weighed well over two hundred pounds without an ounce of fat. He
has one bad eye obscured by a cataract, and heavy, slightly Negroid features, a quiet, gentle voice and manner. He was wearing the plain brown
robe with a slight golden edge that marks royalty in Saudi Arabia and a red
headcloth with golden *igal*.

He was accompanied by a group of nobles, sheikhs, members of his
court and beautifully garbed warriors from his bodyguard carrying rifles,
pistols and gold and silver daggers and scimitars, and wearing crimson,
golden, blue and yellow robes. After his troops had saluted him, Ibn Saud

and his principal courtiers, including his brother, Prince Abdullah Ibn Abdur Rahman, congregated inside the royal tent. The King rested while a northern breeze began to ripple along the desert, curling the palm fronds in the oasis.

While jeeps and other vehicles protected by machine guns drew around the periphery of the encampment to protect the King, Ibn Saud joined his private imam and, facing Mecca, rendered his prayers, kneeling and bowing in the direction of the sacred Kaaba four times. Everybody else including the soldiers did the same. A signal was sent from the royal tent to my tent that the King would receive me. Seated in a large armchair and gazing rather blankly through his dark glasses, the King started a general discussion of world affairs. The basis for this had been prepared in a series of questions I had submitted from Jidda, the answers to which, written in a beautiful Arabic script, were given to me here. The interpreters sat on rugs at the foot of the King and translated while he said, among other things:

There are no basic frontier questions between Saudi Arabia and other states, including Trans-Jordan. "We Arabs, as one family, have the same aims and aspirations. It is not unnatural to find among the members of a family some questions that require conciliation. We believe there are some secondary matters that will be possible to solve cordially and in a fraternal fashion."

He expected to spend the $10 million loan received from the Export-Import Bank as well as accruing oil royalties on projects to develop the country, including railways, harbors, ports and "anything which can serve to raise the living standards of our subjects morally or materially and insure their happiness now or in later years." He specifically said he wanted to build a railroad from the Persian Gulf to Riyadh, capital of the Nejd. He said the camel was outmoded, and the automobile could not withstand the desert.

He said he saw "no need for the restoration of the caliphate and consequently I do not consider either myself or anyone else as a candidate for that office." The only way the Palestine dispute could be settled would be by handing over the country to the Arabs: "Any other solution would be a clear aggression which the conscience of humanity cannot accept." He had sent a new letter to President Truman on this subject.

After a long talk with Ibn Saud, I retired to my tent and typed out an account of the interview which he wanted to have read to him before I could send it. Attendants brought in lanterns. Then I returned and listened while it was translated; he nodded as it was read to him.

Back in my tent, the court chamberlain informed me that Ibn Saud was awaiting me at dinner. I went to the banquet tent where a long table had been set with European-style plates and silverware—as contrasted with the usual bowls of pilaff eaten with the hands according to the dictates of the Koran. Some thirty royal princes and sheikhs were present. It was a nine-course dinner during which the King spoke through an interpreter who stood behind him and translated his remarks and those of his brother, between the two of whom I sat. The interpreter was a large Negro slave who spoke with an English accent.

On the other side of the King was another huge Arab slave with Negroid features who broke morsels of food into small pieces and laid them on the King's plate. These he ate with his fingers—the only man present not to use a knife and fork. He explained to me that he was only "a simple Arab" and ate the way the Koran said he should. He had some difficulty because the middle finger of his right hand (the Arab never eats with his left hand, which is used for other purposes) had a knuckle swollen and broken decades ago by a Turkish bullet.

Conversation did not flow easily. The King made a few remarks such as that his land was barren of all but patriotism and religion; nevertheless, that these sufficed. He remarked that the water which was served at the feast (mainly chicken preparations) was his favorite water; not only was it exceptionally fresh, but it came from the well where the Prophet had drunk.

While sharing with me his plate of sliced oranges from Taif, he spoke of his exploits when, with twenty warriors, he had descended from Kuwait to start his conquest of Arabia by capturing Riyadh in a surprise night raid in 1900. He recalled wounds, including that which has greatly weakened his leg, and pointed to the gnarled finger which had been cut by a Turkish bullet.

As a matter of fact, the Emir Bin Jiluwi told me a few days ago at Dammam the full story of that raid. Bin Jiluwi had been one of the handful of loyal followers exiled to Kuwait with the Saud family and who returned with Abdul Aziz to attack Riyadh. They climbed ladders over the walls of the city and crept over the housetops to overcome the sentries. According to Bin Jiluwi, Ibn Saud was dangerously wounded in a very personal portion of his anatomy during this battle. Old Bin Jiluwi said to his chief, "Ah, Abdul Aziz, you have gained a city, but you have lost something more precious." Ibn Saud, to prove that nothing important had happened to him, ordered one of his soldiers to bring a woman in the middle of the battle and proceeded to demonstrate that he was unimpaired.

At the end of dinner ewers of water were taken around the table, and everyone washed his hands. Ibn Saud then, leaning on his simple cane, limped to another tent, open to the desert on one side. Numerous little cups of coffee flavored with cardamum and poured from long-nosed brass pots were served. We sat on two chairs side by side. The interpreter squatted on a carpet before us. The bodyguards sat in a semicircle outside the one open wall of the tent, and their eyes and teeth and the damascened work on their weapons glistened brightly, reflecting the light of the lanterns. Occasionally a fox barked in the stillness.

Over the coffee Ibn Saud said he had great esteem for the late President Roosevelt. He was touched by the President's gift of a duplicate of his own wheelchair and then by the present of a luxurious airplane. When they had met in Cairo in 1945, they exchanged jokes about their infirmities. Ibn Saud indicated rather directly he did not admire President Truman because of his attitude on Palestine. He said, however, he would not accede to pressure from other Arab states and cancel his oil concessions to the United States. He feels he cannot break his pledged word, and anyway it would be ridiculous to boycott America, which is now only "three days" away by air.

The King has a very interesting way of talking in parables. He told me one he had related to Churchill when the Prime Minister had started to discuss Germany with Ibn Saud. This is the story:

> Once there was an old sheikh. A tiny serpent came to him and said, "There is a wolf hunting me and I crave protection." The sheikh put the serpent in his bosom, but the serpent said he did not feel safe there because the wolf might reach up and scratch him. Therefore he asked to be put in the sheikh's mouth, and the wolf went away. Then the serpent said to the sheikh, "Now I shall reward you for your kindness. I am going to bite you. But I shall offer you a choice as to whether I bite you in the tongue or on the palate." That is the way of an enemy. It is the way of Germany and one must take care.

Finally in the dark night after the audience concluded, I returned to my tent, and a group of attendants came through the door shortly afterwards bearing cushions covered with presents. These were a royal Saudi Arabian costume, a portrait of Ibn Saud with an Arab inscription, and a magnificent gold Swiss wrist watch with gold bracelet with the King's monogram on its face. They dressed me up in the costume and then, finally, my car was brought nearby, and we drove down the road from Mecca to Jidda. Foxes slipped across the desert stalking kangaroo rats in the moonlight, and occasional returning pilgrims wandered towards Jidda and Medina.

CAIRO, *December 4, 1946*

I got out of Saudi Arabia by signing on as navigator of one of King Ibn Saud's airplanes carrying pilgrims out at a clip rate from Jidda to Beirut. The pilot was an American who spoke nothing except English. The co-pilot was an Arab who spoke a few words of Italian, having been trained to fly in Italy at the time of Mussolini's attempt to make headway in the Arab world. I was navigator on the basis of the fact that I spoke a few words of Italian and could translate between pilot and copilot. The plane was overloaded to an excessive degree but the American pilot pointed out this happened every time. He was just about fed up. The King's few planes, used on this pilgrim run, are operated under the control of a colonel whose previous experience has been with the camel cavalry. He had noticed that although a truck filled with benches could hold perhaps twenty people, if you jammed everyone together standing up, it could hold perhaps fifty, and the truck would still operate. He figured aircraft function the same way and would make more money for his king.

We had a hell of a time taking off but finally got into the air. We had hardly gotten up a thousand feet when there was a terrific banging in the back of the bucket-seat DC-3. "They want to know where Mecca is," said the copilot. As navigator, I told them. More banging. The pilot asked me what the hell was going on. I went back and found everybody praying towards Mecca, damn near upsetting the plane. I also noticed right after the prayer that some of the female pilgrims had hauled off their veils and were looking somewhat less Wahhabi now that they were getting away from puritanical influence and going back to the fleshpots of Beirut.

We flew over the Gulf of Aqaba but one of our engines started to fail and we had to come down in a hurry at Lydda. The pilot and I got out and went in to have a drink, but the British sentries at the military airport wouldn't let anybody else out of the plane because Mecca is quarantined against plague. The copilot and all the passengers had to sit in a miserable circle in the middle of the airfield surrounded by bayoneted sentries. The pilot confided that he was ready to quit although he was being paid an enormous salary. He didn't think it was worth it.

When they finally had the plane repaired after a couple of hours, we took off. However, just as we were about to leave the ground, the engine came unstuck again, and we just missed a tree. The pilot turned it around and taxied back in on one engine. He told me to come on out with him, which I did. We walked to the telegraph office and I saw him print out a cable to Ibn Saud telling him that he, the pilot, was quitting and leaving one of His Majesty's planes with about forty-five pilgrims and one busted motor in the middle of Lydda airport in case Ibn Saud wanted to do anything about them. The pilot then asked me if I wanted to come and get drunk with him in Tel Aviv or Jerusalem, but I told him I was going to Cairo. I bummed a ride on an Al Misr biplane just about to take off.

I stayed in Saudi Arabia for a couple of weeks.

Crown Prince Saud is the oldest surviving son. I have seen one family tree which shows well over fifty sons, but I don't know how many are alive. I remarked that two of them were named Türki, but Türki Number One died. There is no record of the number of daughters. Ibn Saud had countless wives, although never more than four at a time. The Koran permits four. Therefore he would always divorce one to leave room for another— in case he saw a pretty girl. The divorced wives had status as princesses and were cared for by him financially. He paid little attention to his daughters but brought up his sons as princes.

The port at Jidda is filled with dhows which have journeyed across the

Red Sea with pilgrims: all kinds of Moslems—Sudanese with scarred cheeks, West Africans in blue robes, Touaregs, Tunisians, Afghans squatting by the roadside over little fires where they broil their meals and exchange news from remote corners of the earth.

Here and there along roads near the Red Sea and many miles from Mecca are occasional dried-up corpses of pilgrims dropped ashore by unscrupulous dhow captains who charge a cheaper rate and don't go to Jidda port where they have to pay quarantine fees. They cruise along the coast and then tell their passengers they are only a few miles from Mecca and leave them off, where most of them wander into the burning sunlight and some die of thirst.

The Souk at Jidda is jammed with pilgrims coming all the way from China to Madagascar who are selling possessions to pay for their eventual trip home and drinking tiny cups of coffee or eating sweets while millions of flies buzz around them. Beyond Jidda's walls a mud-built African village has grown up which is filled with burly black men and unveiled black women, their religious customs being not so strict. These are Africans who do not have funds to return from the pilgrimage.

Last Saturday morning there was a public execution in the square near the Jidda customs house. The victim was a man who had become drunk and run amok murderously. Alcohol is prohibited in Saudi Arabia, and therefore the crime was double. The method of execution is quite simple. The man is stood up, bound, between two executioners. One jabs a knife into his side. As his reflexes make him bend over towards the side from which the pain is coming, the other executioner knocks off his head with a backhand blow of a scimitar.

There are plenty of odd contrasts in Jidda. A few miles from the Africans' mud huts you can see 1946 American automobiles belonging to wealthy sheikhs pulling in at tiny taverns where their owners gather for coffee or the high-priced deep-well water. Heavily veiled women patter down alleys with burdens on their heads and orange henna stains on their bare feet. Behind shuttered harems the less religious puff forbidden cigarettes. As a matter of fact, I remember going into the office of the Syrian foreign minister who handles Ibn Saud's contacts with diplomats. After we had gotten to know each other, one day he locked the door of his office and pulled open a drawer and offered me my choice of cigarettes—Camel, Chesterfield, or Lucky Strike. As we sat and smoked, he took off his headdress and talked longingly of Damascus which he had not seen in thirty years.

The slave trade continues in a dying trickle along the Persian Gulf coast. One day while I was fishing near Bahrein, a little slave vessel came in at Al Khobar, a Saudi Arabian village near the oil centers. It was loaded with children bought or stolen from the Baluchi coast, who were being peddled. The boat found no customers, so it loaded with dates and water and took off. I saw a letter last week written by a sheikh asking the oil company to give jobs to two of his liberated slaves. He granted them freedom because it cost too much to feed them.

While in Jidda I saw St. John Philby several times. Philby is of course a famous English Arabist. He has become a Moslem and is regarded as pretty holy because his beard is red, the sacred color. He has a house in Mecca and is very close to Ibn Saud. He does a good deal of writing, and everybody assumes he also works for British Intelligence. Although Philby pretends to be a good Wahhabi, he drinks like a fish when he can. I first met him in 1938 at the St. James's Club in London and I still recall my hangover. He put down a good deal of whisky when I saw him in Jidda. He is very vain and doesn't consider anybody else knows a thing about the Arab world, but I must say I find him extremely amusing.

The few American oil technicians in town wander around the steaming Jidda Hotel in their undershorts. Aramco headquarters with its excellent mess and air-cooling system is the favorite joint for Westerners. The principal attraction of the American legation comprises its two tethered gazelles and a waddling flock of ducks. Things are developing in Saudi Arabia, but basic life doesn't look very different since the days of Mohammed. Most of the country is desert. Here and there one sees camels grazing on *dikaka* scrub or a caravan wending towards Yenbo. Scavenger birds circle over the occasional corpses of pilgrims. Flies cluster on every edible object in the bazaars. Foxes hunt a scanty life in the desert.

Ibn Saud is accessible to all his subjects in this curious combination of absolute despotism and democracy. A poor man can squat before him and address him directly without any title, saying, "Abdul Aziz. My camels are ill and *mashallah,* praise God, it's the fault of the infidel."

Man here is strikingly adjusted to eternity. Graven images are not permitted. I had great difficulty bringing a horse-headed ebony Eritrean cane to Jidda with me. Bodily death is regarded as immutable and graves are marked only by a rough stone, if anything.

Ibn Saud maintains an extensive information system, picking up a good deal of interesting news from the centers where the pilgrims cluster and exchange gossip from all over the Moslem world. He also has a group of secretaries monitoring his radio in Mecca. Incidentally, I told Harlan Clark, the young American chargé d'affaires at Jidda, I wanted to buy a slave. "Why?" he asked. "Because I want to take him to America and see the immigration officer's face when I fill out the landing card with 'Profession—slave.' "

ATHENS, *December 5, 1946*

CAME back here (via Cairo) to pick up the family and take them to Paris where we have finally managed to find a nice apartment. Things are getting worse. Wrote this evening: "What would appear to be incontrovertible evidence now exists of Albanian, Jugoslav and Bulgarian participation in fomenting informal civil war in northern Greece."

ATHENS, *December 6, 1946*

KING George told me that at the time of the Teheran Conference, he complained to Churchill that Eden had submitted a memorandum claiming George was unpopular in Greece, that he should never go back, and asked him to sign a document stating he wouldn't. He said Churchill told him to pay no attention to Eden; if he ever received any other such documents, he should refer them to Churchill personally. King George said he told this to Roosevelt who was so furious that he actually rose out of his chair and walked a few steps, which George had never seen him do (of course, F.D.R. couldn't!), and that Roosevelt told him the United States was against any such dictatorial intervention in the future of small allied countries.

PARIS, *December 25, 1946*

WE came back by a Greek boat to Marseille, then by train. Never again. They had sold our accommodations to someone else as well. We jammed Marina, Nursie and the two children in one cabin. I shared another with two old ladies but they complained so much at the "indecency" of it that I stayed on deck all day and night. Took David up in his carry-all as the women were sick; terrible storms.

Our apartment is nice but freezing. A glass of water by the bed is frozen each morning, even with the window closed. We had people for Christmas lunch and warned them all to wear long woolies, which they did, and to keep their coats on—despite a log fire. Rations limit gas, electricity, and so on.

And France is in bad shape. Last night I wrote:

Unless the weak, temporary and minority government of Léon Blum can find material ways to implement its leader's pledges to put an end to the Indochinese revolt by positive action during the next month, France faces the possibility not only of losing her prize Far Eastern domain but also of losing eventually a large portion of her overseas empire, especially in North Africa.

PARIS, *January 9, 1947*

I saw Léon Blum, prime minister, this morning in his office at the Hotel Matignon. I arrived a bit early and Blum came out and asked me to wait in the salon while he finished up some work. It is a lovely room with flowers on each table, and a white bowl of roses and ferns on the main table. The furniture is white and gold. There is a thick rug on top of the gray carpet. There are medallions of paintings on the green-colored walls decorated with gold, and gold design on the green-colored ceiling. There is a large crystal chandelier.

Blum looks very delicate but astonishingly healthy for all he has been through. He is very thin. He appears to have shrunk in height, but his walk is brisk and spry.

At the entrance to his own office, he paused to look longingly out over the lovely garden of the Matignon saying it was a pity one had to work and could not just look at the garden. On his desk was a vase of roses with exceptionally long stems and there were two pink azalea plants in his office which is dominated by a huge tapestry.

Blum explained that he could not give an interview, although he might hold a press conference next week when his government terminates—if he thinks such a conference will not do any harm. He was very interested in Byrnes' resignation and a bit uneasy about the prominence of generals in American diplomacy. He had no newspapers this morning because of the current strike. Blum made the following points during our conversation:

He will not accept the position of either prime minster or President when his term of office expires next week. His health would not stand it and he simply does not have the stamina. He used Parisian argot to explain that he was now in a position where, from time to time, he could give his services as an "extra," but he could not take a permanent position of service. The position of President would be just as hard on his health as that of prime minister.

However, he feels that this term as "extra" has left the political situation greatly improved. There is now a very good chance that his cabinet will be succeeded by a coalition government. The Socialists took the leadership and Blum feels the other parties are in a much better frame of mind to cooperate. He thinks it is quite probable that the Socialists might serve as a backbone in such a coalition despite their minority position.

The great thing that has occurred, Blum says, is the reestablishment of France's parliamentary tradition. Perhaps 150 out of the more than six hundred deputies have previous parliamentary experience. Past governments—even that of Gouin—were made up of coalitions and when the majority parties had decided upon a policy, their deputies in the assembly more or less automatically voted to support them without much question. However, Blum's cabinet represented a minority party. Every policy step had to be presented and explained to the deputies and argued out with them. This brought a true resurgence of the best and most useful type of parliamentarianism. Blum thinks this tradition has been firmly reestablished and that no matter what government succeeds, parliament now stands upon its feet in the French political picture.

Blum feels his fight against inflation has caused a remarkable psychological and spiritual renaissance, which will assist France in regaining its European and world position. It is particularly important that this should have come about on the eve of the German peace talks. He said instructions for Couve de Murville on the subject of Germany were now being prepared. Blum speculated on the effect of French Socialist progress upon Socialist parties abroad—but without conclusion. He feels that the heritage of democracy in Germany from before the days of the Nazis is still very powerful. He is extremely worried about the split in Italian Socialism between the factions of Nenni and Saragat. He has a great admiration for the internal policy of the British Socialist government, which, he says, is fully supported by the parliamentary rebels.

PARIS, *January 9, 1947*

BIDAULT, former foreign minister, received me in his apartment at the Hotel Bristol. He was more talkative than any time I have ever seen him. He had a black left eye. I did not ask him where he got it.

Bidault pointed out that France was the first of the Big Four Powers to explain its point of view on Germany in any detail. At London, in 1945, Bidault brought the matter up, but the Council of Foreign Ministers said discussions on Germany must be carried on through the normal diplomatic channels. Bidault said:

Naturally, Frenchmen wonder if the other great powers are waiting for France to make concessions. We did get an accord in principle on the Saar, from an economic point of view. It was not a question of anything except economics and even then we got nothing precise from the Russians. The Saar must be placed under the economic control of France. To do so would in no sense be a concession by the other three powers. We do not ask for territorial annexation. We realize that the 800,000 Saarlanders are Germans but the Saar itself must be linked economically with France.

It should be an independent republic with its own statutes. France does not wish to annex it. After all, the Saar is three times as big as Luxembourg. France should have a relationship with the Saar such as Luxembourg has with Belgium, or Liechtenstein has with Switzerland. It should be taken away from Germany. Its economy, and possibly its financial structure, should be linked to those of France. It should be independent, but within the system of French economy and French customs union.

The Americans even think that we French worry too much about Germany. They have the atom bomb. They are not immediate neighbors. They offer a twenty-five-year treaty to ensure the supervision of demilitarized Germany. I can understand the American point of view. But the Germans are a strong and dangerous people. It is indispensable to reassure France against future aggression. This is not a French obsession; it is good sense. The Germans are numerous, capable, hard working, disciplined, good engineers, good soldiers and dangerous.

The Big Three Powers each privately hope that in the end Germany will be with each of them. France is outside. We entertain no such illusion. We fear that the Big Three will in the end agree to re-create a strong Germany—each of them for its own and different purpose. The British think that Germany will be theirs through the Socialist Party and Dr. Schumacher. The Americans think that Germany will be theirs through propaganda and material assistance. The Russians think that Germany will be theirs. That would put Russia upon the Rhine—in control of Europe.

The control of Europe is at stake. France cannot understand the shortsightedness of Britain on this question. Even Churchill told me on November 11, 1944, that Britain does not change enemies, and yet Mr. Churchill told me one year later that of course enemies must be changed; that his entire career testified to the need of changing enemies.

As far as the Rhine goes—France has asked for the detachment of the Rhineland from Germany. This was originally the idea of General de Gaulle. This, however, is not as vital as the other points at issue. It is mainly a question of strategy in armored warfare. The United States learned such at Bastogne. According to the French plan, France would control the Rhine by supervision south of Cologne and the Dutch and the Belgians would supervise the Rhineland north of Cologne.

Bidault emphasized the desire of France for a federated Germany of a decentralized nature as contrasted with a centralized Germany. He said: "We want a federation of Germany. We do not want a Reich, which we have learned is a natural danger to us. We face a void, however, in the viewpoint of the other three great powers."

LONDON, *January 31, 1947*

HAD a talk with Bob Murphy on Germany. He is still toying with his idea of not having a peace treaty but rather dictating a peace by statute and, instead of having the German government signing, submitting it to the German people by referendum. If they turned it down it would be imposed anyway. The idea would be not to embarrass a democratic government by stigmatizing it with an unhappy peace.

Later, saw General Mark Clark who is handling the Austrian treaty. He is violently anti-Russian and, I believe, rather too pro-Austrian. Although many of his ideas are sound I think he would like to let the Austrians off too easily in the treaty preamble on the subject of war guilt.

LONDON, *February 1, 1947*

HAD a long talk with Chaim Weizmann, Zionist leader. He is most gloomy. He fears the return of six thousand English women and civilians from Palestine will spread anti-Semitism in the British Isles. He deplores the terrorists and says that while there are reasons to believe the Stern gang is made up of misguided idealists, there are many ordinary racketeers in the Irgun. He calls Ben Gurion "that damned fascist."

He thinks the position of the Jews in Palestine is worse than it has been at any time since World War I. He fears the terrorists may force an eventual conflict between the British and the Jews in Palestine and that it would lead to a situation similar to that of the war between the Romans and the Jews. At that time the Jews held out for three years against the Roman Empire and the survivors shut themselves up in the fortress of Massada where they fought for many months and finally slaughtered each other rather than surrender. He says that in the British cabinet, Bevin is becoming increasingly anti-Semitic. He says there is a split in the cabinet and Attlee is Bevin's man. Herbert Morrison and Creech-Jones are more sympathetic. He has not seen Churchill for months. He blames the government for an entire lack of policy and thinks that partition is inevitable but that Britain missed the opportunity to impose it. The Jews would have accepted it and that he is sure Azzam Pasha would have counseled the Arabs to accept it. Now the situation has gone from bad to worse. He says that just at the time Lord Moyne was assassinated the Conservatives, including Churchill and Moyne, were working out a sound plan for partition.

PARIS, *February 9, 1947*

TITO's foreign minister, Stanoje Simić, told me this evening that Jugoslavia will, after all, sign the Italian peace treaty drawn up in last year's conference here. The signature is scheduled for tomorrow. Simić, tall, gray-haired with the usual dish-shaped Serbian face, was formerly ambassador in Moscow and Washington. The decision for him to sign has created unhappiness among the Italians. Their plenipotentiary, Marquis Meli Lupi di Soragna, complained to me: "In reality this is merely a series of conditions of peace imposed upon Italy and to which we perforce must submit. It is not a negotiated treaty."

PARIS, *February 10, 1947*

THE five peace treaties were signed with Italy, Rumania, Hungary, Bulgaria and Finland. Signature was in the Salon de l'Horloge of the Quai d'Orsay on the table where the wounded Robespierre was stretched out before he was guillotined. There was strangely little joy either in the room or in Paris itself which greeted the event with supreme indifference.

PARIS, *February 11, 1947*

THIS afternoon I saw Prime Minister Ramadier, a friendly, unassuming man, with a small pointed beard. He had just come from a long conference with the prefects of France.

Ramadier does not seem at ease in the Matignon. All the flowers that Léon Blum used to keep around his office are gone. While I was waiting in the office of Ramadier's *chef du cabinet,* a former Greek and Latin teacher named Fontanier, the telephone rang, and somebody asked for Monsieur Thorez. Thorez is not yet prime minister!

Ramadier said France would like to see an alliance with the United States negotiated within the over-all framework of the United Nations, thus completing the scheme of pacts represented by the Franco-Soviet alliance and the imminent accord with Britain. Ramadier admitted the United States had always indicated it was averse to alliances. However, now American foreign policy has undergone drastic change.

Discussing the hostilities between French and Vietnam forces (of Ho Chi Minh) Ramadier said:

> The French government was the victim of an aggression. The December 19 attack was premeditated and prepared in advance. It was accompanied by the sudden massacre of French, Eurasians and Indochinese friends of France. Therefore, we cannot treat with Ho Chi Minh until we receive adequate guarantees that the terms will be respected. It would be difficult to undertake any serious negotiations under such conditions and until we have further information on developments within the country and within the Viet Minh. We have made all concessions possible. We are prepared and resolved to adhere to our promises to the Annamite people, but in order to settle this situation we must know who truly speaks for them and we must have guarantees that pledges will be honored.
>
> In the interim, while waiting we must continue our military efforts. These are now showing positive results. Hanoi has been largely cleared and linked to the coast. Consequently, we now have a certain number of bases. We do not wish to reconquer the country. We want to hold a sufficient number of bases to insure the implementation of eventual guarantees.

PARIS, *February 12, 1947*

JAN Masaryk told me Czechoslovakia (of which he's foreign minister) wants to start bilateral negotiations with Hungary now that peace has been signed. He also stressed that Prague intends to hew closely to Moscow's line. He said: "Czechoslovakia is an ally of Soviet Russia which is a Slav country but we are willing to be friends of all nations provided this comes within the scope of our present-day alliance." He admitted this was now "the keystone" of Prague's policy. The statements were made more agreeable by the fact that he expressed them over some Pilsen beer at Brzicki's restaurant, Rue Lincoln (later Chez Louis).

PARIS, *February 21, 1947*

TODAY I visited André Malraux in his apartment at Boulogne s/Seine. It is a rather nice unpretentious apartment, still in the process of being furnished and includes some lovely pieces of furniture and knick-knacks that Malraux picked up in various parts of the world. On his desk was one tulip in an attractive green glass vase.

Malraux is even more nervous than last time I saw him. He smoked one cigarette after the other without even a brief halt. He grunts and sniffs and makes all kinds of strange noises as he talks. Apologizing and saying that an old wound troubles him when he sits down, he spent the entire hour pacing rapidly round the room. He was continually at an extreme point of tension. He is obviously close to de Gaulle.

Maulraux assured me that some kind of understanding has recently been reached between the United States and Russia dividing the world into spheres of influence. He did not "know" if the accord was written or not. Malraux claims the United States has granted a free hand to Russia to act as it desires in all Slavic states and, in return, Russia has granted the United States and England a free hand elsewhere. This covers at least all of Europe, except for Germany, according to Malraux. He says the Russians have now abandoned the Greek guerrillas fighting against the government and, on the other hand, the former Polish government in London has issued orders to the underground in Poland to cease fighting the Bierut (Communist) government.

Malraux sees no likelihood of war between the United States and Russia for a few years. The only possibility of such a war would be an unexpected event in Russia or an inflammatory act by some Russian satellite state disobeying Moscow orders. The superiority of American armaments is far too great and during the last six months, the United States has been spending huge sums upon armament. The Americans now possess a rocket "V-3" that can travel 12,000 kilometers a second carrying an atomic bomb. He is certain that the Russians do not have the atom bomb. The Russians are now demobilizing both abroad and inside Russia, except for such elite units as the air force.

He is convinced the Communists are happy to have Bidault back as foreign minister. He says Bidault is forced by circumstance to play their game and that he can still maintain good relations with the United States whereas, if someone like Thorez were foreign minister, obviously Washington would not play ball.

The colonial phase of history is over. This is not only a result of the change in the relative military strength of imperial countries and colonies. In the eighteenth century the arms of Clive of India were not so incredibly superior to those of the Indian natives. However, at that time, the imperial nations had a great moral advantage. They were convinced they were spreading civilization and they were also convinced of the rightness of their conquests. How can a government in London, which cannot even prevent a strike, expect to hold on to India? How can a government in Paris, which cannot even prevent a strike, hold on to Indochina?

He is convinced the French Communist Party wishes to control France without at the same time taking over full power and responsibilities. He sees as Moscow policy an effort to establish weak governments everywhere, dominated by strong Communist parties; then, when war finally breaks out between Russia and the United States, these parties could immediately take control of the various countries where they operate. However, Malraux says the discipline of the Communist Party in France is not perfect. For example, despite the wishes of the Party, the staff of *L'Humanité* went on strike and fought off the Party when it wished to break the strike.

Malraux said he was now working on a history of art, but he did not really have time to work very much: "These are not times in which to write a history of art." Malraux sees the crisis in France getting continually worse. He says that already there are no newspapers in Paris, no gasoline at gasoline stations, and no *métro*. (The *métro* is working.) Hunger is growing. Some day there might be a general strike.

Obviously speaking for de Gaulle, he saw only four courses of action by which France could face this crisis. The first would be to call in Léon Blum with his vast prestige and personal ability, but this is excluded because of Blum's health. The second is to call upon Herriot to form a government; Herriot will accept, but he will fail. The third is for de Gaulle to take over. Malraux thinks it is likely that de Gaulle will come to power after the failure of a Herriot government. He will come to power in the following way:

More and more newspapers will call upon de Gaulle to take the responsibility for directing France. Then individual groups, representing large bodies of opinion, such as veterans' organizations or delegates from General Leclerc's old army will call upon Auriol to request de Gaulle's assistance. At first, Auriol will merely listen and do nothing, but after fifteen or twenty such visits, he will ask in de Gaulle. De Gaulle will then specify his terms. He will refuse to become prime minister and form another political cabinet. He will state to Auriol that he must have absolute authority for two years in order to achieve certain specific objectives which he will outline in black and white in a fifteen-point program. This must first be submitted to the French people in a referendum and he will come in as a dictator if he wins this referendum.

This does not violate the French constitution, which de Gaulle hates so much, because the constitution makes no provision for or against such a referendum. It is more likely that de Gaulle will come to power than the Communists. First of all, if the Communists came in it might provoke a reaction which means civil war. A civil war, as was the case in Spain, would mean a world war. Russia is not yet ready for a world war. Furthermore, if de Gaulle should fail, the Communists would benefit enormously and they would be much more prepared to assume full responsibility in two years.

France depends too much upon the United States for everything—especially economically. This cannot continue. France cannot pretend to be an important independent country and at the same time behave like a Republic of Panama. The power and morale of Europe are, at present, in a great state of decline, but this is by no means necessarily permanent. In the past, there have been valleys and peaks in European history and all one can say at the moment is that we are now in a valley.

Malraux is convinced that the United States is quietly supporting the continuation of Franco in Spain. The reason for this is that the Americans require a potential air base in Europe and Spain is the only possibility. The Russians are forced by their weakness to accept this situation.

France and many other European countries are suffering now because they lost most of their best men during the war. In World War I, although the slaughter was immense, it was haphazard. In this war, the Germans deliberately killed all the best men and the Communists did the same in the underground movement. Malraux lost two brothers during the war. He had an important position in the French underground. He was the fifth man to hold this position. The four who preceded him had all been killed.

France is weaker than many Frenchmen think, but it is stronger than many foreigners think. These statements are of considerable importance because Malraux is in close contact with de Gaulle and is not only influenced by him, but has considerable influence upon him.

PARIS, *February 25, 1947*

HAD lunch today with King Peter and his wife. He is doing nothing now, except spend money and have a good time. Obviously he is completely finished. He hopes to go the United States in May and to spend at least six months there. He says that the French have assigned two detectives to watch him while he is here and presumably to protect him. One of them spends all his time eating and the other one is so stupid that he gets lost all the time.

Moscow, *March 5, 1947*

ARRIVED here today on Ernest Bevin's special train from London—a memorable trip. The night before we left went on an all-night drinking and dancing party with George Jellicoe. Neither of us was in shape for the journey; but he, not I, had official functions, being a member of the British delegation. We stopped off in Dunkerque where Bevin signed a new alliance treaty with France. Then, in Brussels, Spaak came aboard for a long talk. In Berlin we all had a tour of the ruins, old Bevin heavily tottering about, and then we had a repeat performance in the even more terrible ruins of Warsaw where John Russell, of the British embassy, managed a small reception.

On the stretch through Poland the Poles put on a special restaurant car and I was among those drafted to go and have dinner with Bevin and his Polish hosts (about twenty of us, all told) around an oval table in a very old-fashioned diner. It was an absolutely enormous meal and there were endless quantities of Polish vodka. Bevin's doctor was sitting next to me and kept leaning forward and telling his corpulent patient, who has a bad heart, not to eat, not to drink. Bevin just grinned at him—and gulped. The doctor ended up by determinedly getting plastered.

Am amused to see the British delegation to the Moscow meeting of the Foreign Ministers Council has a kind of uniform of its own—boots (RAF I think) and fur-lined coats, ear-flapped hats. It includes numerous sappers who were in mine-detecting during the war and are going to inspect the snooping devices believed to be in the embassy; the first real sweep they've ever had. Bringing them in as "diplomats" helps. The French, I'm told, have stacked their delegation with intelligence agents including lots of young sons of White Russians who will be able to mingle with the crowds and with university students.

Moscow, *March 10, 1947*

THE council meeting began in the former Yar Restaurant (once beloved of Czarist gay blades: "Oh, Sweetheart, don't go to the Yar . . ."). There was a big crowd as the foreign ministers drove up and entered. No comment on Molotov. On Bidault a woman murmured: "The poor little man, he can't even afford a hat." (He never wears one.) On Marshall: "He looks as if he had an atom bomb in his pocket." On Bevin, admiring his corpulence: "My, what a handsome man." (First time he's ever been called that, I'll bet.)

This is an interesting experiment since we are told there will be no censorship on anything having to do with the Council. I am assigning our people (Middleton and Margie Shaw) to get as much as possible in under that cover, even including such idiotic things banned until now as prices in store windows by getting delegates to go shopping.

### Moscow, *March 14, 1947*

SECRETARY Marshall today made the most revolutionary statement heard for some decades in Moscow when he defined *democracy* as specifying "inalienable rights, that is rights which may not be given or taken away. They include the right of every individual to develop his mind and soul in ways of his own choice, free of fear of coercion—provided only he does not interfere with the like right of others." This was said with respect to Germany, whose future is being discussed, but it applies more sharply to Russia.

### Moscow, *March 16, 1947*

THIS evening had a most interesting conversation with Karl Gruber, the Austrian foreign minister, and almost killed myself en route. I had invited him out for dinner at the Grand Hotel, which is the current gay spot. Gruber is here to hold a watching brief during discussions by the Big Four of the proposed Austrian state treaty. I got tied up by work and therefore was late in picking him up at the Hotel National. I started running from my hotel, the Metropole, and at the broad avenue intersection just across from the National I ran right behind a truck, impatiently not wishing to wait for all traffic to cease. There was another big vehicle coming through the dusk behind the truck. I didn't realize it was a trailer attached by a steel wire until I hit the wire going full steam. Fortunately I was running fast enough so that, when it knocked me off my feet, I dove several yards forward and the wheels of the trailer missed me. But I got a terrific cut on my leg. This I managed to anesthetize with vodka, at the same time anesthetizing Gruber.

### Moscow, *March 17, 1947*

I was sitting quietly in the cold lobby on the mezzanine floor of the Moskva Hotel this morning, hat and coat on, reading a paper when John Foster Dulles, the Republican adviser on Marshall's delegation, came along, nudged me and suggested we go for a walk. Out in the street he reached into his pocket and drew out a paper. It was marked Secret. "Read this," he said, "and be sure to be careful when you return it to me. Give it back to me personally this evening." Later I read it: Marshall's instructions to the American delegation: how to behave, to beware of tapped telephones and devices in the walls, never to discuss important things except in the streets, walking around; not even in the embassy. I wrote a story on it and gave it back to Dulles who was very pleased with his own indiscretion.

This evening Boris Izakov and Yuri Zhukov, diplomatic correspondents of *Pravda,* invited me around to their newspaper. Had a caviar and vodka supper with them and Yakov Viktorov and David Zaslavsky who, despite his vituperative pen, looks like anyone's grandpa. They showed me around the plant and complained bitterly of the newsprint shortage.

Boris, who lost a foot during the war and still suffers pain, told me twenty Russian reporters are covering the Council and are briefed each day by Kosta Zinchenko of the press department. *Pravda,* with its local editions around the country, has a circulation of 3,500,000. Yuri told me: "Our ambition is to get enough newsprint so some day we can print as large a paper as *The New York Times.*"

MOSCOW, *March 18, 1947*

A member of Bidault's delegation gave me the dream scoop, taking me to a room filled with official classified documents of the Moscow meeting of the Council and telling me to take my pick. I went through them and got out several batches, including the draft for an Austrian peace treaty, the draft for a Trieste settlement, position papers on Germany, Japan, and so forth. I made a huge bundle and staggered through the hall, out into the street and the few blocks to the Metropole and our office, edging through the crowds and just peeping over the top of the pile in my arms. Then Middleton and I dealt them out between us and started raining exclusive stories on the *Times*. We had to work fairly fast—fortunately Drew is adept —in order to make up the bundle again and totter back at the end of the day.

MOSCOW, *March 24, 1947*

INVITED Dulles and the Middletons for lunch in my suite: vodka, caviar, Kievski cutlet. Very good. Middleton had cigars and offered them. Poor Dulles took one, sniffed it long and longingly, then handed it back with the explanation they were forbidden to him by his doctor. He talked very authoritatively on foreign affairs. Made it perfectly evident he expects Tom Dewey to be elected President next year and that, when this happens, he expects to be his Secretary of State.

In the afternoon, by special wangle through the foreign ministry, I went off to the Soyuzpushnina (fur trust) to buy for Marina a brother to the platinum fox I got her two years ago in Finland. Took Rosane with me. Waving our permits we arrived at a place as well guarded as Fort Knox, together with Bob Murphy and a few other diplomats. Imagine our astonishment when we were finally conducted into a large store room and there, amid a pile of furs, only his head showing, the grinning Carmel Offie, an American diplomat, heaving pelts about and saying: "I'll take this, not that, not that, this . . ." What an operator. I still don't know how he got there.

MOSCOW, *March 26, 1947*

POLITIS, the Greek ambassador, gave a reception last night and the Russians tried to drown it out by holding a special opera performance at the Bolshoi. Because of Truman's new attitude on Greece and the civil strife there the Russians are increasingly hostile. But all the western ministers, led by Marshall, made a special point of coming to Politis' party right from the theater. It became not only the greatest occasion in Greek embassy history here but a diplomatic event, a deliberate sign by the Western Three that they are behind the Greek government. A very good party indeed, and Politis transported with joy.

MOSCOW, *March 27, 1947*

THERE was a reception for Marshall at the American embassy. Bedell Smith, now ambassador, invited me to his bedroom (which Marshall uses) to look at his trout rods and practice fly casting—which we did. I noticed a pistol by General M's bed table. Marshall is an odd figure. He is quiet, laconic, keeps his cards close to his chest. Very polite when one talks to him, but doesn't light up. An unusually sensitive host, getting up to bring me an ashtray, handing me a drink, and so forth. He calls all his advisers, no matter how well he knows them, by their last names: Smith, Cohen, Bohlen, et cetera. Foster has been promoted from "Mr. Dulles" to "Dulles." Marshall's only small talk seems to be reminiscences of youth or campaigns. He loves to talk about the Franco-Prussian war, on which he is an authority. His besetting sin—nibbling maple sugar occasionally. He is now reading Harold Nicolson's *Congress of Vienna*.

MOSCOW, *March 31, 1947*

LUNCH with Bidault, French foreign minister. That is to say, I had lunch, he had only one glass of wine. And yet this seemed to make him tipsy. He clearly has a very nervous stomach and overwrought system. I suspect he mustered all the courage in his frail body for his wartime record as an audacious underground leader; and that he was shattered by it. Bidault spoke out strongly for a hold on the Saar. He supported the American idea of a four-power alliance, adding: "It is an excellent and vitally important thing to have the United States specifically committed and interested in Europe. We are aware that this would be the first alliance treaty for the United States and realize what a revolutionary significance such an idea has in itself."

MOSCOW, *Early April 1947*

MOLOTOV gave a reception for the foreign ministers at the House of Soviet Aviation. There was little to eat and less to drink. I had a long argument with Vyshinsky who started by saying he was glad to see me, but that he still waited to read an article by me which was favorable to the Soviet Union. I replied that he had no need to worry about that whenever I was in Moscow because the censors took care of it. He said censors were there to help correspondents; to serve as a crutch, to guide them towards the truth.

I said I preferred to agree with Pushkin who wrote: *"Tsensura Doura"* (All censors are idiots). Vyshinsky said of course Pushkin was referring to the Czarist regime. I answered I accepted a literal interpretation of Pushkin's words; that all censors were idiots. I asked if he was a censor.

He replied angrily, his face flushing, that he had many functions in the Soviet government: that he was a member of the Supreme Soviet, was chief prosecutor of the state, was deputy foreign minister, was an editor—and also a censor.

He said I should consider myself lucky that he was only my censor and not my prosecutor. I told him that it was rather easy for a prosecutor here to have a good record of convictions—when there were sufficient bayonets behind every prisoner. Stunned anger. But he started it.

In the end, Vyshinsky became moderately friendly—after approximately forty minutes of debate. He said he would like to help me personally in getting a visa to the Soviet Union whenever I encountered any difficulty. I do not believe that; nor anything else he says.

MOSCOW, *April 4, 1947*

VISITED the Kremlin today. Maybe at last they are going to open it to foreigners. I was last there—and as a very special privilege—in 1945. Apart from the enormous Czar's Bell (which fell down) and Czar's Gun (which was never fired), was much taken by the collection of the Czar's gems and costumes which has now been restored from a wartime haven. For fun I asked a guide where Stalin's apartment was. Horrified, she said she didn't know.

LENINGRAD, *April 5, 1947*

CAME up here last night with a group of French diplomats by the excellent sleeper train from Moscow. To my astonishment I was in a compartment with a Soviet lieutenant general in full uniform. We sparred cautiously in my pidgin Russian and then, as we warmed up on a bottle of vodka he produced, I asked if he spoke anything else. Yes, it turned out, excellent German. We moved from his vodka to my whisky which he relished.

It seemed he had been a naval cadet studying for the Czar's navy in Koenigsberg. When the Revolution came he figured he would stay on, as Russia was his country, but that there was more of a future in the army than the navy; so he switched.

He became more and more unguarded as the whisky disappeared. Complained bitterly about the people in the government who interfered stupidly with military matters they didn't understand. Sounded very much like a Colonel Blimp—but very nice.

In the morning when we woke up he seemed exceedingly nervous and slipped furtively down the car before the train drew to a halt so that he could get out far away from me. Poor fellow, he had to lug a suitcase along also (although, technically, an officer of his rank isn't supposed to carry baggage or even parcels; infra dig). (I never wrote about him, even by inference. Would have been his end.)

Leningrad is absolutely lovely. The Hermitage is one of the most startlingly impressive museums in the world.

Moscow, *April 11, 1947*

TOOK Bohlen (of the American delegation) out for lunch with Vlado and Steve Dedijer and the French Communist correspondents, Pierre Courtade and Georges Soria. Big argument about Communist dogma between Bohlen and Vlado in which Chip definitely had the upper hand. But, on the whole, an agreeable affair.

Moscow, *April 19, 1947*

DROVE out to Zagorsk with Rosane, Offroy, other French delegates. Extraordinary to see the Easter crowd of peasants and priests looking as if they'd stepped out of Tolstoy. A priest showed us around and explained how experts were working to recover old icons threatened with destruction. Some of these experts are from the village of Palekh where they used to make icons, now make lacquer boxes for sale abroad, all painted with the old technique of squirrel-tail brushes and tempera. The police escort broke a way for us through the crowd at each of the chapels, much to our embarrassment.

Moscow, *April 25, 1947*

AFTER forty-five days of increasing stalemate, the Council of Foreign Ministers closed. There is no peace for Germany in sight and relations are pretty abrasive between Russia and the rest. Stalin invited the ministers to dine with him at the Kremlin last night but I warrant I had a better time. It was Boris Izakov's birthday and Yuri Zhukov gave a party for him in his apartment. He invited me and anyone I wished to bring along. So I asked Elisabeth de Miribel, a handsome girl on the French delegation, if she wanted to come. She did.

Elisabeth came around to my rooms while I finished typing and filing my dispatch. Then, well after midnight, we drove to Yuri's. There was a table heaped with food and drink and about sixteen shouting people around it, all plastered. They insisted we pay the "traditional" penalty for being late. This was as follows. Each of us was given a highball glass which was then carefully filled with vodka to the exact brim. We had to stand and lift the glass without spilling a drop, drink it all straight, then turn it upside down on the table. To my astonishment and much to the admiration of the Russians, Elisabeth accomplished this without blinking.

The dinner went on and on. Whenever a Russian passed out two others would pick him up like a log and dump him in the bedroom next door where a stack had already been piled. Yuri made a long toast saying there must be no war. I replied that if there was one, Boris, Yuri and I should look out for each other and families if we fell under the other's sway. We pledged this in another toast.

Elisabeth was taken home relatively early by a relatively sober Soviet diplomat. I stayed on to the end.

A Russian drove me home but it was by then daylight and when we got to the Bolshoi, across the square from my hotel, I hopped out and said goodbye. It seemed an excellent idea to get myself arrested and taken to the Lubyanka prison about which I had heard so much. So I marched (tottered) up to a cop and, startling him, demanded that he arrest me and send me pronto to the Lubyanka. With friendly *politesse* and some amazement he summoned a companion and the two of them delivered me to my suite.

At about 11:30 A.M. Drew came into the room. I stirred, awoke, and asked him if he'd bring me a glass of water. He went to the bathroom and gasped with horror, came out and asked: "What happened? There's blood all over the place." I got up, went in and he was right. Then I noticed broken fragments of glass. I had evidently broken two glasses. I looked at my feet. They were absolutely filled with splinters. But I still had so much vodka inside that I felt nothing.

However, since I knew I was going out that night on Bidault's train (as far as Warsaw) I figured I had better do something. I went over to the embassy doctor's office and he sat me on a hospital table and, after inspecting my feet, suggested a shot of pain killer before he went to work. "Why," I asked, "I don't feel anything at all." So he dug right in and I kept hearing pieces of glass clink into a tray below me; but it was utterly painless.

The doctor wanted to know what had happened. I told him. Then I asked how anyone of his high rank (Navy captain) was assigned to such a job. He winked and explained that we had many new medicines such as sulpha drugs and Russians with sick families sometimes asked if they could obtain access to these. At such a point, he said obliquely, it was useful to have in charge someone of sufficient experience to know how to dispense medicines and what kind of "information" was desired in exchange.

WARSAW, *April 28, 1947*

CAME here from Moscow, my feet starting to throb, aboard the train of Foreign Minister Bidault and was met at the station by John and Aliki Russell (of the British embassy) with whom I'm staying. Impressions: Was struck in Moscow and Leningrad by the fact that people are already better dressed: silk stockings, furs, make-up more prevalent than two years ago. The men have better suits, coats, shoes. Clothing, electric toasters, cameras now creeping into shops.

But from the train windows you could see ravages of the countryside: wrecked bridges along the upper Dnieper, skeletons of rolling stock in White Russia, rusting rails and machinery. Destitute crowds with pale faces jam at the barriers in railway stations at Brest-Litovsk, Minsk, Borisov, Smolensk. One can tell they are still having a hard time and no happiness is mirrored in their eyes.

Here in Warsaw one feels both that one is in the "West" and that a dictatorship and terror are settling in amid the wreckage. It is extraordinary how smashed the capital is and yet, at the same time, how the Poles manage to survive with vitality and determination. But they are very secretive and afraid to show their liking for westerners. The Russells, who have made a charming flat out of the corner of a damaged house, had a nice party with quite a few Poles who, I suppose, were ready to risk trouble with the police in exchange for good food and drink and gay conversation.

WARSAW, *April 30, 1947*

WAS received by Jakob Berman, one of the top Polish Communist bosses. He said that although a disastrous depression will engulf the world within a relatively short time, it will not destroy the Western capitalist system. Capitalism and communism can survive side by side, at peace in this ideologically turbulent era.

Officially, according to himself, Berman is merely under secretary in the Presidium of the Council of Ministers. However, he rates far higher. He is perhaps the second most important man in the hierarchy.

Berman says the boss of the Party is Wladyslaw Gomulka, Communist secretary general. Berman does admit he is a member of the Central Committee. On still closer questioning, Berman says he is a member of the seven-man Politburo, on which he functions as chief of party propaganda.

He is forty-six, stocky, gray-haired, with amiable demeanor. He says he was a prewar Communist but never went to the Soviet Union until 1941, when the Germans attacked Russia. He says the Polish Workers' (Communist) Party has 750,000 registered members.

I asked Berman whether Poland would be prepared to sign as strong an alliance with any Western country as it now has with the Soviet Union. He replied: "Yes, if they would guarantee our frontiers and the security of Poland. It is no secret that we are now carrying on just such negotiations with France."

WARSAW, *May 1, 1947*

TODAY I saw Stanislaw Mikolajczyk, former premier of the London Polish government. He is most unhappy about the way things have worked out since his return and fearful about the future. He said that the Communist-dominated government is now engaged in a final effort to stamp out the opposition Polish Peasant Party. The security police are being employed to terrorize the party's membership throughout the nation. State building commissions are requisitioning party buildings. The government is nationalizing party printing shops. Censors are eliminating Opposition parliamentary speeches from party papers. He continues to maintain the elections were "fraudulent" and that government allegations that his Peasant Party is "finished" are ridiculous.

PRAGUE, *May 4, 1947*

MET Premier Klement Gottwald, the solid, humorless chief of the Communist Party in Czechoslovakia. He said Czechoslovakia's system of bilateral alliances with Russia, Poland and Jugoslavia is aimed solely at a possible recurrence of German aggression and is open to Western nations willing to undertake similar obligations.

Gottwald insisted there was no reason why capitalism and communism should not live side by side in peace. However, he foresaw difficulties between Moscow and Washington as long as the German question remained open. He saw no logic for a "compromise ideology" combining various features of Marxism and capitalism, but he pointed out there were differences between the Communist-led states in Europe and Russia: "each country has its own traditions and requirements and one cannot impose the same system everywhere."

PRAGUE, *May 6, 1947*

HAD a long talk with President Beneš today. He said Czechoslovakia was not interested in an alliance with France. The Czechoslovakian people remember Munich and what happened to their last alliance with France. If France's interests were with Czechoslovakia in another war, France would support Czechoslovakia whether there was an alliance or not. If France's interests were not with Czechoslovakia she would probably not help Czechoslovakia, regardless of any alliance—if Munich could be accepted as a precedent. Actually, Beneš's views are not necessarily final, because Czechoslovak Communists are working hard for such an alliance. Clementis, the under secretary of foreign affairs, was once, according to André Malraux, liaison man between the French Communist Party and Moscow.

Beneš said it was obvious the left wing in France was supporting a Czech alliance as another link with Moscow and the right was opposing it for the same reasons. Prague did not wish to be mixed up in internal French political arguments. Beneš said it was not true he had received a letter from Stalin when he was in London guaranteeing the Czechs would have their 1938 frontiers. Beneš does not recall this, but it was he himself who told me he had received such a letter a few years ago. Beneš now claims that Ruthenia, which was taken by Russia, was willingly given by Prague. He said that in 1918 he and Thomas Masaryk had told Wilson that Ruthenia was not properly a part of Czechoslovakia but was more Ukrainian. However, there was no common frontier between that area and the Soviet Union. Therefore, Czechoslovakia took it over to prevent Hungary from seizing it. Ruthenia was still being held in trust for Russia. In March 1945, Beneš signed an agreement in Moscow with Stalin and Molotov giving this area to Russia. He asked no compensation in view of the great sacrifices of Russia in helping to liberate Czechoslovakia.

Beneš looked sad and worried. Although he was very friendly and recalled our tragic 1938 talks in the same office of the Hradčany Palace, still overlooking the undestroyed and lovely baroque bridges, he spoke with intense deliberation. He insisted Czechoslovakia's democracy was safe and that the country was in no way controlled or dominated by Russia.

Things are going reasonably. You must remember that our trade with Russia had not developed at all before the war. But this country cannot live without the Occident and this must never be forgotten. Our best trade connections are and must remain with the Western world. This country was based and developed upon such a scheme. Those who think we will suddenly turn around and reverse our situation are nonsensical. In the same way our culture is Occidental. It is ridiculous to think that we would turn our back upon the West. This country and its people are absolutely democratic and we will remain so, come what may.

There was a certain stern note of warning in his voice.

PARIS, *May 17, 1947*

LUNCHED with two leading Gaullists, Malraux and Jacques Soustelle who ran the general's wartime secret service. Soustelle is a compact, slightly overweight, bespectacled archeologist who specialized in Mexico. I have a bond with him in that we share an admiration for Nezahualcoyotl (Hungry Wolf), the Toltec king-poet.

Malraux said he thought de Gaulle's RPF (French Popular Rally) was finished if it cannot successfully appeal to the left. He added: "We are embarrassed by some of our right wing supporters. There is nothing we can do about it."

He made a curious confession: If there were a Trotskyist movement in France today, a movement which stood some chance of success instead of the tiny handful of Trotskyites bickering with the Communists, he would be a Trotskyite and not a Gaullist.

PARIS, *May 26, 1947*

TODAY I ran into Princess Aspasia on the street. Marina is away so she invited me to dine informally that night; merely gave me an address on the rue de la Faisanderie. I had no idea if it was a borrowed house or not. Turned out to be that of Paul-Louis Weiller, Aliki Russell's first husband, whom I had never met.

Aspasia was complaining that King Peter and Queen Alexandra are falling into bad company. Some of the envoys of Purić—a reactionary pan-Serb—have gained control of him politically, she says. She says his chauffeur is a spy for them. Furthermore, two English adventurers have become great intimates. Aspasia says they are a bad couple and spend all their time with Peter—usually drinking at Maxim's. She says they are spiritualists and pass on phoney messages to Peter from "spirits" many of which warn him against his mother-in-law, Aspasia (Good idea!).

PARIS, *May 28, 1947*

DINED last night at the residence of Paul de Auer, Hungarian minister. There were two interesting people there. One was Professor Szent-Györgyi who won the Nobel Prize a few years ago for isolating Vitamin C. He is charming, politically rather leftist, seems about sixty-five and is married to his young secretary. He is now working on an analysis of the chemical and electrical differences between relaxed and contracted muscles. If he lives long enough he thinks he can discover the secrets of life; he believes it will take him another ten years.

Also, there were Count and Countess Coudenhove-Kalergi. He is half Japanese and half Hungarian. Ever since 1924 he has been working for "Pan-Europe" or "The United States of Europe." He has been living in America for the last seven years. He and his wife have acquired French passports. Coudenhove-Kalergi assured me there would be a revolution in Italy this week which will be won by the Communists very quickly, and which will establish Russian control of the Mediterranean and invalidate the Truman doctrine in Greece and Turkey.

# 18

---

# DE GAULLE SEEKS

# A COMEBACK

PARIS, *May 30, 1947*

TODAY I HAD A LONG TALK WITH DE GAULLE, THE FIRST SINCE THE war. He is still immensely tall, remote, infinitely courteous, rather gloomy. He received me in his small suite at the Hotel Lapérouse, not too far from the Etoile. He was very friendly and talked quite freely but would not allow me to publish his words. Nevertheless, I took them all down while he waited patiently.

(N.B. That October, I was in America on holiday and de Gaulle began to feature in the news. I prepared a dispatch, based on our talk in May, sent it to my secretary and had her check it out with de Gaulle. He read it, made a few changes of his quoted phraseology—in his own handwriting—and approved it for publication. This was printed on October 28, 1947—one of the very few times an interview with the general has been published.)

De Gaulle said he had found it necessary to create the RPF (Rally of the French People) for the following reasons:

At present there are five parties in France: The Communists, Socialists, Radicals and UDSR (Social Democratic Union of Resistants), the Moderates (the PRL and the Independents) and the MRP. The Communists are not a French party; therefore it is impossible to imagine making a French policy by relying on the Communist Party. There remain four political groups. But these four are continually fighting each other. They make their electors quarrel. No one of these parties has the support of an important part of the French public.

There is a similar situation in Italy. These parties cannot be relied upon when there is a question of framing an important policy and executing it. They cannot be relied upon because they cannot agree on a

356

policy. When an important problem arises none of these parties thinks of how to assume the responsibility to settle the problem instead of which one thinks of how it can selfishly benefit by and take advantage of the problem. The government is composed of four parties and no one of them is capable of settling a program in the interest of the majority of the French people.

The aim of the RPF is to group the French people in such a way as to permit a system whereby policies can be decided and responsibilities assumed in the interests of France, independently of any single political party aspirations. Of course, the Communist Party cannot take part in the RPF for just this reason.

The aim of the RPF is the reconstruction of France to its full productive capacity and power. It is necessary to restore productive capacity, and in order to do so, we must provide for full free enterprise. There are many items, such as bread, for which one cannot yet predict complete unrestricted and nonrationed freedom, but in all branches of activity where it is possible to remove restrictions, this must be done immediately.

In the same way it is possible and necessary to increase the volume of French production. Simultaneously it is necessary to find a solution of the problems relating to the working of capital and labor. For France, it is necessary to organize a system of associations in which labor and capital could participate directly as interested parties. This implies also that labor unions should have no political background. They must be professional and not political organizations. No political party in France should be permitted to interfere in their affairs. And exactly the same should apply to capitalist organizations. We must organize a completely free system to increase the productive capacity of France and prevent political interference among the workers. The associations should include all those who participate in any industry—whether worker, technician or executive. They would all be associated together and not separated into individual organizations. They would all hold stock in their industry.

As far as foreign affairs go—I am convinced that it is necessary to re-create a Europe. If this is not done, the world will be divided into a rivalry between Russia and the United States. That would lead to war—a horrid war.

To re-create Europe the first condition is that France should be on her feet. France is a Western power, and Europe is a symbol of Western civilization. Europe, to be restored, must be built upon occidental civilization. Such a Europe would be an element of strength and equilibrium.

To rebuild such a Europe would be impossible without outside help which, practically speaking, must come from the United States. This American help should take the shape of a treaty and not a bargain. On the French side, the interest is in reconstruction. From the American side, the interest is in the reconstruction of an occidental France and by that I mean an occidental Europe.

I then asked if by this he endorsed the conception of a United States of Europe. He replied:

The name of United States of Europe is not a good one. It implies a federalized Europe. We cannot do that in the same way as the United States has federalized its separate states. But it should be possible to build a Europe on the basis of treaties between the European nations and to establish a system under which they would systematically be meeting at conferences to study common economic, political and social problems. They would also have to study common imperial problems as many European countries have possessions abroad. It has always been impossible to organize such a Europe before. Always in the past one nation has sought to dominate the others. France in the seventeenth and eighteenth centuries attempted to do this. Then England. Then, during the last fifty years, Germany. But such conditions no longer exist, for the first time. No European nation has the ambition or the capacity to dominate.

I asked if the RPF was merely an anticommunist movement as some people contended. He replied: "Of course the Communists will fight us and of course we will fight them. They don't play a French game. But set this question aside. The RPF is something more—it is an organization of Frenchmen to create and promote a French policy."

I asked if political parties would be permitted if the RPF came to power. He replied:

Naturally in a democratic system, such as I favor, there will always be political parties, but what is wrong at present is that the parties have all the powers—executive, legislative, etc. As a result of party disputes, therefore, there is terrible confusion. The RPF is not interested in parties—only in men and in their policies. Naturally, we are willing to receive men from all parties. The RPF addresses itself to all men able to promote a French policy who will come to us as men and not as political representatives.

I asked if the general, returning to power, would dissolve the Communist Party. He answered in the affirmative, adding:

It is indispensable, as the Communists are not playing a French game and therefore must not take part in the French government. Of course, [sardonically] we don't want to shoot them all. It is not at all the doctrinal viewpoint of the Communists on social matters which makes us wish to ban them. It is the fact that they are not French; in the same way we banned collaborators with Germany because they did not follow a French line.

I asked if his movement was not weakening the central parties of the MRP and Socialists and thus aiding the Communists. He replied: "These parties do not represent a force—only voters. Thus only yesterday they succumbed to the CGT and Communists' dictates on electricity. We cannot weaken the MRP and the Socialists. They have no strength. And they are not fighting the Communists."

I asked what appeal his movement had to the left. He replied:

Right now, the appeal of the RPF is largest among people of the left. Those who voted with the Socialists and the Radicals and many from the MRP are coming to us now. We do not have the support of the right. The French right is very bourgeois and mistrustful. Many of them were for Pétain and therefore mistrust General de Gaulle. They have tended to live isolated among themselves. An enormous number of French people tend towards us psychologically, but have not come over yet to the RPF actively. If events prove that we are right, they will. On the other hand, if within a year it is seen that the present system can keep afloat, then they will not have to join the RPF.

This type of reasoning, this spirit and psychology, is that which most of the French displayed towards the Free French movement in 1940 and 1941. They were sentimentally favorable, but they figured that, if the Germans won, General de Gaulle would be wrong. If the Germans lost, General de Gaulle would be right and they would then shout *"Vive de Gaulle."*

Right now we appeal to the left particularly, as well as to all the other elements, by our plans for economic restoration through the system of "association" of which I spoke to you, as well as the idea of national independence.

I asked when he thought the RPF would come to power. He said:

Everything depends upon events. If events keep the present system going, we will not come to power and the movement will no longer interest me. But I fear and believe that the present system cannot survive future events. If that is the case, I think that the principal crisis will come early next winter. At that time, the present system of parties will be paralyzed. At such a moment, France will have only a choice between the Communists and the RPF. I do not believe it will choose the Communists.

By events I mean internal events, the development of the present tendency towards anarchy. Naturally, if a war came, it would precipitate events immediately, but I do not believe there is any serious danger of war before the early winter. [De Gaulle explained that he did not wish to imply that a war would come soon after that.] But international tension influences the French mind and increases the difficulty of our problems.

I asked de Gaulle how he planned to come to power. Would he accept the prime-ministry if Auriol offered it to him early in the winter? He replied: "I cannot forecast such things. That is a question of tactics. If events force such a choice, the Constitution will have to be amended." I said to de Gaulle that would take some time—a few weeks. He answered:

"Some events such as those of 1940 show that a constitution can be changed quickly, even in one afternoon."

I asked if he could tell me something about the organization and membership of the RPF. He said:

> It is hard to do that. I evaluate our membership at about one million now inscribed. But we are creating local movements and committees all the time. It is only six weeks since we began to organize. Hundreds and hundreds of new inscriptions are coming to us daily. Our committees must work fast to take in these inscriptions. Our organizing continues in full force. I do not want to speak of figures. We are not in a hurry. We can take our time. There are no dues to pay. Each member gives what he wants. They usually volunteer something.

PARIS, *May 30, 1947*

A Communist *putsch* seized Hungary today. The Communists did away with the majority Smallholders Party, once and for all. Ferenc Nagy, the prime minister, was in Switzerland on holiday. He agreed to resign. De Auer, the minister here, called up both Budapest and Nagy this evening to get the full story for me. Apparently Nagy is pushing in his chips in exchange for the release of some of his family (small son, I believe) in Hungary. They'll all live abroad. Auer is gloomy but quite courageous; his own fate is sealed.

PARIS, *June 11, 1947*

HAD dinner tonight with Bidault and Ambassador Caffery. They had quite an argument. Caffery accused Bidault of letting the United States down in the United Nations Commission on Greece. Bidault said the French representative on the Commission was independent and without advance instructions. The Commission was shown nothing, and therefore the French delegation had to report this. However, Bidault said he personally was convinced that the revolutionary movement in Greece was being aided by Jugoslavia, Rumania and Bulgaria. He thought the Truman Doctrine on Greece was desirable.

Caffery said the recent *coup d'état* in Hungary was not Russia's reply to the Truman Doctrine and that the United States had been aware for many weeks that it was about to take place. I don't know why, if that was the case, we did not do anything about it. Bidault said France refused to accept the Hungarian coup.

Bidault said de Gaulle's figures on the RPF were a complete lie. The movement had no more than 250,000 members and not the 1,000,000 claimed by de Gaulle. He said de Gaulle was always talking of what was going to happen six months from now and was never right. He and Caffery agreed that Malraux was a "screwball." Bidault said France would always be democratic and would never succumb to communism.

He said France was in a difficult international position. It had no time to develop doctrines as does the United States. France would feel more free if the United States had a few atomic bombs on the Elbe. France has no means of fighting, but if the Russians succeeded in establishing a Communist government in Vienna, the French people would be so frightened that it would put an end to all strikes.

He added, "We must make clear what the menace is—Russia." He said that between now and November, France must make a solemn *démarche* to Moscow in order to ask whether we will have peace or not. France had to "smoke out" Russian policy. France was in the middle. Bidault insisted neither Thorez nor the French Communist Party worked on direct orders from Moscow, but merely followed the pattern by intuition.

Bidault said the United States must realize that France must retain its hold on Indochina and North Africa. He said the alternative there was either France or communism encouraged, in the latter instance, by Mohammedan mysticism. Bidault said he had supreme confidence that France would survive as a democratic nation and that Communists would neither come to power nor be readmitted to the French government.

PARIS, *June 12, 1947*

LUNCHED again with Soustelle and Malraux. Both extremely vague and confused about de Gaulle's movements. Malraux had a few interesting things to say on other subjects, however.

He used to know Maxim Gorki, who was the only "mammoth" he ever knew besides de Gaulle, a heritage from man's ancient past. He said Gorki was a huge man, but had the teeth of a six-year-old child, small, white and evenly spaced. He was astonished when Gorki opened his mouth to laugh.

The one time he met Stalin was at Gorki's house. He said Stalin adores Shakespeare and never misses a performance. His other hobby is the dance—to watch other people dance. Stalin told him that the way he destroyed Trotsky was by making him write.

Malraux said Gorki paid a pension all his life to four old friends. One was a waiter in a café at Capri. Another was a Romanoff princess.

He said the greatest intellect of the revolution was Trotsky's.

NEW YORK, *October 15, 1947*

LONG talk with Ambassador Bedell Smith. He showed me a report sent to Secretary Marshall October 3, twelve days ago. This indicates the belief that an eventual war between the Soviet Union and the United States is probable, although it is not likely to take place for a few (possibly ten) years. In the interim, Russia will push hard for gains in every field. In addition, the USSR by its vicious propaganda will try and prepare public opinion. At present, there is a lot of opposition to the Soviet government within the country and tremendous fear of another war.

It is difficult to know how close Russia is to the necessary level of preparation. There have been some boasts (including one reference by Molotov) of the existence of a Soviet weapon as powerful as the atom bomb. It is believed the very fact that such a weapon was referred to indicates it does not exist. However, Russia is working hard to make the A-bomb.

Some people have thought Russia could not go to war until it has a powerful strategic air force. Actually, the Russians have developed a new four-engine jet bomber. We have pictures of it. They are working hard to develop a large fighter force. Russia hopes to develop self-propelled rocket weapons (V-weapons) in place of a strategic air force.

If a war should start, it would probably be in one of the peripheral areas, the Balkans or the Middle East. Certainly, Russia considers that a war should be prepared for which would be fought in Europe, Asia, or the Middle East and not in the United States. That is excluded. Russia is in an excellent position to control the timing of such a war from the heart of the Eurasian land mass. Soviet policy will continue bullish. But until Moscow is ready, if a crisis verges upon war, a temporary diplomatic retreat is envisaged.

NEW YORK, *October 29, 1947*

LUNCH with Chip Bohlen and Charlie Thayer. Bohlen said Marshal Rokossovsky was in concentration camp in the USSR when the German invasion started in 1941. He was one of the many officers who had been purged. Stalin called Rokossovsky to him. He asked if he would take a command and let bygones be bygones. Rokossovsky said he would if given permission to organize his own staff from among other officers at that time in concentration camps. Stalin agreed. Rokossovsky became one of the great soldiers of the war.

Bohlen said Bidault always emphasized to Byrnes the great fear in France of the possibility of another (Russian) occupation. All Europeans are convinced that if war came between America and Russia the Russians would be on the English Channel in a few days. Bidault explained that it was because of this that sometimes he was not able to support Byrnes as strongly as he desired.

WASHINGTON, *November 4, 1947*

SAW President Truman this morning and talked with him for about three-quarters of an hour. He looked healthy and brisk. He was wearing a gray suit, dark blue socks and a handkerchief. He seemed very sincere and quite self-confident although at times he displayed a rather rural knowledge of the world. He asked me a lot of questions but I tried to keep him answering rather than asking. He asked me if I would inform him directly of my impressions as I traveled around the world. I didn't commit myself but I am no Presidential agent.

When I asked what his basic foreign policy was, he referred me to his speech in New York City on Navy Day, October 27, 1945. He said:

> That is my foreign policy. That was my foreign policy then and it is the same now. It is the same as the foreign policy of President Roosevelt and it is the same as that of Secretary Hull and General Marshall. What I want to do and what we must do is keep our foreign policy bipartisan. That means bipartisan and not nonpartisan. The only way we will accomplish this is by educating the people.

The President sharply criticized Senator Taft and said he was attempting to make a public issue of foreign policy. He did not intend to get drawn into such a fight and would confine his answers only to messages to Congress.

Truman described his policy as: "Peace in the world. Anybody can have any government they want but no one has the right to impose their own form of government upon anyone else. We do not care if Russia wants a totalitarian state. But we do not think that Russia should be allowed to impose such a form of government upon anyone else—such as Poland for example."

This was a perfectly sincere statement but rather naive. In the President's Navy Day speech of 1945 he stated it was American policy not to recognize any government not freely chosen in a free way by the people of that country. He stressed that this was his policy and yet, although he still says it is his policy, it was not American policy in October 1945; it is not American policy in November 1947 (although the President thinks it is); and it never has been American policy.

I asked the President what his view would be if public pressure at some future date should press for a meeting between him and Stalin. He replied: "Stalin can meet me right here. I won't go anywhere to see him. I told him at Potsdam I would like to see him here and if he wants to meet with me he knows where he can do it."

He said the Russians had broken forty-seven treaties since 1922. Later on I tried to obtain a list of these treaties. Neither George Kennan, head of the Policy Planning Division of the State Department and one of its main Russian experts, nor Llewellyn Thompson, chief of the department's Eastern European Division, knew anything about any list of forty-seven treaties to which the President may refer. They suggested that possibly such a list had been sent over by the Combined Intelligence Group but they had not seen it.

Truman said:

Stalin made a number of agreements with me at Potsdam in 1945. He was very amiable and very easy to deal with. The British were far more difficult to deal with. They would make an agreement with me one day and then, the next day, they would start arguing about it. But, since Potsdam, Stalin has broken every single one of these agreements. Maybe it's not his fault. After all, he is only secretary of the Politburo and has his troubles with the other thirteen members just the way I have my trouble here with my Cabinet and the Congress.

This seems a rather simple-minded statement. Truman continued: "How can you negotiate an understanding with people who have no moral responsibility?"

I told the President one of the great fears abroad was the feeling that there was no permanent continuity of American foreign policy. The reason stated was that every four years there is an election and often a new party and a new administration came in and the policy might change completely.

I thought the idea of a permanent under secretary of state would help to allay such doubts but he replied he did not think a career under secretary useful and by making foreign policy bipartisan the same means would be better accomplished. He said, "the striped pants boys are always trying to undercut me. I have enough trouble with them now."

He referred also complainingly to what he calls the "sabotage press" and specifically named the *New York Daily News, Washington Times-Herald, Chicago Tribune* and the Hearst newspapers. I was interested to note that on the top of the heap of seven newspapers on the table behind him was *The New York Times*.

The President said that "Potsdam was an effort to negotiate an understanding." It was evident that President Truman used Potsdam as a symbol of all relations with Russia because this was his one personal experience of Russian methods.

He was very interesting on the subject of Henry Wallace. He said Wallace, during the summer of 1946, just before he resigned, attempted to explain Russian policy by stating that the Russians feel national interests are more important than life itself; that the Russians are that way; that we must accept this as a condition in dealing with them.

Truman said he asked for Wallace's resignation right then and there. He said that this never came out and was still confidential, but that there were two witnesses to the event. He did not say who the witnesses were.

Truman said he considered the Russian system exactly like the Nazi system. He thought it did not require much of a change for a Nazi to become a Communist. That was the big problem in Germany because German nationalists hoped to use Russia in a quest for German world domination.

He defended the Truman Doctrine very strongly. He said: "If Russia gets Greece and Turkey then they would get Italy and then France and the iron curtain would extend all the way to Western Ireland. In that event we would have to go home and prepare for war."

Truman did not expect peace and stability in two or three years. He still hoped it could come about during our lifetime although sometimes he wondered about that. He expressed great concern about the state of leadership in Western Europe. Both Britain and France had lost two generations of leaders during the last two world wars. Their best young people had been heroes. Their old people were now the leaders. They were tired and did not have as much to work for. He asked me: "How can we solve that problem?"

He pointed to a map facing him at the other end of his office across from his desk and he said he always pondered on the centers of trouble, the Middle East (including Greece), China and Germany.

Emphasizing his determination to make foreign policy a bipartisan matter, he said he never made any decision involving foreign affairs, even budgetary matters, without consulting Senator Vandenberg and Congressman Eaton.

Concerning the idea of a permanent under secretary of state, he did not want to change the system of government now prevailing in the United States at all except that he thought it would be a good idea to have Congress elected with the President for four years and not for two years. He said new elections every two years make Congress spend too much time on political matters.

He asked me if I thought the present "attitude" of the Russians, as exemplified by their actions and speeches, was caused by internal pressures and whether such pressures might bring about danger of war. I said I did not think that internal pressures were responsible and I gave the Kremlin full credit for knowing how much the Russian people could stand. The Soviet government did not really respond to pressure as in this country and if the Kremlin felt that temperature was rising too high within the country it would always be possible to abolish bread rationing. This year they have a good harvest but they even had a grain reserve last year when they had a very bad harvest, by maintaining an abnormally low bread ration. I thought it would be possible to restore stability in Europe because Europe had a higher standard of living than Russia, and the United States can set Europe on its feet. Asia is the real problem between Russia and the United States although it is not so much in the news right now.

Truman told me a story about Stalin. He told me that at Potsdam Stalin frequently took pleasure in needling Churchill. At one point when they were discussing Poland, Churchill pointed out that Poland was primarily a Roman Catholic country and he said that the Pope would object to certain of Stalin's plans. According to Truman, Stalin asked Churchill "How many divisions does the Pope have?" Truman said: "That is a true story. I was there."

That afternoon I spent a long time with Byrnes. I asked Byrnes about the story. Byrnes had heard it and had even mentioned it in his book. He said: "It is a good story, but it is not true. I know it is not true because I was there."

WASHINGTON, *November 4, 1947*

I had a long talk with James Byrnes, former Secretary of State. When Byrnes was Secretary he tried to institute a new system to clarify American policy. He had found that usually there was no policy at all. An American ambassador would wire to the State Department and ask "What is American policy on this?" Officials would then meet in Washington and decide what their policy should be and answer the ambassador. That was the way policy was formulated.

Byrnes tried to institute a codified series of policy statements. These would be subject to revision from time to time. (This is somewhat similar to the system employed by European countries three or four centuries ago, when detailed instructions were given through letters to ambassadors.) The Byrnes plan was to have, first of all, basic policy worked out by the American ambassador in each country and then shaped inside the State Department. This was done. For example, policy towards the United Kingdom was stated in about two and one-half pages to which were attached much longer appendices.

This system was completed for countries and to a degree for "areas." It had not yet been worked out for "regions" and continents. As far as Byrnes now knows the whole file has been tucked away in some State Department pigeonhole.

Byrnes said Bohlen wanted the United States to come out strongly in favor of the Social Democratic Party in Germany and to work for it. He and Clay opposed this idea on the grounds that not only would this be interference in the internal affairs of another country, but it might not work out practically. Other German parties might come to power and where would we be?

Byrnes said there has been continual pressure in Washington for a long time to get Caffery out as ambassador in Paris. However, he always felt Caffery was moderately competent and that the political appointee who would probably succeed him would probably make more and worse mistakes. He had been fairly well impressed by Caffery in Potsdam. Caffery came to dinner with Truman and Byrnes and he disagreed flatly with Truman about some point of policy and stated his argument well. Byrnes thought this was a dangerous thing to do since Caffery knew perfectly well many people were already working on Truman to have Caffery replaced. He pointed this out to the President after Caffery left and said both he and Truman had a higher regard for Caffery afterwards.

Byrnes insists the only reason he resigned is health. He submitted his resignation one day after his doctor cautioned him he had to take it easy because of a heart condition and showed Byrnes a cardiogram. Byrnes submitted his resignation with the idea that it would take effect after the five peace treaties were negotiated. He hoped this would be in January 1947. But it took longer. He has not had any heart attacks, however, and is now feeling better.

Byrnes would like to know why Molotov stayed out of the Marshall Plan. He thinks it was a great mistake. However, he figures Molotov was afraid of the position of the Russian satellites. If a country like Czechoslovakia hoped and planned to have a billion dollars, it would be pretty difficult for Molotov to deprive that country of this money later on—taking the candy away. Furthermore, Molotov was very scared of supervision that he thought would go with the Marshall Plan. He saw what supervision went with the Truman Doctrine in Greece and Turkey. He not only did not want such supervision in satellite states but could not tolerate it in Russia. Byrnes wonders if we will change our mind on supervision in Greece and Turkey after the Marshall Plan goes through, in order to be consistent.

Byrnes says there was no Marshall Plan. Bevin started it. Marshall made a speech and Bevin grabbed the ball and got things organized abroad.

WASHINGTON, *November 5, 1947*

I had a long talk this morning with Lieutenant General Lauris Norstad. Norstad thinks the world is in a period of great danger for the next two or three years. The hysteria of one of the satellite countries could conceivably start an incident which would lead to war. Or Russia might present such impossible conditions that the same disaster would result. We are now in the "area of possibility of war." But Norstad does not believe that war will come. He thinks this two- to three-year period will be followed by a period of about fifteen years when war is most unlikely. During that period it would have to be a deliberate and cold-blooded decision on the part of the Russians who would also have to be convinced militarily that they not only could occupy Europe and Asia but could defeat the United States.

NEW YORK, *November 12, 1947*

DULLES told me Byrnes very definitely had expected to go to the Moscow conference because Mrs. Byrnes told Mrs. Dulles she was busy getting her clothes ready. As far as Byrnes' claim that he was quitting because of ill health, Dulles is surprised no newspapers have taken this up. He saw Byrnes the other day and Byrnes told him he was working harder than ever before in his life.

Dulles thinks Byrnes' book was indifferent to moral principles and the tendency toward sharp trading as witness the row about the two-thirds vote at the Paris peace conference in 1946. He argues the peace treaties with Italy and the other satellites constituted at least an implied promise to support all of them for membership in the United Nations, although we and the British opposed all of them except Italy and Finland. He says Bevin was careful at the subsequent London conference to say that Great Britain was not committed, but he doesn't think the United States was that careful.

We were talking about Poland. Dulles said the United States allowed itself to be put in the position of backing the Germans against the Poles on the frontier. As Byrnes afterwards claimed, the armistice terms just said that the boundary would be determined later, but Dulles points out that this provides for moving Germans out of the area assigned to Poland.

As far as Germany is concerned, Dulles thinks the only thing to try for now is the political and economic unity of the American, British and French zones. He believes it's a pity America did not back internationalization of the Ruhr area. The British are the main stumbling block because they do not want this done unless the industries of the Ruhr are socialized, whereas the United States wants to keep existing property rights.

Dulles is very critical of Clay and Murphy and says he understands their desire to make the Germans happy because this simplified their task, but that the policy of the United States should be determined by broader considerations.

About Marshall, he quotes a remark by Vandenberg that Marshall recognizes good advice but cannot recognize bad advice. Marshall has an excellent capacity for judging between rival claims, but if he gets only one point of view, he is as likely to accept it even though it may be wrong.

LONDON, *November 30, 1947*

LUNCHED with Foster Dulles. He says he started his interest in diplomacy in 1907 (when he was nineteen) at the Hague Conference. One of the big worries then was protocol. There was a big argument as to who should leave cards on whom first, and it was finally decided to set aside one hour on a fixed day when all delegates, using their horse-drawn carriages, should simultaneously leave cards on all others.

Dulles again discussed Marshall, calling him a greater man than Byrnes; he is firmer, and a better organizer. He is open-minded and listens to good advice. But again he adds that he does not have sufficient diplomatic knowledge to distinguish between good and bad advice.

LONDON, *December 1, 1947*

SAW Ambassador Lew Douglas this morning. He was very worried about the French and Italian situations and thinks there will be bloodshed. He thinks the big question in France is whether the army will be loyal to the government.

He also thinks the Marshall Plan is suffering greatly as France and Italy economically are being disrupted. However, he says it is necessary to keep pouring money even if there is a leak in the bucket. His worry is that Congress may decide there is no use pouring good money after bad. In order to establish stability, we must simply put England, France, Italy, and Germany on their feet. It is primarily important to aid England and Western Europe first. England because of its empire is most important of all to us. It is difficult to explain to Americans that this little country requires such huge aid, that the empire when it is on its feet will be of paramount importance.

LONDON, *December 4, 1947*

LUNCHED with Maurice Couve de Murville and Hervé Alphand, two of the most brilliant young members of the French delegation. They say France is now advocating a West German state with its own capital at Frankfurt-am-Main. They argue there is no importance staying on in Berlin if the Big Four can't resolve their differences. A divided Germany with the Russians pushing to communize the West may be weakened by Berlin in the center of the Soviet zone. The French occupation area should join the Anglo-American Bizonia. They believe Dulles is going to France tomorrow to get the "exiled" de Gaulle's views on this, since they expect de Gaulle to come back and he won't have Bidault as a Foreign Minister.

Couve told me that Zhdanov has been the man assigned by Moscow to disrupt France by the recent Communist-inspired strikes.

LONDON, *December 4, 1947*

I had a talk with Prime Minister Attlee this afternoon in his office, the cabinet room of Number 10, Downing Street. Attlee is a very small, rather withered man, undistinguished looking with remarkably thin wrists and hands. His speech is sporadic. He halts, then blurts forth quick bursts of words. He thinks extremely rapidly. But it is evident from his conversation why he is such a poor speaker. He is not impressive looking, but is unquestionably intelligent, and very sincere. He has extremely kind eyes in a worn and wrinkled face. He was dressed neatly but not in a distinguished way. He smokes Turkish "Abdulla" cigarettes alternately with a pipe. He fumbles nervously with his hands.

He is a curious figure in this historic house where Disraeli, Gladstone and Churchill lived before him. Attlee said that a socialist revolution had now begun in England. But he said there would always be two parties in England. There would be the Labor Party, and a Party of the Right. He did not think it would change its name from "Conservative" because "here in England we do not change names very often." He did not foresee a future split in the Labor Party or a derivation from such a split in the Labor Party of England's two-party system.

Attlee said he hoped that if the Marshall Plan went through there would be complete recovery in England by 1950, but he said this is of course dependent on other factors such as the harvest, or foreign affairs. Attlee thought there would be no war.

He believed the world tended to sell Great Britain short as a power, and pointed out that not only is the British empire a possessor of the secret of atomic fission, but also influences the vast imperial importance of Africa. He felt that the United States tends to consider England either in terms of George III or Victoria. "We have a different King George now," Attlee said, "and this is the Twentieth Century."

Attlee expressed the hope that when British recovery has been completed, Socialist England, leading the Socialist states of Western Europe, will serve as a bridge between capitalist America, and Communist Russia. England has economic parallels with Russia and parallels of liberty and mutual conception of human rights with the United States. He hopes that some day England will be able to help bring the world together by exercising an economic influence upon the United States and a humanitarian influence upon Russia.

Attlee was very bitter about the American attitude on Palestine. Britain had been well on the way to establishing a satisfactory solution on a cantonal basis in Palestine last year when Truman made his speech demanding the immediate entry of some hundred thousand Jews. He said that now there was no question about any alternative to Britain's intention of withdrawing all troops next year, and furthermore he said the United States had not been exerting pressure on Britain to keep her troops there. He feared considerable bloodshed, and thought it would be very difficult to protect the Jewish colony living inside Arab states, such as the 80,000 Jews in Iraq.

Attlee expressed considerable interest in the Antwerp meeting last week of the Second International. He said it was useful for the Socialist Parties to exchange ideas. But he added that the British Labor Party did not wish to form a joint International Socialist body to control its component members. This could to an extent be done when the Second International was made up of small minority parties but could not be done now that so many Socialist Parties controlled governments.

Russia's great mistake was in controlling the Communist Parties of the world. Communism was more Russian than Communistic. This made all the international Communist Parties conspiracies instead of parties representing national ideas. This conspiratorial aspect of Russia leading Communism was "a fatal mistake."

Attlee pointed out that two years after World War I there were wars and troubles everywhere—Russia, Poland, Greece, Turkey, Ireland. There were housing shortages and disrupted economies. Why did people expect miracles now?

He said the United States had been very fair on its aid to Britain. There had been no implied pressure to oppose Socialism in exchange for aid. America tends to do things very fast but shifts trends. In 1935 we had many socialistic ideas, and he felt that there would be more controls now in America if 1948 were not an election year.

LONDON, *December 5, 1947*

THIS morning I saw Foreign Minister Bevin in the Foreign Office. He looked rather better than in Moscow: neatly dressed in a pin-striped dark blue suit. Throughout the conversation he kept his cigarette in the corner of his mouth and the ash kept falling onto his vest. It did not seem to bother him. He did not offer me a cigarette. Finally I brought out one of my own.

Bevin strikes me as being rather impressed with his own amateur interest in history (one can almost always tell what he has been reading by the way he drags historical comparisons into the conversation), and he made one rather good point. We were discussing the Marshall Plan. He said that, after the Napoleonic wars, Britain had spent a great deal of its wealth facilitating the recovery of Europe, and had sent a large part of its exports to the Continent to accomplish this. As a result of this economic action, which paralleled diplomatic action, Britain had been able to play a very important role in keeping a global peace till 1914 despite local wars in the Crimea, Balkans, Prussia and Russia.

Now the United States was a global power. It was a creditor rather than a debtor nation. Britain at present was not wealthy enough to have a decisive economic influence, nor strong enough to police the world. Such responsibilities were beginning to devolve upon the United States. American foreign policy was definitely maturing as a result of this. Bevin wished that he had had at the disposal of British policy the power which belongs to the United States. He did not mean military power but economic power.

He said there had been no discussion between Britain and the United States along the lines of what became the Marshall Plan before Secretary Marshall made his famous speech at Harvard. However, Bevin had been considering these matters for a long time and was delighted when he heard Marshall's words, and he felt that was the moment to act.

Bevin with great pride recalled that Britain had "stood like a rock" in 1940 and 1941. Britain must now, economically speaking, "stand like a rock."

He expressed great admiration for the resilience of the Latin nations—

France and Italy. He expressed the opinion that the French may emerge from their present travail as once again a great nation. He indicated considerable optimism over the long-range situation in France and Italy. Italy had produced fine new leaders, especially De Gasperi and Sforza.

I asked Bevin if he thought it was feasible for the Western Powers to sign a separate peace with Germany if the Big Four agreement failed, and if Western Germany could be established then under Anglo-French-American supervision with a capital at Frankfort, withdrawing from Berlin. Bevin replied "I refuse to budget for failure."

He said Russia could no more escape the economic consequences of the war than could other countries. But Russia would not go bust. It had too tight a government control on everything.

Bevin said Britain hoped to place at the disposition of the United States its accumulated wisdom and experience in order to facilitate the implementation of the Marshall Plan. This must be done carefully, and without any hint of condescension.

Bevin is a big broad man with a big broad face, and the hands and build of a worker. He repeated, "I have been sitting here dreaming of what I could do for the recovery of the world if I had only had the power, the economic power."

LONDON, *December 8, 1947*

DINED with Bill (Viscount) Harcourt, who was one of the mainsprings of the MO 4 Balkan operation; also Bill Deakin, now Churchill's assistant, who headed the first mission to Tito in May, 1943; and Chip Bohlen.

Bohlen said that in the summer of 1940 the British made a secret offer to Russia through Cripps. Cripps, with government approval, offered the Russians a place at the peace conference if they would remain truly neutral during the war. However, ever since May 23, 1939, the Russians had been lining up with the Germans. Schulenburg continually exceeded his instructions to achieve this after the German-Japanese negotiations failed. Stalin sent word to Hitler not to send anyone to Moscow for signature of a political deal until all details had first been worked out. The British never had a chance. They were really offering Russia war while the Germans were offering her peace—temporarily. There was no choice.

Harcourt said Fitzroy Maclean went to Jugoslavia in September 1943 for Churchill. He had been turned down by Harcourt when he asked for a job as a captain. He went back to England and got himself made a colonel. He returned to Cairo and stayed at the embassy. He dined with Jumbo Wilson and asked to be made a brigadier because the job "merited" it. Jumbo complied next day on the grounds Maclean was close to Churchill. Fitzroy took in a secret radio (the second time he went in) which

Cairo general headquarters didn't even know about—to contact Churchill directly.

Bohlen said that at Teheran in 1943 Molotov was much more pro-Mihailović than the British and talked of the need for "keeping in touch" with all movements.

BRUSSELS, *December 12, 1947*

CAME up here mainly to organize an emergency system in case the strike wave shuts off communications with New York; or even worse, in case it becomes a real political menace and a Communist bid to take over in Europe. I have organized a system of gasoline depots on the Belgian border with France so we can get copy up here by car, refill the tanks and put in extra jerry cans. We have our office in Paris lousy with very flammable jerry cans; it stinks. Am also distributing large chunks of money to correspondents in France, Belgium, Italy, Spain so they can get out their families if necessary, amid chaos, and can keep some currency to handle transmission of copy. I suspect none of this will prove necessary but the money and gas can always be used up over a period of time; and we'd feel like damned fools without it, in the 1 per cent chance that the crisis explodes.

(P.S. Much later. Never did need it. Took months to use up the gas and greenbacks; but no loss).

BRUSSELS, *December 13, 1947*

HAD a good talk with Prime Minister Paul-Henri Spaak, perhaps the wisest statesman in Europe today. He says France definitely requires a "shock" to bring her out of her lethargy. France, as yet, has no real recovery program. Devaluation of the franc alone is no policy. France can never receive the required "shock" by continuation of its traditional prime ministers like Ramadier and Schuman. The only man who can provide this "shock" is de Gaulle. It is necessary for de Gaulle to come to power, but as a previous condition, it is necessary for the Socialists to make a deal with de Gaulle, so that they can serve as a restraining influence upon his autocratic tendencies. He says:

> I am convinced the Communists have chosen a bad battleground in their contest against Western ways. They pose an alternative of "either the Marshall Plan or misery." They have offered no positive alternative. Furthermore, it is evident that the Soviet Union is incapable of affording to Europe the aid that it requires. Therefore it becomes a question of either the United States—or no one.

Ideologically, Spaak says, "The only answer to communism is socialism, not reaction."

PARIS, *January 13, 1948*

LONG lunch with Malraux who says that the Gaullists now have considerably more followers in Paris than the Communists. He believes the Communists will try and start an insurrection in Italy and France between February 20 and March 1. They will not seek power but will try and wreck production in a four-month series of strikes and incidents. They will start with a large number of train derailments during the first five days, in order to bring about raw material shortages. They will also, he says, try a series of political assassinations. The Communists have more than 80,000 organized "shock troops." He indicated de Gaulle's organization has its own private army.

PARIS, *January 15, 1948*

LUNCHED today with Pierre Courtade, one of the leading Communist propagandists in France and member of the Central Committee.

A very cynical young man, thirty-two, he was a school teacher, teaching English before the war. His wife has always been sympathetic to communism, but is not a member of the party. Courtade was a practicing Catholic and not a Communist before the war. After the collapse he joined the Resistance, first as a Gaullist; later he became a Communist.

In many ways I think he is secretly pro-American. He highly overestimates the organization and efficiency of American foreign policy. He made an astonishing suggestion to me: that the United States leave Europe and Asia to Russia and the Communists, and the Communists leave North and South America to the United States. He conceded that many people in the Americas would not like this; nor many people in Europe. Population exchanges should be arranged.

I told him that since he had made such a cynical proposal, I would give him a cynical answer, disregarding the moralities. Every country must look to its own potential for self-defense. An American bloc of 250,000,000 would not be very strong against a Soviet bloc of over 1,000,000,000.

PARIS, *January 15, 1948*

AMBASSADOR Caffery told me during the 1947 Moscow conference of the Foreign Ministers Council a warning was conveyed to the French delegation on a high level by the Soviet government. It was a written document handed to the French, but not on Soviet foreign office paper.

This said France should not make the mistake of allying herself to the United States. The United States was now stronger than the USSR and the USSR did not have the atom bomb. However, the United States was too naive to fight a preventive war. Ten years from now, Russia would be stronger than the United States and would have the atom bomb. It would use it. France should make no error during those ten years.

Caffery said that Robert Schuman is doing very well as premier but he feared if Schuman fell, there would be nothing to prevent de Gaulle from coming to power. Both we and the British would have to support de Gaulle if he came to power by legal means; but we do not relish the prospect. Our relations would not be as close as they are with the present government. De Gaulle does not know how to compromise. He proved this in Syria, in Italy (where French and American troops almost went to battle) and at Metz. He had to back down in Italy and at Metz. France lost Syria because of de Gaulle's refusal to compromise.

PARIS, *January 24, 1948*

MALRAUX told me that the former Communist Victor Serge, shortly before his death, had written to him as follows:

> I want to tell you that I consider the political position you have adopted courageous and probably reasonable. Had I been in France, I would myself have been among the Socialists collaborating with the movement you are in. I consider the electoral victory of your movement a great step toward the immediate salvation of France; although I was foreseeing it, the importance nevertheless surprised me. . . . The real salvation, at a more distant date, will depend on how you and so many others will accomplish what I call your double duty: to fight the enemies of Europe's regeneration and to master the dangers which we all bear in ourselves. . . .

Serge was obviously just as much of an anti-Stalinist as Malraux.

LONDON, *February 1, 1948*

DINED tonight with Bill Deakin. He and Pussy had many stories about Churchill at Marrakesh. Churchill invited himself to the Palace of the Glaoui. Deakin had to insist Churchill should first ask the French military governor and his wife. The military governor explained, "Please tell Mr. Churchill this is not a democratic country but a military area."

Churchill was like a bad boy out of school during the whole vacation. Deakin said he looked very funny sitting cross-legged on a cushion, and eating with his hands at the Glaoui's table, that he and Sarah were in hysterics throughout the whole dinner. Churchill kept talking loudly in bad French. The Glaoui and his two sons were wearing plus fours under their Arab robes.

Churchill ate merrily away with his fingers, waving his right hand around and shouting at Deakin across the table: 'Use your right hand. You cannot use your left." Every now and then the Glaoui reached over and handed

Churchill some particular morsel. After about five or six courses, a huge almond tart was brought in, and Churchill figured this was the end. He ate two or three large pieces and then sat back to wait for coffee, brandy and cigars. However, much to his horror a large copper pot arrived. Churchill, sitting on the ground, looked up and peered into the pot, his little snub nose just over the edge. His eyes almost popped out when he saw a dozen large pigeons floating around inside. However, he had to go on. There were then four or five more courses with Sarah and Deakin laughing so that tears rolled down their cheeks; Churchill speaking worse and worse French, and looking more and more like a strangled man.

LONDON, *February 2, 1948*

THIS afternoon had long talk with Morgan Phillips, secretary of the Labor Party, at his headquarters in Transport House. He came over for drinks later and stayed for hours. Phillips is a nice man, and certainly intelligent but obviously has great weaknesses including thirst and vanity. His face is somewhat self-indulgent. He is a Welsh coal miner who quit school at twelve, and has been in Labor politics since the age of seventeen; he is now forty-four.

He says his is the highest party office and that his position is somewhat like Jim Farley's was in the Democratic Party. He obviously is ambitious and indicated that after the next election, if Labor won, he would seek some big government post.

If anything happens to Attlee, he says the most important rivals to succeed him are Cripps, Dalton and Morrison. Bevin could have the job if he wanted to, but doesn't. Dalton is extremely popular with the rank and file and is playing a successful game by staying out of things now and making speeches around the country. Aneurin Bevan is also a very potent and popular figure.

Phillips says the Conservative Party is finished and the only threat to the Labor Party is from the left, but that this threat is not actual unless the world goes to pot. He travels a great deal and keeps in touch with Socialist movements. He saw Stalin in August, 1946, and says Stalin told him that Great Britain had a higher level of culture than any other European country. Its workers had behind them the tradition of a century in the fight for liberty and economic security. This made it possible for Britain to achieve a planned society by democratic means. It would be a slower method than the method adopted in the Soviet Union, but less bloody and less expensive. Stalin also said Britain was fortunate in not having a big peasant problem. Russia had had a great task dealing with the peasants who were not interested in hearing about socialism.

Phillips is strongly anti-Communist. About six weeks ago he lost a campaign in the Labor Party against Communist infiltration. He says: "The

only way to fight communism is by the democratic Socialist Parties of
Europe effectively pursuing a policy of planning their economic resources
in the interests of their respective nations while preserving individual liberty."

PARIS, *February 6, 1948*

I talked to Maurice Thorez for two hours today. Pierre Courtade came
along. Afterwards had drinks with Courtade and Soria of *Ce Soir*. They
both admire Thorez greatly. They say he is very strong and a good fighter.
When in prison he learned German well. He also speaks good Russian and
can read English.

Thorez, secretary general and leader of the French Communists, is a
hefty man with ready smile and bright blue eyes. He chatted for more than
an hour in his comfortable office, well carpeted and furnished with large
easy chairs and a huge desk of light-colored wood. Behind him was an
intricate model of a locomotive presented to him by friends in the railroad
union; also a tall bust of Karl Marx. In party headquarters, behind a well-
guarded gate on the second floor, an easy informality appears to reign.
Thorez is addressed in the intimate form of "thou" (*tu*) by subordinates.

Thorez said he thought coexistence of communist and noncommunist
states was possible in a world at peace but that the policy of the "governing
class" of the United States was leading the world to war within a relatively
short time. He foresaw a grave economic crisis in the United States, and
soon.

He believes France risks paying too much for such American aid as is
furnished, and that United States influence on the French government is
now so strong that it was on Washington's advice that the Communists
were expelled from the Paris government, because they opposed State Department policy on Germany.

Thorez began the conversation by citing the growth of the Communist
Party here. He said it numbered only 300,000 members when World War
II started but that now there were 1,000,000. He said the party frankly
aspires to assume power some day to make this country a truly "Socialist
state." Thorez contined:

> It is my own conviction that the working class will take its destiny
> into its own hands. We are much more ready than were our fathers or
> our grandfathers. Communism is an old idea in France. We inherit an
> ancient tradition of workers' movements.
>
> It is never those classes on their way to power which take the initiative
> in violence. It is those classes of society doomed by economic develop-
> ments to disappear which seek to maintain themselves in power by
> means of violence and illegality. For example now in France it is not the
> Communist Party which took the initiative in breaking the laws of

the Republic. This was done by the parties of the government. During the strikes a few months ago, they broke the laws of France. They violated one of the fundamental rules of democracy by ejecting the Communists from participation in authority although we are easily the first party.

They have ousted the Communists from essential positions in the National Assembly. They are now employing illegal means even in the economic field. The closing of private banks by decree was in violation of the law. The alteration in the value of 5,000-franc notes by decree was against the law. This causes the working class to think that it is the role of democracy to insure power only to those parties which are working against the interests of the nation and the working class. In that case, this is democracy in the Athenian sense—for the protection of the slave owners.

We have another conception of democracy—that of Condorcet. At the time of the French Revolution Condorcet described this accordingly: "A democracy is a system where all social institutions must aim at the amelioration of the social, moral, intellectual and physical state of the most numerous and poorest class of society." That was his definition and is our definition of democracy.

There is no question of westernizing Soviet communism. There is a general doctrine of Communism. But towards this ideal there are different roads for different peoples, roads which have to be chosen by evolution and according to traditions and the relationships between the political forces of a country and even of surrounding countries. The only thing that is certain in all countries is the implied necessity of fighting those elements which oppose Communism.

I think the United States will soon be involved in a very grave economic crisis. And certainly the states which will suffer least in a resulting world depression would be the Soviet Union and those Eastern European lands now on the path towards Socialism. This is proven by precisely the reason that at present with immense difficulty and strenuous effort, and without American aid—even with strong American opposition—these lands are marching towards reconstruction. And on the contrary, France and other countries will be sucked into the consequences of an American economic crisis just in that measure that their own reconstruction has been dependent upon and subordinated to American help.

I asked Thorez whether he foresaw war, and he answered:

I think the present policy of the ruling class of the United States can lead to war within a relatively short time. I believe official American policy does not take into account the real conditions necessary to establish true democratic and enduring peace. For us Frenchmen, the chief problem is that of Germany. Germany invaded us three times within less than a century. The people of France therefore consider they have a right to insist on real security and reparations. United States policy denies these rights. State Department policy seeks to give priority to the reestablishment of heavy industry in Germany. That constitutes a great danger for France which has no reparations and which will have on its borders a rebirth of German economic power and its attendant military power.

John Foster Dulles, who knew we were opposing State Department policy on Germany, said French Communists were not truly Frenchmen. That is exactly what a Schützstaffel officer said about one of our young heroes who was executed at Chateaubriand after his legs had been broken with iron bars. It is strange that Dulles should use the same words.

We were the first on the soil of France to call for resistance against the German invader. We were the only efficient organization fighting the invaders and were not merely limited to intelligence work. Even now, you can look at a political map of France and see our influence outside of the big industrial cities. It is directly proportional to the strength of our Communist *francs tireurs* during the war. In those places where there were active maquis, today there are Communists.

ROME, *February 18, 1948*

I talked at length with Pope Pius XII this morning. He looked extremely fit and remarkably energetic for a man of his age. Although he is well over seventy he has delicate and extraordinarily youthful hands.

I waited outside in various antechambers about fifteen minutes, watching middle-aged gentlemen of the Noble Guard pacing up and down in their nineteenth-century uniforms. Then I was ushered into the Pope's office. He was seated at a large desk of light wood.

We started talking about communism and nothing he said was very sensational. He expressed considerable worry about the Italian elections especially in view of the vote at Pescara two days ago. I asked him what would be the position of the Vatican if the Communists came to power in Italy. He thought that if the Communists ever did come to power in Italy they would stay long in power, and he admitted quite frankly that the Church was doing everything possible to prevent this. He spoke very enthusiastically about Archbishop Stepinac who is in prison in Jugoslavia and said he was a brave and dignified man. He said the Communists in Jugoslavia were now persecuting the small parish priests and even very religious laymen. He said that in Poland the persecution was not as severe yet as in Jugoslavia, but that the Communists obviously were determined to destroy the Church everywhere. Before the Revolution, although the Czars of Russia were by no means favorable to the Catholic Church, they did permit the establishment of four Catholic bishops in Russia as well as various priests; but now there were only two or three priests in all of the Soviet Union. Persecution in varying degrees was taking place in Poland, Rumania, Hungary and Jugoslavia.

I asked him why he believed that communism was so determined to stamp out the Catholic religion. He said this was because there could never be compromise between catholicism and communism, between materialism and spiritualism. He greatly admired the way the United States was now battling against communism on a temporal basis.

I asked the Pope if it was possible for a good Catholic to be at the same time a Communist, having in mind certain French Communists who said they are believing Catholics. The Pope replied that it was absolutely impossible.

He said that in Italy most of the Socialists were the same as Communists although this was not true in France where the Socialists were still independent and against dictatorship. He said that Saragat was an independent man and against dictatorship but he admitted that from the point of view of the Church Saragat was not welcomed, and that the other Socialists were not very popular either. He spoke warmly of Robert Schuman in France as a good Catholic and also of the MRP, although he indicated that this party was about as far left as the Church liked to see at present.

ROME, *February 19, 1948*

COUNT Sforza, the foreign minister, told me that if the Marshall Plan succeeds, the Soviet Union will some day regret its failure to participate in it, and will recognize that decision as an error.

Who knows that some day when the Marshall Plan has succeeded in the measure we hope, Soviet politicians will admit that the Russian refusal to join the project last summer was a great economic error and an even greater psychological mistake. Believing as I do in the success of the Marshall Plan, I want to express my fervent wish that all doors should be kept open for the Eastern nations to eventually join, as certainly some of them would like to do.

He added: "Proof that the Marshall Plan was really a great historical idea is given by this fact: in Europe now, amid the confusion of languages and ideas which characterizes the political atmosphere everywhere, the only way to determine what a man or a nation really stands for is to know whether he is for the Plan or against it.

Sforza, as always, is consumed by his vanity. A distinguished, noble but crafty-looking man with his white beard and gleaming eyes.

ROME, *February 19, 1948*

THE Communists have adopted Garibaldi as the symbol on their election posters. Garibaldi's only living nephew wrote a letter to *Il Tempo* complaining that his uncle would be horrified by this but nobody has been able to get posters carrying the text of this letter distributed. Previously the

Communists used as symbol a figure of a woman wearing a crown of towers and many ignorant peasants thought they were voting for the queen when they voted for that symbol.

ROME, *February 21, 1948*

TODAY Ambassador Jimmy Dunn sent a telegram to the State Department recommending that the United States publicly point out that Italy will not receive Marshall Plan benefits if it goes Communist. He contended:

At the appropriate period in the electoral campaign (probably a later stage) it seems to us desirable that a high official in the United States should publicly point out that the Soviet Union and the satellite countries have refused to participate in ERP, that Communist propaganda in Italy has constantly attacked the US and American aid to Italy, that therefore there is no reason to believe that a Communist controlled Italy subserviently assimilated into the Soviet orbit of totalitarianism would in any way be willing to participate in ERP or be eligible for US aid which is predicated upon the maintenance of the true democracy and cooperation with other democracies toward general European recovery.

LA NARTELLE, FRANCE, *April 9, 1948*

I had dinner with Norris Chipman tonight on my way to Italy for the elections. He told me that the famous protocol "M" had been proven to be a forgery. The British intelligence service had been duped. They finally found the anti-Communist German who had forged it and obtained a confession from him after giving him a bit of third-degree treatment. Protocol "M" was released by the London Government to the British Press. It allegedly cited secret Cominform instructions to West German Communists to provoke trouble. Considerable fuss was made last winter when the "protocol" was first foisted on the world. This unfortunate incident is characteristic of one phase of present-day nervousness and suspicion in Europe. A network of forgers and falsifiers—some clever and some not—are busily peddling allegedly secret documents to embassies, intelligence officers, ministries and correspondents.

TRIESTE, *April 11, 1948*

I have just completed a drive across Italy from the French frontier to the Free Territory. There are few troops in evidence. The only political demonstration I saw was a group of young royalists at Imperia. They were wearing paper hats with "Long life to the King" printed on them. They looked very harmless, like a bunch of Boy Scouts.

Italy is full of posters—mostly Christian Democrat or Communist.

Obviously both the Russians and the Americans with the Vatican are spending billions of lire. The issue is obviously to vote for Washington or for Moscow. All the propaganda is negative, and vicious.

Two things strike one most about this election campaign. The first is the enormous amount of paper used in placards, posters, circulars and pamphlets. Italy is short on paper and this must have cost a fortune. A second aspect is that no party is bothering much to outline a political program to the voters. Most of the money and paper is being employed to vilify opponents. The Christian Democrat posters advise the population that if they vote for the Communist-led Popular Democratic Front they will be voting for Soviet concentration camps. Leftist-Communist posters proclaim that they support freedom of religion and display large pictures of Milan's Cardinal Schuster blessing the banners of Fascist troops during the war. Schuster recently announced he would refuse sacraments to Communists. Other Communist placards have distorted pictures of Mussolini in one corner and of De Gasperi in another.

The third blatant aspect is the disappearance of the hammer and sickle and the word "Communist" from Togliatti's propaganda machine. The only evidence of that emblem of toil is in painted wall signs, laid on months ago, which nobody has bothered to scrape off. Communism for obvious tactical reasons has gone underground. It has buried itself behind a façade of the Popular Front with Garibaldi's picture replacing the more familiar symbol.

MILAN, *April 17, 1948*

SINCE there is a real threat that in this election crisis the Communists may seek to cut Italy in two (across Tuscany and the Romagna) I am covering the North and leaving our bureau in Rome to cover the South and the government. With my car I am in pretty mobile condition.

Today government officials here showed me what they claim is Communist Plan "K" for an uprising to start in three days. Having just blasted one fake document (Protocol "M"), how much faith should I place in this one?

The security authorities however, believe that Tuesday the Communist Party will announce in its press—before the official election results have been made known—that a solid electoral victory has been obtained by the Communist-led Popular Democratic Front. The fundamental purpose of this tactic would be to denounce the final results tabulated in Rome—which will be known on Tuesday night and Wednesday—as fraudulent and "fixed."

About two dozen well-known Milanese political leaders and journalists have been privately advised by the police to seek refuge on Tuesday with Archbishop Cardinal Schuster, whose properties are believed to be safe from mob attack. Stiff orders have been given to the police and carabinieri and army to take the toughest action if necessary, and to shoot—even against women if trouble comes.

It is expected—if the Communists strike—that they will attempt to seize all trucks available to transport their goon squads. As a result, today the Falck industrial concern, one of the most important in Milan, sold all its trucks en bloc for fear they might be seized.

MILAN, *April 18, 1948*

I had a talk with Luigi Longo today. Longo is head of the Communist Party in the North. He commanded all the international brigades in Spain. He is a Soviet citizen and a graduate of the Frunze Military Academy. He is a short thin man with dark hair and a pale face. I talked with him at the Communist headquarters in Sesto San Giovanni, principal workers' district of Milan. He was in conference with Giancarlo Pajetta when I found him. Pajetta is Communist Party secretary for Lombardy.

I talked to Longo in French. Although this was election morning, he was still predicting the Popular Democratic Front would win at least 40 per cent of the vote and that the most the Christian Democrats would get was 30 per cent. I asked him what the Communists would do if he was wrong, if De Gasperi won and excluded Communists from his government. The answer was: "We will continue to act as we have been doing. We will criticize and attack the government, but we will not promote violence."

A group of friends of mine, including the writer Indro Montanelli, have been running a secret radio station in the home of the Bishop of Novara which is not far away from here. The purpose is to keep on putting out government propaganda despite the official ban on propaganda. Obviously they are helped by the government.

MILAN, *April 19, 1948*

TODAY I saw Achille Marazza, under secretary of the interior. Marazza, who has secret microphones planted at various Communist centers, told me this evening that Communist Party leaders were having a conference in a room of the Milan Town Hall in order to discuss further plans. Among those present, he said, are: Longo, Pajetta, Montagnani (whose sister is married to Togliatti), Mazzali, Alberganti (a tough and battle-minded Communist labor leader) and Troilo. Marazza is the government's boss if military action is needed and the North is isolated from the South. He served drinks and chatted while from time to time, aides rushed in with typed reports from the bugged Communist strategy meeting.

Mazzali, a left-wing Socialist and editor of Milan's *Avanti,* recommended to the meeting that "the Popular Front accept legality of the situation"; but others were for more drastic action.

Marazza says he has been given full authority by the government to command in the provinces of Liguria, Piedmont, Lombardy and Venetia. He said Communist leaders in the North now, in addition to those mentioned, include Moscatelli, who is one of Longo's chief generals, and Valerio, the partisan leader who executed Mussolini and seized the famous Dongo treasure.

Marazza said he thought that because of the strong government position now demonstrated, the Communists would not attempt to put through their "plan K," for forcible takeover of power. He said:

I don't foresee any troubles now. I believe the plan has been abandoned. We obtained a copy of the plan written in Serbo-Croatian when it was slipped to one of our counterespionage agents. It was a very logical plan, but the Communists must fully realize now that if they make any move they will face a most energetic opposition. I have issued tough instructions to our secret forces. We have a counterplan and it is very energetic and severe.

I later saw Cardinal Schuster in his episcopal palace—a hideous building with horrible furniture. He is a lean, blue-eyed old man. He was wearing a red skull cap and black robes trimmed with red. He told me that Mussolini, two days before his execution, was sitting in my chair. He came to pay his respects to Schuster and had a glass of liqueur with him. I asked Schuster if the Duce was seeking sanctuary. He said no.

The Cardinal said he thought there was no chance now that the Communists would attempt a *coup d'état*. Nevertheless he added: "I am ready to give shelter and protection to anyone who wishes to seek it, in case terror is employed. But I simply cannot believe there will be an attempt. The Communists could try such a coup only as part of an over-all international plan and not merely on a local Italian basis."

MILAN, *April 20, 1948*

THERE was a postelectoral riot tonight in the Piazza del Duomo. The Communists were trying to start disorders, but it was settled easily by several jeeps and armored cars, and nobody appeared to be hurt.

Lunched with the Mayor of Milan, Antonio Greppi, who is a right-wing socialist. He told me: "This is not merely an electoral victory. This is the beginning of a new year in Italian democracy. It represents the rebirth of socialism in its national place after years of efforts to destroy it by false socialist theories from left and right."

Later I saw Giancarlo Pajetta, Communist boss for Lombardy. He looked very tired and unhappy. He complained of dishonesty in the elections. He said the Communists would now fight in Parliament for reforms and an additional share in control of production for the workers. He said:

> We won't permit the government to do just as it wishes. We are not entirely beaten. We represent a powerful force in the country. At this moment I see no reason for strikes. However if the employers try to take back gains workers have already won, there will be strikes. Employers may try and translate their electoral victory into an effort to impose a tough social policy. The workers will not permit this. The working class in our country is not defeated.

PARIS, *May 3, 1948*

HAD lunch with Irving Brown, European representative of the American Federation of Labor. He has a very high regard for Kurt Schumacher in Germany. He says Schumacher probably will not live more than another year because he suffers from all forms of vitamin deficiencies as well as thrombosis after almost eleven years in Nazi concentration camps.

Schumacher was a veteran of World War I in which he was decorated. While in concentration camp during the Third Reich, he used to visit the Jewish section of the camp every day. The Nazis punished him for this and put him in solitary confinement. They continually tortured him and suggested he should commit suicide. His reply was: "Gentlemen, I reserve that privilege for yourselves." Probably he was not executed because he was a war veteran.

Brown says the International Transport Federation is the best intelligence service on what is going on in Communist Europe and receives regular information from trains, dock workers and merchant marine workers. The head of the union is a Belgian named Omar Becu and has his headquarters in Antwerp. The general secretary is a Dutchman named Oldenbroeck with headquarters in London.

PARIS, *May 11, 1948*

HAD lunch with Pierre Courtade. He told me he had had a lot to do with formulating the attitude of the French Communist Party on the Palestine question. He said the French were 100 per cent behind the Jews but, on the other hand, did not want to offend the Arabs too much. He said the Jews could have conquered all of Palestine and probably Transjordan if the British had not intervened.

LONDON, *May 25, 1948*

TALK with Ernest Bevin in his private office. He said: "I can get along with the State Department but what can I do when that blessed President of yours and the State Department have different policies?"

In Palestine he had sought a plan calling for four cantons, two Jewish, two Arab, with a central administration in Jerusalem. Bevin wanted this tried for five years without definite commitment by either side and with the right of secession. But in the United States election campaign, Truman decided to issue a Palestine statement to forestall Dewey. The statement asked Britain to grant 100,000 extra immigration certificates to Jewish DPs.

Bevin said partition was won because America told China she wouldn't get a loan if she didn't vote for it in the UN. This was "thoroughly wrong." In the last days before the mandate ended, Bevin had sent in combat troops so as to clear the way for settlement along partition lines—that is to say he stopped the Jews in Jaffa—drove them out of Acre, and restored order in Jerusalem.

Bevin stressed the importance of the Moslems in the Middle East. There are 70,000,000 Moslems in Pakistan. Both for British and American interests, they must not be antagonized.

Zionists want to crush the Arabs, he said. Jews and Arabs can live together, but not Zionists and Arabs. He is convinced the Arabs would not have a chance under the Zionists. He sees the Zionists as Fascists or Communists ruling the Arabs.

He said it would now take five divisions to impose a cease-fire on both sides.

PARIS, *May 31, 1948*

THIS afternoon I saw French Prime Minister Robert Schuman in his office at the Hotel Matignon. Schuman is a tall, grave man, with long nose and sunken cheeks. He speaks very deliberate French and makes an impression of great sincerity and courtly charm.

He said he hoped the discussion on Germany in London would end in sound decisions but explained that there was quite a problem facing France in getting agreement by the National Assembly.

PARIS, *May 31, 1948*

LATER I saw Sir Oliver Harvey, the British ambassador. He thought solution on Western Germany would be reached in London today. He did not believe there was much risk of the Russians being provoked to war or even to a *coup de main* in Berlin. He does not believe there is much danger of war in the near future, nor does he think war between America and Russia is inevitable. The two systems can easily exist side by side.

He thinks de Gaulle is gradually losing popularity, that his chances of coming to power are growing dimmer and that they will be still less after this year's excellent harvest comes in. De Gaulle is a man of crisis and he would come to power if there were an external crisis or an internal crisis, such as a general strike, but France's economy is now good and she is recovering well. France needs as prime minister a man like Schuman, or a man like Monnet who is an economic expert.

Harvey says de Gaulle has no understanding of the American Constitution and thinks a democracy can exist without political parties. De Gaulle is against parties. Also de Gaulle really has no program; he just says he will make things better.

PARIS, *May 31, 1948*

THIS morning I saw the Italian ambassador, Pietro Quaroni. He expressed the belief that war between the United States and Russia was inevitable, unless, after Stalin's death, trouble broke out within the USSR. He thinks Stalin is a wise enough man to prevent war during his lifetime. However, he is very badly informed about the world and the United States because all his diplomats are afraid to tell him the truth. When Stalin dies, the situation could become more rather than less menacing. He cited Malenkov as a particularly dangerous man. Quaroni served in Moscow twice. He said he thinks Litvinov rates 50 per cent below Chicherin and Molotov 30 per cent below Litvinov for brains and ability.

He believes American foreign policy has been clever and successful during the last two years. In 1945, when he was in Moscow, he would have bet that all Western Europe would come under the influence of the Soviet Union. However, American policy—which is now backed by rearmament—had held the Russians to the Lübeck–Trieste line, which was more or less granted to the Russians at Teheran and Yalta. The only country that has ever been able to get on with Russia was Germany in the year 1940–41. The Germans had sixty divisions on the Russian frontier and were ready to use them. The Russians knew this and were prepared to give anything to Germany. Hitler was a fool to attack Russia because he could have had all he needed merely by keeping the sixty divisions there.

The Russians don't change. They remain Asiatic. Communism has not altered them. During the time of Ivan the Terrible, the Danish minister to Moscow married a Russian woman. When he was recalled to Copenhagen, his wife was refused permission to leave Moscow. He complained to the Czar, who told him: "If you like us so much, why don't you remain and we will treat you like a brother? We cannot let a Russian woman brought up in the true religion depart." The Dane left—alone. Molotov used almost the

same words to the Canadian ambassador in Moscow when he refused
permission for Russian women married to Canadians to leave.


PARIS, *May 31, 1948*

DINED with Bidault. He said he had received many reports that Rumania
might become a part of the Soviet Union and he believed the Russians
might possibly arrange this. He was very worried about Western Germany.
He thinks there is serious danger of a strong Russian reaction if the Allies
go too far. Furthermore, he says there is a serious danger that the French
National Assembly may not approve any agreements reached on Germany.
In such a case, the government would fall. This is the last possible government of the center in France and if it falls there will be an extremist
government. Unfortunately, at the present time in France, the mass of the
people tend to vote away from the center in the direction of extreme left or
extreme right instead of from these extremist poles towards the center.


PARIS, *June 1, 1948*

PRESIDENT Vincent Auriol told me in the Elysée that he was deeply
concerned over the question of freedom in France and in Europe and for
the peace of the world. In France he said freedom was threatened by the
Communists, but he also spoke of de Gaulle, saying that he wished a type
of authority that was incompatible with free institutions. Auriol felt obliged
to steer between these two threats, and he endeavors to group all elements
determined to preserve freedom and to keep them from surrendering on
either side.

In this situation, what was most important to France was to have a
period in which to regain strength, economically, morally, and militarily,
and it was for this reason that present negotiations over Germany had
aroused in France the greatest anxiety—the subject that he had now most
at heart and over which there was a very real and well-founded alarm.

He retraced the history of Germany since the war of 1870 and said the
greatest error was in failure to permit the German people to restore
their freedom after World War I. The Allies instead permitted the
magnates of the Ruhr to rebuild their industrial power, and in the process
to destroy the middle classes. All the small industries were shattered and
their force was grouped in the hands of the industrial magnates who had
made the power of Wilhelm II, and who increased that military power and
put it at the service of Hitler.

He said that the mentality of the German industrialists was concentrated
upon power and revenge and that all French who knew them had the
strongest reasons to fear that, if they were allowed to resume the control of
Ruhr industry, it would once again be turned against France. To the Ger-

man people the question of unity was stronger than any other motive, and he said that France felt that if a German state were now created in the West the Germans would hold the allies responsible for breaking Germany in half.

France, he said, fully understood the Germans have to live and that their industry must be restored. France also agreed the United States and Britain could not keep on carrying Germany at their expense. What concerned France was that the industry of Germany should be under strict control.

TRIESTE, *June 7, 1948*

THIS morning General Hoge took over command of TRUST from General Moore. A big ceremony was held for Moore's departure. At eight-thirty o'clock a thirteen-gun salute was fired over Miramare Castle and Moore reviewed a guard of honor. He was then driven to the Italian frontier by British General Airey, and pipers from a Scottish regiment played farewell tunes. Moore was very moved.

ROME, *June 9, 1948*

THIS afternoon I saw Prime Minister Alcide De Gasperi in his private office in the parliament building. De Gasperi looks younger, healthier and more vigorous than ever before. I have never seen him so neatly dressed. He was wearing a new sharkskin suit and a new necktie. He seemed calm and full of confidence.

He said Russia and the satellite states were continuing to exert pressure for political reasons in Italy. There have been no new negotiations on Trieste. Italy cannot defend Trieste. De Gasperi said the April 18 elections represented victory in a battle, but not in a war. The left is attacking the government continuously.

De Gasperi said he thought the Italian press had improved slightly during the last few years, but that there were few good papers. Only a handful, like the *Corriere della Sera, Il Messagero,* and *La Stampa* were actually able to support themselves. The rest were financed by individual political parties.

ROME, *June 9, 1948*

THIS morning I saw Luigi Einaudi, President of the Italian Republic, in the Quirinale Palace. Einaudi was almost twenty-five minutes late for his nine-thirty o'clock appointment, which is not bad for an Italian. He is a short old man with vigorous face and square, flat head, covered with closely cropped hair. He wears glasses and speaks English fairly fluently, but badly. He limps and uses a cane, as a result of an accident a few years ago.

His son, Mario, is a professor at Cornell and is married to an American girl. They have three sons, all of whom were born in the United States. Einaudi used to be a newspaperman. He worked for *La Stampa* several years. In 1906 he was the only man in the editorial office from ten o'clock in the evening on and had to spend considerable time rewriting telegrams on the Dreyfus case.

Einaudi explained the Italian people like to live closely together in towns and cities and like to live in their old houses, so that many destroyed buildings were being restored on the lines of the past rather than in new and modern ways.

ROME, *June 10, 1948*

SAW Pope Pius XII this morning together with Myron Taylor, presidential representative to the Holy See. The pope looked a bit weary. He expressed his usual concern over communism and showed great interest in the American elections. Taylor recalled that in 1936 the Pope, then Cardinal Pacelli, had told him in New York that all religions of the world must unite to combat atheism and Communism.

Taylor has apparently been going around trying to get religious leaders together to work for peace. He says the Protestants in America and Belgium have been most uncooperative. Taylor clearly does not think much of Secretary Marshall and points out he had no experience for the job.

Taylor said he saw Franco on instructions from the White House. He seems to think a lot of Franco and says we may need him "in the war" against Russia. Franco told him: "After all, I am the only man who really fought communism. I fought it and defeated it in my own country."

Had lunch with Myron Taylor. He said that in September 1942 he had a long talk with Franco and warned Franco that the United States had the will to win the war and the means to do so, even if it lasted a long time. Franco, at that time, was hovering on the edge of belligerency. He asked Franco to forget politics and to consider the situation only as a great military general. He pointed out that Russia was on its own supply lines and could provide the basic essentials for its army, such as food, while Germany, which was running short of clothing, had to send its supplies for hundreds of miles. Franco should realize Russia would be able to survive another winter and during this time a great new American ally would be able to deliver a powerful attack against Germany somewhere else. He said that if Franco had any doubt as to the result of the war, he should stay out of it, and especially that he should realize the interests of Spain in a postwar world, above all Latin America. Franco admitted he did have some doubts about the outcome, and at that point Taylor left.

Taylor said he saw Churchill in Rome in 1944 and that Churchill admitted he had been very much opposed to the formula of unconditional surrender. He confirmed that Churchill accepted unconditional surrender at the Casablanca Conference in exchange for Roosevelt's grant of a free hand for Britain in the Eastern Mediterranean.

It is obvious Taylor is working very closely with the Pope on one idea; that is to organize all the religions of the world to present a solid front in moral terms and in terms of force against the spread of communism and against Russian imperialism. Taylor sought to prevail upon the Russians to make a guarantee about freedom of religion and to live up to those guarantees during the war. He saw the Russian ambassador in London, together with Averell Harriman, before Harriman was named ambassador to Moscow, and suggested this idea to him.

Taylor then consulted the Pope and afterwards the President (whom he always refers to as "FR") on the terms of such an agreement. He also talked with several leading American religious leaders, both Protestant and Catholic, including Archbishop Manning. He then suggested to President Roosevelt that he (Taylor) should not be the man to go to Moscow and secure this agreement, because it would represent a rebuff to the Pope and the President, if it failed. Roosevelt then asked him if it would not be a good idea for the President to take Ed Flynn, the Democratic and Catholic politician, with him for the conference with Stalin, and later to send Flynn to Moscow to see what he could do. Flynn went to Moscow (where I saw him) and later returned to Rome, where he conferred with the Pope, together with Taylor. Taylor said Flynn reported he could do nothing and that he got nowhere.

Taylor asked me if I would take a message from him to Ambassador Wilson in Turkey. I wonder if he is now trying to organize the Mohammedan Church!

ATHENS, *June 12, 1948*

LUNCHED with King Paul and Queen Frederika whom I haven't seen since Cairo when I passed out in her arms (only orange juice!) from heat stroke at Casey's. He was then Crown Prince. Among others present were members of various royal families who had attended the wedding of King Michael of Rumania and Princess Anne.

The luncheon was good; the conversation was agreeable. It was dominated by Queen Frederika who is attractive, intelligent but somewhat domineering. Has a way with the men—from Smuts and Marshall on down. When serving cocktails before lunch she gave me a second, with a wink, whispering: "Here. You need it." She was right.

Among other things King Paul and the Queen told me were the following: Should war ever come again, the King and Queen will remain in

Greece no matter what happens. In case of occupation they will send their children abroad but they will stay on. "We are sick of being treated like honorable refugees," the Queen said, referring to their Cairo experiences.

Paul said he had wished to return to Greece by parachute in 1943 and secured Churchill's agreement during the Cairo Conference at the end of that year. However, after his brother, King George, had agreed to the project, Churchill, who was then in England, reneged on his promise. Frederika thinks that possibly the meeting at Teheran after the Cairo Conference changed Churchill's mind. At Teheran the decision was reached to support Tito in Jugoslavia. The excuse given by Churchill was that they could not supply a parachute mission in Greece but Paul says that was silly because there was already a large British mission there.

Both the King and the Queen hate Archbishop Damaskinos, who was Regent of Greece until the return of King George II. They have nothing but contempt for Field Marshal Lord Wilson, who commanded the Allies in the Middle East and Balkans.

Paul said there were three men whom he would never accept as prime minister of Greece and with whom he would never shake hands. These three are General Plastiras, Archbishop Damaskinos, and Tsouderos, who was prime minister of the *émigré* government in Cairo for quite a while.

The King said Plastiras is now seeking an interview with him and he wonders if he has been sent as a possible indirect envoy from General Markos. He suspects Plastiras of left-wing tendencies.

Frederika thinks the present moment is a most dangerous time for Greece. She is very suspicious of Bulgarian efforts to open negotiations with Greece in order to resume diplomatic relations and she also suspects Markos' "peace" offers. The King is extremely anxious to appoint a commander-in-chief of the Greek army and he wants General Papagos for the job. Papagos is at present minister of the court. He commanded the Greek army during the Albanian war. At present there is only a chief of the general staff, General Yadzis, who works with a supreme military committee that includes the prime minister, the foreign minister, and the minister of security. The King complains that as a result no major decisions can be arrived at secretly. There are too many people involved and at least one of them always "leaks."

The Queen makes the point that Greece is simply terrible at propaganda abroad. A few weeks ago she saw Churchill who complained about the "mass executions." She replied to Churchill: "Don't you believe in the law?" He said, yes, and she pointed out that all the men executed had been properly tried and convicted. Churchill replied that it was bad propaganda for Greece. The Queen answered: "There are two countries in the world which are simply terrible at propaganda. One is yours, Mr. Churchill, and the other is mine." The Queen also said there were two countries in the world where it is not necessary for any third country to have an intelligence service. One is Japan where it is impossible to find out anything. The other is Greece, where it is impossible not to find out everything.

The Queen is the dominating personality of the royal couple and her ideas are strong and original. Yet, even when she is expressing these ideas she always refers to "my husband" as if he really were the boss.

The Queen is busily organizing the care of refugee children from the northern areas and seeking to obtain the return of children abducted and sent into Iron Curtain countries. She works very energetically at this and has raised all the necessary funds herself.

She tells an amusing story about a recent visit she and the King made to Corinth. They went by ship but the automobiles that were supposed to meet them near Corinth never showed up. They finally bummed a ride in an ordinary truck from a road repair gang. The driver drove them to Corinth shouting to everybody beside the road, "I've got the King sitting beside me." Everybody replied that he was a fool to say such things and that it was impossible. The driver became worried about the King's white naval uniform on the dirty seat and offered him a newspaper to sit on. The King refused saying, "If I do that, everybody will be able to read the day's news from the seat of my pants."

ATHENS, *June 12, 1948*

I drove out this afternoon to see Dora (my mother-in-law). She has a new Russian servant. He is a White Russian who had been living in Berlin when Soviet forces entered. The day the Russians showed up, he saw a Soviet lieutenant and said he would like to help in any way possible. The Soviet officer looked at him and heard that he was a White Russian. He told him: "Get a horse as quickly as you can and ride as far west as you can as speedily as possible." The Russian got his wife and a horse and did so—and therefore is safe in Greece.

ATHENS, *June 14, 1948*

THE civil war is really on now. General James Van Fleet's staff gave me the following briefing:

The morale of the guerrillas is at best fair. For the last four months they have been constantly on the run and have been defeated in every encounter they have had with the GNA (Greek National Army). Markos is in a position to attack in strength in any direction from the Grammos region and he can also attack in strength from the Bulgarian border in eastern Thrace. But he has always driven back.

The objective of the Greek National Army is to eliminate the rebels— not to drive them back over the frontiers. They must be surrounded. This is extremely difficult in the mountains where all supplies must be carried by men or donkeys and where movement is slow. The bandits have a safe haven in the north to which they can escape and from which they can return. They are supported by fire from the other side of the border. Greek government forces cannot fire back in order to avoid international complications. All major operations are kept five miles away from the border in order to prevent incidents.

The rebel forces of the Communist General Markos receive continual supply of clothing, ammunition and mines from the Balkan states although they appear to live off the country for their food. Their main supply routes are through Albania south of Lake Prespa and through Bulgaria north of Lake Doiran. UN observers have watched trucks coming up to the border in rebel areas from the Albanian side. Markos' officers are trained in Albania and Jugoslavia and his wounded are hospitalized there. There is no evidence that any foreigners are fighting with Markos but there have been foreign advisers reported.

ATHENS, *June 16, 1948*

JUST completed a tour of the forward headquarters lasting two days. Went up with General Van Fleet and General Yadzis, chief of the Greek general staff, in Van Fleet's plane.

Yesterday morning, we flew to Janina. There was a guard of honor at the airfield and another outside divisional headquarters. We were briefed by commanders of two Greek divisions. Two things struck me. The first was the GNA's (Greek National Army) difficulty because it cannot fight near the frontiers under orders of the government. If the rebels get up to the edge of the border, they can usually slip away. The GNA is often shelled from Albania, Jugoslavia, or Bulgaria where guns support the rebels; but it cannot fire back. The other thing which strikes me is the position of the Americans. Actually, they appear to be in charge of operations and there is not much disguising that fact, although everyone pretends it isn't so.

We then flew to Kozani where we visited corps headquarters and had lunch with the chief of staff and a divisional general. Much movement is going on. We inspected a squadron of Spitfires which is giving good support to ground forces.

We flew over the battle areas on the Grammos and Vitsi massifs near the frontiers, circling around, and in misty valleys, then on to Salonika where we dined in the Greek government official house. Lieutenant General Grigoropoulos, who commands "C" Corps, was there, together with the governor general of Macedonia, General Downe of the British, Colonel Holland, who is attached by us to "C" Corps, plus Greek air and naval officers. Good briefing from Grigoropoulos. He wants more artillery and men.

Before dinner, we visited the ancient monastery where St. Paul preached in the first century. Took coffee and rose jam with the bearded old abbot of the monastery. Van Fleet was startled when an eager priest shoved a spoon of sticky jam into his half-open mouth, an old Greek tradition. The abbot later conducted us around the medieval wall and fortifications of the city.

Then to Kavalla and the Seventh Division. There is a new general there now. His predecessor was recently killed by a mine. After briefing, we visited a rocky point beside the old house of Mohammed Ali, whose family now rules Egypt, and ate prawns looking out over the bay at Thassos. Also walked along remnants of the old Roman Appian Way which went from Rome to Constantinople. Spent a wonderful hour skimming around Mt. Athos Peninsula like a huge swallow, inspecting one after another famous old monastery at roof-top level.

ATHENS, *June 18, 1948*

LUNCHED with Winston Burdett of the Columbia Broadcasting System, here investigating the murder of George Polk, an American broadcaster killed while trying to contact the Communist rebels. It is a fascinating story. The body was found almost on the doorstep of the UN commission in Salonika, which includes a weird envoy from Pakistan with huge mustaches and six fingers on each hand. Polk was shot through the back of the head while eating dinner—obviously with friends at least one of whom spoke English. He had eaten four and a half pounds of lobster and green peas. It is very difficult to obtain either of these in Salonika. The investigation is being conducted by a police expert from Salonika who broke up the OPLA (Communist terrorist organization) there by tricking one suspect into believing he was going to be roasted alive.

ANKARA, *July 1, 1948*

THIS afternoon I had a long talk with President Ismet Inönü. He was unusually friendly. His policy is not to give interviews. However, I hauled out my notebook and started taking notes. After a while he smiled and said: "I never give interviews—not even to my own cabinet ministers. But go ahead." And he patted me on the back.

His palace is on a hill above Ankara, a curious modern structure with pools of water and spacious cool rooms. His office is a large rectangular room with light wooden furniture including a large table. It is comfortable. He didn't smoke but his aide and I smoked excellent Turkish cigarettes and drank cherry juice.

Ismet Pasha spoke in fluent if heavily accented French. His aide, who had come to interpret into English, explained later he had learned his French at the Lausanne Conference. Ismet is very deaf and he drew his chair right beside me and asked me to shout at him. I did.

He was cheerful, exceptionally friendly, smiling. He likes Americans although he complains that Turkey is getting a very stingy allotment under the Marshall Plan. He would very much like an alliance with the United States and is afraid that American interest in Turkey is not a permanent factor. That he cannot say publicly though for fear of disturbing people.

Inönü is a small man, once frail and wiry, now thicker set. He has white hair (not much of it), pointed features and humorous eyes. He is a shrewd bridge player (during the war I played with him) and one would never take him for the stern general and military hero he was. He said that despite the present uneasy world situation which forces Turkey to expend an inordinately large portion of its budget on national defense measures, this country is determined not only to defend its frontiers but to push its industrial development and expand its democratic aspirations.

I asked Inönü about the status of the minorities in Turkey. He replied:

There is legal equality for all citizens, and this is strictly upheld, giving no grounds for complaint. Past differences are disappearing and are being forgotten. Turkey is a lay state and the traditions behind the original minority difficulties were religious. Time is required to heal old wounds. But I repeat that in the Turkish state, all citizens have equal and complete legal and religious security.

CAIRO, *July 13, 1948*

I had lunch today with Zaki Saad El Din, a young Arab who was in the United States Army and is the stepson of Nokrashi Pasha. He says two thousand Jews have been put in camps in Egypt as suspects. No Jews without pull can leave the country.

Zaki, who works for Azzam, secretary general of the Arab League, says that Azzam is interested in setting himself up as governor of a dominion of Cyrenaica and has talked this over with Bevin. If and when Azzam quits the Arab League it will collapse. He is fed up with the pressure, disagreements and disappointments. The League was fostered by Eden in 1945, to gain control of the Arabs. Nahas as prime minister of Egypt, which contributes almost half the League budget, was made first head. When the League actually started, Azzam, who had dreamed of it for years, was named secretary general for life and made it clear to the British and others that he was boss.

The Palestine War has already cost Egypt 40,000,000 pounds and is too much of a burden. The League is creaking with disagreement. Emir Abdullah has got most of what he wants—pleasing the British. They control

Abdullah with 2,000,000 pounds a year subsidy for his army. The British want a base in the Negeb. Ibn Saud who gets $180,000 a day from American oil won't cut that off. The Syrians hate Abdullah. Egypt must keep many troops (of her 50,000) at home in case of disorders. Lebanon and Syria have done no fighting. The Iraqis must keep troops at home because of the Kurds. The Lebanese would rather consider themselves French than Arab anyway.

The war will soon grind to a close. Face saving is required; and, afterwards, economic aid to work against the encroachments of communism.

Farouk wants to make himself caliph.

CAIRO, *July 13, 1948*

THIS morning I saw Brigadier Clayton, head of British intelligence here and a first-class man, positive in his opinions but open-minded, an Arab expert since he was with Lawrence. He believes the war in Palestine will cease soon. He has continually recommended to the Arabs that they "acquiesce" in the face of the situation and recognize that the odds are against them and that a Jewish state exists *de facto*. A few days ago he said this to Azzam but Azzam replied, "Where would Britain be if you had followed this line of reasoning in 1940?" Azzam is an idealist who believes in long-range ideas and is willing to die with the other leaders if all is swept aside in defeat.

CAIRO, *July 15, 1948*

HAD a very long talk at Arab League headquarters this afternoon with my old friend Azzam Pasha (he has been promoted from Bey by Farouk) at the League headquarters. Azzam, a slender but tough, wiry man with sternness behind his gentle demeanor, couldn't have been more friendly. After about an hour his aide came in and whispered, somewhat nervous. Azzam grinned and whispered back. When the aide had left Azzam said: "He told me the Grand Mufti is waiting outside for me and is getting impatient. I told him to tell the Mufti I was busy—with an American Jew."

Azzam proposed a three-point formula for the establishment of a long-term truce in Palestine by placing the contested area within an international *cordon sanitaire,* and thereby "freezing" the situation in *status quo* until the basis for a satisfactory permanent settlement can be obtained.

He said the Arab League had guaranteed King Abdullah of Transjordan to pay him the 2,000,000-pound subsidy for his army which Britain had traditionally made over to him, should London stop payment in view of the present situation. He added: "The money is already in the bank."

Azzam said the aim of any new Palestine truce sponsored by the United

Nations "must be to permit development of permanent peace and not merely to prepare for further fighting, by affording advantages to one side.

"My objective would be to let the people of Palestine live together for a while peacefully, totally disarmed and sealed off from the world. With no more arms to fight with, and with therefore an end to fears, a solution could eventually be arrived at by democratic methods even if it took many years."

Azzam Pasha, however, made it utterly clear that the Arabs would not entertain the possibility of any form of Zionist political state within the borders of Palestine as part of such a solution.

Azzam said the present war is

the worst thing I could have feared. We Arabs and Jews have lived side by side for years and there has never been any anti-Semitic or anti-Jewish feeling in the Moslem or Arab worlds. I blame Britain's hypocritical policy and American interference. The British promised the Jews one thing and the Arabs another, and now the mad elements among the Jews of the world have concentrated on Palestine with the illusion that they must create a national state there by a very logical process of force. We can tell from the fortifications we have encountered that they have been preparing for this clash for at least ten years.

Apparently they were convinced that dictatorship and aggression could succeed in what they thought was a vacuum or an area inhabited by degenerate people; that Arab nomads would disappear like your American Indians. That is not true. We have been a center of civilization for five thousand years and despite our ups and downs we have survived and driven back all conquerors—Mongols, Crusaders, Turks, British. Zionist immigrants won't conquer this world. And if they cannot, it means that unless a solution is found there will be an eternal feud of which the present war is only a phase. A new solution and a new approach must be found. There must be no more emotionalism, and no more fanaticism.

CAIRO, *July 16, 1948*

KASHABA Pasha, present Egyptian foreign minister and former minister of justice, told me:

Because of our traditions, our religion and our customs we could never become Communist nor align ourselves with the Soviet Union. On the other hand we are bitterly disappointed with the Western democracies.

The Near East is self-sufficient and we wish to continue so. We have met with so much opposition on the subject of Palestine from the Marshall Plan founders that we have no reason to anticipate or desire its extension to embrace us. The best thing would be if the Western democracies were to leave us alone.

We see almost all the Western powers in coalition today against Egypt and the other Arab countries on this unfortunate Palestine question. The West will have to do much before it can ever reestablish confidence among us, and reestablish a just atmosphere.

# 19

# A NEW STATE
# IS BORN

KYRENIA, *July 19, 1948*

FLEW TO NICOSIA IN AN EFFORT TO GET TO PALESTINE BUT IT'S
pretty tough. Came up here because I heard that (although there is
no regular air or boat service because of the war) it might be possible to charter a plane or caïque. Have banded together with a British
King's messenger to see if our joint forces will do the trick. This evening,
over the bar of the Dome Hotel, we made a deal with the proprietor, chairman, sole pilot and half-owner (the other half-owner is ground crew) of
Hornton Airways, Ltd. He (named Hornton, not so oddly) will see if he
can sell the other two seats and save us some money (it is a four-passenger
plane).

TEL AVIV, *July 20, 1948*

WELL, we made it all right. The plane was of ancient vintage and
flapped its wings like a weary crow. It barely got up above the very low
mountains of Cyprus and we had to fly in by dark because of Hornton's
fear we'd be shot down by the Arabs (or, for that matter, the Jews),
despite the nervous cease-fire. He got two other passengers: an American
B-17 pilot going in on contract to fly for the Irgun, a nervous, scholarly-
looking redhead; and a tough little Scotch demolitions expert who refused
to say just for whom he would be working.

I had bought six bottles of Cyprus brandy for Gene Currivan, our man
in Tel Aviv. But the plane creaked and wobbled so much that we four
passengers drank exactly half the consignment en route.

No room at the inn, as it were; not a single hotel accommodation. So

*400*

Alexis, my brother-in-law, allowed me to share his room at the Kaethe Dan. Alexis is a member of the UN staff here.

TEL AVIV, *July 21, 1948*

THE provisional government of fledgling Israel will not accept any limitation on immigration but is prepared to take in "millions" of new citizens from among world Jews. This statement was made to me today by Prime Minister Ben Gurion. He received me in Israeli general headquarters, an area well guarded by roadblocks, sandbags and bronzed young men and women of the national army carrying Sten guns. He said:

The position of Arab refugees from Palestine would depend in the final settlement on the treatment meted out to Jewish populations in Arab lands.

Israel insists on its claim to the southerly desert area of Negeb and will not barter that area for any other piece of land.

Israel pledges guarantees to all inhabitants of freedom of religion, assembly, and so forth and those civil rights generally accepted by Western democracies.

The government is determined to put down any efforts by extremist minorities to grab power by a *coup d'état*. It will insist by force that if and when a peace is signed and the frontiers for a new state are fixed, these borders will be respected.

Ben Gurion, a big-chinned, little man with flaring white hair, said:

The problem of refugees is naturally one of the main points involved in a final settlement. We must for the moment reserve our position and watch the threats of persecution of Jews in Iraq, Syria, Lebanon and Egypt—not only threats of violence but threats that their property will be taken away.

We will not accept any dictation from abroad or any self-imposed restrictions. We reserve the same rights as any land—such as Egypt for example—to permit anyone who wishes to settle. It would be far better for the Egyptians to mind their own business on this point. They should pay less attention to our immigration problems and more to their own problems such as trying to educate an illiterate people, do something to eliminate their abject poverty, and make efforts to stamp out their horrible record of disease.

He said: "Of course we will keep the Negeb. It is useless to anyone else. It is a desert. Egypt, Transjordan and Saudi-Arabia already have enough deserts. But for us it isn't merely a stretch of sand; it is land and soil which we will cultivate so that we can settle our people there."

Ben Gurion said:

We are a different type of state from others. Our purpose is not only to support our own population but to bring here all those Jews in the world who wish to come. That calls for a partnership between Israel and outside organizations and all the Jews of the world must help. I cannot estimate how many people we can absorb but this I can state—we can take in millions. We prefer to have young people and will certainly encourage the youth, but any Jew who wishes to come to Israel is and will be welcome.

TEL AVIV, *July 22, 1948*

MOSHE Sharett (later Shertok), foreign minister of the provisional government, told me the Tel Aviv administration was prepared to offer free port rights in both Haifa and Jaffa to other Middle Eastern countries requiring such facilities. He said: "Intensity of economic activity in Israel is the highest in the entire Middle Eastern area. By that I do not mean the actual volume of production but the coefficient of intensity. When the present crisis has been surmounted we shall naturally be vitally interested in fostering economic collaboration with our neighbors."

Sharett is quiet, pale, intellectual. He speaks many languages well, including Turkish, having served in Turkey's World War I army. He discussed the future foreign political conceptions of Israel while sitting on a balcony adjoining his office in the governmental quarter of Tel Aviv at the suburban former German colony of Sarona. He said Israel would definitely prefer to see the Arab portion of Palestine become a separate state rather than a part of Transjordan.

TEL AVIV, *July 24, 1948*

A most extraordinary thing happened today. I was typing in our room and Alexis (who is a very late sleeper) was still in bed with the sheet wrapped around his head to keep out the light. A knock at the door and a message was handed to me: a name I didn't recognize. Downstairs were two handsome, tall young fellows in khaki shorts and light-colored shirts. They shook hands and suggested we go out for a coffee because they had something to say. It turned out they were both South African Jews who had come here since the war and were not only ardent Zionists but members of the Stern Gang. They told me not to bother remembering their names (including the one on the message) because the names were phony.

They discussed the aims of the Sternists and, among other things, horrified me by warning that the organization intended to assassinate Count Bernadotte and other advisers on the UN mission just the way Sternists had murdered (my word, not theirs) Lord Moyne because it was necessary to frustrate the UN effort to confine Israel within artificially constricted borders. At first I couldn't believe them. When I was convinced I took them upstairs, awakened Alexis and, as I pulled him up by the hair, said: "This is my brother-in-law. He works for UN and I don't want him murdered by mistake; he's not important enough for any deliberate murdering. Remember this face." Alexis looked bewildered. My visitors nodded amiably and departed. After they left I told Alexis what it was all about. We both inclined to dismiss this as just another one of the absurdities that are so commonplace here. Nevertheless, I suggested he tell the UN people and I intend to pass it on to Reuven Zaslani (later Shiloah), Ben Gurion's high muckamuck in secret service and dirty tricks, if I can get to him on this trip.

Menachem Begin, head of the semisecret extremist organization Irgun Zvai Leumi, refused to see me but sent me a written declaration which included the following points: Irgun claims for Israel *all* of former Palestine plus all of Transjordan as "Eretz Israel." If "Britain's desert puppet, Abdullah," is not removed, "we shall be transformed into something resembling a ghetto, with its curtailed human rights and, in the course of time, even pushed into the sea."

Irgun will try and take control of the government after permanent peace, but "by ballots, not bullets." There is "no possibility of any treaty with England which is still *the* enemy of our people and country."

Irgun respects no territorial limitations imposed by Palestine's partition. "We do not recognize partition nor consent to partition. We consider both to be illegal and in no way binding on our people."

ATHENS, *July 26, 1948*

ARRIVED here last night after the longest (in miles and hours) poker game I ever hope to take part in. It started in a station wagon that drove me to Haifa with John Donovan, Keith Wheeler and two other fellows, dealing on a suitcase stretched on our laps. We didn't even look up for roadblocks or sentry searches. In Haifa, we were dumped in an awful little hotel but it didn't matter as we had our own liquor and cards. Since we were leaving before dawn (to avoid Arab fighter planes in this unrespected truce) we played on all night. We just managed to stop to go through Israeli military red tape and climb aboard the old plane, squatted on the floor, ignored all rules on take-off and played on. Fortunately I was able to quit at Athens. The others were bound onward in another plane. I left ahead—exhausted.

ATHENS, *July 26, 1948*

AMERICAN foreign policy, I wrote today, faces the necessity of careful reconsideration and recasting as a result of the Palestine war and *de facto* establishment of the independent state of Israel. Middle Eastern oil was calculated as a vital raw material necessity for the maturing of the Marshall

Plan as well as an immediate source supply for United States naval and air force requirements. At this particular historical moment, Washington has lost considerable influence in the Arab world where America is regarded as a pro-Jewish whipping boy and simultaneously has not gained sufficient compensatory influence in Israel.

The Soviet attitude toward partition has been outspoken and it has furthered four Muscovite objectives as a result. It unquestionably popularized the USSR among Zionists everywhere. The Russians furthermore have supplied arms—especially from Czechoslovakia—to the state of Israel by underground railway. They have encouraged and abetted immigration. They have placed difficulties before the Marshall Plan—whose obstruction is the primary objective of the Cominform—by blocking off important petroleum resources.

Khashaba Pasha, the Egyptian foreign minister, assured me that Egypt intended to abstain from any western grouping in case of another war. This is also Israeli policy. Therefore at the moment Moscow has managed to some degree to neutralize the Middle East, an area formerly extremely hostile to her.

The backwardness of the Middle East Arab world, with the extreme poverty of the huge masses contrasted to the extreme wealth of the tiny minority in control, leaves a dangerously revolutionary situation if the spark were ever ignited. Mob action occasioned by anti-Jewish demonstrations can be easily turned into broader social protests—as the Cairo government knows and fears. Neither Britain nor America has ever done much to insure that the economic benefits accruing to the Middle East from trade and leases were ever distributed for broad popular benefits.

ATHENS, *July 27, 1948*

I had a long cozy chat and drinks with King Paul today in the air-conditioned little study of his Athens palace, sitting face to face in the armchairs beside the fireplace. He was wearing summer naval uniform and looked tan and fit. He is far from brilliant but has a good deal more common sense than his brother. What he told me—and authorized me to write as an interview—is bound to create a commotion and, above all, a lot of trouble with the British. He suggested that if Cyprus, now a British crown colony, were united with Greece—that is to say, given to Greece by Britain—this country would offer the British rights to establish military bases in Crete or elsewhere, in exchange. The news that the King has asked for Cyprus is bound to inflame both the Cypriots and mainland Greeks. Among other things Paul said:

Greece certainly desires and will continue to desire the union of Cyprus to the rest of Greece. It is difficult to understand why this has not yet been effected. The argument that this might interfere with British security positions is not valid. Were Cyprus to be given to Greece, as the vast majority of its population desires, this would in no way interfere with any military or other bases Britain has established there. Furthermore, if it could be arranged under the United Nations, Greece would be prepared to offer further base facilities to Britain or the United States in Crete or elsewhere. Naturally, this excepts the Dodecanese Islands, which were returned to Greece on the condition of their demilitarization.

The King said the army was near the climax of the second phase of its offensive against General Markos' Communist-led guerrillas in Mount Grammos. The first phase, he declared, developed more slowly than had been expected but, on the whole, was satisfactory in its results. "For the first time Markos has put up a truly tough resistance," he said. "At the beginning we expected he might decamp and go across the borders, but so far he hasn't. Cleaning up of the Grammos area can only have the effect of breaking the back of the guerrilla movement. I fear that for a long time there may still be marauding bands, but I hope they will be on a far smaller scale."

PARIS, *August 24, 1948*

ON July 22 Bernadotte told a few people confidentially in Rhodes that he foresaw the following ultimate solution for Palestine:

There will be a Jewish state, no matter what else happens. Its boundaries will have to be radically altered to provide a more compact and workable state. Its Arab neighbors must be given an ironclad UN guarantee against any move to expand. But he personally does not think there is any danger of such a move. He believes immigration will never prove a source of overpopulation; within a few years emigration from Israel may exceed immigration. Meanwhile, he believes there will be no new outbreak of war.

PARIS, *August 25, 1948*

LONG talk today with Averell Harriman, now of the Marshall Plan. He is no longer as nervous as he was about the possibility the Western powers will make too great concessions during the Moscow talks. He is convinced the Russians will not run the risk of war now. The United States must follow a "tough" policy in insuring that Marshall Plan funds are correctly and efficiently used.

PARIS, *September 2, 1948*

HAD a long talk with Italian Ambassador Quaroni today. He is an extremely intelligent and farsighted man whom I have known since he was named to Moscow after the Italians changed sides. (He had been envoy in Afghanistan where he served as Axis paymaster and inspiration for anti-British activities of the Pathan tribes on the northwest frontier, headed by the Faqir of Ipi.) Quaroni has new false teeth (upper and lower) and his tongue keeps playing with them. It puts one off when the tongue-point suddenly protrudes between teeth and gums. Among other things he said:

The United States is too fond of enthusiastic empty slogans, such as "agrarian reform," "distribution," "democracy." Now one finds that agrarian reform in Italy is very difficult and reduces its crop production, so that American Marshall Plan experts are opposing it. The idea of "better distribution" as a panacea is sometimes ludicrous. If one distributed all the wealth of the relatively small prosperous class in Italy to the poor, it would make no appreciable difference in the national standard of living. When one talks of "democracy" in a country like Egypt, it means only "anticommunism." The present system in Egypt is a reactionary-feudal anachronism.

There is no long-term thinking in American foreign policy. For example, everybody agrees that Italy is overpopulated and there is a permanent problem of trying to find jobs for more than two million unemployed. But there is no capital available to make for new jobs and no big nation like America or Canada is willing to accept a large Italian immigration.

There is a general misconception that the standard of living in Europe must immediately be raised at least to the prewar level. However, this is impossible and the world cannot afford it. We have fought two wars in one generation and we must pay the bill—partially in terms of living standards.

PARIS, *September 8, 1948*

THIS morning I saw a series of State Department telegrams and reports on the Middle East situation. On August 2, the department asked all American missions in the Arab world for comment on a dispatch I wrote July 26, calling for a drastic change in American Middle East policy. The argument voiced by some is that the United States is backing Israel too strongly and that Israel is an aggressive dictatorial state; that the Russians may follow our methods (if the United States supports Israel's request for admission to UN) by setting up dummy Kurdish or Macedonian states and making the same demand. The suggestion that America support forward-looking democratic elements in Israel and the Arab states is dismissed as irrelevant.

In Syria curious things are taking place and the Russians are making headway. Just before returning to Moscow to make a report, the Soviet Minister Solod had several secret midnight conferences with Syrian leaders. Kuwatly, the President, attended one. An entirely new Soviet policy in the Middle East may result from this visit. There are rumors—perhaps planted to scare the United States out of supporting Israel—of a deal in which Syria would grant the USSR bases in exchange for arms to fight Israel. But Syria is studded with Communists. Many are in trusted government posts. Communist organizations of a paramilitary sort are being formed. The British are worried.

PARIS, *September 17, 1948*

I had lunch today with Eliahu Epstein (later Elath), Israeli minister in Washington. He is on his way back from Tel Aviv. He has been instructed to press immediately for a settlement between Israel and Transjordan in order to have peace before the Palestine question arises on the UN agenda. Also, his government wishes to push it at this time (before the American elections) while both parties will be disposed to give Israel more than later on.

Epstein says Egypt wants the war to be renewed in order to see Transjordan's Arab Legion destroyed so that Egypt will be the military master of the Middle East. Egypt is supporting the Mufti against King Abdullah. There have already been serious administrative clashes between Transjordanian and Egyptian authorities near Hebron. Egypt wants to establish a provisional government for all of Palestine centered in Hebron and using the Mufti's men.

The Israeli government is still in regular touch with Abdullah. Abdullah wants peace but the British are preventing him. Abdullah is worried that the Egyptians might make a deal with the British in which he would lose out by making an Anglo-Egyptian barter involving the Sudan and Cyrenaica.

The Lebanese also want peace and are worried about the growing pan-Islamic movement which endangers their Christian population. The Lebanese have been sending feelers to the Israeli government. The British are abandoning their traditional pan-Arab policy, for a pan-Islamic policy that extends all the way to Pakistan. This makes America nervous because we support India. Peace in Palestine would be welcomed by Abdullah, Ibn Saud, the Lebanon and Iraq. The Egyptians and Syrians want war. Egypt wants to weaken Abdullah. The Syrians fear Abdullah's ambition to rule "a greater Syria." Abdullah is not insisting on full rule of Jerusalem. The Syrians therefore fear he might wish to make his capital in Damascus.

Abdullah and Israel are in agreement on Jerusalem. They would put the holy places under international supervision and run the frontier right through the city, thus forming an Arab municipality and Jewish municipality.

(P.S. Flash—Bernadotte was assassinated today: Stern Gang.)

PARIS, *September 30, 1948*

TODAY I had lunch at Franconville with Eugène Schueller, a French industrialist who advocates an economic system called *"Le Salaire Proportionnel."* De Gaulle is said to be somewhat interested in this as one source of inspiration for his new social concepts.

Schueller is a soap, varnish and perfume manufacturer. He has factories at Clichy and Gennevilliers and an office in Paris. He employs four thousand workers. By training he is a chemist. He started out as a simple worker and then went to the Sorbonne. He also is interested in manufacturing prefabricated houses.

He lives in a perfectly hideous but comfortable establishment at Franconville where he appears to be a local squire. The furniture is particularly atrocious. He is an Alsatian, the son of a *patissier,* sixty-six years old and boasts of being a self-made man. He made his first money in the celluloid industry after World War I and then went into the varnish business. He became worried about the world economic situation and the instability of his own enterprises. He saw what inflation did to workers in Germany in 1923 when a worker could not buy a single egg with one month's salary. In 1927 he was forced to close two of his own three factories because of the French inflation.

A *petit bourgeois,* he talks continually of the nineteenth century when money had a stable value. He says that during the accelerated industrial revolution of the twentieth century, all this has changed. The economic means of exchange no longer has a fixed value. Schueller says: "We must alter the form of money, salary and budget. In the old days we could control the ratio of purchasing power and salaries by raising and lowering the price of gold."

He advocates that, rather than seeking lower prices, salaries be fixed proportionately to production. This is the basis of his *"salaire proportionnel"* system.

He hopes, by this system, to arrive at a point in the French economy where prices do not vary much. He has organized a bureau of twenty engineering consultants who advise industrialists on how to establish this system. The bureau is called "Le Bureau d'Etude pour le Salaire Proportionnel." It was started in 1941 (when France was occupied by the Germans).

He says the Gaullists have expressed great interest in his system, but admits he is rather a political lemon because of his career during the Occupation when he was trying to expand French production. Nevertheless, Jacques Baumel and Jacques Soustelle came to see him and discuss his system.

According to Schueller: "If a worker feels that if he is going to make 20 per cent more of the product he is manufacturing, he will earn 20 per cent more, he becomes a member of the firm and personally interested in the enterprise." His idea is to push production and distribution. According to Schueller, the system that de Gaulle is talking of using called *"Le salaire progressif"* is approximately the same as his own *"salaire proportionnel."* He says Baumel admitted this to him.

PARIS, *October 1, 1948*

JACQUES Baumel, one of de Gaulle's principal advisers on economic, labor, and social problems, came to see me this morning. He said the following things concerning de Gaulle's economic program.

The RPF wants independent labor unions but wishes to remove them from politics, government or party. Labor unions may remain in their present form and are free to strike—except for political strikes. Each enterprise would have its "association." This is designed to change the moral basis of relations between capital and labor and to distribute earnings of each industry more fairly. The association would fix the proportion of the worker's share of profits. The idea would be not to establish such associations by order but to encourage industries to form them slowly by persuasion and by example, demonstrating that it was to their advantage.

Salaries would be proportional to production. But if the workers in one factory do in fifty-four minutes what other workers take sixty minutes to do, they should get the benefit. One of the first planks would be to appoint a commission to study ways of raising production and raising salaries proportionately. The system of Eugène Schueller in some industries would be used, but other systems would be applied in other industries.

PARIS, *October 5, 1948*

LUNCHED with Trygve Lie, UN Secretary General. He impresses me as being anti-British. Also, in contrast with the last time I saw him, when he was still foreign minister of Norway, he has become rather anti-Russian. Lie said that there is no longer any debate about putting UN headquarters in New York. The foundations are under way. He hopes to have different nations decorate different rooms in their national styles. This will save money and also make for an interesting building.

The late Count Bernadotte had ascertained both British and American views on Palestine. In effect, Bernadotte based his report on their recommendations. He thought this was the only way to get practicable results. Bernadotte was pro-Jewish by bias, according to Lie.

Lie says Truman promised the Jews the Negeb. The State Department later reversed American policy in the Bernadotte report. Lie insists the Americans should give part of the Negeb to the Jews and should force the British to agree.

He says Gromyko is far more intelligent and able than Vyshinsky. He does not believe Gromyko is in trouble and thinks he will emerge in an important job soon again.

Incidentally, Lie is convinced that Jan Masaryk was murdered and did not commit suicide. He says no man of Masaryk's size could have so few bumps on his body if he had jumped out of the window. He asked: "What do you think I would look like if I were to jump out of a window?"

PARIS, *October 11, 1948*

LUNCHED with Foster Dulles, Republican member of Secretary Marshall's delegation to the UN Assembly. He will almost certainly be Secretary of State if Dewey is elected President—which appears probable. Dulles said if Dewey is elected, the Republicans expect to work out a way of sharing responsibility, especially in foreign affairs, during the period between election day and January, when the new administration is inaugurated. Dulles plans to return to New York on election day to vote and then "work out the take-over" with Dewey.

I asked point blank if Dulles would be Secretary of State. He said: "I haven't yet decided. Nothing has been formally fixed." He was not certain whether he wanted the job. He might prefer a position like Harry Hopkins, under Roosevelt, or Colonel House under Wilson who had "much more fun." Dulles complained the Secretary of State is too tied up with political maneuvers and party obligations. However, he indicated he had the power and would decide probably to be Secretary of State.

Dulles wondered if some of the prominent Americans who have been in Spain have had any confidential missions from President Truman. They have included former Postmaster General James Farley, Eric Johnston, now the boss of Hollywood, and William Pauley, former ambassador in Brazil. Dulles says Truman has the habit of asking distinguished personalities to report directly to him. (He asked me once and I declined.) Dulles said Pauley had been very favorably impressed by Spain.

Dulles was very disturbed by Truman's recent maneuver (almost sending Justice Vinson on a special mission to Moscow). He felt this would have been embarrassing. Once again it made the Americans look as if they wanted to negotiate bilaterally with Moscow without informing Britain and France. This comes after a series of events including Ambassador Bedell

Smith's conversation with Molotov, which the Moscow radio broadcast, that also indicated the Americans were seeking bilateral talks.

PARIS, *October 12, 1948*

REPORTS from Moscow: The influence of Zhdanov, Stalin's apparent dauphin, had waned before his death. He was held responsible for miscalculations in Jugoslavia, Finland, and possibly Berlin.

The reappearance of G. M. Malenkov as a secretary of the Central Committee in mid-July indicates Malenkov is returning to the position he previously held as Stalin's first deputy for internal affairs. Malenkov engineered the loss of influence for Zhdanov and subjected him to tension and humiliation that were probably a factor in his death.

Malenkov's "palace revolution" was accomplished, believe it or not, on genetics. The Soviet seed expert, T. D. Lysenko, with prior approval from the Central Committee, announced that acquired characteristics could be inherited and that adherence to Mendel's law of inheritance was "hearsay." Lysenko, more successful in politics than in biology, has engaged in similar controversies since 1936.

The primary pretext for calling the conference where Lysenko was hailed was the previous denigration of Lysenko by Zhdanov's son, Yuri, on July 10. Yuri Zhdanov had to write Stalin apologizing for his "sharp and public criticism of Academician Lysenko."

Once again with Yuri's father, Andrei, we see that the Politburo is a political blind alley with death providing the only exit. Andrei Zhdanov, often regarded as Stalin's favorite, is said to have been the prime instigator of the first war with Finland.

He presumably died of natural causes, age fifty-two, on August 31. "Paralysis of the heart," however, may have been aggravated by events during the previous two months.

PARIS, *October 13, 1948*

HAD a long talk this morning with Ralph Bunche, the able young American Negro who succeeded Bernadotte as UN representative on Palestine and who before that was Bernadotte's *éminence grise*. Bunche admitted the British had made a drastic change in policy between July and September when they endorsed the conclusions of the Bernadotte report, calling for a state of Israel. This may be the result of American pressure.

The British still want to give ALL the Negeb to Abdullah. They oppose ceding the area north of the thirty-first parallel (dotted with Jewish settlements) to Israel. Nobody can figure out why. They do NOT need that area for a military base. Nobody has yet been able to discover signs of oil deposits there—and the Jews as well as UN observers have been inquiring.

Yet the only logical answer appears to be oil. Britain still regrets the day it let the Saudi Arabian concessions slip from its fingers.

Early last summer the British opposed partition and were calling for settlement between Arabs and Jews. At that time Bernadotte decided to go to Stockholm to allow a cooling-off period. No more heat could be put on the Arabs. The British put pressure on Abdullah. They not only cut off his subsidy but British officers commanded the Arab Legion troops who abandoned the Lydda area leaving only a handful behind. Was that designed to "teach Abdullah a lesson?"

Has there been a deal between the British and the Americans whereby Britain agreed to admit the idea of a Jewish State and in exchange America agreed to support British claims to a Cyrenaican trusteeship? Both shifts took place this summer.

Bernadotte was assassinated on September 17. The next day the Security Council had a silly meeting in which it passed a resolution that his funeral expenses would be paid.

PARIS, *October 15, 1948*

HECTOR McNeil, British minister of state, dined at the house last night. He was indiscreet enough to indicate that one of his jobs is to serve as liaison between the cabinet and British Intelligence. We were talking about Intelligence and he said: "I ought to know about it, it is my job." Later on, I needled him about the way British Intelligence employed newspaper men. He said: "Oh no, we only hire them in the Middle East."

McNeil sneered at the British and American intelligence services and diplomats for not knowing anything about Tito's fight with the Cominform until it was advertised. He said the only information the British had about the row was from "a little priest," and that all the intelligence experts scoffed at his reports.

PARIS, *October 15, 1948*

THIS morning Jim Farley, former member of President Roosevelt's Cabinet, and political expert of the Democratic Party, dropped in to see me. I asked for his election forecast. He predicts Truman will be snowed under.

Farley was extremely angry about the situation we have maneuvered ourselves into in Berlin. He blames this on Roosevelt and Truman—for accepting Roosevelt's decisions. He also blames Marshall and Eisenhower. He says no military man should have accepted such a decision. Roosevelt, Eisenhower and Marshall failed to take into account the necessity of winning the peace as well as the war.

One month ago, Churchill told Farley he had begged Eisenhower to give permission to General Montgomery to move on and capture Berlin before the Russians. That would have allowed the Russians to blame the British and would have exonerated the Americans, as far as the Russians are concerned. Churchill argued that the Russians had already violated the Yalta agreement so much that the British had a justified excuse for going into Berlin. However, Eisenhower refused. Farley says that he is sure if Patton had commanded the Allied Armies, we would have gone into Berlin. He believes that some day we will have to evacuate Berlin. Berlin is an island in the Soviet Zone, and the Soviets are out to communize their zone in Germany.

PARIS, *October 16, 1948*

LUNCHED with Charles Gombault, managing editor of *France Soir*. Gombault is so strongly against de Gaulle that he says that if de Gaulle regains power he and his father will emigrate. His father is the best known political correspondent in France. Gombault says he and his father went to London at the end of June 1940. When his father first met General de Gaulle, he said: "I would never have believed that I would be received in London, in 1940, by General Boulanger." Gombault is convinced de Gaulle is a fascist and surrounded by fascist adventurers. He says that some members of his [de Gaulle's] immediate entourage were outspokenly anti-Semitic in London. He says de Gaulle's background is conservative and slightly monarchist. He says de Gaulle never used the word "democracy" in any of his speeches until 1942. He points out that it was de Gaulle who admitted Thorez to his government and Ramadier who ousted the Communists. He compared de Gaulle's campaign against the government to Hitler's campaign against the *Reichstag*.

PARIS, *October 18, 1948*

LUNCH with Walter White, an adviser to the American delegation to UN, representing the National Association for the Advancement of Colored People. White, who has blue eyes, gray-blond hair and pale skin, looks no more a Negro than I do. He is 5/32 Negro. He told me he resolved to devote his life to improving his race's position when, at the age of thirteen, he saw six Negroes lynched in Atlanta, Georgia. He is strongly anticommunist and has many troubles with Negroes, such as Paul Robeson, who do not believe he is revolutionary enough.

White has great admiration for President Truman. He says Truman told him he was ready to give up his political future if he could help the position of Negroes in America. White says Roosevelt was never so strong or honest in his support of human rights. He distrusts Dewey and Dulles. He says Dewey never did anything for the Negroes in New York City until he was forced to by political pressure and will never do anything that is not politically convenient.

He also has no great admiration for Eisenhower. He says Eisenhower permitted segregation in the Army and always considered his only job was to improve military efficiency and not to work for democracy.

PARIS, *October 21, 1948*

THIS morning I had a long and excellent talk with President Vincent Auriol. He is an unprepossessing little man with a glass left eye. However, he is most impressive, mainly by his sincerity.

During the occupation he was imprisoned. When extremely ill and almost dying, he was transferred to house arrest. He escaped in 1942 and lived in the mountains for a year. During that time, he wrote his book *Hier Demain*.

Auriol said that, internally, he had the great problem of negotiating firmly with the strikers, but not irking them too much and risking civil war. Externally, he said Europe must behave diplomatically and not provoke the Russians. At the same time, Western Europe must prepare its forces as swiftly as possible. However, arms required from America cannot be committed by the US until after the elections. Auriol said Britain will obviously require its own military units to defend the British empire. In Europe, there is nothing to oppose the Russians.

He does not believe there will be a war; nevertheless, if it comes, the Western democracies will win in three or four years, thanks to the United States. However, democracy would be permanently destroyed here. The Russians would occupy all Europe and slaughter free and independent-minded people. Europe could never recover.

Auriol told me about false rumors the Gaullists are spreading about him, designed to undermine the position of the government. One rumor is that Auriol intends to resign as President and head a Popular Front Government. This is utterly untrue. Another rumor is that Soviet Ambassador Bogomolov visited Auriol and told him Russia intended to declare war on December 12, demanding that France should remain neutral. This is equally untrue.

Auriol is furious with de Gaulle. He pointed out that he had worked with de Gaulle both in Algiers and in Paris. De Gaulle has no gift for politics or for economics. De Gaulle had the opportunity to restore France's finances in 1945. He did nothing and that is the reason for the continued inflation and fiscal chaos today.

De Gaulle told Auriol he intended to resign and hold himself in reserve in 1946. Auriol accepted this decision, but de Gaulle has not held himself in reserve and out of politics as he promised. He is deliberately trying to destroy the French Republic. There is a strong Communist bloc on the left and a strong Gaullist bloc on the right. Each one frightens people on the opposite extreme and they serve to build each other up. If de Gaulle were a real patriot, he would dissolve the RPF, so that four-fifths of France would be united against communism.

Auriol thinks the RPF has passed its peak and that a reaction against de Gaulle has set in. The RPF is losing support but Auriol is not sure de Gaulle may not try to take power illegally. He prays that civil war can be avoided.

Auriol invited de Gaulle to see him several times and de Gaulle did not come. De Gaulle wants to be President—not just France's prime minister.

Incidentally, Auriol has a lovely, but not terribly large office in the Elysée Palace with fine furnishings and an old-fashioned desk diary in which he keeps his appointments.

Paris, *October 22, 1948*

When Eric Johnston saw Tito in Belgrade, he told Tito he was acting as a confidential observer for Dulles. Tito told Johnston he did not think there would be a war, but that should there be an outbreak of hostilities, Jugoslavia's position would depend upon internal conditions and who was the aggressor. At no time did Tito mention his treaty commitments to the Soviet Union. In other words, it appears that Tito, as a result of his break with the Cominform, has already decided upon a policy of neutrality despite Belgrade's treaty obligations—which have not been denounced.

Madrid, *October 30, 1948*

This morning I saw Don Luis Maria Lojendio, head of the press bureau, who was extremely friendly. Later in the afternoon a young man named Jaime Torner Cervera from the Falange newspaper *Pueblo* came around with his fiancée who said she was French. Her French was not quite perfect and she had a curious habit of lapsing into German. The alleged purpose was to interview me but they were police stooges. After a few drinks they admitted they had been given a full brief and complete dossier on me by Lojendio who told them that I was an enemy of Spain and that he would see to it that I did not see Franco.

Madrid, *November 1, 1948*

I had lunch with Charles Johnston. He says Galicia is the only province of Spain where there are no gypsies, because gypsies cannot make a living there. The Galicians are too cunning themselves. They are cold, unemotional, astute Celts. The British compare them with the Welsh. Galicia is the home province of Franco.

MADRID, *November 3, 1948*

TODAY I had a talk with one of the American diplomats who is in charge of investigating police methods and the opposition. He is (former Lieutenant Colonel) Clark, a calm, well-balanced man, who was in intelligence here during the war. This is what he had to say:

Despite the fact that Spanish justice is rotten and that people are condemned for no good reason, the prisons are relatively good. This means that after waiting for a year or two before being sentenced, the prisoners are well treated in the formal prisons.

There are two classes of political prisoners: those that have not yet been tried; and those already sentenced. Those already tried and sentenced have a chance to work off their sentence, sometimes at the rate of three days for one. In some prison camps the prisoners are permitted to have their families live with them. They can study and learn trades. However, the picture is pretty grim. Every opponent of the regime except the Monarchists is called a "red" (*Rojo*). There is no distinction between a Communist and someone who is merely antifascist. Meetings of opposition groups—even two or three people—are banned. Participants are jailed. The *Brigadillas sociales* (little social brigade—the same organization existed under the Monarchists and the Republicans) visits the home of the suspect, usually between 2 and 3 A.M. and enters without a search warrant. The man is seized and told nothing of what he is charged with. His home is searched. He is taken away but his family is not told where he is being taken nor why. It is still common, although less than in the past, to beat the person on the way to questioning.

At the police station, the prisoner is told to make a statement. However, he still does not know of what he is accused. Frequently, later on at his trial, the prisoner may be accused of admitting things he never said.

Theoretically the prisoner has a statement read to him which he signs. Normally he is beaten up sufficiently before the declaration is shoved in front of him, so that he signs automatically. Often prisoners stay two or three days without food or toilet facilities, possibly without water, sometimes in solitary confinement and in many cases the prisoner is held incommunicado. If his family inquires at the *Seguridad* it is told he is not there. Under the law the prisoner may be held for only seventy-two hours without being formally charged, but many are held as long as two years without knowing what the charge is.

While still in the Puerta del Sol, the prisoners are questioned by an investigating judge, usually Colonel Enrique Eymar, who is in charge of investigation for communism and freemasonry. No beatings take place in the presence of Eymar but frequently he leaves the room, and when he meets the prisoner again, the latter is usually more ready to talk. It is not uncommon to inject a prisoner with turpentine, which causes a particularly high fever; to hit the prisoner in the face and knock his teeth out; to beat his genitals.

Great efforts are made to ascertain whether any member of the group accused has a weapon in his possession. If so, under a Spanish law of 1927, the whole group is legally liable to capital punishment. Before this law only the leader of an armed band was eligible for death.

In the case of a death sentence, this must be approved by the judge advocate general and by the captain general of the region; then by Franco. Execution is either by shooting or by garroting. It is not public. Only after the execution does the family learn.

Here it must be remembered that political executions also occurred both under the Monarchy and under the Republic. This is a Spanish tradition from days long before Franco, for centuries.

The government admits to a total number of people in jail slightly under 40,000 and claims there are no political prisoners but that these people are involved in blood crimes. The guess is that the actual figure is perhaps 100,000 but this is not large even when compared with pre-Civil War days. It is guessed that between two hundred and three hundred people are executed each year for political opposition. In the Madrid area there have been about thirty since January 1. The figure of executions has shrunk greatly in the last two years.

It can be argued that this is a sign that the spirit of revenge is diminishing. However, one is inclined to remember the story of General Narvaez who was premier in 1844. When Narvaez was on his deathbed the priest asked, "Does your Excellency forgive all his enemies?" Narvaez firmly replied, "I have no enemies. I have had them all shot."

MADRID, *November 10, 1948*

THIS afternoon I saw Franco in the Pardo palace. I went out with the Marques de Lema, an amiable career diplomat, whose father was foreign minister under Alfonso. We were kept waiting a long time and sat chatting in a large waiting room lined with tapestries for which the designs had been made by Goya. The Pardo is a small hunting palace started by Charles V and finished in the eighteenth century.

Franco received me standing up beside a chair before his desk. He was smiling and very amiable and remembered me from last time by saying: "But I know you. You're been to see me before. Welcome back." I think he might not have been so cordial had he remembered fully. We sat down in front of his desk. The desk was sloppy and littered with papers. Franco's heavy-rimmed spectacles were lying on some documents. The room is heavily carpeted and tapestried. Franco seemed less plump, hardier than when I saw him last. His olive complexion appeared slightly wind-burned.

His hands seemed more reposed and stronger. He looked extremely healthy.

Lema told me two stories of "Franquito," as the skinny little major was called in his Morocco days. These are as follows:

There was a mutiny of the Spanish Foreign Legion at Melilla. Franco came to the barracks and ordered formation. He strode along the lineup of angry men who were holding their mess kits. The riot had been about food. One legionnaire took his mess kit and hurled the contents at Franco saying "How do you expect us to eat stuff like this?" Franco calmly drew out his handkerchief, wiped his face and uniform, continued the review. Then, he summoned the captain in charge of the mess and ordered him to bring him a plate of the stew. He tasted it and found it horrible. He then demanded a new meal cooked and fed to the men. After the meal he ordered a new formation. In front of the men he bawled the captain out for serving such foul food and then ordered him to go to the barracks and consider himself under arrest. Franco then reviewed the men again. When he came to the man who had hurled the food he summoned him three paces forward. Then, before the other men, he had him shot.

The other story: General Primo de Rivera, the dictator, worked up a plan for the assault of a certain position held by the Moors. Colonel X was summoned to the general and the plan was outlined to him. He protested it was a bad plan and the unit would be wiped out. Primo was furious, told him the staff had worked it out carefully, that he was relieved of his command and should proceed to Spain. He then summoned Lieutenant Colonel Y. The same thing happened. He then called Major Franco and explained what had happened to the other two officers, then showed it to him and asked: "Well, what do you think, Franquito?" Franco said it was an excellent plan. He started his attack and Primo and the staff watched. They suddenly saw through glasses that Franco was leading his troops another way—following the plan of the two disgraced officers. But they could do nothing to prevent him. Then the Spanish flag appeared on the summit and Franco sent back signaled word the position had been taken.

In our talk, Franco said Spain desired improved ties with the United States. He wanted a loan and suggested $200 million. He also urged a defensive coalition and said: "Spain would be willing to take part in such a Western alliance."

He started chatting about himself. He said: "I started working when I was fourteen years old. By the time I was twenty-one I was commanding 14,000 men. I have always had responsibilities higher than those I have desired."

He went on:

In a certain way we feel ourselves to be American. In these days the seas tend to unite nations more than the land; there is no intervening nation between. Nevertheless, there has been a certain mutual lack of comprehension between our two countries concerning their problems. This has been more true in the case of Americans than with us. The United States has not quite understood the problems we have faced and those we have to face.

The United States has more wealth and a higher standard of living than Spain and this contributes to the difficulty of Americans' understanding us. The same differences in conception apply when Americans judge France. In France one finds instability, strikes and the loss of wealth and energy in a way impossible in the United States where there are more normal channels of life which do not result in the wastage of national energy.

In Spain we have always had sound and cordial relations with the United States in the past and there has never been a reason for them to break down. Even in moments of struggle, when a nation regards only its own interests, we retained cordial relations. Now that the war is over and countries should be more united in peace, when there are no pressing reasons for selfishness, there is still more reason for friendship and such is our desire.

In this world of social crisis there are only two alternatives—Marxism or a way of working out the problems while keeping alive the principles of Western civilization. This is why the Spanish government is seeking to follow a path of social development that conserves traditional national social elements, prosperity, private initiative and accumulated capital wealth. If you destroy these you destroy progress.

He said Spain had suffered much during the Civil War and then lost its commerce with Germany and Central Europe and needed funds to replace outmoded industrial equipment. Its gold reserve had been stolen by Russia (sent there by fleeing Republicans) and Spain needed dollars. When Franco suggested a loan he added: "Spain is a very good investment. Even during our Civil War we paid all our debts promptly." He said Spain didn't want to join the Marshall Plan "for the reason that the other nations participating in it do not seem to want us and make it appear as if we would be stealing their food. The United States is a curious nation. It provides the money but lets the recipients state the conditions. Spain prefers to deal directly with the United States and thus avoid political confusion. When nations help each other they increase mutual love. Spain, as if emerging from a ditch by its own efforts, has felt lonely." He added:

The only way to avoid war with Russia is to make certain that Russia feels she cannot win such a war. If the West is prepared, this condition will be met. Russia will not gamble the outcome of a war on the toss of a coin.

More dangerous than a potential Russian military aggression is Russian political aggression. Until now Russia has preached the contrary of what she has actually accomplished. It has been possible to demonstrate that, despite Russian propaganda about social welfare, the standard of living in Russia is lower than elsewhere. But one must take into account that if, when Russia was economically so much worse off than other countries she was nevertheless able to exert so much international influence, this will become still greater when Russia is better off. Russia sacked and drained the wealth of twelve countries and took their riches and industrial assets, from Europe to Manchuria. She took their mechanical devices and their scientists. Within a few years Russia can raise her standard of living on that basis. Then she will certainly exert a much greater influence. During his recent conversations with visitors, Stalin has said: "I will not permit any country bordering on Russia to have a higher standard of living than that of the Russian people." As Russia develops her wealth she will have an increasing influence not only in Europe and Asia but also in South America, which is not as wealthy as the United States.

To us, socialism and communism are the same thing. If you practice socialism fully you arrive at communism. Therefore, to combat this growing Russian influence, we must meet our social problems ourselves and in non-Marxist ways that will preserve the bases of Western civilization.

We must recognize that Russia has been preparing herself for this contest during thirty years. We must combat this political offensive by bettering social conditions within our own countries in the West. Each nation must develop its social philosophy. No government can afford to be indifferent to social requirements and the needs of the masses. I am convinced that Russia prefers to give battle on political and social grounds. But there is a danger of war if Russia feels that no important resistance will be offered. Certainly an organization must be created to avoid such a potential danger. Spain would be willing to take part in such an alliance of the occident.

LISBON, *November 13, 1948*

SALAZAR runs a benevolent dictatorship. He has been in power two decades. He is a professor of economics at Coimbra. In 1926, he was invited to straighten out the morass of finances wrecked by years of revolutions and changing governments. He demanded *pleins pouvoirs* and was refused. Two years later he was offered them and has been dictator ever since.

Portugal is a corporate state. Economically it resembles Fascist Italy but no strutting, shirted party or posters of Salazar bedeck the place. Salazar has managed for years to keep a balanced budget by trimming expenses. The slight surplus is used to slowly improve the country. But it is a medieval economy. There is some small monarchist feeling. This is one of the few countries in history where the pretender (Braganca) is permitted to visit at will and receives the bows and curtsies of his supporters; that's all.

The balanced budget is costly. Portugal is one of the unhealthiest and most illiterate countries in Europe. More than half the people are illiterate. There is a very high syphilis and tuberculosis rate. To make sweeping improvements would entirely upset the balanced budget, Salazar's great boast. During the war Portugal made lots of money, chiefly by selling wolfram to both sides. Now she is going bust.

The PIDE (secret police) are very efficient. They ferret out Communist and other oppositions. However, the regime is mild. In 1945 there was a military coup planned. PIDE found it out and the leaders were arrested, held in jail a while, given slight sentences. PIDE is sore at the liberality of the courts. Important opposition leaders are generally shipped to prison or a minor concentration camp (where there are said to be little more than a hundred prisoners) without benefit of court (because of PIDE fear they will be released).

The Communists (who receive many propaganda and labor experts from Spain) use the usual tactics of trying to penetrate every opposition organization. They formed a sort of national liberation front movement called MUD behind the facade of well-known liberals. The government merely published confessions of many Communists who had been caught proving this was a "front" organization and the facade members dropped out, scared.

The American attitude is that this is a dictatorship and therefore abhorrent but that nevertheless it is mild and we cannot judge all countries by our standards. Free speech is an ideal not always realizable, especially when there is such a mass of illiteracy.

ESTORIL, *November 14, 1948*

THIS place belongs to another century. It is a hangover from before World War I. At lunch today King Carol of Rumania and Mme. Lupescu sat at the next table. Don Juan, pretender to the Spanish throne, lives in the hotel. Umberto, claimant to Italy, lives a couple of miles away in Cascais. The Comte de Paris, French pretender, is down the line, living with his wife and eleven children in a comfortable farmhouse. The children publish a family newspaper called *Nous Onze*. So confident are they of returning to the French throne, that his wife thought the eleventh child would be born in Paris. They hold a miniature court. Their life is quiet and devout, mass every morning.

Umberto has hired a batch of lawyers to get some of his money out of Italy. Carol still has plenty. Don Juan made a deal with Franco to get some. Juan is scared silly of publicity for fear he might get in trouble with the Portuguese. Madrid complained he was too active.

ESTORIL, *November 16, 1948*

THIS afternoon I talked for about an hour and a half to Don Juan, Count of Barcelona, pretender to the Spanish throne. He is a huge, tough fellow who looks like a football end, with heavy shoulders and a beak of a nose. He has the bluff easy manner of a British naval officer—which he was. Over whisky and soda he expressed his ideas on Franco and on Spain.

He mistrusts Franco and says he is hard to deal with. He talked to Franco (the shipboard meeting late this summer) about the necessity of improving the social and economic lot of the masses. However, Don Juan doesn't want to come out and state this as a program because it would gain him the opposition of some monarchist leaders supporting him in Spain today. Don Juan blames Britain and the United States for ruining his chances of going back in 1946. He said: "I was all ready. Everything had been fixed up."

He says Prieto has learned his lesson the hard way and is now willing to support a monarchy. He expressed a great distaste for the Falange. He doesn't like Franco. He said: "I know these dictators. I knew Mussolini and it was my lot to have a long talk with Hitler once. They all figure that the only thing that counts is themselves. They pay no attention to public opinion. They always reason that the public must want them where they are because they ARE at the top."

He said Franco is a tricky horse trader and continually shifts his position. He believes he impressed Franco greatly for Franco continually told him he had been "misinformed" about Don Juan. Juan believes he will go back within three to five years. It is hard to budge Franco from his position at the top. He says he will not deal with Franco and allow him to keep an important post under the monarchy. Don Juan sees the Spanish as crazy, violent, anarchic people. He doesn't think much of the Portuguese but says his ancestors had to give up Portugal in the seventeenth century (Philip II acquired it in the sixteenth) when faced with the choice of hanging on to Portugal or putting down a French-backed revolution in Catalonia. He adds: "Naturally the King of Spain, as he always is, was too poor to raise a big enough army to face both problems; so he chose Catalonia in order to protect the Pyrenees frontier."

Juan says he wants a liberal constitutional monarchy with full freedoms, freedom of the press, and so on. I doubt this. He is a Bourbon who never forgets and never learns. He assured me: "The only good things ever done in Spain were done by the Kings of Spain."

His wife appears to be intelligent and sweet although no beauty. Juan is quite athletic, sails and golfs. Dan Hanley, who plays with him, says he has a six handicap, but plays nearer fifteen. The Portuguese say he drinks too much in public but after all the Portuguese drink nothing.

LISBON, *November 18, 1948*

THIS afternoon I met Dr. Antonio de Oliveira Salazar, prime minister and for twenty years dictator of Portugal, in his rather simple comfortable office in the parliament building. He is on the short side, thin, very worried and grave-looking although with a nice smile which infrequently lights up. His voice and manner are quiet and careworn. His face is sad and rather religious; he is very devout and was educated by the Jesuits. He has delicate features and shrewd eyes. His hands are fragile, mobile and make expressive gestures. He was simply dressed and, curiously enough, wore high-button shoes.

Salazar was very interested in what is going on in France and Spain. He clearly admires Franco and his governmental theories and has no use for the rather chaotic French methods of democracy which he compares with the anarchy that reigned in Portugal before he took over.

Salazar favors an Atlantic military alliance from the Iberian peninsula to Scandinavia and sees that as "the salvation" of Portugal and the West. He wants the United States to play a dominant role in organizing Europe's resources. When an Atlantic bloc is finally organized he believes the Portuguese empire can offer a valuable contribution. The United States already has a base in the Azores.

CASCAIS, *November 18, 1948*

THIS morning I saw former King Umberto of Italy who lives in a simple seaside house at Cascais. He has with him his three daughters; his son and wife are visiting Switzerland. About him is a small and sycophantic court including General (not Marshal) Graziani and Doctor (Count) Aldo Castellani who used to be a professor at Tulane, and whose daughter is married to Lord Killearn.

Umberto gossiped a great bit. He is lonely, has little to do and few hobbies aside from studying the history of the House of Savoy and going on long hikes (he is a mountain climber). He expressed a fondness for Prince Paul of Jugoslavia. He said his sister, former Queen of Bulgaria, has property in Germany near the Soviet zone and doesn't dare to go there now.

Umberto said he would always be prepared to return to his country as its ruler if the Italian people desired, and that the traditions of Italy clearly did not exclude the possibilities of a future plebiscite on that question despite the present constitutional assertion that the country is permanently a republic. However he would not engage in any "intrigues" or "maneuvers" to encourage his own return.

Umberto, a tall quiet man, has been in Portugal since the Italian referendum of 1946. He says: "If the nation so desires, we are content to remain quiet. We will not participate in any underground manipulations. If the majority wants us we are ready to return and will always be so. If not, we will naturally remain apart as we are. Things are really very simple."

He criticized the referendum which terminated the monarchy, saying:

> The elections were very close. And yet many people did not have the right to vote. Thousands of prisoners had not yet been repatriated. The terms of the referendum were confusing. Electoral problems were mixed in with the institutional question. It was not a clear-cut choice. Furthermore, the holding of the referendum was exceptionally abrupt. Many people did not have their registration papers. The records had been destroyed in bombed and ruined towns. It must be remembered that, because of fascism, the habit of elections had withered. There had been no elections in twenty years.

Umberto admitted that "Italy has been constitutionally declared an eternal republic—a system which cannot be changed." He added, however, "But history has proven that it can be changed. Italy was made through plebiscites. My grandfather introduced the system of plebiscites and built modern Italy out of a series of small states. The tradition of plebiscites is so strong that the possibility of its revival at some future date cannot be entirely ignored."

He complained that all his property had been expropriated. "In other countries there was a division between personal private property and crown property. But in Italy as in Russia, there was no distinction."

### ST. JEAN DE LUZ, FRANCE, *November 23, 1948*

THIS morning I had a long talk with Indalecio Prieto, *émigré* boss of the Spanish Socialists and minister of war in the Spanish Republican government during the Civil War. He now lives simply with his two daughters and his doctor, in a modest apartment, with a magnificent view overlooking the bay. He speaks only Spanish, despite the years he has lived in France. He has a very bad heart and is likely to die almost any day. He is perhaps the most unhealthy looking man I have seen. He is tremendously fat. He has weak, protruding eyes and heavy spectacles with thick lenses. His head is shaven closely, almost bald. His head, face and jaws are of dead-white color as are his soft clammy hands. Obviously he goes out in the air very rarely, although he was in London only last month. It is a great effort for him to move. They say he eats too much and has diabetes.

He is extremely pompous and used to dictate to the little coterie that still hangs around him. On the other hand, he is certainly a sincere, loyal and hard-working idealist. He is almost impossible to interview because he insists on making long speeches through an interpreter instead of answering questions. He was wearing a flannel dressing gown and looked like a disgustingly obese, animated corpse.

PARIS, *December 2, 1948*

THIS afternoon I saw Foster Dulles, who heads the American delegation to the UN Assembly now that Secretary of State Marshall has gone back to the United States. Dulles said the American government is seriously studying the possible effect upon the United Nations of a Communist victory in China. If the Russians recognize a Communist government in China and we continue to recognize the Chiang Kai-shek government, it will split the whole question of the Security Council. The Russians might contend that until the Chinese Communist delegate is seated, the Security Council's actions would be invalid.

PARIS, *December 3, 1948*

TODAY I saw James G. MacDonald, first American minister to Israel. He is impressed with his own importance. He plays the game of Israel more than he represents the United States.

He says Weizmann, curiously enough, has become an extremist after all these years of moderation and is now talking about a State of Israel expanding from the Euphrates to Suez.

PARIS, *December 4, 1948*

LUNCH today with Trygve Lie at his lovely apartment not far from the Palais de Chaillot. He said he has been informed that Chiang Kai-shek plans to move the Chinese government to Formosa. Also, he has been told Chiang offered the United States a military base in Formosa in exchange for new support in the war against the Communists.

Lie said Vyshinsky told him several months ago he expected much more dramatic developments in Asia this year than in Europe. The Chinese Communist drive seems to prove this.

It now appears as if England will not obtain any part of the Negeb through Transjordan. Lie believes the English have been counting upon developing oil in the Negeb. Sir Stafford Cripps had shown in his plans for Britain's economy that England expected to have a huge increase in dollar revenue from oil exports. Perhaps Cripps was counting upon production in the Negeb. If so, Britain's economy will be drastically changed according to present indications, because it now appears unlikely that Britain will (through Transjordan) gain control over any of the Negeb. Lie added:

> I don't attach much importance to the fact that the General Assembly or the Security Council or any other organ of the United Nations may make a bad impression by the slowness of its operations or the apparent deviousness of its methods. I am just as impatient as the next man but in this case we must control our impatience. I think we are over the idea of

preferring railroads that allegedly run on time to human liberties. We are also going to have to get used to the idea of having the United Nations deal with great critical problems which the nations fail to settle by other means. We cannot expect the United Nations to dwell in a hothouse where it will not be bothered by the actualities of the world political situation. It has passed through the incubator stage.

PARIS, *December 5, 1948*

FROM a letter to a friend:
In Madrid we heard one cheerful thing about Eva Peron who recently was the subject of a fine to-do there. She was riding in an open carriage in Buenos Aires accompanied by a retired army general. The crowd, spotting her, booed, screamed and gave her a mighty Bronx cheer. She was furious. They kept calling her *"Puta, Puta, Puta"* (whore). To comfort her, the general stroked her hand and said: "Madame, don't you mind. I retired from the army five years ago but they still call me general."

PARIS, *December 6, 1948*

I had lunch today with my Communist friend, Pierre Courtade. He told me the Jugoslav Communists, such as Dedijer, no longer even speak to him. This year, he was not invited to the regular reception at the Jugoslav embassy.

L'Humanité applied at the Soviet embassy for transit visas for correspondents to go to China to join the Communist forces by traveling across Russia. The Russians replied by refusing the visas and suggesting they should apply directly to the Chinese embassy (Chiang Kai-shek), to go in that way—obviously impossible. Courtade said the Chinese embassy in París was getting more and more nervous and more and more Communist as the Communists continue to advance in China.

PARIS, *December 8, 1948*

A telegram dated today and signed by the head of the Chinese delegation to UN was sent to *The New York Times* in New York categorically denying a dispatch of mine dated December 4 predicting that Chiang Kai-shek's government "planned to establish itself in Formosa." Tingfu F. Tsiang, head of China's United Nations delegation, stated it was untrue that the Chinese government planned to move to Formosa or elsewhere. He requested that his telegram be given "similar prominence" to my original dispatch.

(History did not wait too long to confirm my information!)

PARIS, *December 8, 1948*

BOB Kelly came in to see me. Bob used to be in the American diplomatic service. For a long time he was head of the Russian section of the State Department. He was counselor of the embassy in Ankara, when I knew him last. He told me that Doctor Hanak, former Czechoslovakian diplomatic representative in Turkey, is now in New York. Kelly told me that when Ambassador von Papen was attacked in Ankara during the war, Hanak had been approached by Russian secret agents on the matter of cooperating in an assassination plot against Papen. This apparently confirms that the Russians were behind the attempt on von Papen.

PARIS, *December 8, 1948*

I had lunch today with Dr. Herbert Evatt, president of the United Nations Assembly. Evatt told me he was a strong supporter of President Truman and that he had won several bets on the American elections. Evatt was a successful lawyer and then a judge before he became foreign minister during the war. He is incredibly vain, but intelligent and sincere. Trygve Lie told me the other day that he considered Evatt had a far broader mind than Spaak.

PARIS, *December 20, 1948*

HAD lunch with Averell Harriman. He told me that when he was in Washington, he saw Eric Johnston, who gave him the following report on his talks with Molotov and Tito. Molotov was convinced Dewey would win the elections. He was positive that Wallace would receive more than 6,000,000 votes and would be a major candidate for the presidency in 1952. He was certain a depression would hit the United States before then—but not in 1949. Molotov appeared full of confidence and good humor. Mikoyan was taciturn and cool. Mikoyan asked Johnston if he thought there would be a war arising from the Berlin crisis. Johnston said there would—if the Russians interfered with our planes. Mikoyan could not understand this. He said after all there had been many more serious incidents with Japanese planes before the war.

Tito did not believe there would be a war. If the Western powers attacked Russia, Jugoslavia would fight on the side of the Russians. If a war arose for other reasons, Jugoslavia would have to judge the situation according to national interests. Jugoslavia was very anxious to develop its trade with the West, but would accept no political conditions. Jugoslavia remained a Communist State.

Harriman said also he had heard from "a better source than Johnston," an account of a conversation with Ana Pauker. She said there would be no war, unless Germany were united. In such a case, the Germans would insist on fighting and the Americans would use the Germans to attack Russia.

Harriman said one sign of the success of the Marshall Plan was that the Russians were now on the defensive in the West, in Berlin and Jugoslavia and they had been forced to shift their dynamism eastward into Asia earlier than he had expected.

PARIS, *December 22, 1948*

I saw Ambassador Caffery this morning. He said the American embassy estimates that losses to France from the November coal strike were 25 billion francs in internal losses including lost labor and production, and $60 million in coal imports necessitated by the shortage. He thinks the Queuille government will be in for some time if it wins the test on its proposed fiscal reform. General de Benouville, a Gaullist, has been asking the Americans to withhold the franc counterpart fund from the French government, so that the government will fall, and then the fund could be turned over to de Gaulle.

ATHENS, *January 1, 1949*

AVERELL and Marie Harriman kindly invited Marina and me to fly here with them just after Christmas. Harriman, who runs our end of the Marshall Plan from Paris, came down on that and also to look into the Greek mess. He is worried about Greece. We stayed only a few days (while Harriman flew on briefly to Turkey, before coming back to call for us). The civil war situation is still grim.

ATHENS, *January 3, 1949*

THIS evening I had a talk with King Paul for one hour and a half at his country palace of Tatoi. To my surprise, Paul had sent word asking me to come out for a drink. Tatoi is a simple place in the hills about seventeen miles from Athens. It is well guarded by soldiers, but as a house, is not more luxurious than an average country house of a wealthy American.

Paul was wearing a dark gray flannel suit. He appeared tired and nervous. We sat in front of a log fire and talked. He said that he was going to throw out the present Greek government. He would offer the chance to the political parties of forming a coalition of all parties. If they refuse to agree on this, he would suggest a nonparty cabinet with General Papagos, the hero of the war against the Axis and present minister of court, as prime minister.

If parliament refuses to accept the government, King Paul would dissolve parliament. Legally, he is permitted to dissolve parliament for forty days. However, Paul has resolved to continue this dissolution indefinitely under technical loopholes until the crisis is over.

He would guarantee, in a speech to the nation, that there would be free elections at the end of the crisis. He would like the United States to support his program and to formally guarantee supervision of such free elections at the end of the crisis. King Paul plans to go on the air and explain all this to the nation. The tenure of the present Government expires February 1st. However, Paul would like to take all these steps before then.

He says he told all this to Ambassador Harriman two days ago and that Harriman approved. Harriman told King Paul that congressional committees would commence hearings on the Greek aid program on February 1st. Paul is in a great hurry to get his program started.

He asked me for my opinion and I told him I thought it would be very difficult to "sell" such an unconstitutional move to American public opinion and that it seemed to me to be especially risky to take such a step just at the time Congress was considering the new Greek aid program. I recalled that Communist propaganda links Spain, China and Greece and that there was a risk that the Communists would make many Americans believe that this contemplated step confirmed their accusation of "Monarcho Fascism."

Ambassador Grady, who just returned to Athens today from Washington, has been consulting about these proposed measures, King Paul said. Before going home, Grady told him he would support any move King Paul made.

King Paul said it was imperative to improve administrative efficiency in Greece. He said that if it were necessary to dissolve parliament and name a Papagos government without parliament's approval "this is the last step." If it did not succeed, he implied that the independence of Greece would end.

Paul said that in the contemplated new government Papagos would not only be prime minister, but would have under him the ministries of army, navy and air force. In the past he has tried to obtain for Papagos the position of commander-in-chief of the armed forces. However, as a precondition, Papagos insisted on passage of the 1940 War Emergency Law and the right to veto any government decisions. The political parties refused to agree to this.

Paul thanked me for the article I wrote on an interview with him last summer in which he demanded the return to Greece of Cyprus. He said he had received more "fan mail" on this than anything since he became King. He said that for a day he was worried about the British reaction. However, when Sir Clifford Norton, the British ambassador, returned from London, Paul asked Norton if Bevin had talked to him about Cyprus. Norton said no, but King George VI had asked him why Paul had made such a declaration. Paul explained to Norton that I had asked him to express his views on the subject. Norton said, "But did you authorize him to publish them?" Paul said, "Of course." Paul said *The Economist* had attacked him on the subject and all Greek newspapers arose as one man saying "the time has ended when a British newspaper can overthrow a King of Greece." Later, Paul said, King George sent word berating him for wanting to take apart the British Empire.

My impression of all this is that Paul, urged on by his able but ambitious wife, wants to assume personal rule of the country instead of remaining a figurehead, constitutional monarch. The two chief men in the proposed cabinet would be Papagos and Markezinis. Papagos is minister of court, and therefore one of Paul's closest personal friends. Markezinis would have a key role in the cabinet. His last job was that of a court functionary and he is therefore very closely tied up with the King. It is my belief that Markezinis aspires to be a rightwing dictator in leftwing disguise, and would like to repeat the career of Metaxas riding to power on the coattails of General Papagos.

Obviously Paul hoped I would tell him all this would go down well in America in the name of "efficiency." I didn't. Quite the reverse. I wonder if he will take this view into consideration. After all, he asked for it.

ABOARD HARRIMAN'S AIRPLANE BETWEEN ATHENS AND PARIS
*January 3, 1949*

I had a long talk with Harriman about the Greek situation. He denied that he had approved King Paul's program to dissolve parliament and appoint a nonparty government. He said he hoped for a government with seven ministers and then a sub-cabinet of more ministers, which would improve efficiency. Each minister would head a committee of "sub-ministers" handling programs such as economics or national defense, or security. He hoped such a cabinet would be approved by Paul.

He said the Greek situation was very critical and urgent steps were required. The change in government depends entirely on Ambassador Grady. He doubts if Grady, who is sixty-eight years old, has the ability or drive.

When the Greek aid program was passed, John Steelman, assistant to President Truman, telephoned Harriman in Paris and asked him who should be appointed American ambassador to Athens to head the embassy and ECA. Harriman suggested Paul Hoffman. He said, if necessary, he himself would be willing to go to Athens for a few months to get things started.

I asked him who he thought would be a good Ambassador now. He mentioned Maynard Barnes or Chip Bohlen. They both have important jobs. Barnes is interested in setting up a special listening post in Istanbul, and now is doing intelligence work in Washington.

Harriman denied that Grady had ever told King Paul the US would support him in any move he took. Harriman said he himself had merely agreed with Paul it was necessary to do something immediately to obtain efficient leadership.

Harriman seemed very worried about Greece. I gave him as my opinion that it would be disastrous for the United States to permit Paul to exceed constitutional powers because we would be sacrificing principle for the expedient of efficiency.

PARIS, *January 13, 1949*

THIS afternoon Harriman called me up and indicated that the King of Greece is certainly being tricky. The King, it seems, had told Grady that Harriman supports his program for dictatorial action. Harriman had already denied this to me. In order to make Grady realize how tricky the King had been, he cabled Grady today advising him that the King had told me Grady had pledged United States support of King Paul, no matter what he does, which Harriman also says is incorrect.

PARIS, *January 18, 1949*

TONIGHT, Caffery gave a dinner for delegates to the World Federation of Trade Unions Conference in Paris. I saw some old friends, including Dave McDonald, now secretary treasurer of the United Steel Workers, and Jim Carey, secretary of the CIO. McDonald told me that the CIO was pleased Acheson became Secretary of State but did not request it. They were glad Harriman did not get the job because they still consider him a "big money boy."

At dinner I sat next to a very nice young man named Emile Mazey, who is secretary treasurer of the United Automobile Workers. He is a tough, husky fellow of thirty-five who was born in Canada. He wanted to be a concert violinist. When he graduated from high school, during the depression, he could not get a job with an orchestra. He then learned to play the saxophone and clarinet and played occasionally in jazz bands. He could not make a living, so he became a steel worker and later an auto worker. He began to organize strikes and was fired from the Briggs plant for knocking out a foreman (Mazey used to be an amateur boxer) when the foreman was ordered to provoke him. He is now the right-hand man of Walter Reuther. One thing that impressed me about Mazey is the sincerity of his fight for equal rights for Negroes. He no longer plays the violin and he hopes to go into politics.

PARIS, *January 18, 1949*

THIS afternoon Victor Kravchenko, who wrote *I Chose Freedom,* came in to see me. He is overwhelmed with optimism and conceit about his own self. He is a nervous and enthusiastic young Ukrainian who drapes himself in an air of mystery. He would not even tell me the name of his secretary who came with him to interpret.

Kravchenko claims he is going to strike a great blow at the prestige of the Soviet Union in France and at the French Communist Party by winning a current libel law suit. He is confident of the result. He is bringing about two dozen witnesses in from Germany and claims he is paying all their expenses out of his own pocket and that nobody is helping him financially. I doubt it.

WASHINGTON, *February 3, 1949*

THIS afternoon I had a not very interesting talk with President Truman. He said that if the campaign had continued for two more weeks it would have been a landslide. He seemed full of confidence and said he intended to leave Germany under the control of General Clay and the Army for the moment and not transfer it to the State Department. He asked me if I would occasionally send him my personal impressions. If I gave them to any ambassador marked "Eyes Only," he would get them directly. I demurred.

WASHINGTON, *February 5, 1949*

LONG talk this morning with Sir Oliver Franks, the British ambassador. He is most impressive. It is his feeling that the United States is on the edge of an economic setback, although he doubts if this will be a serious depression. The country is in too healthy a condition to suffer a serious depression. The farmers own more (that is to say, they are less mortgaged) than at any time in history. The stock market is low and the banks are controlled. Nevertheless, it looks as if either a recession, which may last a few months, or something more serious is about to set in.

I asked what effect this would have on foreign policy. He said it might make it more difficult to pass the full Marshall Plan appropriation through Congress this year, although, paradoxically enough, it might make it easier next year when businesses are looking for markets for products they have not been able to sell internally. He doubted whether the latest Russian peace offensive had been launched on an assumption by the Kremlin that the United States was on the edge of a depression and that, therefore, Western civilization was about to collapse.

On the contrary, he thought the Russians were talking like frightened men. The advance of communism in Asia could not change the world balance of power. American steel production is 90,000,000 tons. Russian steel production is 20,000,000 tons. The production of Western Europe, including England, is 40,000,000 tons. The production of the Far East is 1,000,000 tons. Russia is gaining an uncoordinated overpopulated famine area without any of the sinews of power. Russia can become powerful only with the aid of Western Europe and she is being forestalled there.

Franks said there was tremendous need for England and the United States to revise and unlearn much in the Middle East. The British must recognize the change in the balance of power there and must recognize that there is a really solid body of American opinion behind Israel and that it is not just a political phenomenon of New York. The United States must take into account the good Britain has done in the Middle East over past years. Franks said quite plainly he had been embarrassed by Bevin's policy.

He said the greatest change in the Middle East was that two vital new states had emerged at opposite ends of the area in Pakistan and Israel. Pakistan, the most powerful state in the region, has a vast tradition of cultural, intellectual, mechanical and fighting ability. Israel represents the culture and traditions of much of the best in Europe.

WASHINGTON, *February 5, 1949*

THIS afternoon I was talking with Bob Joyce about Jugoslavia. He has just completed a paper for the State Department's policy planning division which will establish a new policy towards Jugoslavia. This is top secret and I cannot write about it yet. Roughly speaking, the policy is as follows:

At all costs Tito must be preserved as an independent heretic in the Communist sphere and this is just as important for Asia as it is for Europe.

In order to achieve this, Tito must not be allowed to starve. We will release necessary goods and equipment to him as recommended by Ambassador Cannon.

We will not attempt to lay down any restrictive political conditions.

However, we will try and secure a blockade of the Greek and Albanian frontiers to prevent military equipment from being sent across Jugoslavia to the Greek Communists.

WASHINGTON, *February 6, 1949*

I spent most of the day with John Paton Davies, who has just completed drawing up a new American policy on China. This was first worked out in discussions between Davies and the other members of the State Department policy planning commission. It was finally passed by the National Security Council and approved by the President. This policy is not entirely new but for a long time was strongly opposed by the Army which, now that

Chiang's central government has collapsed, had more or less withdrawn its objections because it has no alternative ideas.

The State Department position on China is surprisingly unanimous, representing the opinion both of "old China hands" and others. The attitude is this: The Chinese situation is very fluid. A basic revolution is occurring. China is moving from the medieval to the modern world without benefit of an industrial or social revolution. Therefore, the situation is bound to remain fluid for months or even years. In such circumstances there can be no specific spelled-out policy, such as many demand. The "engagement" with Russia over China has not yet really started. We can only lay down certain long-range strategic objectives, but no precise tactical plans. Tactically, we must make decisions from day to day within the framework of our long-term strategic objective.

The long term aims are these: 1. We want a China truly independent and free from foreign control. 2. We do not want a China which is an instrument of Soviet policy. 3. We want a friendly China.

Obviously, fragmentation is taking place. The United States is waiting to see how the process of disintegration in China is finally completed. We don't know definitely whether we wish to meddle with this process or not. The Russians have obviously been benefiting in an imperialistic way from the breakup of China. In northwest Manchuria, near Chita, a Russian controlled unit has been set up. This is the Huilibor Mongol regime with its headquarters at Hialar (an administrative unit consisting of a Stalinist Mongol regime set up by the Outer Mongolian Republic).

In northern Manchuria at Harbin the dominating military leader has been Lin Piao. He is an attractive little man who loves dancing and is an excellent general. The nonmilitary political boss of Manchuria is Li Li-San, the man who wished to base the Chinese revolution on the support of city proletariat. Li Li-San's theory lost out and Mao Tse-tung, who based his theory on the support of the farmers, won. Li Li-San, after losing his dispute with Mao, was in the Moscow "deep freeze" until 1945. He is now believed to be the Stalinist representative in Manchuria.

Mao's agrarian movement gathered momentum during the 1930s. Mao built up his own apparatus of party, secret police and army—fifteen years before Tito did the same thing in Jugoslavia. This insulated him against liquidation: thus Mao is in a position to call his own tune. There is no question but that Mao considers himself a Marxist. Maybe that ideology is the only tie between Mao and the Kremlin and maybe it will not keep him amenable to Kremlin policy. We must wait and find out.

In the north, Stalinist Mongols are in control plus a separatist area in Manchuria. The Russians wish to end the "China salient" and obviously want to establish direct connection from Chita to Vladivostok via Harbin. North China is under the control of Mao and Russian influence is not yet visibly strong. Inner Mongolia was under the control of a Yenan Mongol named Yun Tse. However his administration ran afoul of the Stalinist Mongols. Yun Tse has disappeared from the scene.

In summary, at present there are three belts of influence in China: 1. A Stalinist belt in the north which is still moving. 2. An expanding belt controlled by Mao in the center. 3. The disintegrating belt still under Nationalist control in the south.

Meanwhile, Chiang Kai-shek is waiting for World War III. He retired without resigning. He can operate only from Fukien or Formosa because of provincial opposition in other quarters. Formosa is not a good base. There is a vigorous separatist and freedom movement there; there is also a considerable movement to rejoin Japan. The reason Mao is so adamant in demanding Chiang's surrender is because of a fear of resurgence of Chiang's power from some base.

The speed of the Chinese Communist conquest has been astonishing. Since V-J Day they have conquered more than the Soviet Union has acquired since V-E Day. This was done by their own power with the assistance of captured American equipment.

The Kremlin suspects human nature. It does not want Mao to take all of China without the application of certain checks to be sure he will be kept in line. The Russians fear he might become a massive Tito. Therefore, it is believed they wish to establish a regime in the south to play against Mao and to force the north to depend upon Moscow. Also if the Communists move south they would be in direct contact with the Communists of Southeast Asia. This huge bloc would no longer depend upon Moscow. One must remember that if Stalin opposed a Balkan regime as suggested by Dimitrov, obviously he would be against a huge Asiatic federation which might strike out on its own divergent lines.

The Russians are confused and are taking no chances. Stalin is gun-shy in China and has been so ever since the failure of the Borodin venture in 1927. Stalin, an Asiatic himself, realizes just how slick the Chinese are. The United States in some ways is now in a position in China comparable to the position during the summer of 1948 vis-à-vis Jugoslavia.

The Russians have been embarrassed by China just as much as the United States. They obtained no steel or production centers of importance but only a mass of misery and an area of potential famine. They acquired an area of potential Titoism too large to handle.

The population of China is simply enormous—an estimated 400,000,-000 but actually perhaps even 50 per cent larger. The only way China can ever conquer the demographic problem is by industrialization, but neither the material nor the capital is available to do so. Experience has shown that to industrialize in thirty years time—and even that is a considerable period—half of the population must be moved to the cities. That would mean moving 200,000,000 or more people.

There are many who believe the Chinese Communists will break them-

selves in a morass of misery just as Chiang Kai-shek did. They cannot be
as wasteful and ruthless as the Russians were when they tackled the problems of liquidating property and eliminating the Kulaks because China is
not a rich enough country to support such brutal experiments. If Mao is
going to carry on a program such as that of Stalin in Russia he would have
to be completely ruthless and employ mass brutality, but his own writing
indicates a desire to go slow. In experiments of this kind no compromise is
permissible. One must go ahead ruthlessly or, if one compromises, sink.
The Kuomintang had a revolutionary program but it foundered on the reef
of Chinese realities.

Chinese communism is a vital nationalistic movement. It fought the
Japanese and it fought Chiang when, to the Chinese Communists, he was
an agent of American imperialism. Thus, for ten years Chinese communism fought on a nationalistic basis. This is poison to the present doctrines
of international communism which is against any and all forms of nationalism.

The United States must wait until the distintegration process in China
has been pretty well completed before we know what materials we have to
work with on our Chinese policy. The dust must first settle. We cannot
afford to commit American support to anything yet. We have now virtually
disengaged ourselves from the policy of supporting Chiang which proved
bankrupt. Our military supplies were useless. All they did was to bring us
hatred. In effect we armed the Communists because Mao captured or
bought our material in vast quantities. Since V-J Day, according to American military authorities on the scene, the Nationalists never lost a battle for
lack of equipment. The lack was something else; and the Communists
captured their equipment. The Russians cannot intervene and succeed in
China as exactly that process is what undid the position of America. External forces can influence but not control China.

For a long time the American Army opposed the State Department on
these theories. But the Army now realizes the situation is hopeless and has
abandoned its opposition to the State Department.

By way of summary this may be added: 1. In neither Jugoslavia nor
China can the United States look forward to friendly regimes. 2. Nevertheless, the most effective resistance to Stalinism is not agnosticism but
heresy. What we can hope for is that the heretics will be as unfriendly to
Russia as they are to us and this type of policy already seems to be meeting
with some degree of success in Jugoslavia. It is the long range aim of
Washington to see a parallel on a large scale created in China.

PARIS, *March 2, 1949*

THIS morning I had a talk with Margarethe Buber Faust, formerly
wife of Heinz Neumann, famous Comintern agent who was reputedly shot

during the Moscow purges. She is the sister of Babette Gross, widow of
Willi Münzenberg, who used to be chief Comintern propagandist in Europe
until he was assassinated in 1939, after breaking with the Party.

Mrs. Buber Faust is in Paris (she lives in Stockholm) to testify in the
Kravchenko trial. She detests Kravchenko and says he is a cheap, vain
bully without any moral standards. She described him as a "Neanderthal
man" and a typical product of Stalinism. He has been bullying his witnesses here and warned them that they were to receive no reporters and
write no books because he intended to use all the publicity himself.

In 1937 she was arrested and put in a Siberian concentration camp. In
early 1940, as a sign of friendship for Hitler, the Russians handed her over
to the Germans and she spent the next five years in Ravensbrück concentration camp. She said the Germans were unquestionably more sadistic and
deliberately more cruel than the Russians, but that the Russian system was
more destructive to the soul. A Russian prisoner is merely regarded as an
"object" and so much labor as can be maintained at a minimum cost.
There is no escape. The Germans keep the human combative spirit going
by the constant threat and use of torture which provokes a reaction of
pride and courage.

PARIS, *March 7, 1949*

LUNCH today with Margarethe Buber Faust, widow of Heinz Neumann,
known as "the butcher of Canton" after the failure of his efforts to arrange
a South China *putsch* for the Comintern in 1927.

When Neumann was purged, his wife was arrested. After incarceration
in the Lubianka and Butirka prisons, she was condemned to forced labor at
Karaganda camp in the Siberian Kazakh Republic. Madame Buber Faust
(she is now married to a German poet) worked as a field laborer in
Karaganda where she remained from autumn 1938 until January 1940.
At that time, with several other Germans, she was handed over to the
authorities in Hitler's Third Reich as a gesture of friendship by the Soviet
government under the Hitler–Stalin pact.

The Gestapo sent her to Ravensbrück where she remained until the end
of the war. She is now in the remarkable position of being able to make
valid comparisons between the horrors of Nazi concentration camps and
Soviet "reeducation through labor." Her conclusions may be summarized
as follows:

1. *Torture.* The Russians never in her experience evinced the sadistic
streak of the Nazis. Neither during interrogation nor in the camp was she
beaten by police or guards. She was subjected to mental threats such
as that of permanent imprisonment if she failed to confess to counterrevolutionary activities. The Germans felt no hesitation in beating her
and the other prisoners many of whom were otherwise tortured.

2. *Executions*. The Germans engaged in mass slaughter, shipping thousands of Jews, invalids and others to the Auschwitz gas chambers. The Russians had no equivalent practice. She explains this accordingly: The Germans were incredibly cramped for space and as the war developed they required more and more room for prisoners. To the bestially logical Nazi mind, execution was the solution. The Russians had no such space problem. They have all Siberia to develop. Their solution was to work prisoners on a minimal diet until they died.

3. *Food and Lodging*. The food at Karaganda was a bare subsistence diet. The prisoners received six hundred grams of black bread and one daily meal of soup and salt fish if they fulfilled the scheduled quota of work; half as much if they failed to achieve the norm. Says she: "We were always so hungry that we were on the verge of collapse." There were no blankets and they slept in huts on bare boards. Ravensbrück was clean and warmer. Blankets were provided and the food was far better. The work assigned was unnecessary boondoggling. Of almost five thousand prisoners who died her first year, most succumbed to beatings.

4. *Results*. Deliberate sadistic brutality prevailed in Ravensbrück. In Karaganda prisoners were treated merely as lost objects of potential energy. She says: "There was another form of gassing at Karaganda—starvation. In many ways Karaganda was worse. We existed in apathy knowing we had to work all day to fulfill the norm or die immediately from lack of food. There was no conversation among the prisoners and no energy for it. Our Russian guards were decent men and not sadists but they faithfully fulfilled the requirements of the inhuman system."

NICE, *March 22, 1949*

I dined tonight with Bill and Pussy Deakin. Bill headed the first British mission to Tito and later was chargé d'affaires in Belgrade. He is an Oxford don (Wadham College) and for fifteen years has been a favorite of (and working with) Winston Churchill.

Before the war he was a reserve officer in the territorials. When war came he was called up. His division never got to France. After Dunkirk they were set to guarding a segment of the British coast. Bill's company was typical. Under him (still a lieutenant) he had sixty men with forty rifles. On maneuvers, flags marked antitank guns. The second line of defence included old men like his own one-eyed father with a sporting rifle.

Word got to London that Bill, a talented young gunners' officer who spoke French, German, Italian, was going to waste. He was summoned to London and offered a secret job without knowing what it was. He was not enthusiastic, having no idea what it would be. He asked Churchill, who advised him to "obey orders." He took the job and began to work in a London office on secret reports, guerrilla information, resistance, and so forth. He complained after some months that he had been promised action.

He was reassured and then sent to New York with the promise he would be sent into action later. He was embarrassed because he had to go as a civilian and in civilian clothes. The other eleven passengers on the freighter were RAF pilots who had been shot down so often they were assigned to Canada for a while and merchant marine skippers whose ships had been sunk. In New York, America First was on the rise and Bill was often embarrassed by questions as to why he was not fighting.

In New York he began to deal with reports on Jugoslavia. After screaming for action he was flown back to London on a bomber and almost quit to return to his regiment. Finally, he was put on a slow boat to West Africa, en route for Cairo. Just before leaving he was told he would be going to Jugoslavia. At this time he was still thinking in terms of going to Mihailović.

In Cairo he prepared to go to Jugoslavia. From reports available it became clear that from a purely military point of view the Partisans were doing more than the Cetniks and they were the ones to be visited. At the time there was no contact with them. Several Canadians of Croatian extraction were dropped in blind to areas where it was thought there were Partisans and they had radio sets with them. Then a British officer (who was killed shortly thereafter) was dropped into Croatia. It was planned that Bill and his small mission (four others) should be parachuted to Tito's headquarters much further south.

Bill had already taken his parachute training in England and was working under a group in MO 4 (Middle East SOE) including Keble, Lord Glenconnor and Tamplen. They are all dead now. His direct boss was Tamplen. Before he took off for Derna from where the plane would leave Tamplen told him coldly: "It doesn't matter what you send from Tito, nothing will be done about it." They had had strong indications the Partisans were being desperately pressed. Tito had cabled it was okay for the mission to come but they had better come immediately or it might prove very difficult. The British had not decided yet to give Tito any support so Bill could not load up his plane with arms. He resolved to take medical equipment—drugs and bandages. But at the last minute his superiors canceled his permission to do so. He therefore had to go in an empty plane and was frequently assailed later by the ragged Partisans because he had brought nothing with him.

The first plane took off on schedule. However, over Albania, it ran into a violent electric storm. It was tossed up to 25,000 feet. The three crew members had oxygen masks but the five members of the mission, lying in back in their heavy parachute rigs, had none. They all passed out. They came to hours later, just at dawn, over an island. It proved to be Crete and just over the German fighter base of Herakleion. Bill warned the pilot who dove down to fifty feet and, with all guns pointing upward, thus returned to his base.

The second attempt succeeded. They got over Montenegro, which was then Tito's headquarters. They realized what a crazy thing it was to jump into those incredibly rugged mountains, but that was the spot Tito had laid out. It was a clear night and they finally found a fire marking the spot. They jumped. Bill was within talking distance of his junior officer (Deakin was now a major) and they exchanged impressions as they swung down during the night. They landed without mishap in a valley. They were close enough to each other so they were able to assemble by shouting. They did not dare show lights because they knew there were Germans all around. Suddenly, he bumped into a figure in the dark. He explained in broken Serbian he was an English officer. The figure, a Partisan, embraced him. (Tito had seen them jump and seen the plane blink its good luck signal and sent out patrols looking for them.)

In the morning light, they came upon a barren knoll. There were a few small tents ("like a skiing party") and a group standing there which included Aleksander Ranković and Koča Popović (later respectively minister of the interior and chief of general staff) and Tito. Bill was introduced. Tito was "extremely correct." Almost immediately he was reproached for having brought no medical supplies. Deakin started by talking through a Partisan who had learned English at school in Sarajevo (who was killed a week later). But he discovered Tito spoke German and switched to direct conversation with him.

This was May, 1942. Partisans brought bread and cheese (all the food they had) which was the best fare they had for a month. Tito explained they had to move. They were surrounded by a tight ring of Germans, Ustaši, Bulgarians and Mihailović Cetniks. The Germans had been learning anti-Partisan tactics in Russia and were now determined to wipe Tito out. They almost did. They had herded them with Alpine troops and airforce into barren mountains where there was no shelter from planes and no water. Bombing consisted of fifty-foot descents by small planes that dropped hand grenades with great success. (Bill and Tito were shortly thereafter wounded by the same bomb.) The Cetniks were collaborating fully with the Germans.

Tito resolved to break out. He drove a wedge through one arc of the circle and two Partisan units were assigned to hold either side. They knew they would be slaughtered—and they were. Tito's main force broke through apparently where German and Ustaši units joined and Bill remembers hearing the Ustaši wounded (who of course received no attention) screaming for their mothers. They had to filter through this gap one night. Bill, wounded, wearing a huge white sheepskin coat, was on a horse. They were only a couple of hundred yards from the enemy and went through single file. Artillery fire lit him up like a Christmas tree. About 12,000 managed to get through. Had they not succeeded, there would have been no Partisan movement in Jugoslavia and no Tito. They kept on the move for a month. They lived on mule meat and nettles—nothing else. Water was their greatest craving. The poorest off were the refugees from villages who had joined them and had to live on mule entrails. They were not allowed to light fires, which would attract aircraft. The Partisans shot them promptly if they did. Bill often slept under the same blanket as Tito. Tito's one dream was to disengage himself from the Germans hunting him and to lose himself in the forests of Bosnia. In the end he did. They rode into a burning Bosnian Ustaši village feeling like a Wild West movie, coming to the promised land of food and water. Tito invited Bill to dine that night and they ate well.

After that period Tito really got organized. He had quite an efficient force by the time Fitzroy Maclean came in September 1943, after Bill had suggested a general officer. When the Italians surrendered Tito was furious the allies had given him no advance notice. Nevertheless, he decided to send a force to get the Italian equipment in Split. The Germans were two days' march away on the map; the Partisans four. But Tito sent off a tough outfit which walked without stopping for seventy-two hours and got there in time to accept surrender. Bill went along. The Partisans sent out all the arms they could and then abandoned the Italians (except *carabinieri*, whom they accepted as fighters). The Germans later bombed the place and killed hundreds of Italians.

After Maclean's arrival Bill came out and later went back as a diplomat. He was chargé d'affaires for some time.

TRIESTE, *March 27, 1949*

THIS morning I called on Vittorio Vidali, secretary general of the Trieste Communist Party. I saw him in his office which is decorated with a sailboat model, painting of Stalin, signed photograph of Togliatti.

I asked him if he thought Tito could ever make up his quarrel with the Kremlin and he answered: "He can never come back. He has gone too far. He has burned his boats."

Vidali told me a few facts about his life. He said he was born in Muggia (part of Trieste) in 1900, became a Socialist in 1917 and Communist when that party was formed. In 1923 he went to New York without papers since he could not get documents under Mussolini. In 1927 he was arrested for illegal entry and deported. No country but the USSR would have him so he went to Moscow and remained "a few months." Under the *nom de guerre* Contreras, he fought three years in the Spanish Civil War as a regimental commander (Fifth Regiment) and was wounded. His regiment was the nucleus for an eventual army corps. He went to Mexico in 1939 and remained until 1947. (He is rumored to have played a role in Trotsky's murder.)

Vidali said of Tito: "He will go down this year. This year the problem will be solved. The Jugoslav people will decide it—not the Russians or any foreign interference."

BELGRADE, *April 12, 1949*

TITO is well in the saddle. The revolution has progressed and is here. The top dogs are living in bourgeois luxury. Opposition is broken. Yet I feel Tito may be getting a bit soft and if he ever slips, the tough guys like Djilas and Ranković will jump on him. I felt that strongly, watching their faces while Tito spoke at the People's Front Congress. Tito stuttered and seemed slightly drunk. The disparity between the new rich and the rest is great. There were almost as many large American cars in Topčider for the conference as at Westchester country clubs. Security measures are not very visible and the regime seems confident. There is plenty of food. People are for the most part poorly dressed except for the top level. The army units marching through Belgrade look just the same as before the war and sing well.

The diplomatic colony is a foolish gossip set and few have the guts to ever get out of Belgrade. Delcoin, the Belgian, sent a telegram to Brussels last week predicting a world war in three weeks. The British have broken his code and that's how they (and I) learned of it.

# 2 0

---

# OF COMMUNISTS

# AND KINGS

GENEVA, *May 8, 1949*

LAST NIGHT MARINA AND I DINED WITH KING LEOPOLD OF BELGIUM AND his wife, the Princesse de Réthy, at Leopold's spacious and comfortable house at Pregny, just outside Geneva. Today I went back for lunch and a political chat.

Yesterday his second daughter and the two boys (including eighteen-year-old Crown Prince Baudouin) were at dinner, and the girl stayed afterwards. The boys appear bashful and timid, rather weak. Leopold corrected their homework and called them backward, in front of us; not very tactful. The girl is unattractive and gives the curious impression of resenting her beautiful stepmother. She and Leopold are terrific golf enthusiasts (his handicap is one, hers is six) and they just won a tournament today. They have two shelves of cups. They played a lot at Cannes this winter with his cousin, the Duke of Windsor, who, they say, is pathetically bad, but always eager to win and "tends to forget his score" (Réthy talking). "Once I saw David [Windsor] take three shots in a trap, then give himself a five," said Leopold.

Leopold is quiet and grave, a tall, handsome man. He does not appear to be forceful but I imagine can be quite autocratic. He is extremely badly informed and gives me the impression of being naive and reactionary. For example he asserted that there were so many Communists in England that England could not go to war because there would be crippling strikes in all key industries. Leopold has such an extreme distaste and contempt for political parties that it is unhealthy.

Over cocktails and then coffee and brandy we sat before the fire and gossiped. He has no use for his brother, Prince Regent Charles. He said Charles was supported by groups of Belgians and British because he was weak and they could do what they liked with him. He said Charles' secretary (de Staercke) is his *éminence grise*. He said Charles poses as a liberal and friend of the non-Catholics while he, Leopold, is depicted as a Catholic reactionary, "but the reverse is true."

Leopold told me after lunch today:

I want to go back and put things straight. Then if the people do not want me and are unwilling to cooperate in a government, I am prepared to go away. But it is unconstitutional to forbid me to return. The law which bans me at present was passed in 1945 and refers to the "impossibility" of my reigning because of "enemy action." Such "enemy action" no longer exists and it is up to parliament to recognize this situation.

Leopold said he had requested Prince Charles to meet him in Berne and discuss the situation in view of the impending elections. He added:

He came April 25, together with Spaak and the minister of justice. They reviewed the picture and concluded that the political impasse continued, that a parliamentary majority still opposed my return, but that nobody could predict what new elections would bring. We agreed that it would be wise to wait and see what the vote produced. However, I pointed out to my brother that the present situation is illegal and unconstitutional. I am gravely worried about this. The chief duty of a king is to see that the constitution is observed.

Spaak would like my boy, Prince Baudouin, to return to Belgium—not to succeed me but to study and acquaint himself with the country. But this is difficult. He was only eighteen last September 7 and neither of us wishes to break up our family life. Furthermore it would create an ambiguous situation for the Belgian people. Our enemies, to the embarrassment of both my boy and myself, would exploit this move as a step towards my abdication.

LAUSANNE, *May 9, 1949*

THIS morning I had a talk with Walter Eytan, head of the Israeli delegation at the Lausanne conciliation talks. Eytan is a red-faced man with blue eyes and a retreating shock of dark hair. He is very "English" and used to be a university don.

He is confident of Israel's position. He says it is a matter of indifference to him if Israel is refused admission to UN because that "would leave us with free hands." He says the Arabs make a grave miscalculation there and adds: "If they were smart and really wished to prepare for a long-term friendship, they would be the most ardent supporters of our admission to UN because they could not only gain credit in the world but would insure supervision of our affairs."

Despite the fact the Arabs have announced they are acting as a bloc and will not negotiate directly with the Jews but only through the commission from U.N., the Israelis have already had secret meetings with representatives from Jordan (at Vevey) and Egypt (at Lausanne).

PARIS, *May 21, 1949*

THIS afternoon I had a long talk with Averell Harriman. He had the following bits of information:

Stalin told Harriman once that China requires outside aid and only the United States can provide such aid.

He received the impression at Geneva and Annecy that the Soviet satellites ardently desire trade with the West and both Poles and Czechs want credits from the West to purchase capital goods that Russia cannot supply.

He believes the Russian economy is not going so well and the Russians are prepared to encourage trade with the West. Russia might agree to political unity of Germany provided veto powers for any of the Big Four powers continue. We might agree that a veto is necessary on a few vital issues.

Harriman told Roosevelt in 1945 that he was convinced the United States could never have good relations with Russia while Molotov, an obstructionist, was in power. Now he appears to be out. Nobody knows. . . .

PARIS, *May 23, 1949*

LUNCHED with Foster Dulles. I asked him how he regarded Acheson. He said he was an extremely intelligent man and technically brilliant but it remained to be seen if he had wisdom and judgment. Dulles has been with the last four Secretaries of State at their first international conference—San Francisco with Stettinius, London with Byrnes, Moscow with Marshall, and now Paris with Acheson.

He regards Stettinius as a fool. Byrnes had great political ability, although at first he was far too anxious to compromise. He said Byrnes is not on good terms with Truman. Byrnes appeared to take a rather haughty view of Truman, giving the implication that he thought he should have had Truman's job and was better suited for it. Truman resented this. After some thought, Dulles said he considered Marshall a better Secretary of State than Byrnes, although he had his limitations.

The United States intends to introduce the subject of an Austrian peace treaty immediately in order to embarrass the Russians. The only important thing preventing an Austrian treaty is Soviet support of Jugoslav claims on Austria. If Moscow wants a treaty, it must abandon Belgrade. That is a problem for the eastern bloc to settle and not for the West.

Dulles pointed out that despite a lack of visible success, the Moscow council meeting won France over to the Anglo-American bloc and the London Foreign Ministers Council meeting got the three Western Powers to agree on unilateral action in Germany.

Dulles is very worried about the possibility that Bernard Baruch may go to Moscow this summer. He has asked Gromyko for a visa. Baruch would almost certainly see Stalin. He has told Dulles he favors a settlement with Russia based on dividing the world into spheres of interest between Russia and the United States, including giving Russia an outlet to the Mediterranean through the Dardanelles. If Baruch went to Moscow, it might have a disastrous effect.

PARIS, *June 5, 1949*

AVERELL Harriman told the following story today: Myron Taylor, ambassador to the Vatican, is a trustee of the Metropolitan Museum of Art. He came to lunch with Harriman one day at his Paris apartment. Harriman has a wonderful collection of modern paintings, including Cézanne, Gauguin, Van Gogh, his only personal possessions in the apartment. Taylor came a few moments early. When Harriman arrived, Taylor said: "I suppose you had to take all this 'art' together with the apartment." He pointed at a famous Gauguin and shook his fist saying "It's a crime to hang a painting like that."

PARIS, *June 9, 1949*

HAD lunch today with Secretary of State Acheson. He was very cordial but not particularly informative. Acheson said he had told the Russians he hoped to be able to return to Washington at the end of the second week of June. That is five days from now. He does not anticipate any dramatic developments at this conference. He finds the Council of Foreign Ministers even less interesting than he had anticipated (this is his first session). He expected serious proposals would be put forth and then worked upon. Vyshinsky has produced nothing. He thinks Vyshinsky is very embarrassed because he is forced by the Politburo to argue a policy that is obviously unpopular in Germany. Vyshinsky is even more rigidly bound than Molotov was.

Vyshinsky was very amiable—Acheson said—at the dinner he gave him last week, but he refused to talk any business. He is vain. Vyshinsky was trying to recall when he had met various people for the first time. He told Bohlen he had first met him in 1943. Bohlen said, yes, but he had actually seen Vyshinsky first in 1938—during the Bukharin purge trial. Vyshinsky replied: "Ah yes. Did you think it went off well?"—like an actor talking about a performance.

PARIS, *June 11, 1949*

THIS morning I had a talk with Mark Ethridge who is on his way home from Lausanne, having given up his job as chairman of the Palestine Mediation Commission. Ethridge reported to Secretary of State Acheson today that negotiations for Palestine peace are at a stalemate. Neither side is willing to agree to any basic concessions for fear of internal political repercussions within their own states.

The Arabs, frightened by the Husni Zayim *coup d'état* in Syria, fear internal revolts if they make any move construed as favorable to Israel. Left-wing elements in Israel, such as Mapam, are prepared to try to upset the coalition government in Tel Aviv if the Israeli delegation in Lausanne cedes any positions.

A new United States policy for settling the refugee problem—presently the main stumbling block—and developing the entire Middle East has been elaborated in Washington. This is called the "McGhee Plan," after the new assistant secretary of state in charge of Near Eastern and African Affairs.

While discussions were taking place at Lausanne, Israel, thanks considerably to United States support, was admitted to United Nations membership. Since then, Israeli policy has stiffened. This hampers three-power efforts to get both sides to "bend towards each other."

The first issue tackled by the "McGhee Plan" is that of the refugees. Although some 900,000 Arabs are being fed by international aid, the accepted figure for the refugees among them is 700,000. The rest are just impoverished nonrefugee Arabs. Israel now contains about 120,000 Arabs. Under the Arab proposal it would have to take back about 375,000 more. Even that would leave 325,000 refugees to be settled in Arab lands and Israel certainly will not accept the formula the Arabs put forth.

The "McGhee Plan" recognizes that Egypt is already overpopulated and that neither Lebanon nor Saudi Arabia can handle more than a very few specialized refugees. From this premise it proposes the following: Some will be settled in Arab Palestine (which presumably will go to Jordan) if additional water supplies can be found by drilling artesian wells and developing the Jordan River. A relatively small number can be sent to Jordan itself. However, Jordan is a "remittance state" depending on British contributions. Syria will take a considerable number of refugees if it can get financial aid. Zayim wants more manpower for his army. Iraq can eventually settle some refugees. However, Baghdad is having difficulties resettling its own tribesmen.

PARIS, *June 14, 1949*

I had a long talk with Cavendish Cannon, American Ambassador in Belgrade. He told me that when Fitzroy Maclean was in Belgrade last month, he had lunch with Tito. Tito told him categorically that Jugoslavia was sending no more aid to the Greek rebels. This was told Maclean in great confidence. A cable was sent to London by British Ambassador Sir Charles Peake, reporting this. All copies of the cable were destroyed. Cannon has not even reported it to the State Department because he was enjoined to complete secrecy. However, Cannon showed me a telegram to the State Department sent on June 9 and marked Top Secret, just before he left Belgrade. The telegram reported that Cannon saw Kardelj and Kardelj said no more aid was being sent to the Greek rebels "because we no longer have any friends there."

STOCKHOLM, *June 26, 1949*

DURING the negotiations between the United States and the Scandinavian nations, on the North Atlantic Pact, Sweden made a counter offer to Washington, after having decided to refrain from the pact. Stockholm suggested a secret bilateral agreement which would provide for automatic defense by Sweden against a potential Soviet aggression and automatic American assistance. Furthermore, it was proposed that secret talks should commence immediately on how such defense schemes should be implemented. This was turned down by Washington.

STOCKHOLM, *June 27, 1949*

THIS afternoon I had an interview with Allan Vougt, Swedish minister of defense, a man with a reputation for sticking his neck out. He is not liked by the Americans, who say he gave permission to the Germans to send troops across Sweden during World War II. Also, they complain that Vougt has stated American equipment bought by Sweden would be used to protect Sweden's neutrality and would shoot at American bombers violating that neutrality on their way to Russia. However, Vougt talked very sensibly to me and, although I do not agree with his initial theories of neutrality, I can understand why a country which has not been at war for 135 years still likes to avoid entanglements. Vougt said:

Sweden has reverted to a policy of "automatic neutrality" and now that Denmark and Norway have joined the North Atlantic Pact, the Stockholm government cannot consider any further discussions with those countries on Scandinavian regional defense. Sweden, as a neutral state, will not automatically go to war in case Denmark or Norway should be attacked. Nevertheless Sweden is glad those countries are in a position to improve their defense establishments with American equipment. Sweden will defend its neutrality and resist any violations thereof with force, but at the same time will carefully distinguish between haphazard violations and deliberate attack.

Sweden does not feel that any military threat now exists against her, but in principle considers the Western coalition less threatening than that led by the Soviet Union. We do not regard the West as being as threatening potentially to us as the East. We do not feel that any military threat exists. But we admit the mere fact of communism is a threat which could at a given moment be combined with military threats.

NORWAY, *June 29, 1949*

THIS morning I arrived in Oslo and immediately afterwards went by embassy car to Hankø to visit American Ambassador Charles Bay. I went aboard his twelve-meter yacht by speedboat and stayed later on to dinner. Bay said that Norway is worried about the possibility that the United States military assistance bill may be introduced to Congress and fail to pass or that there will be a continued delay in Congressional action on the North Atlantic Pact.

Two days ago Bay sent a cable to Washington arguing that Norway should be given a specially high priority among Atlantic Pact powers when arms allotments are made. He foresees a fight on this issue and has noticed reference to Norway in American diplomatic cables referring to this as one of the nations "on the periphery." Last night King Haakon had Bay to dinner and told him he certainly preferred the Atlantic Pact to a Nordic pact and wanted to be in a position where he could push a button in times of crisis and feel that two hundred planes would be on their way in a short time to help this country.

OSLO, *June 29, 1949*

THIS morning I had an interview with Einar Gerhardsen, prime minister of Norway. He is a tall, thin man with sharp features, unusually long ears and several gold teeth. He is baldish with graying thatches of hair and sandy eyebrows. He looks like an intellectual workingman. He was in his shirt sleeves but wearing a necktie. His desk is a very large brown table in neat order with a vase of flowers standing on it.

I told Gerhardsen various people had complained to me that the Norwegians were not working hard enough and asked him what he had to say on that. He replied:

Compared to the prewar ratio, the present figures for efficiency and production show up favorably. Naturally, after a war and occupation during which the main purpose was to sabotage production against the occupying power, it takes time for people to readjust themselves—especially the youth. Another difficulty after the war was a great lack of raw materials, especially building materials. This forced building workers, for example, to remain idle. Nevertheless, the present over-all production figure is 25 per cent above that of 1938, whereas the population has only increased from about 3,000,000 in 1939 to about 3,250,000 now.

OSLO, *June 30, 1949*

AT noon today I had a long talk with King Haakon in the royal palace, an awkward building overlooking the town from a slight hill. It is strictly Victorian and encumbered with clumsy furniture, bronze ornaments and statues and little knickknacks. It is the kind of building, on a large scale, one might imagine a rich Norwegian shipowner would have liked to live in, in 1905, when the King came to his throne as Norway separated from Sweden.

King Haakon seemed to have shrunken slightly with age since I last saw him in November, 1945. He appeared a bit shorter. He is as skinny as ever and filled with vitality. He waves his arms around, grins and gesticulates constantly, and at one point imitated the barking of a fox terrier to show how the little *émigré* governments during the war nagged at the British government in London. He has light watery blue eyes, behind a pince-nez, and was wearing an admiral's uniform. His desk was cluttered with papers, photographs of his family and souvenirs. He has his own teeth (it looks as if almost all are there), which is quite evident from their brown color; the upper set is in fairly good shape. He doesn't have a spare ounce of flesh. He is certainly an energetic and healthy man for one who is soon to be an octogenarian. His influence in the country is, however, definitely limited. He is honest and talks frankly with his ministers, who respect him. The people seem to like him greatly. He said he calls the Communists the "Royal Communist Party" because they not only never attack him but local mayors speak flatteringly when he visits them. He recalled a dinner at a hotel in Hankø two days ago in his honor where he said he was surprised the owner had managed to get tablecloths and napkins of linen for everyone. He said all such equipment had disappeared during the war but he supposed the owner had managed to gather enough together from other hotels in his chain. "I am used to paper napkins," he said. He admitted his opinions on the economic situation here were largely shaped by shipowners and industrialists ("because I can't see everyone"), but he certainly appears to do his utmost to speak for all classes and viewpoints.

Haakon said the people weren't working hard enough. He attributed this to the fact that during the occupation it was patriotic not to work for the occupiers and employers congratulated their workers when they did nothing. (This sounds OK, perhaps, but in other countries that were occupied this is not the case. One hears too much of it in Norway. I suspect it is primarily because taxes are too high and consumers goods too few to provide incentive to work and earn.) Haakon complained at length that this government has imposed unreasonably high taxes. He said that as a result industrialists and shipowners cannot lay aside capital for repairs, reinvestment and improvement. The shippers have been hard hit, he said, and have already warned the government that if this continues, small shipping, which handles the coastal services on which this long country's internal transport depends, will be driven out of business. He said hotels and other establishments have had an extremely difficult time in replacing stock and furniture stolen by the Germans.

He said he personally had urged the government strongly to join the North Atlantic Pact. He wants to make it clear to all and sundry who their real friends are now so they can never be fooled during a war. He said it was known who the fifth column was—and there *would* be a fifth column in another war—and in a threatened period they would have to be watched carefully and even locked up. He said he was trying to consider all these questions in terms of a fifty-year period. He would not be here but he was thinking of his son and grandson. His son had seen two wars. His grandson had been forced to leave his country during one; and this had left its effect. But Haakon was not optimistic. He preferred by habit to be rather pessimistic and then he could be surprised by pleasant events. When he left Norway in 1940 and then France fell he warned his cabinet in London the war would last four more years. He told them he didn't want any ups and downs of elation and despair. Whenever such periods came (and the ups were few before 1943) he reminded them of his first statement.

Haakon thought it would take some years of propaganda to get the people truly used to the North Atlantic Pact and happy about it. He said the Swedes were afraid Norway might be taking the lead (in Scandinavia) away from them in foreign policy and were jealous. The Swedes, in 1905 when Norway separated, had opposed Haakon's selection. Only wise King Oskar had prevented war between Norway and Sweden. Haakon obviously isn't too fond of the Swedes.

TURKU, *July 2, 1949*

I spent this afternoon with President Paasikivi at Kultaranda Castle, which is twenty kilometers from Turku. We sat on the terrace under a sun shade. Russian tea was served in glasses together with cakes. He was wearing a gray flannel, old-fashioned suit, a pink shirt with a stiff white collar, and horn-rimmed glasses. After the sun shifted and his head was exposed, a servant rushed out of the large stone house and set a panama hat upon the President's head. It stayed there, awkwardly, for the rest of the afternoon. The President is very old, but demonstrated an extremely shrewd mind. He started to converse in English, but suddenly was paralyzed in a paroxysm of stutters. After a couple of minutes he asked me if I spoke French, and we continued the conversation in that language. His lower set of teeth are false and it is somewhat disconcerting to hear him clacking them like a castanet against his uppers during dull moments in the conversation.

He apparently reads a great deal. He keeps up with political literature in English, French, German, Swedish and Russian. He sleeps seven hours each night and works the rest of the time. He has the same doctor as the composer Sibelius, and the doctor assures him he is in better condition. He is an ugly old man with a wattled throat which shakes when he leans his chin upon his cane. Nevertheless he has an extremely active mind. He will be seventy-nine in November.

The President said, "Our position has always been and of course remains pro-Western despite our geographical proximity to Russia." I asked if Finland had ever been invited by the Soviet Union to join their Council for Mutual Economic Assistance (the so-called "Molotov Plan") and he said, no. Finland does not desire such a relationship and wishes to remain free to trade with the West. He added:

We remain a democratic and occidental country, and the last elections showed that our people are determined we shall remain so.

When the Czechoslovakian coup took place we were again astonished that the Czechoslovakian people were so weak. Of course Beneš, although he was ten years younger than I, was very ill and lacked force. Also the Czechoslovaks are Slavs. We were astonished when Hitler took over Czechoslovakia and was not opposed by a single shot. That could never happen here. They had a good army and an excellent munitions industry. The Czechs made many mistakes. They had maltreated the Sudeten Germans for so long that they turned them into Nazis.

But the Czechs are forced under any circumstances to play closely with the Russians. Both they and the Poles know that it is very doubtful if the Germans will forever accept their present eastern frontiers, and they know that the only way they can defend these areas against the Germans is with Russian help.

Paasikivi said Finland was economically independent of Russia and "will remain so." Between ten and twenty per cent of Sweden's exports went to Russia (I must check this figure). He said that in the future, if the Russians did not require these exports, Finland wished to be free to sell them to other markets. He added:

There are no frontier questions between us and Russia. Russia attacked us aggressively in 1939. We fought twice and we know the results. We have accepted the situation, and the people also have accepted it. The Russians have only strategic interests here and that is all they have ever had. Of course, the Russians also are fostering communism but, as Lenin said, communism must be established in at least one other great European country besides Russia before it can hope to conquer. By this, he meant such a country as Italy or Germany—above all Germany.

Germany remains the ideological objective of Russia. If Germany turns communist, France will follow, and then the entire continent. Of course, if that happens, Finland will become Communist, but in itself it does not matter at this time with the Russians. We have had no indications that the Kremlin intends to communize us. The Russians realize that it is not worth starting a war by subjugating us even through such efforts as an internal coup. It would scandalize the world and they know us; they know we would fight.

We are a homogeneous country. There are no Russians or Russian-speaking people in the country aside from a tiny handful. Culturally, socially, and institutionally we lean towards the West. Economically, we are unimportant to the Russians. There is no possibility of an internal coup. For more than a year we have had a government which does not include the Communists. We have a parliamentary regime. If the Communists are admitted again into the cabinet, they will only have unimportant positions.

(I wonder if this last statement implies that Paasikivi is preparing for the eventuality that Communist ministers may again be appointed sometime.)

Paasikivi said it was difficult to find adequate political leadership in Finland. He added:

The greater number of our leaders are compromised. They supported official policy during World War II. We could not have such a man as president. Kekkonen (the Agrarian leader) was greatly compromised. He wrote anonymous articles for a magazine during the war which were not good. Nevertheless, he is a very clever man. He is still young, about fifty, and definitely a man of the future.

He commented: "I am a good friend of Russia, but I am a Finn. I know Russia. It is another world. The mentality and principles of life are utterly different." He was extremely pleased with Sweden's neutral position, which was comforting to Finland. He said:

I don't believe there will be a war in the near future. Stalin does not want another war, nor do the other gentlemen of the Kremlin. Stalin only attacks little states—the way he attacked Finland in 1939. He knows he cannot do that now and get away with it. And naturally everybody knows, despite Russian propaganda, that the United States is not preparing to wage a war nor does it desire to do so. The greatest danger to the world actually is a resurgence of Germany after it has been restored to its feet. I also believe that if a war ever does break out between Russia and the West, it will hardly touch Finland. All we will know about it is the passage of planes overhead twenty kilometers high in the air.

Following this conversation, Paasikivi took me around the terrace to point out the view over both the Gulf of Bothnia and the direction of the Gulf of Finland. The house is a large, square, Victorian place of gray stone and with small formal gardens. It was built by an industrialist who later gave it to the university at Turku. The state, which had helped the university, was given the house, which is now used as a sort of Finnish Chequers on what is called the "Finnish Riviera." Across the bay is an ancient abbey and church built by the Swedish order of St. Bridget and called Nordendahl. The president says it is more than five centuries old. Standing by the car at the end the President made a few final observations.

He said the Russians owed Hitler a statue. They gained fifty years in their world progress through him. Furthermore, had it not been for Hitler and his disaster, the Russians would not be so conceited now. He thought the United States changes its foreign ministers too often. He said: "Look at the Russians. They always have the Politburo. As ministers they had Chicherin for ten years, then Litvinov for ten years and now Vyshinsky, who was Molotov's assistant. This puts the democracies at a great disadvantage in dealing with questions of foreign affairs."

HELSINKI, *July 3, 1949*

THIS morning Avra Warren, the United States minister (with whom I am staying), was kind enough to drive me to the home of Vaino Tanner, strong man of Finland, leader of the Social Democrats and the cooperative movement. He was convicted as a war criminal but has been completely pardoned after serving a few years in prison. Officially, he takes no part in politics. Actually, however, he is very active.

Tanner lives in the country in a simple wooden house surrounded by wild roses on a lovely hill overlooking a lake. He greeted us at the door in bare feet wearing no collar or necktie. An informal, simple man, he talked quite frankly sitting on his porch puffing a cigar. He is rather elderly with silver hair and mustache, but looks exceptionally alert and shrewd. His wife, who speaks only Finnish and German plus a little Swedish, is a large buxom woman with white hair and a friendly, pleasant face. Actually, her simple exterior masks an excellent mind. She is a soil chemist. She has had eight children, all of whom appear to be specialists—doctors, dentists, engineers.

Tanner began the conversation by saying:

Russia never respects weakness. This government is stronger than its predecessor, which was distinctly pro-Russian. This government does not like the Russians and refuses to accept everything they propose, but it could be more strong. The Russians are always demanding things which are not agreed to in the peace treaty, and this government is yielding. Economically the Russians are taking all they can get. But you must understand that Finland cannot adopt a pro-Western stand now. That would be dangerous. Our situation is bad. The Communists still have thirty-eight representatives in the Diet of two hundred, although the Party probably has only about 40,000 members.

I asked what he thought of Paasikivi. Tanner said:

I have been a good friend of Paasikivi. I have known him for fifty years.
He has been everything in his political career. He studied to serve the
Russians under the Czars and was in the government employ at that
time. Then he was a conservative party member. This was under the
Russians, and he was pro-Russian. Then, at the time of our Civil War,
he was for the Kaiser and the Germans. I was neutral at that time
because I was against Civil War although I was considered "Red" by the
"Whites." When the Germans got out, Paasikivi was a good patriot and
pro-Finn. Then when the Bolsheviks came, he was persona grata with
Stalin and Molotov. He is the only man Finland can find who is a leader
and who did not commit himself against Russia during the war. He
was very weak toward the Russians in the beginning, but he is changing
and developing. He is a very great opportunist."

## (ABOARD *Botnia*), *July 6, 1949*

A recapitulation of some final notes on Finland. This boat goes from
Helsinki to Copenhagen in two nights and a day. The long Baltic sunset is
magnificent to watch; the sun is like an incandescent ball; there is never
really any darkness. The sea is calm and the islands lovely.

One definitely has the feeling that Russia's traditional claims to Baltic
control are pretty logical. As it is, icebreakers are needed in wintertime at
such ports as Helsinki. The Russians are bottled up. One must remember
that the area they have gained around the Baltic so far is traditional. While
they have more in East Prussia they have less in Finland than has been the
case before.

I talked at length with Captain Maano Haaksale, a handsome young
captain in the army who fought in both wars against Russia and was a
battalion commander at the end of World War II. Like most Finns, he is
proud of his *"Sisu"* and dangerous when drunk, as I found out later, when
Warren encouraged us to arm wrestle. He drinks Benedictine in copious
quantities whenever he can and after his first introduction to this went
home and shot up all the books in his family's famous library with a
revolver. A big fellow, he enjoys the favorite Finnish game of arm wrestling
with the local objective of breaking or dislocating the opponent's thumb.

He said he took scarcely any prisoners during the war because of the
way the Russians tortured Finns they captured. He said all the areas taken
over by Russia have been filled with Slavs. The Finns voluntarily evacuated
Carelia—all but five thousand of 450,000. During the war, when he went
in behind Petrozavodsk, he rarely saw civilians and hardly any of them
spoke Finnish. He says that arms are hidden by former soldiers and officers
all over the country. Each regiment when it surrendered its arms tried to
keep the equipment of one battalion to hide away. He has several auto-

matic weapons and machine pistols at home. These weapons are always looked after and kept greased by secret appointees.

I arrived this afternoon by plane from Copenhagen and Hamburg. Obviously, the Americans in Germany are living a far more luxurious life than most of them would be accustomed to in their own country. It is a super-Westchester existence. The Germans must resent this. The unconscious arrogance of such a victorious occupation army must be building up fires of resentment, and this is tactlessness in the highest degree. There is so much destruction in German cities, housing is such a serious problem, there are so many millions of destitute refugees that one cannot help but feel that a more modest and more austere mode of American life would, to say the least, be in better taste.

FRANKFORT, *July 9, 1949*

THIS morning I had a long talk with Professor Ludwig Erhard, director of the Department of Economics of the American-British Bizonal Area [future Chancellor of West Germany]. Erhard is a stocky, pale-faced man with sandy hair, now turning gray. He has a quick, efficient, businesslike manner of speaking and obviously has a good mind. He is clearly a conservative. He puffed cigars throughout our conversation. His office is in a large barracks built by the French after World War I. Erhard, fifty-two, was born in Fuerth, Bavaria. He planned to be a merchant and therefore went only to high school. He was badly wounded in World War I and studied considerably during his convalescence. He liked economics and social sciences. After the war he was a merchant for a while, but soon he became an assistant at an economics institute. He intended to be a university professor, but the Nazis came to power and he was told that he would have to join the Party in order to become a professor. He refused. He remained in scientific research, going into private organizations, because he could not continue any public employment unless he joined the Nazi Labor Front. He says he was in close contact with Karl Goerdeler (of the July 20 plot). Erhard says that in Goerdeler's testament, written in prison and smuggled out, Erhard was recommended by Goerdeler to the German people as a good economist. When the Americans came, Erhard was employed by the Bavarian ministry of economics. Since March 1948, he has been "director of the Department of Economics of the Bizonal Area."

I asked Erhard what he thought of the economic situation. He replied:

At the moment, we can be satisfied. With currency reform, we had a transition to a free trading economy. During the first half-year after the currency reform we had difficulties in revolutionizing the price structure.

Also subsidies were canceled. Combined with this, prices rose. By the end of 1948 a balanced economy was reached. The structure of the German economy was completely wrong under the Nazi regime. For fifteen years under Hitler, economy was not governed by the rules of competition. In all its branches people were employed in utterly unnecessary jobs. There was a needless luxury and waste of manpower. There were too many middle men and bureaucrats. Political connections rather than efficiency were the decisive factor.

Erhard said there was a complete lack of capital available to the German economy. He added:

As long as our currency had no stability, and for the first six months after the currency reform, it was always possible to finance investments with unsound money. This method is no longer possible. Therefore, investment capital is lacking.

Under the present tax laws, it is impossible to raise investment. Therefore, heavy industry and building industries cannot find capital. This makes for unemployment.

FRANKFORT, *July 10, 1949*

THE present German government in Western Germany is collaborationist and is so regarded by the Germans. We and the French as well as the British are willing to play with the Social Democrats in Berlin. Therefore, we accepted the Socialists there for a long time, until they put forth a new economic program there recently. In the American Zone the non-Socialists are strongest. In the British Zone, the Socialists are strongest. This is a natural reflection by local collaborators of the governments of the occupying countries.

The French looted their zone almost as badly as the Russians and lived off it. But the French have mostly lived with the Germans. As a result, while the Germans have hated French policy, they have tended to like individual French people. The Americans cleared out sections to live in and have not really mixed much with the Germans. Therefore, the Germans tend to like American policy, but to dislike Americans.

The salaries the Allies pay to German officials are too high. They are graded too high. The German civil service is the "fifth occupation power." The Germans are at least as powerfully occupied by their own civil service.

Eating has assumed a disproportionate value in German life as a result of the difficulties of recent years. A German with any money will try and eat really well once or twice a week even if he has to pay a good deal for it. He has nothing to do with his savings. He does not trust the banks and has very little incentive to save.

There is plenty of Nazism left in Germany, but not as an organized party. It is rather an attitude of the people. Germans do not talk about

Hitler if they don't have to. They feel about him that he was an unusual man who miscalculated. Both of those statements are certainly true. But people do not have a democratic attitude. The sense of hierarchy remains. Germans are willing to accept authority and even more anxious to exercise it. They misuse authority more than the occupying powers. It is true that they criticize authority. But they expect authority to solve their problems and do not do it themselves.

The Germans are too self-centered and lacking in proportion. They still feel something apart. They don't see themselves as other people in the world. They feel unique. They were at the top of the world when things were going well under Hitler. Today they feel at the bottom. They satisfy their desire for uniqueness by either being better or more miserable than anyone else. Now they feel they are the navel of the world where democracy is being defended, and the fate of mankind is dependent upon the results.

Anti-Semitism remains very strong. Only the Germans express themselves more politely and discreetly. There is anti-Semitism all over Germany. There is more than there was in 1930, because everybody has become Jew-conscious. That was Hitler's contribution. Before Hitler, anti-Semitism was an army and class phenomenon. Now it is a matter of general and primary significance.

Many Germans feel there is always a chance of turning East if the West will not do what they want. This is a blackmail threat. In the old days they said: "If you don't feed us we won't be democrats." Now they say: "If you won't help us, we will turn eastward." German youth is no longer Nazi. But it does not believe in democracy. It inclines to this blackmail threat to turn eastward.


DUESSELDORF, *July 11, 1949*

THIS morning I drove from Frankfurt to Duesseldorf. A faint smog is beginning to hover once again over the industrial regions of the Ruhr and also Frankfurt and Limburg. One can see it over Cologne, Opladen and Duesseldorf. Upon arriving I had a long talk with British Major General W. A. Bishop, regional commissioner for North Rhine–Westphalia, one of the eleven states of Western Germany and the one that includes the Ruhr.

Bishop, who is a thin sincere-looking man with spectacles and not at all military in appearance, said: We are not quite at a full employment level in mining and there is unemployment also in steel, textiles, and agriculture. We are trying to move refugees from Schleswig–Holstein to the Ruhr in order to employ them. The dismantling program will take care of employment vacancies in the steel industry.

I asked if communism presented Bishop with much of a problem. He replied:

Curiously enough it is not such a great problem as you might imagine. The Communists have lost half of their vote since 1947. Last week there were works council elections in the Krupp plant at Essen. The Communists won no seats. In 1947, nine of the thirty-five members were Communists. The stuff we are able to pump in has had a tremendous effect and so have the tales told by prisoners of war returning from Russia.

I asked Bishop for his views on the subject of dismantling. He replied:

Moderate Germans say to us: "If you make it impossible to start up democracy, we will be forced to turn to totalitarianism of either the right or the left." There is a strong feeling that if Germany is permittted to develop a hopeless frame of mind, it will make some desperate moves such as it did in the case of Hitler. I have slowed up the dismantling program a bit. It is not right just to go ahead and dismantle without telling people what we are doing. I have issued orders that before workers enter a plant to begin dismantling, a plan must first be shown listing what must be taken away in order to comply with the decision of the Allied governments.

BAD HOMBURG, *July 13, 1949*

THIS morning I had breakfast with John McCloy, new American High Commissioner for Germany. He said it was a great problem how to integrate into German life former Nazis who have been cleared by the courts or who have served their sentences. We are using all the real democrats we can find. We must let former Nazis play an economic, social, and political role, or otherwise they will sit on the side lines and sulk, perhaps become more dangerous.

Germany was like an infantry company in which ten per cent of the people were heroes, fifteen per cent were cowards and "the rest follow the leader." In the same way, there is a percentage of Communists at one extreme, and a percentage of Nazis at the other.

McCloy is very worried about the lack of coordination and effect of American propaganda here, in terms of educating the Germans for democracy. He intends to do something about this. He believes it is important that German women should gradually absorb the democratic status of American women, especially because there are millions more women in Western Germany than there are men.

BERLIN, *July 15, 1949*

THIS morning I had a talk with Professor Dr. Ernst Reuter, *Oberburgermeister* of Berlin whom I had known in Turkey where he was an anti-Nazi refugee. He is a very amiable intelligent man with gray hair and mobile face. He speaks good English. His manner is extremely informal. He has his office in the new town hall of Schoeneberg, a luxurious wood-paneled room.

Reuter said that perhaps the National Front efforts of the Communists might have some success in West Germany but not in Berlin. There were certainly elements which sought to balance the Allies by playing ball with the Russians or threatening to do so. He said: "Remember that we still have the tradition of Rapallo."

Reuter said: "Officially there is no right-wing party, but it would be an illusion to think the right wing is dead."

He did not see any real danger that the Communists would succeed in forming an important National Front movement. He added:

It is out of the question that such an effort can succeed in Berlin. But in the West there are groups who wish to trade with the East and place commercial orders there. There is certainly a difference in viewpoint between those who are politically conscientious and those who are only interested in their narrow personal efforts to make money.

The Communist Party in Western Germany is weak. It is weaker than the Communist Party in France and it is getting even weaker.

He said that the relationship between the occupying powers and the people of Berlin had changed rapidly as a result of the blockade and the airlift.

Without any question the people of Berlin have felt during the last year that they are fighting for something in common with the West. You can see for yourself that the relationship between American soldiers and the people around Tempelhof is very friendly. It is a great difference. Our people no longer have a feeling that the United States is an occupying power. Now the man in the street feels you are here to defend us. Sometimes we are angry at your policy. But this kind of feeling of anger is quite different from the original fury and resentment at the occupation. We have a much more natural relationship between the people of Berlin and the Allies. It is much better than the relationship in Western Germany.

Reuter hoped some central offices of the new Western *Bundersrepublik* would be established in Berlin. Berlin will remain the psychological capital of Germany and "A real Berliner never for a moment can consider another town as the capital of Germany." He emphasized the desire of Berlin to be included as the twelfth *Land* in the new Republic.

Until that is done, people here and all over the world will always have an uncertain feeling about the future. This hampers recovery. To make Berlin a twelfth *Land* depends only on the determination of the Western powers. Success can only be won if someone wishes success. The airlift is an example. We don't want to be provocative. There are no warmongers in Berlin. But we are convinced that peace can only be established and secured by firmness. The fact that Berlin has not yet been accepted as the twelfth *Land* is the last remnant of an appeasement policy.

Reuter pointed out that the Bonn constitution specified Berlin as the twelfth *Land*. However, this article was suspended as the result of French resistance. The French not only did not wish to antagonize the Russians, but they do not want to encourage a united Germany.

Reuter emphasized that he considered Berlin a key point in the world.

If one said it is not physically possible to link Berlin to the West, that really means you are giving up Berlin. If you give up Berlin, you give up Germany. If you give up Germany, you give up Europe. Therefore, you must start right here and insist firmly upon your rights. As long as Berlin is free and a part of Western Germany, it retains an important influence upon the situation in Poland and Czechoslovakia.

PRAGUE, *July 25, 1949*

AN odd but interesting conversation this afternoon. Luca Dainelli, the ardently religious secretary of the Italian legation, arranged a meeting at his house with the Reverend Father Silar, father provincial of the Jesuit order in Czechoslovakia, who has the clerical rank of archbishop and is the most important man now free and active in the Czechoslovakian Catholic hierarchy. He leads the underground against the government and is organizing a very extensive movement.

Dainelli, who exceeds the usual limits of diplomacy, is most helpful. He brought Silar around. Silar apparently rode on his bicycle to the home of a contact of Dainelli, wearing ordinary civilian clothes, and then was brought here by car with his clerical garb in a briefcase. He went upstairs, changed, and descended clothed as a priest, for a drink and some highly tough talk. It strikes me as rather naive of Dainelli not to assume his place is wired for sound. But this clearly worries neither of them. Silar plunged right in: a fanatical-looking man with thin face, thick glasses, brilliantly red ears and lips. He speaks Italian, French, Dutch and German as well as Czech. We conversed in French.

He said that only twenty of Czechoslovakia's seven to eight thousand priests supported the government's new Catholic Action movement. However, since 1925 the state had been granted the right to pay priests' salaries directly and this gives it a huge advantage today. The government is now demanding that each priest and each church should prepare lists of the faithful and should also prepare complete inventories of church property. So far, the church has refused to do this because it fears confiscation decrees. Realizing that the state is in a position to cease paying salaries of priests when it desires, the church is now organizing the faithful to pay the salaries of the priests. He continued:

The Pope based his excommunication decree upon the effort by the state to take control of the church through a lay organization, the Catholic Action Committee, which was created by the state. The state stole the name and type of organization of Catholic Action in the same way that in other European countries it has taken over the names of the Peasant Party or the Socialist Party.

He said it is only a government lie that Archbishop Beran refuses to see anybody. "The Archbishop desires to see everybody but the police refuse permission."

He said the situation is very difficult and confused. For example, many small local priests in Bohemia do not really understand what is going on. They do not know what they should believe because they are pretty well cut off from the world.

Until now, priests have not been able to receive church news directly except through foreign radios. However, we are now organizing a special secret system for distributing the news and views of the church. For the past ten days, the Vatican radio broadcasts in Czech at ten-thirty o'clock have been jammed and they have been very difficult to hear on local radios. There are nine Czech language broadcasts from the Vatican each week: one daily and two on Tuesdays and Saturdays. One of our most difficult problems is to get news of the situation in Czechoslovakia to the Vatican fast enough for use in their broadcasts.

He said Cepička, the minister of justice, is *the* man in charge of the antichurch drive. Cepička comes from a Catholic family and his father and mother are still believers.

The excommunication decree of the Pope was directed against all members of the false Catholic organization, both priests and laymen, or all those who acted actively in collaboration with them and that such people were excommunicated *ipso facto*. However, only sixteen priests have been excommunicated so far. Yesterday night the Vatican radio said that "a maximum of twenty" had been excommunicated. Probably not more than two hundred or three hundred laymen had been excommunicated. Their names have not been published and nobody really knows who they are. He said:

It will take some time—probably months—to organize an effective underground resistance. At present the people simply do not know who has been excommunicated. All church publications have been cut off. Therefore, they are circulated secretly at great risk to all concerned. Pastoral letters are secretly printed and secretly circulated, and anyone carrying them who is caught by the police is considered to have committed a crime.

The government publishes a bulletin for priests and other false literature pretending to be church literature. There have now been five numbers of the bulletin for priests which is bimonthly. It is very well done. It contains articles on pilgrimages and other church matters but it includes such things as speeches by Cepička which show it up.

He said: "There is now no possibility of an entente with the state. It is clear that there are two ideologies which are completely at odds. The Communists cannot stop now. They have chosen their paths and embarked upon it. The battle must continue. This is a schism. One must obey either Rome or Communism."

He predicted that the Communists would try to build up either the Orthodox Church or the Church of Czechoslovakia to combat the Church of Rome. However, he said both of those churches had already become frightened by the political implication of the dispute and that

the government will probably seek to create an entirely new church based upon the Catholic Action group This will not be done formally under the *name* of a new Catholic Church. They will deny that it is a new church. The Vatican recognizes this as the most dangerous attack in history upon the Catholic Church authority because it is masked under the guise of a loyal movement behind the name of Catholic Action.

He admitted there were many illogical aspects to the present situation. Diplomatic relations continue between the Vatican and Prague. The Czech bishops have not yet been imprisoned. In Slovakia, the faithful protect their priests against the police and in some small encounters both policemen and faithful have been killed. He estimated that between 120 and 130 priests were imprisoned. There were 120 in jail a month ago but some have been released and others have been arrested Archbishop Beran is not under arrest but, juridically speaking, is "under surveillance." He is permitted to leave his palace but only under the "protection" of state police. Therefore, he does not leave. The public is not allowed to visit him. Archbishop Beran is no longer master of his own house. All his mail is scrutinized. There is no effort to hide the fact that his letters are opened. Furthermore, he cannot speak by telephone. He said no priests were allowed to leave the country and as a result there would be no representatives from the Catholic Church in Czechoslovakia at the Holy Year in Rome.

There is a social, political and religious revolution going on in Czechoslovakia now. But it is difficult to really comprehend, even for a Czech. Fundamentally, it is a basic issue between two ideologies which are diametrically opposed. The struggle is against pure materialism, against the negation of God and all concepts of ethics. It is against a totalitarianism which will not admit of any other allegiance except to its own materialist conceptions. Paradoxically, in this country of Jan Huss, the Catholic Church has assumed the role of defender of civic liberties. The church is the great defender of private property and all human rights.

PRAGUE, *July 26, 1949*

THIS morning I had a long talk with Zdenek Fierlinger, vice premier of Czechoslovakia. Fierlinger was extremely friendly and full of confidence. He greeted me like a long lost brother although the last time I saw him in Moscow four years ago (when he was ambassador) he was rather distant.

Fierlinger said that the Social Democratic Party, which he had headed, merged with the Communists in June, 1948. The entire Social Democratic Party, comprising 300,000 members, joined the Communists, who at that time had almost two million members. Fierlinger explained his own position, saying he is a member of the Presidium of the Communist Party of "about twelve members."

The situation was greatly aggravated by the Vatican's decree of excommunication for all Communists. This was a vitally important fact. Why were only the Communists excommunicated? The Pope should have excommunicated all Marxists, all Socialists. By limiting the decree only to the Communist Party, the Vatican demonstrated that the move was purely political. By this medieval conception, the Catholic Church will only lose. It should remember that conditions today are different from what they were in the fifteenth century. Any possibility of compromise depends entirely upon the attitude of the church and upon how the excommunication decree is executed.

But the government will not take advantage of this to act in any way against religion as such. Our attitude towards the Catholic religion will not be changed by the decree of excommunication. It is not true that we are propagating atheism here. Religion is the private affair of the individual. The Czech Church is a liberal, democratic church under a Bishop Patriarch. We are not encouraging the Czechoslovak Church to proselytize. We are absolutely neutral as between religions. Every church is regarded as independent and gets equal support.

I asked him what the attitude was now towards the United States. He replied:

We like the American people. We understand each other well. We admire the democratic traditions of the American people. But the policy of the United States Government, as we see it, is something different. There is no feeling of hostility against your country as such; the only difficulty is that of policy. Your policy is a very determined policy of big capitalist power which is frankly antisocialistic. This prevents true cooperation. Our aim is certainly socialistic and anti-capitalistic. But we are not exporting our socialism. It is only for home consumption. You are trying to export your capitalism.

I told Fierlinger we were not particularly worried about Czechoslovakia's efforts to export her socialism, but that she had a certain neighbor which was of more concern to us. He laughed:

In any case, we don't wish for a war and I do not believe the Soviet Union wants it. We have bright prospects for future prosperity. War would only put a brake on socialist planning. Of course, I realize that our socialist planning has an ideological influence upon other countries. President Truman himself used the words recently "Communist conspiracy." But you must not forget that the capitalist world has an ideological influence that we resent equally. It is certainly possible for the two systems to coexist peacefully. But your government must not talk of conspiracies. It should accept our ideology as a natural fact just as we do. There are two forces in the world today: the force of the old, dying capitalist world and also the ideological force of the new, vigorous socialist world. We must not start a war for this.

PRAGUE, *July 27, 1949*

YESTERDAY I took a walk around town. It is still a beautiful city. People are swimming in the lovely Vltava river and rowing boats by the bathing clubs. It is not a very Communist-looking crowd. The majority of people are well dressed but not chic—they never were. The stores contain considerable consumer goods but prices for the most part are high. Fruits and vegetables are notable by their absence, presumably because of the price structure. The atmosphere is peaceful. Looking at the ordinary crowd and over the bridges towards the towers and spires of the old city, it is hard to remember that you are in a Communist country. However, the screws will certainly be inevitably, if gradually, tightened.

PRAGUE, *July 27, 1949*

LAST night I had dinner with André Simone and his wife who invited me together with Evzen Loebl, deputy minister of foreign trade; a man named Patek who is Clementis's brother-in-law, and several other characters. Simone in reality is Otto Katz but I did not let on that I knew this. Katz is a famous Communist propagandist who worked as a Czech Communist agitator in France for many years. He was born in 1895 in Czechoslovakia. He was a member of the Austrian Communist Party and then the Czechoslovak Communist Party and has always been an agitator and press propagandist. Simone told me he had joined the Communist Party in 1922. He left Czechoslovakia in 1938 for France and England and he spent the war years in Mexico. He returned to France in 1946 and resumed his work as a Communist propaganda writer. He is a small, gray-haired man with a thin, intense face. He started off the evening being very disagreeable and making energetic attacks upon the American press, the American government and above all the Marshall Plan. He said the Marshall Plan is a complete failure and he foresaw this from the start. He admitted that the Marshall Plan was hurting Czechoslovakia's economy but Loebl denied this. Simone

(Katz) is a fanatic and a determined optimist. He is violently anti-American although he pretends to like the "American people." Loebl wouldn't even go that far at the start but by the time we had dined for two hours and drunk *slivovice* and Polish *Kümmel* at Loebl's house for two more hours they were getting quite palsy-walsy.

Simone said the Sudeten Germans would never be permitted to return to the country. He said he had seen Tito in February 1948 but refused to write an interview on him because he felt Tito was insincere. I said I thought he was a lousy newspaperman.

Apparently his position is similar in this country to that of Ilya Ehrenburg in Russia. He knows all the big shots but is not really one himself. He is one of the editors of *Rude Pravo* and also teaches political philosophy. His wife is an unfortunate looking, pleasant, drab woman who I presume imagines herself to be an intellectual.

(P.S., PARIS, *October 1, 1953*

A transcript of the trial for "Titoism" of Slansky and his fellow accused including André Simone has now become available. Simone was sentenced to death. According to the transcript, Simone testified in a deposition [page 241]:

I proposed in the spring [*sic*] of 1949 that Loebl be invited also to the soiree organized for journalists [*sic*], among whom the American agent Sulzberger, at the Hotel Ambassador [*sic*]. The conversation concerned the internal situation of Czechoslovakia and above all the religious problems. Sulzberger interested himself greatly in this question and attacked the position assumed by Czechoslovakia towards the Vatican. After dinner Loebl proposed that we go to his house. There Sulzberger continued to take an aggressive attitude with regard to the religious policy of Czechoslovakia. After his return to the United States [*sic*] Sulzberger wrote a series of articles hostile to Czechoslovakia. In them he made use of the lying and unfavorable information he gathered in the conversation with Loebl and myself.

P.P.S. Loebl was also tried, sentenced to imprisonment, released many years later.)

VIENNA, *August 1, 1949*

I saw Brigadier General Thomas Hickey, American chief of staff here, who said:

In fifteen minutes fifteen thugs could take control of the government and throw the cabinet ministers out of the window. Two years ago a group of hungry women demonstrators got all the way into Chancellor Figl's office before anyone knew what was happening. The police force is infiltrated with Communists. After all, the Russians took this place and set up the government. The government cannot fire a man from a job just because he is a Communist. At one time 50 per cent of the police force was Communist, but it is now down to 25 per cent.

Hickey said he has no use for Foreign Minister Gruber. He thinks Gruber is trying to be a Masaryk and believes he can play with the Russians. He said: "Gruber is first of all ambitious for himself, then for the People's Party, and then for Austria."

VIENNA, *August 1, 1949*

THIS afternoon I had a talk with the American chargé d'affaires, Walter Dowling, and a bright young legation secretary, Ben Kimpel. They said it was impossible for the Communists to stage an internal *coup d'état* in Austria the way they did in Czechoslovakia. In Czechoslovakia they were supported by one third of the population and the trade unions and had control of the police and the army. In Austria they have only four out of 165 deputies.

VIENNA, *August 2, 1949*

THE Russians and the Communists have been busy on the black market here. For example, they purchase huge shipments of American cigarettes at the free port of Antwerp. These are sent to a Communist agency in Budapest and then smuggled to Vienna for American dollars, useful for Communist operations. Another Russian black market operation is as follows: Newsprint is made in Austria and sold at 1,800 schillings a ton. At the legal rate this is $180. But the Russians obtain black market schillings at twenty-five to the dollar. Therefore, they buy the newsprint at $72 a ton. They then export this newsprint. But in order to export they require a certificate of origin. The newsprint is sent to Czechoslovakia as a Soviet military shipment which the Austrian customs cannot touch. In Czechoslovakia it is given a certificate of origin. It is then shipped in transit across Austria to Trieste where it is sold at world prices. Russia gets hard currency out of the transaction. Austria gets only schillings.

This morning I went to the chancellery where I saw Leopold Figl, present chancellor of Austria and one of the principal leaders of the People's Party. Afterwards his aide showed me around the famous building, partially destroyed by the war. Figl uses Metternich's former office. On the same floor is the famous council room where the Congress of Vienna met: a simple well-proportioned chamber with white walls and lovely crystal chandeliers. Later I was taken to the office in which Dollfuss was murdered by the Nazis, left slowly to bleed to death under scowling guards.

Figl is a small, wiry man with red hair and red mustache. He has a brick red face and glasses, a rather amiable, simple manner. He said he did not foresee much change in the present relative strengths of the political parties during the October elections. He said considerable progress has been made in the negotiations in London for the state treaty but that "some definitions are still needed on the subjects of German assets, Danubian shipping and oil properties. But negotiations seem to be very near a settlement. The four foreign ministers will meet in Washington in September and I hope a treaty can be signed there."

ATHENS, *August 9, 1949*

FLEW down here to get a look at the situation now that what seems like a final military offensive has been launched against the Communist rebels under General Van Fleet's guidance, if not his acknowledged direction. Had a long talk with him today: a burly, energetic man, the real dynamo of the war, who looks and acts like an ambitious football coach and has established a remarkable rapport with the subtle Greeks.

My last vivid memory of him is a great chunk of a fellow standing there nonplussed as a Greek priest in Salonika thrust a spoonful of sticky jam into his open mouth, and he could barely get the spoon out. Oddly enough, this excellent officer almost had his career ruined by a ridiculous misunderstanding. General Marshall had it in for another officer, named Van Vliet, whom he believed to be a drunkard. Every time Van Fleet's name came up for promotion to one-star general he was turned down and nobody could argue Marshall out of it—although Van Fleet is an almost complete teetotaller.

This afternoon he said:

Things have improved vastly since we took our trip last year. The army had to be trained and reborn. We now have a new army, except for the officers corps. It is far superior to the army of 1948. Its leadership is splendid. The appointment of General Papagos as commander-in-chief has made a tremendous difference. He now has full authority without any political interference. There is no more political pressure nor rivalry between generals. General Papagos has the real powers of a commander-in-chief.

The country has been fairly well cleaned up. Most of the large bands and the network of intelligence has been cleaned out of central Greece and only remnants are left. The only thing that the rebels, left in Vitsi and Grammos, can now do is to retreat to Albania.

Communism has definitely lost the battle for Greece. The Communist record here is one only of destruction. This has afforded clear evidence to the Greeks that they do not want any of it. Communism will never again get any hold on this country. The Greeks have tested it and denounced it.

ATHENS, *August 9, 1949*

THIS evening I had a talk with Prime Minister Alexandros Diomedes at his house in Kiffissia, a comfortable, large mansion with a garden looking out on Mt. Pentelikon. As we sat and chatted, eating glyco and drinking Turkish coffee, a breeze rustled the trees. He is an elderly gentleman— seventy-eight—of old-fashioned appearance: bald, with gray mustache, and gray temples, a sharp chin and thin nose. He was wearing a green bow tie.

I asked what were the government's terms for peace with the rebels. He replied in an intricate, Oriental way: "This question reappears slowly in our minds, gradually and slowly. From the beginning, I want to say my political origins have been deeply democratic and liberal. I have not deviated one degree from this line during the whole period."

We absolutely wish to reintegrate the misguided youth among the rebels. It is not only a Christian and human duty, but it is in our own interest to educate these boys and girls in an atmosphere of democracy which will again make of them good and useful Greeks. They will be received and treated as people judged in an atmosphere calculated to encourage their tender souls. They are lost sheep who will return to the flock.

ATHENS, *August 9, 1949*

TONIGHT I saw the minister of war, Panayotis Canellopoulos, forty-seven-year-old head of the National Union Party which has twelve members in Parliament. C. is an old friend from the days of the Albanian campaign and, later, Cairo: a thin, intense, clear-eyed decent man.

I asked him what the terms to the rebels are. He said, more precisely than his gabby boss:

Surrender! We will not accept any discussion of terms. Only the leaders and the criminals will be tried. (Of the 11,000 who have surrendered or have been taken prisoner this year only 450 have been convicted.) They will be given a very fair trial before Courts Martial and will be entitled to select their own lawyers. The mass of the soldiers will be treated according to the Geneva Convention although we are not obligated to do so. All those who can prove that they were forcibly recruited will be immediately liberated and restored to full civil rights. All those who surrender voluntarily with their arms will be treated in the same way. No reprisals will be taken against the families of any, even criminals.

BELGRADE, *September 5, 1949*

I had another long talk with Tito today, in his villa at Dedinje, the Belgrade suburb. Tito was rather cool and distant. He made it plain he had no desire to discuss foreign affairs because of the touchy situation. This was his first talk with any newspaperman since the row with Stalin flared. He kept looking at his watch as if he had several pressing engagements. At the end of our conversation he gave me a stony glance and said: "You did not interpret my remarks very accurately last time we met. If you want relations between us to remain as they are, you had better be more accurate this time." Obviously he was referring to a series of articles I wrote criticizing him and his regime. His idea of "accurate" is, I fear, somewhat different from mine.

Tito's villa had its normal small contingent of guards—about the same amount of security as that which safeguards President Truman at the White House during peacetime. There was one sentry at the gate and an officer just within. Inside, only regular military aides-de-camp and secretaries. Our conversation, held through an interpreter in Serbo-Croatian, took place in a broad, long room which the Marshal uses as an office. At one end was a table desk. Another large conference table flanked by chairs was situated beside a row of windows curtained with red velvet. A blue pastel carpet covered the entire floor and atop it were a few excellent Persian rugs. From the white ceiling hung two milky glass chandeliers. At one end of the room was a massive painting of a historical scene. At the other, broad glass doors were open to a rose garden filled with singing birds and a few pieces of statuary.

The painting was completed only a few days ago by Krsto Hegedušić and represents the battle of Stubica in the sixteenth century. In this battle Croatian and Slovenian peasants led by Matija Gubec arose against the German barons who ruled them. To Marshal Tito, Gubec has a special significance not only as a peasant national revolutionary but because he was born in the same Croatian county of Zagorije where, fifty-seven years ago, Tito himself was born as Josip Broz.

Tito appeared fresh, vigorous and in the best of health. He had a good tan from his holiday in Brioni. His hair has grayed slightly; he appeared somewhat slimmer. He was wearing an informal lightweight gray summer suit, gun-metal shoes and socks, a blue shirt and dark-red necktie. On his left wrist he wore a gold watch and on a finger of his left hand a heavy gold ring ornamented with a single diamond. Throughout the conversation he toyed with his favorite pipe-shaped little Bosnian cigarette holder which is inlaid with silver. This is a souvenir from the bitter and dramatic Partisan days. He smoked rarely and sat at his ease on a sofa. This was hardly the picture of a man worried by any particular problem, much less the threats

against his person voiced by Cominform propagandists or the rumors of
war occasioned by massive movements of Soviet troops in Hungary.

Tito said:

> A few days ago I said in a conversation and I still maintain today that I
> do not think there is a possibility of war in the world. I do not for a
> moment suppose that any nation would desire the recurrence of such an
> international conflict as that which ended recently or for that matter one
> which would be even worse. The threat of such a catastrophe prevents
> the possibility of war. The consequences of the last war are still too close
> to us to admit the thought of a new one.

I asked if there was any precise program for collectivization of agriculture. He answered: "In our country there exists something different from
the collective farm. I refer to peasant cooperatives. They are not quite the
same thing. We have no exact program on this question. Furthermore I
would like to make clear that the state is taking no forcible measures to
spread this movement."

BELGRADE, *September 5, 1949*

THIS evening Vlado Dedijer asked me into his office and was very
friendly. He wanted my advice on how to hold press conferences and asked
me in detail how these are held in Washington, London and Paris—
extraordinary, from a veteran Communist *agitprop!*

He wanted to hold two conferences a week himself after he returns from
the United Nations meeting in New York. I told him that this was a good
idea, but that he would have to be completely up-to-date on all events
before each conference and would have to give truthful answers. He said
his conferences would be only for the Western press as the others "don't
count."

I twice saw Vlado Popović, who used to be a general in the Partisan
army, then was ambassador to Moscow and is now deputy minister of
foreign affairs. Another gigantic Serbian egomaniac, he was unusually
friendly. On the whole I have the feeling that the attitude towards the West
has changed greatly. However, Predrag Milojević told me it was still not
healthy for noncommunists to see foreigners. His wife said that last winter
at three o'clock one morning they heard the doorbell ring. They refused to
get up because they thought it was the secret police. Then they heard
somebody rapping on the window. They stuck their head out of the window
and were told "the house is on fire." She said, "You have no idea how
relieved we were."

ATHENS, *September 12, 1949*

RETURNED to Greece for my holiday and this morning I had a very long talk with King Paul at the Royal Palace in Athens. He seemed well and in good spirits, although strangely uninterested in what was going on in the outside world. He looked healthy, calm, sun-tanned, and wore his white, summer admiral's uniform. We smoked, chatted and drank highballs in his library-study.

The King said he had been trying for a year and a half to get Papagos accepted by the government as commander-in-chief. Twenty-four hours after his appointment the situation began to change. All spies were arrested and the enemy was deprived of his intelligence. Before Papagos was appointed Van Fleet had more or less been forced into the position of commander-in-chief which was embarrassing both to him and to the Greeks. Now Van Fleet is again where he should be—chief of the American military mission.

The King made it plain that communism would be banned for a long time as an equal party. I wonder if it will ever be readmitted to equality.

ATHENS, *October 4, 1949*

I learned today that Frank MacAskie has a special assignment from the British intelligence service, aside from his job on *The Times* of London. The King and Queen are determined never to leave Greece in case of war and occupation. His assignment is to arrange for hiding them and moving them around underground.

PARIS, *October 17, 1949*

I had a talk with David Bruce (American ambassador) this afternoon. Bruce was disturbed about policy in Germany. He said that he, for one, mistrusted the Germans. He thought the French were correct to insist that all types of security measures vis-à-vis Germany should be enforced. Furthermore, the French were correct in ascertaining that Germany should enjoy no unfair trade advantages as a result of American aid.

PARIS, *October 19, 1949*

LUNCH with Jo Davidson (the sculptor) who has recently returned from Belgrade where he did an excellent head of Tito. Davidson said Tito told him: "Tell Meštrović (famous Jugoslav sculptor abroad) not to be a fool. Tell him his studio in Split is absolutely intact. All his sculpture has been preserved. Nothing has been destroyed. Tell him to come back. Here is where he belongs."

Davidson views the schism between Tito and Stalin accordingly:

In communism, Marx is Jesus Christ, Lenin is Saint Peter, Stalin is the first Pope and Tito is the first protestant. The Jugoslavs insist the fault clearly lies with the intolerance of the "Pope." They claim that if the "Pope" practiced the approach of Christ the present difficulties would not exist.

When I was in Jugoslavia, I never missed an opportunity of explaining my stand and that of my country which is this, as far as I am concerned: "I am a product of Tom Paine, Thomas Jefferson, Walt Whitman and Franklin D. Roosevelt. Self-determination and liberty of thought are of paramount importance. It is the philosophy of democracy; of Woodrow Wilson and of Franklin D. Roosevelt. You do not impose philosophies on other peoples." According to Tito, Lenin's philosophy did not include the right to dictate to other nations. I went to Jugoslavia to do a bust of Tito. Before I even started to mould the clay, I knew I was doing the head of the first Communist protestant.

PARIS, *October 22, 1949*

THIS evening I had dinner with Joe Jacobs, retiring American ambassador to Czechoslovakia. He said that unquestionably (under Ambassador Steinhardt) we had engaged in establishing espionage networks. The Czechs are now engaged in uncovering this system.

Jacobs says Foreign Minister Clementis now appears to be suspected of deviation and will either be purged, when he returns from the United Nations meeting in New York, or sent as Ambassador to Moscow to be reindoctrinated.

Cominform authorities have been tightening up party discipline in several Eastern European states in an effort to eliminate all traces of "Titoist" heresy. They have not yet quite decided what to do about Clementis, who is considered somewhat too independent-minded.

PARIS, *October 26, 1949*

THIS afternoon I had a long talk with General de Gaulle. He appears a bit milder and mellower and looks somewhat fatigued. He was most cordial and smiling. He looked pale. I saw him in his shabby "exile" headquarters, a dreary building at 5 rue Solferino. The general's own office is bare and that of his aide austere. De Gaulle still talks of himself in conversation in the third person, which certainly gives one an uncomfortable feeling of an autocrat. Whether he is by instinct a diffident dictator or an autocratic democrat, is something impossible to judge.

He started off by saying that naturally his first effort would be to change the constitution in France if and when he comes to power.

The French people are very tired and very fed up with the regime. But they are absorbed in their own difficulties and will wait a bit more. Already the people of France realize that their constitution is not good and is at the root of all present difficulties. The last card of the present regime was the Queuille government. It is now really impossible to reestablish any serious government. Naturally I think we should have a new election as soon as possible, but it won't take place now. The reason is that here—unlike any other country, dissolution of the Assembly depends upon the deputies themselves who so far refuse to dissolve themselves.

De Gaulle said that he believes his RPF would now get 40 per cent of the vote in a national election. He thinks that in six months he would be able to get 55 per cent because of the political and financial deterioration which is coming in France. He said: "Naturally it is better for the RPF to wait six months, but unfortunately it is worse for France."

I asked him if he would agree to participate in the French government if President Auriol requested him to. He replied haughtily:

I have nothing in common with Auriol. Such an idea is a joke. The only way I will participate is after the people have expressed themselves in elections. Unfortunately, there is no way of forcing the deputies to dissolve. The constitution permits the deputies to remain in office right up to the moment of catastrophe, because the constitution was devised by the parties now in control. If catastrophe comes, the deputies will vanish. But they sit waiting for a catastrophe just as in 1940; and that is what I fear.

In an ordinary parliamentary regime as in England (except in the United States where the governmental powers are divided), dissolution comes from the government itself. The English King can dissolve parliament and ask for elections. In France, unfortunately, this depends upon the deputies.

De Gaulle said the first thing he would do when he came to office would be to revise the constitution along the lines he laid down in his Bayeux speech (1947) and along the lines set forth in the Marseille Congress of the RPF. He said it would be almost exactly like the American constitution. The powers of the president and of parliament would be fixed and limited. There would be equilibrium among the legislative, executive and judiciary powers which are confused under the present system. The fundamental differences between the new French constitution and that of the United States would be that the government would be responsible to parliament; the president would be able to choose his cabinet and dissolve parliament. In America the President is not responsible to Congress and cannot dissolve it.

"Dictatorship would be impossible under such a constitution," he said.

"My enemies say I wish to be a dictator. I had all the power in my hand, once. Was I a dictator?"

De Gaulle said the North Atlantic Pact was a good thing in principle but that the aid foreseen under the military assistance program is insufficient. He added: "I told my supporters that France must first count upon itself independent of foreign aid."

He added further: "All of Europe faces insufficient aid from America and we must always live as if war were just around the corner."

He said the Atlantic Pact gives insufficient military responsibility for direction to the French—even inside France—and that this is "an enormous psychological error. It takes away the initiative to build our national defense. This is a result of our present political situation. Because there is no French policy, no foreign government naturally has confidence in France. Therefore, the chief fault for present errors does not lie with the United States. Americans cannot have confidence in France under the present structure."

De Gaulle said, as far as Germany was concerned:

I am for an independent Germany. The Bonn system is not good, but it exists. I am for an arrangement between France and Western Germany on the basis of equality. This has nothing to do with the East German state. I have always had this idea, even before the Russians created the new East German satellite. A French-German accord could balance the effect of the Russians' East German state. This would stabilize the situation. The reason for which I was against the Washington and London agreements on Germany and the Bonn system was because they hinder a direct agreement between Germany and France. The creation of the Bonn system in Western Germany was supported by the British primarily to prevent the strengthening of France.

De Gaulle was very bitter about the attitude of the present French government towards him.

The entire French problem is that the regime considers itself only as an apparatus against General de Gaulle and works exclusively against General de Gaulle. The French ambassador in Washington is the ambassador of that regime and tries to misrepresent my views in the United States. The entire regime is constructed against me. Its papers, its radio, its news agencies and its ambassadors work only against me. When one understands that, one understands the entire problem. Without comprehending that, one comprehends nothing.

LONDON, *November 3, 1949*

DINED last night with Bill Deakin. He tells me that Nasta (his father-in-law and our correspondent in Bucharest) is still in prison and the news not good. He has been under arrest since July and nobody has even been able to find out what jail he is in. His wife has gone on foot to all the prisons in Bucharest and learned nothing. This indicates he is in the hands of the secret police. There is one unconfirmed report that he has already been deported to Russia. Another is that he will soon be brought to trial. It appears they are trying to mix him up with charges of currency deals with an American attaché at the legation and also that he may be charged in connection with his work for *The New York Times*.

Fitzroy Maclean was there. Fitzroy says Tito is in excellent health. He was airsick in a plane between Caserta and Bolsena when Fitzroy (the only other passenger aside from Tito's secretary, Olga Humo) took Tito to see Alexander in Italy; but doctors looked him over afterwards and found his heart in good shape. Two years ago, when Tito was fatter and looked less fit than he does now, he took Fitzroy on a strenuous nineteen-hour day of exercise (riding and walking) including two meals with a good deal of drink. This showed him to be in far better shape than most men his age.

LONDON, *November 7, 1949*

I had lunch with Julian Amery. He is especially gloomy. When referring to the disappearance of the Liberal Party, he said, "You must recognize that the word Liberal is a term of opprobrium nowadays." Julian is discouraged about the situation in the Balkans. He thinks England and America have not only wasted far too much time doing nothing about Albania, but that they may not do anything before spring. If such is the case, he believes it will be too late. Jugoslavia will fall and then Greece will go.

He is convinced that for a small sum in gold, Albania can be saved by promoting a revolution. It would not take a great deal of time to make proper arrangements with some of the northern tribes. He believes this must be done now before the Russians have completed their submarine base at Saseno and before the Russians sign a treaty of military alliance with Hoxha. Otherwise, it will be too late. He thinks there are almost three thousand Russians of all categories in Albania. Julian has a rather high respect for the shrewdness and political ability of King Zog.

Amery says English foreign policy is founded on two principles: that God is an Englishman, and that the road to India must be kept open. So far, God has provided Tito but England is doing very little about capitalizing on this.

LONDON, *November 8, 1949*

LONG talk with Prime Minister Clement Attlee in the cabinet room at 10 Downing Street. He appeared to be in an amiable mood and rather less nervous than the last time I saw him. I like Attlee and feel he has far more quality and tensile strength than indicated by his modest appearance, that of a wise version of Tenniel's dormouse. Tamping his pipe, talking in calm bursts, he made much sense.

I asked Attlee if he thought Britain could really integrate its economy with that of Europe, along the lines desired by Paul Hoffman. He replied:

This is difficult for Britain. We cannot do the whole thing along the lines apparently desired. We are not strictly a European power. We are a member of a Commonwealth. We have to consider that and our responsibilities to it more than Europe and our obligations there. We are in a different position from all European powers, even those with large foreign possessions; different even from a country like Holland. Furthermore, one must always remember that the nations of Europe have long traditions of individuality, and you cannot expect to scramble all these eggs either successfully or in a hurry.

We shall make reasonable progress, but not as much as some optimists in the United States think should be done.

I asked Attlee if there was complete agreement between Britain and the United States in policy toward Jugoslavia, and if this policy could be accurately described as one of "all aid short of war." He answered: "The words 'all aid short of war' are put rather bluntly, but I expect that this is about what it is. Of course, we must never forget that Tito remains a Communist, and his is a National Communist State."

On China, Attlee said:

In international law, one recognizes a new government when it is the effective government in the country. This now is the case, and recognition is to be expected. There is no agreement between the United States and Britain, binding one country not to move ahead of the other, but we do consult.

OXFORD, *November 9, 1949*

SPENT today and yesterday at Oxford, staying at Wadham. Several interesting conversations with my host, Bill Deakin; Maurice Bowra, warden of Wadham; Isaiah Berlin: and others. Here are some random impressions:

Deakin, who collaborates with Churchill on present memoirs, talked about Churchill's work methods. Churchill has immense drive and concentration, and works everybody around him to a frazzle. Generally, when he is down in Kent, Churchill lies in bed in the morning reading newspapers (which he can skim with great speed and precision) and examining his notes. He manages to relax in this way. After lunch, he potters around his farm, feeding swans and amusing himself.

Generally he works in the evening and he may dictate right up until two or three in the morning, wandering around the room puffing cigars and sipping his light but constant stream of highballs. He has four secretaries who work in shifts. Deakin sits in with him and makes suggestions and corrections, some of which are accepted and some of which are snarled down. Churchill tries to get about three thousand words on paper every day. Then he reworks the first draft. He recognizes the necessity for getting something on paper at all costs, although he may revise again and again after he has something to work on.

The various drafts are distributed around among experts on different aspects of recent history—generals, admirals and diplomats. It is Deakin's job to see that they make their comments and that everything is accurate. It is pretty tough for him to ride herd on a cranky old bunch of generals, but he does manage.

Churchill gets into a simply frightful state for the last ten days before the deadline for each volume. He is impossibly grumpy and hysterical. While I was in Oxford he called up Bill twice on most trivial matters. Bill is going over to Paris after this volume is finished next week and is not going to tell Churchill his telephone number. Pussy Deakin says Mrs. Churchill is not only charming but extremely intelligent and has had to submerge her personality a bit to accommodate her cantankerous husband.

Bowra is a brilliant monologist, but his is a very cruel tongue. In rapid succession, he destroys the character and reputation of everybody he mentions, although Deakin says he is actually a good, loyal friend. He cannot bear to be interrupted and conversation with him is merely a matter of keeping your mouth shut and your ears open. But it is worthwhile. He has a precise and crystallized way of talking and an accurate choice of words which is very eighteenth century. He is a professor of poetry and his learning is profound. He can easily quote from Greek, Latin, French or even Armenian poetry. He can deliver magnificent and living addresses in Latin. He is a fat little man, not bad looking, but so bitter under his amusing cynicism that it is obvious he is not happy.

Berlin has a mind of equal brilliance and for me he is far more interesting because one can talk with him and develop ideas. He conducts the conversations of others like a Toscanini. He is an expert on Karl Marx and, in fact, on the whole development of Marxism. He is the son of a Riga timber merchant and apparently his father was able to bring some money out with him. He has a withered left arm and is a plump man with glasses, but both his face and his manner have an attractive warmth. His range of knowledge is incredible; I should say even more impressive than that of Bowra, because it is more catholic in its scope. We had lunch together in the senior Common Room of Wadham, from which Bill had managed to expel eight gloomy dons.

I was amused to go down to the wine cellar of the fellows at Wadham. They drink an extraordinary amount of sweet sherry and vile Chateau Yquem. I talked with quite a few younger fellows and students. They all agreed that the majority of political opinion among undergraduates appears to be rather more Conservative than Labor. They also agreed that, generally, undergraduate opinion tends to be the contrary of the government of the day.

LONDON, *November 10, 1949*

THIS afternoon I had a talk with Herbert Morrison, Lord President of the Council. Affable, friendly, a stocky man of medium height, with unruly shock of hair and thick glasses; he is both humorous and humane.

I asked him if the British Labor Party is Marxist. He replied:

There are Marxists in our party. We have some Marxist doctrines. But the Labor Party was brought up more on Christ than on Marx. You may remember some of our earlier literature, such as "Can a man be a Christian on one pound a week?" The spiritual side of life in England today is probably stronger than before the Labor government came to office. We are not just a materialist party, but we have a strong faith in spiritual values. The Communists use Marx as a stooge. Their doctrine changes continually, just to suit momentary convenience. The Communists are a right-wing party. We are more left wing.

LONDON, *November 10, 1949*

DINED with Bill Harcourt; William Hayter, going to Paris as British minister, was there. Hayter attended Potsdam. He said that Churchill and Stalin had a long argument about the future of Bulgaria. Churchill kept pointing out what bastards the Bulgarians had been during the war. Stalin said he considered it improper to base foreign policy upon motives of revenge. Churchill asked Stalin what he considered foreign policy should be based upon. Everyone expected some vague statement of principle, such as democracy or ethnographical considerations, would be made by Stalin. Stalin, however, replied that foreign policy and settlements in Europe should be based upon "the calculations of forces."

Harcourt talked about Albania. During and just after the war he was mixed up with SOE operations there. He said Enver Hoxha was an extremely disagreeable character: a fat, pudgy, self-indulgent fellow with pink and white face. He speaks good French but has a nasty way about him. At that time (1945, when Harcourt spent a few days in Tirana), Hoxha was surrounded by a mixture of Communists and plain ordinary bandits. Harcourt said it was decided in the end to back Hoxha because his outfit appeared to be the best of a very bad lot.

LONDON, *November 11, 1949*

THIS afternoon I saw Sir Stafford Cripps, chancellor of the exchequer, in his office at the treasury in St. George Street. I used to know him as ambassador in Moscow. He was extraordinarily friendly, warm, suave, urbane and polite, unlike the weird, diffident, puritanical character he was in Russia. Thin as ever, dressed formally in black coat and striped trousers, he seemed in good health, although he has aged visibly and his hair is very gray.

I asked Cripps if he thought that eventually there may not be a fundamental clash between the economic system of Socialist Britain and that of the United States with its laisser faire capitalism. He replied:

> There is no reason why there should be such a fundamental clash. Neither of us is so theoretical-minded that we exclude realities. After all, there are many instances of planning more rigid than ours. Your farm price structure is far more rigid than ours. In many ways, you have a more controlled economic system. There are no absolutes in these relative questions. If we were profound Marxists, and you were equally profound Adam Smithites, there might indeed be such a clash, but neither of us has such a fixed theoretical basis.

LONDON, *November 14, 1949*

LUNCH with General Anders, former commander of the Polish army outside of Poland, Prince Lubomirski, his principal aide, and Lipski, former Polish ambassador in Berlin. We had an excellent meal at the Polish Club in London, which Lubomirski owed me, because he lost a bet we made in Cairo that I would never get back into Russia after General Anders and I had been attacked together, by *Pravda*.

Anders has a pathetically small office in a mews at 7 Waverton Street (off Hill Street). However, he looks astonishingly vigorous and well. He is now about fifty-seven, but has not aged in appearance. He seems to be in good spirits, but is obviously very bitter toward both the British and American governments. He told me that in 1945, shortly after the Yalta Conference, he saw Churchill and told him that war against Russia must be fought immediately (then). He is convinced we must go to war with Russia soon because the longer time passes, the more powerful the Soviet Union becomes, and they are organizing only for war. He admits that American production is far more immense than that of the USSR, but only a small percentage of it is being used as preparation for war, whereas almost all of the present Soviet Five-Year Plan is for that purpose. Moscow is storing up now for war, and America is not.

Of course, all these *émigrés* feel openly and violently in favor of war, because that is the only way they see a chance of returning to their countries.

All three of the men had nothing but contempt for Mikolajczyk and accused him of being too cowardly to admit his mistakes after he had fled from Warsaw.

Much as I like Anders personally, I feel there is far too much internal dissension among the *émigré* Poles, and not enough liberal or left-wing opinion. They are drifting steadily right. They are brave men, and good patriots, but their movement seems to me to lack adequate balance. They are against a Third Force and see no desirable future except for war. They crave return to their country at any cost, no matter how bloody.

LONDON, *November 14, 1949*

THIS afternoon, I saw Eden in Churchill's room in the House of Commons. He was extremely affable and full of good humor: a handsome, vain, slightly overconfident man, suspended between a glamorous past and a still uncertain future.

Eden criticized the government sharply for what we in America would call double talk. He said that on the one hand it keeps boasting how well the export drive is doing. Nevertheless, the exports come almost 100 per cent, with the exception of a little coal, from that 80 per cent of industry which is still in private hands and has not been nationalized by the government. On the other hand, internally the government continues to criticize the efficiency of private industry and campaigns against it.

Eden said he did not really expect the Conservative Party would win with a majority of a hundred or more, but he did not exclude that possibility. He hopes that there will be a sufficient majority to demonstrate the change in public opinion.

He expressed considerable optimism about the Liberal vote. He said Baldwin was a very wise man on internal politics, even if he made serious mistakes elsewhere, and Baldwin had always told him that elections are won or lost north of the Trent. Eden thinks a large body of the Liberal vote in the northern area will come the way of the Conservatives. He admits that south of that line, a good deal of the Liberal vote will go to Labor but he thinks the north will more than overbalance this in favor of the Conservatives. It must be remembered, perhaps, that Eden is even a better politician than he is a foreign affairs expert.

Eden said that, although there was no formal evidence of bipartisan foreign policy in England, actually a pretty good situation prevails. It is not generally known—and he does not want it to be known—but Bevin has remained very friendly with Eden, and calls him in from time to time to talk things over. He has also offered Eden access to the telegrams of the Foreign Office, on any subject in which Eden is interested, and Eden feels the Labor Party in that respect, chiefly because of Bevin, has played the game very straight.

Eden said he himself was violently opposed to any form of rearmament in Germany, or anything which would permit this. He never wanted to see Germany in a position to manufacture aircraft or guns. Furthermore, he felt present British policy tended to separate Britain from Europe too much. The result was that France felt isolated while a strong Germany was being built up, and France envisioned a Western Europe from which Britain would remain apart, and which would be dominated by a strong Germany. Eden is entirely against this and believes it will be necessary, if his party comes to power again, to reassure France in the strongest possible way.

LONDON, *November 16, 1949*

THIS afternoon saw Ambassador Lew Douglas. He has been involved in negotiations on Germany for three years now. He said we must avoid allowing West Germany to get too strong or permitting Schumacher to upset Adenauer. In either case, the French would certainly react violently. Schumacher has now been recognized even by the British as a fervid German nationalist, although it was the British who backed him because he was a Socialist. Douglas believes all Socialists, including British Socialists *per se,* cannot cooperate with European integration, because they are primarily interested in the success of their programs at home.

He sees no danger yet of communism growing in West Germany or of a "deal" between German nationalists and Russia. That will come in the future. The great necessity now is to make it plain to the Germans that they cannot blackmail the Allies into accepting programs we do not want, something they tried to do in the case of dismantling, which they carefully worked up as a separate issue. Douglas believes we can still be tough with the Germans and should be.

PARIS, *November 29, 1949*

VLADO Dedijer came for a drink this afternoon. He is on his way back to Belgrade, after attending the UN Assembly meeting as a delegate. He has obviously become much more pro-American. He said Djilas and Kardelj were extremely impressed by the United States. They visited Detroit and the River Rouge plant and were amazed. Now they realize what a powerful and strong nation the United States is. This should have important effects upon Jugoslavia in the future.

Dedijer has become violently anti-Russian. He now says the Russians supported Mihailović all through 1941; when Tito had Mihailović encircled late that year, he was about to attack and crush him. Then he heard Moscow radio praising him and decided he could not, as a good Communist, carry out his intention. When General Kornyeiev, the first Russian general to go to Jugoslavia in early 1944, came through Cairo in December 1943, he appeared to believe that Mihailović was more important than Tito. The Russians were clearly, at that time, interested in effective military aid in preparation for their Balkan offensive and were suspicious that the British had sold them a pup at Teheran, when it was agreed that all aid in Jugoslavia should be given to Tito.

Dedijer said it was amusing to notice that the delegates from satellite nations never spoke or nodded to any Jugoslavs when Russians were present. However, after any particularly violent speech by a Jugoslav against the Soviet Union, if the Jugoslav encountered some satellite representative in the lavatory, he would whisper "Bravo, keep it up." Dedijer said the Russians were trying to encourage Jugoslavia to invade Albania as a pretext for them to invade Jugoslavia.

LUXEMBOURG, *December 10, 1949*

DROVE here yesterday evening through the Ardennes and Bastogne which now boasts it is the "Nuts" city in honor of General McAuliffe's reply to the Germans during Rundstedt's 1944 counteroffensive.

Today I had lunch with Mrs. Perle Mesta, the new American minister and friend of Truman. She was quite pleasant, modest, sweet and energetic: a most agreeable surprise. She makes no pretense to being a smooth diplomat but is obviously a shrewd and amiable woman who appears to be popular. The prime minister, Dupong, and foreign minister, Bech, were there. Dupong said 10 per cent of the Luxembourg population is Communist, not influential but in a position to threaten. He claims Pavlov, Soviet minister in Brussels, is the boss for this area and the Luxembourg Communist Party works through Brussels, not Germany.

This morning I had a talk with Bech in the pleasant little foreign ministry. The waiting room is decorated with boule tables, tooled leather chairs, and mirrors the top halves of which contain paintings of past rulers. Bech himself is a most amiable rotund man with twinkling eyes, a shock of white hair, and a mustache yellowed by too many cigarettes of strong black tobacco. He loves shooting, fishing and golf for which he has invented what he calls the "pigtail" swing, a circular loop at the top of the swing which seems to confuse him as much as his opponents; his handicap is twenty-eight. He is also minister of viticulture and is not only fond of his Moselles but is an excellent trencherman.

BRUSSELS, *December 12, 1949*

THIS morning I had a long talk with Prince Regent Charles. The palace is a huge sprawling building about a hundred years old, comfortably but not very attractively furnished in Victorian style. The study where Charles received me was very large and oblong, furnished with tables, books, arm-chairs and a comfortable sofa on which we sat.

He is not as big as Leopold; a rather frail-looking, slender man of about six feet, with delicate features, very long upper lip, small selfish mouth, pale skin, light blond hair which is getting thin, and a diffident, shy manner. His voice is extremely quiet. Having spent the years of World War I in England he speaks perfect English, although occasionally at loss for a particular word, which he supplies in French. He appears the apogee of the English public school boy and does not seem to have much force of charac-ter or personality.

The prince had been given a routine briefing on his visitor and therefore somewhat awkwardly, in the middle of the talk, asked me how I happened to write *Sit-Down with John L. Lewis.* Several times he brought up the subject of Lewis and of Jugoslavia but clearly with no particular interest on his own part; definitely none on mine. As a personality he gave me the feeling of being pretty much a cipher.

He said there was no perfect solution to the royal question. Next month a consultative referendum will be held. The King's supporters have agreed that if he gets less than 55 per cent of the votes he ought to abdicate. This is held improbable, however. Charles said the best thing to do, after the vote, would be for Baudouin to come here for a while, postponing the issue of Leopold's return. That could be faced later but Baudouin could start reacquainting himself with Belgium and serve as a link. Charles said Leo-pold's wife, if he comes back, would be queen. There is no provision under Belgian law for a princess-consort or any such thing. She could declare herself queen tomorrow, he says.

BRUSSELS, *December 13, 1949*

LUNCH with Foreign Minister Van Zeeland. He is a smooth man, a Prince-ton graduate who, oddly enough, if he changed his hair-do and the cut of his mustache, would look much like Hitler. We lunched in a private room of the foreign ministry, across from his office, and had coffee and brandy next door.

He favors economic reconstruction of Germany and sees no objection to rearming Germany to a degree. It might prove necessary to use Germans to fight Russians and "when there is an end, one must find a means." (Quite a dandy little Jesuit thought!) All told, he struck me as an amiable, smooth, conceited cold gentleman of no great moral principle.

BAD HOMBURG, *December 18, 1949*

HAD dinner with John J. McCloy, U.S. high commissioner. After dinner, I had a long talk with him. He was very much opposed to German rearmament at this time. He said the British were prodding the Germans to ask the Allies whether they plan to defend the Elbe or the Rhine. McCloy said he did not think we should tell them. I agree.

I told McCloy some Western countries complained that while they had to use a large part of their budget for national and European defense, disarmed Germany had no such expense. This gives Germany an unfair economic advantage. McCloy denied this and pointed out that Germany has heavy occupation costs to support the Allied armies.

Wahn, *December 19, 1949*

This morning I had a long talk with General Sir Brian Robertson, British high commissioner for Germany. The last time I saw him was when I traveled up to Anzio with him and General Alexander on a destroyer in January, 1944. I thought him a rather narrow-minded Colonel Blimp then.

I asked Robertson what he thought about rearming Germany. He answered: "It all depends on France. If Germany is rearmed now, the French won't stomach it. Furthermore, the Russians might be provoked to attack. Finally, we do not yet know in which direction the Germans would turn. They talk differently when they have guns in their hands."

Robertson said the Germans work harder than the other inhabitants of Europe. He pointed out that coal miners have now been working on Sundays to make up for the holidays they will take on Christmas eve and New Year's eve. The solution of the integration problem is: "Germany must be made into a big fish in a bigger pond. Germany will always be a big fish. It cannot be integrated into a small pond. A bigger pond is the only answer."

He said Adenauer was more of a statesman than a politician. "He is working for dreams he will never see. He is working for a peaceful, big, prosperous Germany in a European federation. Even that will be hard for some people to swallow."

Bonn, *December 19, 1949*

Early this afternoon I had a long talk with Konrad Adenauer. I saw him just after one o'clock. An indication of how hard the Germans work is the fact that he and his entire staff were working right through lunchtime. They nibbled sandwiches at their desks.

Adenauer is a tall, elderly man with sad, pale face and inscrutable, red-Indian features, a weary, kind look. His voice is soft. His thin figure was attired in a dark blue suit.

I started the conversation by asking what he considered the role of West Germany in the defense of Western Europe, not as of today, but in the future. He replied:

We must always make a distinction between two things—the cold war and a war which is not cold. In the cold war, the psychological and economic situation of the German population is of importance. In the cold war we can hold our position only if the United States continues to aid us at the same rate as is now the case. In the second instance—a real war, our only wish is that God may prevent it.

The Western powers must give the population of our Republic a feeling that they stand a chance of being defended against aggression. This can only be done by some public assurance that we will be defended.

On one side of us, the Russians are rearming. On the other side, the West is rearming. In between, we are 48,000,000 Germans without arms. We hear that plans are being discussed to defend the Rhine; that only temporary holding operations would start on the Elbe. Everyone would fall back to the Rhine, leaving us exposed. Sometimes I feel that military men are thinking in terms of a war like thirty or forty years ago. The Allies are preparing to blow up the Rhine bridges, but such strategy was proven worthless in the recent war.

I don't want to say a word about rearming Western Germany. However, I think the Western powers already are considering the economic assistance of Germany in European defense and the alteration of the Allied attitude on dismantling is perhaps a part of this. On the subject of rearmament itself, there are many possibilities for eventual development, but the more one speaks, the worse it is both for the Germans and the rest of the world. Therefore, no one should speak of it. We must keep a place for potential war industry, but we hope we will never need it for such a purpose.

I asked Adenauer how the Allies could ever trust Western Germany not to turn Eastward and make a deal with the Russians? He replied: "I believe if you treat the Germans fairly they will never turn to the Russians again."

He said his government fears the new police of the Eastern Zone and added: "We hear they are beginning to rearm. However, there is no use worrying too much about it. If the army of the Soviet Zone becomes actually aggressive, it will mean that the entire Soviet army is behind it and that would be war."

I asked him if his government accepted the present frontiers of Germany, speaking of all Germany. He replied:

Certainly millions of Poles have settled upon territories which once were German. Therefore, the question of the East is *de facto* largely settled. Many of our refugees would never want to return to Poland. But we cannot accept the frontier fixed by the Russians.

In the Sudetenland there is also a problem. The principle of nationality has been highly exaggerated by the mass expulsion of Germans from Eastern Europe. It cannot last permanently. If order can be established in the successor states of the Hapsburg Empire, providing for a federative system, perhaps justice can be found for the Sudeten Germans. Certainly we do not accept the Oder-Neisse Line in the East.

I asked Adenauer what he thought about Germany's role in the integration of Europe. He replied: "I wish the United States would push Europe harder on the path towards integration. I have already expressed in my view that the Americans are the best Europeans."

I pointed out that the people of Western Germany looked well fed and the restaurants were full of food. Adenauer answered: "Don't be deceived by shops and restaurants. You should see how families live. If the Marshall Plan should cease, the result would be catastrophic."

Adenauer said he and Western statesmen were forced to play poker with the Russians until Western Europe is once again rearmed. He said it reminded him of a famous German poem about a man riding across the ice without realizing where he was and then, nearing the opposite bank, suddenly becoming aware that the ice was getting thin and might crack. "Will the ice hold long enough?" he asked.

PARIS, *December 25, 1949*

LAST night I had a long talk with Ambassador Bruce after a dinner party at the Bonbrights. He was very angry at the British and said they are doing more than anyone to sabotage European recovery. They are conducting a deliberate campaign to persuade all nations of the OEEC that Harriman does not represent the opinion of the American government; that his views are not those of Acheson and Truman. This, says Bruce, is utterly untrue and is a very dangerous game.

Bruce insists Germany has an unfair competitive advantage over most other countries because it does not have a military budget. He says one cannot consider Germany's occupation costs as the equivalent because, thanks to American aid, the Germans do not really pay those occupation costs themselves.

PARIS, *January 10, 1950*

I had lunch today with Yuri Zhukov, *Pravda's* only correspondent in the West, and an old friend of mine. He was very amiable. He made the following comments:

He has a high admiration for Philip Jessup, who negotiated with Malik to end the Berlin blockade. He thinks MacArthur did a good job in Japan and "checked progress toward a revolution."

Molotov is a great man with the power to make decisions, something which Vyshinsky has not got. Vyshinsky is as strong as a bull and, incidentally, an excellent swimmer.

Zhukov prefers the political system in the United States to that in England or France. The French people do not know what they want, but the Americans do. History will prove whether the American system or the Russian system is better. He says he is not a chauvinist and will not blindly assert that his system is "perfect." He admits conditions for the foreign press are impossible in Russia, but he advises that we should keep our correspondent there because things will be better.

Russia alone cannot handle the problem of China. It is a thirty-year task for America and Russia together.

Germany remains a great danger point in Europe and Germans will always remain Germans with all that implies. Germany is benefiting from the division between East and West, and both halves of Germany are thereby getting stronger.

PARIS, *January 11, 1950*

I had lunch today with Rosane de Clermont Tonnerre (née Tailleferre). She says Couve de Murville is going to Egypt as ambassador because he wants an embassy for a while and then hopes to become secretary general of the Quai d'Orsay. Incidentally, on behalf of the Quai, where she works, she offered me the *Legion d'Honneur* again and I again refused.

PARIS, *January 12, 1950*

LAST night I had dinner with George Allen, our new ambassador to Jugoslavia. He is not very impressive: nice, clean-cut and youthful (forty-seven), but rather a boy scout. He obviously knows nothing about the Balkans, Russia or Marxism. He started telling me he is afraid Tito is a National Socialist and we must remember that Hitler was a National Socialist. I fear he is going to make a lot of mistakes.

PARIS, *January 16, 1950*

LAST night I had a long talk with Rudolf von Ripper, who is staying with us. He was dropped into Jugoslavia in 1944 and then went up to Austria to work with the underground. He was captured by the Gestapo in a routine roundup at a railway station, but was able to talk his way out of it, although for a while he had a cyanide pill in his mouth ready to crush it with his teeth if they discovered who he was. He had papers as Karl Ritter, a draftsman. He said he was ready to commit suicide because no man who has been tortured once can stand it a second time.

In 1933, as a fellow traveler, he was working in a Communist underground movement against Hitler and Germany. Somebody told on him and he was arrested. An incriminating letter was found in his flat. For days he was kept in solitary confinement at the Gestapo's prison, Columbia Haus, in Berlin. As an Austrian, he demanded that his legation should be informed.

One day, during his interrogation—in which he denied everything—he demanded to know what had happened to his letter to the minister. The interrogator summoned two black-shirted storm troopers. The last von Ripper remembered was seeing one of them raise his arm, as reflected in the glass of a picture of Hitler. He woke up later in his cell, almost paralyzed and in great pain.

Eventually, he was taken to a hospital with a cracked head. He still has a split across the top of his skull. The doctor was a good man and advised him to confess in order to save his life. After three weeks, he was returned. He was tortured considerably. One day, a kind guard offered him a cigarette. Another guard smelled the smoke. He came in with a colleague. They cut two cigarettes into six small butts, lit them, and then threw them into Ripper's mouth. The burning was so great, that tears poured down his cheeks. Then, one guard took a cup and urinated in it; said: "Now we will put out flames," and poured it down Ripper's throat.

Later, he was sent to Oranienburg concentration camp. He was able to smuggle a brief note to his minister by the girl friend of another prisoner who pretended to be his sister. Being an artist, he had been assigned to paint a portrait of Hitler. He used some of the paint to paint a note, the color of an aluminum coffee cup, and put the note in the cup, so that when the girl had coffee with him, she was able to pick the note out on the pretense of cleaning the cup with her handkerchief. The Austrian minister sent one of his staff to the concentration camp without making inquiries at the foreign office and by luck he saw Ripper in the courtyard. Eventually, Ripper was released.

Diehl, the head of the Gestapo, then under Goering, warned Ripper never to mention his experiences because "the arm of the Gestapo is long." In Holland, Ripper wrote a series of articles on what had happened to him. Later, for seven weeks in 1937, he fought in the Spanish Republican Army as a gunner in a Russian Chato twin-engined bomber, as his direct riposte to Fascism.

PARIS, *January 17, 1950*

I had lunch today with Aslan Humbaraçi. He looks like hell, has lost twenty pounds in the last month or two, seems extremely nervous and hysterical. He is living in Paris by selling his possessions—few as they are.

Aslan used to be our correspondent in Turkey. He left in April 1949 and quit *The New York Times* to work for the Communists, first in

London, then in Paris. He has just decided to quit the Communists and is going to announce this in a letter to the press shortly.

Aslan was a secret member of the underground Turkish Communist Party for some time, in contact with the Soviet embassy in Ankara. When he went to London, he was instructed to get in touch with the Tass correspondent who appears to be the man in charge of contact with foreign Communists in England. Aslan was feted and advertised and then sent over to Paris where he was put in charge of Turkish Communist propaganda here. He worked under a committee in charge of all Middle-Eastern propaganda. Aslan went to Budapest and Rome to Communist conferences. He rapidly learned his lesson. He found it was impossible to maintain any opinion except that of Moscow, and that one always had to vote a straight Moscow ticket. He got fed up. He said there is no communism today—only Russian imperialism. He remains very left-wing, and the man he admires most now is Zilliacus, the left socialist member of parliament.

PARIS, *January 20, 1950*

DINNER last night with Averell Harriman. He said Stalin had told him there is only one man who could unify China and that was Chiang Kai-shek. Furthermore, Stalin said the only country which could develop China economically was the United States. What a contrast to present trends.

Harriman said the Russians had made a great mistake by looting Manchuria. Although they had supplied manufactured goods, such as cloth, as well as food to the Manchurian population afterwards, and did not appear to be disliked, they had ruined the capital structure of China's most important industrial province.

Harriman said that for eighteen months he has strongly supported the idea that we must not seek any political concessions from Tito. It is to our interest to keep him internally strong and looking like a communist; his value to us is much greater as a heretic than as a democrat.

PARIS, *January 24, 1950*

THIS afternoon I spent an hour and a half with Elisabeth de Miribel. She is now called Soeur Elisabeth de Jesus and is a novice at the Convent of the Carmelites at Nogent sur Marne, about half an hour from Paris. She was wearing a brown nun's robe with a white headpiece. When she has completed her vows, she will wear a black costume. Next August or September, she takes her first vows as a nun. These last for three years. Then she takes permanent vows.

She looked very well and seemed to be bearing up under the extremely stern regime. She is now thirty-four years old and had an active life in public affairs. She is a granddaughter of Marshal MacMahon and comes from a prominent Faubourg St. Germain family.

During the war, she was de Gaulle's secretary in London for a while and then his representative in Canada. After the war, she was always a strong follower of de Gaulle. She worked in the Quai d'Orsay and passed her career examination in the French foreign office shortly before entering her convent in order to prove that she was not leaving the worldly life because of failure. She claims that she had no long-time previous intention of assuming the contemplative life. It came to her suddenly. She had been working with a Catholic student group called *"l'Eau Vive."* She spent a month in Corsica last summer with a Protestant girl from that group who became converted to Catholicism. The month was spent largely in religious discussions. She visited the Nogent convent a few weekends and finally decided to join. She claims she is very happy, although the routine is severe—above all physically. She is convinced that afterlife is the important thing and therefore she wishes to spend this one in contemplation.

The physical rules are difficult. She suffered severely from the heat last summer wearing her woolen robe; now it is frightfully cold during the winter. The convent is so poor that they can't afford coffee or wine. The order forbids them to eat meat. The rules are largely laid down from Spain and the traditions of Saint Teresa. Visiting hours are between three and five o'clock in the afternoon, but apparently she sees only her family and rare friends. Sunday is the only day she has any time to read or think about mundane things. A friend of hers gave a subscription to *Le Monde* to the convent and that is her only regular contact with daily affairs. She asked if I would send *The New York Times* out because three or four of the nuns, including Count Sforza's niece, read English.

Elisabeth sat in one room by a window which was protected by a double set of bars. The outside bars had blunt spikes about five inches long protruding into my face. For those who are not close friends, the window is shut so that the nun's face can't be seen. Despite all this, she seemed in a good humor and laughed many times.

PARIS, *January 24, 1950*

YESTERDAY Nikola Popović came to see me. He is an old Serbian friend of mine, now a political refugee from Jugoslavia. Despite the fact that his brother, General Koča Popović, is chief of staff in Tito's army, Nikola was never with the Partisans. His friend, Prince George Karageorgević, took him on as secretary at the time Belgrade was liberated, in order to save him from the Germans.

Nikola is disgusted with his brother. He said their brother-in-law was arrested by the Partisans, although he had done nothing. Nikola asked Koča to intervene, pointing out that their brother-in-law was innocent. Koča refused to do anything. He said: "If he is innocent, he will be released; if he is guilty, he will be punished." The brother-in-law was beaten to death.

PARIS, *January 27, 1950*

AMBASSADOR David Bruce asked me to drop around. When I entered his office he laid before me a long telegram marked Top Secret and signed by Secretary Acheson. David said: "I'm not supposed to show you this; only to tell you the substance of its contents. But that's childish and besides I know you wouldn't be satisfied. So read it carefully and then let's talk." I did so. It was a detailed account of secret negotiations between Moscow and Peking for special protocols to the bilateral treaty they are negotiating. Acheson said Washington desired to have the information published but did not want it emanating from there. He asked Bruce to find out if I was interested in writing on the subject and gave his assurances the information was exact as far as the United States government could ascertain. I told David, O.K., that was good enough for me. Acheson was a gent and if he gave his word, that was sufficient. Bruce said it was obviously impossible for him to have told me the contents without showing the text. "You wouldn't have believed me; and you would have been right," said David. "You would have thought it was just propaganda and there was something tricky about it."

The guts of Acheson's message (which I did publish): (1) Russia wants control of seven key North China ports; (2) Russia wants access to Chinese labor and increased grain shipments from Manchuria; (3) Peking must make concessions to Turkoman minorities in Sinkiang; (4) Moscow will give Peking a guarantee of almost $3 billion in financial aid.

PARIS, *January 28, 1950*

TODAY saw General Shanker Shamsher Jang Bahadur Rana, Nepalese Ambassador to London, Paris, and Washington. He is a tiny little man, with smiling amiable face and glasses. However, like so many Ghurkhas, I imagine, he is probably a tough soldier. He was one of the most splendid figures at the official reception of President Auriol, wearing a scarlet coat and more decorations than anyone else.

The general told me his diplomatic secret. It usually takes days for cables from Katmandu to reach him. When a message comes here, he skips to London. When another comes there, he flies to Washington. "A most enjoyable job," he confides happily.

(N.B. The Rana family bosses the King around and really runs feudal Nepal.)

PARIS, *January 27, 1950*

FOLLOWING correspondence:

Ambassador Averell Harriman
c/o ECA
2, rue St. Florentin
Paris

Dear Averell,

I want to pull an old Russian trick on you. I noticed in this morning's New York *Herald Tribune* a report that you are interested in running for Governor of New York State. I have no idea if this is true or not, but either way it is a good story.

I don't like to impinge upon our friendship, but I am a newspaper reporter and this smells like news. Therefore, I am enclosing a formal letter to you posing some questions on this subject. I would be most grateful if you could send me a reply with the idea that I would quote it for publication.

All the best,

Yours,
signed/ Cy

United States of America
Economic Cooperation Administration
Office of the Special Representative in Europe
2, rue St. Florentin

PARIS, *January 30, 1950*

Dear Cy:

Nothing whatsoever to the rumor. Over the years other rumors have been started of similar nature. I never comment. Wasn't it Sam Goldwyn who was quoted as saying about a critic, "Don't pay any attention to him—don't even ignore him." (That doesn't quite fit but it's the idea.)

See you soon.
signed/ Averell

[Harriman was elected Governor of New York in 1954.]

PARIS, *February 11, 1950*

LAST night dined with Averell Harriman. I asked him, since he knows all the great men of our time, who was the greatest. Without any hesitation he said Stalin. He describes Stalin as ruthless, brutal, direct, extremely intelligent, very well informed and expert on many matters, including military affairs. He is ready to sacrifice anything to achieve his objectives, whether millions of men in a battle, or a country. He treats Molotov and his other colleagues the way an autocrat treats servants. Molotov fawns before him. Molotov, incidentally, bullies his own inferiors. Stalin is completely frank. He breaks his word whenever it suits his convenience and openly admits that he has changed his mind. He roared with laughter once when Harriman, in Molotov's presence, told him that Molotov had lied to him. Stalin agreed. He has absolute control of himself and of Russia and, as a result, is not overbearing, pompous or vain the way Hitler or Mussolini were. Frequently he says "I think" or "I have decided." At other times, he refers to "my associates" or "we." When Harriman told Stalin that an atomic bomb had been dropped at Hiroshima, he asked him what he thought this would mean to the future of the world. Stalin said such a weapon might make war impossible. Then he added that this would provide an excuse for the Japanese to capitulate. This was before Russia had invaded Japan.

Stalin is fully aware of the power of America. He indicated this when talking about the atomic bomb. Previously, at Yalta, he openly stated that the Allies could not have won the war without American production. He had great admiration for General Patton and said frequently that the Russian army could never have moved from Normandy to Germany in a similar fashion. He is a real military expert.

Incidentally, Marshal Tolbukhin, at Bucharest in January 1946, offered Harriman a picture of himself and Patton (Patton had just died). Harriman suggested he sign it. The picture never arrived. Obviously someone had prevented it from being sent. The Russian generals were good, straight soldiers who admired their allies. Eisenhower got on beautifully with Zhukov and thought Zhukov would succeed Stalin. However, Stalin has taken care to push this man into the background.

Roosevelt made too much of an effort to get in Stalin's good graces at Teheran and Yalta. However, Roosevelt would have been a good leader after the war because he would have started a tough policy much earlier than has been the case. Roosevelt was already completely aware of the Russian problem at the time of his death. Stalin obviously respected Roosevelt more than Churchill. He admired Churchill as a good, tough fighter and toasted him as a "comrade in arms." However, he toasted Roosevelt as a "leader in war and peace."

# 2 1

# RUSSO-CHINESE

# TROUBLE STARTS

DAVID BRUCE ASKED ME TO COME IN. MORE OF THE SAME. WITH a grin and not a word he handed me another long classified cable from Washington. It gave the gist of secret codicils to the Sino-Soviet treaty and again with assurances that the information was assumed by the United States government to be trustworthy and exact. Soviet "advisers" have been accepted for China's army, party and secret police. (Numbers or terms of service not specified.) The seven ports Russia wanted to control won't be granted; except in time of war when they would come immediately under Soviet supervision. Peking seems to be unyielding in its determination to hang on to complete control of Sinkiang without making concessions to Soviet-sponsored Turki minorities.

PARIS, *February 17, 1950*

LETTER from Moscow:

GEORGIAN JOKE: young man is walking beside a stream when a frog asked him to pick it up, wrap it in a handkerchief and put it in his pocket. He objects but the frog says he will not be sorry. So he does as he is told. When he gets home the frog asks him to put it in his bed. Again he objects. Again he is told he will not be sorry. He puts the frog in his bed. Now, the frog asks him to undress and come to bed, too. He objects, is told he won't be sorry, and gets into bed. "Now," says the frog, "kiss me." "Why should I kiss a frog?" "Never mind. Kiss me and you'll not be sorry." He kisses the frog, which turns into a beautiful woman who throws herself into his arms. At this point his wife walks in.

So . . . Let's drink a toast to wives who *believe* the stories their husbands tell them.

ARMENIAN JOKE: What is it that is long and green and hangs in my living room?—and squeaks? ANSWER: A herring. It is green because I painted it green. It hangs in my living room because I put it there. It is long because it is a herring. And it squeaks—it squeaks so you won't guess what it is.

JEWISH JOKE: a Jewish boy falls through the ice. A Russian jumps in to save him. He dives three times and finally brings up the boy. While the Russian is getting his breath the boy's father appears on the scene. The father says: "You rescued my boy?" "Yes." "You dove in three times to bring him up?" "Yes." "Then why didn't you bring up his cap, too?"

ROME, *February 22, 1950*

I had a good talk with Prime Minister De Gasperi this morning. He considers it would be a good thing if the Conservatives win tomorrow's elections in England. However, he does not think they have a chance. The Conservatives would facilitate integration of Europe (as desired by the United States). Furthermore, they would favor the cause of European union in which Churchill is the outstanding force.

He believes if Labor wins it will turn more to the left in its foreign policy. It will press for socialism in Europe and try to assert more control over the continental Socialist Parties. Already a sign of what London can do in this respect was demonstrated when Denis Healey worked on Saragat to quit the De Gasperi coalition. De Gasperi complained to Bevin about this when he was here.

Cripps told De Gasperi the only way to save Europe from communism was to have socialism. De Gasperi said there was no chance for powerful socialism in Italy unless it controlled the trade unions and there was no chance of that. As a result, the British attitude of trying to force the Socialist parties to refuse to cooperate with others in coalition governments may risk their utter destruction. Furthermore, the lack of union support for socialism forces De Gasperi to depend more and more upon the right and the conservatives for support.

ROME, *February 23, 1950*

THIS morning I had a talk with Monsignor Montini (later Pope Paul VI) who serves as the Pope's acting secretary of state. The Pope is reputed to be somewhat autocratic in this field and has not appointed a successor to his last secretary, a cardinal who died almost six years ago. Montini is young and only a bishop and thus the Pope can dominate him.

The office of Montini is simple and rather ugly. He is a small slender man with thin features and delicate white hands. I said to him that since the world was in a cold war, divided between materialist and nonmaterialist elements, it would seem to me useful if the groups recognizing the spirit could associate themselves more closely; that all religions, Christian and other, should announce agreement to combat materialism. I asked if the Vatican would not take some initiative in this.

He replied that this was extremely difficult and delicate. He explained the Church considered itself the ONLY true church and that naturally this view is combated by Protestants, the Orthodox, Jews, Islam, among others. It was a difficult project to execute and there was no use in embarking upon things which stood no chance of success.

I asked him if any efforts were being made to come closer to the other Christian sects. He said the Roman Curia was now studying means of cooperating better on both lay and clerical levels with the Protestants. But it would be even more difficult to draw nearer to the Orthodox and to heal the schism. Furthermore, there were now two orthodox churches, one of which was subject to the Kremlin.

Montini said the Vatican's relations with the United States had definitely been changed by the withdrawal and resignation of Taylor. They don't know if a new man will be appointed. They considered the abrupt method of Taylor's resignation crude and insulting. They would desire to see a permanent mission accredited to the Vatican rather than a personal envoy from the President and would rather have no mission than another personal one.

BELGRADE, *February 27, 1950*

THIS morning I had a talk with our ambassador, George Allen. Pijade of the Politburo told Allen Jugoslavia is convinced Mao Tse-tung will eventually become a "Titoist" in China and that then Ho Chi Minh will follow him. He criticized American policy in China and said it should have paralleled that in Jugoslavia; that we dropped Mihailović in 1943; that we should have dropped Chiang Kai-shek after the fall of Peiping. At any rate, we should have remained strictly neutral. We have driven Mao into Russia's hands and are therefore responsible for his lack of liberty. It is still not entirely too late to change.

There is *no* change in American policy towards Jugoslavia. However, a bad impression was created by mistake. Allen talked with Harriman before coming here and Harriman pointed out the United States was not a member of OEEC and that if any arrangement between that body and Jugoslavia were to be made it would have to originate from OEEC members. He told this to Sir Charles Peake (British Ambassador). Allen invited Peake and Vladislav Popović, deputy minister of foreign affairs, to dinner soon after his arrival. After dinner (during which Allen had explained

American dislike of communism) Peake turned to Popović and said: "This is a wicked world and nothing is received in exchange for nothing." He then asked Popović why Jugoslavia did not join the Marshall Plan. Allen interceded and said pointedly this question was asked not by himself but by Peake. Popović replied that while he was not stating that a country lost its independence by joining the Marshall Plan, nevertheless, it was politically impossible. He left soon after. Tito shortly thereafter made his speech at Užice announcing Jugoslavia would not make political concessions to the West even if it starved for it. Popović is a close personal friend of the Marshal.

BELGRADE, *February 28, 1950*

LAST November the British landed two teams of Albanian agents, trained in Malta, on the Albanian coast. These were immediately picked up and executed by Hoxha's government. They had been instructed to contact Gani Bey Kryeziu's men who had crossed into eastern Albania from Jugoslavia. Peake advised Robert Reams, American chargé d'affaires, that the mission was going in but never confirmed that it had gone.

(Harold [Kim] Philby, the Soviet spy in Britain's security establishment, described [December, 1967] a talk he had in 1951 in Washington with Allen Dulles, Frank Wisner and Frank Lindsay about organizing an anti-Communist revolt in one of the Socialist countries in the Balkans. This certainly meant Albania, even though there had been several attempted operations in Albania between 1949–1951. I suspect Philby betrayed all of them.)

BELGRADE, *March 2, 1950*

YESTERDAY evening I had a long talk with Archbishop Hurley, Papal Nuncio in Belgrade. I last saw him in the autumn of 1946 at Zagreb during the trial of Archbishop Stepinac. He said the archbishop is visited by his sister regularly and is in good health. The regime has been putting pressure on Stepinac to resign his see but he refuses. He is kept in solitary confinement at Lepoglava prison but is given adequate food, supplies of equipment for mass, books. A priest also in prison is allowed to assist in mass.

Hurley is bitter about the regime but expresses a restrained view. He says there has been no change in the attitude towards the Roman Catholic Church since the Cominform fight; ninety-seven priests were arrested last year. Occasionally they are tortured and sometimes murdered as examples. All ecclesiastical property has been confiscated with the exception of some churches. Nuns have been expelled from convents. The Orthodox Church is similarly but less harshly treated. The two churches have made no effort to get together and fight a common battle.

Hurley admits that American policy towards Jugoslavia now is the only correct one but warns that perhaps in the future national "Titoist" Communism may have more wide appeal than the Stalinist variety (especially in Germany) and then may become an even greater threat.

Yesterday Ambassador Allen gave me a luncheon. He was exceedingly nice but displayed astonishing naïveté. Members of his staff tell an embarrassing story. At a meeting he discussed the question of advertising the American attitude in Jugoslavia. He called for suggestions and himself suggested that perhaps an American "shoulder patch" with a needle should be distributed around the country. The air attaché, Colonel Anderson, cynically proposed we should distribute alphabet soup with the letters in Cyrillic.

ATHENS, *March 5, 1950*

TODAY was election day in Greece. I was extremely impressed by the calm, sober and orderly way in which voting was accomplished. I visited many booths and found the same story everywhere.

Jordanis Dayoglou, a gnarled and weather-beaten man who makes a living taking pictures on the Acropolis, voted a straight liberal ticket. He told me: "I decided to back Venizelos. We Greeks always need a change. Now you take a look at the Parthenon. Twenty-five hundred years ago we threw out Aristides the Just right here. He was a good man and an honest man, but the people wanted something different. That is about the way I feel now."

It was an unusually cold, windy and rainy day. Leaden clouds lumbered overhead like great whales. Below and to the south whitecaps scudded across the slate-colored Aegean Sea. Banks of mist lay along the beehived slopes of Mount Hymettus and distant Pentelicon from whose marble quarries the bones of the famous Parthenon were gouged. Below the antique columns, the usually animated streets of Athens and Piraeus were silent and abnormally tranquil. Banned from their favorite cafés, the men of Greece leaned into the high wind and scurried quickly to and from the polls.

Squinting his eyes across this vista and bracing his battered camera against the storm, Dayoglou pointed proudly saying: "You see after all they have called us we are still democrats and we are doing our duty by choosing our government ourselves. Now I am fifty-eight years old and life has been hard with me. I was born in Ikonion over in Asia Minor, and I had to flee to Athens after the Turkish war twenty-six years ago. I am a poor man. I only make $2 a day. But I am free. This morning I walked past our old Agora down there and I marked my ballot in the little schoolhouse at the corner of Vrissakiou and Kladou Streets. When I came back up here and I looked at the Parthenon—which has been my office for more than a quarter of a century—I began to think. I thought about Aristides and Themistocles, and I thought about why I was voting today. And I said to myself, 'Jordanis, you are a poor man and many poor men have become Communists. Why aren't you?' And I decided it was because I was a man and not a sheep. I have given life a battle and this is proper and is as it should be. A man must struggle. He must fight while he lives. Now Communism makes a man work and sees, they tell me, that he gets paid daily. But he makes no progress. I reflected; isn't that monotonous?

"I am a man of little education. But sometimes I like to think. I have decided that Communism is not the kind of system which suits us Greeks because we must go up and down as we always have gone up and down; one day I am rich and happy and another day I have nothing. But I am not bored. Today I want a change. I want a new government. But I also want always to be able to have that change and this is what matters to me. You who come from a far country, can you understand this?"

Jordanis Dayoglou, who needed a shave badly, rubbed some water off his nose and chin on to a corner of his tattered photographer's smock. With considerable pride, he embraced the horizon in his two thick arms and grime-stained hands.

"You see," he said, "we have all this and if we change our governments we do not change our souls and when I look around me at my place of business up here I understand much that has gone on before us and I place much value on it."

ATHENS, *March 7, 1950*

THIS afternoon I had a long talk with General Nicholas Plastiras, head of the left-wing faction of the Liberal Party. Plastiras, who is seventy-two, is tall for a Greek, with brown skin, and white pointed mustache, brown eyes and an open amiable face. He speaks rather bad French. He described himself as having always been a Liberal and a Venizelist. He said he was an officer but events had pushed him into politics after the disaster of Asia Minor and the expulsion of King George, when Plastiras helped to form a republic. He spent twelve years in exile. He told me:

I remained a republican and therefore in principle I am against monarchy, but the interests of the country are now well served by the royal family. Therefore, I will remain faithful to the regime now and the question of the monarchy does not exist at this moment. I am a liberal and neither for the left nor for the right. I am against communism and against force. I am for individual liberty. You must not forget that it was I who fought the Communists in 1945. Communism does not agree with my character or my thoughts.

ATHENS, *March 8, 1950*

THIS morning I saw King Paul in the palace. He was disturbed that Plastiras had won so many votes. (I recall Paul told me once that Plastiras was one of three men he would never under any circumstances invite to form a government—or shake hands with. It looks as if he will soon have to eat those words.) He said Plastiras was directly responsible for the Asia Minor disaster in 1922. Plastiras was a colonel heading a regiment and fled during the battle, allowing a Turkish penetration which spearheaded the rout. Plastiras then "expelled my father and my brother" and set up a "false plebiscite." He "tried to appease both the Germans and the Communists." The King concluded: "And now I have to shake hands with that man."

Paul expressed the opinion that the American officers in Greece had gotten on with the population better than the British who tended to be reserved, stand-offish, and regarded Greeks often as "colonials."

Paul chatted in his comfortable study, sitting in an armchair, smoking cigarettes in a long holder. He said:

> Some of our enemies have been calling us a Fascist state and ridiculous propaganda to this effect has been spreading about the world. The freedom and fairness of our elections should be a final demonstration to all nations how unjust such allegations have been. This lie should now be considered buried forever. It is fair to say that these have been the calmest elections in all Greek history and this is an incredibly remarkable fact considering the tragedy of our last ten years.

ATHENS, *March 9, 1950*

THIS afternoon I saw Lieutenant General James A. Van Fleet, commander of the American military mission to Greece. He said he is disturbed by the economic and social system that sometimes makes him feel like a Communist (a decent and rather observant thing for him to say). He had recently been to central Greece in a region where there was a fine stand of winter wheat, good herds of sheep and cattle, big flocks of turkeys. Yet the nearest villages were mud hovels. "Where do the profits go?" he asks. Obviously to Athens and the middlemen. Greece is still cursed with corruption and the heritage of Turkish baksheesh.

Van Fleet said he had been up in Thrace just near the frontier with Turkey. The land was rich, magnificent, well cultivated. Yet he saw not a single sign of anything the Greek government had done to benefit the inhabitants since they took over that area from the Turks in 1912. Not a school or a dam or a railway. That is a pretty lousy record. Greece is, indeed, a poor country but there are too many rich people in it (or rich Greeks aboard who have milked it).

CAIRO, *March 11, 1950*

THIS afternoon I had a talk with Abdul Rahman Azzam Pasha, secretary general of the Arab League. As friendly as ever, he seemed a bit downcast. He could see no peaceful solution of the Palestine problem because the Jews were too confident and ambitious. He said the Arabs had suffered a defeat and that, therefore, as a matter of pride, they would have to arm themselves better for a second round.

If Jordan signed a separate agreement with Israel, it would violate the pact of the Arab League. The League would subject Jordan to the same boycott as Israel, in order to prevent leakage of goods from other Arab countries into Israel. However, he said that, until now, Jordan has continued with its negotiations for a settlement with Israel.

He said the Arab states favored the Western and democratic camp. He himself wanted a regional self-defence pact in the Mediterranean to reduce chances of aggression but he opposed a Marshall Plan for the Middle East. The people have their own resources and should help themselves. "We need no charity; we are not paupers. We were here five thousand years before the United States existed and we must solve our problems ourselves. We are doing well; better than people think. We do not want to rely on foreign support."

CAIRO, *March 12, 1950*

A conference of American diplomats from Greece, Turkey and twelve other countries in the Near East ended yesterday.

Arthur L. Richards, embassy counselor in Teheran, made a long speech about the tragic conditions in Iran. He said people were starving in Azerbaijan where bodies actually could be found on the streets of Tabriz. There is misery and economic chaos. He pleaded for quick projects to inspire faith. The Shah came back from America without any dramatic loan and the Tudeh (Communist) Party now says: "See, the Americans aren't going to help you."

William Porter from Cyprus warned that nothing had been done to liberalize the Middle East in the fourteen years since he first came out here. He requested strong swift action to modernize its social policies.

Incidentally, Gordon Clapp, who headed the UN mission to the Middle East, told the conference Israel is not a viable state and could not even be viable if it advanced as far as the Jordan. Israel, which had one $100 million United States loan which it has not even begun to service, has now asked for another even larger one from the Export-Import Bank.

CAIRO, *March 12, 1950*

THIS morning I had a long talk with Abdul Krim el Khatabi, emir of the Riff, who fought Spain and France heroically and is now a refugee here. Abdul Krim, who is sixty-seven, is the hero of the Riff War from 1922 to 1926. In 1926, he was sent to Réunion Island by the French. In 1947, the French permitted him to leave for France. They hoped to use him as a counter to the Sultan of Morocco; but he got off the ship at Port Said and King Farouk gave him refuge. He is now president of the National Liberation Committee of North Africa, which is working for the complete independence of Morocco, Tunisia and Algeria.

He received me in the villa of his brother, Emir Mhamed Abdul Krim, who was present during the interview. My interpreter was a young Tunisian Arab, Taieb Slim (later a distinguished Tunisian ambassador).

Abdul Krim was wearing a light yellow robe, covered with a black mantle. On his head he had a white turban. He has a nice strong face. His eyes are brown and intelligent. His skin is dark tan. He has a quick smile. He wears his gray beard cut extremely short. He has a habit of drumming martial rhythms on the table with his middle finger. He declared:

I am working for the independence and liberty of all North Africa, not just Morocco. We believe in the Atlantic Charter and the United Nations which says that all people have a right to their own destinies. This promise was given by all members, first of all the United States. It is their duty to stick by their promise. When the promises were given, North African soldiers were fighting side by side with the Allies. We earned these pledges and we insist upon our rights.

If France and Spain don't satisfy our claims, we will be obliged to fight them as we have fought before. The situation in all North Africa is desperate. Police states have been created by Spain and France. They are pushing us to use violent means and we are prepared. When the order to revolt is given, it will be answered immediately all over North Africa. My people are waiting for that order. For two years I have been doing everything in my power to restrain them. I have urged them to wait.

No pacific solution is in sight. It is their responsibility if something happens. We have had hopes in the United States, which has been leading the fight for freedom throughout the world. America has strategic and economic interests in North Africa. We do not like to go against you. That is why we have waited until now. But America seems to be on the side of France. Take the example of Indochina. The Americans are against the Nationalist movement, which has been pushed into the hands of the Communists. If we were convinced that the United States would help us, we might avoid a fight which would have repercussions throughout the world.

The French are behaving idiotically in North Africa, just as they did in Indochina. They are opening the way for the Communists. The Communists in North Africa are free to act for liberty, while Nationalists are put in jail. They are allowed to hold meetings and publish newspapers, while we are driven underground. They are acquiring open support.

The French never learn. Ho Chi Minh went to Paris in 1946 from Indochina as a non-Communist Nationalist. He asked the French to change the situation and warned them that otherwise he would fight. No one listened to him. Look at the situation today. America is supporting the puppet government of Bao Dai, while Ho is with the Communists. We do not wish to see a repetition of this in North Africa.

We paused for a moment to drink some small cups of Turkish coffee, followed by glasses of green Arab tea. Then Abdul Krim continued:

Very frankly, we may soon be obliged to fight against France and Spain. We will count only upon ourselves. We are distant from the Communist ideology which is a danger to the Arabs and Moslems. We must achieve independence by our own means. But, if in our struggle, the situation is critical, we would gladly accept arms or support from any quarter, even the Communists and Russia. If we are pushed to a struggle, we will be intransigent.


CAIRO, *March 14, 1950*

THIS evening I had tea with Azzam Pasha. He had just returned from the palace. Farouk whispered to him that this time the rumors about a pact between Israel and Jordan seemed to be true. The pact was supposed to have been signed aboard a British destroyer at Aqaba.

Azzam assured me Egypt was planning no war against Israel nor were the other Arab states. But Israel would have to act with intelligence and moderation and cooperate in settling refugee and other problems.

Azzam says there is a vast range of social development in the Arab world. The Yemen is incredibly backward, but there is enough to eat. Ibn Saud runs a feudal one-man distribution system of his own wealth in Saudi Arabia. Iraq has no need to worry about its future if it will only work hard enough. Neither Jordan nor Israel are viable; both exist by foreign subsidies.

There is a growing social consciousness in Egypt. Conservative cabinets have approved reforms and new taxes. The unorganized force of Islam has helped by pointing out the religious duties to reform. There are no hereditary pashas and few big hereditary estates. There are many rich war profiteers. Now there is a social snobbism for helping the poor; princesses and pashas' wives are working among the peasants and in hospitals. The King is becoming somewhat interested—but not enough. Many people support gradual reform out of fear of communism.

ALEXANDRIA, *March 15, 1950*

TODAY I went to Alexandria to see ex-King Zog of Albania. It was curious to drive along the old desert road between Cairo and this city past what used to be rows of famous base camps during the war. Now nothing is left but a few rusty cans, some barbed wire, occasional foundations for tents, and many camels grazing for desert weeds.

Zog lives in a fancy villa in the suburb of Ramleh. He still seems to keep up "royal" appearances. He has a court chamberlain—a strictly Balkan character named Kemal Bey Messare who used to be Albanian minister in Athens, speaks fluent bad French, expounds on affairs he knows nothing about, and dresses like a bad advertisement from *Esquire*. Messare acted as interpreter for the King, who spoke in Albanian. This in itself is a curious Turkish hangover. (The Turks used to insist on translations even in languages they knew well; they thus had more time to reflect on answers.) Zog's French seemed to me every bit as good as Messare's when we talked directly in it. Then he pleaded that he "had a cold" and therefore wanted to use an interpreter. This makes less than no sense. If he wanted to save his throat, Albanian seems more long-winded than French.

Zog, who ran away when Mussolini attacked Albania early in 1939, taking his gold and jewels with him, appears to have done all right. He was wearing a black frock coat and dark gray trousers and all in all was pretty regal for a man who was a self-made king, and ruled as such only briefly. He still has the ridiculous pointed mustache he had when I saw him last in Tirana, January 1, 1939. He is tall, silly-looking, but not unhandsome; is getting pasty faced, puffy and slightly fat.

Zog shot off his trap at length about world strategy, accused America of stupidity in losing China, and suggested the only way to save Albania quickly was to land a "motorized brigade" by airplane. Otherwise, Greece and Turkey would be cut off by the Russians and we could not "save them by an airlift."

TEL AVIV, *March 17, 1950*

I arrived here this morning after a bumpy flight from Cyprus to Lydda. Tel Aviv looks humming but drab. The buildings give the appearance of being constructed of bad cement and flake off. The whole city needs paint. There is lots of traffic in the streets and no longer any uniforms. The housing problem is tremendous and it is even almost impossible to get a hotel room. A week's meat ration for three people is enough for one meal for all three.

This afternoon I visited our ambassador, James G. MacDonald. He is a gaunt, rather handsome, vain man. He was very friendly and seems to have acquired more wisdom and *savoir-faire* since I last saw him in Paris. He

said American policy was now to encourage bilateral negotiations for peace
but not to stipulate specific terms as before.

MacDonald said Sir Knox Helm, the new British minister, is an able
man. He said Helm personally expressed the idea (and was urging it on the
Foreign Office) that a strong Israel was in the interests of Britain. If Israel
were overrun and defeated by the Arabs there could be one of two results:
Either there would be a vast slaughter and Britain would have to intervene
for humanitarian reasons and incur the wrath of the Arab world; or the
victorious Arabs would set to quarreling among themselves and Britain
would again have to intervene. If MacDonald reports Helm correctly this is
a curious kind of *Machtpolitik* but not unsound.

TIBERIAS, *March 18, 1950*

TODAY I drove down to this ancient town on the Sea of Galilee. It was
a lovely spring day and the fields were full of flowers. In many of them
Arabs in their headdresses were calmly plowing. A pass is still required
to drive through Nazareth, a center of Arab Christians still specially protected. For the rest it appeared completely at peace.

At the little resort hotel in Tiberias I had a long interview with Prime
Minister Ben Gurion. He was much fatter but far more relaxed than when I
last saw him (1948). He is full of visions combined with an energetic
practicality and great will power. He told me he had invited Vlahov, one of
the vice-presidents of Jugoslavia, to visit him. Ben Gurion studied in Salonika under the Turks and Vlahov, as a deputy in Constantinople, defended the Jews when their own representatives were too cowed to speak
up themselves. Ben Gurion knows Turkish well.

He bitterly attacked Communism as "another name for Russian chauvinism." He said there had been a change in British public opinion "but I
don't know if the Foreign Office has changed. Certainly Bevin never will."
He said Israel might eventually face a color problem. Many Jews in Ethiopia were really black and wanted to come here.

Ben Gurion claims Israel wants to negotiate formal peace with all its
Arab neighbors as quickly as possible and on the basis of present de facto
frontiers. He insists it harbors no present or future intention of expanding
into adjoining territory. He said:

Peace is of paramount interest to our policy. We must develop the
country. The North was ruined by the war. The South, Negeb, was
ruined by sixteen hundred years of neglect. It requires a tremendous
effort to rebuild and that in itself is a paramount reason for peace.

Furthermore, we face an urgent problem of immigration. If, for example, Iraq really opens her doors for departure of Jews we must take
them in. Even if there is nothing—no houses, no jobs awaiting them we
must take them in.

Supposing Rumania were suddenly to say "You can have all our Jews who wish to emigrate providing you receive them immediately," we would take them—regardless of economic difficulties. This requires peace.

If there is one Arab state which should fear us it is Jordan. We have no quarrel with Egypt. We do not covet the Sinai Desert or the Suez Canal. Our frontiers with Jordan are long and complicated. Still, there is a real possibility of peace there.

Turning to long range problems, he continued:

Our fundamental policy is one of unlimited immigration. We are especially interested in absorbing as rapidly as possible the Jews from countries where they face persecution or threats their emigration will be restricted in future. Our present population is 1,200,000 of whom 1,050,000 are Jews (the rest Arabs). In ten years, we will probably have a population of 3,000,000. Therefore, we must work to develop our agriculture and industry to provide more jobs.

We will irrigate the Negeb—where experts say there is oil. We are planning to develop chemical, textile and metal industries including steel—for which we will import coal and iron. With hard work and determination our country can support a big population.

Look at the way Switzerland has developed itself with far less riches than are ours. Or Belgium, which is a little bigger than Western Palestine and yet supports 8,000,000 people. We can work as hard and as skillfully. We intend to develop maritime industries—shipping and fishing. Not many Jews have experience in these fields. Yet, a few had had agricultural experience and we proved they could do the job. Experts—even our first pioneers—said it would take generations to make a farmer. We proved you could do it in a year. These things can be done and will be done. In ten years we will have tens of thousands of sailors and fishermen. We will send them to Norway to learn. Everything depends upon brains, ability and determination, not on heritage and habits.

What we still lack—and this is very important—is what you call know-how. Whatever we do must be of the highest quality, demonstrating the best skill and management. We are now sending people to the United States to learn. We may invite some American experts to come and teach us more. We have the required potentials. Having the sea and vast spaces of Negeb which we can and will irrigate—there is plenty of water in Israel—four or five millions can easily live in this country. The output of our workers today is not as high as it ought to be. But it will be, it will be.

He said Israel would never turn Communist, pointing out that in the last election the Communist Party gained only 2 per cent of votes, and in recent local balloting in a region where there were many recent immigrants from East Europe, they dropped below that figure. He added:

Israel stands for democracy and freedom of the individual, although it stands for social justice. We are against any type of dictatorship or totalitarian state. Our people have two characteristics. There is an old Hebrew saying that all Jews are princes. We have a sense of equality as we are all descendants of Abraham, Isaac and Jacob. Everyone breathes a sense of freedom. And while we are more adaptable than other people perhaps, Jews are most patriotic and our population will not easily submit to dictation. They will not submit to ideas foreign to their spirit and communism is foreign to them. Its prior loyalties could never be to this country.

After lunch I crossed the Sea of Galilee in a boat to Ein Geb, a kibbutz (collective farm) on the eastern shore, just off the Syrian border. The British minister, Sir Knox Helm, and a Foreign Office inspector, Sir Alexander Hodgson, went along.

The frontier drawn here by the British and French more than twenty-five years ago is absolutely cockeyed. There were no Jewish settlements on the eastern shore. Yet they awarded the strip of land including Ein Geb and a hill on which the ancient city of Sussita (Hippos) stood to Palestine. For the rest, the frontier is ten meters away from the high water level. This gives Syria (and to the South, Transjordan) absolute strategic domination by commanding every single ridge.

During the war the settlers of Ein Geb resolved not to evacuate. All the adults (about 160) were in the Haganah. Their military boss was a thin, long-nosed blond fellow named Dafni with whom I talked at length. He was born in Zagreb and admires the Serbs, detests the Croats. During the war he joined the American OSS and was parachuted to both the Italian and Jugoslav partisans. His brother, also in OSS, dressed up as a German officer and rescued his own father from prison. He was so well disguised that not even his father recognized him. Other settlers with whom I talked came from Vienna, Bulgaria, London.

Some months before the war started, on Haganah orders, they built a reinforced concrete shelter and command post which I visited. From this a series of communications trenches were dug to the perimeter. The war came suddenly. When they were attacked they rushed all children into the shelter and evacuated them three days later across the lake. They had some automatic weapons. They depended for food and ammunition on boats from Tiberias, several of which were sunk by Arab aircraft. They were shelled by mortars and a few seventy-fives and were also bombed. The Syrians looked down their throats from the heights including the hill of Sussita which they had taken. Twice they broke through but were driven out.

TEL AVIV, *March 19, 1950*

HAD a particularly interesting day today, seeing Moshe Sharett, the foreign minister, and Reuven Shiloah (ex-Zaslani), one of the key men of the government, Ben Gurion's right hand, liaison between the prime ministry, foreign ministry and general staff, reader of all intelligence reports (former chief of intelligence of the Jewish agency) and head of negotiations (secret) with the Hashemite Kingdom of Jordan. Shiloah had plenty to say:

Israel has explored the possibilities of bilateral settlements with the Arab states ever since the war. All sorts of messages have been conveyed to Egypt without result. There is a feeling that the King, foreign ministry and army (in Cairo) are all against settlement and that the Americans are being fooled by private statements to the contrary. Lebanon would like to settle but doesn't dare unless Egypt does. In Jordan, however, there has been much pressure on the King for a deal. Rich farmers, for example, have ordered tractors in America and have paid five times the transportation fee and taxes and waited five times as long to get delivery as would have been the case if these had been sent through Israel, instead of Beirut. Lebanon and Syria have Abdullah at their mercy economically.

Israel put out feelers to Jordan. There have been three stages of the negotiations and Shiloah has been in all. The first was during the Rhodes discussions under Bunche. Israeli delegates kept flying back to "report" to Tel Aviv. Actually they were going to Jordan. Negotiations took place in Abdullah's summer palace at El Shune. Shiloah and those who worked with him went to Jerusalem and were secretly passed through the Arab lines by trusted Arab Legion officers commanded to do so by Abdullah. They were received cordially. Abdullah took part in many of the talks and Rifai, head of the court and briefly prime minister, was always his representative. At first a permanent settlement was sought. Abdullah wanted an outlet on the Mediterranean at Gaza. Various ways of linking Israel with the Negeb were studied including the formula used by Panama across Colon (Canal Zone). These talks broke down but contact remained.

Finally, Abdullah proposed as his own idea that a five-year nonaggression pact should be signed. This would require certain immediate moves. Joint guarantees would be made concerning the holy places, most of which are in Arab hands. An exchange of access to Mt. Scopus (for the Jews) and access to Bethlehem (for the Arabs) would be made. This would be presented immediately to the United Nations. Frontiers would be frozen as of the moment. Haifa free port rights would be granted. Negotiations have been in Arabic, French and English, all of which Shiloah speaks. (Abdullah speaks only Arabic.)

Sharett was as always a bit pontifical and didactic in manner. In terms of personality he is not very diplomatic. He said:

I can see no possibility at all of this country going Communist. It would go against its grain. It would be deadly to the process of economic development which is the very essence of this whole enterprise and without which Israel cannot possibly achieve its mission. I am not aware of a single party in Israel, including the Communist Party, clamoring today for the establishment of one-party rule in Israel.

TEL AVIV, *March 19, 1950*

THIS evening I drove out to Rehovoth to see Dr. Chaim Weizmann, first president of Israel and an old friend. George Weidenfeld, an English Zionist who is serving as volunteer aide to Weizmann for a few months before returning to London, came along. Weizmann's house in Rehovoth, built in 1937, is a lovely place in fine grounds.

Poor Weizmann has been very ill and looked it. He is seventy-five and is just running down. His heart is bad. He received me in his bedroom where he was sitting in an armchair in pyjamas, dressing gown and blanket. He looked like a dying man, thin and with drawn yellow face. His mind is slipping. Three or four times during the course of a forty-minute chat he asked me the same question and showed no signs of remembering when I gave him exactly the same answer. It is a pity to see a great mind failing. I doubt if he will live many more months—or even weeks. The conversation was quite without interest save for one point.

He said Eddy Jacobson, Truman's Jewish friend from Missouri, had told him on the long distance telephone that Truman would welcome a visit by Weizmann. He asked me what I thought about it. I said that he should wait for a better clue as to the President's real desires. He replied that the State Department would try and block it. I added that I thought it was not a propitious time for a visit; that Washington was pressing the Arab states to negotiate with Israel; that if he went to Washington the Arabs would all suspect a Jewish plot. He suggested perhaps it might be better after the Jordan negotiations conclude successfully, but that he would have to go before the Washington heat became too intense. He seems to want very much to go and said his last trip was very profitable for Israel.

CYPRUS, *March 20, 1950*

I arrived here, en route to Turkey, at noon. This evening I had a long chat with Commander Wolfson, formerly head of British intelligence in Turkey, now representative of British European Airways with the various governments where BEA has subsidiary airlines. He told me that the famous "Cicero" story of the Albanian valet of Sir Hughe Knatchbull-Hugessen, ambassador in Ankara during the war, was "unfortunately all true." Hugessen was careless and liked to go out. The valet "Cicero" had a mold made of the key to his office safe (he found the original in the ambassador's pocket one night) and then used to photograph documents. Wolfson said intelligence ascertained there was a bad leak before the end of 1943 and warned Hugessen about his personal staff. He blithely disregarded these warnings. If he had been a Russian, Wolfson said, Moscow would have had him shot—"and quite rightly."

In the afternoon I had a good talk with our old friend and best man Bill Porter, now American consul here. He said Israel is not viable. Gordon Clapp reported at the Istanbul American diplomatic conference: "Gentlemen, if you were going to set up a Jewish state you should at least have given it a chance to exist." Clapp doesn't think it would be viable if it included the entire former mandated territory. Porter and other young diplomats had argued for creating the state at a time when Loy Henderson and others wanted to wait another generation. Porter now thinks Henderson was right.

Porter thinks either King Abdullah or Rifai, his chamberlain and former Prime Minister, may soon be assassinated. There are large discontented elements among the religious, the army, the refugees (Palestine Arabs now in the Hashemite kingdom). (Abdullah was in fact murdered not long afterward.)

Porter says Israel could not exist save as a result of American governmental policy. We are now stuck with it and must recognize the state is not viable. We must be prepared to help it for years.

As for Cyprus, nothing has been done to develop Cyprus into a strategic base. British naval surveys of the ports in 1948 led to nothing. Britain is broke and has so many defense commitments that it is spending nothing here.

Archbishop Makarios, the Nationalist leader, came back to the island in 1948 after studying at Boston. The first time Bill called on him he took off his stove-pipe priest's hat, summoned a bottle of brandy, gave Porter a drink and said: "Why don't you call me 'Mak'?"

ISTANBUL, *March 22, 1950*

I had an interesting time today seeing the Patriarch of the Orthodox Church, Athenogoras. The patriarch lives in the old quarter of the Phanar in a relatively simple home-office. He has a signed picture of Truman beside him—under a cross. He is a huge man—at least six feet three, under a towering black "pope's" hat and wears a long gray beard like Michelangelo's Moses. He speaks good American English, having lived in America almost twenty years.

He was more than friendly. Although I haven't seen him in eight years he greeted me like a long-lost son, embraced me in his vast arms and when I left, kissed me on both cheeks. He gave me a string of amber prayer beads and some Samian wine.

He said it is a tragedy that religion cannot make peace in its own family.

"How can the spiritual world face conflict with the materialist world when it cannot agree with itself? Religion is behaving criminally. It is at war in Christendom." He had sent a message of greeting and regard to Pius XII that was not even answered.

The Orthodox Church is democratic and would like to have a synod of Patriarchs to bring administrative matters up to date. But so much of it is behind the Iron Curtain it cannot summon such a meeting; there would be too many absent.

Athenogoras expressed approval for present treatment of Turkey's Greek minority by the Ankara government and said Greeks here had never before enjoyed such complete freedom and equality. The position of the Orthodox Church had first been established five hundred years ago when Sultan Mohammed captured Constantinople and guaranteed to the Christians the same privileges they enjoyed under Byzantium. "In the past we have of course had bad days," he said, "but they now seem to be over."

ANKARA, *March 23, 1950*

I had drinks with two old friends, Nermine Menemençioglu Streater and Sureya Agaoglu, and dined with Sureya on the train back to Istanbul.

Nermine said the Americans were not too popular. There had been the usual instances of drunkenness, autocratic behavior and an effort to boss "these Turks." She also resented slighting references to Britain by Americans. Nermine and Sureya don't think Wadsworth is a particularly good American ambassador—especially in contrast to his predecessor, Wilson. Wadsworth spends too much time playing golf. At a meeting at the golf club of its committee, of which foreign minister Sadak is an honorary member, Sadak was late. Wadsworth impatiently referred to the lack of promptness of "the Turks." Nermine was furious and said after all the foreign minister had more important things to do even if the ambassador didn't. Furthermore, Wadsworth tactlessly refers to his "long experience" in Turkey when he is really talking of the Arab world, which once belonged to the Ottoman empire and is held in contempt by the Turks. "Sometimes he seems to think we are Arabs," Sureya said.

Sureya said there was still a certain amount of polygamy in the villages. It is illegal but continues. Many of the offspring of these marriages, having no legal rights, are beggar boys in Istanbul. She is trying to help them. Sureya also said the next elections (in May) will probably be the freest ever had in Turkey although possibly not 100 per cent honest. She said the last elections were rigged; that it was a well-known fact that President Inönü was not even reelected to parliament (the *Meçlis*). He has to be elected in order to be voted to the presidency. On the way to the *Meçlis* his car was stopped three times by a hostile crowd.

TEHERAN, *March 28, 1950*

I arrived here from Istanbul Sunday evening March 26. Ambassador John Wiley, a charming individualist whom I first knew in Vienna after the *Anschluss,* was kind enough to give me dinner, put me up for the night, and then get me installed in the home of Spencer and Xenia Barnes, who are being exceedingly pleasant about the "imposed" guest.

Yesterday I had a talk with Shah Rokh, director of information for the Iranian government. He is a shrewd, black-haired young man with rimless spectacles and mustache. He speaks good English as well as German. During the war he broadcast from Germany for Goebbels and against the Allies. He comes from a distinguished Parsee family and his father was assassinated, leaving him somewhat bitter. His voice was quite famous in Iran during the war and apparently he was a rather artful propagandist. I am not yet quite clear as to the circumstances of his return and rise to office. He now has very close relations with the Americans. As one member of the embassy who likes Shah Rokh says: "He may be an SOB but he's ours."

Shah Rokh told me: "Soviet propaganda is increasing in tempo. They say Iran is an instrument of American materialism and is being transformed into a base for aggression against the USSR. The 'ruling class' is denounced as slaves of American imperialism. At heart the Persian is not a Communist. But he would be if he were hungry."

Welles, of the embassy cultural section, an old friend of Joe Upton, who has known this country since 1923, told me:

Nobody can hold Iran together. No one is clever enough to pull it together for cohesive action. But for the sake of expedience the United States must back Iran with an economic program which will at least prevent the country from falling like a ripe plum into the Russian lap.

A real reform would take fifty years. It must be based on educating the young to new aspirations and standards. You can't legislate against corruption and achieve any effect without the backing of the people. We found that out at home under the Volstead Act. The United States wants to do good here. But we must be both realistic and patient.

TEHERAN, *March 28, 1950*

LUNCH with Ambassador and Irina Wiley. John, an endearing, original man with a deep bass voice, proud of his Irish "tribal" ancestry, related the following old Persian proverb: "I and my tribe against the nation. I and my cousins against the tribe. I and my brothers against my cousins. And I against my brothers."

The Persians invented political decentralization with their satrapies. Today they are completely centralized. Nothing can be done in the country without clearing through Teheran. The government is choking with red tape. The Shah acts too hesitantly and slowly. When Wiley urged him to act, at a reception last night, the Shah said: "But if I really act to clean up inefficiency and corruption, your people will call me a dictator." Wiley replied: "We have never had dictatorship in America because we have had leadership."

Our policy is to prevent Iran from falling passively to the Russians. We want to prevent or delay the process and make them "occupy" it rather than appear to absorb it "voluntarily" from within. We want to force the Russians to use more troops than they would plan, if they want to take it, and thus maybe "weaken them in France."

The Russians right now are provoking constant border incidents and inching southwards, about three kilometers a year, in some areas. They merely shoot anyone in the regions they take and thus establish *de facto* territorial control.

TEHERAN, *March 30, 1950*

THIS evening I saw the Shah, Mohammed Reza, in his private city palace. The Shah said there is no indication of any Soviet build-up indicating a threat of aggression against Iran. There is a softening of the Soviet attitude toward Iran, in terms of propaganda. He mistrusts this and thinks such trends sometimes forbode ill.

It is an economic burden to the country to maintain an army of 136,000 men but it is necessary. There are 2,500 kilometers of frontier with Russia alone and even that cannot be manned. The Russians are creeping southward and in fifty years have occupied a strip of about forty kilometers of Iranian territory.

America is under the misconception that Iran is another China—therefore hopeless to defend and salvage. That is ridiculous. The country is in far better and more united shape than China ever was.

Iran has no illusions about being able to form any military alliances with her neighbors. She is too weak. But she hopes some day the United States will extend its already existing commitments and incorporate Greece, Turkey and Iran ("the right flank") into the Atlantic bloc.

Although great undeveloped mineral wealth exists, he said Iran will extend no further concessions to foreign countries or concerns for exploration or exploitation of oil or other raw materials. Iran would, however, welcome foreign investment in development companies—controlled and supervised by Iran.

Britain controls huge Anglo-Iranian oil concessions in the southwestern portion of the country, based on Abadan where is the world's largest petroleum refinery. The Shah said that this concession was unaffected and still has from forty-three to forty-five years to run. New British proposals governing royalties to Iran and operating agreements were presented to the last *Majlis* (parliament) and will again be discussed at the coming session. The Shah said he had been advised the price of oil is declining.

The young Shah was dressed in an admiral's uniform. He spoke in English and smoked an American cigarette. He said: "I must remind you we never begged in our history. But it is a question of world peace for the economic level of this country to be raised to achieve a decent standard of civilization and to avoid threats of internal instability."

Asserting the Iranian people must be given material as well as psychological reasons for defending their national independence if necessary, the Shah said the country needs new social legislation and agrarian reform. He added:

Land reform is not a question of confiscation but of buying and selling the surplus acreage of big estate holders. However, our peasants are not advanced people and need guidance. We must form cooperatives . . .

I expect to commence with tremendously large estates owned by my family's Imperial Welfare Organization. Eight years ago I gave the government all my land for this purpose. But it was not properly exploited. Therefore, about three months ago I took it back and formed a welfare organization named for my family "Pahlevi."

TEHERAN, *March 30, 1950*

AMBASSADOR Wiley is an exceptional kind of diplomat. He keeps his own hours and does all his work in the residence rather than the chancery. He is vain, original, and garrulous. He sent an extraordinarily funny dispatch to the State Department a year ago illustrating his reactions to conversations with the Shah and the foreign minister with cut-out photographs from *Life* of the clown, Fernandel, demonstrating human emotions.

TEHERAN, *March 31, 1950*

WILEY says the Russians are slowly infiltrating across the Gurgan steppes. This is a nomadic area and the Russians are moving southward, extending their control, at the rate of about two kilometers a year. If nomads wander across the southward-shifting "border" they are either shot or arrested. The Russians appear to be gradually ringing the Caspian Sea. The Caspian is the richest area of Iran, its breadbasket.

The Shah is an excellent man. He spends his own money on gifts and contributions—and does it anonymously. He is a religious visionary. When he was six years old he was mortally ill with typhoid, given up for lost. He had a vision of Ali, the Shia saint, before him with a two-edged sword. Next day he began to recover. Some years later he was thrown from a horse but two hands saved him from braining himself on a rock—the hands of Hussein, another Shia saint. One month ago, he had a vision in which Christ appeared to him. (The ambassador thinks the Shah might be considering turning Catholic.)

Iran is in the social condition of late sixteenth century Russia—at the time of Ivan Grozny. The Shah, like Ivan, definitely wants to base the monarchy upon the people. But he wishes to be a Scandinavian monarch rather than another Ivan. His father, Reza (not Mohammed), was Ivan. The *Majlis* is certainly the germ of a democratic process; but actually it is the instrument of the vested interests—and very negative. You cannot impose democracy. You must first make the conditions for its possibility. One need is for an efficient, honest gendarmery. (Here Wiley says, curiously, he wants it like Spain's *Guardia Civil*—a sort of "monastic order" as he puts it.) The gendarmery must protect the people, not exploit them.

The Shah's Swiss upbringing makes him non-Asiatic. He is a hard worker and his main relaxations are movies or sports. He has trouble sleeping at night.

TEHERAN, *April 1, 1950*

JOHN Wiley and Gerry Dooher of our embassy have concocted a fine leprechaun agent and, having let me into the secret, I herewith recount the story as I dispatched it to my newspaper:

The most successful, dramatic, spectacular and romantic secret intelligence agent ever employed by the United States government is Robert (or Roger) T. Lincoln.

Despite the fact that he has been mentioned frequently by the Soviet radio, that he secretly encountered Supreme Court Justice William O. Douglas during the latter's visit to Iran, that a Washington society editor reported spotting him at the capital's Metropolitan Club, that a Teheran newspaper wrote about his marriage to the sister of Syria's army commander, Colonel Shishakli, that the Iranian Government now bans all foreigners from a huge southern area where Lincoln's presence was rumored, he has managed to elude arrest or embarrassing encounters.

His reputation has grown steadily. One Teheran paper wrote of his activities as "by far more active, more clever and more skilled" than those of the late Lawrence of Arabia and said he had worked to neutralize Soviet influence in the north Iranian province of Azerbaijan.

Another journal's reporter, covering the arrival in Teheran sixteen months ago of former United States Ambassador George V. Allen on a visit to the Shah, said that the diplomat was accompanied by Dr. Livingstein Credo, "the tribal expert," and by "Major Lincoln." However, the elusive spy managed to slip away before the very interested Iranian government could find and interrogate him.

The official United States government biographical data on this shadowy but renowned officer lists, as the languages he speaks: French, Turkish, Persian, Uzbek and Kurdish. One might presume from his reputation that he could pass as a native in any of these tongues. Furthermore, his ability to escape detection is certainly facilitated by the the the fact that, as far as is known, no satisfactory photograph of him has ever been published.

Nevertheless, the following information concerning this legendary man can be made public. Now promoted to the rank of lieutenant colonel. Roger (called Robert) Throckmorton Lincoln of the United States Intelligence Service was born in Slippery Rock, Arkansas on October 10, 1909.

According to government records, he was appointed a political agent on September 3, 1943. Clearly an independent-minded eccentric, his prior career is officially listed as: "1930–1933, rum runner; 1933–1939, confidence man; 1939–1943, counterespionage agent." His political affiliation in a confidential report dated January 18, 1949, is listed as "Dixiecrat."

The following biographical data are included in the same document: "Family details, obscure. Major Lincoln is known to have a wife in Springfield, Missouri, from whom he has had one son. He is reliably reported to have at least two Kurdish *sighehs* (concubines)."

These remarks are appended:

"Major Lincoln is a direct descendant (on his father's side) of the famous American writer, Booker T. Lincoln. On his mother's side he is descended from President Thomas Jefferson. He is a member of the Order of the Rosy Cross and a practicing yogi.

"He spent his early years in Poona, Peshawar and Darjeeling, India. In the last city he studied Oriental languages and yogi under the renowned Tibetan scholar, Hilung Hung-lo. In Peshawar he lived with the family of the former Khan of Kokand. He has retained this contact up to now.

"Unfortunately Lincoln's career has been somewhat checkered and he appears to have devoted most of his mature life to shady pursuits. His service in the Intelligence Corps (USIS) dates from 1939 when he led a group of Khorassan Kurds into Bokhara in an effort to subvert the curator of the Bokhara Oriental Museum. His subsequent career is outlined in Secret Report USIS-B-39-T-407, October 4, 1948."

It is possible to quote at such length from highly classified documents because, by a shocking inadvertency, these and other papers were lost in a public place by a United States diplomat whose career thereafter was profoundly altered. It is known that the missing material fell into Iranian and Soviet as well as probably British hands. For that reason permission has been granted to make this information public now.

One of the papers lost by the careless official was one he had no business having in his briefcase at all. This was a top secret cable addressed to Ambassador John Wiley on March 31, 1949, with instructions that, when decoded, it should be shown only to the ambassador and should then be destroyed. This message, of highest classification, came from Major General William J. Donovan, wartime chief of the Office of Strategic Services.

The cable dealt with Donovan's little publicized journey to Iran last year. The parts that can be quoted said: "For publicity purposes my visit is pleasure; actually, I am out to investigate Lincoln's activities. Reports of his excesses among the Kurdish women have reached the President and while he is one of our best operators yet he's got to get on the beam morally. . . . He has got to drop everything, including any women with whom he might be entangled at the moment, and come to Teheran with clean, clean hands."

Of course it was exceptionally embarrassing to the United States government when all these data, not only officially secret but personally embarrassing, fell into foreign hands.

Major Robert (Roger) T. Lincoln does not and never did exist—except in the minds of suspicious Soviet, Iranian, Syrian, Turkish and other inquisitive intelligence services.

Major Lincoln was born about a year and a half ago after the Soviet radio had mentioned the activities of a mysterious American of that name. Ambassador Wiley, a man whose brilliant diplomatic career has never erased his sense of humor, was discussing the Russian broadcast with his political attaché, the genial Gerald F. P. Dooher. Both of Irish antecedents and salty imagination, they decided that, for the good of the United States government and the pleasure of this historical epoch, since Major Lincoln did not already exist, he should be created. He was. This is his story.

TEHERAN, *April 1, 1950*

LUNCH with Geoffrey Keating (of Anglo-Iranian Oil Company) and Shah Rokh. Shah Rokh said he had broadcast for Goebbels until late 1942. He visited the Russian front with the German army and was at Smolensk. He was convinced after the fall of France that Germany would lose the war; the Germans had become ridiculously overconfident. He saw Hitler several times and noticed a great change; he became foolishly optimistic. Shah Rokh said Schulenberg, former ambassador in Russia, had been a great friend of his (Shah Rokh's) father. Schulenberg headed propaganda and planning for the Caucasus and Iran. He slipped word to Shah Rokh to get out in 1942 and Shah Rokh scrammed to Istanbul in early 1943. I wouldn't trust him as far as I could throw Iran but he is bright and entertaining.

Keating said Himmler (disguised as a sergeant) was picked up by British soldiers and interrogated in the house next to his own at Luneberg. When he was stripped naked, a doctor examined him. He got to his mouth. Himmler crushed a capsule of poison between his teeth. Two British officers, fearing a ruined career for letting so valuable a prisoner slip, picked him up and dunked him by his heels in a large tub of water. Thus the man who slaughtered millions died, naked, hanging by his heels in a tub, as his enemies sought to bring life back into him.

TEHERAN, *April 2, 1950*

LONG chat with General Ali Razmara, chief of staff of the Iranian army and its real commander (under the Shah). [Razmara subsequently became Prime Minister—and was assassinated.] Razmara is supposed to be the brains of the Iranian army and a strong man. He says economics is Iran's real problem. There is a Persian proverb: "A man's first country is his stomach." Agitation takes place among the hungry.

# 2 2

---

# ORBIT OF ASIA

DHAHRAN, SAUDI ARABIA, *April 5, 1950*

AIR CONNECTIONS EASTWARD FROM TEHERAN ARE NONEXISTENT SO I bummed a ride down to Bahrein on an American military plane which then took me across the drink to Dhahran, where I hoped to catch a TWA or other liner. I had no visa, which is especially tricky for a Jew in this country that insists no Jews are allowed in. However, Tommy Thompson, vice-president of Aramco, came down to the airport, fixed things up, and took me home to his bungalow for a poker game and quantities of liquor. I don't know if it was real or brewed by Aramco chemists. In theory, no booze can be imported. However, the company's experts can make unusually credible "gin," "scotch," "bourbon," and so on out of petroleum, believe it or not; called "sundowners"—made yesterday evening.

EN ROUTE BOMBAY–KARACHI, *April 6, 1950*

ARRIVED in Bombay April 4, after a flight from Dhahran across Sharja (Trucial Oman) and Muscat, two arid little towns surrounded by desert, verging on the Persian Gulf.

My first evening in Bombay I dined at the Taj Mahal Hotel with Aleco (Marina's uncle) and Leda Sotiriadi and G. Dambala of the Greek merchant firm, Ralli Brothers. The dining room is very formal. I was the only man not in black tie.

The next day (yesterday) I lunched in the Yacht Club, poked around town, visited the Willingdon Club (like Gezira Sporting Club in Cairo but even more luxurious) and dined at the home of another Ralli Brothers official named Paspati (British, despite his Chiote name). Present were Mrs. Wadia, the daughter of Mohammed Ali Jinnah, founder of Pakistan (and her husband), and another girl, Indian, named Santha Rama Rau whose father is governor of the reserve bank and who is a writer and highly intelligent. The Jinnah girl, very tiny but extremely pretty, was disowned by her Moslem father for marrying a Parsee (although Jinnah himself had married a Parsee). Both girls speak perfect English and are very occidental. They were complaining bitterly that prohibition has just been inaugurated (April 5) in Bombay province. The dinner was most alcoholic but only foreigners will be able to buy liquor henceforth with the exception of tiny emergency rations for Indians who have filled out proper applications.

Bombay looks like a big, somewhat more modern Cairo, by the sea instead of the Nile. The Indian navy was drawn up outside the famous "Gateway to India" where President Prasad, here to inaugurate prohibition, reviewed it. Rooks dipped and scared. I noted signs on some restaurants "South Africans not Admitted"—retribution for South African racism and anti-Indian measures. The highest officers in the fleet are still British—training Indians. Blue uniformed Sepoy policemen in shorts, puttees, but no shoes, guarded the city smartly for Prasad, carrying long staves (*lathis*).

Bombay is filled with a medley of costumes and colors: bright saris, turbans and shirts. Down in Crawford Market, the main food bazaar, bearded beggars, squatting basket carriers, blind panhandlers led by small boys with pails for coins—all give a hint of India's poverty. The sidewalks and streets are stained with the blood-red spit of betel nut chewers. In one street a group of laughing Hindus decorated the automobile of a bridal couple with ribbons and jasmine. Tiny bullocks drew big-wheeled carts slowly through the streets and occasionally small-humped sacred cows, strolled aimlessly along.

Breach Candy Baths is still reserved for Europeans only; I don't know how they manage, now that India is independent. Of course, with special segregated baths for Hindus, Moslems, Parsees, and so on, it is pretty complicated. The Parsees, a rich merchant class who have been in India since being expelled from Persia in the twelfth century, mix easily with everyone. They still have their own fire temples.

In the Malabar Hill section where there are still many palaces of Rajahs and Maharajahs, dispossessed but paid off by the new government, Hamals (the lowest form of bearers) walk their masters' dogs in the evening.

When looking at the palaces of Baroda and Kashmir one realizes how fabulously wealthy they are. The government did not even requisition these palaces to house refugees from Pakistan. It still appears somewhat afraid of these princely sovereigns. It bought them off generously in order to avoid having them raise their subjects in revolt. They have been given fat, tax-free fees, but their children will have no such privileges.

I noticed a great red carpet spread out at the entrance to the hanging gardens of Malabar Hill—for President Prasad. This is the sort of thing Indians used to criticize the British for.

In the hotel a Goan from TWA came up and asked to speak to me. He said that Goa, now Portuguese, would soon be absorbed by India. He asked my advice about going to Brazil. Dark as a mulatto, he still considered himself entirely European ("a Portuguese citizen") and wants the chance of living an occidental life.

KARACHI, *April 7, 1950*

I stayed again with Avra Warren, now ambassador here, most amusing, tough and able. He told me an incident of his career here as a young consul almost thirty years ago. The Parsee women are very fertile; their men are not. There was a piper sergeant of the Black Watch stationed here: a huge Scot, six foot four. He used to hire himself out at twenty pounds a throw as stud to the rich Parsee women; payment only when pregnancy was known.

Warren is pretty gloomy about our position in Asia. He pushed Liaquat Ali to go to New Delhi for the present talks with Nehru and Patel. If they succeed, the situation will be easier. If they fail, there may be war. The Indian extremists are spoiling for a fight; they never recognized partition. Many Pakistanis are itching for a crack at "Bharat," which is what Pakistan papers still call India. They were irked when Delhi grabbed the name and propaganda advantages of "India" after it was originally planned it should be called Hindustan.

About 1,000,000 Hindus and Moslems have been slaughtered in the most vile circumstances since independence and partition in 1947. Trains of Moslem refugees going to Lahore or of Hindu refugees leaving Lahore arrived at their destinations filled with blood and scraps of flesh. Babies were brained before their mothers who were then speared. Houses were set afire and the inhabitants mowed down with gunfire as they sought to escape. The Sikhs were particularly savage on the Indian side. The Mahasabha, a secret extremist organization in India, has urged this on. Having assassinated Gandhi, it threatens to do away with Nehru or anyone blocking extreme Hindu nationalism. The streets of Calcutta are now unsafe for Moslem or foreigner. An Englishman was slain a few days ago when he tried to protect his Moslem servants (also killed).

I had a long talk with our string correspondent, Ashiq Ahmad. He used to live in Delhi; his wife comes from the United Provinces and had an estate near Lucknow. They left with only a few belongings and their trunks were robbed by the Moslem servants of the Pakistan high commissioner in Delhi with whom they had taken refuge. His wife used to have five elephants, a sign of considerable wealth. Now they live in two tiny rooms in Karachi, where there is no housing.

Jinnah conceived the idea of Pakistan, a Moslem state, and would have had much difficulty preaching it (as a Shia, himself married to a Parsee— who died years ago) if he had not been harsh with his daughter. The majority of Moslems here are Sunni.

KARACHI, *April 8, 1950*

TEA this afternoon with Al-Haj, Khwaja Nazimuddin, governor general of Pakistan, a renowned Bengal politician and Muslim League leader, first prime minister of East Pakistan. Fifty-six years old, Khwaja Nazimuddin comes from the famous Nawab of Dacca family. He is a Cambridge graduate and married to the daughter of a Zamindar. He is short, very rotund, has an amiable brown face, was wearing a long white coat, looking very cool. The atmosphere of his palace is quite as formal as under the British Raj; saluting guards and aides; formally dressed servants bringing in tea, sweet cakes and spiced hot pastries. He spoke earnestly, gravely, but not excitably.

Nazimuddin was very gloomy on the talks in New Delhi between Nehru and Liaquat Ali, Pakistan's premier. Last night the talks about broke down making the chances of war probable in the near future. Nazimuddin said Pakistan did not fear the population disparity with India so much as the fact that through partition India got a military material superiority of about four to one. America should intervene and "make it clear to India that any act of aggression will be opposed and if attacked Pakistan will be given military aid. War here would become a world war. It would give an ideal chance to communism elsewhere. The whole of Burma, Indochina and Malaya would flare up."

KARACHI, *April 9, 1950*

YESTERDAY morning I had a long talk with Ghulam Muhammad, minister for finance and economic affairs, a strong man in the government. Tall, wearing a white *sherwani* (long coat) and half-lensed glasses, he smoked constantly and talked rapidly and brilliantly except for a speech impediment apparently caused by the loss of his lower teeth, which makes him difficult to understand.

He said: "Just as we imported many things from India we imported communism. The refugees, having lost everything, find succor in the Communist philosophy." He remarked that the leaders were Muslims from India. The Communist Party is legal in Pakistan but "despite chaotic conditions it has not made much headway." West Bengal is the center of Indian communism and in East Bengal "we get the overflow. But there is no problem of communism. This is not an industrial country. There is plenty of food. A full belly and Islam are good insurance against communism."

Regarding Kashmer he said

the only democratic solution is a plebiscite. We have 750,000 refugees from Kashmir now in Pakistan. They have to go back to their homes. The rivers of Kashmir flow mainly into Pakistan. The economy of the West Punjab depends on a canal system out from these rivers. That canal system is the largest in the world. If India were to hold Kashmir she could divert the waters and ruin us. The biggest reasons for requiring Kashmir are economic. Not only the rivers but all trade routes from Kashmir go into Pakistan. West Punjab is the heaviest populated area of West Pakistan and the backbone.

Ghulam Muhammad said American capitalism is "selfish and narrow." It hasn't enough energy or broadness of concept. America hasn't met its global responsibilities properly yet.

You take five years to think about a problem and then three years to act. This process costs too much. Look at China; or at Vietnam. In threatened countries you have two choices; either you must defend them against Russia or you must build up their economies. You are always too late. You are going to lose many things. You are going to link us up in the mess too. You must end your policy of half measures. One curse of capitalism is that it always wants to be efficient in terms of dollars. By the time experts have computed an efficient cost things have already gone too far. You should face the situation boldly. Look at your miserable Point Four. It is wholly inadequate. You must have a bold new plan supplemented by action. Technical advice alone is just tantalizing.

KARACHI, *April 9, 1950*

ASHIQ Ahmad, our local stringer, has been telling me the Pakistanis don't know how to make a proper curry. He and his wife come (Moslems) from India's United Provinces. That's the best curry, he insists, so I went around for some at lunch today.

Unfortunately, I broke my only remaining glasses and had to leave them at an optometrist. Was pretty nearsighted without them. Sat down in Ashiq's modest little flat and he proceeded to pour huge libations of whisky (he's quite a boozer). Finally his wife came in bearing a vast platter of curried rice. I helped myself plentifully as she and Ashiq insisted I take more. I assumed it was what the Turks call *Iç pilaff* because there were plenty of dark specks which I took to be raisins, as in *Iç pilaff*. To my horror, as I was raising about my fifth forkful to my mouth, I saw one of the raisins moving! The specks were flies, so drenched in grease they couldn't fly off.

Il Ministro per gli Affari Esteri.

*Ringrazio molto il signor Sulzberger e il suo autorevolissimo più l'appoggio alla causa giusta dell'Italia*

Il Ministro per gli Affari Esteri.

*2) Durante questo periodo avviare trattative ital-jugoslave; e in caso di disaccordo organizzare un plebiscito intorno alla linea etnica contemporaneamente 3) studiare un progetto d'internazionalizzazione del porto*

Il Ministro per gli Affari Esteri.

*con annessi industriale e con convenzioni ferroviarie la soluzione finale, se non sarà trovata d'accordo, dopo un anno*

The Trieste crisis, brought about by rival Italian and Jugoslav claims, was one of the thorniest after World War II and almost provoked another conflict. This is a suggested formula for solving it as put forth by the Italian Prime Minister Alcide De Gasperi in 1946. At my request he took a red crayon and wrote out the terms of his proposal as outlined above.

PRIME MINISTER TO LORD MOYNE.
Personal and Top Secret.

If you think fit you may hand the following to
Sulzberger: (Begins)

As the grandson of a former owner of the New York
Times, I think I may ask you to be very careful about the
information you have obtained and to consult with Lord Moyne
about its use at this juncture. I should have no difficulty
in defending myself in Parliament about the fullest disclosure
of all telegrams that have passed. You are quite right in
saying that I am (quote) trying to unscramble Yugoslav
puzzles (unquote). Also in Greece I am trying to persuade
the Russians not to use E.A.M. as a disruptive factor. But
this is only a temporary arrangement to help drive the Germans
out of the Balkans. It would be very harmful if you stated
that the Russians were getting the worst of it or anything like
that. As a matter of fact, all is going well between them
and us, unless you tell them the contrary.
I hope therefore that I may count on your aid.

WSC
23.6.44

The above is a top-secret telegram from Churchill to Lord Moyne, Minister of State in the Middle East and a Cabinet member. Churchill was seeking to prevent me from publishing my information about a deal between Moscow and London dividing up southeast Europe. The message, as published above, was corrected in Churchill's own handwriting and initialed by him on June 23, 1944. It was never actually sent.

Memorandum in Churchill's handwriting of his agreement with Stalin in late 1944 when the two divided southeast Europe into specific zones of military influence—along lines earlier arranged between Moscow and London. Stalin checked off the Rumanian aspect of the secret deal.

A Colombo newspaper cartoon following an uproar that resulted from some of the author's newspaper columns after a visit to Ceylon. (above)

Marina in 1942, not long after our marriage, wearing a dress of Damascus brocade.

Marina in a new Paris gown.

In a tent, outside Mecca, with old King Ibn Saud of Saudi Arabia.

After lunch and before bridge at the Eisenhowers' (when he commanded
for NATO in 1951). Left to right: front—Mrs. Gruenther; Mrs. Howard
Snyder (wife of Eisenhower's friend and physician, General Snyder);
Mrs. Eisenhower's sister; Mrs. Eisenhower; Marina. Rear—Mrs. Eisenhower's brother-in-law; CLS; General Gruenther (later NATO commander); Eisenhower.

Fort Custer, Michigan
12 November 1942

Mr. Cyrus L. Sulzberger
Care of New York Times
229 West 43rd Street
New York City, N. Y.

My dear Cy,

As events proceed in Europe and North Africa, my mind goes back to that day in April of this year when you dropped into my office at the Combined Chief of Staff and I asked you your opinion of the Russian capabilities for 1942. As you may recall, we had a little informal gathering with Truman Smith, Herman Kramer and John Ratay. Inasmuch as you had visited the German-Russian Front in the Fall of 1941, you were asked to express your opinion as to the probable turn of events on that front during the current year. I must say, old top, that your 'crystal gazing' fell into the class of good educated guessing. I remember your prophecying that the Germans would attack only on the southern front and that while the drive would go east and southeast, the Russians would be able to hold Stalingrad and prevent the Germans from crossing the Caucasus. You seem to have learned considerable military tactical and strategical calculations during your tour with me in the Balkans. At any rate, your estimate hit the 1942 German effort on the nose.

How do you like the North Africa show? To those of us who live on nervous energy and who like the smell of gunpowder it is quite thrilling. Of course, we still have a long way to go before we strike at the German vitals, but it still is a step in the right direction.

I understand that you will soon be leaving for the theater of operations. When I have completed the job of training a unit that will beat the hell out of Hitler, I shall, I hope, see you there. Best of luck and bon voyage.

Most sincerely,

LOUIS J. FORTIER
Brigadier General, U. S. Army
Commanding.

Letter from General Fortier who was secretary of the Joint Chiefs of Staff in the spring of 1942 and arranged my meeting with Intelligence officers of the War Department when—with their vigorous disapproval—I predicted the Germans would limit their 1942 offensive in Russia to the south and eventually fail at both Stalingrad and the Caucasus. Fortier's letter recalls this prophecy.

KARACHI, *April 9, 1950*

KARACHI is a flat, sandy, hot unattractive city, heavily overcrowded. Refugees have swollen its normal population of 300,000 to 1,300,000. It has no oriental charm or color. It is filled with camel carts and bicycle taxis.

This morning I visited some refugee camps together with a government official. The first was a group of cement one-room huts, supplemented by pitiful shacks of straw and burlap. It was steaming hot but men, women and children squatted inside or around these terrible shacks; it didn't matter because the shelter they provide is minimal. Here and there among them some entrepreneur had established a tiny café or store of flimsy boxes. The community was made up almost entirely of Muslims from Agra, a weaving province of India, so many of them were busily working at looms or spinning thread. Girls promised in marriage had gold studs in the left nostril; married women wore their rings there. The chubby little official with me said quite earnestly: "The refugees are completely settled except they have no houses."

Allauddin, twenty-four years old, from Agra, said: "They put their hands into our pockets." Talking in a monotone, wearing a gold ring in his left ear, the brown little man stood in the baking sun and said: "They put up threatening notices and told us to go to Pakistan or to pay them for protection. There were dacoities. Armed dacoits came and stole all we had."

Aaffoo Beg left Agra March 24. He had all his possessions in seven packages. The Indian authorities took his bundles at the border and gave him a receipt, which he sadly produced for me. The locomotive deserted his train in Jodhpur, near Gadai, and a mob gathered. "They were armed. They had axes and spears and swords. But we put our women and our children in the train and drove them off with rocks." Aaffoo Beg said: "I have no hate. But even before partition they hated us. Now we want to live here in Pakistan—forever. We do not want to go back. They tried to persuade us to become Hindu. They tried to convert us Muslims by all means."

The official with me said: "We need help. Things will be terrible this summer."

KARACHI, *April 10, 1950*

THIS morning I saw Lieutenant Colonel Iskander Mirza, secretary of the ministry of defense (later prime minister and dictator), a large heavy man with friendly manner and obvious intelligence. He said India has been concentrating almost its entire military strength on the Punjab border.

Pakistan was ready to fight at a one-to-three or -four inferiority although the proportion is better in air and armor. Mirza said Pakistan has formally requested arms from America. "All we want is peace. We need peace to develop our country. We need military strength to insure peace. War would be a disaster for both India and Pakistan."

KARACHI, *April 10, 1950*

FOUR tribal leaders are the Wali of Swat, the Wong of Bong, the Faqir of Ipi, and the Nono of Spiti.

The Warrens, with whom I am staying at the embassy, have a mongoose named Charlie, purchased to scout the garden for snakes. A not uncommon snake here is the krait, whose bite is fatal and quick. Charlie is an unattractive creature with the face of a rat and the tail of a squirrel except it doesn't curl. He lives in a cage, is attached to a string, hisses and chatters, moves fast as lightning, and knows one trick—how to jump into his sack.

Every morning and evening myna birds fly into the house to be fed. Two of them are nesting in the house. They chatter and scream at each other. They have yellow bills and a yellow streak from the bill to the eye which gives them a wicked grumpy look. If their tongues are cleft they can be taught to speak like parrots.

The Pakistanis like to wear the fur Jinnah hats because these are the hats which were worn by the great Moguls from whom they claim ancestry. Good Muslims who have made the pilgrimage to Mecca dye their beards and hair red with henna.

The streets are filled with bicycle taxis—a little trailer for two hauled by a bicycle, and rubber tired carts pulled by long-striding camels with tinkling bells on their legs.

KARACHI, *April 11, 1950*

I had a talk for an hour and a half with Liaquat Ali Kahn, prime minister of Pakistan. I saw him in his home and we sat around having highballs, an unusual thing in the Moslem world. He proposed that British Commonwealth nations should issue a collective guarantee of the territorial integrity of Pakistan and India in order to ease tension.

A bland fifty-five-year-old Oxford graduate, Liaquat furthermore suggested it would be "useful" if Britain formally declared that any infringement of the Durand line, Pakistan's border with Afghanistan, would be automatically considered as a violation of a "Commonwealth frontier."

Liaquat is a calm, soft-spoken individual (Pakistan's first prime minister). He thought the United States should encourage guarantees of India and Pakistan territorially in order to allow them to spend more on economic improvement and aid to the poor which would help keep out the potential menace of communism. He admitted that popular feeling in Pakistan against any threat of Indian domination is so strong that some people would rather be conquered by the Soviet Union than reconquered by India.

KABUL, *April 14, 1950*

I flew to Kabul, Afghanistan, with Lieutenant Colonel Miller, American air attaché in Karachi and Kabul. He was flying up about a ton of ammunition and emergency rations because the political situation is believed to be very hot here and foreigners, in an emergency, might have to barricade themselves in their compounds. The Americans have made plans for such an eventuality, choosing a compound that has its own source of water (assigned to Colonel J. F. Mynderse, military attaché) as their fort. The diplomats and a few teachers (who were in the army and know how to shoot) would gather there where there is a store of rations, automatic arms and ammunition.

The flight was exceedingly dramatic over deserts and mountains. We flew over the Hab River, looking for crocodiles through binoculars. Along flat desert wastes. Rugged crags start in Baluchistan, sedimentary strata tilted on edge by ancient earthquakes. Snow capped peaks. Little green valleys here and there. Great sand marshes. Across Southwestern Waziristan, home of the improbably named Faqir of Ipi. Walled villages and little square mud forts. Along the Logar River valley, little cultivated farms and villages as Kabul approaches. Kabul nestling in the hills: pastel shades, beneath ancient walls and forts on crags. In Kabul, many-shaded turbans and women in multicolored veils. Big, rangy, hairy camels. Aristocratic Afghan hounds a rarity. Sloppy-looking soldiers. Poor, ragged-looking sturdy men. Donkeys. Veiled women carrying babies.

Our arrival at Kabul was rather weird. I was Miller's entire crew so when we got to the dirt airstrip which serves the capital Miller asked me to keep an eye out for any American-looking car or jeep as we circled round and round. Not a sign of life of any kind. A tattered wind sock blew but no communication with the control hut or indication of any awareness of our presence. Miller began to wonder if the trouble had already started and the local attaché was unable to get out to the airport because he was commanding the defense of a beleaguered compound. We flew over where Miller believed his house to be, waggling our wings. When we finally got down, a jeep pulled up beside us; no Afghans in sight yet. Apparently Miller's message from Karachi, announcing his imminent arrival, had never been received.

Nevertheless, Louis Dreyfus, the quiet cultivated American envoy, and his charming wife (whom I knew when they were *en poste* in Teheran) insisted on putting me up in the residence. She said the Kabul Hotel wasn't even fit for insects.

The Afghan-Soviet border is more than a thousand miles long. Russia might take over the provinces north of the Hindu Kush if Afghanistan got involved in war with Pakistan, or another country. The Afghan-Indian border area is the invasion gateway to India. Afghan intrigue in the area is continuous since losing Peshawar, to the Sikhs in 1833: the last remnant of Afghan empire in India. The Durand line was fixed in 1893 to "limit Afghan and British spheres of influence."

In 1947 Congress (India) supported a "Red-Shirt" party in Pushtun state called Pushtunistan. Kabul supported this and also offered opportunity of their rejoining "motherland of Afghanistan." In October 1947, when Kashmir fighting broke out, many frontier tribesmen and nomads of Afghanistan were involved. In January 1950, Waziristan created a central Pushtunistan government under the presidency of the Faqir of Ipi. The Faqir received 600,000 rupees from India.

The people of Pushtunistan are a mixture of various invading peoples en route to India from the days of Cyrus of Persia (540 B.C.), Alexander the Great; the Sakas, the Chinese Kushans; the Turanians, Arabs, Mongols, Turkestan Turks, Uzbeks and Moguls.

A national assembly (*Tirah Sangah*) of Pathans published a communiqué in the Afghan press on December 25, 1949, saying:

> Our real brother—Afghanistan— . . . we are coreligionists and the same blood runs in our veins . . . Pushtunistan has been set up in the free and lofty mountains of Tirah. The Islamic, democratic, free and strong state of the entire people of Pushtunistan . . . will grow into a firm rooted and fruitful tree under the shadow of which all the people of Pushtunistan inhabiting this area from Chitral to Baluchistan and from Khyber and Bolan Passes to the banks of the river Indus. . . . Oh powerful youngsters of Pushtunistan. You have invariably fought bravely in order to preserve your religion, honor and self-respect and inherent freedom, in the lofty mountains and in the extensive and fertile valleys of your dear country.

The Durani Afghans call themselves Ben-i-Israil, "Children of Israel," and claim descent from King Saul through a grandson named Afghana. They believe themselves descended from the tribes of Israel carried from Palestine to Media by Nebuchadnezzar. Persian is the language of the nobles and Mullahs. Turki is spoken in the north. Pushtu (like Persian) is the official language. The Nahazaras and some tribes are Shia.

Afghanistan was part of the old Persian empire until conquered by Alexander the Great. The pagan Kaffir tribes still faintly reflect Greek mythology. Later a Central Asian dynasty installed Buddhism in the land. The Arabs and Islam reached Afghanistan in the seventh century. Russia conquered Turkestan and Britain entered India. But Russia never crossed the Oxus whereas the British took former Afghan territory and thrice occupied Kabul, therefore becoming hated.

Afghan *provindahs* (gypsy merchants) travel between Peshawar and Turkestan. Fort Jamrud guards the Indian entrance to the Khyber. It was an old Sikh stronghold when Afghanistan included the Punjab and Kashmir. The Khyber is only 3,700 feet high but it is the most direct route from the north to India and where an invader would have to be met. The center of the pass is commanded by Fort Ali Masjid. The west end of the Khyber is controlled by a fort at Landi Kotal. The Indian border station, thirty-five miles west of Peshawar, is Torkham.

Jalalabad, in a fertile plain of the Kabul River, commands the Kabul-Peshawar road, the gateway to Kaffiristan and the northern trails to Kashgar. Babur laid out Jalalabad before he conquered India four centuries ago and the city was built by his grandson Akbar. The old walled town of Kabul, where the Kabul River cuts through the hills, is a huddle of crooked streets and mud houses. The city has expanded past its former walls but each street is walled as are most houses. Kabul lies beneath the snow-capped Hindu Kush. The name Kabul means "Sheepfold." It became a capital under Babur in 1504.

Local legend says a group of Hindu traders going from Samarkand to India were caught in the mountains by early snow and lost; that is how they got the name Hindu Kush (Hindu death). Alexander the Great found his wife Roxana in the Afghan hills.

Kabul is a brooding city. The bazaars resound with whispered rumors. This is a fanatical Moslem land. At the end of March and in early April the political temperature was extremely high; the King was on his way back; a plot against the cabinet was uncovered.

There is great economic distress and poverty. The Shias were irritated by the arrest of one of their mullahs and demonstrated *en masse* in Kabul. The Hazaras are a miserable downtrodden group. Some of the tribes are restive. Ex-King Amanullah and his collateral relatives are still a potential force to be reckoned with.

The Afghans claim cultural, racial and linguistic ties with Pushtunistan. They claim Pakistan's economic blockade and military threats reinforce their desire for Pushtunistan's independence. They claim Pakistan is continuing Britain's traditional policy of penetrating the tribal areas with the hope eventually of reaching the Hindu Kush.

The Afghan government is dominated by Pathans (all cabinet ministers but one) who do little for their own minorities. The Hazaras and Tadzhiks stride through Kabul in rags. There is no religious freedom.

The Pathan tribes—Waziris, Mohmands, Mahsuds and Afridis—could probably develop better under Pakistan and anyway they have no demonstrated feeling of unity among themselves. There are Mohmands and

Shinwaris on both sides of the Durand line. The Waziris are in Pakistan. The Suleiman Khels are mostly in Afghanistan.

The merchant class and the royal family have most of the national wealth. The royal family is from the Mohammed Zai tribe which is part of the Durani tribe from a region near Kandahar (west of Waziristan). Political power is held by a small group—the royal family plus Abdul Majid's gang. There is no constitution. This is an absolute monarchy and the national assembly was established by royal decree.

Pushtu is the official language, but that of the court is Persian. The Hazaras are Shias and Mongoloid, from the Oxus region.

KABUL, *April 15, 1950*

YESTERDAY at lunch I met the Indian ambassador, Wing Commander Rupchand, and his wife. She is a beautiful woman of about forty-five with magnificent eyes (blue-gray). She was wearing a bracelet of rose petals, other red blossoms in her hair, a white sari with red flowers embroidered on it, huge diamond earrings and a diamond stud in her left nostril. She told me they came from Lahore as penniless refugees after having been multimillionaires. (If ever I am a refugee I hope to salvage an equal number of diamonds.)

In the evening I went to the home of an American geologist named Walsh who is working on explorations for the Afghan government. Walsh showed various color slides he had taken around the country: ancient Arab iron, lead, copper, silver and gold mines and smelters. There are no comparable mines today and the modern Afghan cannot smelt as he could a thousand years ago. The technique was brought from the Mediterranean with Islam but destroyed when the Mongols of Genghis Khan and Timur overran the country.

Walsh, who has traveled all over, said the Uzbeks of Afghanistan cross often into Russian Uzbekistan and vice versa. They pan gold out of the Oxus tributaries and sell it in Russia for teapots—which they can't get here. Their normal gravitation is to the north rather than Kabul. Two-thirds of the Uzbeks live in Russian Uzbekistan, and on both sides of the border they dress alike and are indistinguishable.

From Walsh's photos it was apparent that most Afghans live in appalling circumstances: stone tumble-down huts; hide tents of nomads; and, in some valleys, in mud underground communities with high chimneys that are covered with snow all winter, the chimneys serving as periscopes to obtain air—land-bound snorkels.

KABUL, *April 15, 1950*

TODAY I had a long talk with King Mohammed Zahir Shah. He is a tall, saturnine fellow in his mid-thirties whose French is fluent but perhaps not as good as one might expect of a man educated in France. He was quite friendly but not especially at ease. This was the first interview he—or, for that matter, any Afghan ruler—had ever granted. Mohammed, who was wearing a double-breasted blue suit and striped shirt, had just returned to Kabul five days ago (because of the rumors of conspiracy to oust him) from a long trip in Europe and the Middle East. I suppose one might say he was quite friendly and informal, considering his autocratic powers. He is a dark, lean, brown-faced brooding man with mustache, bald head, crooked features, crooked nose, crooked smile. I would not trust the man behind that face. His voice is very soft. He smoked sparingly as we talked.

The audience occurred in the Royal Palace in the center of Kabul, a large nineteenth-century building in a walled compound guarded by tall Pathan sentries wearing German-type helmets and carrying rifles and packs. The sun was just setting behind the barren crags which surround this city and a blooming apple orchard in the royal compound glowed pink.

I was escorted to the King's study (through a hall carpeted with red Afghan rugs and lined with green-shaded lamps) by formally attired servants wearing karakul caps, a heritage from the days of the Mogul emperors. The King said Afghanistan required assistance, experts and capital from friendly nations, but did not wish to grant any individual concessions. Mixed capital enterprises controlled by Afghanistan would provide a better solution. Exploitation would be started on a limited basis designed to satisfy Afghanistan's own internal requirements at the start.

Turning to foreign affairs, the King said the Saadabad Pact, of which Turkey, Iran, Iraq and Afghanistan are members, still "exists in spirit," but must be "based on reciprocal sentiments." He said that to strengthen the bonds of Islamic countries, however, many mutual problems must first be ironed out. He referred especially to Afghanistan's present dispute with Pakistan. He said relations with Iran were "based on full friendship and we hope in the future will be even better," but that, "an impasse exists at present with Pakistan," which borders both countries.

The King said relations with the Soviet Union were "normal" and that communism had made no headway in Afghanistan because Islam was fundamentally opposed to that political theory and because there was no agrarian problem here or "great difference between the classes" (Nuts!). He said he was seeking to guide Afghanistan along a democratic path but "by little steps," in order to avoid disturbances. Social and economic advances were being gradually registered.

Mohammed Zahir Shah said peace was imperative to Afghanistan "because we need quiet and time to work and make up for our backward economic heritage. We will support all movements working for peace and all international organizations striving to safeguard it," he added. He said Afghanistan had no military alliances and sought none but was by tradition attached to the other nations of Islam.

Mohammed didn't know the techniques of "off the record" but made it clear he wanted to talk about some things that I should not write about. I stopped taking notes and then he burbled ahead quite easily. Here is the substance of this, more meaty conversation:

Russia is happily watching the Pakistan-Afghanistan dispute and would certainly intervene when it considered the right moment came, were things to get worse. Moscow makes propaganda here and when he referred to relations as "normal" he did not mean Kabul was pleased about them.

He favors a Moslem bloc but only after all Moslem states have ironed out difficulties with their neighbors and that is a long way off, unfortunately.

Afghanistan is fundamentally bound not only to Islam but to the West. No country can remain neutral in another war and he would favor the West.

We chatted about Paris, where he once went to school and which he loves. When I expressed admiration for Afghan hounds, the magnificent local dog, he promised me one. What the hell will I do with it?

KABUL, *April 16, 1950*

THIS morning I saw Prime Minister Sardar Shah Mahmud Khan, brother of the last King, uncle of the present one. He is a pleasant, smooth man who does not impress me as a quiz kid. It was curious in a chat after the interview to hear him referring to his family as "My nephew, his Majesty the King; my brother, His Royal Highness so-and-so; my nephew, His Royal Highness so and so."

He urged creation of a new independent country of Pushtunistan (or Pathanistan) embracing all of Pakistan's northwest frontier province and part of Baluchistan including the famous cities of Peshawar and Quetta. He said such a state would extend from Chitral, at the northwestern tip of Kashmir and just below the high Pamir passes, to Chinese Sinkiang and on down to Sind in the south. Its Western frontier would be the Durand line, the present border between Afghanistan and Pakistan. Its eastern frontier would be the Indus River.

The prime minister said no census had ever been taken in the area— which is at present a part of Pakistan—but the population of the state he envisaged would be about 7,000,000. He said the area was entirely inhabited by Pathans and Pathan tribes who are "brothers of the Afghan people."

Sardar Shah Mahmud is a member of the royal Mohammed Zai clan, a branch of the powerful Durani tribe. The reigning dynasty and almost all cabinet ministers and leading Afghan diplomats come from the Mohammed Zai. He is a softspoken, distinguished-looking man of medium height who speaks slow but careful English. He has two sons in the United States. Sardar Shah Mahmud received me in his private office within a compound guarded by soldiers wearing diagonally slung bandoliers of cartridges. The compound, facing towering crags on Kabul's perimeter, is also filled with blossoming apple trees.

"The people of Afghanistan and Pushtunistan are of the same blood," the prime minister said. (Actually less than 45 per cent of Afghanistan's estimated 12,000,000 people are Pathans or their kinfolk; there is a large population of Turki or Mongol origin.) He said:

> We regard the inhabitants of Pushtunistan as our brothers. There is no difference between us in culture or language. Years ago (first by the Sikh Empire, then by the British) they were divided from Afghanistan by force. Now that the entire world favors the freedom and independence of subject peoples, Pushtunistan should benefit. Pakistan, which only recently threw off British subjection, should not wish to be the master of Pushtunistan. The Pathans (Pushtu is the language of the Pathans), don't wish to be the slaves of Pakistan. Afghanistan has the right to champion their cause before the world. By the help of almighty God we hope to gain them their freedom.

The bazaar is filled with tawdry jewelry, silver bangles, lapis lazuli, bad emeralds and ruby chips, fighting partridges in cages, turban cloths and skull caps, rugs, camel bags, stalls where one can buy and eat lentils, kebab or fried entrails. The people are almost universally ragged but clean and colorful.

The last elephant in Afghanistan died about a year and a half ago; the Indians have offered a new one as a gift to the King but because of both India's and Afghanistan's troubles with Pakistan they couldn't get him in. The last two or three elephants were used by the King who liked to shoot ducks in swamps from their backs. That's what he wants a new one for.

In the afternoon I drove around Kabul with Mrs. Dreyfus. When we got back to the residence there was a great clamor going on. The master of the royal kennel had shown up with about fifteen Afghan hounds; I was to take my pick. They were splendid, huge animals but, rather to my astonishment, they were poorly cared for and even had ticks. However, they were marvelous dogs. To my regret I had to refuse (although there was one I dearly wanted: a golden-colored male, lean and shaggy). I got the embassy interpreter to explain my regrets to the puzzled kennel master. Obviously it would have been hard to take a huge hound around the world from Saigon to Tokyo to Alaska to Paris; and I doubt if *The New York*

*Times* would have enjoyed on my expense accounts items listed as food and transportation for One Afghan Hound.

JALALABAD, *April 17, 1950*

I came down here by bus; a hair-raising trip. Broken-down vehicle, overloaded with bearded, ragged, turbaned Afghans; rather high-smelling and given to furious debate, shouts and laughter. The bus spent the night in this eastern Afghanistan town and I found there was a Pakistan consul who was delighted to see me. He is completely isolated and watched like a criminal because of the bad relations over the Pathans. He gave me a burning hot curry, lots of whisky, a bed and a whirlpool of gossip about the Afghans, none of it favorable. His consulate is rather down-at-heels but Jalalabad is a pleasant, ramshackle town with lovely orchards and gardens, a pastel-shaded background.

I confess I am fascinated by the Pathans and their claims to statehood (somewhat like the Kurds or Armenians). Their Pushtunistan propaganda is of a curious sort, generally in poetry. Here are some recent excerpts:

The bulbul is complaining regarding his life. The cruel foreigner does not allow the bee to come near the foreigner . . . Heaven does not permit the lovers to have a sound sleep and a laugh.

I am lying on my sickbed and they do not apply ointment to my wound . . . Why talk of laughing. They do not permit me even to weep.

My sweet friend. I am not allowed to see you. You are a flower and I am a bulbul. They do not allow us to meet.

Pathan. I am addressing you. Get up. Get up with all your gallantry . . . You who are renowned throughout the world as a warrior; whose heritage is a sharp sword.

The most important warrior of the border, who has been raising hell for fifteen years, is Mirza Ali Kahn, Hadji Sahib, the Faqir of Ipi. A splendid name for a little man who lives in a cave.

PESHAWAR, *April 18, 1950*

DROVE into Pakistan from Jalalabad through the Khyber Pass in a screeching, swaying bus. The nomads are swarming over the Khyber from the fertile plains of Pakistan to the high Afghan plateaus.

As they have, since unremembered time; since before Alexander the Great found his wife Roxana in the foothills of the Hindu Kush and marched on to India; long before Genghis Khan and Timur trampled through the mountains with clashing cymbals, the wandering Afghan tribesmen are trudging northward towards Turkestan with their flocks in search of summer grazing.

Each year this vast migration occurs—southward in autumn and northward in spring—disregarding the rise and fall of national states, the creation and destruction of political frontiers. Rich, bearded Moslem chieftains, astride their nodding camels, ride on into the Punjab, pasture their herds, trade their intricately patterned rugs, leave their rifles registered at border checkpoints, and await the next seasonal northward trek.

Their tribesmen, their wives, their children, their flocks, camels and dogs attend them on the grazing grounds until they return from the bazaars of great cities like Peshawar and resume their endless march. To view this great migration in which 3,000,000 people participate annually traversing the rugged passes between Afghanistan and Pakistan, one journeys through dramatic scenery below the Hindu Kush range. Snow-capped peaks protrude into the horizon only occasionally interrupted by tiny green valleys and spreading sand marshes. Below, in Waziristan, the home of the indomitable Faqir of Ipi, little walled mud villages and square fortresses are separated by miles of sheer rock.

Valleys open up abruptly leading past ancient citadels, nestling beneath ruined medieval hillside walls; shaggy, rangy camels, sloppy-looking soldiers and occasional rare graceful long-eared Afghan hounds. Just below Buthkak caravanserai, its gusty courtyard filled with soldiers, donkeys, horses and bins of hay, the nomad caravans come up the road, alternating between tracts of mud and dust. The women wear no veils to hamper their march, trudging along with babies slung pickaback, balancing enormous bundles on their heads.

This is the lambing season for karakul sheep. Fierce bearded men stride along carrying newborn lambs. Donkeys, goats, sheep nibble the roadside grass. Tremendous camels amble forward, their heads nodding, carrying, tied lightly to their humps, sacks of babies—human, lamb, camel: too young to walk this spring, peering with friendly curiosity at the passing world.

Camel after camel, tall and shaggy, littered with lambs and children, tied together with home-made ropes, tassels upon their noses and hanging from their chin halters; ambling donkeys, hens squatting on their backs (the hen is not a peripatetic animal), lean brown men in rags, bearing babies in slings, a black-haired nomad woman in a red shawl, carrying a slender lute. Beside a bend squats a weeping woman head bowed over the sprawling carcass of her donkey, lying with saddle blankets still tied on, flies on its glazed eyes.

High barren peaks rim brown valleys terraced with occasional cultivable patches, from clouds of dust emerge long new strings of camels loaded with nodding karakul lambs staring at hawks circling high above. Turbaned drivers bearing rifles prod their camels with sticks while their womenfolk stagger beneath their head bundles or call aside ferocious sheep dogs. Monkeys chained to trotting donkeys run excitedly on all fours beside camels loaded with sacks of charcoal. Baby camels stagger beside, fur tufts wagging above their undeveloped humps.

The high Lataband Pass winds 10,000 feet above sea level, cutting through a bleak range spattered with snow. A blue-eyed little girl in a pink shawl, wearing a gold stud in her nostril, leads seven placid camels. Behind come six donkeys each bearing six black and gray lambs in saddle bags, followed by frightened donkey, ponies and tiny calves. A sick woman lies sprawled beside the road, her head pillowed in a sobbing crone's lap. Above, threatening clouds hang heavily on the peaks. A cluster of thin hawk-nosed women with stringy hair urges on a flock of goats and minia-ture bullocks carrying babies, gazing round-eyed, their heads covered in many colored skullcaps dangling silver ornaments from chains.

To the left, a family of cliff dwellers sits before the smoke-blackened entrance to their caves, munching a meal of unleavened bread. Unsmilingly a group of tough tribesmen marches by, guarded by armed men bearing rifles and bandoliers ornamented in silver.

In the valley a nomad camp sets up its camel's hair blankets on the mushroom-shaped framework of poles. Rain threatens. Mud-brick hovels look out on the green wheat fields; beady-eyed men sit on the sills of their square windowless homes; a little water mill grinds furiously, watched by a nervous canary in a twig cage hung from a poplar bough. Above stretches a sordid graveyard marked only with rocks at the head and feet of each body.

After crossing a muddy river ford, the road climbs through a gorge hemming in a smoking torrent. Lightning flashes overhead; thunder echoes in the canyons. The bus rushes madly down a narrow cliff-built road through driving sheets of rain. Great hailstones like grapes rattle off the roof and ricochet from the rocks. The nomads trundle on, shrouding their heads in shawls and turban cloths, shivering in sheepskin pushtins or camel's hair cloaks. A startled flight of doves zooms overhead as the downpour ceases and the valley broadens into a wide sandy plain dotted with shrubs. Thick stands of wheat emerge along clusters of trees and square fortress houses pitted with loopholes.

Before a roadside caravanserai sit thoughtful men sipping tiny cups of China tea, fingering Moslem beads and puffing long stems of hookahs. A mound of stones pointed towards Mecca marks a nomad grave on ground too hard to dig. The valley opens up again, green and fertile, beneath great basalt cliffs.

Long before dawn, the nomads break their camps. Sheep stroll darkly through a rocky cemetery. Light exposes the groves of shade trees and the shivering fields of grain as the sun slips up over the Khyber. Patches of purple and yellow flowers take color with the gathering light.

In the sleepy mud village of Dakka a ragged group of men in blue turbans, squatting on rope charpoy beds, sips tea and donkey's milk in a filthy lean-to tavern. Chickens scratch beneath them. A Pathan driver stops, douses his shaven head, then carefully rewinds his turban around a gold-threaded skullcap, squats, fills a hookah, and alternates puffs with two blanketed Afghans.

The green entrance to the Khyber opens up, studded with red poppies. Picket forts—stone-walled blockhouses built in the days of the British raj—mount a guard over the border. Fort Big Ben and Fort Little Ben perch on crags like medieval castles above two white pillars marking the famous Durand line—the Afghan border. Blockhouses strung with wire glower down on the frontier post at Torkham.

Inside Pakistan, toothlike tank barriers remain from the days when Britain feared Germany might drive through the Caucasus towards India. At Landikhana is the terminus of the old military railway where mule teams used to pick up supplies from Peshawar and Rawalpindi. A khassadar, with crossed bandoliers of cartridges, guards the side road near the caravanserai whose courtyard mills with donkeys and Pathan tribesman.

A band of the famous Khyber rifles, Pakistan militia, marches trimly by Landi Kotal as platoons exercise in a nearby field. Afridi villages with mud walls and watchtowers loom above the narrow gorge where Lord Roberts' troops were harried by Pathan marksmen. At Ali Masjid is a tree-girt Moslem shrine. Fort Shagai, once a powerful British base, looms up near the rock cliffs on which are set plaques honoring famous brave regiments of the past: the Second Battalion of the Baluchistan Regiment; the Sixty-second Punjab Regiment; the Second Ghurkhas; the Fifth and Sixth Rajputana Rifles; the Third Brahman Regiment; the Essex Regiment; the Seaforth Highlanders; the Royal Fusiliers.

From Fort Jamrud in the lowest foothills, looking like an earthen battleship, slopes the green Peshawar plain. Turbaned rifle-bearing khassadars lounge by the fortress gate. Nomads camp on the prairie in their mushroom tents, beside feeding camels, waiting for permission to cross the pass.

At journey's end, Peshawar: shade trees, green hedges and banks of flowers surround the overhanging noisy bazaar. Tilted tongas (two-wheel carts) trot by peddlers selling strings of jasmine. The old city smells of hookahs filled with mixed tobacco and molasses.

Caged partridges and fighting quail hang by alleys of silversmiths, goldsmiths, and cobblers working on embroidered shoes. Dominating the old town is the Sikh fort from which an Italian mercenary general used to hang a fresh body almost every day as warning. The Sikh temple tipped with trident nestles close by.

As evening slips along, sitting on the fine grass lawn, heady perfume sweeping out of banks of flowers, taps of hustling horse hooves echoing placidly, the tall Pathan in a karakul cap pours a drink, points at the dust clouds along the road running towards Afghanistan and the setting sun and says: "There go the nomads. It is spring."

PESHAWAR, *April 20, 1950*

HAVE had a fine time here. Major Letts (formerly British intelligence, but now an employee of Pakistan) put me in the Peshawar Club where I spent a couple of evenings when not working in my pleasant hotel bungalow. Letts, an amiable fellow, told me during the war his principal job was keeping tabs on my old friend Quaroni, then Italian envoy in Kabul. Quaroni's main mission was to stir the Pathan tribesmen against the British. Letts intercepted some of Quaroni's correspondence (in Persian) with the Faqir of Ipi. Quaroni was Ipi's paymaster and helped him get arms.

Letts also arranged a car and driver for me to go through the Malakand Pass up to Swat, a semi-independent principality. Its ruler used to be called the Ahkund, leading to a rhyme: "Who or why, or which, or what is the Ahkund of Swat?" Now there is a Wali, with whom I had a long talk.

It is a lovely drive through mountains, past rushing rivers in which I occasionally saw the rising backs of great fish and on to Saidu Sharif, capital of Swat, on the edge of snowy peaks that point toward China. Bees hum amid the honeysuckle. Horses are garlanded in jasmine. Poppies stud rippling wheat fields. Bubbling streams abound in mahseer, a handsome, firm-fleshed fish. Fierce-looking Pathans wear roses behind their ears. Children squat in the bazaars, nibbling sugar cane, while their mothers spin wool that comes from fine Merino sheep. The sun shines brightly in the happy valley of Swat.

All around are mountains, shutting off Pakistan's plains in the south, the little lands of Dir and Chitral in the west and north—and the Soviet Union beyond them—and troubled Kashmir in the east, leading on to China. Swat is not the land of Cockayne where sugar buns grow on trees but it is as near as one can get.

The ruler is the Wali, Mian Gul, Abdul Haq Jahan Zeb. Wali means "ruler" in Arabic. Mian Gul means "descendant of a saint." Jahan Zeb is a glorious Mogul imperial name. Wali Jahan Zeb succeeded to the throne when his father retired last year. The former Wali, now approaching seventy, rises daily at dawn to climb one of the nearby mountains.

The Wali, who is forty-two, received me in his up-to-date little one-story palace which is patrolled by a natty bodyguard of seventy-five men, well drilled and uniformed in British style. From above his desk, Jahan Zeb seemed dressed in ordinary English tweeds but when he rose to offer me a cigarette I discovered that instead of flannel slacks below his jacket he had on something like a large white diaper. He speaks good English and was most affable.

He said 90 per cent of Swat's half million population are Pathans of the Yusuf Zai tribe. Ten per cent are Kohistani Moslem converts from Buddhism. The only national trouble is occasional raids from the hereditary enemies, Dir and Chitral. Swat herdsmen and farmers take rifles to their fields. The main cities are Mingora (12,000) and Saidu Sharif (8,000).

Jahan Zeb says no one in Swat is interested in the Afghan-sponsored Pushtunistan (Pathanistan) movement.

> After all, we are all happy here. That is an Afghan idea and Afghanistan is an autocracy. Who would exchange democracy for autocracy? The trend of the whole world is toward democracy and that is the trend in Swat. We used to have an autocratic state but now it is a true democracy. Our *jirga,* a council of elders, meets whenever it wants and I and my cabinet of four abide by all their wishes. If they wanted a republic I would resign. But they seem happy; and I am pleased.

He has an army of 11,000 who keep their guns and uniforms at home. That's enough to take care of the Nawab of Dir and Mehtar of Chitral. There is no income tax. Exports exceed imports. Education to the tenth grade is free. Fifty new schools and several hospitals have been erected in the last five years.

"My people have more than enough to eat—and good things—wheat, rice, barley, sugar, ghee, honey," said the Wali. "Nobody has any major problems. There are less than ninety people in jail. Everyone comes to me if he has worries."

In Mingora market place my driver bought some ghee. While the shopkeeper was pouring the ghee from a vast iron cauldron, a shepherd came in with a bag of newly shorn wool, which he wanted to sell to purchase some honey. He was carrying his rifle and wearing crossed bandoliers of cartridges. I asked him how the world went. He said: "There is really only one problem of course. If the evil men of Dir covet our possessions, we will drive them off as we have always done. But we would certainly have a worry if Pakistan became involved in war. After all, Pakistan is our ally; and one must help one's friends."

In Saidu Sharif I bought some honey for Avra Warren who claims it is the best honey in the world; a small token of thanks for all his hospitality in Helsinki and Karachi. The honey merchant had no jar. I finally bought a huge jar in the bazaar and brought it back. Very carefully he poured the thick brown honey (filled with the corpses of bees) from a dipper which took it out of a kind of keg. It smells and tastes delicious!

LAHORE, *April 21, 1950*

BUMMED a ride from Peshawar along the northern route which Alexander the Great used as he invaded India from Afghanistan. Lovely spring, fields rippling. Lahore is a splendid city, a great red sandstone Mogul fortress which would have been a far more sensible capital for Pakistan than Karachi. Alas, it is too close to India. Wandered around town, after arranging a ride on to Delhi (there are no flights and the border's closed). It brings back pangs of Kipling to anyone of my generation: the cannon where Kim played, the newspaper office where Kipling wrote; the lovely cool evening; the scents of the bazaar; the jasmine; the lovely women with jewels in their nostrils.

NEW DELHI, *April 22, 1950*

TODAY I had lunch with Ambassador Loy Henderson. He had the following to say:

Nehru went down very well with the American people but not very well with the government during his trip to the United States. He was too vague and theoretical in his talk with Washington officials. He is a curious, vain and petulant man with certain very great qualities. For example he has a way of thinking out loud in a direct and honest manner which he can do to one person or a large crowd and in either case with an astonishing effect of winning support. He also has a direct mass appeal to the broad masses of India and has deliberately cultivated the thinking aloud method, which fascinates them.

Nehru, however, has certain inner secrets. He is strongly anti-American. This stems from several things. His governess when he was a boy came from the British middle classes and regularly hammered into his head the concept that Americans were vulgar, second-rate people. This, as his sister has confided, had an effect. Whenever an American was invited to the house, the governess would alert the children and then comment on the visitor's manners afterwards in a critical way. Secondly, Nehru is by nature a tremendous introvert and automatically resents the normal extrovert manner of Americans. Furthermore, he tends to look down upon them as cheap and nonintellectual. Nehru has been bitterly disturbed by American race attitudes and this has led to a strong and perhaps subconscious reaction of pride. All of this was reinforced in one way or another by his education at Harrow.

Nehru is by conviction a Socialist. He used to be a Marxist but now tends more towards the British form. Harold Laski had a very strong influence upon him. Nehru does not like the autocratic system of Russia but probably in his heart of hearts he is less anti-Russian than he is anti-American.

He is a man of great knowledge and also one who enjoys life. He is more fond of the company of women than of men, probably because he was brought up by and with women. He had a tremendous friendship with Lady Mountbatten which may even have been more than that.

Nehru is passionately loyal to his friends. Although his wife was from Kashmir and his own ancestors came from there, the primary reason for his personal interest in Kashmir is that he is a devoted personal friend of Sheikh Abdulla, whom he has appointed prime minister of Kashmir. In personal conversations Nehru always criticizes the United States and never Russia, but privately he says that if India could not be neutral in another world war, she would be on the side of Western democracy. Nehru opposes Communist tactics in India, but he does not criticize Communism in the broad sense, whereas he frequently criticizes the United States in public. He assails America for colonialism, racial discrimination and unequal distribution of resources. He says America has not yet recognized that European colonialism, no matter what its form, is only the domination of colored people by the West.

Nehru is obviously a complex personality with great and petty qualities. Personally, I have been struck by how badly he writes, but, of course, perhaps it is my own fault because I had expected something more. I find his literary style verbose, loose, disorganized and undistinguished. However, he has a profound amount of knowledge at his disposal. Henderson, in concluding his analysis of Nehru, said that he thought Liaquat Ali Khan would probably go down much better with American government officials than Nehru and much worse with the American people. Liaquat Ali is not a great man or a complex misfit, but he is a good, tough, practical business man, and therefore easier to deal with.

Henderson had two other slight comments on the fascinating character of Nehru. The first was that Nehru's is essentially a feminine personality. Secondly, that Nehru is very vain. He is bald and therefore almost always wears a hat.

NEW DELHI, *April 23, 1950*

THIS morning I had a long talk with Sir Girja Bajpai, who is the equivalent of permanent under secretary for foreign affairs in India (Nehru acts as foreign minister as well as Prime Minister). Sir Girja's exact title is Secretary General, Ministry of External Affairs, Government of India.

I had last seen Bajpai in Washington when I had lunch with him in 1942. Ambassador Henderson said Bajpai had told him he was very irritated with me about what I had written from Pakistan. I taxed Bajpai with this directly. He said he was not irritated; that he realizes a reporter has to report the situation as he finds it, that he merely was disturbed that Pakistan officials had said things which he thought might make implementation of the minority agreement more difficult.

Bajpai is a suave friendly little man, obviously extremely intelligent. He speaks excellent English in a soft voice. He did not look well; he carries too much soft weight for his tiny frame and has some curious disease of the hand; his long thin fingers seem to be shriveling and the skin is peeling off. He said:

We feel that in Indochina there is not one power but two—Bao Dai and Ho Chi Minh. We do not propose to recognize either one until one government is in effective control of the whole territory. We have listened to both sides. The Bao Dai people said they wanted to send a man here to present their point of view; he came and did so. Ho Chi Minh sent a man at the beginning of 1949 for similar reasons, but he sent no one since.

We naturally want to see a fully independent Indochina but our point of view differs from that of other powers, especially those of the West. India only recently won her independence. This enables us to deal more effectively with subversive forces such as Communists, than if we were sharing authority with the United Kingdom. Bao Dai is not generally recognized as representing a truly nationalist Indochina. Many people seem to prefer Communism to French control. The transfer of power by the French to Bao Dai has not been full and complete as was the transfer of power from Britain to India and Pakistan. So long as Bao Dai represents a façade it is impossible for real nationalist Indochina to support him.

We are not champions of Communism but we are champions of Nationalism. If the people of Indochina want Communism that is their business. We are not animated by any spirit of animosity towards the French. But in the year of grace 1950 the world must finish with colonial forms of any sort. Our interests are in nationalism and complete liberty of peoples—not in ideologies. We have already expressed such attitudes in the cases of Burma and Indonesia.

Bajpai said India has no military treaty with any nation. He explained India's relationship with the Commonwealth accordingly:

This is a result of the British genius for the anomalous. As far as we are concerned we made it perfectly clear that there could be no authority vested in the crown for either external or internal affairs of India. We had pledged this to our people years ago. But of course there is a common interest among various members of the Commonwealth, in this disintegrating world. So we proposed to continue as members of the British Commonwealth and to recognize the King as a symbol of free association although, from India's standpoint, he has no authority vested in him.

We are not participants of either side in the cold war. The more the world tends to line up on one side or the other the greater is the risk of conflict; you cannot divide the world politically into black and white or East and West. No useful purpose can be served by our getting involved.

We fully understand the attitude of and sympathize with those countries whose security has been jeopardized by Russian aggressive action. In our heart of hearts we recognize that despite our hopes it will be difficult for us to keep out. We do not like to talk about which side we would come in on, but I think the answer is evident to you.

There is much more of a field for cooperation, economic and otherwise, between us and the West, than between us and Russia. But nothing is to be gained by joining the crusade against Communism. That would simply mean that instead of the mild dose of abuse we now get from the Soviet Union, we should get more. I should think that from the point of view of its own policy it would be useful for the United States to recognize that merely because people do not shout against the Cominform it does not mean that they sympathize with it. The chances of conflict would certainly be greater if the world were to be totally and completely divided in two parts.

NEW DELHI, *April 25, 1950*

YESTERDAY evening I met Sirdar K. M. Pannikkar, India's envoy to China. He is an extremely intelligent man with an active mind. I had met him some years previously in the United States, but he has now grown a beard which appears to be deliberately modeled on that of Lenin and gives him rather a resemblance to that Russian leader.

Pannikkar was very distressed by American policy in Asia and by the manner in which it is presented, which offends Asiatic peoples. He said: "No country in Asia will accept to be bossed by America and any hint of such a desire by the United States causes immediate suspicion and hostility." He said the nations of Europe understood America better and realized that we were not trying to dominate. But they were nations with an older tradition of independence and therefore more self-confident. The peoples of Asia have just been finding their freedom and are extremely sensitive about it. There are frequently times when the United States wishes to sponsor a sensible move in Asia but phrases it in a way offensive to the sensitive people of these countries. Furthermore, statements made by American leaders primarily for local political consumption in the United States frequently boomerang out here.

Pannikkar said India has very little economic relationship with China. This has been the case for nine centuries—since Arabs first conquered India bringing with them not only Islam, but sea connections with the Middle East. In order to link the wealth of India with the Middle East they severed India's former maritime connections with China.

I spent the weekend in Agra, viewing the old fort built by Akbar and Shah Jehan's Taj Mahal constructed as a tomb for his beloved wife, Mumtaz Mahal, who died in 1631 after producing her fourteenth child. I must say I was rather disappointed. I simply don't like Mogul architecture.

The trip by car was fascinating, however. The country is entirely flat and rather sandy but large areas are cultivated. There seem to be many springs forming pools by villages, where water buffalo lie to get cool. The villagers have an astonishingly low standard of living—mud huts and flimsy hovels. There are many trees and huge flocks of cattle, buffalo, sheep, goats and quite a few camels, horses and donkeys. The road is rendered colorful by slowly ambling bullock carts with gaily colored awnings above. The hot dust smells of spice, rhesus monkeys play by the wayside under the trees, their babies clinging beneath them. . . . Shaggy black pigs root beside the road. Huge buzzards sit silently on tree tops looking for carrion. Green parakeets fly from branch to branch. Peacock cries echo at sundown. Cooing pigeons sound in the early evening and early morning. Rose bushes are in full bloom. This is the grain harvesting season and cattle trudge round and round treading on the wheat, threshing for the dusty villagers. At Agra the Jumna River is crowded with huge turtles and dainty cranes picking their way through the mud and crocodiles.

Last night, I saw Indian classical dancing for the first time and found it beautiful. These are sinuous abrupt dances, clanging with heavy jewelry and clashing in rhythm with abrupt musical chords.


NEW DELHI, *April 26, 1950*

YESTERDAY evening I had a talk with Pandit Jawaharlal Nehru, India's Prime Minister, and one of the heroes of the national struggle for independence. He received me in his private residence, a large comfortable building which used to be the home of the commander-in-chief of the Indian Army during the days of the British raj. We sat in a sitting room on the second floor in comfortable armchairs. Orange juice and cigarettes were served.

Nehru was wearing his usual jodhpurs and long coat of linen, but he did not have on his customary Congress cap. His bald head gives him a different appearance from when I saw him last at a Nepalese reception with his hat on. He was fairly friendly in contrast to my first meeting when he was irked about some stories I had written from Pakistan. He has a curious way of talking. It is indecisive and indirect. You ask him a question and he begins to answer it by talking continually in his famous "thinking aloud" method; but just when he seems to have reached the climax he stops. I was not exceptionally impressed. I started off by asking him what he thought should be American policy in Asia and he replied with the following oblique answer:

Our general approach to all these problems is governed by certain idealistic factors. Essentially it is one of having enough troubles to face at home, without taking up burdens elsewhere. Also it is the realistic approach of not saying something you cannot do.

By force of circumstances the United States has an economic responsibility to face. I can only tell you rather generally how we for our part try to act wherever possible. We think that generally speaking the problems of Asia cannot be solved by military means. However, they might be affected by military measures.

It is obvious that the people of Asia are in a state of acute mental change. They are more politically conscious because of the changeover from the period of colonial rule. Their first national reaction is to expect a betterment of their economic conditions. Primary problems of these undeveloped areas are things dealing with the primary essentials of life. Other matters are relatively theoretical.

Another primary urge is what might be called the nationalist urge. This, after the colonial stage, is strong.

That economic urge tends to make people inclined towards any policy or proposition that tends to realize or improve that condition—whether it is or not is another matter.

(I am quoting Nehru directly and as a result this sounds confused.)

Where the nationalist urge and the economic urge join, that produces a powerful movement. Where they tend to split up, there is weakness. It should be our purpose, therefore, to help and encourage the nationalist urge, plus giving it the economic content of future betterment.

The strongest "anti" feeling in these countries is the relic of colonial days and it is against any retention of colonial forms of control. These are the basic factors out of which we feel policy should grow.

Since Nehru had not answered my question on what American policy should be, I repeated it. He replied:

If you apply that it means encouraging national elements as such and helping them in so far as possible towards economic advance. These elements are split up. If sufficient incentive is given to national feeling plus economic advance that would attract many people.

I should imagine most intelligent people don't regard the United States as a colonial power. But I suppose there are plenty of people who have rather vague and undefined suspicions, mainly because the United States is a very powerful country economically and in other ways. Take the relationship of England and India today; there is not a ghost of a chance of their imposing any policy on us. I am not in the slightest degree afraid of such. But past suspicions remain.

I asked him about Russia and he replied:

There has been in India an impression on the one hand that in the past, chiefly in central Asia, the Soviet Union was a liberalizing force that raised the tone. Partly that was because of the frightfully backward conditions prevailing which gave a relative feeling of appreciation for cultural advances in that area. There were many people here who admired the cultural achievements of the Soviet Union but who do not like at all the tendency towards the suppression of individual freedom which apparently is growing more and more into what might be called a nationalist expansionist policy rather than the old style concepts of communism. This has created an adverse reaction among many people in India including many who were previously struck by cultural advances of Russia.

I asked him if Asia felt squeezed between the blocs of the United States and Russia. He said:

It is very difficult to distinguish between pure black and pure white. Maybe in a moment of crisis one would have to choose. That depends on the nature of this crisis. Naturally every country thinks in terms of its own survival and self-interest. Talk of crisis and another war is a council of despair. The prospect of a new war is too terrible to contemplate. Whatever other consequences there might be it would represent the degradation of the world. So one tries to avoid decisions, in terms of a crisis, to the utmost.

Obviously at the present moment our contacts, economic and otherwise, are far more with what might be called the Western countries than with others. They are our trade and support.

"To a good extent our political ideas and constitution have been derived from the West. To some extent also certain political ideas have been influenced by Socialist trends." But Nehru made it clear by implication that he did not mean "Stalinist." He said: "Our constitution may be considered as a kind of epitome of what we have been thinking. Our whole concept has been one of political democracy, but it has been influenced more and more by ideas of economic democracy."

On the subject of Pakistan Nehru said the two countries were so close in terms of geography and tradition that he thought they should draw together even more closely than two friendly countries like the United States and Canada. Partition had cut up a living entity—economic, psychological and cultural. Thousands of people on both sides were related to each other. The quarrel had the bitterness of a family quarrel but ultimately there must be developed common policies for economic, defense, transport, communications and irrigation affairs.

I asked him what he thought of the chances of Titoism in China. He gave me his usual indirect answer: "Countries like China and India, not only by reason of their bigness, but also by reason of the essential national characteristics which are deeply imbedded, can hardly be expected to function on behalf of someone else. They may be affected by outside forces but they are bound to find some kind of level in keeping with the national genius. In the long run this is bound to happen." Nehru said he was certain China could not grant prior allegiance to another country—meaning Russia.

Nehru said the Soviet Union "more and more" is following "a nationalist expansionist policy rather than the old-style concepts of communism." He said the problems of Asia "cannot be solved by military means."

He said "the people of Asia are in a state of acute mental change. They are more politically conscious than ever before as a result of the change-over from the period of colonial rule. Their first reaction is to expect a betterment of their economic condition. I refer to things dealing with the primary essentials of life."

NEW DELHI, *April 26, 1950*

DR. Rajendra Prasad, first President of India, sixty-four, now above politics, talked with me at length. Prasad is affectionately known to most Indians as "Rajen Babu"—a diminutive term. He is a well-built man of medium size and tan complexion with a sweeping gray mustache, twinkling brown eyes and a hawk nose which dominates his handsome countenance. The interview took place in his residence, Government House, last inhabited by India's governor generals before it became a republic. Prasad was wearing cool white thin trousers and a long jacket and the traditional "Gandhi cap."

Commencing an amiable conversation over cups of coffee, Prasad said that India was still suffering from certain food shortages. But he added:

We are working hard to overcome this insufficiency which forces us to import a great deal of rice, wheat, maize, millet. Our program has a twofold aspect. We are increasing production by expanding irrigation and the output and use of artificial fertilizers. Furthermore, we are making extensive use of rationing to insure just the distribution. By the end of 1951, I hope we will no longer have to import any food at all.

Prasad said communism had not been outlawed by the national government but was banned by certain provincial administrations not for ideological reasons but because it was "actively trying to create confusion and overthrow the government." The Communists had sabotaged railways and "murdered hundreds of people." Communist partisans in the hills of Madras and Hyderabad were being hunted down by armed military police.

RANGOON, *April 29, 1950*

THIS will recapitulate the last few days. I left New Delhi on April 27, after spending the final morning sight-seeing in Old Delhi. I wandered

down the Chandni Chowk (silver street). Stark naked Sadhus, burned black
by the sun, swung along on hands and knees on curious pilgrimages. Other
Sadhus, dressed, with wild long hair and beards, gesticulated with continual
emphatic mysterious gestures. Still others pushed through the crowd waving their brass mendicant bowls. Sacred cows lay in the shade of the
bazaars blocking the sidewalks. Public scribes squatted before customers
for whom they wrote letters. Peddlers sold cut, iced sugar cane; candy,
cucumber, nuts. A holy man (*Sanyasi*), dark black, up from the south,
with long white hair and white caste marks on his forehead, pushed along
swinging his brass pot. A Sikh in blue turban stalked morosely along the
street wearing a huge saber in a scabbard. Piles of jasmine and yellow
flowers were heaped up in baskets. Village women hurried by clasping
silver fringed shawls about their heads. Beggar women, screaming "Sahib,
Sahib," extended wriggling babies in their withered arms. At the Shri
Lakshmi Narain (Birla) Temple lazy Hindus slept stretched in the shade
under the bellies of great stone elephants in the garden. The temple is
hideously ugly.

After a flight via Calcutta and a brief stop in Bangkok I arrived in
Rangoon April 28 and was met by George Edman and Ruth Lewis of the
embassy. That evening I dined with Ambassador David Key and a Burmese editor named Ed Law Noon.

Rangoon, paradoxically, considering the situation, means "end of
strife." It is a steaming hot city on the Rangoon River in the midst of the
rice-growing area. It is filled with orange- or yellow-robed monks (*pon-
gyis*) with shaven heads and parasols, hurrying to the magnificent gold
pagodas. Bananas, coconuts, palms, gardenias, jasmine are only part of the
luxuriant foliage. Tomorrow is a Buddhist holiday and crowds danced
slowly through the streets, chanting, waving flags and fans, beating wood
drums and xylophones, playing pipes, parading towards the Big Pagoda,
the women walking straight balancing on their heads pots of water for the
holy tree of Buddha.

Ancient barouches vie with rickshaws in the streets. Beneath the Gold
Pagoda, tinkling in the breeze, monks toy with parasols, shops sell gilded
lacquer gifts for the shrines. Some statues are ornamented with the famous
rubies from the north. Cottages of bamboo thatch stand by lakes filled with
water lilies. Huge palm trees, lavish flowers. Villages of bamboo and lattice
work on stilts. Huge fierce-eyed Buddha looming out of palm tree jungle.
Men in colored cylindrical skirts. Pagoda temples filled with shops. Shwe
Dagon Pagoda, with a huge golden peak, dating back to 585 B.C. Striking
gongs. Offerings of flowers for future world happiness. Umbrella offerings
to avoid danger. Belled tip of pagoda rings in wind. Priests beat gong above
money box. Ornately carved teakwood temple. Bronze and alabaster Buddhas in mosaic temple of colored glass. Priests and women sit on temple

mats smoking cheroots while dogs sleep among naked feet of idlers. Ancient huge bronze ball. Kneeling worshippers intone prayers.

RANGOON, *April 29, 1950*

THIS afternoon I had a long talk with Herbert Spivack, secretary of the American embassy, and his Burmese wife. They said that in February Special Envoy Philip Jessup was here and recommended that Burma be left to "stew in her own juice." There has been a big change in embassy thinking since then and the evaluation of the situation is more optimistic. To some degree this is reflected in Washington but Burma is still low on the global priority list. However, it is recognized in Southeast Asia as the second most dangerous point (after Indochina).

The country is wracked by several civil wars. More of Burma is out of government control than under it. But the government is not as strongly threatened as last year although much sabotage continues. The situation is still very chaotic. The government hasn't defeated the insurgents; it just pushes them away and uses up their ammunition.

No nationwide economic or agricultural program can be carried out yet. There is constant danger of attack. Travel is almost entirely by air.

RANGOON, *April 30, 1950*

LAST night I had dinner with Burma's strong man, General Ne Win (later dictator), who commands all army and police forces. He is a good-looking young man (forty) in the Chinese fashion; clearly very vain and ambitious, by no means brilliant, obviously an opportunist (he fought with both the Japanese and the Allies), certainly energetic. We sat up until 3 A.M. talking and drinking. He is short, stocky, has a good sense of humor and ready laugh, but I am told he has a quick temper and can be cruel and brutal; is given to coarseness.

Also there was his friend, U Aung Than (or Bo Set Kya) and his lovely young wife, a doctor. U Aung Than was also in Japan with Ne Win where they were part of a group of thirty-one who trained with the Japanese army and helped invade Burma after Pearl Harbor. They said the training, mainly in Hainan, was tough but good. The Japanese made a great mistake when they came to Burma, pushed the people around, slapping them frequently, and forcing the priests to climb trees and bring down coconuts. U Aung Than is much like a Ghurkha in appearance. He is a wealthy businessman who is playing in close with Ne Win and the government. He speaks many languages including German which he learned in Japan. Both U Aung Than and Ne Win are strongly anti-British and seem anti-Russian. U Aung Than was extremely interesting on the subject of Buddhism which he says does not believe in God, uses idols only to remind people to do good, does not believe in beginning or end or heaven or hell, believes only in ethics, does not believe in repentance for sins; what you have done is done, whether good or bad. He says it is a most impractical religion and because of its nonresistance credo caused Burma's fall to British rule.

Ne Win predicted that Burma's complex civil war would be ended by a government victory before the end of this year. He said negotiations were now going on secretly between leaders of the Karen rebellion and the government and that "more than half the Karen rebels will come over to our side soon. The Karen revolt will be over before the monsoon ends in September." The monsoon season of heavy rains and bad campaigning starts this month.

Ne Win, who was born in Prome, originally intended to become a doctor. However, he had a dispute with his British biology professor and eventually drifted into left-wing politics. He became a postal clerk and then joined the Thakin party of nationalists. In August 1941, he went to Japan with a group of Burmese nationalists under Bogyoke Aung San, Burma's great hero, and experienced his first military training as infantryman. He gained battle experience in the Burma campaign against the Allies but later turned against the Japanese. He rose rapidly from battalion commander to colonel, then to general and assumed the national command when the Karens revolted and all Karen officers were ousted from Burma's army.

Ne Win spoke openly and willingly in fluent English. He was wearing a light jacket and a cylindrical man's skirt (*longyi*), which is the national garb.

I asked him what Burma would do if the Chinese Communists attacked this country or sought to infiltrate en masse in order to aid the white flag Communists. He replied: "Anybody who tries to come in by force will be opposed by force. We will fight them with everything at our command."

RANGOON, *April 30, 1950*

TODAY I had lunch with Sao Hkun Hkio, Sawbwa of Mongmit, the young Shan foreign minister of Burma. He is a small, bespectacled man with a bland, broad face. He was educated in England. The Sao (prince) is also minister for the Shan States. He is pretty much a figurehead and front man; not a real power.

Discussing the present foreign policy of Burma's Marxist-Socialist but anti-Soviet government, he admitted that no accurate demarcation of the frontier between China and the Kachin portion of Burma had ever been agreed upon, but said the Communist regime in China, which Burma recognized before any other non-Communist nation, had made no claims.

BANGKOK, *May 2, 1950*

THIS afternoon I saw Field Marshal Pleak Phibul Songgram, ex-dictator (and potential new dictator), present premier and former pro-Japanese boss of Thailand. He was very friendly and suave but didn't impress me much. However, I know that beneath his amiable delicate exterior, he is an exceptionally ruthless and tough little man.

Phibul is small, frail, with tiny hands and feet and quick smile. He received me in an office hung with Siamese legendary paintings and filled with large ivory carvings and ornamental elephant tusks. He was wearing a tropical white suit and spoke Siamese through an interpreter in between sips of Coca-Cola. He has one son in Thailand's Washington embassy; another is assistant military attaché in London. He professed great friendship for the West. From 1924 to 1927 he studied military science in France.

The field marshal said he intended to request alliances with the Western powers very shortly. He added that if Thailand is attacked from abroad: "We will fight to the best of our ability—even if China is behind the aggressors. Our people cannot accept a Communist regime or foreign domination willingly. Under existing circumstances the only threat to us could come from the communists."

The prime minister explained that a curious communiqué issued by his office on April 29 announcing "preparations for a possible state of war" was designed to provide a legal basis for the declaration of martial law.

BANGKOK, *May 3, 1950*

ON May 1 and May 3, I had long talks and drinks with Sir Geoffrey Thompson, British ambassador and an old friend. He said the big fear of Thailand is China. The Thais regard the Kuomintang and the Communists as the same—representatives of a dynamic nationalist China.

The Allies must hold Indochina. It is too late to worry about "colonialism" now. Otherwise we will lose Southeast Asia. There are about 30,000 good British troops in Hong Kong. If attacked by China they won't sit tight but will march in and take Canton. The big danger in Hong Kong is that of Trojan horse tactics; hand grenading has already started. The British closed the doors too late on infiltrators.

Phibul is playing well with the Allies. By indirection, the United States hinted to him he would qualify for loans if he recognized Bao Dai. He caught the point and did. However, many American OSS veterans here are anti-Phibul because of his record with the Japanese. Actually he doublecrossed Tokyo but the OSS strongly supported the Free Thai movement, which was valuable in intelligence.

The British planters in Malaya are being magnificently brave and equally stupid. The French are fed up in Indochina and are beginning to think America and Britain want her to "fight to the last Frenchman"; they want more than material aid. The conquest of Hainan by Chinese Communists allows their agents to penetrate more easily into Indochina and Malaya.

World War III is already under way but we don't understand the fact. The Russians have technicians in China; the United States has its arms missions in Asia.

Peking radio is now violently attacking the Thailand government as a "tool" of the western imperialists. It claims the Chinese minority is being oppressed. The Chinese colony in Thailand has always sent large remittances home to relatives in China. Since the fall of Canton they have been buying American dollars here to send to their families. The families are forced by the Peking regime to trade them in at one American dollar for one Hong Kong dollar (instead of one to six).

BANGKOK, *May 4, 1950*

SEVERAL long talks with the American ambassador, Edwin Stanton, an old China hand. He is a pleasant, thin man of calm steady appearance and amiable, confident but modest manner. He said Phibul is a dictator type. Before and during the war he was a definite dictator. He decreed when people should get up and how to dress. He is a great nationalist; he tried to nationalize everything. He is anti-Chinese and during the war introduced restrictive measures against them. He has a big following in the army. He introduced "fascist" type youth movements. He collaborated with the Japanese. He was tried as a war criminal but the whole matter has now been conveniently dropped. Today the Thais say, "The tiger has lost his claws." He talks much about observing democratic principles of government. His administration is fairly liberal. He walks softly in domestic matters and his arms are stretched to the West in foreign affairs.

In 1939 Phibul decided Siam should be changed to Thailand; an emphasis on nationalism, stressing the Thai people as distinct from minorities. After the war it was changed back to Siam, the ancient name, but when Phibul came back in 1948 he pushed for the change and in 1949 it was again Thailand. Thai means "free" in Siamese. The Thais have no inferiority complex compared with ex-colonial countries and their attitude towards whites is quite independent.

BANGKOK, *May 4, 1950*

BANGKOK is a city of canals, rickshaws, lattice-work houses filled with fret-sawn wooden scrolls, and open, Chinese style buildings.

Buddhists bring lighted, incense-tipped joss sticks, often wrapped in gold leaf, to the Wat Prakaeo temple, home of the famous emerald Buddha. . . .

The canals are filled with rushing sampans; this is the Venice of the East and the gondoliers have the same motion as their Italian brothers. . . . The canals are covered by little arched wooden bridges and lined with jerry-built wooden houses lifted on stilts to protect them against the monsoon rains. . . . Open-sided white buses trundle through the main streets. . . . Women stagger along under yokes hanging with buckets of coconut husks by fields of bright green grass and fruit orchards. . . . Little grocers' shacks are heaped with mangoes; durian, a large fruit smelling like rich cheese; burry-skinned rambutan; lotus, famed for its seeds which are eaten like nuts or stuffed in meats as special delicacies. . . .

Wat Prakaeo is a jumble of ornate spires and phallic Phrangs, stretching around the many-tiered temple roof ending in gabled representations of Naga, the sacred King Cobra, looking like the prows of ancient Viking ships. . . . Nearby is the famous Amarin throne hall with its magnificently proportioned roof and mosaics of porcelain tile and colored bits of glass. . . . Each evening, at sundown, millions of frogs begin to croak. . . .

The Wat Poh temple in the palace grounds contains a black Buddha, crowned in gold, seated behind black and gilt lacquer doors. Hindu gods are everywhere mixed with relics of Buddhism, verifying the name of this Indochinese peninsula. The Ramakirti is the Thai version of India's Ramayana. In one temple is a cloister of nineteen golden seated Buddhas. The courtyards are filled with holy and mundane Chinese statuary brought back as ballast in olden days by Siamese rice and teak merchants in their empty ships.

Another door of Wat Poh is inlaid with mother-of-pearl on lacquer, showing the brave fight of Siam's violent ancient gods. . . . The architecture is ornate; the roofs are fantastic mosaics of green, yellow, blue and red. The huge golden reclining Buddha lies on his side, crammed in a claustrophobic temple, lying on a mosaic pillow of blue, green and gold, with his toes and soles made of mother-of-pearl mosaic set in black, traced with designs of Hindu gods, cows, elephants and cobras.

Not far away is a porcelain Phrang of green, yellow and red flowered design. . . . Yellow- and orange-robed priests wander about with paper parasols shielding their shaven heads. . . . The Chao Phya River banks are lined with Buddhist stupas, pagodas and Phrangs. . . . Everywhere are banana and palm orchards, bougainvillea, brilliant orange trees called "Flame of the Forest," jacaranda, hibiscus, planted beside unpainted board houses of curious shape, rambling beside canals filled with sampans and junks.

Peddlers with huge conical hats and yoked trays of goods trot along in the burning sun while passers-by greet each other silently with folded hands in attitude of prayer. . . . Wat Arun (the temple of the dawn) is made of mosaic pottery shards set in loose cement. . . . The streets are full of silversmith shops. In the Thieves Market, where many goods on display were recently stolen, opium dens with wooden bars stink in the corners, filled with almost naked Chinese men, fanning and puffing or languidly dreaming of happiness. . . . In the Sam Peng, wholesale cloth dealers, mostly Chinese, shading their narrow alleys from the sun, while lovely Siamese girls throw entrails to hideous crocodiles basking in a temple pool covered with thick green slime. . . .

At home both men and women wear nothing but cool sarongs but in the streets Western dress is the fashion.

SAIGON, *May 8, 1950*

FRENCH intelligence has received information indicating that Ho Chi Minh's rebel Viet Minh "government" has concluded a secret military agreement with Mao Tse-tung's Communist regime in China. It is believed this provides for accelerated arms deliveries. Chinese Communists captured 60,000 rifles as well as other large stocks of equipment at Hainan, much of which might be useful to the Communist cause in Vietnam. France is strongly urging the United States to speed up deliveries of arms and especially of aircraft to its forces in Vietnam.

The French feel they are the only fighting force on hand to oppose the extension of dynamic communism towards Southeast Asiatic areas of vast interest to the West. Therefore, they argue the least Washington can do is to make available more equipment and economic aid.

SAIGON, *May 9, 1950*

SAIGON is a tranquil city of assassination. A spacious town with wide boulevards, resembling many French Mediterranean settlements, business and pleasure go on as usual, despite the bloody civil war.

Late every afternoon sidewalk cafés fill up. Restaurants, dance halls and gambling establishments do active trade. French and Vietnamese housewives shop in well-stocked stores. Coolies pedal their bicycle rickshaws through complicated patterns of traffic. French, Vietnamese, colonial and foreign legion soldiers stroll leisurely—bearing no sidearms.

And yet, almost daily some individual on Ho Chi Minh's "death list" is suddenly murdered by a chosen executioner. Hand grenades are rolled down movie aisles or pitched into unsuspecting groups of innocents. And at sundown, on the city's outskirts, the crump of mortars and occasional rattle of machine guns remind this nerveless city that right on its borders guerrillas are ready to carry out their nocturnal trade.

From a military point of view this combined "terror" and hovering menace of formal operations is not regarded as important by the commanders of the French and Vietnamese forces. They do not intend to be swayed from their major plan of cleaning up the key Red River valley in Tonkin and strengthening defensive positions near the Chinese border.

But politically, the continual threat of Vietminh reprisals keeps the Vietnamese population in a constant state of agitation. Early this month, when Premier Long and his successor Huu were speaking at Saigon's Town Hall on the anniversary of Bao Dai, a champagne cork popped. Everyone present ducked instinctively. It is that instinctive gesture of fear which is ubiquitous behind the placid exterior of Vietnam's capital.

To eliminate this is more than a military problem. Indeed, despite the successes of General Carpentier's forces, high French civil officials frankly admit the situation is deteriorating.

Recognition of Bao Dai by the Western powers was offset by the Eastern bloc's support of the Vietminh. The rapid collapse of Hainan encouraged Ho's propaganda line that his Communist-led victory is inevitable. There is an increasing number of Frenchmen saying that Paris will eventually have to abandon even any shadow claims to this portion of the world.

The American attitude is to give the Indochinese states of Vietnam, Laos, Cambodia more self confidence—so they can "sell" themselves to their peoples—and to urge them to send diplomats abroad including to the United States. We have been quietly urging the French to liberalize their stand on distribution of American aid, to speed up the transfer of powers as provided under the March 8 agreements, to expand the sectors of Vietnamese control and to give local government authority over the customs and exchange.

The United States attitude appears to be that the French, who are taking heavy casualties, cannot be pushed too hard. The French feel they are defending over-all Western positions in Malaya, Singapore and the Philippines against the Communist juggernaut and are certainly not anxious to see the rich United States grab all credit here as "benefactor" to Vietnam.

SAIGON, *May 10, 1950*

THERE is no doubt that soft-voiced little Ho Chi Minh, a man of simple personal habits, undoubted bravery and vast stubbornness, has captured the mind of a vast number of Southeast Asian peoples still struggling to shrug off the last vestiges of nineteenth-century colonial subjugation. There is also no doubt that Ho Chi Minh is a Communist.

Ho Chi Minh, whose name means "The one who shines," adopted his *nom de guerre* (Asiatic equivalent of Tito or Stalin or Lenin) shortly after Japanese troops occupied French Indochina in 1940. His real name is Nguyen Tat Thanh, and like many other professional revolutionaries he has had various pseudonyms in the past—at least seven of which are known.

He was born about sixty years ago in the small village of Kim Lien in North Annam. Annam, which has been amalgamated by the French together with Tonkin and Cochin China, into Vietnam, is tradionally famous for producing rebels. He was brought up in a revolutionary environment. His sister, Nguyen Thi Thanh, and his brother, Nguyen Tat Dat, were both sentenced by the French for aiding revolts.

In 1911 Ho (Nguyen Tat Thanh) shipped aboard the French merchant-man *D'Artagnan* and visited France, Britain and the United States. In 1919 he settled in Paris and worked as a photographer's assistant. He dabbled in journalism and novels and became acquainted with the French Marxist leftist leaders of the period including Vaillant-Couturier and Marcel Cachin, now dean of the French Communist Party. When the French Socialist Party split, he went with a group joining the Third International (Communists). He left Paris for Moscow in 1923 as a delegate to the Peasants International Congress.

After two years in Moscow he went to Canton as interpreter for the Borodin mission seeking to establish a Soviet state in South China and while there created the "Annamite Section of the League of Oppressed People." Although by then well versed in Marxism, Ho stressed nationalism in his propaganda on the grounds, as he explained in 1927, that "no one would understand the meaning of the word Communism in Indochina."

That same year, Ho returned to Moscow and trained in special Comintern political and military courses. In 1928, he went to Siam (Thailand) and sought to organize an Annamite community there. He then moved to Hong Kong where he headed a South Asia bureau for the Comintern under that body's Oriental bureau. He was arrested and imprisoned eighteen months by the British in Hong Kong after journeying as far as Singapore in his revolutionary pursuits.

In 1940, he reappeared in South China—first in Yunnan, then Kwangsi. He organized his Viet Minh (Viet Nam Doc Lap Dong Minh Hoi) the following year, more or less along the traditional Communist-led "Peoples Front" lines familiar in Eastern Europe.

After the German attack on the Soviet Union, he issued a manifesto on October 25, 1941, summoning all good nationalists to attack the Japanese. There was no mention of France. The Vichy regime was collaborating with the Axis, but the Gaullists were allied to the Great Powers. Viet Minh was given assistance by Chiang Kai-shek's Kwangsi commander, Marshal Chang Fa Kwei.

However, the latter turned against Ho and imprisoned him. After his release, when the Chinese sought to obtain suzerainty over Tonkin—South China's normal outlet to the sea via the Red River—Ho joined as a Minister the "republic" of Vietnam proclaimed in March, 1944, at Liao Chiao. He crossed the border into Tonkin with seven hundred armed partisans and led the local uprising that November.

When the Japanese collapsed, they passed on arms and equipment to the

Viet Minh and sought to encourage civil war. Ho acquired all material possible before making his final play. He was aided at first by Chinese nationalists, awarded the occupation of Northern Indochina by the Potsdam agreement. Emperor Bao Dai, who had remained in office under Vichy and Japan, abdicated on August 28, 1945, "regretting" the twenty years of his reign.

When French troops under Leclerc returned to that country early in 1946, a convention was signed between Ho's "government" and France. However, it was evident from the start that resumption of the French hegemony did not suit the book of the Moscow-trained national revolutionary. The Viet Minh secretly embarked on a program to drive all the French from Vietnam territory and "whatever agreements may be signed . . . the present instructions are the only ones to be complied with."

Likewise, French policy, no matter how dressed up, is as Ramadier (then prime minister) said: "France must remain in Indochina." Between these fundamentals is a gap which cannot well be bridged.

Even if the situation remains only static, it is clearly to Ho's advantage. He has on his side an immensely popular slogan created by the Japanese: "Asia for the Asiatics." The appeal of this to the general public has not yet been affected by realization that the Soviet Union is an imperialist state; or that Stalin is on record as saying "I too am an Asiatic."

SAIGON, *May 11, 1950*

I have been here for several days staying with Ed Gullion, American chargé d'affaires. The situation is very confusing. I have little use for the Indochinese whom I have met and I must say I cannot blame the French for being rather irritated with them although, on the other hand, the French are not being too bright themselves. Several people have told me that most of the troops here are either Foreign Legion (largely Germans) or colonials. The French army seems to be doing pretty well in the north.

The Vietnamese are supposed to handle security around here but don't make much of an effort. Every night we hear machine gun and mortar fire from our house. Catlett and Glazer sleep with pistols beside them. Gullion has a crossbow which probably wouldn't do him much good because it takes him about five minutes to load it. Almost every day some character gets knocked off or a few hand grenades are rolled around the town but it is surprisingly calm and doesn't seem to interfere with normal life in the least.

One evening, after many drinks, I challenged Gullion to show his proficiency with the crossbow which he claims is better as a defensive weapon because it is silent. He brought down the weapon (a Montagnard model), took off his shoes, lay down on his back in the yard (not waking up the sleeping Vietnamese sentry furnished by the French), put the bow against his feet, pulled back the string, aimed at a tree, let go. He missed the tree by a yard and let out a tremendous yell. Somehow he had almost cut off a toe.

SAIGON, *May 12, 1950*

A foolish escapade. After our crossbow interlude Gullion and I decided to tour the Cholon (Chinatown) gambling and night club halls. He, poor fellow, had never been, having worked so hard. I became quite fascinated by a lovely young lady (the Vietnamese girls are entrancing) and also wholly plastered. This morning I woke very early on a palm-lattice bed. When I wanted to leave; she insisted I stay, whispering to be silent and to make no move until the regular daytime bustle started because the Viet Minh was all around. I asked where I was. Discovered myself in a village some miles out of Saigon. Later in the morning she arranged a hitch on a truck and then I got a pedi-cab home. Rather sheepish.

SAIGON, *May 12, 1950*

BAO Dai, chief of state of Vietnam and former Emperor of Annam, told me today that, as soon as this country has been "pacified," he would call for a national referendum on its political future. People would be able to freely express their choice of government. He is prepared to accept any popular decision; republic, monarchy, or other administrative form.

"I don't want to impose any kind of regime" he said. "I left the country in 1945 for precisely that reason; I wished the people to have a chance to decide. I came back only to facilitate the liberation of the nation and when that has been accomplished, the people themselves must decide on the type of regime they want—freely and openly."

Bao Dai said Vietnam regards the March 8, 1949, agreement with France, governing the status of this country, Laos and Cambodia in the French Union, as "a base for relationships, but not a definite treaty." He added that Vietnam accepted participation in the French Union on an independent basis and that any future discussion of such relationships must await complete "pacification."

Bao Dai received me in Lagrandiére Palace. After a hesitant start, he spoke freely in fluent, but accented, French. He is a plump, sleepy-looking man. I wouldn't die for anything he sponsored.

Bao Dai said he thought 80 per cent of the Vietnamese population now supported him. (It is interesting to note that Ho Chi Minh's spokesman claims approximately the same backing.)

He argued the proof was that "populations of villages liberated by operations in the North are demanding arms to protect themselves against Viet

Minh. About 150,000 people a month are now coming over to us from areas the Viet Minh had dominated."

Bao Dai hoped the United States would be able to provide small arms directly to Vietnam in order to provide local defense militias; that, later, heavy weapons and specialists, in accord with the French, would be sent to build up a defensive army.

> The situation is far better than when I returned a year ago. Hanoi has been cleaned up as well as most of the cultivated area in the North. In Hanoi alone, a thousand people daily are coming over from the zone occupied by the Viet Minh. We must have assistance to face economic, medical and social problems. Direct help to us from the United States will be used for such immediate needs while other assistance will come through the French Union.

## TOURANE (LATER DANANG), *May 13, 1950*

WE lunched at 4 P.M. Lingua franca at Tourane is German (Foreign Legion). The French liaison officer explained to me that the place was going to pot (it isn't as bad as all that); that grenades and shells would go off at night (they didn't although there were plenty of noises); that the Germans (legionnaires) were the best troops they had around but that when they came to town they raped, they looted and murdered; that the French army out here was lousy and all spit and polish (I saw regrettably few signs of spit or polish).

An amiable but decidedly suspicious Frog gave me a case of champagne so we drank it eight of us (including an RAF crew) and had a whale of a political argument with the skipper, an old public schoolboy turning out to be a rabid Socialist and the sergeant, a rabid Conservative. We stayed all night. Punctuation of distant mortars, occasional German curses. Staggered into our plane early Saturday morning, and flew silently to Hong Kong through an impossible fog and a rather hair-raising blind landing between hills.

## HONG KONG, *May 15, 1950*

IT has been rather amusing, staying with Karl Rankin and his wife (he is consul general here now), going out to Chinese restaurants. The situation is pretty calm although everybody figures that after Formosa goes maybe the Communists will start some fifth column operations in Hong Kong. Right now occasionally they throw hand grenades around; but it is a big city and this doesn't seem to cause any disturbance.

I had a talk with the governor general, Sir Alexander Grantham. He said he felt the British army was strong enough to "deal with any external attack or any Trojan horse tactics even though things get uncomfortable.

We had the experience of 1925 when the Chinese authorities laid down an economic blockade and we had a general strike. No ship was allowed to go from here to China or to come from a Chinese port. But we survived although we were not then so well prepared for it as we are today."

TOKYO, *May 17, 1950*

I am amazed at the recovery of Tokyo. Today when you drive around you would never know there had been a war—at least in the part I have visited. All the main buildings in the financial center are untouched and the little shacks which are normal in Japanese cities have been completely reconstructed. Tokyo is a bustling, hardworking city and it is clear that at least on the surface American influence is strong. Most people now wear European clothes and the women wander about on the same free and easy basis as Western women, even though some of them still wear kimonos and wooden shoes.

How skin-deep this transformation may be I don't know. Certainly in the hotel the chambermaids and waiters bow and scrape in a particularly fawning fashion. The Imperial Hotel, incidentally, is without doubt one of the most hideous and generally uncomfortable structures ever conceived by an American architect, in this case Frank Lloyd Wright.

I have noticed that Japanese women have misshapen bowlegs. At about the age of six all little girls start carrying their baby brothers around with the result that by the time ten years have gone by they have calves that only a cow could love. Centuries of squatting have helped develop the shape.

Headquarters here impressed me from the start as being organized in a rather Oriental form. I arrived yesterday at five o'clock in the morning and the deputy of the government section of GHQ, as well as a lieutenant colonel, were waiting on the field and took me to my hotel. Later, I met their boss, Brigadier General Courtney Whitney, a Manila lawyer and old pal of MacArthur who has handled a lot of personal affairs for him. You have a feeling that people almost bow when they mention General MacArthur's name.

TOKYO, *May 18, 1950*

THIS morning I had a very long talk with General Douglas MacArthur, former chief of staff, hero of the Pacific war and now Supreme Commander for the Allies in Japan. He is a remarkable physical specimen. Although he is a few months past seventy, he really looks like an exceedingly well-preserved man of fifty. I am told he dyes his hair. Be that as it may, he is a handsome, well set up man filled with youthful energy. He is taller than I expected—being approximately five eleven and looking more. He eats and drinks sparingly but does no exercise. In a uniform he cuts a very lithe figure. He apparently smokes only pipes and cigars because he was gassed in World War I and does not inhale, but he smoked a pipe throughout our conversation, one which continually went out and he kept lighting. In the interim he played in a fidgety way with a box of matches.

He has a very easy, winning and engaging manner. Without any doubt his personality makes one of the most charming first impressions I have encountered. He seems to have a sincere mind but not a particularly profound one. He was clearly irritated by the lack of a coordinated long-range American foreign policy and by the fact that the Pacific has been rather ignored vis-à-vis Europe. However, he was more than decent about restraining his criticisms, which crept into the conversation in only a rather offhand way. What he had to say—which I will repeat forthwith—is a curious cocktail of earnest, decent, hopeful philosophy; a certain amount of rather long-range thinking and a good deal of highly impractical poppycock.

I started off by telling the general I had heard him quoted as saying there was not much chance of a new world war in the near future. He replied that he did not know how accurately he had been quoted but these were his views:

The basic reason I have for concluding that there will not be a war soon is because of the changed nature of war. The scientists of the world have developed to such an extraordinary degree the processes and ways of accomplishing mass killing that war is no longer rationally a means of settling international problems. Its destructiveness has become so great that there can be no winner. Both sides lose. It is almost a form of mutual suicide. Therefore, it is not an acceptable rationalized means of settling international quarrels. [The Korean War came in the next month!]

In this respect you have got to remember that war at the beginning was a sort of gladiatorial contest. You might start with the basis of the fight between David and Goliath. From such an individual contest it became a struggle of professional units fighting gradually in more and more obscure corners of the world. But the results of these military engagements were accepted in peace treaties by the governments represented by these armies and therefore at least some results were accomplished.

However, as the world became more closely integrated and war became a more total concept involving every man, woman and child, and as destruction became so terribly great, war has ceased to be a medium for the settling of quarrels. The opinion of the masses of the world is against it. That is a relatively recent development and it is true of all the masses in all countries of the world.

During the last 150 years, if you look back, you find that international wars were invariably preceded by a period during which one or the other side—and sometimes both sides—became prepared and believed that if they were successful in war they would triumph thereby.

They looked upon war as a short cut to power. Thus always one side or both sides were relatively prepared not only in the sense of military force but in a psychological sense; public opinion approved and that was of great importance.

At the present time that is not the case. The public realizes all too well in terms of the last war that there can be no real victory in a future war. Therefore, on neither side is there psychological preparation. The Russian masses are probably just as opposed to a shooting war as the Anglo-Saxon masses. Therefore, many incidents have taken place during the last few years which in the past would have led to war but which have been passed over.

I don't believe that war is imminent because the people of the world would neither desire it nor would they be willing to permit it. That goes for both sides. That is the basic reason for my belief that war is not upon the doorstep.

We know that we do not intend to start an aggressive war. We have no such thoughts in our national mind and we are only preparing defensively in case of a tragic emergency. It is quite possible that the Russians are preparing in exactly the same way. Russian propaganda indicates their belief that we are preparing an aggressive action. Therefore the Russian is also arming defensively. But there is no indication on either side of preparations for an aggressive, offensive war.

Furthermore I think it is foolish to assume that the Russian would start an aggressive war now. He is doing so well under the present no-shooting war that he would probably and logically wish to continue the present successful system. It is a rare thing, in sports or anything else, when a man changes a winning combination.

These remarks are extremely sensible, it seems to me, and rather unusual coming from the lips of a military leader.

General MacArthur said he thought Russian troop dispositions in the Far East could be described as only defensive. He estimated that the Russians had about 750,000 armed men in the Far East command. However, they had not the industrial basis to support a war. There are practically no bases on this side of Lake Baikal. Between Lake Baikal and the Pacific the Russian forces had to be supplied over a single railway which is being worked to death. The Russians could certainly launch air and submarine attacks but they have not sufficient forces to launch and support a large overseas amphibious operation against such targets as Alaska, Japan, the Philippines or Honolulu. MacArthur pointed out that it takes a long time to build up the necessary communications to support a major military operation—such as the railway, which, he confirmed, the Russians are building from Alma Ata across to North China and the maritime provinces.

However, he argued:

The Soviet is a patient man. He thinks in terms of decades or centuries. He is not an Occidental but an Oriental. He is white; he is partially located in Europe; he has our gregarious instincts. But at heart he is a Tatar. He is like Genghis Khan. It is an Oriental trait to be patient. They deal in decades or centuries. This is against our nature. When we want a thing done we want it done right away or tomorrow. But the Russian will lay down a railway that he wants to use in twenty-five or fifty years.

We must never forget that Asia includes perhaps 1,250,000,000 people and maybe 60 per cent of the assets of the world. Yet it has the lowest standards of living perhaps in the whole world. It is manifest destiny that the effort of future civilization will largely be an Asiatic problem devoted to raising the standards of that huge area.

I wish there was more effort to face the fundamental problem of doing away with war. For example, the United Nations should look squarely at the problem of *abolishing* war. Yet the United Nations continually asks for its own armed forces. It talks of *fighting* to maintain the peace. That is a ridiculous anachronism.

In this respect the Japanese are ahead of their time with the Constitution outlawing armed forces. Someday the rest of the world must catch up. The public opinion of the world is against war because the masses of the world realize its futility.

At several times during the talk, MacArthur, while we were lighting up or changing subjects, indicated his doubts about the wisdom of American national policy. For example, I asked him how he could fit in the idea of a demilitarized Japan with our overall long-range policy of "containing" Russia. He smiled and said he was astonished to hear me refer to an American policy.

To conclude the conversation, I got General MacArthur off on one of his pet subjects—namely the future of communism in Japan. This is what he had to say:

The Japanese people have been for centuries, and if left alone, will continue to be for centuries, conservative. This is not only due to their innate character but it is also due to other reasons. Fifty per cent of the Japanese people are farmers. As a result of the land reform we have put through they own their own land. The Japanese farmer is a landlord. No one is going to become a Communist if he is going to lose in the process.

There is no chance of a spontaneous eruption of communism in Japan. The only chance would be the invasion of an outside disruptive force.

The only real Communists in Japan are the entire criminal class. Every racketeer and criminal espouses Communist causes because they hope to gain by it. This is of course true in Japan and not in other countries. There is a second group belonging to Communists and this is made up of highly educated radicals. They include a small percentage of professors and university students. This is about on the same proportional basis here as in the United States and many other countries and it is a very small percentage. Then there is a group of Koreans from North Korea that likes to follow the ideology of their families in that area which is dominated by Russians. Finally, there is a small element of adventurers who believe that Communism for them would be a short-cut to power: people like certain able and unscrupulous lawyers.

But, all in all, this is a very small number from the total of the Japanese people and I don't think that more than 1 or perhaps 2 per cent of the population can be called Communist. Of course, in the elections they attract a certain additional following which votes with them in order to show criticism of the occupation or the government, or to demonstrate resentment or frustration. The only serious bid the Communists made was in the evolution of labor. Labor had been pretty shamelessly exploited in Japan in the past but we have organized trade unions on a democratic pattern. During the period of evolution from the status of economic exploitation to the development of the power of modern trade unions—a difficult period naturally ensued. The unions, of course, tended to accept power before the accompanying responsibility. During that phase the Communists tried to get hold of the unions, especially those in industry. They prepared a general strike which I was forced to call off in February, 1947. But they failed then and they have been going down ever since.

Just at the last election when the Communists were riding high in China and everything was in their favor the party got a stronger following than was normal.

Finally, there is one other important point. I think practically all Japanese have a fear and hatred of the Russians. Everything emanating from Russia is detested. The fact that communism comes from there makes it impossible to introduce in Japan. I haven't the slightest fear of any internal trouble with the Japanese Communists but one must realize that external pressures are increasing.


TOKYO, *May 18, 1950*

SOME of my conclusions:

1. American policy must avoid any taint of counterrevolutionary or reactionary aspects and must not be caught in such a historical trend as the movement led by Metternich after Napoleon's defeat.

2. American policy should seek to bind together all nations attempting to preserve their independence with the normal common interest of self-defense against imperialism. This is perfectly admissible under the United Nations. By avoiding any ideological taint, such a group can include everything from Tito and the Burmese government on the left to Portugal on the right. It should not be a political alliance—as is the Soviet bloc—but one of purely practical self-preservation. By avoiding ideology, it can thus avoid the spirit of a Habsburg reaction and can honestly promote the type of free nationalism advocated by Mazzini—uninhibited by ideological quarrels.

3. Our propaganda should explain day after day that the main issue is this: Russia is trying to replace one form of colonialism, which had many good as well as bad points, with another form of colonialism which also has many good as well as bad points but which is still colonialism.

4. The United States makes no real effort to win over and educate the youth of the world. All revolutionaries from Mazzini to Stalin have avoided that mistake. What good does it do us to build up support among a lot of disappointed older people or exiles?

5. As Cavour reasoned, in this very imperfect world men must learn to use the tools that come to hand. We have had to do this in countries such as Greece and Italy.

6. We are making the mistake of trying to advertise our concepts of life in terms of lavish gifts, richness, the ECA. At one time in Greece, twenty-six officials of AMAG were receiving salaries of $12,000 a year and some of them were getting a per diem of $60 a day. This makes a horrible impression abroad. Would there not be a stronger appeal to Jeffersonian admirers along the lines of Garibaldi's famous pledge: "I offer neither pay, nor quarters, nor provisions; I offer hunger, thirst, forced marches, battles and death. Let him who loves his country in his heart and not with his lips only, follow me."

7. The American people should realize now that the results of the United States colonial system as demonstrated in the Philippine Islands stink quite as badly as the results of the British, French and Dutch colonial systems.

8. There is a strong need for an extensive military draft in the United States. It is not enough just to entice recruits with promises of movies, travel around the world, etc. The low morale of many American forces abroad has caused some people to refer to our troops as "Russians in pressed pants." Furthermore, our military system is not sufficiently efficient. It takes dozens of men in uniform to support one man with a gun— soldiers who run PXs, laundries, elevators, and so on. Yet, we insistently demand efficiency in our allies. We should cut down the number of administrative soldiers running mimeograph machines.

9. There is too much divided authority among American occupation authorities. In Austria, for example, the high commissioner reports to the Joint Chiefs of Staff. Then he turns his hat around and as commanding general in Austria reports to the defense establishment. Meanwhile the American minister reports to the State Department.

10. Our government promotion lists tend to be stultifying. More of an effort must be made to find young Eisenhowers and promote them—not as aides to political deadheads but in authoritative jobs.

11. We should coordinate all our intelligence services, those of the State Department, the Army, Navy, Air Force, Commerce Department, CIA, Defense, and so on into one quick and efficient department which would have all this information at its fingertips.

12. In Indochina we should not keep hitting the French so critically. We managed to lose China ourselves after a huge investment in energy and money. Yet the Indochinese are less able or educated than the Chinese. We have to work with what we have got; so the French should be encouraged for what they are able to do in Indochina rather than being attacked for what they not able to do.

13. We must encourage the remaining free states of Asia to cooperate against Communist aggression. We must seek joint or at least parallel programs in the area with Britain whose knowledge and experience frequently exceed our own.

14. We should remember that toughness does not always bring about war. Japan, China and Russia all fought large-scale campaigns in recent years without admitting that a "war" was in progress.

15. We have one advantage in Southeast Asia and that is that most of the countries there are at least economically sound, even if they are politically and militarily weak, and they have enough to eat.

16. We continually overstaff our foreign missions. For example, on the huge foreign service list of the Americans in Korea there are the following positions: "Supervisor of Motor Repair Unit," "Supervisor of Solid Fuels Unit," "Assistant Chief of Plumbing and Heating," "Assistant Supervisor of Warehouse Unit," "Supervisor of Carpentering Unit."

17. We should reduce our own concepts of policy to simple basic terms and then simplify those even more and advertise them to both our friends and enemies, repeating them day after day. At present very few Americans or foreigners have the vaguest idea what Washington's policy is in vast areas of the world. We must stress that we are not opposed to communism as a form of government but that we are opposed to Soviet imperialism or any other form of imperialism as we proved by backing Indonesia against Dutch imperialism.

18. The Truman Doctrine should be explained more carefully as a program to protect national individualities. Furthermore, it should be pointed out that it will cease to apply when it is no longer needed for such protection. On this type of basis, it can be used to apply all over the world where small nations are threatened by aggression. The Marshall Plan should be similarly explained as a temporary program to get nations on their feet in terms of their own and our interest. They need industrial recovery and we need it equally in order to promote our concepts of free trade in open world markets.

19. We talk too much in broad loose terms, some of which we don't even understand ourselves and many of which are certainly incomprehensible to foreigners. We assume smugly that every individual in the world craves for the four freedoms and the American way of life. Many foreigners resent this and feel that we are bragging about our gadget civilization.

The Indian or the Chinese is not interested in spring mattresses; he likes to sleep on a hard bed.

20. The Soviet system is more adaptable to the Far East than our form of democracy. The political heritage of the Asiatic people is utterly different from ours. For example, they are not used to voting the way we vote; it is an inefficient and ineffective system in many Asiatic countries. People in most Asiatic countries are far less interested in dogma than in order, stability, and enough to eat.

21. *We* should *encourage* revolutionary concepts such as agrarian reform and social evolution whenever and wherever possible. We must be behind positive liberal concepts and not allow the Russians to monopolize them in propaganda, leaving us holding the bag of counterrevolution. We have allowed ourselves to be pushed into a position where Moscow propaganda says every day that we are reactionaries and many people are beginning to believe this because we don't do much to oppose it. In fact, it is the Russians who are really the counterrevolutionaries and who are seeking to impose dictatorship for the sake of economic democracy.

22. Wherever Russia expands to the south or the east, she introduces a higher standard of living. This is evident all through Central Asia. Certainly the people of Afghanistan would be no worse off if they were administered from Tashkent rather than Kabul.

23. By failing to have a broad but precise program applicable to the whole world and all types of government philosophies, we continually weaken ourselves. We state that we have a strategic interest in a particular section of the world—for example, Greece and Turkey. That indicates gaps in which we imply we have no interest—as in the case of Iran. Similarly, we have indicated that we have a strong interest in Japan and in the Philippine Islands—leaving Formosa exposed and inviting its fall.

24. We should start psychological and economic warfare in Asia on a positive rather than haphazard defensive basis. Economically, our controls are extremely ineffective. We try to blockade China in terms of strategic goods and yet we permit quantities to go to the Philippines and then be reshipped through Hong Kong.

25. When we review our policy and crystalize it both in its formation and in our public statements, we must do it on a global basis. We have allowed ourselves to become too preoccupied with Europe and to have almost forgotten Asia for too long a period.

26. We need coordinators in a position to pull together policy in a single area. The Truman Doctrine succeeded in Greece and Turkey but it could have succeeded much quicker and much more cheaply if it had been more cohesive and directed in terms of the area rather than two separate countries.

27. We need a permanent undersecretary of state in charge of political affairs who would remain regardless of which party was in power. This

would not only insure more continuity to American foreign policy than the rather haphazard so-called "bipartisan" method which at best is only a partial success. Furthermore, it would demonstrate to all foreign nations, both friend and foe, that our policy would be continuous no matter who wins national elections.

28. Right now we are slipshod in the use of titles. There are entirely too many ambassadors and ministers wandering around the world who are not "plenipotentiary."

29. We tend to be influenced by unreal and sentimental notions. For example, we depend entirely too much on Nehru and India. We overrate India's strength and influence.

30. There is a foolish lack of coordination among various American governmental bodies. For example, we have discovered that our broadcasts to China are almost useless because the station in Manila which is used for that purpose is too weak. We wanted a station in Japan. But General MacArthur didn't get on with the national defense establishment in Washington so that didn't work out.

31. We have assumed real responsibilities in pushing colonial empires out—the British, the Dutch and the French. Was it only to create a vacuum and permit the Russians to move in?

32. Our whole Indochinese policy is a matter of hit and miss. An American visitor to Indochina (not a government official) saw Acheson this year. After what he told Acheson, the Secretary of State decided that maybe there was a chance of saving Indochina. He then demanded all the reports on the situation from the Far East Division. He found they confirmed what his visitor had told him. He had not seen them before because they had been held up within the State Department.

33. We have never adequately summarized the lessons of our own past experience. For example, there is much we can learn from our experience in Greece which should be used as a pilot plan. In Greece we learned the need for coordination and a single boss, the ambassador.

34. The Bangkok Conference agreed that our Point IV missions abroad should be as small and inconspicuous as possible to avoid charges of American imperialism. Nevertheless, we are already planning to send too large a mission to Thailand itself. We have too large a mission in Greece. They took the best housing and were far too apparent in public.

35. The American Joint Chiefs of Staff have just reconsidered their attitude on Southeast Asia. It is clear that the installation of a Communist government either by force or by infiltration in Indochina must be resisted by all means short of war. At the same time, we should try and accelerate the rate of independence for the three countries—commensurate with French morale. But if invasion occurs and is resisted by the French and Vietnam, we should help that resistance, including the use of such American armed force as permits the French to continue their resistance. This is

a derivative of the Truman Doctrine idea. The great threat to the United States point of view if Indochina falls to the Communists is the threat of contagion elsewhere in Southeast Asia. This is greater as a danger than the actual loss of Vietnam itself.

TOKYO, *May 19, 1950*

TODAY I had a talk with Lou Fortier, now MacArthur's chief of theater intelligence and my old personal friend. He showed me a staff college report of his, saying:

The Russians are extremely patient and plan in terms of decades. We are extremely impatient and like to get things done tomorrow. We know that we can run and get places but in the cold war the question that remains to be answered is: Can we walk?

Russian policy traditionally has been seeking to obtain outlets on the Mediterranean Sea and the Indian Ocean in the South and to gain control in the southeast and east of the fringes of China. In these gradual and traditional efforts Russia has always been opposed by Britain which has defended actively certain key positions.

The United States is inheriting Britain's role. Britain is gradually allowing America to assume prior responsibility for defending the Middle East and is also no longer trying to store for an indefinite period the oil reserves of that area but is permitting them to be used up more rapidly by allowing American participation in their exploitation—once unthinkable to an Englishman. The Truman Doctrine extricated Britain from its traditional position as defender of the Dardanelles. The British are building up their real new base in Africa behind an American protective line. Perhaps Britain regards the Dardanelles as less important in an age of air power. At any rate, Britain has been engaged in withdrawing from physical contact with Russia in that historic area of conflict and America has been moving in to replace it.

Soviet policy is obviously to continue to build up over-all military strength, to continue to undermine the morale of other nations, to continue to occupy any territorial vacuums where no opposition is met, and in the interim to bide its time.

Already the Soviet successes on the Asiatic mainland appear to have destroyed any subconscious signs of revival by the United States under MacArthur of a new kind of East Asian coprosperity plan.

It appears that by 1952 Russia will have the economic potential to wage a short war of the conventional type with great *initial* ground and air power. By 1960 she will probably have the economic potential to wage a *protracted* war on a *large* scale. By then she may have a considerably more important fleet and will be in better position both to launch amphibious operations and to defend herself against them.

My own conclusions may be appended:

Russian interest in Asia has been so evident for so long a time that it is incredible the United States has not been more prepared in a policy sense to counteract it, especially since the original conception more than three years ago of the doctrine that we must contain Soviet expansion. On May 18, 1945, I wrote the following:

> Some astute observers regard the great half moon stretch of Asia starting at the Turkish straits and running across Iran, India, Tibet, Sinkiang, Mongolia and Manchuria to the Khabarovsk and maritime provinces of the Soviet Union as perhaps the primary zone with which the Kremlin's foreign policy is concerned. . . . There are vast population blocs in Asia to which Soviet influence, contrary to portions of Europe, would introduce a higher standard of living.
>
> Furthermore, it is evident that Moscow, in connection with its over-all security policy, would like to neutralize any potential effort in the future by some antagonistic power to utilize some of these areas as military bases.
>
> The Russians know that some general staffs have always maintained that population masses are the key to the balance of power. Such a mass, nebulous but latent with strength, lies along central and eastern Asia. . . .
>
> Since 1943, the traditional Russian concern with Asia has reasserted itself. This preoccupation is centuries old. . . .
>
> There are many who think that basically Soviet foreign policy regards Europe as a back door, if an exceedingly important one, and Asia as a front door.

This article was written almost three months before the Russians attacked Japan. Since then everything in it has come true. Yet American policy has devoted itself primarily in terms of energy and money to defending the Stettin–Trieste line, which was probably Russia's ultimate aspiration in the West and has permitted the Asiatic advance to continue unchecked until relatively recently. American policy has disregarded the fact of its natural historical advantage in Europe—and that wherever Russia advanced in the occident it introduced a lower standard of living and therefore a counterclockwise historical process. It has ignored the historical disadvantage in Asia of a reverse situation and yet to date the great majority of American dollars spent have been for the purpose of improving European rather than Asiatic living standards.

TOKYO, *May 20, 1950*

THIS morning I had a long talk with Major General Charles W. Willoughby, G-2 of the Far East command. He is a large man who, it is said, is more or less a professional soldier of fortune. Apparently his father, according to rumor, was some sort of a German baron. Some say his mother's name was Willoughby and that he adopted his mother's maiden name during World War I. Others say he changed his name from Weidenbach. He speaks with a slight Germanic accent. He is a man with considerable "manner." He said he has been in the Far East for thirteen years. He is violently anti-Communist and thinks Senator McCarthy, by and large, is doing a good job. He claims he has the names of 180 important agents of international Communism, mainly American, who helped establish Mao in China. He says he seized the records of the Shanghai police and these confirmed his information.

Before discussing specific things, Willoughby said the Japanese middle and wealthier classes had suffered seriously from the war and occupation. He said many of the wealthy call themselves members of an "onion-skin society" because they lived by gradually selling off such heirlooms as fine old kimonos and peeled off layer after layer. He said defeat and taxes caused many middle-class people to say they were down to one *geta* (the Japanese wooden clog).

Discussing the strategic position in the Far East, Willoughby said there was a north-south American defense line that ran from Japan through Okinawa to the Philippines but this was very much weakened by the fact that we had never taken a real stand on Formosa. He said that until very recently there had never been any thought about an east-west line across South Asia.

I asked him if he thought South Korea could hold out. He replied that this depends on how much Russia is willing to support North Korea. Right now he thought the two republics were pretty well balanced in power. However, the Russians had helped revolts in Spain, Greece and China and they might, in the future, be prepared to do the same in Korea. If left alone the two republics would have to reach an agreement and perhaps South Korea "might even have an edge at the moment." He said that the thirty-eighth parallel was a stupid line of demarcation and even split political entities.

On the subject of Formosa, he said the United States had virtually extended an invitation to the Communists to capture that island when we delineated the Japan–Okinawa–Philippines line. A controversy on the American attitude towards the Far East had developed between the State Department and the Defense Department and that Acheson had out-maneuvered Bradley. Willoughby concluded:

Formosa is really an integral part of that north-south island chain. Formosa was the southern base for ground, air and navy from which the Japanese successfully attacked. It has far better ports than Shanghai. It has the largest cluster of operational airfields in this part of Asia. Economically, it is completely self-supporting. Although Okinawa is in the typhoon belt, Formosa is out of it. It is a far better fortification than the Philippines. It is a key. With the Communization of China the Russian potential has moved from Port Arthur to Canton. They have outflanked our Pacific positions.

Willoughby said the only time we had ever asked for Russian aid in Asia was when we were cornered on Bataan and we hoped that Russian pressure would prevent the Japanese from going south. It was a disaster to let the Russians enter the Japanese war. Russian neutrality in 1941 and 1942 enabled the Japanese to move south just the way Russian neutrality in 1939 and 1940 enabled the Germans to move west.

Willoughby said he thought Chiang Kai-shek could hold Formosa but the big question mark was whether the Chinese Nationalists would fight. Recently they have not shown much ability to do so.

He stressed that the Russians were very patient and probably would not encourage the Chinese Communists to attack Formosa until they had air superiority which could destroy Chiang's air force and eventually sink his fleet. He said Chiang Kai-shek has enough troops to cover any beach—provided they fight. Chiang has patched up some of his differences with the Formosan people, providing a better local political attitude.

Willoughby argued that since the conditions of the Cairo conference in 1943 (awarding Formosa to China) no longer prevailed, we should denounce the Cairo agreement and at least give the island back to the Formosans.

He said the Russians were steadily infiltrating into China. They are sending aircraft and special missions which are of large size and have good Kremlin-trained men. The last Soviet military commander from North Korea is now in China as ambassador but his real job is military boss.

He thought the Russians were having a very hard time merely patching up the main Mukden–Harbin–Tientsin Railway and that they even had to rip up tracks to keep the main trunk going. Therefore he did not believe the Russians would be able to build a railway across Sinkiang for many years.

He was not terribly worried about our position in Alaska. He described Alaska as the worst back door for invasion possible, especially in terms of flying. But he did say that the Soviet meteorological service is much better than ours and they were developing Arctic techniques. They have an excellent meteorological service along the northeast coast of Siberia to facilitate shipping.

TOKYO, *May 22, 1950*

THIS morning I had a long talk with W. J. Sebald, head of the diplomatic section of MacArthur's headquarters, political adviser and chief State Department man on the scene, with the rank of minister. He speaks excellent Japanese. He is an Annapolis graduate but quit the Navy when it objected to his half-Japanese wife. He practiced law in Tokyo some years as a member of the Japanese bar. He is very quiet, speaks in a dull monotone. Following are thoughts that occurred to me during our conversation—some my own, some inspired by him.

There is an indication we are losing ground in terms of popularity—if we ever really had any—the longer we remain as an occupying power in Japan. The State Department feels it is a political necessity to produce a peace treaty for Japan as soon as possible; that it is long overdue. The United States cannot keep any good will here if it sits on indefinitely as an occupying power and gives the Japanese no hope of really running themselves. Politically speaking, it is obvious that Japan as an occupied country is a political liability. Japan cannot be expected to rehabilitate itself in its own eyes or in the eyes of other countries in the position in which it now finds itself.

This is from a purely political standpoint. Strategically speaking, the question of bases arises. The American government must decide whether it is possible to execute its over-all policy of "containment" of Russia without having bases in Japan. It would appear impossible to avoid the conclusion that such bases are necessary if such policy is to be followed. Furthermore, without such bases, South Korea, already rotting on the tree, would inevitably fall off or be absorbed like the remaining dry corner of a piece of wet blotting paper.

The question then arises whether bases are necessary on the four main islands of Japan. It is pretty clear that Okinawa is going to remain an American base for an indefinite period of time.

In terms of the four main islands, unless the United States can convince the Japanese that they should have American troops on those islands, we are whistling in the dark when we talk of bases there. It is double-talk to think that the Japanese would not resent it if we informed them that now they had complete sovereignty but we insisted upon retaining troops in their homeland.

It is unrealistic to think of Japan as an unarmed "Switzerland" of the East and this was a foolish dream and public declaration by MacArthur. After all, even if both the United States and Russia guaranteed the security of Japan, we are no longer in a position to believe such a paper pledge by the Russians after our unfortunate experiences in Europe and China.

An occupation is never popular. To begin with, the Americans here, as in Germany and Austria, have been contaminated by their very position of enforced superiority. Inexperienced young men are living higher than they are accustomed to at home and for less money. They are being spoiled by it and assuming an unconscious arrogance which does them no good psychologically and which does the United States no good politically because unconscious arrogance is perhaps an even more dangerous quality than the conscious arrogance of which we used to accuse the English.

We crave popularity too much. We allow ourselves to impress ourselves by the fact that our GIs hold hands with Japanese girls dressed in Western clothes. How many of the Japanese dressed like occidentals go home at night and shift to kimonos? Likewise, how many of them shift to mental kimonos when they are among themselves? At least the British are realistic enough not to worry about this popularity complex.

TOKYO, *May 23, 1950*

THE following ideas occurred to me:

1. The Japanese had been brought up upon the theory that they were invincible. They had never been defeated in war. Now all their history books and school books must be rewritten in order to adjust history to facts. Are we Americans suffering from the same psychological superiority complex that affected Japan in 1941? We have managed to defeat the British in two minor campaigns when they were also fighting the French. We have defeated the Mexicans and the Spaniards who were already coming apart at the seams. We have defeated the Germans and the Japanese when we had great allies who gave us time to get ready. How are we going to do alone?

2. The United States right now is in a condition of war psychosis. A popular song today is "Enjoy Yourself—It's Later than You Think." The fact of the matter is there is no indication that the Russians plan an imminent war. We should put our national head under a cold shower and do some positive planning while we have time instead of working up a great mutual hangover.

3. Our system of government and economy is fundamentally based upon the concept of a small population in a huge country. Yet we are trying to introduce the philosophy engendered by this combination of factors on a small country with a huge population—namely Japan. Perhaps this statement is also applicable to Germany.

PARIS, *June 8, 1950*

AFTER a brief stay in America I returned to Paris by ship. Another passenger was Dr. Vannevar Bush, head of the Carnegie Institute and chairman of the Office of Scientific Development and Research during the war. He told me that we have now sufficient security weapons to insure the preponderance of the defense in a new war. Europe will soon be in a position to defend itself qualitatively against Russian quantity. The only problem now is one of security; how much can we trust the European countries with our secret weapons?

IN the afternoon I had a talk with (American Ambassador) David Bruce. He thinks there is a great need to send some of our secret weapons to our European allies; there is too much emphasis on security. Certainly purely defensive ground weapons, such as new anti-tank devices, should be given to the Europeans. We do not plan any aggressive war, so even if the Russians learn their secrets, it won't matter to us. The Russians will have them some day anyway.

# 23

## COLD WAR EUROPE

PARIS, *June 16, 1950*

L ONG TALK WITH FOREIGN MINISTER ROBERT SCHUMAN, WHO WAS IN HIS usual unflustered mood. He said France had already absorbed several tens of thousands of *Volksdeutsche* in order to make its contribution to the political problem concerning German overpopulation. He had proposed in London, last month, during his talks with Bevin and Acheson, that an international conference should be called to solve the overpopulation and unemployment problems of Italy and Western Germany. Schuman pointed out that France had a special interest in this as a neighbor of both nations. France thinks that transoceanic countries like North and South America and Australia can contribute to the solution. Until now, the Marshall Plan has not occupied itself with this.

On the subject of Europe, he said "we sincerely and strongly hope that Britain can participate. It is impossible to make a Europe without Britain. Especially in this matter—that of iron and coal. Any plan would be unaccomplished and imperfect without British participation." He said the five powers would soon be meeting and agree upon the organism which would then convince the British by realities and facts. British policy is an empirical policy based on experience.

PARIS, *June 17, 1950*

LONG chat with Averell Harriman. His appointment has just been announced as special assistant to President Truman in charge of coordinating American efforts in the cold war. Harriman seems very pleased with the post and I imagine he is glad to be back on the scene in Washington. I would not be surprised if he would like to get into politics while he is still relatively young (fifty-eight).

He explained that his job would be limited to foreign affairs and, in that respect, different from that of Harry Hopkins under Roosevelt. He will not sit in at Cabinet meetings, he said (contrary to reports), but indicated that Truman uses his Cabinet meetings for relatively less important affairs.

Harriman was very interested in MacArthur's views on Japan and a peace treaty there, as well as on Formosa. He was also particularly interested in Indochina and what can be done to improve the situation. He regrets that most of the people who offer themselves for government jobs are not much good in private life, which makes it difficult to find sufficiently able men.

NEW YORK, *June 27, 1950*

ARRIVED in New York yesterday after crossing aboard the *Ile de France*. Aboard ship I had several talks with Lieutenant General Alfred Gruenther and Sumner Welles.

We were playing bridge one day and Al was called to the phone. Gone some time. Came back with a quizzical look. Said nothing. Finished the hand, then, as he was shuffling the cards, remarked with a deadpan: "Cy, you'd better put your soldier suit on, North Korea has invaded South Korea."

Gruenther said he was convinced that, if the Russians did not intervene, the South Korean army would be able to hold its own. I think he is too optimistic. Furthermore, he thinks that if the Russians want to risk a world war, they will do it in Germany—moving there first rather than elsewhere—because it makes a better propaganda issue for them and has more appeal to their satellite allies.

In Indochina, he thinks we must give aid to the French, but that economic aid is perhaps more important than military aid; I disagree. He says General Carpentier, the French commander with whom he talked in Paris, wants to build up a large modern force capable of meeting a full-scale Chinese or Russian invasion if necessary. Gruenther thinks this is impossible. There are already 250,000 Chinese near the Indochinese border. He admitted it might be a good idea to send a squadron of jets to Indochina just to build up French morale. He said it would be ridiculous to send a large force of jets or other similar equipment to Indochina. If the Chinese or Russians intervene it means a world war anyway, and therefore there is no use squandering our limited equipment down there. He expressed the feeling that military operations were not going too well in Indochina, and that the French were not too confident.

Welles told me a few interesting anecdotes. When he was sent by

Roosevelt to Europe in 1940 he asked Mussolini, at Roosevelt's request, to meet the President in the Azores. The idea would have been to put an end to World War II—before Italy was drawn in. Mussolini was very enthusiastic, but Hitler prevented it.

During the summer of 1937, Welles and Roosevelt worked out an idea designed to prevent World War II. On November 11, Armistice Day, Roosevelt was to summon all ambassadors and ministers accredited to the United States and ask them to advise their governments of the need to act energetically to prevent a deterioration of the world situation. Secretary of State Hull prevailed upon Roosevelt not to do this. (Welles and Hull hate each other.)

Welles saw Churchill a few days ago. Churchill spoke very emotionally about Roosevelt, but was furious with Elliott Roosevelt. He claims that at a Teheran dinner party for the Big Three leaders Elliott and some other American officers showed up at the door of the dining room after dinner and Stalin beckoned them in. Stalin made a speech saying that 15,000 German war crimnals should be immediately executed *en masse* after the war. Churchill said he represented the public of Great Britain which would never stand for such a thing. Elliott R. then got up and made a speech— quite uninvited—backing Stalin. Churchill has never forgiven him. Elliott wrote a lot of untrue and unfavorable things about Churchill in his book.

Welles is obviously a disappointed man. He wanted to go into politics in 1940 in his state of Maryland, but Roosevelt wouldn't then permit it. Now he says he has no chance.


WASHINGTON, *October 3, 1950*

THIS morning I had a talk with Tom Finletter, Secretary for the Air Force. He was extremely worried about the possibility that China might intervene almost momentarily in the Korean War. This anxiety was occasioned by reports of a large Chinese convoy headed into North Korea. Finletter said it would be the worst possible thing for the United States to be at war with China, but not with Russia, as we would not be able to attack any primary targets in the Soviet Union.

It is known Russia now has a stockpile of several atomic bombs. However, our lead in the manufacture of atomic bombs is probably permanent. Nevertheless, as Soviet production increases the Russians become increasingly dangerous, especially when one remembers their superiority in other types of weapons.

They now have enough, however, to harm us badly if they so desire. They could deliver the bomb here in the United States. They have the planes. There is no way of ever achieving a perfect air defense. We might, at best, prevent 40 per cent of their bombs coming through, but that is all.

He said we must hold Western Europe. Containment as an over-all policy is impossible. All we can do in Asia is to exercise diplomacy and hope to build resistance. We cannot hope to commit ourselves to a precise containment policy for holding all of non-Communist Asia. We must hold Japan, the Philippines, and Australia, but, if necessary, the rest can go. This presents us with a difficult situation. We must build up strength in Western Europe which includes sending more American troops to Germany and arming the Germans. While this process is being accomplished, obviously a nervous period of history is bound to ensue. The big question is, will Russia react?

Another good talk with (Lieutenant General) Larry Norstad. He said we must arm France and Germany as quickly as possible. Eventually we must have a permanent beachhead force in Western Europe with good tactical air support. However, we can *never* give it greater relative tactical air support than that furnished in South Korea where we were flying seven hundred tactical sorties a day against no opposition and the ground forces were still retreating.

Norstad said it is impossible to build up a successful military coalition in Western Europe without the participation of Germany.

WASHINGTON, *October 5, 1950*

THIS morning I had an excellent and long talk with Dean Rusk, who is in charge of Far Eastern affairs for the State Department. Among other things, he said the following: It is immensely difficult to conduct conversations with the Russians because of the constant danger of leakage to the press. As soon as any hint of such talks appears in print, the Russians drop out. Nevertheless, conversations are taking place very frequently, on various levels and in various ways. Right now, the Russians are prone to make more social engagements. One sort of embarrassment is that whenever an American and a Russian diplomat meet at a cocktail party, everybody rushes away in order to leave them alone to talk, with the result that they become much more prominent and in the spotlight as a result of these good intentions.

The Russians have made it clear in recent conversations that they are particularly worried about what they call "The assumption of world leadership" by the United States. They point out that America has military missions in many countries bordering the Soviet Union, such as Turkey and Iran; that we have military bases in areas much closer to the USSR than they are to the United States. Although we constantly assure them that we have no aggressive intentions, frequently important American officials make jingoistic statements. They understand what we say to them officially, but they really wonder if this is not a trick game, and if the jingoistic statements, in reality, do not represent actual American policy.

Rusk said we have sought through such channels as India's Panikkar to explain our views and policies to the Communist Chinese government despite our lack of diplomatic relationships, but Russia is continually urging China to get into a war with the United States. China has already intervened strongly in Korea, not only with supplies but with troops. The extent of this intervention will probably increase considerably now. China is extremely irritated by the success of the United States in blocking her entry into the United Nations.

We hope gradually to obtain a better balance, both in terms of troops and economic support, of United Nations interest in South Korea. We hope the UN will put fewer American soldiers there and thus will assume a larger share of the burden of security. In this way we hope to extricate the major portion of our forces from Korea.

In Formosa the aim of our policy is to isolate it and to insure that the eventual disposition of the question will be accomplished peaceably while at the same time it will not become a Communist base for potential Soviet aggression against us.

We now have a massive aid ready for Indochina—for the French and Vietnam; however both France and Vietnam must prepare larger contributions of manpower for the army and a greater effort economically. France can contribute many more men to Indochina than she has yet done without reducing her commitments in Europe to the Atlantic Pact. We must never forget that France is a country of more than forty million people. We are irked that Bao Dai remains on the French Riviera and is not back in Indochina. However, as a result of his sit-down strike and refusal to go back, he will probably gain more concessions from the French. We did not put him up to this, but perhaps in the end it will be useful.

Rusk said flatly that Jugoslavia would receive aid from us if attacked by an aggressor despite our distaste for Marshal Tito's ideology. One of our great problems is that of making both our friends and our enemies aware that we would aid any victim of aggression. We cannot have a hard and fast formula on this because of the difficulties in terms of space, communications, and so on. For example, it would be far harder to send American forces to help Iran than it would to get aid to South Korea from Japan.

The fundamentals of our present foreign policy are to work for collective security through the United Nations and at the same time to develop the original concept of containment as implemented by the United States. There is certainly far more faith in the United Nations on the part of the United States government than was the case before Korea. We want the individual members to earmark troops for use by the United Nations when necessary against aggression.

Turning to India Rusk said Nehru is unfortunately doing now what we did for twenty years; that is to lecture us upon our faults without participating in world affairs on a responsible basis, just the way we used to traditionally lecture the British on their administration in India and Ireland. Rusk said we must make Indians aware of what we think of them and not just continue to worry about what they think of us.

In a broad sense our policy today is to build a structure based upon the United Nations, the Rio Pact, the North Atlantic Pact, the British community of dominions and colonies, special alliances (such as that between Britain and Turkey), the colonial possessions (such as those of France, Britain and Belgium), and finally particular commitments (such as that of the United States toward Greece). In the end we hope to shape a broad framework from all of these originally unrelated undertakings.

We are sending more troops to Europe, therefore other nations must share more heavily in the burden of Korea in order to free American military forces. Also, by readjusting the balance of responsibility in Korea, we can more easily convince the Russians and Chinese that we don't want bases there. Strategically, Korea is not of any use as a base to us but, on the other hand, it can be of great use as a base for any enemies pointing against our Pacific possessions.

The fundamentals of the United States containment policy were laid down in the famous eighteen-page Top Secret cable sent on February 22, 1946, by George Kennan, at that time minister and chargé d'affaires in Moscow. This was also the core of Kennan's famous "X" article in *Foreign Affairs*.

In a nutshell, the cable argued that it was impossible to count on the coexistence of the Soviet and capitalistic systems because Soviet ideology refuses to admit such a possibility. However, Kennan was convinced that the Soviet system contained within itself the seeds of its own destruction and if we remain firm we can prevent Soviet expansion and allow those seeds to grow.

This evening I had drinks with Al Gruenther, deputy chief of staff in charge of planning. He said he thought something between fifty and seventy divisions with a very high proportion of armor would be required by the Atlantic Pact on the European scene. This includes American divisions.

BELGRADE, *November 5, 1950*

CHAT with a Serbian peasant working in Belgrade. He said:

*Bogami,* when the Russians came here, they had no culture at all. Their women looked like sows, but you should have seen them when they left. They were all dressed up in our latest Belgrade fashions, with gloves right up to their elbows. Now, I know our culture is maybe a hundred years behind the culture in the West, but, my little mother, I tell you the culture of these Russians is a hundred fifty years behind ours.

I cannot figure these things out, but it seems to me things were better before the war and before the Russians brought these new ideas. Why, in the old days, you could buy ten liters of Dalmatian wine for 20 dinars. Now, all you get for 20 dinars is one liter of piss. When I drink a šlivovica, these days, I wake up with a headache. My God, I wish I knew what they make the stuff from.

This system is good, I suppose, and, of course, I love Marshal Tito. They tell us we are producing 200 per cent more than before the war. But where it all goes, I don't know. Before the war we worked little and ate a lot. You could buy anything you wanted here in Belgrade—even Brazilian coffee and English material. Anybody could go into a shop and buy anything. Nowadays, we work lots and eat little.

*Kuku Majka,* we had these damn Russian films. You could not go to a cinema without seeing a Russian film, so finally nobody went to see the crap at all. Now, we have American films, and, my God, they are good. Ah, I remember that *Tarzan in New York*.

And those Chicago gangster films: you know, we have some gangsters in Belgrade. The real thing. Experts. Bang. They do something and when the police and UDBA come to look for them—*whist*—they are gone. Real Chicago style. Technicians those fellows.

BELGRADE, *November 6, 1950*

I drove to Belgrade from Trieste over the new concrete road laid down between Zagreb and Belgrade; an excellent highway which makes it possible to do the trip in four and a half hours—instead of about fourteen. Lunched in Ljubljana where the food was plentiful and good.

The road through Slovenia was lovely—green fields spread beneath snow-covered mountains; bright pumpkins carefully stacked beside barns; orange ears of corn garlanding the houses, strung out in necklaces to dry. I stopped at one village, Gostilna, to see what they had to eat. There was plenty of bread and sausages. Outside, chickens and turkeys were pecking in the garden. Montenegrin George, my driver said: "You couldn't get food like that in Serbia; no matter how long you waited. But it's always been that way. Life is better here in Slovenia. But the people are better in Serbia."

This evening I had a long and exceedingly interesting interview with Marshal Tito. The talk took place in his simple villa on Užice.

I asked what his country's stand would be should a deteriorating situation bring about hostilities between the United States and Communist China. He replied: "If such a situation as you mention should develop, we would take a stand against any and all aggression. I should not like to be misunderstood. It is the United Nations itself which must decide who is the aggressor. Our stand will be the same—that of the United Nations. We will adhere to that body's decision."

Tito recalled his country had agreed to recognize Peking. There had been no reply from China. "We know why. It is the same in the case of all countries having a close relationship with the Soviet Union. They all have a uniform policy on Jugoslavia, because Soviet policy toward this country has not changed, and they cannot have an independent view."

During the interview, which lasted an hour and a half, Tito spoke in Serbo-Croatian, translated by a government interpreter, but it was evident that his knowledge of English is now fairly considerable. He looked healthy and fit, unworried by the Cominform's political war, its economic blockade or the difficult food situation caused by this year's drought.

He wore a gray army uniform with red stripes on his trousers and no decorations. Coffee, plum brandy and Macedonian cigarettes were served. Two dogs—Tiger, an Alsatian he got from the retreating Germans during the war, and a bird dog—wandered about the antechambers. Beside his desk stood a bust of Lenin—none of Stalin.

He said that if it is in the interest of international relationships and will not cause unrest among Jugoslavia's internal population he would release Archbishop Aloysius Stepinac, at present imprisoned as a war criminal. He might be sent to a monastery, but he would not be permitted to serve as a prelate in the country.

Jugoslavia is ready to purchase arms from the Western powers for national defense, and in an emergency would ask for material aid wherever she could obtain it. Despite Moscow's propaganda, Jugoslavia does not consider that the Marshall Plan has been "catastrophic" for Europe; instead, it has afforded "great help" to certain countries, such as Italy and France.

On Albania, Tito commented:

Press reports that Soviet experts and instructors are being sent there are based upon fact. But they cannot create a large army there because the country is too small. They are certainly strengthening Albania's economy for their own purposes. Albania continues to behave provocatively upon our border and to shoot across at our patrols. Furthermore, Tirana is making plain again its designs on regions of Jugoslavia.

Tito discussed Titoism as an ideology. He said: "It is not true that there is such a new ideology. We merely stand firm upon the precepts of Marx and Lenin and against a revision of them. Ours is a struggle for the correct implementation of these theories applied to the conditions prevailing in this country."

If this country, for its own security, requires material from a Western power, it will seek it. "I can say this," Tito observed, "We won't care what anyone says. If an opportunity comes to obtain arms to defend Jugoslavia—material which we cannot manufacture at home—we will accept it. The Soviet Union has received equipment from Great Britain, including jet planes and strategic raw materials. If it is a question of our own security, we'll buy materials wherever we can, although no negotiations on such matters are going on at present."

I told Tito I had two favors to ask. What were they? First, I wanted to see the chief of staff, Colonel General Koča Popović. Why? To get a briefing on the military situation around Jugoslavia's borders. That was easy, Tito said, but wouldn't I prefer to see Ivan Gosnjak? He was on the Politburo—and also a colonel general. No, I said. In the United States, a "chief of staff" sounded more authoritative. Anyway, the two generals had the same information. OK, said Tito. This pleased me. Our military attaché never sees anyone higher than a colonel.

Favor two: I wanted to see Stepinac. Tito said he was well; I wanted to see for myself. There were millions of Catholics in the United States and all of them were deeply interested.

Tito took this one rather dubiously. He thought a while, then he walked up and down, a stony look in his blue eyes. Finally, "You will hear from me," he said. "One way or the other." We shook hands and I left.

BELGRADE, *November 8, 1950*

THE contact of the Jugoslav party with Moscow has been small. When the party was declared illegal and driven underground in 1920–1921, the center of activities did not shift back to Moscow but to Vienna, Paris, Zurich, Dresden. Unlike the leadership of other Eastern European Communist parties, few of the Jugoslavs were trained in Russia.

The Jugoslav Communist Party was founded in April 1919 as the "Socialist Workers Party of Jugoslavia." Its leader was Sima Marković. Marković was deposed in 1928 and went to Moscow where he subsequently disappeared. The next leader was Djuro Djaković who was slain by the royal Jugoslav police in 1929.

During these early years the party was being continually criticized by the Comintern and Stalin. In 1929 its new leader was Martinović. He was removed in 1932 and succeeded by Gorkić who remained outside the country. Gorkić was removed in 1937 with all his leaders save Tito. Tito was then given a Comintern mandate to purge the Communist Party of Jugoslavia and form a new leadership. In 1937 Tito appointed the present leadership which remains—except for those killed during the war and two defections, Hebrang and Zujović, who were arrested in the spring of 1948 and are still in jail.

BELGRADE, *November 9, 1950*

THEY are really changing things around here and pulling out the stops for me. To begin with, I find all government officials exceptionally friendly. Since Tito I have seen Milentije Popović, now minister of foreign trade and a member of the Communist Central Committee; Colonel General Koča Popović, chief of staff of the armed forces; Vlado Dedijer, chairman of the central committee section on foreign policy; Vlado Ribnikar, publisher of

*Politika,* now organ of the National Front; Makijedo, head of the American section of the foreign office, etc. They have been exceptionally friendly and I should imagine would be even more so after today when both *Politika* and *Borba* (official organ of the Communist Party) devoted their entire front pages to a Jugoslav version of the dialogue between Tito and myself. Furthermore, I saw Predrag Milojević and some other antiregime friends one evening and they were very open and critical but added things had changed and they in no sense feared to be seen with Westerners now.

General Koča Popović is small, dapper, and wears no decorations on his handsome uniform. He received a degree in philosophy at the Sorbonne, speaks fluent French and German and was a surrealist poet before the war. I told him I had heard he was a dadaist poet. He was very offended and made it clear that no, he had been a surrealist. He received me surrounded by great folders of data to which he referred. Every now and then we were interrupted with Turkish coffee.

Popović charged that Bulgaria, Rumania and Hungary, the Danubian states that were allies of Hitler during World War II and are now Soviet satellites, were violating the military clauses of the 1946 Paris peace treaties and building up large armies in excess of the limitations specifically fixed.

BELGRADE, *November 9, 1950*

VLADO Dedijer invited me to his house for lunch, itself an unusual thing. We ate simply—a meat stew with potatoes, an apple, coffee, two shots of šlivovica, bread. Vlado explained this was the one meal of the day and his regular ration.

Clearly Jugoslavia is leaning towards the British type of socialism now. Vlado said the trip of Djilas and Kardelj to America had impressed them enormously. He said the Roosevelt reforms were very "socialistic"; a great change from the Vlado of 1946. He hopes to help the Marshal write his autobiography and wants me to help find a publisher. Indeed I will, and plan to get it for *The New York Times.* Vlado gave me the third volume of his "Dnevnik" which came out recently and in which I figure. He inscribed it in Croatian: "To my eternal enemy, Cy Sulzberger."

ZAGREB, *November 11, 1950*

I had a fascinating yesterday. Late on the previous day, my phone rang and I was told to go to Zagreb to report to the local Interior Ministry and get my permit to see Archbishop Stepinac. Then the phone rang off. I drove

off as early as possible on the new autoroute; and everything worked
O.K.

Even before I was officially advised to go to Zagreb the Jugoslav public,
because of the prominence given in the local press to my conversation with
Marshal Tito, was discussing the projected interview.

Orthodox Serbs of all political shades came up to me and growled:
"Stepinac should have been hanged. It was he who condoned the murder of
thousands of the Orthodox."

"The only good thing this regime has done," said those in opposition to
it, "was to put the rascal in jail."

Croats—virtually homogeneously Roman Catholic—beckoned me aside
in secluded places and whispered. "You should know before you see the
Archbishop that no matter what they tell you we adore him. He is the great
hero of the people and no slanders launched against him are believed. He is
our martyr."

In these antithetical views one sees the basic difficulties that face any
regime in Jugoslavia. I sought to elicit a somewhat less fiery viewpoint in
Slovenia, also a Roman Catholic province.

Of three persons I questioned, two avowed a deep affection for Archbishop Stepinac. The third, who was in no sense a Communist, said: "He
would have been shot by any other government—for example, the royal
government before the war. I am a Catholic, but he was a traitor. Like our
own bishop in Ljubljana, who fled to Argentina, he collaborated with the
Germans and permitted the slaughter of innocent Orthodox Serbs."

After spending a night in Zagreb, I called yesterday morning at the
headquarters of the ministry of interior for the Republic of Croatia. It must
be remembered that this is popularly conceived as a dread organization.
When one mentions the ministry—known locally as the UDBA, a combination of the initials of the ministry's name— it is *sotto voce*. A revolution
always brings with it popular fear of its dynamic and brutal qualities and
this is exceedingly true in Croatia.

At the entry bureau I requested in bad Serbo-Croatian a guide to the
office of the Croatian minister of interior. The young man at the desk was
perplexed by this and asked for my *legitimacia* or identification documents.
I replied that I was an American and had no such papers. An old gentleman, sitting on a bench with a group of petitioners for various favors,
stood up and said: "Comrade. The American comrade has no *legitimacia*
because anyone knows that in America you don't need such things."

This seemed to satisfy. The youthful official showed me politely upstairs
to the office of the minister's cabinet chief. The latter also spoke no
language but Serb-Croatian. "When do you wish to see Stepinac?" he
asked. "Immediately," I replied. "Where is he imprisoned?" The answer
was "Lepoglava."

In Jugoslavia, Lepoglava has deep connotations. It is a prison some fifty miles from Zagreb that was built when Croatia belonged to the Austro-Hungarian empire. Patriots and opponents of all the regimes in the bloody history of this region have suffered there. Under the Hapsburgs, hundreds of Slav nationalists paid for their ideals in Lepoglava. Under the Karageorgević dynasty both Marshal Tito and Moše Pijade, a member of his Politburo today, were incarcerated at Lepoglava. It was there that Pijade, an artist, painted self-portraits with the aid of broken pieces of mirror and also translated Karl Marx's *Das Kapital*.

During World War II the Fascist Croatian Ustaši and the German Gestapo perpetrated horrors within its walls. Since Jugoslavia's liberation by Marshal Tito's Partisans, fearful rumors have seeped through the country about Lepoglava. Its very name throws a dark shadow although it means "beautiful head."

The Croatian minister of interior himself entered the picture at this moment and politely asked me if I knew the way to Lepoglava. I replied that I did not. He asked if he might send someone from his office to escort me and I agreed. Shortly thereafter a young man named Anton Sobotinćić, wearing the long brown leather coat often associated with members of the UDBA, entered the room and we departed.

We drove off through the lovely countryside of the Zagorije region of Croatia, where Tito was born in a small peasant house. It was an exceptionally beautiful autumn day. The sun lay softly on the ruddy mountains and velvet green fields.

The uniformly Roman Catholic peasants of Archbishop Stepinac's own flock took advantage of the fine weather. They busily stored pumpkins, beets and cabbages in bins, strung pepper garlands outside their barns, tended their small herds. The woods were filled with girls in gaily colored costumes gathering faggots. Old women in aprons and kerchiefs beat their washing by purling streams.

After chatting at length with the amiable Sobotinćić, who speaks rudimentary German and who describes himself as not a Communist but a sympathizer (improbable, or modest, for a functionary in the interior ministry), we finally arrived at Lepoglava, a small village nestling below the mountain massif of Ivansčica.

This hamlet is dominated by the prison that has made its name famous. Virtually the first sight is a series of white walls punctuated with square watch towers, each of which is guarded by armed peasant boys in blue militia uniforms.

Sobotinćić told the sergeant of the guard that we wished to see the prison commandant. We were taken to his office and shortly afterward he strode in, a friendly if perplexed, tough-looking functionary wearing jackboots, brown leather overcoat, and the type of visored cap that twenty-five years ago was popular in America among motorists and golfers. Today it is fashionable among some members of the political bureaus of Eastern European countries. He was introduced as Josip Spiranec, a former major in the Partisan army of Marshal Tito, a war hero, and undoubtedly—a member of UDBA.

When the purpose of my visit was described by Sobotinćić, Spiranec appeared a bit doubtful. When I asked him how many prisoners were in Lepoglava he seemed still more so. Sobotinćić then said that, first of all, Marshal Tito had himself approved this trip and, secondly, the government had nothing to hide. At this, Spiranec brightened up.

We went into the sunny courtyard, examined the village church which abuts upon the prison, and he said there were about a thousand persons locked up here with only one "special prisoner"—Archbishop Stepinac. The others live in dormitory rooms, which I did not see, and work eight hours a day, six days a week in neighboring fields and workshops. The archbishop has exceptional quarters and treatment.

Accompanied by the assistant prison director, we walked down the village street past groups of idling militiamen and UDBA troops to the actual prison gate.

A young soldier with a tommygun flung this open saluting the commandant, who entered first. We three followed, passing more guards in blue uniforms in a courtyard, going through still another gate, and then climbing a stairway to a brick building. Just inside the doorway we halted in a corridor on each side of which was a row of wooden doors. In each was inserted a tiny peephole, covered by a wooden disk.

Spiranec said something to his assistant. He then took a key from his pocket and entered the first door on the right. Sobotinćić urged me to follow. I went in.

We found ourselves in a room about nine by fourteen feet. The window was barred but not in such a way as to exclude the light of day. The room was warm. The furniture was simple: a cot with sheets and a pillowcase as well as blankets; one table and one chair; a bureau upon which, among other things, were a wash basin, a pitcher and a tin vacuum bottle. The floor was bare wood. From a series of hooks hung some clothing and a towel.

Having worn dark glasses because of the bright sun in the courtyard, I needed a moment to adjust my vision. Then I saw a slender man of medium height standing behind the table, looking first at Spiranec and then at me. It was Archbishop Stepinac.

The archbishop is a man of pale but evidently healthy countenance, fine features, thin brown hair, and a facial expression that clearly denotes a tremendous inner passion. He stood there for a moment, looking at me, his left hand holding open the pages of a large book upon the table, his reading glasses set beside it. It was then that I realized he had not the faintest idea who I was or why I was there. His contact with everyday affairs is slight, and Spiranec had not had time to explain the circumstances.

The archbishop's four visitors stood awkwardly for a moment, clutching their caps and hats. Then I told the prelate who I was, how I happened to be there, and that with due respect to the circumstances of the interview and to his own desires I wished to report to the world any messages he might care to send on how, in general, he felt about his physical treatment and psychological condition.

We spoke in French, which no one else in the room understood. The archbishop apologized for his mistakes, saying he was far more fluent in Italian and German. Nevertheless, he has mastered the language.

"Monseigneur," I said, "could you tell me what the state of your health is?"

He replied, still standing: "I feel well. I am in no way ill. I have lost no weight since I came here four years ago."

I then asked the archbishop how he occupied his time. He said he devoted many hours to prayer, contemplation and, at the moment, to the translation of a work on the lives of saints. He is studying church history. He showed me the work he was engaged in examining: a Latin tome on the Franciscan order by an Irish prelate named Wadding.

I asked whether it was difficult for him to receive reading material. My three escorts stood silently by and I am convinced they understood not one word of the conversation. As for the archbishop, it became evident as the interview progressed that he could not care less.

He told me he received books continually. Most of them are brought by his sister, who visits him every month, he said. He complained, however, that all the reading material, even ecclesiastical, was first scrutinized by the prison censors. He had no access to newspapers; he especially missed *l'Osservatore Romano,* the journal of the Vatican, which he described as "prohibited."

I asked if he was in touch with the world outside the prison walls. He replied, "Letters are not strictly forbidden. But they are all subjected to censorship. Therefore I do not not write."

I then explained to the archbishop what Marshal Tito had said to me concerning the possibilities of his release either to a Roman Catholic monastery within Jugoslavia or to exile—on condition that he should never return.

He stood there silently for a moment, dressed in his black clerical garb, one hand upon Wadding's ecclesiastical history, absolutely motionless. Then, in a calm and quiet voice, he replied: "Whether I go to a monastery, or whether I remain here, or whatever should happen to me, I am utterly indifferent.

"Such things do not depend upon Marshal Tito. They depend only upon the Holy Father, the Pope and upon no one else."

I asked the archbishop if he had any kind of message he would like to transmit through me to the world outside the walls of Lepoglava. Again, after slight deliberation, he replied: "I have nothing to say. I am content to suffer for the Catholic Church. Whether or not I shall ever resume my office depends only upon the Holy Father."

I then asked, "Monseigneur, are you well treated?"

"There were some difficulties," he replied. "It is better that I should not speak of it." He added that he received plentiful food and that his cell was heated every day.

All this time, the archbishop was standing before the one chair in the room. I asked if he would not please sit down. He remained on his feet and said: "I am sorry that I have nothing to offer you. I regret that I cannot even ask you to seat yourself."

I asked if he was able to perform his religious services and to take communion. He pointed to another wooden door opening on to one wall of his cell and said: "There is my chapel. You may go in." I opened the door and saw another cell, slightly smaller, dominated by one table covered with a white cloth and serving as an altar. Archbishop Stepinac explained that there were two other Roman Catholic priests imprisoned in Lepoglava who were permitted to pray with him daily.

"I am completely indifferent as to the possibilities of my liberty," he said again. "I know what is at the root of this matter. It is a question which only the Holy See can resolve. My freedom, or what I may do afterward, is not for this government to decide. I am completely indifferent concerning any thoughts of my liberation. I know why I suffer. It is for the rights of the Catholic Church. I am ready to die each day for the Church. The Catholic Church cannot be, nor will it ever be the slave of any regime.

"If Marshal Tito wishes to free me he should speak with the Holy See. The Catholic Church cannot be the slave of anyone or any country."

After this conversation we bade each other farewell and, led by Spiranec, walked out of the building, out of the prison compound and into the sunny village street. "What did he say to you?" asked Spiranec with considerable curiosity and a gleam in his hard, intelligent eyes.

I precisely recounted the interview. He thought for a moment. Then he said: "That is not entirely true. For example, he has never asked for that paper, *l'Osservatore Romano*. What he asks for he gets. Why, he lives better than the guard here.

"In the morning he gets coffee, bread and butter. For lunch he has soup, meat, dessert and half a liter of Dalmatian wine. In the evening he is given either a schnitzel or eggs and half a liter of coffee. Every day he has either šlivovica or a liqueur. We give him between one and a half and two liters of šlivovica each month to drink when he wishes.

"How can this man complain? We can never forget the crimes he committed, we who fought this war. It was under him that thousands of Serbs were butchered because they were not Catholics. It was he who collaborated with the enemy. It was he who hid gold and valuables in his church, contravening our laws."

On the way back to Zagreb, after a very considerable silence, a conversation began between myself and Scbotinčić. He described himself as a strongly proregime Catholic who went regularly to church. He contended that Archbishop Stepinac should be where he is and that the Roman Catholic people of Jugoslavia had largely forgotten about him. But he confessed to an admiration for the prelate's obdurate courage. At this moment my Montenegrin chauffeur, who is of the Orthodox faith, muttered: "They should have killed the pig."

When I got back to Zagreb, two men rushed up to me in the street and asked: "Are you the American journalist? Did you see the archbishop?" "Ah, he is a fine man, a saint. Tell the American people he is our hero."

PARIS, *November 21, 1950*

LUNCH yesterday with Vlado Dedijer. The project of Tito's autobiography is going through. At present, it is being called "an authorized biography." I hope in the end it can work out so it will actually be an "autobiography." At the moment, I think Dedijer wants to grab literary glory. Vlado, during the course of our conversation, said he has been with Tito since 1938.

Vlado used to be a newspaper reporter and was fired from *Politika* after he had spent one month in Spain because of his pro-Republican reports. His biggest scoop was an interview with King Edward VIII, who was vacationing on the Dalmatian coast with Mrs. Simpson. Vlado obtained this disguised as a fisherman, and was so excited by his success that he bought himself three ice creams. He is becoming more and more of a regular old-fashioned Serb. Vlado boasts: "We Serbs never change," and is now all for the West—which certainly is a change for him.

He, like the other close friends of Tito, call him "old man" (*Stari*) in private informal meetings with the Marshal.

PARIS, *November 23, 1950*

LUNCH at the embassy. Vangie Bruce told me their chef had recently sent a formal note to the ambassador asking if his excellency did not think that, in view of the situation, they should not cease calling the dessert *"Charlotte Russe"* and call it *"Charlotte à l'Américaine."*

Chip Bohlen said that, in 1946, when Senator Tom Connally was here during the peace conference, he expressed the desire to meet Thorez at one of the receptions. When he was introduced to Thorez, he put the index finger of each hand on his forehead like horns, bent over and shouted at the startled Communist: "Thorez. Taurus. Bull." Then he went away. Thorez, utterly confused, asked Bohlen what the Senator meant. Bohlen hadn't the least idea.

PARIS, *November 27, 1950*

LUNCH with Raymond Laporte of the Eastern European and Russian section of the Quai d'Orsay. I used to know him in Warsaw. He is a very intelligent young fellow whose wife died in Poland. He returned early this year after five years in Warsaw.

Laporte said that when Paillard, previous French ambassador in Belgrade, left, he had a farewell dinner alone with Tito and Madame Paillard. In the past, he and Tito always spoke Russian to each other. This time, Tito insisted on speaking German and whenever he spoke of the Russians, he described them as *"Schweine,"* making due apologies to Madame Paillard.

PARIS, *November 28, 1950*

THIS morning I had a long talk with Prime Minister René Pleven. He was extremely friendly and forthright. He is disturbed by what he considers lack of comprehension by the United States on the whole question of rearming Europe and, above all, Germany.

Pleven is tall, mustachioed, wears glasses, speaks correct English, although with a distinct French accent. His desk is piled with papers and his telephone rings constantly—calls from political leaders and cabinet members which he takes personally.

He claimed France is seeking to cooperate with other North Atlantic powers in working out a compromise formula designed to bring into being as swiftly as possible a European army within which Western German units could participate on a basis of equality.

France is prepared to accept the following bases for accord:

First, a continental defense force would be made up of international divisions. Each division would comprise three regimental combat teams commanded by either a brigadier general or a colonel. Each regimental combat team would represent one participating nation. Thus a division could, for example, contain one French team, one Italian team and one West German team—each with its own officers.

Second, divisional commands and corps commands would be distributed on a basis of individual qualifications and merit to officers of all participating forces. German officers would be accepted on complete equality with those of other nations. Thus, according to this formula, in the eventual European army there could be German generals commanding European divisions, corps or armies. In theory, the day might arrive in the future when a German could command an entire force.

Also, during an interim period NATO nations in Europe having overseas commitments would necessarily continue to safeguard such interests with their own national overseas armies. Thus, for example, France, for some time, would need her own national—as distinct from European—units in Indochina and North Africa. Nevertheless, Pleven hopes the day will come when a European or North Atlantic rather than a French force could be employed for all such special purposes.

Finally, Pleven continues to hope that the Schuman Plan will be adopted before the end of this year. This would establish a supranational control authority over the coal, iron and steel production of Western Europe— above all over the Lorraine–Ruhr coal, coke and iron complex. France considers her proposals a revolutionary step toward European unity, approaching that common goal by fundamental economic means. Through the proposed supranational authority it would insure that neither German nor French heavy industry would ever again be built up for purposes of national aggression.

Pleven feels the United States stirred up a hornets' nest by presenting the issue of German rearmament in an inept fashion. This stimulated many problems both in terms of intra-Allied arguments and German popular reaction that were unnecessary. Says Pleven: "We have always said we were ready to accept German participation in continental defense. But first we Allied powers must be strong—and strong in Germany. The two halves of bisected Germany will inevitably reunite someday. Their natural tendency will be to reunite on the base of the stronger half."

PARIS, *November 28, 1950*

THIS afternoon saw Bob Reams, counselor of our embassy in Belgrade, who has now been appointed to London. Reams told me two important things:

Yesterday, Ambassador Allen requested the release of Archbishop Stepinac. The State Department had advised him it was very much afraid Congress might put a rider on the Jugoslav aid bill demanding the archbishop's release as a precondition. As a result, the State Department recommended to Allen that he should ask Tito to move the archbishop to a monastery immediately. Allen decided to suggest he should be sent out of the country right away, making it clear, of course, that while requesting his liberation, the United States government was in no way requesting the Jugoslav government to restore him to his functions as archbishop of Zagreb.

The CIA and the British are up to another plan to overthrow the regime in Albania. I presume this will be along the lines of the disastrous effort a year ago that resulted in the capture and execution of everyone involved. Personally, I think this is a very dangerous moment for such adventures and might be regarded as very provocative by the Russians; their "provocations," of course, being directed at Jugoslavia.

PARIS, *November 29, 1950*

TODAY I received word concerning Allen's discussion with Tito about Stepinac. Tito said he could not release him now because the man is too "stubborn." He would be glad to let him out three or four months after Congress acts on the Jugoslav aid bill. However, letting him go now would make it appear to the Jugoslav people and the outside world as if Tito were responding to pressure; this he refuses to do.

PARIS, *December 1, 1950*

CHIP Bohlen says there is no doubt that MacArthur made a terrible mistake in pushing this latest Korean offensive. If, as he now claims, he did it to force the Chinese into action before they had built up an even larger force, he was a fool to send isolated units way up to the northeast. He was caught with his pants down and disregards the basic military assumption that the enemy will always do what he appears capable of doing; and it was evident from the last bloody nose we received in Korea from the Chinese a few weeks ago that they were capable of plenty.

Bohlen does not think the Chinese are intervening merely as a result of Soviet pressure and he thinks it is a great mistake on the part of our propaganda to keep asserting this. It is more likely that the Chinese considered the presence of American troops on their border a threat to their regime and reacted accordingly.

It is clear the Chinese were prepared to react physically as soon as we crossed the fortieth parallel. We made a fatal mistake in not stopping at the narrow neck of Korea and fortifying the line there. The South Koreans would have been able to hold this, but clearly could never have held the long frontier along the Manchurian and Soviet borders.

Bohlen says that, were war to start now, it is quite conceivable Russia would not attack Western Europe, but would warn that area to remain neutral and not to offer any bases or other help to the United States. Considering the weak condition of Western Europe, that might, at this moment, be more advantageous to America than to have the Continent overrun.

PARIS, *December 5, 1950*

LONG talk with David Bruce. He also admits it would probably be a good thing, if war breaks out, to have a neutral Europe; but naturally the United States cannot adopt any such policy. Privately he thinks perhaps the best thing that could happen would be for us to get out of Korea if we can save most of our manpower.

He thinks MacArthur has been talking entirely too much and made two fatal errors. The first was insisting Formosa was necessary to protect his lines of communication, even after we were in Korea. As a result, he was able to persuade many American leaders to support him and got us into deep entanglement over Formosa after the seventh fleet was sent there. The second was not to work for a fixed line in Korea and a neutral zone, thus avoiding the frontiers of China and the USSR.

Bruce cannot understand how MacArthur's estimates of Chinese troop strength have been so incredibly wrong. He thinks they are highly exaggerated at the moment (MacArthur now claims there are 800,000 Chinese in Korea or on the Manchurian border).

Bruce envisions no basic difficulties among the British, French and ourselves at the three-power conference starting in Paris Thursday to answer the Russian proposal for a quadripartite meeting on Germany. We all agree on the desirability of meeting with the Russians but we cannot accept the narrow terms of reference laid down by the Russians.

However, we do not want to risk phrasing our reply to the Russians in such a way that Russian propaganda could say we rejected their proposal. We must be very careful in terms of the propaganda effect. We are sincerely willing to meet with the Russians, providing the terms of reference are broad enough.

On the other hand, we must never forget that the Russians announced earlier this year that they would view with great concern any move to rearm Western Germany. The exact words they used were that Moscow "will not tolerate such measures." This means that the Russians could use the pretext of rearming Western Germany to intervene forcibly in Europe whenever they wished.

PARIS, *December 7, 1950*

AT lunch today I had a long talk with General Pierre Elie Jacquot, assistant French chief of staff in charge of intelligence and operations. He is a small dynamic man, very amiable, who talks a bit too much. He rather resembles, in profile, James Landis. Here are some of his ideas:

At the beginning of May, 1940, France had eighty regular, well-equipped divisions in line and twenty-seven other incomplete divisions. This was the best army France has ever had. Its casualties, during the first six weeks of the war, were 15,000 more dead (about 90,000) than during the first six weeks of World War I. However, it was defeated primarily because the Germans broke through four of the twenty-seven phoney divisions at Sedan. The Maginot Line surrendered many days after the armistice and was still intact.

In order to defend Western Europe one must base defense on depth. Positions in depth should be established above all in wooded heights like the Black Forest in Germany where concrete fortifications should be built up to a depth of fifty kilometers. Rivers are not satisfactory defense lines against the Russians. The Russians are plains people; they can cross rivers but mountains disturb them.

If France had forty divisions it could act effectively. Even if the Rhine were lost the Russians could not get to Clermont-Ferrand. To defend Western Europe against Russia it is necessary to have either a French army or a German army; at present we have neither.

The great period of danger will be when the Russians react to the rearming of Germany. However, Stalin is a wise man and realizes we can blow the hell out of his industrial centers. If the Russians attack the Ruhr we can put an "X" over it with the atomic bomb.

The difficulty of France at the moment is that its officers and NCOs are in Indochina, in other words the training cadres are absent.

PARIS, *December 15, 1950*

LUNCH today with Yuri Zhukov, *Pravda* correspondent in Paris. He is having an increasingly difficult time working here as a journalist. He lives in a house on the Boulevard Suchet, which belongs to the Soviet embassy. He telephones his stories. It takes him about four hours to get Moscow on the telephone. Whenever he dictates something antipathetic to the French government, the line goes dead and the operator tells him it is out of order. Then it usually takes twenty-four hours to get Moscow by telephone. In such cases, he calls up his correspondent in Prague to dictate his story for relay. So far, he has had no trouble with that system.

He is having trouble with his *"permis de séjour."* It is renewed on a month-to-month basis. He has to report each month to the Commissariat de Police.

I told him I was delighted he was having the same troubles that I have in Moscow, except he does not have as much trouble yet. Ours was a difficult profession, but interesting. I told him I had applied for a visa to go to Moscow but knew that, even if I got the visa, I wouldn't be able to travel around the country. He said he did not travel around France now because he was afraid of getting into trouble with the police.

Idiotically, he pretended he was not a member of the Communist Party and said many people in Russia would like to think for themselves. I told him it was difficult for me to see what the difference was when he worked for *Pravda* and had previously worked for *Komsomolskaya Pravda* (both CP organs) whether he was a party member or not.

Yuri does not think there will be war. There is a lot of building going on in Moscow, which would not be the case were war imminent. He remembered that in 1939–1940 all such building projects were stopped and everybody, including journalists, was mobilized, long before the German attack.

He said that, realistically speaking, there would be no use rearming France because it would not fight. However, he said there would be no violent Soviet reaction to the rearmament of France because this is not excluded or precluded by any international agreement such as Potsdam.

He is convinced the Germans won't rearm, even if we want them to. But there is no doubt the West Germans would fight and have something to fight for; the East Germans would not fight and are a weak force in comparison.

He was very anxious to have dinner with Chip Bohlen. I said I would try to fix it up, if he promised they would speak French instead of Russian.

He said the United States had stupidly made a great present to Russia, the Chinese market. Senator Austin's speech saying China was a "puppet" of Russia was a propaganda gift to Moscow. It would still take many years to satisfy the needs of China economically, even if we both worked together, which he said would be a good plan.

He was not worried about Korea provoking a world war. A delegation had recently arrived in Paris—Russian intellectuals. They had had no idea how serious the world situation was, and when they read the French newspapers they got frightfully worried. Russian newspapers carry only brief communiqués from Korea and people are not afraid of war. Later, we drank *Pyom na Brüderschaft* (which we had done in 1947 in Moscow), and he said that, no matter what happens, we must always drink to our children and to our friendship.

I asked him how he could imagine there was a chance for peace when, in a Soviet note of October 18, Moscow said it would not "tolerate" rearmament of West Germany; on next Monday, a meeting starts in Brussels for the purpose of incorporating German rearmament into that of the West. He said that I should look up the *Pravda* account of that communiqué and I would find the Russian word was not "tolerate" but something more mild.

(P.S. The word "tolerate" [in Russian "*primiritsia*"] mentioned above would be more exactly translated by "reconciliate" or "resign.")

PARIS, *December 21, 1950*

I got back from Brussels last night after covering the North Atlantic Council meetings. We are prodding Europe to rearm Germany against its will. Immediately, that weakens the morale of European countries who want to be rearmed first. The way we have told the whole world we hope to rearm Germany has managed to get the Russians some popularity for the first time among subject peoples in Poland, Czechoslovakia, etc.

At Brussels, I had talks with various people, but will mention only a few. General Al Gruenther looked tired, but was as always nice and com-

fortingly intelligent. The poor fellow has personal worries. His favorite son
was shot and seriously wounded in Korea. Gruenther asked me if Eisenhower (who will command NATO) should go first to Paris, first to London, travel around, or what? I said for God's sake, Eisenhower should
come to France and stay for at least a few months. We should stop these
hysterical junkets around Europe and should give everybody the impression that this is a real headquarters, even if, for a while, such will be an
illusion. If anybody wants to see Eisenhower, they can come to see him, not
vice versa. And he should not talk with any German leaders yet.

Gruenther will be Eisenhower's chief of staff—thank God. Eisenhower
will probably take over the Hotel Astoria in Paris as his first temporary
headquarters. At present, it belongs to the Graves Registration Service.
Sounds like a gloomy foreboding.

Incidentally, Gruenther definitely hinted the Pentagon has hopes of making some sort of a deal with de Gaulle. He gave these hints by the questions
he asked me, including: What did I think of General Billotte?

Gruenther said he thought the Germans would have to be rearmed because the French won't fight very well. They certainly won't if we rearm the
Germans at this moment.

Chip Bohlen came down on the train with me last night and then came
over for a drink. He said that of the ten divisions France was supposed to
furnish by the end of 1951, she would pay only for the equipment of one.
Actually, the number has gone up, but the proportion remains approximately the same. The United States is paying 60 per cent of the cost
of French rearmament. This year, and probably next, we will pay for the
equipment of nine of the ten divisions to be ready at the end of 1951.

He confirmed that the Pentagon was dealing with de Gaulle but said it
was not behind the back of the State Department and that General Billotte
had come to see the American ambassador before he went to Washington.

Chip told me in great confidence (only Acheson and Perkins know it)
that he had asked Acheson for approval to come to dinner with Zhukov
(who, he says, has a very important secret job). Acheson said O.K. I will
arrange it.

At Brussels Joseph Bech, the little Luxembourg minister, was merry and
fairly shrewd. He said the atmosphere of the conference was definitely not
one of enthusiasm and he thought Acheson must be disappointed no matter
what he said. In my room one night, together with his minister in London,
Clausen, Bech took a Top Secret telegram out of his pocket and read it
with great difficulty because he had forgotten his glasses. The purport of it
was that the Luxembourg minister in Moscow had received reports that
Russia had advised France of a guarantee of French frontiers, if France
opposed German rearmament.

I met Chuck Spofford for the first time and asked him why the hell we could not stop this nonsense of pushing German arming until the French had an army. Why not say to the French: "All right, if you don't want ten German divisions, you give us ten more French divisions, just as quickly." He shook his head silently and said: "The Pentagon thinks the Germans are better soldiers. They had a high regard for German troops during the war." Who's loony now?

PARIS, *December 23, 1950*

TALK with David Bruce. Bruce is irritated by the American Army argument that France won't fight. He says powerful groups in the United States and Britain are urging a tripartite alliance between those two countries and Germany. This would isolate France.

PARIS, *January 2, 1951*

ON Saturday night, December 30, I had a small dinner party at home. Those present were: Chip Bohlen and Bill Tyler of the embassy (later U.S. Ambassador to Holland) and Yuri Zhukov. Zhukov had expressed the desire to meet Bohlen. I told this to Chip. George Perkins, in charge of European affairs at State Department, approved the project at Brussels. I invited Zhukov who apparently called off a New Year's weekend trip in order to come. Tyler was there, so that the dinner party would not look too obviously arranged as a get-together between Zhukov and Bohlen.

During the general conversation in French, and later in a direct talk in Russian with Bohlen, Zhukov indicated that:

1. Russia would like very much to have a two-power talk with the United States.

2. If this is impossible, Russia wants a "real" Big Four conference and not just a propaganda meeting.

3. Russia is not really getting on too well with China and the economic problem of aiding China is enormous. The United States has made a propaganda present to Moscow on the subject of China by continually calling Mao Stalin's stooge.

Zhukov is convinced there will not be a war this year and says that absolutely no preparations are being made in the Soviet Union; that there is far less evidence of such preparations than was true in 1939 and 1940 even after the von Ribbentrop–Molotov Pact.

Bohlen went into a long spiel to the effect that the United States would not discuss anything until first the Russians brought about a cease-fire in Korea. He stressed the determination of the American people not to yield and to go to war if necessary.

Zhukov kept suggesting to Chip that he should visit Moscow again because he knew the language and the governmental leaders.

What will come of this talk, I don't know. I am not sure just what Zhukov's position is in addition to being *Pravda*'s correspondent. Unquestionably both sides will report it at length to their governments and probably attribute more significance to it than is warranted. Zhukov and Chip had a long private *tête-à-tête* in Russian in the corner—on Korea.

I was at Chip's house Sunday evening, New Year's Eve, and he took me in a corner and expressed the feeling that the meeting had been a very useful and interesting evening. Clearly Zhukov was acting as Moscow's messenger and not as a journalist.

LONDON, *January 5, 1951*

HAD a two-hour talk with General Anders. He says war is inevitable and very likely this year. He quite evidently hopes for this as the only possible way to accomplish Poland's liberation. However, he says it is a great mistake to rearm Germany before France and England are rearmed—and also before *émigré* Poles, Czechs and others are given token weapons. War would throw many Polish soldiers into the arms of the Communists if they thought they were fighting the Germans. Much as they hate communism, they have not forgotten the barbarity of the Germans during the last five years.

Anders does not think there is a chance of holding any of Europe north of the Pyrenees if war starts during the next few months. Nevertheless, every month that goes by is in our favor now because Western production is so much greater than Soviet production.

He thinks British morale is extremely good—better than eighteen months ago. The British are not enthusiastic for a war but, nevertheless, they are determined and tough. He has Poles scattered all over England in farms, mines and factories and they report to him that the spirit is resolute.

He claims he could mobilize an army of between 80,000 and 100,000 *émigré* Poles if only they are given equipment. The flag of each *émigré* government must be kept flying so that anti-Communists in East Europe can be encouraged to desert.

LONDON, *January 5, 1951*

LUNCHED with Hector McNeil. He is relatively gloomy, believing war with Russia inevitable, but does not think it imminent in the sense of the next eighteen months. I asked him as a betting man what odds he would give against war this year, and he said four-to-one.

He and Hugh Dalton are in a minority in the cabinet on the question of German rearmament. They both feel it is a great mistake to think of rearming Germany before France. He fears that if this is done the Russians may some day come to a rearmed Germany and offer it Alsace and Lorraine as well as the Saar in exchange for an alliance. He said he last saw General Marshall in 1948 and Marshall had at that time said it was imperative to arm the French with any weapons available as quickly as possible. McNeil wonders what has happened to Marshall's policy.

LONDON, *January 6, 1951*

LUNCHED at White's with Randolph Churchill. He is unreasonably cocky about the war situation and thinks the best thing to do would be to drop an atom bomb on Russia immediately. Fortunately, that is neither the policy of the British government nor the desire of the British people.

Later in the afternoon I had a drink with Sir Geoffrey Thompson, former ambassador to Thailand, now at the Defense College. Tommy was very disturbed about the situation. He said there was a growing feeling in England that the United States is pursuing a terrible and foolhardy policy. He also said Britain's voice in world councils is much weaker than it should be, because of Bevin's ill health and resultant failure to grasp the situation adequately or to speak strongly enough.

Tommy says many British now think there is more chance of the United States starting a war in 1951 than of Russia doing it. They are scared of an "irrevocable hysterical act." Public opinion is not as united as it was in 1914 or 1939. Moreover, the British people are not as terrified of communism as are the Americans, because they are confident they are able to handle it. Britain, with five years of austerity behind it, is fed up with talk of "more sacrifice," coming from fat and prosperous America.

On the way home I was talking with my cockney taxicab driver. He said: "Governor, we are not as frightened of Communists as you people are."

PARIS, *January 11, 1951*

SAW David Bruce this afternoon. Bruce said he dined with Churchill one night and was astonished when, after an Alsatian wine with the first course, a Rhine wine with the second course and a good Burgundy with the third course, Churchill called for a bottle of whisky. He filled a tumbler, putting only a dash of water on the top and then drank it off. He offered Bruce the bottle. Bruce declined. The dinner then went on as usual. Churchill showed no sign of any alcoholic effects.

Bruce said the Schuman Plan was close to conclusion, but was being held up by the French argument that the Germans must not be pushed on decartelization until the high commissioners had agreed on decontrols. The Germans want to know the Allied plans on decentralization by January 15.

Bruce asked: "Will we be able to keep Adenauer in power and anyway, is it worthwhile? What concessions would we have to make for this?"

PARIS, *January 12, 1951*

LUNCHED today with Randolph Churchill. He told me his ambition still is to be Prime Minister of England but he thinks now he has rather less chance in the long run than he optimistically felt last time he proclaimed this desire to me two or three years ago.

He said his father is perhaps not 100 per cent sold on Eisenhower. He never forgave Eisenhower for not sending air support to Jumbo Wilson during the Dodecanese campaign. The campaign had been agreed upon at the Quebec Conference and started just after the conference ended. Wilson, after committing his troops, needed P-51 fighter planes—at that time the only Allied fighter with sufficient range. Eisenhower refused to send them on the grounds that the combined chiefs of staff had not recommended this and he needed them for the Salerno operation.

As a result, Churchill really wanted General Marshall to command "Overlord." However, being a good student of psychology, he allowed the impression to be given that he did not want Marshall and that has become the historical version. When Eisenhower was appointed, Churchill "cottoned up" to him strongly and did a deliberate "snow job" on him.

Randolph thinks Roosevelt was in many ways a greater man than his own father and that, above all, he was the greatest politician who ever lived, one who really *knew* public opinion. Roosevelt was always a little bit hurt that Churchill did not remember him from the days of their first meeting in 1919 when Churchill was first lord of the admiralty and Roosevelt was assistant secretary of the navy. Nevertheless, two days after Britain entered World War II, Roosevelt telephoned Churchill from the White House. Churchill thought it was a spoof, told the butler to keep these "damned correspondents" off the phone. A few minutes later, the butler came back and said: "It is really the President." Over the open wire, Roosevelt said: "Winston, we are all for you and I hope you can keep me informed on what is happening." Churchill reported this to Chamberlain (at that time Prime Minister) and Chamberlain gave him permission to do so. Churchill wrote to Roosevelt almost every week afterwards—long before he became Prime Minister.

Churchill always tried to use Harry Hopkins, of whom he was very fond, to put across ideas toward the latter part of the war. He cabled Hopkins more often than Roosevelt. Hopkins would plant the idea in Roosevelt's mind and then FDR, sold on the project, would try and convince Churchill as if it had been Roosevelt's own idea. That, at any rate, is Randolph's account.

He says his father has a curious reputation for drinking much more than he actually does. He really does not know much about food and nothing about wines; he drinks less than a bottle of spirits a day. However, he used to have a whisky and soda at cabinet meetings, and often calls for one at ten o'clock in the morning, but it is always a very weak highball and it may take him three hours or more to finish it. He merely likes to toy with it. Randolph utterly disbelieves David Bruce's account of the dinner party with his father.

He told me his father recently said to him that he had simplified life at Chartwell by arranging that nothing but champagne should be served at lunch as well as dinner—and only Pol Roger. The old man figured that would save him the trouble of worrying which drink should be served, whether it should be beer, hock, claret or Burgundy. Randolph says his father has a horrible fear of brandy which is, he says, "the drunkards' drink." He will never take more than a couple of brandies.

He said Picasso once stated that Churchill could have earned his living as a painter. Since Picasso was already a Communist, Churchill was grumpy about the compliment, but secretly flattered.

Randolph was the only member of the family to greet his father at the airport when he came back from his first visit to Stalin and he dined on the train with him, returning to London. The old man was pretty irritated by Stalin's remarks that the British navy had an insufficient "love of glory" when a convoy turned back because it feared the *Tirpitz* was out. Stalin complained the British were not fighting and that they should get used to the idea of fighting even if they did not like it.

PARIS, *January 15, 1951*

THIS afternoon had a talk with Senator John Sherman Cooper, who has stayed over here since serving as Acheson's adviser at the Brussels conference. Cooper is very anxious for Senator Taft to come abroad and see things for himself. This might change Taft's views.

Cooper has been surprised to find that in Belgium, Luxembourg, England and France the national leaders worry about a lack of judgment and wisdom in American policy.

He found virtually unanimous agreement that the United States has mishandled the German rearmament question, and he thinks McCloy has been indiscreet and has talked too much. We must rearm our allies first.

MADRID, *January 22, 1951*

LUNCH today with Johnny Jones, United States chargé d'affaires, an alert, bright young man. Johnny is clearly not sympathetic to the regime. Yet he views two questions with great levelheadedness: (1) what will be in the best interests of the United States; (2) what will be in the best eventual interests of the Spanish people. He wonders whether we should merely indicate to the Spaniards that, if they wish to defend themselves we will help them with material or whether we can bring them into a coalition as a useful partner.

I reminded him that Doc Matthews told me in October (in Washington) that our policy is to bring Spanish manpower into the North Atlantic Pact after France is somewhat stronger and the German question has been "settled." He thinks that in any case it will only continue to do harm to the Spanish people if they remain isolated; that Spain has been politically, economically and culturally isolated far too long; that increasingly relationships and exchanges with other nations will have useful repercussions in Spain which tends more and more to regard itself as the center of the earth.

MADRID, *January 23, 1951*

I had lunch (literally from 2:15 until 8:15 P.M.—an old Spanish custom) with Don Luis Maria de Lojendio and Don Antonio d'Olosquagua. They—as ever since my first postwar visit in 1946—run the foreign press section. Both are Basques and friends of Lequerica, new Spanish ambassador in Washington. Never before has Lojendio spoken so strongly and openly about the "totalitarian" state nor has he defended censorship and press control so strongly. He used to talk of the "Spanish type of democracy." Now it is open "totalitarianism." He says that suits Spain; that the prevailing economic ills are not its fault; that Spain was a poor country under the monarchy, the republic and the "totalitarian" system. He boasts now of the value of censorship and says it not only "protects" the Spanish people from getting unduly excited about world crises but also protects France and even the United States by preventing the press from publishing hostile articles that might otherwise appear.

Incidentally, I asked Lojendio what people here thought of de Gaulle. (Of course they all hate France as such and despise it as a weak country.) I got a curious answer. According to him, de Gaulle is unpopular because he imprisoned Pétain. Pétain was the great Frenchman! What a country.

MADRID, *January 24, 1951*

ANOTHER talk with Johnny Jones. He said it was imperative for the United States, even if it could not hope to succeed in major policy objectives vis-à-vis Spain, to try and bring the country out of its isolated state as swiftly as possible. At present Spain and her government don't think AT ALL in terms of European cooperation.

America must, in dealing with Madrid, realize these things: Spain is a fact. Franco is a fact. What do you do about it?

There are rumors that the Pope intends to transfer the Vatican's files and seat—if not his Person—to Spain in case of war. I recalled to Johnny that this most Catholic country was above all nationalist and its most Catholic king had given Rome its worst sacking in history. Johnny hadn't remembered this. So I looked it up in a lousy 1911 edition of the *Encyclopedia Britannica* and found that the imperial troops of Charles V in 1527 had sacked Rome "with a violence which cannot be paralleled even in the days of Alaric and Genseric." On May 6, 1527, "the Eternal City was stormed by Imperial troops and subjected to appalling devastation in the famous sack. Clement (VII) was detained for seven months a prisoner in the castle of St. Angelo."

MADRID, *January 25, 1951*

LONG talk in one of Madrid's snappier clubs with Lieutenant General Don Antonio Aranda, apparently the leader of the Monarchist opposition. He is on the "reserve" list, tantamount to retirement. Aranda said that three years ago he had been sent to the Canary Islands, arrested for a few months; not a particularly tough punishment in Spanish terminology. He claimed he was constantly followed by police. He says he is in regular contact with the other opposition groups within the *"Comite Interior de Coordinacion"*—everyone but the Communists. The general has a renowned and apparently well-earned reputation for great courage. This is what Aranda said: The Communist Party has penetrated the Falange. Furthermore, the Falangists are ideologically extremists. Many, when they disagree with Franco, threaten to go over to the Communists. The Communists are again very active; apparently only a few months ago they redoubled their activity, backed by a considerable amount of money. They appear to be following strict orders to "lie low," in terms of sabotage, and to limit themselves to organization and recruitment. The Communists are organizing resistance centers in the mountains and establishing increasing numbers of arms depots. Some of the arms are stolen from Spanish military depots. Some are sent from Russia to Genoa, then transshipped to the Balearic Islands, then transshipped to the Catalan and Valencian coasts.

Aranda said Franco will never accept Don Juan as king. He won't permit a "real king" to come back; only a puppet.

It is impossible to change the regime as things now are. The only two organized forces in the country are the army and the syndicates. The army is not pro-Franco; but it is passive. It won't move against him. The workers have neither arms nor real organization; they dare not take the risk of moving. None of the exiled political leaders, not even Prieto, has any important influence in the country now.

Aranda says the *Alianza* (former opposition coalition) is only a farce: a camouflaged "popular front" and republican group actually run by the

Communists. He says that today there is a real working agreement between the monarchists and the syndicalists. Monarchists, Socialists, union leaders meet occasionally in secret in the CIC.

Aranda says the workers are very anti-Communist. Nevertheless, they will NOT fight any war with Franco as boss. According to him, Franco has put eight thousand chiefs of the CNT and the UGT in prison; some 250,000 are under conditional and observed liberty. Even if the Atlantic Pact, led by the United States, asks Franco to fight, the people will not follow him. The Communists, well aware of this, are making the attitude useful in their organizational campaign.

It would be impossible to mobilize Spain for war: Franco would not trust the people; the army, as it now exists, could not function. Regular officers today are so badly paid that many of them drive taxis or work at other night jobs so they can support their families; they could not "afford" a war.

PARIS, *January 29, 1951*

THIS evening I saw Ambassador Alan Kirk, American envoy to Moscow. Kirk thinks Russia is still seeking to isolate the United States from all its friends and only when that has succeeded, will Moscow strike with force. He found an attitude of real hysteria back home and jokingly said, "It will be good to return to the calm of Moscow." The hysterical situation in the United States makes for bad policy.

He said we are doing with China exactly what the Russians want us to do: isolating it, calling it a puppet of Moscow, and forcing it to depend entirely upon the Russians. He described this as an unreasoned policy which made no diplomatic sense.

PARIS, *January 30, 1951*

I saw President Auriol this afternoon. He seemed a bit jumpy and nervous. When I asked him why France did not mobilize more men and provide more divisions, he got very angry. He made quite a speech pointing out that France took colossal losses in 1914–1918 and had to rebuild herself by her own efforts and rearm herself for a new war. When the Germans struck in the West in 1940, thanks to the Polish collapse and Russian "treason," France was again alone with an insignificant British contribution. The fall and surrender of Belgium exposed the whole French flank.

During four years of German occupation, plus the process of liberation, plus the campaigns in Africa, France lost more dead than Britain and America combined. A very large number of these were racial or political deportees or people killed during the resistance. The entire French coast was mined and had to be demined. Two million houses were destroyed. France has had to budget 4,000,000,000,000 francs for reconstruction. She had to pay the Germans 500,000,000 francs (at a higher rate than the present value) a day during four years of German occupation.

The French alone are defending Southeast Asia against a drive by Mao Tse-tung towards Singapore.

Despite all this, France has managed to demonstrate its energies in recovery. Its industrial production has risen to a rate of between 133 and 135 per cent as compared to 1939. Her trade is balanced.

French military service is on a completely democratic basis and everyone, no matter what his position, is equally affected. France needs weapons before it can have larger targets in terms of numbers of soldiers. The United States is able to build armies that take relatively small casualties because they are protected by a shell of steel.

France has not been in such a fortunate position. France was occupied. Britain, indeed, was bombed and America fought a brave war, but the Frenchman never knew when a knock was coming on the door to summon him to torture.

The United States should not expect *too* much from France. It will certainly contribute as much of its energy to defense as Britain. But, after all, the United States would not, for example, ask Belgium to mobilize as many divisions as America.

Incidentally, I asked Auriol, after he had calmed down, what he thought of the chances of collaborating in any way with Spain. He asked: "Is there a democratic government there?" By his mobile facial expression he made it more than clear how much he detested the thought of collaborating in any way with Franco.

PARIS, *February 7, 1951*

LAST night, the Jugoslav Ambassador gave a reception for Milovan Djilas, a member of the Jugsolav Politburo. Djilas has aged considerably since I last saw him. Although he is only forty, he has grown gray and thin. He said to me: "You never come to see me in Belgrade. You always go straight to Tito." I told him the reason I did not go to see him was that he had never been very friendly; that in 1946 he had publicly announced his intention of hanging me.

Vlado Dedijer, who was doing the interpreting, laughed heartily while translating this. Djilas said it was true; that I had written that Tito was killing Serbian peasants with American rifles. I reminded him that when Tito had first introduced me to him in the spring of 1945, Djilas had said: "Ah. You are the man who writes that our Tito is slaughtering Serbian peasants with American rifles." He then turned his back. Tito patted me on the back and said: "Don't pay any attention to him."

Djilas remembered this. He said: "Tito remembers the good things as well as the bad things. Maybe I just remember the little things." He suggested that we should have a drink, forget everything and start out afresh. "Times have changed."

Dedijer told me Djilas was very much impressed by England and had decided there was far less bureaucracy in English trade unions than in Jugoslav trade unions.

PARIS, *February 8, 1951*

BILL Deakin came to town for a couple of days. He told me that Fitzroy Maclean had asked him if—should trouble come—he would join Maclean on a new mission in Jugoslavia. Deakin refused. I am interested that Maclean—and presumably the British government—is thinking of such a mission again in Jugoslavia in case of war.

BONN, *February 12, 1951*

THIS afternoon, I visited Dr. Kurt Schumacher, head of the Social Democratic Party and probably the most powerful single man in Western Germany. He is a complete cripple with only one arm and one leg, but obviously has a powerful fighting spirit and lives a very active life. He has a comfortable house outside Bonn, where he seems to keep extremely busy. Thin, with a long face and gray-green eyes, he looked rather well for an invalid in frail health. He wore a bright blue suit. In addition to his other infirmities, several of his front teeth are missing from the lower jaw.

Schumacher said neutrality would be impossible in Germany, unless the Russians and Americans could agree to neutralize their own policies. Furthermore, it would be possible for Germany to be neutral only if it were unified. Schumacher could not accept the terms offered by the Russians for unification because Moscow will not permit, as a prerequisite, free elections. These must be held on the same basis as the elections which have already been held in Western Germany and in the Western sector of Berlin.

Schumacher said if unity proves impossible, West Germany must first gain its complete political freedom before even thinking of rearming. This is a prerequisite. Furthermore, the present international situation makes a German military contribution senseless because it could not ward off a Russian attack. It would take at least four years to establish really effective German forces. It is necessary for strong allied forces to protect West Germany while she is rearming. This must be an "Anglo-Saxon" army because the French aren't reliable.

Schumacher was very elusive when I asked him if he considered himself a Marxist, replying: "Marxism is not a catechism or doctrine, but a method of investigating economic and political developments." However, he added that the best fighters against Stalinism "have come from the Marxist school." He said the labor movement in Western Germany and not the *bourgeoisie* was the strongest force against communism.

BONN, *February 13, 1951*

LUNCH with Chancellor Konrad Adenauer in his office. Also present: Dr. Herbert Blankenhorn (Adenauer's chief of cabinet), Casimir von Tschwardowski (head of the government press section), and Ulrich Noack (a former diplomat, now attached to Blankenhorn's office).

We had a long talk in an antechamber over an *apéritif,* followed by an excellent lunch, and then another long talk over brandy and coffee. The entire performance lasted about 2½ hours.

I must say, I had a feeling that Adenauer is a cunning man, but by no means either a leader or a man of vision. He has almost a Balkan quality of suspicion. He seems always to believe that almost everybody is double-crossing him. I wonder if a man with a character like that is not just as ready to do some double-crossing himself. He has certainly changed from his previous pro-French attitude. I suppose this is a result of the dispute over the Saar in January, 1951.

Adenauer mistrusts the French and believes they have been secretly negotiating with the Russians. When I asked him for the basis of this suspicion, he said: "The French knew entirely too much about Grotewohl's 'Unity' proposals before they were made." He thinks Pavlov, the Soviet ambassador in Paris, was secretely negotiating with members of the French government. Furthermore, Adenauer has a contempt for the French and exaggerates their weakness. He thinks the only possible way they could ever be strengthened would be by General de Gaulle coming to power again. The only member of the present French government Adenauer mentioned in a friendly way was Schuman.

Adenauer says the French have told him they are glad to end the High Commission set-up, but do not wish Bonn to be free—in terms of foreign affairs—to negotiate its own relationships with the East European countries. Adenauer insists Bonn should be permitted to negotiate with complete freedom although it would consult the Western powers.

Adenauer complained that the Western powers want to keep Germany "on hand"; that they wish to negotiate with Russia before the status of the Germans has been decided and turn to Germany as friends only if their talks with Moscow fail.

FRANKFURT, *February 14, 1951*

THIS afternoon I had a talk with Colonel Henry Byroade, head of the German section of the State Department (later assistant secretary of state, and ambassador). He claims the concept of a European army is not French but American. Byroade (who was with Marshall in China and became one of his fair-haired boys) said he himself drew up the first paper on this subject on July 27, 1950. He still hopes a European army can be formed if it is based upon divisional contingents rather than combat teams.

There is a terrible shortage of able German officials. This is too bad because many committees on different aspects will have to negotiate a long time. The refusal of Adenauer to delegate power makes it difficult to negotiate with him. Adenauer has a much weaker position now than a year ago. The parties in the government coalition are now against him on many issues.

WIESBADEN, *February 15, 1951*

LUNCH today with (Lieutenant General) Lauris Norstad, commander of the American Air Force in Europe. At present he is living with his wife and daughter in the palatial home of the Henkel family, champagne merchants, one of whose members married Ribbentrop. He will come to Paris in about a month to become Eisenhower's chief air subordinate.

He said NATO should include Spain, whose air bases would be useful, even if not essential. Very shortly, Ambassador Bruce will present the French government with a coordinated request for American air bases on all French territory in and near Europe and suggesting agreement on specific items such as labor and costs.

Norstad said anything between 60 and 85 percent of Soviet bombers attacking the United States could at present get through to their targets.

PARIS, *February 18, 1951*

TONIGHT Gruenther and his wife came for a quiet dinner. Gruenther admitted that when he went out to Toyko last summer, he had a preconceived prejudice against MacArthur, but by the time he left Toyko, MacArthur's charm and personality had won him over. "How long did he take to get you in his pocket?" Al asked me. "About thirty seconds." "Oh," Al sneered, "it was about thirty minutes for me."

PARIS, *February 19, 1951*

THIS morning I saw Donald Heath, American minister in Indochina, on his way back to Saigon. He says things are much better. An important amount of American war material has now been reaching Indochina; in fact it is not too much to say that it may have saved the situation during the recent battles in Tonkin.

Heath is very favorably impressed with the generalship of De Lattre de Tassigny. He says De Lattre is now back seeking more manpower. He would like to have more than 10,000 new troops—French, not natives. Eventually, troops now in Indochina could be returned to France to help in building up the NATO army. This would be especially important in terms of trained cadres. However, replacements are now needed because of casualties.

Heath says Bao Dai has impressed him as being an intelligent and intricate character. He intends to reread *Hamlet* because of the resemblance in personality of the two princes!

Later I lunched with Phil Bonsal, who told me a basic decision had been reached to try and bring Spain into NATO. Bonsal is worried and thinks the military minds sometimes ignore the more important political and philosophical problems; that we might be using different kinds of "bricks" to build the structure and find they contained a "corrupting" material that might weaken the building. He strongly believes we should pay more attention to the philosophical and political ideals of the alliance than we are doing.

PARIS, *February 22, 1951*

LUNCH with Brigadier General C. T. Lanham, generally known as "Buck." Although a Regular Army officer, he has much wider interests than is usually the case with American military men. Before being assigned to SHAPE, he was military attaché in Brussels. During the war, he commanded a regiment in the Huertgen Forest and made the first deep penetration of the Siegfried Line. He has a first-class collection of ribbons acquired for gallantry. He feels strongly about the idealistic purposes of SHAPE and vigorously opposes the idea of diluting its ideology for pragmatic purposes—such as admitting the Fascist government of Spain for the sake of a few additional divisions.

Lanham is a close friend of Ernest Hemingway, who was with his regiment for some time in Germany. He also visited Hemingway in Cuba. He says Hemingway has the heart of a lion and is first class in war, but horrible in peace. Hemingway used to wander around with two canteens strapped to his belt. One was filled with gin and the other with vermouth. Whenever there was a quiet moment, he would haul out a battered tin cup and suggest: "Let's have a Martini." He was a good fighter with all weapons, although, strictly speaking, he was not permitted to bear arms, because he was there as a war correspondent. Hemingway used to say that he was going to have the Geneva Convention tattooed on his back side in reverse so he could read it looking in a mirror. Lanham says he is entirely fearless.

He and Hemingway made a bet in Normandy as to which one could get into a certain village first. Lanham found a peasant who showed him a side road, and he was there, having a drink, when Hemingway arrived with his French jeep driver, "Michel."* An old peasant come up to the two of them and asked each one: "Are you the general?" At that time, Lanham was still a colonel. Hemingway told the peasant Lanham was the general. The peasant then turned to Hemingway, looking at his graying hair and beard and asked: "How is it that a man of your years is only a captain?" (the rank Hemingway told him was his). Hemingway replied: "It is to my eternal shame and sorrow that I must confess I never learned how to read or write."

The troops in the regiment used to call Hemingway "Mr. Ernie." In battle he is quiet and modest. Yet, when Lanham visited Hemingway in Cuba, he was loud and boastful, surrounded by toadies. He insisted on dominating everyone.

Lanham claims Hemingway drinks gallons of hard liquor—mostly Martinis mixed at the rate of fifteen-to-one. He had a head injury in an automobile accident in England some years ago and every now and then the wound breaks open. He has a bad skin disease on his face, and cannot shave. Although he takes handfuls of sleeping pills, he always wakes up around four-thirty o'clock in the morning. He usually starts drinking right away and writes standing up, with a pencil in one hand and a drink in the other. He mixes his drinks all day long and buys double daiquiris for everybody in a cheap local bar. When he is "in training" he does not drink until noon, but usually around 11 A.M. he starts on the excuse that it is "noon in Miami." Despite this fantastic life, his physique is still good. He has immense biceps and stomach muscles and can swim for miles. Many years ago, friends of his wanted him to seek the heavyweight championship from Jack Johnson.

Hemingway says all he ever learned about writing was from Gertrude Stein. During his youthful years in Paris he lived on starvation rations and frequently earned a little extra money by acting as a sparring partner for boxers, despite the weakness of hunger. Lanham says Hemingway has been badly shot up at various times and is full of lead.

Lanham was partly the model for the Colonel in *Across the River and into the Trees,* but, of course, the real model was Hemingway himself.

PARIS, *February 28, 1951*

LAST night dinner at Chip Bohlen's. Carmel Offie, retired United States diplomat, said that when Ambassador Kirk was home recently, he

* This is a pseudonymn.

warned President Truman to make no mistake about Russia: that Russia could be provoked into war on the subject of German rearmament. He said the CIA had been very disturbed about the article I wrote on Albania last March from Istanbul. There had been an important meeting of CIA and State Department officials in which it was decided to demand from me where I got the story. Offie had refused to sign the cable.

Offie, who is a devout Catholic, thought my articles on Spain were very good and very fair. He is now acting as an official for the Free Labor Organization, but I suspect is also working for CIA.

PARIS, *March 5, 1951*

DINNER last night with Gruenther. He told me Eisenhower is very irked about Secret Service precautions, which limit his movements. It is obvious that it would be useful to the Communists to knock Eisenhower off. As a result, special pains are taken to guard him. Eisenhower would like to play some golf but his guards have so far refused to permit him to do so. He is fretting.

PARIS, *March 6, 1951*

LUNCH with General Eisenhower, Gruenther, Lanham and Colonel Virden. Eisenhower was in an extremely good humor, full of beans. He has gained a bit of weight and aged somewhat since I last saw him but is very vigorous. He chafed at the diet set for him by his doctor, General Snyder. He appears to be on the water wagon and doesn't smoke. He is very anxious to relax a bit and suggested playing bridge Thursday afternoons. He is also anxious to arrange a golf foursome.

He asks: "What would have happened had Moscow started war last year? or the year before?" He answers his own question by citing current military preparations of NATO. Admittedly, SHAPE headquarters is still undergoing birth pangs and has not yet even moved into its permanent buildings. Nevertheless, the basic deterrent exists: American nuclear superiority in atomic fission plus the ability to deliver this where strategically required. Therefore the prospects of a Soviet invasion are in all probability remote. The new NATO armies cannot be considered a threat to Soviet security in any sense.

We are working for a limited number of Western divisions in the general area of the Rhine. At best they could be employed in battle around the Elbe. It is ludicrous to fancy they might be conceived as a force to assault the Oder; still more ludicrous to imagine them fighting on the Vistula; beyond all reason to think of the small army being planned ever getting involved in combat further eastward.

This army is conceived solely as a defensive force safeguarding nations which have reason to feel themselves threatened. In *no* sense can Moscow or anyone else regard it as provocative. Therefore it is not only *not* accelerating the possible imminence of war; it is achieving the opposite. In the end it will serve as a deterrent to any imperialist thoughts entertained by Moscow which might otherwise be attracted westward by a vacuum.

Eisenhower has been painstakingly explaining to political leaders that the Allied forces being assembled have only one fundamental objective: the preservation of peace. The subsidiary *raison d'être* is, of course, to afford the best possible military defensive prospects should war recur.

Eisenhower says NATO protects the *national* freedom of its members and of any nations which may later choose to align themselves, in one way or another, with the alliance. It is not NATO's business to mix in any way into the political or ideological affairs of other countries. It is concerned with the independence of nations as such. But Eisenhower emphasizes the intrinsic importance of personal liberty within the framework of national liberty.

He said he cannot personally approve of governmental systems that make of the individual citizen a slave or servant of the state. But he has a clear idea of the authority he holds as NATO commander and that does not impinge upon the realm of political philosophy. He feels it is absurd for Americans to expect all other nations to model their governing systems upon our own—one which took some three centuries to mature in its special surroundings.

This world cannot be divided into realms of "black" and "white." There are large "gray" areas: regions where for different causes various philosophic concepts and economic conditions have arisen.

Eisenhower has been deeply impressed by all he has heard of the fighting spirit and determination of Greece and Turkey. He thinks it would be excellent, from a strategic point of view, if the Eastern Mediterranean were strongly braced and if any conceivable threat of attack on Western Europe were to be menaced by a problem on Russia's left flank. He recognizes that Jugoslavia is, politically, a Communist state but it has already asserted its intention of defending its *national* integrity. Therefore he favors granting all necessary assistance to Marshal Tito to preserve economic viability, and to improve his military potential. He would like to demonstrate that the United States is doing more to aid the suffering Jugoslavs than the Soviet Union is doing to alleviate Hungary, Rumania and Bulgaria—lands stricken by drought last year.

Eisenhower feels that all nations wishing to join in strengthening Western defenses against aggression should be encouraged. Nevertheless he recognizes special political problems are presented by Spain. One European statesman told Ike that Franco would welcome an invitation to join NATO because it would give him pleasure to spurn it. Eisenhower admits there would be difficulty in associating the Franco government with Britain and

France. It is certainly not worth risking offending two of NATO's principal members on this issue.

Therefore he thinks it might be wise to make some preliminary military arrangements with Spain before any political compact. He would like to coordinate some of Spain's particular defensive problems with the overall common task of Western Europe.

Eisenhower kept stressing that a soldier must have a clear feeling he is fighting for a worthy cause. One of the tasks of NATO governments is to disseminate among their populations the moral principles of NATO: freedom, peace, self-defense. Ike recognizes the immense importance of morale and hopes the NATO governments will coordinate their propaganda.

He says the Italian soldier did not feel he had a worthy cause for which to fight in either world war. During World War I he saw his country sit on the fence until a victor appeared probable, and then join the Allies for selfish reasons. This is what was at the root of the Caporetto disaster. During World War II Mussolini's bravado was not able to instill vigor in the Italian soldier's heart—as demonstrated first in the Albanian campaign. Even during the days of Garibaldi's insurrection the morale question was not adequately met. The hostility of the Piedmontese for the Neapolitan remained a deterrent factor.

But Italy is now building up twelve good divisions—the number permitted within limitations of the Paris Peace Treaty. These will be exceedingly important to NATO because they are strategically placed to protect the Lombard plain and one invasion route to France; to help hold the free sea lanes of the Mediterranean. They are developing into *good* divisions because the soldiery is aware of the values for which it might be called upon to fight.

Ike is bearish on the European army. He emphasizes the technical difficulties of command and organization, the complexities of interplay between governments that might have contingents assigned in mixed units. He recalls that in past history individual national units fought together on foreign soil—such as the mercenary English and Swiss "companies" that sold their services in medieval and Renaissance Italy. But the problem which would be presented today bears no comparison. Good soldiers might indeed be found among *émigrés* in Europe or among adventurous-minded Germans. But they would have to be organized in some form of foreign legion. This is different. A European army would be difficult to work out. In a sense, it would be "putting the cart before the horse" because it would represent a political unity that does not yet exist. If the experiment is attempted, it should start slowly; forming one division of mixed brigade combat teams, assigning to it officers of exceptional quality and political awareness.

Eisenhower complained of intergovernmental wrangling. He said he doesn't care if governments are red-faced. What would distress him would be to see populations white-faced. He does not consider assignment of positions in SHAPE headquarters in the category of political plums or gestures towards national pride. These jobs are not kudos. Rather than being a "wreath of roses" such an assignment is more truly a "crown of thorns."

As each nation has more and more citizens selected for SHAPE, it gains not prestige but added responsibility. SHAPE is an international headquarters and as such as equally responsible to all member governments.

Ike says he is a good soldier and works for an American administration— as well as for Allied governments. But this does not necessarily identify him with the social or political philosophy of the administration. Nevertheless, he is on record, he recalls, as favoring unity among nations menaced by aggression, and as recognizing the necessity of combating communism economically if that threat is to be overcome. He wants the West's workers and farmers to feel that NATO is conceived to help preserve them and their way of life. He once talked with a French peasant who boasted that his plot of land had been tilled for six hundred years by his own family. That peasant's love of his own soil must be encouraged and defended.

When he visited Paris in January, Ike was asked if he would see de Gaulle. He replied that he would seek no such appointment; but, on the other hand, he would never refuse a visit from an old wartime comrade-in-arms.

He confessed that in political prejudices he has a far greater community of views than disparity of views with Herbert Hoover or with Senator Taft, despite their vigorous disagreements on the subject of NATO. But he is not thinking as a political man today, only as commander of an Allied force. He does not believe an army—any army—should mix in politics.

During World War II, it was suggested to him that he should pioneer social reform in the United States by ameliorating relationships between Negroes and whites in his units. Regardless of the good intentions of such a suggestion, Ike felt it was not the role of any army or its commander to spearhead social reform in the government to which it was responsible. Any American general who conceived his duties as such should be fired.

PARIS, *March 12, 1951*

LUNCH with Eisenhower, Chip Bohlen and Bunny Carter at Morfontaine Golf Club; then we played. Ike was in a fine mood. It was the first opportunity he had had to get away from his office. Nevertheless, a French secret police guard followed us around at a discreet distance. Eisenhower plays an amiable, steady, unsensational game. He made an eighty-eight and was very pleased with himself. He has a slight fade on his woods but hits good eight and nine irons and is quite a good putter.

Ike is very enthusiastic about golf. He is also extremely fond of fishing and we had quite a talk on the subject afterwards in the locker room. He was pleased to win five hundred francs because it is the first French money he has had in his hands since 1929. His aides are generally with him and pay for everything.

The general reminisced about various things. He recalled going to the races here in 1929 and making a bet on a horse named "Hot Weed" because it sounded like an American horse. It turned out to be a French horse, but it won and enabled Eisenhower to celebrate that evening.

He said he had been at West Point with Van Fleet and they used to play football together. Van Fleet is a good fighter. Once, when Eisenhower visited him, Van Fleet told him not to expect any signs of bright strategy. He said: "I don't know anything about that sort of thing. I am pretty dumb. All I know is how to fight."

Eisenhower thinks that Zhukov is a really "good" Russian with whom the West might have gotten along, but the Soviet system prevents any such possibility of an individual rising to such a position. In August 1945 Eisenhower was visiting Moscow. As an exceptional honor, he was invited to join Stalin on top of Lenin's tomb during a review in the Red Square of gymnastic formations. Eisenhower was allowed to take Harriman and his military attaché, General Deane, with him. It was killing business to stand up there for five hours, but the review was impressive.

Ike said he thought perhaps the most disastrous decision ever taken by makers of American policy was to abandon Chiang Kai-shek because he refused to allow any Communists in his government. (An oversimplified view, indeed! say I.)

PARIS, *March 14, 1951*

LUNCH at David Bruce's with René Pleven (former prime minister and now vice-premier) and Jean Monnet (inventor and chief proponent of the Schuman Plan). Both Pleven and Monnet are very worried about the American attitude towards Spain. They vigorously urged that the United States should not attempt to spring a unilateral solution *de facto* upon the French just before elections—the way we announced our intentions to rearm Germany in September, 1949. Neither France nor Britain would tolerate this, and there is an extremely strong feeling against Franco. Bruce assured them Washington has no such plans. Nevertheless, they emphasized the fear that the United States might secretly tell Franco it would arrange a deal with him and would "take care" of Paris and London.

Pleven explained that, in French politics, the fall of a government does not mean a change in policy. Under the Third Republic there was a curious sense of responsibility. Ousted politicians agreed to take minor jobs in order to preserve French national policy. That is why Pleven, for example, is now vice-premier and has moved his office from the Hotel Matignon to a small *hotel particulier* across the street. The national policy of France, as far as foreign affairs go, remains unchanged always. The changes in government result continually from internal and local political disputes.

Monnet stressed the conviction that every Frenchman is at least as concerned about his position and renown in his local *pays,* as he is in terms of Paris and France as a nation. Monnet claims French individuality and particularism—which he contends have produced the genius of France—result from the geography of the country with its varied plains, mountains and valleys. America, a country of vast plains, has developed differently and the two-party political system could not apply in France, whose regionalism requires many parties.

Bruce said he was horrified at the way the Ruhr industrialists are behaving. First, they insisted German steel companies should obtain 50 per cent of their coal from their own "captive" mines. This was allowed. Then a new agreement was given them allowing 75 per cent from "captive" holdings. Now they are demanding 100 per cent. They are putting heat on Adenauer not to agree to the Schuman Plan until all their ambitious demands are acceded to. Instead of arguing out their case in the Bonn parliament, after the Plan has been initialed but before it has been ratified, they are exercising direct influence upon the executive branch of the government.

Despite all this, Monnet says he remains optimistic. The only hope is that Germany can be integrated into the West so that eventually the German mentality can be altered.

Pleven said two groups have controlled Germany in the past; the general staff and the Ruhr barons. The Pleven plan and the Schuman plan are designed to eliminate these by preventing the resurgence of a purely German army or a purely German industry, permitting German energy and talent to work for the benefit of Western Europe as a whole.

I asked Monnet if he did not think there was a possibility that some day when Western Germany (integrated into Western Europe) and Eastern Germany (integrated into Eastern Europe) were unified, it might result in a political explosion equivalent to the union of two pieces of U-235, which produces atomic fission. He was startled.

PARIS, *March 16, 1951*

LUNCHED and played golf with Eisenhower today. Morfontaine is usually closed Mondays, but they opened the course for us and arranged caddies. Nobody else there. He made a ninety-one (with a nine); I made an eighty. Incidentally, he straightened out my putting for me. One of his favorite expressions—used when someone hits a long shot—is "a country mile."

The general talked at length about Forrestal. He said that in 1943

Forrestal was the only man in the Cabinet who sized up the Russians properly. Roosevelt always said "I can handle Uncle Joe." The rest of the Cabinet believed the Russians would be peaceful. Eisenhower thought that after the war the Russians would want a period to recover. Furthermore, modern communications would make it easier for us to tell the truth about the democratic world. Unfortunately, communications have helped Russian propaganda more than ours. Forrestal always cited Lenin's and Stalin's writings and said it was impossible to expect collaboration with them. They were our implacable enemies.

At the end of the war Admiral Doenitz, who had succeeded Hitler, proposed to Eisenhower that, despite the German surrender, all German divisions under arms should immediately be placed under Eisenhower's command and used against the Russians. It would not affect the German defeat. Naturally, the proposal was rejected.

Eisenhower, at lunch, compared Montgomery and Patton. He said Patton did not know how to stand and fight a set battle, but was a genius at pursuit. He liked to make headlines and the best way was by registering the deepest advance. Montgomery could fight a methodical, planned battle and knew how to get the utmost out of the British Tommy.

Incidentally, Ike says the Tommy will fight harder under worse conditions than any other soldiers except Germans. Our soldiers have to be convinced that the fate of the nation depends upon this or that particular effort in order to equal the Tommy.

Montgomery is not a good strategist. He moves too slowly. During the Normandy break-out, Montgomery failed to utilize to its full potentialities the Falaise "killing ground." Montgomery thought he had done well but Eisenhower says he missed a great opportunity.

I asked Ike if he would have fought the battle of El Alamein the same way Montgomery did. He said Montgomery protected his tanks with infantry during the initial penetration stages. Eisenhower would have first attacked the German mine field with "scout" forces of tanks. Then, the infantry and reserve tanks would have been used to exploit the opening. This would have saved lives. He got up in the empty Morfontaine dining room, gathered salt and pepper cellars, sketched a battle map on the paper tablecloth and moved his "divisions" around. Like a fool I didn't pinch the table cover map—"Eisenhower's plan for El Alamein."

He used to play halfback on the West Point football team in the early days of the T formation. His playing weight was 174 pounds. Oddly enough, every player of the backfield weighed 174. Ike was very disappointed that he had to give up golf just during the "wrong" years. Naturally, the war prevented him from playing during middle age. He developed arthritis and bursitis which harmed his swing afterwards. Still, he adores the game. In America he likes to play at two courses where Ed Dudley is professional, in Colorado and at the National in Augusta, Georgia. He describes Dudley not only as the best teacher in the game but as "the man with the molasses swing," in terms of sweetness, not slowness. In Georgia, he plays often with Bobby Jones. He admires the way Jones putts. He never hesitates a moment. While walking up to the ball, he studies the line so that all he has to do is to bend over and tap it swiftly.

After the game, we relaxed over Scotch and soda. I asked the general why he gave up smoking. He said he had been very ill two years ago and almost died. The doctor suggested to him each day that he abstain from smoking for another day. He has continued this abstinence although he has not committed himself to swearing off for life. He said he was a chain smoker and used to smoke sometimes five packs a day.

During his Army career he has done a great deal of "military writing." He said most American Army officers write very badly, so that he made quite a study of such books as *Fowler's English Usage*. When writing, he found it very useful always to have a cigarette at hand.

PARIS, *March 17, 1951*

DINNER with General Pierre Billotte, at the home of his fiancée, the former Sybil Esmond (resumed her maiden name after her previous marriage). She has lived in France most of her life—except for ten years in New York and five years in Rome. Used to be the French women's golf champion, but has given up the game. Enormously rich. Also very nice.

Billotte, whom I've known since he was a captain, told me he had resigned his commission to go into politics. He is member of the governing board of the Gaullist party and hopes to stand for the assembly. He estimates de Gaulle has between 40 per cent and 45 per cent of the people behind him. However, he complains the electoral law works in such a way that it requires almost three times as many votes to elect a Gaullist to the assembly as a Radical or a Communist. He says the present system in France is crippling the country. There is too much optimism now concerning Western Europe and the situation remains extremely bad. He has a feeling there is a growing sympathy for de Gaulle in the United States.

Billotte thought France had quite a few good division and corps commanders but was very short on top-flight generals. He had a great admiration for Leclerc. He modestly classified de Gaulle, De Lattre de Tassigny and himself as "the only French generals with a real sense of strategy." He says de Lattre possesses enormous self-confidence, a great sense of instinct, and luck—which is enough to make a good general.

I first met Billotte in the cellar of the Hotel Metropole in Moscow in 1941 during an air raid. Then a captain—son of the famous Billotte who commanded in the north in 1940—Pierre had been taken prisoner but had just managed to escape from Germany with two other officers. When they crossed into Russia, they were arrested, but eventually released after Hitler attacked. The Russians questioned them very intensively on German troop dispositions in Western Europe. Later on so did the British. The British, who did not want a second front at that time, estimated the Germans had a huge number of divisions in France. The Russians, who did want an invasion, said they had hardly any.

BELGRADE, *April 3, 1951*

LONG and excellent chat with Milovan Djilas, minister without portfolio and member of the Politburo, Number Two or Number Three in the country. We met in his office in the prime minister's building, a rather ugly carpeted room with typical central European furniture and a picture of Tito. We drank Turkish coffee. Djilas smoked a curiously shaped fake-amber stemmed pipe and I smoked Jugoslav cigarettes. Vlado Dedijer, good friend of Djilas', translated.

Djilas didn't look well; no longer the tough Montenegrin Partisan leader. He has lost lots of weight. Afterwards Vlado told me Djilas was ill; people were worried about him and wished he would have a complete physical check-up. He was wearing brown golf knickerbockers and a brown tweed coat; a checked shirt open at the collar, no necktie. On his desk were a visored cap and a brief case. Afterwards we drove off (a chauffeur did the driving) in his Buick convertible. We were accompanied by another individual in civilian clothes who might have been his bodyguard. Djilas spoke very frankly and openly, with evident friendship for the United States. This is what he said in substance:

The satellite armies (Bulgaria, Rumania, Hungary) are getting stronger all the time. The Russians are replacing outmoded equipment. They have definite superiority over Jugoslavia in armor, aircraft and vehicles. However, Jugoslavia retains superiority in other weapons, in morale and in officers. Jugoslavia feels confident that, if invaded, it could seize additional weapons from the invaders.

Satellite morale is poor. For example, in Bulgaria, there are no officer cadres. It is improbable that the USSR would risk provoking a direct or satellite war this year. There has been no real change in Soviet military contingents in Danubia since I was last here in November. They are based on air and motorized forces.

Bulgarians are seeking by all means to escape into Jugoslavia and many have succeeded. If the Bulgars hadn't established very strong police and military forces at the border there would be a mass emigration. There is even stronger opposition to the Russians in Poland and Czechoslovakia. In Poland it is based on "nationalist" elements; in Czechoslovakia on "democracy." American propaganda is bad in this respect. It tends to associate the opposition with *émigré* leaders like Mikolajczyk and King Peter.

Admittedly the former means more than the latter but no *émigré* movement can succeed. (I refrained from reminding Djilas of Lenin's success.)

In Albania things are even worse. It is a pitiful little country. Hoxha has lost the support of all elements and merely keeps in the saddle by brutal police methods. The police are loyal because they have been established as a privileged class. Moscow never signed an alliance with Albania for two reasons: (1) because it wished to keep its hands free for the possibility of trading Albania off to the West in exchange for something else; (2) because it wanted to be free to provoke an insurrection there as an excuse to invade Jugoslavia.

Stalin told Djilas in 1947 that Albania was the "weak point" in the Communist structure. Djilas says he now realizes just why Stalin was content to keep it weak. However, he is worried about outside interference in Albania. Jugoslovia would like to see Albania free—but within its present boundaries. It opposes Greek desires to gain southern Albania. What is the use of risking the entire democratic structure (with possible Soviet reaction) for the sake of two poor provinces? Venizelos recently proposed to the new Jugoslav minister in Athens that the two countries should partition Albania. This was vigorously rejected. It was because of this idea that Djilas has encouraged a recent spate of articles opposing foreign meddling in Albania.

Jugoslavia is pleased with American generosity and the way the food assistance program was carried out. It trusts Washington and knows the United States has no intentions on this country, politically, militarily or ideologically. America must follow its policy of giving things for the common interest but not demanding political concessions. That would be fatal. The people would resent it and fail to understand. Jugoslavia has not embarked upon a course of democratizing its political system just to please America or in gratitude for food. Nevertheless, its social system is growing closer to that of ours. It would be foolish for Jugoslavia to join the Atlantic Pact. It is valuable to keep Jugoslavia an independent socialist country. That damages Moscow much more and keeps hope alive among the oppositional elements in satellite countries.

Nevertheless, it is apparent that our countries must work out a basis for mutual aid. In a sense they are already allies. Some day a system can be arranged for joint declarations of mutual policy; this would be different from a formal alliance such as NATO. Negotiations for arms aid from America must come about (I gathered some such talks have started). It is necessary to have certain equipment for training purposes. This army must be modernized. But naturally such negotiations must take place in secret, without publicity. Otherwise great harm might be caused. General Vlatko Velebit returns to Washington tomorrow to resume negotiations for raw material aid from the United States (he handled the food assistance talks).

It is necessary—before a war—for Jugoslavia to work out a common defense plan with Greece and Turkey. Diplomatic relations with those countries are now normal. Each must know how many divisions the other can provide on a particular sector in case of emergency. Such arrangements must be made *before* a war breaks out. Djilas thinks the chances of war this year are remote—because of the popular attitude in the Soviet bloc which cannot be counted on. Therefore he feels there is time to make common defense preparations.

Djilas recognizes there must be a strong Balkan flank to menace a Soviet attack. I told him if he wanted to facilitate things this government should be more open and friendly with the American military attaché, who can't even get to see such men as Colonel General Popović. Djilas apologized, explaining that first of all the tradition of the Communist Party here was secrecy because it had been illegal and underground for so long; secondly, the army itself was extra suspicious; all armies always thought themselves surrounded by spies. He promised to rectify this situation and help our military attaché.

Djilas thought American propaganda suffered bacause it always stressed opposition to communism—rather than Soviet imperialism. Many eastern European people hated Russia but wanted to retain some of the "advantages" brought about since the war—such as nationalization of many industries in Bulgaria or the joint Beneš–Gottwald program of 1945 in Czechoslovakia. The United States should recognize this and stick to the main points. Also, it should rid itself of the continual taint of *émigré* leaders who had lost contact with reality. Jugoslav propaganda had a considerable effect in Eastern Europe despite its weakness both quantitatively and qualitatively, because it stuck to the main point: Soviet imperialism.

The "Titoist," or deviationist, movement was spreading. It will come soon in France and on a *nationalist* basis. The movement was perhaps not as strong as might have been hoped in Italy because of the apathy of the working masses. Nevertheless, when they quit the party structure, Cucchi and Magnani had taken with them the best cadres of the Italian partisans— the only men who knew how to fight. Magnani was a brave man who left the Italian army before the 1943 surrender, had found his way to the Cetniks, escaped to the Partisans and there became chief of staff of a division.

The most important part of our talk came at the end. Djilas said he understood I was going to Greece. I said yes. Would I see the King and the chief of staff? Yes. Would I please tell them Jugoslavia was willing to join in mutual defense talks, perhaps an ultimate alliance? I asked if this was *just* Djilas' personal idea or if he spoke for Tito. "The latter," he said, looking me straight in the eye. "Very well," I said. "It's not my regular work but I'll transmit the message."

A far cry from when Djilas turned his back on me—or offered to have me hanged.

BELGRADE, *April 4, 1951*

ANOTHER talk with Vlado Dedijer. He said the Russians appeared to be stirring up trouble in Albania—possibly seeking an excuse to intervene in Jugoslavia. A bomb was thrown at the Soviet embassy—maybe a Soviet agent provocateur. Leaflets and agents from the *émigré* movement in Italy have been dropped in Albania and the Kossovo Metohia areas of Jugoslavia. Other leaflets were dropped in eastern Jugoslavia—by mistake. They were in Bulgarian and meant for Bulgaria. Dedijer is confused and suspects the Russians. (I suspect C. D. Jackson's amateurish "Free Europe" Committee.)

Dedijer also indicated Jugoslavia is about to change its propaganda line on China and "explain to the people" that China is an imperialist, aggressive power. He wants to send a man to my office in Paris to look through our bound files for data. I said O.K.—when I get back. This will be important. Indeed Ambassadors Peake (British) and Allen (American), when I told them, refused to believe it.

Dedijer says that in the early party days (when it was underground in Jugoslavia) Tito traveled along different routes than those assigned by the Comintern because he suspected rivals or traitors might turn him over.

This evening I dined with Ambassador George Allen after drinks with Sir Charles Peake. When Moše Pijade left for London he told Peake he had three requests: to see the Turners in the National Gallery; to see the Constables; to see Churchill. Odd for a Communist! He spent a day at Chartwell with Churchill. They compared notes on painting.

At Allen's home was Earle Cocke, commander of the American Legion, who has been giving out toys here. How weird we can get! He was accompanied by a character named Norman Dodge who described himself as "the Old Sarge" when introduced. Together they might have come out of a musical comedy. Allen said Cocke had unsuccessfully sought to see Tito (who is ill) and left a questionnaire which he wants to publicize, asking such appalling things as whether Jugoslavia, if attacked, will stand in the flatlands or withdraw immediately to the hills!

BELGRADE, *April 5, 1951*

TODAY I saw Allen again. He told me that on State Department instructions last December he had asked Tito to consider releasing Stepinac. Tito, for the only time in Allen's experience, grew very cold. He said Stepinac had been sentenced for his crimes and forced conversions and not for religious reasons; that "public opinion" would not tolerate his release.

Allen showed me a copy of the leaflet in Bulgarian that had been dropped by mistake in Jugoslavia, much to our embarrassment. It summoned Bulgarians to action against the Communist government; told them to listen carefully to the radio.

Lunched at Vladimir Dedijer's house. He and Vera, his wife, were exceptionally friendly. He said his mother had taught for some years in a girls' college and he studied there; was teased as the "boy from the girls' school." He became a Communist when he was eighteen (about twenty years ago). (He used to deny to me that he was a Communist!) Tito stayed in Vlado's house before the war but for a long time Vlado didn't know he was Communist Party secretary. Djilas, now forty, is Vlado's oldest Party friend. Vlado is obviously confused by the Cominform dispute. He is groping his way towards Western democracy like so many Jugoslavs. England with its socialism seems to be a convenient stepping stone.

ATHENS, *April 10, 1951*

THIS morning I had a long chat with Prime Minister Sophocles Venizelos, an old friend and amiable little man, not too bright and certainly not strong of will. He said it was at Greek initiative that an exchange of military attachés with Belgrade had recently been arranged. The Jugoslav minister, Jovanović, had been to see him three times since his arrival. In one talk Jovanović asked if Greece would aid Jugoslavia should that country be attacked. Venizelos replied with the question: "What will you do if we are attacked?" There the matter rests. But it is obviously in the minds of both parties. Venizelos begged me not to mention this even to his undersecretary for foreign affairs.

Venizelos said it was imperative that the West should fix plans for defense of the Balkans. If they are not going to do so, obviously the Jugoslav army would be exposed and threatened with isolation.

Later this morning I saw Lieutenant General Grigoropoulos, now chief of the Greek general staff. I knew him a few years ago as commander of C Corps in the Macedonia–Thrace area. He is a stocky short man whose once red hair has gone gray. He has small blue eyes, a ruddy complexion, a bullet head, high cheekbones and looks exactly like a typical Russian general. He is very wrought up about Greek children taken to Jugoslavia; mistrusts Tito and doubts if he is sincere in his intentions to aid the West.

When I gave Grigoropoulos the message from Djilas about a possible alliance (which I did *not* tell the gossipy Venizelos), the general almost jumped out of his seat. Then he regarded me sceptically with his shrewd, peasant's eyes. He said nothing, only that I should talk about it to the King.

ATHENS, *April 12, 1951*

I visited King Paul this evening for a lengthy chat. He was wearing a double-breasted pin-stripe suit instead of uniform and had just come back from a trip to Olympia with the British and American ambassadors.

He said Papagos recently told him the Bulgarians had three times as much artillery as Greece and much stronger air and armored forces. Paul thinks Turkey, despite appearances, would like to stay out of a new war and would do its level best to do so. Cyprus is an irritating problem and the British have behaved stupidly. If they would only at least promise to review the situation after the lapse of a certain period of time it would ease the temper of the people. Instead they affirm it is a closed matter—which it isn't.

Paul wants the Balkan area to be considered in terms of a possible offensive base—not just defensive. Generals Cannon and Van Fleet and Admirals Sherman and Carney approve of this concept. But General Collins, Army chief of staff, opposes it.

Paul would like Greece's traditional two big parties to reorganize themselves on a popular basis and put an end to the innumerable splinter groups now confusing Greek politics.

I told Paul about my talk with Djilas and the latter's assurance that the alliance bid comes from Tito himself. The King was excited but wary, much like Grigoropoulos. But he promised to explore the idea with care and discretion.*

ATHENS, *April 13, 1951*

TALK with Ambassador Peurifoy. He said a new American floating broadcasting station is now at Patras, flying a Panama flag (but, stupidly, also flying an American flag). It will cruise about sending propaganda programs to the Balkans. In Athens, we are now doing "black" propaganda broadcasts to Bulgaria and elsewhere from a special radio station geared to shift about continually and avoid the Soviet jammers.

PARIS, *April 23, 1951*

LUNCH with Brigadier General Tony Biddle, formerly ambassador to Poland, now Eisenhower's liaison officer at SHAPE. Biddle said that six months before the Germans attacked Poland, its President, who was a chemist by previous training, called him in and assured him war was coming because his German chemist friends advised him to that effect. The

---

* All this developed into the short-lived Balkan Pact signed among Greece, Turkey and Jugoslavia in 1953.

President asked if he would please remain with the government even if it had to leave Warsaw. Biddle asked President Roosevelt for $5,000 in gold to finance any emergency preparations. He bought one large truck and filled it with food and emergency supplies. This was what the small American diplomatic colony survived on during the evacuation.

# 24

---

# DE GAULLE AND

# EISENHOWER

TALK FOR AN HOUR AND A HALF WITH JULES MOCH, MINISTER OF defense and former prime minister, a member of the Socialist Party.

He said France will not permits its obligations in Indochina to upset commitments in Europe under NATO. French soldiers (never regular conscripts) are sent to Indochina for two years service. Many veterans are now coming back. They have a good deal of experience in Indochina, but it is entirely different from a European kind of war. In Indochina, the French have artillery and aircraft against no air opposition and very little enemy artillery. It is a question of infantry fights and coolies slipping by in the jungle. The Indochina veterans have to be taught new tactics when they return to France. France is weakening its garrison in Africa in order to fill up the necessary complements in Indochina and at the same time not reduce its strength in Europe.

Moch said de Gaulle now only had about thirty seats of the 620 in the Assembly so that obviously he would gain more seats at the next elections. However, his movement has lost popularity during the last two years. Should de Gaulle come back it would be a disaster for the UN and NATO and France would go Communist. De Gaulle still believes France is *the great* power of the world, which is an illusion. He does not know how to cooperate. If he came in, or if a Catholic clerical party came to power and tried to take control of schools, the Communists would be able to propagandize throughout the country "in defense of the Republic." All kinds of fellow traveler organizations would commence to gain new members.

Moch said de Gaulle now had come to represent the extreme right and, paradoxically, 75 per cent of his support came from those who were for Vichy, although Moch admitted de Gaulle still had good patriotic resistance leaders like Malraux with him. Moch recalled that when he escaped from France, he went to see de Gaulle, who was very haughty. At that time, Moch talked with Attlee, then British vice-premier. Attlee complained of the following: Britain had ceded bases to the United States for ninety-nine years in the Western Atlantic in exchange for American destroyers. The United States asked de Gaulle to turn over bases for ninety-nine years in French West Africa to facilitate the air route to Egypt. De Gaulle refused. He said he would turn over such bases only for the duration of the war plus six months, and his conditions were that all installations left by the Americans must be turned over afterwards to the French without compensation and fifty modern American aircraft must be made available immediately to the French. As a result, the United States was irritated and established bases at Lagos and Accra in British colonial territory. Attlee said the British were very embarrassed. He said although the British empire was willing to cede bases for ninety-nine years to its ally, de Gaulle, who had been created and financed by Britain, would not cooperate simultaneously.

Moch said France was now well vaccinated against generals in politics. It had had Napoleon and his nephew, Napoleon III. Then there was Marshal MacMahon who failed. Then there was General Boulanger whose coup had never come off. The French want no more of this type of experiment.

PARIS, *May 11, 1951*

THIS evening Al Gruenther, Eisenhower's chief of staff, said de Gaulle is sending notes continually to Eisenhower assuring him he is in favor of NATO and advising him to disregard some of the things he has been saying in his speeches, which are purely for political consumption in view of forthcoming French elections.

PARIS, *May 11, 1951*

THIS afternoon I had a long talk with de Gaulle. He was extremely gentle, courteous and forthright. He gave the impression of being less arrogant than during previous conversations. He seemed older and tired. His face was gray and lined.

He was wearing a double-breasted black suit, a white shirt and a black necktie. His headquarters at 5 rue de Solferino were bustling with activity. Dozens of RPF workers were wrapping up brochures and sending out letters. It certainly does not give the impression of being a wealthy organization. The furniture is ramshackle and the general's office itself is astonishingly simple and bare. He was leaving town again on an election tour that same afternoon. I noticed he had had only four appointments on his calendar including one with Soustelle, the political organizing expert of the movement.

De Gaulle said he would consider it a big victory if the RPF gained two hundred seats. It would even be a victory if the RPF got 170 seats in the assembly because this is its first presentation on the electoral lists. If he gains 170 or more seats, no government can be organized "except with me or with the Communists—one or the other, that is a fact."

> That is the position: If I win I will make proposals to the others [parties] to make a government. I will propose a government with those who agree to work in participation with me. France must have a government. You cannot have a government without me. I will point out the responsibility of the others; that they must have a government and therefore must join me.

I asked de Gaulle if he hoped to be president of the Council, in other words, prime minister. He said: "The question of title is not important. I will be chief of the government. Of course I would accept the title of president of the council."

He said he had no intention or desire to hold a plebiscite and that he had made that clear before, but that his enemies accused him of desiring a plebiscite. I asked him if he would outlaw or limit the activities of the Communist Party if he came to power. He replied:

> Certainly. They are already illegal in many ways. They are acting in the trade unions, but this is against the law because the law specifies that trade unions must only be professional and not political. It is easy to prove they are political. Up to now, the law permits the expulsion of the Communists from unions. The legislative position vis-à-vis the Communists must be further defined. You cannot have a state within a state. We cannot prevent people from being for the Soviet Union, but we can prevent them from favoring the Soviet Union against France.

De Gaulle said that, if he comes to power, he would certainly seek to establish a new law permitting the creation of labor "associations." He pointed out that the law now permits the creation of *Sociétés Anonymes*. He said he wished to encourage the responsibility of the workers as well as of capital. The question is, he explained, to let the law "permit," not force, the creation of "associations." He thought this would contribute to productivity. The law should encourage productivity and national output. Under "associations" the quality of work would be improved. France has sent special missions to visit the United States and study American industry. These have been struck by the moral interest of the American workers in production. "It is our idea to encourage French productivity. We must establish new contractual relationships between the worker and the owner

and develop their joint interest in output. It is to their common interest."
De Gaulle said these contracts would fix the proportion of profits of workers and owners.

De Gaulle said he agrees it is to the interest not only of the United States, Britain and other powers, but equally of France, to support the concept of NATO and that Eisenhower was the logical commander-in-chief. Nevertheless, it must never be forgotten that various nations have special interests within this alliance. There is, for example, the particular interest of England and likewise, national interests of France and especially of both Britain and France in the Mediterranean. The British are, of course, most interested in a defense of Northern Europe and the United Kingdom. For this reason, they wish that command to be under an Englishman and they have succeeded in putting an Englishman in command of Northern Europe. This northern command includes land, sea and air. The central command includes France's special interests and France is the biggest factor in it. Therefore, it is normal to have a French commanding officer; but Juin does not command the air and sea forces, only land.

France has particular interests in the Mediterranean; so does Britain. British imperial interests are connected with the East and Britain would like to have an eastern Mediterranean command. French interests are preponderant in the western Mediterranean because of North Africa and it would be normal to have a Frenchman in command. De Gaulle said:

> We can accept a British command in the eastern Mediterranean. We recognize that the Americans have general interests in the Mediterranean and we can accept an American commander for the whole Mediterranean on condition that France's special rights in the western Mediterranean are recognized. But the English seek an eastern Mediterranean command and also a preponderant influence in the western Mediterranean. This, France cannot accept. The British are playing a role against France in the Mediterranean. Britain is particularly concerned with such eastern areas as the Suez Canal, Iraq, Jordan and the Sudan, but to retain their influence there the British would be ready to encourage the Arabs to rise up against the French in Morocco, Tunisia and Algeria. If the British obtain control of the entire Mediterranean command, they would work against France for the sake of British interests in the same way as, during World War II, they expelled France from the Levant with the concurrence of Stalin and Roosevelt.

De Gaulle said France must be revived militarily. This was necessary for France and for NATO: "Therefore we must have true responsibility in the Mediterranean. If France has a greater responsibility towards NATO in Europe and in North Africa, it will have more interest in working for the coalition."

I asked if de Gaulle thought France should contribute more divisions for the defense of Europe than are scheduled at present and he replied: "Certainly yes; not only divisions, but also a greater contribution in sea and air power." He explained that France cannot at present make much more war material, but it can certainly produce more manpower units—both active and in reserve—and could also increase its arms production. He asserted that with American equipment many more French divisions could be provided, but that it was necessary that France should have more interest in making this greater contribution by having more responsibilities. He said that France could easily undertake to produce twenty active divisions for Europe, plus twenty reserve divisions. If the equipment were provided, this would give France a strength of forty divisions available within eight days of the outbreak of war. But, in order to do this, the term of military service must be increased to twenty-four months.

I asked de Gaulle if he thought West Germany should be rearmed. He replied that it should, but on condition that West Germany should never be permitted to have an army in Europe stronger than any other army in Europe—above all that of France. He dismissed the idea of a "European army" and said that only national armies could be formed, although an international expeditionary corps could be selected from such armies. The idea of a "European army" was a "joke of the politicians." De Gaulle said he recognized the necessity of NATO bases which must be established in all kinds of countries, but he added: "I believe that France should not grant such bases until France's status in NATO has been regulated and revised to assure the security of France. Only then should the base machinery be applied."

I asked if De Gaulle favored denouncing the Soviet-French Pact. He replied: "The pact I made with the USSR was a wartime pact to prevent Germany from becoming a nuisance. When the fate of Germany is regulated to ensure this, then no longer would any reason exist for a pact against Germany." This was rather elliptical. I pointed that out and he said: "The Franco-Soviet Pact is not important."

I asked de Gaulle if he favored European federation or the Council of Europe. He said he did not favor the idea in its actual form. It was not "serious." But, he said he was for "a true European federation—but first off we need an arrangement between France and Germany. Above all, I am for a direct arrangement with Germany which would be political, economic and strategic. My intention has always been for a direct entente between the French and the German people. The necessary initiatives are ready. On that basis, a European federation can be formed."

He added that England, of course, would oppose this idea and do all it could to prevent it in order to maintain a disequilibrium in the balance of power of the European continent.

I asked if he was in favor of a Mediterranean pact as such. He replied that he wanted Greece and Turkey to be admitted to NATO. NATO should extend into the Mediterranean and include Greece, Turkey and

Jugoslavia. "Certainly Spain should also be included. Spain cannot be excluded from Western strategy—the contrary would be an absurdity—even if one does not like the political regime."

PARIS, *May 12, 1951*

THIS morning I had a talk with Field Marshal Viscount Montgomery of Alamein, Eisenhower's deputy commander. He does not believe in Moch's estimate that only one division can be produced for each million population among Western nations. To begin with, each nation must produce its own kind of divisions. Montgomery has had troops from many nationalities under his command and has discovered that they all fight differently. Divisions must be formed according to the military talents of the country involved. Furthermore, it is nonsense to think that, because England has about 48,000,000 population, it can be counted upon for forty-eight divisions. England's contribution may be much heavier in air force and navy and much lighter in terms of army than that of other nations.

I asked Montgomery what the situation was on the proposed Mediterranean command and he said it was a terrible political mess. However, he had certain personal ideas of his own and he knew that Eisenhower agreed with him because he had discussed them with Ike just a few minutes before. He thought there should be one NATO command (Eisenhower's) directly responsible to the Standing Group in Washington. Then, there should be a METO (Middle Eastern Treaty Organization) command including Greece, Turkey and the Middle-Eastern States which should be placed under another commander, not subordinate to Eisenhower, but directly responsible to the Standing Group. (Obviously Monty wants this himself.) Then, there should be a separate Mediterranean command, which would be entirely air and sea and which would also be directly responsible to the Standing Group. If the NATO commander wished to move troops or ships, for example, to the Aegean, he would advise the Mediterranean commander and the Standing Group, and get clearance. Similarly, if the METO commander wished to send forces to Greece, he would operate in the same fashion. In this way, the Mediterranean commander would carry out the true function of the Mediterranean Sea which is a highway between East and West.

Montgomery said it was imperative to include Spain in NATO. It is ridiculous to leave that country out especially since it is surrounded by NATO members: France, Portugal and French North Africa. Spain may be a Fascist state in the eyes of the politicians, but at any rate it had already fought and defeated communism. It must be brought into NATO as soon as possible.

I asked Montgomery what he thought of the chances of war. He said he did not believe there was any chance of war this year. However, by the end of 1952, there must be a decision one way or another. The Russians believed that they had enough superiority available in the West not to fear Western rearmament until Germany began to rearm in cooperation with the Western powers. At the moment, the question of German rearmament was "under the table" and nothing was being done on it. However, if the subject becomes current again and active steps are taken, the danger of a Russian attack will increase. In such a case he might have to revise his thoughts on war's imminence.

On the other hand, by the end of 1952, some decision is likely to be forced. By that time, the subject of German rearmament will have been faced squarely and steps would have been taken. It is necessary for Europe to be reunited. The day must come when we tell the Russians that we want them to get out of Europe in order to reunite this continent or else we must be prepared to drive them out. One cannot maintain a rearmament program indefinitely. It costs too much. There is no use having a tank on hand once it has become obsolete. Therefore, by the end of next year, a decision must be taken.

Montgomery complained that generals are never given adequate directives. This was the case with MacArthur. First, MacArthur was told to hold onto South Korea and to drive the North Koreans out. Then, he was told to reunite Korea, which meant conquering all of North Korea. One cannot blame him for being confused. The records will show he never received any truly logical instructions.

Right now, the West is fighting three separate wars in the Far East. Britain is fighting in Malaya in order to introduce self-government when the Malayan people are ready for it. The French are fighting in Indochina in order to bring Indochina into the French Union. The United Nations, under American leadership, are fighting in Korea against aggressors with ultimate objectives which are not yet clear. A common policy must be found and must be coordinated. This is equally true in Europe.

My impression of Montgomery, who was wearing his Field Marshal's uniform, was that he has aged considerably since I saw him in the war. He is, of course, very fit for a man of his age, but his eyes appear tired and watery and his face seemed to have new lines. He has great impatience with civilian and political problems. He strikes me as arbitrary and by no means particularly perceptive or intelligent in world terms, even though he is an outstanding general. I should hate to trust any important international decisions to him because he does not impress me as being either profound enough or well enough informed. He tends to bring to my mind Clemenceau's remark that war is entirely too important to be left in the hands of generals.

PARIS, *May 15, 1951*

PLAYED golf with Eisenhower Sunday and dined with him last night at Bunny Carter's (Paris head of Morgan's bank). Mamie Eisenhower— beside whom I sat—said she certainly hoped de Gaulle would not come in if it meant "any more problems for Ike. He has enough already." I could not agree with her more. She was quite charming and youthful looking.

General Ike—as we sat around over coffee and brandy—said the "great debate" going on in Washington over MacArthur's recall has served one very useful purpose: it has certainly proved to the Russians that we are not arming with aggressive intentions. They can have no illusions on that score now.

He said that it was a sad thing that nowadays so many people mistook "bad deportment" for strength. They consider that a man who beats upon the table is a strong man when really tact is more important and often depicts a much stronger attitude.

We had a discussion about cowardice and bravery. The general said he did not think a prize fighter was necessarily a brave man. It did not take much courage to stand up and to hit with a four-ounce glove. Indeed, it took more courage for youngsters who box in college and who often absorb more of a beating than professional prize fighters. It took much more courage to stand up at the plate in baseball and face a pitcher who was going to throw a ball at you at a speed of twelve feet a second. Sometimes it took a lot of courage to play football. But moral courage is the most important thing. By this he referred to men who had to do something they did not want to do and he said the greatest courage was that of the poor GIs fighting in muddy foxholes.

Playing bridge afterwards—which Eisenhower does very enthusi- astically—he said he always followed one basic rule which was particularly useful when he had Gruenther as a partner because they know each other's game so well. This is that if one man bids one of a suit and the opponent interjects a higher bid of one or two of another suit, if his partners doubles it means "business." The way to make money in bridge is by doubling.

PARIS, *May 16, 1951*

I forgot: Eisenhower says he will refuse to go home and testify before Congress in the MacArthur dispute. He recognizes that he is now the servant of twelve countries—the members of NATO—and not only the United States. He would have to get permission of all these countries to get involved in an American debate. He would rather resign his commission than do this.

PARIS, *May 20, 1951*

DINNER with Al and Grace Gruenther. He said that when he arrived in Washington in June, 1950, after a European trip, he was informed by the Pentagon that there was nothing between the North Korean Army and Pusan. If the North Koreans had had an audacious general like Patton, they would have overwhelmed South Korea long before the Americans could have reacted. Fortunately they slowed up because they exaggerated their fears of overextended lines of communications.

PARIS, *May 27, 1951*

I had a letter today from a young Jugoslav friend of mine, lecturer of English at the University of Ljubljana, who used to be with the Jugoslav embassy in London and was an ardent Titoist. He said:

> Our "democracy" is far from being the democracy I imagined. There is no future for me here since I was brought up, studied and prepared myself for tasks other than those one is dictated here to do. A lot of things can be done to remedy the decay here. But the right people should be given a chance to do so. If you can find channels which are safe, will you let me know and help to get me out?

PARIS, *May 28, 1951*

DRINKS with Alan Kirk (ambassador in Moscow). The Poles originally refused to grant clearance for his plane to fly over Poland. Kirk is fed up and would like to get tough with the Poles, Russians and others. He would like to see an able, tough man in the State Department work out a system of making things difficult for Communist diplomats in America, shutting off their lights for ten or fifteen minutes and then explaining that there was a power shortage, and other things of the sort.

Soviet policy seeks to keep the world on the very brink of war. We must be careful not to push the Russians too hard so that they topple over. The Russians do not want war any more than we do. It would wreck their economic system. The longer we hold off, the more we are catching up in strength vis-à-vis the Russians. It is only when we are strong enough that we can really negotiate.

We must be careful in trying to arrange a solution of the Korean crisis to permit China and the Soviet Union to save "face" which is so important in the Orient.

I played golf today with General Eisenhower and General J. Lawton Collins, chief of staff of the United States Army. Collins and I played Eisenhower and Chip Bohlen and beat them. Afterwards, I lunched with Eisenhower, Collins, Gruenther and Biddle.

Collins, Eisenhower and Gruenther were all very concerned about the information and education program of the American Army and its lack of success in explaining to the ordinary GI the political and philosophical reasons for his being in the army and why he might be called upon to fight.

Collins and Eisenhower told me they had agreed the constabulary set up by the American Army in Germany, although it has the strength of an armored division, is not to be considered as a division. This will permit the Army to build itself up stronger than the six-division limitation fixed by Congress. In actuality the Defense Department could build up American strength in Germany to the equivalent of seven combat-strength divisions by including the constabulary and not listing it as a division. Collins begged me not to write anything about this because it would put Congress on its ear and damage the chances of the plan.

Gruenther drove me back and said there will be many difficulties in bringing Greece and Turkey into NATO because Turkey is mainly an Asiatic country and if you read the Atlantic Treaty carefully it refers only to Europe. The Portuguese are opposed to the inclusion of Greece and Turkey unless Spain is also admitted.

Incidentally, Ike told me he took up oil painting three years ago. His first attempt was with a hydrangea plant. He likes to do portraits now. He did one of Gruenther that is not a success, so he is painting it over. Gruenther remarked that when he last heard about it, "Flowers were growing out of my chest." Eisenhower uses canvas over and over again if the first try is unsuccessful.

PLAYED golf with Eisenhower, Winthrop Aldrich and the latter's son-in-law. We all stank. Ike got so angry at himself on the sixteenth tee after poking the ball into the woods that he shouted "God damn it!" and knocked his club against the ground. If I had not been in such distinguished company I would have done the same much earlier. Aldrich is rather dim. I cannot understand how some of these great bankers manage to keep from going broke. Aldrich was completely misinformed about the recent Italian municipal election and thought it was a great victory against the Communists—which it certainly was not.

Eisenhower said he was in favor of some form of official secrets act in the United States. He thought it was shocking the way members of Congress or government officials rushed to be the first to leak something to the Press. However, he is very opposed to censorship and disliked having to enforce military censorship during the war.

PARIS, *June 2, 1951*

GOLFED with Eisenhower, Chip Bohlen and an officer named Lieutenant Mays of the general's headquarters. I got the impression that the lieutenant had been provided by one of Eisenhower's aides because he had the reputation of being a good golf player. He was not, and the general wasn't pleased.

Afterwards, while we were sitting around having a few glasses of beer the Duke of Windsor came along playing with Henry Ford, Jr. and his wife. Among Eisenhower's views over drinks: He thought the German surrender should have been publicized and that it was stupid of Truman to hold it up one day for the benefit of the Russians. However, he thought Ed Kennedy of the Associated Press had let down his journalistic colleagues badly.

PARIS, *June 5, 1951*

FOR the first time I met General of the Army Omar Bradley. He is tall and slender, but strong looking, has an extremely soft, weak voice which—added to his distinct southern accent—makes him difficult to understand. His face is honest and homely with a protruding underlip. He wore no decorations. He seems like a nice decent forthright American who does not impress one either with his personality or superior intelligence.

He said we have been doing very well in Korea since January. The South Koreans do not fight the Chinese successfully. This is probably the result of centuries of domination by the Chinese which has produced a complex. South Korean troops, by and large, are untrustworthy although when given the proper leadership they do all right for a time. But one can never predict their abilities from day to day. During the May 1951 Communist offensive, the losses among UN troops were very small, except for the South Koreans.

There were many North Korean officers and NCOs fighting with the Soviet army at the time of Stalingrad. This was good training—above all for officers.

He said: "If Russia intervenes actively, we will have to get out. We don't want to fight a world war in Korea," Bradley said. *We* certainly would not want any more divisions in Korea in case Moscow intervened. A good defense line could be established on the parallel 38.30 running from the Imjin River to the coast. He hoped that we would settle on a line with more defense capabilities than the thirty-eighth parallel which had been drawn for political reasons. He added: "I think we are fighting under pretty good ground rules now. We don't attack each other's air fields in Pusan and Manchuria. They don't attack our ships, which are very vulnerable. They don't attack our bases in Japan. We can bomb the hell out of their two hundred miles of communications in North Korea leading to the front."

Bradley said the Joint Chiefs of Staff have always looked upon Formosa as of considerable importance. It would be of great use to an enemy but as things stand we don't need it as an American base. The best solution would be to have Chiang Kai-shek hold it. In order to insure this we must reequip his army and build up its morale.

Bradley pointed out that during World War II we bypassed Formosa en route to Japan. Therefore, we demonstrated that the island is not "vital." But in order to connect the Philippines and Okinawa we would run into inconveniences if any enemy held Formosa. Now, our jet fighters can fly between those points easily. But they would need belly tanks if enemy aircraft were in Formosa and they had to fly a circuitous route. That would be a nuisance. But we don't really need Formosa as long as the Communists don't have it.

Bradley's aide, Ted Clifton, said MacArthur ranged from hysterical optimism to deepest pessimism while commanding in Korea. MacArthur started capturing wholesale groups of volunteers from various Chinese divisions beginning November 6. He disregarded the intelligence and refused to recognize the Chinese were committed in force against him. He wanted to start his offensive on November 15. The Joint Chiefs of Staff delayed and delayed this offensive but MacArthur decided to go ahead on November 25 anyhow. By January 10, MacArthur had the blues and said he had to get out of Korea. On the 12th Collins and Vandenberg took off with a plan to stay and also open wider aggressive action against China itself. They arrived on the 14th by which time Ridgway had straightened out the line without help from MacArthur and made a public statement: "I'm staying." Ridgway accomplished what MacArthur had said was impossible. Thus MacArthur proved wrong three times: misinterpreted his intelligence about the Chinese; split his forces unnecessarily; predicted we couldn't hold.

PARIS, *June 5, 1951*

LUNCH with Gaston Palewski, one of the staunchest Gaullists, in his apartment. It is a small ornately furnished flat in which he has lived for seventeen years. I presume the paintings and furniture are quite valuable but I would go mad if I had to live with them. The lunch was excellent.

Palewski believes that under a de Gaulle government he himself will eventually be foreign minister. However, he points out, de Gaulle will always in fact be his own foreign minister. In order to gain the support of other political parties in forming a government the RPF will be "generous" in alloting ministerial posts to members of other parties.

PARIS, *June 12, 1951*

THIS afternoon I had a long talk with Foster Dulles, special representative of the United States now seeking to prepare the way for agreement among the governments of Britain, France and the United States for negotiation of a peace treaty with Japan—minus Soviet participation. Dulles saw Auriol and various Americans including Eisenhower and Bruce.

He wants negotiations as rapidly as possible to draft and sign a peace treaty permitting Tokyo to recreate a land army and employ it for defense against aggression in an overall system of Pacific Ocean collective security pacts.

He envisages three such accords: A bilateral arrangement between the United States and Japan; a bilateral arrangement between the Philippines and us; a trilateral arrangement among Australia, New Zealand and America. This Pacific arrangement envisages further extensions to include both Britain and France.

Washington has suggested that both Chiang Kai-shek's Nationalist Government and Mao Tse-tung's Communist Government should be permitted to sign the Japanese treaty if they accept the terms.

Dulles conferred with Attlee Friday on American-British disagreements and requested that the entire subject be reviewed. The British attitude softened a bit as a result. Britain's principal reluctance to go ahead with our formula is founded upon mistrust of American wisdom and temperance in Asiatic questions of policy and a fear that our impulsiveness might precipitate a new Far Eastern crisis.

Britain, Dulles says, is working strongly to limit sovereignty of the future Japanese government. London would like a modified version of the existing Far Eastern Commission to be established by treaty and given certain powers over Japanese policy.

Washington's view is that the best way to keep Japan's future army under control is to incorporate it as part of an international collective security arrangement in which Japan would provide certain contributions and other countries would provide the rest. Dulles says our view is that the Japanese should re-create a land army but no sizable navy or air force. Japan, being an island, could not employ any army for aggressive purposes without having the ships to transport it.

Dulles assured both Britain and France that no steps taken in connection with the proposed Japanese treaty will be regarded as a precedent in connection with Germany. The problem involved is utterly different.

PARIS, *June 13, 1951*

LUNCH with Pierre de Leusse of the Quai d'Orsay. He said the United States had originally proposed in its treaty draft for a Japanese peace that if the status of the various islands taken away from Japan had not been decided upon within three years of the ratification of a treaty, those islands should return to Tokyo. This included not only Southern Sakhalin and the Kuriles, but also the Ryukyus, the Bonins and also Formosa.

France pointed out to Dulles that this was an impossible clause because it would be bound to bring about a Pacific war. Japan could not reobtain Southern Sakhalin and the Kuriles without attacking Russia. The clause was changed.

PARIS, *June 14, 1951*

EXCERPTS from a letter to Ernest Hemingway:

A fortnight ago I had lunch with Buck [Lanham] and he told me, in broad outline, the story of "Michel Dupont" [Hemingway's wartime jeep driver] from the days he first knew him until the present, including the sad episode of his conviction for collaboration. I have since seen Michel several times and have gotten from him his own account of his personal history.

Buck has told me in some detail of Michel's exceptional courage while he was fighting and driving you around.

I want to write a story about Michel in an effort to show, through his own individual case, the huge problem that still exists in Europe as a result of the psychological scars of the war which have not been eradicated. Also I want to try and help Michel get some sort of a job so that he can try and make a new life for himself. Naturally Buck [a general at SHAPE] cannot permit himself to become involved with a man who has been imprisoned as a confessed collaborator.

I would deeply appreciate it if you could send me a brief account of Michel's behavior as a soldier while he was with you. Furthermore, could you give me your own opinion concerning the psychological reasons for his courage as related to his prior tragedy.

Michel speaks of you with the deepest affection and highest respect but in no sense tries to "build himself up" as a result of the privilege he had of being with you so much during the war.

PARIS, *June 14, 1951*

LUNCH with Buck Lanham. He told me of Hemingway's views on Dupont. Hemingway said Michel was utterly fearless and sometimes he wondered whether he was trying to get killed, except that he was "cheerful brave." Michel had told him he hated the Germans because they had mistreated his Jewish wife. When he heard Michel had been imprisoned for collaboration he was astonished. But, he said, if a man gave away his network in the Resistance he would have been condemned to be shot. Every member of the Resistance was supposed to hold out for twenty-four hours under torture so other members of the network could go into hiding.

The other evening I had dinner with Pierre Bertaux, until recently head of the French *Sureté*. He voiced deep suspicions about Michel when I told him he had been arrested twice by the Gestapo. He said the Gestapo itself would trust none of its agents after they had been in Russian hands more than twenty-four hours; in fact, it was very dubious if a man escaped after the Russians had had him for more than three hours.

PARIS, *June 15, 1951*

LAST night I saw Pierre Bertaux at a party at the British embassy and continued our conversation of the other day. He told me that two of the people present at the party the other evening, which Raymond Laporte gave to celebrate his impending wedding, were Russian agents. Naturally, he did not identify them. There were only about twenty-four people there.

I asked him if he could explain a bit how confessions were extorted by the Russians and the other Communist countries without apparently damaging the accused person physically. He said there were many ways nowadays.

He recalled that when the British had first parachuted some machine pistols in the neighborhood of Toulouse, one of the men with him held up a pistol and said: "Now there are no longer any strong men." In other words, he meant that no man could withstand that weapon.

Bertaux explained that under modern methods of pressure there are no longer any "strong men." Any man can be broken down by ruthless police methods. Drugs and psychoanalysis can be used to change a man's personality completely within three months.

The most horrible and most effective system, however, is a brain operation called lobotomy. An ice pick or an instrument like it can be inserted beneath a man's upper eyelid and a hole leading to the brain passage can be discovered. If the ice pick is pushed in five centimeters and then turned at an angle and inserted seven centimeters and this is done behind both eyes, the victim undergoes a permanent change of personality. He does not know anything has been done to him and he remembers nothing of the process. The operation takes only a few minutes and the patient merely wakes up with swollen eyelids. It is impossible for any medical examination, after such an operation, to detect that anything special has been done.

Lobotomy is of course widely used for purely medical reasons in the Western world and has been employed thousands of times in order to help patients suffering from various disorders.

Bertaux says there is no evidence of a provable sort that the operation is employed for political purposes in Communist countries since, of course, it is impossible to get witnesses who can escape. He is nevertheless convinced it is being used. There was one case of a political prisoner in Poland having undergone a brain operation which was known about. This man was told, when he woke up in the hospital, that he had tried to commit suicide by jumping out of the window. As a result, his head had been trepanned. It is impossible to know whether that was the case or whether he was operated upon for "experimental" reasons.

PARIS, *June 19, 1951*

LUNCH with Manes Sperber, the writer. He hopes to go to America soon because he says it is a pretty stupid way to commit suicide just to be caught here and turned over to the Russians when the war starts. He already has his eldest son over there and hopes to arrange to move the rest of the family as soon as possible. He told me the reason Arthur Koestler has bought an island in the Delaware River is the same—to keep out of the clutches of the Russians.

I had a long talk with Sperber about his life. He is forty-five and was born in a little village in Eastern Galicia which was inhabited almost entirely by Jews. His ancestors were mainly rabbis. His father was a small village banker and very orthodox. He was brought up speaking German, Ukrainian, Polish and Yiddish, more or less interchangeably. When World War I started, the Russians occupied the village and it was pretty rough. Then his family managed to go to Vienna. His father was offered a good position in a bank but refused it because it meant working on Saturday, the Jewish sabbath, so he got a less remunerative job. Sperber became very interested in psychology as a young student. At fifteen the famous Adler became impressed with him and more or less took him over as his protégé.

Manes explains he was named for a cousin because both his grandfathers and great-grandfathers were alive when he was born and tradition dictated that he should be named for one of them, but only after death. He adds that Manes was a Greek name for the founder of the Manichaen heresy, and many Jews used the name to show contempt for Christianity.

He went to the University of Vienna, but his primary interest was studying with Adler. He specialized in crime psychology with particular reference to youth. He was very interested in left-wing movements and joined the Communist Party in Vienna. However, he said, he detested Stalin as did most of his colleagues; but he and they thought Stalin would not last.

In the late 1920s, Sperber went to Germany and became a member of the German Communist Party. He gave many lectures on psychology and in 1930 was put on the black list of the *Voelkischer Beobachter* as a "corrupter of youth."

In 1933 he was arrested by the SS and beaten up. The Polish embassy finally got him out after several weeks. He went back to Vienna. For many years he had spent holidays in Jugoslavia on the Dalmatian coast. He went down to Zagreb and established himself there as a psychoanalyst. He was a close personal friend of Gorkić (real name something like Zymirski), who was head of the Jugoslav Communist Party (in exile) until Tito took over in 1937. Because of this friendship with Gorkić, the underground Communist movement in Jugoslavia used Sperber for many important assignments.

After Gorkić was liquidated in Russia, Sperber went to Paris. He had already broken with the Party, but before that, had refused to continue Cominform work to which he had previously been assigned in Paris—mainly youth work. He met Koestler in those days.

In 1939 he volunteered into the French army. He was with a special group of intellectuals who refused to surrender and managed to get as far down as Grenoble after the collapse. He lived in hiding in the South of France in a small village for a couple of years and then got away to Switzerland where he was locked up as a refugee. He returned to France after the war. His wife, Zenka, is Latvian.

PARIS, *June 20, 1951*

LAST night I saw Averell Harriman at dinner. He was pretty tired from his trip. He described General W. as having a typically Prussian mind which used great logic to arrive at illogical conclusions.

Harriman was oddly disappointed that he had not been summoned to testify in the MacArthur hearing because he had prepared himself for that event by lengthy briefings.

He hinted strongly that General Koča Popović, now in Washington, is not only discussing Jugoslavia's arms requirements, but is also talking over possibilities of joint action with the United States and NATO as well as Greece and Turkey, in case of war.

PARIS, *June 20, 1951*

I just talked on the telephone to Zdenek Fierlinger, vice-premier of Czechoslovakia and a member of the Politburo. Fierlinger is the man who led the Social Democratic Party into the Communist fold.

Madame Houel, our telephonist, asked the post office in Paris to give her Mr. Fierlinger, vice-premier, Prague, without saying who the call came from. When she had Prague on the phone she asked for "Herr Fierlinger"; the person she was speaking to answered something in Czech which she did not understand but presumably they were asking who was calling. She said: "Herr Sulzberger." The other side said: "Schlumberger?" and Mme. Houel replied: *"Ja, ja"* (knowing it was better not to give too many explanations). She then heard a man's voice and asked "Herr Fierlinger?" After he answered *"ja"* she passed him on to me.

Fierlinger was very friendly on the telephone. I told him I wanted to come to Czechoslovakia and asked him to intervene on my behalf for a visa. He told me Vaclav Kopecky was in charge of visas and that he would get in touch with Kopecky and make a favorable recommendation.

Fierlinger said, "You [meaning the United States] are making a very bad policy these days." I told him everybody seemed to be "making a bad policy." I was just a newspaper reporter and I wanted to talk to him and other leaders about the situation. All I could guarantee to him was that I would write a truthful account of what they said. I also added that I did not want to go to jail. This elicited a rather faint chuckle. He said he would talk to Kopecky.

PARIS, *June 21, 1951*

TALK with Averell Harriman. In the spring of 1945, when Harriman was ambassador in Moscow, he had to send a cable asking Washington to warn General Pat Hurley not to believe everything Stalin said. (As a matter of fact, I recall talking to Hurley in Moscow in the spring of 1945, when he said he had had an easy time convincing Stalin on the subject of China, although it was much more difficult with Churchill!)

It would be "appeasement at home" to try and compromise with Taft on foreign policy. Taft, Harriman said, "believes in things I consider dangerous to national security." The United States decision to station troops in Europe was "revolutionary." Even more so was the decision to give aid to Greece and Turkey where we have no direct interests. We still believe Germany must be brought into defense arrangements with the NATO countries and not left in a vacuum. We have been waiting on France in this connection. There is "great impatience" of American public opinion over getting an agreement with Germany and Spain; there is "acceptance" of the principle of aid to Jugoslavia.

When Germany rearms we want no German general staff, but Germany should have an honorable position. Spain could become an effective ally under certain conditions. A fixed number of Spanish divisions would have to be placed at Eisenhower's disposal since they are of no use to Europe sitting on the Pyrenees. It will be a year before we have an adequate supply of arms for secondary priorities such as Spain. Korea has used up a lot of equipment and ammunition.

It will be a slow development to bring closer relations between Jugoslavia and the West. We must not press Tito too hard. He has been very useful. There is no chance of rapprochement between Tito's Belgrade and Stalin's Moscow. Jugoslavia's readiness to fight is a deterrent to war.

Our public opinion talks too much about Spain and makes it difficult for us to urge France and Britain to make reasonable arrangements with that country. We would like Spain to join NATO (after Germany and Jugoslavia) provided it does not weaken the morale factor in Europe. Therefore this would require French and British acceptance of any regime governing Spain. *Au fond,* you cannot get away from geography. Maybe certain adjustments in the Spanish system would have to be made first before Britain and France would agree. But this is quite a problem. Yet, there is no rush about Spain. We don't have the equipment to give her now anyway. The only urgent thing we want from Spain is air bases. Jugoslavia, which is on the front line, and Germany have a higher priority.

On Iran, Harriman said that when we have an interest in an area we must see to it that the entire population benefits. The British cared only for their own workers in Iran; the entire population did not benefit. The situation is now extremely dangerous. We would not support a British effort to hold Abadan by force. The days of landing Marines are over. Henry Wallace was right during the war to insist that when we bought strategical materials in South America, minimum wages in countries benefiting must be lifted.

PARIS, *June 23, 1951*

VLADO Dedijer came to see me this afternoon. He is still working hard on his biography of Tito (my project, which he took over). A few weeks ago he went for a drive with Tito. The Marshal was at the wheel. Dedijer said: "For God's sake, be careful, I have four children and I don't know what they would do without me." Tito replied that Dedijer shouldn't worry; he, Tito, had been a test driver in the Benz factory in 1910.

PARIS, *June 27, 1951*

TODAY I had a long letter from Ernest Hemingway about "Michel Dupont." He called him exceptionally brave, battle-wise, not silly.

PARIS, *June 27, 1951*

LUNCH with Eisenhower, then played golf. He played appallingly badly and was quite grouchy for a while, but finally broke into a few reluctant smiles. We played with Cliff Roberts, an American business man and old friend of the general, and an Englishman named Bentley who is damned good and used to play on the British Walker Cup team.

At lunch Ike said the greatest disaster in American foreign policy was the fumbling which resulted in handing China over to the Russians and giving them 400,000,000 people to use as they saw fit. It now looks as if the second greatest disaster is about to occur—the loss of Iran. Eisenhower recalled his own experience in the Moslem world in North Africa and how strongly he was struck by the misery and poverty of the native Arabs.

He recalled that when he first landed in North Africa in 1942, German propaganda told the Arabs that the "Jew" Roosevelt had sent the "Jew" Eisenhower to conquer North Africa and place the Arabs under Jewish sovereignty. Only a few months previously, the Nazi radio had been saying the Americans were so hard up for generals that they had had to call upon the "Prussian" Eisenhower. He said that when this anti-Jewish propaganda started the British, who knew more about the area than we did, printed thousands of leaflets with a picture of Eisenhower's profile showing "my little snub nose" and a statement of his ancestry tracing back to Germany— in other words, showing that he was not Jewish.

He said Montgomery had done a great thing in reviving the spirit of the defeated Eighth Army in Egypt. Montgomery had something of Cromwell about him. However, he had all kinds of complexes. He did not come from the same top level of society as Alexander. He had not gone to the best public school. He was a little, insignificant fellow as a young man, and had never been popular. Eisenhower preferred Alexander, who was a better man to work with.

Eisenhower said brave men sometimes acted curiously. Patton was always very nervous about bombing and shelling and took great precautions.

Eisenhower said he learned in North Africa that "the Arabs did not follow the desert but that the desert followed the Arabs." They would move into a cultivated area and destroy it. Their goats and camels would eat up all the vegetation and they would foul existing water facilities. He said, however, that it was a difficult social problem to improve their lot. Thus, for example, if you put running water into an Arab village, you eliminate the only social contact available to the women who liked to gather at the village well.

Ike said he is going to London July 2 for the ceremonies in memory of American Air Force personnel who lost their lives in England. He is going to make a speech at the English-Speaking Union in which he will point out that argument and disagreement between democratic allies are necessary and useful, but should not be staged in public. He will recall that during the war he had bitter arguments with some of the people present (at the dinner) but they did no damage because the world never knew about them. He will be referring above all to Churchill. He is going to stress the imperative need to unify Western Europe. He believes the greatest thing Anglo-American policy could accomplish would be this.

He sees no reason to wait for years to accomplish this in a series of slow steps. After all, when a person goes to a hospital for surgery, the doctor does not operate 10 per cent each time. We should set a goal for unification within six months or a year and work hard for that immediately—not talk of the vague and distant future. He is thinking, as a first step, of trying to bring about one state for West Germany, the Benelux states, France and Italy. England could not be included at this time because England remains primarily an imperial rather than a European power. He wants agreement to do away with all customs barriers; to create one currency, one nationality and one passport in a real union of Europe which would then be open to other nations to join.

Even if some countries are in debt and others are not, they should cancel these difficulties and go ahead now with a dynamic move forward. Schuman has the right idea. As it is, many nations are adopting a negative policy. Belgium increased its term of military service to two years and is now complaining that Holland has not raised its own term of service. He tells the Belgians not to pay attention to what the Dutch are not doing. They should feel that Belgium is worth defending as best possible and that it should set an example to Holland.

If this idea could be brought about, "it would make my job much easier," he says. Right now, there are continual arguments among the Allies. Each wants its own factories to make particular weapons in order to benefit economically rather than to work for the over-all scheme of defense.

If Eisenhower makes a speech as strong as he plans, it will cause a great sensation.

Incidentally, I asked how he got the name of "Ike." He told me all the boys in his family had been called "Ike" at one time or another, deriving from Eisenhower. When he went to West Point he did not know a soul, but inside of a day he was called "Ike." His younger brothers now call him Ike, but his older brothers call him Dwight.

As we were walking across the golf course, the general saw a caterpillar and rushed to stamp on it. He said: "I kill the bastards whenever I can because they ruin the trees."

He recalled that a tank skirmish had taken place on part of the golf course. He always impresses me as having an extraordinary knowledge of military history but an extraordinary lack of other knowledge. He is extremely bad at languages and has picked up very little French. He says he speaks a little Spanish.

We got talking about Rommel and Desmond Young's biography of him. I remarked that Brigadier Young must be a pretty naive character if he figures Rommel could once have been chief of Hitler's private bodyguard and at the same time was never a member of the Nazi party. Eisenhower said he knew nothing about this. He added that Young had criticized him for refusing to receive the conquered German generals in North Africa and Europe after their surrender. Eisenhower said the hell with that. War was no longer a private event of gentlemen commanding mercenary armies but a great and brutal effort on the part of entire nations. He was certainly not in the mood to invite a defeated enemy general to lunch on a friendly basis of "let bygones be bygones."

GOLFED and lunched with Eisenhower today. We both stank. The conversation was dull. He told me Mamie had a certain amount of money—"she never had to think of working for her living the way I did." Ike has always made her keep the household accounts so that she knows just how far a dollar will stretch.

He still considers his theoretical home Abilene, Kansas, because, ever since, he has moved all around the world. He is an admirer of the West Point "hazing" system, which he thinks makes a man really stand up to things. He also is a great advocate of the "honor system" at West Point, which his son John says is no longer as strict as it used to be.

From his description, the system sounds detestable. If a cadet is caught telling a lie of any kind or violating any regulation, it is up to any other cadet who finds out about it to report it. This rather shocks me, although he thinks it is a good idea.

Ike unquestionably has some bias against Negroes although I fancy he considers himself fairly liberal in this respect. This may derive only from his days in Kansas, or it may possibly also be connected with his wife's views; I don't know.

At any rate, he said at lunch that things in this connection were getting better in the United States. As an example, he cited the fact that while he was president of Columbia last year, he looked over the list of those receiving honorary degrees and was surprised to see the name of Ralph Bunche. It is the custom for the president of the University to invite those honored for dinner. Apparently, he was a bit puzzled whether he should do this or not and worried lest some of the others awarded degrees might be offended. In the end he did so and he commented that things went off very well and that people made a point of seeking out the Bunches.

I am sure Ike felt he was doing a good thing and was very charming to the Bunches. However, I must say any thought of hesitation would never have occurred to me. I consider Bunche one of the finest Americans of our time.

DINED last night at the home of Henri Laugier, former assistant secretary general of the United Nations. He quit his job recently because he was fed up with Trygve Lie.

Laugier is rather short, fairly thick-set with a most alert intelligent face. He has dark, graying hair and a long nose. He wears heavy rimmed French spectacles which he frequently pushes up on his forehead. He is a chain-smoker of American cigarettes and is not averse to a few drinks of Scotch.

He is stimulating, intelligent and amusing, although, like so many

European intellectuals, his arguments have no practical conclusions. He is perfectly good at saying what is wrong with things, but when it comes to suggesting what should be done about them, he seems pretty weak. For example, he says it is impossible to prepare for peace by arming for war; that brings only war. But when asked what the alternative should be, he says merely that the people of the world must be educated and this will take many years. Unfortunately, that is not a very concrete program.

Laugier is sixty-three and a professor of hygiene who has taught at the Universities of Paris, São Paulo, Lima, Mexico, Montreal and the New School for Social Research in New York, which he helped to found. He was rector of the Academy of Algiers after the liberation of North Africa. He had been deprived of all titles in 1940 by the Vichy government. He was director of cultural relations at the French foreign ministry and professor of physiology at the Sorbonne.

His apartment is fantastic, although I am not sure whether it belongs to him or to his mistress, Mme. Cutoli. Both she and he are old friends of Picasso, and the salon—an enormous room—is filled with magnificent Picassos as well as one lovely Braque. The Picassos are from all periods. Laugier says Picasso is a charming man, stimulating and friendly. He had him once to dinner together with De Lattre de Tassigny.

Among those present was Pierre Mendès-France, French representative on the International Bank. Mendès-France is still a Radical deputy in the Chamber of Deputies. He is a lawyer and professor and has had a great deal of financial experience, having been head of the French mission at the Bretton Woods Conference and minister of national economy in de Gaulle's first postwar government.

He is a small stocky man with a rather sad Spanish-looking face. Mendès-France maintains that a democracy cannot stifle the opposition because then it ceases to be a democracy. Thus he says it is impossible to limit a debate of the Communists or any other deputies on a particular bill, and yet, if you do not limit the debate, it frequently becomes impossible for the government to act. He says he does not yet have any solution for this paradox, but is extremely worried about it.

Laugier bitterly attacked Trygve Lie. He said Lie was stupid, ignorant and vain. He is a Scandinavian with a limited education, has some acquaintance with the Germanic and Anglo-Saxon civilizations, but none whatsoever with that of the Mediterranean basin; nor has he any use for the latter. He is pompous, foolish and given to uttering platitudes.

Laugier bitterly criticized the United States government for its lack of a truly international spirit and Lie for his mishandling of the Malik truce offer (on Korea). This offer had been made by Malik at UN and the United States should have discussed it through its representative there, Warren Austin, rather than through Ambassador Kirk in Moscow. It was an international matter which should not have been taken up on a traditional national diplomatic basis. Lie, who is incredibly lazy, had no business to be on holiday at this time.

Incidentally, Laugier has frequently been accused of being a Communist. I am confident this is utter nonsense. The man is a sincere left-wing liberal intellectual and I am glad he has the courage not to be stampeded by the hysterical McCarthys of our day; that he continues to see such people as Picasso and to disagree with American policy when he sees fit.

PARIS, *June 30, 1951*

LAST night I played bridge and dined with Eisenhower in his apartment at the Hotel Trianon Palace at Versailles. The other players were Al Gruenther and Cliff Roberts.

When I came in Ike was playing with his grandson David, aged three, a sturdy tow-headed little boy who looks very much like the old man. David began to squall when his mother, the general's daughter-in-law, took him away. Ike was surprised and said it was the first time he had heard him cry since David had come over a few weeks ago. He then found out that he was crying because he was not being allowed to have a drink with the men. The general decided this was a valid reason. Apparently every evening little David is given a glass of water with a bit of maraschino juice in it so he can have a cocktail with grandpa.

It is impossible to go up to see Eisenhower without being cleared by an American in civilian clothes who works for the Criminal Investigation Department of the Army. He goes up in person while you wait downstairs and then comes back to escort you to the apartment.

The apartment probably contains a fair number of rooms, but the two I saw were very simple, ordinary hotel rooms. One appears to be a study and that is where we played bridge. The only nonhotel decorations were family pictures. We had dinner in the other room served by Sergeant Moaney, a Negro who apparently has been with the general for many years. His daughter-in-law dined with us but then rushed out for an engagement.

We played bridge for about an hour before dinner and had drinks. Eisenhower had two Scotch highballs. Nothing was served with or after dinner. The drinks were made by Moaney. Obviously the meal came from the hotel kitchen because we all ordered what we wanted. Gruenther is a Catholic and had to have fish. Al had just received from America a portable long-playing phonograph, so we had music throughout the evening.

Eisenhower is a good, tough bridge player who slaps his cards down in a very definite manner. He gambles on his bids but they are good and, on the whole, cautious gambles. He took me to the cleaners. I lost almost 17,000 francs—all of it to Eisenhower.

There was very little conversation. I noticed the general seemed uninterested in music. He said he had little chance to paint nowadays because he

kept too busy; but occasionally he worked at it on Sundays. He said he was
sore (jokingly) at Field Marshal Alexander because they had once agreed
to exchange paintings. Ike sent one of his but never got one from Alexander. Eisenhower said the Duke of Windsor had yesterday given him a
copy of his reminiscences. The general was amused that he wrote an inscription to him, but instead of putting it on the flyleaf, he wrote on a
separate piece of paper and enclosed it.

He said the title "General of the Armies" had been granted only once in
the United States. This was to Pershing. However, Pershing never wore
more than four stars. Eisenhower remarked that the American people
wanted to do something very special for Pershing although he had by no
means commanded the largest army of America's history and that it was
not at war for long. By inference, of course, Ike must have been comparing
Pershing's to his own World War II command.

He said an officer in the regular army could not remain in debt, and if he
was, he was relegated to "Class B," which means that he is merely given an
opportunity to resign. However, when he was young, all officers were considered extremely good security risks by banks and merely showing a West
Point class ring was usually good for cashing a check up to $25.

Ike said he knew two good American ambassadors. One was David
Bruce, here in Paris. The other was Daniel E. Sickles, American ambassador to Spain many years ago. The general said that although Sickles was
getting along in years and weighed three hundred pounds, he managed to
get as his mistress none other than the dowager Queen of Spain. (She was
famous for nymphomania, I may note.)

PARIS, *July 2, 1951*

THIS afternoon I had a valuable talk with Gruenther. He said the French
were doing particularly well economically and if we pressed them too hard,
they would suffer from inflation and "diminishing returns."

He told me Eisenhower is indeed making a very important speech tomorrow night at the English-Speaking Union in London, in which he will
call for a speedy unification of Europe. The last draft of the speech was
being prepared this afternoon and submitted to the State Department.

Ike had Pleven to lunch today and they discussed the speech. Gruenther is not sure how Eisenhower's contemplated shock treatment will work
out in terms of swift European Union.

Gruenther said NATO is planning to start a war college open to officers
of the twelve member nations. This will be situated in Paris and will work
directly under the Standing Group. It appears to be a project both Eisenhower and Gruenther are interested in. It is hoped this staff college will
help develop a NATO spirit.

DINNER last night with Henry Morgenthau Jr., an old friend, who was one of Roosevelt's closest collaborators and his Secretary of the Treasury. He said that, at Casablanca, Roosevelt of his own accord agreed to change the dollar value of the occupation franc in order to please General Giraud. Giraud wanted a different franc rate and also wanted to be commander of all Allied troops in North Africa. Roosevelt compromised by changing the franc rate without even consulting the American experts. Certain wealthy people, above all those with large interests in Morocco, made about $35 million as a result.

Morgenthau has no use for Couve de Murville. Morgenthau says he personally forced the discharge of Couve as de Gaulle's financial aide and arranged his replacement by Mendès-France.

Morgenthau's diaries comprise nine hundred volumes. They are made up of stenographic notes of all meetings that took place in his office while he was in Roosevelt's Cabinet and all his telephone conversations (which he had recorded). He is making these papers available to Arthur Schlesinger Jr. and other qualified historians.

Morgenthau said one of Roosevelt's greatest gifts was to be able to stick a knife into you so adroitly that you smiled while he did it. He referred to the franc deal, for example.

Morgenthau replaced Acheson as undersecretary of the treasury because Roosevelt requested him to. Acheson had done a curious thing leaving a statement of policy available for Elliott Thurston, then correspondent of the *Herald Tribune,* to write a story about. Apparently it was a fake statement of policy. Roosevelt was furious. He told Morgenthau to take the job and that he would move only upward from there on; never down.

Morgenthau said Sumner Welles, when he made his famous trip through Europe, during the early part of World War II, reported to President Roosevelt that Ciano was the "top man" in Europe and that Churchill was nothing but a "sot."

YESTERDAY Eisenhower made the speech he had talked about. I must say he watered it down a lot from his original plan. It was by no means as strong and urgent an appeal for quick action on European unity as he had promised. But he did ask for "the establishment of a workable European federation" and requested that the problem should be attacked "by direct and decisive assault with all available means." He concluded: "We cannot reach maximum security without a united Europe."

PARIS, *July 5, 1951*

DINNER at the home of Jean Laurent, head of the Banque d'Indo-Chine, reputed to be the smartest banker in France today. Among those present was Pierre Bertaux, ex-chief of the *Sureté*.

Both Laurent and Bertaux predict Daladier will be Premier within six months. They say Pleven doesn't rate well with de Gaulle, but that Daladier does and will therefore gain power.

Laurent has a tale about how he helped to launch de Gaulle into the Free French movement in 1940. Laurent was a member of the French mission in London and as a result eventually gave his apartment to de Gaulle although he disliked him. However, before Laurent put de Gaulle on an airplane for England he recalls that near Tours he and several other officers were stationed with de Gaulle at the time of the collapse. One morning they listened to the sad news by radio. They had no communications other than a hand-cranked telephone and not enough gasoline to tour around. De Gaulle gave pompous orders *"à la bataille"* but commanded that they should eat first—standing up because the battle impended. They ate a box of sardines and had some red wine. They heard the battle was over and the Germans were advancing. They retired and sat down.

Madame Bertaux admitted she had a *"faible pour Charles"*—an odd expression to use about de Gaulle.

PARIS, *July 7, 1951*

LAST night Hector McNeil and General Sir Terence Airey came for dinner. McNeil said Guy Burgess was a good friend of his (Burgess is one of the two missing British diplomats), was brilliant but unsteady, an avowed homosexual and a drunkard. Nevertheless, McNeil gave him a job in his own office and Burgess was very useful in preparing briefs on important subjects such as Stalinism. McNeil claims Burgess never saw any defense papers, which were always delivered and returned locked and signed for. He claims Burgess became strongly anti-American because he made a pass at an American "boy friend" who wouldn't have him. Burgess had a pal named "Peter" who was captured during the war and fell in love with an Indian hockey player. The whole business sounds pretty sordid. McNeil thinks Burgess was knocked off by his chum McLean after the two had started off on a toot in Europe.

Airey is horrified by the whole business and recalled somberly that he had to sentence a young English officer in Trieste to two years in prison for homosexuality—after he had been cashiered and his career ruined. Airey wondered how come these Foreign Office boys were promoted at the same time.

LONDON, *July 13, 1951*

AT a dinner party last night Randolph Churchill kept saying the only thing to do to end the cold war would be to send the Prime Minister of Britain and the President of the United States to Moscow immediately and advise the Russians that if they did not pull back to their 1939 frontiers within seventy-two hours, we would blow up all their main cities with the atom bomb; that instructions had been left behind with the commands of the United States and British forces to proceed to do just this, regardless of what happened, unless the Russians accepted this proposal "carte blanche." When I pointed out there was a small matter of legal responsibility under the democratic system, to Parliament and to Congress, Randolph became impatient. When I recall the number of times he has assured me his one, overriding ambition is to become Prime Minister of this country, these remarks give me the creeps.

Randolph told me his father considered Eisenhower's speech at the English-speaking Union one of the finest he ever heard. The old man didn't quite get it at first, as it was delivered, because he is hard of hearing. However, when he read the text the next day he hastened to write to Eisenhower congratulating him and explaining he would have done so that evening in person had he not been deaf.

LONDON, *July 16, 1951*

THIS afternoon I had a good talk with Aneurin Bevan, leader of the left-wing dissident faction of the Labor Party, and only a few months ago minister in the Labor government.

Bevan wants a "supreme effort" to negotiate "a settlement with Russia" in the next two years. I asked him how he suggested such an effort should be made since we had been trying to negotiate for six years. He replied it would be a great mistake to have an agenda including all points on which East and West were in disagreement. The first discussion should be limited to such problems as sharing the world's oil resources, administering international waterways, allocating fair shares of raw materials and improving world trade.

He said many people, above all in the United States, are openly expressing the idea nowadays that eventually there must be a showdown with Russia—meaning war. He added: "We think the generals talk entirely too much and are listened to too much." He asked why, if such a vast rearmament program as is now contemplated has proved to be necessary, was it only found to be necessary in January? If it really was necessary, the Western governments had been betraying their people by leaving themselves helpless for five years.

If by the end of 1951 there is no major war, it will be clear that the existing relative strengths are adequate to maintain peace. Why does not Russia attack us now? If it is a question of the atom bomb, we will still have the atom bomb in 1952. What we are really doing is telling the Russians that we want to get strong enough to take them on in a war. We are talking ourselves into a condition of semihysteria.

He feels the main causes of world trouble do not lie in the military aggressive intentions of Russia, but in the extent to which Russian military power can take advantage of the semistarvation existing in many parts of the world. The Western proposal to meet the Communist challenge only by producing immense military strength ignores the main force of the Russian threat. The expenditure on arms should never be allowed to exceed that on social benefits.

He said apologists for the present scale of Western rearming were paying the Russians the "biggest compliment ever." They were saying that Russia had repaired all the ravages of the war; had built up a colossal military machine with modern weapons and mechanical armaments; had established a huge submarine fleet; and all of this had been accomplished on an annual production of less than 30 million tons of steel. If this really were a fact, it would prove that communism was more efficient than Western governmental methods. The United States would have to give credit for "know-how" to Russia, but it is nonsense to believe that Russia is so strong. The Russians are frightened and this has made them rigid. They fear to grant concessions because this would be interpreted as evidence of weakness. Where the Russians can take military advantage they will, but they won't start a major conflict. Therefore we are fighting communism by incompetent means.

I asked him whether, despite his opposition to German rearmament, he would be willing to see German participation in a European army and he replied, "No."

He advocated "international settlement of control for international waterways including the Suez Canal, the Panama Canal and the Dardanelles." I noted that he did not include the Danube. He replied: "What about the Great Lakes?" I told him I thought that was adequately taken care of by Canada and the United States but he said, "It is not international."

On the subject of Spain, he said he detested Franco, who represented an affront to all Socialist opinion. His regime was established by Fascist aid and existed only through dictatorship. Any attempt by the West to ally itself with Franco would "make nonsense of the NATO claim to be defending the free world. It would create a vital weakening of the Western position and any physical aid from Spain could not make up for this." If there was a bilateral understanding between America and Spain, it would inevitably include Britain because of Britain's direct understandings with the United States.

By and large, Bevan gave me the impression of being a sincere, intelligent but irresponsible and not really well-informed man. I rather liked him, but I think it would be a very dangerous thing if he should come to power. He is friendly but seems to have a rather violent personality just below the surface of an amiable manner. It is quite clear that he is not exactly pro-American; far from it.

He is middle-sized, rather strongly built but definitely podgy and out of condition. He has a low forehead and a shock of thick iron-gray hair, watery blue eyes and a ruddy complexion. On his cheeks the blood vessels stand out very strongly and you have the feeling that he is a man who is not only rather passionate but drinks too much.

LONDON, *July 17, 1951*

THIS morning I had a good talk with Herbert Morrison, the foreign secretary. Morrison said there were many British who kept talking about the United States as a warmongering nation. He would like to point out to them that as a matter of fact the United States was induced to come into World War I only when the *Lusitania* was sunk and into World War II after it was attacked at Pearl Harbor. This was hardly warmongering.

Morrison said Britain was now quite in favor of rearming Germany. It was admittedly a gamble but we certainly could not undertake to defend Germany with British and American troops, while the Germans sat by. There was a split in the Labor Party on this, and Jewish opinion in Britain was opposed to it. Nevertheless, one had to be realistic and go ahead. Britain had not yet made up its mind whether it would be a good idea to seek German rearmament under a European army formula, as desired by the French. This certainly would not be good if there was no equality. Naturally, Britain itself would not be prepared to participate in any European army.

I told Morrison that Montgomery advocated to me the creation of a Middle East Treaty Organization (METO), including Greece and Turkey, rather than admitting these two countries into NATO. Morrison admitted this had been British policy. He said that in response to American pressure, Britain had agreed to accept Greece and Turkey into NATO.

Morrison said he had the "vision" that if this could be worked out, maybe Britain's problems with Egypt could be resolved, providing that Egypt could get in on the "ground floor" of a Middle Eastern treaty arrangement. He said Britain has a good base in the Suez area and he would hate to give it up. He would like to get Israel into such an arrangement because the Israelis had certainly proved themselves to be good fighters, but he admitted this would be extremely difficult because of the relationship between Israel and the Arab states; technically, they are still at war. Clearly Morrison views Turkey as the most eastern member of NATO and at the same time as the most western member of a Middle East defense bloc.

He said he had lunch with Eisenhower early this month and Ike was very unhappy. He felt thwarted by the political complexities of his SHAPE command. Morrison said he often felt like that himself; that foreign policy would be okay "except for the bloody foreigners."

LONDON, *July 18, 1951*

LAST night dined with Eliahu Elath (ex-Epstein), Israeli minister and an old friend. He was very pessimistic about Israel's relations with the Arab world. The Arab states were too weak and as a result lacked the confidence to accept better relationships.

When he was appointed minister in London, following his term as ambassador in Washington, President Weizmann called him to his home at Rehovoth and gave him the following advice:

He should remember that Israel wished to be a truly democratic state and that in many ways it was far closer to England than to the United States and had more to learn from England. He suggested that Elath should never forget old friends in England who helped to bring about the creation of a Jewish state in Palestine. Elath should not only try to see the famous people in England, such as Churchill and cabinet ministers, but should take special pains to cultivate close friendships with the more intelligent young people, because some day these would be the leaders of England. Elath should always remember that Britain produced two opposite types of statesmen in its empire—Smuts and De Valera. He should alway seek to emulate the Smuts type and impress this upon those with whom he worked.

Incidentally, Eliahu told me of his past life. He was born in Russia, near Kiev. As a young fellow, his Jewish religious teacher told him about Zionism and he became converted to it while still in his teens. He was arrested by the GPU and thrown into prison for many months. Finally, he was released and lived underground in Moscow (Zionism was and is considered a dangerously anti-Soviet movement). He decided to leave Moscow and go to Latvia to work for the Zionist underground in that country, which was still independent. The day after he left, the home of the doctor with whom he had been hiding was raided and everybody was sent to Siberia. From Latvia he went to Palestine. He left all his family behind in Russia, including a Communist sister. The last news he heard of any of them was of an uncle and aunt—three years ago.

In Palestine, he decided to learn something about the Arabs who shared the country with the Jews, and he spent years living and working with them, learning fluent Arabic. Lord Samuels, who is a member of the board of the Hebrew University in Jerusalem, has offered him the job of rector, succeeding the late Dr. Magnes. He is enormously flattered by the offer but considers himself unworthy. Furthermore, he feels he must continue to serve the government as a diplomat for a while, since he is only forty-seven.

LONDON, *July 19, 1951*

LUNCH with Lester B. (Mike) Pearson, Canadian secretary of state for external affairs, and Geoffrey Crowther, editor of *The Economist* and one of England's most brilliant men.

Pearson said Canada is now spending about 13 per cent of its total national income on defense. He is convinced that for a period of many years Canada—and other nations—must be prepared to spend an average of 10 per cent every year on defense. This is not merely an emergency but would be a permanent expenditure because of the unfortunate present-day world. He compared the present rearmament program to a mile race. At this phase, we are in the initial sprint seeking an advantageous position. Later on, when we have caught up with the Russians, we can reduce the pace a bit—but not too much.

Crowther agreed. However, Britain was now spending only about 10 per cent of its income. It would have to raise this proportional contribution, perhaps up to 15 per cent before it finally leveled off and reduced the percentage.

Crowther said he personally was in favor of a new partition of Persia, similar to that which was privately arranged between Britain and Russia in 1907. I told him I thought this would be folly. In 1907, Russia agreed to recognize Afghanistan and Tibet as zones of British influence. Tibet is already in the Soviet sphere and Afghanistan could fall like a rotten apple.

Pearson said he was concerned about the prevailing crisis between India and Pakistan. He resents the way Nehru seems to be developing into a regular Hitler vis-à-vis Pakistan.

LONDON, *July 19, 1951*

THIS morning I had a talk with Winston Churchill at his home, 28 Hyde Park Gate, a charming brick house with a lovely garden behind it. I waited for a moment in the library downstairs before being taken up to his bedroom. The library is extremely attractive, paneled, with inset bookcases at both ends and a fireplace in the center of the main wall. I was interested to notice a painting standing on one shelf by Grandma Moses, the American primitivist: a rather gay winter scene. Above the mantel piece was a wash drawing of a Parliament session, which I imagine must have been done around the seventeenth century. There were two portraits, which I should guess were probably the Duke and Duchess of Marlborough, his great ancestors, and a battle scene which I should suspect was Blenheim.

After a moment, I was taken upstairs to Churchill's bedroom by a manservant. The old man was propped up in bed, his arms resting on a bare breakfast tray that had legs on it. He had two sponge pads on which to ease his elbows. He was wearing a cream-colored night shirt and smoking a long cigar. He did not have glasses on. The first thing he did was ask me if I wanted a whisky and soda (this was 11:30 A.M.). I replied in the affirmative and he asked the servant to bring me one and to "bring me another" startling me by handing out an empty glass. However, the highballs were pale and I noticed he sipped his about twice; the drink was really almost full when I left. Likewise, I don't believe he puffed his cigar more than eight or ten times in forty minutes. In fact, I was surprised that it stayed alight. Although on the surface his habits appear to be intemperate—above all for an old man—he is very temperate about applying them. When I left he was just about to get up and have his bath, because he had a luncheon engagement at the House of Lords.

He was extremely courteous and friendly. He has aged a great deal since I first talked with him eight years ago in Cairo. He seemed rather dreamy and not thoroughly alert. I am told he really perks up only in the evening. It is sometimes difficult to follow his conversation. First of all, he speaks very softly and frequently rolls his words around his large cigar. Furthermore, he sometimes begins to talk about something; then remains silent for some seconds and you believe he has finished what he was about to say; then he recommences. As a result you are left with the alternative of risking interruption or just sitting in blank silence while he ruminates.

Churchill said the United States has every right to negotiate a private bilateral agreement with Spain and he intends to say so soon in public. (I may recall that today and all this week there has been a great furore in the British press because of Admiral Sherman's visit to Madrid and the announcement that America intends to seek an agreement with Franco. We are being bitterly criticized by most British papers and Britain is catching it for "interference" in the American press.) Churchill, however, said that Spain should not be admitted to NATO. He thought that the present argument would soon blow over. He warned that America should beware of making any deal with Franco on Gibraltar.

Churchill spoke strongly in favor of a European army. Each of the European members of NATO should have its own national army which would then contribute divisions to an over-all European army. Germany should likewise contribute divisions to such an army. Britain and America would send divisions from their armies to Europe to be added to the European army, which thus would become the force under Eisenhower's command.

He claimed the Labor government was sabotaging projects for European unity and he said, "Of course, you know how I feel about the need for such unity."

He said a European army was necessary, above all, in terms of the day when, if our policy succeeds, the United States will eventually withdraw its troops from Europe, when that continent is strong enough to stand upon its own feet. He thought that 80,000,000 Britons* scattered around the earth, and 150,000,000 Americans together were strong enough to face anyone and to press for the desirable goal of European unity.

Churchill is very worried about the Iranian situation and furthermore about the rumbustiousness of Egypt. He said surely the United States, England and France together should talk to Egypt and point out to the Cairo government the necessity of a sane solution. The United States must take an active part in all Middle Eastern political and defense arrangements. He was very much against any such concept envisioning that Britain should retain the Middle East as its own sphere. Churchill also pointed out that the British dominions had a particular interest in the Middle East (of course, during the last war Australian, New Zealand and South African troops fought in that area and the Anzacs were there during World War I).

He said it was rather a shame the United States had never had any colonies because it did not appreciate the problems posed. The French were doing a very good job in Morocco and it would be most damaging to NATO if French control were removed. The United States criticized England for years about India. Now a disaster is occurring there. A half-million people have been killed in the Punjab alone (I think Churchill's figure is a gross underestimate), and terrible growing pains are being felt. The situation is bound to get worse. There is little advice we can give India and Pakistan because their leaders are intelligent men who were trained and educated in England and "know all the tricks." Churchill also said the situation in Burma was very grim.

British and American policy is, of course, to get strong enough so that eventually we can negotiate a settlement with Russia and force Moscow to abide by it. Russia must evacuate the eight captive capitals of Eastern Europe. But the most dangerous situation is while we are getting stronger— not when we are finally strong. Russia might feel it necessary to risk an attack during the process of our rearmament, before we are really strong.

Russia fears our friendship more than our enmity. The Soviet dictatorship could not stand free intercourse with the West. We must make Moscow fear our enmity more than our friendship.

Churchill thought Eisenhower's speech on July 3 was a great speech. He asked me whether I believed Ike would run for President. I said I thought that would depend upon the other candidates in the field. He said it would be disastrous for Western efforts if Taft should be elected.

I asked Churchill if he was still planning to go to the United States. He

* I presume he included Canadians, Australians, New Zealanders as "Britons."

said that would depend entirely upon whether there was a British general election. He thought it was an even chance there might be an election this autumn. He still hoped to go to America during the winter. He said he had heard from his publishers that the latest volume of memoirs was doing even better than its predecessors.

PARIS, *July 23, 1951*

LUNCH today with Pierre Bertaux. He asked if I could get a message conveyed directly to Marshal Tito. He had tried to send the message through the British, but was not sure the British had direct enough contact. The message is this: The Soviet ambassador in Paris recently told certain French Communist leaders that they need not worry about Titoism. Russia was confident it could have Tito assassinated whenever it wished, but there was no need for it at present. The Russians had agents so close to Tito that the latter could not possibly suspect it. One French Communist leader asked the ambassador if he was not being indiscreet. The ambassador laughed and said: "Not at all. If Tito got suspicious and started a purge he would do half of Russia's job for Moscow."

PARIS, *July 24, 1951*

LUNCH with Hervé Alphand, French Ambassador, who is Chairman of the European Army Conference that has been meeting intermittently in Paris since February. He said the size of units in the future European Army is a matter of secondary importance. For the moment these are not being called divisions or anything else, but "operative units."

General Juin would be the first commander of the European army. There would be a separate European army general staff, similar to that of SHAPE. The Germans will be admitted on an equal basis and could not only hold high staff positions, but actual commands. There will be a common uniform and the same pay rate for all ranks.

PARIS, *July 25, 1951*

THE European army conference has recommended to the governments of France, West Germany, Italy, Belgium and Luxembourg the creation by the beginning of 1953 of an international force equivalent to twenty divisions, which would be placed directly under the command of Eisenhower's SHAPE headquarters. This would include a German contingent furnished by Bonn on a basis of full equality with the other four powers.

*De facto,* if not *de jure,* this plan if adopted would more or less incorporate West Germany into NATO. Obviously also the Italian peace treaty would have to be amended because of military restrictive clauses which would be invalidated by the proposed agreement.

By far the most important agreement is the initial philosophical premise of the interim report: that a "European community" shall be established with "common supranational institutions." This is a remarkable achievement of statesmanship scarcely six years after V-E Day. The report recommends common military expenditures, equal distribution of resources, a common supply and armaments program, the standardization of military equipment and the specialization of production.

As soon as a treaty has been drafted and ratified, the force would be considered the defense force of the "European defense community." The institutional formulas of the Schuman Plan regulating Western European iron, steel and coal production would be used as models.

PARIS, *July 25, 1951*

LUNCH with Bill Deakin. Deakin dined at Winston Churchill's two nights ago. Churchill was telling stories of the Boer War. He said he had been personally captured by Botha, the Boer leader and later commander-in-chief, who ran Churchill down on a horse. Churchill was a war correspondent and therefore had thrown away his revolver but had forgotten to throw away the dumdum bullets he was carrying. He dropped them one by one in the grass as he walked along in front of Botha.

The man who interrogated Churchill, oddly enough, was Smuts. Churchill said Mrs. Smuts never spoke to any Englishman until only very recently. Three of her children had died in British concentration camps after the Boer War. However, when Churchill wrote to her on her husband's death, she sent a magnificent reply. It is all the more tribute to Smuts that he did not allow his bitterness, because of his children's death, to interfere with his later career.

PARIS, *July 27, 1951*

LAST night we and the Deakins (who are staying with us) had dinner at the home of Arthur Forbes (Lord Granard). Arthur was British air attaché in Bucharest at the beginning of the war, and I believe arranged for the Polish gold reserve to be sent out of the country following Poland's collapse. For a short time after the war he was air attaché in France.

Granard said he planned the first American air raid on Ploesti. They made a model of the oil fields and then took a film which gave the appearance for the pilots of their actual low-level approach to the installations.

Deakin said that in May 1944, when I learned in Cairo that the British were negotiating a secret deal with Russia dividing up spheres of influence in the Balkans, the matter was taken up at the highest level. The Foreign

Office protested to the State Department. Bill has recently been reading the records because of his work with Churchill on his memoirs. British records say that I learned about this through the "indiscretion" of the American ambassador to Greece, Lincoln MacVeagh (resident in Cairo because of the occupation). I told Deakin I had never told anyone where I learned it.

This reminded Arthur that it was he, as chief of Royal Air Force intelligence in Greece, who was ordered to cable Belgrade in late March and early April 1941, ordering me to return to Athens to face a court martial. I paid no attention to these commands because at that time I was not accredited to the British forces. I had applied for accreditation in Athens but the British were too slow in acting upon it.

Bill said one of the great difficulties was that Roosevelt was very ignorant of the geography of Eastern Europe. He did not even seem to know where the Balkans were. He did talk vaguely of the Ljubljana Gap, but didn't know what it was. Churchill always wanted to mount an offensive through the Ljubljana Gap. As a compromise, it was finally agreed this should come after the Italian campaign was over. However, the Americans (according to Bill) made a deal with Tito leaving the Jugoslavs in that area.

Permission for the Russians to occupy Prague and Berlin was granted at a low level. It was not a governmental decision, but it was made by Eisenhower—who must bear full responsibility. According to Bill, it was he who commanded Patton's troops to stop west of Prague and who set the Elbe as a meeting place for Russian and Allied troops.

Deakin said that Churchill on his own hook went to Turkey and sought at Adana to persuade the Turks to enter the war. He realized a Balkan front would be impossible without the Turkish army. His mission failed.

PARIS, *July 31, 1951*

LUNCH today with Irving Brown and Jay Lovestone, of the American Federation of Labor. They have just been in Germany and are anxious to strengthen the Social Democratic Party. They say relations between Schumacher and General Heusinger are excellent. Both believe that any new German army must be a "people's army." Brown and Lovestone say relations between McCloy and Schumacher are bad, that McCloy is a fool and does not understand either the Germans or world politics.

PARIS, *July 31, 1951*

EISENHOWER has told a group of United States Senators: "Wars are won by people jumping in, believing in something with all their hearts and doing it right now."

The discussion centered around the mutual security bill and the possibility of spreading it over a two-year period. Eisenhower said the countries of Europe could become dispirited again and an easy prey to communism. He continued: "We would be standing alone as a sort of island of freedom surrounded by a hostile sea of communism—if that becomes the case, the amounts we are talking about ($8.5 billion) would be picayune . . . The sure way to drag this out and get half the results for twice the costs is to make it a longer effort than it has to be."

The world, he continued, is growing more complex and along with it problems are growing; men hate to face them. They would like to find some place on earth, some Tahiti to which they can escape. But, he added: "There is no Tahiti left to go to."

PARIS, *August 14, 1951*

LONG letter from Hemingway on "Dupont" dated August 10 from Finca Vigia, San Francisco de Paula, Cuba. He said "Michel" had been no angel except in bravery.

PARIS, *August 24, 1951*

INTERESTING talk with David Bruce. He said the meeting between Eisenhower and the Jugoslav chief of staff, Colonel General Popović, took place in the embassy. Those present were Eisenhower, Gruenther, Doug MacArthur, Bruce and Lieutenant Colonel Walters, the interpreter; and Popović, the Jugoslav chargé d'affaires and one other Jugoslav.

Popović said Jugoslavia had 400,000 men under arms plus 800,000 men trained as partisans and a mobilizable reserve of 400,000 additional soldiers. He believed the Russians would attack Jugoslavia only if they thought they could get away with it without a world war. He admitted it was impossible to standardize weapons of the Jugoslav Army and also, in case of an attack, they would inevitably be driven back into their mountains. He did not bring up the subject of possible collaboration in planning with Italy, Greece or Turkey.

Eisenhower, who was leery about seeing Popović, limited his questions to the subject of the Jugoslav army and further queries as to which American military leaders Popović had seen in Washington. The meeting has been kept strictly secret.

Bruce believes the British scheme for a Middle East Treaty Organization has been pretty well scrapped. He thinks it does not make political sense and that Egypt, for example, would certainly not join up. He says the United States has given no commitments to Britain supporting such a scheme.

PARIS, *August 24, 1951*

LUNCH with Doug MacArthur, Eisenhower's political adviser. He said Popović saw Eisenhower very secretly in the home of David Bruce. First Eisenhower, Gruenther and MacArthur showed up. Then Popović came with a couple of Jugoslavs, all dressed in civilian clothes. Popović said he was prepared to talk either in French or Spanish. He spoke in French. He impressed the Americans as being a very intelligent, ruthless man who knew more about politics than military organization.

However, he knew his own army very well. He did not, MacArthur said, discuss in any way the possibility of making any secret Jugoslav arrangements for mutual defense with Greece and Turkey. If MacArthur's report is correct I think it is too bad the Americans did not bring this up. We kept this quiet because we do not want to give the impression that Eisenhower is stepping out of his NATO bailiwick in any way.

PARIS, *August 27, 1951*

LONG talk with René Pleven, who is once again prime minister of France at a very difficult moment. As usual, his desk at the Hotel de Matignon was piled high with papers. Nevertheless, also as usual, he was calm, courteous and did not appear to be in the least bit rushed for time. He is an exceptionally tall Frenchman, I should say six foot two and a half. But, despite this, he is very Gallic in appearance; black-rimmed spectacles and a curious pig-like face which, nevertheless, is not disagreeable.

Pleven said France must now see exactly what kind of aid was coming from the United States before it made its own final pledges. France needed assistance badly. She cannot simultaneously bear the cost of the Indochinese war, the cost of reconstruction, the cost of European defense, etc., hampered by insufficient coal for her steel industry.

When I asked him what he thought of Russian policy, he said it was his impression that Moscow wanted neither war nor peace but hoped to be able to disrupt the economy and tranquillity of the democratic nations by its present methods.

PARIS, *August 29, 1951*

LAST night I played bridge with Eisenhower and Gruenther, and Eisenhower's friend, Cliff Roberts. They took me to the cleaners again. I must say I react more or less like a bird terrified by a snake when I get among those characters and my bridge becomes even ten times worse than usual . . . which is bad enough. It is all I can do to follow suit.

Ike's new house is beautifully situated quite near SHAPE headquarters at Rocquencourt. It has a lovely lawn and a pond which the French have stocked with ten-inch trout. He said there is supposed to be a big one there, but he hasn't seen it yet. He got five the other day, in a brief time, for lunch. (Incidentally, he said that when you see fish beginning to swim close to the surface with their heads up, it is time to do something about the water in an artificial pond.)

The house is comfortable and spacious but not pretentious. There is a very large sitting room to the left of the entrance hall. To the right, there are a more formal sitting room and dining room. So far, the place is incompletely furnished.

Mrs. Eisenhower, who, together with her mother, had dinner with us (they played canasta afterwards), took me around. She said it was well suited for entertaining but she is having difficulties with the decorations she wants. Right now, the large sitting room has some rather ugly, but comfortable armchairs and a couple of bridge tables and small chairs and tables around. The bookcases are half-full. The general bought two oil paintings in Germany on his recent vacation and they are hung, one above each bookcase. One is a sea-shore scene at Capri and the other a mountain scene in Bavaria. They are the usual conservative picture-postcard type of painting which I do not care for. He obviously gets great pleasure from the mountain scene.

We had a good American dinner in the middle of our bridge session, and Mrs. Eisenhower, who is not only very nice, but also seems to be a good American housewife, provided all the general's favorites. We had lettuce and tomatoes to start, then some excellent roast beef (from America) and potatoes, followed by custard pie with a graham cracker crust. I noticed that no one took coffee after dinner except myself. I also took the only postprandial high ball.

While we were driving out in Ike's car, he expressed complete pessimism as to the possibilities of ever building up a decent Middle East defense bloc. He saw no possibility of getting Egypt into it and even less of arranging cooperation between the Arabs and Israel. He asked me if I could get an estimate from our correspondent as to the real military strength of Israel. He has not been able to figure it out at all. At the end of the evening, he made some particularly gloomy remarks about France and said he felt that the French situation right now was rather bad.

I drove home with Cliff Roberts. Roberts is a very close friend of Eisenhower and seems to share his confidence. He made it absolutely clear that Eisenhower would not be here next year—in other words that he would run for President. He furthermore made it clear that Eisenhower is doing all he can to build up Gruenther to succeed him in NATO.

PARIS, *August 30, 1951*

DINNER with Averell Harriman who stopped off to see Eisenhower and Pleven on his way back to Washington. He looks very tired and worn out by the Persian negotiations. The only people there were Marie's daughter and her husband and the Bruces. Averell talked quite frankly.

I was particularly interested to hear his account of his meeting with Tito a few days ago. This took place at Tito's summer castle of Brdo. The combination of luncheon and conversations lasted six hours. Harriman said the atmosphere was cheerful, informal and even jocular.

There was a brief discussion of the position of Archbishop Stepinac. Harriman explained the political importance of Catholic opinion in the United States, but got only a "bored" reaction from Tito.

Tito explained to Harriman that Jugoslavia's fundamental policy was one of self-preservation. Harriman said Tito did not seem worried about peasant opposition to the government, which now appears to be pretty strong. Tito emphatically agreed with Harriman that Stalin does not want a war. However, he fears that war might be brought about by Soviet miscalculation.

Lunch with Zhukov. Yuri intimated that Malik's peace-in-Korea speech was a result of the dinner party I had at my house where I brought Zhukov and Bohlen together. He said: "Didn't you see how Malik followed the line Bohlen gave about settlement on the thirty-eighth parallel?" I recalled to Zhukov that for more than a hour he had sat at one end of the room with Bohlen talking in Russian while I sat at the other end of the room chatting with Bill Tyler, the only other person present. Therefore, I did not know all that went on. He then said that Bohlen had intimated a settlement could be reached around the thirty-eighth parallel. I asked if this had anything to do with Malik's reply and he said "of course." Obviously Zhukov passed on all of Bohlen's remarks to Moscow.

I then said I could not understand why Moscow did not produce a settlement. I was convinced that if the United States wished France to do something particularly important that they could persuade Paris. Therefore, I was convinced that with a disciplined dictatorial system like that of Russia, Moscow could surely accomplish whatever it wanted. He replied: "That is not so simple. It is not a question of Vyshinsky picking up the telephone and calling Peking and telling them what to do."

From there on—always by innuendo—he indicated that Russia was having a great deal of trouble with the Chinese. I said I thought the Chinese wanted a settlement in Korea. They were losing a lot of blood and their best human cadres just at the moment they needed such elements to carry out the final processes of their revolution. I had heard through Indian sources that the Chinese really wanted a settlement. He agreed that China needed such a settlement. I could not understand why the disciplined Russian Communist system did not order it. He said there were difficulties—but I "could not understand."

Zhukov was extremely worried about Jugoslavia. He was convinced the United States was planning an attack on Russia through Jugoslavia. Not less than three times he asked me if Harriman had not gone to Belgrade to arrange such an attack. I said he was crazy and I was sure the situation was the reverse, that there was every reason to fear a Communist attack on Jugoslavia. He said that was ridiculous and was entirely against Russian interests. I reminded him that even if Moscow did not want such an attack, the Russians were dealing with volcanic Balkan people and had better be sure to control them. Zhukov admitted that a war involving Jugoslavia would certainly produce a world war.

On the other hand, he seemed absolutely convinced not only that there would not be a world war, but that the situation would become more and more relaxed in the near future. I said it was silly to count on such a thing in terms of words; that acts were necessary. He said Gromyko had gone through the United States en route to San Francisco and had hoped to see Truman, but had been advised only that Truman would be prepared to see him if he "requested" such an interview. Zhukov seemed puzzled by that. I told him to get off his "high horse" and remember that Gromyko was an assistant minister of foreign affairs and that Truman was our Stalin; that if Gromyko wanted to see Truman he had damned well better request it; that if there were only two great powers in the world today, the United States of America was certainly one of them.

I am convinced that Zhukov—as Chip Bohlen believed—has a pretty important governmental job. For that reason, I am interested by the fact that he complained to me his relations with the Soviet embassy are perfectly cordial and correct, but not in the least bit intimate. For example, he says (which may or may not be true) that he can never have a pleasant informal evening with Ambassador Pavlov. He even remarked that his wife was very lonely because his little boy has now joined his older daughter at school in Moscow.

At one point I said it seemed obvious that Russia would like to keep the Korean war going. He asked me why. I said it should be to Russia's advantage to keep American divisions and American equipment occupied in Korea while no Russian troops were tied up. He asked me if, after all, I did not think it would not be more advantageous to Russia to give China a period of detente to get stronger. I said I did not think China would be very strong for twenty years. He replied: "Let's say five."

PARIS, *September 3, 1951*

HECTOR McNeil (British minister of state) and his wife Sheila came over for the weekend. Hector said there was a quarrel between NATO and OEEC. The European countries regarded OEEC as Santa Claus but NATO made them spend their money on arming.

PARIS, *September 3, 1951*

OVER the weekend I also saw a lot of Eisenhower and Gruenther with whom I played bridge three hours Saturday afternoon and seven hours Sunday afternoon and evening, dining briefly in between at Gruenther's.

I asked Eisenhower just exactly how he set about painting a picture: whether he drew an outline of the face he was portraying, or what? He said he first covered the canvas with paint of some bland color. Then he tried to shape out approximately the form of the head he was painting. Then he would paint in very roughly the position of the mouth and eyes. Then he would begin to work more carefully on colors than on the actual features. He says he draws very badly and that it is impossible for him to sketch things out in advance. He was very pleased that he had been able to complete a portrait in six hours recently. It normally takes him much longer. He said he had to move the left eye bodily three times on this painting— a somewhat difficult process I should imagine.

PARIS, *September 20, 1951*

ANOTHER letter from Hemingway about "Dupont." He said he had heard stories in his life that made him feel awful but this made him feel worse than any of them.

PARIS, *September 25, 1951*

LUNCH today with Eisenhower. Others present were: Gruenther, Prince Makinsky (a big shot in the Coca-Cola business and a friend of Jim Farley), Bernard Gimbel (wealthy New York businessman and a pal of Gene Tunney) and Louis Marx (a New york toy manufacturer who is apparently an old friend of Eisenhower). Marx, an ebullient, round little man who talks with quite a marked accent, waving his hands excitedly, was absolutely delighted with a portrait of him done by Eisenhower. I must say it was quite good. After lunch, Lieutenant Colonel Schulz, Eisenhower's aide, took some pictures of us with Marx proudly holding the painting in front of him, his face absolutely devoured by one big smile.

This was the first time I had lunch in the general's dining room at the new SHAPE headquarters in Rocquencourt. It is pleasant, with wide walls decorated with some simply framed hunting prints. The carpet is green and the chairs have dull red leather seats. I noticed that all the match boxes were from the Brown Palace Hotel in Denver.

Ike said he had been very strongly influenced by General Fox Connor, with whom he worked as a young officer. Connor apparently was a remarkable officer and one of Pershing's principal staff members during World War I. Eisenhower said he is conscious of certain traits in his own character which had been developed under the influence of Connor. For example, Connor told him: "Always take your job seriously and never take yourself seriously." I think this is a fair description of Eisenhower's remarkable humility which is certainly a trait that has endeared him to millions.

Eisenhower made one point on the press. He said he was in agreement with the theory that in a newspaper the editorial page belongs to the editors but the news columns belong to the public.

He is distressed at the way the American public permits politicians to bring about national policies on a basis of purely selfish personal interests of individuals thinking of votes. He said he would like very much to see committees or centers established in cities and towns throughout the country where businessmen, lawyers, farmers and other citizens would get together and discuss issues and make up their own minds what is in the national interest, then try and exert public pressure accordingly. He said he had established such a center on a large scale at Columbia University.

Eisenhower said it was a shocking notion on the part of some American politicians that the United States should cease all trade with Russia and her allies. It was similarly ridiculous to expect other nations to cut off trade with the Russian bloc. The only result of such a policy would be to force all foreign nations to make a choice between trading with Russia or trading with us and in the end possibly to choose the Soviet bloc. In order to survive, all nations must have foreign commerce. Bernard Baruch, during World War I, even maintained a secret trade for certain vital materials with Germany. It is folly to assume that we can force other nations to cut all foreign trade to suit our political interests. Furthermore, it is suicide; it is playing the Russian game.

Gimbel asked Eisenhower if it would not be a good idea to smuggle an atom bomb to some friendly country and then have them drop it in North Korea or elsewhere. Eisenhower speculated that it might conceivably be more practical to advertise that a certain number of bombs had been sold or given to our allies and then perhaps let someone drop it; Washington would proclaim that we had no responsibility. However, I must emphasize he was talking in terms of pure speculation. I am confident, fundamentally, he would be strongly opposed to any such gamble and that he firmly believes we must continue our policy of restrained, unprovocative strength.

We talked at length about General Marshall. Eisenhower said Marshall had been very strongly influenced by "Black Jack" Pershing, a stern disciplinarian. This, he thought, was the reason that Marshall's staff was always personally terrified of him. As a result, Marshall was horseback riding on December 7 when the Japanese attacked Pearl Harbor, and his own staff was afraid to notify him as quickly as should have been the case. Eisenhower said Marshall was shocked when he first heard his staff was afraid of him. Eisenhower said loyalty was not a sufficient quality to introduce into one's staff; an element of personal friendship and contact on a human basis was also required.

We discussed General MacArthur. Eisenhower admitted that when he served with MacArthur in the Philippine Islands, MacArthur always underestimated the role of airpower in war. Apparently this was true even during the initial period of World War II; but MacArthur learned thoroughly and quickly the value of air. Queson told Eisenhower that when the Japanese attacked Pearl Harbor MacArthur was convinced for some strange reason that the Philippines would remain neutral and would not be attacked by the Japanese. For that reason, presumably, MacArthur refused permission to General Brereton to bomb Japanese bases on Formosa immediately after the attack on Pearl Harbor. As a result, the American airfields in the Philippines were badly bombed by the Japanese, more than twenty-four hours after Pearl Harbor, because all our planes were still on the ground.

He said the biggest problem facing the world today was one simple question: Are the fourteen men on the Politburo truly ambitious dictators or ideological fanatics? If the former is the case, their primary ambition would be to retain personal power. If the latter is the case, it means inevitable war.

One visitor mentioned a recent newspaper report that Eisenhower should seek the Republican nomination for President now if he wanted to stand any chance of getting it. He replied that he would never "work" to get any job. Nevertheless, although I cannot put my finger on any particular statement, I have an increasing feeling that the general definitely wants to be elected President on a Republican ticket. I cannot prove this, but I know him well enough to feel my instinct is correct.

Eisenhower expressed considerable worry about the Middle East and above all Iran. He said that those foolish politicians who would like to boycott Iran would suddenly wake up finding gasoline rationing on the East Coast of the United States. Some kind of agreement must finally be arrived at between Britain and Iran.

PARIS, *September 27, 1951*

I had a drink this evening with Stanton Griffis, American ambassador to Madrid. He is returning to Spain in two days, after going home on a brief trip for medical reasons. Griffis is an ugly, tough-looking man with a mouth like a rat trap, but he was extremely courteous and friendly.

He was convinced the only possible government in Spain today was that of Franco. He said if Franco had to go, instead of having ten parties as in France, there would be twenty parties in Spain—and no government at all. Furthermore, he said that the government changes in Spain this summer definitely marked an advance towards liberalism and pro-Americanism. He said he could talk frankly and seriously with several of the new cabinet ministers.

PARIS, *October 2, 1951*

LAST night, at the home of Margaret Biddle, dined with the Duke and Duchess of Windsor (formerly King Edward VIII). I had met him a few times before, but never had the opportunity for a really good talk. He is a curious, somewhat pathetic fellow. Although he has, of course, given up any rights to the throne he still maintains a strict atmosphere of court etiquette; there is much curtseying and bowing despite the fact that he is extremely informal and friendly. What I cannot figure out is the fact that on his station wagon, in metal letters, he has "The Duke of Windsor" displayed on both doors. This I saw several times in Biarritz where he spent part of the summer.

She is very nice and rather attractive with a warm and pleasant personality. She had fallen downstairs a day or so ago and was wearing a black handerchief around her arm to hide a bruise. I sat next to her at dinner and she talked at great length about her stay in China in 1924. She adored Shanghai and above all Peking but admitted she knew no Chinese people. She blamed this on the Chinese who, she said, were terrible snobs. I asked if she had learned any of the Chinese language. She replied: "Yes, I studied it a little, but all I learned were a few phrases such as 'Could I have a bit more champagne please?' "

The Duke clearly adores her. He had just come back from London where he stayed during the critical operation on the lung of his brother, King George VI. After dinner we were sitting together talking and every now and then he would look across the room at the Duchess and say: "It's so wonderful to see her. You know, I have not seen her for a week. Isn't she charming?"

After dinner there was a pianist. The Duke was transported with joy. He sang a few songs rather badly and joyfully imitated the playing of various instruments such as the cello and the violin, waving his arms around like a happy schoolboy. He knew a few Spanish and German songs partially. I asked him what languages he spoke and he said: "German, a little Spanish and a little French."

The Duke drank a bit and seemed just slightly tight at the end of the evening. He talked steadily during dinner. At one point the Duchess leaned over the table and said: "You promised you were going to listen tonight because there are a lot of brains around but you are talking all the time." He replied: "I have to talk or otherwise I would fall asleep."

He thought it imperative for the United States and Britain to continually strengthen their relationships and stay together; that this was something he had always worked for. There remained a great residue of prejudice against Britain in some parts of the States and against the United States in some parts of Britain, but he thought that during World War II we had learned to know and respect each other. He regretted that during World War I he was not able to get to the front and see more of the Americans in action.

He thought it would be "an admirable education for a British prince to go to an English public school and then to go to an American university like Harvard." He had been interested in talking with people in the States about their experiences in England during the war. Many said to him: "You know, you English have an institution we have not got, called the pub. That makes us feel at home." He added regretfully to me: "You know what I mean. Of course I can't use them."

On the subject of golf he said he took a lesson every day in Biarritz, but added he was not very good, that he rarely broke ninety. He said his handicap was fourteen in Europe and eighteen in America.

The Duke was worried about the British elections. He feared the Conservatives might be overconfident. He said it would be "disastrous" if they did not come in; if they were defeated this time they would never get back to power and people like Aneurin Bevan would take over the destiny of England. He did not think the policy of the Conservative Party was made by Churchill now but by younger men such as Eden who were much more important. In a sense it was too bad that Eden would not come in as prime minister. Nevertheless, the Duke made it clear that he has enormous admiration for Churchill.

He said the United States had made two tremendous mistakes in policy. The first was insisting on unconditional surrender during the war and the second was pressing for the trial of war criminals. He said unconditional surrender forced any decent German man to fight to the end. He thought the real criminal Nazi leaders should have been shot immediately when they were captured and the rest should not have been arrested and tried. The precedent was bad and it meant that nowadays, if the Russians defeated us in a war, they could execute the King of England and President Truman.

He made it clear that he still feels strong sympathy for the Germans as a people. He recalled that he has German blood and many German relatives. He appears to speak German better than any other foreign language. He said he understood the Germans and that "we must have them as allies."

PARIS, *October 8, 1951*

LUNCH today with General Pierre Billotte, now one of de Gaulle's deputies in the National Assembly and a member of the Commission on Foreign Affairs.

Billotte says there is no way of rearming Germany except as a German national army and that the European army is a joke. He thinks the only thing preventing Russia from starting a war is American rearmament.

Incidentally, he said that at a meeting two weeks ago of the assembly's foreign affairs commission practically all deputies on the commission voted that France must now choose between continuing the war in Indochina or rearming in Europe; it could not do both. Billotte maintains that he was the only one who insisted both must continue.

PARIS, *October 12, 1951*

SPENT the afternoon with Gruenther. Al said his father used to run a newspaper in Platte Center, Nebraska. It was a weekly newspaper called the *Platte Center Signal*. His father was also clerk of the district court in the county seat, fifteen miles away. In those days it was a train ride, and trains were few. Therefore, his father spent many days away from home in order to handle his job at the County Seat. Platte Center only had a population of 370, so the paper was pretty small. Al used to help with setting type, writing articles. He and his family moved to Omaha in 1917, and the paper folded in 1920. Al once wrote an editorial for the *Signal* criticizing large appropriations for the military.

Gruenther hardly ever takes a day off except for Sundays. He goes to bed at 11 P.M. and reads until eleven-thirty or eleven-forty-five. He wakes up at 7 A.M. He says he can go to sleep immediately within five minutes and would never dream of using a pill. He reads a good deal of his regular allotment of newspapers before 8:45 A.M. He tries to keep up with non-official reading over the weekends. At this moment, he is reading *The Caine Mutiny* by Herman Wouk, *Modern France* edited by Edward Earles and *The Outline of History* by H. G. Wells.

Gruenther said he was extremely interested in history but that Eisenhower knew it even better than he did, although he admits he, Gruenther, is better on dates. Today at lunch, Ike was talking about the Crusades. Gruenther, as a result, is now reading up on them because "Ike knows he cannot dare risk being inaccurate next time he mentions the Crusades; I will be checking him."

He said Eisenhower had served as a staff officer in Panama under General Fox Connor. Connor had an extraordinary intellect with a great knowledge of history, politics, philosophy, religion. This experience inspired Eisenhower and left a permanent influence upon him.

Gruenther learned bridge in an unusual way. His class graduated twice from West Point because of World War I. They were graduated as second lieutenants on November 1, 1918. On November 11, the Armistice ended World War I. Then, the class went back until 1919. It was sent around to various service schools. Gruenther went to Camp Knox for a year. He was selected as an instructor and "had to work like hell." He was assigned under a major in the "department of miscellaneous subjects." These included such unrelated topics as bookkeeping, law, hygiene, military courtesy.

He had to work extremely hard and at night, when he saw his fellow bachelors playing bridge, he looked upon them with scorn. However, one night he was invited to his major's house for dinner. After supper, three card tables were brought out. Gruenther noticed there were only twelve people including himself. The major asked him if he knew how to play bridge and he said no. The major told him he would have to play. The only card game Gruenther knew was called "high five." The Major said: "Don't worry, it's just like 'high five.' " To Gruenther's great embarrassment he spent a good deal of the evening with the major's wife as his partner and played extremely badly. He decided to study it in order to prevent future embarrassment.

He was ordered to serve in the Philippines, where he studied some more. Then he went to West Point, which was near the bridge center of New York. He attended a tournament with a friend one day and did quite well. The next autumn he invited some friends of his to West Point for a tournament and did even better. By 1929, he was in the top flight. He was invited to run a tournament in New York and was told there would be some prima donnas among the players and that, although he was a young fellow, he should be tough and make no exceptions. The man who gave him those instructions showed up late at the tournament. Despite the fact that he was Gruenther's mentor and was giving the cup to the winners, Gruenther refused to let him play because he was late. For some time he was a tournament referee and he put an end to "coffee-housing"—a practice in which the players used to insult their opponents.

In 1920, with the war over, it looked to Gruenther as if the military profession was going to become a dead end. He worried whether by the time he reached retirement age the United States Army would be big enough to include nine colonels. There were eight younger men at that time who outranked him. He thought very seriously of going to the Harvard School of Business Administration and actually sent for the catalogues. However, his father talked him out of it and persuaded him that the army was a worthwhile and patriotic career for a young man.

PARIS, *October 15, 1951*

YESTERDAY we went to a surprise birthday party for Eisenhower, who was sixty-one. The whole thing was a plot by Gruenther. Ike is a great lover of birthday parties and regularly celebrates. Al decided to kid him. When General Ike woke up yesterday morning, nobody congratulated him. He was astonished when Moaney, the Negro sergeant who has been with them for years and adores him, seemed to have forgotten his birthday. Mamie said nothing. When the general got up he asked whether she wanted him to wear anything special. She said no, anything that would be comfortable to play bridge in. Gruenther had invited him for bridge that afternoon.

The general was kind of sulky and sat around painting all day until 3 P.M. when he was due to go next door to the Gruenthers. Although he has a pretty large house at Marnes-la-Coquette, the only place he can paint— because of space and light requirements—is at the head of the stairs by the sitting room. Mamie says she has a lot of trouble because he keeps messing the place up and won't put things away. However, yesterday she let him fuss around and stayed in her own room all day, so that she would not give away the conspiracy by her behavior.

Meanwhile Gruenther had fixed everything. Averell Harriman, Secretary of the Navy Dan Kimball, and I had been invited to play bridge at 3 P.M. at the Gruenthers. We were all in on the plot. When Eisenhower came in nobody mentioned his birthday. We just sat down and played bridge. Both generals were wearing ordinary civilian clothes. Grace Gruenther was downstairs in the kitchen supervising the cooking of the turkeys, etc. Gruenther had seen to it that no letters or telegrams congratulating Ike were delivered. All telephone messages, including trans-Atlantic calls, had been stopped.

As we were playing bridge, the plot took shape. A few other friends, including Marie Harriman, Marina, Mrs. Perle Mesta (American minister in Luxembourg, who came down with a birthday cake she'd baked) gathered at the Eisenhowers'. Here they learned a song which a member of SHAPE had written for him.

At 6 o'clock sharp, while we were playing bridge, and Eisenhower—with his back to the surprise—was sitting gloomily as dummy, the whole group tiptoed to the entrance of the room and suddenly began singing the following song: To the tune of "When You Wore a Tulip":

> Oh, Ike had a birthday, a big, happy birthday,
>     But nobody told him so.
> Not even Moaney, Admiral Capponi,
>     Or Mamie seemed to know;
> Instead of being cheery, the day seemed so dreary,
>     And poor Ike felt so alone.
> We're sorry we ignored you, for really we adore you,
>     Happy birthday from one and all.

The general was astounded. He turned around blushing a little with delight and surprise. Then the party started. Cocktails were distributed while Eisenhower sat in an armchair and his presents were brought in, plus his cables, letters, and so forth. I gave him a bottle of Przovka (pepper vodka). He said the last and the only time he drank it was with Stalin. The Gruenthers gave him an apparatus with which to make sauerkraut out of cabbage. The Harrimans gave him a book, *The Cruel Sea*. Among the cables he received was one from President Truman. He sat like a little boy grinning from ear to ear as he went through his presents and messages. It was a curious mixture of gifts, including a rather odd porcelain parrot, an ornate picture frame, etc.

While all this was going on, Lieutenant Colonel Schulz, Ike's aide, wandered around taking snapshots. Then we had a buffet supper, which, as usual at the Gruenthers, was excellent and copious, and where the guest of honor demonstrated with considerable appetite his belief that the best part of the turkey is the wing. After dinner we resumed our bridge game and the women played canasta.

On the whole it was a pleasant and rather endearing party. If I had not had an incipient attack of grippe coming on I would have enjoyed it more. As a footnote, I would like to add a few things I recollect about serious moments of conversation.

Harriman said Truman had asked him to be sure and find out if Eisenhower was "happy" over here and to do all he could to make him happy. This obviously pleased the general although it is a curious commentary in the sense that he and Truman may be running against each other next autumn.

Eisenhower said that he remembered that Henry Wallace wanted to have a permanent civilian head of the Atomic Energy Commission, not only to take it out of politics or interservice rivalries, but also because he thought it would be better for security. The general said that if he were called upon to testify upon that period he would have to support Wallace.

At this point, he added that no diary is ever a very accurate document. He was referring specifically to Forrestal's diary which claimed that Wallace wanted to give the atom bomb to the Russians. Although Eisenhower had a very high regard for Forrestal, he says there are many things in his diary which he knows are quite untrue.

Gruenther was worried about the Middle Eastern situation. He said information had come in that day (October 14) indicating that the Egyptians would not accept the new Anglo-American proposals for an Allied command in the Near East. Both he and Harriman said the sad thing about our policy was that we were always much too slow and too late. We would not be in the fix we are in now concerning German rearmament if we had moved expeditiously a year ago. If the British had acted with sense in Iran a couple of years ago, that whole crisis could have been avoided. The same is true about the Suez Canal. Gruenther is also worried about what may happen in French North Africa. The big problem—they both agree—was that we had to make up our minds very speedily and then act with the utmost swiftness. Further delay now might be very costly. Harriman and Gruenther considered that the most important question, philosophically speaking, was: How could democracies (founded upon the principle of proportional representation) be tough enough or quick enough or single-minded enough to protect themselves during times of crisis when they are threatened by dictatorial systems?

Eisenhower said the thing that bothered him most was the complete absence of any real leader in Western Europe who, "in the manner of Peter the Hermit," is willing to crusade for our ideals and can enlist the enthusiastic support of the democratic populations. He saw no indication that any such leadership was being developed.

Gruenther thought there was probably only one possible solution for the jam we are in in Egypt. This would be to appoint an American supreme commander for the Middle East command. The Turks would welcome this and the Egyptians might be persuaded to accept it. But it would be an incredibly sharp blow to British prestige abroad and pride at home and it is most unlikely that we can persuade the British to accept it.

LONDON, *October 19, 1951*

YESTERDAY evening drinks and chat with Lord Salisbury, one of the Conservative leaders and almost certainly an important member of the next Churchill cabinet if the Tories win the election. Should Churchill fall ill or retire and Eden succeed him, Salisbury may very well be secretary of state for foreign affairs.

He is tall, thin, ugly, with a remarkably mobile face, long nose and spectacles; extremely talkative and informal. His wife has great warmth and charm. They live in a rambling, comfortable but far from luxurious house in Chelsea.

Most of our conversation dealt with foreign policy under a Tory government. Salisbury says a Conservative government would desire the closest possible relations with the United States. While this was also true of Labor, the Tories think it would be easier to work on a close and harmonious basis with men like Eden and Churchill, who have old, personal connections with Washington.

Churchill would wish to revive something like the Combined Chiefs of Staff. This body would probably include France but would be controlled by Britain and the United States. It would be much more directly under the heads of government than the existing NATO structure which operates through the ministers of defense.

He said it was possible the Conservatives would decide eventually to break off diplomatic relations with China. Salisbury himself had been firmly against *de jure* recognition of Peking from the start. Recognition had been a complete failure.

The Conservatives would almost certainly request full membership in a Pacific pact. Australia and New Zealand now have defensive agreements with the United States in that area and there is a similar bilateral accord between the United States and Japan. It was obvious if war started in the Pacific, Britain would be involved immediately because of alliances of two of her dominions. Therefore she wanted full partnership herself. Salisbury thinks a Pacific pact should be developed which would be equivalent to the Atlantic Pact.

LUNCH with Trygve Lie, Secretary General of the United Nations. He seems to get fatter every time I see him. I was fascinated by the structure of his ears, which are shaped almost like those of an elephant. He was very friendly; a man of good will, good intentions and steadily increasing vanity.

He thinks the Kashmir dispute is the most dangerous quarrel now going on—outside of Korea. Nehru—despite his smooth talk—is a dictator. Nehru has admitted to him in the past that his policy is to do nothing about settling the Kashmir question because he is convinced Pakistan cannot survive as an independent state and will some day have to come "crawling back" to India.

Lie expressed horror over the fact that for many years the British Oil Company in Iran had paid several times as much in taxes to the British government as it had paid in revenues to the Iranian government. A proof of how medieval the Anglo-Iranian administration had been was that the British had trained not one single competent engineer or expert of Persian nationality; that is why the Iranians are in a difficult position now.

TALK with Field Marshal Montgomery of Alamein. He is convinced Eisenhower would remain here in NATO—if he possibly could—rather than return to the United States to run for President. Eisenhower has a "very high sense of duty" and recognizes that "he is the only man who can accomplish this job—indeed if anyone can." Montgomery described Ike as "the greatest American of this time."

He said he was a very close friend of Eisenhower and knew Ike was now exchanging letters with Senator Taft trying to assure himself that Taft would support NATO if Taft is elected President. I cannot imagine Eisenhower will be satisfied with a mere statement from Taft on this subject.

# 2 5

# EISENHOWER

# ENTERS POLITICS

LUNCH OUT AT SHAPE. AMONG THOSE PRESENT WERE: GRUENTHER; Jean Monnet; Major General George Olmstead, an ordnance expert; Major General Schuyler (special assistant to Gruenther); Harry Labouisse (head of the Marshall Plan mission to France).

Gruenther thought if the Russians attacked, they could certainly still win a first phase and occupy most or all of Europe; but that they could not face phases two and three—a long war. There was not yet any satisfactory defense against long-range, high-level strategic air attack if you do not know in advance from which direction the planes are coming. We could smash Russia itself while its armies were occupying Europe.

Gruenther said he did not think Russia at present has enough infantry available to constitute an occupying force in a conquered Europe. Most Soviet strength is now in armored units which could crush forward. We would get some advance notice of Russian intentions if they started train loads of infantry westward. But it would not give us enough notice to do much about it yet. The Russians would not have to do very much defense stockpiling for a sudden surprise attack.

Monnet said it was a great danger ever to talk in terms of a date such as 1954 when the West would be strong enough to take on Russia or defend itself against Russia. Such gives the impression that by that time we will be ready for anything and some people might therefore want to start a war; others might want to cease the defense effort. The West must be prepared to pay for its defense for an indefinite period of time.

Gruenther had serious doubts about the wisdom of including Spain in

NATO. It would cause a bad political reaction which would not be advisable at this time. We could never count on getting a couple of Spanish divisions available to be transported to Germany within seven days of the outbreak of war. Spain was only a matter of a geographically available space for planes and ships. In this sense it is useful to have a bilateral deal between the United States and Spain—provided the price is not too high. It is interesting to hear the sensible and moderate opinion offered by a devout American Catholic who is not stampeded into political hysteria when talking about Spain.

Monnet was convinced the European army plan will go through and that eventually there will be a federation of Europe. He has a bet with Field Marshal Montgomery that the latter will take place within three years (I agree with Montgomery that it won't).

Monnet says the Indochina war is so unpopular that the French government could never send conscripts there. As a result, practically the whole French army is fighting in Indochina, which means that cadres for training are not available in Europe. It would be easier to send conscripts to Korea.

Monnet thinks de Gaulle no longer has any chance of coming to power. It was a tragedy that de Gaulle did not work harder to produce a good constitution after the war. French governments must be weak as things now are because of the terrible constitution. But France has several exceptionally able men among its leaders.

PARIS, *October 26, 1951*

LAST night the Gruenthers, Harrimans and Bruces came for dinner. Gruenther and Bruce said I was a cynic when I maintained the real policy of France in supporting the European army project is to keep Germany divided and the real policy of the United States was to back it in order to get some German divisions armed as quickly as possible. Bruce, who acts as the American observer at the European army talks, is convinced there will be a real federation of Europe within the next few years. I hope his idealism proves more correct than my skepticism.

After dinner Harriman said he was forced to admit that the Socialist government in England has been able to distribute funds received from the Marshall Plan on a more just basis—giving the workers a greater cut—than had been the case in France and Germany.

Gruenther said that the men—aside from himself—who might be chosen to succeed Eisenhower as NATO Commander, if he runs for President, were the following: Bradley, Clark, Collins, Ridgway. He would have to be an American.

I spent the morning and lunched with Larry Norstad, commander of NATO's central Air Command. Norstad was willing to bet fifty to one that Eisenhower would not be here in December 1952. If he did not go into politics he would leave anyway and let some other man take over the job while it was still "building up" so his successor could get some of the credit.

Larry said the greatest quality Ike has as an administrator was that nobody ever feels he is working for him; rather one is working with him; he supports his subordinates. He allows them considerable free rein. If he disagrees, he does so in a gentle and tactful way. He has an incredible sense of subtle tactfulness.

Norstad is impressive in his conviction that NATO's most important aspect is moral and that it must succeed in keeping the peace rather than in making an efficient military machine to prosecute a war. There is nothing to replace its concepts of collective security should it fail. It is the only alliance in history which was clearly postulated upon the philosophical concept of maintaining peace.

Lunch and long talk—lasting almost three hours—with Eisenhower at his SHAPE private dining room. Ike gave the impression of being in a nervous mood. He seemed to have gained weight during his holiday in Scotland. While there he was not able to play any golf because of his bad wrist. I noticed he had an iron in his office and he occasionally takes a couple of swings with it.

He is under immense pressure to run for President. He pointed to a pack of letters on his desk, either congratulating him upon his alleged decision to run—which has not been made—or begging him to run. The mail also included brochures from various "Ike for President" clubs. He joked about the latter that they were not printed at government expense.

He pointed affectionately to some pressed columbines which he had received from Denver. The columbine is the state flower of Colorado and he has named his new plane for it. We had a glass of sherry with Gruenther before lunch. At lunch Eisenhower, who has to watch his weight, had only consommé, a bowl of fruit and milk, and one piece of Swiss cheese. He used saccharin in his coffee.

Luncheon started on a joking basis when Eisenhower had to pay off a bet to Gruenther on the British election. Knowing about Al's other bets, I presume Eisenhower wagered the Conservatives would have a majority of sixty or more seats.

Ike said that before he announced his decision not to run for the Presidency in 1948 (by a letter to a New Hampshire newspaper editor) President Truman offered him the opportunity to run on the Democratic ticket and added to this that he, Truman, would step down and run for Vice-President. After Eisenhower's public announcement that he would not run for political office, he said that he ranked about "as high as Saint Peter" with Truman.

Eisenhower again said he was astonished at how inaccurate diaries kept by important men can be. He was referring once more to the recently published Secretary of Defense Forrestal's diary. According to Ike, this says Forrestal talked with Truman who told him that he did not want to keep Eisenhower as Chief of Staff and that he was planning to bring Bradley back to Washington. Ike would then take the hint and quit— according to Truman (as reported by Forrestal). Eisenhower says this is utterly untrue.

Eisenhower looks back with horror upon the confusion and lack of coordination in our planning and defense spending immediately after the war. He recalls that Admiral Ernie King visited him at his SHEAF Headquarters during the spring of 1945. Eisenhower said to him: "Well, Ernie, you will be glad to know that this show is going to be over soon and that you can have the whole damn British fleet to help you out in the Pacific." King replied that he did not want a single British ship. Since he (King) had been a little boy, the British had been trying to plant the white ensign on the islands of the central Pacific and he damned well was going to prevent it. Eisenhower asked him if he meant by this that the United States was planning to build the huge tonnage in extra shipping to do the job all alone without British aid. King said that was exactly what he meant. Eisenhower was horrified by the enormous waste of money required to build these strategically unnecessary ships and said: "That certainly is a hell of a way to build a democratic system in the world."

He continually criticizes waste in the country's economy and in defense planning. For example, he said it was a shame that so much money was now being spent to develop the Marine Corps. As a result of Truman's unfortunate public reference to the Marines some time ago, they are now being permitted to expand beyond all reason, not only into new divisions but into corps. They were forming what was tantamount to a "private army" of the Navy. This is utterly uneconomic and useless. Until World War II the most Marines ever in action at a time was one brigade serving as part of a division during World War I. Right now, SHAPE planners are not reckoning on the use of a single United States Marine.

Again on the subject of waste and bad planning, Eisenhower recalled that the United States Navy alone had 34,000 planes available when World War II ended. This massive force had been permitted to disintegrate. In 1946 President Truman had promised Eisenhower there would be an annual defense budget of $15 billion. He thinks that would have been enough to continue maintaining an adequate defense force. But Truman reneged on this pledge. Now, even with the present annual defense budget of $60 billion, we may not be able to accomplish our current defense requirements because of the huge rise in prices.

The general said the organization of the American government was inefficient and wasteful. Such impartial reports as that of the Hoover Commission were ignored. He felt the President was unwilling to delegate sufficient authority to any one man because he did not wish to see "another sun emerge on the horizon." Eisenhower feels there is a terrible overlapping and waste in the government. This led him to recall that early in the war, when Ike was chief of operations, General Brehon Somerville (in charge of supply) put up a project to build a concrete road from the United States right down to South America in order to ship goods without risking destruction by the German submarines that were then ravaging our coast. Eisenhower opposed this on the grounds that it would have no effect on the outcome of World War II, which would be over long before the road was finished. Somerville was furious. Eisenhower finally got the project shuttled over to the logistics section. However, he pointed out that sometimes imaginative projects of this sort were very useful. Everybody sneered at General Hap Arnold when he first started the construction of a line of air bases across the North Atlantic via Newfoundland, Greenland and Iceland. Yet, this visionary plan enabled us to send thousands of fighter planes to Europe under their own power, thus saving enormous sums of money which would have had to be put into shipping to transport them.

On the subject of rearming Germany, Eisenhower said he had told Hallstein, secretary of state at the Bonn ministry of foreign affairs; General Adolf Heusinger, military adviser to Adenauer; and General Hans Speidel, formerly Rommel's chief of staff and now one of Adenauer's military advisers, that there must be no attempted German blackmail seeking to get better terms out of the West by playing off the threat of the East. The Germans must realize that their bread is buttered on the western side; they must take a real part in the western community. Eisenhower said he had told the German generals they must remain absolutely confident that Germany would have a fair chance as part of the western world. We had no desire to create a bunch of Hesses. (By this Ike meant we did not wish to break Germany into a group of small states.) In fact, Eisenhower jokingly said to the Germans that we would hate such an idea because we recalled the role played by Hessian mercenaries serving the British against Washington during the American Revolution.

Eisenhower admitted he was disturbed by General MacArthur's speech at the recent American Legion convention in Florida although he pointed out quickly that he was far more disturbed by the antics of Senator McCarthy. However, today Eisenhower said MacArthur now, as always, was an opportunist seeking to ride the crest of the wave.

We talked about the hysterical folly of the present witch hunt against anybody suspected of harboring pro-Russian, pro-Communist (or even liberal) sentiments during the past twenty years. Eisenhower, for example, spoke of the case of a Columbia professor, George Counts, who perhaps twenty years ago saw some good things in communism and some dangers in the historical trend of democracy. It was ridiculous that Counts should be handicapped now because of what he had thought two decades ago. Eisenhower asked where the churches of the world would be if there had been no sinners. He thought it would be a good idea to have a sort of statute of limitations in terms of time, setting a date before which a man's loyalty could not be questioned.

He said General Bedell Smith had recently visited him here. (Smith is now chief of the Central Intelligence Agency.) Ike said he told him he thought the Voice of America should limit itself strictly to presenting, without commentary, the point of view of the American government in its news broadcasts. Other types of propaganda should be handled by private agencies but the Voice should have as its sole mission the presentation of a truthful version of American policy. As far as other types of foreign operations go, Eisenhower thought the CIA should have its men here and there working quietly in foreign countries fostering political movements and propaganda. He told this to Bedell who replied: "What the hell do you think I've been doing for the last year?" Eisenhower said this type of propaganda had certainly operated during the last French elections. (I presume he was referring to the anti-Communist posters and literature of *"Paix et Liberté."*)

Eisenhower thought it was necessary to explain day after day with enough repetition to drive the point home just what American foreign policy is. He recalls that after the British advised us they could no longer support Greece and Turkey, Truman decided we would have to do so—the so-called "Truman Doctrine." But Truman told Eisenhower we wanted to announce he would support any country against communism. Ike told the President it was the wrong way to go about it; we should promise support to any country prepared to defend itself. We could not embark on a straight anti-Communist campaign around the world but we must encourage independent nations to fight for their independence against aggression.

Eisenhower admitted he was a member of the Republican Party; that he had voted for Dewey as President in 1948 against Truman; that he had voted for Dulles in 1950 as senator against Lehman. He agreed to allow a statement to this effect to be put out in America by his brother Milton. He does not seem to wish to run for President. However, he may be forced to do so.

PARIS, *November 5, 1951*

LUNCH with Vladimir Dedijer, who is here as a member of the Jugoslav delegation to the UN Assembly. Vlado told me Jugoslavia is preparing to introduce a resolution charging the Soviet Union with threatening world peace. In preliminary talks the Americans have been supporting the idea strongly but the British are negative.

PARIS, *November 7, 1951*

LAST night dinner at Harriman's. Senator William Benton, Connecticut Democrat, and Admiral Kirk, ambassador to Russia, were there.

Kirk said the Russians were having considerable economic difficulties as a result of rearmament. He added, however, that the Soviet Union was going to have exceptionally good crops this year. This places them in a better military position for 1952.

Harriman said he had been surprised in Washington to find a "peace offensive" planned, but everybody assured him it was imperative for us to seize the initiative in propaganda. I told him I foresaw pitfalls since we were still committed to a policy of "facts not words" and "negotiating from strength."

Harriman recalled how, in 1950, he was urged to run on the Democratic ticket for governor of New York state. He said Ed Flynn told him he could have the nomination if he wanted it. At that point Marie Harriman said she would jump off a bridge if Averell ever ran for political office. Averell remarked with a smile: "How do you think Marie would fit in in Albany?" We agreed that it was not her type of town.

PARIS, *November 10, 1951*

LAST night I attended the annual reception at the Soviet Embassy in honor of the October Revolution. It was crowded with Russians, satellite diplomats, and various Communist delegations to the United Nations Assembly. General Slavin, a member of the Soviet delegation and a burly, thick-set man with hands like a blacksmith, forced me into a corner with an overly affable vodka toast, saying: "You people want war and if you insist we will give you war—and smash you." I thought this was a somewhat eccentric bit of hospitality in the middle of a peaceable-minded gathering.

PARIS, *November 10, 1951*

LUNCH today with Lester (Mike) Pearson, Canadian foreign minister. He saw MacArthur in Tokyo in February 1950 and at that time the general gave him a briefing on Pacific defense. He showed him our defense line from the Aleutians through Japan to the Philippines. It included Okinawa, but excluded Formosa. Pearson said MacArthur told him Formosa had no value as a strategic base and could be blanketed by air from Okinawa. This certainly disagrees with what MacArthur told me in May, 1950.

PARIS, *November 12, 1951*

LUNCH at the home of Henri Laugier and Mme. Cutoli, a shrewd-looking and extraordinarily intelligent (also obviously wealthy) woman who must be in her mid-sixties. I enjoy visiting them enormously. You are likely to run into anyone from Picasso, their dear personal friend, to Miro or General De Lattre de Tassigny.

This time, those present—in addition to wives—were Torres Bodet (former Mexican foreign minister and now head of UNESCO), Parodi (French ambassador who is now secretary general of the foreign office) and a little old man named Montel who is supposed to be one of the most brilliant living mathematicians.

The apartment is chock full of Picassos from all periods. Mme. Torres Bodet remarked: "I never understood Picasso until I came to this flat. You really appreciate the scope of the man when you're here."

Mme. Cutoli said Picasso had confided that he likes to try any style of art until he gets bored with it; then he wants to start off again with a new style. She told Picasso once, "You're killing painting for a hundred years." What she meant was that he could paint better than anybody in any style. She says Picasso continually begs her to send him "an artist who'll kill me," meaning someone who has a new and original genius.

Our host is referred to as "Laugier" and not "Henri" by his oldest friends and by his mistress. He has lived openly for years in the utmost respectability with Mme. Cutoli. When he was sent to New York as Assistant Secretary General of the United Nations, Mme. Cutoli—plus a few Picassos—went along. They have never deemed it necessary to take out a marriage license, although both must be pushing seventy. I find this delightful.

PARIS, *November 12, 1951*

THIS afternoon I had a very good talk with Eden. He seems in excellent health and humor. He said that in his speech before the Assembly today he had demanded that Italy be admitted to UN in order to "rehabilitate" his own name in Rome. He is not yet too popular on account of his noble attitude during the Ethiopian War. Eden admitted he would be happy to see a "package settlement" on UN admissions, letting in such Western countries as Italy, Portugal and Eire, together with such Russian puppets as Rumania, Hungary and Bulgaria. However, he drew the line at Outer Mongolia.

Eden amused me by referring twice to "Borgia" when he meant Count Sforza, the Italian foreign minister. He wasn't aware of this slip.

He said Britain was in a far worse fix than he had suspected before the elections, and he had to blame Attlee, whom he described as a good friend, for misrepresenting the situation. (He described Attlee as "very naughty.") Britain is economically in the soup. Eden said the Conservatives had lost many seats as the result of the Labor campaign to smear them as "warmongers."

Eden said Churchill would visit Truman in Washington on January 3. The big topic will be a request by Churchill for reestablishment of something like the Combined Chiefs of Staff that operated during the war—in other words, a sort of "super committee" to coordinate Allied strategy and policy all over the world—Europe, Middle East, Far East. The French would have to be included in such a committee, although Eden remarked certain aspects of this would be "inconvenient." He said Britain would not change its attitude towards China at this moment but the British were fighting China in Malaya just as hard as the French were in Indochina. He said the Malayan war was going very badly. Eden was astonished—coming back to the job—at how much traveling there is. Everything was topsy-turvy. He remembered the good old days when he was foreign secretary before the war, and when all he was expected to do was to go to Geneva a few weeks a year.

Nuri el Said, Iraqi prime minister, came to see Eden two days ago and assured him that Iraq wanted to join the Western defense scheme for the Middle East. I remarked to Eden that all this was O.K. provided nobody bumped Nuri off. He replied: "Yes, this new business of assassination by selection is somewhat embarrassing."

Eden said opinion in Syria was generally in favor of the proposed pact, but he could not understand why the prime minister had just resigned because his foreign minister disagreed with the proposal. He said: "After all, I have heard of other cases where the foreign minister, rather than the prime minister, was forced to resign." He was grinning and obviously referred to the time when he resigned from Neville Chamberlain's cabinet during the Anglo-Italian crisis of the Ethiopian War.

Eden said the great difficulty in the Middle East was Palestine—not so much the mere fact of Israel's existence as an independent state, but the tragic situation of the Arab refugees. Now that King Abdullah of Jordan was dead, it was more difficult to deal with this. However, Eden said Sir Alec Kirkbride, British resident minister in Amman, had sent very reassuring reports about the new King Talal. This is good news because Talal was not only rumored insane, but was said to be a violent Anglophobe. Eden was inclined to believe that it was "just another case" of a royal father who did not get on with his son and railroaded him to an asylum.

By the way, Eden hinted that secret negotiations now going on between the Italians and the Jugoslavs on Trieste are proceeding well, and he looked for success.

PARIS, *November 13, 1951*

LAST night I attended one of the most extraordinary dinner parties I have ever been to. It was given by the Duke and Duchess of Windsor. Aside from Senator Warren Austin of the UN delegation and his wife and Prime Minister René Pleven and his wife, a weird collection of social derelicts was there.

The dinner itself was lavish in the extreme. Cocktails were accompanied by *pâtés* spread with caviar or covered with slices of lobster. The dinner comprised about ten courses and was heavily spliced with sherry, white wine, red wine, pink champagne and huge slugs of brandy. During course Number Seven, a complete string orchestra popped in and started playing away in a fashion reminiscent of prewar Vienna. The Duke got up and made an affectionate little speech in honor of Austin, whose birthday it was. The senator replied with a toast. Everybody sang "Happy Birthday to You" in somewhat embarrassed fashion. From then on, the Duke couldn't eat because he was too busy waving his arms around in time to the music— his favorite habit. Whenever I have seen him anywhere near music, out comes his conductor's complex.

After dinner and dull conversation, Pleven departed, rapidly followed by Austin and the rest of the company. I was anxious to go but the Windsors insisted we stay. Some other character, whose name I never did get and who looked like an old rakehell, hung around but was given the bum's rush.

The Duchess caught Marina by the hand and said, "Don't go, it's so nice to have brains to talk to." She sat down and we began speaking of the world situation. She kept repeating, "I do hope really nothing is going to happen, because we do want so to buy a house."

Then Marina and I were treated to an extraordinary conversation. In essence, it comprised a tragic lament about the British royal family. The Duchess kept insisting she would never go back to England because "the Duke," as she always calls her husband, had been treated so shabbily.

They told the following story. The Duke had worked nobly and patrioti-cally for Britain while Prince of Wales and, briefly, as King Edward VIII. Between 1918 and 1936, he averaged one speech every day. It was untrue to say that Winston Churchill had been his "ghost." He had no ghost, wrote all his speeches himself, and was very proud of it. This, he insisted, was true of his famous speech of farewell to the British nation—

although I must say I have heard from other eminently responsible sources that he got a good deal of help from Churchill on that one, at any rate.

The Duke was furious over the following incident. He had prepared a lengthy speech designed to boost his book of memoirs. The thing was recorded for a publishers' dinner but Buckingham Palace ordered it stopped on the grounds that it was no time to make such a speech because of the King's illness. On the afternoon before the speech was to have been delivered, Princesses Elizabeth and Margaret went to the races. Both the Duke and the Duchess kept repeating that the two "nieces" had gone "to the races," while, at the same time, the speech was banned because of King George's illness.

The Duchess said: "Why don't your play them your record?" The Duke protested: "Oh, no, no, I can't." Then we were escorted downstairs where they have a long-playing phonograph.

The Duke's speech said he now "knew why Job said 'I wish my enemies had written a book.' " It was a great honor for him because "it is the first time in fifteen years that I have spoken in England, which, in spite of everything, is my country and my home." The speech continued: A lot of people had been nasty about the book, there had been criticism, but he didn't see why, just because he is an ex-king, he wasn't allowed to write. He brought in a lot of examples of English rulers who had written books— Charles II, Henry VIII and Queen Victoria. The speech ends with the remark: "My book is not a novel, but it is a romance, and all I can say is that I hope it can end like most fairy tales—'and they lived happily ever after.' "

The speech was very pleasant but we were told he had never been allowed to make it. The Duchess kept saying, "What nonsense! What hypocrisy! What jealousy! When I think that that very day, the girls went to the races and the Duke of Gloucester went to a dinner party!"

The Duke said his only real "home" was in Canada where he had acquired several thousand acres because he deliberately sought as Prince of Wales to cement the trans-Atlantic bond.

I observed that the Duke had been born a king with all the disadvantages and none of the advantages. He said: "Of course, of course, unless, of course, there is a revolution or a 'civil war'—if there is a change or civil war."

The Duke kept referring to their lands in Canada. Speaking of Elizabeth's Canadian tour, he said: "We drilled for oil on our land and didn't find any. It would be just our luck if they found oil." The Duke said crossly that the Canadians acted as if they never had a member of the royal family in Canada before "when, after all, it is my second home—but of course they don't consider me a member of the royal family." The Duke kept referring to "the lovely lady I married," and I had the impression he is mad about her.

PARIS, *November 16, 1951*

REMARKABLE dinner party last night given by Marie Harriman in honor of Averell's sixtieth birthday. Averell looked extremely happy and nowhere near his age. He kept wandering around like a little boy saying: "I'm astonished to be sixty. I am not sixty. I won't be sixty."

It was a pretty distinguished gathering, way out of my league. Present were Dean Acheson and his wife, General Eisenhower and his wife, General Bradley (Chairman of the Joint Chiefs of Staff) and his wife, General Gruenther and his wife, Ambassador Bruce, Admiral Kirk, ambassador to Moscow, and a few others.

Everybody brought presents. Grace Gruenther had baked a cake which she brought along and also had written a little poem to Averell, which she intended to read. However, she was rather embarrassed and, on Al's advice, decided against it. She showed me the poem afterwards. Thank heaven it wasn't read aloud.

When the champagne and birthday cake arrived, a Hungarian Gypsy orchestra from Monseigneur came busily fiddling into the room playing "Happy Birthday to You"—the same that had plowed into the Duke of Windsor's dining room, playing the same tune to Senator Austin this week. They winked at Marina and me. They must think we are professional birthday party-goers, like the mourners one hires for funerals.

Kirk told me that Pavlov, Soviet ambassador in France, who used to be envoy in Brussels, told the Belgian ambassador here that Acheson's speech last week meant "This is war." Kirk was inclined to laugh at this. He considers Pavlov small potatoes in the Soviet line-up, having known him in Brussels. Lydia Kirk said, "Mme. Pavlov is much more terrifying; she is a Soviet pistol champion."

Mrs. Kirk was talking with Acheson over a postprandial glass of champagne and remarked that, of course, Harriman had always wanted to be Secretary of State, much as he liked Acheson. Acheson replied he had known this; he had known Averell since they were in school together, although they had never been really close friends; yet despite Averell's secret aspiration he had always been the most loyal friend and faithful servant any Secretary could ever ask for.

Marie Harriman told Marina that just before dinner General Bradley's wife whispered to her, when she saw me talking to Eisenhower, "For goodness sake, why doesn't the press leave him alone." Marie said she replied to Mrs. Bradley, " 'The press' happens to be Ike's best friend in Paris." (I wish that were true.)

After Averell had blown out the birthday cake candles, Acheson made a very pleasant little speech on behalf of "all of us around the table who have come together this evening because we are so fond of him." He recalled that he had first met Averell in 1905. (They were schoolboys together at

Groton. Acheson told me afterwards that Averell was two years ahead of him. He had regarded Averell as one of the older boys and viewed him with appropriate awe. It was Averell's advice which had taught him how to row, both in school and college.) Then he went on and talked about what a great public servant Averell was.

Harriman got up and recalled that he had coached the Yale varsity crew while Acheson coached the Yale freshmen. He said Acheson rowed Number Seven on the freshmen at 149 pounds, and that he was willing to wager there had been nobody that light on the Yale freshman crew before or since. He said Acheson's advice had always been good, although it was once responsible for the two of them getting "fired" together in Paris when they were youngsters. I didn't quite catch this one.

Then Averell turned to Eisenhower and said he wanted to take particular notice of him, as he was the most important man here and the most important man in Europe today. Averell has been a Democrat since the days of Al Smith. I think the party bosses would have run him out of the ranks after hearing this—although Averell was sincerely talking about Ike's value to western defense and had no thoughts concerning politics.

Both before and after dinner I had good talks with Eisenhower—first over a Martini, which he admitted is a very rare drink for him—and afterwards over a glass of champagne while most of the party was gathered around the piano singing sentimental songs.

Eisenhower said he was still strongly opposed to the idea of bringing to Paris all the various NATO headquarters such as the production committee, the deputies' council, and so on. He had enough headaches now and nobody would do a thing without calling him up and asking for his opinion; it would be impossible if all these other outfits showed up.

He said when he was home on his recent trip, he was hounded by the press so much that he was really "glad to get in my old plane again and leave." He had been advised that he wouldn't see the press until Fort Knox, but at every airfield where the plane put down for fuel, there were dozens of reporters and photographers. At Washington an officer came aboard while he was relaxing with a detective story and told him, "General, there are forty reporters outside." Shrugging his shoulders, Eisenhower said, "After all, you can't be discourteous to forty people."

He told me Arthur Krock's story that Truman had offered him the Democratic candidacy in 1952 wasn't really true. He told me this twice—before dinner and after dinner. When he first met Truman on this trip, they winked at each other and by mutual agreement said right away there was one subject they weren't going to talk about, and that was the closest they ever came to politics.

I told him Montgomery had recently told me that Ike was corresponding with Senator Taft and that Monty felt Eisenhower would support Taft if he

(Taft) pledged himself to back NATO. The general remarked that a promise from Taft on this subject didn't strike him as being worth very much.

PARIS, *November 17, 1951*

DOUG MacArthur told me today that certainly if Spain were to become part of the "Western community," three conditions must be met: (1) a new minister of labor should be appointed; (2) exiled trade unionists, many of whom wish to go back to Spain, should be invited back by Franco; (3) new labor legislation should be written permitting unions full freedom, except specifically excluding them from politics.

This would be similar to legislation passed in Peru after the coup against Haya de la Torre. It would hurt things if this were written up ahead of time, because everybody would like it to look as if Franco had dreamed these ideas up himself. Obviously, the mission of George Meany (AFL) has had a big effect. MacArthur implied that instructions along this line were being given to Ambassador Griffis, who returns to Madrid tomorrow after seeing Acheson, Harriman and Eisenhower.

PARIS, *November 17, 1951*

LUNCH with George Meany, old-time plumber and one of the main leaders of the American Federation of Labor; Mrs. Meany; Irving Brown, AFL representative in Europe; and Harvey Retz, AFL representative in Germany. I must say that although Mr. and Mrs. Meany still talk like a plumber and his wife, they look and dress more like big business. She was wearing a mink cape.

Meany and Brown had just seen General Ike. Eisenhower began the conversation by saying: "I wish I were in a position just to take a simple straight line like you fellows and stand by it. Now, for example, I have just seen a fellow [Ambassador Griffis] who would like me to do things that would make you very red in the neck. I have to take a middle course and hew to it." Meany then said American labor recognized Eisenhower had to make certain deals for purely military reasons and appreciated that position. However, American labor thought this should be done on a purely practical basis. Speaking nonpolitically, all labor wanted was to get its own men back in Spain.

They discussed European labor and Meany said he thought Eisenhower showed a very intelligent grasp of the situation, "although we told him a few new things." I asked if labor would oppose Eisenhower as the Republican candidate against Truman—reminding him that Dubinsky had forecast many weeks ago that such would be the case. Meany replied this would depend entirely upon the attitude Eisenhower took on his internal program if he should run. If Eisenhower adopted a liberal point of view, he could gain much labor support.

I asked Meany to tell me, as a good Catholic union leader, why it was that so many American Catholics associated the Franco regime with the Vatican and kept attacking any politicians or journalists who spoke out against Franco. He said they made the mistake of being "more Catholic than the Pope."

Paris, *November 17, 1951*

This evening I saw Ambassador Stanton Griffis who is returning to Spain tomorrow. He said: "If you want to quote me, you can say I told Franco last spring that the United States insists on the right of free worship as well as the right of labor to strike." He said he had told Franco the United States was founded upon the principle of free religion and that all sects should have an equal right to worship. Franco remarked that this was a very unimportant question in Spain where there was only a handful of Protestants and Jews. Griffis said he told Franco: "Even if there are only six Protestants and two Jews, we want them to have the right to be buried according to their own religious rites."

Paris, *November 19, 1951*

Lunch at the Jugoslav embassy with Milovan Djilas. He looked thin and somewhat shrunken in stature. I remember him originally as a man about my size and weight, with a very strong constitution. Now he seems little. He has a keen, rather sad, if passionate, intellectual face. If you met him under any other circumstances, you would think he was a Left Bank poet. As a matter of fact, he is a poet. He became Stalin's favorite foreign Communist and used to sit at Uncle Joe's feet reciting Montenegrin epics. He is a member of the Jugoslav Politboro and one of the top men in the country.

I can't forget that Djilas, in 1946, publicly announced he would have me hanged as a friend of Mihailović if I ever came back to Jugoslavia. I came back a few weeks after that and nothing happened. A year or so again, when I was talking with Djilas I reminded him about this threat. He said with a rather endearing smile: "Times have changed now."

Paris, *November 19, 1951*

A hell of a day. Richard G. Casey, Australian minister for external affairs, kept calling up to deny a story by our correspondent in The Hague and claiming he was misquoted. The story didn't quote Casey at all, as I pointed out to him. Later I saw Casey at an official Australian reception to which Sir Keith Officer had invited me. Casey has been going around Paris saying that he saved me from being expelled from the Middle East during the war. The truth is that when Chester Morrison of NBC was about to be expelled, as president of the Middle East Correspondents Association, I prevented Casey from heaving out Morrison and made him eat his words on the whole matter.

This evening I talked for an hour and a half with Azzam Pasha, head of the Arab League. He is an old friend but seems to me to be going downhill. He talks more and more like an Egyptian and less and less like an Arab; more and more like a Pasha and less and less like a social reformer, which he used to be. Azzam thought that if the Egyptian crown served as a symbol of the Sudan, it would help the Sudanese. I wonder if he is really serious.

He claims the Suez Canal has no strategic value and quotes Captain Liddell Hart. He claims Eisenhower told him he could bomb Suez from Chicago. I happen to know that Eisenhower thinks the canal of great strategic value.

Azzam said Jordan wasn't a country but only a "collection of Bedouin tribes" who really formed part of Syria. They had to subsist by means of a British subsidy—unlike Egypt which was economically independent. He added that the true defense of the Suez was up near the Russian border or in Syria and Palestine.

ROME, *November 22, 1951*

I asked Al Gruenther about his job as Eisenhower's chief of staff. He gossiped:

> Take a briefing of visitors, for example. We do a team job. I do the analytical presentation. I present the problems and tell them what we are doing about them. Then Ike comes on and refers to me as "my brilliant chief of staff—at least I guess he's brilliant because he always tries to impress that on me." Then he will say he assumes I've covered all the details of problems, and so on, so "I'll go on with the spiritual side." He explains that we need unity to accomplish our goals. But this is particularly difficult to obtain; we need unity by cooperation and not, like the Russians, by sticking a dagger into another country's back.

Gruenther says he and Eisenhower are "a team" and he couldn't possibly do the job Ike does. He thinks when Ike goes that Bradley probably wouldn't be too good at it but that Ridgway or Collins would. Eisenhower's successor must be an extrovert. "Ike exudes leadership; he makes a tremendous impression," says Gruenther.

When Eisenhower went back to Washington this month, Al told him he didn't think that he (Gruenther) was the man for the job as the general's successor. Ike replied: "Thanks for your view. I'm glad to have your opinion. We all have our views and I have mine."

Al says to succeed Eisenhower "you need a man with a big prestige in Europe. It would be easier to put me in a high position on the United States side than on the European side. Also, you don't generally put younger men in on a job like this. Juin and Monty are well along in their sixties. It would be difficult to put a man more than ten years their junior in over them."

Al said the "relationship between Ike and Monty is just about perfect." He admitted that if Bradley succeeded Eisenhower, he would have difficulties with Montgomery but added that Bradley "has great prestige with the Europeans."

"Ike dominates this show," Al said. Everybody points only to Ike. Harriman, Plowden and Monnet (the three "wise men") always say concerning a particular problem: "We want this to be satisfactory for Ike." If you ask them: "How about the standing group?" they'll reply: "To hell with the standing group."

ROME, *November 24, 1951*

THIS morning I drove out to Castel Gandolfo and saw the Pope at his summer residence. The drive and the experience were pleasant. But the interview with him was a flop. I had been promised a "private" talk. Instead I was granted a "special" audience. This is supposed to mean that three or four other people are in the room and he goes from group to group but chats a while with each visitor. This "special" turned out to be a dud. There were no less than sixty people in the room, ranging down from a three-star American general (Coulter).

The general is a Catholic and was at the head of the line. He genuflected and kissed the Pope's ring. The result was that all sorts of embarrassed heathen heaved and creaked their paunches down until a sturdy Baptist remained aloft. From there on, the line was predominantly erect.

It was curious, looking out across at the lovely lake and the silhouette of the Alban hills, to hear the conversation of the group (mostly American) waiting:

These Europeans are strange people. There's no use our trying to change their system. They have the rich and the working people. This seems to suit them so let's leave it alone.

I can't stand England. You freeze to death. You can't talk and you can't eat. And they're so dirty.

The French are filthy too. And these Italians. How do they live in it?

Well, I'll say one thing. The Japs have sure got the Europeans licked. They're real honest. You can leave anything around without having it swiped. And that Dai Ichi building. Why it's as good as anything in New York. Maybe not as big. But as good.

A cup of coffee would sure go good right now. . . . Yeah, it sure would.

NAPLES, *December 1, 1951*

THIS morning good talk with Admiral Carney, commander of NATO forces in Southern Europe. Carney, who had with him his chief of staff, Major General Gavin, former commander of the Eighty-Second Airborne Division, said it was absolutely imperative that the Suez Canal should be controlled and defended by the Allies—not merely by the Egyptians. He said it was possible there were a few "maverick" Soviet submarines in the Mediterranean and they might be able to push in some others in preparation for a war, but they couldn't support them long; such submarines could cause trouble at the beginning of a war but "We can control them." Bases in Albania would be insufficient to keep submarines going very long.

He believes the Mediterranean—second only to England—is the most important area to be held by the West in case of war. We can lose all of Germany, France and the rest of Western Europe, but we must hold onto the Mediterranean in order to maintain our East-West communications and to mount counterattacks up towards the Danube when we are ready. Gavin told me he considered the Ljubljana Gap was probably the most important single European point to be held.

PARIS, *December 6, 1951*

LUNCH with Paddy Leigh Fermor. I got him to tell me how he got started on his rather strange career. He was thrown out of public school in England because of a teen-age love affair. His father insisted he should go into the army and he was sent to a cram school for that purpose. At eighteen, he said the hell with it and decided to take a trip through Europe. He arrived at the Hook of Holland with about 20 pounds of borrowed money and a guaranteed income of a pound a week that his father couldn't touch. He hitchhiked from there to Istanbul. That took about a year. Sometimes he slept in ditches and sometimes in palaces.

Paddy is related to the Taafe family—a branch of the Irish nobility which settled down with the Hapsburgs in Vienna a couple of centuries ago and they took care of him in what was left of Eastern Europe before the war. He fell in love with a Rumanian princess and lived with her in a water mill in Greece until they went broke and then moved up to the ramshackle remnants of her estate in Moldavia.

He was there when World War II started and applied to join the British army. Lady Hoare, wife of the British minister in Bucharest, was asked to look after him and another young fellow. Lady Hoare was a real eccentric and somehow developed the illusion that these two rather tough youngsters were children. She would send them to bed at night at seven-thirty o'clock with milk toast and they had to sleep in cribs with their knees folded up so they could fit. As soon as Lady Hoare had kissed them good night to go down to a legation dinner party, they would slip out the back door and hit the nightclubs of Bucharest until about 7 A.M. and then stagger back to their cribs. After four days of this, Lady Hoare saw them off at the railway station. She gave Paddy a rag book with pictures of animals and gave a toy horse to his colleague.

Paddy joined the Irish Guards and was drafted into SOE. He was sent to the Albanian front, after the Greek-Italian campaign started in 1940, as an intelligence officer. When the Germans attacked Greece, he went to Jumbo Wilson's headquarters at Ellascna. He was given a caïque which he armed to the teeth. It was assigned to go to the Peloponnesus and pick up big shots like Wilson, Prince Peter and others, in case the British navy was unable to do its job. The VIPs were successfully removed in a Sunderland flying boat, so Paddy was left with a pack of admirals and brigadier generals. One brigadier had a lot of valuable wireless equipment which he ordered Paddy's crew to take on. It was loaded aboard the caïque during a Stuka divebombing attack. The brigadier stood at one side of the boat commanding everybody to lift heavy cases aboard. An admiral stood at the other side and insisted the caïque would sink if all this "useless" equipment was loaded. He ordered the crew to drop it overboard. As a result, hours were spent lifting heavy cases onto one side of the boat and dropping them into the Aegean Sea on the other side.

In the end, Paddy went down to Crete, which he had to leave in short order when the Germans occupied it. Later he went back with Billy Moss and the two of them (under Paddy's command) captured General Kreipe, the German commanding officer, kidnapped him and took him off to Egypt.

PARIS, *December 11, 1951*

THIS morning I had a talk for an hour and a quarter with Eisenhower. He was sitting in a little room right off his office, with his left arm wrapped in a towel and baking in a special heating apparatus that General Snyder, his doctor, has procured for him to try and cure his left wrist. He was as relaxed as anybody could be in that position, with his coat off and his sleeves rolled up. We had several cups of coffee as I sat in the hall at the edge of this little antechamber and after he had baked for twenty-three minutes and he put his jacket on, we moved into his office.

I said I wanted to talk off the record about a very important question. He smiled and said, "All right, as long as it isn't politics." I replied that unfortunately that was the one thing I.wanted to ask him about and told him there were so many rumors concerning his intentions that I really wanted to get things straight. Then he talked—straight from the shoulder—and kept on for more than an hour.

He does *not* want to run for President. He has never wanted to run for that office. From a personal point of view he has nothing to gain from it, but that, of course, is not the fundamental reason for his attitude. It's a hell of a life and would be very grim for his grandchildren. He detests the idea that they would always have to be followed around by Secret Service men.

Eisenhower said, furthermore, that being in politics placed a man in a very uncomfortable personal position. He said, for example, that he had recently given a few thousand dollars to an old friend of his in the oil business to invest in a new well. Some of this money had been invested in the name of his son and grandchildren. He did this just as a "fling," he said. What would happen if the well came in and he made many times his original investment? Were he in politics, people could attack him and attempt to create a scandal, although he was merely taking a gamble and hoping to make something for his family.

He would like to continue the job he is doing and eventually to become a sort of "elder statesman" who would be completely free from any political attachments and therefore would be in a position, if necessary, to advise or influence people and events for the sake of his country. He feels that it would be a useful thing in our political system to have two or three such men utterly free from politics, who would thus be in a position to speak for the United States and the American people, rather than for any political party.

When he came over here, he took the job with the understanding that he would remain as SHAPE commander until the NATO armed forces were "on the rails." But lord knows when that will be. It might be a question of three or five years. The job was first mentioned to him in October, 1949. President Truman named him at the request of the Brussels NATO Council meeting. He came over briefly in January and then returned to stay in February. At one time, he admits, he probably had the idea that he might only have to stay on for about a year. But actually he has really had the job for more than a year now, although he will have been permanently in Europe for a year only in February, 1952. He has no intention of returning to the United States again while he has this job. His last visit caused too much speculation and too many headaches.

He is now determined to stay on as commander in SHAPE unless he is given another responsibility. In other words, he has no intention of resign-ing and returning to Columbia or to any other civilian job unless he is drafted as a candidate for the Presidency. (In the past Eisenhower has said that he does not believe an Army officer should run for the Presidency and indicated he might therefore resign this position and return to America to permit his nomination. He no longer feels this way.)

He has no intention of making any move to help those political leaders who are seeking to draft him as the Republican candidate. He is, of course, a Republican and always has been. He is against many aspects of the New Deal and particularly the trend toward centralization of government power. However, he does not believe the clock can be turned back, even to the days of Calvin Coolidge. Our Constitution is a living thing, but it must adjust itself to changing circumstances as the world evolves.

He is fully aware that there are many people who would like him to run for the Presidency, but he feels there are many possible candidates and he does not intend to make any move in that direction, either covert or overt. Many of the political leaders of the Republican Party, such as Dewey, Taft and Lodge, are continually requesting him to come out and declare his colors. He will not do this. If the American people draft him as a candidate, he would respond to a call of duty, but he hopes this will not occur. He has no interest in politics or political machines.

A recent political visitor said the trouble with Eisenhower's possible candidacy was that the Republicans would have no idea who he would name to his Cabinet. This visitor (a Taft supporter) said to him that, after all, if Taft is elected, the Republicans would know not only everybody who would be named to Taft's Cabinet, but how all the spoils would be shared right on down to the county level.

Eisenhower understands how the politicians feel, but he will not give them any comfort. That is their racket and not his. He wants to remain entirely aside from politics.

Since 1943, there have been various movements trying to get him interested in politics. In 1948 (he told me before that Truman offered to stand down and run as Vice-President if Eisenhower would accept the Presidential nomination for the Democratic Party in that year) all he had to do was to promise political leaders that he would "keep my mouth shut." The situation now has altered only in the sense that "I'll keep my mouth utterly and permanently shut." Now he has a position of vast responsibilities to the American people and to their European allies. He does not intend in any way to jeopardize the movement towards constructing the democratic alliance.

If he were to make a statement now that he was a Republican, it would immediately split American opinion in terms of backing NATO. As I know—he has said this to me often—he is strongly in favor of changing the regime in America because twenty years is too long for any party to be in power. Corruption has set in. Although Truman is a fine man in many ways, the only thing he knows is politics. Every inch he has moved up the ladder has been on the basis of winning elections. As a result, men have been appointed to offices who are not fit for those offices. For example, George E. Allen is a very close friend of Eisenhower. He feels that Allen is as honest as a man can be. Although he has the reputation of being a jester with a magnificent sense of humor, he continually "drops pearls of wisdom." But he is no man to head the RFC and this was a great mistake by Truman. The man to head the RFC should be someone who knows something about finance. (Incidentally, Eisenhower said Allen told him on his last visit over here that he thinks the general would be the best President the American people could possibly have, but that he—Allen—was a Mississippi Democrat, and if Eisenhower ran, Allen would have to vote for Truman, "the way I always do.") Eisenhower asked me if I knew Allen and I told him no. He said, "By golly, next time he comes over here, I'm going to get ahold of you because I want you to meet him. He is a wonderful fellow, as well as a lot of fun to be with."

It would be a good thing to "clean out the stable," Eisenhower thinks. I remarked that I thought Truman had at least shown good judgment in appointing Acheson and standing by him, and that it seemed rather gallant on the part of the President to remain loyal to the one member of his Cabinet who was a great political liability. Eisenhower smiled and pointed out very shrewdly that if the President were to fire Acheson now, it would be an admission of failure of his own policy—which Acheson was pursuing.

Eisenhower talked strongly against Taft. He said Taft was a very stupid man. He might have a memory—that, the general did not pretend to know—but he had no intellectual ability, nor any comprehension of the issues of the world. Eisenhower had talked with him several times and saw how little Taft was able to grasp the basic problems.

I told him that Montgomery had told me Taft and Eisenhower were corresponding; that Taft had agreed to support Eisenhower's views on foreign policy and the building up of Europe; that in exchange Eisenhower had agreed to back Taft. Ike said he was amazed to hear this, but "of course, Monty is scared stiff that I might leave this job."

He said he had in his possession a letter Taft had sent to somebody else that said Taft was prepared to back the principle that six American divisions should be stationed in Europe and that even this amount could be increased by "bits and pieces." But Eisenhower said he would not place his trust in Taft as a man; Taft's own record showed how weak and confused he was.

Eisenhower said some of the liberal Republicans were very worried about the way Taft was muscling in on the party machine and lining up delegates. Eisenhower could not help this. The politicians told him he would have to make some move pretty soon to give them a clue. He refused to do this. I pointed out that Willkie had managed to gain the nomination in a whirlwind last-minute finish without benefit of the political machines. Ike remarked, "That, of course, was a different matter," and he went on to say that the party was looking for anybody at that time who could possibly capture public imagination and gain office on behalf of the politicians. (Of course, it was also very different because Willkie campaigned strongly for the nomination.)

Eisenhower said that he would respond to a "call of duty" only if it were demonstrated by the country, forcing a convention to nominate him. He knew the limitations of the American political system and that sometimes politics was a pretty "sordid" business, and big issues were settled in "smoke-filled rooms," but, nevertheless, it was our system and he had no intention of making any move himself.

He said there were some Republicans who felt that if Taft was nominated as the candidate of their party, the Democrats would then draft Eisenhower immediately afterwards at their convention. At this point he repeated that he was a Republican, even though he would make no statement to that effect now because he wanted to remain entirely outside the political picture.

Eisenhower admitted that Dewey, Lodge and Duff were all fine men working for a selfless purpose—especially Dewey, who is still the "titular head of the Republican Party." But he added, "They should have another string to their bow." He meant by this that he does not intend to help them in any way to promote his own candidacy and they should find someone else to represent the liberal attitude in the Republican Party. He regretted very much that they had not built up anyone else, but he hoped they would do so during the "next two or three weeks." I wonder what he is getting at. I am having dinner at Ike's house tomorrow night and I know that Stassen will be present. I wonder if the general is trying to promote Stassen as the liberal Republican candidate.

Eisenhower regretted very much that no other man had been built up to succeed him in the command here. He said that he thought in principle he should leave here when he becomes sixty-two years old next October, because there is no use in having a "superannuated" fellow like himself staying on. Room must be made for the younger military leaders. Nevertheless, nobody had been built up by the American government. "I got a fourth star for Al Gruenther," he said, "in order to give someone else some stature around here." Eisenhower wondered if this reluctance to build up any possible successor for him might perhaps not be a deliberate policy. I presume by this he means that Truman wanted to keep him here and out of the political arena.

He said he had hoped during his period of initial command of SHAPE that new men would be developed—possibly even non-Americans—to succeed in the command. Nevertheless, he recognized now that this was his responsibility and he was going to stick with it.

He said that when he had gone to Rome to address the NATO Council, he made three speeches in one day—one to the military committee, one to the civilian ministers and one to the correspondents. He was astonished when many people and some newspapers like Le Monde interpreted his remarks as his "first political speech as a candidate." On the contrary, he had been ready to tell the ministers that he would agree to stay on here as their commander in Europe for three or five years if he could only "get some fire into them" and galvanize the NATO movement.

Arthur Krock's story about Truman offering him the candidacy on the Democratic ticket was inaccurate. As a matter of fact, the only hint of politics was when the President showed him some architect's drawing and pictures of the interior of the remodeled White House. When the President held these out, he looked at the general and smiled and he grinned back.

He was extremely irked at John Gunther who wrote a piece for *Look* magazine. He had seen Gunther twice here and had invited him out to his house. Gunther "violated all decency" by mentioning this fact in his article and then went ahead and attacked Ike as "a stupid, nonintellectual man who is incapable of grasping abstract ideas." Eisenhower was not only furious but deeply hurt; he feels that one of his main jobs here has been dealing with the basic abstractions.

This whole political cloud is a tremendous headache to him. In fact, for some time he used to wake up at night "in a cold sweat." He has now gotten over that and refuses to let it bother him. Events will take their course.

I wondered if I could not sit down some day and write exactly what his position was, without attribution. He said for the moment he did not want this. He hoped the wave of speculation concerning him and politics would die down. Someday, however, it might be advisable to have "an authoritative piece" written and then he would call upon me.

Right now it was a constant source of embarrassment even if he sought to ignore it. Representative Celler of New York, for example, has been over here trying to prod various European governments to inquire of Eisenhower concerning his political intentions. The idea, of course, is to try and force him to tell these governments whether he is staying on or not, and thus smoke out Eisenhower in terms of American politics.

Many Republicans say to him the trouble is nobody knows whether he is a Republican or a Democrat. As a matter of fact, he is a Republican and has been one all his life. But he doesn't want to divide American opinion in two by proclaiming his political allegiance so that he would be supported by only half the country in his efforts over here.

At one moment, reflecting upon the service he could render as an "elder statesman," Eisenhower said he figured he had "about fifteen more years during which my brain ought to be working pretty well" and he thought he could serve his country during that time. Continually, he stressed the idea of "service," and I know from dozens of other conversations that he means this in the most sincere way.

On and off during the conversation, he got up and started to swing the heavy practice driver (twenty-two ounces) Larry Norstad has lent him. The general is eager to get back to playing golf but says he feels an awful pull and strain on his wrist. I remarked that anybody but a giant would feel such a strain swinging that club.

Before leaving I asked him if he would give me an inscribed photograph. He called in Bob Schulz, his aide, and gave him holy hell. He said they had been taking pictures of him by the thousands "and here I am still signing a picture taken five years ago." Why the hell, he wanted to know, couldn't he get some of these new pictures and have them on tap. A fellow had been in just a few days ago from *Vogue* in London and "took me in the God-damnedest poses. All these photographers try and get you in the God-damnedest poses." (The "fellow" he was referring to was Cecil Beaton, probably the best-known photographer alive, but it is one of Ike's endearing qualities that he wasn't aware of this ) He got quite worked up and red in the face and it was embarrassing to poor Schulz, who told him that he had already arranged to have a considerable set of the Beaton photographs available. After Schulz had left, Eisenhower strode up and down and said, "After all, I know I'm getting old and I look different than I did five years ago." (As a matter of fact, I don't think he does.) He said, "I know this because painters who painted my picture five years ago and have painted it again recently paint it different, and they know what they're doing. After all, a man gets old and it might as well be recorded." I must say that I was more than ever impressed with the sincerity and fineness of character of Eisenhower by this conversation. Despite all he said, it is my hope that he is drafted at the Republican convention, runs and is elected.

PARIS, *December 13, 1951*

DINNER last night at the Eisenhowers'. Those present were the Averell Harrimans, the David Bruces, Governor and Mrs. Harold Stassen, Brigadier General and Mrs. Arthur Nevins and Bunny and Hope Carter. Under normal circumstances I would call it a dull dinner party. However, it was extremely interesting when the men got together afterwards and the big shots began to talk.

Before dinner we stood around and had a few drinks. Ike had just hung two new landscapes he had painted. He gets a great bang out of it if somebody tells him he likes them. When Averell came in, he looked ghastly. He is visibly overtired and thin. He had worked so late he didn't have time to shave before dinner. When Ike looked at him, he said, "By golly, I think you've lost about seven pounds on this job." Averell said he had lost the weight last summer, but Eisenhower said he is sure he has lost still more. He asked him when he was going home, and Averell said he hoped to leave Tuesday in a plane being sent for him by Washington. Ike begged him to stay on three or four days after he had finished his work and promised to give him a good vacation. He said he would send him back in his own plane if Averell could have it back in Paris by Christmas because Eisenhower has promised the pilot he can spend Christmas with his wife here. Apparently, the fellow has been married five years and never had a chance to spend Christmas with his family. Averell said he had to go Tuesday anyway. He really looked bushed. Last week when his committee of "wise men" finished their work on the final day, he worked straight through from 8 A.M. until 7 A.M. the following morning. That's too much for a man of sixty.

David Bruce was extremely happy about Pleven's tremendous victory in the vote of confidence Tuesday on the Schuman plan. Stassen didn't talk very much. Although he calls himself "a good friend of Ike" in public, I noticed the general always referred to him as "Governor" instead of by his first name, as he calls everybody else.

I first met Stassen in Moscow in 1945 where I saw him a few times. At that time, he made a very dreary impression on me and I didn't like him. I tried to come out last night with an open mind and I had more or less talked myself into being ready to like and respect him because I think Eisenhower has a high regard for him. However, he made a very sad impression all over again. He has a face like a baby pig and seemed to make nothing but banal remarks. He is not suffering from any overwhelming modesty either. I hope to God he never is elected President of the United States. I don't think I'd care for Mrs. Stassen in the White House either.

General Nevins is an extremely nice and rather shy individual. He is retired from the Army and lives on Eisenhower's farm in Gettysburg, Pa., where he sort of acts as caretaker for the place (about 170 acres) and George Allen's farm next door. Eisenhower has a dairy farm, and apparently he has quite a valuable herd and some expensive equipment such as electrical milking machines, tractors, harvester-combines. It had never occurred to me before, but I suppose he is really pretty well off.

The dinner was pleasant but not very interesting. Marie Harriman sat on my deaf side so I couldn't hear her, and Mrs. Nevins is hardly scintillating. Unfortunately, as is the custom in both the Eisenhower and Gruenther households, after the brandy there was nothing, which has the effect on me of making me want to go to sleep by around ten o'clock. The dinner actually broke up about eleven-thirty.

The interesting part was when the seven men sat around for about two hours afterwards, chatting. There was no mention of politics despite the fact that this is, of course, the only reason Stassen is in Paris, so far as I can figure out. I shall try to summarize some of the remarks made.

Eisenhower said we had to assume the Russians were dominated by a group of men following one of two possible philosophies. Either they were dictators who were out to hang on to their jobs and stabilize them; or they were fanatics whose actions could never be predicted and who would inevitably force another war. His own thought was that the former is the case. He remembered when he was in Moscow during the summer of 1945, he received the impression that the Russians wanted to play along with us and were still hoping for friendship with the United States; that they really needed our help. He thought the real break came later that year.

Eisenhower blames Churchill entirely for the political division of Germany which gave Russia such a large share. He said Churchill never had any faith in "Overlord"—the invasion of Normandy. Churchill had already told Eisenhower that the capture of Pantelleria in the Mediterranean was a "miraculous" military operation. When they were planning "Overlord" in England during the spring of 1944, Churchill said that if Eisenhower moved thirty-six divisions across the Channel into France to control the Brest and Cherbourg peninsulas, it would be the greatest military operation in all history; that if he also gained control of Le Havre, it would be an operation without any historical comparison and that he (Churchill) would be the first to get up and announce this. Eisenhower said that he expected to be on the frontiers of Germany by Christmas. Churchill kept shaking his head and said that this was entirely out of the question.

As a result of Churchill's skeptical attitude, unsound political decisions were taken. In fact, in a final briefing Eisenhower had before the start of "Overlord," Churchill was extremely pessimistic. All the high Allied officers plus the King of England and Churchill were present. After Eisenhower had finished his briefing, Churchill said before the group that his attitude towards "Overlord" was "hardening." Eisenhower commented: "That was a hell of a way to inspire faith in my officers."

Eisenhower said he had absolute confidence in the ultimate success of his plans but he could never convince Churchill. Churchill came to him once and started explaining what a terrible tragedy it would be if the operation failed. Tears began to roll down his cheeks and he said that in such a case, he would have to present his resignation as Prime Minister to His Majesty. Churchill kept building up logical arguments as to why the operation would fail, but he always based them upon an unsound initial premise.

Unfortunately, Eisenhower said, Churchill forgot all about his promise to get up and announce what a great victory and unprecedented success "Overlord" had been, after France was overrun. In March of 1945, the Allies were all ready to close in on Germany. They were still about three hundred miles from Berlin. The Russians had no more rivers to cross and had a powerful bridgehead across the Oder. As a matter of fact, the Allies could have gone much further east then they actually did. When they met the Russians, the latter proved to be a battered, rag-tag, bobtail outfit, and,

Eisenhower said, "We could have licked the hell out of them." But he had to stop at the Elbe, which was already far to the east of the political line dividing Germany which had been fixed by the political leaders.

This line was chosen largely because of Churchill's pessimism. Churchill refused to believe that the Western armies could even get that far into Germany. If Churchill had had confidence in Eisenhower's armies, the line dividing Germany between east and west could have been moved much nearer to the Elbe or on the Elbe itself. Eisenhower could not have taken Berlin because the Russians were in a position to surround the city before he could get there. He had to draw a battleline where the Eastern and Western armies would meet in order to avoid confusion because there was a tremendous paucity of interpreters on both sides, and friction had to be avoided at all costs.

The Russians told him when he was in Moscow that the Russian soldier always fought well for his motherland. In fact Eisenhower said he thought there was more patriotic love of country in Russia than in any other land. While he stood on Lenin's tomb beside Stalin, reviewing Red Army units, Stalin kept saying to him that America and Russia must be friends because Russia needed help from the United States.

Eisenhower said the Russians would certainly not be provoked into attacking the West by the defensive preparations of NATO. They had a marvelous intelligence system and they knew perfectly well that the scale of our preparations was only defensive and could never be considered useful for an offensive. He cited as an example the fact that when he was in Moscow, he saw in one of the offices in the Kremlin a group of American magazines and newspapers which had just appeared in the United States. They had been flown over immediately by the Soviet intelligence. He said he would not have received the same publications in Berlin (his headquarters at that time) until three or four days later. All the Russians had to do was comb the American press and they could see perfectly plainly what we were after.

Furthermore, he added that a preventive war or an attack on Russia would be insane because Russia could never be defeated by an invasion. He cited the cases of both Hitler and Napoleon.

Eisenhower said there was, of course, no doubt that Russia could overrun Europe very swiftly at present. However, he was confident the Russians were sufficiently realistic to recognize that this was inadequate in terms of winning a war. They would embark upon a war only if they were confident of swift and total victory. This was out of the question. The Russians were fully aware that a long war would be a question of relative production ability, and we alone had three times their economic capacities. For that reason they would certainly not start a war.

The general said he had two of the most brilliant officers he had ever run into on his staff—two young Americans. One of them is Lieutenant Colonel Andrew J. Goodpaster, an economics specialist in the office of the special assistant to the chief of staff. The other is Lieutenant Colonel Pete Carroll. He said that "by golly" if he were president of General Motors, he would hire the two of them and give them each a salary of $50,000 a year even if they didn't know a damned thing about the business, because in no time they would prove invaluable. He added with a smile that, of course, he did not "gyp" himself when he was selecting his staff.

Eisenhower remarked that he had suddenly gotten the idea last summer that the only solution to the basic problem in Europe was federation—the first step towards which would be the creation of a European army. He worked out his approach on this, which was crystallized in the speech of July 3. Afterwards, fortunately, he began to get increased support that finally solidified into a stand of the United States Government.

Eisenhower said he was really puzzled by Churchill's attitude on the European army. After he made his London speech on July 3, Churchill wrote to him praising to the skies the address, the choice of words and the logic. Yet in that speech Eisenhower had come out flatly in favor of European federation.

He is going to give Churchill hell on the eighteenth when he comes to Paris. Eisenhower had invited him out to lunch because he wanted him to see SHAPE headquarters, to see an example of the type of cooperation the European army is working for. Yet Churchill said he couldn't come out to SHAPE and asked him to come and have lunch with him at the embassy. Eisenhower sent word back in a deliberately grumpy way that, of course, he would always go and see his old friend, but he was very disappointed he didn't have the time to come out and see SHAPE. Unfortunately, Sir Oliver Harvey, the British ambassador, isn't in Paris at the moment, and the general wonders if the minister (Hayter) had the guts to transmit the message in the same tone as he had delivered it. Eisenhower is really going to put the bite on Churchill to stop his blocking attitude on the European army. Both Harriman and Bruce were delighted to hear this.

Eisenhower said he had had breakfast with Eden in Rome and they talked about the project, and Eden seemed all for it. He wrote "Anthony" just a few days ago and urged him to get his boss into a more cooperative mood.

Bruce said Churchill was now the key man on the European army project. It was necessary to keep up the momentum in favor of federation which had been gained by Pleven's victory on the Schuman plan and Spaak's resignation as president of the European assembly in order to fight for federation. However, Churchill was balking at the project. Churchill had always envisioned a European army in terms of a loose coalition, such as NATO actually is. He did not want to see the kind of integrated force now being planned. Only last week he had prepared a speech which was going to come out against this project. Thanks largely to Eden, he tore the speech up. Eden favors the idea.

Bruce is now urging Churchill—and Harriman did the same thing when he saw him a few days ago—to come out and back the project in the following way. He could announce that Britain would not contribute any troops to the integrated force. However, he could offer the cooperation of British civilian experts in the nonmilitary administration of the European army. He could promise Britain's favorable attitude and say that in some future year Britain would be willing to reconsider the possibility of joining the force actively itself.

Eisenhower interjected that the European army was absolutely necessary from a military point of view because it was cheaper and more efficient to have a common budget and procurement program. He said, however, the divisions had to be on a national basis because the efficiency of a division depended on the tight cooperation of infantry and artillery teams. These fellows invented their own telephone codes every day and kept in the closest touch with each other. This would be impossible if two languages were spoken by the small combat units within a division.

David said he had talked with Guy Mollet of the Socialist Party, and Mollet had explained to him that it was absolutely imperative in order to obtain Socialist backing in the National Assembly vote on the European army to get some form of English cooperation.

Incidentally, Bruce thinks that if the European Army project goes through—and he thinks if the vote were held tomorrow, it would certainly fail; that the odds are still only four-to-six that it will go through during the next three or four weeks—it will mean the end of de Gaulle.

Harriman said that in 1942 Stalin told him he was not at all sure the Russian soldiers would fight for "us" (meaning the Communist Party), but he knew they would always fight well and die for their mother country. Stalin also expressed great skepticism about the ability of the Russian army to conduct an offensive outside of Soviet territory. (Eisenhower interrupted at this point and pointed out that when the Russians finally crossed their own western border during their counteroffensive, the German army had really been destroyed.)

Harriman is convinced the Russians halted on the Vistula for military reasons and not merely to permit the Germans to destroy Warsaw and the Polish home army uprising of General Bor-Komorowski. (Eisenhower tended to agree with this. He said the Russian method of conducting an offensive was to line up as many pieces of artillery as could possibly be gotten together on a single front. Then these guns fired every single shell available, and then the infantry and tanks attacked. When the offensive ran out of momentum, it had to stop. They not only had to bring up the guns again, but factories had to manufacture more shells and these had to be shipped to the front. Thus, the Russians could mount an enormous offensive and then, when it stalled, they would have to wait six months to get another one going.)

Harriman said that a group of Polish leaders was in Moscow just before the Vistula offensive was supposed to start. These included Mikolajczyk. Stalin promised there would be such an offensive. However, the Germans shifted two divisions from the West to the East and strengthened their position on the west bank of the Vistula. Harriman thinks the Russians were really embarrassed when they found they were not in a position to cross the river. They had been announcing to the Poles that they were coming. A few days later the Moscow radio suddenly started talking about the "traitor" Bor-Komorowski who was destroying Poland by his "premature" rebellion. Harriman thinks the Russians were truly embarrassed about this because it showed up their military abilities. (I am a bit skeptical about this viewpoint because the Russians were so obdurate in their refusal to permit Allied bombers to shuttle across to Soviet territory after bombing the Germans in Warsaw.)

Harriman said he believed the Russian attitude towards us had definitely shifted after Yalta and this crystallized when they secretly rounded up the Polish resistance leaders in March, 1945. The thing became absolutely firm, however, when he visited Stalin at the Black Sea resort of Sochi in October, 1945. Stalin told him point blank then that Russia had decided to "go it alone" without the United States and to pursue an independent policy regardless of consequences.

Harriman said it would always be possible to threaten the Germans—if they ask too high a price for cooperation in Western defense—with the prospect of giving "end item" goods such as tanks to the French; or, vice versa, menacing the French with the idea of building up the German army with similar goods if they don't go along on a European army project.

Stassen contributed very little to the conversation. To me, he didn't even seem to understand some of the basic points involved. This was evident from the questions he asked.

PARIS, *December 17, 1951*

LUNCHED and played golf with Eisenhower. When I arrived at his headquarters, he was looking anxiously at the fog outside and swinging Larry Norstad's superheavy practice driver. We had a quick and simple lunch— the others were General Ed Clark (retired), who used to be in the Middle East and then with SHAEF; Brigadier Jimmy Gault (Eisenhower's British aide), Bunny Carter and myself. Before lunch Al Gruenther joined us for a glass of sherry. He complained rather strongly that the newspapers placed the whole NATO program in a difficult position by breaking the story of the Harriman committee report in advance. He said he guessed it demonstrated it was pretty hard to maintain security among twelve nations. I said I thought it was impossible and that the Rome conference had proven it. At this Eisenhower laughed affirmatively.

During lunch we spent most of the time discussing the idiosyncrasies of women doing finances. Eisenhower said that when he was a second lieutenant, he told his wife she would have to run the bank account. His future was assured because he would always receive a salary from the Army even after he had retired. Therefore, it was up to her to keep the accounts and see if she could put any money away. He said she is very careful about this and sometimes struggles for hours if she is seven cents out at the end of the month.

The golf game was extraordinary, but rather good fun. We played in a thick fog and you couldn't see ten yards ahead. As a matter of fact, Ike played rather well and seemed pleased by the experience, but we managed only nine holes—all five of us. I stank. He was frightfully bored at the prospect of having to go to a stag officers' dinner at SHAPE. He said the only times he liked to go out nowadays were to small dinners with friends. On all other occasions people asked him questions—obviously he was referring both to SHAPE and American politics. As a matter of fact, he said he had a horrible time the other night during the Stassen dinner because Harriman and Bruce kept coming up to him and whispering "How'm I doing?" out of the corner of their mouths—referring, of course, to the impact upon Stassen.

PARIS, *December 19, 1951*

LUNCH with Senator John Sherman Cooper, who is here on the UN delegation, and Mayor Ernst Reuter of Berlin, whom I knew as an anti-Nazi refugee in Turkey. Reuter, who is a Socialist, nevertheless does not have any particular admiration for Schumacher, the party leader. He said the real reason why Schumacher opposes the European army plan is that Schumacher "would like to be the commanding general." Reuter dislikes Adenauer intensely and says he has an autocratic and eighteenth-century, dictatorial-type mind. He has surrounded himself with yes-men and does not like to consult with others on an equal basis. He thinks one of the great difficulties in rearming Germany is going to be the difficulty of persuading the German people to pay for it. They are *treheitig herzen,* or lazy-hearted. They would rather make money and rebuild their cities in the west than do anything about protecting Western civilization. Immediately after saying this, Reuter proposed a toast to German rearmament. Cooper said, "I'll sure join in on that one."

PARIS, *December 20, 1951*

LAST night went to a reception at the Soviet embassy. I arrived fairly late and noticed Vyshinsky having a talk with French Foreign Minister Schuman and trying to press him to drink another vodka—without success. The moment their conversation lapsed, I butted in, shook hands with Vyshinsky and started chatting with him in French. He was extremely cordial. Then I said, "How about a visa? I have been waiting for fourteen months and can't get any answer out of your government." Immediately he stopped talking French, and some little character popped up from the crowd and started translating. Vyshinsky explained that he didn't deal with visas and it was entirely out of his hands. I said this was rather curious because he had told me in 1947 in Moscow when he was only a deputy foreign minister that his section was in charge of visas. Then he tried a new line and said there were too many American correspondents in Moscow anyway. I told him there were five to the best of my knowledge. He said that they were worth five divisions to the United States. I said I took this as a great compliment to my profession. He then explained that he liked me but didn't like my newspaper or my editors. At any rate, he concluded by promising that he would personally take the matter up upon his return to Moscow in February.

PARIS, *December 21, 1951*

LUNCH with Yuri Zhukov. He was extremely amiable. Not only did he pay for the lunch but he called for me with his own car and chauffeur—both rather unprecedented. Then he asked me to fix a date now to meet him again—setting January 7. Surely he is after something.

He said he thought peace could really be arranged in the world. Our preliminary objective—that Korea should be settled by a cease-fire—is about to be met. The real problem is Germany, and he thinks a solution can be found there. He then said, "Why do you think we are having our economic international conference in Moscow in April, except to try and arrange peace?" He said that if Charles E. Wilson, defense production director, were to go to Moscow in April, he would be received by Mikoyan and others and they could really talk seriously. He thought that once the businessmen started discussing markets and purchases they could lay a foundation for peace.

Yuri said *Pravda*'s editor, Ilitchev, used to be secretary general of the paper—which is about the same as a combination of business manager and managing editor in American terms. The post of editor is chosen by the Central Committee of the Communist Party. The Soviet Cabinet chooses the editor of *Izvestia*. Zhukov is paid 3,000 rubles a month plus approximately 300 rubles per article that he sends in. The editor is paid approximately 5,000 rubles a month. Yuri says he makes more than 5,000 rubles a month as a result of the articles he writes. He complained that *Pravda* has only four pages, so many of his articles are killed and many others are cut to ribbons—frequently stupidly. I asked him what happened to his money and how he changed it into francs. He told me he received about 100,000 francs a month to live on in Paris and the rest of his salary was deposited in rubles in Moscow. He wouldn't tell me what the exchange rate was.

PARIS, *January 3, 1952*

A considerable amount of speculation is going on these days as a result of Harold Stassen's announcement that he is a candidate for the Republican nomination for the Presidency. In this morning's Paris *Herald Tribune,* Bert Andrews writes that Stassen's "evasive" answers to the press on the subject of what he and Eisenhower said to each other have caused confusion. I don't know what Stassen is after. He is certainly doing his best to imply that he and Eisenhower exchanged important confidences, and at the same time he indicates he is not free to reveal what these were. This is a pretty cheap trick. I was present throughout the Stassen–Eisenhower talks at Eisenhower's house. In other words, Stassen is trying to imply that many secrets were exchanged. This is not true.

PARIS, *January 4, 1952*

LUNCH today at Ambassador Kirk's apartment. He has now officially resigned as our envoy to Moscow. George Kennan, who has been accepted by the Russians, will be going there around April. Kirk said that in September, 1950, Vyshinsky had called him to the foreign office to deliver a note protesting the shooting down of a Soviet plane over the Yellow Sea. Kirk said he had to sit for about three-quarters of an hour with his arms folded and not even touch the note while he insisted that Vyshinsky must deliver it to the UN and not to the United States.

He also recalled that when the Russians changed the rate of the ruble, he protested to Gromyko that this doubled the rent he had to pay for the American embassy. He pointed out that he wished he could double the rent of the Soviet embassy in Washington. Gromyko smiled and said, "But you gave it to us in 1933." Kirk admitted there was no answer to that.

Both Kirk and Bruce (who was also there) are very worried about the Indochina situation. Kirk says he believes the Chinese may very well intervene in Indochina within "a few weeks." He said there is a blind spot in Pentagon thinking on this problem, and he is not at all sure what we are ready to do. Kirk insisted, however, that it is utterly untrue that we are transporting Chinese Nationalists from Formosa to Burma to invade Communist China by the back door.

SENATOR Lodge has caused a great sensation by announcing that Eisenhower has given permission to have his name listed in the New Hampshire primary as a member of the Republican Party. Thus, the story I have been sitting on for many weeks has broken. Today Eisenhower issued a statement confirming that he was a Republican and adding that although he would not campaign for political office, he was prepared to accept the nomination if he is chosen by the party convention. I have had a hell of a time all day getting permission to write some of what I know about the general's own personal views. Jimmy Gault suggested the only man who could give me the green light was Al Gruenther.

I called Al and explained the situation. I told him I did not want to break any confidences and I certainly did not wish to jeopardize my own friendship with General Ike. On the other hand, I pointed out that I was under great pressure to write a story. I said I would phrase it in such a way that it appeared to come from visitors to the general. At that moment Eisenhower called him on the other line. Al told me to write the story and call him later at home. I have written a hell of a long story. I included the guts of a year's conversations. I called Gruenther and he told me to come on out and see him when I had finished. I drove out in the fog and arrived at Al's house at about nine-thirty o'clock. He was doing some "homework" alone at a card table in his sitting room. He asked me if I wanted anything to eat, but I told him all I needed was a drink, so he got himself an old-fashioned and me a Scotch highball. Then he read the story through. After a few comments here and there he said the whole thing was O.K. He had ridden home from the office with Eisenhower.

Afterwards we sat around, I had another drink, and we talked a bit about various things. He said that he had hoped to see the Pope when he was in Rome for the NATO meeting. He had arranged an interview but unfortunately it came on Gruenther's busiest day and he had to cancel it. He wanted to talk to the Pope about the necessity for arranging some kind of spiritual NATO, in which the Catholic Church would try to muster the spiritual forces of the world.

Gruenther said Eisenhower asked him on the way home in the car, "Do you think I'm going to be bothered a hell of a lot after this statement today?" Gruenther said he was afraid he would be. Eisenhower grunted. Gruenther said that Eisenhower definitely does not intend to say anything further on the subject of politics.

Pleven fell today with a thump. It looks as if there will be a cabinet crisis for about four weeks which will indefinitely delay the next meeting of the European Army conference scheduled for the end of this month. Gruenther said he talked with David Bruce this evening, and David said he was going to pull his foxhole in on top of him.

PARIS, *January 9, 1952*

YESTERDAY afternoon I had talk with Trygve Lie at his office in the
Palais de Chaillot. Lie was very critical of the British on their dealings in
the Middle East—above all Iran and Egypt.

I asked if there was nothing the UN could do ahead of time to forestall
Chinese intervention in Indochina. He replied they could do nothing unless
France requested UN action. Several times in private conversations he has
suggested to the French that they should do so—in fact, he told this to
Schuman last year. But the French are against it. Lie cannot make up his
mind whether reports of Chinese intentions result from French propaganda, because the French want more aid, or whether it is the real stuff.

PARIS, *January 10, 1952*

LUNCH with General Pierre Billotte who is a Gaullist member of the
National Assembly. Billotte was recently in the United States and finds that
de Gaulle is at a peak of unpopularity there. He has been trying to persuade de Gaulle to see more Americans and to take more of an interest in
the United States, but without success. De Gaulle has so many complexes
and is so touchy that he keeps himself isolated and "provincial." He was
hurt when David Bruce asked to see him after years of avoiding him.
Likewise he has conceived a grudge against Eisenhower.

Billotte thinks it tragic that a plan has been drafted for a so-called
European army, which means the abandonment of the French Army, although other nations such as Switzerland and Spain would retain their
national forces. This plan was drafted by four men—Monnet, Pleven,
Schuman and Alphand. Monnet, according to Billotte, was not in the French
army in World War I or II. Pleven was a young soldier in World War I and
most undistinguished. He had no military experience—despite his youth—
in World War II. Schuman was a soldier in World War I—but in the German army, not the French army. Alphand has no military experience. Yet
these are the four men who are drafting a plan to do away with the French
army.

PARIS, *January 15, 1952*

LUNCH with Pierre Bertaux, former head of the *Sureté*—French counterintelligence. He told me there was no hard evidence of the Communists
using lobotomy as an operation to produce confessions. However, a French
citizen arrested in Poland was finally released with a strange story. He said
he had undergone a brain operation (which he thought was trepanning)
after having jumped out of a train to escape the Polish police. He was told
by the Poles that he had sought to escape them by jumping out of the train.

There is no evidence to this effect aside from his testimony. Medical experts believe he really had been subjected to lobotomy. This type of operation not only inclines one to forget what happened immediately before the operation, but leaves the subject apparently ready to believe anything he is told concerning that period.

Bertaux told me there was positive evidence that the Communists used "truth serums" in interrogations. He said the usual form was to inject Pentothal and scopolamine simultaneously into the victim. This happened, it is believed, to members of the crew of a British boat which appeared to have been sent to a Polish port to help certain agents to escape. However, MI-5 refused to admit a thing to the French.

PARIS, *January 17, 1952*

I spent about four hours with Larry Norstad today and then lunched with him. He has an interesting idea: a conference of chaplains of the various NATO countries so they will be able to appreciate the spiritual things our alliance represents and will be better able to point this out to troops of their own nations. Like Eisenhower, he is more concerned about the spiritual and philosophical aspects of this alliance than the purely military ones.

Discussing the cold war, he said, "We have one great asset—the appeal of a free system of government to the hearts and minds of men. In the end, this appeal will shatter the hold of Communism. We should seek military equilibrium as cheaply as we can and then make this a simple struggle between two ideologies, trusting to the decency and justice of our cause."

MADRID, *January 23, 1952*

THIS morning I had a long interview with Generalissimo Franco. My interpreter was a foreign office official named Juan de las Barcenas, an amiable but rather pompous individual who speaks extremely good Oxonian English. We drove out to the Pardo together in a foreign office car and were passed by the security officials at the outer gate guarded by blue-caped Moors bearing lances and sitting on gray Arab steeds.

Barcenas took me into the council room where Franco meets with his cabinet. It is a lovely long, narrow room hung with many Goya and other tapestries and with a lovely painted ceiling. There are no ashtrays before the places of the cabinet members; only notebooks and pencils. Franco doesn't permit smoking. As a result, there is a constant shuffle in and out of the meetings as ministers wander out to grab a quick cigarette.

I knew that this interview was really being drummed up for propaganda purposes when a group of newspaper photographers showed up in the antechamber and started taking pictures of me talking with Barcenas and other officials. A gang of photographers snapped pictures of Franco and myself for almost five minutes.

Franco was extremely affable. It is very difficult for one to turn him off once he gets started on a particular subject. I had been asked to submit some questions in advance. I didn't do this but instead submitted a list of subjects I would like to discuss. The foreign office, presumably, had prepared a long written statement supposedly coming from Franco's own lips. Franco insisted that Barcenas should translate this to me before we went on with our conversation. While Barcenas was laboring over the job and Franco alertly regarded him to be sure he didn't skip a word of this wisdom, I gazed around the room. I noticed that Franco's desk was piled high and rather messily with papers. There were several photographs including one inscribed picture of the present Pope.

Among the most important views expressed by Franco were the following:

Spain would welcome the stationing of United States military missions here to instruct this country's armed forces in the use of new weapons and new techniques if the proposed bilateral agreement between Washington and Madrid is enacted.

Spain would be willing to accept the philosophical premises of our Mutual Security Act and the Benton amendment (providing for acceptance of the principles of free trade unionism, encouragement of private enterprise and discouragement of cartels). Franco said Spain already fostered private enterprise and sought to check cartels. He thought support of free trade unions was "merely a matter of definition." However, he said later on that he regarded such American labor institutions as the right to strike as "archaic," so I think that little point of "definition" is going to raise a bigger stink than he foresees.

Franco thought a bilateral agreement with the United States would be a step on the road to fuller cooperation between Spain and NATO. He said the Iberian peninsula was a "natural geographical area" of Western Europe. Britain was another. France, Germany and Benelux comprised still another. They all had fundamental common interests. A bilateral Hispano-American accord would serve as an "indirect agreement with other NATO members." Franco said there would be little difficulty if a NATO naval unit, including non-American ships, wanted to use Spanish port facilities. He was confident that vessels of all Allied nations could enter Spanish harbors.

My conversation lasted for about an hour and a half. Franco was clearly in no hurry to encourage development of new bonds between Spain and the European members of NATO but recognized their basic interests coincided. *De facto,* these would be tightened by a Hispano-American agreement even if political differences still prevailed between this country and such nations as France and England.

He stressed that it was to Spain's interest to assure the defenses of western Europe as far to the east as possible and dismissed the idea that any neutrality in a war between the United States and Russia would be respected by Moscow or that "neutralism" as a concept had any validity. However, he added that the possibility that Spanish armed forces could be contributed to any defensive coalition north of the Pyrenees would depend upon conditions yet to be reviewed.

He said Gibraltar must inevitably return to Spanish sovereignty, but that Spain would be prepared to lease base rights there to Britain on a short-term basis to ease the political embarrassment of effecting such a transfer. He argued that the value of Gibraltar as a base is now reduced especially since "all of Spain" is being made available—if the American bilateral agreement goes through.

He extended a verbal invitation to "representatives of United States trade unions" to visit Spain to study "the social evolution of our nation" and "the advances made by our workers." He said that last year's Spanish strikes in Barcelona and Vittoria had been engineered for political reasons by foreign Communist agents.

Franco said Spain "keeps her borders generously open" to political *émigrés* who left the country as a result of the Civil War "provided they are not guilty of crimes or other grave deeds during the Red Revolution."

The Caudillo was dressed in his generalissimo's uniform with a red sash about the waist. He said that throughout his life—even long before he became a political figure—it had been his fate to intervene in labor disputes and revolutions. He was convinced union leaders sought to accomplish their own "revolutionary" aims rather than to improve the social welfare of workers. Spain had now established workers courts under the ministry of justice and inspections under the ministry of labor which sought to meet the requirements of workers long before disputes reached a "strike" stage.

He admitted that the worker members of Spanish syndicates do not have the right to strike but explained that he thought this was a good thing because Spain is a poor country on a marginal economy. According to him, the national welfare of everybody would be damaged if strikes were permitted.

He considered either a workers' strike or an employers' lockout illegal because it would mean that individuals were taking the nation's law and welfare into their own hands. He added that this was an "outmoded method" of solving social problems and he thought other nations would have to organize similar systems to avoid the possibility of strikes.

He said the Spanish strikes last year were led by Communists sent from abroad. For the first period of its existence the Cominform had sent considerable sums of money to its underground in Spain, he said. Then, he continued, they sought to finance underground operations on a pay-as-you-go basis by staging a series of bank robberies and thefts.

MADRID, *January 25, 1952*

I must say this place does not change much.

Denis McEvoy, who is here trying to work out a deal for the *Reader's Digest* to be published in Spain, showed me a letter sent to him on January 10 by Juan Aparicio, director general of the press. This letter had the effrontery to suggest the following bases for an agreement to publish an edition in Spanish:

1. The price of the magazine was to be 50 per cent more than that for any similar magazine published in Spanish.

2. The edition would be subject to Spanish censorship.

3. The *Reader's Digest* would promise to refrain from publishing articles, in *any* of its editions throughout the world that the Franco regime considered hostile or which could be deemed as "praise of any kind" for Russia, any of its statesmen, the satellites or any Communist parties (presumably including that of Jugoslavia).

4. The *Reader's Digest* would promise to print, in *all* its editions, articles on "the real Spain." These would be selected by the government in Madrid.

5. The *Reader's Digest* would agree to publish, in *all* its editions (despite the fact that it is not a photographic magazine), four full pages of photos of Spain, selected by the General Press Directorate.

This gives a real clue to the Madrid mentality.

MADRID, *January 25, 1952*

THIS afternoon I had a talk with Lieutenant General Agustin Muñoz Grandes, Spanish minister of the army and former commander of the "blue" division which fought with the Germans at the Russian front during World War II. My interpreter was Lieutenant Colonel Garcia Rollan, a man who speaks good English and is generally used as a liaison officer with the Americans.

Muñoz Grandes is a dark, black-haired fellow with a rather saturnine, evil expression. He is of middle height and thin but wiry. His manner is very direct and I must say that on the whole I rather liked him. I told him that we were neighbors in 1941 when his division was fighting under von Leeb and I was with Vlassov's army near Volokolamsk.

Muñoz Grandes talked freely while we exchanged Spanish and American cigarettes. Although he was direct, I must say I thought some of his opinions pretty stupid. For example, he said Spain was preparing to adjust its national railway network to that of the rest of Europe where the gauge is narrower. He said this had already been done between Spain and Gibraltar, but there is no railway between Spain and Gibraltar.

He said Spain would welcome the presence of American technical missions here to instruct Spaniards in the use of new weapons, but he showed an astonishing ignorance of the length of time that would be required. He thought that in a few days Spanish soldiers could be taught the use of any new weapon. Furthermore, he did not think Spanish officers required tactical instruction on the basis of such weapons; only teaching on how they should best be used and repaired.

After he had outlined Spain's military requirements from the United States, I asked him what, in effect, America could expect to gain in return for the possible investment of millions of dollars in aid and equipment to this nation. He replied that a tough and spirited Spanish Army was the basic answer.

MADRID, *January 25, 1952*

LAST night I attended a dinner at the foreign office given by Foreign Minister Martin-Artajo in honor of Ambassador Griffis, who leaves the day after tomorrow for Gibraltar and then the United States. Very stuffed-shirt—white tie and decorations. I was glad to notice that pretty nearly every other man present seemed a bit too big for his tailcoat, as was I. There were about twenty men and a dozen women at dinner. It was preceded by a ceremony in which Martin-Artajo decorated Griffis with the Order of Charles II. The foreign minister is an enormous fellow and had a difficult time stooping over and getting the ribbon around little Griffis' neck. He made a long, flowery speech about what a wonderful character Griffis was and what a great gentleman. Then Griffis, who has a face like a potato, made a sentimental speech about Spain and America, ending up with Rudyard Kipling. The poor fellow was so moved he actually had tears in his eyes.

The suite in the foreign office palace where we dined was most attractive. I sat next to a fellow named Lucas de Oriel. His family is perhaps the richest in Spain with the possible exception of Juan March. They own and operate the Talgo streamlined train which goes between Irun and Madrid, and they also own huge hydroelectric properties and orange groves in Spanish Morocco, as well as all kinds of other enterprises. After dinner when the party broke up around I A.M., we sat around in my hotel drinking whisky and gassing until about four o'clock. Oddly enough, he appears to be strongly anti-Franco on the grounds that Franco is too "left-wing." Oriel is a Carlist and fought as a Requetes during the Civil War. (One of the Carlist factions still thinks it would be a good idea to reintroduce the Inquisition. My chum Oriel is just a tiny bit to the left of that.)

GIBRALTAR, *January 28, 1952*

ARRIVED last night after a train journey from Madrid to Algeciras. From Ronda, made famous by Garcia Lorca's poems, on south through Andalusia, the trip was magnificent: almond trees in full blossom, neat vineyards, pastel green cactus plants, swollen brown freshets pouring through valleys dotted with white houses, olive orchards silhouetted against red earth, orange trees studded with gleaming fruit, tawny goats, pigs and cattle grazing below woods of cork oak, peasants ambling along behind their donkeys, clumps of white wild narcissus, and always at every village, dour looking civil guards with lacquered flat-backed cardboard hats, carrying tommyguns or rifles. These are apparently prevalent in southern Andalusia to thwart widespread smuggling from Africa.

At Algeciras, I was met by Rowland Winn (later Lord St. Oswald), wearing a blue British cavalry officer's dress coat. He has bought a house near Algeciras at Pelayo, called Las Colunas, where he now lives as Don Rolando in the country of his adoption. Rowland just got back from a year in Korea with his hussars regiment (now equipped with Centurion tanks). It was pretty grim, he says. All the Allies detested MacArthur, but Ridgway has made a big difference. Inter-Allied feeling has improved immensely and American troop morale and efficiency are now far better.

Later I dined in my Gibraltar hotel, the Rock, which has a wonderful situation above the harbor, and then went to bed. This morning I wandered around the town a bit (really a village). There are about 25,000 civilians plus the military, air and naval population.

I had a good talk with General Sir Kenneth A. N. Anderson. I knew him slightly in 1943 when he commanded the British First Army in Tunisia. He told me that a few weeks ago he dined with the captain general of Andalusia who told him that, of course, no Spaniard liked to see the British flag waving over Gibraltar. However, he admitted it was to the interest of Spain and the Western world that Gibraltar should be efficiently run for the benefit of the West during these critical days. He regretted that there was a much better chance of this being done under the British than under the Spanish.

This evening I had drinks at the home of Commander Underhill, naval aide to Lord Ashbourne. Admiral John, son of Augustus John (the painter) and commander of the carrier group now in Gibraltar, was also there. Mrs. Underhill showed me the room in their house where Nelson's body was laid out after the battle of Trafalgar. On the walls hang a replica of one of Nelson's last letters and another of Collingwood's dying letter handing over command to his successor.

This evening I had dinner with Griffis and Johnny Jones, minister in our Madrid embassy. This was Griffis' final meal in Europe as he sails at six o'clock in the morning for home and retirement. After dinner I read him the copy of the story I sent last night as we sat around in his bedroom. He said he agreed with every fact I mentioned, but that it was a "poisonous" argument against aid to Spain.

GIBRALTAR, *January 29, 1952*

LONG tour of the Rock today, including everything from the subterranean tunnels and gun sites to a view of the little colony of Barbary apes.

I must say Gibraltar would be pretty hard to take but, with a hostile Spain, it would be awfully difficult to hold for long because of the inadequate and unprotected airfield running across the neutral zone.

Legend has it that when the last of the Barbary apes has died or quit the Rock, Britain will be driven out. On his way to Casablanca, Churchill inquired about the strength of the ape population and was told it was low. Promptly he cabled Sir Alan Brooke in London and told him to take "urgent measures."

Today the ape colony is prospering and the British are here in force. Anderson includes on his table of organization for the Rock an "OC" (officer in command of) apes.

Neither the apes nor the British are indigenous. The former came during the uncharted past from Mount Abyla in Morocco across the way, the other pillar of Hercules dominating the entrance to the Mediterranean. The British arrived in 1704 when Admiral Sir George Rooke captured the Rock in a surprise assault. Twenty years before Rooke's successful attack, Samuel Pepys, a naval commissioner as well as diarist, recommended seizing Gibraltar, which could be "fortified for a mere trifle against all the fleets and armies in the world."

TANGIER, *February 2, 1952*

I have been seeing various odd characters—most of them Arab nationalists who use this place as a center for agitation in both French and Spanish Morocco. I also saw my old friend Colonel W. F. Stirling, Lawrence's former chief of staff, and had him to lunch on his seventy-second birthday. He still carries within his aging carcass four bullets fired into him a couple of years ago by what he claims were French agents. Poor old Stirling was living quietly in Egypt after he recovered but has been bounced out as a result of anti-British feeling.

Had a long talk with Abdel Khalek Torres, forty-year-old leader of the Islah Party, which is the nationalist group for the Spanish zone. He is a rather charming individual who looks like any prosperous, well-educated Spaniard and strikes me as being about as revolutionary as Herbert Hoover. He used to be minister for Moslem affairs in the puppet government in the Spanish zone but resigned in 1943 and went to Cairo in 1947 to work with the Arab League. He came to Tangier in 1948 and has just recently been permitted to enter the Spanish zone again. He has an extremely comfortable house in Tetuan, which I visited, and which is now being prepared for his permanent return.

In a nutshell, Torres told me over innumerable cups of mint tea that the aspirations of Tunisia and Egypt receive the full support of the Moroccans, "but our hopes are that in both cases things can be solved peaceably with neither Christian nor Moslem blood shed." He said he hoped Egypt would participate "on an equal basis with the Western powers to save world peace." He said most of the people of North Africa hope to attain their aspirations without bloodshed and would like to see Egypt as a leading power in a Middle East command associated with the West.

I went to Tetuan by automobile and first had a long talk with General Garcia Valiño, governor of Spanish Morocco, who is an amiable but tough and certainly conservative officer. He is a stocky little man with blue eyes and a rather non-Spanish appearance, whose favorite relaxation is hunting. I asked him a great many straight questions through a ludicrously pompous interpreter who twisted both questions and answers. Garcia Valiño indicated that no changes in attitude towards the nationalists were contemplated. He said, "My policy is to turn the tap on very slowly," and emphasized with his hand just how slowly that would be.

I told Garcia Valiño I wanted to see the caliph, and he told me that would be impossible. Right afterwards, I saw an Arab friend of mine, Mehdi Bennouna, from one of the wealthiest and most prominent Tetuan families, who has just returned. He called up a secret contact with the caliph to find that the caliph left town right after I left Garcia Valiño's office apparently instructed that under no circumstances should he receive me.

FEZ, *February 11, 1952*

JUST wound up a fairly brief tour of French Morocco and am jotting this down in the Palais Jamai, which the French tourist agency has remodeled from a prosperous Arab's palace into one of the most delightful hotels in the world—especially now when you can sit out by the orange and lemon trees drinking mint tea on a spring afternoon, or beneath the full moon on a warm spring night.

I spent a good deal of my time traipsing around among American officers who have been building five strategic bombing bases, and I not only went to the Fifth Air Division headquarters of General Archie J. Old, Jr., but also to one of the two operational bases, the main one at Nouasseur.

A congressional investigation on waste in these bases has been going on, but I must say I was fairly well convinced that the waste was no more than should be expected on any cost-plus contract where completion was ordered at the earliest moment on a sort of cost-be-damned basis. Old did not impress me in the least. He is a pretty uncultivated character, but I suppose he knows how to bomb people.

In Rabat I dined with General Augustin Guillaume, the resident general, an extraordinarily egocentric and pompous little man, very vain about his linguistic abilities. He says he speaks German, Russian, Serbian, Arabic and Berber. I suppose he really is good, but his Serbian, judging from the efforts he produced, is something less than rudimentary. He tried to give me the impression that there was no Arab nationalist movement and that anyway the Berbers were the people to be counted on.

I was equally disappointed with Ahmed Balafrej, secretary general of Istiqlal, the Moroccan nationalist party. I lunched at Balafrej's home, having an excellent Arab meal with plenty of coffee, mint tea and orange juice. He is quiet, unprepossessing, speaks fairly good French and voiced bitter complaints against France as a breaker of promises and a brutal tyrant. He claimed that Morocco was now a police state and that he did not dare to leave his home, which was continually watched. When he took me to the gate through his garden, I asked him where the watchers were, and he pointed to a house about four hundred yards away with shuttered windows, and said there was a fellow peering through the shutters. I could not confirm this but it didn't strike me as terribly effective—if true.

From Rabat to Meknes to Fez fine roads curl past recently planted forests, vineyards and grain fields. Banks of gold and orange wild flowers stretch below blossoming almond trees. Storks solemnly regard blue-caped riders on their Arab steeds and veiled women selling bunches of wild asparagus.

In the native quarter of this medieval town—with minarets and crenelated walls etched against snow-capped Atlas peaks in the distance—the pace of life appears unchanged since the days when an independent Sheriffian empire scorned the heathen foreigner. Half blindfolded, sweating horses circle millstones grinding olive oil. The faithful wash their feet in a pool at the entrance to the ancient Kairouine Mosque, while children's voices chanting Koranic texts echo through lattices from the school across the alley.

One sees drink peddlers with goatskin bags, children with trachoma or shaven scabrous heads, unveiled Berber women with tattooed foreheads and with babies slung upon their backs. Outside the many mosque gates stand Arab women, eyes peering above their veils, and beggars singing prayers while worshippers squat in the sunlit courtyards. Up and down the winding alleys shoppers stroll purchasing copper pans, wool, golden belts and perfumed amber extract.

It is a romantic prospect and today a peaceful one. Members of the city's venerable colony of Jews chat amiably with Moslems. Bargaining thrives in the bazaars. Yet one cannot forget such peace is relatively new to the traditionally dour and fanatical Fassi people. Forty-three years ago a rebel pretender to the Sheriffian throne was publicly displayed here in an iron cage for more than a month before being thrown to the sultan's menagerie. Chaos and bloodshed were the norm for centuries.

Not even Moroccan nationalists will deny that the French protectorate has brought with it order and quiet. Casablanca, a dilapidated fishing village four decades ago, is now the sixth largest port of the French union. Electricity, railroads, airports, highways, public health installations and tractors have been introduced. Nevertheless, nationlist leaders complain that the price they have had to pay is unacceptable, that in exchange for order they have lost their independence.

Road signs throughout the protectorate are in French—not Arabic. Frenchmen live in comfortable European quarters while the countryside and city suburbs are dotted with native shacks of thatch or beaten tin cans. There are no poor French here, the nationalists say—only poor Moroccans. The sultan is powerless to enact any laws without General Guillaume's countersignature. The resident general is foreign minister and war minister. He appoints Frenchmen to head administrative branches, Frenchmen to govern provinces in paternalistic but firm fashion.

The nationalists assert that most of the new schools are for the growing French colony; that thousands of native children, but no French, are condemned to illiteracy. Although the French contended when they established the protectorate that they were merely assuming the obligation to prepare Morocco for an independent place in the modern world, the Moors argue not a single school for training native administrators had been established until December, 1949.

Moroccans are not permitted to form their own trade unions, but must join those of France, including the General Confederation of Labor led by French Communists. The Moors cannot travel freely and require France's permission even to visit Tangier. While press censorship was removed last year when signs were increasing that the Moroccan issue would be raised before the United Nations, the nationalists detect signs of its return. Editors of two Arabic papers are now facing fines or prison for publishing articles the French interpret as likely to foment unrest.


LISBON, *February 12, 1952*

THIS evening I had dinner with Ambassador Lincoln MacVeagh, a friend for fourteen years and a first-class fellow. He is going to Spain as ambassador shortly.

He called my attention to an observation by Lord Macaulay when that historian discussed the Monmouth and Argyll rebellions against King James II. Macaulay said the military movement was organized like a "debating club" and it made the mistake of trying to organize an army as if it were a commonwealth.

There is a certain aptness to these remarks in connection with the NATO meeting here.

LISBON, *February 16, 1952*

LUNCH today with King Carol, former sovereign of Rumania, and his wife, Magda Lupescu, who now calls herself Princess Helen. Also present was Urdareanu—who used to be minister of the Court. He is married to a moderately attractive English girl, twenty-six years younger then he. This is astonishing because Urdareanu has a face pock-marked like the map of the moon. I found him neither intelligent nor agreeable. Princess Helen seems amiable but far from being a quiz kid. She seems to be a sympathetic, "womanly" type.

King Carol is in no sense impressive. He has a slightly missing chin and an obstinate face. His forehead is exceptionally narrow. He is a fairly big man, who inclines to plumpness. He speaks English with a noticeable German accent and has the unfortunate habit of spitting and drooling. I talked with him at length and he has everything worked out very simply in world affairs. According to him, the United States is much stronger than Russia so we should send Moscow an ultimatum, in a year or two or, otherwise, attack. He considers himself the ruler of Rumania because he never abdicated as did his son and successor, Michael. When we were discussing the German situation, he said the only solution for Germany was monarchy and the obvious choice was the eldest son of the late crown prince.

Carol said there was a good type of democracy in Rumania where the peasants were not servile but were respectful and took their hats off. He thought it would be better if there was more of this type of democracy in the United States. It strikes me as a good thing that men like this are no longer ruling, but it is a tragedy that they have been replaced by something even worse.

Carol did not even seem to know much about his own country's history. I asked him if he could tell me something about the Dacian people and their language. (They were the original inhabitants of Rumania—before it was conquered by the Romans.) He knew absolutely nothing.

Carol told me he had been brought up in the Orthodox religion but that his father was a Roman Catholic. Obviously his father had to square that with the Vatican for political reasons because Orthodoxy is the official religion of Rumania.

In the afternoon I went to a cocktail party given by MacVeagh. Quite a collection of relics was there including former King Umberto of Italy, who seems just as amiable and simple-witted as when I last saw him, and

Admiral Horthy of Hungary with his wife and daughter-in-law. Horthy, the former Regent, is now about eighty. He does not look it physically, but mentally shows his age. He was very affable when I told him I had last seen him riding a white horse into Koloszvar (Cluj), the capital of Transylvania. He told me he had a lot of trouble wth that steed because it kept growing bigger and bigger. As a matter of fact, it looked like a plow horse.

LISBON, *February 18, 1952*

MACVEAGH points out that the origin of present-day American foreign policy was all conceived in Greece. The UNRRA experiment was first applied there. American aid to Greece became the military assistance program. The American effort there, in fighting communism, was also a precedent for Korea. The Truman Doctrine developed into the Marshall Plan and the North Atlantic Pact. It was the first area where Russian expansion was contained. MacVeagh said President Truman had told him that his (MacVeagh's) testimony before congressional committees and his reporting on the situation from Greece were instrumental in bringing about this policy. MacVeagh showed me a letter from the President, in effect confirming this. He recalled his dispute with Griswold, a Republican and former governor of Nebraska. MacVeagh insisted that the ambassador should be in charge of all American representation in Greece. Griswold wished to run the show himself. MacVeagh was backed by the President, but then, for political reasons, during the election year of 1948, Truman had to reverse his policy in order to gain bipartisan support. It was after this that Mac-Veagh left Athens and came to Lisbon.

I had lunch with Averell Harriman. Harriman said much progress must be made here on the European Army because "Adenauer is a diminishing asset" as he grows older and politically weaker—we must move fast. He said that the biggest problems at the NATO meeting here were caused by financial difficulties in Italy and France which had, respectively, suffered from the Po Valley flood and the Indochina war. The French are still antiwar-minded. This mood is kept alive by the Indochina campaign. Furthermore, there remains widespread hatred of the Germans among the French. He recalled the horrible alternative to success at this conference: de Gaulle in France, Schumacher in Germany, Bevan in England and Taft in the United States.

This afternoon I had a couple of drinks with Secretary of Defense Lovett. We were talking about the importance of our bases in Morocco. He remarked that they would not be worth a damn if the local population is against us.

LISBON, *February 21, 1952*

RANDOLPH Churchill was present during the NATO Council meeting on assignment from the *Daily Telegraph*. He had just concluded another one of his diets to win a bet, having lost thirty-four pounds, and seemed to be doing his best to gain it all back in about ten days—mainly with alcohol. His gossip was nevertheless interesting. Among other things he said his father had always been convinced Roosevelt was jealous of him. He also told me his grandfather, Lord Randolph Churchill, had died of syphilis at the age of forty-seven. He said that Winston more than anything else would like to be made an honorary citizen of the United States before his death.

He said anti-Semitism of a social sort was still fairly evident in England. Every club had three or four Jews as members just in order to "prove" that it wasn't anti-Semitic.

He said that Winston was now getting fairly gaga except when he pulled himself together for public appearances. At a recent cabinet meeting he turned to Eden when Rab Butler was speaking and asked Eden, "Who is that fellow?"—an odd comment on his chancellor of the exchequer. Randolph said he recently spent a family weekend with his father who failed to recognize several of his grandchildren. The last time his father saw King George VI was when they went to the airport to see Princess (now Queen) Elizabeth off on her world tour. At the airport the King saw Churchill having a glass of champagne and remarked that he was surprised because he thought Churchill never drank before lunch. Winston replied that his rule was merely not to drink before breakfast.

Bob Lovett, whom I saw every evening for nightcaps, said it was absolutely essential to Western defense to get German troops armed as soon as possible. At the end of the meeting he was by no means 100 per cent sure how successful the conference had been and asked me if I would "put on his hat" and draft a statement of what he ought to say to the press when he returned to Washington. To my embarrassment I found this was far from easy.

PARIS, *March 1, 1952*

RECENTLY Hugh Cumming, our chargé d'affaires in Moscow, received a cable from Washington asking him why so many Russian generals seem to be dying these days. The implication was that maybe there is a purge on. As a matter of fact, Hugh thinks it is merely a result of the fact that they overwork incessantly and that, after all, there are so many generals in Russia and every one of them gets some kind of a little death notice when he kicks off.

PARIS, *March 5, 1952*

FAREWELL chat at the embassy with David Bruce. He thinks Acheson is now probably an asset to Truman, rather than a deficit. David makes no bones about being unhappy at the thought of leaving Paris. He is confused about Eden. He simply cannot understand how the British managed to do such a sloppy job on Sir Oliver Franks. He said that three days before Franks was offered the job as secretary general of NATO, Eden said he wasn't at all sure that Franks would take it. Yet Franks was offered the job without ever having an official inquiry ahead of time—and Franks turned it down. Schuman told David only yesterday it was his impression the deal on NATO's permanent headquarters coming to Paris hinged upon either a British or Canadian secretary general. Schuman is beginning to think that the British really don't want the position and that this was all a trick to disentangle them from European obligations; in other words, that they named Franks for the position, knowing that Franks wouldn't take the job. Bruce feels Eden has been a disappointment as foreign minister. He is too slipshod. He has an easygoing, nineteenth-century manner and asks in an offhand fashion, "Well, Bob, what do we think about this?" (Presumably referring to Pierson Dixon). That "doesn't go," David says. I asked Bruce who the next ambassador in Washington would be and said I had heard Lord Salisbury might be the fellow. David said Churchill would do anything for Salisbury, and he recalled when Salisbury was offered the job of viceroy of India. He says Malcolm Macdonald is detested by Churchill and would not be considered either for Washington or the NATO job; in fact, Churchill exiled Macdonald to Canada. He didn't know whether Salisbury's health would stand up to the Washington job. He thought Salisbury might have been foreign secretary instead of Eden, and that Eden might have been deputy prime minister, except Eden told Churchill that he would either be foreign secretary or nothing; in other words, Eden would not settle just to be deputy premier.

PARIS, *March 6, 1952*

GOOD chat this morning with Field Marshal Montgomery. He seemed in a rather calm and affable mood.

No deals are going on between Jugoslavia and any of the NATO powers as far as Montgomery knows. However, he is convinced that Jugoslavia would defend itself in case of attack. It is not an inconvenience to have a neutral country situated there. It is somewhat like Switzerland: a neutral country in a key position which is willing to repel aggression.

Straightening out the Mediterranean command is going to take a long time—probably even longer than the agreement over the Atlantic command. First of all, it has not been decided whether it will all be regarded as one lake or whether it will be divided into separate commands. The British would like it to be one lake and commanded by an Englishman. On the other hand, Montgomery admits the United States would never agree to place its Sixth Fleet under an English admiral.

The announcement at Lisbon that NATO hopes to have fifty divisions by the end of this year was "nonsense—utter nonsense." *The* (London) *Times'* editorial describing this as a "phantom army" which afforded more provocation than protection was very sensible. Indeed, many people asked Monty whether he had written it himself. Whether NATO is a "fifty-div NATO" or some other figure doesn't matter. We can never afford to establish a permanent combat-ready force equivalent to the Russians' 175 divisions. That would destroy our economy and social structure.

What we need is enough combat-ready divisions to hold—even if they give in various areas—until reserve forces are brought into position. There are no adequate reserves in Europe. The British territorial army is useful, and British national service soldiers are sent to Korea or Malaya after only six months' training. But the French won't send their national service soldiers to Indochina. As a result, France's professional army is engaged in Indochina. The eighteen months' military service in France is inadequate because there are no professional soldiers here; they are all in Vietnam. With this situation, the length of service should be raised to two years. "Look around Europe," Montgomery said, "and you will find no reserves."

Montgomery said the Germans were very much needed in the western defense force, but it was by no means certain they would get in. It will be very difficult to pass the project through the French parliament and also through the *Bundestag*. He said there was no flat Allied agreement to rearm the Germans under any circumstances; in other words, to incorporate them in western defense if the European army project flops.

PARIS, *March 10, 1952*

THIS morning I had a talk with Eisenhower. The general got back Friday from his visit to Greece and Turkey. He looks in pretty good health, but now is having that same sort of rheumatic pain in his right wrist that he used to have with his left wrist, and he is worried that it may prevent him from playing golf again. He is starting to take baking treatments in the morning, the way he used to do for his left wrist.

While we were talking, Kevin McCann came in with letters for Eisenhower to sign. McCann is over here temporarily again, presumably on leave from his job as president of Defiance College in Ohio. Obviously he is handling a good deal of Eisenhower's political correspondence. Cliff Roberts is also back in town, so I imagine he is doing some courier work between the general and his political backers.

Eisenhower didn't have much time to sight-see. He had one hour on the

Acropolis which he enjoyed immensely, and about an hour and a half in Istanbul, which also fascinated him. Mamie thought Athens was the most beautiful city she had ever seen; he didn't and did not like the modern architecture in either Greece or Turkey. The Turks gave him two Oriental rugs which he reluctantly accepted because they were of value. He didn't want to hurt their feelings. In Athens, he was given a little rug and chair made by wounded Greek war veterans. This touched him very deeply. Mamie liked them so much that she wants two bigger rugs to make a bedroom set.

He and Gruenther were much embarrassed by the Greeks. When they went to the royal palace for dinner, they were each handed a box. When they opened these up, they found they contained decorations. Since Eisenhower has refused decorations from other NATO countries, he was obliged to refuse this. When they left Athens, they left the decorations with the ambassador, asking him to return them. Unfortunately, the Greeks had announced to the press that these decorations were being given. Incidentally, Eisenhower said the French had offered him the *Medaille Militaire* after the war, but he had declined it.

He was clearly depressed by all the political intrigue going on in Greece. He saw General Papagos, who explained to him that he had gone into politics reluctantly in order to keep the palace from messing around in the army; that he didn't really want to be in the political picture at all. Eisenhower wasn't quite sure how straightforward Papagos was. He thought King Paul was a nice fellow, but completely controlled by his wife. He was convinced the Queen is intriguing much too much. A woman sitting next to Gruenther when they dined at the Palace said to Al: "Our host is a very fine fellow, but he is going to lose his job soon if the Queen doesn't stop her manipulations."

Eisenhower said he was very disappointed because the arrangements for his visit to Athens gave him the best car available in the place which was a large closed Cadillac. The crowds had poured out into the streets "to demonstrate friendship for an old fool like me," and he was almost invisible. He leaned forward in the car to wave his hand, but he didn't think many people saw him. He was amused by the Greek hand wave, which is in reverse of the usual one we know.

Incidentally, I told Eisenhower I had heard rumors that we were about to tighten up our Jugoslav policy and insist on more "quo" for our "quid." He said he hadn't heard that, but he favored the idea. He thought that in general we should insist on commitments in exchange for our aid; we were too often ready to offer aid free and for nothing.

Eisenhower was very apologetic because his aide had mixed things up and forgot to notify me about my appointment. He suggested we should get together on the golf course and have a long talk as soon as his wrist feels better.

AL Gruenther sent me Eisenhower's first and surely only annual report to the standing group of NATO. He wants my comments. I have read it very carefully this afternoon and am going up to see Gruenther with some suggestions for alterations. Then we are going on to the Eisenhowers' for bridge and dinner.

YESTERDAY afternoon after I had finished working on Eisenhower's report. I drove out to SHAPE and spent thirty-five minutes going over it with Gruenther and Colonel Pete Carroll, one of the bright young colonels Eisenhower brought over with him when SHAPE was created. I had several minor and a few major suggestions and I think they are going to be incorporated into the final version of the report. Gruenther and Carroll agreed with my insistence that we should stress defense against "aggression" and "Soviet imperialism" instead of the draft's mention of "communism." The latter, after all, includes Tito.

Gruenther and I then drove over to Eisenhower's house, where there was a female canasta game and a male bridge game organized. We started playing at six o'clock, stayed on for an excellent steak dinner, and then played again until half past eleven. This was pretty late because Eisenhower and Gruenther had to leave at 8 A.M. for Germany, where they are having a conference today. The only people present were the Eisenhowers, the Gruenthers, General Snyder (Ike's doctor and one of his best friends) and his wife, and Cliff Roberts.

Roberts obviously is doing some political work for the general. He is, of course, an old personal friend and handles his investments. But this is the third time he has been over during the past year. He is staying for only a brief visit, and then flying back. During our bridge game, at one point, Eisenhower referred to the 1948 elections and then said, "By golly, I think that was the first time you ever talked to me about politics, Cliff." Roberts then said, "Yes. I always told you to stay out, but now I'm not so sure I was right." (Obviously Roberts was referring to his previous belief that Dewey would defeat Truman in the 1948 vote.)

Yesterday was the day of the New Hampshire primaries. The eyes of the entire United States and a good deal of the world were turned on this small political test. Nevertheless, we never mentioned the subject last night except to make a couple of kidding remarks to the general. Al asked me what my forecast was, and I told him I heard MacArthur would sweep up all fourteen delegates. Apparently Gruenther has got a bet on concerning the plurality in the popular vote that he expects Eisenhower to get.

General Snyder went home early to listen to the radio and said he would call us if there was anything exciting. Ike said, "Don't call me. I'm not interested. Call Al if you want to speak with anyone. He's got some money on it."

As a matter of fact, Eisenhower was remarkably self-controlled and, although he must have been genuinely interested, he really kept the fact well hidden. His right wrist was bothering him a bit, and he complained to Snyder several times that it was swollen thicker than it had ever been, but Snyder reassured him that the swelling was going down. He looked a bit tired and a tiny bit overweight compared to his normal weight—possibly because his wrist has been keeping him off the golf course. His bifocal rimless glasses bothered him during the bridge game, and at one point he overtook his own queen and thereby lost a couple of tricks and was set one, which didn't exactly improve his temper. I may add that his temper justifiably was pretty well strained because I was his partner at that point, and, in all my years of bad bridge playing, I don't think I ever played worse. Fortunately for the equanimity of the other three, my talents were shared around equally—followed by a pretty generous distribution of my wealth.

I must say that although Ike is a mild and amiable fellow, one can easily see the drive, dynamism and force within him when he gets thoroughly interested in a bridge hand. He sort of leans forward, and he is a much bigger man than he sometimes appears, with a very large frame—and begins to bang the cards down on the table, as his whole face lights up with interest in an operational plan for playing that particular hand.

Incidentally, Snyder almost inevitably sits around and kibitzes at these bridge games. He clearly knows how to play, and I have wondered why he doesn't. Mrs. Snyder told Marina today that actually he plays quite well, but some years ago at Miami he was playing with Eisenhower and they had such a terrible fight that he swore he would never play with him again.

We talked a bit about Greece and Italy at dinner. Eisenhower clearly didn't like Queen Frederika and complained that she always whispered to him behind her hand while at the table. He did not like the atmosphere of intrigue, and he felt that the Queen was scheming too much.

Eisenhower asked me why Pacciardi was unpopular in Rome and I explained that he had been on the Republican side in the Spanish Civil War; that he had been a political *émigré* during World War II and had constantly broadcast to Italy, calling upon Fascist soldiers to desert Mussolini. Eisenhower remarked that if he had known that, he would have taken special pains to be even more cordial to him. He had not realized that he was on our side throughout the war.

PARIS, *March 12, 1952*

THE New Hampshire primary results came in with an extremely good victory for Eisenhower over Taft. I was surprised in view of what all the so-called experts have been writing. Ike told reporters at the airport, coming back from Germany—where he spent the day in conferences—that he was very "moved" and "deeply touched."

PARIS, *March 16, 1952*

I spent two hours this afternoon with General Lucius Clay, who is going back to New York tonight after a flying weekend trip devoted to advising Eisenhower to return between May 16 and June 1. Officially Clay said that he had come over on business for the Continental Can Company, of which he is now president, but that is, of course, a lot of hogwash. We had an extremely frank talk sitting around in his hotel suite with a couple of whiskies, and in his usual straightforward way he said the following.

Eisenhower is at present weakest in the Middle West, above all in Ohio and Illinois. (Clay's observations on these political nuances are pretty accurate as was proven by the fact that he made successful bets that Eisenhower would win the New Hampshire primaries on a five-to-four population ratio and that Kefauver would defeat Truman.)

Clay said he was particularly anxious to avoid personal publicity in connection with his work for Eisenhower's campaign because he doesn't want anybody to get the idea that this is a generals' "cabal" trying to put Ike into power.

Clay intends to remain behind the scenes all the way through on the campaign, but he definitely will go to Chicago when the Republican convention is on. He has known Eisenhower for more than twenty years and they are close personal friends, so that he feels he is in a good position to be able to advise the leaders back home on the general's probable reactions.

He said Ike is now visibly more eager to get the Republican nomination because he deeply fears the potential results to American policy and the world should Taft be elected.

Laughingly, Clay said that about the only way Ike could really be hurt now would be if Colonel McCormick came out in open support of him. Yesterday McCormick visited Eisenhower here and begrudgingly admitted that if Eisenhower were nominated, he would back him because "I even supported Dewey in 1948—for God's sake."

PARIS, *March 17, 1952*

I spent the morning with Larry Norstad and lunched with him and Isabelle out at Fontainebleau. Most of our conversation dealt with politics, which is becoming the main subject on the peripheries of SHAPE nowadays. By politics, of course, is meant whether Ike will go home this spring and whether he will be nominated.

When Norstad was home last week, he discovered to his amazement that a lot of dirty politics was now being applied against Eisenhower. The method seems to be that either anonymous pamphlets or rumor campaigns are launched against the general clearly by his Republican opponents, who then go around saying, "Isn't it too bad that the Democrats are doing this." Among the slanderous things being said are: that Mrs. Eisenhower is a drunk; that Eisenhower is still very much in love with Kay Summersby, with an implication that a divorce is in the offing; that Eisenhower's health is failing and he is rarely around the office now. The Summersby diary is quoted extensively to prove that his health was bad during the war (referring to such things as arthritic pains in the shoulder).

PARIS, *March 18, 1952*

IT is extraordinary how Paris has become the magnetic center of American politics. This morning I spent an hour with Paul Hoffman, head of the Ford Foundation and former chief of the Marshall Plan, who has been over talking political facts with Eisenhower. He leaves for New York tonight. Hoffman, who is an energetic, forthright fellow, said he is going to request the trustees of the Ford Foundation at their meeting on April 10 to grant him a leave of absence without pay until July 7, when the Republican convention meets in Chicago. Cabot Lodge has been asking him to devote more time to the Eisenhower campaign. So far he has been giving his Sundays and evenings to the movement but has had to spend his days working for the Foundation. From tomorrow—when he arrives in New York—until April 10, he expects to give about half his time to the Eisenhower movement.

PARIS, *March 20, 1952*

EISENHOWER is going to return to the States in May or June and "run." That is the big news today. I had lunch with him.

He was still furious and red in the face over the Malmédy slaughter of American troops during the German counteroffensive in December of 1944. He said he could quite understand how it might be embarrassing for patrols or armor to have too many prisoners and not know what to do with them, but the Malmédy massacre was a coldblooded affair in which the Germans had tied the hands of their captives first and then shot them. He could never forgive that. He recalled that there had been incidents during the war when American soldiers had exceeded their military prerogatives and it had caused him grave concern. There had been a case in eastern Tunisia where a fellow had lost his closest buddy, had gone berserk and finally had been responsible for the loss of life of several of the enemy in inexplicable circumstances. Nevertheless, after the court had sentenced the culprit to death, Eisenhower suspended the sentence in review, then gave him a life sentence in suspension, then sent him back to active duty. The man in the end had received an honorable discharge from the Army, but the death sentence had been advertised, so that the North Africans and the French could realize how determined we were to condemn irregularities.

For some time Eisenhower spoke about President Roosevelt and indicated much more of an antipathy than I had suspected. He said Roosevelt, whenever he (Eisenhower) had talked to him, had used the "vertical pronoun" far too much. At the time of Casablanca, Roosevelt kept telling Eisenhower what "I" plan to do. Roosevelt had said that "I" do not know what "I" will recommend for the future of such capitals as Algiers and Tunis because "I" don't know what France will be capable of after this war. To Roosevelt it seemed like a potentially weak power. He gave Eisenhower certain "orders" for North Africa and West Africa which Eisenhower said he could not accept because he was an Allied commander and not merely an American commander. Roosevelt then agreed with Eisenhower and said he was right, but within a few minutes started talking in terms of "my" wishes again. Nevertheless, Eisenhower admitted he was *for* Roosevelt in the 1944 election; he had been against him in 1932, 1936, and 1940. He had been against the third term above all, but when it came to the fourth term Eisenhower felt so many things were at stake that it was too risky to change leadership at that juncture.

Eisenhower admitted he had more or less made up his mind to ask for relief from his job but did not quite know how to do it. He admitted that President Truman—who he said had always been very square with him—should have sufficient advance notice of the general's departure date in order to choose a successor and have enough time to get agreement in the United States and from the other NATO Allies. At this juncture, Eisenhower said he thought Al Gruenther was obviously the man and he had found an increasing acceptance of that point of view from the European countries recently. He said Truman in October, 1949, had admitted to him (when Eisenhower asked for Gruenther as his chief of staff) that Al had always given the President the best and most precise briefings on the situation. When Eisenhower had asked for a fourth star for Gruenther, the President had come through immediately. Only yesterday, Field Marshal Montgomery had told Eisenhower he thought Gruenther was an excellent man for the position and assured Ike that he, Montgomery, would be delighted to serve under Gruenther as NATO commander.

Eisenhower was worried about the best way of putting in his request for relief. He thought he should come home between the middle of May and June 1, and he admitted that he had to give the President a great deal of advance notice. I suggested to him that when he submitted his first annual report as NATO commander on April 2 (the anniversary of SHAPE's activation), he should send a separate letter to Washington requesting relief on the grounds that he was no longer able to separate his military capacity as an international civil servant and NATO commander from his political position. He wants to send that letter to Bob Lovett. I think he has now been convinced the letter should go to Truman in the form of a sealed communication, submitted together with a letter from him to Lovett, stating approximately what is in that sealed communication. Lovett would give the enclosed sealed letter to the President. I gather Eisenhower would have to have the letter made public around April 5, 6 or 7 and to plan his departure as of approximately May 15.

Eisenhower made it very clear that he now really feels an obligation to run for the job on the basis, above all, of the Minnesota vote for him, because he doesn't want to let down the thousands of people in the United States who seem to be for him. He said he had really never aspired to that honor, and in fact he had always tried to plan for his later years in life on the basis of his family. His wife has a heart condition which prevents her from going back to Denver. Therefore, he had hoped to live in the foothills of the Appalachians near Gettysburg. Mamie was now asking where she should park their luggage "when the Republicans make up their minds."

Eisenhower said Senator Vandenberg had urged him to run for the Republican nomination for the Presidency in 1948 and that this will appear in the currently serialized book by Arthur H. Vandenberg Jr. on his father's diaries.

Eisenhower talked at considerable length about his political ideas. He was against centralization of government and, above all, against overwhelming federal taxation; for example, state schools should be supported by state taxation rather than federal grants for education. I told him he sounded very much like a Jeffersonian Democrat, rather than a Republican, and he replied that he thought it would be better to describe him as a "Jeffersonian American" and that the Democrats had diverged too far from Jefferson's ideas.

He said his greatest hope was to achieve a form of cooperation between labor and capital in the United States, with the government remaining in the position of "referee" between the two forces, because they simply had to collaborate with each other in order to preserve a common front against the Soviet danger.

He thought there was a great danger of the military messing in politics in the United States, and that was one of his most serious problems at present, since he remained a military man. His conscience troubled him considerably, and it was clear from listening to him that this is the primary reason why he has now decided to quit his present NATO job and eventually to resign his commission. He thought it would be disastrous if there was ever a chance of American officers being appointed to commands on the grounds of their political opinions. He intimated during the conversation a fairly considerable dislike for MacArthur's politics and policies, and also the same for General W., although he said that General W. had been a good soldier in the past.

Eisenhower was in a pretty good frame of mind. He had had two whiskies and soda before lunch and a glass of wine at lunch. He ate rather better than General Snyder would have liked and had an especially good helping of mushrooms with the main course of chicken, remarking that he was extremely fond of that vegetable. When he left, he told me that his right wrist was in much better shape and that he hoped to be able to play golf soon again.

PARIS, *March 21, 1952*

I had a talk with Al Gruenther early this afternoon shortly before his departure by air for Washington where he will testify on SHAPE requirements before congressional committees now holding hearings on the President's foreign aid program. Gruenther is forging ahead as the most likely candidate to succeed Eisenhower. He told me he is going to make a strong appeal to the Pentagon and the White House to nominate a European to succeed Eisenhower as NATO commander-in-chief. This is a pretty modest thing to do because he would be weakening his own chances. He feels very strongly that either a Frenchman or an Englishman should succeed Eisenhower and indicated that it should be either Juin or Montgomery. He feels there are too many Americans connected with the show now and he wishes to avoid the impression that it is an American rather than an Allied affair.

PARIS, *March 28, 1952*

YESTERDAY afternoon I went out to see Buck Lanham and pick up a couple of advance copies of Eisenhower's first NATO report. Buck then asked me to have a couple of drinks with him and his wife at their hotel in Paris. They destroyed any vestige of reputation remaining to Bob Schulz, Eisenhower's aide, and said he hated my guts and did his best to block my contacts with Eisenhower. Buck said Montgomery was violently anti-French and at a recent conference had ordered, "I won't have any bloody Frenchmen in here," with the result that a crisis had been precipitated.

PARIS, *April 1, 1952*

LANHAM called up in a dither this afternoon. Two thousand copies of Eisenhower's report to NATO had been sent by special plane to Washington for distribution by the Pentagon. It was to be published at midnight. The plane went by way of Iceland where it was forced to land because of weather conditions. The pilot, wanting extra gasoline, ordered some of the cargo unloaded, including Eisenhower's reports. Nobody had bothered to tell him what was in the packages. As a result, the plane landed in Washington, minus the reports. I had received an advance copy which I sent to New York a few days ago. Lanham asked me to arrange to have it teletyped from New York to Washington, which I did. This is sure a hell of a way to run a railroad. The report is the most important document SHAPE has put out so far.

PARIS, *April 2, 1952*

LAST night Eisenhower's report was finally made public. It is a firstclass document. I noticed that several of the changes I had suggested were incorporated, including a final philosophical round-up statement, as well as a reference to the NATO staff college and a long section on the necessity of building up a permanent program of reserves because the West could never support large standing armies. One suggestion I had made was that the adjective "Communist" should not be used throughout when describing the Soviet threat, but that "Stalinist" and "Soviet imperialist" should be substituted. Al Gruenther, last week, showed me a semifinal draft which had followed this suggestion also, but I find the final version reverted to the original and stuck fairly generally by "Communist" and "Communistic." (Later I found this was for political—Republican Party—reasons.)

PARIS, *April 3, 1952*

I had a talk this evening with Senator Cabot Lodge, manager of the Eisenhower-for-President movement, who flew in from Washington. He claims all he is going to do is report on the current situation and make no recommendations. Lodge is obviously brimful of enthusiasm. He claims that before the New Hampshire primary nobody wanted the job, because the experts thought Ike didn't have much chance, but since then all kinds of people have been trying to get Lodge's position away from him. He also says all kinds of fellows are now offering money or votes in exchange for promises of jobs such as embassies, but he is laying off them. He claims Eisenhower will have more than five hundred votes pledged to him by the time the convention opens July 7 and that Taft will have less than half that amount. He doesn't think there is any chance of making a deal with either Warren or Stassen before the convention to get their delegates, but it doesn't matter. Stassen has been double-crossing the Eisenhower movement all along, and when he came back from Paris he implied that Eisenhower had told him he didn't want to run.

PARIS, *April 3, 1952*

THIS morning I talked with Eisenhower for about three-quarters of an hour in his office. I told him I was coming as Mr. Hyde, the newspaper reporter, rather than as Dr. Jekyll, the friend. The general seemed rather preoccupied and a little bit crotchety. The strain of his double role is clearly telling on him these days—I mean as SHAPE commander and as Republican candidate. Furthermore, his wrist is still bad, which means he cannot relax out on the golf course. It will certainly do him good when he can start getting exercise again. He looked a little bit puffy. When I came in, he was discussing with an aide how to prepare a roast beef to send to a friend in England. (Although it's frozen meat, it has to be at least slightly cooked in order to get by English customs.)

I told him I was going to ask him a pretty embarrassing question. When I had done so, he explained that he could not answer it—the question being, had he already submitted a request for relief?—because he did not want to embarrass the President in any way. He did not want this information to leak over here; the President could do with it as he desired. I have a pretty strong hunch the request has already been made.

He said that as a matter of fact the question of how to request relief was very interesting because there was no precedent. "Administratively and by citizenship I am an American. But operationally I am responsible to fourteen Allies. That raises the question of to whom I should apply for relief."

Eisenhower would not recommend a successor personally unless he was asked to do so. However, he is prepared to report his opinions of what others think on this subject.

PARIS, *April 7, 1952*

I had lunch today with Bob Thayer (CIA station chief). He told me he has strongly recommended to Washington that there should be no more flapdoodle about listing the head of the CIA in each country under a phony title. Bob at present is supposed to be liaison officer between the embassy and SHAPE. He thinks it would be far better to have his real job known open and aboveboard. It would have the advantage that people wanting to pass on information would know to whom they should go.

Incidentally, Bob, who was in naval intelligence during the war, claims it was as a result of Stassen's advice that Admiral Halsey made a mistake during the battle of the Leyte Gulf and chased a Japanese fleet north seeking "glory" rather than making a proper kill. He thinks this should be known more generally during this political campaign. Of course, Bob is strongly pro-Eisenhower, politically speaking. He has only one worry and that is that Eisenhower may not be a completely good judge on civilian appointments.

PARIS, *April 18, 1952*

THIS morning Walter Lippmann came in for a chat. He said Dunn had expressed great alarm to him about the Trieste situation and thought it was a very serious crisis. I told Lippmann I was convinced both the Jugoslavs and Italians were happy to have the British and the Americans stay on in there but could not admit this for national political reasons.

He also said that two days ago, Norstad assured him that Gruenther would succeed Eisenhower despite all the newspaper articles backing Ridgway. Lippmann was worried about the vague and foggy way Eisenhower's mind worked when discussing European problems.

BERNE, *April 22, 1952*

TODAY I had an extremely interesting talk with Alfred Zehnder, head of the political division of the Swiss foreign office. Switzerland is against the Schuman Plan because it doesn't like integration of large communities. It wants to stay out of them. Furthermore, Switzerland as a coal and steel importer doesn't want to see established what would be in effect an international cartel.

Intellectually Swiss neutrality dates back to the days of Nikolaus von der Flue who, in 1481, warned the early cantons not to mix up in foreign quarrels or ally themselves with foreign powers. During the Thirty Years War (1618–1648) the Swiss remained neutral. Those were religious wars, and Switzerland had to stay out in order to survive because her population was 60 per cent Protestant and 40 per cent Catholic.

Switzerland has a customs union with Liechtenstein, and Swiss economic laws apply there. Switzerland represents Liechtenstein in foreign affairs but has no commitment to defend that country. In 1920, the Austrian province of Vorarlberg voted to join Switzerland, but the Berne Council of Ministers decided to reject this. Above all, the Swiss didn't want to change the present balance of Protestants versus Catholics and German versus French- and Italian-speaking elements.

Zehnder said, discussing the role of a neutral state, that the Swedes and some of the Arab states had asked the Swiss to explain their technique of neutrality. It is not a policy of equilibrium between power blocs. The Swiss follow a hardheaded policy of their own. If they give a credit to France, it doesn't mean they are also going to give a credit to Czechoslovakia. If they ban exports of strategic materials to the East, it doesn't mean they will also do so to the West. Zehnder said Switzerland acts in its own interests and according to the way it judges the situation at the moment. Thus, the Swiss joined the Marshall Plan despite Russian protests that this was not neutral. Switzerland would be prepared to join a bloc during a war if it thought the situation demanded such. But it believes in keeping its hand free during peacetime.

He thought it would be a fine idea to form a neutral bloc of truly neutral states, but the trouble was you couldn't find the others. They would not have to be geographically contiguous but philosophically harmonious. Switzerland won't join the United Nations because that means accepting sanctions. The Swiss have renounced war as an instrument of policy, but they are prepared to defend themselves. Zehnder said that, on the contrary, the French have not renounced war but won't fight to defend themselves— have to be protected.

Afterwards I saw Colonel Hans Bracher, director of the military administration of the military department of the government. He outlined the fundamentals of the Swiss military system to me. The fundamental requirement is a very swift mobilization. Since 1900 a new system of recruiting and training has grown up. Infantry units are developed in geographic regions all over the country so that every reservist when called up can reach his mobilization point by foot or bicycle rapidly. The soldier must be equipped as speedily as possible. For that reason he keeps his uniform, helmet, rifle, gas mask, musette pack and sixty to eighty rounds of ammunition at home. When called up, he reports to a unit depot where automatic weapons, mortars, machine guns, blankets and other supplies are kept.

According to Bracher, an army of 600,000 men can be called up within forty-eight hours and dispersed in units. That includes all able-bodied Swiss men between the ages of twenty and sixty. The system worked three times during World War II—when the Germans attacked Poland, when they invaded France and the Low Countries, and on D-Day.

As a neutral state with extensive frontiers, Switzerland found it necessary to have as many men under arms as possible. Six hundred thousand men was a large figure for a nation with less than 4,500,000 population. To this total must be added 100,000 local guards and 100,000 civil air defense.

Although there are three hundred full colonels in Switzerland, there is no general. A full colonel is elected general whenever a war starts in Europe and made commander of the army.

During the last two days I have been visiting Swiss military installations. I spent most of one day at Dübendorf airport, north of Zurich, and the better part of another day in the vicinity of Solothurn where a militia regiment was having its refresher course. Incidentally, Solothurn is a lovely old town which used to provide the best mercenary soldiers in Europe and, therefore, at one time had a French embassy there to pick up good fighting men.

At Solothurn I watched infantry units scramble around declivities. They are certainly a sturdy-looking lot—farmers, lawyers, accountants, mechanics and two regular officers. The colonel remarked that his chauffeur, an industrialist during forty-nine weeks of the year when he is not on military duty, earns ten times as much as his commander. The exercises were largely taken up with practicing with a new Swiss bazooka and a new heavy machine gun, just issued to the army, with a firing rate of a thousand rounds per minute. A signals company staged a maneuver communicating over the radio entirely in English.

Afterwards, with much satisfaction, an officer remarked: "You can see we might just as well be in SHAPE." Another added, "Even if we are not, Eisenhower can certainly figure in his plans that Switzerland will be well defended." A third produced a tiny American flag. He lifted a glass of burning *kirschwasser*. "To democracy," he said, and drank it.

MUNICH, *April 28, 1952*

I talked with a group of Czech refugees. They contended that the recent rather minor and not very widely publicized trials in Czechoslovakia are probably a preparation for the big trials of Slansky, Clementis and others. However, there is a difference of opinion even among the *émigré* Czechs on this. Everybody admits that Slansky has a very strong personality and it will take a very long time to break him down. They believe that Clementis was prepared for public trial even last year and had been carefully nourished and barbered for a public appearance. He then reneged and they have been working on him all over again. The general impression is that these people will not be broken down in time to hold any publicized trial before this autumn.

PARIS, *May 2, 1952*

I spent yesterday from 4 P.M. until midnight at Gruenther's, playing bridge with him and Eisenhower. Bill Robinson was the fourth. Also there were Mamie, Grace Gruenther, Marina, General and Mrs. Snyder, Mrs. Moore (Mrs. Eisenhower's sister) and Captain René Chesnais, Gruenther's French aide. It is somewhat dreary to play bridge almost eight solid hours. I played my usual exceptionally bad game which I always produce for that distinguished company, incurring a couple of bawlings out from the two generals when they were inflicted with me as their partner.

Eisenhower was tired and pale and a bit crotchety. Around midnight we were sitting around waiting for the ladies to finish their canasta and he asked Snyder (his doctor) for some more of that "cold medicine." He complained that his chest was still stopped up, but Snyder told him he would feel that way for some time. Eisenhower said he was getting tired "seeing all these people" and traveling around. He said he could rest all right on airplanes, but he finds he is not getting any work done and sometimes comes into his office and discovers papers he saw there three weeks ago. He was going to Germany today to have dinner with Adenauer. At one moment during the bridge game he said, "God damn it, I've got to go up and see the Dutchman tomorrow," and I thought he was referring to The Hague.

Before dinner we had drinks and he had three stiff highballs instead of his usual ration of two. As a result, he got a bit tight and was singing quite merrily and somewhat off key. At one point the group sang "Auld Lang

Syne" and Ike was rather emotional and recalled with some sadness that he would be gone in a month. It was Marina's birthday, so Grace produced a cake with candles and everybody kissed her.

I'm fascinated by the joy Snyder gets out of these evenings of relaxation in which he does nothing but kibitz at the bridge game or read newspapers or books. He told me that from World War I until 1936 he worked an average of seventeen hours a day as a surgeon and rarely had an uninterrupted night's sleep. Despite this he looks exceptionally fit and is a remarkably handsome and even-tempered man. He is very interested in horses and loves to go to the races.

Ike said the review and march-past of American troops in Frankfurt on April 30 were the finest he had ever seen and he was exceptionally impressed. When we were sitting around chatting afterwards, Gruenther brought up the subject of our extra edition on April 12 when Eisenhower had a press conference at 10 A.M. and we held the presses and had it in that same morning's paper. I told Eisenhower I was disappointed because he didn't say very much and that we would really have caught the *Herald Tribune* with its pants down if he had gotten up and announced he was giving up his American citizenship and was becoming a Swiss. "Not a Swiss," he replied with a chuckle, "but maybe a Spaniard."

The generals both donned civilian jackets—Eisenhower's being brought over from his house next door by Moaney, his sergeant and valet. When he left, he would have been a rare pictorial shot with his general's hat and pants on and an old tweed jacket. Chesnais, incidentally, took several photos of the group. The general was fascinated by a little German camera the size of a cigarette lighter that Chesnais wears on a chain in his pocket now and that he says takes good pictures. Incidentally, Ike told me that the pond outside his house still has plenty of trout in it but they are very wise now and hard to catch.

We kidded him about the Massachusetts primary vote in which he won a smashing victory, but he didn't bite, just grinned and kept on playing cards. On the whole he gave me the impression of showing the nervous strain he has been under during the last couple of months. He was pale, a little bit drawn, a little bit crochety and rather tired-looking. His few drinks hit him harder than I have ever seen but did not seem to really relax him. The case of grippe he had a couple of weeks ago is probably as responsible as anything for his fatigue. He looked a bit thicker around the middle. He likes to eat a good solid dinner and was having a grand time wandering around gnawing a bone from the roast lamb Grace produced.

PARIS, *May 2, 1952*

THIS morning I had a long talk with Pug (General, Lord) Ismay, who is the first permanent secretary general of NATO. He was rather apologetic about his offices in the Palais de Chaillot, which, I must say, are not very comfortable. They hope to have something better before a year has expired but it is going to be pretty difficult because of finances.

Ismay is a cozy, informal fellow, a large man about sixty-five, with an affable manner. We talked at length about the selection of Ridgway to succeed Eisenhower. The way it worked was this. Ismay was formally notified by NATO's Standing Group when the latter received Ike's letter requesting relief. He then advised the fourteen governments. He talked to each permanent representative briefly and ascertained that they all wanted an American. Then a meeting was held and President Truman was formally asked to nominate an American general. Fifty-seven minutes later— after Draper had talked with Washington—Ridgway's name came through. Most of the member countries had already instructed their delegates to accept any man put forward by the United States. Truman never submitted any names for consideration by the NATO countries. However, the British and French and possibly some others had made informal inquiries and ascertained ahead of time that Ridgway would be named.

The French insisted vigorously to Ismay that Gruenther should remain at SHAPE. He asked whether they meant as commander-in-chief or as chief of staff and they said they would be content either way as long as he was there. The British war office was delighted with Ridgway. They wanted a man with command experience because, as Ismay says, the war office is still dominated by "stuffed shirts" who emphasize the need of command experience. To Ismay's own mind, this is quite unnecessary for such a job. Naturally a divisional commander should have had command experience, but not the leader of an Allied coalition. If such had been the case, Eisenhower never would have commanded "Torch." The British were very pleased with the selection. Eisenhower himself told Ismay some time before the selection was made that he thought an ideal team would be Ridgway and Gruenther.

PARIS, *May 3, 1952*

THIS evening I had a couple of drinks with Foster Dulles, who is very likely to be Secretary of State if Eisenhower wins the next election. He told me he has not yet announced whom he will support for the Republican candidacy. He wishes to reserve his position in order to make some speeches on policy with a free hand, not implicating any particular faction of American political opinion. Afterwards he will announce his support of Eisenhower. However, he apparently has gone through a considerable analysis, and I gather he did not in any sense think it was an open-and-shut case against Taft.

Dulles reveals himself as even more conservative than I had thought him. Nevertheless, he said he considered Taft too intellectually arrogant.

He added: "He thinks he knows all the answers." Dulles said he had had a good talk with Eisenhower today. In the past, he feared Eisenhower stressed Europe too much in his thinking and did not consider the whole world. Dulles poses as rather an expert on Asia now, as a result of his few months' experience negotiating the Japanese treaty. He said he thought Eisenhower was engrossed in Europe, that he was developing a policy somewhat like Hoover's.

Dulles is making an important policy speech on Monday. He will discuss colonialism and Indochina. He explained to me his policy, which he says advocates warning the Communist bloc that we will not necessarily reply to aggression at whatever point it occurs, but will hit back where and when we desire. He has discussed this point at length with Admiral Radford. He emphasized the need of preparing to strike back at points where a blow is not expected. In the case of China we might bomb and use naval action against ports and islands. But never again can we use American troops on the Asiatic mainland. He said he talked to Eisenhower for about five hours using a globe to discuss specific geographic policies. He found Ike's answers "satisfactory."

Dulles said Dewey now wants to go back to private life. He needs money desperately because all he has is a fairly modest farm that is barely on a self-paying basis. Dewey has no capital savings. He can get a big salary as a lawyer, but he can't save much of this because of taxes. A lawyer doesn't get any expense account perquisite like a businessman. Dulles said that in the plane coming over, General Clay told him that in the Continental Can Company expense accounts had gone up 300 per cent during the last two or three years as more and more use of perquisites is made.

Dulles thought American taxes have surpassed the level of logic. The government would take in more if individual taxes were lower. He said the budget was now too high. The military budget could easily be reduced. There are not enough competent people in the United States to know how to disburse $60 billion a year for defenses. There is uncoordinated defense planning in Washington. No branch of the service knows how to plan for which kind of a war.

PARIS, *May 4, 1952*

LUCIUS Clay complained that Mrs. Eisenhower's friends airmail her all the dirty pamphlets attacking her and the general, causing her considerable distress. It is a pretty filthy campaign. She is labeled a dipsomaniac. He is supposed to be so ill that he couldn't handle the job. Some pamphlets call him a Jew. Others say he was baptized a Catholic by the Pope. Still others say he is a Soviet agent. Clarence Brown, Number Two man in the Taft machine, told the Women's National Press Club in Washington that there was "no breath of scandal" attached to the name of his candidate, Taft, by implication saying that there was in connection with Eisenhower.

Clay said Taft had virtually promised Dulles the secretaryship of state if Dulles would support him. It was at Clay's initiative that Dulles came over here to meet Eisenhower because Clay thought it would be good for the two men to get to know each other, and that Dulles was the obvious candidate for that position if Eisenhower won. Dulles is now an expert on foreign policy and had been devoting all his time to study. He hoped Eisenhower and Dulles would be seeing each other often from now on.

Clay said Harriman was dead serious now about his candidacy for the Democratic nomination. "He has been bitten by the bug." Clay thought he would have several eastern delegations. Nevertheless, he didn't think Harriman stood a chance for the nomination. He thought things would work out with Kefauver against Eisenhower or Stevenson against Taft. None of the best runners on the Democratic side wanted to oppose Ike.

I asked Clay how Ridgway happened to get the nomination to succeed Eisenhower. He said the most important reason was that the State Department wanted Ridgway out of Tokyo when the peace treaty was ratified and the new American ambassador arrived. Nevertheless, Clay thought there was another important factor in making the decision. Truman had been advised by the politicians to oppose Gruenther because he was Eisenhower's man and the politicians didn't want any successor over here to redound to his credit. Bradley's faction, recognizing that Bradley couldn't get the job, wanted somebody who wasn't Eisenhower's candidate.

PARIS, *May 5, 1952*

MAURICE Schumann invited me for lunch at the Quai d'Orsay given in honor of Foster Dulles. I was able to eavesdrop on the conversation, sitting, as I was, across the table from the guest of honor. Schumann speaks excellent English but made the mistake of saying to Dulles that, of course, the latter spoke French. Dulles smugly agreed and from there on a criss-cross of misunderstanding developed with conversations like: "Do you think German rearmament is a good thing?" being answered with observations such as "I am sorry she isn't here." I was sitting next to André Maurois who was equally fascinated.

PARIS, *May 5, 1952*

LUNCH with Randolph Churchill. Randolph is now working on a television program for his sister, Sarah, which seems to be a pretty good bet. The idea is to do movie recordings of interviews with well-known statesmen and world leaders. He has already got Tito, De Gasperi, and Togliatti.

Randolph told me about the only time he met Stalin. It was at his father's birthday party during the Teheran Conference, sitting at the bottom of the table between General Marshall and Admiral King. Roosevelt mixed the cocktails and Randolph handed them around. He offered one to Pavlov, Stalin's interpreter. Stalin heard the English conversation between Churchill and Pavlov and asked Pavlov what had been said. Pavlov replied that Mr. Churchill had offered him a drink. Stalin then asked if he was going to take it. Pavlov interpreted this back to Churchill. Churchill asked him if he would have it. Stalin demanded a translation. The upshot was Stalin said Pavlov could have the cocktail if he was pressed. Churchill pressed him. Pavlov took the cocktail, sipped one sip and put it down very gingerly. He was taking no risk of becoming plastered by foreign drinks in front of his boss.

PARIS, *May 6, 1952*

INTERESTING talk with Dulles this afternoon. I had written that he would probably be Eisenhower's Secretary of State. He said this would be embarrassing at the moment. I agreed to hold it up in exchange for a promise of an interview when he gets in. He said he isn't nearly so sure now as he had been in previous years that he wanted to be Secretary of State. It had always been an ambition ever since he was a little boy. It was sort of a family tradition because of his relatives, Lansing and John Foster. However, a Secretary of State had to be certain the President had the same views on foreign policy as he himself. Under the Constitution the President makes foreign policy. Therefore he was still waiting to get some answers to questions he had left with Eisenhower. He is seeing the general tomorrow morning and will get those answers. I am having lunch with Dulles tomorrow, so I ought to get the upshot of it all.

Dulles also feels the Secretary of State nowadays doesn't have nearly enough time to really create policy. He is tied up on administration and he is always going up to Congressional committees. Acheson spends far too much of his time on Capitol Hill. Of course that may be Acheson's fault, and anyway Acheson seems to enjoy the badinage of Congressional committees.

Dulles said he did not exclude Dewey from the job. I had written that Dewey wanted to go back to private life and make some money. He thought Dewey still might change his mind, although Dewey has always told him he would like to see Dulles Secretary of State. Dulles then said, of course Dewey did not know anything about foreign affairs "except what he learned from me." He got into trouble when he spoke out on his own. By and large I'm convinced Dulles very much wants the job. He said his support would not really help Eisenhower much since most of the people who were for Dulles were also for Eisenhower. Had he supported Taft, it would have been an enormous asset for Taft and might even have swayed the balance. I am confident Dulles will come out for Eisenhower as soon as Herbert Brownell or the Eisenhower campaign managers advise him to.

Dulles was very critical about American policy, and I find it rather strange that his criticisms—coming from a staunch Republican—rather parallel those I have been feeling recently, and I consider myself a fairly leftish Democrat. He was very disturbed about the German situation and shocked by the fact that we have no alternative policy to the inclusion of Germany in the Western rearmament scheme. We have made the mistake of putting integration of Western Germany with Western Europe ahead of unification of Germany. The Germans will never take this. In Korea the South Koreans will give up the fight immediately if they lose faith in our determination to unify the country. Yet we depend upon holding that line with 250,000 South Korean troops. We must commit ourselves to unifying Korea and likewise to unifying Germany.

Incidentally, Dulles said he had been informed here that we could have a revolution in Czechoslovakia any day we wanted, but he said, "What on earth could we do with it under present circumstances?" He said our policy must not be one of containment, but one of preparation to retaliate against aggression by striking the aggressor where and when it suits us, rather than holding any point of the perimeter he attacks.

He said the only solid way of making policy in Europe would be to make Western Europe so prosperous and powerful that Germany would normally be desirous of joining it and attracted to it. We must recognize the need for German markets in places like Poland, Czechoslovakia and the Balkans. Likewise, we must recognize the need of some settlement someday in China because otherwise we can never hold Indochina, Korea or Japan. Their livelihood depends upon trade with China. Our policy has been maladroit and insufficiently farsighted.

PARIS, *May 6, 1952*

GRUENTHER called up late in the afternoon with a problem that was, namely, what would be the best date for Eisenhower to hand over to Ridgway, in terms of public opinion. The present plan is that the ceremony should take place on the morning of Saturday, May 31. However, June 1 is a Sunday, and June 2 (a Monday) is a holiday in England and many other European countries. Gruenther wanted to know if there wouldn't be a pretty strong reaction by reporters having to come out on Saturday morning and spoiling their long weekend. I said I didn't think that was very important, but it was far more important that most European daily papers including those in England, did not print Sunday editions. With June 2 being a holiday, there also would not be Monday papers. I suggested the ceremony should take place on Friday, May 30, which would allow the daily papers to have it on Saturday and the Sunday papers to have it on

Sunday. He said he understood that, but then there was a difficulty with the principal actor—meaning Eisenhower. He would have to get out right away. I said, why doesn't he spend the weekend in Iceland, which is a pleasant place where he can eat a lot of herring. Gruenther agreed that this might be a very agreeable experience, but he thought the principal party might not enjoy it. I recommended that the turnover should take place on Friday, May 30; and that Eisenhower should arrive in Washington on Saturday, May 31. Then all the American reporters could have it for their Sunday papers and all the European reporters could have it for their Saturday and Sunday papers. It now remains to be seen what will happen.

PARIS, *May 9, 1952*

LUNCH with Bill Deakin. He told me a rather pathetic story about Randolph Churchill. Several years ago when he (Bill) first became closely associated with old man Churchill he was staying at the house. Very late one night, Randolph came into his room, a bit stewed, and sat down for a chat. All he said was, "Under a great tree nothing can grow." Bill figures that despite Randolph's tremendous affection for his father and his immense admiration, he, at the same time, has subconsciously what amounts to a resentment. He has always been in the shadow, and it represents a challenge he can never meet. Winston Churchill used to admire Randolph greatly in an amused way because when Randolph was a very young man he was extraordinarily handsome and had a great success with the ladies. For example, the two of them were staying at San Simeon, Hearst's California home, once when Randolph sneaked out late at night with a young girl guest, and came tottering back rather noisily at five o'clock in the morning. Winston later on that morning remonstrated in a somewhat amused, paternal fashion: "Randolph, don't you think you have been violating the rules of hospitality?"

PARIS, *May 9, 1952*

LAST night I had dinner with Gruenther and Alphand, among others. Gruenther said the Russian effort in Korea is extremely large. It is costing them plenty although they are getting a lot of training and apparently are rotating a great many of their own pilots, giving them combat experience in MIGs. This is one reason why they are very careful not to lose fighters except in their own territory. Of course, we could trap them there. Whenever they establish a forward airfield, we bomb the hell out of it, forcing them to keep their main bases up around China. If we let them establish a few forward bases, we could probably suck a few MIGs into combat over our lines. The Russians have about nine hundred jets available there and can put a hell of a lot of them into the air. The most we can ever put in the

air at any one time is eighty, and even that represents an extensive effort on
our part.

I asked Alphand how we could reconcile the French hold on the Saar
with the so-called "equality" in which Germany was being admitted to the
Western family of nations. He said, "We are negotiating a treaty for the
European Defense Community. We are not negotiating about the Saar."
That attitude doesn't lead to any solution.

PARIS, *May 12, 1952*

LUNCH with Eisenhower today and then we played golf out at Morfontaine. The poor fellow played exceptionally badly and was sore as a boil
about it. He kept saying, "You'd think I'd never seen a golf course." He
worries about what he is doing with his hands and his hips and his head,
and is pleased as punch when suddenly he gets a good shot. I only wish the
stakes were higher at golf and lower at bridge. We play for 100 francs a
hole and I give him a few strokes.

Afterwards in the locker room he was saying rather regretfully, "Anybody is a damn fool if he actually seeks to be President. You give up four
of the very best years of your life. Lord knows it's a sacrifice. Some people
think there's a lot of power and glory attached to the job. On the contrary,
the very workings of a democratic system see to it that the job has very
little power."

While we were at lunch, he said it was odd that his boyhood friend
Larsen had gotten the most important fact wrong in an article he wrote
recently for the *Saturday Evening Post,* trying to tell the "final and true"
story of Eisenhower's boyhood. That had to do with an injury he received
on his leg. He scraped it, and then it got infected. The doctors wanted to
amputate it, but he wouldn't let them do it. He said, "My brother and I
were brought up to be athletes. We loved games and were good at them.
My brother understood how I felt—losing a leg was like being murdered."
He said that, as a matter of fact, he missed the whole rest of the year of
school after his injury—despite Larsen's assertion that he was back at
school a day or two later. He said, "By God, Larsen should remember that
because, as I recall, that's the year I worked for his father."

Later on, we started talking about the article printed in *Le Monde* last
week, contending the Fechteler had made a secret report to the National
Security Council. This allegedly had been intercepted by the British Intelligence service a few days later—still in January. In February a French
newsletter, called *Information et Conjecture,* printed this alleged report. *Le
Monde* put it out last week. In a nutshell it says that war with Russia is
inevitable by 1960, that Europe can't be held, that fifty-two western divisions could be overrun in three days by the Russians, that England could
be isolated from Scotland by a Soviet attack of 150,000 paratroopers, that

as long as the West holds the Mediterranean including Gibraltar, Malta and the Dardanelles, it can mount a counterattack and defeat Russia, and that, therefore, America should ally itself with the Arab states and not worry too much about Europe.

Eisenhower said he hadn't read the account in *Le Monde* but it sounded awfully cockeyed to him. He admitted that the Navy has some pretty weird ideas about the Middle East and said Fechteler wasn't very endowed with brains. He pointed out that at the time referred to, January, 1952, Fechteler was still commanding in the Atlantic. He said it was ludicrous to talk about holding the Dardanelles, Malta and Gibraltar without holding Europe. Gibraltar had no value unless a good bit of the Spanish hinterland was defended, in which case it was admittedly a strong point. Malta could not be held without part of Italy. Obviously the Dardanelles couldn't be held if Europe fell. It was ludicrous to talk of a Russian attack upon England of 150,000 paratroopers. "Where would they get the planes to drop them and supply them?" he asked. I asked him how many men he had at Nijmegen and Arnhem, and he estimated between 20,000 and 30,000 pointing out that this was a major airborne effort. He also scoffed at the idea that such an operation might have as its goal the separation of England from Scotland. He didn't pretend to know whether it was a phony or not as far as the document went. I get the impression that if there was any doubt in his mind, it was because of his opinion of Fechteler's stupidity. He remarked that if a document of the National Security Council could be picked up like that, it was a "fine state of affairs.

By the way, I gave my girl caddy a ride back from the golf club to the little village of Thiers where she lives. She said she thought the general didn't look very well and that his face had become quite drawn since last year. Undoubtedly this is true. That is to say, he has aged visibly during the past twelve months. However, he surely doesn't look any older than his age and possibly a bit younger, and is in pretty vigorous shape despite all the dirty political gossip in America trying to spread the rumor that he is in seriously bad health. I noticed in the locker room that he is still a sturdily built man with squarely set shoulders, although he has put on a few pounds about the middle since a year ago. He ate with particular restraint today. Although I had beer, he stuck to a glass of water, and all he wanted to drink after the game was mineral water (Evian).

PARIS, *May 20, 1952*

LUNCHED today with Ismay. He had one amusing tale about Churchill. Just before the Normandy invasion Churchill was doing his best to get himself accommodation on the first wave going over to France, and nobody was cooperating with the old man. Ismay wandered into Churchill's office one day and found him talking with Admiral Ramsay (who was killed later), who was handling the British naval side. Churchill was obviously most displeased to see Ismay enter the room. Finally he had to explain to Ismay in front of Ramsay that he was arranging to get aboard a destroyer going in on D-Day. Ismay then voiced the opinion that this was a rather unseemly prospect because the Prime Minister might be needed to participate in vital and urgent decisions. At that point Churchill muttered out of the corner of his mouth, "Shut up, you damn fool. I promise you if I get aboard, I'll find a place for you too."

PARIS, *May 21, 1952*

I spent all day and evening yesterday with Eisenhower. We started off at 9 A.M. and I left at 11:30 P.M. In the morning I played golf with him and General Ted Curtis, once Tooey Spaatz's chief of staff and now one of the big wheels in Eastman Kodak, and General Fred Anderson, one of the three American NATO ambassadors over here. It was a fine day and Ike played fairly well so he was in excellent spirits. He still has a trick knee which goes out every so often and stems from a football injury he had at West Point, but he said, "Except for my knee, I never felt better in my life." He was grinning and sun-tanned, tranquil and in good spirits.

We stayed for lunch in his dining room at SHAPE, and he was as excited as a kid when ripe cherries were served for dessert. He said, "By golly, these are the first cherries I've ever had in Europe." He was pleased to let his diet go by the boards a bit on the grounds that he had been out exercising. He remarked that at least every year he gets his weight down to 170 pounds or less. He does this by betting more money than he can afford to lose that he will do so, and then he is stuck with it and has to comply. He said that during his term over here as SHAPE commander—especially while he was wandering around on farewell tours—he got up above 180. He said, "After all, when you go to some of these countries and you have to attend formal luncheons and dinners and you don't speak the language, all you can do is show an exceptional interest in your food and limit conversation that way."

Starting at four o'clock in the afternoon, Curtis and I played bridge over at the Gruenthers with Al and Eisenhower. I am glad to report to myself that I cleaned them out last night, finishing up with a grand slam which Ted and I made against the two generals.

I was amused to note that when they served drinks before dinner, General Snyder, who, as usual, was amiably and quietly kibitzing, saw to it that Eisenhower's were sufficiently strong. In fact, he came around with a bottle of whisky at one point and said, "Ike, I don't think your drink is strong enough so I'm going to pour some more in it." Quite obviously Snyder is trying to keep the general completely relaxed as part of this last round in Europe and in preparation for the strain of the political campaign. In fact,

Snyder told me, "I'm resting him up now and I think he will be in good shape." As a result of this medical treatment, Eisenhower again got a little bit high before dinner, but in a gay and pleasant mood. I noticed that when he gets a tiny bit tight, he likes to hum or sing songs. I may add neither his voice nor his sense of tune is very good.

In addition to the Curtises and the Snyders, the only other people present were Senator Fred A. Seaton, Republican of Nebraska, and his wife. Al Gruenther, who comes from Nebraska, muttered to us as the Senator was making his way around being introduced that he supports Eisenhower. The Senator and his wife are young and rather pleasant. Apparently he owns several newspapers in Nebraska. He told me that he had come to Europe in order to adopt two German children. He had a seven-year-old daughter who died a few years ago, and after that he adopted two children; now he wants two more and thinks this is a good opportunity to give a chance to a couple of German youngsters. He has already picked them out but hasn't seen them yet. He said it is going to be rather curious for him and his wife when they take them back because they don't speak any German. Poor Seaton had very little to do except to talk to Snyder and such of the women as were not playing canasta, because we were all tied up in our bridge game.

Nothing much of interest was said during the day, and I can record only that it was pleasant and relaxing for all concerned. When we went back to Ike's office after golf and sat around having a sherry, he spent about ten minutes at his desk signing various papers and letters. At one point he looked up and remarked, "You know, it's a damn good thing not to want anything. When people tell me that Taft is going to have so many delegates from such-and-such a state, I simply don't care." I am still convinced as I always have been that he does *not* want to be President and is merely running as a public service.

As Snyder was sitting quietly reading beside the bridge players, he suddenly began to read aloud from an American history book some of the savage press attacks on Washington at the time he concluded his first term. The implication was very clear. Ike just grunted.

At lunch we had a long discussion about such amiable subjects as shooting and fishing. Eisenhower complained that he can't shoot ducks. He says he's a pretty good quail shot and has done all right against other birds such as turkeys. "But by golly, for the life of me I can't hit a duck." He recalled that although King George VI had been known as a drinker, he was one of the finest wing shots in England and was especially good at high pheasant shooting.

When we went over to the Gruenthers, Ike boasted with considerable pride about the way the four of us had played the fifteenth hole today. We had two pars and two birdies. The first thing he said to his wife was, "Mamie, why don't you ask me how we played the fifteenth hole?" He was quite amused when he was told the Communists had been putting posters around in some of the villages near SHAPE saying in English, "We don't like Ike but we hate Ridgway."

I had lunch today with Ike and played golf with him and Fred Anderson and Jimmy Gault. We lunched out at SHAPE and ate some of the trout from Eisenhower's pond. They had to drain the pond and netted all the trout first. They are good-sized fish. He said they had become very hard to catch. They wouldn't take a fly. Then he and Moaney, his sergeant, caught a couple with pieces of liver as bait. They got one after chumming the water with bread.

When Eisenhower came back from his tour of visits this morning, he was wearing a light tan summer uniform. He complained that he had to treat it with the greatest of care because it was falling apart. "But," he added, "I only have to keep it going for twelve more days."

During lunch he asked Anderson what he had been doing in civilian life after quitting the Army in 1947, and Fred replied that he had been mixed up with various companies and also had done some wildcat oil gambling. The general said that some time ago a friend of his had let him in on a wildcatting operation when he had a little money and he thought he would take a fling. He bought a large interest in some previously barren acreage. Luck was with him, and they struck oil. He realized late last year that he was just going to have to be involved in politics, so he asked his colleagues to sell him out and to be sure that he got no more from his property than he had originally invested in it. This proved to be pretty difficult because it had made quite a lot of money. Nevertheless, he had to unload in order to be able to discuss oil questions freely.

The thing that interested me was that he said his bosom friend and Gettysburg, Pennsylvania, neighbor, George Allen, was the man who bought him out. I kind of suspect that Allen will insist, when Eisenhower finally winds up his political career, on returning the property to him. Incidentally, Eisenhower said, "By golly, when my children and grandchildren find out what I have been doing with the little money they might have inherited, they are sure going to cuss me."

He looked quite bad today, drawn and tired. He said when he woke up this morning he felt quite ill. As a matter of fact, he called in General Snyder after lunch and had him look at his throat. He quit golf after playing nine holes and went home to bed. It is extraordinary how he varies from day to day physically. Yesterday he was in tip-top shape and full of energy. Today he was overtired and looked at least as old as he is. His golf wasn't bad, but he was quiet and his mind seemed to be on other things. I wouldn't be surprised if he fell ill for a couple of days again. His attention seemed to be wandering and he admitted he wasn't feeling right.

Incidentally, Ike had more to say about how he keeps his weight down. The man he bets with every year is George Allen. Allen also has to lose a fixed amount, which is pretty difficult for him as he is an exceptionally fat man. Ike's theory is that every additional pound added to his frame means that more capillaries are spread around his system to feed the additional poundage, and this adds extra strain to his heart.

On the way to St. Germain, Jimmy Gault told me Eisenhower had been irked and hurt by Harry Butcher's book. Jimmy has nothing but contempt for Butcher and said he utilized his position deliberately to make money out of the war. He said he completely violated Eisenhower's confidence and, furthermore, summarized things inaccurately so as to put Eisenhower in an unfavorable light on many subjects. Jimmy admitted that Butcher was a charming and attractive fellow, but said he was not wholly reliable. During the last eighteen months of the war he, Jimmy, kept all really confidential material out of Butcher's reach. He said that since Butcher's book came out, Eisenhower has never once mentioned his name to Jimmy.

I asked Jimmy how he first got with Eisenhower. He said that after having a battalion in the desert in North Africa, he was assigned to Jock Whitney's staff. When King George visited North Africa as "Colonel Lyon," Jimmy was assigned to look after him (coming from the Grenadier Guards as he does, the regiment of which the King is colonel). After that job, Eisenhower asked him to join his staff, and he stayed with him until the war ended. They became very close personal friends.

PARIS, *May 25, 1952*

I hear that Winthrop Aldrich is going around telling people that if Eisenhower wins, he thinks he will have to accept a job himself in Washington to "keep Ike on the beam." That fatuity is calculated to do the general nothing but harm.

PARIS, *May 26, 1952*

LUNCH today with Billotte. He is livid with rage against de Gaulle and thinks de Gaulle has just about had it. Apparently when he came back from America, Billotte contacted de Gaulle and the general refused to see him. This, of course, irks him, particularly since he gave up his military career to join de Gaulle's political movement.

Furthermore, Billotte has been trying to get de Gaulle into contact with leading personalities of the West. When Selwyn Lloyd was over here, he asked Billotte to arrange for him to meet de Gaulle. Billotte saw the general about it. The general said, "Why did he apply to you? Why didn't he come directly to me?" Billotte replied that, after all, he knew Lloyd, and de Gaulle didn't. De Gaulle refused to receive him. Billotte was horrified and pointed out that this is the first time in six years that a British minister had sought out de Gaulle.

Again, when ceremonies were held in Paris mourning for the King of England, de Gaulle was invited. He inquired where his position would be in the church. When he found it was after President Auriol, he refused to go.

All this winter Billotte has been working with Tony Biddle to bring de Gaulle together with Eisenhower. Eisenhower once invited him for lunch at SHAPE headquarters, but de Gaulle refused to go, arguing that since this was France, Eisenhower should come to him. Billotte and Biddle tried to repair the damage and worked out the project that both generals should attend a dinner of the Order of Liberation. An invitation to attend was left with Biddle to present to Eisenhower at what he considered a propitious moment. The meeting took place. Among the others present were Juin and Thierry d'Argenlieu. Billotte had just come back from America but wasn't invited, which also made him furious. I asked him what happened. He said he doesn't know except that the next day de Gaulle made a speech violently attacking the European army, and two days later Eisenhower made one strongly supporting it.

PARIS, *May 27, 1952*

TODAY the six foreign ministers of the European Defense Community signed the EDC (European army) treaty, and Acheson and Eden, who were also present in the Clock Room at the Quai d'Orsay, signed the separate guarantees the English-speaking world is giving to that organization. The regular NATO representatives were also there to sign the cross-guarantees between the EDC and NATO. Since Ridgway arrived in town today, it was a particularly historic occasion. If the EDC is ever ratified, it will change European history; and it will probably change it just as much if it is not. In either event, if the Russians react, Ridgway is the man who is going to have to direct the fighting.

Adenauer sat stonily throughout the whole performance. His expression did not change except when Eden, who was in the neighboring chair, leaned across and made a wisecrack which caused a faint, Mona Lisa-type smile to flicker for a second on the German's face. It was odd to recall that Schuman, who was the principal figure at the ceremony, served in the German army during World War I.

Afterward, during a champagne celebration of the event, I talked with Adenauer, who said he considered the occasion a "brilliant success" for American policy. All through Western Germany everything can be made— once the treaty is ratified—on order from the European Community, except for atomic, bacteriological and chemical weapons, long-range guided missiles, heavy warships and military aircraft. Adenauer in a separate guarantee to the British and Americans promises that no civil aircraft will be made. The limitations are theoretically based on the assumption that Germany is an "exposed area" that might be overrun during a Russian attack. West of the Rhine the Germans will be permitted to make explosive and antiaircraft (short-range) guided missiles.

PARIS, *May 29, 1952*

I had lunch today with Lieutenant General Hans Speidel, former chief of staff for Field Marshal Erwin Rommel and one of the brightest generals in the German army. Speidel talked about World War II military operations. He was extremely amiable—so much so that when we parted company, he sent his regards to my wife—whom he has never met—and promised to bring me a bottle of the "best *kirsch*" from the Black Forest. Nowadays, in addition to his job as an EDC advisor and expert, he is professor of modern history at the University of Tübingen. Like Rommel, he is a Württemberger and they served in the same unit during World War I. The present course he is teaching stresses mutual defense efforts since the Holy Alliance of 1815.

Speidel is a schoolteacherish type of man. He has an intellectual face and wears glasses. He studied French, Latin and ancient Greek in university and says he still reads and writes both Latin and Greek. He reads and understands English but doesn't speak it much. We conversed in French. He was wearing a tweed jacket and gray pants and looked very little like a general.

He said the most important thing in Germany was to sell the youth on the necessity of defending their homes and families and defending the civilization to which they were accustomed. It is no longer a matter of national patriotism to defend the borders of a country which can be flown over by a jet plane in less than an hour. Something bigger is required. He thinks the young men understand this fairly well. They are violently against war and don't want to join any army, but they see no other choice. The only alternative would be to be occupied by Russia and sent off to Siberia without a fight. Speidel is not so optimistic about speedy EDC ratification, but he thinks it will be done in a matter of months. He says Schumacher is intellectually not as opposed to the project as he is emotionally because he has become so bitter against the Americans as a result of our inept treatment of him. Schumacher, incidentally, he says, is a very ill man, and Heusinger, who saw him a couple of weeks ago, warned Speidel that he is dying. Speidel keeps in regular contact with Schumacher and says he has great personal admiration for him although he disagrees with him.

He told me that during the Russian campaign he was first on the central front around Viazma, then took part in the Kharkov offensive in the early months of 1943, then commanded the northwest sector at Stalingrad. There he had Italian, Rumanian and Hungarian troops under him. He said the Rumanians, who came mostly from Transylvania, were good fighters but their officers were riddled with corruption. One general who had been in the Crimea with the Rumanians had sold all the food and material for his division, transporting it back to Rumania to make a black market profit. The Hungarian units with him were pretty bad but the Hungarians are good soldiers and, according to his information, the best satellite army the Russians have today is the Hungarian army. The northern Italians such as the Alpini were extremely good, but the southern Italians from around Naples were appallingly bad. One fault he noted throughout the Italian army was the big difference in privilege between officers, noncommissioned officers and enlisted men. This was true even among the good troops. He has talked with present-day Italian generals about this. He said the Neapolitans were pathetic and it was slaughter when they were involved in a battle. They had neither equipment, morale nor interest. They threw themselves into the snow and voluntarily died of frostbite.

He said the two best American generals were Patton and Bradley. The Germans never knew what they were going to do, and they handled their troops extremely well although Patton made a fool of himself in the public declarations he made. Montgomery, he thought, was a terrible general. You could always predict exactly what he would do, and you knew that he would rest and draw things together always after so many days of battle. He had only one maneuver—a left hook. He is a charming man but a lousy general, Speidel thinks. He thought Zhukov and Koniev were the best Soviet generals. Timoshenko and Budenny were awful.

Speidel said the Americans were better than the British on the attack, but the British were better on the defense and held fast more doggedly. He had no way of judging the French. In 1940 the Germans went through France much faster than he expected. He thought the campaign would last at least six months. When the French were reorganized and came back into the war in 1944, Juin's troops fought well, but they were mainly North African, so it is difficult to prove anything by that. Incidentally, he expressed a high regard for Juin. He said Rommel was a fine, clean-cut fellow, straight and honest and not a Nazi. Guderian was a brilliant military man and the best tank leader the Germans had—better even than Rommel, but politically he was a sap and a Nazi until almost the last minute.

PARIS, *May 30, 1952*

TODAY Ike held a farewell press conference and then turned over the SHAPE command to Ridgway. It was a moving ceremony. Ike looked worse

than I've ever seen him. He appears to be just about over his con-
junctivitis; General Snyder told me he more or less recovered from it last
night. Therefore he didn't have to wear dark glasses. But I wish he had.
You could see his eye was still bothering him with the result that it seemed
to draw up his face rather tightly. He looked pale and exceptionally tired.
Ridgway, on the other hand, is a hefty, healthy-looking fellow. He is only
fifty-seven but looks much younger, while Ike looked considerably more
than his sixty-one years. Mrs. Ridgway, who is in her thirties, attended the
ceremony: quite a babe.

Eisenhower is scheduled to go off tomorrow and arrive in Washington
late Sunday afternoon. He will get out of uniform Tuesday evening and
from then on will be a general on the inactive list. If he is nominated, he
will resign his commission.

PARIS, *June 5, 1952*

LUNCH today with Reuven Shiloah, who is passing through on his way
to the United States. Shiloah, who heads Israel's intelligence and who is
sort of a hatchet man for Ben Gurion, is now making an inspection of the
various Israeli diplomatic missions around the world. He is only forty-two
and is clearly one of the coming men. Incidentally, Shiloah (and for the
purposes of the index in this diary I must point out that his name used to
be Zaslani, and British MI-5 also had him listed as Raphael) told me that
Weizmann is in terribly bad shape now. He is conscious only about 20 percent of the time and is thoroughly lucid during those moments but is just
coming apart physically.

Shiloah told me he had had information from an "A-1 source—classified
according to conservative intelligence classifications"—that at a Cominform meeting in March instructions had been issued by Moscow to reduce the influence of Jews in the Communist Party throughout the world.
This information was received through a delegate at the meeting from one
of the Western European parties. He reported "in a document" (which
shows how efficiently the Israeli service works) that the instructions compared the influence of Israel (and the Jews) with that of the Vatican (and
the Roman Catholics). In other words, when it was pointed out in the
meeting that Israel was a small state and could do very little, it was
immediately recalled that the Vatican had no military forces but had vast
power.

PARIS, *June 6, 1952*

I had dinner last night with Hank Byroade, who is now assistant secretary of state in charge of Near Eastern affairs. He has just completed a tour
around his bailiwick from Morocco right across the Arab states to Israel

and up through Turkey, Greece and Admiral Carney's headquarters in Naples. Hank is very worried about the situation. He thinks we must force the British and French to modify their "colonial" policies sufficiently so that we will not blush to support them—which, in the end, we obviously now do. He thinks Israel is pretty well on the rocks. If there is even a slight depression in the United States, the country will go bust. The only way it can survive is by expanding, and the Arabs know this. Thus, ultimately, it means a new Middle Eastern War.

King Ibn Saud is now absolutely senile. Hank talked with him four times during his trips to Jidda and Riadh and couldn't really have one useful conversation because the old man's mind was wandering. The Aramco oil company is in a very difficult position. A group of Syrian and Palestine Arabs have gained the ear of the old man and are souping up anti-American sentiment. Hank foresees a big row between Saud and Feisal when their father dies.

He is worried about Morocco also. From what he was told, if that place blows up, it will make the present Tunisian situation look like nothing at all. We are up to the ears in Morocco, but we have not formulated any sensible policy there. The American businessmen down there are a bunch of carpetbaggers.

BONN, *June 9, 1952*

I had a long talk with Chancellor Adenauer in the Palais Schaumburg. He was extremely friendly and fairly forthright for such a careful, shrewd man. I must say he is remarkably well preserved and doesn't look anything like his seventy-odd years. He has a strangely wooden face that every now and then breaks into a restrained half-smile.

He discussed his policy towards the Oder–Neisse territory. He pointed out that the United States did not wish him to discuss that area at present on the grounds that it would stir a bad reaction in Poland. He thought that when future events had removed the tension now existing between Germany and Poland (I'm not quite sure what he means by "future events"), good relations must be created between a reunited Germany and Poland. The Russian danger would continue to exist. Poland has an innate anti-Russian feeling and therefore would want to tie up with the West. We should regard Poland eventually as the easternmost bastion of the Western world. The Oder–Neisse territories might some day be placed under a condominium between Poland and Germany. Otherwise they might be put under the United Nations in the form of a trusteeship, presumably awarded to Germany.

Personally, I can see in this type of thinking a distinct desire by Adenauer to employ NATO, EDC and even UN to restore German territories to Germany under the guise of building a stronger Western "Europe." I think this is the key to his present foreign policy, and I don't believe our government realizes it.

At the end of our talk, Adenauer asked me to answer a few questions for him on American election prospects. Of course I knew nothing. He expressed the hope that either Eisenhower or a Democrat would be elected on the grounds that—according to his information—they would both favor continued strong aid to Europe. He feared the election of Taft would mean either a return of American isolationism or an "Asia first" policy.

BERLIN, *June 12, 1952*

TALK today with Ernst Reuter, the mayor of West Berlin, in his dark, paneled and rather ugly office. Reuter was as nice as ever, but of all the times I have seen him this was the least interesting.

He started off by saying, apropos of the European Army treaty: "I am not a child. Obviously, from these papers you hope to get twelve divisions. That is all they mean."

Reuter said Stalin was very cautious and wants to get everything but has a great respect for power. He fears war. Everyone is the prisoner of his own ideology. Stalin is deeply convinced of the decline and fall of monopoly capitalism. He sees divisions in France, weakness in Britain, and the elections with their disputes in the United States. Therefore he figures, "Why have a war?"

He thought the Russians, no matter what they said, could not go very far towards building up an East German army because it would be too untrustworthy. They *will* try when West Germany forms its divisions but will take no drastic moves until then. Ninety per cent of the East Germans are opposed to the regime, and any units they form would be unreliable.

The West Germans did not want to fight but would be prepared to fight against Russia. The East Germans don't want to fight and would feel that they would have to fight against other Germans. As a result, young people are now fleeing East Germany in order to avoid military service under the Russians.

Incidentally, Reuter frequently showed an anti-French bias. He particularly dislikes François-Poncet and says the latter hates all Germans, seeing in them the evil that "exists within himself."

PARIS, *June 23, 1952*

SAW Al Gruenther and Jimmy Gault this afternoon, in that order. Both—and God knows they are fond of the man—are worried, not only about Ike's situation and chances of getting the nomination, but about what he has been saying and what advice he has been getting. Gruenther asked me what I thought would be the effect upon his historical stature if he fails to obtain the nomination. I said that undoubtedly for a year or so it would have an adverse effect, but that afterwards I thought Eisenhower would really be doing what he had always wanted to do, namely, be a retired figure always available for consultation or service as a nonpolitical elder statesman. I thought he would have many years in which to give further nonpolitical service, and that ultimately his stature would not be affected historically—regardless of an immediate drop—if he loses the nomination.

Gruenther was frankly worried about who was giving him advice now. For example, he said, "I know damn well it isn't like Ike to come out and say he wants a $40 billion budget reduction." Again, he remarked that the general surely could not have meant what he said when advocating the retirement of all the top State Department people. Gruenther recalled that Eisenhower depended heavily upon people like David Bruce, Chip Bohlen and George Kennan and had the highest regard for them.

Gruenther praised Ridgway as a man of incredible physical and mental energy. He said there were no plans at present to change either the staff or any of the commands in SHAPE. I can't help feeling when I talk to Gruenther on such subjects that he is a remarkably good sport and working with exceptional loyalty to assist a man who holds the job which I think rightfully should be Al's.

In Washington, says Al, we still figure that 1954 will be our most nervous year. In 1950 it was generally felt that 1952 would be our most difficult year; now we think it probably won't. In 1954 the Russians will have a long-range air force and an adequate stockpile and would be in a position to wage long-term war. The Joint Chiefs of Staff have reaffirmed that 1954 is the danger point.


PARIS, *June 25, 1952*

LAST night we dined at Gruenthers' and played bridge with him and Grace and Ely J. Culbertson. I was rather amused to notice Culbertson make a couple of glaring mistakes. For example, on one occasion when he was my partner, we had a part score of thirty. I opened with three hearts. Culbertson, with a lousy hand, raised me to four hearts. Instead of making the game which would have been ours thanks to the part score, we went down one.

He is far more anxious to acquire a reputation as an expert on international affairs and foreign policy than as *the* authority on bridge (although he admits he has a new book coming out soon with an original and simplified system of point count). He is convinced that war with Russia is inevitable and argues that we are foolish to permit the Russians to build up an atomic stockpile now which will condemn twenty or thirty American cities to be laid waste in the future. On the whole, he talks like most

Russian *émigrés* although he is not actually an *émigré* himself. As a matter of fact, he boasts that he is the only seventh-generation American who speaks Russian with no accent and English with a Russian accent. The reason for this is that his father was in the oil business and went to the Caucasus (Maikop and Grozny) in the 1880s, where he married a Russian woman. Culbertson spent his childhood in Russia, although he went to college at Yale. He has a marked accent still.

### ABOARD THE *Mauretania, June 27, 1952*

TED Curtis is aboard, and we are eating together. He told me a rather interesting story. Ted was in the Lafayette Escadrille during World War I, and when the United States entered the conflict, he shifted to the new American Air Force. He recalls that this small unit was commanded by a certain Major Spaatz and a certain Captain Weidenbach. All the boys hated their commanding officers. They had no planes and therefore couldn't do any flying. As a result they were subjected to a lot of drill, and so forth. They didn't like the names or personalities of Spaatz and Weidenbach and used to refer to them as "the Prussians." The French likewise were pretty suspicious of those two officers.

After the war Ted became a great friend of Tooey Spaatz (and still is), but he lost all track of Weidenbach. The next he heard of him was when Spaatz told him one day that Major General Charles Willoughby, MacArthur's chief intelligence officer, was his (Spaatz's) old World War I adjutant, Captain Weidenbach.

# 26

# FROM GENERAL

# TO PRESIDENT

CHICAGO, *July 6, 1952*

I ARRRIVED HERE THIS MORNING—THE DAY BEFORE THE REPUBLICAN convention starts. It is hot as hell but there is a real atmosphere of excitement. The hotels are jammed. The huge Conrad Hilton contains both the headquarters of Eisenhower and Taft as well as the Republican National Committee. Furthermore, committee meetings are being held here with the result that you have to queue up and wait in line as much as ten minutes to get in an elevator. Practically every important room has a tray of drinks and a television set. I have rapidly discovered an organization called the "Key Club," which is in a large suite on the fourth floor of the Hilton. It is an exclusive organization made up of the big contributors of the Eisenhower campaign. Ike got so few campaign tickets, thanks to the way the Taft party stacked the operation, that the "Key Club" was invented for a big group who were unable to get in the convention hall. There are three television sets and a very busy bar operating all the time, and the place is filled with characters like Howard Petersen, chairman of Ike's finance committee, Jock and Betsey Whitney, Tex McCrary, General Ted Curtis, General Pier Hamilton.

The first thing I did after checking in at my hotel—which took an hour and a half because of the queue—was to go over and see General Lucius Clay at his suite in the Blackstone, which is where Ike is living. The usual trays of drinks were well in evidence. People kept telephoning, and I was rather amazed that in the middle of all the political hocus-pocus, a big wheel from the Continental Can Company, of which Clay is now president, called up and they did a rather large transaction which, as far as I could gather, affected canned soup.

Clay was very disturbed about the use of the words "retaliatory striking power" in the draft of the national defense plank of the proposed platform. He thinks this implies that a Republican administration would rely solely on long-range atomic bombing or, in other words, the "fortress America" concept of Herbert Hoover. Clay wants a more active foreign and strategic policy expressed. For example, last autumn, word was received through Radio Free Europe that we could stage a revolution in Czechoslovakia any day we wanted to. We had to tell our friends in Czechoslovakia to lay off because they would have been crushed and there was nothing we could do about it. We must evolve a policy warning the Russians that if there is any revolt by free forces in a satellite nation, we will not permit the Soviet army to intervene. We cannot keep calling off possible revolutions, or all our friends will either get fed up with us and give up the ghost or get locked up by the Communists.

I gather that Clay, in his own quiet and efficient way, is really a kind of chief of staff for the Eisenhower forces. He stays in the background very deliberately, above all to avoid having Eisenhower tarred with the brush of an Army "cabal." As a matter of fact, Ike is so worried about this that he has left his closest aide, Colonel Bob Schulz, in Denver and has left General Howard Snyder, one of his best friends and his doctor, in Washington to avoid having military folks around.

Clay told me Foster Dulles was now enthusiastically for Ike and actually would have declared so publicly had it been so desired by the Eisenhower strategy board. He said Dulles was the Number One choice for Secretary of State as things now stand. He doesn't think Dewey really wants the job, although I have heard remarks that Dewey might accept it or might also take the position of Attorney General.

After leaving Clay's office, I went upstairs one floor to Eisenhower's suite. I was just making myself known when Ike and Mamie came down the corridor returning from church, and they asked me in for a drink which developed into a couple of drinks and a buffet luncheon. All told, I was there about two and a half hours. The only other people there were Milton and Earl Eisenhower (two of his brothers), Senator Carlson who bobbed in and out, and a certain character named Dr. Strickman, who was apparently a great Pennsylvania buddy of Earl Eisenhower. Ike looked fine—far better than when he left Paris last month. He said his weight was 177 pounds which is only three pounds more than when he was a halfback at West Point. He had good color and a lot of energy. He didn't seem nervous, although from time to time he would get up and walk around for a minute or so and then sit down. Mamie admitted to me, however, that both of them needed a rest. He was very impressed by the preacher at the Presbyterian Church (whom he described as "the finest speaker I've ever heard") but irritated that his own picture was taken on the church steps, because he felt it was indecent to be advertised in a religious sense. Ike, who was wearing a neat blue suit, commented upon the fact that he bought all his clothes very cheap from a Jewish friend in New York. They certainly were not a "super-tailored" job, but much to his amusement he was included once on a list of the country's best-dressed men. He had once painted a portrait of this fellow who was, therefore, extremely devoted to him.

I asked Ike what he thought of the foreign policy and national defense planks of the platform draft. He said he had not seen the actual text but that Dulles had come to see him yesterday, shortly after Eisenhower had arrived in Chicago, and had given him a verbal outline. As far as I could gather, particular reference was made to the theory of "retaliation." Eisenhower is dead set against this and said he simply would not accept it. When carefully interpreted, it really means abandoning the concept of NATO in favor of sole reliance on strategic air power. He went so far as to say that he not only would not take it in the platform, but that he would rather not run than accept it. He made no secret of the fact that he is very worried about this critical issue, which is one very few people seem to understand. He got red in the face as he does when he's angry, put his tray aside, walked up and down and said: "I'll be damned if I run on that." Wow. Here was the candidate saying he wouldn't run on the party platform. His brothers looked puzzled.

He repeated once again that he is not "running for" or "seeking" public office. Personally, I don't think he means this quite as sincerely as he did when he used to tell me that in Paris some months ago.

After I left, I hunted up Foster Dulles. He asked me in for a drink and I told him about Ike's reaction on the retaliation business. He was very surprised and said, "Does he still feel that way after what I outlined to him?" I said, yes, and I expect Dulles will be hearing more about it. Dulles, of course, is really the author of the theory of "retaliation," but he explained to me that he conceived it in a broader sense as merely "one of the means" of safeguarding the free world and preventing Russian expansion. In other words, in an area where we have troops and allies *sur place* we can enforce an immediate reaction on the scene to any efforts at aggression including political aggression. However, in the Middle East where there is a military vacuum, retaliation and the threat of the atom bomb is the best protection. Dulles said that he was, of course, for Ike but had not declared himself publicly because he wanted to assume a neutral position, which he thought would help him to get through a satisfactory foreign affairs plank. He said he had absolutely no fear that Taft would be nominated. I finally persuaded him to agree to let me violate his confidence and write a story stating that Dulles was flatly for Eisenhower.

CHICAGO, *July 7, 1952*

I was amused to run into General Bonner Fellers, who has been stuck by Taft in a job on the Republican National Committee in Chicago on veterans' affairs. Bonner is, of course, all out for MacArthur, but would not be unhappy if Taft got it. He hates Ike's guts and is now completely of the "fortress America" and "Asia first" isolationist philosophy. Then, of all fellows, I ran into General Louis Fortier who is up here working hard for MacArthur, but, of course, ready to accept Taft. What the hell he is doing or what he can do, I don't know. It is always pleasant to see Lou, but our political ideas are very different. Arthur Lane, former ambassador to Jugoslavia and Poland, is also up here working hard for Taft. He told me he is trying to propagandize "minority groups," by which I gather he means mainly Poles.

Tonight General MacArthur made his keynote speech. A tremendous demonstration preceded his arrival on the dais, and there was enormous excitement during the first fifteen minutes of his address. However, although he gave it fairly well from an oratorical point of view, he said nothing but sheer baloney. One could feel the electricity gradually running out of the room. I think he cooked his own goose and didn't do much to help Taft. I was amused to see little, roly-poly General Courtney Whitney strutting along with MacArthur and sitting right behind him on the platform. MacArthur, the man who has publicly stated the army should keep out of politics, has managed to bring up here Generals Whitney, Fellers, and Fortier, while Ike keeps his close buddies Colonel Schulz and General Snyder out of Chicago.

CHICAGO, *July 8, 1952*

AT last Doc Snyder has been permitted to come up to Chicago and is happy as a lark, but Schulz isn't coming. I had a long talk today with Mamie and her mother. Later on I had drinks with Oveta Culp Hobby, whom I have seen several times and who is exceptionally charming as well as intelligent. She had a hell of a lot to do with the clever publicity at Mineral Wells, Texas, where the issue of Taft's stealing southern delegates was developed.

Incidentally, Edgar and Arthur Eisenhower, the other two surviving brothers, arrived today. I asked Earl what was Edgar's political point of view. "Extreme reactionary," he replied. Of course, he is nevertheless working for Ike.

CHICAGO, *July 9, 1952*

ASIDE from all the drifting around and gossiping today, I had an extremely interesting talk with Dulles. He told me that, at last, reference to "retaliation" has been taken out of the platform draft, although the latter has not been made public.

Dulles saw Senator Millikin, chairman of the Resolutions Committee, and asked him what the national defense subcommittee had recommended. Millikin told him. Dulles said Ike would insist on eliminating reference to retaliation.

The national defense plank as it then stood commenced as follows:

On the prudent assumption that Communist Russia may not accommodate our own disgracefully lagging preparedness, we should develop with utmost speed a force in being, as distinguished from paper plans, of such *retaliatory striking* power as to deter sudden attack or promptly and decisively defeat it. [The italics are my own.]

Dulles explained that Millikin did not understand the importance of the reference to retaliation. "He was too dumb to know what it was all about and thought it was only a matter of semantics," Dulles said. Of course, in fact, it was the difference between the foreign policy advocated by Eisenhower and Hoover's concept of "fortress America." Millikin agreed to get the offending words removed.

Dulles felt he personally had achieved a great success in obtaining the inclusion in the foreign policy plank of the following paragraph referring to Western Europe:

We shall encourage and aid the development of collective security forces there, as elsewhere, so as to end the Soviet power to intimidate directly or by satellites and so that the free governments will be sturdy to resist Communist inroads.

There was quite a battle on that paragraph. MacArthur, Hoover and Taft were all strongly opposed to it. The preponderant sentiment of the foreign policy subcommittee was against it, but Dulles in the end was able to get it through.

(P.S. Much later. Dulles is a confusing man. Together with Admiral Radford, he invented the policy of "massive retaliation." He got it into the platform. Then, when Ike balked, he got it out again. But when the campaign developed, most of Foster's declarations advocated "massive retaliation" once more. Ike, who was ready to withdraw on the issue, either didn't notice or didn't care.)

CHICAGO, *July 10, 1952*

I talked to Ike again for a moment today, but although he was pleased about his victory on the question of "retaliation," he was not completely happy with the foreign affairs and defense planks. He admitted that the negative aspects—meaning the attacks on the Truman administration—were a bit savage, but he thought that, by and large, the constructive aspects were acceptable.

This evening I went out to the convention to hear nominating speeches. Senator Dirksen nominated Taft. Among those seconding him was Mrs. Bolton, representative from Ohio. Poor woman; I happen to know she privately favors Ike. However, not only is she running for reelection, but one of her sons is standing for Congress and would be murdered if Taft jumped on him.

All day long it has been apparent that Taft's chances are sinking. He called up General MacArthur in New York. There is a rumor that he offered to throw his votes to MacArthur in an effort to stop Ike. There is another rumor that MacArthur would come out again, make a dramatic appearance on the convention floor, refuse the offer and ask the delegates to nominate Taft. There is still another rumor that Taft will throw all his delegates to Governor Warren of California. Dewey's gang—which is violently hated by the Taftites—deliberately spread this phony Warren rumor in order (1) to demonstrate that Taft is slipping and desperate; (2) to spike any Taft effort to use MacArthur.

Eisenhower was nominated by Governor McKeldin of Maryland who is a ham orator, although I don't think speeches matter if you've got the delegates. McKeldin was threatening to try and get the vice-presidency. I am told he was allowed to nominate Ike in order to give him some kudos without having trouble on the vice-presidency.

At the last minute MacArthur's name was put in by Oklahoma, and a gang of thugs picked up in saloons or around the stockyards was brought in to make a "popular" demonstration in MacArthur's favor. It didn't take.

CHICAGO, *July 11, 1952*

EISENHOWER was nominated today as the Republican candidate for President. When the morning session of the convention started, I went over to Clay's suite in the Blackstone Hotel and watched the performance on television together with Clay, Cliff Roberts and Harold Talbot, who is one of the team put together by Ike's staff. Midway in the balloting, a message came down from Ike's suite (one floor up) asking Clay to go upstairs. He went up together with Roberts and Talbot, and I sat around as the voting proceeded. When Ike got up to 595—just before Minnesota swung its delegation from Stassen to Eisenhower—I rushed up one floor and Homer

Gruenther shoved me in the door to Eisenhower's apartment and said, "Why don't you see the show?" Victory came with the Minnesota change, thus nominating Ike on the first ballot. I must say I felt a little unhappy that the double-dealing Stassen should have received the credit for this last-minute swing since I know how he has been behaving during the past few months, not in any way helping Ike, but on the contrary hindering him.

Ike seemed to be in a curious mood of dazed elation. He rushed in to see Mamie who was in bed with a bad case of neuritis, which kept her up all night. Then in a few minutes he went over to see Taft on a courtesy visit, which also represented an appeal for party unity that the two men made on television. The few of us who were in his suite started drinking to his victory although it was probably not even luncheon time. They included Clay, Bill Robinson, Cliff Roberts, Senator Carlson, Senator Seaton and the four Eisenhower brothers. In the middle of our toasting, Ike came back. Curiously enough, there was a moment when he was sitting all alone on the sofa as if he were an invisible man. For a couple of minutes he sat there looking rather pale and stunned with his thoughts obviously far, far away, while we all drank to him as if we didn't even know he was there. I went in to see Mamie, who was sitting up in bed in a pink bed jacket, and gave her a victory kiss. Although she had obviously been suffering pain from her neuritis, she was visibly elated. Her mother was sitting beside her. General Snyder, their doctor, told me he was not yet sure if she would be able to go to the convention hall, but he planned to rest her up during the afternoon. As a matter of fact, she not only went but looked very well and made a fine appearance on television.

On the table where the daily buffet was set they had a bucket filled with several bottles of champagne. Snyder rushed about and saw to it that everybody had a glass to make a victory toast.

I hung around for about three hours just to watch the performance. All kinds of characters drifted in such as Roy Roberts, publisher of the *Kansas City Star,* and Mrs. Oveta Culp Hobby, who worked so hard in Texas advertising the "steal" at Mineral Wells. The Cowles brothers and Fleur Cowles drifted in. Everybody got a little bit tight by the time I left. I gathered from talking to the "boys" that it has already been agreed that Richard Nixon of California will be the vice-presidential nominee. Cliff Roberts was working hard to find a place for Ike to spend a holiday doing some fishing and golfing and at the same time starting to bone up on his "homework." He asked me where the general should go, and I said I had no idea but for God's sake keep him away from the private estates of any millionaires.

Ike and his advisers worked during the early afternoon on his acceptance speech. While this was going on, I talked at length with the Eisenhower brothers. Edgar recalled that he had been a back during their old football days and Ike was in the line. His big problem he said, was to get the slow

Ike "out of the way" on plays. As a matter of fact, Ike became back when he went to West Point.

Ike got an enormous reception when he went to the convention this evening, as did Mamie. I think he made a very dignified and simple speech. Everybody is now saying, however, that he should start swinging a bit to the liberal side of the Republican philosophy. The old die-hards have no place to go and will have to vote for Eisenhower anyway. He will lose votes and respect if he tries to cater to the Taft boys.

CHICAGO, *July 12, 1952*

NIXON was nominated today as Vice-President and there was no speech. I understand that Ike likes him primarily because he is young (only thirty-nine) and the general wants to capture the imagination of American youth—an idea he has expressed to me before in Europe. I dropped in late in the afternoon to say goodbye to Ike and Mamie. She was exceptionally sweet and reminded me once again to be sure and send her love to Marina.

CHICAGO, *July 21, 1952*

I flew in here at lunchtime for the Democratic convention which opened this morning. I was amused that the first demonstration I should see was a rather motley-looking band followed by a gang of singing youngsters waving Harriman flags and singing "I've Been Working On the Railroad." Averell must have spent quite a lot of money on this campaign. The next two buttons I saw read: "Win With Williams," (an apparently forlorn hope for Governor Soapy Williams of Michigan) and "Dan's the Man." As far as I can find out, "Dan" is a fictitious character and merely a joke.

After dropping my luggage, I went around to Averell's suite and saw Marie Harriman, Grace Tulley (Roosevelt's old White House secretary who is now helping Harriman) and Averell's two daughters. They are all working very earnestly for the Harriman nomination, but nobody outside of his immediate entourage gives him a Chinaman's chance. He is dead earnest and seems strangely hopeful. Then I dropped in on Jim Farley, who gave me a ticket to the convention as "assistant chairman of the Democratic National Committee," which allows me to go anywhere including the speaker's platform. Jim is holding a sort of open house here and really seems like a fish back in the swim. He is strong for the nomination of Vice-President Barkley.

It was odd to watch a group of delegates propose to Jim Farley that Eleanor Roosevelt should be put into nomination for the Vice-Presidency. Jim, who hates all the Roosevelts and has no use for the "left wing" of the party, said that of course he thought this might be a noble gesture but it would mean nothing. He was extremely smooth.

I dined with Governor Ernest Gruening, of Alaska, who is still pushing hard to get statehood for that territory. He invited me to come up fishing next year.

CHICAGO, *July 22, 1952*

I spent two hours today watching Averell Harriman work as a politician. His set-up is really pretty disorganized and amateurish. For example, his machine is now working feverishly to stop a boom shaping up for Adlai Stevenson. Yet none of his henchmen seem to be able to contact each other by telephone when needed or to reach state delegations who must be swung immediately to prevent the boom from materializing. Grace Tulley told me they were even unable to reach Frankie Roosevelt—Harriman's floor manager—by telephone. I spent some time in Averell's headquarters and then rode with him in his official car behind a police escort to the Palmer House. His personal bodyguard, assigned by the City of Chicago, had been Taft's bodyguard at the Republican convention. He told me Taft had openly broken into tears the minute Eisenhower was nominated; the detective swore he had seen this with his own eyes.

At the Palmer House, Averell dropped in at a meeting of Negro delegates and told them how strongly he felt about an adequate civil rights program. He made a good impression on them, but I noticed many of them were wearing buttons favoring other candidates.

I asked Harriman, as we were riding back to the Blackstone, if he would agree to run as Vice-President on a ticket headed by Kefauver or if he would serve as Secretary of State were Stevenson to be nominated and elected. He turned on me with a very pale face saying, "Don't insult me by thinking I would make any deals for second place or any other position. I am in this fight to the finish. I am the man to put through this program." Later he cooled off. Of course, what he is trying to do today is to persuade Kefauver to come out and run for Vice-President on a ticket headed by Harriman. I don't think either Kefauver or Harriman will be able to hold together a large enough bloc of votes to prevent Stevenson from getting the nomination if the boom continues for the Illinois Governor. Barkley has now withdrawn his candidacy in an atmosphere of some bitterness after a group of labor leaders informed him they could not support him because he was too old.

Mrs. Perle Mesta, our minister in Luxembourg, is here and invited me to one of her really fancy parties tonight. I decided to go to bed instead.

CHICAGO, *July 23, 1952*

THERE still seems to be an argument over the final wording of the Democratic platform. The main discussion apparently continues to center about civil rights and also the insistence of the labor unions that the word "repeal" should be included with reference to the Taft–Hartley Act.

Jim Farley told me he was now supporting Stevenson. He said the reason Stevenson was not running openly was that he had promised Harriman a couple of months ago that he would not run and that he would support Averell and does not like to go back on his word. I saw Harriman afterwards. He was lying down on the sofa absolutely pooped but strangely enough still optimistic about his chances—probably the only man in Chicago who is. He said he will continue to push his candidacy despite the fact that Truman is now believed to support Stevenson. He said Farley's story about Stevenson was not true. He said the Democrats need a man and not a wishy-washy character to beat Ike this autumn. He thought Stevenson was definitely wishy-washy and, as he himself said, was not physically, mentally or morally fit for the job. I was quite surprised at the bitterness in Averell, who in the past has been described as a friend of Stevenson.

Farley predicted that Stevenson would get the nomination on the first or second ballot, thanks to a swing of votes after an initial expression of support for such favorite sons as Harriman in New York. No matter what kind of a deal Kefauver and Harriman make between themselves, they cannot hold on to a large enough bloc of delegates to stop Stevenson.

Jim said young Frank Roosevelt is smart and has a lot of the old man's charm but that he is very ambitious and unreliable. Neither Frankie nor Blair Moody (Senator from Michigan), who have been aiding the left-wing drive here trying to force through Southern acceptance of a strong civil rights plank, have handled themselves well and they have made a great many enemies.

Louis Bromfield, the novelist, came in and joined Jim and me in Farley's suite. They agree that Stevenson is not beholden to Truman and that if Russell is selected for the vice-presidency to run with him, they can lick the Republicans. Farley says he would like to make one of the speeches seconding Russell's nomination for the vice-presidency—"because I am a Northern Catholic and that should be a help to him."

NEW YORK, *July 25, 1952*

I had to come back to New York early to go into hospital, but I saw the nomination take place on television tonight. Stevenson got it on the first ballot. I must say I am fascinated by this boom for Stevenson and the assurances from everybody that he is an exceptionally intelligent, able and strong man. I used to know Adlai a few years ago, and I thought he was a weak sister, rather naive. My main impression then was of a wishy-washy character, and I must say his actions during this convention only confirm that previous idea. If a man can't make up his mind to run or not to run, I would hate to have to have him in a position where he has to make a fatal decision such as what to do about a North Korean invasion of South Korea. As a party, I like the Democrats; but as a man, I like Ike.

I was astounded to see Harriman interviewed on television and strongly supporting Stevenson as a wonderful choice. That is quite a change from a couple of days ago.

NEW YORK, *August 5, 1952*

I have been in Harkness Pavilion getting chopped up. Before the conventions, when I had a routine checkup, my doctor suspected an intestinal block, had me X-rayed and confirmed it. It was a major operation and they didn't know whether it was cancer or not until they opened me and, in the end, removed several inches of gut.

Not wishing to worry anyone, I simply disappeared and confided my address and the reason for it only to Orvil Dryfoos of the *Times*. Then I got a portable record player, a television, a collection of records by Bach, Vivaldi and Albenoni; plus Plato's *Dialogues* and Donne's poems; and went off.

I instructed the doctor to mention my presence to no one and if he found me cancerous to sew me up again as I needed several weeks to clear up my affairs. Fortunately, I was O.K., except that they kept giving me the wrong kind of sleeping pills (without asking me) and these woke me up so that I was wheeled into the operating room yammering in Serbian to the White Russian intern who did the wheeling.

When I came to, they made me walk around my bed, held up by two doctors. Quite unpleasant but it cures you fast. I'll be working again soon and holidaying thereafter (many pounds lighter, *dei gratia*).

NEW YORK, *August 6, 1952*

I had a letter from Adlai Stevenson today: I quote one bit in view of the fact that he may be our next President: "I shall do my best, limited by such meager talents as I have and I hope we can keep it on a level that will serve some public service. I shall try."

WASHINGTON, *August 21, 1952*

LAST night the Joyces gave me a dinner party and among those present were Averell Harriman, David Bruce, Chip Bohlen, Frank Wisner, and wives. Hank Byroade, assistant secretary of state for Near Eastern affairs, dropped in briefly for coffee afterwards.

Averell was very loquacious and seemed in excellent spirits. Among other things, he said that in 1944 Roosevelt seemed to think the Republicans would have a good chance of coming in in 1948, and, therefore, expressed the opinion that the salvation of the GOP would be for it to turn to a liberal leader. He specifically mentioned either Stassen or Saltonstall.

Averell said flatly he is not going to run for Senator this year. He clearly hopes to be Secretary of State if Stevenson is elected, but he didn't state this in so many words. He thinks in case of a Republican victory that the Secretary of State would be either Dewey or Dulles. Averell hates Dulles and thinks he is ambitious and dishonest. Tonight he is having a debate with him on television and has been briefed by the State Department and the Mutual Security Agency on certain aspects. I fear that Dulles, a shrewd lawyer, may provoke him. Averell thinks McCloy would be an excellent Secretary of State under Ike. Right now A. is very irked with Ike and says very many unkind things about him. He regards him as a captive of the Republican right wing and a political babe in the woods.

Harriman recalls that in 1945, when he was ambassador to the USSR, the Russians demanded that a Soviet commander-in-chief with powers equal to those of MacArthur should sign the surrender terms of Japan at the same time that MacArthur did so. Before even communicating this request to Washington, Averell flatly turned it down. The Russians then withdrew the demand. At the same time, as Bohlen recalled, Moscow desired a military occupation zone on the island of Hokkaido.

Averell says de Gaulle behaved pretty well, by and large, during his wartime Moscow visit. The Russians deliberately offended him at a Kremlin dinner where Stalin first toasted Churchill as a "great comrade in arms" and then Roosevelt as a "comrade in both war and peace"—but no word of France. When a draft treaty between Russia and France was drawn up, Averell requested the French ambassador to show it to him. He warned him that if it was agreed on as drafted, it would mean that France was choosing between the United States and the Soviet Union. The French got frightened and pulled in their horns.

Bruce and Wisner spent a large part of the evening recalling some of the screwballs who messed up OSS activities in the Middle East and Balkans during the war. David was fascinated by the operations of Colonel Amoss who, although he knew nothing and messed up everything he touched, actually ended up as a one-star general and chief-of-staff for General Brereton. Wisner confirmed that another officer had actually recommended himself for a Silver Star and signed the recommendation. All told, a pretty picture when you consider these were the men operating our important secret activities in the occupied Balkans.

Chip believes the announcement of a Bolshevik party congress in October and the decision to turn the Politburo and Orgburo into a Presidium is not of major significance. He thinks it merely harmonizes the Soviet propaganda position by officially confirming that a "classless" society now exists and, therefore, basing policies on the dictatorship of the "proletariat" or "working" class—implying existence of different social classes—is no

longer required. Personally, I disagree and think this means the party
Secretariat is assuming even greater powers and that, therefore, Malenkov
is now moving into the open as Stalin's heir apparent. Molotov may be
eased out of the picture since he isn't on the Secretariat and is not likely
to be named to the new one.

WASHINGTON, *August 22, 1952*

I had a particularly good talk with Bedell Smith over in his office at
the CIA. Bedell looked like hell; thin and drawn and pale. However, he
told me he was feeling much better now that he had had two-thirds of his
stomach cut out, and as far as he knows he has no more ulcers.

He is very concerned about the possibility that Moscow might use its
huge gold reserves as an economic weapon to smash western economy. He
agrees that the Russians have a vast annual production and don't use much
of their gold. The hoard is mounting. We know they use it occasionally to
finance foreign missions, including the UN, and to pay for subversive activities. Once a shipment in a box broke open at the Paris airport and gold
coins spilled all over the place. Whether the Russians use bar gold or mint
their own fake sovereigns or Napoleons (the way the Bank of England
mints sovereigns for the Greek government) we don't know. However, a
good deal of these costs listed above are handled by the Russians with
platinum. This is smuggled abroad from Moscow in Soviet diplomatic
pouches.

The Soviet gold supply is enormous. They could do two things with it.
Moscow could suddenly establish a gold backing to the ruble, making it a
real currency which would then attract foreign investments and could also
be used to make purchases abroad, breaking the Allied blockade on strategic materials. Or the Kremlin could order the dumping of huge quantities
of gold on foreign markets at an artificially low price. This would break the
economies of many countries with vital but dwindling gold reserves such as
England or France. Bedell admitted this was an important problem with
which he has concerned himself since 1947 when he was ambassador in
Moscow. He said he thought it might be a good idea to have a new CIA
study made on the matter.

There were no new alarming indications of a Soviet plan of a general all-
out attack. In late 1950, at the time of the Korean debacle, we were scared
and put our armed forces on the alert when there was a very considerable
Soviet build-up in the Far East. Nothing of the sort is now evident.

Bedell, while agreeing with David Bruce that the Sino-Russian talks
were of extreme importance, thought the proposed changes in the party
structure were also of great significance. The Chinese are obviously coming
to Moscow to ask for more help because they are losing a great deal of
material and energy in Korea. The Russians will drive a hard price. At all

costs they do not intend to see built up on their eastern frontier a Chinese military Frankenstein monster.

Bedell thinks that the change from a Politburo to a Presidium means increased powers for the party secretariat and a still stronger position for Malenkov. He thinks it is possible that Stalin might resign as first secretary of the party Secretariat and become president of the Presidium. Malenkov would become first secretary, and Molotov could become president of the Presidium when Stalin dies. Or Stalin might even become president of the USSR and at least give that office some importance—providing an eventual niche for Malenkov.

NEW YORK, *August 25, 1952*

I talked on the telephone today with Lieutenant Colonel Bob Schulz. He has been Eisenhower's aide for years but has now been reassigned by the Army, after being released by Ike. He has been replaced by Ed Green, whom I used to know in Italy and Germany as a naval commander working for the OSS and a very bright young man.

Paul Hoffman had said a few days ago that Schulz was released because Ike didn't want to stand in the way of his Army seniority rights and promotion. Today, Bob told me this is not the case. He said the group now around Eisenhower resented having intimates around the general whom they could not "control." Since we were talking by telephone, Bob did not identify the group to whom he referred, but my guess would be Arthur Summerfield typifies it. Kevin McCann is still with the general but Bob implied he was rather unhappy. Bob definitely said he had been eased out. He also implied, very strongly, that Eisenhower is unhappy and that neither he nor anyone else knew what he was getting into when he went into politics. He thought the people around him would be sincere, straightforward and honest. They are not. It is still Bob's belief that the general will get the bit in his teeth and reassert himself.

ROCQUENCOURT, *August 27, 1952*

AL Gruenther says that in order to start a war the Russians would have to organize extensively and move additional units into Germany. By causing this requirement for the Soviets, we have registered a very definite achievement. Of course the Russians could bring in more troops to Germany gradually and then not attack. For example, if they moved ten divisions into Germany, we would be faced with the problem as to whether we would have to increase our protective shield by calling up some of our reserve divisions. That would be partial mobilization and a big question. If the Soviets started a slow build-up, it is difficult to know how we would react. Some people might feel that we would be provoking Moscow if we started to mobilize.

However, since the Russians have not increased their forces opposed to ours in Germany, it would at present be far more difficult for them to launch a surprise attack than was the case last year.

Gruenther admitted to me that unfortunately there was now no single man with the prestige of Eisenhower to beat down the dry rot of propaganda which has been spreading pessimism concerning NATO. Ike used to go into the economic side and philosophize on things, although this is not truly the job of the military to do.

ROCQUENCOURT, *August 28, 1952*

TODAY I had my first talk with General Ridgway, who replaced Eisenhower as SHAPE commander last June. He makes an exceptionally good impression. He is a large, bulky but very fit and muscular man who looks a bit younger than his fifty-seven years. His uniform is extremely neat and so is his appearance; for example, his hands. He does not smoke but is scrupulously careful to offer cigarettes. I have a feeling that he probably never uses bad language because there seemed to be a tiny and momentary hiatus in the conversation when I used the phrase "hell of a situation," discussing the anti-NATO propaganda now going on. All in all, Ridgway seems an extremely high-minded—one might almost say noble—sincere democrat who takes his responsibilities with immense seriousness. He gives the impression of being exceptionally moral and religious, which I have heard he is. I doubt if he has much sense of humor or a light side. I did not have the feeling that he was an intelligent man or comprehended in the fullest degree many of the important problems related to his job, such as politics and economics. However, his character is clearly unimpeachable and must surely have a profound effect on some of those who deal with him. As long as he has the brilliance of Gruenther at his right hand, he should be able to avoid any major problems. He clearly recognizes that SHAPE is no longer the tail which wags the NATO dog—a situation that obviously prevailed under the more glamorous Eisenhower.

We discussed Korea and the Russians. He thought Russian divisions had a very high fire power (meaning first-line divisions such as those now in Germany), probably equal to our own. When they were ready for a fight and their army artillery was moved forward, they were pretty strong units. Therefore, it would be impossible to use against them any Allied reserve division which was only, let us say, 60 per cent ready according to SHAPE standards because such a unit would merely "disintegrate." He said that in Korea we had benefited a great deal in learning how to fight in cold weather conditions. We now had truly good clothing for our troops. The new cold weather boots made of glass fiber prevented frostbite. He compared these with the leather boots used by his corps during the bitter winter fighting of 1944–1945 where there was a lot of frostbite. Unfortunately these boots cost $26 a pair. We might be able to provide them for our own troops in Europe, but surely the European powers would be unable to do so for obvious economic reasons.

On the whole, Ridgway impressed me sympathetically as a fine and admirable man. His possible shortcoming would be in terms of intellect. Surely he and Gruenther make a pretty good team. And after all, I must recollect that, as Lord Ismay told me on May 2 of this year, Eisenhower had once told him—long before his successor was chosen—that he thought an ideal combination at SHAPE would be Ridgway and Gruenther.

PARIS, *August 29, 1952*

DINNER last night with Jimmy and Peggy Gault. Gault asked me what I thought of Ridgway and I told him. He thought Ridgway was an exceedingly fine man and used the same word "noble" about his character. He also thought he was neither brilliant nor excessively intelligent and had difficulty in mastering all the various aspects of NATO. He is a simple fellow who lives an extremely quiet life here. He gets up around six o'clock in the morning and starts work at home. He comes to the office around eight-thirty and works methodically through whatever problems have piled up on his desk, tackling them one by one and listening patiently to arguments and explanations. He goes home for lunch with his wife and little boy every day. Jimmy is trying to get him in the habit of staying on and using his private dining room in order to invite distinguished visitors and get the general to know a few more people. He goes home in the late afternoon and plays badminton vigorously for about forty-five minutes. Then he dines quietly and retires around half past nine.

He simply never goes out aside from the minimal required invitations such as from the President of France. He completely skips both Paris and SHAPE social contacts. He doesn't smoke and doesn't drink but is scrupulously polite about offering drinks to his occasional guests. He does not appear to have any sort of light side. He is not gifted conversationally, and talks with him produce many dead moments. However, Jimmy says he does not feel "nervous" with him when he sits in silence; in fact, he is quite restful to be with.

PARIS, *October 4, 1952*

GEORGE Kennan is not wanted back by the Russians. They have demanded his recall as ambassador as a result of his Tempelhof Airport statement comparing the life of a western diplomat in Moscow to internment in Germany during Nazi days. I must say this was ill advised and indiscreet for George to have said. He had hoped to use his personal arts of diplomacy to try to ease tension between the USSR and the USA. He thought the arts of old-fashioned diplomacy would help, but surely no old-fashioned diplomat would have made these remarks.

PARIS, *October 15, 1952*

THIS evening I had a good talk with Foreign Minister Robert Schuman in his office at the Quai d'Orsay. He said the recent Communist Party congress made it evident that Moscow will redouble its efforts to divide the democratic powers. "Our strength and security is in the unity of the West." He expressed confidence that the Kremlin's efforts would fail.

"Several of the speeches at the nineteenth Bolshevik party congress plainly sought to distinguish between the United States on the one hand and Britain and France on the other in an effort to divide us and split our common policy," he added.

Schuman denied that any secret talks had been going on between representatives of the French and Soviet Governments as widely rumored recently. French intelligence services had traced the origin of such reports and located them in Germany and Switzerland. There were three original sources in Germany. Each turned out to be a left-wing Socialist who had formally quit the Communist Party three or four years ago. It appeared evident that Communist agents had deliberately fomented an entirely false story with the purpose of embarrassing France in its relationships with its allies. Fabricated "documents" had been distributed. Rumors had been deliberately spread that Soviet representatives in Switzerland had held conversations there with a French general. The only foundation for such a report was the presence in Switzerland of "General" Alfred Joinville, a French Communist deputy whose military "rank" was a wartime Partisan courtesy and who was passing through there in connection with a Communist front peace congress.

At the present time France will make no effort to link the possibility of an armistice in Korea directly to truce prospects in Indochina. More than a year ago when Marshal De Lattre de Tassigny sought to join the two issues, France felt "more menaced by the possibility of direct Chinese intervention" than is now the case.

He said Moscow has made no official threat to denounce the Franco-Soviet mutual defense treaty of December, 1944, although it has frequently stated in notes to this government that it considers France's adhesion to NATO contrary to that pact. The French position is that NATO is a purely defensive alliance and in no sense aimed against the USSR.

PARIS, *October 17, 1952*

THIS afternoon I had an excellent talk with Montgomery. He was looking rather old and tired but seemed very keen. He is plunking for the establishment of an Allied propaganda directorate to coordinate all cold war attitudes and psychological warfare and says he is going to do as much as he can to promote this idea. As soon as he begins talking about it, he comes very much alive.

Monty, who has a gift for getting to the heart of the matter rapidly, said he felt the West was not doing enough to win the cold war and that, after all, "if we win the cold war, we won't have a hot war." He said:

> We are today at war. It is called the cold war. No one knows how long it will go on. Yet no one handles this problem. We handle a hot war. We have armies and headquarters and commanders and councils dealing with that possibility. But there isn't any Allied organization for the cold war.
>
> Why don't the nations come together with a declared unity of purpose and coordinate their psychological warfare and propaganda? Of course, this is a civilian thing. It has nothing to do with us soldiers. But we must get the truth over to the enslaved peoples—and get it over quickly. Right now look at the situation. The other side puts out something—say the Moscow radio. All our nations have to hold meetings and consultations on how to answer. They ask each other. Finally they reply a month later. By the time we answer the effect of the other side has sunk in. That's no good.
>
> We should answer the same night—at once. But you can't do this unless you have a setup handling it. Right now fourteen nations are handling it in fourteen different ways. There is no single directing mind of the free nations to fight this insidious enemy.

I asked Montgomery how he would propose to create and organize the directorate he recommended. He replied:

> To tell you the truth, I haven't given much thought to how it should be done. I only know that it should be done. I'm a soldier and concerned with hot wars. I'm no expert on this type of thing. It would require a very experienced international political figure who would have to get all nations to coordinate their propaganda and funnel it through the same trumpet, play the same tune or song. I repeat. If you win the cold war, there won't be a hot war.

PARIS, *October 22, 1952*

LAST night we dined with the Norstads at Fontainebleau. Larry has just come back from a brief trip to the States. He saw Eisenhower Saturday night (October 18). He said Ike looks very well and is full of beans, but seems nervous and fidgety. They didn't talk politics. However, several times during their conversation, Ike referred to "the old guard" in the Republican Party, which Larry takes as a very good sign. In other words, Eisenhower still considers the old guard an old guard and presumably intends to do something about them if he gets in. He kept saying that he thought America should move straight ahead—neither to the right nor to the left. He also agreed with Norstad that regardless of the expense of establishing a satisfactory defense, it had to be done.

PARIS, *October 24, 1952*

LAST night dined at Bill Tyler's. He told me that Louis Joxe, French ambassador to Moscow, who is in Paris on leave, was very unhappy about the Kennan incident and felt it would weaken the Western team in Moscow. He thought Kennan had been a damn fool to make the Templehof statement. The moment he read in the papers that Kennan had referred to the Nazis, he was convinced he could never come back to the USSR.

Joxe said that the one time he met Stalin, the latter inquired about the Atlantic Pact and why France belonged. Joxe painstakingly explained that the Atlantic Pact was purely a defensive, peaceful alliance without any aggressive intentions. Stalin laughed and turned to Vyshinsky, saying, "If that is the case, why don't we join, Vyshinsky?"

PARIS, *October 29, 1952*

DURING the course of a chat I had this afternoon with Ambassador William F. Draper Jr., just returned from America, I asked him who would be Secretary of State, and he said most of the gossip indicated it would be Dulles under Eisenhower or Harriman under Stevenson. He didn't appear to think much of Dulles and said he was afraid it was Dulles who had been selling Ike all this moonshine about let Asians fight Asians, and so on, plus the idea of announcing he would go to Korea. I told him I really didn't think Dulles believed all the stuff he'd been saying, and Draper said he hoped to God he didn't. Draper, of course, is a Republican.

PARIS, *October 30, 1952*

LUNCHED today with the two Rothschild brothers at the bank on the rue Laffitte. I must say one has the feeling in that not very lavish but extremely old-fashioned building filled with retainers that this is a very stable world indeed. I remarked upon that to Alain and Elie, and they said the trouble was that sometimes they suffered from the same illusion.

I asked what they thought the Russians did with their gold and they admitted they had no idea. Alain was of the opinion that the Soviet ruble is actually a very solid and orthodox currency, but Elie agreed with me that it had no value and no orthodoxy because it simply could not be exchanged abroad; nobody, for example, could buy or sell rubles in a place like Tangier. I asked them if they thought the Russians could not wreck Western economies by suddenly dumping a couple of billion dollars' worth of gold in bullion or other forms in the various world markets and offering it at, for example, $20 an ounce instead of the legal American price of $35 an ounce or the approximate current world price of $36 an ounce. They both felt this would be quite illogical and could do no harm to the West. The French government through its banks could buy up huge quantities of such gold at the hypothetical price of $20 and then print— free for nothing—more money with the $15-per-ounce profit. As long as the purchasers of such gold were in a position to print money with the profit—in other words, governments—it wouldn't affect world economy in the least, and in the end Russia would lose by such an endeavor.

They said the price of gold has fallen a great deal recently. Right after the war many people thought gold would have to be revalued at perhaps $80 an ounce, and therefore they bought a great deal and this demand drove the price up. The gold has been sterile; it has produced no income such as securities would. As a result, people got fed up and started dumping their holdings, thus bringing the price down.

Alain said an important meeting would be held between the English and the Americans, probably in April, to discuss the possibility of revaluing the price of gold upward. The English favor this. The American attitude is likely to depend upon the situation at the time.

TRIESTE, *November 3, 1952*

TODAY I had a very interesting conversation with Stanislaus Joyce. He is the brother of James Joyce and has been living here for many years. James spent twelve years in Trieste teaching English, also the profession of his brother. I asked Stanislaus how he got his name. He said his father had been named John Stanislaus Joyce (for the Polish King Stanislaus Leszczynski), and was called Jack. His son is called "Stanny." He showed me letters from James addressed "Dear Stanny" and signed "Jim." He loaned me the manuscript of the first part of a book on his brother and a very violent attack on Oliver St. J. Gogarty, the original for Malachi Mulligan of *Ulysses*. Joyce lives only in the memory of his adored brother. Curiously enough he started keeping a diary while still a youngster in his early teens and devoted largely to "Jim."

BELGRADE, *November 8, 1952*

I had a conversation with Marshal Tito this morning in his villa on the Rumunska which lasted about an hour and a half. Tito spoke in Serbo-Croatian through his interpreter, Madame Kveder, wife of a Jugoslav general, but he made it very clear that he now understands some English well by interrupting the translation frequently. He is still taking lessons. He was wearing a green tweed suit with a slight red check and cuffs on the sleeves, brown suede shoes and a purple tie. he was very affable and served šlivovica and coffee. He smoked constantly through his little pipe-shaped cigarette holder.

I asked him first why, since Jugoslavia founded its policy on the UN and strongly supported collective security, it did not send at least a token force to fight in Korea. He replied that it would do more political harm than good since "no other country is as threatened as we are."

I pointed out that Turkey was certainly menaced, having a long frontier with the USSR, but nevertheless the Turks had sent troops to Korea. Tito replied: "Our position is different from that of the Turks. Turkey is threatened only as a territorial unit but not politically."

I asked him if he had any thought on how the Korean War should be ended since Jugoslavia maintained that as long as it continued, China would remain dependent on the USSR. He replied:

I have no concrete proposals. Korea should be returned to the *status quo* so that the Korean peoples can settle their own destiny under UN supervision. I wish to emphasize that the UN should supervise this and insure against further aggression.

I believe that China's participation in the Korean War was partly the result of faulty Western policy. The West's support of Chiang helped Russia to push China into the Korean conflict. It is difficult to say how this can be rectified now. We think it would be a good idea to recognize the Chinese Government in order to make international cooperation possible and stop China from being a tool of the Soviet imperialists.

Talks on regional security measures with Greece and Turkey will start soon. In a sense military talks have already begun. We are trying to reach agreement on what should be done to defend the Balkans. This involves what kind of mutual help should be pledged, which bases conceded, and technical preparations and plans.

After such agreements have been reached, it will be perfectly easy for us to write down such obligations. I would like to say also that people looking at these problems from the outside naturally want speedy results. But it should be remembered that we have not had friendly relations with each of these countries for a considerable period of time. But great progress has been made recently.

I think developments should follow a pattern like this: first, preparations must be made for friendship and cooperation, above all on economic and cultural levels; then diplomatic and defense agreements. This requires time. When the third phase comes about, it should start with talks on broad strategical questions and then discussions of details on a tactical level.

The basis is to maintain peace by a strong collective defense.

I asked if Jugoslavia was prepared to accept obligations vis-à-vis Asiatic Turkey as well as European Turkey. He replied: "There is no difference, for there is no real boundary between Asia and Europe as aggression is not limited to geographical frontiers. We consider Turkey as a whole."

I asked Tito if he favored denouncing the Teheran, Yalta, and Potsdam agreements. He said they should not be denounced as a whole, but the following portions he thought should be specifically annulled: The agreement on the boundaries between Poland and East Germany; the agreement concerning the frontier between Poland and the USSR; the agreement placing Germany under Soviet military occupation; and the agreement to permit the right of veto in the UN Security Council.

I asked if his new "Socialist Front of Working People" intended to join the Second International or to try and sponsor any international movement of its own. He said that the "latter was entirely out of the question," but it was not precluded that the "front" would join the Second International if such were "considered beneficial."

Tito said the Cominform was "gradually being liquidated." This was clearly demonstrated at the Nineteenth Bolshevik Congress where all foreign parties were called upon to support Moscow and the Cominform wasn't even mentioned.

BELGRADE, *November 11, 1952*

I am very much impressed by the visible recovery in Belgrade and Zagreb. There is much more in the shops to buy, plenty of food in the restaurants and gypsy orchestras have returned to the *kafanas*. Thanks to the revaluation of the dinar (now three hundred to the American dollar), prices are cheap for foreigners. There seems to be plenty to eat despite this year's drought. Apparently its pinch will be felt mostly in around February or March. At that no famine is expected. It will hurt more economically. I received the impression that in a gradual and reluctant way the Communist system is tending increasingly towards decentralization and modification in a democratic direction. Everyone assures me this is not a temporary NEP phase but permanent.

ZAGREB, *November 12, 1952*

I went to the Sixth Congress of the Jugoslav Communist Party today. An extraordinary event occurred. Djurić, secretary general of the
government and therefore a pretty important man, got up and made a
rambling speech criticizing the personal behavior of the Communist leadership. He then accused Stambolić, a member of the Politburo of stealing his wife. At that point the Congress started shouting at Djurić and he
was expelled from the hall. Tito then got up and made a violent speech
implying that he was a Cominform agent. Obviously poor Djurić is now in
the coop.

ATHENS, *November 14, 1952*

I talked with Field Marshal Papagos today at his home in Ekali. The
conversation was in French, which he speaks fluently. He was wearing very
well-tailored civilian clothes and seemed in good health and exceptionally
youthful for a man of seventy. He was confident he would win Sunday's
elections. His suburban home is comfortable but not pretentious. The sitting room features signed photos from Van Fleet and Nimitz.

I asked him what he intended to do (if he headed the next government)
against the Communist Party. He replied, "I will continue a policy of
conciliation. It is my hope that by education and economic improvement I
can bring the bulk of Communist sympathizers back into the nation. But
this does not apply to the militants, the convinced fanatics from whom
there is no hope. Those who are dangerous must be interned in the islands."

I asked Papagos if he intended to modify the present legal structure in
order to take such action and he answered, "No, the present laws are
sufficient."

I then asked what his attitude was towards the monarchy in view of
previous reports that there had been friction between him and the palace.
He replied:

I am very attached to the person of the King and the regime, which I
believe is very necessary. In the past I thought it my duty to tell His
Majesty certain truths which were perhaps irritating. These concerned
his entourage. However, now that is all over.

I entered politics not in order to form a party or to be prime minister.
I had been offered that post several times before by the King, but I had
refused. I wish only to be put in power by the people in order to work
for them.

I told him many of his enemies said he had dictatorial or Fascist tendencies. He replied,

The proof that I am not dictatorially inclined is in the record. I could easily have made myself dictator when I was commander-in-chief of the Greek armed forces. I always refused the prime ministry when it was offered to me in the past. The King proposed that I should take that post at least three or four times, but I declined. One should make careful distinctions. There is a big difference between a strong government and a dictatorship. I want a strong government, but only in order to apply the constitutional laws of the country. The law will be dictator.

ATHENS, *November 15, 1952*

I had a long talk with King Paul today at Tatoi Palace. Despite the fact that tomorrow is election day, he seemed very unconcerned and relaxed. He was dressed in an admiral's uniform, and we sat around informally before the fireplace in his study. These are the main points the King had to make:

If Papagos is elected, he will purge the leadership of the Greek army. Papagos has a personal grudge against all the officers from corps commander up and will certainly replace them. I asked the King if he thought this would damage the efficiency of the army, and he admitted that probably such would be the case.

The King expressed absolute confidence that the Communist underground was now licked in Greece. He said the police are very efficient and kept a sharp eye on all conspiracies, moving in on the plotters if and when necessary. He expressed the belief that there was a definite split between the EDA (existing legal *locum tenens* of the Communist Party) and the Moscow Cominform leadership. EDA continually disobeyed Moscow orders and took independent action. I asked if by this he meant that they were "Titoists." He didn't seem to know much about this, but thought it was just a question of disobedience.

I asked if in view of the differences he had had in the past with Papagos, he cared very much whether Plastiras or Papagos won the election tomorrow. He said that quite frankly he did not think it made much difference and that it would not affect the country's future very much either way.

"Many times" the King had asked Papagos to assume political leadership in the country. He had planned to form a coalition government under Papagos including Venizelos and other factional leaders. The task of this government would have been to call for national elections. Papagos would have had the opportunity of forming a political organization as prime minister and could have swept to power as a national hero. At the very last minute, to the astonishment of the King, Papagos asked for six more months before giving a decision. The King tried to dissuade him unsuccessfully. Then he said, "My wife tried afterwards, with equal lack of success." Papagos swore he did not want to go into politics at that time. Then

Papagos resigned his post as head of national defense forces on the basis of what the King called rumor and gossip contained in a letter to the field marshal from a Greek military attaché in Washington. At the time he resigned, he assured the King he had no intention of going into politics, "but ten days later he did enter politics."

He said the Jugoslav mission, which had visited Greece in September, was made up of "a bunch of thugs." He was obviously very sceptical about Tito, and at least three times asked, "Can we trust him?" He said the Queen had had a very interesting conversation with Moše Pijade, the Politburo member who was on the delegation. She said to him that she could not understand how Pijade, a Jew, could reconcile his philosophy of materialism with his religion. Pijade replied that he saw no conflict. The Queen then said she thought materialism was a very old-fashioned philosophy. Pijade asked why. She replied, "Ever since atomic fission was discovered, materialism makes no sense. By splitting the atom we have proven that you can destroy matter. Therefore, there is no basis for materialism."

The King said he was rather embarrassed by having to entertain General Tempo, who had been the Jugoslav representative with the Greek Communist rebel army, but, he added, Tempo had the tact not to mention the subject. The King said he expected he would probably be entertaining Tito in the Palace one of these days, but added, "I certainly shan't like it."

In concluding, the King expressed the opinion that Papagos has learned a lot, politically speaking, during the past year. When the King had first suggested that he become prime minister, he had immense prestige as a national hero. He had lost this prestige now because he had been tarnished as an extremely bad leader of the opposition in parliament. But he was a wiser and more experienced man.

ATHENS, *November 17, 1952*

THE Greek elections were held yesterday and Papagos won in a landslide. The American embassy, which has been quite frankly favoring Papagos, was not in the least surprised, but everybody else was. As a matter of fact, we intervened strongly in Greek politics (although not as much as in Italy in 1948), more or less forced the adoption of the majority voting system, and urged the King to call the present election.

NEW DELHI, *November 20, 1952*

IT is a long flight to India. At Istanbul I watch Turkish officers bid farewell to their families. No tears; few embraces; merely some proud looks as if welcoming heroes home. And then, a few salutes to the officiating generals, and all follow the fat, old, bull-necked colonel to the plane.

"What branch is your colonel in?" I inquire of the young lieutenant as we loosen seat belts. "Oh, the colonel. Why he is taking over as second in command."

"Yes, but what branch of the army? He's pretty old?"

"I don't know what you call his branch in America," he answers. "He has been running our commando school at Izmir. He's not so very old. Why, the colonel got his parachute wings two years ago. Now he's been teaching underwater demolitions."

I regard the colonel: fat, gray-haired, heavy nosed, easing his paunch comfortably: anybody's amiable grandpa. Yes, I suppose age is relative.

Many hours later, over the Sind Desert, cloaked in night, all four engines fail together: splut, splutter, silence. The huge plane noses downward through the night. The sign flashes on. "Fasten Seat Belts" the sign says.

I regard the lieutenant as he stirs his highball idly. He takes a tranquil sip. There is a sputter, a grunt, a hum: we begin to climb again. "Somewhat inconvenient," says the Turk.

NEW DELHI, *November 21, 1952*

THIS morning I had a very long and especially valuable talk with our ambassador here, Chester Bowles. I must say, upon conclusion of the conversation I had the feeling that he was one of the ablest and most useful representatives of Washington I have met abroad in some years. He is a rather tall, affable, informal man who is known, as a matter of fact, in India for his disregard of the restrictive protocol of normal diplomatic life. For example, it is not unusual, apparently, for him to ride home from a dinner party on a bicycle.

But he is by no means a "dumb farmer." He is a man of considerable cultivation who is familiar with the main currents of history and the basic elements of the conflicting thoughts of our time. One can, for example, talk to him intelligently on Karl Marx or Russian ideology or Tito or materialism or the curious psychopathic condition of the Moslem world. He has many interesting ideas and acute observations. Apparently he gets on well with Nehru; unusually well. I make reference specifically to his predecessor, Loy Henderson. Henderson is an able man with a first-class mind, although rather more traditional in a diplomatic sense, but Henderson detested Nehru and Nehru knew it. The reverse is true in the present case.

Our conversation commenced on a level of platitudes but developed from there. Bowles remarked that

Asia after all is not a town. One cannot frame one policy for Asia. In its most simplified form you need two policies. One would be for the Far East. There is an active military threat there and a defense has been erected to face it. But in India, Burma, Indochina, Ceylon and Pakistan, we are not thinking in terms of military terror. There is a huge economic problem which requires careful long-range handling. We are trying to get through with India a standard treaty of friendship and commerce. There have been two years of negotiations, mainly involved in quibbling over words. But we cannot be impatient with India.

(At this point I would like to insert an apt, if corny, poem by Rudyard Kipling:

> Now it is not good for the Christian's health
> To hustle the Aryan brown,
> For the Christian riles, and the Aryan smiles,
> And he weareth the Christian down.
> And the end of the fight is a tombstone white
> With the name of the late deceased,
> And the epitaph drear, "A fool lies here
> Who tried to hurry the East.")

Bowles read me a letter he recently wrote to Secretary of State Acheson requesting the formulation of a long-range policy for India. The letter said substantially as follows: We are not facing up to the fundamental crises in Asia. A free India is vital to world peace and to our own security. We must build a program to meet the requirements of the situation. The choice in India is between the present democratic government and communism. There is no other organized force. It would be a catastrophe if the present government fails. One-sixth of the world's population lives here. In the last war India provided an army of three million. A Communist India would help communism to dominate southeast Asia. India has rich mineral resources and a strategically important location. It defends South Asia. In Communist hands it would block the Suez Canal route to the East. India's loss to the West would cause Moscow's prestige to soar. Millions around the world would join the Communist bandwagon. Europe's confidence in us would be deflated and Africa would blow up. The prospects of a free world would be jeopardized.

What are the chances of India remaining free? Paul Hoffman said that India in 1952 is like China in 1946. This is too simple. There are certain favorable factors. India has a good civil service. Most of its leaders have a western tradition and are non-Communists. They have an Anglo-Saxon respect for the law. The Army is free from politics. Nehru has vast prestige. The five-year plan is a good program for growth. During the last seven years the United States has been improving its Asian relationships.

But there are also negative factors. There is considerable graft among the minor politicians. The Communists use this politically. The older leaders are tired. Some of the younger leaders have drifted towards Communism. When Nehru dies, the Congress Party will splinter. Nehru is the only cohesive force. He cannot force through reform because of the complicated situation. There is a great need for land reform and the servicing of the debts of the poor, and the Communists stress these facts.

The Indian educational system turns out streams of cynical youths. The caste system causes frustrations. There is a psychopathic fear of colonialism and antiracism. Furthermore, the Chinese have sold themselves well here. India needs United States aid to accomplish its five-year plan. This should come on the scale of aid to Greece. It would take less than $1 billion to get the five-year plan through. There is a need for village and land reform before communism goes into the villages. And communism *is* moving in. The youth must be given a sense of participation in progress. But the Congress Party is too far removed from the people.

The Chinese have given their people a sense of participation. For example, they build their own schools, physically speaking. *We* don't understand the appeal of communism out here. At the lower levels the Communists do a good job of what passes for democratic participation. The people ask, "What shall we do?" For those with their own political ideas, and therefore oppositional forces, there is the whip. But most people want only to build a better ditch. *Their* opinion is asked in terms of how can a better ditch be dug. But their opinion is asked for the first time. The Indian universities are turning out Communists.

Discussing the situation in Indochina, Bowles said Nehru used to be very violently agsinst French colonialism. Now his attitude is somewhat softer. In fact, he would probably be disturbed if the French got out of French Indochina. Nevertheless Nehru has been more anxious about nineteenth-century (British) colonialism than twentieth-century (Soviet) colonialism.

Nehru has been extremely worried during the last few days by our apparent turndown of the Indian proposal on Korea. He sees in this an indication of new trends in our policy; an ascendance of Republican belligerency. He thinks the outgoing Democratic administration has been influenced by the recent elections. Nehru recognizes that China is as hard to deal with as Russia. He now admits that it will take much longer before China breaks loose from Russia than he had originally calculated.

By 1956 Nehru hopes India will be self-supporting in food. Now, however, the annual deficit is about 4,000,000 tons (primarily wheat and rice), approximately 9 per cent of the annual food output of India.

If the country keeps healthy, the population will, of course, zoom. But the output per acre right now is only, for example, one-third of that in Japan. There is no use of fertilizers. Available cow dung is burned for fuel. Thus obviously there is a terrific potential agricultural output increase. It would be simple to double agricultural output in fifteen years. As the farmers' income goes up, it has been found the size of the families decreases; therefore it is hoped that the population will finally reach a static level. Also India is interested in fostering birth control (despite the fact that the woman minister of health is a Catholic). The Indians would like to have an American factory here making contraceptive equipment. When

India's food deficit is cleared up, this will result in between $500 million and $600 million a year being turned loose for industrial improvement.

India, it may be seen, is being stirred up with a great stick. All types of traditional systems are undergoing change: the caste system; the educational system; the old relationship between the landowner and the tenant. A Pandora's box is being opened and nobody knows what will flow out. For example, as the illiterates are being educated, they learn to read Communist propaganda which unfortunately is better than ours. Nobody can foresee if and when a period of violence will ensue. In the United States when we had 15,000,000 out of work just after the depression began, there was no violence; but by 1936 when the workers had food in their stomachs the sit-down strikes began.

Old structures are cracking up in India. The minds and the hearts of the population must be filled as well as their stomachs. Obviously the first stage in this great social development will create immense new problems. We must do more than help the Indian people fill their stomachs; we must also influence their minds. India is not a "Socialist" state. Her leaders do not think socialism will work. Thus, for example, India has guaranteed that three new refineries we are helping to open up here will not be nationalized for at least twenty-five years. But although they are skeptical about socialism, the Indians don't like British scarcity capitalism. We Americans would like to introduce our own incentive system and high wages rather than the restrictive British system of capitalism.

This evening I had an interesting talk for about an hour and a half with Jawaharlal Nehru, Indian prime minister and the only dynamic force in the country. I saw him in his residence, former home of the British commanders-in-chief. We sat in a relatively small study decorated with carved ivory. The two of us were perched upon a comfortable stuffed sofa. Nehru is so delicate and graceful that he makes one feel awkward. He was dressed in a long russet-brown Indian jacket and white leggings. He seemed relaxed and far more affable than the last time I saw him two and a half years ago. Coffee was served and we smoked occasional cigarettes.

But although he was quite cordial in his curiously diffident way, what he had to say was not of penetrating interest. Furthermore, I had a constant feeling of his mental arrogance and assumed contempt for the intellectual capacities of most Americans. (Later on Bowles told me this is a fair observation.) Time and again I asked him questions concerning ideologies, Marxism, and so on, and he gave me rather childish and, I thought, contemptuous—certainly unsatisfactory—replies. He is a confused man who is unquestionably enveloped in a cloud of his own egotism, which is obviously kept charged by surrounding admirers. That he is sincere, intelligent and potentially dynamic is beyond a doubt. Nevertheless, I had the feeling that he is groping his way through many difficult problems without a very clear idea of where he is going and without any preconceived plan, either moral, political or economic. In addition, I received the impression (and Bowles again confirmed this) that he is so tied up in the weary process of day-to-day administration that he no longer has a chance to feed a mind which requires the stimulation of continual new intellectual intake.

We started off with a discussion of Marxism. He said that when he had read Marx and other books by Soviet leaders, he had been very impressed, but it was "not the dogma I adopted." He continued:

Marxism is an analysis of history. The present-day Communists have changed this about a lot. Therefore I take what helps me from Marxism and discard the rest. Socialism as such is naturally making its way in the world through economic doctrines. Progressively in each country there is more and more social control by the state—even in the United States.

Thus in India there is a definite tendency for the state to assume increasing control. But this is limited by a paucity of financial resources and of available administrative personnel. The state needs to control the key strategic vital sectors such as transportation. Thus the railways are owned by the state. Motor transport is largely state-owned. Air India is one-half state-owned although privately operated.

This was a rather vague and amateurish definition—if such it may be called—of socialism, and I remarked as much to Nehru. I asked him if he felt himself socialistically inclined, whether he considered having the Congress Party adhere to the Second (Socialist) International; I pointed out that Marshal Tito had just told me he was contemplating having his People's Front join it. Nehru answered that the Second International was merely a trade union organization. (Of course, he is wrong there, but I didn't want to get into a debate with him.) He said, "Our trade unions might some day join it, but the question has never come up."

I asked if India thought of signing any strictly defensive alliances with any powers or joining a mutual defense coalition of a regional nature. He answered, "No alliance is contemplated. After all, what is a strictly defensive alliance? A defensive alliance automatically becomes a military alliance, and the purpose of a military alliance is to deal with preparations for war. We are obviously interested in what happens along the regions near our borders; thus, for example, we are interested in what happens in Burma or Pakistan, but we are not resolved on any concrete policy of what to do."

I asked Nehru if he had any information on the Peking government's attitude towards the new Indian peace plan for Korea. He replied evasively, "There is nothing definite from China, nothing definite means something good." I asked him to please elucidate because this made no sense to me. He answered: "It is obvious we hoped our proposal would be accepted. Otherwise we would not have made it. Clearly the Chinese are waiting to see what other people's reactions are. At least they have not reacted against it." From all of this doubletalk I gathered that at least some hint had been given the new Indian ambassador in Peking that China was favorably inclined. (Bowles later confirmed this guess.)

I asked if Nehru could explain to me in his own words just what it was that held India together as a state against the various centrifugal forces operating in this newly independent country. He replied:

In one word, it is a certain nationalistic sentiment. This goes deeply into the past. Throughout history you will find that, politically, India was often divided but it remained more or less a unit. The same ideas coursed through India, the same background of culture. The people never attached too much importance to politics. That was for the kings and emperors. Now to this matrix of a common past two or three germs of politics have been grafted. I must say that one of the politically unifying forces was the British occupation.

I asked what he thought of the possibility ultimately, in long-range terms, of India federating in some fashion with Pakistan and perhaps Burma. I pointed out that after all they shared the same common "matrix" of the subcontinent's cultural past. He answered:

Yes, that common matrix of culture is also applicable to Pakistan. We share the same community of history despite present differences on a purely political level. When Pakistanis and Indians meet—aside from politics—they do not meet as nationals from two different countries. They have the same background and speak the same languages. We are often misled by publicity given to extremist opinions in both Pakistan and India. But the masses of the people do not feel this.

I do hope that India and Pakistan will cooperate in a very large measure. They should not lose their common tradition. They cannot reverse history. They must increase the area of mutual cooperation. Groups of Pakistanis come here—refugees from the Punjab. They are not bitter. They weep together with their old friends and discuss old memories.

In the modern world unless we destroy each other by war, there must inevitably be larger spheres of cooperation; regional cooperation and ultimately world cooperation. India, Pakistan and Burma ultimately should cooperate in that way. Perhaps they might form some kind of superfederation but always keeping their identities. However, these things must develop automatically—not artificially.

After a while I thought it was about time to go, but Nehru was in a mood to talk some more in that curious and occasionally effective manner of his that some describe as "thinking aloud." He said:

India is a big country. It is frightfully difficult to define its ideas and conceptions in a single phrase. But generally speaking, our approach to problems—economic, political, and so on—is pragmatic, not dogmatic. Our new five-year plan will soon be out—in a month or so. It may well be varied considerably from the original project as it is carried out. There are many uncertain factors.

We based our five-year plan upon what I might call present advantage. The choice is between present advantage or future development. The Russians, in their five-year plans, have chosen the latter. But to do this requires an authoritarian government. We also want to plan for the future but our first requirement is to plan for the present and this makes for a sort of juggling act. We must deal with a heavily populated country. There is not enough land to go around as there is in Russia.

This, as Nehru indicated in this rather complex way, was the reason that India is not planning for heavy investment in capital industry to anything like the degree of Marxist five-year planners such as in Russia and the satellites. Nehru meant that India must satisfy popular requirements for such things as consumer goods and keep the people happy. It was not a monolithic state which could order its helots around as does the Soviet dictatorship.

Later, after an inconclusive conversation held standing up, Nehru guided me to the door and shook hands in a rather nervous and diffident way. Going down the stairs, I noticed passing through one of the salons a curious mélange of signed photos inscribed to Nehru. Standing on a table side by side were the pictures of the prime minister of Afghanistan, President Truman and Haile Selassie of Ethiopia. Truman was in the middle— whatever that signifies.

NEW DELHI, *November 22, 1952*

ANOTHER equally interesting talk with Bowles today at his house. He sat around in his shirt sleeves brimful of enthusiasm and ideas. He started off by saying it would be easy to finance a new Indian railway through the Export-Import Bank. This would be a self-liquidating project. It would facilitate the shipment of raw materials from India to Japan. One hitch is that India would like to process its ore and make pig iron in order to create more jobs for its own labor pool. But Japan has its own pig iron industry. There must be a compromise on this subject. One of the most important resources of India is its quantity of monazite sands. This is a uranium ore and useful for atom bombs. We have been buying all of India's output, but now we have discovered other sources in South America. Nevertheless, Bowles hopes we will continue preemptive purchases if necessary to prevent anybody else from getting this valuable resource.

Nehru thinks that in the end China and Russia will split. He says he will only admit he's wrong if and when Stalin (or his successor) goes to Peking. Nevertheless, Bowles feels that Nehru is now getting discouraged on China. He recognizes that the pressure of the cold war will weld the friendship between China and Russia.

Bowles told Nehru in March that if China intervened in the Indochinese civil war, the United States will hit China. He did this on his own initiative and not as a result of Washington's instructions. He requested Nehru to inform Peking of this view. He feels that in all probability this helped restrain China from interfering.

Discussing Korea, Bowles said he had recently told Nehru that there are now only two choices. Either there will be a truce or there will be an all-out war. The United States is not prepared to continue for an indefinite period the process of bleeding. Bowles hopes Nehru is passing this on to Peking.

Furthermore, Bowles has explained to Nehru his belief that if the Communist-imperialist menace continues in the Far East, the United States must inevitably rearm Japan. That would include giving Japan a fleet, and it is quite evident that Japan has a motive for war—to reestablish itself on the continent of Asia. Therefore such a process would be extremely dangerous. The only alternative is a truce in Korea followed by a peace. That in turn would have to be followed by a peace settlement in Asia including Indochina. Only when this comes, would we be prepared to abandon the concept of making a militarily strong Japan. Of course, we would insist on hanging on to Formosa, but in the case of a peace, Formosa would cease to be a threat to China. Then China would open up again for trade. Once it began to resume commercial relationships with the West, it would be less dependent upon Russia. Bowles has urged Nehru to pass on to the Chinese the warning that dictators "fall into wars." By this he means that they become involved in wars they do not calculate on. Thus Hitler was surprised after gobbling up large chunks of Europe to find England and France making a stand in Poland.

And now we will dine at Moti Mahal in old Delhi where Hindu refugees from Peshawar and the northwest frontier still prepare their food in Pathan fashion and whole chickens, dipped in spices, are lowered for but a moment on an iron spit into the flaming tandoor ovens and emerge roasted crisp, to be seized with the ten fingers and consumed with voracity; and the grease drips from your face as you dab a drumstick into dishes of still hotter sauces; and you wipe your lips with half-cooked unleavened bread called *nan;* and you nibble crystallized sugar and cardamon and silvered betel leaves containing betel nuts, called *pan;* until, sated with the delicacies of the Khyber Pass, you lurch and belch your way into the steaming hot night of Asia. . . .

KARACHI, *November 27, 1952*

THE papers today announce that the Czechoslovakian purge trials are over. All but three have been sentenced to death. I cannot help recalling a few facts. Clementis, the former foreign minister, was in New York at the

UN when it was first clear he would be purged. In fact I wrote an article that was published on the front page saying he would be "in for it" if he went home. But he did—on Gottwald's guarantee. Of course Gottwald is just a weak drunk. Clementis now will die. André Simon, after publicly stating he wanted to hang, will do so. I had a long evening with him in Prague in 1949. Simon was a rabid toady of the Soviets and rude to an unbearable degree, both in print (*Rude Pravo* and *Parallèle 50*) and in person.

KARACHI, *November 27, 1952*

YESTERDAY, shortly after arriving, I went over to the embassy for a drink with my old friend Avra Warren, who was leaving that afternoon after almost three years here as ambassador, and then he took me on to lunch at the home of a wealthy Pakistani friend of his, Wajid Ali. Wajid, a millionaire, originally made a fortune as a contractor for the British army in the days of the *raj*. He is now not only rich but well connected. Among those at the lunch were the minister of interior and governor of Sind, secretary for defense. Each of us had his own separate little table and sat back to guzzle partridge, curry, sweet—well laced with champagne. The building where we ate was of American design: a globe of concrete poured around a balloon that was later removed. It was extremely cool and comfortable. After lunch we all went down to see the Warrens off on a seedy ship for Bombay, the BI boat *Dara* which was loaded with odd customers including the Sheikh of Kuwait. A magnificent Pakistani band of pipers marched up and down the pier drumming and piping the Warrens away.

Today I had a long talk with Lt. Col. Iskander Mirza, Secretary of Defense (later dictator). Kashmir and water are the two big problems with India. "Get us a Kashmir decision and water," he said, "and I'll be the first to approach India on staff talks for joint defense of the subcontinent. We want to be friends with India. The future of each of our economies and everything else depends on the two countries pulling together. We would have staff talks and plan a regional defense—save for that blasted Kashmir thing."

It would be ideal if there could be federation of Pakistan, India and Afghanistan. But that's impossible.

BEIRUT, *November 29, 1952*

I spent an unforeseen night and day here when we developed trouble en route to Istanbul after a Beirut stop-off and had to turn back. As a result I had long talks with Harold Minor, our ambassador; Armin Meyer, his political officer; Musa Bey el Alami, a chief of the Palestine Arab community, now visiting from Jerusalem, and others.

Minor and Meyer are very discouraged. They say the situation gets worse rather than better. Palestine peace is further off than ever. There won't be a shooting war; but chaos and economic blockade coupled with increasing anti-Americanism.

I lunched aboard the carrier *Franklin Delano Roosevelt,* which is here on a diplomatic visit. Its jets have been flying over Lebanon, Syria and Jordan. The President of Lebanon came on board and proudly got his picture snapped in a jet cockpit. Captain Anderson of the *F.D.R.* (who used to be at SHAPE) says he could get four fighters in the air within thirty minutes despite the present jumbled decks, crowded with sightseers.

ANKARA, *December 1, 1952*

THIS morning I had a talk with Major General Arnold, head of the Joint American Military Mission for Aid to Turkey (JAMMAT). It is astonishing to see his group, all in uniform, working side by side with Turks all over the country on an equal basis, when one recalls that only a few years ago widespread xenophobia and above all military suspicion were directed at all foreigners.

Arnold says there isn't much hope of organizing a meaningful defensive alliance in the Middle East. The fighting would have to be done by the Turks and the West. South of here is "just a can of worms." It would be desirable to have bases in the Arab world but they mistrust us on Israel and our "colonial" allies.

The general claims: "The Turk is the finest soldier in the world. He is ready to die. Life is hard and death is a ticket to the Moslem heaven. The ignorant peasant doesn't know the good things of life. He has a great love of country and respect for his superior."

ANKARA, *December 1, 1952*

LONG talk with Fuad Köprülü, foreign minister of Turkey, in his dark-paneled office of the new foreign affairs ministry, and then I went to his house for lunch—the rather ugly but comfortable residence of the foreign ministers on the Çankaya heights, where we ate lavishly from a golden service. Köprülü, a small, amiable fellow, speaks fluent, rather bad French.

He told me Tito has stated he would consider an attack on Greece or Turkey as an aggression against Jugoslavia. K. said, "My conviction is if there is a war, it will be a total war; war and peace are today total conceptions. Therefore it is very necessary to have a regional arrangement for immediate reaction to an attack. We are still preparing the terrain. I foresee definite results fairly soon." He added such must be "co-related" with NATO. Turkey is sending a military mission to Belgrade in a few days. "We have the same destiny before any aggression. The collaboration between our three countries is sincere. And it is necessary. Aggression does not accept neutrality any more."

He despairs about Iran. Mossadegh is now the slave of the hysteria and xenophobia he created. There is financial and economic chaos. If Russia gains Iran, Iraq may well go.

TEL AVIV, *December 6, 1952*

THE blond hatchet-faced, collective farmer in Israel is explaining that it really was quite easy for him to rescue his father during the war from a German concentration camp in Jugoslavia.

> You see, I am a Croat. That is to say, of course I'm Jewish but I come from Zagreb. I was in Palestine when war came so I volunteered and was attached to your OSS. When they dropped me in I heard about my father . . . where he was. So I put cn a German officer's uniform and with two other colleagues drove to the camp and told the authorities I had been sent to pick him up for new examination. The Germans are very impressed if you are wearing a uniform and your forged papers are adequately stamped. Really it was simple. The only thing that worried me was father. Did he give the show away? Why, no. He didn't even recognize me.

Very interesting talk for a couple of hours today with Ben Gurion, the Israeli prime minister, in his Tel Aviv house which is crammed with books in many languages on many subjects. He seemed in vigorous shape for a man his age (sixty-six) who works so hard and who is said to sleep only four hours nightly.

He told me not only that he had won money on the American elections but had a deep admiration for Eisenhower's "humanity and understanding" (although he intimated he would have preferred a Stevenson victory).

Ben Gurion thought Israel would be self-sufficient in food in from four to six years (which I vastly doubt, above all if the population increases the way the Government wants). Right now it is about 10 per cent self-sufficient in meat and from 30 to 40 per cent in bread. He also spoke with visionary enthusiasm about developing exports from copper, phosphate, manganese and iron resources and new "basic industries."

He said the population is now 1,600,000 with four thousand monthly still coming in. He expects much more immigration—above all from French North Africa. In ten years, he says, the population should be 4,000,-000 (which I think is nonsense) and this can "easily" be supported by the present territory of Israel, above all the Negeb (which is patently out of the question).

He said Israel desperately wanted peace with the Arabs and then economic and military cooperation. He first thought Naguib was conciliatory but now doubts it. Ben Gurion won't tolerate the return of any of the Arab refugees or any territorial changes except minor frontier adjustment trades. He fears the recent Prague trials mean official anti-Semitism by Moscow under the guise of "cosmopolitanism" and that in case of war the Russians will "exterminate" their 2,000,000 Jews. "After all, they killed millions of their own peasants when it was deemed convenient."

He said the Arabs were rearming, above all Egypt and Syria which are getting jets and tanks from Britain.

CAIRO, *December 9, 1952*

I saw Couve de Murville, French Ambassador, today. Couve thinks it is foolish of us to include the Turks in any Middle East Defense Organization (MEDO) project. They are still heartily disliked by Egypt as former "occupiers."

The overall project, of course, is to establish a MEDO agreement. At the start, this would include the United States, Britain, France, Turkey and Egypt. But the other Arab states would come in shortly if Egypt joined. A separate Allied agreement would have to be made with Israel, whose army is useful, as the Arab nations would never sign a peace recognizing Israel's legal position. In fact, although the Egyptians and others don't want to resume war with Israel and fear her as much as she fears them, they also don't want formal peace or a termination of the blockade.

In a MEDO it would not be valuable to build up local armies. What is desired is a positive rather than a negative political attitude: infrastructure, communications, local labor. All Egypt wants militarily is a few more tanks and planes for parade purposes. Britain, Couve thinks, is being too stingy in supplying arms.

CAIRO, *December 10, 1952*

I had an excellent talk with Ambassador Caffery this morning. Although he is now about sixty-six, he looked better than in years and seems very much on the *qui vive*. He has just come back from a visit to the army along the Palestine border (Gaza Strip, and so forth). I doubt if Caffery will be here much after Ike gets in because I recall very well Ike doesn't care for him. He was close to King Farouk, and, despite this, seems to have become close with General Naguib, who gave Farouk the bounce.

Caffery described himself as a "restrained, long-range optimist" on Egypt. He thinks the Sudanese negotiations will end well soon. The British are bucking hard but they have to give and we are pushing them. This is too bad in many ways. They have done very well in the Sudan. It was a jewel of colonialism. Nevertheless it *is* colonialism, Caffery points out, and that is just *démodé*. It won't help Egypt, the Sudanese or England, but it must be done to get anything else accomplished.

After that, Caffery thinks the Suez negotiations and a MEDO arrangement can be concluded within six months or less. MEDO would include participation of British Commonwealth troops; therefore it could not be subordinate to NATO. It's too bad, Caffery thinks, that the Turks are in it; but that can't be changed. Turkey is unpopular here as a former occupier. Britain is detested. The French are disliked. And our Palestine policy has been unpopular. So it makes an odd bunch of allies.

He has the feeling that Naguib and the men around him *want* to join up in a defense arrangement with us—and therefore are prepared to take our allies as we have insisted they must. They also want military and economic aid. They are not, as Couve thinks, truly "neutrality" minded. They know what Russia means. The Russians weren't active here prior to the coup because they regarded Egypt as a ripe pear ready to fall to them. Now, however, the Communists are getting more active despite the fact they have few leaders and these are mostly in jail. Their agents sit around in cafes about the country and spread rumors such as "life is lousy in Egypt; it is equally lousy in the USA; but it's heavenly in Russia." And of course the fellah has no means of judging.

Naguib, Caffery thinks, definitely wants an eventual Palestine peace. But this must go slowly. MEDO must come first. There is no fanaticism on the Palestine question.

CAIRO, *December 13, 1952*

I have had a pretty packed time during the past few days. Among those I have talked with were General Mohammed Naguib, who ousted King Farouk last July and established a semidictatorship; British Ambassador Stevenson; and, on a trip to the Suez Canal Zone, General Sir Brian Robertson, British Middle East land forces commander, at his headquarters in Fayid.

I saw Naguib on December 10 in his office at the presidency of the Council. He is a small, stocky, dark man of unmistakable African ancestry, with a rather kindly face, a lined, worried expression, and exceptionally warm brown eyes. He was wearing his general's uniform with a few ribbon decorations. He seemed a simple, unpretentious man.

He explained to me that his job was very hard work, that he went to bed at midnight every night and arose at 6 A.M.; that Friday (the Moslem sabbath) was his only day off and that even then, after going to the mosque, he received people at his house. Despite his appearance of modesty, he obviously likes publicity and seems to put himself out to see reporters and get his pictures printed in the papers.

At the end of our talk (after an hour) I made a move to get away, but he kept on chatting, smoking his pipe, sipping lemonade. He hauled a silver Torah out of his desk drawer and explained it had been given him by the

Jewish community. He stressed that despite the Palestine war he believed in brotherhood regardless of race or creed, adding: "Egyptian Jews are like any other Egyptians, they have all the rights and respect of everyone else. They and the Christians like me as much as anyone does. I believe in liberty in every way. Anybody is free to adopt the religion he likes."

During our talk Naguib spoke in English, which he seems to know quite well but certainly not perfectly. Time and again he said, "Now I am going to tell you the truth, but you must be kind to me and soften it when you write it." Just what he means or what he expects a reporter to do, I can't say.

In brief, he said negotiations with Britain on the Sudan were going better. But then he launched into a long diatribe against the British. This lasted a half-hour. He said the British had deliberately fostered differences between the South Sudanese and the northerners, had prevented the former from becoming Moslem. He promised he would never exploit South Sudan. Since the Egyptians originally moved into the Sudan only to find a cheap slave market; since the South Sudanese are mostly naked pagans or at best phoney Christians and illiterate savages who never heard of either England or Egypt, it is odd to think Cairo and London are now arguing about what voting procedures they should have in a plebiscite three years from now.

He asked for American military aid and said Egypt should be treated like Turkey "because we are more important than Turkey"—not too modest a remark. I asked if he would accept an American military mission of 1,300 men the way the Turks had. That gave him pause.

He complained about Western support for Israel; said we had created a state of 1,000,000 and thus lost the friendship of 50,000,000 Arabs and their oil. He said he didn't trust the Israelis, who had ignored UN resolutions and created a "bad stain" by expelling 1,000,000 Arab refugees. Egypt could trust Israel only if it paid the refugees an indemnity and returned them to Israel—which is, of course, out of the question. He complained bitterly that the US had pushed Germany to pay reparations to Israel for the Nazi Jewish victims, and with this money Israel was getting stronger militarily while Britain held back even on delivering jet planes which Egypt had paid for on the excuse of priority delays.

He said he opposed change and did not favor a republic; change damaged economic stability. He had abrogated the constitution to modernize it and limit the future powers of the monarch to those of the English sovereign. But he favored a king because that represented national unity. On the whole I had the impression that Naguib is a most honest, decent man but rather limited and not the "strong man" he is made out to be. I would not be surprised to see more revolution and more fireworks before the next year has passed.

Sir Ralph Stevenson, whom I've known for years, spoke freely about the need for evacuating Suez in order to reach final agreement. But the Egyptians would have to make certain guarantees to keep the base in order with the aid of foreign (British or American) technicians; promise to permit British or MEDO return in case war was imminent; and join MEDO.

Stevenson thought the Sudan negotiations would end with agreement soon and that the Suez talks wouldn't take too long. I wonder. I think Stevenson is slowing things up and I'm not sure he's wrong. After all, returning the Sudan to a jungle and Suez to a dust heap isn't going to help humanity even if it honors nationalist emotions.

I drove down to Fayid yesterday and saw Robertson, with whom I had voyaged to Anzio in the same destroyer wardroom as Field Marshal Alexander. Robertson is a nice guy but damned old-fashioned. He also talked of evacuating Suez but said it would be necessary to maintain British technicians "numbering in the thousands" here to insure that the infrastructure and radar kept going. The Egyptians aren't going to take that. He also said the Suez talks had "nothing to do with MEDO" (just the opposite of Stevenson).

In other words, he wants a hard and fast British toehold on Suez. It certainly is the only existing good base for Middle East defense. It cost about $1 billion to put in the military installations. It has ports, railways, roads, water, communications, barracks, and so forth. Britain is now negotiating new base rights in Libya and building new barracks in Cyprus, but this will take time and cost more money. Robertson maintains the Middle East can't be defended without the participation of at least one great power (Britain is the only one to have stepped up) and without an adequate base (Suez). He said the United States established huge bases in the Pacific swiftly during World War II. But we were at the peak of production and didn't care about expense. There is no other good base in the region than Suez.

Just as Stevenson did, Robertson emphasized the need for us to support Britain in her talks with Egypt. Stevenson had complained that although Caffery and McClintock (the counselor) were helpful, the rest of the Americans were too desirous to be liked by the Egyptians and were disturbing things by vague promises in quest of popularity. Robertson thought we should help the Egyptians buy military equipment.

Caffery was exceptionally talkative. I saw him once in his office and dined with him twice. He recounted at length the events of last July when Naguib bounced Farouk. Farouk called Caffery by telephone in terror; said the palace was surrounded, asked Caffery to have British troops sent to save him. Caffery kept trying to get him to shut up on the telephone, which was obviously tapped, but Farouk was too scared to pay attention.

All this stuff Farouk has been publishing in his memoirs about bullets whistling around him is a lot of crap. Farouk is so greedy that, although he needs no money, he is publishing phony memoirs (ghost written by an English publicity agent) for sheer greed. Caffery said he has evidence from women he knows that despite his lusty reputation Farouk is almost impotent. He had an extensive and foul collection of movies and pictures in the palace, some of which Caffery has seen.

He confirms my guess that the British are dragging their feet on the Sudan and Suez negotiations, trying to hang on and see what comes. Caffery thinks Naguib is truly strong. He was selected by the junta; was not a conspirator himself until the very last minute. Aly Maher turned traitor against the King and was one of the key plotters.

An odd thing happened on our last night when the Cafferys had Marina and me to dinner. I was lighting a cigarette and the box of paper matches accidentally caught fire and exploded in my hand. Caffery thought this was hysterically funny and roared with laughter; the only time I've ever seen him lose control. I wasn't exactly pleased: the whole palm of my hand was badly burned.

# 2 7

---

# THE NEW AFRICA

THERE IS NO CONNECTION BETWEEN THE MAU MAU TROUBLES IN Kenya and Addis or other Soviet centers. Rumors are sometimes spread through Italian truck and mule train drivers, but most Ethiopians are illiterate and can't remember things long. Certain discontented tribal leaders with an education indirectly pick up the Russian line. But there are no known Moscow-trained Communists south of Suez. Of course, there are big potentialities—so far undeveloped.

Last November 7 the Russians had a relatively modest celebration of their national holiday—but gave the same food and drink to the servants and chauffeurs as to the diplomats—and stressed this fact. Soviet propaganda has paid remarkably little attention to East Africa but has been concentrating on those areas which will pay a dividend soonest—Egypt and North Africa. In Addis Ababa they seem to be short on funds.

One Kikuyu did try to get to Ethiopia over the extremely tough border country. He was picked up near Neghelli, about a hundred miles from Kenya, and imprisoned last month. He is suspected of Mau Mau affiliations.

There is no Communist Party in Ethiopia, so it never had to be declared illegal. There is none in Kenya although a few pamphlets from the British party have been circulated.

Russia is not so omniscient and powerful that she has the necessary apparatus at hand yet for African operations. We should not overestimate them. But there is a potential. We must avoid the dangerous drift to a white-versus-black feud instead of all decent people against savagery.

The East Africans are beginning to hear about the Gold Coast, Nigeria and Liberia where the populations are much more advanced. In those areas, after an initial leftist trend, the swing has been more towards conservatism and away from Communism.

I have had several talks with J. Rives Childs, our ambassador, an old hand in the Arab and Middle Eastern world, who is retiring to Nice next January to write an authoritative book on Casanova. He is an amiable chap and craves to be an author, friendly but rather discouraged with the State Department and hardly a ball of fire. He thinks we have mishandled the French in North Africa from the word go and should back them more strongly.

My impressions of Addis Ababa are mixed. It is a beautifully situated town (selected only some sixty years ago as a capital by Menelik after he whipped the Italians, and developed when it became the terminal for the French railway to Djibouti). Most of its relatively decent buildings were constructed by the Italians and started collapsing when they left. The majority of the population—and no one has any idea of its size—lives in wattle and mud huts or shacks with corrugated iron roofs. A weird mixture of people strolls through the streets or rides about in tiny gharries like trotting race sulkies, drawn by ponies and filled with typhus-bearing fleas. Many of the women, with dark faces, aquiline features, massed bound hair, luminous black eyes, and multicolored turbans setting off their white robes, are lovely. The better class men ride donkeys or stroll about, often carrying umbrellas, wearing white togas and jodhpurs, weird hats ranging from topees to black homburgs, but with grave, bearded, dignified faces.

The people are somewhat pathetic. We are staying in a hotel called the Filwoha Palace which was once an imperial bath house and looks it, with tiled floors, walls, ceilings. But it is quite comfortable. The servants speak a rather useless form of English. Their better sentences are something like this: "Some wants see you on telephone please." Or "Your wife she bathing her body upstairs." I caught one pathetic man dressed in blue trying desperately to teach himself to read Amharic from a primer, sitting muttering letters of the alphabet aloud with great effort. Practically everybody I run into says what a tragedy it was the Italians were ever kicked out.

Oddest of all is an American Negro named Homer Smith. I used to know Homer in Moscow. He had gone there as a sympathizer, married a Russian wife, and I remembered him as an office boy and assistant in the AP office. He once drank like a fish—now it's like a whale, starting at 9 A.M. He was never quite bright but his mind does not function too well now.

Homer came from the South and was deeply and understandably embittered by American racism, so when Soviet propaganda, during depression and postdepression years, appealed to American immigrants, he went to the USSR where he had to give up his passport (as was the rule) to get a job. To his horror he discovered that, quite apart from the discomforts of the climate and the repressions of the dictatorship, the Russians themselves were even worse racists than white Americans. All this helped encourage in him a fondness for vodka. Once a week (after pay day) he used to totter in the AP office, reeking and dead gray.

During World War II, when Ethiopia reestablished relations with Russia (broken at the time of the Bolshevik Revolution) a chargé d'affaires was initially sent by Addis Ababa and he, being also of dusky complexion, became Homer's friend. After the war the Ethiopians were pressed by the Russians to accept a small aid mission of four persons and Homer persuaded his pal (so he could finally escape from the USSR) to specify his name as the press and cultural affairs expert who was one of the four to go. Homer, of course, qualified because he was a Soviet citizen.

So off he went with his Russian wife and he's been here ever since. In no time he discovered that the Ethiopians (whose upper class pretends to be Amharic and looks down on Negroes as *Shankalla* or "niggers") were the most racist of all people he had known; and the Ethiopians discovered that an alcoholic ex-AP office boy wasn't much of a buy as a cultural expert.

Ambassador Childs has been trying to get Homer out—back home to dear old racist America—but the State Department expressed prompt and astonished horror that a distinguished envoy should even think of asking our government to let back a man who gave up his citizenship in order to go to Russia and become a Communist!

Homer now works for the propaganda ministry, the English language weekly, and strings for *Time* and the AP. He has a busted down old car which he doesn't know how to drive. It is quite a sport rattling along with him over the rotting roads between trotting gharries and herds of cattle. He got his white, Soviet wife out but she's miserable too.

Because of Ethiopian prejudice, Homer is more popular with the foreign set than the locals. He keeps grumbling about how terrible it was the Italians got out; that everything has collapsed since. He's writing a book on a Negro's experiences in Russia, which isn't as bad as it might be; could be quite good if he'd sober up and finish it. I've hired Homer to drive me around and help—but he's a pretty fumbling aid.

The red tape of the local bureaucracy is beyond belief. The Ethiopian legation in Cairo gave us transit visas valid three days, saying otherwise it would take weeks as they'd have to get authorization from Addis. They said it would be easy to fix things up in Addis. What a joke.

We arrived at the airport (Cairo, Port Sudan, Asmara, Addis) and first got a real going-over from customs who went through everything despite the fact we were met by a bevy of embassy and TWA (Ethiopian Airlines) officials. We were later told they had been very easy on us. They howled like hell because Marina's smallpox vaccination certificate didn't have a rubber stamp on it. In the end we got in, and a young chap from the embassy said he'd send the passports and certificate to the proper authorities to have them okayed. The embassy driver took us off. He dropped us at an Ethiopian bath. We finally got him to take us to the hotel. There we were dumped in our room with someone else's luggage. I had to search the entire hotel to find ours. God knows what happened to the other fellow's bags.

We spent two and a half days getting our documents fixed up because the bureaucrats refused to help out the Embassy. They complained about our passports and demanded letters from the ministry of foreign affairs, and so on. Marina had to get a new vaccination at the Ras Desta hospital (given by an Italian linotypist who does parttime work as a doctor), and they wanted to keep her here fourteen days to test the reaction. This required twenty-four hours more maneuvering and documents and the aid of a Swedish doctor advising the public health ministry.

I was asked by Childs to pay courtesy calls on the Emperor's secretary and the minister of finance, press and propaganda (yes, it's all one). They even have a minister of the pen here. The latter was out. His office called back three days later and said if I would come see some minor functionary and explain why I wanted to see the minister, perhaps it might be arranged. I told them the hell with it; I was leaving. What should we do, they asked. I said it was their problem. The secretary of the secretary of the Emperor told me the secretary himself was too busy to see me. I told him I didn't want to see him anyway, but was merely calling at the ambassador's request.

I have now got it fixed to see the Emperor tomorrow morning and *must* see the secretary this afternoon. I had to borrow a cutaway from a guy in our embassy (fortunately my size) because that is mandatory for seeing the boss. Prince Henri of Orléans, visiting here some years ago, appeared before the Emperor in ordinary clothes. Result: the Emperor demanded: "Who is this foreigner who doesn't know how to appear before a king?"

ADDIS ABABA, *December 17, 1952*

TODAY I decided to kill two birds with one stone. My hand (burned in Cairo when a box of matches exploded in it) has been festering and needs treatment. And everyone is talking about the Russian Hospital (established long ago under the Czars) as a nest of Soviet spies. So I had myself driven there and walked right in.

Nobody paid the slightest attention. I wandered around clusters of dusky in-patients, poked my head into wards crammed with beds, finally asked an agreeable nurse (in my best Old Slavonic) where I could get my hand treated. I was taken to a doctor handling visitors. He asked no questions, spoke briefly to a nurse, put some kind of disinfectant on it, then a balm, and the nurse tied it up while chattering pleasantly, showing only mild curiosity in the fact I was American and spoke a few words of Russian. They couldn't have been nicer—and refused all payment.

I then strolled about, picking up several propaganda pamphlets in a waiting room, from the table (they were in English, boring, not in the least inflammatory but more in the nature of dull travel brochures on Russia) and wandered from one ward to the next. Since my hand was in a sling (which I didn't keep there many hours) I guess my presence was accepted as normal.

On the whole I was impressed by the niceness and efficiency of the Russian medical staff, by the nonpolitical aspect of the place, and by the utterly normal relationship among doctors, nurses and patients—like an American missionary hospital.

Obviously it is naive to draw serious conclusions from such a visit, but if that hospital is a hotbed of Soviet agents and propagandists, I'll eat my hat.

ADDIS ABABA, *December 17, 1952*

AT a cocktail party Childs gave for us, British Ambassador Busk told me he had received from Nairobi an official denial that Sir Percy Sillitoe, head of intelligence, had ever stated that the Soviet Hospital in Addis Ababa was the center of Communist African activity and had sent agents to stir up the Mau Mau in Kenya.

French Ambassador Roux told me one Allied diplomat is very suspect as a Communist. He sees a lot of Soviet diplomats here and is suspected of working on Cominform matters.

Judge Marein, a Palestinian Jew who used to handle the Emperor's legal and church affairs in Jerusalem (Haile Selassie has personal property in Palestine) and is now a judge on the Ethiopian high tribunal, told me some interesting facts about justice here. There is still a law on the statute books providing that a man's hand is knocked off if he is heard cursing a bishop. But, although the statute hasn't been replaced, it is not used and such amputation is no longer practiced. If anyone is heard complaining about the Emperor, he is sentenced to prison promptly. Flogging and hanging are common, but it is very rare that they are done in public.

The prisons are foul. A man sentenced to three or four years has slight chance of surviving if he has no friends or relatives to send food. Not only are the jails foul (in some, prisoners are shackled) and generally all the prisoners are in one cell (in the provinces men and women together), but death from malnutrition is commonplace. Under an agreement with Britain when Ethiopia was liberated, Europeans—although they have no capitulatory rights—are never put in jail unless they are run by Europeans or army officers. Also they have special food and housing privileges. Prisoners are used to operate the state gold mines—and are paid nothing.

Yesterday I drove through this odd town with its lovely flowers, gaudily beautiful birds, white-togaed inhabitants (and chieftains with black capes over their togas, riding donkeys and carrying umbrellas), to the office of Ato (Mr.) Tafara Worq, secretary to the Emperor. He is a rather surly and very Negroid individual, although he claims to be Amharic. He used to be interpreter to the British legation and had his office in a little thatch hut the Busk children now use as a playhouse. Busk says he can see "T. Worq" (as he calls him) regarding the shack askance whenever he comes to the embassy. His life was saved by Eden's personal intervention during the Italian occupation. He is a gruff individual with a superiority (inferiority?) complex, but has the reputation of being relatively honest as well as extremely important because he controls access to the Emperor.

The other day when I paid a courtesy call on T. Worq, his secretary said Worq was too busy to see me. Worq's secretary is a twenty-seven-year-old utterly black, Negroid type from Harar who was a wireless operator with the British during their attack on Italian-held Ethiopia. He is not very well educated nor very bright and is absurdly pompous and full of himself.

I am told the press (which means to say the weeklies) have strict censorship instructions including the stipulation the Emperor's name must always appear before anyone else's in a sentence and any pronoun referring to him such as "His" or "Him" must be capitalized.

Everybody here admits there is a certain amount of slavery still in the country. Most of this, it is said, is probably on a "humane" basis; that is to say, old slaves prefer to remain with their masters. In the hinterland there may well be some more brutal slavery. It is, of course, now against the law.

ADDIS ABABA, *December 18, 1952*

THIS morning I had an audience with His Imperial Majesty, Haile Selassie I, the Conquering Lion of the Tribe of Judah, Elect of God, and Emperor of Ethiopia. This is a very formal business. I had to borrow a cutaway from a fellow at the embassy. My taxi driver, Michael, a young man from Tigre who drove a Honey tank in the Eighth Army, chauffered me to the Green Gate of the New Palace (not the Emperor's residence but where he receives), past chained, mangy lions and sentries in battledress and topees, bearing bayoneted rifles, who saluted stiffly. We drove past a lovely rose garden where some officers in summer tan uniforms took charge of me. I sat a few minutes in a hall while white-garbed servants regarded me curiously. Then Ato Tafara Worq, the Emperor's secretary, came along and escorted me to H.I.M. On the way he explained to me I must bow three times: at the entrance, half-way through the room, and finally when shaking hands. This I did, without too much grace, and then the Emperor motioned me to sit on his right-hand side while Tafara Worq sat on my other side.

The Emperor knows English quite well, thanks to his exile in Bath, and speaks fluent French. Nevertheless the interview was gravely held in Amharic. I looked at Haile Selassie and addressed my questions. Then T. Worq translated them, translated the answers, and so on. His Imperial Majesty is a small man. I should say he was about five feet five. He is thin and has a dark, rather handsome countenance, with black beard, aquiline features, rather sad eyes, and a thinning mane of black hair which, as with so many Ethiopians, seems to grow out like a bush of wire. He was wearing the summer tan uniform of commander-in-chief, spattered with ribbon decorations. He sat on a sofa and beside him were two small tan and white dogs, something like spaniels, who slept throughout most of the audience.

There was one rather lovely rug at the Emperor's feet. The rest of the carpets were garish. The furniture was a curious mixture of French-type green brocaded chairs and sofas and objects made locally including a table with three sides, each of which was decorated with primitive drawings from the Emperor's life history. Other objects I noticed were a large silver elephant on a black pedestal, two silver microphones (why, I'm sure I don't know), a picture of what I took to be either the Emperor Menelik or one of the Coptic Abunas (rather Negroid), some family photos and silhouette drawings. Haile Selassie sat quietly, occasionally smiling and gesticulating with his fine thin hands.

The Emperor declared that his country not only wished to join any projected Middle East defense organization, but was anxious to have an American military aid mission established here in order to modernize the army and help establish a navy. This country, although not strictly Middle Eastern in a geographic sense, thus becomes the first nation of the region to apply for MEDO membership without any prior conditions.

The Emperor said that were Ethiopia to receive aid from friendly countries it could be more useful to the outside world. It now had access to the sea through federated Eritrea but required assistance to develop communications with its ports. He specifically said he desired a military mission to train his troops, and some ships with which to create and instruct a navy so that Ethiopia could become a more effective ally.

Speaking as head of the Coptic Christian Church, he said that while

the forces of materialism are at present increasing in the world, they are still weaker than those led by people dominated with spiritual beliefs. According to my understanding, the religion first preached in this world was to serve the purpose of God and preach His word. Unfortunately its ways have changed. Religion is frequently used by different countries for their own national purposes.

It is a fact that the materialist philosophy of communism is a grave danger to world peace. But it is very hard for the Russians to prosper here in Ethiopia. Communism succeeds where there is poverty. Thank God we are not so poor.

OUTSIDE ADDIS ABABA, *December 19, 1952*

IN rural Ethiopia the popular court is that of the *chika shum* and today there are three score people gathered beneath a fig tree preparing to argue the case long before the *chika shum* himself, the local mayor, has called the session to order. First, after all, the *chika shum* must finish his lunch, and this he proceeds to do, washing it down with several gulps of *tej,* the local mead, fermented honey. He dunks a piece of *injera* in a cup of *wat,* sucks his fingers heartily, wipes them upon his white toga. Finally he opens a battered old book in Amharic writing and spreads it on the table before him.

The case is about a cow, one of those small humped zebu cattle, which wandered into the complainant's garden, devouring his grain. This is wrong, avers the complainant, amid the contrapuntal babble of supporters; he should be paid a fine in silver dollars.

The *chika shum* deliberates. He discusses the matter with the village elders. He shares some *talla,* barley beer, with these wise men.

Who, argues the defendant, can prove the cow was his? And if it was, can he be responsible for the fact that the plaintiff is too lazy to construct a fence? And, as far as that goes, anybody here knows this grain was inferior and therefore valueless.

Such assertions are provocative. While the *chika shum* regards with interest, the friends and families of both parties stage their own discussion. It is assisted by the use of sticks. Wearily, the *chika shum* and elders retire to another fig tree. There, with a jug of *tej,* they consider the matter further. The law is evidently somewhat complex. Interpretation requires still more *tej.*

The *chika shum* lifts his gaze. He indicates to the assemblage, now silent, that the time has come for a verdict. Compromise is clearly the essence of justice. The *chika shum* therefore decrees the plaintiff has won his argument. However, his demand for silver payment is excessive. The defendant shall indeed be fined. Penalty will be a jug of *tej.* Case dismissed.

NAIROBI, *December 25, 1952*

WE have been in Kenya several days. There is only one topic of conversation—Mau Mau. Almost everyone we know carries a hand gun; either in his wife's bag or strapped around his middle, in a shoulder holster or even a pocket. Everyone locks his doors and windows at night and locks the servants out (they live in separate huts anyway) until morning. Nevertheless, life seems surprisingly normal.

There are plenty of holiday parties in a typically colonial atmosphere: dinner jackets, pink gins; highballs; characters muttering that "The Portuguese and Belgians don't stand for any nonsense like this. You see plenty of Africans with only one hand in their colonies. Those chaps know how to run a show."

In the streets there is a strange medley of ordinary Europeans, sunburned farmers in from the country, wearing khaki shorts and bush jackets, broad-brimmed hats and often beards and monocles; Indians, including many turbaned Sikhs; various Kenya tribesmen: tough-looking Masai and Kikuyus, their men and women with their ears punctured, torn into fleshy lace, or filled with strange ornaments.

On December 20 we lunched at Governor Sir Evelyn Baring's, a harassed-looking man, rather typically British and hard to figure out; courteous, grave, and I suspect rather tough under a languid, pale exterior. He suggested a long list of people for me to see and, when I checked this with others later, I found it was a generously impartial group of names.

Baring said that to date there was no evidence of direct Communist organization in Mau Mau or that Communists were prime movers. It doesn't follow from this, he added, that the Communists won't move in. Jomo Kenyatta is THE big figure of the troubles. He spent some time in Moscow in the thirties and obviously remembers what he learned. Jomo fused modern techniques of agitation with an appeal to superstition. He has a personal witch-doctory appeal with a hypnotic stare and "charm" stick.

Lady Baring told me they suspected their Kikuyu servants passed on information to Mau Mau "but good servants are so hard to get."

One of the most interesting, and indeed brilliant, men I met is Apa Pant, the Indian high commissioner, whose enemies call him a Communist but who impresses me as being an imaginative liberal. He takes a broad view and points out that the Commonwealth in Africa has seen the simultaneous development of two extremes—Malanism in the South and liberalism in the Gold Coast.

Pant points out that the African has difficulty in understanding abstract things such as death or justice or loyalty. Furthermore, exchange of ideas is hampered by the use of an artificial language, Swahili, a bastard mixture of Bantu and Arabic.

The change from barter economy to money brought violent repercussions in the East African mind. The old pattern of tribal life went. A new society came, to which blacks did not belong; frustration set in.

No one ever bothered to think of creating a "nation" here. There are three racial groups: European, Asian, African. These distinctions are kept in schools, clubs, residential areas, political institutions. This lack of synthesis is thus being perpetuated.

Among other people I saw was Eliud Wambu Mathu, a very black Kikuyu, educated in Cambridge, who is the leading tame Kikuyu politician and a member of the legislative council (first African appointed) and the

governor's executive council. He has the reputation of being a hard drinker
(as so many Africans are) and went to bed with some brandy for a few
days at the time the emergency was declared, presumably to avoid the Mau
Mau. Many suspect he is playing a double game and really working for
Mau Mau. I must say after talking with him I would not be surprised. One
thing is sure: he is not a very courageous or firm man; and as such he
should logically be a sucker for Mau Mau terrorism tactics.

Mathu, continually rolling his eyes which have extraordinarily large and
gleaming whites, said land hunger was a main Kikuyu grievance. The tribal
population had increased as land available shrank. Urban workers are
dissatisfied with wages and housing conditions. They have no social security. There are not enough schools or jobs. There is political frustration.

The British, he said, have as usual been too little and too late. Some
emergency reforms must be made immediately. Then a royal commission is
scheduled to arrive next year and plan for long-term reforms. Mathu says,
"Africa is boiling. This is not a local affair."

NAIROBI, *December 26, 1952*

ED DORZ, the United States consul general, very kindly asked us to a
Christmas party. Good, old-fashioned colonial style; all the men in white
dinner jackets, women in summer evening dress; lovely and friendly, plenty
to drink; the decorations looking a bit out of place in the tropical air of a
prosperous Nairobi suburb. Next morning we learned that three native
Kenyans had been murdered by Mau Mau within a three-hundred-yard
radius of our party. Most of the murders are against natives—to instill
fear.

Mike Dunford, an old friend of mine whom I knew as a wartime British
officer in the Middle East War, is now married to a lovely Greek girl and
lives here. He is part of one of the local defense units, going off in uniform
on night Mau Mau hunts. Cleo, his wife, always packs a gun in her handbag. When they are home at night they always have at least one gun right
beside them, on the table or by the bed, so that their servants can't surprise
them. Not a nice atmosphere!

ZANZIBAR, *December 27, 1952*

I have taken the following notes. As we left Nairobi, was again
impressed by the curiously sliced up and extended ears of the Kenya
tribesmen. The great hanging gaps of flesh are filled with ornaments on
occasion. . . . At Mombasa on the coast, the altitude drops a mile and the
temperature rises accordingly. The vegetation is tropical with heavily laden
pawpaw and mango trees. . . . At Tanga, the northernmost Tanganyika
port, I chatted with a tough stocky, sweating man who operates mobile

movies; he drives three thousand miles a month showing Wild West films to native workers in sisal plantations. . . .

Zanzibar is filled with clove forests, but many clusters of trees instead of being heavy green have gone gray with a blight called "sudden death" that has destroyed thousands of pounds worth. . . . The fruit trees are incredible: jackfruit, baobab, vast mango trees, coconut palms, lemon, all set off by brilliant red flamboyants . . . The first dhows are now coming in on the northeast monsoon from Muscat and other Arabian ports (they go back in a few months on the southwest wind). . . . Dhow captains with silver J-shaped daggers in silver scabbards thrust into their belts, bearded and fierce looking, stroll about the streets or wander past squatting Indian and Parsee shopkeepers in the narrow bazaars. . . . Humped Zebu cattle graze amid banana clumps. . . . African workmen, with colorful skirts and white skullcaps, walk in and out of the forests near their villages of daub and wattle huts, thatched with palm leaves. . . . In the bazaars the first African agitators from the mainland are said to be stirring up whispers of racial resentment. . . . Fazel Nasser Mawji, an unofficial member of the legislative council, at that body's last meeting (earlier this month) demanded that Britain pay a higher rent for the Kenya coastal strip rented from the Sultan. At present the rent is only 11,000 pounds a year. Mawji asked that this be raised to 400,000 pounds. This created a lot of talk but for the present won't do anything else, in all probability, because the government "official" majority controls the Legislative Council.

I went to the British residency for a talk with the resident, a slow-talking character named J. D. Rankine. He explained that the ten-mile coastal strip of Kenya is rented by the Sultan at 11,000 pounds and an additional six thousand pounds is received annually as interest on a loan made about four decades ago. Zanzibar is a British protectorate. The Sultan asked for a protectorate in 1890. This guarantees the throne to him. He can nominate his own successor subject to British agreement. His government is administered for him by the British resident.

The Arabs here originated for the most part in Muscat and Oman. There is still a large dhow traffic back and forth with Arabia. The Arabs bring to the bazaars the latest Middle Eastern politics. Thus, an argument is now going on between Ibn Saud and the Sultan of Muscat, cousin of Zanzibar's ruler, and everyone's interested.

The common language is Swahili. The Sultan's other principal domain is the nearby island of Pemba. He is sixty-four and his official title is His Highness, Seyyid Sir Khalifa bin Harub bin Thuweini.

DAR ES SALAAM, *December 28, 1952*

THIS really is rather a hell-hole. Tanganyika's economic future may be good, thanks to diamond finds and sisal plantations (largely owned by

Greeks) but the capital city is dismal and dank (unlike Nairobi) and without charm (unlike Zanzibar). A sad American consul general from the deep South (who is soon retiring) looked after us (sadly) and gave us a party to meet *le tout* Dar es Salaam. There is no Mau Mau type movement but the usual preindependence stirrings and simmerings of hatred between white, black and Asian, to which one can add the spice of tribal rivalries.

SALISBURY, *December 30, 1952*

NORTHERN Rhodesia has gone further ahead politically than Southern Rhodesia, where I am writing, but is far behind economically. In Northern Rhodesia and Nyasaland the colonial office has pushed the political advance of the native; therefore, there is more African antifederation feeling; a desire not to be "pulled down" by federation with the South. But on the whole there is no real "African" opinion. This has been confirmed by surveys by missionaries who aver the Africans don't care or know what federation means.

One has the feeling of a boom town in Salisbury. The immigration was up to a thousand whites a month and is now being held somewhat lower because of lack of housing. The wide streets of Salisbury and Bulawayo, which look as if designed for big city growth (and there already are real skyscrapers) come from the original settlement days when the long ox teams required wide avenues to turn. Indian immigration is carefully restricted.

On December 29 I went to a luncheon given by John Hoover, our consul general, attended by G. A. Davenport, acting prime minister; Lionel Powys-Jones, secretary for native affairs; Colin Kirkpatrick, an investment trust man and active proponent of federation; Sir Ernest Lucas Guest, lawyer and politician who opposes federation on its present terms; Brigadier Appleby, commander of the British South African Police (much like the Canadian Mounties); and two bankers named Jeffreys (Standard Bank) and Skipper (Barclay's). They are a definitely conservative group, completely confident that the present system of handling race relations here is correct.

Sir Godfrey Huggins, who has been prime minister for nineteen years (and is now in London for Central African federation talks), is head of the United Party. He is on record for "Partnership between the various races." No color bar to ability or culture. "We can only develop and hold this country as partners." But the African is on the lowest rung of the firm's ladder. For the foreseeable future, control must remain in white hands. Right now only about 450 Africans are on the voting lists.

Federation of Southern and Northern Rhodesia and Nyasaland is the hot issue: Europeans fear a future British government may force through universal suffrage for the Africans; therefore they want federation now, before the blacks get a break, yet everyone knows their ability. In 1946, the Goromonzi secondary school was established for Africans. In Cambridge examinations the Bantu boys did better than the whites.

The Capricorn African Society wants immediate federation for British Central Africa and almost immediate inclusion of British East Africa. Ultimately it wants inclusion of the Belgian Congo and Portuguese East and West Africa. The federation would be within the British Commonwealth and would be based upon "partnership" with the Africans. The movement is led by N. H. Wilson and Colonel David Stirling. Wilson is an elderly Southern Rhodesian whose son was a prisoner of war with Stirling. Wilson seems to be the speech writer, Stirling the promoter and contact man.

Capricorn believes that in Africa north of the Limpopo a great gulf is developing between the Union and the rest of the area on race relationships. Wilson wants no imperialistic adventures or grabs of territory; instead a voluntary association of territories for mutual advantage. He says even the Belgian and Portuguese territories, while in the British Commonwealth under federation, could retain affiliations with Brussels and Lisbon.

SALISBURY, *January 1, 1953*

I spent the day at the Chinamora Reserve of the Vashawasha clan of the Mzezuru tribe (part of the Mashona people). It is named for Chinamora, chief of the tribe. Chinamora is the hereditary name of the chief. Before he got the job this chief was called Kahari. The title is handed on from brother to brother, descending from the eldest, and then from son to son providing the son's father has himself been a chief. Somewhat complicated.

Chief Chinamora has five wives. He had six but divorced one. Native law applies on civil matters along basic Bantu lines with some tribal variations. The criminal code is based on Britain's. There are no open witch doctors. They are subject to legal penalty under the "witchcraft suppression act."

This reserve of approximately 75,000 acres contains around nine thousand people, settled in little kraals of mud brick and thatch huts. The chief is the principal native authority as head of the tribe. He is responsible to the Southern Rhodesian government for tribal well-being and order. He arrests offenders, reports the presence of locusts, and so on.

I visited this reserve (a tribal area approximately equivalent to an American Indian reservation) in order to discuss affairs with the local chief, accompanied by Waldemar von Memerty, a Southern Rhodesian, who represents the native affairs office. Von Memerty said this tribe's chief, who speaks English and once worked in Salisbury, the capital, is considerably better informed than the average.

Chief Chinamora, for whom the reserve is named, is a short, plump man with smiling face. The *kraal* (or village) of mud brick and thatched huts in which he lives is situated in lovely fertile country near two hulking rock mountains, Domboshawa, where witches were once cured by being marched round and round the top, and Mgoma Kurira, inside which it is said drumbeats can be heard.

When we arrived at his *kraal,* the chief sent word we should wait while he dressed, and we stood under a wild loquat tree looking about unsuccessfully for signs of the baboons, hyena and leopard which inhabit this reserve. The only edible "game" I saw were huge white termites which the tribe traps in their anthills and eats either raw or cooked. In the distance were flat rock surfaces we visited later where there are ancient bushman's paintings of animals strikingly similar to the Cromagnon paintings in Pyrenees caves.

Chief Chinamora received us in his home, a mansion compared to the rest of the *kraal,* for, although built of mud brick, it had seven rooms. Decorations included two pairs of handcuffs, used for criminals and hanging from a hook; a wooden table, a garage calendar, some native-made clay pots shaped like animals, a set of "willow pattern" plates and an empty Coca-Cola bottle.

When we entered, the chief stood up. He was wearing a flashy, checked tweed coat, yellow polo shirt open at the neck, gray slacks and brown shoes. Before starting our conversation, he proudly showed me a cheap silver medal given him in 1947 by the late King George VI when he visited Southern Rhodesia and a brass badge and chain made in Birmingham, England, and presented by the British South Africa Company some years ago.

Noticing that I was interested in his possessions, the chief shouted to one of his wives to bring in his royal robes and crown. These were produced with the bow which each wife always addresses to her sovereign lord.

Chief Chinamora told me the normal life of the reserve was to rise at 6 A M. when the natives started work on the land. Around nine o'clock they returned for the first of two daily meals: *sadza* or boiled *mealiemeal* (corn) and tea. After a day's work the dinner is *sadza* and vegetable stew, sometimes with meat.

Many of his people are not Christian but believe in a supreme god called Mwari and a series of lesser divinities comprising the spirits of tribal ancestors. I asked the chief if he resented the fact he had no vote under Southern Rhodesian law. He replied, "I don't want to vote. I don't understand it." He told me he had never heard of the following: Stalin, Communism, Eisenhower, the Archbishop of Canterbury (he is Anglican himself), Moscow, Washington or London. He had heard of Churchill whom he described as "a member of Parliament." He knew America was "a big country."

I asked him if he favored the project for federating Southern Rhodesia, Northern Rhodesia and Nyasaland, now being discussed in London. He replied, "No, I am against it. I don't understand it. I don't support things I don't know about."

I asked the chief how old he was. He said, "I think I must be fifty-six." I asked him if there were any *Muroyi* (witch doctors) practicing in his reserve, and he said no. They are banned under the witchcraft suppression act but are not uncommon.

The only drink (European alcoholic beverages are not permitted here for the native) is a native beer called *ropoko*. I asked the chief if his tribesmen liked to get drunk, and he replied happily, "Oh yes."

Chief Chinamora explained to me that he had five wives named Jessica, Shaiko, Gertrude, Estancia and Eulalia. He had a sixth but divorced her because "she was naughty."

He told me he was Christian; that three of his wives were Roman Catholic and two Anglican. I asked von Memerty later how Chief Chinamora was able to square such polygamy with the Pope and Archbishop of Canterbury. He replied, "Oh, these are native marriages, not church marriages. Each native considers himself a member of the sect of any mission that has helped him."

The chief told me he had to pay each wife's father a sort of reverse dowry called *lobola*. They all cost the same: eight head of cattle and twenty-five pounds sterling each. He has seventeen sons and eighteen daughters (five babies died). I asked which was the eldest and youngest.

The chief then hauled out a dilapidated old bank accountant's book where were registered his progeny under the name of each wife. The eldest child is thirty-two. The youngest is ten months.

I asked him if he liked Europeans (this continent's euphemism for white men). He answered, "Yes. They help my people. I live a European life. I have seven rooms in my house. The Europeans brought us a new method of plowing. We have many crops."

As a special favor the chief then dressed up in his royal regalia, explaining, "I wear my crown only at big meetings." The crown was a shabby hat of otter fur trimmed with leopard. Over his tweeds he pulled a tawdry bright red and blue robe given him when King George was in Salisbury.

He showed me his two black wooden scepters, about four and a half feet long, one bearing in gilt the arms of England and the other a broad silver ring with the names of previous chiefs engraved on it. He explained that when he goes to assemblies of tribal chiefs in Salisbury, he wears a white sun helmet instead of his crown.

PRETORIA, *January 3, 1953*

WALDEMAR Gallman, our ambassador here, has the following views: Prime Minister Malan is concerned at the extent to which Britain is "eliminating" itself in Africa. He refers in this connection to the Gold Coast. He tells Gallman he wants Britain to remain in Africa, and wants to keep the connection between the Union and Britain. Britain must save Africa for the West. Gallman is of the opinion that Malan is by no means as "anti-British" as he is depicted. I am a bit sceptical about Gallman's faith on this score.

Malan, according to Gallman, feels a community of interest with the United States. He points out how the Afrikaners pushed back their frontier and also had their own struggle against Britain. But as Gallman points out, there is still a very strong feeling among Afrikaners against Britain. This is why the Nationalists place so much stress upon the question of language.

The European element in South Africa is determined, regardless of party, to maintain white supremacy. Apartheid is just a slogan. The native is too intermingled in the various strata of society to be easily extricated.

Gallman feels that there is no reason to think that an explosion is imminent here. Neither the natives nor the Indians are well enough organized to threaten security of the economy on a nationwide basis by means of strikes, and so on.

Of course, the natives are so worked into the various levels of society that in theory they could tie up the country in twenty-four hours. They are in the mines, transport, household servants, post offices, etc. But they are not yet adequately organized. When that will come about remains to be seen.

When Gallman first arrived in the Union, he thought it would be a matter of twenty-five to fifty years before there could be an explosion. Now he thinks it is more likely to be between five and ten years, as a result of the efficient way in which the Indians, above all, have organized a resistance campaign. They showed considerable discipline in protests against the segregation laws.

This is the largest European population in sub-Saharan Africa. There has never been a question, as in the Gold Coast, of "native" government. The Nationalist Party is strong. It looks as if it cannot be ousted for years. The United Party suffered from the fact of Smuts' long leadership, which prevented the youth from coming into positions of authority. The United Party has no dynamic leaders now. There is much apathy in the party— even in its stronghold of Natal.

PRETORIA, *January 5, 1953*

THIS morning I had a long talk with D. D. Forsyth, secretary of state for external affairs. Despite his name, Forsyth is an Afrikaans-speaking South African. His position is the equivalent of the British permanent undersecretary for foreign affairs, and he served in the Smuts government.

Forsyth is a lean, rather dour-looking individual, but has an appealing frankness and deliberative quality about him. We started talking about the issue of Southwest Africa. He explained that the Union does not seek to incorporate Southwest Africa into itself. It did in 1946, but this is no longer official policy.

I asked Forsyth for his comments on the new UN group appointed to investigate South African race problems and policy. He said this commission would be completely ignored, because its validity is not recognized. He added that South Africa resented the role of the United States in this matter. He asked: "What would the United States have felt if a commission had been appointed to investigate American policy towards the Negroes in the South?" He contended that such efforts on the part of UN represented interference in internal affairs.

PRETORIA, *January 6, 1953*

THE *Broederbond* is a secret organization, founded in 1919. Its main purpose is to ensure that Afrikaners are appointed in preference to English-speaking South Africans in all fields of government service. Today it has developed into a shadow government. The extent of its influence is unknown, but is undoubtedly great. It has only a few thousand members. It is not open to all Afrikaners. Only members of the Dutch Reformed Church are admitted, and they are carefully selected by the *broers* (brothers). During World War II the military intelligence of the Smuts government wired a room in which the *Broederbond* was meeting, and gathered considerable information. At that time it was reported that the head of the organization was Professor J. C. van Rooy, rector of Potchefstroom University (about sixty miles from Johannesburg); it is likely he still is. He is the leader of the Dopper faction of the Dutch Reformed Church—a very fundamentalist group, which is strongly republican and which gives money to the *Broederbond*. Certainly in the *Broederbond* are Prime Minister Malan; J. G. Strydom, minister of lands; T. E. Donges, minister of the interior; and C. R. Swart, minister of justice. Malan is probably more moderate than Strydom. Strydom is determined to see established here a republic having no connection with the Commonwealth, and some think he wants to be its first president.

During the war there was a good deal of pro-Nazi feeling among the

Nationalists. The police were pro-Nazi and sometimes fought uniformed soldiers in the streets. The Dutch Reformed Church would not allow uniformed soldiers inside the church, and their pastors would not marry men in uniform. Of immigrants today, the Nationalists definitely prefer Germans. They feel Germans will automatically give support to their views on the color bar. Nationalists have misgivings about the Dutch, because they are skilled workers, confirmed trade unionists, frequently Socialists, and have an international point of view. Furthermore, the Dutchman tends to look down upon the Afrikaans language, which he regards as a crude form of Dutch.

The governmental form here is English parliamentarianism, but there is an authoritarian trend in the Nationalist Party. There appears to be an inner cabinet, and some ministers have reported in confidence that when they go to Cabinet meetings, decisions appear to have been taken already by the inner circle, which is very likely the *Broederbond*. The government's attitude on the constitutional issue of the high court showed an authoritarian trend. However, fascism has not in the past been in the Afrikaner's nature; he is not by instinct a disciplined and easily controlled type.

There is no doubt that the British have tended to look down upon the Afrikaners in the past, and this built up a current of dislike which is now being overcompensated by the Nationalists. This country was always supposed to be bilingual, but in the past the language which really counted was English. The Nationalists are now struggling to put Afrikaans on an *equal* basis with English, and maybe they will eventually try to make it superior.

PRETORIA, *January 7, 1953*

I had a long talk today with British High Commissioner Sir John Le Rougetel. Le Rougetel says Malan has gained considerable wisdom with experience. He knows that any attempt to force a republic would split the Union from end to end. Therefore he is taking it easy, although the Dutch Reformed Church would like to split off from the Commonwealth. He recognizes that the English-speaking South Africans have a very strong attachment to the Crown. This is, of course, irritating to the Afrikaners.

Extreme Nationalists would like to get out of the Commonwealth. There are not many outright Nazis among the Nationalists. However, there is a large proportion of Afrikaners of at least partial German descent. Many of them are farmers in the backwoods and isolated from the current of world events. The main influx of English came in search of diamonds and gold. Their arrival and ensuing industrialization transformed the economics of the region.

Le Rougetel says the *Broederbond* is largely the instrument of the Dutch Reformed Church, and in a sense operates for it the way the Jesuits once acted for the Catholics.

I think it is inevitable that there will be an eventual blowup in the Union if no solution is found to the racial question, but this crisis will probably not arise for years. The resistance campaign here against apartheid was stronger last summer and autumn than it is now.

The African National Congress represents the natives in this campaign. The present head is Chief Albert Luthuli. He is a tribal chief who was removed by the government for being too much opposed to it. The previous head of the congress was Moroka, who was considered by the leaders of the agitation as too moderate.

There are two essentially different white viewpoints towards the Negroes here. The right-wing Afrikaners contend that all natives are animals, and that there is an intellectual ceiling beyond which they cannot aspire. Liberal thinkers contend that the 8,000,000-odd natives are potentially the equals of the whites although the great majority at present is extremely backward.

Chief Luthuli is head of one of the Zulu tribes. He was educated by an American mission, and has been to the United States. He is a true intellectual—a great rarity among the more than 8,000,000 natives.

Circumstances have forced a great proportion of the natives to become good linguists. They talk Afrikaans and English as well as their own language. Much of their education is in the hands of missions, and there are also government schools.

The African here has progressed greatly, and he is treading close on the heels of the white man. Some people think that the greatest resource of South Africa is the advanced status of its native labor.

South African Jews are very uneasy. There is a noticeable Zionist feeling among them, and this is usually ascribed to a desire for an "insurance policy." To date the Nationalist government has done nothing of an anti-Semitic nature, but the Jews remember when the Nationalists were in opposition, some of their leaders made anti-Semitic speeches. The Nationalists regard the Jews as an opposition bloc, because they are supporters of the United Party and contribute quite a lot of money to it. The Jews are in a peculiar position because many of them feel that as a group the Afrikaners have been individually more decent to them than many of the old-fashioned colonial-minded British.

The psychological effect of apartheid has been tremendous. The native feels that a permanent collar of inferiority has been clamped upon him. The government is trying to freeze a feudal system of life. The Nationalists have intensified bad relationships.

Marina visited a native village today, and this is her report:

I went to a little native village on a farm. Actually it is more of a settlement, like gypsies. The people are called Mapoch, are related to the Zulus and come originally from Central Africa. They settle on some land and the farmer usually allows them to build their houses there and also allows them to cultivate maize and things like that near their houses.

The houses are rondovals made of tightly packed mud and painted all over with designs—squares, spots, lines—in pretty colors. Apparently they are the only tribe that does that. We went into the house which has a yard outside with mud floor over which they spread cow dung and pat it down and then sweep it off and it makes a very hard, tidy, clean-looking earth floor. In the yard of each house were two trees, and one had a vine growing on poles, just like a European house might have.

The house inside is one large room with thatched roof (some have started building square houses). It was spotless; the walls were all decorated in pale gray and red and black and brown. In the middle of the room set into the earth floor is a large iron circle in which they make the fire in the winter and cook. In the summer it is out of doors. We saw a great big pot cooking and it was wild spinach. On one side of the room were straw mats neatly folded, and from the ceiling hung a sort of coathanger thing, one stick hung from two wires, and on it were the family blankets on which they sleep at night.

When the children are small, they all sleep in this room. As they grow older, a second outer house is built around the first rondoval; the boys sleep on one side of the door and the girls on the other. When they marry, they build another rondoval for themselves. The blankets, mats, some cups made of pumpkins cut in two (round ones for water, long ones for their beer), one aluminum plate and a small, very long, thin, home-made guitar were the only things in the house. In a sort of cubby-hole thing in the outer house we saw a sack of mealie, some more mats, all terribly tidy, and some more cloths.

I was amazed at the cleanliness, the tidiness and the extraordinary simplicity and purity of life. Work, eat, sleep and have children. The men and women were all away at work, but two older girls were there looking after some twenty naked babies. They wear stiff bead bracelets around their legs, arms and necks, which are woven on them. When they outgrow them, they are cut off and new ones put on. One of the girls had her legs covered up to the knees. They also wear a tiny G-string beaded skirt. The older girls had a bit of sacking thrown over their bosoms. Apparently on ceremonial days the sacking is replaced by beads also which covers them all up. There are blonde and dark Africans, and this was very noticeable among the babies. Some were real black and others brown. Their hair is shaved except for a few strands on the forehead which have beads worked into them.

They feel no tremendous ties for either their home or land and are apt suddenly to just get up and move somewhere else. Actually these had been there for many, many years. Some of the inhabitants come and work in town, but most of them stay on the farm. This is out of the municipal area, so nobody says anything to them about not having a right to be there. Some of the farmers take advantage of the squatters, and one apparently had six hundred of them on his farm charging ten shillings a head rent. By the time the authorities found out, he was a rich man and the natives had to be moved somewhere else and nobody knew where to put them and it was quite a problem. I did not find out how it was solved. They say this kind of native never causes any trouble; he is liked and likes the farmer and all is cozy and nice. It is only the ones who comes to town who cause problems.

The women who rioted in Bechuanaland over the Seretse Khama difficulty used hat pins as weapons and it was most effective. Hat pins have gone up in price tremendously and you can't buy one anywhere.

CAPE TOWN, *January 17, 1953*

THIS morning I had a two-hour talk with Dr. Daniel F. Malan, seventy-eight-year-old prime minister and head of the Nationalist Party, in Groote Schuur, a few miles out of Cape Town. It is a lovely house, built in the old Dutch style, with magnificent grounds. The original house was built in the eighteenth century for the Dutch East India Company. Cecil Rhodes lived there and he bequeathed it and his estate to the Union as a residence for prime ministers.

Malan, a large heavy man, was sitting in a dark brown leather armchair in his study when I came in. He was very friendly and talked for about two hours. After the first hour his secretary came in and asked if we wanted drinks. We each took a Southwest Africa Windhoek beer.

I asked Malan if he intended to establish a republic should the Nationalists be reelected, and if so, whether such a republic would remain within the British Commonwealth. He replied:

Do you think it abhorrent for a party to desire a republic in South Africa? Is it not only natural? The most important parts of South Africa, the Transvaal and the Orange Free State were republics. A very considerable number of people alive today took part in the struggle for these republics and independence. Thousands died for it. Is it strange, or only natural, that a considerable number desire a republic? I think it is not strange.

I asked what restrictions were being placed on immigration. He replied: "There is no restriction in regard to numbers. That depends on available space. But our immigration is selective. An immigration board examines applications. We have screening committees in various countries. We prefer applications from the Christian civilization of Western Europe. There is nothing in the law or its practice against Roman Catholics.

I asked him about relationships between the Union and Pakistan and India. He said:

On the whole, Pakistan is friendly. It has not boycotted us because of the "Indian question" here. Indians as "persons of color" are debarred from entering the Union. But there is a large number here, especially in

Natal. They are restricted in their movements, and always have been so. The Indians of Natal cannot move to another province. They have never been allowed in the Orange Free State. They are in overwhelming numbers in Natal. They were originally imported to work on sugar plantations. They came as indentured labor. Today they outnumber by thousands the Europeans in Natal. The Indian knows how to make money cheaply. The European cannot compete with him. In trading the Indians have already largely ousted the Europeans, and they are increasing three times as fast in population as the European community. Nehru insists they be given equal rights, including political rights. If we did this, our beautiful Natal would be lost to Europeans.

I then asked Malan if race tension was not mounting. He replied:

Race tension has mounted, unfortunately. Why? The cause is that it is only natural for a party, the opposition, when it loses ground, to try to strengthen its position by appealing to racial feeling. The English-speaking people in the country cannot complain that any of their rights have been infringed upon, either language or political rights. Is there a single English-speaking person with any complaint? No. The Communists thrive on trouble that they themselves make. I would not be surprised if they had their hand in the stove. They certainly want trouble between whites and blacks.

Of course at the root of racial feeling [I must note that Malan kept confusing the color question with the Anglo-Boer question] is the difference of language. It goes back to the Anglo-Boer War when the republics were conquered. For seventy years at least, outside of the republics, in the old Cape Colony, the Afrikaners were in the vast majority, but had no language rights. Only English was used in the schools. This, of course, is at the root of it all. We are overcoming these difficulties. Political and language equality now exist. No priority is insisted upon for Afrikaans, all civil servants must be bilingual. Every section of the population must be equally served. You know from your own history that there was a section of your opinion which would not submit to the American government, and that migrated north to Canada. So, in South Africa there is a section that cannot bear the idea that South Africa is no longer a British possession. It does not *belong* to the British *empire*. It is only a member of the Commonwealth, which is a combination of independent countries.

England, as far as South Africa is concerned, won the Anglo-Boer War but lost the peace. Her original idea, as expressed by Lord Milner, (who together with Joseph Chamberlain, was the chief instigator of war), wanted to break the back of Afrikanerdom. This is not abandoned.

I asked Malan if he had any thoughts concerning a sound racial policy for the entire African continent. He answered:

Africa must belong to the Africans, just like Europe for the Europeans, America for the Americans and Asia for the Asians. The first claim to a large part of Africa, anyway, belongs to the indigenous people. Of course, they are divided into tribes, as Europe is into countries. They are primitive. We see, from recent events, that they are even more primitive than some countries thought. To a large extent they are not far removed from barbarism. We see this in Kenya. We saw it in the Port Elizabeth and East London riots. They murdered, above all, those people who had been doing good for them, and only because they were white. They were murdered in a savage manner not known for generations.

You cannot expect a primitive people to rise to a European level in one or even in many generations. Africa must develop, but the African must be assisted and guided in the direction of European Christian civilization. He must be protected against the infiltration of the Asiatic.

I have been introduced to A. H. Jonker, an Afrikaner who has become fed up with the right-wing secret organization called the *Broederbond* which really runs the Afrikaans-speaking population. As far as I can reckon from what Jonker tells me, the *Broederbond* controls this country in just about the same way that another secret organization—the Communist Party—controls Eastern European countries.

It is a dead secret group indeed. As he describes it,

The objectives of the AB (Afrikaner *Broederbond*) are to Afrikanerize the public life of the Union, to turn the Union into an Afrikaner republic, with a constitution which will insure Afrikaner domination. The AB infiltrates into key positions in the same way as the Communists. Eleven of the fourteen cabinet ministers are *broers* [brothers] and at least two-thirds of the government MPs and senators. All editors of Nationalist newspapers are *broers,* and today most of the heads of government departments are *broers.* Once in these key positions, the *broers* advance other *broers* until they have a tight grip of the machinery of government, schools, defense, and so on. The Red parallel is strikingly complete.

The constitution, of which Jonker has a copy, describes the *Broederbond* as a brotherhood based on "Christian-National" foundations and having the motto "Be Strong." Its objects are:

(a) The bringing about of a healthy and progressive unanimity among all Afrikaners who strive after the well-being of the Afrikaner nation. (b) The stimulation of national self-consciousness in the Afrikaner and inculcation of love for his language, religion, traditions, people and land. (c) Promotion of all interests of the Afrikaner nation.

The constitution says of the membership:

The *bond* consists of *broers* [brothers]. Only a white male person of twenty-five years or more can become a *broer,* provided he (a) is Afrikaans-speaking (b) is of Protestant faith (c) is clean of character and firm of principle, also in the maintenance of his Afrikanership (d) accepts South Africa as his only fatherland.

Jonker says "critics of the *Broederbond* say that in 1935, General Hertzog, then prime minister, publicly castigated the *bond* in these words:

They are sworn not to entertain any cooperation with the English-speaking population and thereby they stand in direct racial conflict with our fellow English Africans, and are striving by way of domination on the part of the Africaans-speaking section to put their foot on the neck of English-speaking South Africa. . . . The *Broederbond* has become a grave menace to the rest and peace of our social community, even where it operates in the economic-cultural sphere.

CAPE TOWN, *January 18, 1953*

I had lunch today with Jacobus G. N. Strauss, head of the United Party and successor to the mantle of Smuts. He is an exceptionally youthful-appearing fellow, who looks only in his middle thirties, although he is fifty-two. He is decent and amiable, but no ball of fire. He confirms by his own personality what I have been hearing about the Opposition—*viz.* that they have no adequate leadership. We lunched in the City Club, which was virtually empty over the weekend.

Strauss said that he personally thought it would be a good idea to advocate once again reestablishment of the "Cape" formula allowing the vote to all persons, regardless of race, provided they satisfied minimum educational requirements. However, he would not dream of saying so in public, because he would lose the election immediately. I asked if there were any members of the United Party who would take this stand during the forthcoming election campaign, and he replied: "Of course not." Obviously a party which is even afraid to take a stand on this critical issue because of the elections is not going to do anything drastic about it even if it regains power.

Strauss was quite optimistic about his party's chances in the elections. I am not.

LOURENÇO MARQUES, *January 20, 1953*

FROM a letter: This is a fine town, very European as compared with the South African blend of megalopolis and racist megalomania. We came to Mozambique by train from Johannesburg, rolling comfortably through Krueger Game Park looking for rhinoceros, hopefully and unsuccessfully. Incidentally, the trains in this part of the world are fabulous.

We took one from Jo'burg to Capetown that is probably the most comfortable I've ever ridden: huge stateroom with two beds, table, chairs, tastefully painted in blue; excellent dinner, etc.

In Jo'burg we dined at Harry Oppenheimer's whom we'd met at Margaret Biddle's in Paris. He and his wife most agreeable, modest, intelligent, liberal. H. is a shortish, thick-set dark fellow with definite political interests but not much hope. He owns most of the gold, all the diamonds and much uranium of South Africa. He arranged for us to visit one of his mines (the first I'd been in since, almost eighteen years ago, I accompanied Mrs. Roosevelt into a West Virginia coal pit and thus made a *New Yorker* cartoon come true). Strange tan piles of ore tailings for miles: dark, deep holes into which lightning fast elevators drop; sweating blacks, most of them recruited as real slave labor (except, after their term, they can go home) in Mozambique (the wages available here are even lower than in the Union!). Once a week the various tribes are allowed to form up in a special arena and beat the hell out of each other, supervised by company policemen who try and prevent killings but spur on old tribal hostilities. The idea is that this release of pent-up energy is good for the amiable savages! Wandered through their living quarters and inspected their paybooks; appalled that this should occur in my time.

The odd thing is that the Afrikaners for the most part are such fine, decent people. I had known some of them when they went to the desert and Italy during the war and Shorty Lessing, a six-foot-four war correspondent, greeted us and took charge with his wife while we were in Capetown. Absolutely charming and open-minded pair, infuriated with their regime. While in Capetown I met another Afrikaner who is fighting the government tooth and nail and who used himself to be a member of the Boer secret society, *Broederbond*. His life is now threatened by the *bond*. He gave me a photostat of the charter and secret oath including signatures of the principal officials. Our embassy didn't have this stuff and was pining for it so I let them have it (making me a copy). *Broederbond* is a kind of dour, respectable, unflamboyant Ku Klux Klan which already damned near runs the country and controls the armed forces and police.

In Pretoria, a quiet Dutch town, I played golf a few times with Wally Gallman, our ambassador. An odd experience. South Africa is not only far huger than it appears on the map (a thousand miles from Jo'burg to Capetown) but much higher, over a mile above sea level. On the second hole, about 490 yards long, the score card said par was four. "Isn't this a bit ambitious even for your mighty Boers?" I asked Wally. "Hit the ball and see." I did. It goes a mile in this rarefied atmosphere.

But Lourenço Marques is a pleasant contrast. The Portuguese, who have an authoritarian kind of fascism at home, also impose it here but it is relatively easygoing and relaxed. There is at least a small loophole permitting advancement of Negroes and their assimilation into the white ruling society. You see Negroes (a few) at restaurants and some parties—which would make neighboring South Africa shiver. The food, thank God, is neither English nor Dutch by antecedent and it is pleasant to have garlic, spices, rather good wine. The American consul took us out to a seaside tavern north of town where monkeys raced through the trees and we dined off a local shrimp preparation called *piri-piri,* devastatingly hot and delicious. Incidentally, Don Lamm, the consul, and his vice consul are the entire American diplomatic establishment (with their wives) and the happiest I've ever seen. They both intend to put in for a repeat assignment in this, which is considered a hardship post. Why? One is a big game hunter, the other a bird hunter who takes specimens for the Smithsonian. They carefully arrange the work schedules so first one can go off for several days with his rifle after a rare rhinoceros and then, when he gets back, the other is off with his shotguns for even rarer hummingbirds. And the wives adore each other. Ideal, ain't it?

Lourenço Marques, *January 21, 1953*

I had a talk this afternoon with Don Lamm, American Consul. He points out that Portuguese colonial policy has everywhere gotten rid of the word "colony." In 1951 Mozambique was changed from a "colony" to a "province" of Portugal. All Portugal is divided into provinces. The former minister of colonies is now called minister for overseas. The Portuguese theory is that these overseas provinces are a part of Portugal, just as if they were on the mainland. The people of Mozambique are inhabitants of Portugal under this theory.

Not all inhabitants here have citizenship rights. But anybody, regardless of color, can become *civilizado* or "a civilized one." If he becomes *civilizado,* he is just as eligible for citizenship as if he were a white man living in Lisbon. The *indigena,* or native, is governed by a different set of laws. He is not regarded as "civilized." Everyone in Mozambique is in one of two groups:

1. All whites, all Portuguese citizens, all Indians who are Portuguese (Goans), all Macaoans who are "civilized," all mixed bloods recognized as "civilized," all the civil administration.

2. The others—meaning the overwhelming majority of blacks.

A native who meets certain requirements is recognized as "civilized"; he becomes what is called *assimilado*. He must have certain educational qualifications, including secondary or commercial school. He must also demonstrate that he lives in European style, and presumably speaks Portuguese at home. These claims must be approved by a Native Affairs Board in his district. The board includes natives as well as whites, and many of the natives on the boards are not themselves assimilated. To be regarded as assimilated a mixed blood must show that he lives like a European, but he does not have to pass any educational tests. The *assimilado* or *civilizado* have the same rights as a white man. They also have the same obligations, such as taxes. They are no longer eligible for the social and medical benefits of native law, and cannot take refuge in such law.

There are certain fundamental differences between the Portuguese system and apartheid. One never sees here benches marked "Europeans only" as in Durban. There is no segregation on the buses. Natives nevertheless stay out of restaurants, although the latter cannot legally bar the *assimilado*. Distinctions are not thrown in the natives' faces. There is no open color line as in South Africa or southern United States. The situation here is by no means ideal, but there is no sentiment against repression working up as in South Africa.

The government is not keen on very much assimilation. Neither, for that matter, are the natives. For the most part they do not want to divorce themselves from their tribes.

The *assimilado* can get a passport, which a native cannot. He can send his children to European schools, and is eligible for better Government jobs. Nevertheless, most natives do not like to break their tribal connections. Family and tribal bonds tend to induce parents to keep their children "native." This is a tribal country. Most of the people are Shangaans, a collection of tribes who, for the most part, live between the Natal border, Zululand and Beira.

The Portuguese have always been somewhat nervous about the Union of South Africa. They claim Smuts planned to seize Mozambique before World War II, and also early during the war. Britain formally attempted to buy Lourenço Marques early this century for 400,000,000 pounds sterling. There is a fear and mistrust of South Africa as an expansionist country. Furthermore, the Portuguese are angry about apartheid. They feel it represents a danger to all Africa. They recognize that any serious native trouble in the Union is bound to spill over the borders.

LOURENÇO MARQUES, *January 22, 1953*

TODAY I went out to see a witch doctor and soothsayer. The "witch doctor" (*shikwembo*) is legally forbidden but at least 75 per cent of the natives go to them. The one I saw was a woman named Mahigo. I took along two interpreters in order to communicate via three languages: Ma-Ronga, Shangaan, Portuguese. She lived in a village west of Lourenço Marques called Mefalalla. We walked through several sandy alleys, some of which smelled sweet with fermenting cashew wine, by palisades and cornpatches with stalks ten feet high. There were many cashew trees.

Mahigo was lying on a reed mat under a manioc (cassava) tree in her yard. Her little black grandchildren were sprawling around in the sand, playing with baby chickens. Two of her daughters, Isabel and Maria, were sitting with her. Both of them wore headscarves, and all three wore colored shirts and skirts. Mahigo, a large elderly woman, had a bald spot in her close-shaven kinky hair. She told me she learned her trade as a girl. She fell ill, and a woman witch doctor named Mwagulane, called in to attend her, discovered that she had a *shikwembo* in her. She told her she was destined to be a *shikwembo*. She took her off to the forest, where she learned about herbs and how to use animal blood in preparing mixtures. They lived by the banks of a river in her native Inhambane district.

Mahigo described to me how she cured aches, fevers and pains with various herb concoctions. She apparently was not quite so good at setting broken bones. Each treatment was accompanied by prayers addressed to the god Kulukumba, and the spirits of her ancestors, the Unguluve. Her prices were 200 escudos to cure a broken leg, 50 escudos for a headache and 10 escudos for a hangover. The last named is cured by putting hot *zilongo* pods on the patient's tongue (no prayers needed). I took the 10-escudo hangover treatment. Very effective. But Mahigo insisted, after much deliberation, that she could not do any reverse witchcraft—in other words, casting spells. I wanted her to do an overseas hexing job on *The New York Times* cable desk. I gave minute descriptions of the principal targets and offered a fat fee. Reluctantly, Mahigo turned me down, suspected I was a police agent.

Then I went to another village, Shamankulu, where I saw a soothsayer named Joaquim Mafumo, a gentleman with a bad left eye, a wispy mustache and a good business sense; he made me put 20 escudos on the line before he would go to work. He was sitting on the floor in his undershirt. His performance included a divining stick, which he gnawed, some flat bone chips with holes in them, and a wicker basket containing two old dice, some sea shells and a bunch of wild goats' teeth with wire around them. He spent a lot of time muttering mumbo-jumbo and shaking his equipment about, but he was no good as a fortune teller and claimed the only spells he could cast for a European were those to break up friendship. He also spurned my request to hex the *Times* cable desk. Said he could only do local jobs. So, in the appalling heat, my hangover returning despite Mahigo's *zilongo,* I staggered off with my two interpreters and left Mafumo muttering over his dice.

LEOPOLDVILLE, *January 27, 1953*

A glimpse of the Belgian Congo has proven disappointing and pessimistic. We stayed with Mulloy, a very nice United States consul general, and wife who put us up in great comfort. They talked admiringly of the Belgian colonial officials but I was depressed and felt the contact with the vast native population was almost nonexistent. Despite Mulloy's assurances that the natives were happy, had a high standard of living and vast numbers of bicycles, I sensed disquiet. Blacks must be locked up in their native quarter each night. The Belgians have given them absolutely no preparation for self-rule. This is a powderkeg. It looks nice on the surface, but appearances are deceptive. Like the day I played golf with Mulloy and hooked a ball into the rough. When I went in after it I noticed my caddy stayed on the fairway so I shouted at him. "That place may look all right to you," hollered Mulloy, "But watch out for the spitting mambas." So should the Belgians.

One day we went across the sluggish, vast Congo river, filled with islands of floating vegetation, to see our old friend Bob Mason, now British consul general in Brazzaville (French Congo). The French may not give as good a life to their charges as the Belgians in terms of economic statistics, but they treat them as human beings. Saw a most interesting modern cathedral, like one of those wooden viking churches at Bergen, Norway. Also went to an art school where some French intellectual pansies rounded up youngsters from the hinterland villages—absolutely illiterate kids—gave them paints and brushes and canvas and watched what they could do. Quite remarkable: dozens of brightly talented dark Douanier-Rousseaus.

It was nice to get back to a sleepy French café for an *apéritif*. Mason, who goes across the river often, says he invariably shocks the Belgian businessmen there. At one after another party someone inevitably comes up, as Topic A is discussed, and says to Bob: "Quite right, monsieur, but after all, how would you feel if your sister married one of these types?" Bob's reply: "As a matter of fact she did."

ACCRA, *January 30, 1953*

I saw Sir Charles Arden Clarke, Governor of the Gold Coast, today in the old Danish Christiansborg castle (used to protect slave traders). He has thirty-two years in colonial service, starting in Nigeria. Even then, he says, the policy was to build local government so the native could eventually stand on his own feet, always hoping he would elect to remain in the Commonwealth—although nothing could stop them from leaving, as Burma did. He hopes when the Gold Coast reaches the stage of independence, it will have reasonable standards of efficiency and integrity. He observes:

> Where you have plural societies, a number of mixed races as in East Africa, it will take longer to put nations on their feet as natural units; one race tries to dominate the other. In West Africa the problem is simple. There are about 5,000,000 reasonably homogeneous Africans in the Gold Coast: about 5,000 nonAfricans (including a few Syrians and Indians). There are few foreign "settlers"; thus land was not taken and a clash was avoided on that issue.
>
> We are trying to overcome Soviet propaganda by showing there is no

racial prejudice here and that the African is becoming master in his own house. We are deliberately committing our own political suicide as far as control goes. We are trying to show that African and European can live together as long as the European doesn't insist on being the senior partner; the African won't stand for alien domination.

Arden-Clarke said the Nkrumah government is paying lip service to the idea of a United States of West Africa and a general theory of pan-Africanism. However, he thought it would take a generation or two to bring about. Tribalism is still very much alive in the Gold Coast, and it will be a full-time job to make a truly united people even in this small area. Nkrumah is now trying to use nationalism to destroy tribalism. But the northern territories, which represent a quarter of the population, are split up into a number of jealous tribes. They are united only in fear and suspicion of the people in the south, which is a better developed group and in a position to dominate. Furthermore, there is no love lost between the Ashantis in the center and the coastal tribes. The Government is trying to amalgamate them behind a belief in Ghana, the entire nation. Ghana is the name of an ancient West African kingdom to which the Gold Coast did not even belong. The opposition calls itself the Ghana Congress Party.

Nkrumah gets his reason confused with his emotionalism. If Africans oppose federation as in the Rhodesias, he opposes it with clichés such as, "It is a device to rivet the shackles of imperialism."

Arden-Clarke maintained that "We are showing the way—under conditions infinitely easier than in East or South Africa—two races can live together in amity and work together effectively, and that the African, given a chance, is capable of managing his own affairs with such advice as he himself seeks from his European friends."

He admitted that witchcraft and secret fetish societies continue in the Gold Coast and ritual murder has not yet been blotted out entirely.

In conclusion, Arden-Clarke said that the problem of Africa is entirely one of race, and until that is solved, there can be no solution of other questions.

Ho, TOGOLAND, *January 31, 1953*

TOGBE Sri II, the Awoamefia of Anlo, paramount chief of Togoland, a barren sandspit along the Guinea Gulf, lies miserably dying. Togbe Sri II is eighty-seven, blind and eaten by a cancer. For forty-six years he has held the mystical *stool* (a tribal throne) in his rustic palace at Anloga, looking across the rolling Atlantic breakers. Aided by his faithful wing chiefs, the Awadada, Chief Anthonio of Weh, and Chief Tamakloo of Wuti, he has ruled 200,000 subjects: fishermen, boat builders, net repairers and, above all, smugglers.

The Awoamefia has had a good life. A huge, sturdy man with ebony skin, he levied quantities of champagne and whisky from the smugglers and consumed it with his friends. No formal loyalties to the Christian faith inhibited the number of his wives or loyalty to the Nyigbla fetish grove where unknown gods gave counsel. His word was law. Far and wide, it was conveyed by trumpeting of the Ynikpo war horn and the thunderous voice of the Nyikor drums, so massive that to move each requires eight strong men.

But now Togbe Sri II, member of the Most Excellent Order of Saint Michael and Saint George and Commander of the British Empire, is bed-ridden. He has lost his power to a palace revolution. The cabal of wily Kukubor has proclaimed a regency and the old chief can but groan. Kukubor and a new-fangled political clique called the "Anloga Youth Association" has taken power. It refuses to pay taxes. It has murdered collection agents, burned houses and fomented riots.

Armed, British-officered police, sturdy Akans and Ashanti, moved in to reestablish order. They chopped the groves around the Nyigbla fetish to prevent dark scheming in the woods. The Nyikor drums were carried groaning to the "protective custody" of a common prison cell to end their false and cabalistic messages.

Well, why do the forces of law and order still patrol in Anloga: sixty big policemen bearing guns? Peace has been reestablished by the government in the name of Togbe Sri II.

The answer is simple. The chief lies dying. And back to the beginning of time, when an Awoamefia has died, at least two hundred of his subjects are slain with him—to journey as companions into the unknown.

Togbe Sri II lingers on. And old times linger with him. Up and down the paths of Anloga stride policemen—to insure the Awoamefia dies alone.

ACCRA, *February 1, 1953*

THIS is a most interesting town, the center of the first successful independence movement in Black Africa. Hot, malarial, on the verge of civilization, it poses many problems. The natives are still close to the jungle—men with green, maroon and yellow togas swung over their shoulders, brilliantly dressed women bearing burdens on their heads, drums beating throughout the night (it is from here that the famous talking drums of the Ashanti come).

There has been no nation living here much longer than the European; the Adansi, Akwamu and Accra came in the sixteenth century; the Denkyera in the seventeenth; the Ewe and Gonje in the seventeenth. Trade in gold, slaves, ivory and pepper attracted the first whites.

The Ga arrived at the beginning of the sixteenth century and came to Accra about one hundred years later. In 1660 a decisive battle took place at Nyantrabi, twelve miles north of Accra, between the Akwamu and the Gas of Accra. Okai Koi, the Ga king, saw that all was lost. He summoned his chiefs and painted one side of his body with white clay, one with charcoal. He then cursed his chiefs for treachery (turning against him in battle by private understanding with the enemy). He said if his white side fell up, Accra would have victory and prosperity. Black side up and Accra would forever be disunited before its enemies. He shot himself, seated on his throne. The black side fell up. Everyone fled.

The poem chanted by warriors after that battle said, "We are pressing forward to gore." One of the old Accra military bands, called "the invincible," beat on its drums, *"Mogya regu, mogya regu, mogya regu"* (Blood is being spilled).

ACCRA, *February 3, 1953*

## ALL THE GOLD COAST NEWS
## THAT'S FIT TO PRINT

Here are some quotes from current Gold Coast newspapers:

*The African Morning Post,* Accra (Letter to the editor): "Gentlemen. Diffusing Kremlin tang: I hear of a crusade of purges which you are allegedly to be carrying into your rank soon Not good enough People will say you would brandish the purge sabre when you got into power Drop the idea Of course the rotten eggs should be disposed of."

*Ashanti Pioneer,* Kumasi (Editorial): "We should all of us be now cognizant of the multifarious ills of the present Government, owing, of course, to the glaring inefficiency of the people manning it."

Obituary notice: "Talking drums announced at Wiawso the death of Mr. Archer Kwabena Bretu— . . ."

*The West African Monitor,* Cape Coast (News item): "Rumor is afloat that Small Pox is juggling in some villages around this area it may eventually opened to this town if prevention is not taken . . ."

Court report: "One Madam Kyekyeh, wife of Mr. T. K. Mensah, pleaded guilty to a criminal charge against her for having unlawfully assaulted one Madam Assor (also a wife of Mr. T. K. Mensah) and she was sentenced to a fine of 6 pounds sterling . . . The accused, leaving the husband, suddenly jumped on Madam Assor who was sitting unconcerned in the struggle and gave her on the ears some repeated slaps and subsequently held her by her hairs with such a force likely to endanger her life who became unconscious when she was out from the grip of the accused."

Letter: "Dance Fans: Fighting is becoming too rampant with you these days. . . . This practice must give way to strict discipline."

Advertisement:

"FLASH GRAND HOTEL" (The City Hall Calling)
"A strictly Evening Dress Dance will be staged at the City Hall with
E. T. Mensah and his Tempos Band and the Rockies Band on Sat. February 7. Discipline assured. Bar Excellent."

ABIDJAN, *February 3, 1953*

HEREWITH I append a dispatch sent today from Abidjan, Ivory Coast,
and a United Press follow-up story:

ABIDJAN, IVORY COAST—An interesting constitutional question is posed
in the instance of Senator Victor Biaka-Boda who disappeared in the
jungle here three years ago and may have been eaten by his constituents.

The Ivory Coast is part of French West Africa and as such is entitled
to parliamentary representation in Paris. M. Biaka-Boda was one of
three senators elected to the Council of the Republic in metropolitan
France.

But since the day, early in 1950, when he vanished on a stump-speaking tour of the bush, it has not been decided by the French system
of jurisprudence whether the senator can be considered legally dead.

Therefore he has not been replaced and his Negro constituents are *de
facto* if not *de jure* disenfranchised. This gives rise to the philosophical
reflection that you cannot have your senator and eat him too.

Just exactly what became of the statesman has never been decided.
His body was not found—as such—and under French law a man cannot
be adjudged dead unless there is a *corpus delicti.*

In the case of the missing senator, the only remains which may or
may not have once represented the Ivory Coast on the River Seine were
a few bones, utterly devoid of flesh. These were discovered in the vicinity of Bouaflé, near where M. Biaka-Boda was last heard commenting
upon the political scene.

They were carefully assembled by police agents and mailed to the
principal laboratory of the justice department in Paris for identification.
Analysts, after careful examination, reported that they could not be sure
the bones were those of M. Biaka-Boda; nor that they were not. Nor
could it be stated what caused the death of the bones or how the flesh
happened to be removed from them.

The Ivory Coast police meanwhile did their best to inquire of the
African tribesmen dwelling in the neighborhood of Bouaflé. They met
with universal bland silence and a mass profession of ignorance.

Intimates of the statesman have described him as frail, small, and
exceptionally thin; by no means a tempting morsel. Nevertheless, despite
a stern legal embargo, ritual murder including the devouring of portions
of the victim is not unheard of in the remote areas inland from the Gulf
of Guinea. Can this have been the fate of the missing senator? Is that

why only a parcel of clean bones was discovered a few months after he disappeared?

Nobody from the governor down knows the answer to this question. In the meantime the Negro population here has no senator of its own race. M. Biaka-Boda's two colleagues are white.

All this makes for interesting café talk in Abidjan, capital of the Ivory Coast. "How," one is asked, "can there be a new senator until it is decided if the old one is dead?"

One acquaintance of M. Biaka-Boda says that although formally a Christian, the senator is (or was) privately a pagan animist. This man suspects there was (or is) more than one Madame Biaka-Boda. He adds that a wife of the senator lives in French Guinea now and to the best of his knowledge still receives the senator's salary—since he is legally alive.

Another source of information on the subject scoffs at the idea that M. Biaka-Boda was devoured. "When they eat them," he remarks with an air of authority, "they don't leave any bones."

WASHINGTON, Feb. 4—(UP) The United States Senate was deeply stirred today by a report that a senator in French West Africa may have been eaten by his constitutents.

The report, published in *The New York Times,* was the subject of intense scrutiny on the Senate floor.

According to the report, a Senator Victor Biaka-Boda disappeared in the jungles and was never heard from again. When last seen alive, he was "commenting on the political scene."

Later, a few bones believed to have belonged to Biaka-Boda were found. They had been picked clean.

Although the African Gold (*sic*) Coast is outside the jurisdiction of the United States Senate, there was some talk of investigating the incident.

Senator Homer Ferguson (R-Mich.) suggested it might come under the Corrupt Practices Act.

Senator James E. Murray of the cattle-raising state of Montana noted that Biaka-Boda was described as "frail, small and exceptionally thin—by no means a tempting morsel."

"If beef cattle prices keep dropping," said Murray, "there'll be a lot of Americans eating their senators, too."

Senator Alexander Wiley, both as chairman of the Foreign Relations Committee and as a citizen of Wisconsin, was interested in Biaka-Boda's fate.

"They'd never have trapped Biaka-Boda if only they had first tasted America's premier farm product—Wisconsin cheese," said Wiley.

Senate Democratic Leader Lyndon B. Johnson of Texas thought Biaka-Boda had set an example in the highest tradition of statesmanship.

"It's really amazing what a senator will do for his constituents," Johnson commented.

But another senator, who asked not to be identified, said there was nothing unusual in the Biaka-Boda case.

United States senators, he said, have been giving their constituents indigestion for years.

ABIDJAN, *February 4, 1953*

WE dined last night at the home of the governor general. He and his wife were charming, friendly, delighted to get even our ancient news from Paris. But what a curious meal. The GG had assembled all the principal members of his staff, who were in uniform, and their wives. It was appallingly hot and humid but we had the full treatment: believe it or not, this was the menu: *pâté de foie gras, potage, civet de lièvre,* salad and cheese, a soufflé, all with wines (the main one a heavy red burgundy) and postprandial brandy. I was touched—and almost murdered. The GG was courtly and agreeable but clearly irked and embarrassed by my interest in Biaka-Boda.

We walked home through the stagnant night. I must say Abidjan is a nice town, except for the awful climate and the high costs. (Like all French colonies everything costs double what it is in the Metropole but the local franc and officials' salaries are pegged to this rate). The hotel is pleasant, the atmosphere is not tense, there is an active small industry and timber trade, the relationships seem affable.

ACCRA, *February 5, 1953*

I had a talk today with Kwame Nkrumah, prime minister of the Gold Coast, in his office. He is an affable, youthful chap with a rich chocolate complexion and a loose-lipped mouth. He seemed quite amiable but did not impress me very much as an intellectual. Among the things he said worth noting were the following:

He wants to work for a West African federation extending from the Congo to Dakar, but this is obviously an eventual hope and there is nothing imminent about it.

I asked him why parliamentary democracy was assumed to be the best form of government here. He said no other form had ever occurred to him, but he favored parliamentary democracy because it was workable, lasting and guaranteed free speech, press and religion.

He said he wants independence for the Gold Coast as soon as possible and that steps are being taken to negotiate constitutional changes. He wants the Gold Coast to stay in the Commonwealth as an independent state because then it would benefit from the advantages of mutual defense, economic assistance and participation in the sterling bloc.

In the Commonwealth Nkrumah thought the Gold Coast could exert an influence over some of the colonial areas through the Commonwealth conferences, and in such a way it could spearhead the West African liberation movement.

He said he would keep on white advisers as long as they were needed, but meanwhile he was intensifying a program for Africanization. He thought it would be between five and ten years before the administration was entirely African on all levels.

I asked him why among the world's Negroes the leading ones were American despite race prejudice in America. He said he had found through his own experience that the most vocal Negroes were from the United States despite the question of the racial problem there. He thought this was because students are left to themselves and initiative and responsibility are encouraged despite prejudice. Despite all the handicaps of the Negro, there is an opportunity for ability in America.

LISBON, *February 12, 1953*

WE came here more or less by accident. As we wound up our stay in West Africa I got a violent attack of gout. From Accra we were scheduled to fly by Pan American to Liberia. But I hobbled on to the plane with Marina. Fortunately, there was a free berth so I stretched out on it with a sleeping pill and told poor Marina to inform those who were meeting us in Liberia that I was simply too ill to get out. The plane had seats available all the way to Lisbon.

The plane sent a wire ahead to Cavendish Cannon, who is now ambassador in Lisbon, and he had a car at the airport and a lovely room in the Aviz, perhaps the best hotel in the world. So we arrived in style, I collapsed into bed, and Cavendish sent his most excellent doctor who filled me with a new kind of injection. So am slowly improving—and not working. Have seen a lot of the Cannons and have driven around sight-seeing with Lily in their immense car. Our sole conversation has been made up of reminiscences of Bulgaria, Greece and Jugoslavia.

PARIS, *February 18, 1953*

THIS morning I had a talk with René Mayer, prime minister since early in January (succeeding Pinay). He was very friendly and certainly gives the impression of being an efficient, businesslike chap. Of course his record in the field of transportation, finance and economics is impressive. It is probably a good stroke of fortune that he should be French prime minister at this moment just as a "businessman's" government takes over in the United States. He is the most near equivalent to the American "businessman-politician" available in France today and has the additional advantage of speaking very fluent English.

Mayer, a fairly heavy-set man of medium height, told me that Al Gruenther yesterday had informed him he had received a letter from President Eisenhower asking Al to pass on a message to Mayer: namely, that Ike hoped Mayer could make his visit to America as soon as possible in order to discuss pressing problems.

LONDON, *March 1, 1953*

LAST night I dined at the embassy with Mrs. Aldrich (her husband is back in the States with Eden and Butler on some bilateral negotiations). Although she has been here only a fortnight, she already has a tough job. A letter has just been received from Colonel and Mrs. McCormick, advising that the McCormicks are coming to London shortly, and wish to be received at the embassy. Only recently Aldrich had been considering suing McCormick for libel as a result of an attack written about him during the Republican convention. The *Chicago Tribune* accused Aldrich of bribing delegates. Apparently the ambassador has consented to receive the McCormicks since he is, after all, a distinguished American, but they can't quite figure out who should be invited with them.

LONDON, *March 2, 1953*

DINNER at the Harcourts. Nigel Birch, under secretary for defense, was there. He complained bitterly that Caffery was working against the British all the time during the Cairo negotiations, and encouraging the Egyptians to set us against each other. He said he thought Caffery was absolutely no good. It was urgently necessary that we name a good American ambassador who would not only be a well-known envoy but one who understood the necessity of Anglo-American friendship and the vital importance of Suez to the West.

LONDON, *March 3, 1953*

EXTREMELY good long talk and tea with Field Marshal Earl Alexander at his office in the ministry of defense. Alexander is now secretary of state for defense. I have not seen him since we went to Anzio together in January, 1944, so our conversation roved over a considerable field. When we got to the subject of Russia, Alexander picked up the telephone and asked General Strong, head of British intelligence, to come in, and he was with us for at least forty-five minutes of the conversation.

Alexander said (and Strong agreed) that Russia would not be provoked into war. They simply were not ready to accept provocation. They intended to go along in search of their goals in a patient, long-sighted, Asiatic way. They wouldn't be provoked even if we bombed Manchuria or even if China and the United States formally went to war or even if the EDC treaty started to rearm Germany—unless they were ready for and desired war at the time. Then they wouldn't wait for provocation. What Alexander fears as a possibility, however, is that a series of incidents might lead into each other. We might bomb Manchuria and finally decide this wasn't achieving enough; then decide to bomb closer and closer to Russian territory until we begin to hit it.

The two men had no faith in Chiang Kai-shek or his strength. Alexander made the point that much of Chiang's army was made up of overage soldiers; many had served with Alex himself in Burma during World War II. If they ever landed on the mainland, a great number would simply desert and disappear.

They were not unduly alarmist over Iran. They thought Russia would certainly occupy Iran in case of another world war. They would not risk moving in physically otherwise, for fear of igniting such a war. But, in a war, they would certainly want Iran, to deprive us of the oil—even though Alex and Strong didn't think the Russians themselves would be able to transport the oil and make use of it themselves. In the meantime the Russians, of course, were happy to see more and more chaos created by the Iranians themselves and would, of course, not object to any gaining of power by the Tudeh Party. Alexander, however, thought Mossadegh (who both agreed was the best man available in Teheran right now, unfortunately) could keep going for at least another year with the resources he had. The Americans, Alex thought, were too impressed by Mossadegh's financial crisis and kept wrongly insisting that we had to provide him with aid now and pronto. Alex recognized that it was more than unlikely that any Iranian individual or government could or would dare to sign any oil agreement with Britain; they feared rule by assassination.

For these reasons, it was absolutely imperative that an agreement on Suez be reached. The Suez base had cost 300,000,000 pounds (then close to $1.5 billion) and even if another piece of geography could be found for another such base, there is neither the time nor money to build it. Furthermore, there is no such other piece of geography. Suez can be approached from west or east by sea and from north or south by land. Of course Alexander, who has troops all over the earth (he kept referring to the fact that "I have troops"), would like to get the two divisions out of Suez for use elsewhere. But a very large number of technicians and experts would have to remain in Suez to keep the base going. The Egyptians simply aren't competent in terms of engineers. This goes for the operation of the French canal company as well as the base itself. Not only must the Egyptians agree to leave foreign technicians in adequate numbers, but they must make firm agreements on MEDO before a Suez evacuation is accepted.

I asked Alexander if he could trust Naguib or what would happen if Naguib died and someone else came in and broke his word. He replied that he thought it would probably be necessary in such an event "for us to go back again." He talked at length of the absolute necessity for Britain and America to stand together on the Suez issue. Again (as from Nigel Birch) I inferred that Britain is extremely distressed not only with the general American attitude on Suez but specifically with that of Caffery. Alexander said he hoped Ike would personally make clear America's fundamental unity with Britain on this point and would send a strong man as ambassador to Cairo. Alexander was convinced Suez was necessary for any defense of the Middle East and directly related it to the Iranian situation.

Both Alex and Strong felt that as long as Stalin was around there was very little risk of war. Stalin undoubtedly knew not only of America's atomic superiority but of the immense destructive power of the bomb and the fact that we had the means of delivering it. No man of seventy-three was going to start a war and risk seeing all he had built up around him destroyed. Neither general thought Russia was undergoing any particularly serious economic strain. Such things simply didn't happen. The Russian might be just about starving for bread; then the government doubled the ration and everything looked good—even though doubling zero is still zero. (Of course, this is fictitious and theoretical since bread is one of the things there is enough of.) The new purges, Strong thought, were not on an anti-Semitic basis; furthermore their popularity among Germans and Arabs was a mere happy bonus, from Moscow's viewpoint. They were actually devised as a simple security measure to eliminate one more mass of people in whom trust could not be placed 100 per cent, since they had foreign connections and sympathies with Israel.

Alexander considered Zhukov "a good chap" and Strong added the same about Sokolovsky. Alexander said that Tolbukhin (the marshal who liberated the Balkans and is now dead) was a fine fellow. When Alexander visited him in 1944, Tolbukhin scanned Alex's row of medals. He saw the old Czarist decoration of St. Andrew. He went up to him and whispered, "You know, I have it too, but, of course, I cannot wear it." Alex said he seemed deeply regretful. Tolbukhin had been a Czarist officer.

Alex met Stalin twice at conferences. He said the man had great charm unless he was irked about something; then you could see the force of his anger come out on his face. Such was the case when Stalin (quite unfairly, says Alex) complained about the way Soviet officers and missions were being treated in Italy. He has two menu cards signed by Stalin. He said he was interested to note that despite the mass of hair starting just above Stalin's brow and covering his head, he has a growing bald spot on the crown.

Strong thought the great improvement in the Malayan situation would have important repercussions. The habit of victory in their adventures led the Communists on to new adventures. Now, in this case, they were being badly licked. Alexander thought the mopping-up of Malaya would be completed within a year.

He remarked that the English were not aware enough of the extent of

American effort and casualties in Korea and neither of us of the French effort in Indochina. The policy Ike had of building up Asian armies was sound. When the Russians find the Korean war has developed into primarily an Asian fracas, not tying up Western manpower, they might call it off. The French were doing their utmost to get as much money out of America as they could—too much. "The French are always trying to make money out of others," Alexander said. "I can't understand it. It's certainly a wealthy enough country. Maybe it's just because they don't pay their taxes."

LONDON, *March 4, 1953*

I had a talk this morning with Frank Roberts (Sir Frank Roberts, later successively ambassador to Jugoslavia, NATO, and Germany) at the Foreign Office. Frank is quite gloomy about the prospects of the European army. He thinks the only way the French could be induced to approve it speedily would be if the Russians were to make aggressive moves in Europe, and there is no sign of this. The only other way perhaps to get the French to approve the project at all is to revive the thought of creating a German national army and bring Germany into NATO. Frank thinks all the talk now beginning to appear in the press about the search for an alternative to the European army is unfortunate. After all, we have the EDC treaty already initialed and workable, and it would be tragic to lose so much more time. Furthermore, if the European army does not go through, Adenauer would almost certainly lose the next elections.

Most of our conversation, however, dealt with the question of Russia, now that it is clear from this morning's news that Stalin is dying. Frank thinks that the initial period following Stalin's death is bound to be a very uneasy one for the world at large, although afterwards this might work out for our benefit. There will almost certainly be some kind of internal struggle for power in Russia, although the outside world might well not know about this for a long time. It is Frank's guess that Stalin will be succeeded by some form of triumvirate, probably Molotov, Malenkov and Beria. Who will win out in the end as the actual dominating force remains to be seen. After all, following Lenin's death, the rule of Russia was really a committee rule with Stalin as the dominant individual. There would be open discussions in the Politburo that would finally come to the point, after everyone had expressed his views, when there would be silence. Then Stalin would utter his own opinion and everyone would agree. It was only during World War II that Stalin openly seized the visible symbols of power and became prime minister and marshal.

Now it is quite probable that a period of committee rule will again come about. There might be considerable differences of opinion among the members of the Politburo with no dictatorial arbiter like Stalin available at first to end these. If any contest develops between rival factions, this might in the long run prove useful to us by weakening Russian power. However, in the short run it might very well be dangerous. To begin with, there is always the possibility that someone might seek to unite the country in the face of internal squabbles by bringing the people together against external dangers in war. Secondly, the conservative, cautious hand of Stalin will be missing.

PARIS, *March 24, 1953*

I had lunch and a fascinating conversation today with David Bruce. He is now living in the house previously occupied by Harry Labouisse and before then by Barry Bingham. He has just moved in and is so short on furniture that he is even lacking in such things as wastebaskets and ashtrays. Vangie is coming with the children on Saturday, and I suppose she will take over. David is very proud of a bust of Voltaire he has just obtained on approval that shows the old bird, shortly before his death, dressed in a Roman costume with all his humorous, wicked wrinkles well outlined. He doesn't think Vangie is going to permit him to keep it around long. We lunched on a little table wheeled into a small room off the sitting room, and our conversation ranged over many subjects.

David had been called in and asked to take his present job representing the United States on European army discussions and Schuman plan affairs somewhat to his surprise. He said he asked only one question of Eisenhower and Dulles, and that was: "Is support of the European army American policy now?" He was told yes and then immediately accepted the job. He admits it is by no means a perfect solution, but he thinks it is the only one. The sole way Germany can be rearmed is through something like the EDC or NATO, and France would never accept Germany as an equal in NATO; therefore EDC is the only thing. David admits he had a lot to do with selling Eisenhower on the necessity of EDC in the spring of 1951. Instead of taking the line that it was militarily impracticable, Eisenhower saw that it was the only possible political solution and therefore instructed his officers to adjust their military thinking according to existing realities.

The English have really made a remarkably large number of concessions and cannot be expected to do any more. In fact they have done just about everything the Socialists ever wanted, but they did it step by step and so slowly and with such inept advertising that they never really got credit for their concessions. The only thing Bruce would like to see now, which he thinks would clinch the issue, would be to have Eden persuade Churchill to come out in a speech saying that upon mature consideration he had changed his mind and in order to insure the defendability of Europe and to honor the "Grand Alliance" he supported EDC.

If the project is not passed, David foresees an extremely bad reaction and a revision in American thinking to peripheral defense. By this he means "Fortress America" plus holding such positions as the Pyrenees, Gibraltar, and the like. Europe simply cannot be defended without the Germans and there is no other way of obtaining German rearmament.

Bruce is most impressed with Adenauer. He said Adenauer told him that he would never personally stomach a German national army even if EDC fails. He was thoroughly European-minded and in favor of EDC not as the only politically acceptable solution, but as the obvious and logically necessary solution. He bitterly opposed any conception of a revival of German nationalism. Furthermore, Adenauer assured him he quite understood French suspicions of and fears of Germany, although sometimes he was a little puzzled by the French politicians.

Bruce expressed considerable admiration for Caffery's ability as ambassador in Cairo. Caffery is, of course, ready to retire, but David assumes he will remain until the Suez talks are over. He admits that Caffery is somewhat unusual in manner. I gather that such allegations, which are not astonishing in view of Caffery's obviously eccentric personality, have been made during the recent fluster of McCarthyism in the State Department.

PARIS, *March 24, 1953*

I was up at the Soviet consulate today trying to speed up action—if any—on my request for a visa to visit Moscow. A fish-faced blond character I talked with made one rather startling observation (for a Russian). Looking at the picture of Stalin hanging on the wall (there is none of Malenkov yet in sight), he remarked that there had recently been a *"changement de direction"* in Moscow and perhaps this might affect the policy on visas.

PARIS, *March 24, 1953*

THIS evening I had a couple of whiskies and a long talk with Eden. He was in an exceptionally affable mood. You cannot help liking him, and despite the fact that he is now for the first time really beginning to show his age and is thin and drawn as well as white, there is something appealingly boyish about him. He bounced in to the Embassy study full of beans and bubbling over with enthusiasm as a result of today's luncheon, in which he had a long heart-to-heart talk with Mayer. Several times during the course of our conversation Eden said he now felt exceedingly optimistic about Europe—although he always qualified this with pessimism concerning other areas. He said that one week ago he could not have imagined being as sanguine in his attitude towards the future of this continent in general and of the European army project in particular.

Apparently at lunch today he calmed the last lingering suspicion that some kind of an Anglo-American deal might have been made without due regard to France's interests. He said he told Mayer he would find on his trip to Washington that the American attitude was now fully comprehensive and sympathetic concerning France's difficulties in Indochina. Nevertheless, he warned Mayer that there was grave disappointment concerning France's lack of action on the European Army, and this was the most important issue. Mayer assured Eden that he was going to put the EDC through and Eden is really optimistic. He said the French had asked once again for further British support. Eden explained that really there was nothing else that could be done of any major sort. I told Eden I had heard it suggested that it might be a very good thing if Churchill were to make a speech saying nothing new but merely throwing his support verbally to the EDC and stipulating in the form of a résumé what Britain is prepared to do to support it; that this would not have to promise a single new thing, but by merely summing up the individual pledges Britain has made at various times it would carry great weight. To my surprise Eden said he had already suggested this to Churchill, but he did not seem very optimistic about the old man's doing it. Eden admitted quite frankly that the PM was not very enthusiastic and also that he, Eden, had been working on him very hard.

Incidentally we were interrupted a couple of times by Eden's secretary coming in and reporting on the French cabinet crisis which was going on at that moment and which almost unseated Mayer just as he was about to take off for Washington. The Assembly damn near refused him permission to borrow 80 billion more francs from the national bank. Eden kicked his secretary out and said, "After all, I can't give them 80 billion, can I?"

He said his visit to Washington had been highly satisfactory and that full agreement had been reached on the Middle East. Dulles had reassured Eden that if Mossadegh turned down the latest offer on Iran, the United States would stand together with England. Furthermore Eden and Dulles agreed that the United States should formally take part in the Suez negotiations in Egypt. As a result, Caffery and Stevenson called jointly and formally upon Naguib and told him that it was considered a good idea to broaden the talks to tripartite negotiations. Naguib seemed very pleased. However, he saw his junta afterwards, and the next day he called in Stevenson and Caffery separately and very sheepishly said there was no go; he admitted that the junta did not like it. As a result there are no tripartite talks. Eden was rather irked with Caffery, who made a statement explaining merely that the United States was trying to offer its good services to both sides.

Now things are going badly and Eden is worried about a new crisis in Egypt. This is of vital importance to the whole world. We must keep Suez defended and open to the West. The French, for example, are particularly interested in this. If Egypt had full control of Suez and decided one day not to permit French ships to traverse it, that would mean that all vessels bound for Indochina would have to go around Africa, and there simply is not enough shipping to support the Indochinese war in that event.

Britain is absolutely adamant on insisting that while it is completely prepared to evacuate Suez, guarantees must be made. It must be arranged that the evacuation should be progressive, step by step. Provision must be made to retain the necesary number of technicians—and this will be a large number. Not only must the canal be defended, but provision must be made for the return of Allied forces in case of war. This course of action means MEDO. Eden said it was necessary to have "what you people call a package deal." He said that he personally did not care at all how the agenda was worked out and whether MEDO was put off till the very end in the discussions. However, he added, although he had no feeling of pride and prestige in the order of discussions, he was not going to sign anything until everything had been wrapped up.

He recognizes this is going to be exceedingly difficult. Furthermore, he feels that Naguib is in a much weaker position than most people realize. He thought this recent business about the tripartite talks has shown that Naguib is really a prisoner of the junta. As a result, Naguib is going around making his newest spate of anti-British speeches quite obviously to gain popular support and backing. This is making the situation worse rather than better. Eden wonders if there may not very well be some kind of dramatic disaster in Cairo.

He also thinks that now that the United States is not going to take part in the talks, we must make it absolutely clear beyond any doubt to the Egyptians that we stand with the British on the basic idea of a package deal. Despite the Washington agreement, Eden is rather worried that we may not make this clear enough to them. It would have been one thing with us taking full part in the negotiations, but since we are not going to be directly involved, he is afraid that our stand may not be sufficiently clear to Cairo.

Eden said that optimistic as he is about Europe, he is very seriously worried now about the Middle East. He would like to settle Egypt first and then Israel. He thinks that's the only way to handle things. However, he is certainly gloomy at the moment about any prospect of settling Egypt.

Many times he repeated how important Suez was both as a base and as a canal to the United States and France as well as England. He said the President certainly realized this, and he thought Dulles did. But he is clearly worried that the Egyptians are going to try and play us off against the British and that they still harbor the delusion that they can expel the British from Suez and then get American military and economic aid to build themselves up.

Eden has no worries now on our stand on Iran. He thinks now the only thing to do is to let Mossadegh stew in his own juice. After all, we really never have tried this. We have always come forth with a new proposal every time he said no. Now we simply must leave him alone.

He said the Tito visit had gone off quite well and that it had been a very good thing for Tito to get to England. I asked him if Tito either directly or indirectly indicated a desire to join NATO as a full member. Eden said he never gave Tito a chance to bring the matter up. He thought with a bit of encouragement that Tito would very much have liked to introduce the subject, but Eden kept the conversation away from it because he thought it was most impractical. He said that after all NATO is a kind of club with certain rules and regulations and that at this juncture Tito certainly would not be accepted as a member. He was very surprised to notice Tito's real concern with the possibility that if there were a Soviet attack on Jugoslavia, the Western world might permit this to remain an isolated Balkan war or European version of a "Korean incident." Eden strongly reassured Tito that to his way of thinking this was absolutely impossible and no such attack could be isolated. This seemed to comfort Tito a great deal. Eden admitted he was puzzled why Tito should have such a worry just after signing a treaty with Turkey and Greece.

Eden did point out that, of course, it would be far easier to protect Tito if he came to an arrangement with Italy on the subject of Trieste because the main American bases were in Italy. Tito was thoroughly realistic on this subject and said he would like to make an arrangement on Trieste. He recognized that it would be difficult to do anything prior to the Italian elections. He did think it would be a good idea for him to see De Gasperi and to try to arrange a "temporary solution" based upon Italian occupation and administration of Zone A and continued Jugoslav "temporary" administration of Zone B. Then perhaps two or three years later a formal and permanent solution could be reached. But even such a temporary deal would have to follow the Italian elections.

Incidentally, Eden said there would be no question this year of trying to help De Gasperi win his elections by any kind of Allied commitments on Trieste. We'd made a mistake in 1948 and we were still paying for it. He also said the Italians were nervous about Jugoslav intentions in Albania. I remarked that Jugoslavia was far more nervous about Italy's intentions there, and he added that, of course, the Albanians were convinced that the Jugoslavs and the Greeks wanted to partition the place. In any event, he said, Tito fully recognized the need for not doing anything in Albania at the moment and strongly opposed any effort at a *coup de main* there.

At one point in our conversation, which kept wandering rapidly around the world, Eden made an interesting remark. Reverting temporarily to Suez, he described it as the only real Allied base between Belgium and Japan. I wonder why he picked Belgium.

REUVEN Shiloah, head of the Israeli intelligence and counterintelligence services, came to see me this afternoon for a chat. Shiloah says the Egyptians have sent feelers to Israel for new negotiations, but Tel Aviv is not yet convinced Cairo is serious. According to his tale, Ralph Bunche stopped off in Cairo on his way back from a visit to India in February. Bunche saw Mahmoud Fawzi, Egyptian foreign minister. They had a long talk and Bunche did not mention the subject of Israel. However, after a considerable conversation, Fawzi remarked to him that it would be strange for Ralph Bunche to pay a call upon him and not to mention the Palestine question to which Bunche had devoted so much time. Bunche then remarked: "Well, how about it?" He added to Fawzi that he was going to Tel Aviv on a brief visit after his Cairo trip. Fawzi, without asking Bunche to keep it confidential (in other words, by implication, suggesting that he pass the message on to Israel), said Egypt would be interested in negotiating a settlement. As far as Egypt could see, there were three main questions:

1. The Arab refugee issue. This, Egypt felt, need not be settled along the lines of repatriation, but rather the refugees should be resettled, and Israel should contribute financially to such resettlement.

2. The internationalization of Jerusalem. Fawzi thought that this should be accomplished but added that it was not an essential prerequisite to any settlement—in other words, by implication indicating Egypt would not make an all out stand for this rather improbable solution.

3. The "contiguity" of the Arab world; in other words, an overland connection between Egypt and Jordan. What Fawzi meant by this was the desire that Egypt should be awarded some of the Negeb in order to have a common frontier with Jordan.

Bunche then went to Tel Aviv and passed this on to the authorities. They expressed great interest. Bunche said he was going back to Cairo to take a plane on westward. The Israelis gave him the following reaction to report back to Fawzi:

1. They were in basic agreement on the first point mentioned by Fawzi.

2. There was no insurmountable difficulty on the second point (although, of course, Israel is not going to accept internationalization of Jerusalem).

3. Differences on the third point should not represent an insurmountable barrier at least to negotiations. Therefore Israel suggested that talks should be held between Egyptian and Israeli representatives on any level and at any place and in any fashion desired by Fawzi. Furthermore, the Israelis explained to Bunche, permitting him to pass this on to Fawzi, that while they were not prepared to cede any portion of the Negeb, they were ready to consider some other type of solution, such as perhaps the estab-

lishment of an international road or the granting of access to a free zone across the Negeb so as to link the two Arab states of Egypt and Jordan.

According to Shiloah, at approximately the same time as these informal soundings were taking place an official of an Egyptian embassy in Europe—presumably with the approval of Naguib—advised an Israeli envoy that Egypt was considering the possibility of trying to reach a settlement with Israel; no more than this, but the Israelis interpret this as indicative of the fact that Egypt has not yet made up its mind how to respond to the possibility of new negotiations.

Shiloah pointed out that when Bunche returned to Cairo and told Fawzi what the Israelis had said, Fawzi in no way reproached him for having conveyed his original message to Tel Aviv and, furthermore, assumed Bunche would keep the State Department advised of all these details.

PARIS, *March 30, 1953*

I went out to SHAPE today and had a talk with General Ridgway; we covered a broad range of topics. I must say that although Ridgway continues to impress me as being an exceptionally decent fellow, he also continues to impress me as being not very bright.

I asked him whether he was disturbed by the spate of articles in the Allied press recently attacking his command as being a purely American show. He said he did not know where these articles originated and he was not bothered by them personally. He was doing the best he could and as long as his conscience and his wife's conscience were all right, he wasn't bothered and could sleep well at night. He added that he slept very well. There had been some criticism of the fact that he did not have among his aides an officer from this or that Allied nation. He said that this was his own private affair and he intended to have as aides those people he thought best suited for the job. Criticisms had been heard that not enough Allied officers had been given high positions in this or that section of his own headquarters or subsidiary headquarters for reasons of national prestige for this or that nation. It was his policy to name suitable and efficient officers to each post and it would be uneconomic to appoint additional men for reasons of national prestige and he did not intend to do so.

By and large I was impressed by the fact that Ridgway regards his operation as a purely military show and does not seem to take into account—unlike Eisenhower—the immense political importance of the whole SHAPE and NATO operation. Incidentally, he referred to the fact that it had been his lot to succeed two geniuses—MacArthur in the Far East and Eisenhower at SHAPE—and he would merely do the best he possibly could, but he recognized he could never truly fulfill the role of his predecessors.

I noticed that since I last saw Ridgway at the end of last summer, he has changed his office around and it is no longer decorated or organized the way Ike had it. He has moved his desk to the end of the room near the door and has rearranged the chairs. He has taken away the collection of national flags that Ike had and he has had a lot of maps added and removed the few pictures that used to be there.

Afterward I had a good talk with Colonel Bernard Fergusson, who is Number Two in intelligence. Fergusson, incidentally, used to be Number Two in the Palestine police after he finished his wartime career under Wingate in Burma. He told me that eighteen months ago he had had a confidential meeting with Friedman Yellin, head of the Stern Gang in Palestine, and they had had a long talk after Fergusson, pretending to be joking, had frisked both Yellin and his bodyguard. Yellin explained at length how the Stern gang had assassinated Lord Moyne and Bernadotte. He said they had rehearsed the Lord Moyne operation very carefully and had a practice operation on a street in Jerusalem before sending the assassins to Cairo. Yellin inquired after Moyne's family and said he regretted that "we had to do the job."

Yellin contended he had not officially sponsored the assassination of Bernadotte, which had been carried out, he said, by three members of the Stern Gang without official approval; but afterwards they had sought shelter with the Stern Gang, which had protected them. Yellin claimed the Israeli authorities never found the real assassins and had arrested the wrong people at the time.

Fergusson asked me if I thought there was any real knowledge on Malenkov or what was going on in Russia, and I said I didn't think so. He agreed heartily and then told me a shattering story about how Allied intelligence operates. He said an American officer had just been talking with him and had told him he had been ordered to draw up a report on the significance of Stalin's death and Malenkov's succession. The officer complained he had absolutely no facts and Fergusson said he had none to give him. Nevertheless, since he was ordered to do it, the officer did draw up a report, starting off with the premise that Stalin had been murdered by Malenkov and ending up with the deduction that this made peace more likely.

By and large, as a result of my day I was rather depressed. I had the feeling that the intellectual level of SHAPE is deteriorating and that there is some substance to the criticism in Allied newspapers that the thing is becoming too much of an American show; that, furthermore, the intellectual level of the Americans there is not rising.

PARIS, *April 1, 1953*

I had a good talk with Douglas Dillon, our new ambassador, this morning, and then Marina and I lunched with him and his wife at their hotel

suite. They are not moving into the embassy residence for another fortnight, although Dillon warned his wife he is giving his first luncheon there
on April 15 for a bunch of congressmen and that she had better be ready.
They have had a lot of trouble with the interior decorator hired by the
Foreign Buildings Administration. He had done some horrible things, including painting the stone hall chocolate colored, putting a marble table in
it with a searchlight to be focused on it to show off any flowers placed
there, and painting two gold consoles dark brown. The Dillons put an end
to these monstrosities, but they have not been able to fire the guy because
he is employed by Washington.

We first discussed the new Soviet peace offensive. Dillon has the impression it is rather sincere, as a tactical maneuver, and that it comes at a
highly inconvenient time. It is bound to affect budget allocations. His
feeling is that in order to get approval of Congress, the Administration is
going to cut its own budget estimates considerably and possibly too much, to
avoid a congressional row, and this tendency may become even worse as a
result of the Soviet peace offensive. Furthermore, if there is an armistice in
Korea, it may completely erase the pledges of new aid to Indochina because the American people may figure that the Far Eastern problem has
been resolved and therefore they should save money.

We then talked about the Mayer visit. I asked Dillon what the French
got out of it. He said they hadn't asked for anything in terms of specific
pledges or money, but that they were very pleased by recognition of
France's status as a global power. We promised that if there is an armistice
in Korea, we would regard any direct Chinese intervention in Indochina
afterwards as a violation of that armistice. We promised to consult the
French on any world problems in which they were even indirectly affected.
The French have left a couple of experts behind to consult with the Pentagon on their plans in Indochina. We have pledged considerably more aid in
Indochina if French plans for increased use of Indochinese units and their
actual military plans satisfy the Pentagon. To date they have not satisfied
the Pentagon, but it is expected the present conversations will produce
results. In that case the French have agreed to accept an American military
mission in Indochina to help coordinate the anti-Communist war.

I remarked to Dillon that Churchill some time ago had an idea that a
supercommittee should be formed similar to the Standing Group in Washington but competent to handle world planning and strategy, and I asked if
this had come up. Dillon said that when the French first got wind of this,
they rushed to London to get reassurances that this would not be a purely
Anglo-American affair similar to the wartime Combined Chiefs of Staff.
The British promised the French they would be included. Mayer brought
this up in Washington and was told that the United States was against such
a scheme on the grounds that such a tripartite supercommittee would be
suspect by the rest of the world which would resent the Big Three making

plans on what other people should do. However, we promised the French
to consult them whenever they were affected and to have future talks like
the recent conversations in Washington, and this apparently pleased them.

The French raised the question of the Suez Canal and pointed out that if
an unfriendly control were established over that area and someday barred
French ships, it would seriously complicate the Indochina war because
there weren't enough ships available to send equipment and manpower
around the long Cape of Good Hope route. I suspect that Eden brought
this up with Mayer during his visit last week just before Mayer took off for
Washington. At any rate it echoed Eden's views and it was favorably
received in Washington.

I asked Dillon if we were still putting the heat on the French to correct
their system of tax collections. He said that Mayer had come over with a
lot of figures proving that the proportion of their revenue derived from
taxes was satisfactorily high, and he also added that collections of income
taxes had improved markedly. Dillon said the Treasury has now recognized
that it is tactless to interfere in other nations' internal problems of this
sort and the only thing we were concerned with officially now was the
extent to which France should make pledges in NATO. Dillon admitted
that it was his impression that still far too much French revenue came
from invisible taxes which hit the poor and allowed the rich off the hook.

Dillon said that Cabot Lodge is feeling a little bit big for his breeches
and is intervening directly in State Department affairs. For example, Lodge
has written to Dillon several times—bypassing Dulles—giving his ideas to
Dillon of what the United States should be doing in France and making
specific suggestions for acts by Dillon. Dillon finds this very embarrassing
and has advised Dulles of what Lodge is up to.


PARIS, *April 8, 1953*

LAST night we dined at David Bruce's. The Bohlens were there. Bruce
said he was now for the first time worried about the future of EDC because
of developments in Moscow. He said that prior to the new peace offensive
he had arranged a "deal" and had everything fixed up. I don't quite know
what he means by this, but I expect it has something to do with the
uncertain bloc of Socialist votes.

Chip is still hot under the collar about Senator McCarthy and I don't
blame him. He claims that the President has now missed three good oppor-
tunities to crack McCarthy and get rid of the creeping menace. Things in
Washington are really terrible. Everybody agreed with Chip. I argued
that perhaps the President was holding his fire until after the budget debate
in order to avoid any risk of disaster to his foreign aid program. Nobody
agreed with me. Chip said he was particularly irked with Dulles. At one
point during the McCarthy attack on Bohlen, Dulles said cozily to Chip

that he should be very careful because "you know, we're sticking our necks out for you." Chip was furious and said to the Secretary that he had no desire to be beholden to anyone and if Dulles felt he was sticking his neck out, Chip would be quite happy not to accept the Moscow appointment and relieve Dulles of any embarrassment. Chip also said Dulles tricked him in the Charlie Thayer affair. He got Charlie to sign some kind of a paper on what Chip regards as a phony and immoral basis of trickery. He says that all the known enemies of McCarthy in America now are receiving letters and postcards—frequently unsigned—generally addressed "Dear Commie-Lover" or "Dear Jew-Boy."

Chip says the situation in Washington is appalling now and that there is real administrative chaos. He claims the new government simply does not understand politics. It thinks that everything in government runs the way a business operates, and it doesn't. Nobody in Washington seems to realize that there is a basic fight on now in which Congress is trying to steal the executive power from the administration while the President, envisioning Congress as a corporate body, works for harmony without recognizing the basic issue.

Chip has a theory that in Russia the Communist Party administration had secret cells in every single branch of the Soviet government including the army, the security police and the party apparatus, and now a real struggle for power is taking place at all levels inside those cells.

PARIS, *April 8, 1953*

LUNCH with Dillon. He said two of McCarthy's investigators (Cohn and Schine) were here over Easter weekend. They asked some people at the embassy, including security officers, to come and call upon them in their hotel. They had a curious system whereby one of the two investigators would disappear into the next room while his colleague was interviewing someone. The door would be left ajar. Then the two would exchange posts when a new subject arrived to be interviewed. Obviously they were either taking shorthand notes or running a dictaphone. Dillon said they seemed very disappointed when they kept asking people what their problems were and were told that there were none. They kept hammering away at the security people at the embassy, asking time and again if they were getting sufficient backing from the ambassador.

PARIS, *April 10, 1953*

LUNCH with Randolph Churchill. He is very worried about what he considers appeasement tendencies in the Western world as a result of the Russian peace offensive. He says that when Sumner Welles was taking a trip in 1940 at the behest of President Roosevelt, trying to find a way of ending World War II, he called upon Randolph's father (not yet Prime Minister) after visiting Rome and Berlin. He said his father, trying to dodge any compromise or appeasement maneuvers, kept the conversation for a long time on the subject of the New Deal, arguing that England had accomplished similar reforms three decades earlier. Welles finally got to his subject. Churchill replied, according to Randolph, that England would require specific guarantees from the United States as well as from the Axis powers before it would consider peace. Welles supposedly asked what type of guarantee was involved. Churchill said, "Well, we might commence with Hitler's scalp." That, apparently, ended the topic.

Randolph said he has gotten friendly with Eden again now that the latter has married his cousin Pamela. He added, "I'm going around telling everybody to sell their Butlers (Rab Butler) and buy Edens now, because obviously Anthony is the man to succeed as PM. After all, we want to keep the Churchill family in 10 Downing Street."

PARIS, *April 13, 1953*

LONG and interesting talk with Al Gruenther who has just returned from a trip of several weeks to the States.

Before going in to see him, I was chatting with his aides when Colonel Walters came in and told some amusing stories about Mossadegh. When Mossadegh was checked over at a New York hospital, the doctors confided to Walters that the old man was the healthiest specimen they had ever run into for his age—despite his political fainting fits. Also Walters said he had twice seen Mossadegh spring out of his chair and stride halfway across a room without his cane when suddenly his aide whispered to him, reminding him of his act, and he doubled over and hobbled the rest of the way. Just before Mossadegh left Washington at the end of his official visit, Walters had gone in to say good-by to him, and the old man as usual was sitting up in bed muttering *"infiniment"* and *"je prie."* (Walters says he always uses those phrases, but Walters has never found out what the hell they refer to or what he was praying for.) Walters asked Mossadegh if he wasn't disappointed in going home empty-handed to Iran. Mossadegh replied on the contrary that he would be much stronger politically going home empty-handed. If he'd made any kind of a deal, everybody would have said he had sold out Iran's oil to foreign interests. He then said to Walters that he wanted to kiss him good-by. Walters thought, my God, I'm ready to do anything for the fatherland, but must I do this? At last he said, "Your Excellency, all right, if you promise that's all there is to it." He said Mossadegh roared with laughter, embraced him on both cheeks and sent him off.

Walters' monologue was interrupted when the button buzzed and I went in to see Gruenther. He started talking about his trip back home and said

Eisenhower was doing a very smart thing by inviting every member of Congress at one time or another in group luncheons and then taking them on personal tours through the White House. Some of them had never before seen it, Al said. He said the President looks extremely well and vigorous and is in good form. Incidentally, he said at a bridge game he had there with Phil Reed, Bill Robinson and the President, Al hauled out a letter I had written him asking for his opinion on the bidding of two rather unusual bridge hands which had cropped up recently in a game. He said nobody got the right answers, but "Ike's solution was the worst of all."

Al said that quite frankly SHAPE could not plan to have enough forces for a long time to meet a Soviet threat if such should develop unless there were very sizable increases in Allied commitments, and these are not expected. If Russia attacked now, we would definitely be weak. That, however, he said, "represents a purely military point of view. The NATO powers have adopted as a basic principle the precept that the economic viability of a country is the fact of primary importance. We must not spend ourselves into ruin. SHAPE, of course, wants more forces—but not at the expense of basic economic requirements."

SHAPE does not specify the number of divisions each country should produce. It did, however, desire a minimal period of military service of twenty-four months, which was approved at the Lisbon meeting in 1952. It takes twenty-four months to train a man and if he has less training than that, it means the Allied armies would suffer increased casualties if and when the chips were down. A shorter term of military service means a reduction both in the number of men and the quality of troops available. The present situation is dangerous because France has decided for political reasons (and Gruenther said that he frankly never expected the French to do anything else) that they cannot raise their term of service from eighteen months to twenty-four months. As a result, it is feared the Dutch will come down from twenty months to eighteen months and that the Belgians will reduce their term of service. The cumulative effect of these reductions would certainly be bad for NATO.

I asked Gruenther if the Allies had now abandoned their belief that 1954 would be the critical year for which special emergency preparations must be made. He argued that such a "critical year figure" had always been a misnomer. American thinking on this subject had been undergoing change for some time. The year 1954 was an arbitrary date set up in order to establish a suitable defense posture in the swiftest possible period of time. Montgomery as a matter of fact always used to use 1952 as the figure for a critical year. If Gruenther had to choose one year, he thinks he probably would select 1960 on the theory that Russia won't start a war unless it is sure it can win it ultimately, and it cannot be certain of that unless it is fully prepared. The Russians won't gamble. Right now they know they could win the first phase, but they couldn't come through in the end. By

1960 their industrial production, however, should be sufficient to give them more confidence. He admitted he was basing this logic only on industrial production figures.

If there is no EDC, the task of SHAPE planning will be extremely difficult and it means that a "defensive" and "rearward" type of strategy would have to be developed. A neutralized Germany with all occupying forces withdrawn would give a certain cushion in between the West and the Soviet bloc. However, there would really be no place to which British and American forces now in Germany could be withdrawn. There is no room in Western Europe for them, and they might have to go home.

Gruenther said it was a very difficult political problem to arrange a specific military agreement between Jugoslavia on the one hand and Greece and Turkey on the other. A deal would have to be worked out with the Jugoslavs that fits into NATO plans. That is a pretty tricky thing to do especially with the Italian elections coming on because obviously anything involving Jugoslavia has an immediate effect in Italy. No truly effective arrangement between Jugoslavia and any NATO members can be worked out until there is some measure of cooperation between Jugoslavia and Italy.

He said there would be a measurable improvement in the defense picture as far as air bases and naval facilities were concerned if the United States manages to conclude its bilateral agreement for military assistance and bases with Spain. Nevertheless SHAPE could never count in its planning on getting Spanish troops on the perimeter opposite the Russians, which is where they would be needed as a deterrent and to force the enemy to concentrate. That is where Germany would be so important if we could get divisions there. It would be a terrific political problem (even if there were trained and equipped Spanish divisions, which there aren't) to move such divisions into France. Nevertheless SHAPE would like to be able to count on some specified number of Spanish units which could be ready to move by a specified date in case of war. But it is doubtful any such arrangement could ever be worked out until Spain is actively in NATO.

PARIS, *April 14, 1953*

I had a chat with Bill Tyler this afternoon. We were talking about the security-mindedness now so evident in the State Department. Marine guards go around and check the desks and offices of everybody in the embassy at the end of the day after the staff has gone home. Recently Bill had in an unlocked desk drawer a few sheets of paper stamped "confidential"; but they were blank and nothing was written upon them. Bill was reported to the security officer of the embassy by a Marine for violating security by having a classified document in his possession that was not locked up. He had to spend twenty minutes with the security officer arguing that a blank sheet of paper marked "confidential" was not really a security document. The security people kept rebutting that it was a "confidential paper."

PARIS, *April 15, 1953*

I had a very long talk with Pug (General, Lord) Ismay this afternoon. Ismay not only thinks that it is highly unlikely the European Army will ever materialize—because it will not be ratified by the French parliament—but he thinks it a crackpot scheme anyway. However, the difficulty is that French public opinion and even a large part of European public opinion has been focused on EDC. As a result there are many French now who would reluctantly agree to rearming the Germans in a European Army but who would not agree to the "naked inclusion of Germany in NATO."

Ismay said that, speaking personally, he was opposed to EDC. Naturally the United Kingdom would never join it. The French generals frankly prefer German rearmament to an EDC. But we must not let arguments on this subject divide us because Russia is doing her utmost to split the alliance. Five years ago Ismay said that he wanted to rearm Germany because it was quite obvious you could not keep that energetic nation forever disarmed. But he wanted the basic condition that while Germany could have her own armed forces, she could not manufacture any war materials. Now, unfortunately, we are doing just the reverse. A German war industry is gradually reviving, but Germany doesn't have an army. Someday she will have an army—*with* a war industry, and then it will be much more difficult to control her. Ismay's perpetual nightmare is the thought of a rearmed, independent Germany tying itself up with Russia and using its organizing ability and energy together with Russia's vast manpower and fighting ability.

He recalled that recently Bidault had suggested to him that England should join the EDC. Ismay had replied that England could not do so because, among other things, it could not sacrifice the traditions of its armed forces, which had been built up over hundreds of years. Bidault replied, "Of course you're perfectly willing to sacrifice the traditions of the armies of Napoleon and Blücher but not those of Wellington." Ismay admitted that Bidault was absolutely right.

When he was in Washington on his recent trip Pug saw Eisenhower alone for only a brief period. He had a feeling that Ike remained fervently behind NATO and also the EDC concept. In fact he wrote Ismay after the latter had left Washington saying that he could always count upon Eisenhower's support for himself and NATO.

Ismay clearly has no use for Dulles. In fact he indicated a belief that the conversations he had with Eisenhower might have been freer and franker if Dulles had not been present most of the time. He said Dulles had made a terrific mistake in setting up the ANZUS treaty scheme in the Pacific without including England. He thought Dulles was an amateur who thought all problems were easy until he had to handle them.

PARIS, *April 15, 1953*

MARCEL Boussac, the French millionaire, is starting a private endowment to acertain what would be the implications and results for France— economically, politically, socially and militarily—if the French were to shift their policy and base it upon Atlantic Union rather than Western Europe. In other words, this would more or less revive Churchill's offer in the spring of 1940 to unite with France both in terms of overseas and European possessions. The theory is that France and Britain are still both imperial powers but are not in any form of colonial competition with each other. Boussac apparently wants to have a complementary study done in England of the proposition. If this is carried out, it might in the end result in very important fundamental changes for all of Europe and eventually the United States.

PARIS, *April 19, 1953*

LAST night I had a long talk with Ismay again. He was exceptionally interesting on the subject of Anglo-French negotiations in the spring of 1940, just before France signed the armistice. At that time Pug was acting as Churchill's right-hand man, and they were doing everything possible to prevent France from signing a separate peace. De Gaulle, then undersecretary in the cabinet, had already been sent by Reynaud to London. Ismay and Churchill flew over to consult Reynaud after Paris had been evacuated. They and Lord Halifax made the trip in a dilapidated old plane without any fighter escort. As they passed over the Channel Islands, they saw below them the Luftwaffe bombing away, but fortunately for the world the Germans did not look up, and the plane arrived safely at the airport in Tours just after it had been bombed. They circled around to find a path between the craters and finally came down. There was nobody there to greet them. They descended and Churchill looked around, announcing in his bad French, *"Moi, je suis le premier ministre d'Angleterre. Je veux une automobile."* They finally got a little rumble-seat roadster and squeezed in. They drove to town, and finally one of Georges Mandel's assistants spotted them. Churchill said he wanted a good lunch, so the Frenchman cleared a room in a little hotel and they sat down to cold chicken, Vouvray wine and cognac. They then conferred with Reynaud, Weygand and others.

Already it was clear the wind was blowing badly in a political sense—as badly as the military campaign. The British were still fighting hard and had actually started moving divisions to Cherbourg (including a Canadian division) to try and keep a foothold. Nevertheless Pétain already had his surrender terms in his pocket although he had not yet disclosed them, and Weygand had clearly pushed his chips in. Reynaud looked shamefacedly at Churchill and asked if he could send over more RAF squadrons without which the French could not hold out. At that moment, Ismay said, there were only twenty-five squadrons of the RAF in England, and this was the absolute minimum fixed by the general staff as necessary to insure the safety of the country. Knowing how generous and bold Churchill was by instinct, Pug was terrified that he would agree to send over even one squadron. Reynaud argued that this was the decisive battle. However, Churchill thought for a moment and then said, no, he could not send any more planes, and this was not the decisive battle; the decisive battle would be the battle for Britain. Reynaud still at that time was determined to fight on, even in North Africa if necessary.

The Englishmen flew back to London, but the situation kept getting worse. Finally in a cabinet meeting Halifax suggested Britain should offer France a union of the two countries. (This was really Jean Monnet's idea.) Churchill seized this idea and asked de Gaulle to telephone the offer to Reynaud. Reynaud discussed this on the telephone with de Gaulle, but it was later found out that Weygand personally monitored the telephone conversation and told all of Reynaud's cabinet, so that when the subject was discussed by the fleeing French cabinet, Reynaud was in a minority of one.

Churchill and Ismay flew over once more to see Reynaud, and Reynaud asked Churchill if Britain would release France from its pledge not to sign a separate peace. Ismay and Churchill walked around in a garden discussing this and then went back where Churchill said no. He was prepared to recognize that France might consider it necessary to surrender its army as a result of defeats, but no separate peace could be tolerated. He pointed out that the loss of the French fleet and North Africa would completely alter the balance of power. Therefore a separate peace was not signed.

PARIS, *April 19, 1953*

I spent today playing golf with General Omar Bradley. Bradley played extremely well and was quite pleased with himself. He is a curious and rather colorless fellow but very simple and amiable. His face is of the Grant Wood variety and doesn't appear particularly strong until you regard his turtle-like mouth. Bradley said Bedell Smith is trying to get a new deputy to head up the CIA. Bradley suggested General Cabell, head of Air Force intelligence, and this is now being considered. Bradley was a boy in the town of Moberly, Mo., whose population was about 16,000. He said he had always been interested in history and biography, especially of generals.

He was hoping to work his way through college and become a lawyer when somebody suggested to him that he should go to West Point. He didn't know that he could go there free and replied, "I can't afford it." When he found out the terms, he wrote to his congressman (Rucker) and finally got the appointment.

He was in the same class as Eisenhower and Van Fleet and says his class had more stars (in terms of the numbers on general's shoulders) than any other in West Point history. He played football on the same team as Van Fleet (Eisenhower had already been injured and didn't play in his last year) and was in Eisenhower's company. He said that he and Van Fleet and Eisenhower had been close friends at the academy.

He said he was responsible for getting Van Fleet his battlefield promotion after the Normandy invasion in which Van Fleet was only a colonel heading a combat team. He spoke to McNair about getting this promotion for Van Fleet, and—the same old story—McNair replied, "Yes, Van's doing fine; isn't it too bad he has a drinking record." Bradley said he replied, "Jeesus Christ," that Van Fleet was almost a teetotaler.

PARIS, *April 21, 1953*

LAST night as I was rushing home rather late, a voice shouted across the Rue de Verneuil, "Hey Sulz." I looked across the street and there was Pierre Courtade, smiling and extremely affable. I went over and chatted with him. "I don't see any reason why we shouldn't coexist," he said. "Not at all," I replied. I suggested he call me up any day next week and we could arrange to have lunch or dinner together. I pointed out that I was completely occupied this week because of the NATO meeting. "We are making plans against you," I added. He said he would certainly call me up Monday or Tuesday, but he thought lunch or dinner was carrying it a bit too far; that maybe just a drink would be enough. With that, we parted.

(P.S. Courtade, who is foreign editor of *L'Humanité* and a fairly important wheel in the French Communist Party [on the Central Committee], was in Indochina a few months ago visiting the Viet Minh, and there is good reason to believe he snuck up into China and saw the boys in Peking.*)

PARIS, *April 21, 1953*

LUNCH today with General Speidel (once Rommel's chief of staff), who as usual was extremely affable. He has invited me to go to Tübingen with him this spring where he will arrange for me to meet a group of students taking his modern history lecture course, in order to have a frank

* He later admitted he had.

discussion on how German youth feels. Speidel says it is a very critical generation. Apparently the only other Americans to whom he has afforded this privilege were Charles Lindbergh and his wife who came to Tübingen in 1948.

Speidel told me he had been in Russia in 1930, when Germany was secretly manufacturing tanks and aircraft there. In 1932, Marshal Tukhachevsky attended German maneuvers on the Oder River and Speidel was with him all the time. He was very impressed by Tukhachevsky. Tukhachevsky spoke good French and was very free in his observations, which were extremely intelligent. Tukhachevsky always wore an immaculate uniform and was a very smart officer. At a party one night he got drunk and announced he would lead the Russian army into Istanbul and he did not care a damn whether it was under the Red Star or the Cross of St. Andrew.

Speidel said German intelligence information was so good at the time that when Stalin purged Tukhachevsky and most of the principal Red Army leaders, the Germans never believed that this crippled Soviet military potential. He said it was a mistake to consider the Russians rigid and unimaginative in military strategy; Zhukov was a first-class general and Koniev was also good.

Speidel again got in a few digs about the British. He said they are magnificent soldiers, but the Imperial General Staff is hidebound and that is why their generals—such as Montgomery—never know how to exploit an opportunity.

Speidel thought that a national German army with bilateral arrangements with Britain and the United States (which in turn could give individual guarantees to France) might be set up if EDC fails. From a military point of view there would be no problem as all the planning has been done.

If Russia offers a reunified Germany with completely free elections in the eastern zone—even if she stipulates that such a Germany must be neutral and sign no military alliances—it will be impossible for the West German government to turn this down. This could indeed wreck NATO and Speidel wonders why the Russians have not made such a move before. There is no room in Europe for the ten British and American divisions now in Germany once they have to evacuate.

Speidel confirms that Major General Remer, leader of the new Nazi Socialist Reichspartei, is now in Egypt at the invitation of General Naguib. Remer is a good friend of Voss, the former SS leader who heads a German mission of experts in Cairo. Speidel professes complete contempt for Remer's military abilities and says he never even heard of him—he was only a major of relatively junior rank—until July 20, 1944.

Speidel said Germany would never accept de Gaulle's theories on a German national army because de Gaulle "only wants a satellite army from us." Most of the French generals working on the European Army project privately feel a German national army would probably be more satisfactory.

Speidel, who is certainly an intellectual officer, told me that he could still read books in Latin and ancient Greek, although now he requires a dictionary. French is his best foreign language, but he can read English easily.

PARIS, *April 23, 1953*

TODAY Carl McCardle, now assistant secretary of state, told me that when he got on the plane to fly from Washington to New York with Dulles and Humphrey, he picked up *The New York Times* and was startled to read on page seventeen my story saying NATO was now giving up the "critical-year" philosophy in favor of a "stretch-out." He showed it to Dulles and Humphrey and they were both irked that the story should have gotten out ahead of time since this is one of the principal things they want to emphasize and publicize at the NATO Council meeting. However, McCardle said they need not worry since obviously the *Times* didn't know a good story when it saw it and had buried it on page seventeen. I told McCardle that he was even more fortunate than he thought because at least 50 per cent of the story had been killed.

PARIS, *April 27, 1953*

I played golf yesterday afternoon with General Bradley and afterwards sat around and had drinks with him at Fred Anderson's house. Bradley, incidentally, played exceptionally well and came in even par for the second nine, which pleased him no end.

Bradley said it had taken him and his aide about five years to prepare his (Bradley's) book. The aide had kept a diary which totaled around 250,000 words. Bradley used to spend evening after evening (following the war) with his aide and a dictagraph. His aide, Colonel Chester Hanson, would ask questions and then Bradley would reply. This process was then transcribed in a total of about 1,000,000 words. Then Bradley used to work on it a bit over weekends, and Hanson was assigned to spend a good deal of time on it by Bradley. The final book was cut down to about 170,000 words. Bradley says he has a mass of unpublished and interesting stuff, mainly anecdotes, and is thinking of possibly, someday, putting together a second book. I told him and Anderson I thought the NATO communiqué was a miserable mess. They both agreed—vigorously.

I just talked with Bob Thayer (CIA man at the embassy). He told me he now has a report on the recent book *My Uncle Joe*. The report says the book is a complete phony put out by a former Soviet diplomat in France.

His outfit is supposed to have been responsible for *"Les Maréchaux Sovietiques Vous Parlent"* and is now working on some fake memoirs by Litvinov.

PARIS, *April 28, 1953*

I had a chat and a drink this evening with my old friend Panayotis Canellopoulos, Greece's defense minister. He was astonishingly indiscreet. I asked him how the negotiations with Turkey and Jugoslavia were going. He told me:

In case of war there will be no joint Greek-Jugoslav offensive against Albania. Rather, it is hoped that within between two and nine months a *coup de main* can be staged there (this year) getting rid of Hoxha and prying the country from Soviet grip. I gather American troops, if necessary, will be used to "maintain order" after a local coup. The Greeks have agreed to keep out and the Jugoslavs have been more or less warned to do so. The Jugoslavs are suspicious.

Nevertheless, even if the coup doesn't come off, it is figured (and Admiral Carney approves) that no occupation of Albania is necessary. Thus a large number of Jugoslav and Greek divisions are being freed for use to the north and east—troops that otherwise would have to invade and do occupation duty.

At the end of the NATO Council meeting Dulles urged the Greeks to press through their military negotiations with Turkey and Jugoslavia to a firm and successful conclusion as fast as possible on the grounds that the Soviet peace offensive so far cannot be assumed to mean anything and strength is required.

It has been decided, in accord with Carney, that *offensive* operations will be necessary *immediately* in the event of war in order to hold Thrace and the link between Greece and Turkey. Formerly evacuation of Thrace had been the primary planning problem. This has now been relegated to a secondary consideration. The Turks and Jugoslavs would push into Bulgaria while the bulk of the Greek army (released from Albania) held.

Carney promised the Greeks and the Turks secretly that they would receive immediate atomic support (both strategic and tactical) in case of war.

PARIS, *April 29, 1953*

LUNCHED with Gaspard de Villelume, head of the East European section of the Quai d'Orsay. This does not include Russia, a separate section under Laloy.

Villelume said there have been no signs of any change in policy or propaganda in the satellite countries since Stalin's death. The only exception is an apparent cessation of violent attacks on Jews and Zionists in most of the satellite press.

Perhaps the only single "fact" in the satellite area showing repercussions of the peace offensive is this: Twenty-three months after his first request for an interview, the French minister in Albania was received by the vice-minister of foreign affairs. The Albanian dignitary apologized to the Frenchman for the fact that all notes and démarches the latter had submitted during more than two years had never been answered and said the Albanian government would shortly get around to it. He also gave the French Minister permission to have a camera. This does not do the diplomat much good since he is not allowed out of Tirana, cannot walk across the street to the American legation (which he protects) without being followed by a police agent.

PARIS, *May 6, 1953*

I am now for the umpteenth time in the process of being investigated by irate authorities for a security leak. I remember this happened in 1944, in 1945 and in 1950. A newspaper reporter's life is sometimes inconvenient, to say the least. As far as I know, the 1944 and 1945 investigations wound up and died, but to the best of my knowledge several people including the Americans and the British are still actively trying to find out the source of a story I wrote about Albania from Istanbul in 1950. Occasionally somebody still drops an idle question at a cocktail party on that line.

The subject this time is a story I wrote quoting from a NATO report on China which was classified as Secret. The report was entirely harmless and arrived at no conclusions either positive or negative. Nevertheless a security check is being made in the State Department, the American embassy in Paris, the office of the Special Representative in Europe, and so forth. For more than a half an hour at today's meeting of the permanent NATO Council the subject was discussed. I went to a cocktail party this afternoon at Parmely Herrick's and Ben Bradlee of the American embassy told me they had a staff meeting on the subject. He had been assigned to ask me where I got the story. He told the embassy not to be damn fools, that obviously I wasn't going to tell him. They were astonished and said, "Do you really think he won't tell you if you ask him?" Ted Achilles, the American minister, was at the party and said with a smile, "I haven't even seen you and I don't know you." Brose Chambers of SRE greeted me with, "I thought the next time I'd see you, you would be wearing handcuffs."

I dined with Ismay and Bill Batt (also of SRE). Ismay told me I was certainly not in his doghouse and that he agreed the paper was utterly harmless. He did say, however, that it presented a problem to him because of the irate American security boys and also because the smaller countries were complaining that although they were told to keep things secret the

Americans leaked to *The New York Times*. I told Ismay I could appreciate his problem and that he would probably be horrified to know that in the case of one particular classified document of the last NATO meeting, *The New York Times* received three copies of the same document.

Ismay was extremely amusing about the coronation ceremonies. He is going in privy councillor's attire, which is a complicated robe faced in gold and worn over another complicated uniform. He got his from what he termed a "deceased peer." When the late King died, Churchill announced to the cabinet, "Naturally we must all attend the funeral in privy council-lor's dress." Ismay said a horrified cabinet responded unanimously, "You don't really mean that, do you, Winston? None of us has got it." Lady Ismay said she has to wear a complicated gown plus all the jewelry she can borrow. She's already busily at work borrowing. Ismay himself was worried about the innumerable square yards that make up his costume, about the problem of walking in it, and about the problem of sitting in it for an interminable number of hours.

FONTAINEBLEAU, *May 9, 1953*

LUNCH with Harold Hoskins, an old friend from Middle Eastern days, who has just completed an extensive trip through the Arab world and Israel. Hoskins is now probably the driving force of the American Near Eastern College Association. I would not be surprised if he were doing some "separate" work for the government. He saw a great many people during his trip, including Stevenson (in a hospital in Cairo), Caffery and a batch of Arab and Israeli leaders.

He is very pessimistic. Suez Canal negotiations in Cairo have broken down. Hoskins is convinced the British intend to stay there indefinitely. The British contend they need five thousand civilian technicians in the zone, and the Egyptians have agreed to leave on only eighty. Negotiations are waiting for Dulles' arrival next week, but Dulles isn't going to have any ideas; he's just on a fact-finding trip.

Hoskins doesn't admire Dulles. They are distant cousins and after World War I they took a tour of Europe together. Hoskins says Dulles is brilliant and after their extensive trip, on which Dulles took no notes, he sat down and dictated an eighteen-page report on his impressions which was so intelligent that Hoskins read it with wonder and said not a single phrase could have been changed without damaging the report. Nevertheless he thinks Dulles suffers from the same arrogance and cocksuredness as Ache-son, although expressed in a different and perhaps even less agreeable way. He thinks he has the cure-all for everything, and, of course, adds Hoskins, he hasn't.

Ben Gurion keeps trying to negotiate with Naguib. There is no chance of succeeding because Naguib is losing power continually to the extremists in the junta headed by Colonel Gamal Abdel Nasser. Furthermore, there is an increasingly powerful Nazi German faction working behind the scenes in Egypt, headed by SS *Obergruppenführer* Voss and including Major General Otto Remer of the neo-Nazi Socialist Reichspartei. To Hoskins' knowledge they now have representatives in all government ministries except foreign affairs, and they may have one there. Obviously they are not working for the West. You can see the results in the form of the red, white and black flag which has been adopted by the Liberation Party and the increasing resemblance between demonstrations staged by the extremists and those the Nazis used to organize.

FONTAINEBLEAU, *May 9, 1953*

LAST night we dined at Norstad's with the Ridgways, the Drapers and Ted and Marion Achilles. The conversation ranged over a great many subjects, and at one point I shot my own trap off too much, claiming that the world was being deceived by present NATO policy. It was being advertised as scheduled to be 30 per cent stronger at the end of this year despite the stretch-out, and this was untrue. Before he left, Ridgway came up to me and took me in a corner and asked me for goodness' sake to push that idea, which was true, and it was necessary that the United States should know it.

Norstad insisted that 1954, when it was selected as a "critical year," was selected only in order to fix target goals and not because it was really felt from a military point of view it was going to be critical. He said he attended all the meetings which decided on fixing that date. He said that 1952 was a very bad year because the United States had to exert so much pressure on its allies to keep them pushing for rearmament. Now everybody is going to be happy and we will be much more popular because we are not pushing. But the West is not preparing its defenses either. It was much better when we were hated and forced things through and got things done.

Norstad claims there is absolutely no military chain of command in Indochina and no connection between the French command there and the Paris general staff. Salan has been directly responsible to Letourneau, minister of the Associated States. Letourneau in turn, whenever there is a military query from Paris, answers only that he "has full confidence in my generals." There is no order to the situation. (I happen to know, for example, that the intelligence branch of the services has never permitted the regular French Intelligence to operate in Indochina.) Norstad has complained to Juin.

SATURDAY night we had dinner at Givry with Melvin Hall and his wife, and yesterday we had drinks before lunch with them at their little fourteenth-century house just outside of Vezelay. Hall is an old friend of mine from Turkey, Washington and other odd places. He is an adventurer and soldier of fortune who was a staff captain in the British army during World War I (attached to the Royal Flying Corps); received the DSO from the British for a commando-type demolitions operation; transferred to the American Air Force as chief of staff to Billy Mitchell and ended up a lieutenant colonel; later was a general in the Persian army and governor of East Persia; when I first knew him, was a commander in the United States Navy and assistant naval attaché for air in Turkey, Rumania and Bulgaria; later was in the American Air Force as a full colonel. He just returned last autumn from eight months in Indochina where he was officially listed as an assistant to the ambassador but was actually on a CIA assignment. He is surely over sixty, and yet just last year was riding around in dilapidated transport planes along the Chinese border, pitching cargoes out to French outposts and coming back time after time in planes riddled with Chinese antiaircraft fire.

He thinks the Indochinese situation is pretty hopeless, and yet we must continue to support the French because nobody else is available to hold the sagging dike. Were we to let it go, all of Southeast Asia would fall to the Communists and eventually India—and in the long run the Middle East would crumble. Yet the French are certainly not doing well. Their military strategy and tactics are not good and their training, both of French and local troops, is inadequate for guerrilla warfare. The French colonial administration and settlers are riddled by corruption and have been profiteering to a disgraceful degree on black market exchanges of the piaster, the French franc and the dollar.

Very recently Hall gave a lecture in London, and he said he was asked a question which is quite unanswerable by Commander Stephen King-Hall. King-Hall asked, "Supposing the Viet Minh takes a village. Supposing they come up to a peasant and they ask him, are you against the landlord who is charging you a preposterously unfair rent and keeping you permanently in debt? The peasant says yes. Then they ask him, are you against the local usurer who charges you 200 per cent interest on the money you borrow to pay your landlord? The peasant replied yes. Then they say to the peasant, well you are a Communist. You are one of us. We are against the landlord and the usurer." King-Hall asked, what do you tell that peasant?

PARIS, 5:15 P.M., *May 12, 1953*

JUST called Grace Gruenther to congratulate her and send her kisses on both cheeks. "Why?" she asked. I told her that to the best of my information, in about an hour's time it would be announced in public that Al was going to be commander-in-chief of SHAPE, NATO, and so on. She said, "I've been fishing around trying to get solid information from him for four months." I said, "For God's sake, don't tell him I told you."

PARIS, *May 13, 1953*

YESTERDAY Eisenhower announced his new general staff. Ridgway is going as head of the Army, and Al Gruenther will take his place as Supreme Allied Commander in Europe. Last night General Gene Beebe dropped around at the office while I was writing my story on all this, and then we went out to dinner later. Gene was one of the five men in the United States (or, in fact, the world) who knew all this during the past week. He saw the President twice about drafting the letters to the various individuals involved, and the President instructed him to be sure and arrange that all the men were informed as simultaneously as possible— including Admiral Fechteler, who, I believe, is going out two years early. Radford as new chairman of the Joint Chiefs of Staff terrifies Europe because of his dynamic policy towards China and infuriates the air boys, who don't like the Navy anyway.

Beebe was given one week within which to accomplish his mission. He came over here by commercial airline, and nobody in Paris was advised he was coming in order to keep the thing super hush-hush. He arrived Saturday bearing various letters from the President to Gruenther, Ridgway, the NATO Council. He wasn't allowed to tell anybody what his mission was. He dined at Gruenther's Saturday night with some of the staff officers, and after dinner he raised his glass in a toast to "a new star to be born in Paris." Grace Gruenther, who knew something was up, tried to pry the information out of Al that night. Gruenther later told Beebe that he never told her.

Monday morning at nine o'clock Beebe went in to Ridgway's office escorted by Gruenther. At the doorway Gruenther said, "Am I allowed in also?" Ridgway nodded and then Beebe handed the two men their two letters from the President. He said their faces did not change expression as they read them, but he saw Gruenther's blood pressure rise visibly as he flushed. He couldn't tell whether Gruenther was pleased or displeased. To my mind the NATO job is probably the most important command an American can have, but in the hierarchy, chief of staff is higher. Ridgway must have mixed feelings because, although he is fifty-eight, he is a remarkably young-looking man, and he must know that this is the last step in his career before retirement.

Beebe and I had a long, rambling discussion throughout the evening. He told me he is going to get together a complete file on the origin of the European Army plan drafted in the United States and Marshall's role in it. He was astonished at Wilson's ignorance when he became Secretary of Defense. He rode over on the same plane as Wilson to the NATO conference and had to brief him. It was all Wilson could do to remember that England and France were members of NATO. He couldn't master the rest of the alliance roster. Nevertheless Wilson is learning very rapidly and is doing things in an efficient, businesslike way. Furthermore, if he says something will be done, it is done quickly and methodically. He has high hopes for Wilson but thinks the period of learning is going to be tough.

Beebe is right up at the top echelon in the United States armed forces and sees everything and should remember them. I was therefore amazed at his limitations (although he is a very bright, as well as nice, fellow), when we started discussing specifics on a map, such as the Middle East and the Balkans. For example, he envisions the possibility of an Allied thrust into the Caucasus from Iran, with the Turks holding their side of the Caucasus, although losing Thrace during the initial period of a war. I told him I thought it would be infinitely more important for Turkey and Greece to knock out Bulgaria right away while the Turks retreated to the west of Erzurum. I think he is nuts to think of any kind of a drive from Iran, which will fall like a ripe apple. I told him it would obviously be the easiest thing on earth for the Russians to figure out what our Balkan plans were just by reading published material. I then showed him Marshal Papagos' book containing all the secret plans and papers up until 1941, and he was astounded when he read the draft for a proposed military pact between Greece and Turkey and the detailed plan of attack drawn up by Papagos as Greek chief of staff.

PARIS, *May 15, 1953*

LUNCH today with Bill Hayter who has just been knighted and made ambassador to Moscow. He thought Churchill's speech was a disaster. Churchill unfortunately now is an old man in a hurry trying to get things done. Presumably by this he means to get the label of peace attached to his name before he dies. He thought it was a great shame that Eden is sick because Eden's influence on a thing like this would have been very useful. He hopes the speech has not been shown to Eden, who will have another relapse if he reads it. Incidentally, he says Eden is much more seriously ill than has been indicated, but it isn't cancer. However, he will probably be out until about September. Hayter doesn't think Butler is very bright. Butler is getting kind of anti-American as a result of the failure of his "trade not aid" campaign and his tiff with Dulles.

PARIS, *May 17, 1953*

LAST night we dined with Walter Lippmann. Lippmann is tremendously discouraged by the strength of McCarthy and McCarthyism. He thinks things are getting worse. He blames Eisenhower for being "a pacifist by nature. He always wants to make peace, which is funny because he is a soldier. Therefore he simply refuses to believe that he cannot make peace with McCarthy." Lippmann also thinks Dulles is doing badly. He said he never sees Eisenhower himself.

Lippmann claims the office of Secretary of State traditionally does not go to a statesman but to the man who failed to get the presidential nomination. Therefore he thinks Dulles will be replaced when he goes—and he predicts Dulles will be gone within eight months—by Senator Taft and that would be a logical appointment. If Taft has the responsibility, he will probably be a good Secretary of State. (I think Lippmann is loony.)

PARIS, *May 25, 1953*

I spent yesterday afternoon and evening at the Gruenthers' playing bridge. Phil Reed, chairman of the board of General Electric, was there. After the game we sat around for about an hour and a half gassing. Gruenther was very disturbed about the failure to give a British concern the contract to build the Chief Joseph Dam in the state of Washington after the English had submitted the lowest bid. He said it is only an $8 million contract but it is costing us $16 billion worth of bad publicity. The English, and in fact all of Europe, are furious.

Gruenther was deeply worried about the effect of McCarthyism abroad. Reed said Llewellyn Thompson, our ambassador in Vienna, had told him confidentially that foreign service officers no longer dared to report the flat truth to the State Department because all their cables were submitted to Scott McLeod, McCarthy's man, who is at the head of State Department security checks. Gruenther thought this was shocking, and he feared the State Department was getting into a frame of mind where they were afraid to report the truth just the way Russian diplomats feared to tell the truth to the Kremlin. If truthful patriotism and loyalty of service were to be endangered by McCarthyism, we would go down the drain just the way the Romans did when patriotism was no longer the paramount quality.

A few days ago several dozen young American men and women studying in France under a special arrangement run by Sweetbriar Women's College came out to SHAPE, and Gruenther made a speech to them stressing that the most important thing for young Americans today was to try and find careers in which they would serve their country; he didn't care whether it was in the Army, the State Department or any other service. He got nowhere. He received letters afterwards in which the young students indicated they had no desire to go into the foreign service and be crucified by Mc-Carthy.

Gruenther hopes something can be done to buck up sagging morale in the State Department—an organization that has always been lambasted by Congress but never as is now the case. To his way of thinking, Senator Taft should put forth a resolution expressing faith and confidence in the whole United States foreign service on a broad basis and get it through Congress. He did not think this was up to the President but would be more suitably done by Taft. He is frightfully worried about McCarthy who, he says, is a very clever man and although he has no organization behind him, no one can "get him." He has a popular subject—namely, the hunt for Communists—and he handles himself exceptionally shrewdly.

PARIS, *May 26, 1953*

WE had a lot of brass to dinner last night: the Ismays, the Gruenthers, the Norstads and the Andersons. Ten minutes before anybody was due to arrive somebody called up from SHAPE and asked if Gruenther was there yet because there was a call from Washington. I told them to call back in twenty minutes. Al was just settling down to an old-fashioned when the call came, and I put him upstairs in our bedroom so he could take it uninterruptedly. He was gone about forty-five minutes.

When he came down, he told me what had happened. Washington had appointed Admiral Fechteler, until now chief of naval operations, to replace Admiral Carney as NATO commander in Southern Europe. I expressed astonishment and said I thought it was a pretty cheesy appointment. Gruenther just smiled and didn't react. After dinner he took Ismay aside and had a talk with him for quite some time. Ismay told me later on that Gruenther was furious. The appointment was made under Ridgway while Ridgway was still NATO commander. Ridgway, incidentally, is still in Washington. Apparently Gruenther is not only sore at the way the appointment was made but does not like the appointment. It seems to me a hell of a way to run a railroad. For better or worse, Fechteler's name is known all through the Mediterranean area in connection with the forged "Fechteler report" that was published last year, which advocated backing the Arabs against the French and abandoning Europe. Of course, this was a completely fake document, but unfortunately Fechteler's name is associated with it in the minds of many ill-informed people.

Ismay thought it would be a good thing if Eden (who, he says, will not be well enough to return to work until October) were to give up the foreign ministry and become Lord President of the Council for a while. Eden is still heir apparent to Churchill but has never had any experience in the cabinet outside of the Foreign Office except for a very brief tenure in the War Office. Ismay thinks Harold Macmillan would be the logical foreign secretary if Eden gets out of the post. Churchill is really quite happy (since Eden is ill) to take over the foreign ministry. He loves playing with it. That is the only cabinet post Churchill has never held so he feels as if he had a new toy.

There was a long round robin on McCarthy and his dire effects. Anderson said he was afraid there just weren't enough senators with guts in the Republican Party to stand up and fight McCarthy. He doubted there were ten senators in the party who would really stand up for the count. Norstad, rather angrily, said that he was a Republican and had been all his life, but, by God, if there weren't ten Senators ready to get up and fight McCarthy, he thought the Democrats should come back as soon as possible. Gruenther ventured the opinion that Taft had sold Eisenhower on the idea that the Republicans could not win the 1954 congressional elections if they split over McCarthy.

PARIS, *May 27, 1953*

THIS morning I had a long and excellent talk with René Mayer, who is still acting as prime minister until a new government is formed. He expects Paul Reynaud will probably get the approval of the Assembly this afternoon.

Mayer says there is only one basic question in France today. This is the necessity of a constitutional reform that would permit the executive to dissolve the Assembly when it does not approve of the government—in other words, the English system. Until this is done, the Assembly can continue to dictate French policy and maintain an interminable procession of governments rising and falling.

De Gaulle made a grave political error, although he is a great man, when he failed to leave the constitution of the Third Republic alone. There was no need to establish the Fourth Republic in 1946. As Poincaré had pointed out before the war, the only requirement for modification of the constitution of the Third Republic was to eliminate the authority the Senate then held to approve of any dissolution of parliament and call for elections. The lower house, then the chamber of Deputies, did not have any such veto power.

LONDON, *June 3, 1953*

HAD a talk with Winthrop Aldrich, now our ambassador here. He suspects Churchill will try to get the Commonwealth prime ministers to give him a mandate to request a four-power conference (with Russia) at the Bermuda meeting in order to strengthen his hand. Churchill is very anxious to have a meeting with Malenkov and is doing all he can to force this through. He wants to be known as a "man of peace" before he dies.

Aldrich thinks both Caffery and Byroade have been pursuing a disastrous policy in Egypt. He obviously reflects the British view. Aldrich says he spends most of his time disagreeing with the State Department on the Middle East.

Aldrich says he hasn't the vaguest idea what American policy is because every time Eisenhower sets it out in a speech, Dulles makes another speech modifying it.

Aldrich has been trying to sell Churchill and Eden on a *quid pro quo* deal that the United States will back Britain in the Middle East if Britain backs the United States in the Far East. Churchill likes the idea and has come out strongly for us.

Eden is very, very ill. They found about thirty-three gallstones in him and several of them were lodged in a duct which has not healed since it was cut open. Aldrich thinks he will probably never be foreign minister again although he may be able to stay in politics. He thinks either Macmillan or Lord Salisbury will succeed him. He hopes it will be Salisbury, but unfortunately the latter also suffers bad health.

Aldrich complains he was beleaguered with requests for invitations to palace and other snob functions here from various Americans. There were very few American invitations allotted by the British, who wanted to make of this coronation primarily a Commonwealth affair. Aldrich had to intervene with Churchill personally to get a larger batch of invitations for Americans. He did his best to have friends of balky senators and recalcitrant newspaper publishers invited in order to avoid having their anti-British sentiments still further fanned by being ignored.

The British, in response to South African urging, agreed with the Union to request us to raise the price of gold. However this was purely routine as we had already told the British in advance that the answer would be no. The British did it just to stay in with Malan's boys.

Eisenhower has told the British there will be *no* agenda for Bermuda. If the conference is not held before July 1, Churchill is going to get very restive. He is anxious to seize this chance of meeting with Malenkov and he is "an old man in a hurry."

LONDON, *June 3, 1953*

QUEEN Elizabeth was crowned yesterday in an extraordinary ceremony. I must say that despite the discomfort of sitting in the Abbey from 6 A.M. until after 3 P.M., hungry and thirsty and cold, in a tailcoat, I was extremely moved.

At almost precisely half past twelve the Archbishop of Canterbury, wearing a cope of cloth of gold faced in cobalt, placed the heavy crown of Edward the Confessor upon Elizabeth's head. For a brief moment a hush fell across Westminster. Then a fanfare of trumpets sounded. The peers and peeresses of the realm donned their coronets and a sharp chorus broke forth, "God save Queen Elizabeth." And through the tall gothic windows, over the heads of those determined servants of the crown—the Queen's field and air marshals, generals, admirals, and, most redoubtable of all, the Queen's prime minister, Sir Winston Churchill—came the dull boom of guns from the venerable tower fortress down the Thames.

Hardly a soul entering the Abbey doors today looks as if he or she had stepped in from the humdrum twentieth century world. Yet there was effective living reality to the solemn contract negotiated between Elizabeth, the lovely young Queen, and her people by this deeply religious ceremony. And eleven Commonwealth prime ministers in addition to twenty-three princes and princesses from foreign lands and eight colonial rulers gave both color and political meaning to the rites.

At precisely six o'clock this cold spring morning the Duke of Norfolk, leading Roman Catholic layman in this Protestant nation but Earl Marshal by hereditary right, ordered the Abbey doors thrown open.

From that moment a protracted drama of rich imagery and spiritual significance commenced. No better stage has ever been prepared than the great perpendicular Abbey with its buttressed vaults, marble floors and pillars of mellowed shades of brown, and pastel-tinted rose windows in the transepts.

Lords and ladies in red velvet, banded with ermine and miniver, swept in carrying coronets and followed in many cases by satin-clad pages. Tiered rows in specially constructed transept galleries filled gradually with changing bands of colored dress. In one large bloc sat Britain's leading judges in crimson robes and wigs of long, white wool. On the cornices above them were blue and gold drapes adorned with the Tudor rose. Below, upon a golden-hued carpet, placed upon a dais in the center where the transepts meet the sacristy, stood the royal throne upon which the Queen eventually received her homage. Eastward, toward the altar, rested the gnarled, brown oaken chair of King Edward I, built over the Stone of Scone, upon which she was crowned.

Shortly before eleven o'clock, while members of Europe's ever-dwindling royal families were still proceeding down the nave, Elizabeth's coach drew up before the Abbey's annex gate and the sovereign was greeted by her earl marshal. Slowly she walked below the carved effigies of her royal beasts with ferociously aristocratic miens: the lion of England, the unicorn of Scotland, the greyhound of the Tudors, the dragon of the Tudors, the falcon of the Plantagenets, the griffin of King Edward III, the white horse of Hanover, the bull of Lionel Duke of Clarence, the white lion of Mortimer, and the yale of the Beauforts, silver with gold spots, hooves, horns, tusks and tufts of hair.

In scarlet cassocks the beadle and chaplains of the Abbey entered followed by representatives of the free Protestant churches of the United

Kingdom, leaders of knightly orders in flowing robes of blue, scarlet, white and darkest green, standard bearers, and the officers of the heralds' college and the Scottish court of chivalry, wearing square gold and crimson tabards and bearing these proud names of bygone chivalry: Bluemantle, Clarenceux king of arms, Portcullis, Norry and Ulster king of arms, Rouge Dragon, Rouge Croix and the heralds of Somerset, Windsor, Richmond, York, Lancaster and Chester; the Lord Lyon king of arms (an elderly Scot who fainted at the dress rehearsal Friday), Carrick Pursuivant, Lion Macer; Marchmont, Albany and Rothesay heralds, and Kintyre and Unicorn Pursuivants.

The prime ministers of Ceylon, Pakistan, India, South Africa, New Zealand, Australia and Canada, followed by Sir Winston, resplendent in the garb of garter knight, took seats along the aisle behind a beaming Lady Churchill, visibly pleased with her husband, her son, Randolph (a gold staff usher), and her grandson, little Winston, serving as a page.

Elizabeth, who symbolizes both Britain's unity and future hopes, was pale but beautiful. She walked with pondered grace as six noble maids of honor and a duchess struggled to balance her long velvet train. Her royal robe of crimson, trimmed with ermine and bordered with gold lace, covered a white satin dress embroidered in diamonds, crystals, amethysts, rose-colored stones, colored silks and gold thread in the emblems of the Tudor rose, the shamrock and thistle of the British Isles, the maple leaf of Canada, the wattle and fern of Australia and New Zealand, the protea flower of South Africa, the lotus blossoms of India and Ceylon, and the wheat, cotton and jute of Pakistan.

Then began those extraordinary rites that establish the sovereignty of an English king or queen. The Archbishop of Canterbury, together with the Lord Chancellor in black and gold gown and with a white wig, the earl marshal in his ducal robes and the garter king at arms walked to the east side of the theatre formed at the transepts' intersection. As the Queen stood up behind him, straight, simple and alone, the primate asked the people in a resonant, clear voice:

"Sirs, I here present unto you Queen Elizabeth, your undoubted Queen: wherefore all you who are come this day to do your homage and service, are you willing to do the same?"

Four times he asked this to the four points of the compass. Four times the Queen curtsied humbly to the nation's representatives. And four times, preceded by the loud flourish of trumpets, came the shouted answer: "God save Queen Elizabeth."

Having concluded the series of interrogatories which comprise her oath, the Queen laid her right hand on a great Bible and swore upon it, "The things which I have here before promised I will perform and keep. So help me God."

Then, as sovereign and subjects knelt, the Archbishop of Canterbury commenced the communion service which is so fundamental to this rite. "O God, who providest for thy people by thy power, and rulest over them in love," he prayed, "grant unto thy servant Elizabeth, our Queen, the spirit of wisdom and government, that being devoted unto thee with her whole heart, she may so wisely govern, that in her time thy church may be in safety, and Christian devotion may continue in peace."

While the music Handel wrote for George III's coronation resounded through the Abbey where the composer himself lies buried, the primate anointed his sovereign on the hands, breast and head, saying: "And as Solomon was anointed king by Zadok the priest and Nathan the prophet, so be thou anointed, blessed and consecrated Queen over the peoples." This is the most mystical aspect of the rite. The holy oil separates monarch from subject. In medieval times the argument held that it made of the sovereign a "mixed person," both layman and priest.

The Archbishop of Canterbury turned to the altar, lifted St. Edward's crown and blessed it. The Dean of Westminster, a gothic-faced man in crimson cassock, brought it to him. For a moment he held it above Elizabeth, then placed it upon her brow. Until that moment no noble in the great assemblage wore a coronet upon his head. But, as the tower guns thundered in the distance and the trumpets blared; as the entire Abbey resounded with echoing shouts of "God save the Queen!" the great lords and ladies of Britain, their arms swaying in one ballet of fluid ruby red and ermine motion, placed upon their own heads their own aristocratic circlets.

Then, as the Abbey stilled, the archbishop told his now acknowledged ruler, spiritual and temporal: "God crown you with a crown of glory and righteousness, that having a right faith and manifold fruit of good works, you may obtain the crown of an everlasting kingdom by the gift of him whose kingdom endureth forever." He blessed her. He wished her: "Faithful parliaments and quiet realms; sure defense against all enemies; fruitful lands and a prosperous industry; wise counselors and upright magistrates; leaders of integrity in learning and labor; a devout, learned and useful clergy; honest, peaceable and dutiful citizens."

OXFORD, *June 5, 1953*

WE came down here yesterday afternoon and spent the night with the Deakins. Bill is now warden of St. Antony's. At drinks yesterday a bunch of Jugoslavs arrived, including Djilas, Koča Popović (now foreign minister), Velebit (now ambassador in London) and others. They all professed to be highly unimpressed with the coronation, which they regarded as a medieval ceremony and a waste of time.

They roasted an ox at St. Antony's College in accordance with an old English tradition. It was hard cutting through red tape in order to get the ox. The Danes took occasion of Elizabeth's coronation to send a roasting ox to their British friends for cooking and devouring in the manner customary at the time of King Canute. The gift was made by Professor H. M. Hansen, rector magnificus of the University of Copenhagen. But Britain's Ministry of Food, more versed in twentieth-century red tape than medieval custom, was not happy. Indeed, until the animal was eaten this evening to the accompaniment of substantial liquid refreshment on the farm of a fellow of St. Antony's, the ministry never seemed entirely convinced that Deakin wasn't going to lug the carcass out and sell it on the black market.

May 7 Count Eduard Reventlow, Denmark's ambassador in London, wrote Deakin on behalf of the rector magnificus and advised him: "The ox will be delivered to you entirely free of cost at the proper time, as all the formalities with the various ministries have been cleared. If you accept the offer of the Copenhagen University, you will be approached by an official of the Ministry of Food."

The next day Hans Bang of the Danish Bacon Factories Export Association advised the ox was being sent and a permit to roast it requested. He added: "Roasting an ox is quite a complicated matter, and I am trying to get some expert advice supplied to you from the Butcher's Company in London."

The bursar of St. Antony's placed an order for some hundreds of "bread rolls" with the reputable Oxford bakery, Messrs. Cooper and Boffin. He told the ministry that the ox "is presumably in the custody of Her Majesty's customs and at the disposal of the Danish Bacon Factories Export Association." On May 16, Mr. Bang, with evident embarrassment, wrote to Deakin:

Re: Coronation Ox: The Ministry of Food informed me that I required an import license from the Board of Trade for the importation of your ox. The Board of Trade has now informed me that an import license can only be granted provided they receive from you a letter stating that this ox is for roasting for the coronation and that no charge will be made for the meal.

Unaware of legal restrictions on ox-importing. A. A. Van Zwanenberg of the Medieval Company of Butchers wrote Deakin giving him certain technical details on how to split, dress and roast an ox. The nub was:

Build a wood fire (not resinous) on an area sufficiently large to cover the spread carcass. A minimum of one ton of wood will be required for the cooking which, all told, will take approximately fifteen hours. After two to three hours, spread the fire in a horseshoe shape, lay the carcass flank downwards and pulled open (chine bone should be split from the inside to make this easy) on a harrow. . . . We understand that this is a most extravagant way of eating meat but it is reputed to have a flavor second to none.

In the same mail as Van Zwanenberg's recipe arrived a note from the ministry telling Deakin, "I should be glad to hear further from you as soon as possible as to whether the ox is already slaughtered." Bill replied that it had indeed for some days been very dead in an exceptionally large refrigerator. The ministry then wrote to say that a special import license would be required.

The Board of Trade advised Deakin, "An import license has been issued exceptionally on this occasion on the understanding that the ox is roasted and used as indicated in your letter." The president of St. Antony's student association then received this message from Bang: "The ox left London in a frozen state yesterday and was scheduled to arrive this afternoon."

The bursar arranged with the St. John's Ambulance Brigade "to send two ambulance men to the ox roasting ceremony" in case anything occurred to the diners—who have been on a strict meat ration for a decade. He arranged with the commander of the local Royal Air Force squadron to borrow "latrine seats, surrounds, hessian, et cetera, for the ox roasting"— an outdoors affair. The Ministry of Food telephoned. A female voice complained that to date the ministry had not yet seen an import license. "Anyway," she added, "I hope you enjoy the beast."

This evening the beast was eaten.


PARIS, *June 12, 1953*

DINNER last night with the Halbans (Hans von Halban, nuclear scientist). I was horrified that when Sam Reber was forced to resign from the foreign service by the McCarthy gang, Conant (American high commissioner in Bonn) refused to make any statement. I asked our correspondent to call up Conant and have him say something to the effect that he regretted to have his great friend and able assistant, Mr. Reber, retire. Conant refused. Halban said Conant was a son of a bitch. During the war when he, Halban, had been working on the British atomic scientists team, Conant, the great liberal, had gotten up and made a speech saying: "In this business it is necessary to double-cross your own brother." Later Halban saw Conant on behalf of the British government to arrange to have American heavy water sent to Canada to help the British experiments. Conant was most affable and promised to do everything possible to cooperate and send an adequate supply immediately. Halban found later that Conant had gone to see Vannevar Bush afterward and arranged that no single drop of heavy water would be sent.

Afterwards we went to a ball at the British embassy where I saw David Bruce. He has just returned from Washington. He said the climate there is incredibly worse than anyone imagines here; it is frightening. He said the President is isolated from what is going on. One can talk to him but he doesn't think the full impact of the situation reaches him. Incidentally,

Bruce said he had inquired about his proposed joint Bruce-plus-Sulzberger visit to Moscow this summer, and he added, "I'm afraid there's not much chance of getting any visas until the climate changes."

Yesterday the American embassy called me up and told me they were having difficulty getting my passport validated for Hungary. I have just received a Hungarian visa to go to a Communist peace council. The embassy is being rather naive and has demanded of the Hungarian government assurances that I will not be molested. Obviously if the Hungarians want to do something, they are going to do it regardless of any guarantees, and I think the United States looks rather simple-minded asking for such things. At any rate the embassy was instructed to read me part of the telegram warning me that I would be violating United States law if I go without validation.

BUDAPEST, *June 18, 1953*

SEEDY group of reporters from Communist countries crowd in dilapidated bus to visit Apprentice Home Number Twenty-one. This apprentice school includes a dormitory for 560 students. They are totally cared for and receive an allowance or small amount of pay. It is the first "Soviet" institute of its sort in Hungary. The term is two years and the workers are prepared for the Lang Mechanical Plant. Students first must finish eight years of primary school before they are accepted for entry. This is all explained by a blue-smocked director of the institute with an amiable face and cracked leather shoes. In 90 per cent of the rooms the principal decorations comprise pictures of Lenin, Stalin and Rakosi with Rakosi in the center. Second language learned by these and other students is Russian. Few of them now speak German.

We then visit the Rakosi House of Culture, a sort of community center. Our guide is an earnest-looking girl with dark blond hair who is the "artistic" leader of the house. This, too, is plentifully decorated with pictures of Lenin, Stalin and Rakosi, as well as plenty of red stars and red draperies with slogans about production and politics. The building was built only in 1949 but already large strips of ceiling in the movie hall are peeling off. The principal slogan in the movie hall is "Hungarian workers desire peace and will defend it with all their strength."

The next place is an apartment building called a "Peace House." In order to qualify to get an apartment here, everybody has to have done something for "peace." We visit an apartment for a family of four—a Stakhanovite worker (the second-best lathe turner in the country), his wife, his divorced daughter of twenty-seven and another child of eight. The apartment comprises one bedroom about twelve by fifteen feet, a small kitchenette with a gas stove, a small bathroom with a gas water heater, and another small bedroom in which the daughter lives. The head of the family makes 2,000 forints a month. He pays rent of 125 forints a month. Over his large double bed is a picture of his father (in Austro-Hungarian uniform) and his grandmother (taken at their wedding). He has a pretty good radio and a bedside clock. There are flowers and an ashtray on the table. In his daughter's little bedroom are various books (all in Hungarian) by Pearl Buck, Selma Lagerlof, Robert Louis Stevenson, Boccaccio, John Steinbeck, Frances Brett Young, H. Rider Haggard, A. H. Cronin and Flaubert's Madame Bovary.

On June 15, I had lunch with Ivan Boldizsar, editor in chief of *Magyar Nemzet* (The Hungarian Nation) and former chief of information for Foreign Minister Ivan Rajk. Boldizsar contends the Voice of America program is very bad and has no effect on the Hungarian people. It uses the wrong people to prepare and broadcast its program. It is too warmongering and makes wild statements like promising that gallows will be set up for the four main leaders of Hungary.

That night I had dinner with Boldizsar at a restaurant called Rozsadom Ettevan where a gypsy orchestra plays but loudspeakers spoil the effect. Boldizsar makes the rather odd suggestion that it would be a good thing for the world if a people's republic were to be established in Western Europe, either Italy or France, preferably France, in order to set up another magnetic pole of attraction for a country like Hungary. Right now the Hungarians, who are ideologically in harmony with Russia, must depend entirely upon Russia for their cultural relationships. Yet the tradition of Hungary inclines toward the West. Therefore it would be sensible to have a French people's republic so that the Hungarians would continue to lean towards the West and would have an alternative to Moscow.

I tell Boldizsar my feeling is that Petöfi was correct, when he wrote his poem about independent wolves and dependent dogs, to prefer the life of the wolf. Boldizsar says perhaps this is true in a romantic sense but the people of Hungary need protection. The feudal system was abolished here only fourteen years ago and the country was completely ravaged by war. They want security above all. He admits there have been mistakes in the regime but he argues you cannot make an omelet without breaking the eggs—a familiar platitude! Furthermore, he says that before the war patriotism was primarily a class affair and did not interest the workers and peasants; but now all the people feel the interests of the country. He argues the people are ready to risk encounters with the secret police in exchange for the land-sharing program.

Boldizsar contended the Rosenbergs had been unfairly convicted—at least Mrs. Rosenberg. I told him I personally opposed capital punishment in any country but, after all, if they considered Rajk should have been executed for betraying state secrets, that showed the United States was more than justified in executing the Rosenbergs for betraying more than state secrets. Boldizsar claimed Eisenhower was popular on the basis of his April 16 speech but that Dulles was detested. I recall that a short time ago they were calling Eisenhower "cannibal," not a customary term of endearment.

Boldizsar professed to think it was reasonable for the United States to want to negotiate from strength and not want to weaken itself at this moment, but he wondered if the United States was not actually preparing for war. He did not think Eisenhower's Cabinet could represent the true point of view of the American people because it was comprised mainly of millionaires. I answered that this was precisely the point of the American dream where everybody hopes he or she might be a millionaire and that most of the millionaires in the cabinet were self-made men.

BUDAPEST, *June 19, 1953*

ATTENDED a couple of dreary sessions of the World Peace Council. In speech after speech, regardless of the orator's language, there were continual references to "Li Sin Man" and that always brought the house down with roars of rage. Finally discovered this was Syngman Rhee (South Korean president). Ilya Ehrenburg was the hottest Soviet contribution. I have known him for years, been on friendly terms (although I dislike him) and he has entertained me at his Moscow apartment. But when I went over to chat with him he gave me a disdainful, fishy stare. Obviously it is not the chic thing to speak to Americans now, and he goes with the wind.

Took a trip to Sztalinvaros with a group of Hungarian writers. They proceeded to get amiably drunk and became increasingly friendly, after a slow start. One of them, Karinthy, is the son of a great writer but not so hot himself. They had all asked me about Albert Maltz (an American I never heard of—later discovered he's a Hollywood script writer who they think is the greatest American author along with Mark Twain, Jack London and Upton Sinclair). When I finally convinced them I had never heard of him and he was a nonentity they promptly dubbed Karinthy "The Hungarian Albert Maltz."

PARIS, *July 7, 1953*

LAST night I dined with Al Gruenther and Paul Hoffman. Gruenther takes over the SHAPE command Saturday.

Hoffman was very much disturbed by the impression received on this hurried European trip, of the extent of damage done to the United States' reputation by McCarthyism. He also thought Dulles had made a great mistake in compromising with his principles and accepting McLeod (Bridges' spy) as head of State Department security. Hoffman said he had sincere admiration for Dulles, who was a high-minded man, but nobody should ever compromise that way. Dulles was seeking to prove he was a "regular" Republican, but he would be destroyed by his concessions. Hoffman said he too had found out that the morale of the American foreign service is at an all-time low. Nevertheless, he is optimistic about the administration. He said Eisenhower was making a very real effort to get everybody to work together. This had to be done. It was in the character of the man. Only if that failed, would he make any other type of move.

Hoffman swore he had never wanted any public office in this administration and that he had told this to Eisenhower right after the convention in Chicago. He had heard that Taft laid down as a condition for his own cooperation with Eisenhower that Hoffman should receive no government post. However, he did not think this was true and certainly Eisenhower would never make a deal on that basis. Hoffman was proud of the part he had played in defeating Taft's efforts to obtain the Republican nomination and added: "If I don't get any thanks for it on this earth, I will get my reward in heaven."

Hoffman said Harold Stassen was really doing a first-class job now. He too had been furious at Stassen for the way he double-crossed Eisenhower during the preconvention campaign last year. He said that, unfortunately, like so many men, Stassen was poisoned by his own ambition. However, he no longer has any immediate ambitions and is doing a fine job. He is one of the very best young leaders of the Republican Party.

Hoffman said he had been out in India and Pakistan last April. He was not on any official mission but, unofficially, he sought to harmonize relationships between New Delhi and Karachi. He saw Nehru on the very evening Eisenhower made his April 16 speech, and took the occasion to read him large sections from an advance copy. Nehru was very impressed.

Hoffman said it is absolutely imperative for the United States to support Nehru. The basic contest is between Nehru and Mao Tse-tung for the leadership of Asia. Nehru is essentially a believer in democratic procedure and we must back him. Hoffman believes we will probably have to lend India about $200 million a year for the next three years to see Nehru over the hump.

PARIS, *July 10, 1953*

EARLY this morning it was announced that Beria had been arrested. I spent last night and most of today with Chip Bohlen (ambassador to Russia) talking with him about it. They had an advance clue in Moscow. On the afternoon of June 27 quite a few tanks and trucks loaded with soldiers suddenly appeared in the streets. A few hours later they disappeared. That night Malenkov and the top political bosses appeared at the Bolshoi theater. Beria was not there. A list of dignitaries, minus Beria's name, was printed in all government papers. On June 28 rumors commenced that Beria was in trouble.

Bohlen thinks this is directly related to the East German troubles. Either Beria was held responsible for the lack of security or for the repression which touched off the explosion. At any rate, he was arrested ten days after the East Berlin riots. Since then, there have been various softening measures—the reverse of a tough policy in Germany, Czechoslovakia, Hungary and Rumania. Thus, it is unlikely that this means a new "get tough" era.

Furthermore, Bohlen does not believe this is the beginning of a great new purge. He pointed out that the *Pravda* editorial today attacks Beria in a highly individual sense, but not as the leader of a great conspiracy. It is his guess that Malenkov remains top dog, but as "chairman of the board" and not as dictator. He believes that committee rule will continue in the Communist Party rather than individual dictatorship. He points out that the Stalin legend has been deliberately vitiated by the present government.

Bohlen is not inclined to believe the present situation is more likely to produce danger of war. He discounts the possibility that some new aspiring dictator may seek to rally public opinion by starting a war. Wars are nowadays too dangerous and the Soviet army could not risk a hostile and uncontrolled population along its lines of communication.

PARIS, *July 11, 1953*

LAST night I dined was the Bohlens again. Poor Chip has had to call off his plan to drive down with me to Majorca on Tuesday (where our two families are sharing a house). He was summoned back to Washington urgently and had to leave from Orly at 11:30 P.M. He thinks Washington's reaction to the Beria purge is wrong. Washington is saying that Beria represented a "soft" policy and that this now means a tougher dictatorship and cold war. Chip points out that since Beria's arrest on June 27, there has been a continued series of events indicating that the "soft" policy has been accelerated rather than dropped.

PARIS, *July 17, 1953*

THIS morning I had a good chat with Adlai Stevenson. He is very worried about the internationally bad effect on the United States reputation of McCarthyism. He should know whereof he speaks since he just completed a worldwide tour.

He was surprised at the extent of French disillusionment on Indochina and their desire to get out of that situation. He is trying to point out to the French that now particularly they must keep containing Soviet dynamism in that quarter. We have neutralized Russian pressure in Europe. We must prevent the Sino-Soviet bloc from outflanking India.

The Germans told Adlai that now was the time for the West to tell Russia to fish or cut bait in East Germany. But Stevenson fears we will be embarrassed if the Russians offer German unity in exchange for guarantees of its neutralization.

PARIS, *August 5, 1953*

I had a long talk this afternoon with Lieutenant General Cortlandt Van R. Schuyler who has come back to SHAPE, this time as Al Gruenther's chief of staff. Schuyler, who is a nice, intelligent man, was frank and voluble. Among other things he said that the French are taking 15,000 regular soldiers from their divisions in Germany and sending them to Indochina to provide additional troops for General Navarre. These regulars have most of the key jobs in the three divisions in Germany. Their departure will temporarily lower the training level and battle efficiency of French forces in Europe.

Schuyler said the tendency of our intelligence agencies now is to credit the satellite armies in Eastern Europe with real offensive strength. They are much better than they were two years ago, although not yet up to parity with the Russians.

I asked Schuyler where American troops could be stationed in Europe if it was ever agreed to evacuate occupation forces from Germany. He said he simply could not see any alternative area at present and the problem keeps him awake at nights. Possibly the American and British troops will have to withdraw to enclaves, the British around Hamburg and the Americans in the southwest border area.

# 2 8

---

# GERMANY RECOVERS

BONN, *August 15, 1953*

THIS MORNING I HAD A TALK WITH JAMES B. CONANT, FORMER
president of Harvard and now American high commissioner in
Germany. Conant said he thought the elections next month would
not change the political picture here much. He foresaw that the next
*Bundestag* would be about the same as the present one.

The United States is officially neutral in the election. If there are any
"covert" operations, they must of necessity be denied. Conant has been
advised by John Slocum, his information man, to pay no heed to any
rumors or charges by parties during the campaign.

Conant admitted there were two outstandingly grave theoretical questions before him. What would happen if the Karlsruhe court declared EDC
unconstitutional in October? Conant believes the court will probably follow
the election returns.

What would happen if Adenauer, now almost eighty, dies? Conant thinks
he might be succeeded by one of the *Laender* minister presidents rather
than by Hermann Ehlers, Fritz Schaeffer or some other cabinet or *Bundestag* leader. In the *Laender* Conant is impressed by Hans Erhard and Karl
Arnold of the Christian Democratic Union (in Bavaria and North Rhine–
Westphalia respectively) and by Ernst Reuter, Max Brauer and Wilhelm
Kaisen of the Social Democratic Party in Berlin, Hamburg and Bremen
respectively.

Concerning the German attitude on national unity, he said:

This is like civil liberties in the United States. Everyone is in favor of it.
That is true of civil liberties also—until a special case involving some

Negro in a southern state arises. Here also everyone is in favor of unity. But what price must we pay for it? Where are the boundaries of East Germany to be fixed? It is obvious the United States will never maintain troops here to protect a neutral Germany. Unity is a very emotional issue. No German politician dares to oppose it.

Turning to the present situation in Berlin and Allied disagreements concerning the food program, Conant said that Berlin presents a great long-range program replete with dangers to both ideological blocs. There does not seem to be any long-range policy for Berlin in the event that unification is delayed.

I asked Conant what chances he gave for the success of the European Defense Community. He thought it was a fair even-money bet that the project would succeed by January 1. However, to obtain this there must be stable governments in France and Italy. Conant sees no alternative to EDC, because France could veto any changes in the occupation statutes if we sought to make a deal giving Germany some sort of national army.

Conant said that so far there was no important open political movement of neo-Naziism, but he thought it was necessary to watch Werner Naumann and his party carefully. Conant admitted it is impossible to know the extent of any secret underground Nazi movement. He thought that if EDC fails or unemployment grows seriously, things might change for the worse.

I asked Conant whether there had been a serious effect upon the morale of the High Commission staff as a result of McCarthyism, and whether Germans were claiming we had no right to claim the privilege of "teaching" democracy? He replied: "The hurricane is now by. Morale is gradually improving. Reports from home have shown that McCarthy's position with the American public is less important than we here had originally thought." (I'm not entirely convinced about this.)

BONN, *August 17, 1953*

THIS evening I talked for more than an hour and a half with Adenauer in the Schaumburg Palais. I must say he is a remarkable old man. Despite his seventy-seven years he looked young and vigorous, and despite the political campaign he looked calm and rested. He was wearing a gray suit, blue tie, black shoes. We sat in armchairs around a table. He had along with him a young interpreter who was with him in the United States, as well as Georg von Lilienfeld, head of the American section in the foreign office, and von Eckardt, his press adviser. I noticed behind his desk in the background four signed photographs from Churchill, De Gasperi, Eisenhower and somebody whose features I could not make out, but I suspect it is probably Robert Schuman.

The Chancellor started out by referring to a message put out today by Eisenhower on the significance and meaning of Europe for the United

States. Actually this comprised a report on the first six months of this year's foreign aid program. Adenauer said the President had emphasized the strength of the United States, but pointed out that America cannot do everything alone. Adenauer said this message stressed the industrial potential of Western Europe, insisting that this should and must be added to that of the United States.

Adenauer continued: "I might summarize it this way. The President pointed out that the policy of the United States towards Europe is governed by the self-interest of the United States. I am under the impression that he wanted to stress this point because of the present internal mood of the United States."

Adenauer said: "I welcome this statement greatly. It will bring home to the responsible leaders of the United States the fact that the policy of the President is not only founded upon emotional reasons but on a cool, clear-sighted policy."

I asked Adenauer to comment on the Soviet proposal that from January 1, 1954, Germany should be freed from reparations payments and that all postwar debts except trade treaty obligations should be canceled. He replied that this idea was "a foul trick. For a long time we have been paying no reparations. The eastern zone has been bled white and is in no position to pay any more." As to the canceling of debts, Adenauer said—and this did not impress me as a terribly good answer, politically speaking—"If we have received something, we should pay for it. This was provided for under the Bonn convention and the London External Debt Convention."

I asked Adenauer what he thought of the Soviet suggestion that occupation troops should cost the Germans no more that 5 per cent of the country's total revenues. Adenauer replied that he was not interested in that idea, but wanted the establishment of the European army as soon as possible and that the EDC treaty provided for the German contribution. At present occupation costs in West Germany total 7,200,000,000 marks a year out of a total revenue in the West of 24,000,000,000 marks.

Adenauer thought that politically the most important part of the Soviet note was the threat that there could be no unification of Germany if the Federal Republic is a member of an active EDC. He thought the West German parties opposing EDC would use this Soviet threat in the election campaign. He referred specifically to the SPD and Heinemann's Neutralist Party.

I interrupted to ask the Chancellor what he thought the final eastern boundaries of Germany should be. He replied:

I think the question of the eastern border cannot be settled until there is a general decrease of tension. First there must be a free Poland. We must find a solution for Germans to return to their homeland beyond the Oder–Neisse without causing a war. We must seek a solution for general understanding by further development of the *European* idea. But this must await events. There must by no means be any hostility between a free Poland and a united Germany. Free Poland will be the eastern outpost of the Western world. Therefore there must be solution by negotiation agreeable to both sides.

I then asked if, when he referred to the return of German refugees to their "homeland" in the east, he meant that the territory they returned to would be under a German flag or under a Polish flag. He realized he was getting into rather deep waters. He did not want to deal with "tricky subjects of this sort. The basic question is how to decrease general tension and solve one problem after another."

I asked what he thought should be the eventual frontiers between Germany and Czechoslovakia. He admitted that refugees from Czechoslovakia and the Sudetenland were in negotiation with each other, but he refused to talk any more on this subject of borders. I was very much struck by the way he distinguished between "Czechoslovakia" and "Sudetenland." I made him repeat it, and again he said "Czechoslovakia and the Sudetenland." Quite obviously he regards them as different areas.

For my money, Adenauer, in his shrewd, quiet way and under the camouflage of his so-called "European" formula, is out to get back for Germany everything between the Saar and East Prussia. Who can blame him? He is a German statesman, after all. But very few American diplomats seem to realize this.

I asked Adenauer what he thought of Eisenhower's "liberation" policy. He replied obliquely by saying that the purpose of Soviet control of Eastern Europe was to protect the USSR from the menace of the West. Therefore we must eliminate such fears from the Soviet mind.

Adenauer then went back and continued a long spiel about the European Army. He said:

The only enemy of Soviet Russia is the United States. Other countries are too weak to be considered such. The American war potential in coal, iron and steel is much higher than Russia's. The Soviets do not have sufficient resources to attain the United States level.

In Western Europe we have the considerable potential of Germany, France and Belgium. If Russia were to obtain this potential undamaged, overnight the Soviet war potential would be stronger than that of the United States. That is why Soviet Russia tries by its cold war to gain this potential in an undamaged condition. A hot war with a scorched-earth policy would do Russia no good.

If the European political community and EDC become effective, there would remain no more chance for Soviet Russia to lay hold on Western European war potential. That is why Moscow is trying to prevent EDC and the integration of Western Europe. Moscow is not doing this for fear of a few German divisions, but in order to avoid losing the cold war. If Western Europe is integrated, the political situation of the world will be basically altered. Then it will be necessary to rid Soviet Russia of its fears of an American attack and to reach a solution of all global problems.

Soviet Russia spends vast amounts on armaments. This reduces its industrial capacity for consumers' goods. The consumers' goods output in the Soviet Union is far from adequate. Likewise the arable land in the USSR is not enough to feed its population. These factors combine to weaken the Soviet Union.

Therefore, when EDC becomes a fact, the Soviet government will have to face the problem of whether it is worth continuing the cold war when Moscow no longer has a chance to win it. Surely the Russians will deem it better to meet with the Americans, and probably to receive help from the United States of the sort mentioned by the President in his April 16 speech.

I then asked him if the McCarthyist purge of American officials in Germany had in any way affected German regard for American democracy or the German opinion of American qualifications to teach democracy. He replied:

The American occupation Army here at first had a number of Communists in important positions. Then there was a purge—prior to and without McCarthy. It is certainly true that neither the regard for nor the respect for the United States and its democracy suffered from this.

Now there are some things going on which we cannot understand. I met a number of very honorable men recently in Chicago who admired McCarthy greatly. I met a number of equally honorable men in New York and Washington who condemned him strongly. Here in Germany we have a proverb that one should not wash one's dirty linen in public.

All in all, Adenauer impresses me as being a shrewd, patient and determined man, autocratic and arrogant. Some of the things he said and the assumption of my ignorance on his part were quite incredible. I wonder if he gets away with some of the twaddle he talks when he receives men like Conant. Of course he pulled plenty of wool over McCloy's eyes, but that is not a very difficult task because McCloy is not as bright as he thinks he is.

GRAFENWOEHR, *August 23, 1953*

I have seen three American generals during the last week, and it is interesting to make a comparison among them in terms of John Marquand's *Melville Goodwin*. Major General Timberman, commander of the American forces in Berlin, is a very affable guy but seems to spend much of his time socially. However, Barney Koren, who is serving as more or less the equivalent of his chairman of the combined chiefs of staff, tells me that

Timberman actually is extremely shrewd and a very good negotiator. Timberman spent a good deal of his career in China and is a Chinese language officer. He shared a room for some time during the war with one of the leading Chinese Communist generals. He thinks Chiang Kai-shek is a fool and a disaster and simply cannot understand our policy in the Far East.

The next was General Thomas Handy. Handy is a typical American Army soldier—much more the Goodwin type. I saw him in Frankfurt. He was very cautious about saying anything which was difficult for him because he likes to talk, but quite obviously doesn't like talking to the press. He said there has been a complete plan drawn up on what to do about arming German contingents as soon as the final political decision has been made to arm them either in a European army or on some other basis. He didn't think the build-up of German forces would be delayed for a moment by lack of equipment. We have promised the Germans all the heavy equipment they require. He said that the American forces in Germany comprised five divisions and three armored cavalry regiments. At one time it was wanted to have another armored division here.

Handy remarked—as had Timberman in Berlin—that the Russians must surely have learned one thing from the Berlin riots. When they called their tanks out to put down the rioting, there was no infantry with the tanks. This crippled the tanks, which were subject to being attacked by men with poles or homemade bombs or anything. For riot control the Russians must now have discovered that a good deal of infantry is required with tanks.

Finally, here at Grafenwoehr I have spent a couple of days with Major General C. T. Lanham, who is now commanding the First Infantry Division. Buck is delighted to be away from SHAPE headquarters and to have his own unit. He is extremely enthusiastic and apparently has improved the division a lot. Oddly enough, Timberman had it before Buck. I must say I am impressed at the amount of equipment that goes with a modern infantry division, including lots of heavy tanks (I was allowed to drive an M-47, which in some ways handles easier than a Buick), airplanes, helicopters.

PARIS, *September 1, 1953*

THIS morning I saw Dillon, who has just returned to Paris from his holiday. He said the *coup d'état* by which General Guillaume ousted the Sultan in Morocco had gone off very efficiently, much to everyone's surprise. Guillaume had always maintained the former Sultan was highly unpopular, and apparently this view was confirmed by events. There were no riots or demonstrations. Now we are urging the French to put through reforms as rapidly as possible (within the next week, it is hoped) so that they will make a better showing when the subject is raised in debate before the United Nations.

Dillon seemed completely confused by the complicated United States position in Morocco and did not realize that our minister there was accredited to the Sultan. As a matter of fact, I believe the arrangement is for our minister always to deal through the French with the Sultan. Dillon said it was politically impossible for the United States to alter its legal right to capitulations in Morocco thanks to the effective American businessmen's lobby in Casablanca which had sold Senator Hickenlooper and a bunch of other politicos on this screwy deal.

Dillon said the Navarre plan for Indochina is going to be paid for by the United States. The initial take will be out of foreign operations administration funds. Indochina now has top priority. The necessary amount will be earmarked for Indochina, and funds for all other countries will be proportionately cut. If this is still not sufficient, it is probable that a bill will be presented to the next Congress demanding special funds for Indochina on an all-out-aid basis and emphasizing how much France has done in the fight. The idea would be to have a sort of "Truman Doctrine" for Southeast Asia emphasizing the great need to dam the Communist tide there. In fact, Dillon seems to think that even if the initial funds requested under the Navarre program are met, the dramatized special Indochina aid bill will have to be prepared and exacted.

PARIS, *September 2, 1953*

THIS morning I had a long talk with Larry Norstad which, until he got on the subject of golf, was quite interesting. He told me that at present the general plan of operations and statement of Allied requirements need no modification because of Soviet acquisition of the hydrogen bomb secret. However, additional defensive measures will obviously be required. More antiaircraft must be installed, and improvements must be pushed in the surface-to-air missile field. Better radar coverage is needed. The Soviet H-bomb announcement must push us to do things we had already figured we ought to do.

PARIS, *September 4, 1953*

THIS afternoon I visited the Carmelite convent at Nogent-sur-Marne to see Elisabeth de Miribel, now Sister Elisabeth of Jesus. She completed her final vows only a few weeks ago. The convent is a most unattractive looking place and I must say gives me the creeps. I was conducted up to a visitors' room by a dwarf nun who must have been considerably less than three feet high but looked very efficient and nun-like in her cowl. I sat on an armchair facing a curtained window protected by three sets of bars, the last of which pointed out horizontally so that it would be impossible for anyone even to reach to the other side of the curtain with his arm.

Elisabeth came in and drew the curtains aside. I must say she looked well and happy. She says the life is very tough. At best she has only an hour a day to read, although she has finished writing a book which took her two years. It is about a German Jewish woman named Edith Stein, who became a Carmelite and was finally burned by Hitler at Auschwitz. Aside from a great deal of time spent in prayers every day, she has to work in the garden and in some kind of home industry setup; her convent has to make a bit of money in order to keep going. Elisabeth (who was once de Gaulle's secretary) said she had heard from friends that he was now leading a completely retired life. She said he had always had two different personalities—one the arch-conservative, Jansenist, minor aristocrat, family man, and the other the thinker and philosopher. His wife always sees to it that the first aspect is never forgotten. Now he is just leading the life of a retired officer and grandfather. De Gaulle's great fault, Elisabeth thinks, was that he never quite found the secret of translating his phase as a thinker into the requisite qualities of a man of action. He always remained somewhat of a mystery even to those closest to him.

PARIS, *September 11, 1953*

LAST night I dined with Hardit Singh Malik, the Indian ambassador. He had a small dinner party for Mrs. Vijaya Lakshmi Pandit (Nehru's sister), who is passing through Paris. Mrs. Pandit was very nice but by no means completely trustworthy. For example, she was announcing to one and all how well she knew Malenkov and how often she had seen him in Moscow. She could not remember why it was that she had seen him, but on several occasions he substituted for the man she was supposed to see. This is obviously untrue. Her business was with the foreign office except when she was received by Stalin, and Malenkov never substituted for anybody in the foreign office. Mrs. Pandit laid great stress on how critical the forthcoming United Nations Assembly will be. I expect she is rather interested in emphasizing that point because she will certainly be its president.

Also present was Sardar K. M. Panikkar, now Indian ambassador in Egypt and previously Indian ambassador in Communist China. He is a very vain, evil-looking character with red lips showing the habit of betel nut chewing, a little pointed beard and the general appearance of a cartoon of Lenin. He is incredibly conceited and full of his own importance. Practically everything he says is hogwash. Yet the man is undoubtedly intelligent, and it was he who first warned the United States that if our troops crossed the dividing line in Korea, Communist China would intervene. Panikkar assured me that General Naguib has no backing in Egypt. He says his regime has no stability and indicated he thought it would inevitably collapse. Panikkar said that Egyptian security is run by Voss, the former SS general who heads the group of former Nazi "experts" now in Cairo.

Pawelka, the present West German ambassador in Cairo, told Panikkar that Voss had threatened to take out an East German passport if the Bonn government withdrew Voss' papers. Panikkar said he knew Mao Tse-tung very well. I wonder if this is just another version of Mrs. Pandit's "friendship" with Malenkov. Panikkar made the interesting observation that Chiang Kai-shek "is a very great man—but of the early nineteenth century."

MADRID, *October 2, 1953*

THIS morning I had a long talk with Major General August Kissner (Air Force), who heads the American military mission here. Kissner was in Germany before. He is an energetic, pushing, rather nice chap, but with the typical Air Force mentality which has absolutely no patience with the idea that there is a moral issue involved in an agreement with Franco. He thinks the Spanish government is fine and cannot understand why anybody had any question about it. He thinks the Spanish are good mechanics, fine soldiers and airmen and that we are getting a good thing with this agreement. He said that since Spain is not in NATO the United States can lay down its own specifications for the air bases and naval bases, and therefore they will not have to conform to NATO standards. Kissner, an airman, thinks the air aspect of Spain is strategically even more important than the naval aspect. We can get B-47 medium bombers well into Russia from here.

PARIS, *October 7, 1953*

I had drinks before lunch with Dave McDonald, president of the United Steelworkers Union and an old friend from Pittsburgh days. I asked Dave why Durkin (Labor Secretary) had resigned. He told me that not even Durkin knew the real story, which was as follows: According to McDonald, the steelworkers have a secret agreement with the White House that nothing will be done in terms of applying or amending the Taft–Hartley Act without first being subjected to the approval of the steelworkers union. Furthermore key appointments have to be cleared with the steelworkers. Durkin, who is an AFL veteran and therefore anti-CIO, did not know of this agreement. He wanted to appoint certain men who were not approved by the steelworkers and were therefore rejected by the White House. Durkin was furthermore irritated when McDonald was appointed on a White House employer–labor committee. Vin Sweeney, another old friend from the *Pittsburgh Press* and public relations director for the steelworkers, chimed in and said Durkin was pretty fed up by the Coventry treatment he was receiving from the President's cabinet. He said Durkin complained that whenever he arrived at a cabinet meeting the conversation suddenly hushed. When dinner parties were being given at which cabinet members were present, the Durkins were rarely invited. This got under his skin.

I asked McDonald if there had been much disappointment among the steelworkers or labor in general at the election results last November. McDonald replied: "Why should there be any disappointment? Labor voted for Ike."

PARIS, *October 8, 1953*

THIS morning I had a chat with Bob Joyce, and he told me that Bohlen, judging by his reports from Moscow, is increasingly impressed with the abilities of Malenkov. He thinks Malenkov is an extremely able man and a far more dangerous enemy than Stalin, who was almost insane with egomania during the last few years of his life. Bohlen refers to him as "Warren G. Malenkov" who is emphasizing a "back-to-normalcy" movement in Russia. He has got everybody working normal occidental hours instead of the cockeyed system that followed Stalin's habits and saw people starting work in the late afternoon and finishing in the early hours of the morning.

Bohlen thought it would be a good thing if the American people stopped worrying about who is purging whom in Russia and abandoned the idea that the Kremlin is filled with a bunch of Keystone cops shooting each other up in the halls. The regime is obviously strongly in the saddle, and there had been no wholesale purge aside from individual officials of Beria's police machine.

LONDON, *October 13, 1953*

CHURCHILL does not plan to relinquish the post of Prime Minister despite his stroke. He told a visitor: "There are so many things to do—the *History of the English-Speaking People* (a book Churchill is planning), sunshine, painting and, of course, politics. I shall not give up my seat." He said the recent Margate speech was a strain for him, but he was not worried about debates in the House of Commons, where he felt as much at home as a child in the nursery.

Churchill said, concerning his health, that he had had a stroke a few years ago, but this had been kept very secret. His stroke last summer, however, interfered with the proposed Bermuda conference and therefore became known. One leg still bothers him, but his mind and speech are okay. Churchill said he was keeping Eden well informed and recalled that it was "a black mark" against Roosevelt that the latter had not kept Truman completely *au courant* when the President knew his physical condition was failing. Churchill said Eden's health was improving daily.

DÜSSELDORF, *October 16, 1953*

I had lunch today with a group of Ruhr characters in a most extraordinary setting, the home of Dr. Schneider, president of the Düsseldorf Chamber of Industry and Commerce. Schneider lives in a dilapidated, gray stucco apartment house in a quarter that looks half-industrial and half-tenement. The cracked walls of the apartment house are propped up with wooden beams. To get to his apartment, you climb one flight of dirty gray stairs, a door opens and you are in a hallway absolutely lined with Meissen china. His sitting room-office is next door—not very large and cluttered up with hideous overstuffed furniture, odd knickknacks like a Japanese sword, walls lined with assorted Meissen ware and two of the most magnificent Holbeins I have ever seen. The Holbeins hang between the windows and against the light so you can hardly see them. I congratulated Schneider upon them, but he didn't seem very interested. He is much more interested in his porcelain collection which is lovely and very valuable but displayed with an absolute minimum of taste.

The luncheon was arranged by Martin Liebes, who used to be a director of the Salamander works, Germany's largest shoe manufacturer. He was never a Nazi and actually was involved in the July 20 plot and was detained by the Gestapo for some time. He is now public relations adviser to the big businessmen of the Ruhr. He is a very oily and horrible type, but I guess he is pretty successful. I inquired about him afterwards and found out the kind of operation he seems to specialize in. Under decartelization two subsidiaries of I. G. Farben were separated. He wrote a letter objecting to this. Later on, for purely economic reasons, the High Commission agreed that the subsidiaries could again be merged.

Schneider owns half the shares of Hain, Lehmann & Company, one of Germany's biggest bridge builders, and is also a shareholder in many other companies. He was also involved in the July 20 plot and was never a Nazi.

Another fellow there was Dr. Günter Henle, a former diplomat who was in the foreign office during the Weimar Republic and resigned from a post in the London embassy when the Nazis came to power. He is married to the only daughter of Peter Klöckner, owner of one of Germany's largest steel empires, which has now been taken over by Henle. He was a CDU deputy in the first *Bundestag* and is a close friend of Adenauer. The other magnate present was Helmuth Wohltat, who worked for the Nazis as one of the senior officials in Hitler's economic ministry and was in charge of international trade talks, especially in the Far East. He is now a member of various big business boards of directors including that of Bayer Leverkusen, one of Germany's largest chemical concerns.

Wohltat was by all odds the most impressive of those present in terms of his keen intelligence. He talked about the way Germany was edging England out of the markets of South and Western Asia in a regretful tone of voice similar to that I once heard a German diplomat use in saying what a shame it was that Coventry had been bombed because the stupid British insisted on keeping the war going. Wohltat said quite outright that France was finished and that he thought Germany should make a direct alliance with Britain and the United States which should be completed by a pact between Tokyo and Washington. That was the only way to keep the world balance of power, and NATO was worthless. Germany could not be kept down by French hesitations over EDC.

I have checked up on Wohltat and find the following: He was born in 1893. He was an artillery officer in World War I and lived in New York from 1929 to 1933. He got an MA degree at Columbia. Starting in 1933 he had a series of jobs under the Hitler regime and was a high official in the economic ministry and also in the Prussian ministry of state.

BONN, *October 17, 1953*

I lunched today with James Bryant Conant, former president of Harvard and American high commissioner in Germany. He talks glibly and quickly, says nothing. I have a horrible feeling that the more I see him and the better I get to know him, the more depressed I am going to be. I don't think he stacks up against shrewd, tough Germans like Adenauer, and he gives me the impression of being an even worse United States representative than McCloy, whom I never admired although he built up quite a reputation both at home and in Germany.

I asked Conant what he thought the United States should do if EDC failed. His reply was that this would open a Pandora's box. With rather sad humor he said he guessed about the only thing to do would be to install a Communist government in France and then occupy the country on that excuse. He said that France's real estate in terms of Indochina and Morocco and the position of France in Europe enabled the French to blackmail the United States for help. He didn't see any solution or anything to do if EDC failed except to return to Petersberg (Allied negotiating center) and start talking again to negotiate a brand new set of contractual agreements since the present agreements, which would come into effect only if EDC is ratified, would have to be replaced. Obviously this would take a couple of years. If Conant really believes this, it is hogwash.

BONN, *October 19, 1953*

I lunched with Adenauer today in the Schaumburg Palais. Blankenhorn was present. Adenauer as usual looked incredibly fit for a man of almost eighty. He was in fine humor and ate heartily, taking two courses of everything but ignoring his excellent Bordeaux and only tasting a good Rhine

wine. He is going to make his speech at the *Bundestag* tomorrow and says
it is fifty-seven pages long and will take ninety-seven minutes: quite a
speech.

He and Blankenhorn acted out a little piece. They denied, after raising
the subject themselves, that there was any "list" of people in the United
States High Commission and American press *persona non grata* to the
government here. A rumor has been floating around for two days that such
a list had been drawn up and would be presented to McCloy (now head of
the Chase National Bank), who is coming here Wednesday. Presumably, at
least it so is implied, McCloy would be asked to get action on it. Also,
presumably, Conant is being bypassed. There was a lot of heavy-handed
humor attempting to smear the yarn as a phony, but I must say it strikes
me as probably true, remembering Adenauer's rather clumsy way of trying
to set up a propaganda ministry here after last month's elections—which
he later abandoned, denying it was even contemplated.

Adenauer, after lunch, took us in the next room for coffee and brandy
and waited until the waiters had finished serving and actually left before
anything was said of a serious nature. He explained *sotto voce* later that
the Soviet intelligence service was exceptionally good and might well have
one of the waiters in its employ. He said during the war the British had the
best service, then the Germans. The Americans had too little experience.
To my surprise he said that now the Germans, thanks to their experience in
Russia, had the best intelligence. He added there were many patriotic
Germans in East Germany who provided information for no payment at
all. I was amazed that he should in effect say that this demilitarized country
had the best intelligence in the world—which he did.

Adenauer said the September elections had been a great victory for his
pro-American policy. This would be disastrously set back if EDC is not
ratified. In that case it would be necessary to improvise a substitute (not
alternative but substitute, he emphasized) swiftly or Germany would turn
eastward towards Russia. He had secured modification of the Big Three
note sent yesterday to Moscow, separating EDC discussions from the Locarno and nonaggression idea. He didn't want EDC talked to death. The
only way to force it through would be by isolating France. If France is the
last country not to ratify, it will do so, he thinks. Italy and Benelux must
now finish the job. Adenauer is afraid Bidault isn't very sincere about EDC
and is using the Saar as a fake issue to hide behind. He doesn't think
Bidault will be elected President of France. He believes Auriol will be
reelected and doesn't like the idea much because he considers Auriol an
enemy of EDC—although not as violent as his fellow Socialist Jules Moch.

Adenauer said he would "think aloud" and speak deliberately vaguely
when I asked him what should be done if EDC fails. He said he had in his
mind a map including the USA, Germany, England, Spain and Turkey. In
other words he was for busting up NATO and for a separate scheme of

alliances—although he didn't say so. He implied France should not be permitted to frustrate a United States–Germany alliance. Although France was in NATO and an occupying power in Germany (with those two vetoes), Adenauer recalled there had once been four Allied occupiers in Germany; they split but the Big Three kept on with their policy. The Big Two, if necessary, he implied, should go ahead regardless of France. He said if France doesn't ratify EDC, there must be an immediate alliance between Germany and the USA. It would be better if England joined also. But if there is any indication England would delay the project and slow things up, the USA should go ahead anyway because delay would be fatal to the psychological atmosphere in Germany.

Adenauer said in 1948 there was absolutely no gold or foreign currency backing—literally zero—for the West German mark issue. Now the backing was 60 per cent. I am sure this is true and it is astonishing. As a matter of fact the Chancellor said the *Bank Deutscher Länder* now had $1,000,-000,000 in gold.

Incidentally, Adenauer said he agreed heartily with the objectives of the McCarthy investigations although he didn't agree with the methods. He thought Soviet espionage was magnificently organized and widespread and had to be dug out.

I am impressed by the great interest the Germans take in any developments in France and by the vast amount of erroneous and so-called inside information they have. Thus, with a knowing look, Adenauer asked me what I thought about Laniel's "list" of politicians who have been bribed by industry to support him. When I replied I'd never heard of it, he and Blankenhorn thought this a great joke.

Adenauer said he had had a full agreement on the Saar with Schuman. Then the government fell and Bidault became foreign minister. When he asked Bidault about the agreement, Bidault claimed there was no such paper in the Quai d'Orsay files. (Adenauer describes these as being full of dust and waste.) Adenauer feels Bidault double-crossed him and clearly has no use for him. He also told me that the last time he had seen Schuman (he was out of office then), Schuman told Adenauer that Bidault had not conferred with him (Schuman) one single time since Bidault took over this last tour as foreign minister; nor had he filled in Schuman on a single development.

Incidentally, I was struck by occasional references Adenauer made to the reading he is now doing. Apparently he is in the midst of some work on the French Revolution and another one on the early history of the United States. It rather impresses me to see this old man who is so busy running the most dynamic country in Europe still finding time to do such reading. I think of it particularly in contrast with a recent article in *Time* Magazine saying that all John Foster Dulles reads is a half-hour's worth of the Bible or detective stories every evening. Ike sticks to westerns.

BONN, *October 20, 1953*

YESTERDAY evening I dined with Theodor Blank, head of the West German defense office and, in fact, minister of war although he has no cabinet title. General Heusinger, Blank's principal military expert, was there as well as Konrad Ahlers, the young former paratroop officer who does their high-level interpreting and press relations. Blank is a most unimpressive-looking little man. He seems nervous and emotional as well as very egocentric. He complained long and loud that he had not yet been given the "rank" and title of minister so that he would be able to vote in cabinet meetings which, he says, he already attends as an observer. He wants to speak and vote to counterbalance Finance Minister Schäffer. I observed that if he had Adenauer's agreement on any issue, it didn't seem necessary for him to vote. Adenauer, after all, really runs this show.

The dinner took place in a small room of the Bonn Press Club. It was on a simple basis although the food and drink, for Germany, were excellent. Blank got very excited because the lights kept failing. I noticed he and Heusinger also always waited until the waiters had left the room and closed the door before saying anything of interest. Obviously German government secrets have been penetrated and the order has come down to take extra precautions. After dinner we sat in another room over coffee and drinks including Black Forest framboise.

Heusinger is small and undistinguished looking; like a very small-town functionary. However he is obviously bright (which is more than Blank seems) and has mastered quite fluent English. Heusinger is a regular staff officer. He was chief of operations on the *Oberkommando des Heeres* during World War II. Since 1933 he had been an operations officer on the general staff. He drafted the plans for the campaigns in Poland, France, the Balkans, Russia. He complained he was greatly surprised by the vigor of the Greek resistance; this set the timetable back. He also criticized Mussolini for his attack on Greece, saying a Balkan offensive had never been envisioned—until they had to bail the Duce out. However he said Mussolini was a good man for Italy—until he made the mistake of lining up with Hitler.

Heusinger was present when the briefcase bomb went off at Hitler's headquarters on July 20, 1944. He said he had been substituting at the briefings for a few weeks because General Zeitzler, chief of staff, was ill. Heusinger says he knew there was a plot being concocted against Hitler. Tresckow, his army contact in the plot, tried to sign him up. Heusinger refused to go along unless the plotters got a flat guarantee from Britain and America that they would stop the war as soon as Hitler was dead and Naziism overthrown; that they would then pitch in with Germany against Russia. I observed to Heusinger that this was a difficult pledge to expect enemies to make against an ally, which Russia then was. Heusinger didn't join. He fought on and was a prisoner at Nuremberg for two years where his testimony was valuable in the war criminals trial.

He said when Colonel Stauffenberg (who carried the bomb) entered headquarters on July 20, he was confident this was the day. Heusinger was standing next to Hitler when the bomb in the briefcase left by Stauffenberg beneath the table went off. Fortunately, he says, they were in a temporary headquarters above ground while Hitler's underground bunker was having more concrete added. Also there was a heavy oak table which absorbed the shock of some of the blast. Heusinger's aide was killed. But he found himself on his back with a map burning above his head. He fumbled about and felt his hand in a mass of hair as he struggled to rise and get out. The hair was Hitler's. He complained that Stauffenberg hadn't tipped him off on the bomb. "Why should he?" I asked, astonished. "You had refused to join."

Heusinger admitted to me that it would be far handier to have twelve German divisions in national corps and armies than an EDC—from the point of view of military efficiency. He also admitted that from the standpoint of plans it would take no time at all to shift the blueprint for remilitarization from a supranational to a national basis. The only important thing would be supplies, said he. Since the United States is going to provide the basic equipment anyway, I don't see the problem there.

By the way, Heusinger continually used the figure of six American divisions here. I told him our people still used five. He replied, "What about the constabulary?" Of course he's right.

Heusinger thinks 1956 is the critical year of danger. The satellite economic plans are all geared to be at their peak that year. The satellite armies will be ready for modern war by then, with a brand new officers corps of reliables finally trained. The USSR will by then have a powerful stock of atom and hydrogen bombs and planes to deliver them. And in both the West and the Soviet bloc the economic burden of the arms race will by then be so strong that the economies will want a dynamic shift.

Heusinger and Blank both insisted France *must* ratify EDC. If the United States is strong enough to contemplate possibly establishing separate military relationships with Germany, it is strong enough to *force* French ratification. Heusinger says that Western Europe already (with the six American and four British divisions) is strong enough to prevent Russia from invading with only the twenty-four divisions she has in East Germany. She would require the bringing up of other units and this we could detect.

Heusinger insists Czechoslovakia is the most important point in Central Europe. Frankfort is only a three-hour drive from there. There can be no "neutral" zone in Europe's heart without including Czechoslovakia. (He obviously follows the old Bismarck and general staff line about the master of Bohemia being the master of Europe.)

Both Heusinger and Blank think the earliest EDC can be ratified is February, 1954. The other powers won't ratify until France does—despite pressure. Bidault, they say, made a secret deal with de Gasperi when he was still Premier, promising to support Italy on Trieste if Italy held off ratification until after the French. (Always the anti-French line. Obviously Germany is either going to boss EDC or have a national army.) Heusinger assured me the French were way below the strength pledged by them as a force goal in Lisbon, but were trying to keep it secret. For this reason the French were trying to get new protocols guaranteeing that the Germans could never have more troops than the French in EDC—as long as it lasts.

I must say it is obvious to me that the best the French can hope is to delay things a bit more. Obviously the Germans are on the move again. They are either going to get EDC and gain control of it or pull out and act on their own if such control isn't granted. Or they are going to set up a national army with full American approval.

VIENNA, *October 24, 1953*

LAST night I dined at Tommy (Llewellyn) Thompson's; he is now ambassador here. I must say he remains affable, simple and quite unambassadorial. Karl Gruber, the foreign minister, came in after dinner. He has just returned from a political tour of the Tyrol where local elections are to be held tomorrow. Gruber told me that if there is any plebiscite around Trieste, there must also be a plebiscite in the South Tyrol to decide whether that area should remain Italian or go to Austria. This rather astonished me because it was Gruber who personally negotiated with De Gasperi the settlement allowing the South Tyrol to remain Italian after World War II and merely securing certain autonomy rights for the German-speaking population and a sharing of such things as hydroelectric power.

After Gruber left, I talked with (Sir) Harold Caccia, British ambassador. Harold thinks a little less than nothing of Gruber. He says he is unreliable and tricky. When Gruber went off to see Nehru in Switzerland earlier this year, he didn't even tell his closest advisors at the foreign office where he was going or why. Caccia called up the foreign office to ask if it was true that Gruber had gone to Switzerland to see Nehru and the foreign office denied this—in good faith because they didn't even know Gruber had left Vienna. Caccia asked me if I knew anything about Gruber's war record. I told him that to the best of my recollection he was still an engineer in a German factory making communications equipment for tanks as late as February, 1945, although he had once boasted to me that he used to listen to the BBC.

VIENNA, *October 25, 1953*

INTERESTING day driving around the Burgenland up to the barbed wire fence that separates Hungary from Austria. The Soviet occupation zone is exactly like the rest of Austria, and Hans Kronhuber of Chancellor Raab's office, who was along, explained that there is no difference in prosperity, standard of living or anything else between the zones of occupation. The only difference is that about once a month someone is picked up and carted off by the Russians. On the whole the Russians are very little in evidence and seem to be allowing the Austrians a remarkable amount of freedom. There is absolutely no comparison between East Austria and East Germany. The country is not partitioned off the way Germany is. The few Russian soldiers I saw were astonishingly nice-looking, spic-and-span youngsters.

We lunched in a little town called Eisenstadt where the Esterhazy family had its main palace—a huge yellow baroque affair which is now a Soviet administration building. After lunch we visited a rather extraordinary house in the old ghetto which belonged to a wealthy wine merchant named Wolf. Apparently the Wolfs had been very prosperous for some generations and had been rather close to the Esterhazys in the curious way that prevailed in the old Austrian empire. Judging from the house, which was quite attractive, they lived extremely well. The last Wolf had become a collector—indeed a collector of just about anything he could lay his hands on from old bones to tombstones and locks. He turned his house into a weird museum like an old curiosity shop, but there are some lovely things mixed up with the junk. Among his collections was one of Jewish religious objects—silver scrolls, and so forth. When the Nazis took over, they used this house as the central assembly point in which all the silver and other objects they took from Jewish synagogues were stored. For one or another odd reason, the Gestapo left all this in Wolf's house, and when the Russians came in, they also left it untouched. These objects seized by the Gestapo are being returned to the few surviving Jewish Communities of Austria (there are now only 12,000 Jews in the country out of the 200,000 in 1938). The house is now being run as a town museum.

PARIS, *October 28, 1953*

LUNCHED with Ismay. He is worried about NATO; he says it needs a new wave to regain momentum—something like enactment of EDC. Oddly enough, he seemed to think EDC was all right today, although in the past he has assured me it was a crackpot scheme. I told him I really didn't think EDC stood much chance. He agreed that now that Adenauer had been reelected he was being more demanding on the Saar than had been anticipated. Adenauer's excuse is that he must take a sterner attitude to satisfy his *Bundestag* backing. Personally I think he's just fooling everybody; that he always wanted to really take over the Saar again and that in the end this is what he will accomplish.

Talking about Churchill, Ismay said he had told the old man last August that he would be good for another five years as Prime Minister if he would only work eight or ten hours a day instead of sixteen hours a day, but at the same time he knew Churchill would never confine himself to that degree. Ismay said he insists on keeping his nose in everything and wears himself out messing around in things he knows nothing about like questions of transport subsidies, and so forth.

Pug is absolutely confident that Churchill intends to remain Prime Minister and also that Eden is the heir apparent. As a matter of fact, I don't believe Churchill ever talks about Rab Butler, but only refers to Eden. I have never thought that Butler would succeed Churchill.

Ismay said Churchill was taking great pains to keep Eden effectively briefed as his possible successor although he thinks Churchill is still remarkably well and vital. He recalled that at the Yalta Conference it was very evident that Roosevelt was failing rapidly. Ismay said that although the President had just recently been reelected, he looked like a doomed man. After about an hour in conferences his jaw would fall open like that of a corpse. Ismay said he had remarked to one of his English friends at the time that it was certain the President would either be dead or "no longer in possession of his faculties" within six months.

PARIS, *October 29, 1953*

THIS morning I had a long talk with Foreign Minister Bidault, who started out by complaining about a piece I had written recently saying his political ambitions constituted one of the blocks in the way of EDC ratification. He denied that he had any ambitions to be President of France. He admitted, however, that political rivalries over the campaign were tending to help delay ratification. He still thought there would be ratification sometime during the first three months of 1954, but that it would be a very difficult thing to achieve.

By and large I must say I had the feeling that ratification is rather unlikely despite what he said. He obviously still mistrusts the Germans and has little faith in the French political system. He said it was ridiculous that a conservative government like the present French cabinet should have to depend upon the divided Socialist Party to achieve the main aim of its foreign policy, namely EDC. He said that when he came into office this last time as foreign minister, EDC was absolutely dead and it was largely through his efforts that its chances had been revived. Therefore he resented the fact that many people and above all the Germans kept blaming him for delays.

I told him the Germans (I did not mention Adenauer) had informed me Schuman had written a letter to Adenauer when Schuman was foreign minister formally agreeing to a Saar settlement. The Germans complained that Bidault had omitted this from the dossier of the Quai d'Orsay and had claimed no such letter exists.

Bidault was very irked. He said that indeed Schuman had written a letter. The letter was merely a bit of equivocation and did not really represent any agreement. The story came about this way. Shortly after Bidault had come back into office, he met Adenauer for a first discussion on the Saar. After they had talked things over, Adenauer complained the French dossier was incomplete. Bidault asked what he meant, and Adenauer replied that the Schuman letter was missing. Bidault then said to Adenauer, "Surely you must have the letter if you know that my dossier is incomplete." Adenauer admitted he had the letter, and later Bidault was able to read it. There is something fuzzy about all this.

Bidault had very snide remarks to make about Adenauer. He would start off praising him as a great European-minded statesman and then hasten to say that he was a slippery political operator. He said Adenauer always said unkind things to Bidault about Schuman and unkind things to Schuman about Bidault. He said there had to be agreement on the Saar before any EDC ratification—that is to say, agreement between Bonn and Paris. After all, the western frontiers of Germany had to be definitely settled even if the eastern ones remained in limbo. There had to be a European settlement, and Saarlanders would march in the European Army in units from the Saar, not German units. Now that Adenauer had a big majority in the Bundestag the Germans appeared to be far less conciliatory about the Saar. Adenauer had guaranteed that he would be able to reach an agreement after the election. Now he was apologizing that his deputies were making things difficult for him.

Bidault emphasized how difficult the whole job of European integration was. He recalled that when he had been in Washington with René Mayer, they had been invited out on the presidential yacht *Williamsburg.* Sam Rayburn happened to tell him that ever since the Declaration of Independence the states of Maryland and Virginia had been scrapping over Chesapeake Bay fishing rights and fishermen continually shot at each other. If that is the case, Bidault asked, how can anybody expect to have a Franco-German agreement in one or two years and French and Germans marching side by side in the same red Zouave pants?

PARIS, *October 30, 1953*

THIS morning I had a talk with Prime Minister Joseph Laniel at the Hotel Matignon. Laniel is a stocky, fat, red-faced character of medium height, who looks like a big Normandy butter-and-egg man, is, and talks like one. He started off by uttering a lot of unoriginal platitudes on the subject of Indochina. I don't mean to be cynical, but there wasn't a single word that I haven't been hearing for the last two years.

He said the war was difficult, that France had lost and suffered a lot, that without the Indochina war the French would have a magnificent army in Europe and would not fear German rearmament so much, that there was nobody to negotiate a peace with because you need two to negotiate. He could not tell whether the Korean armistice had made the situation in Indochina more dangerous because so far there had been no concrete reaction by the Chinese. He said the morale of the Vietnamese (Saigon) troops had been greatly lifted. They were the same people as the Vietminh, but there was no doubt that the Vietminh had far more fighting spirit. He thought that General Navarre's current operation had forestalled a Vietminh offensive. If China were to invade Indochina or interfere in a more direct way, the war would be internationalized; he had obtained agreement to that by his trip to Washington.

All in all, Laniel was affable but unimpressive. He was very polite and kept apologizing for the fact that he didn't speak English. I cannot think of him as any great shakes in terms of France's future.

PARIS, *October 30, 1953*

LAST night Douglas Dillon came to dinner. In his boyish way he blurted out several opinions of interest. He thinks Adenauer is toying with the French now. His belief is that Adenauer is using the new unconciliatory attitude of the recently elected *Bundestag* majority (on the Saar issue) as an excuse for being less conciliatory to the French. Dillon suspects Adenauer may be secretly encouraging his deputies to be more recalcitrant.

Dillon is convinced that Queuille will be the next President of France. His logic, which is rather entertaining, works this way. Queuille and Laniel are the outstanding candidates. Laniel, who is a conservative businessman, will never be able to get the necessary support from the Socialists and the left wing in general. The greatest disadvantage generally attributed to Queuille is that he is very ill, failing more and more every month, and bound to die within a year or so. Dillon figures that is his greatest vote appeal. Every other candidate is going to vote for him and then, while the old man is dying, try and negotiate new alliances with different deputies and senators so that they can replace him.

Despite what everybody tells him and what he himself is saying, Dillon admits that he is getting a little bit sceptical about the chances of EDC. He is particularly worried about the Saar negotiations.

To my surprise he said that he thought Bidault was a first-rate man and had behaved very well in all negotiations during the last three or four months. Dillon does not share the previous suspicion of Bidault that so many American ambassadors have felt; and I am glad to hear this because I think Bidault is pretty smart. Dillon admits that he's a damn sight more intelligent than Robert Schuman.

PARIS, *October 30, 1953*

I lunched with Norstad who has been up to the ears during the last few days with visiting American brass including Admiral Radford, chairman of the Joint Chiefs of Staff, General Twining, chief of staff for the Air Force, and Harold Talbot, Secretary of the Air Force. Norstad remarks with a twinkle that this is the first visit Radford has paid to Europe in forty years.

Larry is still somewhat worried about the effect of the spate of stories that came out from Washington at the end of last week to the effect that the United States was going to reduce its overseas forces and the size of its over-all defense forces. The remainder would be armed with new atomic weapons. Conventional weapons would be supplied to the Europeans. This was publicly denied by Radford when he arrived here. Gruenther requested that the President himself deny this, and that was done a few days afterwards. However, Norstad still fears repercussions of this apparently calculated leak may help to scotch EDC when the worried Europeans argue that despite denials the United States is going to reduce its forces here.

Norstad dined at Pleven's last night (in honor of Radford). He asked Pleven if he was a candidate for President of France. Pleven replied that he thought he was still too young (he is only fifty-three) but might be ready to run at the age of sixty. When Pleven is sixty, the term of the next President (seven years) will just be expiring. Pleven also said that he was too closely linked with EDC and that if he were defeated as President, it might hurt EDC's chances. Personally I don't think Pleven has any more chance of being elected President of France than I have.

Incidentally, Norstad said that until a year ago he was opposed to the idea of a base agreement with Spain because the Spaniards were holding us up for too much money. However, when they got more reasonable, he was glad to see a deal go through. Nevertheless he thinks similar bases might be even more useful elsewhere. He said that the decision has now been taken to build one of the remaining two Moroccan airbases, but probably not to build the other. There isn't so much pressure for the Moroccan bases any more, and any remaining funds could better be expended elsewhere.

PARIS, *November 4, 1953*

I had lunch today with Hervé Alphand of the Quai, who keeps up a bold front about EDC. He continues to say he is confident it will pass in the end. He thinks the critical period will be between February 1 and 15. Following the elections of the President, the present cabinet will resign in the middle of January, and it should take about a fortnight to get a new cabinet. Then it will plunge right into EDC. Alphand thinks either Laniel or Queuille will be President. He thinks Auriol, the great enemy of EDC, may try and become prime minister of a leftist coalition.

Alphand says there is absolutely no alternative to EDC. If the project fails, he intends not only to resign from the French diplomatic service, but will probably move abroad. He said that he could not continue to serve a government which did not support this program because it is the only salvation for France. Only a few weeks ago in the United States, where he was on a brief trip, he saw Hallstein (Adenauer's principal assistant in foreign affairs). Hallstein confided to Alphand that he also intended to resign from the German diplomatic service if EDC does not come about.

Hervé spent an hour and a half with Bedell Smith in Washington. Bedell told him there was absolutely no intention by America to modify present strategic commitments or to reduce military strength in Europe. There was only one possibility which would bring about reconsideration of our present strategy; that would be the failure of EDC. Bedell explained he wasn't trying in any sense to hold a cudgel over the head of France, but that obviously it would be necessary to reexamine the implications of present American strategy if EDC fails.

Alphand said the enemies of EDC in France are now widely advertising the theory that American troops will be withdrawn from Europe as soon as German divisions are formed in EDC. The reverse is the case and the Germans would not agree to form their divisions except behind the protection of American and British divisions.

I asked Alphand how French policy was actually formulated; whether there was a "policy planning board" in the Quai d'Orsay or not. He said there was nothing so formal and that it was largely empirical. For example, on the question of EDC he was almost alone in the career service of the Quai d'Orsay. He had many enemies who opposed him. However, he had had the full cooperation of both his foreign ministers, Robert Schuman and Georges Bidault. He had largely made policy together with Schuman and Bidault on this critical matter. But he thought it did represent the popular view of the French people.

I said to him that I had talked recently with a high official of the British Foreign Office who thought French foreign policy was very successful. His view was that the French had brilliantly achieved three basic objectives: obtained military support from the United States and Britain against the threat of Soviet aggression; obtained financial support of the United States; managed this without permitting the reascendancy in Europe of the Germans.

Alphand admitted there were indeed people who saw in EDC a possibility of keeping Germany permanently divided. He grinned and his eyes twinkled when he said this, but I haven't the vaguest idea if he referred to himself or not. It was of course lunacy on the part of the Germans to believe the Adenauer theory that EDC was the only way to unify Germany. However, he did not think the tradition of national entity was as deeply rooted or as vital among the Germans as among the French. As a result, many of the West Germans actually didn't give a damn what happened to their cousins in East Germany as long as they were well off, comfortable and protected.

Alphand waxed quite eloquent on the subject of the grim future if EDC fails. It was obvious that Germany could never be admitted into NATO. It was equally obvious that a third force could not be formed in Europe with the support of Britain because Britain would remain aligned with the United States and with Germany. It was impossible to conceive of a successful alliance between West Germany and the English-speaking powers minus the aid of France. Therefore the United States would have to withdraw to a peripheral defense and permit Europe, seeking to be neutral, to be overrun by communism. This was the only alternative. The United States might maintain bases in Spain, French Morocco and the Middle East, but the bulk of Western Europe would be undermined and taken over by pro-Soviet elements.

PARIS, *November 6, 1953*

ERIC JOHNSTON came in to see me this afternoon. Eric has now been named Eisenhower's special ambassador in the Middle East to make peace between Arabs and Jews. He gave me a long speech about the proposed plan for a Jordan Valley authority which, at an over-all cost of less than $150 million, would provide about 180,000 more irrigated acres in Israel and about 200,000 for Jordan plus a small amount for Syria. Hydroelectric power would be provided for the area. Certain minor frontier rectifications would have to be made. This is a State Department plan which would serve as the gimmick for making over-all peace. Eric says all four riparian states—Israel, Jordan, Lebanon, and Syria—have promised to consider the plan, although none of them gave it outright support. He also went to Cairo where Naguib implied mildly favorable interest.

After Johnston had made his long spiel, I apologized and said that I was paid to ask direct questions and inquired just why he had come to tell me all this. Did he want a story written about it, and if so, what was the story? He said he had come to tell me merely because he thought I might be interested. I said I was interested but it was really not very much of a story to say that all the governments had promised to consider accepting this gift from Santa Claus—especially if I couldn't quote him; and he had stipulated that this was "background" information. He said, "Well, under those circumstances maybe you can quote me." I still don't see any story in it.

PARIS, *November 9, 1953*

BY the way, I saw Ben Bradlee, the embassy press attaché, today. Ben told me that last Friday Eric Johnston had dropped in at the American embassy together with George Barnes, his press attaché, and asked for a list of the prominent correspondents in Paris. Bradlee had furnished him the list. Barnes asked if he thought it would be a good idea for Johnston to have a press conference. Bradlee, having had a bad experience with a press conference Johnston gave here a couple of years ago, said no. Barnes then called up a series of newspaper offices. According to Bradlee, Johnston not only came to this office but also went to the *Herald Tribune* and *The Times* and *Daily Telegraph* of London. Maurice Ferro of *Paris Presse* came to see Johnston. Apparently Johnston also saw the Associated Press, trying to peddle his story everywhere. As far as Bradlee knows, the only outfit to fall for it was the *Herald Tribune*. He thinks Johnston is about the lowest piece of work that has yet come into the embassy.

PARIS, *November 10, 1953*

GRIGORE GAFENCU, former foreign minister of Rumania, came in today. He told me it was the partition of Eastern Europe which had always provoked war and that by his 1944 deal with Stalin, Churchill had "contributed to the moral disarmament of the West." In so doing, Sir Winston had in fact helped stimulate the cold war, Gafencu thought. Bitterly he observed, "These revelations are of a sort to shatter the confidence of East Europeans in the democratic powers and even in the principle of democracy."

PARIS, *November 12, 1953*

I DINED last night with Chip Bohlen, who just came in from Moscow with Brose and Virginia Chambers. Chip is going to spend a few days here in order to testify before the Randall Commission, which is holding hearings on foreign trade. Incidentally, he had to leave his plane at Frankfort because if it goes west of Wiesbaden, the Air Force bills the State Department. In other words, had he continued on to Paris, the State Department would have been asked to pay the Air Force about $1,500, and the State Department damn well would have told Bohlen to pay it.

Chip had a lot of interesting gossip about things in Russia these days. The November 7 reception given by Molotov on the anniversary of the October Revolution was absolutely incredible. Molotov insisted that the American, British and French ambassadors and their wives, as well as the Chinese Communist, Burmese and Argentine ambassadors and Walter Ulbricht, boss of Communist East Germany, should sit together at his table, where Bulganin, Mikoyan, Kaganovitch and Pervukhin were also seated. Incidentally, Chip said that Pervukhin behaves very much like a junior boy in school and hardly opened his mouth. Molotov was extremely affable, and a great deal of hooch was poured. Bulganin got so plastered he had to be taken away before the evening had terminated. Joxe, the French ambassador, was sitting next to Bulganin and had to absorb some of the shock treatment. As a result he got quite polluted and towards the end of the evening was making some long and flowery speeches in very polished phrases but without any point whatsoever. The satellite and other diplomats were apparently furious at the joviality with which the Big Three Westerners were received. The Burmese and Argentine envoys were rather confused at being present in this collection. Chip didn't even recognize Ulbricht. He had been talking across the table in Russian with Kaganovitch when Ulbricht turned to him and passed the bottle of *Perzovka,* saying to him that it was the favorite drink of the Ukraine. As a matter of fact, this is not true. Chip thought Ulbricht was a Ukrainian party boss. He asked, "Are you Ukrainian?", and to his horrified embarrassment Ulbricht replied, "Oh no, I'm German."

Chip feels it is crazy to think that Soviet policy is deliberately trying to divide the West if this is any indication. On the contrary, it was the satellites and the other diplomatic representatives who were offended. The Italian ambassador stalked off in a rage and said, "I represent a great power also and should have been invited to Molotov's table." Apparently dozens of other guests at the party just gathered around this table of stars, eavesdropping and listening to every quip and sally. Chip said you couldn't even turn around without brushing people who were bending over the table and kibitzing: ambassadors, Russians, newspaper reporters, and so on.

As the evening wandered on, Molotov sent word that he wanted Marshal Zhukov to join the table. Chip says Zhukov is by far the most popular man in Russia, and feels that he actually outranks Vassilievsky in importance although Vassilievsky is listed as ranking higher in the army set-up. Zhukov joined the group and behaved with extraordinary dignity. He did not participate in the vodka-drinking race, and Chip had the impression that he was looking with great disapproval at some of the others who were throwing the stuff down. Several toasts were exchanged and Chip made a toast in favor of "justice among the peoples of the world." Zhukov was later on asked if he would make a toast. Chip overheard him replying to his neighbor and saying, no, he would not make a toast, but he was glad to associate himself with the toast of the American ambassador. This is a very extraordinary statement even though it was just muttered in an aside to one of the party boys.

Chip is convinced the Russians are stuck with their foreign policy whether they want it or not. Even if they are trying to change over from Stalinism, they have to hang on to the basic essentials of his policy. They cannot possibly discuss getting out of Germany because if they lose East

Germany, they are likely to lose their satellites. They don't want war, but they can't have real peace. As far as Stalin himself goes, Chip says the process of deflating him now seems to have ended. He makes this analogy. He refers to the Peruvian Indian habit of shrinking human heads. Stalin's head has now been shrunken to its final size. He is no longer a god but just one of the idols of a series of idols in the Soviet Valhalla. He is now Stalin, the great successor of Lenin and part of the Marx–Engels–Lenin–Stalin legend; but no more.

Another extraordinary development in Russia is the fact that the secret police have stopped following ambassadors. Ever since Bullitt first went to Moscow in 1933 the American ambassador (and all other ambassadors for that matter) had been openly followed by a police car, generally with four cops in it. Now the MVD tails have stopped.

Chip has a very interesting theory about Voroshilov's savage speech last week attacking the West. He said it was quite clear that Voroshilov was chosen to make this speech even though he is an old man and an insignificant figure because he is absolutely uncontroversial as far as Russia goes. In that speech there are two paragraphs praising Stalin. This is the first public praise of Stalin there has been since Stalin's funeral. Chip believes Voroshilov made this his price for agreeing to speak; in other words, he said all right, he would speak on condition he was permitted to praise his old friend.

We discussed the deal between England and Russia to divide up the Balkans. Chip agrees we gave Britain the authority to control policy and decisions in the Eastern Mediterranean and the Balkans for the duration of the war. This was done at Casablanca. Chip says he doesn't think it was done in exchange for Britain's agreement to the "unconditional surrender" theory, but I still think that's the case. As a result of this agreement in May, 1944, the British made their first deal with the Russians on the Balkans, granting Russia "military" control over Rumania in exchange for British "military" control over Greece. Theoretically this was supposed to be just military, but Hull protested about it because he saw the political implications. We granted our reluctant approval to the arrangement on the grounds that these spheres were only on a wartime basis. It was later that year that Churchill and Stalin actually divided up the Balkans in a more precise way; at Moscow in October, 1944.

Chip recalled that General Marshall, while he was still Secretary of State in April, 1948, was extremely unhappy about the March 20 agreement on Trieste, promising it to Italy, announced that year by the Big Three. Chip said that once when Marshall was congratulated by some Congressmen on that "fine act" in Trieste, he replied that he wasn't at all proud of it and that he had reached a decision on the subject with great difficulty. The United States was breaking its word by the March 20 compact and it would pay for it.

PARIS, *November 13, 1953*

I had drinks with Chip Bohlen and Jock Whitney this afternoon. We were discussing ambassadors. Chip said that at the Luxembourg meeting of ambassadors which took place in September, Clare Luce horrified a dinner party at which a great many European dignitaries were present. She said she had been asked to write a review of the new Kinsey report on women for some well-known American woman's magazine. After serious consideration she decided she couldn't do it in her present position. Then she added in a loud voice that it wouldn't have taken her any 480 pages to prove that all men are dopes. All conversation ceased, and her male colleagues perked up their ears. After all, she said, women are not interested in sex. All they want is babies and security from men. Men are just too stupid to know it.

Whitney told me Eisenhower had told him that Aldrich had absolutely insisted on getting the London embassy once he learned he was not going to be made Secretary of the Treasury. Ike said that after he learned he wasn't going to get it, he actually beat the table and said that he wanted to go as ambassador to London and he was determined to get the job. This was right after the election. He got it.

Incidentally, Jock indicated to me that had he really pushed at all to be ambassador in Paris, he might very well have gotten it. However Jock, when asked if he wanted anything, said no (which he may regret now). Furthermore, he told the President and others that he didn't think it was a good idea to stuff the diplomatic service with big contributors.

PARIS, *November 16, 1953*

I spent the weekend with Bohlen playing profitable but bad golf. He had some interesting things to say about Russia.

In his view Russia is a country of many secrets but few mysteries. It is a great mistake for people to keep harping on the old clichés about the sphinx and the enigma of Russia.

In some strange way Laurence Steinhardt became a great buddy of Matsuoka when Matsuoka was Japanese foreign minister. When General Tatekawa, an old cavalry officer, was named Japanese ambassador to Moscow, Matsuoka told him to be sure and look up Steinhardt, a good friend, and tell him everything. Tatekawa, who was an affable officer and liked to drink a bottle of whisky every day, was also very stupid and took the instructions literally. He used to drop around and see Steinhardt whenever he learned anything. If he was at the Kremlin where the Russians were trying to negotiate a pact with Japan, he would drop in at the American embassy before going back to his own embassy to draft a telegram for Tokyo. He was thus a magnificent source of information.

The Russians had a "neutrality pact" with Japan. The Japanese wanted to change this into a "nonaggression pact." The Russians had just signed a nonaggression pact with Hitler. Molotov therefore pointed out to Tatekawa that Russia might be willing to consider a nonaggression pact with Japan if the Japanese made a territorial settlement and gave Russia a little piece of ground, the way the Germans gave part of Poland and the Baltic states. The Japanese were rather horrified, but Molotov kept telling them how many islands they had and surely they could spare a few.

The only instructions Bohlen had from Eisenhower when he went to Moscow were, literally, "Watch your stomach and don't let them get you."

Chip says that the army in Russia now has a "higher specific gravity" but is not a coherent political force as such. Nevertheless one can see its influence creeping back. Zhukov is definitely back in the picture. The army is bound to be pleased by the present program of the Malenkov government which is seeking to incur popular favor by more consumers goods and benefits for the farmers. This is bound to make the peasant recruit a more contented man and therefore better soldier material, and that's what the Army likes.

The basic reason for the recent Beria purge was to reduce the power and authority of the MVD. One example of how this is working out has been the dropping of "tails" that used to follow all the ambassadors. Reports from Moscow indicate that there will soon be news on Beria's fate.

At the famous November 7 reception Molotov gave, Avis Bohlen made a toast (which was translated by Chip) to the housewives of Russia who had been mentioned in Mikoyan's speech this autumn as needing consumers goods, gadgets, and so forth. Mikoyan asked if Chip had really read his speech and he replied yes. Molotov then leaned across the table and said, "That certainly is a rare experience for you, Anastasias."

The Burmese ambassador made a toast to peace. Kaganovitch, who is a tough, old Bolshevik with huge hamlike hands and who was then nicely plastered, leaned forward and muttered after the Burmese had concluded, "None of that stuff. What we need is to get those Kuomintang troops out of Burma."

WASHINGTON, *November 23, 1953*

THIS afternoon I had an extremely interesting set of visits in the White House. I had written the President from Paris that I was going to be in the United States for a few days and was planning to come down to Washington on Monday, November 23; that I hoped to get a chance to say hello to him if possible. Almost immediately after my arrival in New York, I received a telephone call from Tom Stephens, appointments secretary. I was out when the call came, so I called back directly to Bob Schulz, one of the President's several military aides. Bob explained the President was

going away Monday evening and that three o'clock was the only time I
could see him. I suggested that I would like to come in a few minutes early
in order to say hello to other friends in the White House. It was therefore
agreed I should arrive at two o'clock and gas with others before being
taken in to see the boss. I was told that this was an unofficial visit and not
to talk about it. I was taken into a waiting room, and the first people to
appear were Pete (Brigadier General P. T. ) Carroll, Slick (Major General Wilton) Persons, and Major General Howard Snyder, the President's
doctor and close personal friend. We sat around a table shooting the bull.
Carroll asked me what I thought were the chances of EDC going through. I
told him I didn't think there was any chance at all. This surprised both
Persons and Carroll, who said they had had two visitors who had recently
come back from Europe and assured the President EDC was in the bag. I
said I had no way of really knowing but this was my impression and they
could take it or leave it.

At that point Snyder interjected, "Maybe Cy is the only person who is
telling you the truth."

Persons pointed out that if EDC doesn't go through, Congress will stop
all military aid to the five NATO powers who are to be members of EDC.
However, both Persons and Carroll were absolutely convinced that the
European army is going to be ratified—and soon.

Carroll then gave me a sort of briefing on the set-up at the White House
and who does what. As he describes his own job, it sounds as if he were a
kind of minor chairman of the Joint Chiefs of Staff for Eisenhower. All
kinds of important papers on all kinds of subjects go through him, and he
deals them out to the proper people for attention. Of course, he is not in
any sense as high-ranking as fellows like Governor Sherman Adams but I
expect his invisible influence is extremely great. Among other things, he
decides on how all important letters shall be answered.

Both Carroll and Persons were of the opinion that if there is no EDC,
the United States simply must back the Germans directly. However, Carroll
agreed there was no way of giving air support in such a situation except
through France where most of the new airbases have been built under the
infrastructure program.

Snyder then asked if the bases existing in Italy, Spain and Morocco
could not be substituted for those in France in the hypothetical situation
we were discussing. Snyder added that Morocco would not remain under
French control if we, the United States, were not protecting it on behalf of
Paris.

Snyder then asked me if I wouldn't like to go up and see Mamie. He
took me along with him and in his affable way paraded me through a whole
series of offices where he flirted with the young secretaries and made
friendly cracks to everybody. I may point out that he is well over seventy
years old, so the flirtations were strictly of a witty and platonic nature—

although he is still an extraordinarily handsome and well-preserved fellow. In one little office lots of fishing tackle was hanging all over the place. Snyder explained to me that President Roosevelt had been a great fisherman. When this became known to the public, various friends and sporting goods establishments sent him tackle that he didn't know what to do with, so a good deal of it has just been scattered around the walls of this particular office.

We rode up in an elevator to the floor where the private living quarters are and went through a hall on the walls of which were a couple of recent paintings by Ike—not so hot, but then the hall was not so brilliantly lit that they were too visible. Mamie greeted me like a long-lost friend. She was sitting up in bed in a pink bedjacket. She stretched out her arms and kissed me on both cheeks, sat me down beside her and we started to chat. The bedroom which she shares with the President (although he has his own bedroom and study next door) is the room where Abe Lincoln used to sleep. Lincoln's bed has been replaced by her pink double bed. The walls have been painted green—a rather nice hue of light green which she takes to all the houses she successively occupies and refers to as "my green, you know." She pointed out to me a plaque above the fireplace which I read and which merely stated that this was the room where President Lincoln had slept. Outside the window is the nice small park and lawn where the President practices his golf shots. Right below the window was a large tree that Mamie said had been planted by Andrew Jackson.

Our conversation was certainly of no particular interest but was extremely pleasant. She told me that the President had had a special set of miniature golf clubs made for David, his five-year-old grandson, and had just finished painting a portrait of the youngster with his clubs. She told me about a new card game called "Bolivia," a version of canasta that she plays with great enthusiasm.

She loves the job of running the White House. She finds she can handle all the work. She dictates two or three hours a day to her secretary. She has to make arrangements as to whom she will see from among the hundreds of applications that come from wives of politicians, important people, etc. She is bored by the fact that sometimes she has to change her clothes as often as four times a day. She insists on running the house herself and not just leaving it to the staff. She approves all the menus herself (and claims that Mrs. Truman left all this to the housekeeper). She goes through the house often, checking up to be sure there is no dust in the corners. She says she enjoys living in the house and enjoys showing it to people.

When Montgomery was their guest, she took him all through it. Monty showed great and eager curiosity about everything, but when he had finished his sight-seeing tour, he said, "Mamie, it's certainly a fine house. But you know, it is smaller than Buckingham." She said that the children's quarters are upstairs, one floor above, where they can raise hell whenever they are staying with them. At present her son is a major at Fort Benning, and the kids are down there. The Eisenhowers themselves live in what is called the west wing. The east wing is reserved for formal guests such as state visitors. There is a room for Mrs. Doud, Mamie's mother, in the west wing.

She said she gets a massage three times a week to keep her in shape and she tries to do a good deal of her work in bed. I noticed two of the books on her bedside table were *The Robe* and a detective story. She told me that when she plays Bolivia, the stakes are one-fortieth of a cent a point. That certainly doesn't sound extravagant. She said she loved the campaign last year, but it was pretty tiring and she had to take three weeks' rest after it was over.

She said Ike has to work extremely hard. His best relaxation around the White House is painting. Often after a full day's work he will go into the studio they have fixed up for him in the White House. Unfortunately it doesn't have a northern exposure and therefore a constant light, but he doesn't need that. She regrets she can't relax completely at golf or painting, the way he does. But they both benefit enormously from their fairly frequent trips to Augusta, Georgia, and their cottage at the golf club there.

She said John, their son, is proud of his new battalion at Fort Benning. She obviously adores young David and says he has a temper "just like Ike. You really have to watch out if either of them loses his temper."

While we were chatting away (she wanted to know all about Paris), her secretary came in several times with various sorts of messages, but each time she sent her away. Then all of a sudden she came in and said the President was waiting for me, so I had to rush off.

I went down the elevator and then was rapidly conducted along the hall to the business offices where Pete Carroll was waiting in Stephens' room and took me in to the President. He was sitting at his desk—the old familiar desk at which I have seen Roosevelt and Truman. The desk was much less cluttered up than in Roosevelt's time. The President looked well but has aged very visibly in the months since I have seen him. His face is more lined and a little bit more grim. His neck has gotten much heavier, and so has his midriff. He looks bigger, thicker across, older and less bouncy. He told me he had had a bad elbow which had prevented him from playing golf for some time, but that he was going off tomorrow to Augusta and hoped to try it out and see if the elbow would allow him to play.

I told him I just dropped in to say hello and I certainly didn't want to disturb him. But he seemed quite relaxed and started gassing about all kinds of things. Pete Carroll sat there and said nothing. Among other things he talked about the following:

Pakistan wants to help the cause of the United States and the Western powers, but in order to do so needs military aid. The Pakistanis are vital, brave people like the Turks and the Greeks. However, India and Afghanistan object to the thought of our giving help to Pakistan. Afghanistan is worried that Russia might use this as a provocation and excuse to do something against the Afghans. India, on the other hand, is just being "a nuisance." Several times the President referred to "Nehru and his tribe." He obviously has no patience with the Indian point of view and resents the fact that Indian objections may conceivably delay or hamper the project for helping Pakistan.

The President said, "We must have EDC." He emphasized the vital importance of the European Army project to Congress. "I have had two visitors in the past two days who told me that it will go through—shortly after the French elections," he said. I told him I was pessimistic about its chances. This irked him. He expressed great confidence. Ike got all red in the face at my gloom, got up and walked around. He did, however, add that "It is too bad Moch is the *rapporteur* of the project" in the French parliament.

He said he didn't expect any news at all or any real developments at Bermuda. The whole idea was Churchill's, and he was merely trying to be agreeable. He said he couldn't imagine why I wanted to go down there because there certainly wouldn't be anything doing. He said he had investigated and heard the weather was bad. As a result, Mamie was not going. He began to wonder aloud as to whether he should take his golf clubs or not. I suggested no, recalling his clouding political mirror. Finally he said he guessed he wouldn't do it, although he had heard the Mid-Ocean course was pretty good.

The President at some length developed an idea I've never heard him express before. He said he wanted to outlaw the Communist Party. The Communist deputies should be taken out of the French Chamber. He thought there was no point in keeping the Communist Party respectable and allowing it senators and deputies. The Communist Party was like an iceberg and only a bit of it showed above the surface; the really important part was invisible and secret. Nevertheless he thought it would be useful to render illegal and destroy the "respectable" part that was "visible." He had not made up his mind whether to talk to Laniel and Churchill about this or not.

He said he had had a letter from Al Gruenther today. In this letter Al wrote to him that whenever he felt discouraged about NATO and its problems, he looked back to where we all were three years ago, and the rate of progress that was so visible made him feel much better.

Eisenhower then went back to the subject of the dangers of communism. He shoved his chair back and got up and started to walk around. He said he detested the methods of McCarthyism, but nevertheless it certainly was necessary to fight communism and fight it hard. It was silly to think that the liberties of the United States were being endangered merely because we were trying to squash communism, but he disapproved very strongly of the methods by which McCarthy himself was trying to conduct that battle. Again, as he strode up and down, the President said that at Bermuda he would like to suggest that the Big Three should severally and together outlaw the Communist Party.

That got him back onto the subject of Bermuda. He guessed it was necessary for the Big Three to talk things over even if they didn't decide anything. It was sort of the equivalent of an international cabinet meeting.

I suggested that it was really high time I should be going because he obviously was very busy, but he waved me back to my seat and started rambling along on other subjects. Among other things he asked me, "What is Arthur Krock doing these days?" I replied that he was writing a column three times a week and every Sunday for *The New York Times*. "Is that so?" asked the President. "I didn't realize that." Clearly the President doesn't read *The New York Times* and probably little else save westerns and state papers. He went on to say that Krock was a good man and tried to be objective about things. (I later found out from Leviero, our White House reporter, that Krock had been trying to see the President ever since he was inaugurated but had been flatly turned down—as had Scotty Reston.) The President then said, "And you know who another good reporter is—that's that little fellow—what's his name—that little fellow who works—" I asked him if he meant Roscoe Drummond of the *Herald Tribune* (and who pretends to have Ike's ear). He said, "Yes, that's right, Roscoe, that's the fellow I meant." I suppose actually the President merely gets some kind of a White House clipping service and doesn't really read any newspaper.

Finally the President, who was still striding around, began in a rather diplomatic way to walk sort of nearer to the door. I got up and we stood chatting for a few more minutes, and we finally shook hands and I departed.

On the way out I had a brief chat with Tom Stephens. He told me all kinds of screwballs are always trying to get in to the President or to write him letters. Stephens himself had received a letter recently from Pakistan. A Pakistani had read in a newspaper that Stephens was a member of Eisenhower's "kitchen cabinet." He recommended himself as a very good cook and asked if he couldn't come and be Stephens' assistant.

Another time, Stephens said, an extremely presentable and sane-seeming man was brought in by the Secret Service with a note. The Secret Service said the man was obviously screwy, but Stephens wanted to talk with him. The fellow talked with great seriousness and sanity until he developed the subject that he wanted to be President and he thought that Eisenhower should resign immediately in order to make way for him.

WASHINGTON, *November 24, 1953*

THIS afternoon I had a talk with General Matthew Ridgway, the first time I saw him since he took office as Army chief of staff. He looks fit and completely self-contained and sure of himself. He has an enormous topographical map of Europe and the Near East in his office, to which he referred several times during the course of our discussion.

He told me it is absolutely essential for Jugoslavia, Greece and Turkey to coordinate their military planning, and in the end to tie it up with Italy so that Southern Europe can be properly defended. Taking me over to the map, Ridgway pointed out that Salonika and Istanbul must be held against any possible attack. But, to my surprise, he said it was not essential to hold Thrace. In other words, it is obvious the Bulgarians might be permitted to surge through to the Aegean Sea as long as we are in a position to build up pincers on both sides and eventually chop them off.

He emphasized that it was also essential to have Italo-Jugoslav cooperation on planning. Of course, this is still a long way off. Ridgway pointed out that even if and when the Trieste argument is settled, no closer cooperation than joint planning could be expected because Jugoslavia is not in NATO. The same, of course, concerns Jugoslav planning with the NATO members to its south—Greece and Turkey. Likewise, it is imperative to prevent enemy penetration of the Ljubljana Gap in northwestern Jugoslavia. Italy is in no position to try and defend itself again on the Isonzo.

Ridgway said that the old Middle East Defense Organization project has been shelved for good as far as he knows. He also said that no bases have been requested by the United States in Pakistan although we are trying to work out an agreement to strengthen their armed forces.

WASHINGTON, *November 24, 1953*

I dropped in at the Pentagon for a talk with Joe Collins (General J. Lawton Collins), now permanent American representative with the NATO Standing Group, and formerly United States Army Chief of Staff.

He told me there is a secret agreement between the United States and NATO providing that there will be no withdrawals of combat troops now stationed in Europe for a period of ten or twenty years (he didn't know which) without prior consultation between the United States government and NATO's commander-in-chief at the time.

WASHINGTON, *November 24, 1953*

I had a long talk and lunch today with Hank Byroade (Henry A. Byroade, assistant secretary of state in charge of the Near East, Africa and Asia). Among other things, he told me the United States is not asking for any bases in Pakistan. The only thing we are trying to do is to build up Pakistan's military defenses in order to bolster a friendly state. India seems to think that an Asiatic equivalent of our recent Spanish aid-for-bases agreement is contemplated with Pakistan. The Indians have even been talking about an American base in Gilgit, which is a lot of baloney.

There can be no British deals with either Iran (on oil) or Egypt (on Suez) without the United States. We are the people who are trying to mediate and build agreement. We are trying to act as friends of both parties in each case, and it has been rather difficult. There is a very serious fear that if the Suez negotiations do not succeed, an actual war may break out between Egypt and Great Britain. This would presumably commence with guerrilla operations against the British in the Suez area and then spread into formal war. General Naguib realizes that Egypt couldn't win such a war, but he might consider himself forced into it for political reasons and because of the hysterical condition of some of his advisors. This would place the United States in a terribly difficult position. In the end, it is obvious, we would have to support Britain. This might mean the necessity for armed occupation of the whole Arab world with absolutely unforeseeable consequences. Obviously, Russia would make the best of it, and it could indeed mean the beginning of World War III—a beginning under most unfavorable circumstances.

Despite all this, we are frequently being undercut by the British in the Middle East. Certain Englishmen have been assiduously spreading reports throughout Western Asia and Northern Africa that the United States backs Britain in the Middle East under a deal in which Britain has agreed to back the United States in the Far East. This, according to Byroade, is absolutely untrue. I told Hank that he should be aware of the fact that Winthrop Aldrich, now our ambassador in England, told me last spring that he was working for precisely such an overall agreement—namely British support for us in China and the Far East in exchange for our support of them in the Near East. Byroade did know Aldrich was involved in this. My own conclusion is that British policy is clearly aimed at such an overall barter arrangement, and it is likely to be tried out at Bermuda.

Byroade gave me a precise analysis of the status of the negotiations in Suez between Britain and Egypt. He said if the British had only moved fast after the conclusion of the negotiations with Cairo on the Sudan, a Suez agreement could have been arranged easily and some time ago.

The present tentative draft agreement worked out between the Egyptian and British negotiators, but waiting for approval by both governments, provides as follows:

1. A seven-year pact. During this period of seven years from the date of signature, 3,000 British technicians would be permitted to remain in the base area. There is as yet, however, no agreement as to whether these technicians would be allowed to wear British military uniforms or not. The

Egyptians are insisting that they wear mufti. The British are insisting that they wear uniforms, claiming this is necessary, both for reasons of discipline and prestige. We have been counseling the British that perhaps the matter could be solved by having the technicians wear uniforms without any insignia or badge of rank.

2. The present tentative draft envisions the return of the British military to the Suez base in case of an attack by a third power against any Arab state.

3. It envisages immediate consultation between Great Britain and Egypt in case of an attack by a third power on either Turkey or Iran.

4. It has been suggested the United Nations should be permitted to request Egypt to make the base available to Britain in case of emergency. There is a big debate between the British and the Egyptians on this particular point. The Egyptians are very reluctant to give any kind of authority to the UN on this, and the British also foresee potential difficulties.

Israel is now using shrewd diplomacy in an effort to have blame attached to the Arab states for turning down the latest American proposal aimed at paving a way for a Palestine settlement, namely the new Jordan Valley authority that was recently peddled around the Middle East by Eric Johnston. The Israelis are very clever and will always have an advantage over the Arab states on economic know-how. But the Arabs are getting wise to this diplomatic maneuver and therefore are playing a smarter diplomatic game on the JVA business.

Byroade says that one basic change of American policy in the Middle East is that the United States has now ceased the *unconditional* support of Israel, right or wrong, that previously prevailed. He thinks there is more awareness in all American groups, even including American Jewish groups, of the responsibilities of the United States in the Middle East and the need for an unbiased policy. Even the American Zionists understand American responsibilities better now, Byroade says.

One basic requirement of our Middle East policy is to avoid having our European commitments outflanked by a hostile North Africa and Western Asia. Our extensive and costly commitments in Europe would be useless under such conditions.

Israel is already planning long-range irrigation programs as far down as the Negeb, with water from the Jordan, and hopes to go ahead on this regardless of the JVA suggestion. Jordan, on the other hand, is scared that it is not going to get enough water from the Jordan under the American scheme and that Israel is getting too much. Jordan depends upon the Yarmak for its water to a large degree.

Incidentally, Byroade indicated there is some thought of trying to build an eventual alliance bloc—Turkey, Iraq, Iran, Pakistan. I said this was lunacy. Pakistani adherence would automatically throw India (and Afghanistan) against it. This hadn't occurred to Hank. Why not, I suggested, put muscle in a revived Saadabad Pact (Turkey, Iraq, Iran, Afghanistan)? Russia had accepted this group and it would avoid choosing sides in partitioned India.

To my dismay, the assistant secretary had never heard of the Saadabad Pact—which has neither expired nor been denounced.

WASHINGTON, *November 24, 1953*

I had a talk with Bedell (General Walter Bedell Smith, under secretary of state) today. He looked god-awful. Not only does he seem to be sinking every time I see him, in terms of his nonexistent stomach, but he had a bad cold and sore throat. Bedell used to be a stocky man of about 155 pounds. I doubt if he weighs more than 115 today. I don't think I've ever seen a living man who looks so close to being dead.

He hopes that at the Bermuda meeting four basic agreements of a practical nature can be arranged, aside from any tactical decisions vis-à-vis Moscow. He wants agreements on EDC and the relationships of Britain and the United States to the defense community; on a common Anglo-American policy towards China; on a common approach to Suez; and on a settlement with Iran on oil.

I told Bedell I had heard he was about to quit government service and join a private company. He told me he had been offered a job some time ago, but had taken a leave of absence to accept his present job. He said he will terminate that leave of absence, but he is not yet sure when. He figures he has six or seven more years of active work left in his system, and he really needs some money.

I asked him if he was going to Bermuda. He said no, that he had to be the "shopkeeper" while Foster Dulles is away. He then went on and described his job as primarily that of the State Department "shopkeeper."

He asked me what I thought of the chances of EDC and I said I didn't think it would ever get enacted. He then went on to say that he personally thought it would get through, but it was a pretty tough prospect and we had to keep pressing.

I was surprised, incidentally, to see on Bedell's wall an inscribed photograph of the unappetizing Scott McLeod, McCarthy's stooge in the State Department. Maybe the military shouldn't be in government, after all!

WASHINGTON, *November 24, 1953*

THIS afternoon I had a long talk with Foster Dulles. This is the first time I have seen him since he became Secretary of State. He has been in Europe a couple of times as Secretary, but each time I was wandering and missed him. He seemed very relaxed and in good health and humor, although he always has that permanent twitch of the left eye which puts one off a bit. He said he was feeling fine and that hard work agreed with him. This is what he told me:

The United States does not intend to admit Britain into the ANZUS agreement. What Senator Jenner calls "PATO" (a Pacific treaty organization) is not going to be agreed to by this government. We don't want to band together with the old colonial powers in any kind of regional agreement that would lay us open to the charge of joining up with the imperialists. What we are hoping for now is the emergence of some Asian leader who could take the initiative in bringing together an alliance of the free Asian nations which we could support, but which would not be dominated by the western powers.

Syngman Rhee is far too involved politically and emotionally to qualify. Chiang Kai-shek is an *émigré*. After all, he has to demonstrate leadership at home before he can try to be a leader of an international group. The mere fact that he got tossed out of his own country disqualifies him for leadership of an international coalition. Yet there must be someone who can tie together the anti-Communist nations of Asia, Japan, Formosa, Korea, the Associated States of Indochina, and even Indonesia, with its incredibly long set of islands and increasingly feeble central government. Perhaps the best and indeed only, man for the job is Ramon Magsaysay, who has now emerged as a definite Asian personality. He is getting good support from Carlos Romulo who is far better known abroad than he is back in the Philippine Islands and who has considerable foreign experience. However, it is premature to think of counting on Magsaysay. He has lots of homework to do first, cleaning up corruption and trouble in the Philippines.

I asked Dulles if there was any truth in the rumor that we were shifting our policy on China more to accord with the British in the hopes of a split between Mao and Moscow. He said emphatically that we are *not* changing our policy at all and that sharp differences remain between Britain and the United States on the subject of China.

I asked what he foresaw in the nature of agreements at Bermuda. He said he doubted if there would be any important understandings arrived at there. He pointed out that he is not taking any of his State Department regional experts along with him, and that he does not like to make deals or agreements without prior consultation with his experts. Dulles said he is not bound to take the advice of these experts, but he likes to ask it first. He thought that probably the main value of Bermuda would be to give the three sets of leaders a chance to talk things over. Churchill, said Dulles, sprang the idea of Bermuda as a "surprise package," and we "don't yet know what he wants."

Dulles said we expect Bidault to raise the issue of an American pledge to keep our troops in Europe for a specified period of time in order to help the French government to get the EDC treaty ratified by their parliament.

Dulles today assigned some State Department experts to study American commitments in NATO and to review the current debate on NATO in Congress in order to see how far the United States can go in any pledge to France. Dulles doesn't want to make any pledge without the support of Congress. He claimed that President Truman held Congress "in contempt" and the present administration doesn't intend to make any commitments which are not within its legal prerogative and which will not be supported by Congress. Dulles said it might be possible to reword existing United States pledges concerning troops in Europe, such as one not to withdraw contingents now there without first discussing any such proposed withdrawal with the commander-in-chief at SHAPE. Dulles said we would never do that without prior consultation.

Dulles said that it is absolutely essential to American foreign policy that the EDC treaty should be enacted. Under existing United States law (the Richards Amendment) 50 per cent of the present aid program pledged to the six countries supposed to be united under the European Defense Community is pledged to EDC itself as an organization. Not even Eisenhower's prestige can get more aid out of Congress if EDC fails. If it is not enacted, a definite revision of United States foreign policy—especially as it applied to Europe—would almost inevitably be brought about.

Dulles said that as far as Southern Europe goes, we have definitely worked out a policy. As soon as a Trieste settlement can be arranged, every effort will be made to bring about full cooperation between Italy and Jugoslavia and to get Italy's complete adherence to the existing treaty between Greece, Turkey and Jugoslavia. In that way a true link could be established between the East Mediterranean area and the rest of NATO and a political as well as military arrangement.

WASHINGTON, *November 24, 1953*

AT dinner tonight I saw Alice Roosevelt Longworth, and during the course of our chat I mentioned the fact that I had always looked upon her father, Theodore Roosevelt, as the American equivalent to Churchill since he was an author, an adventurer, a soldier and an explorer, to say nothing of having a particular personality flair. She agreed with me, and then added something interesting. She said her father had always hated Churchill during the years he knew him. This was not only because Roosevelt and Churchill fought on different sides during the Spanish-American War, but because Churchill in his younger days had been arrogant, rude and generally insufferable—very much as Randolph is, unfortunately, so much of the time nowadays. This, above all, Teddy Roosevelt detested.

NEW YORK, *November 27, 1953*

AVERELL Harriman gave a lunch for King Paul and Queen Frederika, who are making a propaganda tour. I must say the Queen is getting pretty good at putting on a snow job suited to the country she is in. She ought to work for Batten, Barton, Durstine & Osborne. She said she had been greatly impressed by the unity of the United States, and she made the good point that although differences among us may appear great to Americans, they are not very great to Europeans. She emphasized that despite the immensity of the United States, the accent, the appearance and the standard of living were remarkably harmonious. She thought the spiritual faith of the United States was much greater than we ourselves realized, and that we were the only country to give the "power and the glory" to the free world which was necessary to achieve its unity.

The King had relatively little to say because although the Queen always referred to the opinion of "my husband," she did most of the talking. Nevertheless, he did tell one story about his trip to California. He said that at one small town a boy had come up to him and asked him, dead earnest, "Say, King, who's going to be king when you're out?"

The King and Queen were not very interesting; but that is not their business. The King recalled, as the gents sipped brandy together afterwards, a conversation between "my wife" and Moše Pijade of Jugoslavia. He said Pijade had described himself to the Queen as a materialist. According to King Paul, the Queen replied that she understood this very well; she had had the same beliefs when she was fifteen years old; but she got over them. I somehow think that in an intellectual battle the Greek royal family would not overwhelm the Jugoslav Politburo.

Averell was quite interesting on politics. He and Marie wanted to know all about my visit with the Eisenhowers. They were both still affectionately inclined to Ike and Mamie despite the rather bitter political dispute that has arisen. They recalled the sixtieth birthday parties of each of them (which I attended) and would clearly like to be buddies again. But that seems a long way off. He said the last political talk he had had with Eisenhower was in October 1951 when they were both in Paris. He says he told Ike at the time that if Truman or another good Democrat were to run for President, he, Harriman, would back him. Ike had told Averell he was a Republican. Averell said he appreciated this and that he hoped that if they had to arrive on opposite sides during the election they would remain friends.

He says that in June 1952, he spoke on the telephone with Ike for the last time. That was in Denver when Averell was campaigning for the Democratic nomination. He said Ike was very warm on the telephone, but his political advisors counseled him not to see Harriman.

Averell said he had utter contempt for Foster Dulles as an individual and as a Secretary of State although he admired and liked Allen. He considers Bedell Smith an excellent and loyal public servant who sometimes, thanks to his army training, blindly follows policies he personally does not believe in.

Averell claims that Dulles has been forced to support a foreign policy which is that of the previous Democratic administrations. Nevertheless, he thinks Dulles has been shockingly bad in the cases of Israel and Trieste. Furthermore, he can't forgive Dulles for "handing over the foreign service to McCarthy—through McLeod."

TUCKER'S TOWN, *December 3, 1953*

HERE in Bermuda with a large staff on the strange mission of covering a secret conference for a strike-bound newspaper. All I learn is useless.

I had a drink with Frank Roberts yesterday evening and a walk with him and Denis Allen, British East Asia expert, this afternoon. Frank said the British delegation had carefully ascertained whether Ike was bringing his golf clubs. When they learned to their disappointment he wasn't, no Englishman brought his; and Churchill left his paints behind.

Frank said the Russians "made" this conference. There would have been virtually nothing to do if they hadn't proposed the four-power Berlin meeting. Now Bermuda can produce an answer. It is interesting to hear Roberts, an Englishman, say: "otherwise the conference would be purposeless; it is Winston's baby." Roberts said the agreement for Britain's "association" with EDC has been just about negotiated. It doesn't satisfy the French but is the best that can be produced. He thinks it is pretty good.

Hervé Alphand says what France wants from the United States is not a written pledge that our six divisions will remain for a fixed period in Europe but an announcement that ours is a "European strategy" and that we are committed to the defense of Europe. This of course is implicit in NATO. Alphand confirms that in 1951 NATO agreed that no member nation could reduce its forces without prior "consultation" with the commander-in-chief. However, there is a difference between consultation and approval.

TUCKER'S TOWN, *December 5, 1953*

I had drinks today with Walter Robertson, the State Department's Far Eastern expert. Robertson says he was called here suddenly and to his great surprise. Apparently things are so badly coordinated that nobody knows who is around. Robertson said the first time he saw Eisenhower, the President shook hands with him and said, "Hello, Robbie, it's good to see you. I had no idea that you were coming."

Incidentally, Hank Byroade, who is also here, was called upon at the last minute. Dulles told me last week in Washington he was not going to take any experts. Obviously he changed his mind. But both Byroade and Robertson say they weren't told until about forty-eight hours before their arrival.

TUCKER'S TOWN, *December 6, 1953*

SIR Frank Roberts told me today the Big Three have advised Russia they are prepared to meet at a foreign ministers' conference in Berlin on January 4. Adenauer cabled the Bermuda conferees through their capitals today that he was in accord with the idea. It is rather interesting to note how big a role he plays even in his absence.

Roberts says Churchill and Eisenhower are the ones who have insisted on absolute secrecy concerning the conversations here. The Frenchman Baeyens (Quai d'Orsay spokesman) leaked like a sieve to the French correspondents on the first evening of the conference, so the Big Two administered a proper bawling out to Bidault and Laniel. Laniel promptly fell ill, but I believe his fever is real, not diplomatic.

TUCKER'S TOWN, *December 8, 1953*

HERVÉ Alphand dropped into the room this morning. He said that what France really wants is some form of assurance from the United States and Britain that we will not denounce the NATO treaty after its automatic features terminate following the first twenty years of its existence. France is not asking that the NATO treaty be renegotiated to run for fifty years and thus be equivalent to EDC. The French realize this might be difficult, above all in terms of the United States Senate. But they do want some kind of a pledge not to make use of the privilege of denouncing after twenty years.

Hervé says Bidault has been very strong on NATO and adapting the treaty to the new situation of the world. NATO, he thinks, should recognize existing capabilities and take into account the effect of new weapons. Bidault told the British and the Americans that France would insist on retaining its membership in the three-power Standing Group of NATO even after EDC is ratified. He argued that the Standing Group coordinates European strategy with that of Asia and Africa as well, and that France as a world power therefore would have to keep its position there.

TUCKER'S TOWN, *December 8, 1953*

THIS morning Dulles said there had been few concrete issues "to which we could direct ourselves" during these Bermuda talks. He described the conference as "Churchill's inspiration." He said it wasn't designed to resolve concrete problems. After the conference was called, the Soviet Union reversed its tactics on a proposed four-power meeting in Berlin, and therefore this became the one concrete issue of the Bermuda talks. It was resolved, and agreed texts were sent on by the three Western powers. The character of their reply was such as to indicate that an early meeting is probable. It leaves few excuses for evasion by Moscow.

The other concrete matter was the President's United Nations address. The present Assembly is to recess shortly, and Eisenhower had been under strong pressure to speak there. The British and the French approved the idea of his speech, although they did not edit the text. In fact, the text still remains to be completed aboard the plane today. However, the approach and subject both pleased the British and the French.

TUCKER'S TOWN, *December 8, 1953*

HANK Byroade dropped by for a drink. He said Eden and Dulles will again discuss Egypt on the side in Paris during the NATO meeting. Byroade warned Dulles that this question has got to be solved within the next few weeks or otherwise the Egyptians are going to stir up trouble. Byroade admits this is a serious political problem for Churchill because of the fight in the Tory party. There is still a wide area of disagreement between the United States and Britain on the Middle East. Byroade says Nasser is getting stronger all the time in Egypt. However Hank is convinced that Nasser wants a deal on Suez.

Later Ismay stopped in. He says the trouble with this Bermuda conference is that it has no agenda, nor has it any conference secretariat to keep people advised as to what is going on. As a result all kinds of important delegates spend hours cooling their heels and twiddling their thumbs without knowing whether they are wanted during the day's proceedings or not. Ismay is here for the purpose of protecting the other eleven NATO members against any decisions which might affect them when the Big Three discuss NATO matters. Ismay complained there are not even any official minutes taken of the conference.

Ismay says Britain and the United States cannot give France an absolute guarantee concerning the pledge to maintain a fixed number of divisions in Europe until the French do something concrete about EDC. You cannot put the cart before the horse. He recalls that as France was collapsing, the French government requested Britain to make available to France *all* its squadrons of fighters in the Royal Air Force. If it could have been proven to the British that this would have won the battle of France, it would have been worth doing. However, the British calculated that by acceding to the French request both the battle of France and the eventual battle of Britain would be lost. Therefore they turned it down. In a like fashion, some sort of positive French action and guarantee is required before further Anglo-American pledges should be made.

Ismay does not think this Bermuda conference is useful. He calls it vague and inconclusive and adds that it cannot guarantee anything. In his own inimitable argot he remarks, "This meeting is a sod."

Ismay said it is terribly dangerous to depend upon intelligence reports for estimates of the enemy's strength or intentions. He cites as an example the case of Italian Northeast Africa. During that campaign it was discovered that the Italian defenses were nowhere near as strong as British intelligence had estimated. To confirm and emphasize this point, Churchill ordered that a one-page study be made. In one column was a most concise statement of British estimates of Italian defenses at particular strategic points. In the other column was an equally concise statement of what the British actually found after they conquered these points. The contrast was remarkable.

TUCKER'S TOWN, *December 9, 1953*

LUNCH with Hank Byroade, assistant secretary of state for the Middle East and Africa. He is very discouraged and foresees a gloomy future in his area.

Byroade fears imminent disaster in Egypt. He has only had a chance to speak briefly to Dulles since he came to Bermuda and saw the President but for a moment at a large dinner party. In other words, he really didn't get his views across to anybody. Nor does he quite know the President's views—above all, whether Eisenhower really wants to push for a military assistance agreement with Pakistan or not. Byroade was wondering whether he shouldn't stay here another day in order to confer with Eden and settle things which he hasn't had a chance to discuss yet. He says he gets on very well with Eden and knows him well; that they understand each other. He very much fears that before January 1 the Egyptians are going to start guerrilla operations against the British forces in the Canal Zone, and the situation might very well deteriorate into formal war. In that case, of course, we would have to stand by the British who are our allies. Byroade muttered the last with singular regret.

He said the subject of the Middle East had only been discussed briefly at France's request here. Bidault said France would like to be present during the discussion. France is, of course, interested in the Suez Canal as a major owner of the company. At this Big Three session Eden briefly stated the British position. Eisenhower then asked, "Does anybody else have anything to say?" There was silence. The President then said, "Okay, let's have lunch. I'm hungry."

Byroade said he deeply mistrusted the series of secret tête-à-tête conversations in bathing suits on the beach between Dulles and Eden. He feared Dulles was too ignorant on the subject of the Middle East and that Eden might get away with things.

This evening I had a chat with Captain Christopher Soames, Churchill's son-in-law and parliamentary private secretary. I last saw Soames at his house on Churchill's estate at Chartwell. His wife, Mary Churchill, is extremely agreeable and attractive. I cannot say the same for Soames. He has a petulant, arrogant manner, is very touchy.

He told me Churchill was extremely angry at a story he saw today that said Churchill and Lord Cherwell had given complete approval to the text of Eisenhower's speech on atomic energy. The story quoted Jim Hagerty on this. Churchill immediately saw the danger that would be created in American minds at the thought that a British Prime Minister was having American Presidents' speeches submitted to him for approval before they were made.

Soames also said Churchill was furious at the official French "leak" a couple of days ago. Baeyens, former French ambassador to Chile and now press officer at the Quai d'Orsay, told French correspondents here in some detail and with quotes the main substance of the first day's discussion on Soviet Russia. According to Soames, the old man really blew his top at this, and he and Eisenhower not only bawled out the French for leaking but clamped down strict orders to all delegation members that everything discussed must be kept secret.

I had drinks and a long talk this evening with Anthony Eden. He looks exceptionally thin but on the whole rather healthy, full of energy and with good color. I would estimate that he has lost fifteen or twenty pounds since I last saw him, but he is possibly in better health, despite the fact that he never was in the least bit stout. This evening he was full of enthusiasm and talk and was slightly pickled. He had the following to say:

Eisenhower's speech is really a great speech. Churchill did not like some phrases in it. He considered them a bit too menacing. He told this to Ike and they were eliminated. The general purport of the speech was given by Eisenhower to the British and French together here. But the text was not shown to the French. The text was sent up to Churchill in his suite. Then Sir Winston lay down on his bed, and Eden stretched out on a sofa while a member of their staff read the whole text. Churchill agreed with Eden that it was a fine address.

This Bermuda conference has accomplished little. The bathing parties of Eden and Dulles together were actually much more important. The two men got to know each other increasingly well. Eden professes to like Dulles a lot and finds him a good man to work with. Their exchange of views has been exceedingly valuable. Eden however confided that he detests Hank Byroade. He says Byroade knows absolutely nothing about the Middle East. "He has only spent five minutes there." (Eden, after all, majored and took honors in the Persian language when he was at Oxford and has been dealing with the Middle East for many, many years.) He regards Byroade as rather a smart aleck. He also strongly dislikes Jefferson Caffery, our ambassador in Cairo, and contends he is anti-British. I argued this point with him, but he says he is convinced of it. On the other hand, he has great respect and liking for Loy Henderson, our ambassador in Iran.

Eden said he and Dulles had actually reached an essential agreement on China. Each recognizes the other's internal political problems. Dulles saw clearly that Britain cannot "de-recognize" the Peking government. On the other hand, Eden saw perfectly clearly why the United States could not "re-recognize" China. Eden said he quite understood what an important role China had always played in American history since the days of the Yankee Clippers. Many American individual traders and clergymen had spent their lives in China. Many fortunes had been made there. In a sense it was like the British tradition in the Sudan over the years—something, Eden added, that was not generally understood in the United States.

Returning to the subject of the meeting, he described it as "Winston's conference." He said it had no real use. Most of the time, as far as three-power meetings had been concerned, was devoted to the tripartite note replying to the Russians on the proposed Berlin conference and to Ike's speech. Eden said Bidault spoke too much, too often and for too long a time on subjects "we all knew about anyway."

When I brought up the subject of Egypt, Eden half jumped off the sofa we were sitting on, splashing his drink on his suit. It is obviously something he is really worked up on. He admitted that there were only two points at issue between London and Cairo, but he said these were all-important and Britain could make no further concessions. He said the issue of uniforms for the British technicians to remain in the base area if an agreement is signed is not merely a matter of prestige. He did admit that it was very important in terms of the political situation at home where Julian Amery and other young Tories are making a terrific fight and threatening to split the Conservative Party over the subject of concessions to Egypt, which they oppose. But, Eden went on, uniforms are important in order to protect the troops. Status-of-forces agreements must be signed between Britain and Egypt to cover these technicians. These would protect them from being arrested arbitrarily and otherwise molested by the Egyptians. Obviously the technicians would have to be military men because the British government simply could not afford to pay high enough wages to attract technicians from private concerns to live in the disagreeable Suez area. After all, American airmen in Libya wore uniforms and were protected by similar status-of-forces agreements. Eden argues that Egypt would accept this point of view if the United States really pushed them.

He says this is not the basic issue but is being used by Egypt to obscure the most important point which is the agreement on Britain's military "reentry" into the Zone in case of crisis. The Egyptians are trying to obscure the latter with all kinds of phrases about "consultation," and so forth. This means nothing. Dulles, Eden said, had written out a formula last spring governing reentry which would still be perfectly acceptable to Britain. But it is no longer acceptable to Cairo, and American policy seems to have changed. He admitted that Byroade had shown a new formula for reentry to Sir Pierson Dixon, but he dismissed this with a gesture as "silly."

He said Britain would indeed be glad to have its troops out of Egypt. More than two divisions (totaling approximately 80,000 men) are now stationed in the Suez Canal Zone, while the United Kingdom itself is bare of defense.

Eden said the only alternative base to Suez in the whole area is Cyprus. (In my opinion this is a lot of crap. It is impossible to make a decent base on Cyprus. It would mean that every time a truck had to be repaired it would have to be shipped out. The four main ports of Cyprus—none of which is any good—are all dominated by Communists. The British obviously know that no decent base can be made in Cyprus, and that is why, despite a couple of survey parties, they have never built a single decent installation there since the end of World War II.)

LONDON, *December 11, 1953*

I flew back from Bermuda today on the same plane with Ismay. We had several conversations aboard. He told me Great Britain admired General Marshall enormously and felt he was more responsible than any single man for the build-up of the United States forces that fought in World War II. Nevertheless, Pug thought Marshall was a very bad strategist. He had old-fashioned ideas of always wanting to get straight at the enemy regardless of over-all strategic requirements. Thus, Marshall opposed the North African campaign, although Ismay considers it was probably the most important strategic campaign conducted by the West during the war. Incidentally, Ismay commented regretfully that he thought Eisenhower had aged ten years during his less than one year in the White House.

PARIS, *December 15, 1953*

THIS evening Dulles said the reaction of the French press to his press conference of December 13 was about what he had expected. He threatened an "agonizing reappraisal" of American policy if EDC fails. He had arrived at the conclusion that EDC was dead unless shock treatment was administered. It was necessary to get across to the French people that this is a serious state of affairs. The government and parliament had allowed the project to drag along. "I was advised to use shock treatment," he said, "in order to get across to the country and to parliament."

Dulles pointed out that almost nine years have elapsed since the armistice.

Germany is still occupied. France has not yet even ratified the proposed contractual agreements with Germany, much less EDC. There are an increasing number of French people who say they would rather have Germany in NATO than have an EDC. But this is a mere excuse. Once EDC is out, they would change their minds. They also say they would like Germany in NATO under certain restrictions. But the Germans won't accept such restrictions which would make them a second-class power. Anyway, Chancellor Adenauer is against all thoughts of a German national army.

He insisted the United States was not just thinking of German divisions, but was primarily interested in ending the suicidal strife between France and Germany which had so often undermined Europe. If a European political community (EPC) came through, there would be no trouble in getting Congress to change the Richards Amendment. An EPC could then act as a roof for EDC and the European Coal and Steel Community (Schuman Plan). As now conceived, however, EDC and EPC are interlocked, and it is too late to change.

He thought that if Europe became available to the Soviet Union, it would shift the balance of world power and "menace our safety." He described Europe as, in the past, "the world's worst fire hazard." He said that always "others" had been called to put it out. He said it was imperative to prevent another war. That would disclose the "bankruptcy of our statesmanship." However, he added, "We cannot lightly abandon Europe. But we cannot cling to a Europe which will again be a source of war."

Paris, *December 16, 1953*

I had a chat with Paul Van Zeeland, Belgian foreign minister, this morning. He told me at great length about his so-called "Van Zeeland Plan" to neutralize Germany. The idea would be to withdraw all British and American troops to positions west of the Rhine and all Soviet troops to positions east of the Vistula. Germany would be garrisoned by EDC troops.

I pointed out that there is no room in Europe west of the Rhine for ten and a half British and American divisions. He said his plan would allow for that. The dividing line could be moved twenty-five miles east of the Rhine, and commensurately the Soviet strategic border could be moved twenty-five miles west of the Vistula; or any other agreed distances. He said the plan would have the virtue of guaranteeing not to increase the strength of EDC for a fixed period of years. It would reassure Russia that Germany was not going to have more than twelve divisions (within EDC), and France would likewise be comforted. On the other hand, it would represent *de facto* Russian recognition of EDC.

Van Zeeland said it was imperative to do something quickly about EDC, or Germany, more than eight years after the end of World War II, was going to assert its national rights regardless of the wishes of other countries. He said the present German government was sincerely desirous of avoiding militarism or excessive nationalism. However, the trend in Germany was to the right and if we were to check it, we would have to move now.

Van Zeeland says he hasn't officially submitted his plan to NATO or anyone else but has distributed it to "friends." He says the only copy he gave Americans he gave to Dulles. He claims his plan is being considered by the Big Three working party preparing for the quadripartite Foreign Ministers' Council meeting in Berlin.

PARIS, *December 16, 1953*

I lunched today with Panayotis Canellopoulos, Greek Minister of Defense. He told me that last month in their meeting in Belgrade the Jugoslavs, Greeks, and Turks had agreed in substance on a vitally important military understanding. For purposes of defense the three countries agreed that they will react together against any aggression within an area of "common interest." This area means the frontier of any one of the three states with Bulgaria. In other words, if there is an attack by Bulgaria or through Bulgaria against any one of the three members, the three will act together against such an attack.

The understanding is quite precise. For example, if Russia should attack Turkey on its Caucasus border, Jugoslavia would not be bound to help Turkey although Greece, as a NATO ally, would. Similarly, if Russia through Rumania and Hungary (or either of those countries) should attack Jugoslavia directly and not through Bulgaria, Greece and Turkey would not be obligated automatically to help Jugoslavia.

Although Albania has common frontiers with both Greece and Jugoslavia, it is deliberately left out of the agreement. It is not felt that there is any threat from Albania nor is there any possibility, even with Russian aid, of an attack coming from there.

Another point of the accord is that there is now an informal but pretty precise arrangement which in effect eliminates the "military frontier" between Greece and Jugoslavia. That means, for example, that Greek reconnaissance teams can come up and survey the Jugoslav-Bulgarian border whenever they want to. This is of particular interest because it was primarily by penetration of Jugoslavia from Southern Bulgaria that Germany was able to come in 1941 and attack Salonika and Florina directly.

PARIS, *December 17, 1953*

I went out to Versailles today to see the rat race involving election of France's new President for seven years. Unlike most countries, in France the whole performance is preceded by a magnificent lunch; all the big shots except for the party whips gathered in the Hotel Trianon Palace to eat lobster and drink champagne. Afterwards most leading figures in parliament took care to wander in and out of the press corridors of the palace to hobnob with assembled journalists. When I left at about 3:45 P.M., the first ballot had started. The general dope was that the Catholic Church had decided at the last minute that they simply had to have Bidault. None of the other candidates in the lists could be tolerated by the church. Therefore priests were running madly in all directions lining up votes in the hope that he would either crash through on the first ballot or at any rate establish such a huge lead that he would inevitably win through on the second ballot. As a result, all the supporters of Vincent Auriol, who, no matter what he says, seems to be ready to run for reelection, were rushing around trying to persuade people who under no circumstances would want him to be elected to throw their ballots to Joseph Laniel. The idea would be that any vote cast for Laniel would steal a vote from Bidault. When the deadlock was established, Auriol could forge through. It is interesting to recollect that the last time I had a good talk with Bidault, October 29, he berated me for writing that he was a candidate for the presidency and swore up and down that he wouldn't dream of becoming a candidate. (René Coty was elected as a compromise.)

I had a long talk with Robert Schuman. He was worried and angered by Dulles' remarks here on "agonizing reappraisal" and only hoped they wouldn't do much harm. He hoped that in fifteen days they would be forgotten and after all there won't be a government for another month. It was very lacking in taste for Dulles to make these remarks in the manner he did in the capital of France, laying down the law to Frenchmen in their own country, more or less as if they were subject people. He deeply resented such "interference" and tears came into his rheumy eyes.

Nevertheless Schuman said he remained quite optimistic about EDC. A united front government must and would be formed in January comprising MRP, Socialist, Radical and Independent–Peasant ministers. This government would have to announce in the most forthright fashion that its priority task was ratification of EDC, and it could then be pushed through. But, for heaven's sake, Schuman said, the Americans must leave us alone to do this ourselves. We will get the ratification through even though we may not be able to do it in quite as much of a hurry as Washington hopes. I told Schuman the story of what Adenauer had related to me last time I was in Bonn concerning a missing letter that Schuman had written to Adenauer, pledging a solution of the Saar. Schuman said this was not true. He said Adenauer had written to him on March 18, 1952, outlining a solution of the Saar dispute on which France and Germany should agree. This was fairly early in the negotiations and the situation had evolved a great deal

since then. He was sure Adenauer could not possibly adhere to the solution
he outlined in March of 1952, nor would it be acceptable to France at
present. Schuman said he did not reply to this letter in writing but merely
gave his views to Adenauer orally a few times afterwards. He retained the
copy of Adenauer's letter which was personal and therefore not in French
government files.

PARIS, *December 21, 1953*

I had dinner last night at Sardar Hardit Singh Malik's (he is Indian
ambassador). As I was leaving, he took me into a corner for a long
discussion of Pakistani-Indian relationships and stressed how unwise India
thought it was for the United States to make any kind of a military aid
agreement with Pakistan. Malik said anything that upset the military balance of power existing between India and Pakistan was dangerous and the
Pakistanis were openly talking about their desire to march on to Delhi. I
asked him if it was true that India was actually seeking arms from Russia
in the event of an American-Pakistani agreement. He implied the affirmative.

PARIS, *December 21, 1953*

I had lunch today with Bob Barnes (later an American ambassador),
assistant secretary general of NATO. He agreed with me that if Russia
doesn't make any hostile move within eighteen months, NATO will probably collapse. The United States is cutting its budget ruthlessly, and regardless of what lip service they pay, the European countries are ready to
follow suit. Barnes said there is no leadership in NATO today.

He remembers when Dean Acheson used to come to NATO meetings
and exerted a magnetic influence upon the proceedings. If a discussion took
place, for example, between the Dutch and the Belgians on some minor
point Acheson would sit there taking notes and when it was all over, he
would contribute his brilliant analysis of the point of view of each participant and then add his own third point of view. Nowadays if there is a
debate of that sort, Dulles sits there with a dead look on his face, doodling.

Nobody—and that includes Eden, Mike Pearson, Lange or any of the
other so-called bright boys—contributes anything. Everybody is just glad
to get the meeting over and done with. Everybody makes a lot of promises,
few of which are likely to materialize. The thing that appalled Barnes more
than anything was the sweet and reasonable American promises on defense and financial contributions and the clear-cut American pledges in the
annual review which, according to every indication coming out from Washington, aren't going to be carried through.

Another complication of NATO's legal cobweb involves the use of atomic weapons for defense. For example, if Bulgaria were to attack Jugo-slavia (and Greece and Turkey came to the aid of Jugoslavia) NATO would not be obliged automatically to help its allies, Greece and Turkey. However, if the Bulgars, deciding to attack Jugoslavia, also attacked Greek Thrace, NATO would be obliged to come in under Article 5.

In those terms General Gruenther could order Admiral Fechteler to give the fullest support immediately to the Greeks and the Turks. He could do this as Supreme Allied Commander, Europe. However, he could not give Fechteler any orders to use atomic weapons in defense of the Greeks and the Turks. Permission to do as much would have to be given him by President Eisenhower, instructing General Gruenther as Commander-in-Chief of United States Forces, Europe. Therefore a series of legalistic problems still remains in the alliance structure and could conceivably slow up action for a period of fatal duration in case of war.

PARIS, *December 30, 1953*

THIS afternoon I had an excellent talk and a cup of tea with René Pleven, minister of defense, over in his office in the defense ministry on the rue St. Dominique. He said France is cutting its budgetary contributions to NATO by less than 1 per cent although the over-all defense budget has been considerably reduced. The main reductions are in Indochina where the United States has taken over an increasing share of expenses. Pleven said:

I am worried about the trend of United States policy—but not more than I was a year ago. Eisenhower was elected on a program of reduced expenditures. A year ago at the NATO meeting I warned the American representatives of the difficulty of preventing Europe from following such a trend. I recognize that any budget of the size of the United States defense budget can be reduced by many millions without touching essentials. You can cut away the fat. But the United States should not reduce its expenditures on research. Furthermore you must adhere to your NATO commitments. Under such conditions I am watchful but not panicky.

Pleven is convinced there cannot be a purely military decision in Indo-china. He said he did not know exactly what Dulles meant when the Secretary of State said he had military information that the Indochina war would be ended sometime in 1954.

PARIS, *January 3, 1954*

I dined last night with Al Gruenther. It was a most informal, bridge-playing evening, but during the course of it Gruenther expressed a few views of interest, for example:

Italy is now definitely the weak link in NATO. The Italian political crisis is causing serious concern. There is worry about whether Italy will be able to establish a strong and truly democratic government without depending to some degree upon extreme left-wing support. Al recalls that when he saw the Duke of Edinburgh at the time of the coronation in England, he told him jokingly that he and the Queen had been sabotaging NATO by performing their job so well. Al pointed out that the Italian election came right after the coronation and De Gasperi failed to obtain the necessary majority by only a few thousand votes. The Monarchist vote was many times higher than had been predicted, and some people thought this was a result of the highly advertised British coronation. Gruenther thinks it is absolutely imperative for the Trieste question to be settled so that Jugoslav and Italian defense plans can be coordinated.

Gruenther is very impressed by former King Leopold of Belgium and his wife, the Princess de Réthy. When Al and Grace were up in Brussels, the Belgian Embassy here had arranged that he should express the desire to King Baudouin to meet Baudouin's "family." He didn't even have to make this suggestion, as Baudouin raised the subject himself. The Gruenthers then met Leopold and his wife and liked them a great deal.

PARIS, *January 5, 1954*

A top-level security meeting was held yesterday by the permanent NATO staff to investigate a story I wrote concerning a NATO analysis of Soviet policy. The story was published just after the last NATO Council meeting in December. Richard (Lord) Coleridge, the permanent secretary in the Secretariat, wanted to request the American government to have me prosecuted for security violations. He insisted there must be some American law on the books under which they could "get" me. It was pointed out to Coleridge that no such law existed and that the culprit, if any, would be the person who made the document available. It was decided that the story as read probably indicated that I had had access to the document in question, but it couldn't be proved in court. The general consensus seemed to be that I had gotten the information from the American delegation, so a strong protest is now being forwarded to Ambassador John C. Hughes.

Ismay is away sick, and Deputy Secretary General Henri Van Vredenbruch, who acts as boss when the secretary general is absent, was thumbing through some press clippings of the last few weeks and came upon my own by accident. He sent it on to the security chief, Brunet, a former Royal Canadian Mounted Policeman, demanding action.

THIS morning I went to the Bank of France and had a good talk with Wilfrid Baumgartner, the governor and one of the leading Protestants of this predominantly Catholic country. He has been a government official ever since he was an inspector of finance in 1925. He received his present job in 1949. He said there were some people who wanted to get him out of the Bank of France because his policy has been inconveniently tough as far as certain politicians are concerned.

We had a long discussion about Soviet gold sales in Western Europe. He said that for more than three months these sales had been taking place in bulk. The Russians started off by buying agricultural produce, above all in Denmark, the Netherlands and France. They are also acquiring sterling in the United Kingdom. They had few dollars available and therefore had to pay gold for all this. Original calculations by the Russians, who, he said, are good bankers, were made on the basis of then prevailing gold prices in Tangier, Zurich and Beirut. Gold was then on a premium in those markets. Since then the Russians have had to sell more gold and at Bank of England parity rates. He thought the consequences of the Russian sales, which have now totaled well over $100 million, were on the whole good. These he described as: (1) The premium of gold over the dollar has disappeared. Thus, Moscow has strengthened the dollar in Europe. (2) A small but definite reenforcement has been given to Europe's gold reserves. (3) The weak trend in various gold markets as prices dropped with Russian sales has resulted in making hoarding less profitable.

Baumgartner doesn't think the Russian action is designed to hurt the capitalistic world. As a matter of fact, it only serves to reenforce the position of Western banks. None of Europe's central banks are accepting Soviet bar gold, which first has to be transformed into ingots approved by reputable firms in either Amsterdam or London.

LONG talk this morning with the affable but not very inspiring Laniel, who remains prime minister. He was extremely cordial, although throughout his conversation rather bitter references to his recent defeat at the Versailles elections for the presidency of the Republic crept in. I arrived at the Hotel de Matignon twenty-five minutes early, but much to my surprise was immediately received. I gather the prime minister doesn't have a great deal to do these days. His health seemed to be entirely restored (after the Bermuda breakdown), and he sat talking away, puffing one of those heavy yellow-papered French cigarettes out of the corner of his mouth with ashes occasionally drifting down over his more than ample chest and belly.

I told him that when I had seen President Eisenhower just before the

Bermuda conference, he had spoken of his feeling that the Communist Party should be outlawed. The President had later taken some action on this in the United States. I asked him if Eisenhower had brought the matter up in any way at Bermuda. Laniel said that of course he had been ill at Bermuda, but surely on a matter of such importance Bidault would have mentioned the subject to him. He said that during the meetings he attended with Eisenhower and Churchill it certainly had not been discussed and that he was confident it had not been mentioned during his absence on a sick-bed. He went on to say that the Communist problem was a very grave menace in France but he didn't see what could be done about it right now. Under existing laws the Communist Party was entirely legal, and he did not think it was possible to change France's legal structure. The Communists had many friends and allies now, as had appeared during the Versailles presidential election. Whenever there was a secret ballot these friendships and alliances showed up, although they did not appear in open votes. By implication Laniel was a bit sour on the system of secret ballots. He thought the Communists were working very hard to promote some form of popular front here and again referred to their support of Naegelen in the elections.

He said that nothing serious had emerged so far in the form of official Russian hints to official French representatives that they could make a peace for France in Indochina or do other favors in order to split France off from the West. Laniel had read a good deal on this subject in the newspapers but nothing had come through in any talks with the Russians. However the new Soviet ambassador here, Vinogradov, was the most smiling Russian envoy that has been seen around here in years. Furthermore, he gave a large box of caviar to Laniel during the recent holidays. The prime minister thought that Bidault and all the cabinet members had received similar gifts. However Laniel said he was not going to fall for any of this soft Russian line. He thought the Russians would tend to devote a good deal of time at Berlin to trying to split France and the United States. For the rest he thought the conference in Berlin was going to be a propaganda contest.

He said that at Bermuda he and Bidault had explained to the British and the Americans that they required some form of official guarantee that the Americans and the British were not going to pull their troops out of Europe when EDC was formed. Furthermore, they wanted some form of assurance that the United States and Britain were not going to denounce NATO which expires thirty years earlier than EDC. These things have not been crystallized and will have to be negotiated. It was agreed that such promises would be most valuable if made public when the question of ratification finally arose in the assembly. Laniel said he intends to push for ratification right after Berlin. He said he told Sir Winston at Bermuda that had the British pledged only one division as part of the EDC ground forces, the whole project would have gone through now. He could not understand why the British, who are only a little further away from the danger of aggression than France, could not commit themselves to this one symbolic contribution. Churchill replied rather grumpily that at the moment the British had only one brigade in the United Kingdom.

He said the military situation in Indochina was going a bit better now. He thought that in five or six months new Vietnamese units would be available for operation. (This seems to contradict a bit what Pleven said to me the other day on the subject.) Laniel said he certainly hoped to be able to get a negotiated peace in Indochina, but until such a peace was likely, the French had to fight as hard as possible. He did not think it would be possible to negotiate with either Ho Chi Minh or the Chinese. You would have to go right up to the Russians. After all, he said, that is what happened in the case of Korea. He complained that if it were not for Indochina France would not have an inferiority complex vis-à-vis Germany in the European army. However, he added, "all my cadres" are tied up in Indochina. He said that the Vietminh had absolutely no air power and therefore France must make the best possible use of its advantage in the air. For this reason he was requesting more bombers and transport aircraft from the United States. There was no question whatsoever of asking for American troops or personnel.

PARIS, *January 15, 1954*

I had lunch today with an extraordinary American who, I must say, strengthens my faith in the country. He is Gerold M. Lauck, an elderly, retired advertising man and friend of my father, who, incidentally, was responsible (by introducing me to the head of Scripps-Howard) for getting me my first newspaper job in Pittsburgh. Lauck is a rotund, merry-looking little man who resembles Santa Claus without a beard. I should guess he is about seventy years old. Fourteen years ago he decided he would learn French. Therefore at his home in Princeton, he taught himself the language by reading a French edition of Franz Werfel's *The Song of Bernadette* with the aid of a dictionary. Although he speaks with an atrocious accent, he obviously knows the language pretty well now because, during the last few years, he has translated several books from French into English. When he was snowbound by a blizzard a few years after the war, he read a story in a French magazine by the Dominican priest Father Bruckberger. He was so taken with the story that he wanted his wife to read it. His wife speaks no French so he translated it. He wrote Bruckberger asking if he could have the translation printed privately to send out as a Christmas present. Bruckberger said of course but suggested that he have it printed by a regular publisher. He knew one of the McGraw-Hill people and sent him the manuscript. The book was published and sold more than 35,000 copies. Since then he has translated some of Bruckberger's other writings and has become a good friend of the remarkable French priest and Maquis leader who is now living in the United States. (Apparently Bruckberger was far too much of an individualist for the Catholic hierarchy in France and especially for the Dominican order, so they exiled him first to Morocco and then to the United States.) I was also interested to note that Lauck, who has been living in Spain for the last several months, knew all about Pio Baroja and his writings. Lauck is an unpretentious little man but absolutely first class and is now enjoying his old age with great enthusiasm in an apartment on the Ile St. Louis filled with Rouaults.

PARIS, *January 15, 1954*

I had a talk this afternoon with Hervé Alphand concerning the future of EDC. If EDC fails, Alphand says his career is wrecked, so he certainly takes more than a passing interest in it. He said he hoped there could be some kind of an arrangement between the Big Three and NATO for consultation in case at any future date one or the other wished to reduce the number of troops it had stationed in Europe. France also wants some form of American public statement committing the United States to a "forward strategy" to defend Europe on the continent itself rather than liberate it after an occupation. The matter was raised in Bermuda rather indefinitely. Alphand hopes to get some kind of American statement at the time EDC ratification is ready for discussion before the National Assembly. Also the French want a pledge from all NATO members, but above all the United States and Britain, not to avail themselves of the privilege that is theirs after twenty years to denounce NATO on the basis of one year's notice. This, Alphand admits, would make NATO into an "eternal" treaty.

PARIS, *January 15, 1954*

LAST night I had dinner at the Norstads. Gruenther was there and also Captain (Lord) Coleridge of the Royal Navy who is Ismay's right-hand man and the guy who is always trying to get me thrown into jail for writing stories he considers confidential. Also Malik. I must hand it to Malik. He really gets around more than almost any ambassador here in Paris as far as circles useful to India are concerned.

Coleridge could not have been friendlier. In fact I was quite amused at the extent of his cordiality. He asked if *The New York Times* was planning to publish a special section about NATO on its fifth anniversary next April. I told him with a broad smile that I thought *The New York Times* gave

NATO very complete coverage as things are. Norstad who was listening in roared with laughter. Coleridge later on kept sidling up to me and asking me how well I knew Barnes, who is his assistant. Obviously he has now got the idea that Barnes is the fellow who is leaking everything to me. I must call Bob up and warn him.

# 2 9

---

# GIANTS CAN DO
# NOTHING NOW

PARIS, *January 21, 1954*

I HAD NOT SEEN GENERAL DE GAULLE IN A LONG TIME, SO THIS AFTER-
noon I spent an hour with him at his RPF headquarters at 5 rue
Solferino. The headquarters are, if anything, shabbier than ever before. Some of the lights don't work. The furniture is rickety. The general's
office itself is extra simple with a desk and a few not particularly comfortable chairs. De Gaulle has aged a great deal during the last year or two. He
is gray and lined and getting just a bit more jowly. He was dressed in a well-
fitted, double-breasted, dark, pin-stripe suit with a stiff collar and gray tie.
He looks far more distinguished in civilian clothes than uniform, unlike
most military men. His face seemed somewhat lined and he looked a little
tired. However, he said he felt fine and had recovered well from the eye
operation he had last year. For him, he was extremely affable and almost
courtly. He was also, for him, about as informal as I suppose he ever gets.
He offered cigarettes and told me to go ahead and take notes if I wanted to,
even though he stressed that this was off the record. He said, "It is you,
and I have confidence in you."

We started talking about Morocco and Spain's hanky-panky in Tetuan
where Franco is drumming up trouble by not recognizing the new sultan
and sticking to the old one, now exiled by the French to Corsica. De Gaulle
said,

I knew the old sultan well. I regretted that he had to leave. When I was
in Africa last year, I had originally planned to return to France via
Morocco, but I called off this trip because of the political situation
resulting from his removal. Evidently Spain is not trying to please

France by what it is doing in its zone. On the contrary. But after the war we did not establish the relations with Madrid that Spain expected. I started to work in the direction of good relationships even while I was in Algiers. However, things did not pan out. The Spaniards quite clearly are now trying to found an "Arab policy." They sent their foreign minister, Martin-Artajo, to Egypt, Iraq and Saudi Arabia. They are using this moment to flatter the Arab League. They have called this Tetuan manifestation against us in order to flatter the Arab League. But the Spaniards won't go very far. They don't want this to become an "international affair." If it remains only an affair of the *caids* and between the two zones of Morocco, it will still serve their purpose without causing an international crisis. There has always been a Spanish Morocco at Tetuan and an international city at Tangier. When the French went to Morocco we inherited that situation and we had to make a treaty along those lines. There is no great divergence between France and Spain, and this affair should not be exaggerated. I fear the Spaniards will keep playing this card—pro-Arab and anti-French. But I am confident it will not go too far.

I then turned the conversation to the subject of Indochina. I asked him what solution he could see. "Solution?" he asked, shrugging his shoulders.

I can't see anything but evacuation of Indochina or a continuation of the present situation. For a military solution a new method and a new effort would be required. But France does not want to make that effort. We have no really direct interest in Indochina. That is a reality. What is taking place there now is merely a prestige war. Not even the prestige of France is involved any more. Indochina is of international interest more and more and of French interest less and less. There are only two real authorities in Indochina—France and Ho Chi Minh. There is nothing else. There are no other "authorities." The dynasties of Bao Dai, Cambodia and Laos are nothing now. They are only an appearance. Ho is a reality. He represents independence, nationalism, communism, Asia. France is a reality. She represents the occident. Now there is no more French authority in the country. Everything has been given up. Therefore, inevitably the French must get out. They will get out when they have had enough. We will regret it greatly, but we must go. In 1863 Napoleon III went to Mexico. He supported Maximilian. But all the United States was against him. He had to get out. It is the same thing in Indochina.

I asked him what he thought might come out of the Berlin conference starting next week. He said,

I don't think any *real* entente is possible between the East and West as things now are. But I think for a certain time each can coexist with the other and trade with the other. Neither the United States nor Russia wants to make war now. As a result the cold war has become insupportable. It costs too much. It weighs on the budget, business, the spirit. A cold war cannot be continued if nobody wants it to lead to a hot war. There must be a *modus vivendi* even if nothing is signed. It will provide for more exchanges—tourists, students, athletes and goods, and it can last a long time. After Berlin there will be many other conferences. A détente is beginning, a *modus vivendi*. It started already in Korea. The dangers of war at present are less and less. The decisive point in Korea was the quarrel between MacArthur and Truman. This showed that the United States did not want war. After Truman said no to MacArthur's proposal to attack China, war was excluded. The English want business with Russia. The French want an arrangement in Indochina. The United States wants export markets. These are the imponderables that make for a *modus vivendi.* This is not an entente; it is armed peace.

I may say this is the first time since 1946 or 1947 that I have heard de Gaulle talk about the chances of some form of peace or, at any rate, not war. In the past, he has always talked about the imminence of world war and how, when it comes, France will need him.

I asked him if he had any new proposals on how to deal with Germany. He said, "The first question is to finish with EDC." He said that this was an

*entreprise manquée,* an error, a stupidity. It was invented by some French politicians who aren't France. When it was submitted, France said no. Finish with the system. That is the first thing. It is absurd from a national, an international and a military point of view. Finish with it. It is absurd.

But we must incorporate Germany into the West. I have always said that. How? By a very wide European arrangement—Britain, France, Germany, Scandinavia, all of free Europe in an alliance, a confeder-ation, in which each would safeguard its own individuality. You cannot suppress nationalities. Within such an organization you can have com-mon arms. See the way Britain has just accepted the NATO rifle. You can have a progressive rearmament of Germany. But it is an absurdity, a dream, a fantasy to think that you can suppress France and French nationality.

The United States has walked along with this idiocy. Now you must extricate yourselves. If you put your money on a bad horse, you are lunatics if you keep throwing it away on the same horse. I guarantee that EDC will not go through. I will do everything against it. I will work with the Communists to block it. I will make revolution against it. I would rather go with the Russians to stop it. It won't go through. It won't go through. I repeat, I will make revolution to prevent it.

At this point I asked de Gaulle what reliance he thought France should place upon the Soviet Pact he signed in Moscow in 1944. He replied, "France must not lose its independence to anyone. I prevented the Com-munists from grabbing power in France in 1944 and also in 1947 when I started the RPF. We cannot lose our sovereignty to Russia." This is rather a doubletalk reply.

He then continued by saying the Germans would be rearmed without French permission if the French held back too long. He thought that on this issue the Soviet pact could have a useful influence. He then said another curious thing: "If one rearms Germany and France does not approve of such rearmament, the Soviets also will object. Then the Soviets may occupy West Berlin. What would the French do? The French would not object, under the Franco-Soviet pact." I pointed out that if West Berlin were occupied, the Allied garrison would be taken prisoners by the Russians. The general replied, "France could have its troops repatriated by the Russians."

He continued that there was "no chance of any serious policy being based upon the Soviet pact. We must have the United States' alliance. We also want Germany with the western world—but without the simultaneous disappearance of France. Everything but that."

I asked him what he thought of Eisenhower's proposal to take citizenship away from persons accused of conspiring against the government—namely, Communists—and asked him whether he thought the Communist Party should be outlawed in France. He replied, "You in the United States have a different problem. You have not been invaded as often or had as many revolutions as we have. You don't have as many Communists because you have not had fourteen revolutions and thirteen invasions in 150 years." (I must say, I don't quite follow his history when he uses these fourteen and thirteen statistics.)

The real remedy in France is a great France, *une grandeur française.* Now there is despair here. Those Frenchmen who are despairing go to the Communist Party. That is why you need a great French policy to eliminate communism. This is not easy. But on this we have not received much support from our allies.

During the war I made war. I finished by success. Now France is divided again. In 1947 when the Communist Party was dangerous, I made the RPF to stop them. Now that they are not so dangerous, the French are again dispersed—the RPF also. [This latter was a curious admission.] Now all I want to do is to prevent stupidities like EDC. I cannot achieve *positive* progress all alone, but I can block absurdities.

I asked de Gaulle what his personal program was now. He said, "The age of giants is over. Giants can do nothing now. Churchill is the only survivor and he can do nothing. I like Eisenhower. But he is not a giant. Roosevelt is dead. Stalin died—too late. This is the epoch of Malenkov, Fanfani and Queuille."

BERLIN, *January 24, 1954*

THIS afternoon Dulles expounded his views of the Big Four conference opening tomorrow. He did it with an air of considerable assurance, an

easy manner and great fluency. On the surface it sounded pretty good, but
when analyzed there was some rather dangerous crackpot stuff in it. He
said:

> I suppose the Russians will inject a proposal for a five-power conference
> here—including Communist China. The United States sees no basis for
> such a five-power conference. Neither the five powers wanted by Russia
> for such a conference nor any other five powers have a mandate to settle
> the problems of the world. At any point where particular issues should
> be discussed in which the United States is involved, we are prepared to
> sit down and discuss them. But I don't accept the theory that any group
> of powers should settle the fate of the world. It is grotesque that the
> Chinese Communists should have anything to do with settling the future
> of Germany.

Dulles says he wants the French to carry the ball here. A secret poll of
German opinion taken only last week showed that 62 per cent of the West
German people mistrust the French and their aims at this conference. Furthermore, 64 per cent of the West Germans are convinced that if the
United States has to choose between Germany and France as an ally, it will
pick Germany. Only 7 per cent thought America would favor France. In
other words, the Germans hate and mistrust the French. Dulles may think
he is going to get back some popularity in France and remove the irritation
produced last month when he read them his famous "agonizing reappraisal"
lecture. But he is surely going to stir up a hornets' nest in Germany when
he tries to hand the torch to Bidault. Furthermore, Bidault is not the
staunchest and most reliable champion. He is quite a tricky little man. And
right behind him on the French delegation here as Number Two and Number Three are Parodi and de Margerie of the Quai d'Orsay, both of whom
are fanatical enemies of EDC. They will do anything to spike it.


BERLIN, *January 25, 1954*

I had lunch today with David Bruce. He is completely puzzled by Dulles.
He says the only man who will be happy will be Bidault, who is being
permitted to make the first statement of the foreign ministers at today's
meeting. The Germans will obviously be furious. The French will be bewildered. Parodi will probably try and use the opportunity to still further bitch
up EDC. Bruce can't figure out for the life of him what Dulles is up to.

I asked him about security guarantees. He said a working paper had
been agreed upon by the low-level working party in Paris of the three
powers, but nothing had been accepted by the three foreign ministers. The
idea was merely to have something ready in case the Russians raised the
question of security guarantees. Bruce himself is all against the idea and
doesn't think it is necessary. The Russians are realists and are not going to
be fooled by any verbal pledges. If they are out to prevent German rearma-

ment and EDC they are not going to be prevailed upon to change their mind merely because of some nicely worded promises.

The whole issue was produced as a result of Churchill's speech last year suggesting a kind of Locarno agreement. Only three methods were considered. One was the Adenauer idea that after an EDC had been formed, that same EDC would exchange nonaggression pledges with the Soviet Union. The second was the Van Zeeland plan. The third was the suggestion that the government of a reunited Germany should make a formal promise in an official document that it would never seek to revise its existing frontiers by forceful means.

The first, or Adenauer, version was scrapped by the working party. It is recognized that if the Russians are against EDC, they are not going to buy it any quicker because of such a promise. The second, or Van Zeeland, theory was scrapped as impossible and illogical. However, the third theory was crystallized in a paper adopted by all three delegates on the working party. Bruce thinks it would be idiotic for any German government to sign such a paper. But the French are very much in favor of it because they figure if they can get the Germans to pledge themselves not to use force to change their frontiers, that will mean that the Germans will be committed never to try to seize the Saar; also that in any future arrangement tying France to Germany, it would not drag France and the rest of Europe into a war on the question of the Oder-Neisse line.

Both David and Evangeline, who are staying with the Conants, were delighted to get out of that atmosphere. They have had only one meal outside the official entourage since they arrived in Berlin several days ago and they are fed up with talking polite doubletalk to the German officials who have been gathering around the high commissioner's dining room table.

Bruce is very afraid that the French have now missed their last opportunity of holding the Germans in check. He thinks that if EDC has not passed within about three months, the Germans will demand a separation between the contractual agreements and EDC. At present the two are mutually dependent upon each other. If and when the Germans make such a demand, the United States and Britain will have to agree with them and will support the German point of view. The French will then be furious and turn their rage against us.

BERLIN, *January 27, 1954*

I lunched with Chip Bohlen. He said he thought the conference would last only about three weeks. I said how about Molotov trying to drag it on in order to delay action on EDC. He thought even Molotov would be prepared to make it a fairly short conference. Molotov's entire tactic is to develop the thesis of Europe for the Europeans (Russia, of course, to be considered a European power). The idea would be to isolate the United States—that is to say, to drive it back into isolation. This became very clear in Molotov's speech yesterday replying to Dulles. Molotov actually was rather afraid for a time that Dulles was not going to speak. He didn't like the idea of Britain and France putting forth the Western point of view, with the United States lurking in the background. He wanted our cards on the table before he moved.

BERLIN, *January 28, 1954*

LUNCH today with Yuri Zhukov, who is now assistant director of *Pravda*. He explained to me that there are two assistant directors. When the director is away, the other one, who handles internal news, acts as "chargé d'affaires." He said Pospelov is indeed a very important man in the Soviet hierarchy now and that he still keeps good contacts with his old friends in *Pravda*. I offered Yuri some vodka, but he said he thought not. I was interested to notice that although I offered him plenty of white wine and red wine, he drank very moderately—which is not always the case.

After sparring around with some polite opening remarks, Zhukov suddenly dove in. He said: "Well, it is quite a while since you and Bohlen and I arranged the Korean armistice."

I replied obliquely that I remembered an interesting dinner party at my house at which he and Bohlen had been present. He said, "Yes, we arranged the armistice quite successfully. After all, they followed the terms that we discussed. Don't you think it is about time that we should have a similar agreement on present problems?"

I asked Zhukov, appearing to change the subject, whether he saw Molotov often here in Berlin, and whether he had good contacts with the rest of his delegation. He told me he didn't see Molotov at all but that he could see Gromyko, Malik or any of the other delegates whenever he wished. However, he told me he was confident what he was saying was the viewpoint of all the "principal leaders" in Moscow with whom he was in contact.

He thought that what was needed to make this meeting a success was a realization by both the United States and Russia—the only two really great powers here—that neither one nor the other wanted war. This meeting could achieve an armistice in the cold war and future meetings could achieve real peace. He thought that bilateral talks between the Russians and the Americans were absolutely imperative in order to arrive at a real understanding. I asked if he meant by this talks between Dulles and Molotov, and he replied either between Dulles and Molotov or between Bohlen and Molotov. He then stressed that conversations could be held under the cover of being negotiations on atomic issues such as have already started between Russia and the United States. Under this guise of "atomic affairs" everything could be talked over from Indochina to East-West trade.

He assured me that Russia had *no* desire for further territorial expansion. I said to him that this might indeed be true, but surely anyone reading the newspapers would be fully aware that the United States was concerned about the expansionist tendencies of the Soviet bloc and international communism. I pointed out, for example, that even if he thought a Ho Chi Minh Indochina would not be another republic in the Soviet Union, from the United States point of view it would be a gain for the Communist bloc and in my opinion surely would not be tolerated.

He said such things could be arranged. I remarked that as far as I could see, the only way they could be arranged would be by Russia telling China to stop sending arms to Indochina. He said after all, Russia could not tell the people of other countries and the Communist Parties of other countries what to do and could not order them to cease fighting for their independence. I replied that this might be true but that in my opinion a basic fact remained, and that was if Russia told China to stop sending arms to Ho Chi Minh, it was probable a solution could be arranged in Indochina. Zhukov replied, "Maybe such things can be arranged."

He emphasized that the Soviet Union did not insist the United States should destroy its stocks of atomic weapons as part of any settlement on the armaments and atomic questions. He said all that the USSR wanted was for the United States to sign some kind of an agreement like the Geneva Convention on gas which would pledge the United States not to use atomic weapons in case of war. He said that in such a case the United States could conserve all the weapons it has, and if it felt the Soviet Union was aggressing in an unfair war, it would still be in a position to use its "superiority in stocks of these weapons" in such a war. I made him repeat the phrase "superiority in stocks of these weapons."

I then pointed out that it would be a very difficult thing, it seemed to me as a journalist, for the United States to embark on two-power negotiations with the USSR because after all it had obligations to its allies, France and Great Britain. Zhukov replied that he understood this, but after all France and Great Britain were not really great powers as were the USSR and the United States. I then said that it seemed to me pretty evident that the Soviet Union was just trying to split France and Britain off from the United States and to divide us. He said, "You mean to drive you into isolationism?" I said, "Precisely." He said, "Well, one must always have alternatives. If our negotiations with you do not succeed, naturally we must seek alternative policies."

I remarked that I didn't think it would be possible under any conditions to come to an agreement on the unification of Germany because I felt, among other things, that the Soviet Union was too scared of a unified Germany to permit it, even if it was a Communist Germany. Zhukov then started on a tangent and said the Russians had lost 17,000,000 persons killed during the war (this is the first time I personally heard a Russian give a precise figure for their losses in dead) and that naturally they were afraid of Germany.

He took off on a long talk about the EDC. I said that I honestly couldn't understand why they were against EDC because it seemed to me to offer all the kinds of guarantees that they appeared to want. He talked about German rearmament in the EDC. He said he couldn't understand why we were so anxious to get twelve German divisions anyway because they really wouldn't make any difference. He said that we must understand the Russian psychological attitude towards a rearmed Germany.

I asked, "Then, as I understand it, the only objection you have to EDC is the fact that the West Germans would be rearmed even in a limited sense?"

He said yes, that was the only objection they had. He added, "If you take the trouble to read all our notes during the last few months, you will see that we don't even have any objection to NATO. There is no Russian opposition to the North Atlantic Treaty Organization, and we understand your point of view." I told him I was astonished to hear this and that I had been reading continually about the objection to American bases overseas. He said yes, there was an objection to American bases and a feeling of encirclement, but as far as NATO itself went, I as a journalist should be able to distinguish between facts and propaganda and that the facts were contained in Soviet notes on the matter and that these did not object to NATO.

Quite obviously Zhukov had something to do with shaping up the Russian decision on the Korean armistice. Also quite obviously he figures that I am a kind of Jeffersonian Zhukov because I happened to be the host when he was talking with Bohlen. Therefore he is putting out what appears to me to be a most important Soviet "line," although naturally I am in no position to judge whether this is for propaganda purposes, for the purpose of trying to get us to swallow some bait and divide the Allies, or in a sincere effort to arrage a *modus vivendi* along the only lines the Russians understand, namely, power politics.

He stressed the fact that there had been a big change in Moscow and that there were major problems now. What Russia wanted was to improve the standard of living of its own people. It needed peace and had to have security. It wanted to expand East-West trade. The Russians were not kidding themselves that there would be a depression in America. They knew we were a great power and that our economy was not in any great danger. We should recognize the Soviet situation and the reality of changes that had taken place and we should act accordingly.

I pointed out that after all, as Zhukov could see from reading American newspapers (he interjected that he didn't read English, and I rebutted that there were surely enough bureaucrats who did), we were seriously concerned about the USSR's insistence on keeping a huge army, air force and navy in being, including 175 divisions and an immense force in Eastern Europe. He replied that things could be arranged—a rather nebulous response.

He emphasized that he thought bipartite negotiations must be started; that they should be held in the completest secrecy; that it should not even be known that such negotiations were taking place at all, much less what was occurring in them; that they could take place at various levels, speaking in terms of governmental hierarchy. He said that on different points different individuals could get together to talk things over.

My own impression of this extremely interesting conversation is dual:

1. I truly think that Zhukov has surely been put up to this by persons in the highest positions, although I cannot guess who they are. My guess is that they sincerely would like to work out a *modus vivendi* based upon carving out spheres of influence in the world and that they would be genuinely prepared to go along on such a basis.

2. On the other hand, I think they are just about equally desirous of starting negotiations for carving out spheres of influence in order to be able, if things don't go the way they would like, to betray the fact of such negotiations to the British, French and others in order to help them in their efforts to split the United States from its allies.

BERLIN, *January 30, 1954*

I had lunch today with C. D. Jackson. He claims the Russians are back on their heels. They simply don't know what has happened to them, and Molotov "has met his master" in Foster Dulles. The Soviet "fly wheel" has been turned into a reverse direction. I think C. D. is getting a bit naive and I fear this type of thinking may lead to overoptimism and also may encourage somewhat dangerous "rollback" tendencies that are always latent.

BERLIN, *January 31, 1954*

LAST night I dined with Chip Bohlen. He gave me a rather good definition of democracy—a word the Russians flaunt all the time. He said that in the Soviet lexicon a "democratic government" is one with at least 20 per cent Communists in its composition. A "progressive democratic government" is one with at least 40 per cent Communists in its make-up. A "people's democratic government" is a Communist dictatorship.

Chip, like all the other Americans, says Bidault's speech was magnificent. He thinks the Russians are on the defensive but that this is a gradual development and must not in any sense be exaggerated.

Chip is clearly a bit discouraged—although he masks this very well—by not being one of the inner circle on American policy any more. He says Doug MacArthur is the man who is closest to the Secretary now. At a later stage in the conversation Bohlen remarked that Dulles doesn't like people around him who know more than he does.

BERLIN, *January 31, 1954*

THIS afternoon Dulles summed up his impressions of the first week of the Big Four conference. I must say they were not very interesting. I also have a feeling that we are somewhat overconfident of our position and too impressed with the extent to which Molotov is allegedly on the defensive. He is a pretty smart operator and he may be leading us up the garden path. Dulles said:

I told Molotov that we had not come to a conference just to arrange other conferences.* I hinted that unless this first Big Four meeting in five years achieved some concrete results, it would be hard to see the utility for further such meetings. As a result Molotov didn't press his proposal for new conferences.

Of Molotov he said,

I have an extremely high opinion of Molotov as a diplomat. I have personally known most of the diplomats of this century. As a boy I attended the second Hague Peace Conference in 1907. I would classify Molotov as tops. He is very skillful. But his skill is directed against two things he cannot surmount—the pretty solid unity of the West and the fact that world opinion is sick and tired of Soviet propaganda. [Of course, Dulles hopes to master Molotov, outdo the "best."]
A few years ago we would have had to stop, look and listen on the Soviet world disarmament conference proposal. But now no one gets excited about it when it is pulled out of the drawer again. Molotov's skill hasn't declined. But the environment is less susceptible.

He said during Stalin's lifetime Stalin controlled all fields, but "now there is more of a committee form of government. Power is more decentralized. Molotov has a greater measure of authority in the field of foreign affairs." He said some of Molotov's remarks yesterday were "susceptible to a slight optimism. He made some slightly more hopeful allusions to free elections in Germany, but these were rather obscure."

---

* Later: This in fact is all we did; "Berlin" arranged "Geneva"—with Peking's presence.

BERLIN, *February 1, 1954*

I had lunch today with (Sir) William Hayter. This is the first time I have
seen him since he was named British ambassador in Moscow. He says he is
enjoying his job a lot.

He often wonders what he would do if he were walking down a street in
Moscow and suddenly ran into Donald MacLean. He is sure that he would
forget himself and shake hands and say, "Hello, Donald, what are you
doing here?" He knew MacLean well, thought he was very able and liked
him a lot. He is sure that he would be so absent-minded that he would
quite forget, at first glimpse, everything that had happened. Hayter's own
theory—and he says he hasn't the slightest bit of evidence but still believes
it—is that Burgess was a "talent spotter" for the Communists already by
the time he got to university. He believes Burgess got ahold of MacLean
back in those days and signed MacLean up for the party. The party told
MacLean to go into the diplomatic service. He thinks MacLean was a
double agent—that is to say, was working as a diplomat and reporting to
the Russians—throughout his career with the foreign office. It is William's
hunch that during the last year the strain became too great for MacLean—
that is to say, the strain of leading two lives. He felt things closing in on
him and got ahold of Burgess and told him to get him out of all that. That,
Hayter thinks, was the reason for their flight. Hayter has no use for Burgess who, he says, was a rotter, although a clever one.

Hayter doesn't believe there have been any changes at all in Soviet basic
policy although there has been a change in method and external appearances.

Hayter had the rare privilege of seeing Malenkov. Since he arrived after
Malenkov was already prime minister—unlike Bohlen and Joxe—he requested of Molotov the privilege of meeting Malenkov. He spent about a
half an hour with him. He said Malenkov is a pretty sloppy specimen
physically but was very agreeable and rather impressive. He seemed like an
efficient big businessman, in western terms. He says Malenkov has never
been out of the country except for a few postwar trips to the satellite area
like Warsaw and Bucharest when he was in the Cominform business. Malenkov was wearing the rather shapeless tunic he is photographed in so
frequently when he received William. Molotov and an interpreter were
there.

Hayter agrees with Bohlen's analysis of Russian policy—they want
"peace at no price." That is to say, they want peace but aren't ready to give
anything for it.

Hayter thinks the Big Four—and in this order—are Malenkov, Khrushchev, Molotov and Bulganin. Soviet picture displays always have Lenin
and Stalin in extra-large-size posters in the middle. Malenkov is then immediately above to the left, Molotov immediately below to the left, Khru-

shchev immediately above to the right and Bulganin immediately below to the right. Then the rest of the boys are spread on the flanks.

BERLIN, *February 3, 1954*

YESTERDAY I had a fairly full day. Chip Bohlen told me there had been quite a flap in the United States delegation when reports came in of a story I had written (published Monday morning, the day before yesterday) saying that Soviet sources were seeking to convince the Americans they wanted an agreement on the atom and an over-all accommodation. Dulles called in Bohlen and asked him if he had been leaking to me. Of course Bohlen was the interpreter between Dulles and Molotov Saturday at the conversations on the atom. Naturally Bohlen had not been leaking to me, but I must say the mere fact that Dulles asked him such seems to lend special authority to the story that I wrote.

I had lunch with Anthony Nutting, British parliamentary under secretary for foreign affairs. He is just a youngster and seems to be a favorite of Eden's. I have met him several times before, and he impresses me less each time. He seems to be exceptionally conceited with a minimum knowledge of foreign affairs. He rejoices in the current nickname of "Minipots" which he and his English diplomatic friends seem to think uproariously funny and keep iterating and reiterating with giggles.

Last night I dined in the east sector on caviar plus some bad food in a new restaurant called the Budapest, with David and Evangeline Bruce. Our conversation ranged considerably, but among other things David said the following:

He thinks the United States diplomatic team is undoubtedly much better than that of any of the other powers at this conference. Upon reflection, he considers the United States has been very fortunate in its Secretaries of State during the past fifteen years. Our top-level team is a much more rounded and skillful one than are those of the rest of the Big Four. He has no high regard for Gromyko or Malik and thinks Molotov's reputation is exaggerated. He says Dulles has been bowling over the Russians with the sheer weight and force of his arguments. He gets up the momentum of a bull. Bidault has been exceptionally skillful and sharp. Furthermore, his speeches have been prepared in beautiful French. The French are justly proud of his presentation even if some of them, including his diplomatic opponents and his political enemies, disagree with what he is saying. Bruce says Eden is a fine and gentlemanly fellow who has had a beautiful record on the main issues of his career, such as appeasement, etc., before the war, but that he is a lightweight, not really intelligent and doesn't stand up to the others. He considers him the weak sister of the Big Four here.

We got onto a discussion of the moral blot on Dulles' record as Secretary of State—namely, his failure to prevent unfair persecution within the

State Department and to stem the advance of McCarthyism and Scott McLeod (who, Bruce says, is reputedly a very attractive fellow no matter how much of a witch-hunter he is). I said I could never understand how Bedell Smith could remain under secretary with all this McLeodism under his nose. Bruce said Bedell had explained to him last time he was home that he was a mere staff officer by training and that his whole career had been that of a staff officer who carried out orders. He pointed out that he had had two wonderful chiefs—George Marshall and Eisenhower—and that he had learned that it was the function of a staff officer to follow directives.

BERLIN, *February 3, 1954*

I lunched again today—this time as his guest—with Zhukov. I met him at the Adlon Hotel. The back end of the hotel is inhabited; the front, on the Unter den Linden, is gone. It looks kind of seedy. I asked him if he was comfortable, and he said, oh yes, that he had a sitting room and a bedroom. I asked him to take me to the bar for a drink. He was very reluctant to do this, but I insisted, explaining that I had known the bar in its former splendor. We went up one flight of stairs to a restaurant that is a combined bar-restaurant and looks very much like a Russian factory mess for the highest echelon of officials. Then we drove off in his car—a Pobieda (they are made in the Molotov factory) to the Budapest restaurant. He had made no advance arrangements so, somewhat to his embarrassment, we were forced to sit down with a couple of rather seedy-looking Krauts. However, after twenty minutes or so another table emptied and we moved over. He started fencing around but wasn't very illuminating.

He asked me what I thought about the Dulles–Molotov meetings. I replied, "You mean their talk on Saturday on atomic procedures?" He countered, "But there were two meetings, weren't there?" I said I didn't know about that, I had only heard about one. He shrugged his shoulders and said, "Maybe, who knows." I am a bit puzzled by this and rather suspect that there may actually have been two meetings.

No less than three times during our conversation Zhukov voiced the idea that Molotov and Dulles didn't have to confine themselves to discussion of atomic problems when they meet together but could talk about Germany or anything else. It seems to me he must know something to be so insistent on that.

I asked him about the economics of writing in the Soviet Union. He explained to me that if a man wrote a book, he made a special contract with the publisher and was paid a fixed rate on the understanding that a precise number of copies would be printed in the first edition. He did not get any royalties. Then, if a second edition was printed, it was on the basis of a new contract and he would get 60 per cent as much as the first time. I asked him what a writer did if he happened to hit the jackpot and have a great success. He said he put his money in the bank where he got a small amount of interest on it or bought state bonds. He showed me his own bank book from the national bank. It has a provision in it specifying what the depositor wants done with the money in case of his death—to whom it would be left. I remarked that after all, this was pretty close to capitalism and he agreed. I asked him what benefits a writer received if his book was published in a foreign language. He said that generally he received no benefits because Russia had never signed the international conventions on copyrights. Therefore Russian books could be pirated and the Soviets could pirate foreign books. However, he said, there were frequently gentleman's agreements to avoid this.

I asked how he handled his finances when he traveled. He said most people didn't have check books or checking accounts but that he, as an assistant director of *Pravda,* found that one was useful. When he traveled abroad, he used a letter of credit. Thus, when he went to Paris, his letter of credit was able to draw funds from the Banque Commerciale pour l'Europe du Nord.

I asked Yuri how his little boy, who is now eleven, was getting on in Moscow. He said school is very difficult for youngsters there and they have to work extremely hard. His boy goes to school from 2 P.M. to 7 P.M. Yuri says there are not enough school buildings in Moscow so they operate on two shifts a day, and his kid has the afternoon shift. He also takes French lessons twice a week at home. Yuri says they have a television set at home and his kid is crazy about it, spending all his spare time watching it.

Incidentally, Yuri said another interesting thing: in his own articles he has now stopped using insulting terms about the West. He said he hasn't changed his opinions and doesn't write from a different basic point of view, but he no longer uses offensive epithets. He suggested I look at his article of last Monday. I remarked, "You mean you no longer call me a Fascist or a wolf of Wall Street?" He didn't smile.

Yuri told me that a new express train has just started to run between Moscow and Peking. He didn't know how long it took but thought it was something like a week or more. He said the line had been double tracked. I asked how long it took by airplane, and he said he thought about three days. I expressed astonishment and said that, after all, with a four-engine plane it shouldn't take nearly that long. He told me that in the Soviet Union no four-engine planes were used for transport purposes; they were all the rather old-fashioned twin-engined planes.

BERLIN, *February 4, 1954*

I had lunch today with Pierre Courtade, foreign editor of *L'Humanité.* I have known Pierre for a long time. At all of these conferences he is always very friendly, but generally when he gets back to Paris he freezes up. I mentioned that to him and he denied it vigorously. I told him I was anxious to see Duclos when I got back to Paris, and he replied, "Why not?" He volunteered to help arrange it for me after this conference is over.

Incidentally, our luncheon featured a dessert that shatters even my recent experiences in the attempts of the German gourmet to excel. Our dessert was "Swabian onion cake." It is exactly what it sounds like. It is a kind of hot, sweet pie crammed with onions. It looks like onions, tastes of onions and stinks like onions. Even Courtade, who had been telling me how necessary it was nowadays for everybody to become peace-loving and friendly and for the Germans and French to make up, became chauvinistic as he munched his first slug of onion cake.

We discussed various things during the course of this affable, if not delectable luncheon. He assured me that Yuri Zhukov had access to the best Russian sources and really knew what was going on. However, he said that he himself got no favored treatment from the Communists and received exactly the same briefings from Ilichev as *The New York Times* or any other Western newspaper—nothing special for the Communist journalists.

I told him I had bought some Chinese champagne and whisky in East Berlin. He shuddered. He said to me that he had discovered in China that the champagne industry was organized and run by a Belgian Jesuit father. He said it was incredibly foul stuff; the Chinese didn't drink it but exported it. He said he had had a sad experience with Chinese whisky himself. He had seen a bottle of apparently first-class Scotch whisky with a Johnny Walker label on it in a shop in Shanghai. The bottle had really impressed him and the label was perfect. He was a little skeptical because it cost only one dollar. He took it home, had one drink, and vomited as soon as he had recovered his breath. He said he never in his life has tasted anything like it, nor ever will again, he hopes. He took the bottle back to the shop owner and complained. The shop owner explained with great Chinese logic that the bottle did not say on it that it contained real Scotch whisky; it only purported to be a real Scotch whisky bottle. Pierre says that Shanghai is filled with American goods despite the blockade. He said you cannot keep down the combination of a shrewd Chinese merchant plus a hard-boiled British blockade runner plus an unscrupulous American businessman. He said Chinese ports are jammed with British and Panamanian ships; or were, at any rate, when he was there.

Pierre says he is convinced that neither France nor Russia wants a united Germany. After all, he adds, Germany is unlike France and has only a very shortlived tradition of unity. Furthermore there is a basic difference between largely Catholic and modern Western Germany and largely Protestant and feudal Eastern Germany.

PARIS, *February 10, 1954*

THE Berlin Conference is a fraud and I left Clif Daniel in charge of our large staff there and beat it. Dulles keeps insisting the one thing he won't agree to is a Far East conference and dealings with China; yet it is evident this is about all Berlin will produce. He goes out of his way to build up Molotov as the greatest diplomat since Talleyrand—so, if he, Dulles, manages to worst him, he'll look even better. And he acts as a kind of P. T. Barnum presenting Bidault as a brilliant statesman and chief spokesman for the West—even comparing him to Abe Lincoln, a ridiculous *non sequitur*. Bidault goes along with us, above all on Indochina, but French politics are shifting sands and it is silly to build any policy castles on them. The Russians are working for a French sellout; and they'll get it. The French don't even dare draft recruits for Asia.

I have decided to make a tour of Italy to confirm or deny Clare Luce's asseverations to Washington that it is going Communist unless we intervene. I think she's nuts and merely wants to make a big name for herself as an activist in her first diplomatic job. I mistrust her judgment and think she bullies the regular career men on her staff who have been rendered gutless by McCarthyism. I don't intend to see her and discuss her views until I have first completed a survey of my own; so as to be completely objective.

Incidentally, before taking off, I have conducted another survey here in Paris. I brought with me a collection of menus from some of the more distinguished restaurants in West Berlin. I have gone to Lucas-Carton, Le Grand Vefour, Maxim's, La Crémaillère and other highly rated eateries here. After ordering lunch and wine I ask the sommelier, showing him a Berlin *carte,* "What kind of wine would you recommend with this?" Then I point to such tasty monstrosities as oysters with sauerkraut; or roast beef and caviar. This produces an initial reaction of stunned surprise or suspicion that I may be making a poor joke. I then point out that the menu is genuine, from a well-known establishment. That produces consultation between sommelier and maître d'hôtel or other experts and sneering remarks such as: "Only a Boche could eat such garbage." I think German culinary habits are less forgivable here than the savageries of the occupation!

TURIN, *February 17, 1954*

HAD long talk with Professor Vittorio Valletta, general manager of Fiat, and the real boss of this enormous operation. He is small, cocky, with dark face and gray-white hair, large teeth and abrupt gestures. He is obviously a very energetic old man. He received me in his ugly but comfortable house and talked at length in fluent, bad French.

The Communist Party, he said, is extremely well organized. "I think both the Italian and the United States press are damaging relations between our two countries by the news they publish, which exaggerates the importance of communism." (Obviously Valletta is worried about the possibility he may lose some contracts.) He said the Communists are now spreading rumors that he, Valletta, is their friend, and thus trying to get him ousted.

He thought it was a good idea for the United States to cut off aid contracts where actual Communists dominate a factory, but only if the direction of the factory is communistic. He didn't think it was possible to work this thing out just on the basis of a percentage of the workers who might be Communist.

He said Fiat workers had an organization formed in 1906—the Federation of Italian Metallurgical and Engineering Workers. It is now a member of CGIL, the federation controlled by the Communist Party. However, Valletta insists the federation is not a Communist union. But if the United States were to cut off contracts on the basis of the number of workers in CGIL, it would affect this particular union.

Valletta says the Allies themselves bear a heavy responsibility for the situation. At the time of the armistice they brought with them such Communist leaders as Togliatti and Longo. These "liberators" took over the trade unions.

The tradition of the Italian worker, according to Valletta, is Socialist. The Communist Party, as such, is not really strong in Italy. It has unfortunately, however, been greatly aided by Nenni, who "betrayed the true cause of socialism and is the most evil man in Italy. We must separate those at Nenni's side and bring them over to democratic socialism. We must continue along the same lines by which we split off Saragat and Romito from the CGIL. One must act though, not just talk about it. Press campaigns only help the Communists."

BOLOGNA, *February 22, 1954*

ALDO Cucchi, one of the two Communist intellectuals (and deputies) who quit the party in 1951, is a fat, sleek, well-dressed, pale-faced man. At first glimpse he appears indolent and inactive. It is only when one looks carefully and sees the especially cruel expression of his mouth that one credits his ruthless reputation as the most brutal and cold-blooded resistance leader in all of Italy during the war. He headed the underground in Bologna under the name of Giacoppo. I dined with Cucchi and we talked for some hours afterwards. He said that the peasants of Italy are only temporary Communists. They all hope to own their own land in the end. Already some of the sharecroppers who got land with the aid of the Communist Party are turning against communism as they adopt the property owner's viewpoint. But the industrial worker is much more reliable Communist material because he does not dream of becoming his own boss.

Cucchi told me that he and Magnani (the other renegade) had been considering quitting the party for some time when they left in January, 1951

for the same reasons we joined it. I joined the party with Magnani in 1936 because we thought it was the only way to solve Italy's great problem by establishing socialism. During the struggle against Mussolini and during the war, there was real elementary democracy in the party. I and the other officials of the resistance were elected, not named from above. Until the Cominform was established, there was always the possibility in communism of real independence for all the Communist Parties, with each following its own line. The Cominform's creation caused us to start an opposition within our party. The oppositionist element were mainly partisan veterans and union leaders. We argued: How could Russia decide Italy's labor policy, for example? Until the election of 1948 we had the impression that Togliatti would soon be a Titoist and would break with Moscow. In the party Togliatti was then always changing the appearance of his policy from day to day. But after the 1948 elections we lost such hopes and we then tried to form a faction within the party.

In 1950 I was sent to Moscow to persuade me to get rid of my doubts about Soviet wisdom on Italian affairs. I was there three weeks. Then I was given a post as a functionary in the Soviet-Italian society. I came back entirely disillusioned. I am not a Leninist. We must return to Marx. Marxism is fundamentally democratic. The dictatorship of the proletariat cannot succeed in Western Europe except in Spain which is as backward as Russia was at the time of the revolution. It won't even succeed in Czechoslovakia as far as Eastern Europe is concerned.

BOLOGNA, *February 23, 1954*

CARDINAL Lercaro, Bishop of Bologna, is a short, slightly overweight man with a rather undistinguished face and manner. Nevertheless he has the reputation of being exceptionally intelligent and forceful. He is seen by many as leader of the left-wing faction in the church. He is very ambitious to be the next Pope and is held by many to have an excellent chance. At Ravenna four years ago there was an incident when the rich and poor priests appeared to be in dispute. Lercaro ordered them to pool their property entirely and then to redivide it in equal shares. He had the permission of the Pope to do this.

I saw the cardinal in his bishop's palace. He sat in a stiff armchair with a huge amethyst ring on his right hand with which he played as he talked. He said the main reasons for Communist strength in Italy were: economic and social problems; Italian psychological nature; and the country's religious feeling.

The economic and social problems were self-evident, he said. He said psychologically the Italian character always sought "quick" solutions to problems, like fascism or communism. As for religion, the cardinal said that unfortunately the religiosity of the Italian people was very shallow. Italian Catholics were Catholic more by tradition and heritage than by belief.

The Communists were able to avail themselves of this situation through the efficiency of their total organization. They penetrated all forms of life. Communism is actually a religion with its own religious forms (pictures of Stalin, Lenin and Togliatti), its own marriage and burial customs. It must be fought in all fields, including that of religion. The Cardinal explained that the twenty-two friars of Fraternitas (his so-called "flying squads") are "the assault troops or *arditi* of anticommunism." He claimed that they had had one outstanding "conversion" of a militant Communist who returned to Catholicism. He said that Fraternitas was doing what the Jesuits had done in the days of the counter-Reformation and that a counter-Reformation was necessary in Italy to take a stand and erect a dam against communism. He warned that one of the great dangers of communism was its attraction to youth, which must be offset.

I asked Cardinal Lercaro if the Communists had ever sought to penetrate the Catholic Church hierarchy itself, and he replied in the affirmative. He said a Jesuit priest in Rome was attached to the Vatican secretariat working in the political section. He remained there until just before the 1953 elections when he quit and publicly joined the Communist Party, for which he was now writing and working. There was evidence that he had had access to a great deal of confidential material which he had passed on to the Communists.

BOLOGNA, *February 23, 1954*

GIUSEPPE Dozza is the mayor of Bologna and president of a League of Democratic Communities which, in effect, means Communist municipalities. He is one of the handful of top Communists in Italy. He is an extremely popular and intelligent man. He received me in his mayor's office in the Palazzo del Municipio, a beautiful medieval building on the main square of Bologna. He is heavy-set, smiling, with sharp features, a shock of white hair and the powerful nose and jaw of a *condottiere*.

When I asked Dozza why communism was so strong in Italy, he replied that the tradition of Italy's labor movement had been violently interrupted by fascism. When communism started here, it was small and weak and had no great force in the unions. But during the twenty years of fascism, the Communists were always at the head of the struggle leading strikes, trials and fights against fascism, and later on against the Germans. This process formed a cadre of experienced leaders. They were all in a position to exert the influence of their experience during the wartime resistance. He said:

If I were an anti-Communist, I would not counsel anyone to take exceptional measures against the party such as outlawing it. Look at the way the Communist Party grew during the fascist repression. We never gave up the struggle and by our sacrifices we gained leadership of all antifascist movements, not just our own. Unknown youths imprisoned for ten or fifteen years educated themselves in their cell and assumed leadership over older and better-known prisoners. When these people emerged from prisons and from hiding, they gained the confidence of the masses.

FLORENCE, *February 26, 1954*

BERNARD Berenson is an extraordinary old man. A Lithuanian Jew who was brought up in Boston and graduated from Harvard, he came to Florence as the purchasing agent of Mrs. Jack Gardner and finally settled down here, becoming the world's most famous authority on Florentine and Sienese art. He is also rather a philosopher and a collector. Having started out with nothing, he now lives in a magnificent house filled with wonderful fourteenth- and fifteenth-century paintings, surrounded by cypresses and a lovely garden. His personal collection includes paintings by Lippo Memi, Sassetta, Luca Signorelli. He has also acquired various pieces of Oriental art including Khmer and Siamese heads. And he has assembled an unequaled art and archeology library which he is leaving to Harvard University in his will. He is proudest of this library which he thinks will still be of concrete use a century from now. He came to Florence about sixty-five years ago, his friends say, and most of his paintings were bought around the turn of the century for a song. He moved into this house, *I Tatti*, fifty-four years ago. His secretary, Miss Nicki Mariano, has been with him for years, and they are supposed to adore each other. During the war the German consul in Florence helped to save his possessions from the Nazis. He went into hiding in the hills. He is now eighty-eight years old and says he is living on his capital, that it will be a race between his capital and death. He still works every day. He wakes up at six o'clock and works in bed. He is now producing a book on Giorgione and plans to go to Venice in April for a long trip of investigation.

He is extraordinary-looking: very small and frail, neat and erect, dapper with a pointed beard; rather handsome, and resembles a figure out of a Henry James book with a definitely Bostonian-cut suit and a flower in his buttonhole. His accent and his manner are exceedingly courtly. He has a curious habit when he meets someone of standing off on the side and examining him carefully as if he were a painting. His vocabulary is rather old-fashioned and he is a definite snob, continually referring to people as "well born" or the opposite. He is clearly delighted at the social success he has had, as a little Jewish emigrant. He is a close friend of former Prince

Paul of Jugoslavia and the darling of Florentine society, one of the "sights" of Italy. Almost anyone with intellectual pretensions who comes to Florence visits him—people like Sinclair Lewis or Cyril Connolly. Despite his age he continually entertains at luncheon, tea or dinner. One of his favorite hobbies is to try and befuddle and embarrass pretty young women with impertinent questions. These are some of his observations:

Italians care only for their pride, not for their national interests. If before the war the British and French parliaments had voted that the Italians had the best army in the world, Mussolini would have been overthrown immediately.

Berenson says he has a deep mistrust of mobs, any mob. Even a Century Club mob would be dangerous, he says. Italian mobs are brutal and cruel.

He claims Trieste is of no earthly interest or importance, but merely a question of alliteration. Hundreds of thousands of Italians died for "Trento and Trieste." If the Italians had given Tito Trieste at the start, the question would now be forgotten. The truth is that the Italians are terrible soldiers and cannot be relied upon, whereas the opposite is true of the Jugoslavs. We should warn the Italians that if their government goes Communist, we will base all our Mediterranean defenses in Jugoslavia.

The Italians dislike the British and have a contempt for the United States. They view us as intellectual barbarians, their opinion being based largely upon our magazines and our movies. They feel as if they were pressed between the Soviet and American millstones. They don't have any idea what the Russians are, so they are drawn to them. Many Italian intellectuals are revolted by United States culture and, therefore, with no other reason, become pro-Communist. Some of them go behind the iron curtain where they are impressed by carefully conducted propaganda tours.

"The big task is to make the Italians realize that communism is a one-way street and that it represents Soviet dictatorship and not an Italian ideological experiment," he argues.

CONSUMA, *February 27, 1954*

I drove to Consuma on the comb of the snow-powdered Tuscan hills in order to see Professor Giorgio LaPira, mayor of Florence, who is taking a brief vacation here. He is an extraordinary phenomenon of modern politics: a saintly little man who lives permanently in Florence's San Marco, the Dominican monastery with frescoes by Fra Angelico, where Savonarola lived. Incidentally, LaPira is a professor of Roman law. Nuns are taking care of him while he is mayor. He came to a simple, freezing, little pension over the weekend in order to get some work done uninterrupted. We sat by a small fire with our overcoats on as he chattered away, occasionally looking up, like a little insect, above his glasses with an inquisitive, humorous face. This is what he said:

Democracy has different aspects in different lands. So does communism. Without doubt, Italy is in a situation where numberless masses of the people, above all in the South, need to be liberated from the uncertainty of life. They require food, housing and the essentials of life. This is not Marxism or theory. It is a fact. Democracy must give these people hope. In the United States there is both hope for greater production and spiritual values.

I am impressed by what I read of the writings of Thomas Merton and see the quest for contemplation in the United States. The elementary problems in your country have already been solved, and there is a high standard of living which permits religions and contemplation to develop. But in Italy the people are immediately occupied with the task of finding bread.

Christian Democracy and all Italian democracy have been too wrapped up in political affairs and have lost time in dealing with pressing social problems. The problems of life have grown more rapidly than corrective measures. The parties succeeding fascism have unfortunately adopted pre-Fascist habits. They are more Machiavellian than liberal in spirit. The same aristocrats and landlords are in power; the same feudalism in the south. The people are fed up and want something new and communism is making the most of it. Democracy must present a new and spiritual vitality. The Italian ruling classes have failed in this responsibility.

Florence is a citadel of the spirit and culture and therefore of particular importance as a symbol. It is a citadel of the West, and that is why we had to defend it in municipal elections and win it back from Communist control. I am now experimenting there on a small scale, trying to give work and housing and to end unemployment; to help the hungry and the jobless in special canteens. The industrialists showed insensitivity to the basic problems and selfishly closed down their factories without thinking of the human or political consequences. . . .

There are only two choices in Italy at present—Christian Democracy or communism. We must polarize Christian Democracy towards the left. You cannot apply pre-Fascist democracy to post-Fascist people. The need now is for dynamic democracy. Unfortunately the leaders of our party mistrust the ability of the younger people. We must rely more upon youth.

Communism is a danger to Italy, but not yet a mortal danger. We must be aware of it and take steps to curb it, but we have time and ability.

Unemployment is like slavery. Jobs and houses are necessary regardless of the cost. Liberty and spirituality together with practical care are the essentials of democracy and those who do not recognize and accept this are not true democrats. We Left-Christian Democrats are not visionaries, but realists. To see the basic necessities of the situation is not to be visionary. We are not poets but realists who see the realities of life. There must be a purification of the ruling classes, political, social and economic. Gandhi, after all, achieved this in India.

ROME, *March 2, 1954*

GIUSSEPPE Saragat, head of the Democratic Socialist faction (future President of Italy), is tall and youthful with a gentle manner. He has an exceptionally high forehead. He is affable but has a rather disagreeable way of rarely looking you in the eye. This is what he said:

> To combat communism a good social policy must be instituted. The problem in Italy is not like the United States where communism is merely a small police problem, and not social and human, as it is here. The difference of standard of living between the classes is far too sharp in Italy. It is hard to know what can be done because this is not a laboratory where you can do what you want. We are dealing with people and history. The Italian *bourgeoisie* is unenlightened and backward. The proof of the matter is that this is the bourgeoisie that created fascism in order to fight communism.
>
> Italy has no liberal traditions in politics like Britain nor in the proletariat like France. We had nothing like the English revolution of the 17th century nor the French revolution of the 18th century. The only revolution here was national and intellectual, and the masses never participated. The mob has no tradition of liberty. And there were no religious revolutions here as elsewhere in the northern countries of Europe. All we had was the Counterreformation. History weighs heavily upon us. Then there was fascism, which was not thrown off by the people but by war. Democracy was foisted upon us, not won.
>
> [Pietro] Nenni [the left-socialist] is more pro-Russian than he is pro-Communist. Also he plays a double game. He speaks to crowds in virtually the language of European socialism—like Bevan or Guy Mollet—but in inner party circles he talks like a Communist. The masses follow Nenni because Italian socialism has always had a strong left-wing maximalist tradition. Its fundamental idea is class warfare. It is a primary form of socialism which exists only in Italy.

Saragat said that Nenni has a remarkable personality and is the most powerful orator in Italy. Many capitalists join Nenni's movement because it represents a guarantee for the future. They can tell the Americans, "I am not a Communist" if the Americans win. And they can tell the Russians, "I am pro-Russian" if the Russians win. Therefore industrialists give money to Nenni as insurance.

ROME, *March 4, 1954*

IGNAZIO Silone is a fairly big, middle-aged man with a mustache. He was very affable and was wearing a dapper tan suit. His rather attractive Irish wife sat beside us while we talked and kept passing whisky and port.

Silone says there are no simple, easy answers to the question of the strength of Communism in Italy, and there are many paradoxes. In some areas where there is misery there is little communism, and in other rich areas there is much Communism. Communism conquered a majority among the workers because it lacked organized opposition there. There has been a strong syndicalist tradition in Italy since the days of the First International. After World War II the labor movement was reconstituted with three controlling bodies—Catholic, Communist and Socialist. But the schism in the Socialist Party was badly handled and without prior discussion with the trade union leaders whose majority were anti-Communist. The union leaders were irked and did not go along with the right-wing Socialists.

While other parties devoted themselves to parliamentary struggles, the Communists carefully organized the factories and unions without adversaries. When American labor leaders tried to intervene and set up a new labor movement, opposite results were often obtained. The Americans should have refrained from external pressure and waited until there was a real schism in the labor movement instead of doing what they did in 1948 when they helped the Catholics to quit the labor federation and at the same time formed a Social Democratic federation. Catholic syndicalist traditions are different from those of the Socialists, and the Catholics are often regarded as strikebreakers. But American labor leaders didn't understand the situation and thought simply of Communist and anti-Communist. They helped to liquidate the real Socialist strength by breaking the unity of action among anti-Communists.

Silone said from personal experience he found that Communist crowds here are not concerned about vague things like liberty and morality, but are very impressed by statistics of power and relative forces. He said:

> Communism's exaltation in its own force is its most important strength. The Communist likes to feel that the future belongs to Russia, and therefore he must be with it; not that Russia is right. Every argument that reinforces the impression of the horrible and inevitable power of Russia reinforces communism in Italy. When Communist propaganda complained about the American atomic bomb, it weakened the party's position in Italy because people realized that the United States was strong. Twenty years of fascism has developed a cult of force.

Silone believes that behind the campaign now going on to emphasize the strength of communism is the preparation by the extreme right for a *coup de force* against the Communists. He thinks the military want to see something like a Reichstag fire to use as an excuse. Silone fears this and thinks it is not the solution. He adds, "I fear the trend among the right where the cult of force also has influence and which says, If all they respect is force, let's give them force."

Ignazio Silone, whose real name is Secondo Tranquilli, is the author of *Fontamara, Bread and Wine,* and *A Handful of Strawberries,* for all of which his native Abruzzi region in the central Apennine mountains provides the setting. He is now fifty-three. During the past thirty-five years he has covered the whole range of Marxism: a leader of the extreme left-wing youth organization of the Socialist Party after World War I, he advocated Communist secession at the famous Leghorn Congress of 1921 and was then made a charter member of Italy's Communist Party at a time when Palmiro Togliatti was still obscure.

Until 1930 Silone was one of the leading lights of western communism, prominent in the *émigré* organization in Paris and a frequent visitor to Moscow. He broke with the party in 1930. In 1945 Silone returned to Italy as a Nenni Socialist, became deputy of the Constituent Assembly (1946–1947) and editor-in-chief of the party organ, *Avanti*. In the latter capacity he had a row with Nenni and has ever since been loosely affiliated with Saragat's right-wing Socialist Party.

ROME, *March 4, 1954*

AMINTORE Fanfani (past and future prime minister) is the leader of the extreme left-wing group of the Christian Democratic Party. Industrialists attack him as being a "white Communist." He was prime minister for a few days early this year, but his government was not confirmed by the parliament. He proved to be entirely different from anything I had expected. He resembled a Tammany Hall ward heeler a great deal more than a left-wing idealist. Fanfani is a small, affable man, stocky, with a shrewd face. He speaks fluent bad French—which seems to be the trademark of the educated Italian.

He said the maximum strength of the Communist Party in Italy had been reached before the June, 1953, elections. It was now dangerous to give the impression that either Russia or communism was too strong. That helped the possibilities of communism conquering the country. The Italian people were frightened and weak and were much impressed by appearances of strength. He himself did not agree with those who see an imminent Communist Party victory. Furthermore, he said, such an impression aids Communist propaganda. He added, "Togliatti must be very happy about it."

One of the greatest strengths of communism in Italy is that it does not present itself as communism. The leaders of the party realize that communism as such is unpalatable. Thus, when Togliatti came back to Italy during the war, he supported the King and accepted a concordat with the Pope. The Communists actually pretended to be more friendly to religion than other groups such as the Socialists.

ROME, *March 5, 1954*

I dined last night with Ambassador Clare Booth Luce and spent the entire evening until after midnight talking to her—that is to say, listening to her. I was appalled. She is an exceptionally beautiful woman—quite astonishingly so when one considers her age. She has the (lifted) skin of a girl and an excellent figure. But this exterior conceals the most arrogant conceit and the most ruthlessly hard-boiled self-assurance it has ever been my privilege to come up against. Furthermore, Mrs. Luce blandly assumes that she has everybody eating out of her hand in a few minutes' time. At one point in our conversation she said that an American newspaper columnist had written, "Poor Clare Luce thinks she can save the situation in Italy by charm alone." "If he only knew," she said with mock *Weltschmerz*.

She started off the evening by assuring me with an earnestly appealing look in her eyes that she kept a scrapbook of things of particular interest and that it was filled with my articles. From that moment on she seemed to assume that I was 100 per cent on her side. In fact, when we left some time after midnight, she said, "And now I am counting on you to help me out by explaining the situation as I outlined it."

It was a small dinner party at which Harry Luce played the part of hostess. That is to say, after dinner he sat in one room with the ladies and a couple of characters from an advertising agency that presumably does big business with *Time* and *Life,* while Mrs. Luce, the ambassador, sat in a small room over the brandy (she didn't smoke a cigar) with Cortesi (our correspondent), myself and Elbridge Durbrow, embassy minister. As she explained the intricacies of the situation and her own brilliance in handling it, she would occasionally turn to Durbrow and say, "Durby, isn't that so?" Whereupon Durbrow would nod sagely and add a platitude like, "Yes, the ambassador really handled that one well." With a claque like that it is easy to see why her self-esteem floats blandly along.

I have a feeling that she is now messing with some really bad scheme, having tried to climb aboard the bandwagon of an anticipated De Gasperi election victory last summer—which did not materialize—by warning that American aid would be withdrawn from Italy unless the proper party won. Two days ago she called on Scelba, the new prime minister, and spent a couple of hours with him although he hasn't yet been confirmed by parliament. She also flew down to Naples to see Admiral Fechteler. I have a dreary suspicion she is trying to cook up some kind of violent action to insure that the Communists are not going to gain power in Italy. And if she has a hand in it, I gravely fear it is going to be a fiasco.

Our evening started off with a conversation about the Vatican (Mrs. Luce is a converted Catholic). She told me the Vatican was in complete chaos and confusion because the Pope has always insisted upon being his own secretary of state and would never let anybody else assume the functions. Now he is too ill to act himself. The two assistants who help him in these secular fields are Msgr. Montini and Msgr. Tardini. She describes Montini (later Pope Paul VI) as left-wing and pro-American and Tardini as right-wing and pro-Spanish. If Montini is even remotely left-wing, I will eat my hat covered with chocolate sauce. I know him and have often talked with him. She said that it was Tardini who sent, in the Pope's name, a message of congratulations to Senator McCarthy when he was married; that this never would have been done if the Pope had been healthy and active.

She then turned—for the benefit of Lily Cannon, wife of the American ambassador in Greece (and Lily was gnashing her teeth throughout the performance)—to the subject of the difficulties of being American ambassador in Italy. One of these difficulties is entertaining the thousands of Americans who pour through. Therefore, Mrs. Luce said that for the first time in American diplomatic history she has organized a system to take care of it. The lowest category is treated to a performance which Mrs. Luce kindly calls "four o'clock shadow." These characters are invited to the embassy chancery at four o'clock in the afternoon, and Mrs. Luce goes down the line shaking hands with them as they stand around in the hallway. The people in this category she described as persons with letters from Congressmen she doesn't know, who are obviously also unknown to the Congressmen, and people who write in to her merely expressing curiosity to meet her, or people of no importance who assure her they voted for her in the Connecticut elections. The second category are people who are honored by invitations to cocktail parties. These are people recommended by more important political figures back home or by friends of hers, but who have no importance in themselves. The third category is invited to dinner. These, she said, looking at me with a soupy expression in her eyes, are "friends."

At dinner I sat next to Mrs. Luce and had an extremely interesting time listening to her. I am rather fascinated at the way in which she acquires knowledge here. I presume it must be by osmosis because surely she does not listen to what anybody has to say. She is not interested in listening because she is talking all the time herself. She assured me that the problem in Italy was decidedly complex. Forty-nine per cent of the people had supported the De Gasperi coalition—that is to say, the way the votes were counted (1,300,000 votes were thrown out as the result of Communist challenges). This coalition included the Christian Democratic Party, the Saragat Socialists, the Liberals and the Republicans. Fifty-one per cent of the people were either in the left-wing bloc of Communists and Nenni Socialists or the neo-Fascists and the Monarchists. In parliament this percentage applies.

That meant that 49 per cent of the people were trying to govern "the other 61 per cent." (Throughout the evening she kept referring to the other 61 per cent—meaning, of course, 51 per cent.) Therefore the problem was quite simple. The problem was how can an arrangement be made with the right to bring the right into the government. I asked Mrs. Luce if by this she meant just the Monarchists or the Monarchists and the neo-Fascist MSI. She said it would have to be just the Monarchists. However, they simply had to be brought in in order to make a government that could really function. The Scelba government could never succeed, she felt.

She very much regretted, but she did not think that real democracy could work in Italy at present. Perhaps one had to jam the wig of Thomas Jefferson on the head of Mussolini. She regretted that there was no man around like General Naguib, Colonel Gamal Abdel Nasser (she continually refers to this new subject of knowledge as "Nasseer") or Kemal Ataturk because a man like that could rule Italy with a strong hand and then turn it over to democracy on his death. At this point she interrupted her steady stream to say that her husband had just come back from Egypt. He had arrived just before the recent *coup d'état* but had stayed long enough to straighten things out and, she added with a giggle, to get Naguib back in. She said he had had a long talk with Colonel Nasser trying to persuade him to institute freedom of the press. I have not noticed any success along these lines. She also said that despite the miserable gap between poverty and wealth in Italy, Harry had told her that in Egypt the "fellowhens" (here, of course, she meant the fellahin) were worse off than the Italian peasants.

It was absolutely necessary, in order to save Italy from communism, to get a large appropriation out of Congress to give Italy large off-shore procurement contracts and other direct injections of economic aid. She regretted that she no longer had the club that had been so badly used by the Democratic envoys here, Dunn and Bunker. Now, instead of the enormous club they had represented by "New Deal billions," she only had a tiny little "matchstick." Yet she would do her best with that matchstick. But it was not enough, and if Italy was to be saved, there had to be a large appropriation.

In order to get this appropriation, however, Congress had to be awakened to the dangers of the situation in Italy. Italy was its own Indochina. Congress had to realize that it was going to fall to communism unless Congress acted. But the art was to scare Congress sufficiently without scaring Italy too much. The Italians were great bandwagon riders. As soon as they thought communism was going to win or Russia was going to win, they all jumped on the Soviet bandwagon. The task was, therefore, to scare Congress but not scare the Italians too much. She thought Congress had now been scared enough by recent articles and the appropriation would come through.

Last week Senator Styles Bridges (Republican) and Senator Stuart Symington (Democrat) came through here. They were investigating off-shore procurement contracts. They arrived simply horrified by some of the contracts that had been let in Italy and determined to block a project for establishment of an F-86 (Sabre) plant at Turin, which Fiat is trying to get. Bridges argued it was ridiculous to establish such a factory in dangerously exposed North Italy which might fall to the Communists. Symington argued that it was economically absurd because the same planes could be manufactured cheaper at home, and the necessary materials were not available here.

But Mrs. Luce said without any pretence of modesty that she had taken care of them and here Durbrow faithfully nodded and echoed his assent. Mrs. Luce said she had prepared a very large chart showing the dangers to the United States and the cost to the United States if Italy went Communist, as compared with the cost of carrying out off-shore procurement and other commitments here. These were shown to the senators and she had some of her experts around to brief them on details.

Then she hauled out the gimmick. She said she warns all Republican legislators who come through that if Italy goes Communist, not only will it be a disaster to the United States, but it will be an incredible political defeat for the Republican Party. It would make the loss of China look small by comparison. The loss of Italy would have a profound effect on Americans of Italian descent and on Catholics in the United States. The Republicans could never win an election after losing Italy. She said this produced a grim effect on Bridges and changed his views entirely.

I asked her what she did for Democrats. She said she then turned to Symington—and this is her formula for all Democrats—and said, "Of course I would be forced to report to the American people that Communism gained power in Italy because of the help of Democratic administrations from 1943 to 1952, who brought Togliatti back."

Mrs. Luce has the most extraordinary contempt, which she does not bother to conceal, for the intellectual acuteness of apparently everybody. She says the Italians are corrupt cowards who are unable to govern themselves by democratic means. She says there is no chance of a third-force government such as the present one continuing for any long period, as has been the case in France, and anybody who thinks so simply does not understand Italy. The only thing is for the right to come in.

She has contempt for the moral values of the Italians. She says one of the largest companies in Italy has bought several deputies and corrupts the government. The government never passes any decent tax laws or slaps tax cases against the rich because it is bribed by the rich. She has contempt for the real workings of democracy as displayed by her remarks on the subject of Bridges and Symington. And she surely must have contempt for the Italian mentality if she thinks she can play this game of scaring Congress up to fever temperature while not scaring the Italians "too much."

It was obvious from names she dropped here and there during our four-hour conversation that the people she sees most of in Italy are—as is so often the case among our envoys abroad—those who speak English. She was talking to me about an evening she had spent the other week with a group of "intellectuals." It turned out to be a dinner at Luigi Barzini's house.

She says the Italians have been firmly convinced that they can blackmail help out of the United States because we cannot afford to give Italy up. Therefore she is assuring them that this is not the case. She sent Durbrow out the other day to pass along word that with American bases in Spain and Turkey, and with Wheelus Field in Libya, and with the new weapons now available, it was quite possible for the United States to withdraw from Italy and still maintain its NATO commitments.

She said Italian industrialists have no idea of what modern labor-capital relations are. Costa, the head of the Italian industrialists' federation, assured her he was an anti-Communist because for two years he has resisted every effort by the labor unions to get a raise.

Mrs. Luce is very intrigued by the appointment of Bogomolov as Soviet ambassador to Italy. She has some strange theory based upon an eclectic version of all the rumors one hears among the Italians (who like to flatter themselves that Moscow sends its best hatchet men to Rome). Her assumption is that Bogomolov has been sent here to make the basic decision as to whether Russia will encourage the Italian Communists to make a decisive move to capture Italy or to refuse any challenge in case the issue comes to a fight. I think she has a rather simplified idea that a Russian ambassador can make up his mind on the scene and (1) can commit the Soviet government one way or the other on issues of major policy, or (2) can issue orders to a disciplined local Communist Party to follow one or another party line. She seems to have absorbed the current Italian theory that Bogomolov is a Soviet hatchet man who, among other things, arranged the Czechoslovakian *coup d'état*. I pointed out to her that Bogomolov had nothing to do with the Czechoslovakian *coup d'état* (to which Durbrow was reluctantly forced to accede).

Several times during our conversation Mrs. Luce referred loosely to the danger that the conflict between Communists and anti-Communists might erupt "into the piazzas." I asked her if this would not be a good thing, from an American point of view, since she was convinced that the Communists themselves were a minority of the nation and the militant Communists were a very small minority within the party. She seemed to think it would be a good thing but only when there was a strong government firmly in the saddle. That government would not be, she said, the Scelba government, but a government based upon Monarchist support.

Mrs. Luce said it was a shame that we had not been able to do something dramatic for Italy on the subject of Trieste. If the October 8 decision had gone through, the Italians would have been pleased, but we allowed ourselves to be blocked by Tito. She admitted, upon prodding, that even the October 8 decision might have lost popularity some months later if its opponents had continually attacked the government in terms of what had happened to Italians in Zone B, abandoned to Jugoslavia.

She blamed the government for never taking adequate steps against the Communists. She said she had a list of dozens of moves taken by the

French government against the Communists—things like eliminating them from positions of influence in the communications setup, and so forth. But the Italian government of past years had done scarcely anything along similar lines.

Mrs. Luce contends that she is taking the "unprecedented step" of using the information from American consulates around Italy to assess embassy views on the condition of the country rather than depending solely upon information acquired in Rome. Such an assertion is, I believe, unwarranted; I certainly hope so, at any rate. She said she sends out questionnaires to consular officials every so often requesting information on specific matters. The last one was a question asking whether it would be a good thing from a United States point of view to have national elections in Italy at this time. She said that from all over the country United States consular officials replied in the negative.

She professed to be horrified by the medieval attitude of many of the wealthy society people here and the great gap between the rich and the poor of Italy. She says that sometimes she finds herself reacting subconsciously to the effect, "that almost makes a Communist out of me."

The evening, which certainly was an interesting one objectively, if not subjectively, terminated shortly after midnight. Ambassador Luce, Durbrow, Cortesi and I were still sitting in a small room with the beautiful blonde envoy talking away at a great clip. Durbrow, looking up, saw the other guests filing into the hall shepherded by Mr. Luce and told the ambassador that some of her guests appeared to be leaving. We all got up and said farewell; and nobody restrained us. Marina told me afterwards, in a blaze of white fury, that Mr. Luce looked at his watch as he was jabbering away with the ladies and suddenly said: "It is twelve o'clock. The embassy car is here waiting for you, Mrs. Cannon." Lily Cannon was apparently in the middle of a story. There was a dead, embarrassed silence all around. Then everybody got up and Mr. Luce practically pushed them out the door.

Mrs. Luce in the course of her remarks during the evening had said that basic American policy was to arrange some kind of a *quid pro quo* with Italy in exchange for aid. She is confident that in the end she will be able to secure the aid she wants. In exchange for this she wants a commitment from the Italian government to put through certain specific reforms in the social and economic field. In order to get a government strong enough to enact such reforms, she feels it is necessary to call upon support from the right—namely, the Monarchists. She describes this as not "an American *quid*" for "an American *quo*" but for "an Italian *quo*." What she means by this is that Italy would be doing itself good. This is a pretty sane idea, and while it is interference in the internal affairs of another country, it is benevolent interference and based upon direct aid also. However, what I would question is the wisdom of calling upon the right.

ROME, *March 5, 1954*

DE Gasperi, now just running the Christian Democratic Party, survives
remarkably. He is almost eighty and I must say he looks a good deal
younger than his comrade, Adenauer. He is full of energy, health and good
humor. He said he is now limiting himself to party affairs because it is of
paramount importance in the struggle against communism to get the party
into good shape.

De Gasperi said the problem now is not so much the revival of communism as it is the strengthening of the extreme right. "The two together
represent a return to the shadows of the past. In a sense, what has hurt the
center has been anticommunism (the right) rather than communism." He
almost wept when complaining of Mrs. Luce's efforts to encourage the
right in a misguided anti-Communist move.

It is difficult for us to form a government with the Monarchists, as
your ambassador wants. That poses the question of the regime which is
very important. The danger comes more from a rightist revival than
from communism. You cannot expect us democrats who fought fascism
to join with fascism. There are two methods of defense against communism. Either all the moderate anti-Communist votes should be rallied, or
we must depend upon the Monarchists. It is a question of one or the
other. But, if the Monarchists come in, the Saragat Socialists and
Republicans will work with the Communists, and they will be lost
forever.

De Gasperi said that in the south, even in Bourbon times, the poor
people were with the King against the aristocracy, and this tradition still
continues. That is one of the appeals that monarchism has, politically
speaking.

He said it would be unconstitutional to outlaw the Communist Party.
Mrs. Luce once discussed this matter with De Gasperi and explained that
communism could not be outlawed in the United States because it would be
against the Constitution. He pointed out it would be even more against the
Italian Constitution, which had been made in 1946 with the collaboration
of the Communist Party.

De Gasperi recalled mournfully that the Communists had captured the
resistance movement during the war. "We were schoolboys compared to
the leaders Moscow sent us," he said.

ROME, *March 5, 1954*

I saw Pietro Nenni, former foreign minister (for a brief moment) in one
of the early postwar De Gasperi cabinets and leader of the fellow-traveling
left-wing Socialist Party, in his office in the parliament building. He is a
pale, almost bald man with spectacles and a rather unimpressive physique.

He has the reputation of being an exceptionally powerful orator who is able to sway crowds. He is also said to be astonishingly intelligent. I must admit he made no particular impression upon me, either positive or negative.

He said the Socialist Party was a considerable force in Italy before the advent of fascism. At the 1919 elections 156 Socialist deputies, or about one-third of the parliamentary seats, were elected by the party. The Communist Party started in Italy only in 1920. At first it was very sectarian and weak. In the 1921 elections only a small minority of the working class voted for the Communists.

However during twenty years of fascism there was a very large development of Communist "opinion" in Italy. Mussolini made the mistake of posing a choice to the Italian people as between "Rome (the Church) or Moscow." This helped to swing many anti-Fascists, above all the most vigorous enemies of the system, towards the Communist camp.

When fascism collapsed, the relationship of power between the Communist Party and the Socialists had been reversed. Nenni personally had made a great effort to reorganize the Socialist Party, he said, and to bring hundreds of thousands of workers back from the idea of communism into socialism. He said that in the 1946 elections his party had a considerable success and more votes than the Communists. But the schism within the Socialist Party had enfeebled it. Today the relative strength of the Socialists plus the Communists—that is to say, the left-wing bloc—compared to the rest of the country was in no sense miraculous if one looked back to the strength of the working class movement in 1920.

He said he and Togliatti had had their differences. While he was in exile in Paris, he had quarreled with the Communists. But their struggle ended in 1933–1934 when Hitler came to power in Germany and the Communists realized how dangerous sectarian disputes were for the workers. Unity of action was agreed upon. The present Italian government and its predecessors were not truly democratic. There was only a veneer of democracy, liberty and freedom of speech, but no substance of democracy. He said:

> My relations with the Communist Party are based on sentiment. We struggled together; we were imprisoned together; we were sent to the same concentration camps together. But our collaboration is also based upon the facts of the situation. I am not a Communist. But I think we must continue our fight for success in solving political and social problems. I don't believe Togliatti is a foreign agent. But the Italian Communist Party has made an effort to be a moderate nonsectarian party. We are not bound to the Communists in any way, and if they err, we will withdraw our support. Furthermore, I am the first to recognize that many Socialists disagree with me. But when Saragat split off from the Party, many of our members quit and joined the Communists because they were fed up with rivalry among the leaders. I regard myself as

always independent and free to abandon collaboration with the Communists.

I asked Nenni if it was true that he had been a Fascist and had organized fascism for Bologna. He replied that fascism had come from the extreme left interventionists of the World War I period. He had been in the Republican Party at that time. During the war he had been a member of the *"Fasci Revoluzionari della Guerra"* from which the Fascist Party eventually came. He said he had been in these *"Fasci"* until the point had been reached where he had to either join the Fascist Party or another party. Then he joined the Socialists in 1920.

ROME, *March 6, 1954*

PRIME Minister Mario Scelba received me in his private law office where he spends the evening whenever possible, winding up his attorney's business now that he is back in politics. He is a bald, chubby, short man with long nose and a shrewd, ugly, humorous face. He looks something like a pudgy Roman emperor. We started right off talking about communism, and he remarked that this was a question that must be regarded with calm serenity. Unfortunately it had been sensationalized by the foreign press.

There is no danger of Communist conquest of power in Italy either by legal democratic means or by violence. Communism remains a distinct factor in the national life that makes government actions and the social situation difficult; but it has no chance of taking power, and that is fundamental. The press of the world, as well as the governments of some nations, should remember this in formulating attitudes towards Italy. The forces at the disposal of the state are such as to prevent any attempt at conquest by violence. At any time in recent years that the Communist Party tried a test of strength it was immediately repelled. The government must be and is resolute in its determination to use its strength to check Communist violence or any attempts at seizing authority.

NAPLES, *March 8, 1954*

THIS morning visited Admiral William M. Fechteler at his headquarters of the Allied Command for Southern Europe. Fechteler is an amiable but rather stupid-looking old man. Perhaps appearances are deceiving. We started off talking about communism in Italy, and he was very reluctant to talk until I assured him that everything he said would be considered off the record. He said the Communists, he had been told, had gained control of the Italian labor movement largely by default. They were using money on a widespread basis seeking political control. Fechteler had been told that the Communists had invited Valletta back to run the Fiat works after the war.

He said he didn't believe Italy would go Communist because, "The Catholic conscience of the people would be aroused—at least that's the way it is explained to me." He said, "My interest lies in a strong democratic government in Italy, pro-Western and pro-NATO."

ROME, *March 14, 1954*

FROM A LETTER:

Marina and I have now toured Italy from Turin to Venice to Calabria and talked with Communists, capitalists, priests, labor leaders, etc. I have seen people as far apart as the Cardinals of Genoa and Bologna and Saragat and Nenni or de Gasperi and Mrs. Luce. De Gasperi is almost heartbroken by her manipulations and her ignorant efforts to bring the right wing into a governing coalition thus wrecking his hopes for a moderate, center Christian Democratic Party. But, as Gastone Guidotti, head of the foreign ministry political section, says: "Mrs. Luce is the most important ambassador you have ever had here because she is a member of your Politburo. If there is anything we really want done we persuade her—she circumvents the State Department and telephones the White House. *Time* and *Life* are more valuable to us than experience."

I must say, after working very hard on this trip, I basically and profoundly disagree with Mrs. Luce. She is convinced Communism will take over Italy unless we bring the right into the government. I am convinced Communism will not take over Italy—unless we bring the right into the government. I fear Mrs. L has been listening too much to the liberal leaders who are charming, for the most part English-speaking gentlemen of the old school, exceedingly conservative despite the name of their party.

PARIS, *March 25, 1954*

I had lunch today with Exintaris (Greek Envoy to NATO). He told me America policy on a Balkan alliance has changed embarrassingly. In January Washington suddenly began to exert diplomatic pressure on Greece and Turkey *not* to sign a military pact with Jugoslavia right away. The United States—and Britain seconded the motion as the result of Washington's pressure—suggested to Athens and Ankara that the project be staved off for awhile. This was very embarrassing to the Greeks and the Turks.

The United States wants things delayed in order to point out to the Jugoslavs that it would be easier to get such an agreement if the Trieste question first were settled. Exintaris thinks the Italian government has exercised influence upon Mrs. Luce, the United States Ambassador, who in turn has applied pressure on the State Department. Exintaris thinks this is a disastrous move. He says the Jugoslavs certainly know what's going on. The United States would not have risked such a change in its policy except

for the conviction that the Russians are not now threatening war, thanks to
the Malenkov "new look" policy. Therefore they are willing to try and put
the heat on the Jugoslavs. But the Jugoslavs know this full well. Exintaris
thinks the only way to get the Jugoslavs over on our side for sure is to sign
them up in a Balkan military alliance. If we keep up this kind of dilly-
dallying policy, they may change their minds and succumb to the "new
look."

PARIS, *March 25, 1954*

I had a chat with Ambassador Douglas Dillon this afternoon. It is the first
time I have seen him in months because he has been laid up with a bad
back. Dillon says that early this month David Bruce's office worked out a
schedule of what would be necessary to accomplish by which dates if EDC
was to be ratified before the Geneva conference started April 26. This
tackled the subject from all angles and was shown to certain Frenchmen as
a purely private sort of working paper. It was apparently greeted with
interest and enthusiasm. It was in no sense an official American document
handed to the French. Specifically the paper was shown to Hervé Alphand,
Paul Reynaud and Antoine Pinay. It leaked. The best dope is that the leak
came out of the Hotel de Matignon. Bidault personally was furious that it
was shown to Reynaud because Bidault says Reynaud talks too much and
leaks everything. Herriot picked it up at a Radical Party conference and
called it an American "timetable" which was laying down the law to
France.

Herriot is now very embittered and savage on the subject of EDC. He is
no longer in the least bit reasonable. This has had one good effect, according to Dillon, because some members of his party figure the old man is
going a little bit gaga and are no longer influenced by him.

PARIS, *March 25, 1954*

I spent an hour and three-quarters with Clare Luce this evening. I
must say she was quite interesting. She claims that the October 8 decree
on Trieste went sour because of Eden. She claims that her own formula
which was accepted by the State Department and the British provided for
partition along the lines of Zone A and Zone B without hard and fast
agreement that such a boundary was final—in other words, permitting both
the Jugoslavs and Italians to negotiate minor adjustments later. Finally it
called for a five-power conference—the Jugoslavs and Italians plus the
Western Big Three—to arrive at final solution.

Mrs. Luce says she was horrified when she was advised first by the State
Department that it had been decided that no conference was necessary and
then when she received advice from the British that instructions for Sir

Victor Mallet and Mrs. Luce had been received merely to notify Belgrade and Rome by fiat that partition had been decided upon. None of the other sugar coating for the pill was mentioned. She says Eden had been confident that Tito would accept this.

I asked her if she believed that there was an agreement between the French and the Italians providing that Italy would not ratify EDC until after the French did and providing that the French would support Italy on Trieste. She said yes, that she was convinced there was such an agreement which had been made at Santa Margherita, but she couldn't prove that it existed, nor could she prove exactly what it specified. However, she said that every evidence indicated it did exist.

I asked her whether the Italians had been putting the heat on us to keep the Greeks and the Turks from signing up with the Jugoslavs in a formal military alliance. She said the Italians had certainly been trying every possible thing to get at Tito. She finds among the NATO and SHAPE folks here a general disposition to believe that regardless of Trieste or politics, the Jugoslavs are far better fighting material than the Italians.

While I was talking to her, her husband rang up from London. He had just seen Churchill. Churchill told him that he was planning to retire within the next three months. She was very saddened by this news I wonder if Churchill means it. He has certainly been changing his mind often enough.

I talked with Geoff Parsons today. He said there is going to be a new report on Soviet policy and intentions for the NATO conference in April that is now being drafted and is known up at NATO as the "Sulzberger Report."

PARIS, *March 26, 1954*

LUNCH with Freddy Reinhardt. He said that Dulles' neck was right in a noose on Geneva. There will be no French ratification of EDC before then. Whatever agreement is made on China will be the end of Dulles politically. In order to get French ratification of EDC, there will have to be some help for France on Indochina, which almost inevitably means some kind of concession to Peking. And that would mean the end of Dulles. Yet EDC is the most important point of the adminstration's foreign policy, and China is the most vulnerable political point of that same foreign policy.

PARIS, *March 29, 1954*

LATE this afternoon I had a chat with Hervé Alphand. He went to Berlin for a few days at the end of the Big Four meeting last month, and at a recess of one of the meetings he attended Molotov spotted him and signaled to him to come around and have a glass of vodka. Through an interpreter he told Alphand how glad he was to see him, and then sent word to the French that he wanted Alphand to attend the next Franco-Russian dinner party there because Hervé was "an old friend" and also because he sympathized with him since he had to "defend a difficult cause." When he greeted Alphand, he said "Ah, you are the hero of EDC." Hervé claims he modestly protested that he merely advocated that project. Molotov asked him why. Hervé says he replied, "Because I am seeking the same thing as you are—the prevention of German militarization." He says he explained to Molotov that EDC was a way of preventing a German national army and that the Soviet Union was embarking upon just the wrong course.

Aphand says Molotov undoubtedly scored a great success at Berlin. Hervé says he is now convinced that the most important objective Molotov sought to gain at Berlin was a five-power conference including Communist China. He managed by his brilliant if awkward diplomacy not only to obtain this, but to get the West to propose the meeting.

PARIS, *March 30, 1954*

VERY pleasant talk with Ismay this morning. He says that undoubtedly the latest hydrogen bomb explosion a few weeks ago has completely changed strategic thinking. To his way of thinking, the atom bomb, terrible as it was, was still, relatively speaking, a conservative weapon—just a bigger and more horrible one. The atom bomb meant that you could eradicate cities like Paris or London. Nevertheless, it meant that you had to keep regular troop formations so that if the Russians attacked and wanted, for example, to cross the Rhine River, you could resist and drive them into a concentration that could then be atom-bombed. The effects of the hydrogen bomb are still not to be calculated. It is possible that ultimately it may change all kinds of military thinking. As things now are, however, it is still essential to get a German contribution to NATO—and the best means is EDC.

Ismay is furious with Marshal Juin, who made a speech a few days ago at Auxerre attacking EDC. He thinks such indiscipline should not be tolerated. It would not be tolerated in England. Juin should be retired at the very least.

Ismay told me he spent an hour with Eisenhower in Bermuda and that Eisenhower would talk about nothing but EDC and the necessity of getting it through. Ismay now says he is similarly convinced (I recall in the past when he has referred to it as a silly project), but he stresses that failure of EDC would not in any sense mean failure of NATO.

Ismay says he hopes someday NATO can just become a piece of an overall world alliance which would include ANZUS, Middle East defense areas, and so on; NATO would merely be the biggest piece.

PARIS, *April 1, 1954*

LUNCH with David Bruce. Among other things he told me had heard persistent and serious reports that the *Herald Tribune* was prepared to sell its Paris edition and David urged that *The New York Times* should buy it.

David said there was a great deal of worry among the smaller nations of NATO about the *de facto* existence of what was tantamount to a political standing group—in other words, a controlling committee of the Big Three. In the past the small countries had always talked about it privately and on the side, but now they were actually discussing it in NATO Council meetings.

Regarding this morning's news that Moscow last night had proposed the Soviet Union should join NATO, I recalled to David that I had mentioned this possibility to him more than two months ago in Berlin. He thought it would be fatal if the United States were to say no quickly and unilaterally to Moscow's proposal. We should leave discussion and decision on this matter to the smaller nations, and he hoped we would refer it to the NATO Council. Obviously the whole thing is a trap and a fake, but we should get all of the Allies involved in drafting a means of turning it down.

He said he was now convinced I was right, that there is a secret deal between the French and the Italians providing that the Italians will not act on EDC until after France. He admitted that he had denied this often in the past to me, but he said there was too much evidence in favor of its existence and that he had received information that there had been leaks confirming the existence of this deal.

David says Chip Bohlen is the finest career diplomat in the American foreign service. He only hopes that in a year or so when Chip is eligible to full pension rights, he will retire and get into business or lecturing or writing and stay out of the diplomatic service for a couple of years. He can make some money doing that and will come back in with a fresh mind.

Bruce thinks George Kennan is far too emotional and egocentric. When David was under secretary of state, he got to the point where he simply could not read Kennan's reports and telegrams because they were so long-winded and so blatantly seeking to be literary rather than to provide information.

This afternoon I had a talk with Larry Norstad out at SHAPE. He had been seeing Juin who is out there getting his comeuppance from Al Gruenther. He told me that accounts in this morning's press about Juin spurning a command from prime minister Laniel to show up yesterday evening are a little bit inaccurate. Juin did not just ignore the prime minister's summons. He sent word back when he received the summons that he did not wish to go to the Hotel Matignon because the doorway was completely besieged by reporters and photographers and he thought it would do no good for

France to advertise the situation. Laniel then sent word back to Juin that there was a back door to the Matignon. He told him how it could be used and promised him nobody would know of his arrival. Juin never answered this. Norstad concludes that actually the situation is just a little bit worse than the newspapers made out. He says that as far as Gruenther goes, it is none of Gruenther's business to bawl out Juin on the matter because Juin is a French Marshal, although in the NATO structure Gruenther is his commanding officer. It is up to the French to discipline Juin. Norstad thinks he is a nice guy but also thinks it is appalling and shocking that he should be allowed to get away with his public criticism of French policy on EDC.

I remarked to Larry that it seemed to me that since the March 1 hydrogen bomb explosion showing how incredibly terrible that weapon is, the arguments about relative divisional strengths of potential enemies and the need for West Germany's twelve divisions (promised to the EDC) seemed to have lost point. Norstad replied that in terms of actually winning a war these twelve new divisions probably were not now needed. But the question is how to win without having a war, and to do this you do need the divisions. The only possible victory is to win a peace. For a combination of political and psychological reasons we must have these German divisions. Furthermore to defend Europe (not to "wage war" against the Russians), the German divisions are needed to help prevent overrunning the continent. Local air and ground forces are required for such protective purposes. Western Europe must be defended against being overrun and this cannot be done without some ground forces. The plans set out by NATO for minimum D-Day forces are really a minimum of what is necessary, and they include always the assumption that the German troops will be contributed. After all, if the Russians were able to occupy France, for example—even for a short time—it is very questionable whether it would be "worth taking back."

Norstad says it will be an absolute disaster in terms of our position at Geneva if Dienbienphu falls. There is a French column secretly marching for the relief of the fortress, but it doesn't seem to be doing too well. The fortress was established in a geographical area which was folly from an air point of view. It is in a basin, and the only way it can be supplied is for DC-3s to swoop down over the hills to the flat lands. They are like sitting ducks for antiaircraft and small arms fire as they dip low over the hills, and four or five planes have just been lost during the last two days. This is pretty expensive. The latest news doesn't look good. Norstad thinks there is "a chance" of holding out, but he obviously isn't very optimistic.

PARIS, *April 3, 1954*

WE had a curious group of people for dinner last night. Among them was Lieutenant General Hans Speidel. He was extremely agreeable, but, curiously enough, the French, while appearing to be interested in everything he had to say, seemed to resent anything nice he said about France. After he had left, the French all confided they resented it deeply when he told them about various beautiful spots in France he admired. Did they expect him to say France is ugly?

Gilles de Boisgelin kept murmuring: "You know, this is the first time I have spoken to a German since 1944." I didn't ask him what the circumstances were in 1944. Since Boisgelin is one of Ismay's assistants, I suppose he will have to get used to the idea of speaking to the Germans nine years after the war—especially since NATO's official policy favors a European Army.

I must say that although intellectually I like Speidel and respect him and I believe in his sincerity, I cannot help still feeling uncomfortable with him. Curiously enough, although the West Germans are practically our allies now and there is a climate of hysteria vis-à-vis the Soviet Union, I still think I would probably feel more comfortable sitting down having dinner with a Russian general.

Speidel himself said very little of interest. He claimed the German general staff had not really been influenced to alter its strategic dispositions very much by "Operation Mincemeat." That was the floating ashore of a fake dead marine officer with phony papers attached to his body, designed to give the impression that the first campaign after North Africa would be in Sardinia and Greece, rather than Sicily. Despite Speidel there is evidence the Germans sent at least one extra division to Greece instead of Sicily because of "Mincemeat." Speidel, who was Rommel's chief of staff, said that a much more important deception was that which kept the Germans from launching an all out counterattack in Normandy after the June 1944 landings. They had been completely fooled into believing there were several extra United States divisions still in England ready to make another landing further north, and for that reason the Germans kept strong forces along the coast to the north until it was much too late to make use of them in Normandy. These American "divisions" actually never existed, but a very clever camouflage scheme was worked out to give the impression that they were already disposed in England for a landing on the Continent.

It was amusing to hear Quaroni talking rather contemptuously of the British and of the success he had had in raising a rebellion against them in India by using the Pathan forces of the Faqir of Ipi. At that time Quaroni was Italian minister in Afghanistan. He learned to read and write Persian and sent his messages to the Faqir directly in that language.

Norstad was a little bit moody because right after his arrival his aide called up to tell him that General Vandenberg had just died. Norstad said the situation in Dienbienphu was slightly better; that it had been desperate the night before. He kept observing with some bitterness that it was an idiotic site to choose as a fortress because it could not be properly supplied from the air.

PARIS, *April 7, 1954*

LUNCH today with Gaston Palewski, who regretted very much that our meal wasn't for tomorrow so that we could discuss the reactions to General de Gaulle's press conference. De Gaulle is speaking at 3 P.M. this afternoon. Palewski was disappointed that I was not attending. He said de Gaulle was going to be quite optimistic about the world situation. We will see.

He told me he first met de Gaulle in 1934 when de Gaulle was a major and was drawing up a scheme for armored divisions for the French war ministry. Palewski at the time was working with Reynaud. He said de Gaulle was somewhat more affable and less distant in those days. He also said at that time de Gaulle was rather fond of women. I asked him if he meant that de Gaulle actually was able to carry on a badinage and flirtation in the approved French fashion, and he replied that the badinage was more in the nature of a cavalry charge and that de Gaulle seemed more intent on proving himself than in enjoying the process. His was "the technique of the heavy cavalry."

Palewski said the famous Dienbienphu commander, Colonel de Castries, would have been a general ten years ago except that he was such a playboy and roughneck that he had always failed to be promoted. His family wouldn't even recognize him. All he liked was horses and card playing and fooling around on a pretty tough basis. Now that he is being made a general his family is proud to acknowledge him.

Palewski thought the three most interesting men in France today were de Gaulle, Malraux and Picasso. He says he is a great personal friend of Picasso. He claims Picasso hasn't the vaguest idea what communism means and is purely and simply an anarchist. Despite the fact that Picasso is listed as a member of the Communist Party, he and Palewski have remained good friends—according to Gaston.

PARIS, *April 7, 1954*

TODAY I paid a call on my old friend, Numan Menemençioglu, who has been Turkish ambassador in Paris now for almost ten years. He is really a remarkable man. He has been in Turkish diplomacy since the days of the Sultan. Although he is virtually stone-deaf and depends on a hearing aid, he has a facility for hearing things affecting Turkish interests even when they are spoken in whispers. I have great respect for his judgment and wisdom. For years he was permanent undersecretary for foreign affairs in Turkey and then later was foreign minister. Therefore I was impressed today when he said he was still confident that EDC would be ratified by France despite all the difficulties of the moment, because he felt a sufficient majority had finally, if regretfully, made up its mind to vote for ratification as the best way out of a difficult situation and for fear of the repercussions in America if the project fails.

While waiting to see Numan, I noticed he had three signed photographs in the reception room outside his office. One was signed Qazi M. Kemal. It was a very early picture of Ataturk who dropped that form of signature a long time ago. A second was from Çelal Bayar, who is now President of Turkey. A few years ago Çelal and Numan were bitter political enemies. The third was signed by "His friend, Franklin D. Roosevelt" and was dated Cairo, December 1943. It amuses me to look back on that date, which is when Ismet Inönü, then President of Turkey, and his entourage came down to Cairo to get the Dutch rub from Roosevelt and Churchill who were trying to force them into the war.

Numan said that when China and Russia signed their alliance back in 1950 he was impressed by the rudimentary simplicity of the terms of the pact. He therefore calculated there were a great many secret clauses but that their contents would not become known because of rigid Communist discipline. Therefore at the time he reported as much to his government and informed Ankara of his conviction that one of the clauses of the secret understanding guaranteed to China a free sway in Southeast Asia. He thinks the present situation in Indochina confirms his original views.

Numan says that what de Gaulle is now seeking is to establish a position for France as a leader on the continent of Europe that would aspire to be the arbiter between the United States and Russia. Numan says the ultimate decision on the world balance of power must be taken in free Europe. If the Russians were to gain Europe, it would mean that any future war would be lost ahead of time by the United States. De Gaulle recognizes that and may try to play the card in a search for a new policy establishing a diplomatic and political role for France able to swing the balance one way or the other. The trouble with De Gaulle, according to Numan, is that he still thinks France is as strong in world affairs as it was in 1914—which unfortunately is no longer the case.

Numan is convinced the Soviet Union now really wants peace. Russia fears encirclement by Germany and Japan, backed up by the United States. The Russians want time to gain economic advantages and to catch up in the race for new weapons—above all to improve their present hydrogen bomb position. They have the great advantage of knowing that the United States will not use its present edge on the hydrogen bomb to start a war and destroy them. Therefore they can afford to sit back and try to disorganize Europe and play for time.

Numan believes there is much less danger of world war now than two years ago. However, the situation is even more complicated perhaps. Obviously there must be a real war or a formula must be found for coexistence, and that is extremely difficult. The day that Moscow resigns itself to a position for Russia as a great power in the world instead of the dominating power of the world a formula for coexistence can really be found.

PARIS, *April 11, 1954*

LAST night we dined and spent the evening at the Gruenthers. It was just a family bridge party, very pleasant and informal and the first chance I have had in some time to chat with Al. He is having the tennis court on the place repaired and hopes to resume playing soon. He promised to take me apart on the court. He undoubtedly will. I am told he plays a most unstylish game but stays in very good shape and is fairly efficient. Incidentally we noticed a red fox wandering around the flower beds when we arrived and a couple of trout rising in the pond that was stocked for Ike.

I am surprised to see how well Gruenther looks considering the life he leads. Grace says he simply never takes a day off and has only had one week off (Garmisch–Partenkirchen) during the four years they have been abroad. Apparently they have played bridge only once since the last time we played with them.

Throughout our game the nonstop long-playing phonograph played. It was a curious mixture of music including shifts from Beethoven to Tchaikovsky to hillbilly "corn music." One of the two Gruenther boys (both are in the army) apparently likes to sing hillbilly music and play the banjo. In West Point he had his own hillbilly orchestra.

Gruenther during the evening chatted about many things. Here are some of the observations he made:

The only way of relieving Dienbienphu is to expand the area under French control so that the airfield can be made operable again. It would be very difficult to get a ground column in.

Gruenther had the feeling Mrs. Luce talks too much. When she dined at the Gruenthers with twenty people, she announced to everybody that her husband had seen Churchill that afternoon and Churchill had told him he was going to retire. Gruenther was appalled by her indiscretion.

Both Al and Grace were absolutely delighted with the Catholic bishop in Chicago who made a strong speech against McCarthy. They are terribly disturbed about McCarthy's influence. They were also very disturbed about an appearance McCarthy made at the Hotel Astor before a group of New York policemen at some kind of a dinner. Apparently McCarthy got a tremendous reception. Then some monsignor (apparently one of the New York priests) got up and made a speech all in favor of McCarthy. Cardinal Spellman arrived a little bit late, just in time to get the tail end of the priest's speech. He had clearly not heard the significant portions of it. Spellman was asked for a few words and replied amid great applause that he thought the monsignor had expressed his views well enough and there was nothing to add.

Gruenther said there was no getting around it but this was a very bad spring from American and Allied points of view, and Geneva was going to be an awfully tough operation with not much prospect of any kind of success for us.

I told him I had seen Jim Farley last week. This reminded Al of a story according to which two high-powered salesmen from the United States, who were Catholics, had a private audience with the Pope. Vatican officials, knowing how important these men were and also having advance information that they were prepared to offer an enormous sum to the church, decided to eavesdrop and listened at the keyhole. They couldn't hear the whole conversation, but they kept hearing the loud voices of the salesmen saying, "Okay, Your Holinesss, if 3,000,000 isn't enough, we are willing to go up to 4,000,000." The Pope muttered a few words in reply which they couldn't hear. The businessmen whispered to each other and then said, "Okay, our final offer is 5,000,000, Your Holiness." A little while later the businessmen came out. The acting secretary of state rushed in and asked His Holiness whether he had accepted. The Pope replied in the negative. The Vatican official was very disappointed and pointed out to the Pope that the treasury of the Holy See was in poor shape. He asked what it was that the two salesmen wanted. The Pope replied, "All they wanted was for me to interject one word into the regular service." The official asked what this was. The Pope replied, "Instead of saying just '*Dominus vobiscum*,' they wanted me to agree to say '*Dominus vobiscum* Coca-Cola.' "

PARIS, *April 12, 1954*

LUNCH today at General Pierre Billotte's with General Paul Ely, chief of the French general staff. Madame Ely is apparently now at last moderately recovered from her tragic wartime experiences. She was a prisoner in Buchenwald and was tortured by the Germans for more than two years. Until very recently she has been in a wheelchair. She still looks a little bit strange and strained. Ely is minus his right hand which he lost during the last war. Apparently he was in the Resistance after the collapse of France. Incidentally, he was born in Salonika and lived in Greece as a little child, was there again during the Balkan front of World War I.

Ely said it was impossible for France now to lose Dienbienphu. The place had no military value. Its only military importance was during the invasion of Laos last year. However it has become a political symbol of such importance that it cannot at any cost be lost. It is impossible to relieve Dienbienphu by ground. Ely says there are only two directions from which a column could approach overland, Luang Prabang (Laos) or the Tonkin delta. It is a distance of about three hundred kilometers from the delta, and it would be impossible to send an expedition from there overland because it would be subjected to crippling guerrilla attacks. It is virtually impossible to send a column from Luang Prabang. The operation would be exceedingly difficult. There are few troops at Luang Prabang now, and it would be a very complicated process to build up a force in Luang Prabang and then send it up to the relief of Dienbienphu.

As a result, the only possible way of holding on in Dienbienphu is by expanding the area held by the French. Ely estimates the Communists have lost, in terms of permanent casualties (either dead or totally crippled) 12,000. In order to expand the French position it is necessary initially to get a large enough area to reopen the airfield so that troops can be flown in. Billotte told me there is now only one parachute battalion in reserve. In other words the troops now at Dienbienphu have to be sufficient to open up the airfield so that more aid can be flown in. This means that more air support is necessary.

Ely is going to see Premier Laniel this afternoon, in anticipation of the Dulles visit (Dulles arrives tomorrow) to request that the French be prepared to accept American air assistance. That does not mean merely aircraft but also crews. Although the French carrier Arromanches is already in Indochina waters and backing up Dienbienphu, and another carrier (formerly American) the Bois Belleau, is about to arrive there, still further air assistance must be prepared for. That means agreement must be achieved between France and the United States so that in case of emergency American carriers and land-based aircraft are already prepared to move immediately. This will be one of the most important aspects of the Dulles meeting.

Incidentally Ely explained to me why Colonel de Castries has not been given a field promotion to general. Not only is it an old French tradition not to grant such a promotion in the field until a battle is over, but also the French remember Hitler's promotion of Paulus from general to field marshal during the battle of Stalingrad—and what happened then to the German army and Paulus himself at Stalingrad. (Events later proved Ely sadly right!)

PARIS, *April 13, 1954*

ISMAY and Gruenther were at dinner last night. I had borrowed a book from Al on Saturday with some Kipling stories in it and called to his attention the first paragraph of *The Man Who Was.* I recommended that all American diplomats should be made to read that. It points out that there is a great difference between the Russian as the most western of the Oriental peoples as against the Russian's own estimate of himself as the most eastern of the western peoples. Apparently Ismay has always been impressed by this particular observation. This set him off into a slightly bibulous and considerably incorrect quotation of "The Bear That Walks Like a Man."

Incidentally, Pug plays joyfully atrocious bridge, managing even to trump his own aces, but gets a great bang out of the game.

PARIS, *April 14, 1954*

SAW Dulles this evening before he took off for Washington on the conclusion of a two-day trip to London and a one-day visit in Paris trying to straighten out Big Three teamwork on the eve of the Geneva conference. By and large I think he has done a pretty good job, considering that the situation is hopeless. His neck is in a noose still, but he has got some soap on the rope.

Before Dulles, I had a chat with Walter Robertson, assistant secretary of state for the Far East. I remarked on the communiqué issued this evening that there is a paragraph saying, "The independence of the three Associated States within the French Union, which new agreements are to complete, is at stake in these battles."

I guessed the reference to new agreements must have been a hard one to get through. He admitted that it was the toughest wrangle of the whole deal. We objected to the words "within the French Union" and the French objected to the words "which new agreements are to complete."

I asked Robertson whether the French had finally requested American land-based and sea-based air support and told him about my conversation with General Ely. He said they hadn't really clarified their own point of view yet. He was very distressed by French ineptitude. At hysterically urgent French prodding he and a group of American civil and military experts had sat up until three o'clock this morning arranging a special airlift to Dienbienphu because the French said it would fall otherwise. When everything was arranged, they got word from Pleven that it really couldn't start operating until the middle of May because it would interfere with vacation schedules of pilots.

I have the impression that the new Southeast Asia alliance Dulles has worked out with the British and the French is a radical change of policy from that Dulles described to me in Washington last November 24.

Dulles looked tired but in good humor. He is going to be back here next week. I must say he stands up to this travel pretty well. Over a whisky and soda he said the reason for his trip was that: "We foresaw at Berlin that if the subject of Indochina was put on the agenda of the Geneva Conference, it would probably lead to intensified military efforts by the Communists in Indochina in order to try and help their bargaining position at Geneva. Precisely that has happened, and they have been pushing hard with extravagant wastage."

Without a defense agreement in that area it is quite conceivable that the countries of the region would be lost to communism one by one—first Vietnam, then Laos, then Cambodia, then Thailand, then Indonesia. A threat to the Philippines, New Zealand and Australia would develop, and the entire Western Pacific position would be menaced if there were no agreement on unity of action covering the area.

Dulles said that in England prior to this trip of his, many people appeared to think he was advocating an ultimatum to the Chinese Communists that would order them to take certain action by a specific date or else face the menace of war and atomic bombing. He never had such an idea in his mind, but because misinterpretation was prevalent he thought it would be useful for him to fly to London, and obviously he did not want to go to London and not visit Paris.

There could be no peace in Indochina just by surrendering a part of the area and then establishing an armistice line. After a time the Communists would attack again and take over more and more piecemeal. We might gain peace for a few weeks or months, but such an arrangement would in the end bring a war of even greater consequence and scope than the present one.

Dulles said the Communists must be made to realize that they are up against "something strong enough" to force them to abandon their plans to extend their rule over Southeast Asia. He did not think this would precipitate a war. On the contrary, the Communists were capable of starting a war whenever it suited their book. They would not be provoked into a war. He recalled that some people had thought the North Atlantic Treaty would stimulate a warlike reaction by Moscow—and it didn't. There was a much greater danger of war coming as a result of Soviet miscalculation concerning Western determination to resist, which might lead them to overstep a line unless we specified what we were prepared to defend. Dulles hoped practical arrangements to prepare for a Southeast Asia Alliance could be started very soon, at least in the form of working committees, etc. It was of the utmost importance that "the stigma of colonialism" be removed from this enterprise. (Personally I don't see how on earth he is going to remove such a stigma with the French and the British as partners. After all, the British have Malaya and nearby Hong-Kong which is a crown colony; and the French have Indochina. I don't think Nehru, for example, is going to fall for the idea that this is not a colonial enterprise.) Dulles said he was convinced the French sincerely plan to give independence to the Associated States of Indochina "and I am satisfied there will be such independence for the Associated States."

Dulles has always been a sincere opponent of colonialism, but I am afraid that since he has become Secretary of State he finds it isn't possible to be practical about such pleasant but theoretical concepts during a cold war. He said the kind of collective defense envisioned for Southeast Asia was important whether the Geneva Conference succeeded or failed. He added: "You may recall I negotiated the security treaties with Australia, New Zealand and the Philippines, and all of these included language stipulating that the treaties were valid pending over-all security arrangements for the area."

I must say it seems to me that Britain has gained two important points as a result of these negotiations. The first one is bolstering up her position in Malaya and in Hong Kong. Even though Hong Kong is not specifically included in the Southeast Asia area—which it may not be—obviously if there is an alliance in Asia and Hong Kong is attacked and Britain resists, it is going to be very difficult not to help her out.

The second point is this. Britain has been trying hard to get into the ANZUS pact ever since it was signed, and the United States has kept her out—primarily with the argument that it is an association of independent countries and doesn't want to mix up with colonialism. Now overnight Britain is coming into something even bigger than the ANZUS pact. Churchill has always wanted this. What this represents is a triumph of the Churchillian theory of an over-all global association in which Britain is an equal partner of the United States.

PARIS, *April 14, 1954*

THIS afternoon I had an excellent talk with Al Gruenther out at SHAPE. Al said there was a growing feeling that our (NATO) divisions, in view of the menace of atomic or hydrogen attack, had to be more mobile, equipped with better communications and better able to conceal themselves. There was a big discussion as to what to do about this question. Should the divisional unit be done away entirely and replaced by mere combat teams, or what? There were great differences of opinion on this.

Eisenhower had been complaining for some time that American divisions were much too heavy. Yet Gruenther pointed out the structure of these divisions had been approved when Eisenhower was chief of staff.

One of the questions to be surveyed is whether reserve units as well as active units would be made smaller, and if so, by how much. Major General James M. Gavin, now assistant chief of staff in charge of operations, believes more rather than less ground troops are needed in this atomic era than was the case before. He also envisions the development of guerrilla-type warfare.

Gruenther thinks one effect of the atomic era will probably be to establish the need for many more airfields. Another will be to develop planes that do not need nearly as much space on airfields. Already certain groups of experts believe that from now on we must build nothing but underground airbases from which aircraft would be ejected. When they return to their bases, they would land in small areas with the aid of arrester devices such as those employed on aircraft carriers. Gruenther believes it is futile to try to seek absolute protection militarily speaking. NATO is still weak in air defense, but, after all, so is the United States.

American possession of the hydrogen bomb and its lead in atomic weapons do not diminish the need for German divisions. In fact, the strongest proponent in favor of including German divisions in Western defense is

Marshal Juin, although he opposes the framework of EDC. Juin insists you cannot begin to hold a 500-mile front without the aid of the Germans.

Gruenther says it is clear we are evolving toward a changed attitude on global strategy. In the past we were content to base ourselves on the idea of a NATO for Europe and some kind of arrangement in the Western Pacific. Now with the Turkey–Pakistan agreement and the development of thinking towards a Southeast Asia alliance, we may be working up towards an overall global alliance structure. Many people are thinking along these lines. Ismay for some time has been arguing for an overall global organization. However, the big question is who shall be the members.

PARIS, *April 15, 1954*

THIS morning I am in the rather extraordinary and certainly anomalous position of having in my American passport a Bulgarian visa valid for entry to Bulgaria which is illegal in the United States and which is also illegal in Bulgaria. I applied in December for a Bulgarian visa although the United States has not recognized that country for four years and no American has been there since our legation was kicked out. This week to my astonishment I received a letter from the Bulgarian legation in Paris advising me that authorization had arrived to issue me a visa. I have made all my plans to go there. I advised our embassy confidentially of my plan, and although officially they were forced to warn me against such a trip, unofficially they have been friendly and helpful and have asked the Swiss to look after me. The Swiss are handling United States interests in Bulgaria during the period of the diplomatic break.

This morning I went to see Nedelkov, the Bulgarian minister in Paris, in order to request him to arrange interviews with the prime minister and the foreign minister for me next week. He is a friendly, stocky, little man who looks like the average Bulgarian peasant and, in his bad but fluent French, could not have been nicer. He assured me that there would be no difficulty whatsoever about arranging the interviews. However, he added that he had just received some news *"un peu désagréable."* I asked him what he meant. He told me that he had been advised in Sofia that it was all a big mistake and that he shouldn't have issued me a visa.

He then said something very curious and was rather pathetic about my request for a valid visa. "I examined your passport with great interest, Mr. Sulzberger, and I see that of course you have traveled a great deal. You are head of the foreign correspondents of *The New York Times* and therefore you are a man of wide experience. Surely you must realize that this question of issuing you a visa does not depend only upon *my* foreign ministry."

Obviously what he was telling me was that the Russians have put the kibosh on it. It isn't a question of the Bulgarian secret police organization. My application was made last December and the secret police have had plenty of time to make up their minds one way or another. Quite clearly what occurred was that the Russians thought it over and told the Bulgarians flatly *"nyet."*

SENLIS, *April 17, 1954*

SIR Gladwyn Jebb, the new British ambassador to France, came to lunch today at the Carters' where we are staying. Jebb said he was astonished at the way Dulles had been changing his policy. He said that when he left the United Nations a little more than a month ago, Dulles was still vigorously opposing any thought of Britain entering ANZUS; now he favors an overall Southeast Asia alliance including the Big Three as well as the Asian countries.

Jebb thought American policy was idiotic towards China and that sooner or later we are just going to have to realize the necessity of granting diplomatic recognition. He advised me in Geneva to get in touch with the man who will probably be the chief official interpreter for the Chinese whose name is Pu. Jebb said he met him at the United Nations and managed to talk to him privately. He claims that Pu is "a good liberal" who told him that he saw no other future for himself. He hated the idea of Formosa and he didn't like the idea of the Communists, but he follows the latter as the lesser of two evil futures.

PARIS, *April 22, 1954*

TODAY appears to have been a historically tragic day in terms of the position of Western democracy and the United States. I don't quite know what the full news is, but I can gather something dreadful seems about to happen. Obviously the United States is now convinced Dienbienphu is going to fall and nothing can save it; that as a result either Indochina will be conquered or we will have to intervene—and nobody wants to intervene with us. We feel that the loss of Southeast Asia would cripple our world position.

I saw Foster Dulles this evening at the Dillons. He was in an astonishingly good humor—largely engendered, I think, by about three stiff highballs. We had a rather extensive conversation about nothing—mainly fishing. He told me when he flew back home last week, he got his plane to land him at Syracuse where a Grumman amphibian picked him up to fly him to his place at Duck Island, where Lake Ontario joins the St. Lawrence River. For years he has been going up there for an Easter weekend of fishing. I asked him what kind of fish he got this time of the year, and he said perch and pike. I sneered at the idea of catching perch, but this touched him to the quick and he assured me that perch caught in cold water were very delicious eating. I asked him what bait he used and he said worms. I shivered. I asked him how he got the pike and he said with spoons. I observed that it was awfully early in the year for pike to be close enough inland to be attracted by artificial bait, but he claims he caught some good ones. It was only after the conclusion of a lengthy but uninteresting conversation along these lines that he said he would see me in Geneva, and then he went off saying that the discussions today had been unfortunate, and the situation was "awful, awful."

I had dinner with Walter Robertson, assistant secretary of state for Far Eastern Affairs. He also had had a couple of drinks and was highly charged with an explosive mixture of emotion and alcohol. He said that April 22 had been one of the worst days in United States history. He compared the present situation in a rather illogical way with that of Washington at Valley Forge and said we simply could not abandon our position. What he was referring to was news that had been received that Dienbienphu is apparently gone. It hasn't actually fallen, but the area is now so small that aid cannot be effectively sent to it. In other words, the airlift we arranged last week with the French is too late—if not too little.

As a result we face a tremendous problem. We must recognize that it is impossible for us to lose Southeast Asia which would follow the loss of Indochina. Our whole civilization would be affected. We must intervene. The loss of Southeast Asia would not only represent an enormous loss of face, but also of vital raw materials and rice coveted by China. What is the difference, Robertson asked, whether the Communists start a war of aggression or we lose our civilization because we have failed to take a sufficiently powerful stand? He was a little fuzzy on this but seemed on the verge of advocating a preventive war. Yet from that position he hastened on to say that any kind of war means the end of our civilization—even in budgetary terms, quite apart from the destructive power of new weapons. He remarked that the national debt is now $275 billion, and another war would bankrupt the country.

Nevertheless—and if these recollections appear confused, they are a faithful portrait of Robertson's mind—he feels the United States must intervene. There is no point in our arguing that we will intervene in one way but not in another way. If we are going to intervene, we have to intervene wholeheartedly. This is a time to tighten our belts, for unpopular decisions and higher taxes—not for a soft, easy, luxurious life.

The Navarre Plan in Indochina has been a complete failure. The Indochinese hate the French and with reason. Robertson recalled the bombardment in 1946 of innocent Indochinese civilians by a French cruiser which killed "thousands" of them. We are stuck, he said, with the "horrid little Bao Dai," whom he described as useless and cowardly. He said that although Bao Dai claims that malaria keeps him away from visiting the front, it does not keep him away from big-game hunting and the Riviera. He is a "rotten little Japanese collaborator," and if he, Robertson, were an

Indochinese, he would have no use for him at all. If only Ho Chi Minh were on our side, we could do something about the situation; but unfortunately he is the enemy.

Robertson said we cannot abandon our position concerning the role of China in the Geneva Conference which opens Monday. We are not going to recognize China as one of the great powers. It is going to remain a four-power conference. We are prepared to see the chairmanship rotate among the four great powers who agreed at Berlin to call the conference, but we will not admit the Chinese as a peer. If that formula is not acceptable, we are prepared to see a distinguished and neutral Swiss appointed as permanent chairman of the conference. We do not think that Dag Hammarskjöld, Secretary General of the United Nations, would qualify because he is obviously not neutral as the United Nations is a combatant in Korea.

We would rather walk out on the conference than accept the idea of a five-power meeting. Robertson said that on this question "Bidault is on our side—I hope."

Robertson said Dulles scored "a great diplomatic victory" at Berlin in getting a conference on Korea (the Geneva Conference) at which no neutrals are to be represented. He complained that unfortunately even members of Dulles' own party failed to recognize this achievement upon the Secretary's return to the United States.

Robertson talked at length of Chou En-lai, who is coming to Geneva as head of the Communist Chinese delegation. He said he is one of the most charming, intelligent and attractive men of any race he has ever known—"But he'll cut your throat." Robertson said he knew Chou in Peking and Nanking just after World War II and found him extraordinarily attractive. Chou talks in terms understandable by anyone with whom he is conversing. Incidentally he is a fine linguist with a magnificent education and speaks excellent French and English. Robertson says he warned General Marshall about Chou's charm and untrustworthiness. Despite this, Marshall fell for him hook, line and sinker. Ten months later Robertson went to see Marshall just after the General had read the news of the cold-blooded murder of American Marines by the Communists. Marshall had taken this up with Chou who rebuffed him completely. According to Robertson, Marshall never got over this shock.

PARIS, *April 24, 1954*

I had lunch today with Assistant Secretary of State Carl McArdle. Dulles is doing his best to prevent disaster on the eve of Geneva. He is meeting with Bidault and Eden this afternnon. Each minister will have only one adviser with him. Dulles is taking Walter Robertson.

The guts of Dulles' position is, "If you don't quit, we won't quit." He is trying to bolster up the French at all costs. The French have asked for "massive" American air assistance so they can strike back. McArdle is not clear as to whether this includes American crews or just aircraft. I told him I was positive it meant crews as well.

Apparently Dulles intends to stress that agreement in principle must be reached on a Southeast Asia alliance *before* the Geneva conference opens. He is pointing out to the French that it is impossible for the United States to take on intervention alone. Thus it can be done only within the framework of an alliance which he wants to see concluded urgently. The alliance would be under the United Nations. In other words, what he is really saying is, "If you sign up on the Southeast Asia pact, we will give you the airplanes you are asking for." However, he is pointing out that we cannot grant the aircraft without first consulting Congress.

There is considerable fear among the Americans that we are hovering on the verge of World War III.

This evening I had a talk with Dulles, who, I must say, is bearing up with remarkable good humor. I saw him over at the American embassy where the top members of the American delegation for Geneva had gathered for a quick buffet supper before taking off a half-hour later in Dulles' plane. Admirable Radford, chairman of the Joint Chiefs of Staff, had just finished conferring with Dulles when I saw the Secretary. Radford, with whom I had a rather uninteresting but pleasant chat, is much less sturdy-looking than I had expected.

Dulles told me the French had requested the intervention of American aircraft manned by American crews. It had been explained to them that it was impossible under United States Constitutional authority to intervene that directly. Such would be an act of war, and the President could not take such a step under his peacetime executive powers. Dulles said the French simply didn't seem to understand American law very well.

He had pointed out to them, however, that the request might be regarded differently if there were actually an operational Southeast Asia alliance with France and the United States as members. Congress would have to approve American participation—probably by a resolution. Then, perhaps in a fashion similar to Korea where the United Nations intervened, the United States might be able to intervene.

Dulles admitted the prospects for Geneva were by no means good.

PARIS, *April 24, 1954*

TONIGHT I wrote:

France has asked for direct large-scale intervention in the Indochina war by United States aircraft manned by American crews.

However, she has been told it is impossible for President Eisenhower to sanction such a grave move in peacetime.

It has been explained that the United States has gone to the limit of assistance within the prerogatives of the President's existing peacetime authority in furnishing technicians to keep aircraft operational and in flying paratroopers from metropolitan France to Indochina bases outside the combat area.

There was no mention of ground forces in the request but it included both land- and carrier-based aircraft.

The French have been advised that if a united front can be established through the creation of a Southeast Asian Alliance, as suggested by Secretary of State John Foster Dulles, the legal status of their request for wholesale "air assistance" may be regarded differently.

If such an alliance is agreed to, it is believed the United States Congress will be asked to approve a resolution approving American participation.

France, Britain and other countries whose membership in such a pact has been tentatively discussed have been reluctant so far to adhere until after the Geneva conference has indicated whether peace in Indochina is possible.

GENEVA, *April 25, 1954*

SAW Dulles this afternoon—on the eve of the Geneva Asian conference which is supposed to open tomorrow. Right now there is absolute confusion on policy among the Big Three and on procedure among the Big Four.

He doesn't expect to stay here long and hopes Bedell Smith can take over the delegation leadership within a week. He admits to no optimism on the conference. He warned that whenever the USSR gains a "temporary" advantage over an area, it doesn't relax its grip; and therefore partition would be a dangerous solution in Indochina. There is also little hope of expelling the Communists from North Korea. But it is worth exploring possibilities.

Dulles thinks he'll be gone before Indochina comes up as a topic. It will be mainly up to the French to decide whether priority should be given to consideration of Indochina because they are doing the fighting. The United States will be guided primarily by French views. In Korea we always insisted that those with troops on the battlefield should be responsible for basic decisions. We will thus be guided largely by the French on whether they want the Viet Minh represented here or not. Of course the French will consult us.

Dulles explained the United States had taken all steps short of war to aid France in Indochina, but there was no present reason to foresee that we would cross the line of belligerency. We don't want to see Indochina fall, but sometimes things *do* occur that we don't like. The administration's policy is to avoid belligerency.

Dulles said he didn't expect to see Chou En-lai here "unless our automobiles collide."

Dulles said he didn't think Indochina lent itself to possible partition as does Korea. The fighting shifts about and there is no demarcation line. It also involves Laos and Cambodia—not just Vietnam.

He said the French seemed at the moment too preoccupied with immediate problems to develop long-range planning such as the Southeast Asia alliance scheme Dulles is pushing. He added that pact cannot be applied to these daily problems (meaning the war) until it is brought into being. It would not take long to create. A formal treaty is not required (together with Senate ratification). A joint congressional resolution would do the trick, from the United States' point of view.


GENEVA, *April 25, 1954*

LUNCHED today with Elisabeth de Miribel. She is out of her Carmelite nunnery—for good. Officially it is because her health wouldn't stand the gaff. However, asking her no questions, I gathered it was a much deeper thing. She said it was like a concentration camp, iron dictatorship accompanied by espionage. The first mother superior was all right, but she was succeeded by terror. Elisabeth said all her mail was opened and censored—even letters to priests about spiritual matters. All her conversations (for example, my visits to the Carmelite convent) were listened to. This violates the code of the convent, she said. She said it was impossible to form friendships. The nuns cannot speak to each other except briefly during recreation hours on a few limited subjects and in groups. Only three days a year can they converse to any greater extent. The life is terribly difficult, physically. Her liver apparently suffered. The poor girl looks thin, unwell, her hair still showing signs of convent barbering, and she has a broken leg from skiing.


GENEVA, *April 28, 1954*

I had lunch today with Humphrey Trevelyan (later Lord Trevelyan and ambassador), British chargé d'affaires in Communist China. He left there April 3 (via Hong Kong). He says that the Communist government, broadly speaking, is succeeding. It has restored order out of chaos, stabilized the currency at an approximately fair rate, built up an industrial base which is definitely being helped by Russia. The Chinese people don't seem to like the Russians much, and there is grumbling about some of the payment rates for goods exchanged, but there is fundamental unity between the two. Trevelyan can travel to Shanghai and Canton when he desires, after asking for a permit. He takes many walks around Peking and strolls through the city, eats in restaurants. Everyone is very friendly. Sometimes they ask if he's Russian, and he feels they are even more friendly when they find he isn't.

He thinks the United States' policy is insane. It is far more important to have representatives in a country you dislike than one you like. He can do little for British subjects held by the Chinese and even less for Americans. America must expect no favors after its savage attacks on China. Chiang has no more influence in China; he is finished and done for, even as a symbol.

GENEVA, *April 29, 1954*

I lunched today with Yuri Zhukov. He assured me he was confident I would eventually get a Soviet visa. He counseled me to see Vinogradov when I next went to Paris. He said he would speak to Vinogradov himself about it when Vinogradov comes back here.

Zhukov describes Molotov as a "theorist" and says that in contrast Khrushchev is a practical man. He has a very high regard for Khrushchev, who is a Ukrainian also. Zhukov first met Khrushchev during the war in the spring of 1943 (I think this must have been July) in the salient of Bielgorod during the German attack. Zhukov says Khrushchev was then an advisor of Vatutin, the marshal who died later.

Zhukov admits that Khrushchev's recent speech (early this week) signifies the development of a Tough Line in Soviet policy. However, he claims this is "party" rather than "government" stuff and is prompted by reaction to Dulles' tough speeches.

There was only one global point of danger, Zhukov said. This was Indochina. I asked how about Korea and Formosa. He said Korea would remain divided and nobody would care; as for Formosa, this was unimportant. I asked: "How about your ally Chou," and he repeated, "That is unimportant." I asked how he proposed to settle Indochina, and he said he was sure this could be worked out if there was good will on both sides.

Zhukov said it would never be permitted for any individual to gain control of power again in Russia; that collective rule was now the mode. He explained that since Stalin's death, for example, speeches by men like Malenkov were *read* into the radio by commentators instead of being repeated from disks, in the original voice—although Malenkov is an excellent speaker.

I have a deep hunch actually that there is a new struggle for power in Moscow. I think Khrushchev is rapidly easing Malenkov out and there will be a break soon. I can also smell that Zhukov is strongly on Khrushchev's side.

BELGRADE, *May 6, 1954*

TONIGHT I dined with Jimmy Riddleberger, who is now American ambassador here. I showed him a story I am sending tonight on the new secret formula for Trieste. He confirmed it entirely, was too discreet to ask where I got it, and delightedly said, "I'll bet this will send Luce into a tizzy." He makes it plain he has no use for her. Apparently Durbrow told him it is all he (Durby) can do to stop her from sending instructions to other ambassadors including Aldrich, Dillon and Riddleberger. The idea was to sit on this Trieste deal while she sold it to the Italians. But, as I explained to Jimmy, you can't sit on things forever. He agreed and said he was surprised it hadn't leaked already. He said the story would create a tremendous stir.

BLED, *May 7, 1954*

TODAY I saw Tito at his summer house in Bled. He is up here for a fortnight or so, following his official visit to Turkey, shooting *auerhahn* (capercaillie); the season is in the beginning of May. He resents the lousy weather; it has been cold and rainy. I remarked that it was good fishing weather, at least, but this brought the rueful observation that he was a hunter, not a fisherman.

I rode up on the overnight train from Belgrade and spent the morning at the hotel. It hasn't changed much from prewar days. Today it was packed with rather cheesy English tourists, apparently on some kind of fixed-price trip basis. The rain was coming down in sheets on the lake and the mountains were obscured by clouds.

I had never seen Tito's summer place here before. It is on the lake (he sent an open Chevrolet for me—the top was up, fortunately) about a mile from the hotel. It is a hideous, large, square stone residence that embodies all that is worst in *mitteleuropa* architecture. There was one guard at the gate and that was all. Over the entrance were two flags, that of Jugoslavia and the red banner of communism, with hammer and sickle on it.

Tito's dog Tiger is now dead and I saw no animals. He received me in an awful-looking salon, the walls of which were all hung in heavy dark blue velvet curtains. The furniture was massive, square and certainly not comfortable for my build. Tito was wearing a blue suit with a modest figured necktie clasped to his shirt with a ruby and diamond bar pin. He had a large solitaire diamond ring on his left hand and a gold bracelet wristwatch. He smoked Yeni Harman Turkish cigarettes in a little pipe-holder; not his wartime Bosnian one but a new one of the same sort. He talked readily on every subject I raised.

He was "satisfied with my Turkish visit which definitely proved what progress had been made by the two allies already in the economic, military and political fields." (Incidentally he spoke Serbo-Croatian through an interpreter—Mme. Kveder, the same pretty woman, a general's wife, who has translated before for me. Tito said a word or two in English which he claims to be learning.)

He said there were "no more obstacles" in the way of a full military alliance between Jugoslavia, Turkey and Greece and that this would be a "firm guarantee of peace in this part of the world."

Neither we nor the Turks see any reason why such a full alliance should not be formed. That is why I am going to Greece next month. Everything has already been done by the three general staffs preparing for the alliance. All that is needed now are formal arrangements to give formal approval to what already exists.

Tito said the alliance would have to come in the form of a military annex to the Treaty of Ankara and that this would have to be ratified by the parliaments of the three countries. The annex, he said, would of course be "the most important part of the treaty." It would "give it its true character and be a binding obligation."

He said: "If the base of EDC is broadened, Jugoslavia will be ready to join it." This is all, of course, a lot of crap. Tito clearly doesn't even understand just what EDC is (or was) but he is being very shrewd about using it for propaganda.

I asked Tito, considering that he was pressing for alliance with Greece and Turkey, both members of NATO, and was talking of maybe joining EDC which would be part of NATO, why he didn't wish to join NATO himself directly. He said that while it was necessary for Jugoslavia to cooperate with NATO "to a certain extent," he didn't want to join that organization. He recognized Jugoslavia did have certain obligations to NATO and was receiving arms from some of its members. Jugoslavia had discussed mutual problems with NATO both in talks at Washington with the Americans, British and French and in Belgrade when General Handy visited there.

Tito said China should be admitted to the UN. This would end Peking's isolation and make it easier to discuss eastern problems with her. It might help convince China to abandon a warlike policy. There was no new intention for Belgrade to seek diplomatic relations with Peking.

Tito said, apropos of Djilas: "We have forgotten him already." He said Djilas had no influence; that he would never be permitted to rejoin the Communist Party which he had voluntarily quit. Obviously Tito now dislikes Djilas personally.

He did say, however, that Vlado Dedijer was still in the party and parliament, and "We hold nothing against him although the masses might find it difficult to understand why he supported Djilas. Time will iron out his position and there is no threat to his political future." He said Dedijer's health was bad and "We did our best to see he got some rest."

Tito remarked with relish that in "other eastern countries" Djilas and Dedijer wouldn't have lived twenty-four hours. He concluded: "We have an entirely different attitude to deviation from other eastern lands."

BELGRADE, *May 8, 1954*

STEVE Dedijer dropped in and bought me a drink. Steve is Vlado's brother and is now head of the Jugoslav atomic energy commission. (He is still quite American in appearance although gaining a foreign accent. Steve graduated from the Hill School and Princeton, where he rowed on the crew, and was an American paratrooper.) He says Vlado is quite well now and working four or five hours a day, writing. He is down at Split. The Djilas row had a bad effect on Vlado's wound, and he had a stroke of sorts and was unconscious several hours.

Steve says he has great difficulty getting enough money for his atomic project from the government. The Government seems to think of it only in terms of "When are we going to have an A-bomb." Steve tells them, of course, never. He says, however, Jugoslavia pools its work with other European countries including Norway, Sweden and Italy and has made some good progress. None of their material is classified except when they deliberately classify some information merely to use it on a trading basis with some other country. He says it is ridiculous how much the United States classifies. But Russia classifies absolutely everything. The Russians have now stopped sending the Jugoslavs even the most routine scientific publications—but the Jugs pick them up elsewhere in Europe. Steve judges that America is way, way ahead of Russia.

He recently visited France and went through their pile, etc. He estimated that despite the ouster of Joliot-Curie there were still some 60 per cent Communists in the French atomic business. He told this to the French who admitted it (he says) and were astonished at his estimate. He replied: "I'm a Communist; I ought to know." He claims he based his estimates on such clues as pictures of Joliot-Curie, Picasso doves, etc., he saw in the various offices and laboratories.

ATHENS, *May 13, 1954*

TODAY I lunched with King Paul at his country residence in Tatoi, about twenty-three miles out of Athens near the old civil air field which is now a military air base. Here the royal family has a very large farm—enormous for Greece—where they produce rather bad wine and are trying to develop a good strain of cattle from Danish breeds, seeking to market the butter and milk. The King leads a country gentleman's life. However, he told me he is no longer riding—which he used to do every day. He still has a little paddock and jumps. The Queen isn't here, being in Austria and Germany attending a christening and visiting her family.

The King told me his kids are now between thirteen and sixteen. The boy, Constantine, is fourteen and goes to a modern boarding school near Maroussi. It is run along the lines of the Hahn school at Gordonstoun where Prince Philip, Duke of Edinburgh, went. Hahn was a German Jew who opened a modern character-building school in Hanover and took it to Scotland after Hitler came in.

King Paul was very simple and slightly ill at ease. The sitting room was comfortable and plain, with large armchairs, pleasant and unpretentious, books, a pretty Bokhara embroidery spread across the top of the piano. Lunch comprised a cheese soufflé, steak with imitation béarnaise sauce, asparagus, and éclairs. There were three wines—a white, a red and a tawny dessert wine. They were all Greek and lousy. The white wine was extra-sweet and, I guess, from Samos. The red wine was heavy and sweet and the dessert wine was, I suppose, Mavrodaphne. I noticed the King ate a plate of vegetables instead of meat, but everything else was the same.

He said he was very unenthusiastic personally about Tito's visit, but it was one of those things he had to put up with. I asked him if on visits of that sort any indiscreet questions were ever asked. He said he was afraid his wife would ask some. (He always refers to "my wife" or "my house," and so on.) He said Tito would stay in a government guest house, the former American embassy residence "which is next to my house in Athens."

King Paul was very irked with the British on Cyprus. With a smile and a puff at his cigarette holder, he then looked at me and said: "Remember, we started that one, didn't we? King George of England sent me word that he didn't want me breaking up his empire. He sent word by Norton" (former British ambassador here). King Paul was referring to an interview I had with him a long time ago on the matter.

He blamed Eden largely for the present crisis but then added: "Of course everybody knows how disagreeable Eden is." He said that when Eden was recuperating from his operation here last year, Papagos had asked to see him on Cyprus and Eden had been exceptionally rude. That had put Papagos' back up.

King Paul made it more than plain that he is still very irked with Papagos and doesn't care much for him. However, he is sore at the British and particularly with Eden and Sir Charles Peake on Cyprus.

The King said he thought Papagos had bitten off more than he could chew in the way he was handling the Cyprus business. The British insisted Cyprus was an "internal affair" because Cyprus was a colony. Therefore they refused to discuss it. Papagos would only get embarrassment if he insisted in bringing the matter before the United Nations.

I asked King Paul if he didn't consider that his title as "King of the Hellenes" did not make him automatically King of the Cypriotes since they are 80 per cent Greek. He replied that technically at present they were British subjects.

He said Adlai Stevenson had lunched with him and his family here and had recalled this in a dinner in Chicago, during the visits of the King and

Queen last year. Adlai had said he was distressed to learn from the little princess that her favorite animal was the elephant (Republican symbol).

ATHENS, *May 17, 1954*

I had a good talk this morning with Field Marshal Papagos, the prime minister, in his office at the parliament building. Papagos' office is dark, large, comfortably furnished, decorated with large photographs of the King and Queen. Papagos looked exceedingly well and nothing like as old as he is. He was wearing a very sporty and well tailored gray suit. We chatted in French. He was in no hurry. After I finished my questions he kept me there an additional thirty-five minutes, assuring me he had nothing to do.

Papagos said he had always been "a partisan of military alliance" with Jugoslavia and Turkey and that a political understanding—as under the Ankara Treaty—was not enough. I told him what Tito had told me about his hopes for a military annex providing for automatic assistance if any party were attacked and he said: "I am completely in accord with Tito." He also said he agreed that the proposed military annex must be ratified by each participating parliament.

ATHENS, *May 19, 1954*

ALL today and yesterday there has been a stink about the story I wrote after my interview with Papagos. The result is that I am about as irked with the Greeks as I can be. The government issued a series of denials on the story—based on a garbled and abbreviated version printed in *Eleftheria*. I remarked to the press minister that it was an odd way of doing business; at least before they deny something they should have the text and read it. A foreign office denial was issued yesterday. Yet the first text of my story was received at noon today. They deny that the United States has asked Greece to postpone agreement to a military annex on the Ankara pact; that there was a Greek-Italian démarche; and so forth. The press minister explained that Marshal Papagos didn't know what he was saying because he speaks very bad English. I told him (the minister) he at least should ascertain his own facts, that Papagos used French which he speaks excellently.

This evening I had a good chat with Ambassador Cavendish Cannon. He complains that the State Department, kowtowing to Clare Luce, has put him in an awful position. He was forced to follow instructions to ask the Greeks to postpone agreement on the military annex. Now they have been isolated and irked with him. Yet the military pact is something he personally has been advocating for years. He hopes the State Department will stop catering to the Italians on Trieste and tell the Greeks to go ahead now—before the Tito visit. I told him he had better push it because Tito isn't going to be satisfied with a lot of soft soap about good intentions. Furthermore, anybody with a grain of sense can foresee a deterioration of Greco-Turkish relations next summer as the Cyprus crisis between Athens and London comes to a head. The Turks will vote against Greece, despite their alliance, if it is brought to the UN.

Cannon blames Peake, Eden and Papagos for the Cyprus mess. When Eden was here last autumn, recuperating, Peake could have informally suggested to the Greeks not to raise the matter. But Papagos came to the embassy and saw Eden. He hauled out a paper outlining the Greek claim to Cyprus. Before he got started Eden arose, almost turned his back, and said he would refuse to listen because there was no Cyprus question and he refused to admit its existence. In a cold rage Papagos put his paper back in his pocket. But he will never forget what he terms a personal insult. And he has great pride as Greece's only field marshal, national hero and prime minister.

ANKARA, *May 25, 1954*

THIS evening I went to see the prime minister, Adnan Menderes (later hanged). He is handsome, exceptionally smooth, smiling and youthful looking. He has the appearance of a man of forty-five or less although he is over fifty. He is reputed to be a tough, clever politician. Obviously he has no understanding of the function of the press nor any use for it, either foreign or local. While especially friendly, the replies he gave to my questions would have made the Oracle of Delphi appear to be sticking its neck out. Menderes is going off to Washington Sunday to try and get some dough to pay for his four-year economic program. But he wouldn't give me any answers either on the cost or scope of the program or his requests in Washington. He speaks fairly good Americanized English but we had an interpreter present (Eralp of the foreign office who jotted down notes in Arabic script—showing that old-fashioned customs have not yet been eliminated).

About the only thing Menderes said of interest was that he believed it would be useful to exchange ideas in Washington concerning Turkey's armed forces as well as economic matters. He expressed desire to expand the Balkan and Pakistan pacts and to conclude any bilateral agreements desired by the United States. He also spoke strongly in favor of maintaining the status quo in Palestine.

ANKARA, *May 26, 1954*

THIS morning I visited President Çelal Bayar at his residence, the Çankaya Palace. The last time I was there Ismet Pasha (Inönü) was boss man and Çelal was leader of the relatively small opposition. Now the roles are reversed. I inquired about Ismet of Bayar. He admitted he had worked with him thirty years and that he had held various cabinet posts under him in the old days. But he indicated rather plainly that that was that; he was not seeing him these days nor was he giving him any kind of job as an elder statesman or consultant. There were some fairly sharp recriminations exchanged during the recent election campaign.

The palace is astonishingly ugly; I had forgotten how much so. However, it is situated on a lovely location atop a hill outside the city. The rooms are square, ornately marbled and paneled, furnished with cumbersome awkward square chairs and tables, combining the worst taste of the Balkans, the Middle East and modern Russia. But there are some magnificent pieces of blue Chinese porcelain displayed on the walls. These were brought up from the Sultan's collection in Istanbul.

President Bayar is now over seventy but still a sturdy-looking character. He has a square head, stocky frame and brown, somewhat Asiatic appearance. He is clearly a shrewd, careful man who had a good deal of economic as well as political experience. We talked in Turkish through an interpreter. As we sat around a table chatting, we sipped large glasses of orange juice set before us on silver plates. The conversation was scarcely fascinating.

Internally Turkey was completely stable. The Communists had made no headway with their propaganda attacks on Turkish policy abroad and at home. The right-wing "Gray Wolf" fanatics had been squashed. (At any rate, that is what he said. I believe he minimized the strength of the right, at least.) Bayar claimed there were only "one or two" Pan-Turanians left.


IZMIR, TURKEY, *May 27, 1954*

HAVEN'T been here since I left Greece in a sponge-fishing caïque thirteen years ago to get away from the occupying Nazis. This time we flew down in a U. S. Air Force plane at the invitation of General Eaton, NATO air commander in this Southeast Europe sector (which is made up of Turkish and Greek forces under American command).

In Ankara I had expressed a desire to take Marina and my cousins sightseeing so I was astounded to be greeted by a large military delegation of brass who handed in a mimeographed "proposed itinerary" which somehow sandwiched in between cocktail parties and briefings by generals, trips to Ephesus, holy places, museums, air bases and included such items as: "14:30 arrive Parking area near the Home of the Virgin Mary. Walk to the Shrine with a Coffee Stop enroute." God bless the military.

IZMIR, *May 28, 1954*

LONG talk with Lt. Gen. Paul Kendall commander of headquarters Allied Land Forces, South East Europe (ALFSEE) here in Izmir. Kendall is like a tactless bulldog.

Kendall, who is friendly, rather overbearing, and by no means subtle, continually referred to the Turks and Greeks as "the best damned mercenaries I know. We've bought ourselves some damned fine mercenaries and they're cheap at the price. We get five times as much soldier for our money here than at home." Et cetera. Later he gave a cocktail party for me and introduced me to his senior officers and their wives. He took me aside and all over again told me what a fine group of mercenaries they were. He thought the Turks were better mercenaries than the Greeks because there were more of them and they were cheaper: they got paid (the *"Asker"* or private) only about 15 cents a month plus two uniforms, one winter and one summer, for their two-year service. They ate little and when told to stay in a hole they remained there and fought until they died.

Kendall said the Turks had no softies like America and in Korea there were no instances of Turkish prisoners collaborating with the enemy. Kendall commanded a corps there, where he said the finest battalion was the French (40 per cent Foreign Legion) and the next two, the Turks and Greeks. All three were volunteer. He said there was much worse collaboration by American prisoners than is yet known. He said the best American was better than the Turk because he had initiative and imagination when left to himself. But the Turk was dogged, determined, and not afraid to die.

Kendall complained loudly about the foreign exchange situation. He said all his officers and men changed their money at the 5-or-more-to-1 rate of liras to the dollar as compared with the legal 2.8-to-1 rate. This was as impossible to stop as drinking during prohibition and he made no effort to.

KYRENIA, *June 1, 1954*

CAME to Cyprus from Izmir (courtesy United States Air Force) for brief consultation with our Middle East correspondents. Got out of Nicosia pronto for the cool beaches of Kyrenia and the agreeable Dome Hotel.

What would merely have been a pleasant interlude was rendered sad: Anne McCormick has died. Poor Anne. I never really knew just how old she was but apparently she was well into her seventies. She was always sweet, feminine and rather girlish as well as very wise and understanding. Last trip I had with her was to Bermuda. It was the first trip she'd ever taken without Frank (who is in his eighties, was then ailing, now survives her) and she held my hand in the plane, later insisted on buying me some neckties.

PARIS, *June 12, 1954*

I have heard from friends in the embassy that it is now known among top American diplomats here that Dulles gave me the story last April 24 that France had requested American air intervention and we had turned it down. What disturbs me is that Dillon told this to his top embassy staff people and embellished the truth. I don't know whether Dillon made the mistake or whether Dulles told Dillon a cockeyed story.

The story Dillon told his staff was that Dulles was very concerned about the situation and about the attitude of the British. Therefore, according to the yarn, Dulles called me in as the most respected and reliable American newspaperman in Paris and volunteered the information that France had requested American air intervention and that the United States had told the French this could be supplied only if the British agreed to go along on a collective basis, but that the British had refused. This is a lie. The fact is I sought Foster out and probed hard. I am trying to trace the whole thing down in order to ascertain whether it is the fault of Dillon's misinformation or a somewhat tricky effort on the part of Dulles.

PARIS, *June 12, 1954*

I had a most extraordinary lunch with Stavros Niarchos. Niarchos is one of the wealthiest men in the world, and either he or his brother-in-law Aristotle Onassis is the largest single shipping owner. Surely the two together own a larger tonnage than any country except the United States and Britain. Although they are brothers-in-law, they hate each other's guts.

Onassis has recently gotten a lot of publicity through two coups. He bought controlling interest in the holding company of the Monte Carlo casino. And he established a private shipping company with the government of Saudi Arabia in which he owns a 75 per cent interest and then got the King of Saudi Arabia to publish a decree stating that all petroleum from that country must be sent in tankers belonging to that particular shipping line. Niarchos claims Onassis spent mere chicken feed to buy up Monte Carlo—only "a few million dollars"—in order to bribe and subvert people. Thus a diplomat or a businessman can come down to Monte Carlo and he will be given the royal treatment and a free ride because Onassis instructs accordingly. In exchange for such flattery, Onassis can do big business. Niarchos seemed to resent this and thought it highly immoral.

It was rather odd that we were having lunch in a private room at Maxim's—although there were only two of us—and the whole damn staff of Maxim's was lined up to fawn upon us. Niarchos said that, after all, Onassis was spending no more money on the subversion project in Monte Carlo than if I (CLS) were to buy a good lunch for somebody in exchange for a story.

He then gave me a very thick envelope stuffed with folders and papers purporting to show what a bastard Onassis was to make this deal with Saudi Arabia. Niarchos complained that it was highly unethical and was destroying all standard business practices. He thought this shocking. He explained he had no personal business interest in proclaiming this view because he personally was not affected and had more business on hand than he could possibly carry out for some years to come. He said that he was the only shipping man still ordering new tankers. Everybody else had too many tankers already for the business on hand, and the shipyards were idle—even in Japan and Germany. He assured me earnestly that he was talking to me only because he knew I was interested in the morals of the situation.

Towards the end of the excellent lunch and a rather repetitious conversation, the maître d'hôtel, a fat snob who loves to lord it over the poor folk who come to Maxim's, came up in person and said to Stavros, *"Monsieur Onassis est en bas et voudrait vous voir."* Stavros blushed purple. I roared with laughter and said, "For God's sake, invite him up because he must have had agents hearing everything you've been saying." Stavros, who had been complaining throughout the lunch that he was spied upon and who had gone to the door four times and suddenly pulled it open to find a waiter standing right outside with flapping ears, did not think this remark funny. He said he didn't consider it a good idea to invite Onassis up and went down for five minutes to see him. He came back still looking rather flushed and said, "After all, he is my brother-in-law, and he heard I was here so he just wanted to say hello."

When we finished our lunch, I remarked to Niarchos that, although the file he gave me was very thick on the subject of the Onassis–Saudi Arabia business deal, it seemed to comprise mostly newspaper clippings and other public material. I expressed the opinion that a business on the scale of his (Niarchos') surely could not rely upon such meager information, and I thought this was a very incomplete file. Stavros then hastily told me I was right and that there were certain documents missing which he had not wanted to give me originally because he had no business having them and he was a bit embarrassed about them. When I pressed him, he said they included a telegram from Ambassador Aldrich in London and another telegram from Ambassador Wadsworth in Jidda, both to the State Department. He promised to supply the documents.

PARIS, *June 15, 1954*

LUNCH with Bill Gibson of the American embassy.

He says there is cleavage between the reports of the American embassy in Paris to the State Department and the public pronouncements of the State Department. Thus, yesterday Livingston Merchant, assistant secretary of state for Western Europe, told Congress the chances of France ratifying EDC were "excellent." This absolutely contradicts what the embassy in Paris is telling Washington. Dillon, who is by tradition a Wall Street Republican, is completely disenchanted with Dulles and the State Department. His telegrams are becoming so sharp these days that Gibson fears very much that he may be removed and withdrawn from Paris.

Gibson says Donald Heath, ambassador in Indochina, gets things so balled up that he seems to have a gift for reconciling seemingly irreconcilable points of view. General O'Daniel, head of the military mission in Indochina, believes the answer to everything is just to arm native troops—even if the natives, once armed, immediately desert to the enemy. But Heath manages to reconcile O'Daniel's recommendations to those of his bitterest opponent, the counselor of embassy. Recently upon instructions from Washington—as the result of the sharpest kind of prodding from Dillon—Bedell Smith conferred with Emperor Bao Dai at Evian. The purpose of the meeting was to urge Bao Dai to get back to Indochina. Nothing whatsoever came of it. Bao Dai returned to the Riviera, and Heath was allowed to make an insipid statement to the press contending that Bao Dai was being very useful by staying near to the Geneva Conference.

The military situation in Indochina is absolutely disastrous. It is far worse, says Bill, than it looks. It is a ridiculous joke to think that Cambodia and Laos can be saved even if Vietnam goes. There is no will to resist anywhere in Southeast Asia. Almost certainly Thailand will make a deal for collaboration with the Communists just the way they collaborated with the victorious Japanese during World War II. The French are in desperate straits in the Delta. Chinese intervention is now on a massive scale with convoys of thousands of vehicles coming over the border. The Vietminh not only gained a tremendous moral ascendancy after Dienbienphu but acquired a vast new amount of equipment which they know how to use very efficiently. Vietnamese troops fighting for the French are virtually useless. The way the French use them, Vietnamese soldiers are mixed up with French soldiers in the same units. This makes it all the easier in times of crisis for an entire unit to disintegrate and collapse.

The new prime minister just chosen for Vietnam, Ngo Dinh Diem, is a virtually unknown individual. By sheer chance Gibson knows him well and is probably the only Westerner who does. Ngo Dinh Diem is a rather mystical Catholic of an impractical sort. He has been studying at a Catholic retreat in Bruges recently and is now in Paris very much incognito. The ministry of the Associated States here didn't even know a thing about him when he was named. He is staying at a third-class hotel in Paris, and Gibson is his only contact. He calls up Gibson under a code name and they meet in places like park benches. He is a completely unreal figure, but at least he is scrupulously honest. Gibson offered to put me in touch with him if I want to see him.

I had lunch today with Douglas Dillon, and I must say it was interesting. Dillon told me it was the second time since he has come to Paris as ambassador that he has had lunch in a restaurant. The first time, he said, was a complete failure. He went to La Méditerranée with Phyllis one Saturday evening. He had hardly sat down when Henri Laugier started making faces at him and finally moved over to his table. He didn't quite know who Laugier was, except that he remembered he had seen him at a reception at the American embassy. Then just as Laugier muscled in, François Mauriac seemed to be sitting at the next table, and what was supposed to be a quiet family view of Paris turned into a violent debate between Mauriac and Laugier.

Dillon seemed absolutely delighted to get out and relax in Paris. He apparently is not terribly well. Although the operation on his back was a success last autumn, the doctors seem to have made a mistake and bruised a nerve. As a result, his right arm lost its feeling and began to atrophy— just as if he had had infantile paralysis. He has been taking a series of very painful exercises for many months now—two hours a day—in order to get it back in shape. He says (rather proudly) that it is now back to 40 per cent of normal use. Apparently it was down to 5 or 10 per cent at the beginning.

Douglas is very disillusioned with the job of being an ambassador for the Republican administration. He thinks the White House team is extraordinarily bad. Furthermore, he is frank to say that the blame for the present mistakes in American foreign policy should not rest upon the State Department and Dulles but should go right on up to the White House. He says he knew Eisenhower when he was president of Columbia University and used to come to his father's (Dillon Sr.'s) house for dinner. In those days Eisenhower was a sincere, decent, relaxed man. Now he has sold out to the politicians. He simply doesn't know how to operate without a good chief of staff.

Dillon believes Acheson made great mistakes in foreign policy because he never took the country and the Congress into his confidence. Dulles has tried earnestly to correct this. But the result has been he has been taking Congress and the whole world into his confidence on every single move. He doesn't seem to know how to say "No comment" at a press conference. It has been disastrous to have continually conflicting statements uttered on basic issues by Dulles and other American leaders.

Thus, for example, yesterday's papers carried a statement to the effect that Livy Merchant thought the chances of France ratifying EDC "excellent." Today's papers quoted Dulles as saying the chances of any action at all in the near future were rather gloomy. Dillon says he is continually embarrassed by such conflicts in public statements. Everybody back home is talking all the time, and they are always expressing a point of view rather than being noncommittal.

Furthermore, Dillon is furious at the immorality of the State Department in terms of defending its employees. He thinks it was a great disaster to allow so many public servants to be pilloried and forced out of office on highly publicized and frequently fake charges of procommunism and homosexuality. Dillon has had many fights on his hands concerning his own embassy. For example, he said that the father-in-law of his aide was bounced under the Scott McLeod program and has now been relegated to some minor job.

Dillon was furious at the way Clare Luce is able to operate and influence decisions against the interests of the United States. He said, "She hasn't got anything except *Time, Life* and *Fortune.*" He adds that if she didn't have these instruments, she wouldn't be able to get away with the political pressure that she now is able to apply. He says she is merely trying to prove that her original first guesses are correct and is damaging American foreign policy thereby. Thus, for example, Dillon is convinced Mrs. Luce desperately hopes there will be no French parliamentary action on EDC so that she can avoid having the issue put forth in front of the Italian parliament because that would make her look silly.

Dillon says the State Department pays absolutely no attention to the recommendations it gets from the embassy in Paris. The people in Washington are entirely convinced that the only way to make the French react is to hit them over the head with a baseball bat. Although time and again the embassy here gives them evidence that this produces the wrong results, they continue to follow that technique. Dillon said he is sending more and more cables merely quoting reactions to this policy as printed in French editorials or as voiced in conversations by distinguished French leaders, but he is convinced nobody of importance ever gets these reactions.

He said Eisenhower never reads the newspapers and therefore doesn't know what goes on, and the apparatus around him sees to it that he doesn't know what goes on. The President's information nowadays is limited to what he is allowed to see by his entourage. He doesn't read newspapers himself but sees only the clippings that are sent up to him by Jim Hagerty and others of that ilk. It was quite clear that Dillon has absolutely no use for Hagerty. Incidentally, it is also clear Dillon thinks the President should have acted in a drastic way about Senator McCarthy long ago.

I must say I was fascinated to hear all these observations, particularly since Dillon is a political appointee and a lifelong Republican. (He later became Kennedy's Treasury Secretary in a Democratic administration.) I asked whether he kept any kind of notebook or diary in order to remember his reactions, and he said no, he didn't. He simply didn't have the time because all of his extra time was now taken up with physical exercise attempting to recover the use of his right arm completely.

Incidentally, Dillon said a tragic misunderstanding had taken place between Dulles and Eden last April. Eden had agreed to go along with Dulles and accepted a communiqué after their meeting—one week prior to the NATO conference—in which it was stated that the possibilities of joint intervention in Southeast Asia would be examined. As a result of this communiqué a meeting was called the following Monday morning in the State Department by Dulles with six nations interested in Indochina. The Sunday night immediately prior to the suggested meeting Makins, British ambassador in Washington, with much embarrassment had to report to Dulles that the British government refused to go along. Dulles was furious. He had not only received the agreement of Eden, but the two of them had dined with Churchill, and the Prime Minister had also gone along on the program. Makins told Dulles the British government had meant that the problem would be "examined" in the distant future—after Geneva. As a quick, face-saving measure, the projected Monday meeting was transformed into a meeting of all nations interested in the Korean problem, and ten additional countries were invited pronto. But Dulles was absolutely enraged and has been taking it out on the British and Eden ever since.

PARIS, *June 22, 1954*

LAST night I had dinner at Laugier's. Yvon Delbos was there as well as Henri Longchambon, a junior member of the new Mendès-France Cabinet. He is Secretary of State for Scientific Research and Technical Progress as well as senator from the RGR (Radical group).

I was very interested to hear Laugier, who is regarded as a left winger, and Delbos discussing Mendès-France and his cabinet. Laugier said the premier had placed himself completely at the mercy of Moscow because if Moscow did not agree to an Indochina armistice within the time limit set by Mendès-France, he was finished.

Both Laugier and Delbos said Mendès-France had almost betrayed himself by establishing a right-wing government. There is an unusual number of Gaullists in the cabinet. The general, of course, is a sworn enemy of EDC. Delbos estimates that twenty-three of the cabinet ministers are opposed to EDC. Both he and Laugier say de Gaulle would not permit his main supporters, like Soustelle and Palewski, to take cabinet jobs—only second raters. Neither one thinks the cabinet can last very long.

Delbos is convinced the great majority of the French people want EDC, but that the politicians are not going to let them have it.

PARIS, *June 23, 1954*

I had lunch with Lieutenant General Hans Speidel. He was very gloomy about the prospects of EDC. That very morning General Edgard de

Larminat, president of the military committee for the organization of EDC, with much embarrassment, for the first time in the history of these Franco-German negotiations at the military level suggested a "solution de re-change" for EDC. As Speidel understands the Larminat suggestion, it would be to ratify EDC with a simultaneous codicil that actually fundamentally changes and in a sense negates EDC. It would provide for a coalition army and no high commissariat. In other words, it would be an end of the supranational army idea.

Speidel foresees a serious crisis this summer. He says Adenauer is slipping steadily in Germany. The United States is increasingly unpopular in Germany. It is felt that the Americans continue to promise much and do nothing. The British are gaining in popularity while we lose. The Germans are fed up with the French. Neutralism is increasing, but so far Speidel doesn't think that Russia's popularity is gaining much. Speidel says that if the French assembly does not ratify EDC before it adjourns this summer, the Bonn government will be forced to demand immediate and full sovereignty.

Speidel is very disturbed about one of the military aspects of the delay. He says all the equipment earmarked for the German divisions under EDC and piled up by the United States is now becoming obsolete. It will still take two years to produce the German divisions. If German rearmament had been agreed upon in 1951, there would be eighteen German divisions now. Speidel added, after mentioning this figure, "that would include reserves." I asked him if it would require much new planning to work for a German national army rather than divisions in a supranational army in case EDC fails. He replied with pride, "No. Not a single minute has been wasted. Our plans have been made so that it is merely a question of changing hats." In other words the German planners for EDC have blueprinted a German National Army as Heusinger implied to me.

Speidel said the Germans have absolutely no respect for the French army or for many of its commanders. The Germans cannot forget that the French did not fight in the last war. He regards Marshal Juin as an incompetent. He says General Navarre was a complete disaster in Indochina. He considers General Guillaume a braggart and a fool. Guillaume's book on the Red Army was incredibly stupid. Its only sources, according to Speidel, were *Pravda* and the *Red Star*. It was absolute nonsense, Speidel says, adding, "I know. I fought in Russia." He says General de Castries, who was captured at Dienbienphu, is most unpopular in Germany where, as a colonel in charge of Moroccan troops, his unit was renowned for brutal looting during and after the war. He said de Castries behaved with incredible stupidity at Dienbienphu. Furthermore it was in bad taste for him to don his best uniform and medals in order to be taken prisoner. The braggadocio of de Castries' communiqués from Dienbienphu was embarrassingly ridiculous. The whole affair, both militarily and in terms of propaganda, was folly. Speidel, however, says he has a great admiration for General Ely, who is a first-class and sincere man as well as an excellent operations officer—"a real expert."

The most important thing Speidel said to me today was that if Germany had to start planning a national army instead of European Army divisions it would take only about "a couple of hours" to change the blueprints around. But the most significant event of our meeting was an extraordinary kind of ballet in which all the players were unaware of their roles.

I arrived at Lucas Carton a few moments ahead of him and told the waiters to send "Le Général Speidel" to my regular table. So they knew who he was (although he always wears a gray double-breasted suit and looks like a well-fed professor, with his glasses and earnest expression). Some of the waiters must have known him from the war when the principal occupation officers including Goering, Rundstedt, Rommel, Choltitz, Speidel and others often ate at Lucas. Malraux once told me the ground floor here was the favorite restaurant of the Nazi military brass so Resistance leaders often gathered in the private dining rooms one floor up. Gestapo tails were put off if they followed a suspect through the revolving doors and came face to face with Goering. For Lucas Carton it was a war between the first floor and the second floor.

Because of Larminat's ominous news, Speidel was flustered, nervous and did the rare thing for him, accepted a preprandial cocktail. This was unusual enough and confirmed his conviction that EDC was finished. But then his nervousness showed as he was eating his soup later and spilled a bit on his lapel.

Immediately, before my astounded eyes, the occupation was reenacted. Speidel grew taller and taller, straighter and straighter, his belly drawing inward, his chest expanding, as he sat up stiff and summoned the maître d'hôtel, the sommelier, the waiters, as if he owned the place, ordering salt, hot water, vinegar, and so on to remove the foul spot. And the waiters, for their part, became smaller, and smaller, stooping and cringing obsequiously before this suddenly military figure. They formed a kind of parade, each with his napkin, salt or lemon, performing menial services and whispering apologies as if it had all been their fault. Finally, the stain was out. Speidel relaxed, his chest caved in, his stomach sagged out, he subsided into civilian comfort. And the waiters, pleased with themselves, grew taller, cockier, more self-confident.

I sat there with my eyes popping. Nobody playing his role in that sad and grim enactment had the faintest idea of what a spectacle was taking place.

PARIS, *June 25, 1954*

LUNCHED with Randolph Churchill, who, poor fellow, has swollen up an extra twenty pounds since I last saw him. He told me he has less and less interest in politics. This is a far cry from the days when he was assuring me that his one undying ambition was to be Prime Minister of England. Now he says he prefers to write about politics. Actually he is doing very little. He writes a column in a seedy publication and has just written a book about fifteen stately English homes.

He told me his father is exceptionally well these days. He thinks his mother will have the final influence in inducing his father to retire. His own guess is that the old man will probably get out in July. But he says the Prime Minister loves to change his mind. He told me that when Henry Luce saw his father, the PM suggested to Luce that Clare Luce should be transferred from Rome to Paris "because she can do more harm there." I told him I was sitting in Mrs. Luce's boudoir when Harry called up to report that the Prime Minister was retiring in a few weeks' time.

He said that one thing undoubtedly in his father's mind is that if a Prime Minister announces he is going to retire in advance—the way Baldwin made plain he intended to do—he loses all influence. Secondly, Randolph is convinced his father has received intimations from Malenkov that the latter might be prepared to meet with him. (God forbid that this is the case. I hope Malenkov is not toying with old Churchill.) Apparently, according to Randolph, he still has this tremendous desire to die as a "man of peace."

PARIS, *June 28, 1954*

I had a long talk with Al Gruenther this afternoon. He looked very fit and relaxed. He has taken up playing tennis again, and I suppose it does him a bit of good. He told me about his recent visit to England and the speech he made before the English-Speaking Union on June 8. He said he had referred to the fact that he came from an anti-British section of the United States (Nebraska) and that one of his grandparents was Irish, named Shea, and "had left Ireland as a result of a dispute with the British about potatoes." Churchill didn't quite understand this and kept nudging the Duke of Edinburgh, inquiring in a loud voice, "What was the dispute about?"

Gruenther said also that in principle he would still favor a European getting the commanding job of NATO. However, he added that it would be difficult at this moment because of the frame of mind of the United States. It would be unwise to relieve America of its responsibility at the moment and to let the United States "off the hook." Gruenther recalled that two weeks ago today he testified before the Senate and House Foreign Affairs

Committees and that they were in a bad frame of mind. Thus there was considerable sentiment for preventing the dispatch of *any* equipment to *any* European allies until after EDC was ratified.

I asked Gruenther how it happened that in 1950 the United States government thought there was no critical importance to the United States in Indochina and that now the United States government considered its loss would be critically important. He said that was fundamentally a question of definitions and semantics. For example, when he was at the Pentagon, there had been a great argument as to whether, in case of war, the Middle East would be "critical" or "vital." Vital to us means an area that must be defended because if it falls we would lose the war. Critical means highly important but not that important. Therefore, in case of a war, when you are faced with a tremendous choice, you may have to move forces from the defense of a critical area to the defense of a vital area. It is quite possible that there has been some muddy thinking on semantics in Washington.

PARIS, *June 29, 1954*

LAST night at dinner party I picked up some interesting gossip. Bill Gibson of the American embassy told me he had spent the day with Don Heath, who has now flown to Washington with the mission of shaking the United States loose from its support of Bao Dai and shaking Bao Dai loose from Indochina. Bao Dai now claims he is ill and has to go to Vittel for a cure. The French apparently are in agreement and it appears that Bao Dai is never going to go back home. Why the hell we couldn't have done this five or six years ago, I don't know.

PARIS, *July 1, 1954*

I had a good talk with David Bruce this morning. Bruce took apart the Radford theory of strategy very neatly. He said some of its advocates had obviously wanted to intervene with tactical atom bombs at Dienbienphu as a way of getting the United States engaged first in Indochina and then in China; that to conquer China more than the forces of Chiang Kai-shek now on Formosa would be necessary. This meant engaging American land troops. If the Soviet Union were to intervene in this war between the United States and China, these people wanted to blow up the Soviet Union with hydrogen bombs. Bruce said that if one wished to accept the logic of Radford's theory, it didn't make sense anyway. Radford's theory was that the relative advantage now held by the United States was slipping and the Russians were gaining every year, holding their own advantage in conservative forces and weapons and catching up on new weapons. Therefore, according to some theorists, a preventive war was necessary. However, as Bruce points out, if this logic is sound, there is no sense in going through the performance of intervening steps involving China. If the theory is sound, war should be started right away against Russia. The other approach is dishonest because it seeks to get the United States involved in a war with China without letting the people know that.

NEW YORK, *September 8, 1954*

I had lunch today with Marie Harriman. Averell was supposed to be there, but he got hung up at the last minute and came in after lunch looking very fit and excited. He told me confidentially that everything is now in the bag for his nomination for Governor. This morning apparently the bosses agreed. Senator Lehman and Mayor Wagner of New York City are going to make public statements in the near future supporting Harriman.

Averell says Frankie Roosevelt does not have nearly the number of committed delegates he thinks he has. He now hopes Frankie will gracefully accept the facts as they are and realize that he has a long political career ahead of him and will loyally work for the party and the committee. Harriman thinks Ives will probably be easier to beat than Dewey, who announced last night that he will not run again.

Harriman is bitterly upset about the failure of our foreign policy and its inept administration by Dulles. He claims this largely stems from the desire of Dulles to please isolationist elements in the Republican Party while ignoring the bad effect abroad of many of his statements.

# A SEMICOLON

I N OCTOBER, 1954 I CEASED BEING A REPORTER AND BECAME A JOUR-
nalist. In other words I got pompous and started writing a column. But
if I also stopped being an executive and running the foreign service
of *The New York Times,* serving as its ambassador at home and arguing for
its raises, transfers, expenses, etc., I hope I did not stop doing my own legwork, chasing down my own information, developing my own sources. In
other words, remaining a newspaperman.

When Anne McCormick died her column on the editorial page became
available and I applied for the privilege. Nobody could hope to fill Anne's
shoes but somebody had to fill her space. In 1952 Arthur Krock, then head
of the *Times'* Washington bureau, had offered me the job of eventually succeeding him there—although, technically, this was not his right. I declined
his suggestion politely, telling him my life had been spent abroad acquiring a
specialized knowledge of foreign affairs so I thought I might as well pursue
that destiny. Later Krock's Washington job went to James Reston. But
when Mrs. McCormick died I was awarded her column and, after my
summer holiday, took off a couple of weeks preparing myself for the
task.

I went up to the Adirondack mountains that September and lived alone
in a tent, fishing and trying to decide what kind of column I was best fitted
to produce. Since I was neither as wise as Anne nor as gifted in literary
style I decided the way to overcome these shortcomings was to exploit my
own advantages: wide travel and extensive acquaintanceship in the world.
I would continue to move about constantly, taking advantage of the jet age.
Anne had preferred to live in New York and take one trip a year to
Europe, generally by ship. I decided to remain in Paris and to fly around

from there, at least initially, until my children might go to school in the United States.

Secondly, I resolved to try and substitute information, first-hand news and exclusive background for the polished periods of Mrs. McCormick that I could not hope to equal. I would seek to provoke people into reading my column instead of politely persuading them. And, to start this formula off, I determined to ask the help of my old friends, President Eisenhower and Secretary of State Dulles, in providing material for my initial columns.

Having thus made up my mind and chosen the innocuous if accurate title "Foreign Affairs" for my new project, I called my wife, who drove up to join me with the children. The four of us spent an additional week in the tent. It was getting cold. The boreal wind blew down from Canada. Waves lapped on the shore and a wildcat livened each night by wailing like a banshee from a bough above the canvas roof. A porcupine ate our butter and bacon from the stone cache in the lake which constituted our ice-box.

As I prepared to embark on this new life—which is a much greater journalistic change than it sounds—I contemplated many things. All the people in my organization intent on scrambling up the power ladder would probably be pleased by my evident withdrawal from a competition that had never interested me. This was good; but it is harder to preserve one's independence if one cannot fight from a power base. And if I was losing enemies, I would also lose friends: the fair-weather variety. This might complicate my job since a columnist must take a stand, a position on policies and events, and I could not always guarantee my views would mirror those of my paper. Indeed, I suspected the contrary.

I reviewed events of the decade during which I had organized and run our foreign service and was proud that, before the postwar world had frozen, I had foreseen certain of its patterns. I had divided up East European coverage in such a way that Tito's split with Moscow did not interfere with our operations; nor the Greek civil war. We anticipated the Truman Doctrine by making Greece and Turkey a single beat in 1945. Likewise, we split the Arab world from Palestine and also from Iran as soon as World War II was over. And we created an organization to cover free Africa before it was decolonized.

I realized that the period of my stewardship of *Times* reporting abroad had seen division of world power between two superstates, the United States and the USSR, but that we had dammed the westward flow of Communist influence. However, where it offered improvement in living standards, to the East and South, that influence remained dynamic. I also realized, if then only dimly, that two major events had begun to shape up in this ideological struggle on which the United States was perhaps unwittingly embarked. The first was the rearmament of West Germany, which began under the ill-fated European Defense Community scheme. And the second was the growing American involvement in Indochina which became a precise commitment in 1954 after the Pentagon decided the area was of "critical" importance to the United States.

Here I put semicolon to these memoirs—in late September, 1954.

# Index

# INDEX